1,000,000 Books

are available to read at

Forgotten Books

www.ForgottenBooks.com

Read online
Download PDF
Purchase in print

ISBN 978-1-332-94719-5
PIBN 10441524

This book is a reproduction of an important historical work. Forgotten Books uses state-of-the-art technology to digitally reconstruct the work, preserving the original format whilst repairing imperfections present in the aged copy. In rare cases, an imperfection in the original, such as a blemish or missing page, may be replicated in our edition. We do, however, repair the vast majority of imperfections successfully; any imperfections that remain are intentionally left to preserve the state of such historical works.

Forgotten Books is a registered trademark of FB &c Ltd.
Copyright © 2018 FB &c Ltd.
FB &c Ltd, Dalton House, 60 Windsor Avenue, London, SW19 2RR.
Company number 08720141. Registered in England and Wales.

For support please visit www.forgottenbooks.com

1 MONTH OF FREE READING

at

www.ForgottenBooks.com

By purchasing this book you are eligible for one month membership to ForgottenBooks.com, giving you unlimited access to our entire collection of over 1,000,000 titles via our web site and mobile apps.

To claim your free month visit:

www.forgottenbooks.com/free441524

* Offer is valid for 45 days from date of purchase. Terms and conditions apply.

English
Français
Deutsche
Italiano
Español
Português

www.forgottenbooks.com

Mythology Photography **Fiction** Fishing Christianity **Art** Cooking Essays Buddhism Freemasonry Medicine **Biology** Music **Ancient Egypt** Evolution Carpentry Physics Dance Geology **Mathematics** Fitness Shakespeare **Folklore** Yoga Marketing **Confidence** Immortality Biographies Poetry **Psychology** Witchcraft Electronics Chemistry History **Law** Accounting **Philosophy** Anthropology Alchemy Drama Quantum Mechanics Atheism Sexual Health **Ancient History Entrepreneurship** Languages Sport Paleontology Needlework Islam **Metaphysics** Investment Archaeology Parenting Statistics Criminology **Motivational**

RICH. BAXTERS APOLOGY

Against the Modest

EXCEPTIONS

OF

Mr T. BLAKE.

AND THE

DIGRESSION

OF

Mr G. KENDALL.

Whereunto is added

ANIMADVERSIONS

on a late

DISSERTATION

OF

Ludiomæus Colvinus, aliàs, *Ludovicus Molinæus*, M. Dr OXON.

AND AN

Admonition of Mr *W. Eyre* of *Salisbury*.

WITH

Mr *Crandon's* Anatomy for satisfaction of Mr *Caryl*.

Phil.1.15.16,17,18,19. *Some preach Christ even of Envy and Strife, and some also of Good Will: The one preach Christ of Contention, not sincerely, supposing to adde Affliction to my bonds: But the other of Love, knowing that I am set for the Defence of the Gospel. What then? Notwithstanding every way, whether in pretence or in truth, Christ is preached, and I therein do Rejoyce, yea, and will Rejoyce. For I know that this shall turn to my salvation through your Prayer, and the supply of the Spirit of Jesus Christ.*

London, Printed by *A.M.* for *Thomas Underhill*, at the Anchor and Bible in *Pauls* Church-yard, and *Francis Tyton* at the three Daggers in Fleetstreet. 1654.

TO THE
Honourable Commiſſary General
EDWARD WHALLEY.

SIR,

THough Weakneſs and diſtance have prohibited me that converſe with you which ſometime I did enjoy, yet have they not excuſſed your former Kindeneſs out of my Remembrance. Received Benefits ſhould not Die before us: If the Donor kill them not by Retraction, the Receiver muſt not ſuffocate them by Oblivion; nor prove their Grave; who was intended for a Storehouſe; if not a Garden where they may be Rooted and be fruitfull. In thoſe hearts where Benefits Live, the Benefactor Liveth. And thoſe that Live in our Eſtimation and Affection, we deſire their Names may be inſcribed on our Monuments, and ſurvive with ours, when we are Dead. While we live alſo we more regard their Judgements of us, then other mens; and are more ambitious of ſtanding right in their eſteem; and therefore are willing that our juſt Apologies may be in their hands, to hinder miſapprehenſions, and reſiſt unjuſt Accuſers. May theſe Reaſons excuſe my prefixing your Name to theſe Papers, and directing them firſt to your Hand: (Cuſtom having led me into that Road, wherein I do not unwillingly follow.) It is not

[* 2]   for

for Protection or Patronage of my Opinions: For that I referre them wholly to the Father of Lights, the Illuminating Spirit, and the Light of that Truth Which they contain and Vindicate. Nor do I desire that you should make these things your Studies; they being more fitted to the use of those Students, that can lay out much of their time on such things. I confess I had rather see in your Hands, the Holy Scriptures, and Books of Practical Divinity, then these Controversies: and had rather hear such Practical Discourses from your Mouth. So farre am I from soliciting you to any singular Opinion of mine, that I solicit you not once to read these Books; save onely When any Opinion in them shall be Accused, to turn to the Words, and see what is said. It is the Practical Christian that holds fast the Truth, which many eager Disputers soon lose. Doting about Questions that engender strife, is not the Religiousness that God approves; What ever the Professours of this Age may imagine. It is the most Practical Teachers and People in England *commonly that are the most Orthodox. I have oft noted many mens Prayers to be much freer from Libertinism, then their Sermons; and their Sermons then their Writings and Disputes. That's a mans Judgement indeed, which he dare reduce to Practice, and own before God.*

The Work of these Papers have been to my minde somewhat like those sad Employments wherein I attended you: of themselves, grievous and ungratefull; exasperating others, and not pleasing my self (besides the ruinating of my bodily health) And as the Remembrance of those years is so little delightfull to me, that I look back upon them as the saddest part of my life; so the Review of this Apologie, is but the renewing of my trouble: to think of our Common frailty and darkness, and what Reverend and much valued Brethren I contradict; but especially for fear lest men should make this Collision an occasion of Division, and by receiving the sparks into Combustible Affections, should turn that to a Conflagration which I intended but for Illumination. If you say, I should then have let it alone: The same answer must serve, as in the former Cause we were wont to use. Some say, that I who pretend so much for Peace, should not Write of Controversies. For my self it is not much Matter: but must Gods Truth (for such I take it) stand as a Butt for every man to shoot at? Must there be such Liberty of opposing it, and none of Defending? One party cannot have Peace without the others Consent. To be Buffeted and Assaulted, and Commanded to Deliver up the Truth of God, and called Unpeaceable if I defend it and resist, this is such Equi-

ty as we were wont to finde. In a word, both works were ungratefull to me, and are so in the Review ; but in both, as Providence and mens onset imposed a Necessity, and drove me to that strait, that I must Defend or do worse; so did the same Providence so clear my way, and draw me on, and sweeten unusual Troubles with unusual Mercies, and Issue all in Testimonies of Grace, that as I had great mixtures of Comfort with Sorrow in the Performance, so have I in the Review : And as I had more eminent Deliverances and other Mercies in those years and wayes of Bloud and Dolour, then in most of my Life beside; so have I had more encouraging Light since I was engaged in these Controversies. (For I speak not of these few Papers onely, but of many more of the like Nature that have taken up my time.) And as I still retain'd a Hope, that the End of all our Calamities and strange Disposings of Providence, would be somewhat Better then was Threatned of late : so Experience hath taught me to think, that the Issue of my most ungratefull Labours shall not be vain; but that Providence which extracted them hath some use to make of them, better then I am yet aware of ; if not in this Age, yet in times to come. The best is, We now draw no bloud : and honest hearts will not take themselves wounded, with that blow which is given onely to their Errours. However, God must be served when he cals for it, though by the harshest and most unpleasing work. Onely the Lord teach us to Watch carefully over our Deceitfull Hearts, least we should serve our selves while we think and say, we are serving him; and lest we should Militate for our own Honour and Interest, when we pretend to do it for his Truth and Glory !

I hope, Sir, the Diversity of Opinions in these dayes, will not diminish your Estimation of Christianity, nor make you suspect that all is Doubtfull, because so much is Doubted of. Though the Tempter seems to be playing such a Game in the world, God will go beyond him, and turn that to Illustration and Confirmation, which he intended for Confusion and Extirpation of the Truth. You know its no news to hear of some Ignorant, Proud and Licentious, of what Religion soever they be. And this Trinity is the Creator of Heresies. And as for the sober and Godly, it is but in lesser things that they disagree : and mostly about words and Methods more then Matter (though the smallest things of God are not Contemptible.) He that wonders to see wise men differ, doth but wonder that they are yet Imperfect, and know but in part ; that is, that they are yet Mortal sinners, and not Glorified on Earth ! And such wonderers know not what man is, and it seems are too great strangers to themselves.

And

And if they turn these differences to the prejudice of Gods Truth, or dishonour of Godliness, they shew themselves yet more unreasonable, to blame the Sunne that men are purblinde. And indeed were Pride and Passion laid aside in our Disputes, and men could gently suffer contradiction, and heartily love and correspond with those that in lower matters do gainsay them, I see not but such friendly debates might edifie.

For your self, Sir, as you were a friend to sound Doctrine, to Unity and to Piety, and to the Preachers, Defenders and Practisers thereof, while I converst with you, and as fame informeth us, have continued such; so I hope that God who hath so long preserved you, will preserve you to the end; and he that hath been your Shield in corporal dangers, will be so in spirituall.

Your great Warfare is not yet accomplished: The Worms of Corruption that breed in our bowels, will live in some measure till we die our selves. Your Conquest of your self is yet Imperfect. To fight with your self, you will finde the hardest, but most necessary Conflict that ever yet you were engaged in; and to overcome your self the most honourable and gainfull Victory. And think not that your greatest trials are all over. Prosperity hath its peculiar Temptations, by which it hath foiled many that stood unshaken in the storms of adversity. The Tempter who hath had you on the waves, will now assault you in the calm; and hath his last game to play on the Mountain, till nature cause you to descend. Stand this Charge and you win the day. To which, as one that is faithful to you, I shall acquaint you in a few words, what his temptations are like to be, and how you should resist them: If you are already provided, a Remembrancer will do you no harm.

1. The first and great Assault will be, to entice you to Overvalue your present Prosperity, and to Judge the Creature to be better then it is, and to grasp after a fulness of Honour and Wealth, and then to say, Soul, take thy Rest. As you love your Peace, your Life, your Soul, your God, take heed of this. Judge of Prosperity as one that must go Naked out of the world: Esteem of earthly Greatness and Glory as that which will shortly leave you in the dust. Why should it be proper to Dying men to be Wise, and to Judge truly of this world, when all the living undoubtedly know that they must Die?

2. At least the Tempter will perswade with you to enjoy your Prosperity to the satisfying of your flesh; and tell you that the free use of the Creatures is your Christian Liberty, and therefore you need not deny your selves those Delights that God affordeth you. But remember that it is the seem-

ing

ing sweetness of the Creature that draws men from God: The Pleasantest Condition is the most dangerous. If ever you would have your soul Prosper, make no provision for the flesh to satisfie its lusts: *A better man then any of us, was fain to tame his body and bring it into subjection. Mortification is a necessary, but much neglected part of the Christian Religion.*

3. Should the *Tempter* prevail in these, it would follow, that God would be much forgotten, former Engagements violated, and the Invisible things of the Life to come would be seldom thought on, and less esteemed. O think on him that remembred you in your greatest straits! Its a provoking sin to break those Engagements which depth of Extremity, or Greatness of Deliverance, did formerly constrain us to make with our God! Ingratitude makes a forfeiture of all we have. And think not well of your own heart, when you cannot think more sweetly of another world then of this. Its unhappy prosperity that makes God to be more sleighted, and the Glory to come more unsavoury to our thoughts, and makes us say, It is best to be here.

4. Another dangerous *Temptation* that will attend these, will be, to disregard *Chrifts Interest* through an over-minding of their own: To play your own game, and lay out your chiefest care for your self, and make Gods businefs to stoop unto your own. Where this prevails, the hearts of such are false to Christ: While they pretend to serve him, they do but serve themselves upon him. They will honour Christ no longer then he will honour them. And when they are once false to Christ, they can be true to no one else. Their friends are esteemed but as stepping stones to their Ends. When they can serve them no longer they reject them as unprofitable. Ever Remember, that man stands safest that espouseth no Interest contradictory to Chrifts; I had almost said, None but Chrifts: For even Chrifts must be made his own, and then his own will be Chrifts. God is more engaged to secure his own Interest then ours. There is no Policy therefore comparable to this, to Engage most deeply where Chrifts chiefest Interest lieth, and to Unite our own to his, in a just subordination. He that will needs have a standing divided from Christ, Independent on him, or Equal with him, much more in Opposition to him, is sure to fall. It will break the greatest Prince on Earth to espouse an Interest inconsistent with Chrifts, when he doth but arise to plead his Cause. Study therefore where Chrifts Interest most lieth, and then devote all your own to the promoting of it: and hold none that lives not as the Vine on the Wall, or rather as the branch in the Vine, in Dependance upon his. And upon Enquiry you will finde, that

Chrifts

Chrifts Intereft lies much in thefe two things, the Piety and the Peace of his People. The Reformation of his Churches, and the Uniting of them (at home and abroad) are the greateft works that any can be Imployed in. To which ends Gods chiefeft means, is an Able, Godly, Diligent Miniftry; to Teach and Rule his flocks according to his Word. All the Intereft that God hath Given you, he expecteth fhould be fpeedily, diligently and undefervedly imployed to thefe Ends. Delay not, you have but your time. Think it not enough to do no harm, or no more good then thofe below you. Your ftanding is unfafe when you do little or nothing for God. He is not bound to hold you the Candle to do nothing, or to work for your felf. Work therefore while it is day: the night comes when none can work.

5. Another Temptation that you muft expect, will be, to have your minde fwell with your Condition: and to difrefpect the inferiour fort of your Brethren. But I hope the Lord will keep you fmall in your own eyes; as remembring that you are the fame in the eyes of your Judge, and your fhadow is not lengthened by your fucceffes, and that you muft lie down with the Vulgar in the common duft.

Sir, Becaufe the matter of this Book may be lefs ufeful to you, I could not direct it to your hand, without fome words that might be more ufeful. I do not fear leaft you fhould take my faithful dealing for an injury, or interpret my Monition to be an Accufation; as long as you fo well know the Affections of your Monitor. The Lord be your Teacher and Defence, and Direct, Excite, Encourage and Succeed you, and all that have Opportunity to do any thing to the Repairing of our Breaches, by furthering The Reformation and Unity of the Churches: Which is the earneft Defire, and daily Prayer of

Your Servant in the work of Chrift

Kederminfter, Marc. 8th
1653.

RICHARD BAXTER.

RICH. BAXTERS ACCOUNT

Given to his Reverend Brother
Mr T. BLAKE.
OF THE
Reasons of his Dissent
FROM
The Doctrine of his Exceptions
in his late
TREATISE of the COVENANTS.

JOHN 3. 7.
Little Children, let no man Deceive you: He that doth Righteousness, is Righteous, even as he is Righteous.

1 TIM. 4. 8.
Godliness is Profitable unto All things, having Promise of the Life that now is, and of that Which is to come.

LONDON,
Printed by *A. M.* for *Thomas Underhill* at the Anchor and Bible in *Pauls* Church-yard, and *Francis Tyton* at the three Daggers in *Fleetstreet*, 1 6 5 4.

The Preface Apologetical.

SO sweet a thing is Christian Love and Concord, and so precious are the thoughts of Peace to my Soul, that I think it unmeet in this contentious Age, to publish such a Controversie as this, without an Apology: which, its likely, may be needful, both as to the Matter and the Manner. Not that I dare rather choose to Excuse a fault, then to forbear the committing of it: But that I would have the Reader judge of things as they are. Just Apologies are not a cover to our faults, but for removal of mis-representations, and healing of misapprehensions, that those may not be taken for faults which are none, or those to be of the greater size, which are but ordinary infirmities. Whether my Apology be Just, the Reader must judge.

I do so heartily Love Peace, that I have hard thoughts of Controversie: yet do I so Love the Truth, that I refuse not to contend for it. Though the strait be great, yet its no other then we are usually put to, even in lower things. The most noble and excellent ends, may have some distastful means: which as none that is in his right senses will choose for themselves, so none but a slave to his senses will refuse when they are necessary. It is no Contradiction in such a case, but true Discretion, to Choose the thing which at the same time we do Abhor: To choose it as a necessary Means, and yet to abhorre it for its Ungrateful Nature. We are contented to seek, and buy, and take that Physick which we so abhorre, that we have much ado to get it down or to retain it. The Lord knows, that contending is distastful to my soul: though my corrupt nature is too prone to it. Much studying of Controversies hath oft discomposed my minde, and interrupted my more sweet and heavenly thoughts, and unfitted me for publick and private duties; so that I as sensibly finde my self a loser by it, as by some other avocations of a more aliene nature. Yet dare I not be so selfish as to cast it off. That must be endured, which may not be desired. We may not pretend the disadvantages to our souls (much less any lower) against apparent duty, and service to the truth of God. Many wayes hath our Master to make us a full reparation for our losses. What then shall I resolve on? Neither to Delight in Controversie; nor totally to Refuse it. Not to rush upon it unadvisedly, nor to be carried into it by blinde Passion and partiality, nor yet to cast away my Captains Colours, nor to draw back when I am prest. Not to militate for any Faction, but for the Faith; nor for vain-glory and credit, but for Christ: And this with such a differencing the Person from the Cause, that as it respecteth the errour, it shall be bitter and contentious; but as to my Brother, it shall be a Conference of Love. I abhorre almost nothing more in Divines, then laying too much upon the smaller controvertible Doctrinals, and making too much of our Religion, to consist in curious and unnecessary speculations, if not unsearchable, unrevealed things; contradicting one of their first Maxims, that [*Theology is a Practical Science.*] An honest Philosopher saw the evil of this *. Yet must Gods commands be obeyed, and the Truth defended, and the Church confirmed and edified, and the soul of an erring Brother be relieved, though at a dearer rate then a verbal Disputation.

*² Seneca *Epist. ad Luc.* 102. *Non debuit hoc nobis esse propositum, argutias serere; & Philosophiam in has angustias, ex sua Majestate detrahere.*
Quanto satius est ire aperta via, & recta, quam sibi ipsi flexus disponere, quos cum magna molestia debeas relegere? Neque enim quicquam aliud ista Disputationes sunt, quam inter se perite captantium lusus.

It is about five years since I wrote a small book about Justification, and being in great weakness and expectation of death, I was forced to deliberate, Whether to publish it with its many Imperfections, or not at all? I chose the former, supposing the Defects and Crudities would be charged only on the Author, and that some Light might notwithstanding appear to the Reader, which might further him in the understanding of several truths. I durst not so far value reputation, as to be injurious to Verity, for fear of discovering my own infirmity: Its no time to be solicitous about the esteem of men, when

when we are drawing near to the Judgement Seat of God. When this Book came abroad, it fell under very different Censures, as most things use to do that seem to go out of the ordinary road. Too many overvalued it : Some were offended at it. Hereupon being afraid lest by Ignorance or Rashness I should wrong the Church and Truth, I did in the end of my Book of Baptism, desire my Brethrens animadversions, and advice : which accordingly many of the most pious and Learned men that I know in the Land, were pleased to afford me; and that with so much Ingenuity, Love and Gentleness, as I must needs confess my self their Debtor, as having no way deserved so great a favour : and I do hereby return them my most hearty thanks. After this my Reverend and Dear Brother Mr *Blake* in a Treatise of the Covenants, did publish a Confutation of some things in my Book (among many others whom he deals with, Mr *Powell*, Mr. *Tombes*, Mr. *Owen*, Mr. *Firmin*, &c.) wherein I found nothing but tenderness and brotherly Love, as to my person; and no such inclination to extreams in his Doctrine, as I found in some others; but much Moderation and Sobriety, as indeed the Gravity, Piety and Integrity of the man, would promise to any that know him. Only I thought it might have been more convenient to him, to me, and to others, if I had seen his exceptions before they had been published; that so having known what I would reply, he might have published only so much as he remained unsatisfied in. But as it seems, his Judgement was otherwise, so is it no whit to me offensive. Yet when I had read his Book, it was my Resolution, to send him privately my Reply, that so we might consider how farre we were agreed, and how farre the difference was onely seeming and about words, and might publish only the remainder to the world, by joynt Consent. The Reasons of this Resolution were these : First, Because I was loath by tedious altercations, to hinder the Reader from discerning the Truth : It is the course of most voluminous Disputers, to tire their Readers with Contendings about words, that they can hardly finde out the true state of the Controversie; much less discern on which side is the Truth. Which might be much remedied if men would but lovingly first debate the matter in private, and cut off all the superfluities and verbal Quarrels; and then put out only the material differences by joynt Consent, having Corrected even in the language and manner of debating, whatsoever was displeasing or seemed injurious to either party. Secondly, Because I unfeignedly abhorre contending, and never wrote any thing that way, but when

I was

I was unavoidably necessitated. Thirdly, Because I so well know my own frailty, and proneness to be over-eager and keen, and unmannerly in my stile, and the frailty of most Brethren in being Impatient hereof; yea of many in judging themselves wronged when they are not, and making some plain speeches which were but necessary or innocent, to seem proud, contemptuous, and sleighting as to mens persons, racking them to a sense that was never intended, I therefore thought it safest to avoid all occasions of such mistakes, which may be injurious to themselves, as well as to me. Fourthly, Because the Lord hath of late years by a strange, unresistible work of his power, fastned in my soul so deep an Apprehension of the Evil of Dissentions, and of the Excellency and Necessity of the Unity of Brethren, and the Peace of the Church; and in order hereto, of the healing of our Divisions, that it sticks in my thoughts night and day, and the Zeal of such a Reconciliation doth eat me up; so that I make it the main study and businefs of my Meditations, which way I might do any thing towards its accomplishment. And I was much afraid, lest if I wrote by way of Controversie, I might, by exasperating my Brethren, hinder this happy work. He that knoweth my heart, knoweth that these were my thoughts. Hereupon I did in the first Page signifie to M. *Blake*, this my Resolution, which when I was forced to alter, I would not alter the words of my writing, but having given this account of the reason of them, I shall let them go as I wrote them.

Before I had finished my Reply to Mr. *Blake*, comes out Mr. *Kendal*'s Book against M. *Goodwin*, with his Digression against me: After this, I was informed of divers others that were ready to write against my Doctrine, and some that had written, and were ready to publish it, and divers others that were desirous to send me their Animadversions. I did therefore apprehend (and so did many learned Friends) an unavoidable Necessity of appearing more publickly, both to spare my Friends the labour of writing the same things to me over and over, which so many others had written before; and to spare my self the time and pains of endless private Replies (which have this three years taken me up, and hindered me from more profitable work:) and also to prevent mens publication of more such writings as have already been published; seeing when none know what I can say against them, the rest may go on in the way as these have done, and trouble themselves and the world in vain. Besides, I understood that some were offended at my silence, as mis-interpreting

preting it to be from contempt. Being therefore necessitated to do something of this kinde, I could not (according to the Laws of Justice or Friendship) deal publickly with any, but those that had begun to deal publickly with me. Its true, there hath been long unanswered, a Book of Mr. *Owens* against some things which I had wrote which concerned him. But I never thought fit (nor yet do) to Reply to that: 1. Partly because it containeth so little matter of reall difference between him and me (and most of that is answered by Mr. *Blake*, and in my Reply to Mr. *Kendall*:) The main Points being, Whether Christ suffered the same which the Law threatned, or the Value, or that which was equivalent? (wherein he yieldeth as much as I need) and, Whether the Covenant be Conditional? and, Whether the Obligation to Punishment be dissolved before we Believed, sinned, or were born? And to vindicate the Truth in these two or three Points, I conceive it not so meet a way, to do it in Answer to that Book, wherein ten times more words would be bestowed in altercations, and upon the by. 2. Besides, I was never never necessitated to a Reply to that Book, nor once desired, and I will do nothing of that kinde, which I know how to avoid. 3. But indeed my greatest reason, was the consciousness of my temerity in being so foolishly drawn to begin with him; and the consciousness of my fault in one or two unmannerly words of him, and consequently the consciousness of my duty to be first silent. It is not fit that I should both begin and end. But these Brethren that I here Reply to, did begin with me.

Upon these Reasons, I sent not my papers to Mr. *Blake*, but resolved to publish them, with my Reply to Mr. *K*.

As for Mr. *K*. himself, I know not the man; but by his writings he appears to be a Learned man: And I will hope his humility may be answerable to his Learning, though he here express it not: We are all poor frail sinners; and above all do hardly Master our Pride; the fire whereof in an unmortified soul, doth make fewell to it self of Gods excellent Gifts, till it have turned them all into salt and ashes. That which this Learned man hath troubled himself to write concerning my self, I will not insist on: It is not for my self that I am disputing, but for the Truth, so farre as I know it: I can truly say as *Augustine* to *Hierom*, *Obsecro te per mansuetudinem Christi, ut si te læsi, dimittas mihi; nec me vicissim lædendo malum pro malo reddas. Lædes enim si mihi tacueris errorem meum, quem forte inveneris in Scriptis, vel in dictis meis. Nam si ea in me reprehenderis, quæ*

re-

reprehendenda non sunt, te potius lædis quàm me; quod absit à moribus, & sancto proposito tuo, ut hoc facias voluntate lædendi culpans in me aliquid dente malevolo, quod mente veridica scis non esse culpandum,&c. Fieri potest ut tibi videatur aliud quam veritas habet; dum tamen aliud abs te non fiat quam charitas habet. Nam & ego amicissimam reprehensionem tuam gratissime accipiam, etiamsi reprehendi non meruit, quod recte defendi potest : Aut agnoscam simul & benevolentiam tuam & culpam meam; & quantum Dominus donat, in alio gratus, in alio emendatus inveniar. Quid ergo? fortasse dura, sed certè salubria verba tua tanquam cestus Entelli pertimescam. Cædebatur ille : non curabatur : Et ideo vincebatur, non sanabatur. Ego autem si medicinalem correptionem tuam, tranquillus accepero, non dolebo. Si vero infirmitas vel humana, vel mea, etiam cum veraciter arguitur, non potest non aliquantulum contristari; Melius tumor Capitis dolet cum curatur, quam dum ei parcitur, & non sanatur. Hoc est enim quod acutè vidit, qui dixit, Utiliores esse plerumque inimicos objurgantes, quàm amicos objurgare metuentes. Illi enim dum rixantur dicunt aliquando vera, quæ corrigamus : isti autem minorem quam oportet exhibent Justitiæ libertatem, dum amicitiæ timent exasperare dulcedinem. Non mihi esse debet molestum pondus ætatis tuæ, dummodo conteratur palea culpæ meæ. I do not feel my self hurt by the words of Mr. *K.* against my self, much less by any free disclosure of my faults. But I confess I desired more Clemency to his Adversary, and more humble sense of his own frailty, when I read some passages in him against Mr. *Goodwin.* For example, part. 3. pag. 112, 113. much of two pages are taken up in [* *A solemn Profession of his discerning the Just hand of heaven, and the spirit of slumber on* Mr. *Goodwin, and the pompous display of his folly, to appear most ridiculous,* &c.] even daring to [*adore the hand of God in infatuating his parts, that* Balaams *Ass may see the hand of the Angel against the Prophet*] with more of the like. And what is the matter? Why Mr. *Goodwin* overseeingly wrote the word [*Antecedent*] for [*Consequent*] and [*Consequent*] for [*Antecedent.*] A hainous crime! When I read such passages as these in him, I began to think, how well I had sped, and *tantum non,* did owe him thanks for handling me so gently, even in those passages that others most blamed. But I

* Yet (if you be able to believe him) he tels his Reader he is sure there is no Pepper sprinkled throughout his Discourse, nor is he Conscious to himself of the least bitterness, &c.

saw

saw it was no wonder, if all my words were sifted to the bran *. *] Indeed I more desired in Mr. K. a conscience so tender as would have strained at some of all those palpable untruths in matter of fact, then a milder language to my self. But he tels us in his Epistle, that *Aliquando innocentius delinquendum erat, ne deessent in quibus condonandis*, &c. *Et quidni mihi gratuler fælicia quædam erratula*, &c. Whether he think also that he should *innocentius delinquere, & fæliciter errare*, that there may be matter for the honour of Gods Grace, as well as mans, I cannot tell.

2. As for the Manner of my handling these Controversies (which is the next thing that (more) needeth an Apology,) I expect to be blamed for these three things: 1. For unprofitable Altercations and Repetitions. 2. For too much curiosity and obscurity in some distinctions. 3. For too course and sharp a stile.

1. For the first, I knew not how to avoid it, without inconvenience. I must follow the leading of them that I reply to. I must not digress too farre, to fetch in more usefull matter then they put into my hands. Yet I think I have done somewhat in that kinde, as far as I saw fit. And when the same words of theirs, require the same answers, I am forced sometime to repeat them, where the occasion is repeated. Yet I can promise the Reader that I will not go near so far in this way of repetition, as more learned disputants do, and in particular Dr. *Twiss*.

2. For the second Exception, I must say, that many are mistaken in my way, in that they discern not the difference, 1. Between Necessary distinguishing and unnecessary. 2. Between Curiosity in the main Cause, and in the Means of discussing it. 3. Between curious Notions that are thrust on the Church and poor ignorant people, as Necessary and Certain; and such as we are forced to use with Learned men to discover their mistakes, and to expugne curiosity of Errour or Uncertainty, by exactness of indagation, and as curious an explication of the Truth. I am somewhat confident that my curious distinguishing (as some call it) is but of the later sort, in all these respects. For example, In the present Controversie about the Instrumentality of faith to Justification, that which offendeth me is, that Divines should be so dangerously curious, as to make a Logical Notion of such Necessity, which Gods Word never used, nor for ought I know, the Church for many a hundred year; and which poor people cannot comprehend: Yea and that they may lay so much of the difference between us and the Papists on this point,

(a) thereby

thereby moſt dangerouſly hardening them, when they ſhall diſcover our Errour; and occaſion them to triumph over us, and to think, that the reſt of our Doctrine is like this? And that this Inſtrumentality is ſtill ſo contradiſtinguiſhed from Merit, as if there were no third way of Faiths Intereſt in our Juſtification, but it muſt needs be the one or the other. Yea and the moſt Learned in the upſhot flie to this, that *Credere* is not *Agere,* but *Pati,* and is but *Actio Grammatica,* or the name of Action, but Phyſically or hyperphyſically a ſuffering. Is not here a curious Doctrine of Faith and Juſtification? If *Ariſtotle* had been a Chriſtian he could not have comprehended it: Much more is it too fine for vulgar wits (as well as too falſe for lovers of the Truth.) In oppoſition to this, and in compaſſion of plain Chriſtians, I only ſay, that faith is the Condition of our Juſtification; or that the reaſon why we are Juſtified by it (ſuppoſing its Object, and its Aptitude) is, becauſe the Free Donor, Law-giver and Juſtifier will have it ſo, and hath deſigned it to this Office in his Promiſe or Teſtament. I think this is plain Doctrine, and fit for plain men. There's ſcarce the ſimpleſt man in the Town, if one offer him the Soveraigns pardon for Rebellion, on Condition he will thankfully Accept it, and promiſe to Rebell no more, but he knows this to be the reaſon why his Acceptance hath an Intereſt in his pardoning (*viz.* as the fitteſt Condition freely determined on by the Soveraign) without any more ado. And I think to reade him a Logick Lecture about Active or Paſſive Inſtrumentality, would more abuſe then enlighten his underſtanding. Yet the ſubtilties of thoſe whom I oppoſe, doth force me oft to diſtinguiſh, to expugne their Sophiſtry: and I am forced to uſe more accurate means to defend a plain Truth. And indeed, he that Defineth and Diſtinguiſheth well teacheth well. Confuſion is the Mother and Nurſe of Errour. Truth loves the Light. It is not ſound Diſtinction that I blame in any, but fancies and vain curioſities, and carrying us from Matter to Words, and making an appearance of difference, where there is none, and calling Confuſion by the name of diſtinction or explication. I am ſure a few obvious Diſtinctions, have been a Key to let many a truth into my underſtanding.

 Moreover I muſt deſire the Reader to conſider, when things ſeem too curious to him, and hard to be underſtood, whether it be not from the Nature of the ſubject matter, rather then from any unneceſſary Curioſity in me: If the matter be ſuch as will bear no more familiar and plain enodations and explications, I cannot help that.

As

As *Seneca* faith, *Epist. 58: Platoni imputes, non mihi hanc rerum difficultatem. Nulla est autem sine difficultate subtilitas.* I cannot better speak my minde then in the words of *Austin, li. 5. de Trinit. c. 1. Ab his etiam qui ista lecturi sunt, ut ignoscant peto ubi me magis voluisse quam potuisse dicere animadverterint, quod vel ipsi melius Intelligunt, vel propter mei eloquii difficultatem non intelligunt: Sicut ego eis ignosco; ubi propter suam tarditatem intelligere non possunt.* Pardon my obscure difficult expressions, and I will pardon your dulness of apprehension.

3. For the third Exception, *viz.* the sharpness of my stile, I have these things to say, 1. I dare not, nor will not wholly excuse it. I am too conscious of my frailty, to think my self innocent in this. I confessed my fault as to one even now; and I confess as to another (Mr *Walker*) I committed the same fault, by too unmannerly provoking expressions (Though I will take none for a competent Judge of the degree of my fault, that hath not read his Answer to *J. Goodwin*, and Mr *Gatakers* Vindication of Mr *Wottons* Defence.) The other passages that some accuse me of, are, I think, upon a forced mistaken sense of my words. The most real sharpness that ever I was guilty of, was against Mr *Tombes* in my Book of Baptism: and its too probable that in this against M^r *K*. I have transgressed: which if I have done, I heartily desire him, as I do all other Brethren whom I have offended, in compassion of humane frailty, to remit it; as I heartily do all those passages of his, which his Readers do generally judge so unsavoury. However I do adjure every Reader, that would not break the ninth Commandment, and wrong God and themselves and me by false censures, that they impute not my sharp expressions to a disesteem of Christian Unity and Peace, or a hatred to my Brother: and that by too impatient reception, they make it not an occasion of disaffection, or breach of peace in themselves. For the Lord knows, that, though my words may be too rough and earnest, yet my soul longeth after the Unity and Peace of the Church. And I never yet wrote against any Brother so sharply, but I could heartily live with him in dear Love and Communion; as I am confident I should do with these, if they were near me: For sure I am, I disagree not with those with whom I do converse; nor ever fell out with any Brother, to my remembrance, since I was a childe. Charge me with unmeet expressions if you please; but with no further Unpeaceableness, Disaffection, or Con-

(a 2) tempt

tempt of my Brethren, then you can prove. 2. I muſt intreat the Reader to diſtinguiſh carefully, between my ſpeeches againſt the Perſon, and againſt the Errour or Cauſe which I oppoſe. I confeſs, when I am confident that it is Errour that I ſpeak againſt, eſpecially if it appear to be foul or dangerous, I am apt to ſhame it, and load it with Abſurdities, and ſhew the nakedneſs of it to the Reader: In this caſe, I finde many take it as if I ſpoke all this of the Perſon, and cenſured him as abſurd, as I do his Opinion: which is an injurious charge; ſeeing a wiſe man may hold an abſurd Opinion. And I think, as I muſt not ſpeak contemptuouſly of my Brother for a leſſer Errour, ſo neither muſt I for his ſake, ſpeak lightly and favourably of his faults. Errour is not like confeſſed ſins, which none dare own, or encourage others in: but it is a Vice that diſpoſeth men to Infect all they can; and emboldneth them to defend it, and fearleſly to draw all others into the guilt. And therefore it needeth the moſt potent oppoſition, and the ſouls of our Brethren need the moſt effectual preſervative: And that muſt not be only by a naked, dull Confutation; but alſo by a diſcovery of the foulneſs, the ſinfulneſs and dangerouſneſs of the Errour. The Affections have need to be awaked, as well as the Underſtanding informed, in the preſent caſe; as well as againſt common moral Vices. I am ſure Seducers make no ſmall advantage, by moving the Affections, and why they that ſpeak Truth ſhould not do ſo, I cannot tell. If we muſt do ſo in Preaching, ſo muſt we in ſome Diſputings, ſtill ſuppoſing that Information go firſt, and exciting application be but ſubſervient, and be not the leading, or the principall part. Thoſe that take intellectuall Errour to be no ſinne, muſt deny the underſtanding to be under a Law, and its acts to be *participative* voluntary, and being commanded by the Will. And if Errour be ſinne, we may have leave to diſgrace it and deal with it as ſinne; provided that we maintain our Charity to the erring Brother. I am bound not to hate my Brother in my heart, but plainly to Rebuke him, and not ſuffer ſin to reſt upon him. If he take it ill, that makes not me the offendor, nor will diſcharge me from my duty. 3. I confeſs I think we are commonly too tender ear'd in ſuch caſes: of which I have ſpoken my minde already in the end of the Preface to my Book of Baptiſm. I have oft wondered to think what patience we expect (and juſtly) yea and finde, in many of the worſt of our hearers, when we ſpeak to them as cuttingly as poſſibly we can (and all too little:) and how

little

little we exercise or can allow to one another! and what silken ears the Preachers of humility have themselves? And I cannot but observe the strange partiality of the best: how zealous they are against a Toleration of Errours; and yet how impatient of being told of their own. Other mens should be cut down with the Sword, and theirs may not be plainly confuted by the Word: nor can we so skilfully butter and oyl our words, but that we shall be taken for contemners of our Brethren. Not that I am free from the same disease: but (though proud hearers judge him a proud speaker that deals plainly with them, yet) I can truly say of that sin, to the praise of my Physition, as *Seneca Epist. 8. Salutares admonitiones velut medicamentorum utilium compositiones litteris mando, esse illas efficaces in meis ulceribus expertus: quæ etiamsi persanata non sunt, serpere desierunt. Rectum iter quod serò cognovi, & lassus errando, aliis monstro.* And for my own stile in writing, it is but such as I would use in free speaking, if any Brethren were present: and I think they would then bear it. I would not be furious, nor yet would I be blockish; nor speak as without life about the matters of life. I say of earnestness as *Seneca* of wit, *Epist. 75. Qualis sermo meus esset si unà sederemus, aut ambularemus, tales esse Epistolas meas volo, quæ nihil habeant accersitum, aut fictum. Si fieri posset quid sentiam ostendere, quam loqui, mallem. Etiamsi disputarem, nec supploderem pedem,* &c. *hoc unum plane tibi approbare vellem, omnia me illa sentire quæ dicerem, nec tantum sentire sed amare. Non jejuna esse & arida volo, quæ de rebus tam magnis dicentur. Neq; enim Philosophia ingenio renuntiat. Hæc sit propositi nostri summa: quod sentimus, loquamur; quod loquimur sentiamus.*

4. One thing more I desire: that if my words be any where offensive, the Reader will do me that right, as to consider diligently the words that I Reply to: for without that, you cannot equally judge of mine. Though I do not feel my self smart by any words of Mr *K*'s, yet I knew not well how sufficiently to Reply to them, without manifesting them to be as they are. I remember *Hierom*, speaking of one *Evagrius* that pleaded for the Stoical impassionateness, saith he was, *Aut Deus, aut Saxum*: I am neither: and therefore must speak as I am. Yet this I will promise my most offended Brethren, that in the harshest of my Writings, I will not give my adversaries half so hard language, as did either *Hierom* the most Learned of the Fathers, or *Calvin* the most Judicious and

(a 3) Happy

Happy of the Reformers, no nor as D: *Twiſſe* the moſt Learned oppoſer of the Arminians. And I remember what it was that *Hierom* complained of (*adverſ. Ruffinum*) *Canino dente me rodunt, in publico detrahentes, legentes in angulis: Iidem Accuſatores & Defenſores; cum in aliis probent, quod in me reprobant: quaſi Virtus & Vitium non in Rebus ſit, ſed cum Authore mutetur.*

   I cannot blame the Reader if he be weary of this long Apologie, and ask, To what purpoſe are all theſe words? To whom I truly anſwer; More for thy ſake then mine own: becauſe ſome angry Divines that diſſent, do raiſe ſuch an *odium* againſt my Writings, upon the pretenſes before intimated, that they may thereby hinder thee from receiving any benefit, and entertaining the Truth. For my own ſake, I confeſs it little troubleth me; for I know it hath been the caſe of my betters, and I have greater matters to be troubled for. I can ſay as *Vict. Strigelius Epiſt. ad Weſenbech.* a little before his death, *Ego editione talium pagellarum nec nominis mei vanam gloriolam quæro, nec aucupium pecuniæ exerceo: Sed cupio Deo declarare meam gratitudinem pro maximis beneficiis; & Ecсleſiæ oſtendere meam confeſſionem, deniq; mediocribus ingeniis aliqua ex parte prodeſſe. Horum finium cum mihi optime ſim Conſcius; non metuo quorundam inſulſas aut venenatas reprehenſiones, ſed me & meos labores Filio Dei commendo. Scio meum Vitæ curriculum & breve & exiguum eſſe: Quare in hac brevitate peregrinationis ea dicam, ſcribam & faciam, quæ migrationem in vitam æternam non impediunt.* This Learned Divine (*Strigelius*) himſelf, and before him *Melancthon*, as peaceable as Learned (and many another beſides them alſo) have been ſo tired with the cenſures and reproaches of Divines, that it made them, if not weary of living, yet more willing to die: So that *Melancthon* thus wrote down before his death, the motives of his willingneſs to leave this world.

	A dextris.
A ſiniſtris.	*Venies in Lucem:*
Diſcedes a Peccatis:	*Videbis Deum:*
Liberaberis ab ærumnis &	*Intueberis Filium Dei:*
a Rabie Theologorum.	*Diſces illâ mira arcana quæ in hac vita intelligere non potuiſti: Cur ſic ſimus conditi: Qualis ſit copulatio duarum naturarum in Chriſto.*

Nay

Nay it is not only Dissenters, that do terrifie people from reading what I have written, by telling them of I know not what latent dangerous Errours; but even they that are of the same opinion with me: For example, I lately wrote, that [the Doctrine of Infallible perseverance of all the sanctified, was my strong opinion, and I was perswaded of its truth,] and I argued for it from Scripture; yet because I so far acknowledged my own weakness, as to say, that I was not so fully certain of it, as of the Articles of the Creed, and because I say, I think it unsafe for a backsliding scandalous Christian, to venture his salvation meerly on this controverted Point,] what offence is taken? what reports spread abroad? some proclaiming that I wrote against Perseverance (even when I wrote for it;) Others that I am turn'd Arminian: Others that I am dangerously warping! In so much that some of my nearest friends, for whose good I published that Book, were ready to throw it by for fear of being infected with my doctrine against Perseverance! The enemies Instruments be not all unlearned nor ungodly.

For my part, I commend their zeal against Errour, so it be Errour indeed, and so they will moderate it with Charity and Humility. I am as strongly perswaded that its the Dissenters that erre, as they are that its I. And were they as zealous against Errour indeed, I think I might have spared the labour of such Writings as these. But I remember how they reprehended *Beatus Rhenanus* for his supposed covetousness, *Beatus est Beatus: attamen sibi.* So are such Brethren charitable, *sibi & suis.* And all this comes *a studio partium*, and because the Doctrine of the Unity of Christs Body, and the Communion of Saints (as Saints) is not reduced to practice; and we love not men so much for being of the same Body, as for being of the same Side or Party with us; nor for being in the same Christ, as for being of the same Opinion. If he that knows Christ knows all things; and if Interest in Christ alone be enough to make us Happy; then is it enough to make our Brother Amiable; though still we may be allowed the dislike of his faults.

Which side the Truth lies on, in the Points here debated, I willingly leave the Reader to judge according to the evidence that shall appear to him in the perusal. I desire no more of him, but Diligence, Impartiality, and Patience in his studying it: And I again intreat my Brethren to believe that I write this in an unfained Love of Peace and them: and that accordingly they will receive it: and where they meet with any of the effects of my infirmity, which may seem provoking and injurious to them, they will compassionately remit them; remembring that Heaven will shortly Reconcile our differences.

Kederminster, Aug. 1. 1653.

THE CONTENTS.

The Prologue to *Mr.* Blake, pag. 1
Certain Distinctions and Propositions explaining my sense, How Christ as King is the Object of Justifying Faith, §. 1. 3
Ten Arguments proving that Christ as King and Head is the object of the Justifying Act of Faith, §. 1. 3, 4
The common Distinction between Fides Quæ, *and* Fides Quâ Justificat, examined, §. 1. 7
The danger of the contrary Doctrine, §. 1. 8
The former Doctrine defended against *Mr.* Blakes Exceptions, §. 1. 9
The same defended against more of his Exceptions: and the faith Heb. 11, explained, §. 2. 10
James 2. about Justification by Works, explained and vindicated, §. 3. 12
How far Works Justifie, §. 3, & 4. 14, 15
Why I wrote against the Instrumentality of Faith in Justifying, §. 5. ibid
Ethical Active improper Receiving, distinguished from Physical Passive proper Receiving, §. 5. 17
How Christ dwels in us by Faith, §. 5. ibid
Mr. Bl's Exceptions against my opposition of Faiths Instrumentality in Receiving Christ, considered, §. 6. 18
Mr. Bl's dangerous Doctrine, That God is not the sole efficient, nor any Act of God the sole Instrument of Justification, §. 7, & 8. 19
Mr. Bl's contradiction, that faith is the Instrument of man, and yet man doth not Justifie himself, §. 9. 20
Whether Faith be both Gods Instrument and mans in Justification, §. 10. 21
Further, how Christ is said to Dwell in us by Faith, §. 10. 22
The common opinion of Faiths Instrumentality opened: and the Truth further explained, §. 11. 23
More of *Mr,* Bl's reasoning on this, confuted, §. 12. 27

(b) *Whether*

Whether God make use of our Faith as his Instrument to Justifie us, §.13
                                                                    28
Whether the Covenant of God be his Instrument of Justification, §.14.28
Mr.Bl's arguing against the Instrumentality of the Promise confuted, §
                                                                    15,& 16. 29
Mr.Bl's dangerous Doctrine confuted, that [the Efficacy that is in the Gospel to Justification it receives by their Faith to whom it is tendred,
                                                                    §.17,& 18. 30
Whether Mr.Bl. say truly, that the Word hath much less an Influx to the producing of the Effect by a proper. Causality, then faith, §.19. 31
In what Way of Causality the Word worketh, §.20. 32
Whether the Word be a Passive Instrument, §.21, 33
Mr.Bl's strange Doctrine examined, that [the Word is a Passive Instrument of Justification, §.22,& 23. 34
More against Mr.Bl's Doctrine, that [Faith through the Spirit gives efficacy and power of Working, to the Gospel, in forgiving sins] §.24. 35
Fuller proof of the most proper Instrumentality of the Gospel in Justification, §.25. 36
Mr.Bl. Contradiction, in making Faith and the Gospel two Instruments, both making up one compleat Instrument, §.25. 37
More against Mr.Bl. strange doctrine, that [Faith gives efficacy as an Instrument to the Word, §.25. 37
A Condition, what; and how differing from meer Duty, §.27. 38
The difference between us compromized or narrowed, §.27, 40
Of Evangelical personal Righteousness, §.28. 41
What Righteousness is, §.28. 43
In what sense our personal Righteousness is Imperfect and perfect, §.28. 44
Isa. 64.6. explained, Our Righteousness is as filthy rags, § 29. 46
How Holiness is perfect or Imperfect, §.30. 47
Whether Holiness or Righteousness be capable neither of perfection nor Imperfection, but in relation to a Rule, §.31,& 32. 48
Concerning my charging learned Divines with Ignorance and other harsh speeches, §.33. 49
We are not denominated personally righteous for our conformity to the Law of Works only, or properly, proved, §.33. 50
Whether as Mr.Bl. saith, the old Rule, the Moral Law be a perfect Rule, and the only Rule, §.33. 51
A Vindication of the Author from the imputation of Arrogance, for charging some Divines with Ignorance, §.33. 49

Whether

whether Imperfect Conformity to the Law be Righteousnefs, an Image lefs like the patern is an Image, §.35. 54
How fairly Mr.Bl.chargeth me to fay [Sincerity is the New Rule, §.36. 55
An Anfwer to Davenants Teftimony cited by Mr.Bl. §.37. 56
How far Unbelief and Impenitency in profeffed Chriftians are violations of the New Covenant, §.38. 57
How many forts of Promifes or Covenants there are in Scripture mentioned, §.39. 58
How far Hypocrites and wicked men, are, or are not in Covenant with God; in feveral Propofitions, §.39. 60
An enquiry into Mr.Bl's meaning, of Dogmatical faith, and being in Covenant, §.39. 64
Of the Outward Covenant (as they call it) and how far the Unbeliever or Hypocrites may have right to Baptifm and other Ordinances, §.3. ibid
Mr Bl's Abfurdities fuppofed to follow the reftraint of the Covenant to the Elect, confidered, §.41. 80
Our own Covenanting is the principal part of the Condition of Gods promife or Covenant of Grace, §.41. 81
Whether I make the Seal of Baptifm, and of the Spirit, to be of equal latitude, §.42. 84
Mr.Bl's dangerous argument, anfwered [The great Condition to which Baptifm engageth, is not a prerequifite in Baptifm: But Juftifying Faith is fuch: Therefore] §.43. ibid
More of Mr.Bl's Arguments anfwered, §.44.& 45. 8(
My Arguments Vindicated from Mr.Bl's Exception, §.46.to 52. 8;
26 Arguments to prove, that it is Juftifying faith which God requires of them that come to Baptifm, and that Mr.Bl's doctrine in this is unfound and unfafe, §.52. 9.
Of Mr.Bl's Controverfie with Mr.Firmin, §.53. 10;
My afferting of the Abfolute promife of the firft Grace, vindicated, §.55 108
Whether our Faith and Repentance be Gods Works, §.55. 109
What Life was promifed to Adam in the firft Covenant, §.56. 111
Of the Death threatned by the firft Covenant, §.57. 112
Whether the Death of the body by feparation of the foul were determinately threatned, §.58. 113
Of the Law as made to Chrift, §.59. 115
Whether the Sacrament feal the Conditional promife Abfolutely? or the Conclufion

Conclusion [*I am Justified and shall be saved*] *Conditionally*, §.60, 61,62,63. 115
The Nature of sealing opened, §.64. 118
20 Propositions shewing how God sealeth, §.64. 119
That the minor being sealed, the Conclusion is not eo nomine sealed, as Mr.Bl.affirmeth, §.65. 123
How Sacraments seal with particular Application, §.67. 125
Mr.Bl's doctrine untrue, that [*If the Conclusion be not sealed, then no Proposition is sealed*] §.68. 126
Whether it be Virtually written in Scripture that Mr.Bl. is Justified, §.69. 126
More about Conditional sealing, §§.70,71. 128
Whether it is de fide that Mr.Bl. is Justified, 72,73,74. 129
In what sense we deny that Conclusion to be de fide, §.75. 133
That Divine Faith hath Evidence, as well as Certainty. Rob. Baronius and Rada's *words to the contrary, examined*, §.75. 134
The difference between Mr.Bl. and me contracted, and a plain cogent Argument added, to prove that the Conclusion fore-mentioned is not sealed, §.76. 139
The possibility but vanity of Conditional sealing, §.77. 140
More of Mr.Bl's Reasons answered, §.78,to 81. 141
The danger of teaching men, that they are bound to believe that they are Justified, and shall be saved, §.81. 142
In what sense the Covenant commandeth perfect obedience, §.82. 144
Mr.Bl's Reasons examined, concerning the Covenants commanding perfection, §.82,to 91. 144
How far true believers are Covenant-breakers, §.84. 148
The Covenant is Gods Law, §.91. 152
The Conclusion Apologetical against the charge of singularity, §.92. 152

The

The Prologue.

MY Reverend and dearly beloved Brother, I remember that when I met you last at *Shrewsbury*, you told me that you had sent to the Presse a Treatise of the *Covenants*, and desired me not to be offended, if you published in it some things against my Judgement: Your Treatise is since come to my hands, and upon a brief perusall of some part of it, I am bold to let you know this much of my thoughts, 1. That I very much value and honour your Learned Labours, and had I been M*r* *Vines* or M*r* *Fisher*, I might rather have given (in some respects) a higher commendations of your Book: And especially I love it for its sound discoveries of the Vanity of the Antinomians. 2. So farre am I from being offended at your Writing against my Writings, that (as I have oft said concerning M*r* *Owen*, since I saw his Book against me, even so do I by you) I never honoured you so much (though much) nor loved you so dearly (though dearly) before as since; for I see more of your worth then I saw before. For where I erre, why should I be offended with any brother for loving Gods Truth and mens souls, above my Errours, or any seeming Reputation of mine that may be ingaged in them, and for seeking to cure the hurt that I have done? God forbid that I should seek to maintain a Reputation obtained by, or held in an opposition to the Truth. I take all my Errors in Theology (even in the highest revealed points, *particulaliter*) to be my sinnes; but especially my divulged Errors: And I take him for my best friend, that is the greatest enemy to my sins. And where I erre not, I have little cause for my own sake to be offended at your opposition. For as you are pleased to honour me too highly both in your Epithetes and tender dealing, yea in being at so much pains with any thing of mine, and in stooping to a publick opposition of that which you might have thought more worthy of your contempt, so I know you did it in a zeal for God and Truth, and you thought all was Error that you opposed; so that in the general we fight under one Master, and for one Cause, and against one Enemy: You are for Christ, 1. For Truth and against Errors, so farre as you know it, and so am I. I know you wrote not against Me, but against my Errors, reall or supposed. And truly, though I wou'd not be shamelesse or impenitent, nor go so far as *Seneca*, to say we should not object a common fault to singular persons (*Vid.Cor.de Iri*, l.3. c.26.p. (*mihi*) 452. no more then to reproach a Blackmore with his colour; yet I

B see

see so much by the most Learned and Judicious, to assure me that *humanum est errare*, and that we know but in part, that I take it for no more dishonour, to have the world know that I erre, then for them to know that I am one of their Brethren, a son of *Adam*, and not yet arrived at that blessed state where that which is childish shall cease, and all that is imperfect shall be done away. Only if my Errors be greater then ordinary, I must be humbled more then ordinary, as knowing that my sin is the cause that I have no greater illumination of the Spirit. I have truly published to the world my indignation against the proud indignation of those men, that account him their enemy that shall publiquely contradict them.

2. Yet must I needs tell you, that in the points which you contradict, I finde no great alteration upon my understanding by your Writings; whether it be from the want of evidence of truth in your Confutation, or through the dulnesse of my Apprehension, I hope I shall better be able to judge, when I have heard from you next. I think I may safely say, It is not from an unwillingnesse to know the Truth. And one further difference there is in our Judgements: For my Judgement is, that it is not so convenient nor safe a way to publish suddenly a reply to your opposition, as to tell you my thoughts privately (seeing we live so near) and to bring the Points in difference by friendly collations to as narrow a compass as we can, and make as clear a discovery of each others meanings as may be; and then by joynt consent to tell the world our several Judgements, and our Reasons, as lovers of the Truth and of each other; that so others may have the benefit of our friendly Collations and Enquiries; and may be thereby advantaged for the more facile discovery of the Truth. Truly I would have all such Controversies so handled, that all the vain altercations might lye in the dust in our studies, and that which is published might be in one Volume friendly subscribed by both parties. In this I perceive by your practise, your Judgement differs from mine; and that you rather judge it fittest to speak first by the Presse, that the world may hear us. I crave your acceptance of these Papers, rather in this private way, and that you will signifie to me in what way I shall expect your return, wherein I think it fitter you please your self then me. I shall faithfully give you an account of the effect of your Arguments on my weak understanding; but not in the order as they lye in your Book, but I will begin with those Points which I judge to be of greatest moment.

---

§. 1.

Mr *Blake* Treat. of Covenants, *pag.* 79.

IT is also true that faith accepts Christ as a Lord, as well as a Saviour: But it is the Acceptation of him as a Saviour, not as a Lord, that Justifies: Christ Rules his People as a King, Teacheth them as a Prophet, but makes Atonement for them only as a Priest, by giving himself in Sacrifice, his blood for Remission of sins: These must be distinguished, but not divided: Faith hath an eye at all, the blood of Christ, the command of Christ, the doctrine of Christ, but as it lies and fastens on his blood, so it Justifies. He is set out a propitiation through faith in his blood, Rom. 3. 24. not through faith in his command. It is the blood of Christ that cleanseth all sin, and not the Soveraignty of Christ. These confusions of the distinct parts of Christs Mediatorship, and the speciall offices of faith may not be suffered. Scripture assignes each its particular place and work; Soveraignty doth not cleanse us; nor doth blood command us: Faith in his blood, not faith yielding to his Soveraignty doth Justifie us.

§. 1.

§. 1.

R. B. THis is a Point of so great moment in my eyes, that I resolve to begin with it. I doubt not but the difference between you and me is only about the bare methodizing of our Notions, and not *de Substantia rei*: But I doubt left your doctrine being received by common heads, according to the true importance of your expressions, may do more against their salvation then is yet well thought on: And that not *per accidens*, but from its proper nature; supposing the impression of the soul to be but answerable to the objective doctrinal seal. I am no friend to the confusion that you here speak against; and I am glad to find you so little in love with it, as to pass your judgement that it is not to be suffered: For now I rest assured that you will not be offended, when here or hereafter, I shall open your guiltiness of it; and that you will not be unwilling of what may tend to your cure. These two or three necessary distinctions I must first here premise, before I can give a clear answer to your words.

1. I distinguish still between constitutive Justification or Remission by the Gospel grant or Covenant, called by most *Justificatio Juris*, and Justification *per sententiam Judicis*. 2. I distinguish between constitutive Legal Justification as begun, and as continued or consummate. 3. Between the Physical operation of Christ and his Benefits on the intellect of the Beleever *per modum objecti apprehensi*, as an intelligible *species*; and the moral conveyance of Right to Christ and his Benefits, which is by an act of Law or Covenant-donation. 4. Between these two questions, 'What justifieth *ex parte Christi?* and What justifieth, or is required to our Justification *ex parte peccatoris?* 5. Between the true efficient causes of our Justification, and the meer condition, *sine qua non, & cum qua*. 6. Between Christs Meriting mans Justification, and his actual justifying him, by constitution or sentence.

Hereupon I will lay down what I maintain in these Propositions, which (some of them) shall speak further then the present Point in Question, for a preparation to what followeth.

Prop. 1. Christ did Merit our Justification (or a power to justifie) not as a King, but by satisfying the justice of God in the form of a servant.

Prop. 2. Christ doth justifie *Constitutivè* as King and Lord, *viz. ut Dominus Redemptor*, i.e. *quoad valorem rei*, he conferreth it, *ut Dominus gratiæ beneficiens*: but *quoad modum conditionalem conferendi, ut Rector & Benefactor*. For it is Christs enacting the new Law or Covenant, by which he doth legally pardon or confer Remission, and constitute us Righteous, supposing the condition performed on our part. And this is not an act of Christ as a Priest or Satisfier; but joyntly, *ut Benefactor & Rector*.

Prop. 3. Christ doth justifie by sentence, as he is Judge and King, and not as Priest.

Prop. 4. Sentential Justification, is the most full, compleat and eminent Justification; that in Law being *quoad sententiam*, but virtual Justification; though *quoad constitutionem debiti & relationis*, it be actual Justification.

Prop. 5. Faith justifieth not by receiving Christ as an object which is to make a real impression and mutation on the intellect, according to the nature of the *species*: I say, To justifie, is not to make such a real change: Though some joyn with the Papists in this, and tell me, that as the Divine Attributes make their several moral Impressions on the soul according to their several natures, so do the satisfaction and merits of Christ, apprehended, procure comfort and joy, and a justifying sentence to be pronounced in the soul it self: and so the apprehension of Christs Soveraignty causeth our subjection (which last is true.)

Prop. 6 Faith therefore can have no Physical Causation or Efficiency in justifying; seeing that the work to be done by us, is not *nosmetipsos Justificare*, in whole or in part, but only *Jus acquirere ad Beneficium gratis sed conditionaliter collatum*: It is a Relative change that is made by Justification, and not a Real or Physical.

Prop. 7. The Legal, formal interest, or conducibility of Faith to our Justification, cannot therefore be any other then that of a Condition, in the proper Law-sense, as the word [Condition] is used, *viz.* that *species* of conditions which they call *Voluntariæ vel Potestativæ*, and not *Casuales vel Mixtæ*.

Prop. 8. Scripture doth not say (that I can finde) that Faith justifieth; but that *we are justified by Faith*: I therefore use the later phrase rather then the former, both because it is safest to speak with the Scripture, and because the former speech seemeth to import an Efficiency; but the later frequently imports no more then a meer condition. Yet I will not quarrell with any that speaks otherwise, nor refuse to speak in their phrase while I dispute with them, as long as I first tell them my meaning.

Prop. 9. Though, *ex parte Christi*, our several changes proceed from his several Benefits, and parts of his Office exercised for us; yet, *ex parte nostri, i.e. fidei*, it is one entire apprehension or receiving of Christ as he is offered in the Gospel, which is the Condition of our interest in Christ, and his several Benefits; and the effect is not parcelled or diversified or distinguished from the several distinct respects that faith hath to its object. Christ meriteth Remission for us as Satisfier of Justice; and he actually justifieth us as Benefactor King and Judge, and he teacheth us as Prophet, and ruleth us as King. The real mutations here on us, receive their diversification partly from our faith, because there faith doth *efficere* or *causare*; As we learn of Christ because we Beleeve him, or Take him for our Teacher: We obey him because we Take him for our King, *&c.* But it is not so with the Conveyance of meer Right or Title to Christ and his Benefits. Faith doth not obtain Right to Remission and Justification distinctly as it receiveth his Righteousness, or himself as Priest; and so Right to the Priviledges of Christs Government, distinctly as it taketh him as King; nor Right to Adoption, as it taketh him as a Father; nor Right to Glory, as it taketh him as Glorifier: no more then all inferiour benefits (as Title to Magistracy, Ministry, Health, House, Lands, *&c.*) proceed and are diversified by the divers aspects of our faith on Christ. The true Reason of which is this; That Right to a benefit is the meer effect of the Gift (Donation) or Revealed Will of the Giver: And therefore no Act of the Receiver hath any more interest, or any other then it pleaseth the Donor to assign or appoint it to have. So that (*supposita actus natura*) all the formall Civil interest comes from Gods meer Will, as Donor: (for to the Absolute Benefactor doth it belong, as to conferre all Right to his freely-given Benefits, so to determine of the Time and Manner of Conveyance, and so of the Conditions on the Receivers part.) The nature of the Act of Faith is caused by God, as Creator of the old and new Creature; I mean of our natural faculties, and their supernatural endowments or dispositions: And therefore this is presupposed *in ordine naturæ* to faiths Legal interest: As God is first the Maker of faith, before he is the Maker of

Adams.

Adams body: Faith is to be considered as being Faith (*i. e.* such acts exercised about such objects) in order of nature, before it can be rightly considered as justifying or the condition of Justification: Seeing therefore it receives all its formal Legal interest from God, as Legislator and Donor of Christ and his benefits, which is after its material aptitude *ad hoc officium*; its interest must not be gathered directly, *ex natura actus*, but *ex constitutione donantis & ordinantis*: And therefore you must first prove out of the Gospel, that *It is the Ordination of God,* that as Christs several actions have their several effects for us and on us, so our faith shall be the proper condition of each of these various effects, *quâ apprehendit,* as it Beleeveth or Accepteth each distinct effect, or Christ distinctly as the cause of that effect, *& etiam consideratum in modo causandi.* But, alas, how invisible is the Proof of this in all your Writings? (I will leave the rest of the Propositions, by which I intended here together to have opened some more of my sense, till afterwards, because I will not interrupt the present business.) Here, either my Understanding is too shallow to reach your sense, or else you are guilty, *quoad literam,* of very great confusion; (which one would think should have befallen you at any time, rather then when you are blaming others of unsufferable confusion:) and yet *quoad sensum involutum,* of more dangerous, unscriptural, unproved Distinction.

1. Your expressions confound Christ and his Actions, with mans faith in our Justification: Or, these two Questions [By what are we justified *ex parte Christi?*] and [By what are we justified *ex parte nostri?*]

2. Your implied sense, even the heart of your reasoning, consisteth in this assertion, that [As our Right, as to the several benefits received, is to be ascribed distinctly to several distinct Causes on Christs part, so also as distinctly are the particular Benefits, *quoad Debitum vel Titulum,* to be ascribed to the several distinct apprehensions of these Benefits (as most say) or of Christ as diversly causing them (as some say.)] And here I cannot but complain of a treble injustice that you seem to me guilty of (even in this elaborate Treat. wherein you correct the Errors of so many others.)

1. Against the Truth and Word of God, in implying it to have done that, even in the great Point, the Constitution of the Condition of Justification and Salvation, which is nor to be found done in all the Scripture.

2. Against the souls of men: 1. In such nice mincing and cutting the Condition of their salvation, to their great perplexity, if they receive your doctrine. 2. And also in not affording them one word of Scripture or Reason for the proof of it, which is injustice, when you are Confuting others and Rectifying the world in so great a Point. 3. Lastly (and leastly) it is evident injustice to your Friend, to Accuse him (for it is no hard matter to know whom you mean) with confounding the distinct parts of Christs Mediatorship, which he still distinguisheth as exactly as he can: though he do not distribute as many offices to Faith, as there are objects for it, or as he doth to Christs several Works. Why did you not name one line where I do confound the parts of Christs Offices? I pray you do it for me in your next.

I will not trouble you much with Arguments for my opinion in this Point, seeing you meddle with none already laid down, and seeing I have done it over and over to others, and because I am now but Answering to your Confutation. Only let me tell you, that the Proof lieth on your part. For when I have once proved, that God giveth Christ and his Benefits to man, on Condition he will Beleeve in Christ or Accept him: If you will now distinguish, and say, It is Accepting his satisfaction, which is the Condition of Justification, and Accepting him as King, which is the Condition of Sanctification or Glorification, &c. you must prove this to be true. For *non est distinguendum vel limitandum ubi Lex non distinguit vel limitat.* If God say [Beleeve in the Lord Jesus, and thou shalt be saved,] and you say, [Beleeving in him as Priest is the only Condition of saving thee from guilt: and Beleeving in him as King, is the only Condition of saving thee from the power of sin, &c.] you must prove this which you say. Or if you will not say [It is the only Condition] but [the only instrument] you give up the Cause. For the word [Condition] is it that expresseth its neerest Legal Interest in justifying or conveying any Right: and that which you call its Instrumentality, is but the natural Aptitude and Remote Interest.

1. It is the Receiving of Christ as Christ that justifieth (as the Condition of Justification) But he is not received as Christ, if not as Lord-Redeemer.

2. Justifying faith is (say the Assembly) the Receiving of Christ as he is offered in the Gospel: But he is offered in the Gospel as Saviour and Lord, and not as Saviour only: Therefore, &c.

3. Justifying faith is the Receiving of Christ as a full Saviour: But that cannot be except he be received as Lord. For to save from the power of sin, is as true a part of the Saviours Office, as to save from the guilt.

4. Justifying faith receiveth Christ as he justifieth us, or as he is to justifie us: But he doth justifie us as King and Judge and Benefactor; as he satisfieth and meriteth in the form of a servant under the Law.

5. If receiving Christ as a Satisfier and Meriter, be the only faith that gives right to Justification, then on the same grounds you must say, It is the only faith that gives right to further Sanctification and to Glorification: For Christ Merited one as well as the other.

6. Rejecting Christ as King, is the condemning sin: Therefore receiving him as King is the justifying faith, *Luk.* 19.27. *Those mine enemies that would not that I should reign over them, bring,* &c. The reason of the consequent is, because unbelief condemneth (at least partly) as it is the privation of the justifying faith: I speak of that condemnation or peremptory sentence which is proper to the new Law, and its peculiar condemning sin, eminently so called.

7. *Psal.* 2. Kissing the Son and submitting to him as King, is made the condition of escaping his wrath.

8. *Matth.* 11.28,29,30. The condition of Ease and Rest (from guilt, as well as power of sin) is our coming to Christ as a Teacher and Example of meeknefs and lowliness, and our Learning of him, and Taking on us his yoke and burden.

9. That faith which is the Condition of Salvation, is the Condition of Justification or Remission: But it is the receiving of Christ as King, as well as Satisfier, that is the Condition of Salvation: Therefore, &c. 1. Justification at judgement, and Salvation (from hell, and adjudication to Glory) are all on the same conditions, *Mat.* 25. *& ubique.* 2. Justification is but the justifying of our Right to Salvation; *i.e.* sentencing us as *Non reos Pœnæ* (*quia Dissoluta est obligatio*) *& quibus debetur præmium*; Therefore Justification and Salvation must needs have the same conditions on our part. 3. Scripture no where makes our faith, or act of faith, the Condition of Justification, and another of Salvation. But contrarily ascribeth both to one. 4. When *Paul* argueth most zealously against Works and for Faith only, it is in respect to Salvation generally, and not to Justification only. *Eph.* 2.8,9. *By grace ye are saved through faith,* &c. *Not of works, left*

any man should boast. Tit. 3. 5. *Not by works of righteousness which we have done, but according to his Mercy he saved us,* &c. Never more was said against Justification by Works (which *Paul* excludes) then against Salvation by them : Nor is it any more dishonour to Christ that he should give Justification or Remission on Condition of our Accepting him as King, then that he should give Salvation on that Condition. 5. Pardon of sin and freedom from hell, must needs have the same Condition : For pardon respecteth the punishment as truly as the sin. *Pæna & Vænia sunt adversæ :* Pardon dissolveth guilt ; Guilt is the obligation to punishment. Yet I speak here only of a plenary and continued pardon.

10. Lastly, If Accepting Christ as Lord-Redeemer, be the *Fides quæ Justificat,* i.e. *quæ est conditio Justificationis,* then it is neerly, strictly and properly the justifying act of faith, as the accepting of Christs Righteousness is : But the Antecedent is granted by all Divines that I have had to do with : Therefore,&c. For the general cheat is by the distinction of *Fides quæ Justificat* (that is, say they, the Accepting of Christ as Saviour and Lord, by a faith disposed to fruitfulness in obedience) and *Fides quâ Justificat* (and that is the Accepting of Christs Righteousness as our formal Righteousness, say some : Or the Accepting of Christs Righteousness as the meritorious cause of our Righteousness, say others : Or the Accepting of Christ himself as Priest, say others :) Now this *Fides* [*Quâ*] either respecteth the meer matter of faith, or it respecteth the formality of the effect, or it respecteth the Formal Reason of faiths interest in the effect, *ut medium, vel causa.* 1. If [*quâ*] respect only the matter of faith, then 1. it is an unfit phrase ; for [*quâ*] and [*quatenus*] are strictly used to express the formal Reason of things. 2. And then the Accepting of Christ as Lord must be the *Fides Quâ* too : for that is confessed to be materially an act of that faith which justifieth. 2. If [*Quâ*] respect the formality of the effect, and so the respect of faith to that effect rather then another ; then faith is not [justifying] *quâ recipit Christum, sed quâ justificat :* And so the distinction containeth this truth, That *fides quæ sanctificat etiam justificat, sed non quâ sanctificat : & è contra.* But neither of these can be the sense of them that use this distinction in our case. 3. It must therefore be the former reason of faiths interest in justifying that is expressed by [*Quâ :*] and then it implieth the begging of the Question, or this false supposition [that *Fides quâ fides justificat*] I mean not *quâ fides in genere,* but *quâ hæc fides, viz. quæ est fiducia in Christum satisfactorem, vel acceptatio Christi.* Indeed the term [Accepting] implieth the gift and offer, and the constitution of that acceptance for the condition : But the Act it self is but the Matter apt to be the condition : If Christ had been given (or pardon) absolutely, or on some other condition ; then beleeving in him would not have justified. Therefore *fides in Christum quâ talis* doth not justifie ; but *quâ conditio Testamenti præstita :* though *fides in Christum quâ talis* had in its nature a singular aptitude to be chosen and appointed to this Honour and Office. So much to shew the vanity of that distinction (of much more that might be said.) Further the consequence of the *major* Proposition of my Argument, is made past all dispute, to them that will but well consider this ? To (be the condition of our Justification) speaks the nearest interest of faith in our Justification, that is, as it is *medium legale ;* or that kinde of causality which it hath ; which is to be *causa sine qua non, & cum qua :* Therefore it is a meer impossibility that the Receiving Christ as Lord should be the condition of our Justification (or the *fides quæ est conditio,* as they speak) and yet that we should not be justified by it as a condition, when performed ? It is no sounder speech, then to say, that is an efficient cause, which doth

not

not effect. Some Conditions (and most among men) are Moral impulsive causes: Faith is rather a *removens prohibens*, and each nothing in it that so well deserves the title of a Cause, as of a Condition: though unbelief may be said to be the Cause of our Not-being justified, as such causes are said to move God, when we speak according to the manner of men: Indeed if they will say (according to their principles) that *Fides in Christum Dominum que est conditio non justificat per modum instrumenti*; I shall grant it: But then 1. I shall say as much *de fide in Christum satisfacientem*. 2. Thus they grant it the interest of a Condition in our Justification: and I intend no more. We are justified by faith *as* the Condition of Justification: Therefore we are justified by every act of faith *which* is the Condition: For, *A quatenus ad omne valet consequentia*. Thus I have given you a few of those many reasons which might be given, to prove that the Accepting of Christ for Lord-Redeemer, and not only as Satisfier, or not only his Righteousness, is that Faith by which as a Condition we are justified. And what sad effects it may produce to teach the world that the only justifying act of faith is, The Accepting of Justification as merited by Christs blood, or the Accepting of Christs Righteousness to justifie them; it is not hard for an unprejudiced man to discern. For my part, in all my experience of the case of the ungodly that I have trial of, I can finde no commoner cause of their general delusion and perdition, then this very doctrine; which they have generally received, though not in such exact terms as it is taught them. I never met with the most rebellious wretch (except now and then one under terrors) but when they have sinned their worst, they still think to be saved, because they believe: And what is their beleeving? why they beleeve that Christ died for them, and therefore God will forgive them, and they trust for pardon and salvation to Christs death and Gods mercy: This were good, if this were not all; but if Christ were also received as their Sovereign and Sanctifier and Teacher: But if this were the only justifying act (as they usually speak) then I should not know how to disprove him that should tell me that all men in the world shall be saved that beleeve the Gospel to be true: or at least, the far greatest part of the most wicked men: For I am certain that they are willing not to be damned, and therefore Accept, or are Willing of Christ to save them from damnation: and I am sure they are Willing to be pardoned as fast as they sin, and that is, to be justified: and therefore must needs be Willing of Christ to pardon them (supposing that they beleeve the Gospel to be true) What therefore shall I say if a wicked wretch thus argue: He that hath the only justifying act of faith is justified: But that have I; for I Accept of Christ to forgive and justifie me by his blood: Therefore, *&c?* Shall I tell him that he dissembleth, and is not Willing? Why 1. Long may I so tell him before he will beleeve me, when he feels that I speak falsly and slander him. 2. And I should know that I slander him my self: Supposing that he beleeve that there is no pardon but by Christs blood, (as the devils and many millions of wicked men do beleeve:) For I know no man in his wits can be willing to be unpardoned and to burn in hell. Shall I give him the common answer (the best that ever was given to me,) that though the only justifying act be the receiving Christ or his Righteousness to justifie us, yet this must be ever accompanied with the receiving him as Sovereign, and a resolution to obey him? Perhaps I may so puzzle him for want of Logick or Reason; but else how easily may he tell me, that this receiving Christ as Lord, hath either the nature of a *medium ad finem*, or not? If it be no *medium*, the want of it in this case cannot hinder the Justification of that man that is sure he hath the sole justifying act it self: For as

meer

meer signs or idle concomitants do nothing to the effect, so the want of them hinders not the effect where all causes and means are present: But if I say, that this act of faith is a *means* to Justification; then I must either make it a Cause, or a Condition, or invent some new *medium* not yet known.

But you say [Soveraignty doth not cleanse us, nor doth blood command us.] *Ans.* 1. How ill is Soveraignty put in stead of the Soveraign? I say not that the reception of Chrifts Soveraignty doth justifie (those words may have an ill sense) but we are justified by receiving Christ as our Soveraign (which much differs from the former.) 2. Christ as Soveraign doth cleanse us, both from the guilt and power of sinne, by actual Remission or Justification, and by Sanctification. 3. Suppose you speak true, as you do, if you mean it only of Meriting our cleansing: What is this to our Question? But you adde [Faith in his blood, not faith yeelding to his Soveraignty doth justifie us.] *Ans.* This is something to the purpose, if it had been proved. But will a nude and crude Assertion change mens judgements? or should you have expected it? A text you cite, and therefore it might seem that you thought it some proof of this, Rom. 3. 24. But all the force of your Argument is from your dangerous addition, which, who will take for good Exposition? The text faith, He is set forth to be a propitiation, *through faith in his Blood.* And you adde [Not through faith in his Command.] 1. *Sed quo jure nescio.* Your exclusion is either upon supposition, that *faith in his Blood* is equipollent to *faith in his Blood only*; or else it is on some mysterious ground, which you should the rather have revealed, because it is not obvious to your ordinary Reader to discover it, without your revelation. If the former; 1. By what authority do you adde [only] in your interpretation? 2. Will you exclude also his Obedience, Resurrection, Intercession, &c? When *by the obedience of one many are made righteous?* and Rom. 8. 33, 34. *It is God that justifieth, who is he that condemneth? It is Christ that died, yea rather that is risen again; who is even at the right hand of God, who also maketh intercession for us.* 2. But the thing that you had to prove was not the exclusion of [faith in his Command] but of [faith in Christ as Lord and Teacher] or either: Receiving Christ as Ruler, goeth before the receiving of his particular Commands. And for the text, *Rom.* 3. 24. It was fittest for *Paul* to say [by faith in his blood] because he intends to connote both what we are justified by, *ex parte Christi,* and what *ex parte nostri,* but the former principally. I will explain my thoughts by a similitude or two.

Suppose a Rebell be Condemned, and lye in prison waiting for Execution; and the Kings Son being to raise an Army, buyeth this Rebell, with all his fellow prisoners, from the hand of Justice, and sendeth to them this message; If you will thankfully acknowledge my favours, and take me hereafter for your Prince or General, and lift your selves under me, I will pardon you (or give you the pardon which I have purchased) and moreover will give you places of Honour and Profit in my Army:] Here now if the Question be, What it is on the Princes part that doth deliver the prisoner? It is his ransom, as to the Impetration or Preparation: and it is his free-Grant, which doth it, as to the actual Deliverance. If it be askt What is it that Honoureth or Enricheth him? It is the place of Honour and Riches that by the Prince is freely given him. But if you ask on the offenders part, What it is that delivereth him as the condition? It is not his accepting Pardon and Deliverance (or the Prince as a Pardoner or Ransomer) that is the sole Condition of his pardon and deliverance from death: Nor is it the Accepting of the Honour (or of the Prince as one to honour him) that is the sole condition of his Honour: Nor is it accepting of Riches, that is the sole condition of enriching him. But it is entirely the accepting of the Prince for his General, and thankfull acknowledging his Ransom, that is the Condition of all together, and hath as near an interest in one part of the Benefit, as another.

Or suppose the condemned prisoner be a woman, and the Prince having Ransomed her, doth send this offer to her, That if she will thankfully acknowledge his favour, and take him for her Redeemer and Husband and Prince (to love, honour and obey him) he will deliver her, and make her his Queen, and she shall partake of all his Honour and Riches.] Here now if the Question be, What it is on his part that Redeemed her? What that Delivered her? What that honoured her? What that enriched her? each effect must be ascribed to its proper cause, and the causes not confounded: And she must distinctly apprehend, by what way and cause each priviledge comes. But if you ask only, What it is on her part that is the condition of enjoying these Benefits? Why it is but one entire, undivided Condition before mentioned: Will you here subtilly distinguish and say, that her taking him to deliver her, is the sole act which is the condition of her Deliverance? and her taking him to Dignifie her, is the sole condition of her Dignity? and her taking him as Rich, or to enrich her, is the sole condition of her enriching? No, It is one undivided condition that equally gives her interest in all. Much less is it the Accepting of his Riches, that is the sole condition of enriching her. Yet if any should in one Question include both, What on his part did save her from death? and what on her part? then it must be exprest as *Paul* did in the forementioned text, in our case: It is her Marrying or Accepting a Mercifull Redeemer. I should wrong you, by seeming to imply a doubt of your Apprehensiveness, if I should spend words in application of this to our case. Having been so much too tedious already, I will only adde; That the common doctrine in this Point, requires that there be as many acts of faith as there are Benefits from Christ to be received; and that each one is the Instrument of receiving that particular benefit: and so one act of faith Justifieth, another Adopteth, &c. And that act which receiveth Justification, which they call the Passive instrument thereof, in the upshot of all their Disputes they so describe, that it is apparent they mean *ipsam Justificationem passivam*: And so with them *Credere & Justificari* must be Synonimall termes: For so to receive Justification, is nothing but to be Justified.

---

§. 2.

Mr *Bl.* THere are several *acts of Justifying faith*, Heb. 11. *but those are not acts of Justification. It is not* Abrahams *obedience*, Moses *self-deniall*, Gideon *or* Sampsons *valour, that were their Justification: but his Blood who did enable them in these duties by his spirit.* Paul *went in these duties as high as they, living in more clear light and under more abundant grace. I doubt not but he out-topt them, and yet he was not thereby Justified; as* 1 Cor. 4. 4.

---

§. 2.

R. B. 1. IT is a strange phrase to call any act of faith [An act of Justification.] If you speak properly, you must mean it *efficienter vel constitutivè*: either that some act of faith is an act of Justification, as the efficient (but thats farre
from

from truth, to beleeve and to juftifie differ) or elfe that it is an act conftituting Juftification: But that is as far from truth; for then *Credere* fhould be *Juftificari*. If you fpeak improperly, you muft mean, either [An act effecting Juftification] as it feems you do; which is unfound, as well as improper: or elfe [An act which is the Condition of Juftification] which is found, though improper.

2. Who knows whether you mean that [none of thofe acts, *Heb.* 11. are acts of Juftification] or [not all of them] The proper importance of your words is for the former. But that is a dangerous untruth: for *verf.* 13. is judged by our Divines to contain a proper defcription of juftifying faith [they faw the promifes (*i.e.* the good promifed) a farre off, and were perfwaded of them, and embraced them, *&c.*] But which foever you mean, you fhould have proved your affertion. It will be eafily acknowledged that many there mentioned, were not the great and principall act which is the Condition of Juftification, as begun: But yet they may be leffer acts which are fecondary parts of the condition of continuing their Juftification. I do not think but that act [by which *Noah* became the heir of the righteoufnefs which is by faith,] *v.* 7. had a hand in continuing his Juftification, though it were the preparing the Ark, being moved with fear. I think that act by which *Abel* obtained witneffe that he was righteous, and that by which *Enoch* pleafed God, and without which it is impoffible to pleafe him, had fome hand in Juftification: I think thefe four great acts mentioned, *v.* 6. are part of the condition of Juftification. 1. To beleeve that God is (*viz.* that he is God, the Chief Good, the firft and laft, the principal efficient and Ultimate End, *&c.*) 2. The diligent feeking of him. 3. Beleeving that he is a rewarder of them that do fo. 4. Coming to him. (If this be diftinct from the fecond.) When the holy Ghoft doth of purpofe in the whole Chapter fet forth the glory and excellency of faith, I dare not be one that fhall imagine that he fpeaks all this of a lower fort of faith, and quite left out the noblest part which juftifieth, from his praifes.

3. Yet you fhould not (in my judgement) have called [*Abrahams* obedience, *Mofes* felf-denial, *Gideons* valour] acts of Juftifying faith: Are thefe acts of faith? If you mean that thefe acts are fruits of faith, its true: Or if you mean that an act of faith did excite the foul to each of thefe acts, and fo you mean not the obedience, valour, *&c.* but the act of faith which excited it, then you might call thofe acts of juftifying faith: But if I had called valour and obedience fo, I fhould have been blamed.

4. What mean you to fay Obedience and Valour was not their Juftification? Do you think that any act of faith is Juftification? You mean (if I may conjecture from your after-doctrine) the inftrument of Juftification.

5. But then how come you to fay next, that it is Chrifts blood? The blood of Chrift is the meritorious caufe of our Juftification, which improperly may be called alfo, the Matter of it: But I think it is neither our Juftification formally, nor the inftrument of it in proper fpeech.

6. But I thought the conteft in your Difpute had been, Which is the juftifying act of faith, and which not? and therefore when you denied thofe in *Heb.* 11. to be acts of Juftification (which I am forced to interpret [juftifying acts]) I expected to finde the true act afferted; but in ftead of that I finde the oppofite member, is [The blood of Chrift.] Is this indeed the Controverfie? Whether it be [Accepting Chrift as Lord] or [the blood of Chrift] that juftifieth? Never was fuch a Queftion debated by me, in the way here intimated. I am wholly for you, if this be the doubt: It is Chrifts blood that juftifieth meritoriously. But yet

we are juſtified by faith too, as the condition of our intereſt in free Juſtification. And why ſhould theſe two be put in oppoſition ? I lookt when you had aſſerted and well proved that it is not taking Chriſt as Lord, but only faith in his blood, that is the condition on our part, of our attaining Juſtification.

7. It would prove a hard task to make good, that there are ſeveral acts of juſtifying faith, by which we are not juſtified; without flying to great impropriety of ſpeech. By [juſtifying faith] you muſt mean, the Act, Habit, or renewed Faculty: If the act, then I think you will ſay, it is but one, or not many: Or at leaſt every act, which is juſtifying faith, muſt needs be ſuch as we are juſtified by: Or elſe why ſhould that act be called [juſtifying faith.] 2. But I doubt not but you mean the habit: And then 1. you confeſs that the habit is [juſtifying faith] which is true; not only as it helpeth to produce the act, but even as it is in it ſelf; But that will overthrow the doctrine of inſtrumentality. 2. It requireth another kinde of Diſputing then I here meet with, to prove that acts and habits of mans ſoul, are of ſo different a nature; that where the acts are ſpecifically diſtinct by the great diſtance and variety of objects, yet the habit producing all theſe is one and the ſame, and not diſtinct as the acts: and that obedience, ſelf-denial and valour, are acts of the ſame habit of faith, as is the accepting an offered Chriſt. 3. If you ſhould mean by [juſtifying faith] the faculty as ſanctified, then all other acts of that faculty as ſanctified, or of the Spirit there reſiding, might as well be called Acts of juſtifying faith. But I will not imagine that this is your ſenſe.

8. 1 *Cor.*4.4. is nothing to our buſineſs. *Paul* was not his own juſtifier: Though he knew not matter of condemnation.(*ſenſu Evangelico*, for no doubt he knew himſelf to be a ſinner) yet that did not juſtifie him, becauſe it is God only that is his Judge. Can you hence prove, that accepting Chriſt as Lord, is not the condition of our Juſtification? Then you may prove the ſame of the accepting him as Saviour. For *Paul* knew nothing by himſelf, as if he were guilty of not performing the one or the other: yet was he not thereby juſtified.

---

§. 3.

Mr *Bl.* JAmes *indeed ſaith, that* Abraham *was juſtified by works, when he had offered* Iſaac *his ſon on the Altar,* Jam.2.21. *but either there we muſt underſtand a working-faith, with* Piſcator, Paræus, Pemble, *and confeſs that* Paul *and* James *handle two diſtinct queſtions, The one, Whether faith alone Juſtifies without works? which he concludes in the Affirmative: The other, What faith juſtifieth? Whether a working faith only, and not a faith that is dead and idle? Or elſe I know not how to make ſenſe of the Apoſtle, who ſtreight inferres from* Abrahams *Juſtification by the offer of his ſon, And the Scripture was fulfilled, which ſaith,* Abraham beleeved God and it was imputed to him for righteouſneſs. *How otherwiſe do theſe accord? He was juſtified by works: and the Scripture was fulfilled, which ſaith, he was juſtified by faith?*

---

§. 3.

R.B. 1. IF *James* muſt uſe the term [Works] twelve times in thirteen verſes, (a thing not uſual) as if he had foreſeen how men would queſtion his meaning, and yet for all that we muſt beleeve that by [Works] *James* doth not mean [Works] it will prove as hard a thing to underſtand the Scripture, as the Papists would perswade us that it is: and that there is as great a necessity of a living deciding Judge.

2. Do but reade over all those verses, and put [working-faith] in stead of [Works] and try what sense you will make.

3. No doubt but *Paul* and *James* handle two distinct Questions, but not the two that you here expresse. *Paul* speaks of Meritorious Works, which make the Reward of Debt, and not of Grace, if you will beleeve his own description of them, *Rom.* 4. 4. But *James* speaks of no such Works, but of such as have a consistency with Grace, and necessary subordination to it: I prove it: The Works that *James* speaks of, we must endeavour for and perform, or perish (supposing time) But the works that *Paul* speaks of, no man must endeavour, or once imagine that he can perform, *viz.* such as make the reward to be of Debt and not of Grace. *Paul* speaks indeed of faith collaterally, but of Chrifts Merits and free-Grace, directly and purposely: So that the chief part of *Pauls* controversie was, Whether we are justified freely through Chrifts Merits? or through our own meritorious Works? But *James*'s question is, Whether we are justified by faith alone, or by faith with obedience accompanying it; and both as subordinate to Chrifts Merits? *Paul*'s question is, Of the meritorious Cause of our Justification: *James*'s question is, Of the condition on our parts, of our interest in a free Remission; supposing *Pauls* question determined, that Christ only is the Meriter. *Paul* speaks of Justification in *toto*, both in the beginning and progress, but especially the beginning: But *James* speaks only of Justification as continued and consummate, and not as begun: For both *Abrahams* and every mans was begun, before Works of Obedience: Though a disposition and resolution, and engagement to obey do go before.

4. If with the named Expositors, you understand by [Works] a working-faith; either you grant as much as I affirm, in sense; or else you must utterly null all the Apostle's arguing, from *verf.* 13. to the end. For if by [Working-faith] you suppose that *James* meant that God did not only make [Faith it self] to be the principall condition, but also [its Working] in obedience, when there is opportunity, to be the secondary condition (or part of the condition) of Justification as continued; as being the necessary *modus*, or effect (both which it is in several respects) then you say the same in sense as I do, only changing the Scripture terms without and against reason. It is ordinary to make the *modus* or quality of that matter which is the substance of the condition, to be as real a part of the condition as the matter it self. As when you oblige your Debtor to pay you so much currant English money; it is here as necessary that it be [English] and [Currant] as that it be money. If you promise your servant his wages, on condition he serve you faithfully: here [Faithfulness] is as real a part of the Condition, as [Service.] If a man take a woman in Marriage, and estate her in all his Lands, on condition that she will be to him [a chast, faithfull Wife:] here her chast fidelity is as true a part of the condition, as to be his Wife. So if God say, [He that hath a Working faith shall be justified and saved, and he that hath not, shall perish.] Here as faith is the principall part of the condition, so that it be a [Working] is the secondary, and as real a part of the condition, as that it be faith. And if Satan accuse you for not-beleeving (at Judgement) you must be justified, by producing your faith it self, so if he accuse you as having a faith that was not Working; how will you be justified but by the Works or Working disposition of that faith?

, §. 5. As for your single Argument here, I answer, 1. It is a weak ground to maintain that *James* twelve times in thirteen verses, by [Works] means not [Works;] and by faith alone (which he still opposeth) doth not mean faith alone, and all this because you cannot see the connexion of one verse to the former, or the force of one cited Scripture. Others may see it, and be able to shew sense in the Apostles words, though you or I could not. If every time we are at a losse in analysing or discerning the reason of a cited Text, we shall presume to make so great an alteration, meerly to bring all to hang together in our apprehensions, we shall finde Analyzers the greatest corrupters of Scripture. It is easie to imagine and fain a false Analysis with much plausiblenesse.

I conceive that *James* citeth these words expositorily: *q.d.* [And thus or in this sense the Scripture was fulfilled, *i.e.* historically, spoke truly of that which was long before done, *Abraham beleeved God, i.e.* so as to second his faith with actual obedience, *and it* (*i.e.* beleeving and so obeying, or trusting Gods promise and power so farre as to offer his son to death) *was imputed to him*, &c. 2. Or why may not *James* by concession preoccupate an objection? knowing that this would be objected he might say, *q.d.* I grant that the Scripture was fulfilled, which saith, *&c.* but yet though he were initially justified by faith only, yet when he was called to works, he was justified also by his obedience. 3. And is it not as hard to discern the reason of this citation, according to your exposition as mine? For you may as well say, [How do these accord, He was justified by a working faith; and The Scripture was fulfilled which saith, He was justified by faith?] For *James* is not proving that *Abraham* was justified by faith, and yet this is it the Text speaks: but that he was justified by works seconding faith, or, as you say, by a Working-faith: Where, if you put any emphasis on the term [Working] and account it to superadde any thing to meer beleeving, you say as much as I; and then *James* must cite that Text expositorily; and then whether according to my exposition or yours, varies not the case, seeing one faith as much for Works as the other.

But I suppose you will say, Faith which justifieth must be working; but it justifieth not *qua operans*. *Ans.* 1. True: nor *qua fides*, i.e. *qua apprehendit objectum*, if the *qua* speaks the formall reason of its interest in Justification. 2. But why cannot faith justifie unless it be working? If you say [Because that God hath made it the condition of Justification, that we beleeve with a working faith] and so that it be working is part of the Condition, you say the same in sense as I. If you say, either that working is necessary as a sign, that faith is true; or that the nature of true faith will work; both are truth: but to say this is the Apostle's sense, is to null all his Argumentation: For he pleads not for a meer necessity of signification or discovery, but for a necessity *ut medij ad Justificationem*; even that Justification which he cals [Imputing of Righteousnesse] and that by God. And he argueth not only Physically, what the nature of faith will produce; but morally, what men must do to such ends. And it is only as a condition that faith or its working nature can be necessary *ad finem ut media moralia*; if you speak of such an absolute necessity as the Text doth.

---

§. 4.

M^r *Bl.* ALL works before or after conversion, inherent in us, or wrought by us, are excluded from *Justification*.

§. 4.

§. 4.

R. B. 1. THe term [Works] signifieth either such as a Workman doth to deserve his wages for the value of his Work; which make the reward to be of Debt and not of Grace; and so its true: Or it signifieth all good actions; and so this saying is contrary to the scope of the Scripture. 1. Faith and Repentance are such works and wrought by us. 2. *James* asserteth the inclusion of such works. If you say, But faith and repentance justifie not as Good works: I easily grant it: That they be Good, floweth from the Precept: That they Justifie, floweth from the Promise, constituting them the Condition. If they should justifie because Good, their goodness must be such as may accrue to a Meritoriousness: But yet they must be Good, before they can justifie as Conditions of the free Gift: yea and have a peculiar eminent goodness, consisting in their aptitude to this work, and to Glorifie the free Justifier. *Mat.* 25. *Rom.* 2. *James* 2. with the greatest part of Scripture, look not with such a face as your Proposition. This may serve to your following words.

§. 5.

Mr Bl. *ANd these things considered, I am truly sorry that faith should now be denied to have the office or place of an instrument in our Justification: nay scarce allowed to be called the instrument of our receiving Christ that justifies us; because the act of faith (which is that which justifieth us) is our actual receiving Christ, and therefore cannot be the instrument of receiving. This is too subtle a Notion: We use to speak otherwise of faith. Faith is the eye of the soul whereby we see Christ, and the eye is not sight. Faith is the hand of the soul, whereby it receives Christ, and the hand is not receiving. And Scripture speaks otherwise: We receive remission of sins by faith, and an inheritance among them that are sanctified is received by faith,* Act. 18. 26. *Why else is this righteousness sometime called the righteousness of faith, and sometime the righteousness of God which is by faith, but that it is a righteousness which faith receives? Christ dwels in us by faith,* Eph. 3. 17. *By faith we take him in and give him entertainment: We receive the promise of the Spirit through faith,* Gal. 3. 14. *These Scriptures speak of faith as the souls instrument to receive Christ Jesus, to receive the Spirit from Christ Jesus.*

Whether faith be the Instrument of Justification.

§. 5.

R. B. 1. I Know not how to meddle with Controversies, but some body will be sorry or angry, which side soever I take. I am sorry that I have made you sorry, but not for that Doctrine which caused it; which yet I shall be, as soon as I can see cause for it.

2. Why would you not here attempt to prove, that which you are so sorry should be denied, *viz.* That faith is the instrument of Justification? Will all your Readers take your complaint for a demonstration of the errour of what you complain of?

3. I was as sorry that men called, and so called faith the instrument of Justification, as you are that I deny it: And as your sorrow urged you to publish it, so

did

did mine urge me. And my sorrow had these causes (which I am content may be well compared with yours, that it may appear which were the juster and greater.)
1. No Scripture doth either in the letter or sense call faith an instrument of Justification. 2. I knew I had much Scripture and reason against it. 3. I thought it of dangerous consequence, to say, that man is the efficient cause of justifying and pardoning himself, and so doth forgive his own sins.

4. Yet all this had never caused me to open my mouth against it (for I truly abhor the making of new quarrels.) But for the next, viz. I found that many Learned Divines did not only assert this instrumentality, but they laid so great a stresse upon it; as if the main difference between us and the Papists lay here. For in the doctrine of Justification, say they, it is that they Fundamentally erre, and we Principally differ: And that in these four Points.

1. About the formall cause of our Righteousnesse, which, say these Divines, is the formall Righteousnesse of Jesus Christ, as suffering and perfectly obeying for us (or as others adde, In the habitual Righteousnesse of his humane nature; and others, The natural Righteousnesse of the Divine nature.

2. About the way and manner of our participation herein; which as to Gods act, they say is imputation (which is true) and that in this sense, that *Legaliter* we are esteemed to have fulfilled the Law in Christ.

3. About the nature of that faith which Justifieth, which, say most of our forreign Reformers, is an assurance, or full perswasion of the pardon of my sins by Christs blood.

4. About the formal reason of faiths interest in Justification, which, say they, is as the instrument thereof.

I doubt not but all these four are great Errors. Yet for these must we contend as the Reformed Religion; and here must lye the difference between us and the Papists. That which troubled me was this: To think how many thousand might be confirmed in Popery by this course, and what a blow it gave to the Reformed Religion. For who can imagine but that the young Popish Students will be confirmed in the rest of their Religion, when they finde that we erre in these? and will judge by these of the rest of our Doctrine? Especially when they finde us making this the main part of the Protestant Cause, what wonder if they judge our Cause naught? This is no fancy, nor any needless fears, but such a real blow to the Protestant Cause, as will not easily be healed. Had Divines only in a way of freedom used this phrase, and not made it so great a part of our Religion, to the hazarding of the whole, I had never mentioned the unsoundnesse or other inconvenience of it. Now to the thing it self, Your Arguments for faiths instrumentality to Justification, I will consider when I can finde them: You begin with (and say more for) faiths instrumentality in receiving Christ. You can say no more of me concerning this, but that [it will be scarce allowed to be so called.] This intimates that I make it no matter of contention: nor do I know how I could have said less, if any thing; when its only the unfitness or impropriety of the phrase that I mention, and not the sense: which I thought with so much tendernesse I might do, upon reason given, it being no Scripture phrase. If faith be the instrument of receiving Christ, then it is either the Act or the Habit of Faith that is the instrument: They that say, the Habit is the instrument, (speak not properly, but far more tolerably then the others do. If gracious Habits are properly called instruments of the soul, then so may other Habits: And why is not this language more in use among Logicians? if it be so unquestionably proper? But I

perceive

perceive it is the Act of faith that you call the inſtrument: for you anſwer only to what I ſay againſt that. I drew up a Scheme of the ſeveral ſorts of Giving and Receiving, in Anſwer to another Learned Brother: which, for the neceſſity of diſtinguiſhing here, I would have added, but that ſo operous a Reply would be unſutable to your brief Exceptions. Receiving ſtrictly taken is ever Paſſive: Receiving in a Civil, Ethical, leſs proper ſenſe, is but the Act of accepting what is offered: When it is only a Relation, or *Jus ad rem* that is offered, Conſent or Acceptance is an act ſo neceſſary ordinarily to the poſſeſſion (or proper Paſſive reception) that it is therefore called Receiving it ſelf: yet is indeed no efficient cauſe of the Paſſive reception or poſſeſſion: but a *conditio ſine qua non*, and a ſubjective diſpoſition; and ſo makes the ſubject capable of the benefit: but being no efficient it can be no inſtrument. Yet ſtill I ſay, that if any will pleaſe to call it an inſtrument in this ſenſe, I will not quarrel with him, for the impropriety of a phraſe; ſpecially if ſome men had the ſame ingenuity as others have, that ſay, it is but *inſtrumentum metaphoricum*. But to ſay, that the act of faith is the inſtrument of Ethical Active reception (which is it that I argued againſt,) is to ſay, Receiving Chriſt is the inſtrument of it ſelf. Now let's ſee what you ſay to this. 1. You ſay, Its too ſubtill a Notion: That deſerves no Reply. 2. You ſay [We uſe to ſpeak otherwiſe of faith.] Thats no proof that you ſpeak properly. You ſay [Faith is the eye of the ſoul; and the eye is not ſight. Faith is the hand, &c.] *Anſ.* 1. Strange proof! not only by Metaphors, but by metaphors of meer humane uſe. 2. Is the act of faith the eye of the ſoul as diſtinct from ſight? and the hand as diſtinct from receiving? Tell us then what actual ſeeing and receiving is? To ſpeak metaphors and contradictions is no proving your Aſſertion. Next you ſay [Scripture ſpeaks otherwiſe.] Thats to the purpoſe indeed, if true. You cite, *Act.* 18. 26. where is no ſuch matter. If [By] ſignifie an inſtrumentall cauſe, It is either Alwaies or Sometimes: You would not ſure have your Reader believe that it is Alwaies. If but ſometimes, Why do you take it for granted that it ſo ſignifies here? Why did you not offer ſome proof? This is eaſie Diſputing. Next you ſay [Why elſe is this Righteouſneſs ſometime called the Righteouſneſs' of faith? Sometimes the Righteouſneſs of God which is by faith; but that it is a Righteouſneſs which faith receives?] *Anſ.* 1. Its properer to ſay, *Credens recipit credendo*, The Believer by beleeving receives it: Then to ſay, Faith (eſpecially the act) receives it: But if you will uſe that ſpeech, it muſt expreſs but *formalem rationem credendi* expoſitorily, and not the efficiency of faith, and therefore no inſtrumentality. It is the Righteouſneſs of God by faith, becauſe God gives it freely (Chriſt having merited it) upon condition of mans faith. You adde [*Eph.* 3. 17. Chriſt dwels in us by faith. By faith we take him in, &c.] *Anſ.* You odly change the queſtion: We are ſpeaking of faiths inſtrumentality in receiving Right to Chriſt, or Chriſt in relation: and you go about to prove the reception of his Spirit, or graces really, or himſelf objectively: For Chriſt is ſaid to dwell in us, 1. By his Spirit and Graces. 2. Objectively, as my friend dwels in my heart when I love him. The text being meant of either of theſe, is nothing to the purpoſe. 2. Yet here you do not prove that [by] ſignifieth a proper inſtrument: no more then your actual intellection is ſaid to be the inſtrument of Truths abode in you; when it is ſaid that Truth dwelleth in you by intellection. The ſame Anſwer ſerves to your following words about receiving the Spirit. 1. Its nothing to our Queſtion. 2. You give us but your bare word that Scripture ſpeaks of faith as the ſouls inſtrument, even in receiving the Spirit of Chriſt, much leſs in receiving Right to Chriſt.

Christ. But still remember that from first to last, I profess not to contend with any about the use of this phrase, of faiths instrumentality in receiving Christ. It is its being really the proper instrumentall efficient cause of Justification, which I denied, and resolvedly more then ever do deny. This you next come to, and say,

§. 6.

Mr Bl. THe instrumentality of it in the work of Justification is denied, because the nature of an Instrument (as considered in Physical operations) doth not exactly belong to it; which if it must be alwaies rigidly followed, will often put us to a stand in the assignation of causes of any kinde in Moral actions. The material and formal causes in Justification are scarce agreed upon, and no marvell then in case men minde to contend about it, that some question is raised about the Instrument. But in case we shall consider the nature and kinde of this work, about which faith is imploied, and examine the reason and ground, upon the which faith is disabled from the office of an instrument in our Justification, and withall look into that which is brought in as an instrument in this work in the stead of it, I do not doubt but it will easily appear, that those Divines, that with a concurrent judgement (without almost a dissenting voice, have made faith an instrument in this work) speak most aptly, and most agreeably to the nature of an instrument.

§. 6.

R. B. BUt is this certain? Do I therefore deny faith to be the instrument of Justification, because the nature of an instrument [as considered in Physical operations] doth not exactly belong to it? I said 1. The action of the principal Cause and of the instrument is one action. Is not this true of moral operations as well as Physical? If it be not, you must make us a new Logick before you can reasonably expect that we receive your Logical Theology. 2. I said, the instrument must have Influx to the producing of the effect of the principal cause, by a proper causality: that is, *in suo genere*. Is not this true of Moral operations as well as Physical? Its true, Moral causes may be said to have a less proper causation then Physical: But 1. The instrumental must be as proper as that of the principal. 2. There is a wide difference between, *causam Moralem*, and *causam Moralitatis*. *Effecti naturalis potest esse causa moralis, vel imputativa: Et effecti moralis scilicet Ethici, (ut Debiti, Juris, Meriti,) potest esse causa remotior naturalis.* It may well be called a proper causation, when the effect is produced by as full a causation as the nature of the thing will admit (as in relations that are by meer resultancy.)

2. You say [the material and formal causes of Justification are scarce agreed on.] But doth that give you a liberty to assert what you list, or what cannot be proved true, because all men see not the truth? I should have thought you should rather have thus concluded: [Seeing Divines themselves cannot agree about the assignation of these Logical, unscriptural notions in the businels of Justification, therefore it is a meer Church-dividing course, to place so much of the Protestant Cause in such notions, and insist upon them as matters of such necessity and weight, as is done in asserting faiths instrumentality to Justification.] Your argument (in the issue and tendency) is like that of plundering souldiers in time of fight; that say, Now they are altogether by the ears, we may take that we light on: why should they

they question us, till they agree among themselves? 3. Whether this phrase be so apt as you affirm, we shall better know when you have said something to prove it. If Divines have been so concurrent in it as you say, that there is scarce a dissenting voice, I hope I am the more excusable, if it prove an error, for opposing it: For it is pity to let so many mistake themselves, mislead others, and make us part of a new Religion.

But Sir, whats the cause of this sudden change? Through their great condescension, I have received Animadversions from many of the most Learned, Judicious Divines that I know in *England*: And of all these, there is but one man that doth own the Doctrine of faiths Instrumentality; but they disclaim it all; some with distast, others with a modest excuse of them that use it, and the gentle interpretation of [a Metaphorical instrument] and that remote: for so they would have me interpret our Divines. I told you this when I saw you, and you asked me, Whether Mr C. were against it? To which I Answer, Not so much as divers others that write to me; but judge you by his own words, which are these, [*Obj.* But though faith be not the instrument of our Justification, may it not be called the instrument of receiving *Christ*? *Ans.* I think they mean so and no more, who call faith the instrument of our Justification, &c. I shall not be unwilling to yield to you, that to speak exactly, faith may better be called a Condition, then an Instrument of our Justification.] So far M^r C.

§. 7.

M^r Bl. *THe work about which faith is imploied, is not an absolute, but a relative work: a work of God towards man: not without the actual concurrence of man: such in which neither God nor man are sole efficients; nor any act of God or man can be sole instruments; but there must be a mutual concurrence of both.*

§. 7.

R. B. A Dangerous Doctrine, in my Judgement, to be so nakedly affirmed: No doubt but Justification is a Relative change: and it is past Controversie, that it is not without the actual concurrence of man: for he must perform the Condition, on which God will justifie him: But that God is not the sole Efficient, nor any * Act of God, the sole Instrument, I durst not have affirmed without proof: and much less have undertaken to prove.

* *I suppose the word* [*Act*] *is used so largely, as to include the Law it self.*

§. 8.

M^r Bl. *THis must needs be granted, unless we will bring in Dr Crispes passive recipiency of Christ: Christs abode in man without man, in spite of man, and suppose him to be justified in unbelief.*

§. 8.

R. B. This is very naked asserting. Why did you not shew some reason of this ill consequence? Its past my reach to see the least. 2. Why do you still confound Christs real abode in us by his Spirit, with the relation we have upon Justification? when even now you affirmed, it was a relative work (as you call it) I pray, by the next shew us more clearly, how these absurdities follow that doctrine which affirmeth, That God is the sole Efficient cause of our Justification, but having made mans Belief and Consent the Condition (whose nature is to suspend the effect, till performed) he will not justifie us till we first believe and consent. This is my Doctrine plainly.

§. 9.

Mr Bl. And faith is disabled from this office in Justification, by this Argument: If faith be an instrument, it is the instrument of God or man, &c. I Ans. It is the instrument of man: and though man do not justifie himself, yet he concurres, as a willing ready Agent with God in it. God is a justifier of those that beleeve in Jesus, Rom. 3. 26. God hath set Christ forth a propitiation through faith, Rom. 3. 25.

§. 9.

R. B. If this be not palpable contradiction, saying and unsaying, my Logick is less then I thought it had been. If it be [Mans instrument] of Justification; and yet [Man do not justifie himself.] Then either Man is not Man, or an Instrument is not an Instrument, or Justifying is not Justifying. Had you only affirmed it to be mans act, and Gods instrument (how absurd soever otherwise yet) you might have said, Man doth not justifie himself. But if it be mans instrument, then man is the principal cause (in respect of the instrumentall.) For *omne instrumentum est causæ principalis instrumentum*. And can he be the efficient cause, and yet not effect? Is not that to be a Cause and no Cause? In my judgement this doctrine should not be made part of our Religion; nor much stress laid on it if it were true; because its so obscure: That man concurres as a ready Agent, who doubts? but doth that prove him or his faith the efficient cause of his own pardon and Justification? Is the performer of the condition of [Gratefull consent] no willing Agent, unless an efficient Cause? The text you cite doth not speak of instruments, for ought I can finde.

§. 10.

Mr Bl. And because it is the instrument of man in a work of this nature, it is also the instrument of God. As some have observed a communication of Titles between Christ and his Church (the Church being called by his Name) so there is a communication of actions in these relative works. Christ dwels in our hearts by faith, Eph. 3. 17. We believe and not Christ: and yet faith there is Christs instrument, whereby he takes up his abode. God purifies the hearts of the Gentiles by faith, Act. 15. 17. They believed and not God: yet faith is Gods instrument in the work of their purification. So on the other side, the Spirit is Gods work: yet we by the Spirit do mortifie the deeds of the flesh, Rom. 8. 13.

§. 10.

§. 10.

R. B. IF this be indeed true, That it is mans instrument of Justification and Gods both; then both God and man are both *Causæ principales partiales*, by coordination making up one principal cause. This I hope you will not downright affirm: I deny it on this reason: Every absolute Donor (I mean, who is absolutely owner of what he gives) is the totall cause-efficient-principal, of his own Donation: But God in justifying is an absolute Donor (giving remission and Righteousness) Therefore,*&c*. 2. Or else God and man must be principal causes one subordinate to the other; and each total in his own kinde. This must be your meaning, by your first words: But then which of these is the most principal cause, and which the subordinate ? It is hard for a better wit then mine to know your minde by your words: For when you say [Because it is mans instrument,it is also Gods instrument.] It may seem that you take it to be mans instrument first, or else how can it be therefore Gods instrument [because] it is mans ? But yet whether you speak *de ordine consequentis vel consequentiæ, de ordine essendi & efficiendi,vel de ordine dicendi & colligendi,* I know not. However, I will not be so uncharitable as to imagine that you take man for the most principal cause, and God for the subordinate; but contrarily. But then you do not only make man the pardoner and justifier of himself, but you make him the nearest total cause of it: and so it would be as proper to say, Man forgives himself, as that God forgives him: And so faith would be only mans instrument directly, as being the nearest cause-principal; and Gods instrument remotely. As if I hold my pen, and you hold my hand, the pen is *proximè* my instrument, and *remotiùs* yours. And so God should justifie and pardon man, by himself, as Gods instrument: As if a Judge had committed Treason, and the King should give him authority to Judge, Pardon and Absolve himself. But how much might be said against this ? To justifie *efficienter* is *actus Rectoris: Sed homo non est rector sui ipsius* (in the sense in hand :) Therefore he cannot justifie himself. Indeed if you had spoke only of the Justification *in foro conscientiæ* you might well have ascribed it to man as the efficient cause: but that you speak not of.

2. The communication of Titles that you speak of, is 1. very rare. 2. Uncertain whether at all found in Scripture. That Text 1 *Cor.*12.12. seemeth rather to leave out [the Church] as understood, then to communicate Christs Name to it: *q.d.* [So is Christ and the Church.] I would advise all friends of mine to take heed that they presume not on this slight ground to communicate Christs Name to the Church in their ordinary speech. 3. But who can tell what you mean by a communication of actions ? Your putting [Communication of actions] in contradistinction from [Communication of Titles] makes the proper sense of your words be, that Christ doth as really communicate actions themselves, as he doth Titles themselves. But that is no better then a plain impossibility: For the communication will make it another action. The accident perisheth, when separated from its subject: and therefore the same accident cannot be communicated. But its like you intended to have said, That there is a common or mutual attribution of each others actions, or one is entitled to the actions of the other; and so mean only a communication of the Name *quoad modum producendi*, and not of the actions themselves. But then, either this is an improper figurative way of speech; or it is proper, and grounded in the nature of the thing. If the former,

D 3 then

then it is nothing to our Queſtion, who are not enquiring whether there may not be found ſome Figure in Rhetorick according to which faith may be ſaid to be mans inſtrument of Juſtification and Gods ? but whether it be ſo properly and indeed ? And if you could finde any Scripture that ſo ſpeaks figuratively, calling faith mans inſtrument and Gods in juſtifying; (as you cannot) this would do nothing to the deciding of our Controverſie. It is therefore a grounded attribution that you muſt prove, where there is alſo a real inſtrumentality, and ſo the Name fitted to the Thing. And how prove you this ? Why, as before, *Eph.* 3. 17. you ſay, [We beleeve and not Chriſt ; yet faith is Chriſts inſtrument, whereby he takes up his abode.] But this is too facil diſputing to ſatisfie. 1. Here is not a word to prove that it is a relative In-dwelling that is here ſpoken of. I need not tell you how ſingular you are in this Expoſition (if you ſo expound : If not, you ſay nothing.) 2. If that had been proved, yet here is no proof that [by] ſignifieth inſtrumentality. 3. Much leſs that it is Chriſts inſtrument. How eaſily are all theſe affirmed ? I think Chriſt dwels in our hearts, as I ſaid, 1. By his Spirit and Graces ; and ſo he is ſaid to dwell in us [by faith.] 1. *Formaliter,* faith being the principal part of that grace which dwelleth in us. 2. *Conditionaliter,* Faith being a condition of our right to the Spirits abode. 3. *Efficienter,* as the act of faith doth directly cauſe the increaſe, and ſo the abode of the habit ; and alſo as it exciteth other graces. If you will call this efficiency an inſtrumental efficiency, I think it is no proper ſpeech : We do not uſe to call the act of intellection, Mans inſtrument of knowing or increaſing the habits of knowledge : but I will not contend with you about this : Nor yet if you ſay, This act of beleeving is Mans inſtrument (of exciting and increaſing grace in himſelf) directly, and Gods inſtrument remotely : As my pen is immediatly my inſtrument, and remotely his that holds my hand. Or rather I ſhould ſay, as my action in writing is improperly called my inſtrument, and his. And thus man may be ſaid (yea more properly then thus) to ſanctifie himſelf, and God to ſanctifie man by himſelf : But in Juſtification the matter is far otherwiſe : Man doth neither Juſtifie himſelf, nor God juſtifies man by himſelf. The ſecond way of Chriſts dwelling in us, is Objectively. And here if you will ſpeak ſo improperly, as to ſay that mans act of believing is his inſtrument of receiving Chriſt as an Object, or of the Objects abode in the ſoul, I will not contend with you about it : Only as I would deſire you to make this phraſe no great part of Religion, nor lay too great a ſtreſs upon it, ſo alſo to remember, 1. That it is but the *ſpecies* and not Chriſt himſelf that is objectively received, and thus dwelleth in us. 2. That every other grace that hath Chriſt for its object, is thus far an inſtrument of receiving him, and of his abode in us, as well as faith : but none ſo properly and fully as knowledge. And 3. That thus Chriſt dwels objectively in every wicked man that thinketh of him : Though doubtleſſe not in that deep and ſpeciall manner as in his choſen.

3. And yet further, as a conſequent of the firſt ſort of indwelling, Chriſt himſelf may be ſaid to dwell in us *Civiliter, vel Moraliter,* that is, *Reputative,* becauſe his Spirit or Graces dwell in us *Naturaliter :* As a man that keeps poſſeſſion of a houſe by his ſon or ſervant, or by his goods : And here alſo, if you have a minde to the term Inſtrument, you may, for me, ſay that Chriſt keeps poſſeſſion by faith or the Spirit as his inſtruments : But then you muſt conſider, 1. That this is by no communication of Actions and Titles : but here is a real ground for this ſpeech. 2. That it is not faith as mans act, but faith as Gods grace wrought and maintained

[23]

rained in us, by which he may in this sense be said to dwell in us, or keep possession of us. 3. That thus every grace may as truly be said to be Christs instrument of possession or indwelling, as faith: so he dwelleth in us by love, hope, trust, desire, joy, &c. but most properly by the Spirit or new Creature, or whole body of Sanctification.

4 That all this is nothing to prove faith to be mans instrument and Gods (yea or either alone) to effect our Justification.

The same answer serves to *Act.* 15. 17. God purifieth mans heart by faith: 1. From the power of sin, and that is by faith: 1. *Formaliter.* 2. *Efficienter*, as is before expressed. 2. From the guilt of sin; and that is by faith as a condition on mans part (and not as an instrument:) By or through which God is said to purifie or pardon us; 1. In that he conferreth remission only on this condition; and so doth constitute the formall office of faith in justifying. 2. In that by his Spirit he causeth or giveth faith it self, and effecteth the matter. Though, whether this Text reach to Justification, I will not Dispute. So that you do but nakedly affirm, and not prove that faith is Gods instrument or mans in justifying.

Lastly to what you say from *Rom.*8.13. I reply, 1. An Adjutor or Concause is ill called an instrument. Must the Spirit needs be our instrument, because it is [By] the Spirit? As if [By] signified only an instrument?

2. All this is nothing to the business of Justification. Prove but this, that man is as true an efficient of his own pardon or Justification, as he is of mortifying the deeds of the body, or of Progressive Sanctification, and you shall carry the Cause: I will not then contend whether the term [instrument] be proper or improper.

---

§. 11.

Mr *Bl.* MAn neither justifies nor sanctifies himself, yet by faith he is raised to close with God in both: And so faith as an instrument receives Righteousness to Justification: and therefore is called, The righteousness of faith, which is our Justification, and works Sanctification; provided you understand not the first work, which is properly Regeneration, and precedent to faith; but the further progress and increase of it, &c.

---

§. 11.

R. B. 1. IF man justifie not himself, and yet faith be his instrument of justifying, then farewell old Logick.

2. If man sanctifie not himself, under God, as to the progress and acts of sanctification, then farewell old Theology. God bids men wash them, and purifie their hearts, and cleanse their hands, and make them new hearts, &c and *Peter* saith, *Ye have purified your souls in obeying the truth through the Spirit*, &c. 1 Pet. 1. 22. And we must cleanse our selves from all filthiness of flesh and spirit, *perfecting holiness in the fear of God*, 2 Cor. 7. 1. with many the like.

3. [To close with God] in pardoning me, signifieth not that I pardon my self, or that I or any act of mine is an efficient cause of pardon.

4. When you say, that [Faith as an instrument receiveth righteousness to Justification] you speak exactly the conceptions of most Divines that I have met with,

or read, that go your way; and therefore these words deserve a little further consideration. Their meaning, as far as I can understand of the whole business is this: 1. They conceive of Christs own righteousness, wherewith himself was righteous, as given to us. 2. They conceive of the act of faith, as the instrument of receiving this. 3. Upon the receiving of this, they conceive we are Justified, as a man that receiveth Riches is Rich, or that receiveth Honour is Honourable. 4. Because faith is the instrument of receiving righteousness, therefore say they, It is the instrument of Justification. For Justification *Constitutive*, is but a relation resulting from righteousness received. This is the summe of the common Judgement of most that I have read.

But these things must be more accurately considered, I think. And 1. It must be known, that the Righteousness given us, is not the Righteousness whereby Christs person was Righteous: (for accidents perish being removed from the subject:) but it is a Righteousness merited by Christs satisfaction and obedience, for us.

2. It must needs be known that the faith which is the Justifying condition, is terminated on Christ himself as the object, and not on his Righteousness which he gives us in Remission: Remission or Righteousness may be the end of the sinner in receiving Christ; but Righteousness or Remission is not the object received by that act which is made the condition of Justification: or at least but a secondary remote object; even as a woman doth not marry a mans Riches, but the Man; though it may be her end in marrying the man, to be enriched by him: nor is her receiving his riches the condition of her first Legal right to them; but her taking the man for her husband. And as a Patient being promised to be cured, if he will take such a man for his Physitian, and wholly trust him, renouncing all other: Here it is not receiving Health, or a Cure that is the proper Condition of the Cure: Health and Cure is the end for which the Physitian is Accepted and Trusted: but it is himself as a sufficient faithfull Physitian which is the object of that receiving, which is the condition of the Cure. The like may be shewed in other Relations, of a Master and Scholar, Prince and Subjects, Master and Servants, &c. Receiving the persons into relation, from whom we expect the benefit, goes before receiving the benefit it self by them; which is usually the remote end, and not the object of that first reception which is the condition. Our Divines therefore of the Assembly do perfectly define justifying faith to be, *A receiving and resting on Christ alone for salvation, as he is offered in the Gospel* It is of dangerous consequence to define justifying Faith to be the Receiving of Justification or Righteousness.

3. In my judgement, it is a meer fancy and delusion, to speak of the receiving a righteousness that we may be justified *Constitutive* thereby, in such a sense, as if the righteousness were first to be made ours, in order of nature before our Justification, and then Justification follow because we are righteous; and so these were two things: For to receive Righteousness, and to receive Justification is one thing. Gods justifying us, and pardoning our sin, and his constituting us righteous, and his giving us righteousness, is all one thing under severall notions. Yet as God giveth, 1. Conditionally. 2. Actually: so man receiveth, 1. *Receptione Ethica activâ*, figuratively called receiving. 2. *Receptione Physica, propriâ, passivâ*: The former goes before Justification: but only as a small, and secondary part of the condition, if properly any (it being the accepting of Christ himself that is the main condition:) The later is nothing at all but *Justificari*, commonly called, Passive Justification.

4. Christs

4. Chrifts Satisfaction or Redemption (*folvendo pretium*) and merit, cannot be properly received by us: For they are not in themfelves given to us (but as Tropically they may be faid to be given to us, becaufe the fruit of them is given us.) It was not to us, but to God, that Chrift gave fatisfaction, and the price of our Redemption. And yet juftifying faith doth as neceffarily refpect Chrifts fatisfaction and merit, as it doth our Juftification thereby procured. It is therefore the *acknowledging* of this Redemption, Satisfaction or Merit, and the receiving of Chrift *as one that hath redeemed us by fatisfaction and merit*, and not the *receiving that Redemption or Satisfaction* our felves. To fay therefore, that the juftifying act of faith, is only the receiving of Chrifts Righteoufnefs or of Juftification, is to exclude the receiving of Chrift himfelf any way; even to exclude him as fatisfier from the juftifying act: and to exclude from that act, his Redemption, by bloodfhed, fatisfaction and merit: For if it be only the receiving of righteoufnefs, that is the juftifying act, then it is neither the receiving of Chrift himfelf, nor yet the acknowledgement of his Satisfaction and Redemption by his blood; and fo they muft fay of thefe as they do of the reception of Chrift as Lord, that it is the *fides qua juftificat, fed non quâ juftificans*.

5. If faith fhall be faid to be the inftrument of Juftification *eo nomine*, becaufe it is the receiving of that *Righteoufnefs* whereby we are juftified, then it will follow that faith muft alfo be called the inftrument of our *enjoying* Chrift, *eo nomine*; becaufe it receiveth *him*, and the inftrument of our *Adoption*, *eo nomine*, becaufe it receiveth *Adoption*; and fo the fame act of faith which entitles us to Juftification, doth not entitle us to any other bleffing; nor that act that entitles us to Chrift, doth entitle us to Juftification (unlefs there be feveral juftifying acts:) but every particular mercy hath a particular act of faith as the inftrument of receiving it: which is no Scripture doctrine.

6. It muft be remembred that the thing that faith receives naturally and properly, is not Chrift himfelf, or his righteoufnefs; but the *fpecies* of what is reprefented as its object. And that faiths reception of Chrift himfelf and his righteoufnefs, or of right to Chrift, is but *Receptio metaphorica; vel actio ad receptionem propriam neceffaria:* and that the true reception, which is *pati, non agere*, doth follow faith, and therefore Chrift himfelf is received only *Receptione fidei ethicâ, activa, metaphoricâ: Species Chrifti predicati recipiatur receptione naturali, intelligendo: Jus ad Chriftum recipitur receptione naturali paffivâ, propriâ:* That which is conditionally given (on condition of acceptance or the like) and offered to be accepted; this is received, *Receptione fidei ethicâ:* whereupon followeth the actual efficacious giving of that thing, (the condition being performed, which fufpended it:) and this the beleever receiveth, *Receptione paffivâ, propriâ*; but it is not his *Faith* that receiveth it.

7. The great thing therefore that I would defire to be obferved is this; that though faith were an inftrument of the forefaid objective, or of the Ethical, Metaphorical reception of Chrift (which yet is not properly, being *ipfa Receptio*,) yet it is not therefore the inftrumental caufe of the paffive, proper reception of Right to Chrift or Righteoufnefs. Of this it is only the condition and not the proper inftrument. (For I fhall fhew hereafter that it is impoffible it fhould be both:) It doth morally qualifie the fubject to be a fit patient to be juftified, as M. *Benjam. Woodbridge* faith truly, in his excellent Sermon of *Juftification*. The reafon of this is, That it is only Donation or the will of the Donor fignified, that can efficiently convey a right to his own Benefits. The Receiver is not the Giver, and therefore

fore not the conveyer of Right. Every instrument is an efficient cause, and therefore must effect: and it is only *giving* that effecteth this right. Now if the giving (the donation) had been absolute, it had absolutely conveyed right; and faith would have had no hand in it, as being no condition: Or if the gift had constituted another condition, that other would have had the causing interest that faith now hath (*ut causa sine qua non*.) So that the nearest and formal interest of faith is, Its being the condition; and its apprehension of its object, is but the remote aptitudinal reason, being *ipsa fides*. The great thing therefore that I affirm is this, That if you will needs call faith the instrument of apprehending Christ, or righteousness, yet doth it not justifie *proximè & formaliter, As* such; but *As* the condition of the gift performed.

8. And if you will speak improperly, and call faith as it is the performed-condition [*instrumentum Receptionis*] it is not therefore *instrumentum Justificationis*: In a few words, this is the summe: 1. Faith is an Ethical, Metaphorical reception of Christ. 2. If any will speak so improperly as to call this, The instrument of this Ethical reception; I will not contend with him. 3. This Ethical reception Active, is constituted by Christs Testament, the condition of Passive proper reception of Right to Christ, and with him to his Benefits. Faith must first be faith, *i.e. apprehensio Christi*, in order of nature before it can be the condition of Right. 4. It justifies therefore *quâ conditio*, and not *quâ fides in Christum:* or as they improperly speak, *quâ instrumentum Christum apprehendens*. 5. If any will take the word Instrument so improperly and largely, as to comprehend the condition, then you may so further say, [Faith is not only the instrument of Active reception, but of true Passive reception of Right to Christ, and so of receiving Justification.] 6. But this is *quâ conditio præstita*, and not *quâ apprehensio Christi*. 7. And therefore every act that is part of this condition, may so be called, *instrumentum recipiendi*. 8. And if it were, as they would have it, that faith is the instrument *eo nomine quia Christum apprehendit*, then every grace that apprehendeth Christ must be the instrument too: And doubtless Knowledge, Love, Hope, Delight, &c. do apprehend, or receive Christ in some sort; and have him for their object. 9. Though I will not contend with him that will say, [*Fides non quâ fides, sed quâ conditio præstita, est instrumentum morale recipiendi jus ad Christum & justitiam ab ipso promeritam*.] Yet (as I think he laieth a snare for himself and others, in turning the plain and proper term [Condition] into an improper term [*instrumentum Recipiendi*,] so) I think it not to be endured that therefore faith or any act of man, should be called the instrument of Justification. For though you may in a strained speech say, that *Receptio moralis activa* being made the *medium* or condition *Receptionis physicæ passivæ*, may therefore be called *instrumentum recipiendi*, and *Credere vel acceptare* said to be *moraliter vel reputativè pati*; (and so every condition *quâ* condition be termed a Receptive instrument) I say, though I will not quarrell with this speech for meer unfitness; yet it is a higher and more dangerous errour to say That faith or any condition is therefore *instrumentum Justificationis*. It is not an instrumental efficient cause of the effect, because it is *medium sine quo non recipitur*: As *Realis vel naturalis receptio Justificationis*, is not *Justificare, sed Justificari*; so much more evident is it that *Moralis & imputativa Receptio Justificationis, non est Justificare, sed medium necessarium ad* [*Justificari.*]
10. Lastly, I say again what I said in my Aphorismes; These two Questions must be distinguished: What is the nearest reason of faiths interest in Justification? And, what is the remote reason? or why did God assign faith to this office?

To

[27]

To the first, this is the only true Answer: Faith Justifies rather then any thing else, because God in framing his deed of gift, was pleased to make faith the condition: The meer constitution of the Donor is the cause. To the second, this is my Answer: God chose faith to this office of being the justifying condition, rather then other duties, because it was fittest: as being in its own nature, An acceptance of a freely given Christ, and Life with him (which men call the instrumentality.) I have the more fully opened my meaning here together about this point (though with some repetitions) that I might leave no room for doubting of it, and misunderstanding me.

§. 12.

Mr Bl. *The Spirit will do nothing without our faith, and our faith can do nothing without the Spirit. Man cannot justifie himself by beleeving without God, and God will not justifie an unbeleeving man. Faith then is the act of man; man beleeves, yet the instrument of God, that justifies only beleevers.*

§. 12.

R.B. 1. The Spirits working in Sanctification, is nothing to our question of Justification. 2. The Spirit worketh our first faith without faiths co-working; and that is more then nothing. 3. The Spirit moveth faith to action, before faith move it self: and that is more then nothing. 4. It is not so easily proved as said, that the Spirit never exciteth any good act in the soul, nor yet restraineth from any evil, without the co-working or instrumentality of faith. But these are beside the point. 5. When you have laid down one Proposition [Man cannot justifie himself by beleeving, without God,] how fairly do you lay down this as the disjunct Proposition? [and God will not justifie an unbeleeving man.] *Concedo totum.* Is that your Conclusion? Would you have no more? Who would have thought but you would rather have said [Nor will God justifie man, unless his faith be the instrument of it?] And do you not seem to imply that man with God doth justifie himself, when you say [Man cannot justifie himself by beleeving without God?] No, nor with him neither? For none can forgive sins but God only, even to another: but who can forgive himself? Indeed I have thought what a sad case the Pope is in, that is the only man on earth that hath no visible pardoner of his sin: he can forgive others; but who shall forgive him? But I forgot that every beleever forgiveth himself; for I did not beleeve it. 6. How nakedly is it again affirmed, without the least proof, that our faith is Gods instrument in justifying? Doth God effect our Justification by the instrumentall, efficient causation of our faith? Let him beleeve it that is so happy as to see it proved, and not barely affirmed.

§. 13.

Mr Bl. *So that which is here spoken, by way of exception, against faith as an instrument, holds of efficients and instruments, sole and absolute in their work and causality. But where there is a concurrence of Agents, and one makes use of the act of another to produce the effect that in such causality is wrought, it will not hold.*

E 2 §. 13.

§. 13.

R. B. HE that will or can make him a Religion of words and syllables, that either signifie nothing, or are never like to be understood by the learner, let him make this an Article of his faith. 1. What you mean by [absolute] I cannot certainly aviolate, unless that which is never a principall. 2. Nor know I whether by [sole] you mean *Materialiter, Formaliter, vel Respective quoad causam principalem.* 1. Two materials may concurre to make one formal instrument: Here the instrument is but one, though the matter of it may be of divers parts. Sure this is not your sense, that faith and something else materially concurre to make one instrument. 2. An instrument may be called [sole] formally, when it is the only instrument, and there is no other concurreth to the effect. If you mean that my exceptions hold against none but such sole instruments, then it is more nakedly, then truly asserted: nor do they hold ever the more or less, whether the instrument be sole or not: else they would hold against few instruments in the world. For it is not usual to have an effect produced by a sole instrument: especially of subordinate instruments, though it may be usual as to coordinate. 3. An instrument may be called [sole] *Respective,* as to the principal cause: *viz.* It is not the instrument of many principals, but of one only. Is this your meaning, that my exceptions would hold, if faith were only mans instrument, or only Gods; but not when it is both? If so 1. This is affirmed without the least shew of proof, or reason; why my exceptions hold not as much against that instrument of a double principal, as of a single? surely the nature of an instrument is not varied by that. 2. If God and man be both principals (as they must be, if faith be the instrument of both) then either coordinate or subordinate; but neither of these, as I have argued before. Man neither forgives himself under God, or with God, if you speak of one and the same forgiveness. Though I know there is another kinde of forgiveness, whereby a man may forgive himself: whereof *Seneca* speaks, *de Ira,* when he saith, [*Why should I fear any of my Errors, when I can say, See thou do so no more, I now forgive thee.*] *lib. 3. cap. 36.* O for one proof among all these affirmations, that [here is such a concurrence of Agents, that God makes use of the act of man, to produce the effect of Remission] and that as an instrument, and not only as a meer condition, *sine qua non.*

§. 14.

Mr Bl. THe *Promise or Grant of the New Covenant in the Gospel, is (instead of faith) made the instrument in the work of Justification. This is indeed Gods, and not mans. It is the Covenant of God, the promise of God, the Gospel of God: but of it self unable to raise man up to Justification.*

Of the instrumentality of the Covenant.

§. 14.

R. B. YOu have been farre from satisfying me in asserting the instrumentality of faith in Justification. You here come more short of satisfying me, against the sufficiency of the Gospel-grant as Gods instrument. You say, This indeed is Gods, not mans. I say, There is none but Gods: for *non datur instrumentum, quod*

quod non est causæ principalis instrumentum. You say, It is of it self unable to raise man up to Justification. I answer, 1. It is not of it self able to do all other works antecedent to Justification, as to humble, to give faith, to Regenerate, &c. But thats nothing to our business. 2. But as to the act of Justification, or conveying right to Christ, pardon, and righteousness, I say, It is able of it self as the *signum voluntatis divinæ* to do it. And you will never be able to make good your accusation of its disability. 3. If you should mean that [of it self] *i. e.* without the concomitancy of faith as a condition, it is not able: I answer, thats not fitly called disability: Or if you will so call it; the reason of that disability, is not because there is a necessity of faiths instrumentall coefficiency; but of its presence as the performed condition: It being the will of the donor that his grant should not *efficere actualiter*, till the condition were performed.

§. 15.

M^r Bl.] *IT is often tendered and Justification not alwaies wrought, and so disabled from the office of an instrument; by* Keckerman *in his Comment on his first Canon concerning an instrument. As soon as the instrument serves not the principall agent, so soon it loseth the nature of an instrument. He instanceth in an horse which obeyeth not the reins of his rider, but grows refractory: then he ceaseth to be an instrument for travell. A sword is not an instrument of slaughter, where it slayes not: nor an ax an instrument to hew, when it cuts not. Neither is the Gospel an instrument of Justification, where it justifies not.*

§. 15.

R. B.] I Am too shallow to reach the reason of these words. I know you had not leasure to write them in vain, and meerly to fill paper. And I will not be so uncharitable as to think you willing to intimate to the world, that I had wrote or thought that the Gospel was the instrument of justifying a man that was never justified. Do you think I know not a Cause and Effect are so related, that *formaliter* it is not an efficient before it doth effect? Though it may still be the same Thing, and have the same Aptitude to produce the Effect, even when it is not applied: and therefore by many Logicians is laxly termed a Cause still. 3. Nor can I perceive you make this a *medium* of any argument: except you would argue thus: The grant of the Covenant is not an Instrument of justifying unbelievers that never were justified: Therefore it is not a full or proper instrument of justifying believers that are justified.] Or else, therefore faith is an instrument as well as the Gospel. To your Reader that is no wiser then I, these words therefore, are at the best but lost labour. For I suppose this Argumentation you will not own.

§. 16.

M^r Bl. WHen the Minister is a Minister of condemnation, the savour of death to death, there the Gospel becomes an instrument of condemnation and death.

§. 16.

R. B. 1. So it is, if there be no Minister where it is known any way. 2. I speak of Gods grant or promise in the Gospel: you speak of his commination. 3. If the threat be the proper instrument of condemnation, *à pari*, the promise or gift is the proper instrument of Justification. Saw you not this when you wrote it?

§. 17.

Mr Bl. The efficacy that is in the Gospel for Justification, it receives by their faith to whom it is tendred.

§. 17.

R. B. Darkly, but dangerously spoken. Darkly, for its possible you may mean, that it receives it by faith as by a condition *sine quâ homo non est subjectum proximè capax:* and so I grant the sense: dangerously, For the words will seem to any impartial Reader to import more; specially finding what you say for faiths instrumentality before: *viz.* That the Gospel receives its efficacy from faith, or by faith as the instrument which conveyeth that efficacy to the Gospel: which if you mean, I would for the Truth's sake, and your own, that these words had never been seen. For if faith give the Gospel its efficacy; 1. It cannot be as a concause-instrumentall, coordinate; but as a superiour, more principal cause to the subordinate. 2. If it were the former that is meant, yet were it intollerable.

1. Nothing but a superiour cause doth convey *efficaciam causandi* to another. And this must be either, 1. *Influendo in potentiam inferioris.* 2. *Vel in actum.* To say that mans faith doth either of these to the Gospel-grant, is such a doctrine as I will not dare to argue against, lest you take me thereby to accuse you of being guilty of it.

2. Faith cannot as a concause, convey any efficacy into the Gospel: For a coordinate concause doth *influere immediatè in ipsum effectum, at non in concausæ potentiam vel actum.*

3. If you had only said that faith doth concurre in efficiency with the Gospel, to Justification; you had said more then you bring any proof for: But let's see what you bring in stead of proof.

§. 18.

Mr Bl. Heb. 4. 2. *Unto us was the Gospel preached as well as unto them: but the Word preached, did not profit them, not being mixed with faith in them that heard it.* 1 Thes. 2. 11, 13. *You received not the Word of God, as the word of men, but (as it is in truth) the Word of God, which effectually worketh in you that believe.*

§. 18.

§. 18.

R. B. But where's your conclusion? or any shew of advantage to your Cause? 1. In the first Text, the Apostle speaks of the words profiting in the real change of the soul; and our question is of the Relative. The Scripture meaneth, The word had not that further work on the heart, as it hath in them that mix it with faith: will you interpret it thus: [The Word did not justifie them.] 2. Its true, that the Word did not justifie them: but thats consequential only of the former unprofitableness. Once prove that man is but as much efficient in justifying himself, as he is in the obedience and change of his minde or actions; and then you do something. 3. Is here ever a word for the Gospels receiving its efficacy to Justification by faith? no nor of its so receiving that real profit of sanctification, which is here meant, neither. Its weak arguing to say, The Word profited not, because it was not mixt with faith: therefore faith conveys to it its efficacy of sanctifying, yea of justifying. You cannot but know the sequel would be denied. In progressive sanctification, and obedience, and exercise of graces, the word and faith are concauses, and one will not effect without the other: But it followeth not that therefore faith gives efficacy to the Word in this (much less to Justification where faith is no efficient.) For concauses have not influence on each other, but both on the effect. The want of faith may hinder the Word from that further work on the soul, which presupposeth faith (for faith is not wrought with faith's cooperation:) and thats all that the Text saith: But may not the absence of faith hinder, unless when present it doth effect? I am sure in Justification, where it is but a condition, it may. The nature of a condition, when the gift is free and full, is not to effect the thing, but to suspend the efficacy of the instrument, till it be performed. As (if I may use so gross a similitude) the clicket of a Cross-bow doth hinder the bow from shooting, till you stir it; but doth not adde any force to it, when you do stir it.

The second Text I know not how you mean to make use of; unless you argue thus: The Word worketh effectually only in Beleevers: therefore faith conveyeth efficacy to the Word. I think I need not tell you, that I deny the sequel (not to speak of the antecedent:) nor yet to tell you that this speaks not of working the relative change of Justification.

§. 19.

Mr Bl. So that the Gospel, in it self considered, is wanting in that honour assigned to an instrument, to have influx to the producing of the effect of the principall cause, by a proper causality. If none dare say, that faith hath such an influx, they may much less say that the Word hath such an influx.

§. 19.

R. B. The Gospel in it self considered, without the coordinate or subordinate, or superiour causality of faith, hath this honour so fully, clearly, beyond all doubt, that no man that is a preacher of this Gospel should question it: Much less should prefer the causality of faith, in saying, that [we may much less give this honour to the Word,] or say this of the Word, then of our own faith. Yet

the

the Gospel without the concomitancy of faith, doth not actually justifie: else faith were no condition or *causa sine qua non*: But that is no dishonour to the Gospel; nor defect of power which faith must supply. But the force of the instrument being meerly from the Donors will, he willeth that it shall then (and not till then) *efficere*, when the condition is performed. I appeal to all the Divines, Lawyers and Logicians in the world; when the thing to be conveyed is but *Debitum vel jus ad rem*, and the effect is but a Transcendental relation (as *debitum* is,) Is not the *Voluntas constituentis vel Donantis* the only principal proper efficient? And is not the *signum voluntatis constituens*, the properest instrument that the wit of man can imagine. Is not the Testament of a man the most strict and proper instrument of conveying right of the Legacy to the Legatary? Is not a Covenant, Contract, Deed of gift, the most proper instrumental efficient cause of the duness of the thing given or conveyed? It is not only a Law term, but a term of the strictest Logick, to call these a mans instrument for conveyance. Is not a præmiant or priviledging law, in the most strict and proper sense the Legislators instrument, effecting the *debitum præmii vel privelegii*? It is evident that the fullest definition of an instrumental efficient cause doth agree to these: as far as the nature of the effect (*Relatio debiti vel juris*) will admit of full or proper efficiency. For these instruments are the very *fundamenta proxima* of these relations. Can you prove the like, (yea and more) of faith, and will not? But I pray once more remember that it is not the effecting of a Physical change, but a relative, the conveying of Right that we are speaking of: so full an instrument is each of these that the very name of the effect is oft given to them. So a pardoning instrument is called A pardon: the instrument of donation is called A deed of gift. The Law is said, *præmiare & punire, quia constituit debitum præmii & pænæ*.

---

§. 20.

Mr Bl. PEmble therefore affirming the Word to be an instrument of Gods Spirit, presently addes, *Now instruments are either cooperative or passive, and the Word must be one of these two: Cooperative, he saith it is not, and gives his reason: It is therefore, saith he, a passive instrument, working only per modum objecti, as it contains a declaration of the Divine Will, and it proposeth to the understanding and will the things to be known, beleeved and practised.*

---

§. 20.

R.B. Mr *Pemble* speaks of the Word effecting, or as the instrument of sanctification. We speak of it as conveying right to Christ, and as justifying. Whats that to this? 2. When did Mr *Pemble* prove that the Word or other objects are passive instruments? You know he goes against the stream of Philosophers: and then his reasons must sway more then his authority: And his reason, which you say he gives, is but this, It cannot be declared what operative force there should be in the bare declaration of Gods will, *&c.*] But I will undertake to declare that an operation there is by the agency of this declaration; though not punctually how it operates: I have read many that say that *objectum operatur in genere causæ finalis*: and others that say it worketh *in genere causæ efficientis*, some saying it effecteth Physically, others that it effecteth morally, others that *objectum*

operatur

operatur naturaliter, at proponens objectum est tantum causa moralis; others that it is *causa efficiens objectiva protatarctita respectu earum operationum quæ ab illa immediate exercentur; sed causa finalis respectu aliorum operationum quæ ab illa sunt priorum interventu,* as *Burgersdis* speaks: But I remember none that call it *Instrumentum passivum:* yea not only the object, but declaration and all, *Instrumentum passivum.* For my part I am of *Scotus* minde, that *Objectum operatur efficienter & per modum naturæ in intellectum; sed moraliter tantum in voluntatem;* irresistibly and necessitatingly on the intellect (considering it as an intellect, and not so far as it is *sub imperio voluntatis & ita ejus operationes sunt participativè voluntariæ;)* but on the will not so. And I am sure this passive instrumentality of the Word in sanctifying, doth very ill agree with the language of Scripture; which makes the Word to be mighty, powerfull, pulling down strong holds, sharp, dividing, *&c.* The seed of God by which we are begotten, lively, the Word of life, saving mens souls, quickning, sanctifying, cleansing, *&c.* But what's all this to Justification?

---

§. 21.

Mr Bl. SO that if Burgersdicius *his* gladius *and* culter *be active instruments, and* Keckerman's Incus instrumentum fabricationis, *and his* scamnum & mensa accubitus, & terra ambulationis; *yet it followeth not, as is thence inferred, that there is no passive instrument. Here is an instrument that is passive.*

---

§. 21.

R.B. THese words import an intimation that I said all these were active instruments, which should not have been done, when I manifested that I took some of them for no instruments. 2. These words intimate, as if I concluded hence (if not only hence) that there are no passive instruments; which should not be, when I only brought in these as Objections to be answered, and argued with *Schibler* against passive instruments thus: Every instrument is an efficient cause: All efficiency is by action: Therefore every instrument is active. If you chose rather (as ordinarily you do) to silence my reasons then answer them, yet you should not have intimated, as if I had given you none, or but such as I gave not. 3. I look for your proof of a passive instrument; and not to say [Here is an instrument that is passive] as if you were demonstrating it to my eyes, when you bring nothing but singular Mr. *Pembles* singular word. And I doubt whether you beleeve him or your self throughly; for if you did, I think you would preach but coldly. I am perswaded you look your preaching should operate actively: And indeed so it must or not at all; for *pati non est operari;* and therefore *Pemble* denieth it to cooperate, and to operate. Be not offended if I doubt whether you beleeve this your self, in your Studies, Preaching, Writing and Exhortations. 4. I doubt not but that which doth only *realiter pati,* may be called an instrument *moraliter vel reputativè:* but then its reputative instrumentality, consisteth in a reputative activity. 5. And I doubt not but the *dispositio materiæ* may, by a borrowed speech be called *instrumentum recipiendi;* and so *instrumentum passivum,* i.e. *Passionis,* i.e. *Receptionis:* but all this is nothing to the business. 6. If it were proved that there were a hundred passive instruments, it would never be proved that faith is one (as an instrument signifieth an efficient cause) of Gods work of justifying us: neither Really nor Reputatively is it such.

F

§. 22.

§ 22.

Mr Bl. *THat which is produced by an efficient or principall agent to the producing of an effect, and receives activity and power from some other, is a passive iustrument and not active.*

§. 22.

R. B. STranger yet! 1. Its nothing to the nature of an instrument active or passive, whether [it be produced by the principal agent] or not, so it do but subserve that agent. 2. If this proposition be true, there is never an active instrument *in rerum natura*: For Angels and men, *calor, frigus*, and all creatures are produced by God as the principal cause to the producing of some effects (except there be any *ultimi effectus* found out which are not causes of other effects) and they all receive activity and power from God. Those that are most for passive instruments say, *calor* is an active instrument. But if I use fire to warm my beer, or burn any thing, this receives its activity and power from another, and therefore must be no active instrument, with you. If there be no active instrument, when I thought there had been no passive instrument, I was far wide. 3. But what mean these strange words of [Activity and power received] if the instrument be not active? Is not the *Potentia* here meant, *Potentia efficiendi*? and is not all effection by action? And is not the activity here mentioned, an activity in causing? What? and yet no active instrument? Be not offended with me, Dear brother, if I confess, that you and I differ in more points then one, and in our Philosophy as well as Theology.

§. 23.

Mr Bl. *BUt the Word is produced and held forth of God for the work of Justification, and hath its power of working elsewhere.*

§. 23.

R. B. YEt more strange! 1. Is it not enough that you take the Word to be a passive instrument of Confirmation and Conversion? and all the work that it doth on the souls of your hearers really? but you must feign the Word to be the passive instrument of Justification too? Is there any thing in the whole world that can more unfitly be called a passive instrument, then the Covenant of Justification? Why, it is Gods only instrument of active Constitution of the dueness of the benefit? Though it be but *actione morali, ut signum voluntatis donatoris*. The *Debitum* results from the Grant, Deed of Gift, Testament, or Instrument of Donation or Conveyance, as from its *fundamentum proximum*: And is the *fundamentum proximum Relationis* a passive Instrument?

2. The Word hath its power of working elsewhere, that is, from God; but not from mans faith: Farre be such a thought from my soul.

3. I suspect by your words, when you say [the Word is produced and held forth of God] and by your discourse all along, that you all this while understand not

not what I mean by the Covenants juftifying : (yet I had hoped you had underſtood the thing it felf.) You feem to think that the Covenant juftifies by fome real operation on the foul, as the Papifts fay; and our Divines fay, It fanctifies; or as it juftifies in *foro confcientiæ*, by giving affurance and comfort. But Sir, I opened my thoughts of this fully in *Aphor*. pag. 173, 174, 175, 176, 177, 178, 179. I fcarce beftowed fo many words of any one particular point. I fpeak not of the effect of Gods Word, as preached to mens hearts: but as it is *Lex promulgata, & Fædus, & Teftamentum*, and fo doth convey Right, or Conftitute the duenefs of the benefit? *This is the Record that God hath given us, eternall Life, and this Life is in his Son*, &c. 1 *Joh*. 5. 11, 12. This Gofpel-donation doth conftitute the dunefs of the thing given, to us; and thus the Covenant juftifies, as a written pardon under the Kings hand, or an act of grace or oblivion, doth pardon. Do you not oft read in Divines of *Juftificatio Juris, vel Legis*, as diftinct from *Juftificatio Judicis, vel per fententiam*? I referre you to what I faid in the cited place.

§. 24.

Mr *Bl.* FOrgivenefs *of fins is preached in the Gofpel*, Act. 13. 32. *But it is thofe that beleeve that are juftified. Faith through the Spirit gives efficacy and power of working to it.*

§. 24.

R. B. I Should tremble to fay fo: What *Romanift* by the doctrine of merit gives more to man in the work of Juftification! If our faith give efficacy and power to the Gofpel to juftifie us, then we juftifie our felves when the Gofpel juftifies us! then the Gofpel is our inftrument of Juftification! And can this be unlefs it be alfo faid that we made the Gofpel? Then God and we are concaufes in the Gofpels act of Donation: And is it the fame power and efficacy for juftifying, which the Gofpel receives from God, and which it receives from faith? or are they divers? If divers, fhew us what they are; and which part of its power and efficacy the Gofpel receives from faith, and which from God? If they are the fame, then God muft convey juftifying efficacy and power into faith firft, and by faith into the Gofpel: which who imagineth? or why fhould I be fo vain as to ftand to confute it? O that you had condefcended fo far to your Readers weaknefs, as to have deigned to fhew him, *Quomodo patitur Evangelium recipiendo? & Quid recipit ut fiat potens & efficax? & quomodo hæc potentia & efficacia fuit in fide? utrum eminenter an formaliter? aut utrum fides id communicavit quod nunquam habuit? & quomodo agit fides in hoc influxu caufativo in Evangelium?* with many more of the like, which you make neceffary to be enquired after. And why gave you no proof from Scripture or reafon for a point that is fo new, that I think never man printed before you, for fo far as I can learn at prefent: That faith gives efficacy and power of fanctifying or exciting Grace, perhaps fome before you have delivered: but that it gives efficacy and power of juftifying, I think not any.

2. And fure you do not take the foregoing words for proof: If you do, I defire your Reader may not do fo, What though only Believers are juftified by the Covenant? Doth it follow that faith gives efficacy and power to the Covenant to juftifie? Then either there are no conditions or caufes *fine quibus non*; or elfe

F 2 they

they all are efficients, and give efficacy and power to other efficients: What if your father bequeath by his Testament 110^l a piece to each of his sons? to one on condition he will ask it of his elder brother, and thank him for it: to another, if he be married by such a time: to a third, if he will promise not to wast it in prodigality: Do any of these conditions give efficacy and power to the Testament? No: Yet the Testament doth not *efficaciter agere* till they are performed. Why is that? Because all such instruments work morally, only by expressing *ut signa* the Will of the Agent: and therefore they work both when and how he will; and it is his Will that they shall not work till such a time, and but on such terms; and so he frames the conditions himself, as *obices* to suspend his Testament or other instrument from acting or effecting, till they are performed: but not to give efficacy and power to his Testament. If the gift be *in diem*, the instrument receives not efficacy and power from the Time, *quando venit dies*: no more doth it *per præstationem conditionis*.

3. Your terms of [Faiths giving power through the Spirit] tell me, that sure you still look at the wrong act of the Gospel; not at its moral act of Conveyance or Donation, but at its real operation on mans heart: For neither Scripture nor Divines use to say, The Gospel remitteth sin, or justifieth by the Spirit: Nor doth the Spirit otherwise do it, then by enditing the Gospel; unless by the Spirit you mean the Godhead in Essence, and not in Personality. Sanctification is ascribed to the Spirit as the efficient, but so is not forgiveness and Justification: Nor do I like your phrase, as to sanctification it self, That faith conveys efficacy and power to the Gospel through the Spirit: For 1. I had rather say, The Gospel and Spirit, or the Spirit by the Gospel, convey efficacy and power to faith, then faith to the Gospel. 2. How faith should convey this through the Spirit, is quite beyond my reach: Doth the Spirit receive any influx from faith, and thereby a power, and then convey this to the Gospel from our faith? But its like you mean, the Spirit doth it through faith.

§. 25.

Mr BL. *SO that neither the Gospel, nor faith in the Gospel, should in this office of an instrument in Justification be denied their due honour. The Gospel received by faith, is a plenary instrument in this work: and faith embracing the tender and promise of the Gospel. The Gospel is an outward instrument, saith* Ravanelly: *faith an inward: they both make up one instrument full and compleat: yet faith is more aptly and fitly called an instrument: Seeing that faith gives efficacy, as an instrument to the Word: the Word may be without faith, and so no instrument at all: but faith alway presupposeth the Word of promise: it is not without its object.*

---

§. 25.

R.B. 1. HAd you first proved any such honour due to faith, and so to man, as to be the instrument of Justification, yea and more fitly then the Gospel, so to be called, then you might fairly have thus concluded. But I like not Arguments that have but one part, being all Conclusion. I will say more for the Gospels instrumentality. *Signum voluntatis Donatoris constituens jus ad beneficium Donatum (etsi in diem vel sub conditione) est Donatoris instrumentum maxime proprium: Sed Testamentum Christi est signum voluntatis divinæ jus nostrum ad Christum*

& Justificationem passivam constituens, (viz. sub conditione, & actualiter quando præstatur conditio:) Ergo Testamentum Christi est instrumentum hujus donationis, maximè proprium. For the *major*, examine it by all the qualifications of an instrument, and it will appear undoubted. 1. *Subservit causæ principali, scilicet voluntati donatoris.* 2. *Actio ejus & principalis sunt eadem actio: scilicet Donatio, vel constituere debitum beneficii.* 3. The true definition of an instrument agrees to it: *Instrumentum est quod ex directione alterius principalis agentis influit ad producendum effectum se nobiliorem: Vel, per quod causa alia operatur, sic, ut hoc elevetur ad effectum se nobiliorem, seu ultra perfectionem & suam & actionis suæ.* 4. Yea it is the most perfect instrument; for *instrumentum eo melius est quanto magis est fini proportionatum:* ut Aquin. 1.2ae. q. 188. a. 7. But Gods Legal giant is most perfectly proportioned to the conveyance of right to Christ, and his benefits. Prove this much of faith, as to Justification, before you again tell the world that faith is more fitly called an instrument of Justification.

2. If the Gospel received by faith be a plenary instrument of justifying, as you say: Then 1. How is faith more fitly called an instrument? 2. Then *Recipere Evangelium* is *instrumentum justificandi maximè proprium* (as you think) making the Gospel a compleat instrument.

3. If faith and the Gospel be both full compleat instruments, then either *ejusdem effecti per eandem actionem, vel per diversas:* not *per eandem actionem*, For 1. Then they should be one instrument. 2. Their *esse* is so different that their *operari* must needs be different. 2. If *per diversas actiones*, then coordinate or subordinate: You think subordinate, it seems, and that faith gives power and efficacy to the Gospel; If so, then faith doth *modo & sensu nobiliore Justificare quam Testamentum:* But thats farre from truth: For 1. It is most proper to say, The Covenant-grant justifieth: or the Law of grace justifieth; but it is less proper to say, Faith justifieth: and Scripture never saith so that I know of; but that we are justified by faith. 2. You say your self that faith is but a passive instrument: but the Testament is active, (morally in its kinde.) 3. *Recipere Evangelium* is not so properly *Justificare*, as is *immediate Justificare, Remittere, Jus ad Christum & remissionem constituere*, which is the Gospels act: *(Credere non est tam propriè Justificare.* Much more might be said of this, if necessary.

4. How plain a contradiction do you speak, that faith and the Gospel are two instruments: and that both make one compleat instrument. They might have been said to be materially two things, making one instrument without contradiction; but not without notorious untruth.

5. For it is no better when you say, they make up one compleat instrument. For 1. You said before that faith gives power and efficacy to the Gospel: which if true, then the Gospel is an instrument subordinate to faith, and therefore not one with it. 2. The Gospel is *causa totalis in suo genere*, fully as an instrument conveying right, *quando vel venit dies, vel præstatur conditio:* therefore it is not *causa partialis, vel pars causæ.* 3. There is such a disparity in the actions of each, viz. *Credere*, and *Remittere vel donare Christum & Remissionem*, that they cannot possibly as *causæ partiales*, constitute one compleat cause: For one immediatly and properly produceth the effect: the other not so. 4. You say, that they are both passive instruments: But so they cannot make one instrument: For surely *nec patiuntur idem, nec ab eodem; nec formam Justificationis Evangelium patiendo recipit.* Though indeed your authority must do more then your reasons, to prove it of either.

6. If faith be more aptly and fitly (as you speak) called, an instrument, then it is a properer speech to say, Faith, or man by faith, forgiveth sins; then that The Covenant-grant or Condonation, or act of pardon doth forgive them. *Sed Absit!*

7. When you have well proved that repeated dangerous assertion, [That faith gives efficacy as an instrument to the Word;] you may next take the boldness to speak out its consequents, and say, Gods Word is the Believers words: the Believer enableth Gods Law of grace to forgive him: *Credere non est actus subditi, vel Legatarij, sed Rectoris, Judicis, & Testatoris: Ergo Homo habet authoritatem seipsum Justificandi, & sibi ipsi condonandi, & credendo hanc exercet authoritatem.*

8. Your strange proof is oft answered. What though the Word without faith is no instrument? Doth it follow that therefore either faith makes it an instrument, or is an instrument it self? The King grants an Act of Oblivion or Pardon to a thousand Traytors, on condition that by such a day they come and seek and thankfully accept it: Doth their seeking or thankfull Acceptance, give power and efficacy as an instrument to the Kings Pardon? Or are the Pardon and Acceptance one compleat instrument? Or is it more fit to call the Traytors Acceptance, the instrument of his Pardon, then the Kings Act? *Credat qui credere potis est.*

Twisse saith, *An audebit Arminianus aliquis affirmare Remissionem peccatorum esse effectionem fidei? tametsi nisi credentibus contingat ista Remissio. Dices, fidem saltem prærequisitum quiddam esse ad Remissionem peccatorum consequendam. Esto; atque hac ratione dicatur effectio fidei, sed in genere tantum causa dispositivæ.* Twiss. *Vind. Grat.* l.1.part.2.§.25.p. mihi 173. So he oft saith both of Faith and Works, that they justifie only *ut causa dispositivæ:* and therefore in one kinde of causality; and not as instruments properly so called.

---

§. 26.

Mr Bl. T*Herefore to winde up this whole Dispute in which I have studied to be brief, (though I fear some will think I have been too tedious:) seeing that those that make faith the instrument in Justification, make the Gospel an instrument likewise, and dare not go about to strip it of its honour: I hope that they that make the Gospel an instrument, will acknowledge faith to be an instrument in like manner, being in their efficacy as instruments so inseparably joyned, and so all the Controversie will be fairly ended and concluded.* Amen.

---

§. 27.

R.B. 1. IF this be a Dispute, I am none of those that think it too long: I scarce finde a line in many Pages: It is in my eyes so short, that it seems as nothing.

2. Your motion for decision will take, when man is proved to be God: then mans act of Beleeving may fairly share of the same honour with Gods act of Legal forgiving: And yet then I shall demurre on the preferring it: But till then, I love Peace and Unity, but not on such a compromising, as to share the honour of the Redeemer with the redeemed, of the Creator with the creature, of the Soveraign pardoning, with the Traytor pardoned.

3. I

3. I like *Amen* better then *Ergo*: and *Herberts* transformation I much applaud; but not the substitution of *Amen*, for a necessary *Ergo*. This *nimium felix disputandi genus*, that can prove all with a word, an *ipse dico*, and wipe off all that is opposed with a wet finger, I never liked. I must next take in what you adde afterwards.

§. 27.

Mr Bl. Pag. 91.

Obj. *IT is said by another, If faith be a condition of the Covenant of Grace, then it can be no instrument of our Justification: If it be a condition in this Covenant, it justifies as a condition, and then it cannot justifie as an instrument, and so I pull down what I build, and run upon contradictions.*

Answ. *I answer, I should rather judge on the contrary, that because it is a condition of the Covenant in the way as it is before exprest, that it is therefore an instrument in our Justification. God tenders the gift of righteousness to be received by faith: He Covenants for this faith; for acceptation of it: By beleeving then we keep Covenant and receive Christ for Justification; we as well do what God requires, as receive what he tenders; we do our duty, and take Gods gift; and therely keep Covenant, and receive life, and so faith is both a condition and an instrument.*

§. 27.

R. B. But do you take *officium* and *conditio* to be all one? I easily yield that we may do our duty in beleeving, though it were an instrument: But a condition is more then a duty: yea then a duty to be performed for the obtaining of a benefit. *Cujacius* saith, *Conditio est Lex addita negotio quæ donec præstetur eventum suspendit; Vel est modus vel causa quæ suspendit id quod agitur, donec ex post-facto confirmetur.* Or as *Mynsinger, Cum quid in casum incertum (i.e. contingens) qui potest tendere ad esse vel non esse confertur.* And they are divided into *Potestativas, Casuales, Mixtas*: Ours is of the former sort, and I define it, *viz.* the condition of the Covenant to be, *Actio voluntaria de futuro, a Deo Legislatore & Christo Testatore in nova Lege, Fœdere, Testamento requisita, ut ex ejus præstatione constituatur jus actuale ad beneficium: vel, ut obligationem & eventum suspendat donec præstetur.* For *ex stipulatione conditionali neque obligatio neque actio ulla est, antequam conditio eveniat: Quia quod est in conditione, non est in obligatione. Ut. Mynsing. in Instit. Schol. pag. 523.*)

2. You must consider that it is not *de conditione contractus venditionis & emptionis, vel emphyteusis, vel locationis,* or any the like, that is *propter pretium*: but it is the condition *puræ donationis,* but somewhat partaking *naturæ Feudi,* as to some of the Benefits. This being premised, it is evident that faith cannot justifie both as a condition, and as an instrument of Justification. For 1. Either of them importeth the *proximam & causalem rationem* of faith, as to the effect: But it is utterly inconsistent with its nature to have two such different nearest causal interests. To be an instrument of justifying, is to effect it *per medum instrumenti*: To be the condition, is to be the *causa sine qua non,* which doth not effect, but suspend the effect till performed: It hath the name of a cause, (and sometime is *ex materia* a moral impulsive, and sometime not) but it hath the true nature of such a *medium*

ad

ad finem, as is no cause. As faith cannot be both *efficiens effecti, & effectum ejusdem efficientis*, nor be both the efficient and constitutive cause (material or formal,) no more can it produce one and the same effect of Justification *per modum instrumenti efficientis*, and *per modum conditionis sine qua non*: 2. Else you must feign the pardoning act to run thus [I will pardon thee on condition thou wilt pardon thy self by beleeving, as the instrument] and not only [on condition thou accept Christ.] 3. It belongeth to the pardoning instrument to conferre the right to the thing, that is, to dissolve the obligation to punishment, and to constitute the condition of this Right or Pardon: For *Donantis est constituere conditionem etiam in ipsa instrumentali Donatione*. But faith doth not conferre Right; for your self say, It doth but receive it: It doth not dissolve the obligation, but accept a Saviour to dissolve it: It doth not constitute the condition of right; for you acknowledge it is the condition it self.

To conclude this Point, for the compromising or shortening this difference between you and me, I will take your fairer offer, *pag.* 75. or else give you as fair an offer of my own. Yours is this: [Faith is considered under a double notion. First as an instrument (or if that word will not be allowed) as the way of our interest in Christ, and priviledges by Christ.] In this general I easily agree with you.

If that satisfie not, I propound this, Call you it an instrument of receiving Christ, and consequently righteousness; and give me leave to call it precisely a condition, or a moral disposition of the subject to be justified; and I will not contend with you: So be it, you will 1. not lay too great a stress on your own notion, nor make it of flat necessity, nor joyn with them that have made the Papists believe that its a great part of the Protestant Religion, and consequently that in confuting it, they refell the Protestants. 2. Nor say any more that it gives efficacy and power to the Gospel to justifie us, and is more fitly then the Gospel called an instrument. 3. Yea, I must desire that you will forbear calling it at all an instrument of Justification, and be content to call it an instrument of receiving Justification: and I would you would confess that too to be an improper speech. If you resolve to go further, let me desire you hereafter 1. To remember that its you that have the Affirmative, that faith is the instrument of justifying us: and I say, It is not written, you adde to Scripture: Therefore shew where it is written, expressely or by consequence. 2. Do not blame me for making sincere obedience part of the meer condition (wherein I think you say as much as I) and so as giving too much to man, when you give intollerably so much more as to make him the instrumental efficient cause of forgiving and justifying himself. 3. Above that I have yet said, I pray forget not one thing: to prove faith to be the instrumental efficient of sentential Justification (which is most properly and fully so called) as well as of Legal constitutive Justification. For thats the great point of which you have just nothing (*pace tui si ita dicam*) of which you should have said much. And so much for the Controversie.

§. 28.

§ 28.

Of Evangelical Personal Righteousness.

Mr Bl. Pag. 110, &c.

THere is yet a third opinion, which I may well doubt whether I understand, but so far as I do understand, I am as far from assent to it as either of the former: and that is of those, who do not only assert a personal inherent Righteousness, as well as imputed, against the Antinomians; but also affirm that this Righteousness is compleat and perfect: which if it were meant only of the perfection of the subject, as opposed to hypocrisie, dissimulation, or doubleness, implying that they do not only pretend for God, but are really for him; that they do not turn to him feignedly (as Israel was sometime charged, Jer. 3.10) but with an upright heart: Or of the perfection or entireness of the object: (respecting not one, or only some, but all Commandments) which is called a perfection of parts; we might readily assent to it. The Covenant cals for such perfection, Gen. 17.1. Walk before me and be thou perfect: and many have their witness in Scripture that they have attained to it, as Noah, Gen. 7.9. Job 1.1. Hezekiah, Isa. 38.3. But a perfection above these is maintained; a perfection compleat and full. [Righteousness signifies (as is said) a conformity to the Rule, and a conformity with a quatenus or an imperfect rectitude is not a true conformity or rectitude at all: Imperfect Righteousness is not Righteousness but unrighteousness. It is a contradiction in adjecto; Though holiness be acknowledged to be imperfect in all respects, where perfection is expected, in reference to the degree that it should obtain, or the degree which it shall obtain, or in reference to the excellent object, about which it is exercised, or in reference to the old Covenant, or the directive, and in some sense the preceptive part of the new Covenant; In all these respects it is imperfect; and Righteousness materially considered is holiness, and therefore thus imperfect: but formally considered, it is perfect Righteousness or none; this not in relation to the old Rule, but the new Covenant.] Upon this account they are charged with gross ignorance, that use and understand the word Righteous and Righteousness as they relate to the old Rule; as if the godly were called Righteous (besides their imputed Righteousness) only because their sanctification and good works have some imperfect agreement with the Law of works. This and much more to assert a personal perfect inherent Righteousness, as is said: all which as it is here held out, is new to me, and I must confess my self in ignorance all over. I never took imperfect Righteousness to imply any such contradiction, any more then imperfect holiness.

---

§. 28.

R. B. THe third opinion you rise against, is that which you take to be mine, as your citing my words doth manifest: but you confess your self uncertain whether you understand it or not. There is a possibility then that when you do understand me, you may prove your self of the same Opinion.

In the mean time it is your Reasons which must justifie your strong dissent, which I shall be bold to examine. Where you say, I [do not only assert a personal inherent Righteousness, as well as imputed, against the Antinomians, but also affirm that this Righteousness is perfect.] I Reply: Either you suppose the

G later

later propofition to be an addition to the former, in terms only, or in fenfe alfo: If only in terms, the fenfe being the fame, I fuppofe you would not oppofe it. If in fenfe, then it is either fomewhat real, or fomewhat modal, which you fuppofe the later to adde to the former: Real it is not, for *Res & perfectio Rei*, are not diftinguifhed as *Res & Res*, but as *Res & Modus*. It is therefore but a modal addition. And it is fuch a *Modus* as is convertible with *Ens*. And therefore there is as much imported in the firft Propofition [We have a perfonal inherent Righteoufnefs] as in the fecond [We have a perfect perfonal inherent Righteoufnefs.] For *Ens & Perfectum* are as convertible as *Ens & Bonum*, or *Ens & Verum*.

You adde [If it were meant only of the perfection of the fubject, as oppofed to hypocrifie, &c. or of the perfection or entirenefs of the object (refpecting not only One or Some, but All Commandments) which is called a perfection of parts, we might readily affent to it.]

To which I Reply: 1. Your terms are uncouth to me, but I will do my beft to guefs at your meaning. A perfection of the fubject is *perfectio effentialis vel accidentalis*. The former is no more but *effe fubjectum, vere & proprie*. The later may be varioufly taken, according to the variety of accidents: But certain I am that the fubject is imperfect, *quod ad perfectionem accidentalem*. And therefore in this large expreffion, you feem to fay much more then I. You and I, who are the fubjects of Righteoufnefs, are imperfect, though perfectly fubjects.

2. That which you call here *perfectio fubjecti*, is nothing but the truth of the immediate fubject, as I underftand you. *Juftitia eft vel caufæ, vel perfonæ, vel faltem confiderata vel ut caufæ vel ut perfonæ. Caufa eft fubjectum proximum: Perfona eft fubjectum primum & principale. Juftitia caufæ, eft vel actionum vel habituum aut difpofitionum. Perfecti funt habitus & difpofitiones, & actiones vel perfectione effentiali Tranfcendentali, (& ita perfecti funt, quia vere funt,& vere funt tales:) vel perfectione accidentali: & ita aliquo modo perfecti, & alio imperfecti funt.* It feems therefore that you here fay as much at leaft as I, for the perfection of the *matter* of our inherent Righteoufnefs, (if not more) for I am fure you fpeak more unlimitedly.

3. I do charitably conjecture, that when you fpeak of [a perfection of the object] you do not mean as you fpeak, but you mean a perfection of our Acts as they refpect the object, extenfively (for whether you include or exclude intenfion, I know not.) Here muft I diftinguifh between objects of abfolute neceffity, (and fo of the acts about thofe objects) which a man cannot be juftified or faved without: and 2. Objects of lefs neceffity (and fo acts) which its poffible to be juftified and faved without. In regard of the former, I confefs our acts may be faid to be [Truly acts that are exercifed about fuch objects] if you will call that perfection (as in a larger fenfe you may:) But as to the later, I acknowledge no fuch perfection. And therefore (for that which you call [A perfection of parts] I acknowledge that every righteous man, hath a perfection of the effential parts (that is, he wants them not) but not of the integral alwaies; much lefs of accidents, which are improperly called parts.

Next you repeat fome of my words, and then adde [All which as it is here held out, is new to me, and I muft confefs my felf in ignorance all over.] Reply: I cannot help that, but I will do towards it what I can, that it may be none of my fault: and therefore will let you know my meaning. And in opening the fenfe and nature of [Perfection] I cannot give you more of my minde

in

in a narrow room, then *Schibler* hath laid down in *Metaph.*l.1.c.11. *Perfectum est cui ad essentiam nihil deest.* 'Scaliger *Exercit.*140. p.470. *Omne quod est, sibi est, & bonum, & totum, & perfectum.*' It is a Metaphisical Transcendental Perfection that I speak of, which hath no contrary in Being; which consisteth in the presence of all things necessary to Being: and that only of an inferiour, derived Being, such as the creature is; for we meddle not with the infinite Divine Being or perfection; Nor do we take it in a comparative sense, but in an absolute: this being a Righteousness perfect in its kinde, though a more perfect kinde accidentally, may be found out: I take it rather *nominaliter* then *participaliter:* but still remember that I take it not *de perfectione accidentali, sed essentiali.* And therefore I still maintain that in several accidental respects our Righteousness is imperfect.

Now to know how our Righteousness is essentially perfect, let us consider what is essential to it. Its form is a Relation of our actions and dispositions immediatly, and our selves remotely, as compared with the Law or Rule. This Law (besides the constitution of the reward and punishment considered in themselves, of which we now speak not) doth 1. Constitute (I mean efficiently determine) what shall be our duty in general. 2. It determineth more specially, what part of this duty, shall be the condition of our Justification and salvation, *sine qua non.* When we come to be judged at Gods barre, he that hath performed the condition shall be justified, though he have omitted much of the other duty: but all that have not performed the condition shall be condemned. (But remember of what it is that this is the condition: viz. of the new Law of grace, whose office is to make over to us Free remission of sins, and salvation through the satisfaction and merits of Christ: and not the condition of that Law, which gives the reward directly for the work.) Take up altogether then, and you will see that 1. Righteousness is formally a relation: 2. And that not of our Actions or dispositions to the meer precept of the Law, determining of duty as such, (commonly called the moral Law;) but 1. to the Law, as determining of the condition of life or death; 2. to the promise and threatning of that Law, which are joyned to the condition. So that [to be righteous] signifieth (*quoad legem novam*) these two things: 1. [*Non obligatus ad pænam, & cui debetur præmium.*] 2. [*Qui conditionem impunitatis, & præmii præstitit.*] The first question in judgement being [*An sit obligatus ad pænam, vel non? & an præmium sit debitum?*] therefore the former is our first and principal righteousness, and here to be pleaded. But before the first question can be determined, the second must be raised and resolved, [*Utrum præstitit conditionem?*] And here the second is our Righteousness (*conditionis præstatio*) by which we must answer the accusation [*Conditionem non præstitit.*] That is, [He lived and died an unbeliever or impenitent.] So that 3. You see that our first Righteousness [*Non reatus pænæ: vel jus ad impunitatem & ad præmium,*] as it requireth Christs perfect satisfaction, as a *medium* to it, by which all the charge of the Law of works, must be answered; so it requires our performance of the condition of the Law of grace, as another *medium*, by which Christ and his benefits are made ours, and by which the false accusation of [being unbelievers and impenitent, and so to be condemned by the Law of grace it self, as having no part in Christ] must be answered, and we justified against it. 4. It is not only the form of our righteousness, that is *transcendenter* perfect, but also the matter, as such, as it is the matter: that is, the subject actions and dispositions, are subjects truly capable of that relation. All this is no more but that it is a

G 2 true

true Righteousness, and not equivocally or falsly so called: and so that even the matter or subject, is really the matter or subject of such a Righteousness. 5. The form here being a relation, in it self, admits not of degrees. 4. The matter or subject (our dispositions and actions) though *qua materia*, they have the foresaid metaphysical perfection, yet considered in it self, or considered in reference to the meer precept of the Law, and so in its meer morality, it is imperfect. As *Schibler* saith, *Omne perfectum est ens: & omne ens est perfectum transcendentali, & essentiali perfectione: Duobus tamen modis adhuc possunt entia vocari imperfecta. 1. Accidentaliter, quod scilicet desit id quod ad integritatem vel Ornamentum, vel altiorem & intentiorem statum pertinet. Et sub hac imperfectione etiam continetur imperfectio, quæ est in defectu partium materiæ minus principalium. Nam materia pertinet ad essentialem perfectionem, sed id completur satis secundum partes principales in toto heterogeneo, quæ sufficientes sunt ad radicandam & sustentandam formam, manifesto indicio, quod ablatis partibus minus principalibus, manet prior species. Veluti si homo & careat pedibus, & brachiis & vaso & oculis, adhuc tamen est homo, &c. Atque ita per ablationem partium minus principalium nihil adhuc deest quod pertineat ad transcendentalem perfectionem, quæ essentialis est ipsius hominis. Atque ita homo adhuc est perfecte homo, & perfecte ens: indeque nec hac imperfectione tollitur perfectio transcendentalis, &c. 2. Possunt vocari entia [Imperfecta] comparatè, quod scilicet non habeant essentiam tam perfectam & nobilem, quam alia. Ita materia est imperfecta, quia non sit, tam nobile ens ac forma, &c. Hæc igitur imperfectio iterum non tollit perfectionem transcendentalem, quo minus transcendenter, perfecta dicantur quæ sic sunt imperfecta,* l. 1. c. 11.

In both these respects I confess and maintain that our Righteousness is imperfect: that is 1. Our graces, holiness, obedience, good works, are gradually imperfect, yea oft *numero*, as well as *gradu*. 2. The Righteousness which we have in or from Christs perfect satisfaction and merits, is a Righteousness of a more noble and perfect kinde, then this inherent Righteousness required by the Law of grace: for the later stands in subordination to the former, as a necessary means, *i. e.* condition to make it ours. *Omne tamen ens est perfectum, non solum in genere entis, sed etiam in genere talis entis,* &c. *Et sic etiam materia, etsi in comparatione ad alia entia, sit satis imperfecta, tamen in suo genere habet omnino perfectionem, neque sic deest ei quicquam eorum, quæ ad ipsius esse pertinent.* Schib. ubi sup. n. 7, 8.

The like doctrine hath *Calovius Metaphys. Divin.* p. 246, &c. *de perfectione,* fully: where of our imputed and inherent Righteousness, he saith, *Prior denominatione extrinseca, posterior intrinseca, utraque verè, & realiter, ipsis competit.* And these are two of his Positions, *Perfectio non admittit magis & minus:* and *Perfecto nihil potest accedere vel decedere.* Multitudes might quickly be cited to the same purpose with these abovesaid, but that it is so known a case.

And thus I have done what at present I thought my duty, that it might not be my fault that you are [in ignorance all over.] But I have said the less because I have lately more exactly opened the nature of our Righteousness, in Answer to the Animadversions of another Learned Brother.

You adde [I never took imperfect Righteousness to imply any such contradiction, any more then imperfect holiness.] Reply: 1. Holiness is taken 1. For [the relation of a Person or Thing dedicated to God:] and so I confess it admits not of a *magis* or *minus* any more then Righteousness. 2. But our common use of the word [Holiness] when about persons, is for the qualities or actions of a spiritually-renewed man: and so I further say: 2. That this also hath its transcendental perfection, as well as Righteousness. But here's the difference (which if you

you adde to what is said before, you will more fully see my thoughts.) Holiness thus taken is a quality, which though it have the truth of Being, yet is intended and remitted, or doth *recipere magis & minus*. Righteousness is a relation, which in *suo formali* is not intended or remitted. Nay if you will exactly open it, it will appear that the Righteousness in question is a Relation founded in a Relation (the real conformity of our Acts to the Law or Rule, as it determineth what shall be the condition.) Yea more, that the very *subjectum proximum hujus relationis, nec intenditur nec remittitur:* and this is it that I mean by perfection, besides the foresaid transcendental perfection. But (because these things are *exactioris indagationis*) understand that the reason of this my assertion lies here: The Law as it is the rule of obedience, doth require perfect obedience in degree; and so here is an imperfection in our actions in the degree, as being short of what the Rule requireth; and it being these actions with their habits that we call our holiness (*ab efficiente & fine*) therefore we must needs say, Our holiness is imperfect: And if our Righteousness were to be denominated from this Law, commanding perfection, we must say, not that such Righteousness were imperfect, because the holiness or obedience is imperfect; but it is none at all, because they are imperfect: For imperfect obedience or holiness is not a subject or matter capable of the relation of [Righteous] according to that perfect Law which condemneth them, and admitteth only gradually-perfect obedience, as capable matter, without which the form cannot be received. And so our faith, repentance, and sincere Gospel-obedience, as compared to this perfect Law, are no perfect Righteousness, nor any Righteousness at all: And so this being the matter of our inherent Righteousness, I say, our faith and obedience are imperfect (though not imperfect Righteousness, because none) as thus compared. But then the Law as it is the determiner of the conditions, on which Christ and life shall be ours, hath made the matter or immediate subject, to be *in puncto*, as it were, so that it cannot be more or less, because it is the sincerity only of our faith and obedience, that is made the condition of Life, and not the gradual perfection. So that when we must be justified, the Question will not be, [Hast thou believed and obeyed perfectly?] but [Hast thou done it Truly.] So that no imperfection of the matter consistent with sincerity, makes it less capable of the form, nor no perfection of degrees makes it capable of more of the form. The condition here is as truly performed, by true believing and obedience, in a lower measure, as in a higher: yea and this true performance is as full a Righteousness (in relation to this part of the Law) as if the matter of faith and obedience were more perfect: The strongest faith doth not make you Righteous in a higher degree, then the weakest that is true: For the strongest is but *præstatio conditionis* (which is the Righteousness in question) and so is the weakest. It is not therefore from this act of the Law (determination of the condition) that our graces or duties, are diversified as more or less perfect in degree, but it is in respect to the other act or part of the Law (determination of duty, as such.) So that in a word, Duty simply as duty, and holiness, or supernatural grace, as such, may be more or less. But holiness and duty, as the *Materia requisita vel subjectum proximum Justitiæ, consistit in indivisibili.*

Only let it be remembred, that I speak this of the promise of impunity and glory everlasting absolutely considered, and not of a comparative degree of glory: For it may be yet consistent with this, that a greater faith, love and obedience, may have a promise of greater glory.

Remember also I pray you (if you will do me justice) 1. That I did only assert in my Aphorismes [1. A metaphysical perfection of Being, and 2. A perfection of sufficiency in order to it's end] in our righteousness : 2. And the same transcendental perfection of Being, I affirmed of holiness it self, only adding, that it being a Quality may be intended and remitted, but Righteousness being a Relation cannot *ex parte sui*. Now which of these perfections of Righteousness do you deny ? Not that of sufficiency as to the end, as you expresly affirm. It must therefore be the transcendental perfection of Essence. And if that be denied, then righteousness is no righteousness : for so *omne ens perfectum est*: And then you must maintain that it is but equivocally called righteousness, but indeed is not so. But yet this I finde you not about, but rather confess the contrary, not only by affirming inherent Righteousness, but also affirming a double perfection of it, which you are pleased to call subjective and objective, and which can be no less then I here affirmed.

§. 29.

Mr Bl.[1] [Saiah *I am sure saith*, All our Righteousness are as filthy rags, *Isa.64.6.* *No greater charge of imperfection can lye against the most imperfect holiness, then the Prophet laies upon our Righteousness.* [2] *Neither do I understand how holiness should be imperfect taken materially, and righteousness perfect, taken formally in reference to a Rule.*

---

§. 29.

R.B. 1. WIll not all the imperfections of our Righteousness which in the Aphor. I asserted, serve to warrant the Prophets comparison, without our denying the perfection of Being ? That is, that it is truly Righteousness ?

2. My opinion of that Text is, that the Prophet means plainly, [We are an unrighteous people,] or [we have no other Righteousness to glory of, but what is indeed no righteousness at all, no more then the filthy rags are clean] no nor so much ; for they may possibly have some part clean. Yet that this is called Righteousness, is no wonder, when the next words are Negative, *q.d.* [our Righteousness is none ; or is unrighteousness :] yea it is not unusual to give the name either from common estimation, or the persons profession, and especially from those actions which use to be the matter of Righteousness, though the form being wanting, they are not now actually the matter. So I think *Solomon* forbiddeth overmuch Righteousness. Further, it's considerable, what Righteousness it is that the Prophet there speaks of, whether universal or particular ? and whether Legal, consisting in absolute perfection ; or Evangelical, consisting in sincerity ? and also whether he speak of himself and each individual; or only of the Jewish Nation described according to the generality or main part of them.

3. As for that next passage, where you tell us what [you understand not] I confess it seems strange to me : but I hope you make it no argument against the opinion which you oppose. If it were a good argument indeed, then the less a man understands, the better he might dispute. But let us see what it is that you understand not. 1. [How holiness should be imperfect taken materially ?] Sure you understand that : for what else did you mean in the foregoing words, [No greater

greater charge of imperfection can lye against the most imperfect holiness?] 2. It is therefore, no doubt, the other branch that you mean, how [Righteousness is perfect taken formally in reference to a Rule.] 1. That Righteousness *in sensu Legali & forensi* is a relation consisting in a conformity, or congruency to the Rule, I suppose you understand, seeing both Schoolmen, and Protestant Divines do so commonly affirm it: *e. g. Scotus* and Dr *Twiss* oft. 2. That *omne ens est essentialiter perfectum*, I suppose also you understand: and so that this Relation must be a perfect Relation, or none at all: where there is the form, there is the being; and therefore the word [Righteousness] spoken *formaliter* of our Righteousness, must needs express that which is truly Righteousness, and not equivocally so called. 3. Yea I suppose you understand, that Relations do not admit of *magis* and *minus ex parte sui*, but only when they are founded in quality, *ex parte fundamenti vel subjecti:* At least if any would deny that, yet the relation in question, being of the nature of [Parity,] and not of similitude only, (which are both implied in conformity) doth not so much as *ratione fundamenti* admit of intension or remission. These things being all so generally acknowledged, you leave me only to admire that you should say, You understand them not.

---

§. 30.

Mr Bl: WE may (for ought I know) as well make holiness *formall*, and referre it to a Rule; and Righteousness *materiall*, in an absolute consideration, without reference to any Rule at all.

---

§. 30.

R.B. 1. WHether you take holiness as signifying a Quality or Relation, there is no doubt but it hath its form, or else it could not have a Being? Did you indeed imagine that I had denied that? 2. But that holiness in our common use of the word, doth formally consist in the relation of our qualities or acts to the Law, especially in that relation of conformity, that we are now speaking of, I finde not yet proved. Holiness taken for the qualities and acts themselves, is no relation. Holiness taken for Dedication to God, is such a kinde of Relation as Donation is: It referres to God as the *terminus:* For *omne sanctum est Deo sanctum.* But to be [Dedicated to God] and to be [conformed to the Law or Rule] are not all one. 3. If you or any man resolve to use holiness in the same sense as righteousness, if I once know your mindes, I will not contradict you, for I finde no pleasure in contending about words. But for my self I must use them in the common sense, if I will be understood. 4. That you may use the word [Righteousness] materially, without relation to any Rule, is as much as to say, We may denominate *a materia sine forma*. The form is relative. If you mean, We may denominate that which hath a form, from the matter, and not from the form, then I Reply, 1. Then you must not denominate properly and logically: 2. And then you must not call it Righteousness; except you mean *ludere aequivocis*, and speak *de Justitia particulari ethica qua suum cuique tribuimus*, when we are speaking *de Justitia Legali, Civili, Forensi*, called by the Schoolmen *Justitia universali* in our case. I am not of the Papists minde that make our Righteousness to be our new qualities, and confound *Justitiam & Sanctitatem, & inde Justificationem & Sanctificationem.*

§. 31.

§. 31.

Mr *Bl.* AND in such consideration I do not know how there can be perfection or imperfection either in holiness or righteousness: It is as they come up to, or fall short of the Rule, that they have the denomination of perfection or imperfection.

§. 31.

R.B. 1. AT the first view, the first sentence seemed so strange to me, that I thought it meetest to say nothing, because it is scarce capable of any apt answer but what will seem sharp or unmannerly. For that which you say you may consider, is something or nothing: If something, and yet not capable of perfection or imperfection, it is such a something as the world never knew till now. But upon second thoughts I finde that *de justitia* your words may be born: For it is *nothing* that you speak of. Legal Righteousness not related to the Law or Rule, is *Nothing*: And *Nothing* cannot be more perfect or less; *nisi negative*. But that holiness taken for spiritual habits and acts, can have neither perfection or imperfection; or that they are capable of no perfection or imperfection in any other sense, but as related; nor yet in any Relations to God, or the person dedicating, save only in the relation to the Rule; all these for the first reason shall have no answer but a recital.

§. 32.

Mr *Bl.* PAul's *Gospel frame, whether you will call it righteousness or holiness is set out I am sure,* Rom. 7. *full of imperfection; yet all this as in reference to the Rule, as is answered, or fell short in conformity to it,* vers. 22. *I delight in the Law of God after the inner man.*

§. 32.

R. B. 1. IS not [Righteousness] or [Holiness] as Scriptural, as Logical, as plain a term, and as fit for Disputants, as [Gospel-frame?] Till I know whether by [Gospel-frame] you mean, Habits, Acts, Relations (and what Relations) or what else, I shall pass it as uncapable of a better Reply. 2. Did not I acknowledge expresly as much imperfection as you here affirm of *Paul's* frame? Why then do you intimate by your arguing as if I did not? 3. There is a twofold Rule, or action of the Law, which our Habits and Actions do respect, as I have oft said. The first is the Precept determining of Duty simply. This all our Actions and Habits come short of, and therefore no man hath a Righteousness consisting in this conformity. The second is the promise, or that act going along with the promise, whereby God determineth of the condition. This is twofold: One of the Law of Nature and Works; and according to this no man is Righteous: for the condition and the duty are of the same extent, it being obedience gradually perfect, that is here the condition. The other is of the Law of Grace; which determineth what shall be the condition of our Right to Christ and Life. *Paul* never complaineth of an imperfection of Essence, of this last. It is of the former that he speaks. These necessary things should not be

hidden,

hidden, by confounding the several Rules, or Offices of Gods Law, which so apparently differ.

§. 33.

Mr Bl. ANd whereas a charge of ignorance is laid even upon learned Teachers, that commonly understand the word [*Righteousneß*] and [*Righteous*] as it refers to the old Rule, I profeß my self to have little of their Learning, but I am wholly theirs in this ignorance. I know no other Rule, but the old Rule, the Rule of the Moral Law; that is with me a Rule, a perfect Rule, and the only Rule.

§. 33.

R:B. Either I am an incompetent judge, through partiality, or else you had done but the part of a friend, yea of a candid adversary, to have taken in the rest of my words, which must make up the sense; which were these [*As if the godly were called Righteous (besides their imputed righteousneß) only because their sanctification and good works have some imperfect agreement to the Law of works.*] I pray let the word [*only*] be remembred. 2. It is but in this one point that I charge them with Ignorance. And who is not ignorant in more points then one? If it be so proud and arrogant a speech as some other Brethren have affirmed it to be, then every man is proud and arrogant that differs from another, and disputeth the difference. For I cannot differ from any man unless I suppose him to Erre: And doubtless every man is so farre Ignorant as he Erreth. Must I then differ from none? yea from no Learned Divines? Why then when one affirmeth and another denieth, I must be of both sides, for fear of censuring one side as Ignorant or Erroneous. 3. I confess I was not well acquainted with the *genius* of many of my Reverend and truly Honoured Brethren. I thought that no godly man would have taken himself wronged, if a man told him, he had Error, no more then to tell him he had Sin. I took it for granted that *humanum est errare*, and that we know but in part, and that sanctifying grace had so farre destroyed pride, and made the soul apprehensive of its imperfection, that, at least, men of eminent godliness could have endured patiently to hear that they are not omniscient nor infallible, and that they have some ignorance with their eminent knowledge? and why not in this point as well as another? If any think that I arrogate that knowledge to my self which I deny to them: I reply, So I do in every case wherein I differ from any man living: For if I thought not my judgement right, it were not indeed my judgement: and if I thought not his opinion wrong, I did not differ from him. But if they will affirm that therefore I do either vilifie them, or prefer my self in other things, I hope they will bring better proof of their affirmation. For my own part I unfeignedly profess my self conscious of much more ignorance then ever I charged on any of my Brethren in the Ministry: yea I must profess my self ignorant in a very great part of those Controversies, which are most commonly and confidently determined by my Brethren. I speak not all this as to Mr Bl. but to other Brethren that have made so strange an exposition of this one word, and of one more *pag.* 51. [*Vulgar Divines*] as that they can thence conclude and publish me a slighter and contemner of my Brethren: As if they that know *England*, could be ignorant, that the Churches among us have many such guides, as may well be called Vulgar Divines: Take them by number, and

H judge

judge (in those Counties that I am acquainted in) whether the greater number be of the Profound, or Subtill, or Angelical, or Seraphical, or Irrefragable sort of Doctors? or equal to some of these Reverend Excepters, whose worth I confess so far beyond my measure, that had I spoke of *them* as Vulgar Divines, they might well have been offended. But O that it were not true that there are such, through most of *England, Wales,* and *Ireland* (if any) on condition I were bound to Recant at every Market Cross in *England*, with a fagot on my back; so be it there were the same number of such choice men, as some of these my offended Brethren are in their stead. And then who knows not that the Vulgar or ordinary weaker Teachers, do take up that opinion, which is most in credit, and which is delivered by the most Learned Doctors whom they most reverence? So that the summe of my speech can be no worse then this: [It is the most common opinion] which is all one as to say [It is the opinion of the Vulgar Divines and some of the Learned, the other part of the Learned going the other way,] which is it that men censure for such an approbrious, injurious speech. Yet I will not wholly excuse it, nor this that M*r* Bl. toucheth upon. I confess it was spoken too carelessly, unmannerly, harshly, and I should better have considered how it might be taken.

As for M*r* *Blake*'s profession [That he hath little of their Learning, but is wholly theirs in this ignorance.] I did still think otherwise of him, and durst not so have described him: but yet my acquaintance with him is not so great, as that I should pretend to know him better then he knows himself; and I dare not judge but that he speaks as he thinks. Let me be bold to shew him part of that which he saith he is wholly ignorant of: That [our personal inherent Righteousness, is not denominated from the old Law or Covenant, as if we were called Righteous (besides our imputed Righteousness) only because our sanctification and good works have some imperfect agreement to the Law of Works] I prove thus:

1. If no man be called Righteous by the Law of Works, but he that perfectly obeyeth (so as never to sin) then no imperfect obeyer is called Righteous (*nisi æquivoce*) by that Law. But the Antecedent is true; Therefore so is the consequent.

2. If the Law of Works do curse and condemn all men, then it doth not judge them Righteous (*nisi æquivoce*.) But it doth curse and condemn all men: Therefore, *&c.*

3. If the Law of Works do judge us Righteous for our works (taking *righteous* properly and not equivocally) then we must be justified by our works, according to that Law: *Lex (n.) est norma judicii: & omnis vere justus, est justificandus. Justificatio Legis est virtualiter justificatio judicis.* He that condemneth the Just is an abomination to God. But we must not by the Law of Works be justified by our works: Therefore, *&c.*

4. He that is guilty of the breach of all Gods Laws, is not denominated Righteous (*nisi æquivoce*) by that Law: But we break all Gods Laws: Therefore. Yea he that offendeth in one is guilty of all. Reade *Brochmond in Jac.*2.10. and *Jacob, Laurentius*, and *Paulus Burgensis* (*in Lyra*) on the same Text. *Vid. & Placæum in Thesib. Salmurienf.* Vol.1.pag.29.§.13,*&c. Wotton de Reconcil.* Part.2. l.1. c.5.n.16. *Twiss. Vindic. Grat.* li.2. part.1.c.15. pag.(*vol. minore*) 214. col.2. See whether yours or mine be the Protestants doctrine. Here, if ever, its true, that *Bonum est ex causis integris.*

5. If

5. If imperfect works are all sinnes or sinfull, then they are not our Righteousness according to the Law of works. (For it justifieth no man for his sins.) But the former is true: Therefore the later. I doubt not but you know the state of the Controversie on this point, between us and the Papists.

6. If the Law of works do denominate a man righteous, for imperfect works (which truly and properly are but a less degree of unrighteousness) then it seems that all wicked men (if not the damned) are legally righteous: For they committed not every act of sin that was forbidden them, and therefore are not unrighteous in the utmost possible degree. And the Law of works doth not call one degree of obedience [Righteousness] more then another, except it be perfect. But certainly all the wicked are not Legally Righteous (*nisi æquivocè*) Therefore, &c.

7. If our Faith, Repentance and sincere Obedience, may be, must be, and is, called our Righteousness, as it is the performance of the conditions of the new Covenant, or Law of Grace, then (at least) not only as they have an imperfect agreement with the Law of Works. But the antecedent is true: Therefore the consequent.

Let us next peruse Mr. *Blake*'s Reasons, why [He is wholly theirs in this ignorance.] He saith [*I know no other Rule, but the old Rule, the Rule of the morall Law; that is with me a Rule, a perfect Rule, and the only Rule.*] Rep. *Sed distinguendum est.* The morall Law is taken either for the entire Law of works consisting of Precept and Sanction (and that either as it is the meer Law of nature, or as containing also what to *Adam* was superadded) or else it is taken only for the meer preceptive part of a Law, which is not the whole Law. In the later sense, it is taken 1. For the preceptive part of the Law given to *Adam*. 2. For the preceptive part of the Law of nature redelivered by *Moses*. 3. For the preceptive part of the Law of nature, now used by Christ the Mediator, as part of his own Law. 2. We must distinguish of a Rule. 1. There is the Rule of obedience, or what shall be *due from us*: This is the precept (under which I comprehend the prohibition, it being but *præceptum de non agendis.*) 2. There is the Rule of reward, determining what shall be due to us: This is the conditional promise or gift, so far forth as it determineth *de ipso præmio*. 3. There is the Rule of punishment, determining what shall be due to man upon his sin: This is the threatning. 4. There is the Rule of the condition of the reward or punishment, and of judging to whom they do belong, determining on what conditions or terms on their parts, men shall be saved, or else damned; (though the same acts were before commanded in the precept as they are duties, yet to constitute them conditions of the promise, is a further thing.) This is the promise and threatning, as they are conditional, or as they constitute their own conditions. I think the solidity and great necessity of all these distinctions, is beyond Dispute. These things being thus, 1. What confusion is it to talk of the moral Law being the only Rule, when it is not one thing that is called the moral Law? and who knows what you mean? 2. How strange a thing is it to my ears, that you, even you, should so wholly own this, and so heartily profess that you take the Moral Law for the *only Rule*? For suppose you take it for the preceptive part of the Law of nature only (as I think you do:) 1. That is but part of that very Law of nature: Doth not the Law of nature, as well as the positive Law, determine *de Debito pœnæ*, as well as *de Debito officii*? and is a Rule of punishment as well as duty. 2. Or if you took it for the whole Law of nature, is that the only Rule? 1. What say you for matter of of duty, to the positive Precepts of the Gospel? of Baptism, the Lords Supper, the Lords day, the Officers and Government of the Church, &c. Is the Law of nature the only Rule for these? If you say, They are reducible to the second Commandment: I demand 1. What is the second Commandment for the Affirmative part, but a general precept to worship God according to his Positive Institution? And doth this alone suffice? Doth it not plainly imply that there are and must be positive Laws instituting a way of worship? 2. Do you take the Precept *de genere*, to be equivalent to the Precepts *de speciebus*? or to be a sufficient Rule without them? If the Moral Law, or Law of Nature, be to you, *the only Rule*, and a *perfect Rule*, then you need no other. And if God had only written the ten Commandments, or only said in general, [Thou shalt worship God according to his positive Institutions] would it have been your duty to have Baptized, administred the Lords Supper? &c. Doth the general Precept constitute this particular Ordinance as my duty? If not (as nothing more certain) then the general Law, is not the only Rule, nor sufficient in *omni parte* (though sufficient in *suo genere, & ad partem propriam*) for the constitution of Worship, Ordinances, Church, Offices, &c. or acquainting us with our duty therein. Moreover, did Christ in Instituting these Ordinances and Officers, do any more then was done before, or not? If no more, 1. It is superfluous. 2. Shew where it was done before. 3. Sure the fourth Commandment did not at once command both the seventh day of the week and the first. If more, then the former was not sufficient, nor is now the only Rule.

Moreover, doth not the Scripture call Christ a Lawgiver? and say, *The Law shall go out of Zion*, &c. *Isa.* 2. 3. And is he not the Anointed King of the Church; and therefore hath Legislative power? And will he not use the principal part of his Prerogative?

2. I think the Moral Law, taken either for the Law given to *Adam* or written in Tables of stone, is not a sufficient Rule to us now for beleeving in Jesus Christ; no nor the same Law of nature, as still in force under Christ. For a general command of beleeving all that God revealeth, is not the only Rule of our faith; but the particular revelation and precept are part. And a general command to submit to what way God shall prescribe for our justification and salvation, is not the only Rule, but that particular prescript is part. And a general command, of receiving every offered benefit, is not the only or sufficient Rule for receiving Christ, without the Gospel-offer of him and his benefits.

3. And I suppose you grant that as mans soul hath an understanding and a will, the former being a passage to the later, in the former practical receptions being but initiate and imperfect, and in the later perfected; so Laws have their prefaces declaring the grounds and occasions of them, oft times; and so, the Laws of God have their Narratives, Histories and Doctrines, concerning the grounds, the subject, the occasion, &c. as well as the more essential parts, viz. Precepts and Sanction. These I spoke not of before in the distinctions. Now do you indeed think that the Law of nature, or what ever you now mean by the old Rule and Moral Law, is the sufficient and only Rule of Knowledge, Judgement and Faith? I take it for granted that you will acknowledge the assenting act of faith to be in the understanding: and that the Word of God is the rule of this assent. Had you in the old Rule or Moral Law, a sufficient and only Rule for your faith, in the Article of Christs Incarnation, Birth, Life, Innocency, Miracles, Death, Burial, Resurrection, Assension, full Dominion in his humane nature? &c. Was this Article

Article in the Creed before Chrifts coming [*Except ye beleeve that I am he, ye shall die in your sinnes?*] Befides, matter of faith is alfo matter of duty: for it is our duty to beleeve all thefe Truths. But I think it was then no mans duty to believe that this Jefus the Son of *Mary* was the Saviour, before he was Incarnate; or to believe that Chrift was Dead, Afcended, &c. Therefore that which you call the Old Rule, is not as you fay the Only Rule of our Duty in Beleeving.

4. But what if all this had been left out, and you had proved the Moral Law, the only Rule of duty? doth it follow that therefore it is the *only Rule*? Sure it is not the only Rule of rewarding! For if you take the Moral Law, for the meer preceptive part of the Law of nature, then it is no Rule at all of rewarding; for it is the promife, and not the precept that doth make due the reward. And if you take the moral Law for the whole Law of nature, it is a very great Difpute whether it be *Regula præmiandi* at all; much more as to that great reward which is now given in the Law of grace by Chrift (your felf deny it, *pag.* 74.) I dare not fay that if we had perfectly obeyed, Everlafting Glory in Heaven had been naturally our due. And for Remiffion of fin, and the Juftification of a finner, and fuch like, they are fuch mercies, as I never heard the Law of nature, made the only Rule of our right to them.

5. The fame I may fay of the Rule of punifhment. The privation of a purchafed, offered Remiffion and Salvation, is one part of the penalty of the new Law, of which the Moral Law can fcarce be faid the only Rule. (*None of them that were bidden shall tafte of the Supper.*)

6. But the principal thing that I intend, is that the Moral Law is not the only Rule what fhall be the condition of Life or Death: and therefore not the only Rule according to which we muft now be denominated, and hereafter fentenced Juft or Unjuft. For if the accufer fay He hath not performed the conditions of the Law of grace, and therefore hath no right to Chrift and Life] or fay fimply that [we have no right to Remiffion and Salvation;] if we can deny the charge, and produce our performance of the faid conditions, we are then *non-condemnandi*, and the Law of grace, which giveth Chrift and Life on thofe conditions, will juftifie us againft that charge, of having no right to Chrift and Life: But I think fo will not the Moral Law. The Law of works juftifieth no man but Chrift: therefore it is not the Law of works by which we are to be juftified in judgement. But fome Law we muft be juftified by: for the Law is the Rule of judgement: and the word that Chrift hath fpoken fhall judge us: therefore it muft be by the perfect Law of Grace and Liberty. If it be then faid againft us that we are finners againft the Law of nature; we fhall all have an anfwer ready [Chrift hath made fufficient fatisfaction.] But if it be faid that we have no right to the pardon and righteoufnefs which is given out by vertue of that fatisfaction, then it is the Law of Grace, and not the Moral Law, that muft juftifie us: Even that Law which faith [*Whofoever beleeveth shall not perish*, &c.] Moreover doth not the Apoftle fay plainly, that [*Chrift is the Mediator of a better Covenant; eftablished on better promifes: and if that firft Covenant had been faultleß, then should no place have been fought for the fecond: but finding fault with them he faith; Behold the daies come faith the Lord that I will make a new Covenant*, &c.] *Heb.* 8. 6, 7, 8. which fpeaks not only of Ceremonial precepts, but principally of the promifory part.

If you fhould fay, This is the Covenant and not the law. I Reply 1. Then the law is not the only Rule. 2. Its the fame thing in feveral refpects that we call a Law & a

H 3 Covenant

Covenant (except you mean it of our Covenant act to God, of which we speak not.) Who knows not that *præmiare & punire* are acts of a Law? and that an act of oblivion or general pardon on certain terms, is a Law: and that the promise is the principal part of the Law of grace. So that I have now given you some of my Reasons, why I presumed to call that [Ignorance] which I did not then know that you would so Wholly own.

§. 34.

Mr. Bl. *The perfection of this holiness and righteousness in mans integrity, stood in the perfect conformity to this Law; and the reparation of this in our regenerate estate (in which the Apostle placeth the Image of God) must have reference as to God for a pattern, so to his Law as a Rule.*

§. 34.

R. B. 1. It was the very transcendentall perfection which is convertible with its being (as to Righteousness) which then stood in a perfect conformity to the Law. Adam after his first sin, was not only less righteous, but *reus mortis, condemnandus*, and not righteous in *sensu forensi* according to that Law. For I hope you observe that we speak not of that called Moral Righteousness, consisting in a habit of giving every man his own: but of *Justitia forensis*.

2. There is a partial reparation of our holiness in regeneration, but no reparation of our personal inherent legal Righteousness at all. Is Righteousness by the Law of works? I take this for dangerous doctrine.

§. 35.

Mr. Bl. *As an Image carrying an imperfect resemblance of its Samplar, is an Image; so conformity imperfectly answering the Rule, is conformity likewise.*

§. 35.

R. B. 1. Either that Image is like the Samplar (as you call it) in some parts and unlike in others, or else it is like in no part, but near to like. If the later, then it is but near to a true Image of that thing, and not one indeed. If the former, then it is nothing to our case. 1. Because it is *Justitia universalis*, and not *particularis*, that according to the Law of works must denominate the person righteous, and not-condemnable. 2. Because indeed no one word, action, or thought of ours is truly conform to the Law of works.

2. Similitude, as *Schibler* tels you truly, doth lie in *puncto* as it were, and *ex parte sui* admits not of *magis* or *minus*: and therefore *strictè & philosophicè loquendo* (saith he) that only is *simile*, which is perfectly so: but *vulgariter loquendo* that is called *simile*, which properly is but *minus dissimile*. Scripture speaks *vulgariter* often, and not *strictè* and *philosophicè*, as speaking to vulgar wits, to whom it must speak as they can understand. And so that may be called the Image or likeness of God, which participateth of so much of his excellency as that it demonstrateth it to others, as the effect doth its cause, and so is less unlike God. I dare

not

not once imagine, that a Saint in heaven is like God in a strict and proper sense.

3. If all this were otherwise, it is little to your purpose. For in this conformity of ours, there is something of Quantitative resemblance, as well as Qualitative; and so it hath a kinde of parity and equality in it, as well as similitude to the Rule. And I hope you will yield it past doubt, that parity admits not of *magis & minus*, what ever similitude doth.

§. 36.

M^r. *Bl.* SIncerity is said to be the new Rule, or the Rule of the new Covenant. But this is no rule, but our duty, taking the abstract for the concrete, sincerity, for the sincere walking, and this according to the rule of the Law, not to reach it, but in all parts to aim at, and have respect to it. Then sha'l I not be ashamed when I have respect to all thy Commandments, *Psal.* 119.6. And this is our inherent righteousness, which in reference to its rule, labours under many imperfections. C

§. 36.

R. B. WHen I first reade these words, which you write in a different character, and father on me, I was ashamed of my *non*-sense, for they are no better: but it came not into my thoughts, once to suspect a forgery in your charge: Far was I from imagining that so Reverend, Pious and Dear a Friend, would tell the world in Print, that I said that which never came into my thoughts, and confute that soberly and deliberately, as mine, which I never wrote; and which any man that would reade my Book might finde, is wrongfully charged on me. And truly I dare not yet say that you are guilty of this: For though I have read my Book over and over of purpose in those parts that treat of this subject, and can finde no such word as you here charge me with; yet, before I will lay such a thing to your charge, I will suspect that it may possibly be in some odd corner where I overlookt it, or cannot finde it. But I see (if I am not overseen) how unsafe it is to report mens words themselves, much more their opinions, from the reports of another, how Grave, Sober, Pious and Friendly soever. If when we are dead, men shall reade Mr. *Blake's* Book that never read mine, and there see it written that I said [Sincerity is the new Rule, or the rule of the new Covenant.] Can any blame them to believe it, and report it of me, as from him, and say [*What, shall I not bekeeve such and such a man, that reports it in express words?*] But let eth's go, with this conclusion: If indeed I have spoken any such words, I retract them as *non*-sense, and when I finde them I shall expunge them: If I have not, patience is my duty and relief; and I have long been learning, that we must suffer from Godly and Friends, as well as from ungodly and enemies; and till I had learned that lesson, I never knew what it was to live quietly and contentedly.

The rest of this Section hath answer enough already. No doubt but sincere obedience consisteth in a faithfull endeavour to obey the whole preceptive part of Gods Law, both natural and positive: But no man can by it be denominated righteous (*nisi æquivoce*) but he that perfectly obeyeth in degree.

§. 37.

§. 37.

Mr. Bl. A *Perfection of sufficiency to attain the end, I willingly grant, God condescending through rich grace, to crown weak obedience: in this sense, our imperfection hath its perfectness: otherwise I must say that our inherent righteousness is an imperfect righteousness, in an imperfect conformity to the rule of righteousness, and without this reference to the rule, there is neither perfection nor imperfection in any action.* See *D.* Davenant *disputing against Justification by inherent righteousnesse upon the account of the imperfection of it, de instit. habit. p. 349. and how fully he was perswaded of the imperfection of this righteousnesse appears by sentences prefixt before two Treatises, as may be seen in the margent.*

§. 37.

R.B. 1. YOur term [otherwise] is ambiguous. If you mean that in some other respects you take righteousness to be imperfect, so do I, and that a little more then you acknowledge. If you mean that in [all] other respects you take this righteousness to be imperfect; why then do you wrong your Reader with equivocation, in calling it [Righteousness] when you know that transcendental perfection is convertible with its Being? 2. A natural perfection or imperfection, actions are capable of without a relation to the Rule: though that be nothing to our business, yet you should not conclude so largely. 3. Many a School Divine hath Written (and *Gibieuf* at large) that our actions are specified *a fine,* and denominated Good or Evil, and so perfect or imperfect *a fine* more specially and principally, then *a Lege.* But this requires more subtilty and accuratenesse for the decision, then you or I in these loose Disputes do shew our selves guilty of.

As for what you say from Reverend *Davenant,* I Reply, 1. Do you not observe that I affirm that which you call Our righteousness inherent, to be imperfect, as well as Bishop *Davenant,* and that in more respects then one? yet one would think by your words that you had a minde to intimate the contrary. 2. Yea I say more, that in reference to the Law of works, our works are no true righteousnesse at all: And I think he that saith, They are no righteousness, saith as little for them, as he that saith they are an imperfect righteousness. Yet, if the truth were known, I do not think but both *Davenant,* and you and I agree in sense, and differ only in manner of speaking. My sense is this: Our obedience to the Law of God is so imperfect, that we are not just but guilty, and condemnable in the sense of the Law of works: therefore speaking strictly, we are not righteous at all *in sensu forensi* according to this Law: but speaking improperly, and giving the denomination *à materia,* or *ab accidente aliqua, & non à forma,* so we may be said to have an imperfect legal righteousness, while equivocally we call him just, that is but comparatively less unjust then another. For though righteousness *in sensu forensi,* have no degrees, yet unrighteousness hath many. And I suppose you know that Bishop *Davenant* doth not only say as much as I concerning the interest of works in Justification, but also speaks it in the very same notions as I did. If you have not observed it, I pray reade him *de Just. Hab. & Act. cap. 30. pag. 384. & c. 31. p. 403, 404, 405. & 570, 571, 572, 633.*

And then I would ask you but this Question: If the accusation charge us to have

have no right in Christ and Life, because we died unbelievers and impenitent, or rebels against Christ; must not we be justified against that accusation, by producing our faith, repentance, and sincere obedience it self? and if so (then which nothing more certain) are not these then so farre our righteousness against that accusation to be pleaded? And if it be not a true righteousness, and metaphysically perfect, and such as will perfectly vindicate us against the accusation of being prevalently and finally unbelievers, impenitent or rebels against Christ, there is no Justification to be hoped for from the Judge, but condemnation to endless misery.

Moreover, the *Thesis* that *Davenant* proves in the Chapter which you cite, is *inhaerentem justitiam non esse causam formalem justificationis nostrae coram Deo*. And if that be true, then it is impossible that it should have the formal reason of righteousness in it. For if there be *vera forma*, there must needs be the *formatum*, and he that hath true formall rigteousness, must needs be thereby constituted Righteous, or justified *constitutivè*, and then he must needs be sentenced Just, who is Just.

But then note that *Davenant* speaks of that universal righteousness, whereby we are justified against the accusation of being sinners condemnable by the Law of works; (and here Christs satisfaction is our righteousness) and not of that particular Righteousness whereby we must be justified against the accusation of finall *non*-performance of the conditions of the Covenant or Law of grace: For there it is the performance of those conditions, which must it self be our righteousness, and so far justifie us.

Doctor *Twisse* against Doctor *Jackson*, pag. 687. saith, [*Yet I willingly grant that every sin is against Gods good will and pleasure, as it signifieth his pleasure what shall be our duty to do; which is nothing else but his commandment. And it is as true that herein are no degrees; every sin is equally against the Commandment of God.*] I think I may with much more evidence of truth and necessity, say it as I did of Personal Gospel-righteousness, then he can do of sinne. And so much be spoken of that Controversie.

§. 38.

How farre unbelief and impenitency in professed Christians are Violations of the New Covenant.

R.B. Mr. *Bl. pag.*245. *c.*33. doth lay down a Corollary, That *Impenitence and Unbelief in professed Christians, is a breach of Covenant.* Though I take that to be intended as against me, yet I am uncertain, because he reciteth no words of mine. I have no more to do in this therefore but to clear my own meaning. 1. The word [Covenant] is sometime taken for Gods Law made to his creature, containing Precepts, Promises and Threatnings: Sometime for mans promise to God. [Violation] is taken either rigidly for one that in judgement is esteemed a *non* performer of the conditions: Or laxly, for one that in judgement is found a true performer of the conditions, but did neglect or refuse the performance for a time. Taking the word [Covenant] in the later sense, I have affirmed that man breaks many a Covenant with God, yea even the Baptismal vow it self is so broken, till men do truly repent and believe. But taking the word

I [Cove-

[Covenant] in the former sense, and [Violation] in the stricter sense, I say that so none violate the Covenant but finall unbelievers and impenitent; that is, no other are the proper subjects of its peremptory curse or threatning. I think not my self called to give any further answer to that Chapter of Mr. *Blakes.*

R. B. **M**r. *Blake's* 32. Chap. I take to be wholly against me, and though I know nothing in it that I have not sufficiently answered, either in the place of my Book of Baptism, whence he fetcheth my words, in the Appendix in the Animadversions on Doctor *Ward*, or before to Mr. *Tombes*, yet because I take it to contain doctrine of a very dangerous nature, I will more fully Answer it.

Whether justifying faith be prerequisite to Baptism.

§. 39.

M^r *Bl. Ch.*32. A Dogmatical faith entitles to Baptism.

3. *IT further follows by way of Consectary, what a Dogmatical faith (ordinarily called by the name of faith Historical, such that assents to Gospel truths, though not affecting the heart to a full choice of Christ, and therefore was short of faith which was justifying and saving) gives title to Baptism. The Covenant is the ground on which Baptism is bottomed: otherwise Church-membership would evince no title, either in infants or in men of years to Baptism: But the Covenant (as we have proved) is entered with men of faith not saving: and therefore to them Baptism is to be administred. How the consequent can be denied by those that grant the antecedent; Baptism denied in foro Dei, to men short of saving faith, when they are in Covenant, I cannot imagine: Yet some that confess their interest in the Covenant, deny their title to Baptism, and affirm,* [*If men be once taught that it is a faith, that is short of justifying and saving faith, which admitteth men to Baptism, it will make foul work in the Church.*

§. 39.

R. B. **B**Efore I give a direct Reply to these words, I think it necessary that I tell you, How farre I take Unregenerate men to be In Covenant with God, and how farre not: and that I also discover as farre as I can Mr. *Blake's* minde in this Point; that it may be known wherein the difference lieth.

The [Covenant] is sometime taken for Gods part alone, sometime for our part alone, sometime for both conjunct, even for a mutual Covenanting. As it is taken for Gods act, it signifieth 1. Either some absolute promise of God, made 1. Either to Christ concerning men, or on their behalf (and so the elect may be said to be in Covenant before they are born, because Christ hath a promise that they shall be saved, and the *non*-elect are in Covenant before they are born, because Christ hath a promise of some good to them.) 2. Or to men themselves: And that is either 1. Common, or 2. Peculiar to some. 1. Common: as the promise made to fallen mankinde that a Saviour should be sent to Redeem them. The promise made to the people of *Israel* that the Messiah should be of them.

them according to the flesh, and personally live among them, and preach the Gospel to them. The promise made to *Noah* and the world, that the earth should no more be drowned with water: The promise of preaching the Gospel to all Nations (which is common, though not absolutely universal:) the promise of a Resurrection to all the world, and that they shall be judged by Christ the Redeemer, and (at least those that heard the Gospel) on the terms of the new Law, and not on the meer rigorous terms of the Law of entire nature: the promise of a fuller and clearer promulgation and explication of the Law of grace, when Christ should come in the flesh: the promise of a fuller measure of the Spirit to be poured out, for Miracles to confirm the Christian Doctrine to the beholders, hearers and actors; that there shall be a Ministry Commissioned to Disciple and Baptize all Nations, maintained to the end of the world (which gives Ministers right and authority to Baptize them;) and if there be any other the like promise of the *means necessarily anteceding faith*. Thus farre many thousands that are unregenerate, and *non-elect*, may be said to be in Covenant, that is under these promises. 2. Some of these absolute promises are peculiar to some: as to one Sex (though common as to that Sex) as the mans superiority: to one Age: to one Degree in order of nativity (as to the elder brother to have some superiority over the younger, *Gen.*4.7.) to one Nation, as to the Israelites were made many peculiar promises; and those before mentioned which I called common as to all *Israel*, were peculiar to them (some of them) in exclusion of other Nations. And some to particular persons, good or bad: as for success in battell, or other enterprises; for aversion of some threatned judgement; for the abating of some inflicted punishment; for some temporal or common blessing; of which sort we finde many particular promises which God by some Prophet made with particular men. In all these respects I say wicked men have been under a promise, yea men not elect to salvation: and thus far they may be said to be in Covenant with God. But this is but a lax and improper speech, to say (such are in Covenant) to be used now among Christians that have used to give the name [Covenant] by an excellency, to another thing. Also now wicked men are not under peculiar personal promises of temporal things, as then they were, because now there are no extraordinary Prophets, or other the like Messengers or Revelations from God to make such particular promises to men. (Yet I will not say God hath restrained himself from this, or cannot, or will not do it at all, or that no man hath such Revelations; but only 1. That it is not usual. 2. Nor is God engaged to do it.)

So for the absolute promise of the first special grace (first faith and repentance) to be given to all the Elect (supposing that there is such a promise:) this is made to none but the ungodly and unregenerate, though elect (unless you will say, it is made to Christ for them, or rather is a prediction of good eventually to be conferred on them.)

But though in all these respects wicked men are under a promise, yet it is none of all these that gives them right to Baptism. There is no question of any but the last: and for that I have proved in my Appendix against Mr. *Bedford*, that it is not that Covenant that Baptism sealeth, Whither I refer you to avoid Repetition: much more easie is it to prove, that it is not that bare promise that gives right to Baptism. For many are Pagans and Infidels to whom that promise belongs. So much for the Absolute promise.

2. As for Conditional promises to man, they are either

1. Pecu-

1. *Peculiar*: as extraordinary promises of temporal blessings conditionally made to some particular persons heretofore. Of these I say, as of the former: Wicked men may be under such promises; but these give not right to Baptism.

2. *Common*: such as are not made to this or that man more then others, but to all, at least in the tenour of the grant, though it be not promulgate to all. Of this sort 1. Some suppose certain promises to go before the great Law of grace. 2. But I yet know not of any but the Law of grace it self, (anon to be described.) 1. Those that do suppose some such antecedaneous promise, are of two sorts: 1. The Arminians and Jesuites. 2. Such as Mr. *Blake* about Church-Ordinances. 1. The Jesuites and Arminians speak of two such common promises. 1. One is of the giving of supernatural means of Revelation, to men, on condition of the right use of natural Revelation. As if God had promised to all Heathen and Infidels that never heard of Christ, that they shall have the Gospel sent them, if they will use the light of nature well, or will seek out for the Gospel. 2. The other promise which they imagine is, that God will give supernatural or special grace (*viz.* the first grace of faith and repentance) to men, on condition they will use well their common grace and means. I know of no such promise as either of these in Scripture (of which see *Davenant* in his Dissertation of Universal Redemption.) When any Arminian will shew such a promise in Scripture, we shall yield. But yet I will tell you how far I yield. 1. I yield that God doth actually give temporal blessings to wicked men: But this is no Covenant or promise. Yet it gives them a right to enjoy them *de præsenti* while they do enjoy them; so that it is not sound Doctrine of them that say, Wicked men have no right to the creature, in whatsoever they possess, and that they are but usurpers. For if you see one naked in the street, and put him on a garment; he hath right to wear that and enjoy it, while you permit him: But yet because you promise him nothing for the future, he is not certain a moment of the continuance of that right or possession, for you may take it off him again when you will. So wicked men have right and possession of Gods mercies by actual collation *de præsenti*, but not by promise *de futuro*, or by such proper donation; as gives them the full propriety (for so God useth not to part with the propriety of his creatures to any.) 2. I yield that God doth give to Heathens, who have but natural light, some helps which have a tendency to their further advancement, and doth appoint them certain means to be used for the obtaining of a higher light, and that he giveth them sufficient encouragement to go on in the chearfull use of those means, in possibilities and probabilities of success; so that they are unexcusable that use them not. These Mr. *Cotton* cals half promises (as who knows but the Lord may do thus and thus? *Pray therefore if perhaps the thoughts of thy heart may be forgiven thee*, &c.) But promises properly they are not. God hath thought meet to keep himself disengaged from this sort of men. 3. The very same I yield of men in the visible Church using common grace, as well as they can: that is, that God hath appointed certain means which such men are to use for the getting of special grace: that those that perish, do justly perish, for not using those means so well as they could, and so for not beleeving: that he hath given them sufficient incouragement to use such means by examples, experiences, the nature of the means, and some half promises of success: but no promise properly so called. 4. I yield that he actually gives saving grace to wicked men: or else none could have it. But this they can plead no right to before they have it.

2. The

2. The second sort of promises before the great Covenant of grace, is feigned by Mr. *Blake* (and if there be any other that go that way, as some do, and that with some difference among themselves:) and that is A promise of Church-priviledges upon condition of a faith not justifying or saving. Here some annex special grace to these Church-priviledges, and so fall into the Arminian strain. So Dr. *Ward* against Mr. *Gataker,* doth make a common (not-justifying) faith, the condition of Baptism, and then that Baptism a means *non ponenti obicem* of the certain Justification of all the Baptized, and so, at least, the infants of all common professors, baptized, should be certainly justified. But I finde not Mr. *Blake* any where owning this connexion of special grace, and efficacy of Baptism on such : therefore I suppose it is but some common mercies that he supposeth this promise to make over to the Baptized. But I will enquire further into his opinion anon.

2. The common or general promise-conditional, which I acknowledge, is the new Law of grace, or of faith, wherein God promiseth [to be our God, so we will take him for our God, and will be his people] and [to give us Christ and Life, if we will accept him as he is offered in the Gospel] or [that he that repenteth and beleeveth, shall be justified and saved] and he that doth not shall be damned : Whereto is also annexed, the promise of temporal mercies, so far as they are good for us ; as appurtenances to the main blessings of the Covenant. Now I will tell you how far wicked men are under this great promise or Covenant. 1. As it is a conditional promise on Gods part, or a Law of grace enacted conditionally giving Christ and Life to all men, so All men are under it, or the subjects of it : that is, All the whole world, as to the tenour of the Law of grace, following the meer enacting ; and all that hear the Gospel, as to the promulgation. 2. So as it hath a precept conjunct, requiring them to believe and repent for remission and salvation, so all are under it, that hear it. 3. So are they as to the annexed threatning upon their unbelief and impenitency. 4. So as the Preachers of the Gospel do by Commission from Christ, apply all this to them, and intreat them by name to repent and believe, and offer them Christ and the other benefits of the Covenant, if they will repent and believe ; so wicked men are still under the promise or Covenant, as to the Nunciative offers and exhortations, which is somewhat mere then a meer Promulgation of it as a Law. All these waies, or in these respects, I yield that wicked men, or unregenerate men, may be under promise, or Gods Covenant. But this is not strictly to [be in Covenant :] nor is this it that the right of Baptism belongs to : For all this belongs not only to *Pagans,* but even to *obstinate Pagans* that persecute this Gospel, and draw out the blood of those that thus Preach it to them : whom I suppose, few Divines judge meet subjects for Baptism.

And thus we have spoken of Gods act in the conditional promise, before the condition be performed by man, and so before Gods promise do actually conferre right to the sinner. As for the act of Gods Covenant afterwards, I shall speak of it anon.

2. Having said thus much of Gods act of promise or Covenant, and seen how far the wicked may be said to be under that promise or Covenant, we must next consider of their own promise to God, or the act of Covenanting on their own part. Mans Covenanting with God, or his entring the Covenant of God propounded to him, is either 1. to be considered in respect of the efficient ; 2. or of the object. As to the efficient, it is either 1. The act of the whole man, *i.e.* of

mind

minde and body: 2. Or of part only: and that 1. either of the minde alone: 2. or of the outward man alone. 2. Objectively considered, it is either 1. A true proper consent agreeable to the formall object (or to the object in its absolute necessary respects and nature.) 2. Or it is an imperfect consent, analogically or equivocally called [Covenanting] when it is not suited to the formall nature of the object. This errour is 1. About the object simply in it self considered. 2. About the object comparatively considered: as God compared with the creature. And both or either of these errours is 1. Either in the intellect: when it doth not understand the nature of the object, and Gods terms on which only he offers his blessings; or at least doth not practically understand it, but speculatively only. 2. Or of the Will: when it doth not really consent to the object, and terms of God, though they be understood, at least, speculatively. 3. Or it is, both the errour of the understanding and the will.

Having thus necessarily distinguished, I will lay down in these Conclusions, how far man is in Covenant with God as to his own act. 1. Man may oblige himself by Vows to particular duties, that are not of the substance of the Covenant, and yet be wicked. 2. Yea man may oblige himself to things indifferent, and some think to evil, as *Jeptha*, so far as to ensnare himself in a necessity of sinning, whether he perform it or not. 3. That which God requireth of man on his part, as a necessary condition, to his right in the benefits promised by God, and that God may be, as it were, obliged actually to man, is the sincere resolved consent of the Heart or Will. 4. Yet he requireth for several reasons, that the external profession of consent be added, where there is capacity and opportunity. 5. God doth as absolutely require to our participation of his blessings, and that his Covenant may be in force actually to give us right to them, and he, as it were, obliged to give us the things promised, that we understand the absolutely necessary part of the object of our consent, or acceptance; and that with a practical knowledge. 6. As absolutely doth he require that we do really consent according to that practical understanding. 7. It is essential to God as the object of mans faith, to be his supream Lord and Rector as Creator, and his ultimate end and chiefest good: and so must he be apprehended and willed by all that indeed take him for their God: as also to be perfect in Being, Wisdom, Goodness and Power, and of perfect Veracity. 8. It is essential to Christ as the object of our faith, to be God-man, that in our nature hath Ransomed us, by the Sacrifice of himself on the Cross for us, and Died, and Rose again, and is now Ascended in Glory with the Father, and is Lord of us all, and will Judge according to his Word to Everlasting Joy or Punishment. 9. It is essential to the object of our faith, as such, to be considered comparatively. As that God be taken not only as our good, but our chief Good, to be preferred before every creature: that he be taken not only as our Lord, but as Sovereign Lord, to be obeyed before all other: that Christ be taken for our only Saviour, and for our Lord-Redeemer, to be also obeyed before all creatures; particularly before and against the devil, the flesh, and the world. 10. Where these essentials are not in the apprehension of the object, there is not truly the consent, or faith, or covenanting which God hath made the condition of his Promise; and therefore such are said (as to the Faith, Consent and Covenant so required) but equivocally or analogically to Consent, Covenant or Believe: when truly and properly it is to be said, that they do not Consent or Covenant. Consent hath relation to the offer: and if it be not the offered thing that is consented to, but somewhat else under that name, then it is

not

not indeed Confent: for there is no Relate without its Correlate. Covenanting (in the prefent, fenfe) implies Gods propounded Covenant and terms. For our entring the Covenant, is not a Making of terms, but an Accepting of the terms made to our hands and tendered (with a command to accept them.) Now if we do not confent to the fame terms propounded, it is truly no Accepting, nor no Covenanting: For God never offered to enter into Covenant on fuch terms, and that which was never offered, cannot be properly accepted; nor can we Covenant with God in a mutual Covenant, on terms contrary to thofe which he propounded. The Civil Law faith, *Ignorantis non eft Confenfus*. A God that is inferiour to creatures in Rule, or in Goodnefs and Defirablenefs, is not God indeed. And therefore he that takes God in this fenfe for his God, takes but the Name of God, and not God himfelf, but an Idol of his brain. A Chrift that is only a Juftifier and not a King and Governour, is not the Chrift that is offered us of God; and therefore no man is called to accept fuch a Chrift. To erre therefore about the very effence of the Object, as fuch, is to null the Act, it can be no Confent or Covenant or Acceptance truly at all, but equivocally only. 11. The fame may be faid of counterfeit Covenanting, when it is only *ore tenus*, with the mouth and not the heart. 12. Yet may an oral counterfeit Covenanting oblige the party to the duty promifed (in our cafe) though it give him no right to the benefit offered, nor is God as it were obliged to perform his Covenant to fuch. 13. The like may be faid of the forefaid equivocal erroneous Confenting, Accepting, Covenanting. If the errour be through the fault of the man himfelf, his act may oblige himfelf, though God remain difobliged, and though he have no right to the thing promifed by God. Thus much I thought meet to fay, for the opening of that branch of the Queftion, How far men unregenerate may be in Covenant, as to their own act.

But the great Queftion is yet behind, Whether thefe men be in Covenant with God, as to Gods actual engagement to them: fo far as that Gods promife is in force for conveying actual right to them as to the promifed bleffings? and fo whether it be a mutual Covenant, and both parties be actually obliged? And thus I fay that wicked men are not in Covenant with God, that is, God is not in Covenant with them: Neither have they any right to the main bleffings given by the Covenant, viz. Chrift, Pardon, Juftification, Adoption, Glory: Nor yet to the common bleffings of this Covenant, for they are given by the fame Covenant and on the fame conditions as the fpecial bleffings: So that though they may have right to them at prefent on the ground of Gods prefent collation, or trufting them with them (as a fervant hath in his Mafters ftock) yet have they no right by Covenant: For it is Godlinefs that hath the promife of this life, and of that to come, as being the condition of both; and it is feeking firft Gods Kingdom and Righteoufnefs, that is the condition on which other things fhall be added to us. The fame holds of Church-priviledges and Ordinances *quoad poffeffionem* not proper to the faithfull.

So that in the conclufion, I fay, that though wicked men have many promifes from God, efpecially the great conditional promife of Life, if they will repent and believe; and though they are alfo obliged by their own imperfect, equivocal Covenanting with God; yet God remaineth ftill unobliged to them, and they have no actual right to the benefits of his promife; becaufe they have not performed the condition of their firft right, that is, have not Covenanted truly with God, or entred the Covenant which he propounded; having not confented to his terms,

nos

not accepted Chrift and Life as offered in the Gofpel: And therefore it is the moft proper language to fay, that none but fincere beleevers are in Covenant with God: For the reft have but equivocally Covenanted with God, and God not actually engaged in Covenant with them (for while the condition is unperformed there is no actual obligation on the promifes) and fo it is no proper mutual Covenant. And confequently thefe men in proper ftrict fenfe, are no true Chriftians, but analogically only.

Yet becaufe we have no accefs to their hearts, and therefore muft judge of the heart by the profeffion and outward fignes, therefore we muft judge thefe probably to Covenant with the heart, who do profefs to do fo with the tongue; and thofe to Covenant entirely and without errour in the effentials, who profefs fo to do: and therefore we muft judge them probably to be true Chriftians, and truly godly men (till they retract that profeffion by word or deed:) and therefore we muft judge them probably to be truly in Covenant with God, and fuch as God is, as it were, obliged to juftifie: and therefore we muft give them the name of Chriftians, and men in Covenant with God: and therefore we muft ufe them as Chriftians in works of charity, and in Ordinances, and Church communion: and fo muft ufe their children as Chriftians children. The warrant for this ufage and Judgement, I muft defire the Reader to take notice of, in what I have written to Mr *Tombes* Objections on 1 *Cor.* 7.14. and to Dr. *Ward*, and againft Mr. *Tombes* Precurfor more fully: For to repeat all here again would be tedious and unneceffary. When Chrift faith to us, [*If a Brother repent, forgive him*] here by [Repenting] doth Chrift mean plainly *Repenting*, or the profeffion of it? No doubt, repenting it felf. Why, but how can we that know not the heart, know here when our Brother repenteth? Will Mr. *Bl.* fay therefore that none is obliged to forgive? Rather we know that man muft judge him to repent that profeffeth fo to do: and therefore forgive him that profeffeth it. Not becaufe profeffing was the affigned requifite condition: but a fign of that condition: and therefore we are to accept of no profeffion, but what probably fignifieth true repentance. For if we knew a man diffembled, or jeered us in profeffing repentance, we are not bound to do by him as a penitent. So God commandeth us to love and honour them that fear the Lord, that are faithfull, that love Chrift, &c. But we know not who thefe be: Are we therefore difobliged from loving and honouring them? Or will Mr. *Bl.* fay that we muft not honour them, left we miftake and give that honour to one that hath no right to it? (as he faith about the Sacrament; herein joyning with Mr. *Tombes.*) Thofe that profefs to fear God and love him, we muft love and honour as men that do fear and love him: yet in different degrees, as the fignes of their graces are more or lefs propable. In fome common profeffing Chriftians, we fee but fmall probability: yet dare we not exclude them from the Church, nor the number of true believers, as long as there is any probability: Others that are more judicious, zealous, diligent, and upright of life, we have far ftronger probability of; and therefore love and honour them much more.

Mr. *Blake* therefore in my judgement had done better; if, with that moderate, Reverend, Godly man Mr. *Stephen Marfhall*, he had diftinguifhed between thefe two Queftions, [Who are Chriftians or Church-members?] and [Whom are we to judge fuch and ufe as fuch?] and to bring in the unregenerate in the later rank only.

Next we are to fee what is Mr. *Blakes* judgement herein, that we may not argue againft him before we underftand: which yet I think I fhall in fome meafure be

forced

forced to do, or say nothing, 1. I finde it very hard to understand what persons they be that he takes to be in Covenant: 2. And as hard to understand what Covenant he means. For the first, I finde it clear that negatively he means, They are not truly Regenerate persons, but Positively how they must be qualified I finde not so clear. *Pag.*189. he saith it was with all that bore the name of *Israel* (which is no further true then I have laid down in the former Conclusions) so that it may seem that he takes all to be in Covenant that bear the name of Christians. What? though they know not what Christ or Christianity is? Is taking a name, entering into Covenant? The poor *Indians* that by thousands are forced by the *Spaniards* to be baptized, are said to know so little what they do, that some of them forget the name of [a Christian] which they assumed.

*Pag.*192. he saith [All professed Christians, so called, are in an outward and single Covenant] 1. What? those that are called professed Christians, and are not? No: sure that's not the meaning: else mens miscalling might put them in Covenant. It is then those that are so, and are called so: But will it not serve, if they are so, unless called so? 2. He means either those that profess the name of Christianity, or the Thing. Of the insufficiency of the first, I spoke before. For the second, if they profess the whole Essence of Christianity undissembledly, I think they are truly Regenerate. If they profess but part (as to the Matter both of Assent and Consent, of which I spoke before in the Conclusions, and which we have in this County lately set down in our Profession of Faith) then it is not Christianity which they profess: for part of the essence is not the Thing: where an essential part is wanting, the form is absent. If it be the whole matter of Christianity that is professed, but Dissembledly; then as he is equivocally or analogically a Believer or Christian, so I yield he is a member of the Visible Church, which so far as it is only Visible, is equivocally called The Church: of which I have fullier spoken in Answer to M*r* *Tombes Præcursor*. I know M*r* *Bl.* thinks, that there may be an undissembled Profession, which yet may not be of a saving Faith. But then I yet conceive it is not an entire Profession of the whole essential object of Christian faith, *viz.* of Assent and Consent. It will be a hard saying to many honest Christians to say, that a man not justified may believe every fundamental Article, and withall truly profess Repentance of all his sins, and to Take God for his Soveraign to Rule him, and his chief Good to be enjoyed to his happiness; and to take Christ for his Lord and only Saviour, and his Word for his Law and Rule, and the holy Ghost for his Guide and Sanctifier, and the rest which is essential to Christianity.

Pag. 192. He saith of all that externally make Profession (These engage themselves upon Gods terms.) But if they do so sincerely they are sincere Christians: If not sincerely, they are but equivocally Christians. Some think that in the 11*th* Chapter of the 3*d* part of my Book of Rest, I gave too much to an unregenerate estate: and yet I think there is nothing contrary to this that I now say. He that professeth not to preferre God and the Redeemer before all other things, professeth not Christianity: and he that professeth this and lieth not, is a Regenerate justified Christian.

Pag. 200. he describeth his unregenerate Christians to be such [as Accept the terms of the Covenant.] And this none doth indeed but the sanctified. If Mr. *Bl.* will say, that the unregenerate may do it, he will make them true believers: For what is true faith but an Accepting of Christ and his Benefits on the Covenant terms? Though I confess others may falsly say, they Accept him.

K
Pag.

Pag. 220. he faith [Laws tendred by a Prince, and received by a People, make up the Relation of King and people (yet indeed, that's not true, for it is the Receiving the man to be our King which is antecedent to the receiving his Laws, that makes the Relation.) A marriage Covenant tendred by a man, and accepted by a Virgin, makes up the Relation of Husband and Wife: Covenant draughts between man and man for service, make up the Relation of Master and Servant: Now the Gospel Covenant is all of these between God and a People.] Rep. The Accepting Christ in this Covenant is true Justifying Faith: If an unregenerate man have this indeed, then he is justified, and Faith and Justification are common things, which I will not believe. If Mr. *Bl.* mean that the external profession of this Acceptance, alone, doth make up the Relation, I say, as before; It may oblige the Professour, but makes not up the Relation of Real Christians, because God consenteth not, nor is actually in Covenant and obliged. The differences Mr. *Bl.* must take notice of, between his humane Covenants, and ours with God, or else he will marre all. Men know not one anothers hearts, and therefore make not Laws for hearts, nor impose Conditions on hearts: and therefore if both parties do profess Consent, though dissemblingly, they are both obliged, and the Covenant is mutual. But God offers to Consent, only on Condition that our hearts Consent to his terms; and therefore if we profess Consent, and do not Consent, God Consenteth not, nor is, as it were obliged.

Next Mr. *Bl.* proceeds there to tell us, that the Accepting the Word preached, is the note of the Church. But that is a more lax ambiguous term then the former. Some call it an accepting the Word, when they are content to hear it: Some when they speculatively believe the truth of it. These are no true notes of true Christians, or Churches (in the first sense of the word Church.) Others Accept but part of that word, which is the necessary object of Faith, of whom the like may be said. It is the Accepting Christ and Life in him, offered by this word, which is Christianity it self, or true Faith: and the profession of this, is that which makes a man a Member of the Visible Church (He may accept it for his Infants also.) So much for the indagation of Mr. *Bl.*'s meaning about the description of his visible Christians.

Next, what he means by [Covenant] I confess I despair of knowing. Sometime he speaks as if he meant it but of their own act of Covenant, whereby they oblige themselves. But ordinarily, it is evident, that he speaks of a mutual Covenant, and makes God to be also in Covenant with them. But what Covenant of God is this? *Pag.* 192. He saith [they are in an outward and single Covenant.] But what he means by a single Covenant, I know not. He there also chooseth to express himself in *Paræus* words; who distinguisheth *inter beneficia fœderis* (which he denieth them) and *Jus fœderis* (which he alloweth them.) But I confess I know not what *Jus fœderis* is, except one of these two things: 1. A Right to enter Covenant with Christ: and so have Infidels. 2. Or a Right to the Benefits promised in the Covenant: and this he denieth them. If he meaneth (as *Par us* seems) a Right to be esteemed as Covenanters, and used as Covenanters, by the Church (though indeed God is not in Covenant with them) this we easily grant.

But Mr. *Bl.*'s common phrase is, that they are [in the outward Covenant] and what that is, I cannot tell. I know what it is to covenant *ore tenus*, only outwardly, or by a dissembled profession, or else a profession maimed, or not understood; and I have said, that hereby they may further oblige themselves (so far as the creature can be said to oblige it self, who is not *sui Juris*, but wholly Gods, and is under his absolute

solute obligation already.) But it is Gods Covenant act that we are enquiring after. In what sense is that called Outward? 1. It cannot be as if God did as the dissembling creature, *ore tenus*, with the mouth only covenant with them, and not with the heart, as they deal with him: 2. I know therefore no possible sense but this, that it is called [Outward] from the Blessings promised which are outward. Here therefore, 1. I should have thought it but reasonable for Mr. *Bl.* to have told us what those outward Blessings are that this Covenant promiseth. 2. That he would have proved out of Scripture that God hath such a Covenant, distinct from the Covenant of Grace, which promiseth Justification and Salvation, and having other Conditions on our part. For both these I cannot finde what outward blessings he means but Church Ordinances and Priviledges. These consist in the Word, Sacraments, Prayer, Discipline. For the Word, God oft bestoweth it on Infidels, and in *England* there are men that deride the truth of Scripture, and esteem it a fiction, and yet for credit of men, come ordinarily to the Congregation. These have the Word given them, and so have other unregenerate men: but not by Covenant that I know of. Even the godly have no Covenant assuring them that for the future they shall enjoy the Word, further then it is in their hearts (except that promise with a reserve, If God see it Good, &c.) Where hath God said, If thou wilt with thy mouth profess to believe, I will give thee my Word preached? 2. For Baptism, It is part of our profession it self. And though God hath commissioned us to Baptize such professours and their seed, yet that is not a Covenant with them: Nor do I know where God saith, I will give thee Baptism, if thou wilt but say, thou believest, or if thou wilt profess seriously a half faith: More shall be said against this anon. 3. For the Lords Supper the same may be said. God hath no where made a Covenant, that they shall have the Lords Supper that will profess faith. To feign God to make a Covenant with man, whose condition shall be orall profession, and whose Blessing promised, is only the *nudum signum*, a little water to wash men, and a little bread and wine, without that Christ, and Remission of sin, Mortification and Spiritual Life, which these Sacraments are in their Institution appointed to signifie, seal and exhibit, this is, I think a groundless and presumptuous course. 4. The same may be said of Discipline: which, alas few Churches do enjoy. I desire therefore that those words of Scripture may be produced where any such outward Covenant is contained. I take outward Ordinances and other blessings to be a second part of, or certain appurtenances to the blessings of the great Covenant of Grace, and given by Covenant on the same condition (of true faith) as Justification it self is: but allowed or given by Providence, where and when God pleaseth, and sometime to Infidels that never made profession, as to some of them (the Word and temporal mercies) and not assured by promise to any ungodly man, that from Providence receiveth them.

At last, after this necessary explication, I come to Mr. *Bl.*'s words which I propounded to Reply to. And first, when he saith [A dogmatical faith entitleth to Baptism] I reply, 1. A meer Dogmatical, Historical faith, is only in the understanding; and that not Practical neither: Now if this be the condition of the outward Covenant, then it may consist with a Renouncing Christ, and open disclaiming him, yea a persecuting the very Christian name: For a man may speculatively and sleightly believe the word of God to be true, and yet may openly profess [I love the world, and my pleasure, and honour, so much better then Christ, that I am resolved I will be no Christian, nor be baptized, nor take Christ on the terms that he is offered on.] At least, he that professeth Assent only, and will not

K 2   profess

profess consent also, doth not profess Christianity: For Christianity and true faith lieth in the Wils consent, as well as the understandings Assent. 2. And how can Mr. *Bl* call this Dogmatical faith, a covenanting? when covenanting is known to be the expression of the Wils consent, and not the profession of an opinion. 3. If a Dogmatical faith be the condition, and make a man a Christian, then he may be a Christian against his Will: which was yet never affirmed.

But Mr. *Bl.* in his explication of this Dogmatical faith, addeth by way of exclusion [though not affecting the heart to a full choice of Christ.] Where he seems to imply (though he express it not) that the faith which he meaneth doth affect the heart to a choice of Christ which is not full. But if so, then 1. It is much more then Assent, or a meer Historical Dogmatical faith. 2. But is the choice which he intimateth Real, as to the Act, and suited to the Object? That is, the real choice of such a Christ as is offered, and on such terms? If so, it is Justifying faith. If not, either it is counterfeit as to the Act, or but nominal as to the Object, and is indeed no choosing of Christ. Though perhaps, it may not be suited to the Accidentals of the object, yet to the Essentials it must, or else it hath but equivocally the name as a corps hath the name of a man.

He saith, [The Covenant is the Ground of Baptism, otherwise Church-membership would evince no Title, *&c.*] Repl. 1. I take Gods precept to be the Ground of Baptism, as it is *officium* a Duty, both as to the baptizer and the baptized: and his Promise, or his Covenant Grant, to be the Ground of mens Right to it, as it is a Benefit given directly by God: and their own true consent, faith or covenanting (which with me are all one, for all that you say against it) to be the condition of that Right. But then I think that *in foro Ecclesiæ* a dissembler may claim that Right which strictly he hath not, and we must grant him what he claims when he brings a Probable ground of his claim: And in that it is Ministers duty to Baptize such, they may indirectly, and *quoad Ecclesiam* be said to have Right to be Baptized. I say Indirectly, yea and improperly: for it is not the result of Gods Covenant Grant to them; but of his precept to his Ministers, and his Instructions, whom they ought to Baptize.

2. I argued from Right of admission to Church-membership, with Mr. *T.* and that Right I take the heart-covenant (of Parent or parties themselves) to be the condition of, as to the Invisible Church-state, and the Profession of that Covenant, not alone, but joyned with it, to be the condition of true Right before God to Visible-membership; though men are but to use him as one that hath true Right, who by an hypocritical profession seems to have Right.

Where he takes me to grant his Antecedent, that [the Covenant is entred with men of faith not saving] he doth me wrong: For in the properest sense (*i.e.* as if God were actually, as it were, obliged to such, in the Covenant of Grace, I never said it: But how far such are in Covenant or under promise, I have by necessary distinction explained before: and I think it beseems not a serious Treatise of the Covenants, wherein this Question is so largely of purpose handled to have confounded those several considerations, and dispute so seriously before the Reader can tell about what.

The words which Mr. *Bl.* questioneth, I confess are mine, against Dr. *Ward*, and I did not think in so gross an opinion Dr. *Ward* would have found any second to undertake that cause.

§. 40.

§. 40.

Mr. Bl. 1. ALL that hath been said for the latitude of the Covenant, may fitly be applyed in opposition to this Tenent, for the like latitude of Baptism.

§. 40.

R. B. THerefore did I say the more of the Covenant before, to shew your confusion and mistake in that. It is not every Covenant or Promise that Baptism is the Seal of.

§. 41.

Mr. Bl. ALL the Absurdities following the restraint of the Covenant to the Elect, to men of faith saving and justifying, follow upon this restraint of interest in Baptism.

§. 41.

R. B. WHat Absurdities follow such a restraint of it to sound believers, as I have asserted, I should be willing to know, though with some labor I searched for it. Bear with me therefore, while I examine what you refer me to. It is pag. 209. where you charge those Absurdities. And the first is this, 1. *This restriction of the Covenant (to shut out all the non-regenerate) makes an utter confusion between the Covenant it self and the conditions of it : or (if the expression do not please) the Covenant it self and the duties required in it; between our entrance into Covenant, and our observation of it, or walking up in faithfulness to it. All know that a bargain for a summe of money, and the payment of that summe ; the covenant with a servant for labor, and the labor according to this covenant, are different things. Faithful men that make a bargain, keep it ; enter covenant, and stand to it : But the making and keeping; the entring and observing are not the same ; and now according to this opinion, Regeneration is our entrance into Covenant, and Regeneration is our keeping of Covenant : before Regeneration we make no Covenant, after Regeneration we break no Covenant, there is no such thing as Covenant-breaking. All this makes an utter confusion in the Covenant.*

Reply 1. I have seldom met with a complaint of confusion, more unseasonably, where the guilt of it in the plaintiffe is so visible as to marr all the work so much. 2. I cannot give my judgment of the intolerableness and great danger of your mistake here manifested, without unmannerliness. I will therefore say but this; It is in a very weighty point, neer the foundation, wherein to erre, cannot be safe. In my Aphorisms I gave my reasons *(pag. 265)* for the contrarie. It is a truth so far beyond all doubt, that *our own Covenanting is a principal part of the condition of the Covenant of Grace*, as that it is, in other terms a great part of the substance of the Gospel. 1. The conditions are imposed

A a

posed by God, and to be performed by us ; the same act therefore is called *our conditions* as the performers, and *Gods conditions* as the Imposer and Promiser, giving his blessings onely on these imposed conditions. Most properly they are called the conditions of Gods Covenant or Promise, rather then of ours: for our own Promise is the first part of them, and our performance of that Promise but a secondary part. For 2. Gods Covenant is *a free gift of Christ and Life to the world on condition of their Acceptance:* this our Divines against the Papists on the Doctrine of merit, have fully proved. Onely this Acceptance must have these necessary modifications, which may constitute it sutable to the quality of the object, and state of the receiver. It must be a Loving, Thankfull Acceptance: and it being the Acceptance of a Soveraign, and Sanctifier, it contains a Resolution to obey him. Our Acceptance, or Consent, is our Covenanting, and our faith. So that our Covenanting with Christ, and our faith is the same thing: that is, our accepting an offered Saviour on his terms: Or a Consent that he be ours and we his on his terms. And who knows not that this Faith, or Covenanting, or Consent, is the condition by us to be performed, that we may have right to Christ and Life offered? 3. Indeed there is herewith joyned a promise for future duty: but mark 1. what; 2. and to what end; 1. It is principally but a promise of the same consent to be continued, which we already give: and secondarily, a promise of sincere obedience. 2. It is not that these future promised acts shall be the condition of our first Justification, or right to Christ ; but onely the condition of the continuance of our Justification, it being certainly begun, and we put into a state of favor and acceptance, meerly on our first consent or covenanting, that is, believing or receiving Christ.

That all this is no strange thing, (that our own Covenant Act should be also the Primary condition of Gods Covenant) may appear by your forementioned similitudes, and all other cases, wherein such Relations are contracted. If a King will offer his Son in marriage to a condemned woman and a beggar, on condition that she will but have him, that is consent, and so covenant and marry him : here her covenanting, consenting or marrying him, is the performance of the condition on her part, for obtaining her first Right in him and his : but for the continuance of that Right, is further requisite, Primarily the continuance of that consent ; secondarily the addition of subjection and marriage-faithfulness. Yet though consent begun, and consent continued, be both called consent, and are the same thing, it is only the beginning that is called marriage : so is it only begun faith, which is our marriage with Christ, and constitutes us Regenerate, or converted. And therefore you do not well to talk of *Regeneration being the keeping of our Covenant.* If by *Regeneration* you mean not Gods Act, but our repenting and believing, then it is our keeping Gods Covenant, by performing the condition. *i. e.* Our obeying him in entring his Covenant ; but it is not the keeping of our own Covenant: for our making or entering Covenant, is our principal condition, on performance whereof we are justified ; yet in so doing, we promise to continue that consent or faith : and so the continuance is our Covenant-keeping.

As for your instances of the Covenant of paying money, and doing work, had I used such instances, what should I have heard from those men that already charge me with giving too much to works in Justification ? you should have considered, that our Covenant 1. is not principally to pay, and to labor, but to receive. 2. nor is it onely *de futuro,* but *de præsenti :* A consent to have Christ

fo.

for our Lord, Redeemer, Saviour, Head and Husband in present and for the time to come; though the very relation consented to, doth indeed oblige us to the future duties of that Relation. By this time, I leave it to the Reader to judge, who it is that introduceth confusion about the Covenant, and whether this be an error of the lower size?

As for that you adde, that *then there is no Covenant-breaking*; I Reply, 1. *Quoad essentiam & possibilitatem* there is. 2. *Quoad existentiam*, there is a breaking of meer Verbal and of Erring half Covenants. But if you think that sound Covenanting may be utterly broken, then you are against the certaintie of perseverance. As for the texts you cite, I say 1. The Israelites broke Gods commands, which are called his Covenants. 2. They broke their particular Covenants, about reforming Idolatrie and such particular sins. 3. They broke their Verbal and equivocal Covenant or Promise to God, whereby they seemed to Accept him on his terms, but did not; and therefore had not his obligation again to them, but yet thereby obliged themselves.

Your 2. Absurditie is, that *then there are no Hypocrites*. Reply; Rather, *Then all unregenerate professors are Hypocrites*. They pretend meerly to real proper Covenanting, and they do Covenant but Verbally, and equivocally. Your Answers to the objection therefore, *pag.* 211, 212. have not the least strength, where you say, The Covenant which they enter is their pretence for God; I Reply, they do therefore but pretend to take God for their God, which is the proper Covenanting. How else could you next say, that they are guiltie of hypocrisie? Doubtless they had hypocrisie as well in entering the Covenant, as after in pretending to stand to it. Is it not you rather, that consequentially say, There is no Hypocrites (among these at least) in Covenanting, who make them all to Covenant truly and unfeignedly? And where you say, that *then they do but pretend to the stage, and to hypocrisie*: It is a strange feigned consequence, without the least shew of proof. What! is he but a pretender to Hypocrisie, that takes on him a Christian, when he is none? (Suppose he never Covenanted) or he that takes on him to consent or covenant in heart, when he doth it but in words, and wilfully dissembles? Yea, if they think they Accept Christ, not knowing what Christ is, and so do not Accept him as he is offered them, and yet go on in a supposition that they are Christians; these seem to have done what they did not, and to be what they are not: and therefore are Hypocrites, though not purposely dissembling.

For your 3. Absurdity, I have said enough against that charge to Mr. *Tombes*, which shall stand, till you confute it, as the confutation of yours. And so much for your feigned Absurdities.

---

§. 42.

Mr. Bl. TO *make the Visible Seal of Baptism, which is the Priviledge of the Church Visible, to be of equal latitude with the Seal of the Spirit, which is peculiar to invisible members, is a Paradox.*

A 2 §. 42.

§. 42.

R. B. But you take it for granted that we do so; which is too easie disputing. We give the Seal of Baptism to all that *seem* sound Believers, and their seed; and we say, the Seal of the sanctifying Spirit, is onely theirs that *Are* such Believers. But if you speak onely of Covenant-Right to Baptism, *Coram Deo*, by his gift of Covenant, then I make them of the same extent: supposing that by the Seal of the Spirit, you mean somewhat common to every true believer. 3. But if it be the *formalis Ratio* of Sealing, that you look at; I say, God sealeth to the wicked his Covenant or Promise as it is made to them, (of which before): He sealed the conditional Covenant, which they seemed to Accept, (which if they had not seemed to Accept, he would not have commanded the annexing of the Seal): and so God may be said to do it, in that he commandeth his Ministers to do it. But it is not such a sealing, as leaves God actually obliged to fulfill the promise, as he is to them that perform the condition. But of this more in its own place.

§. 43.

Mr. Bl. The great condition to which Baptism engageth, is not a pre-requisite in baptism. This is plain; no man is bound to make good his condition, before engagement to conditions: no servant is tyed to do his work, before he hath received his earnest: no Souldier to fight before he is listed, or hath given in his name. But faith that is Justifying to Accept Christ, is the Condition to which Baptism engageth.

§. 43.

R. B. What is the conclusion? therefore *Justifying faith is not a prerequisite in Baptism:* or according to the simile, *therefore no man is bound to accept Christ to Justification before he is baptized.* I confess, the reading of such passages in Grave, Learned, Godly Divines, and that with such confidence uttered as undoubted truth, and that in zeal to save the Church from the errors of us that are contrarie minded, doth very much convince me of humane frailtie, and that the best of men do know but in part, and in a little part too: and it makes me less angrie at those unlearned mistaken men, that have of late so troubled the Church: and to say with *Seneca, Iniquus est qui commune vitium singulis objicit, &c. quanto in his Justior Venia sit, quæ per totum genus humanum vulgata sunt? Omnes inconsulti, & improvidi sumus; omnes incerti, queruli, ambitiosi. Quid lenioribus verbis ulcus publicum abscondam? Omnes mali sumus. Quicquid itaque in alio reprehenditur, id unusquisque in suo sinu inveniet. Quid illius pallorem? illius maciem notas? Pestilentia est. Placidiores itaque invicem sumus. Mali inter malos vivimus.* But to the matter.

1. Then it seems, if a man believe sincerely and savingly, the main use of Baptism, as engaging, is past already. Must any sound believer then be Baptised? or onely unsound believers and Infidels that will promise to believe hereafter?

after ? But I will shew the foulness of this error anon, and therefore let it pass now. 2. But you say, *This is plain*; to whom? all men have not the truth, that are confident that they have it ; I see that you say, *No man is bound to make good his Condition before engagement*, &c. very dangerous: It is not our condition only nor principally, as to the efficient obligation, nor at all as to the Justification. Are we poor worms, our own Gods and Lords, that we should be disobliged till we will be pleased to oblige our selves ? Our faith is Gods Condition as the Imposer ;. three several Bonds hath he laid upon us. 1. As Legislator of the Law of Grace, he hath commanded us to believe in, and accept an offered Christ. And is Gods command insufficient to oblige us, till we oblige our selves ? then more happy are Pagans then I imagined. 2. As the Donor of Christ and Life, and the Author of the Promise or Deed of gift (and so Christ as Testator) he hath made our sincere faith the condition; saying, *If thou believe, thou shalt be saved*. Hereby we are bound to believe, as a necessary means to salvation. This is but a sanction of the first obligation. 3. The like may be said of the threatning, *He that believeth not shall be damned*; which God addeth as Legislator to this Law, so that every man is bound to sound Believing, as the necessarie condition of salvation, before he doth consent himself, or oblige himself to it: even by an obligation which is ten thousand fold stronger then any that he is capable of laying on himself.

3. It is also a very high mistake, to think that our Covenanting or Consent, (which is our actual believing) is none of our condition, when it is the great and principal part of our condition; yea all the condition of our begun Justification (not taking the word Faith too narrowly). You will perhaps say; These are our conditions as subjects, but not as Covenanters. Reply. They are our conditions as subjects called to Covenant, as we are the persons to whom the Covenant is offered: They are constituted by God as Donor, Benefactor, and Author of the Covenant or Promise, and not meerly as Rector. It belongeth to the Donor to determine of the conditions of his own gift, on which they shall become due or not. Yet doth God make no transactions with men but as with subjects; and therefore even when he deals with us as Benefactor and Donor in free gifts, it is still as *Dominus & Rector Beuefaciens*: he lays not by his Dominion or Soveraigntie, nor these Relations to us.

4. For your instance of servants and souldiers, they leave out the great part of the condition of the Covenant of Grace: which is, that we consent to be servants and souldiers. The Relation must first be entered; God must be taken for our God, and Christ for our Redeemer, Lord, and Saviour; the Holy Ghost for our Guide and Sanctifyer : This is Faith and Covenanting. This goes before working and fighting. But this Covenanting is the great condition of Gods Covenant. As when the forementioned Prince is offered in marriage (with his Dignities and Riches) to a condemned beggar; as it is a gift, and covenant propounded on his part, and actually to be entered, it is consent, or marriage-covenanting on her part that is the condition ; yea, and all the condition of her first right to him and his riches and honors. So in your instance: It is the servants consent or covenant to have such a man for his master ; and the souldiers consent and covenanting to have such a man for his General ; that is the condition on which one hath all his first right to the Priviledges of the family, and the other to the Priviledges of the Armie. Is not this consent necessarie in our present case ? If you would have spoke to the point, you should have said thus,

No servant is tyed sincerely to consent or covenant to be a servant, before he have received his earnest: No souldier is tyed to consent or covenant truly to be a souldier, till he be listed; which are both plainly false. Baptism is as the listing; Consent (which is saving Faith) is the heart covenant, prerequisite to listing, and not the work to be done after, except you speak of the continuance of consent. Baptism is the solemnizing our marriage with Christ. And it is a strange marriage, wherein the woman doth only promise that she will begin hereafter to take that man for her husband, but not at present. Nay where such present consent is not Requisite, is a feigned or nominal, or half-consent, the condition on which a woman hath Right to the man and his estate, and a full consent hereafter the thing that she is engaged to.

5. In your minor, *But faith that is Justifying to accept Christ, is the condition to which Baptism engageth*; either you mean only the continuance of that faith, and that is true, (but not your meaning I think). Or you mean, the beginning of that faith (as doubtless the foregoing words shew that you do); and then why had we not one word tending to the proof, which would in this place have been very acceptable to me. I will anon make an argument of the contrarie.

You seem to me in all this to mistake the very formal nature of a condition, as if it received its denomination from our promise to perform it; when as, by the consent of all Lawyers that I have read of it, it is denominated from the determination of the Donor, Testator, or other Imposer; and most evidently and unquestionably it is so, in unequal contracts, where one is the Benefactor, and hath the absolute power of disposing his own favors.

---

§. 44.

Mr. Bl. THat Faith upon which Simon Magus *in the Primitive times was baptized, is that which admitteth to Baptism;* Simon himself believed and was Baptized, Act. 8. 13. *But* Simons *Faith fell short of saving and justifying.*

---

§. 44.

R. B. COncedo totum; *sed desideratur Conclusio;* That may be said to admit to Baptism, which so qualifieth the person as that we are bound to Baptize him, as being one that seemeth sound in believing, as *Simon* did. But this is not *Entituling*, or, having *Coram Deo & à foedere*, Right to Baptism: nor doth prove that it is not saving Faith which God in his Covenant makes the condition prerequisite to such a Right to Baptism.

---

§. 45.

Mr. Bl. 6. *IN Case only justifying Faith give admission to Baptism, then none is able to baptize, seeing this by none is discerned: and to leave it to our charity, affirming that we may admit upon presumption of a title when God denies, I have spoken somewhat*

what, Chap. *and I refer to Mr.* Hudson *in his Vindication, whom learned Mr.*Baxter *so highly commends, to shew the unreasonableness of it.*

§. 45.

*R.B.*1. SEing you have read what I have said to Mr. *Tombes* against this Objection, I shall take it as needless to say more, till you confute it: 2. I say not that *onely justifying Faith gives Admission to Baptism.* I say that the seeming, or Probable Profession of such a faith gives Admittance. 3. Nor is it left to our Charity, but imposed on us as a Duty to Baptize those that profess sound belief: but whether the profession be probably serious, or not, our understanding, and not our Charity must judge. And if you go not that way too, then it seems you would Baptize a man that should apparently jest or deride Christ under colour of professing: which were to Accept that as a profession which is no profession. For it is no further a profession then it seems to be serious and express what is in the heart. 4. Though God deny the justness of the hypocrites Title *in foro Dei*, yet he doth not deny it to be our duty to deal with them, for their profession, as with those whose Title is just. 5. I know not what Chapter it is that you refer us to for more. 6. Having lent Mr. *Hudsons* book out, I have it not now by me, and therefore cannot consult him: but I suppose you would use the Arguments which you thought strongest.

§. 46.

Mr.Bl. HEre it is objected: 1. When Christ saith, *Make me Disciples of all Nations, baptizing them,* he meant sincere Disciples, though we cannot ever know them to be sincere. *I Answer, In Case I make this first Objection brought against me, my seventh and last Argument for me, it will fully discover the weakness of it; and thus I form it. All that are Disciples unto Christ, and made Disciples for Christ, are to be baptized: But some are made Disciples to Christ, that are short of Faith saving and justifying, as hath been proved at large: This Discipleship that Christ here mentions, is such of which whole Nations are in capacity, as is plain in the Commission; to which this Nation (with others) hath happily attained according to the manifold Prophesies before cited: Of these the whole Universal visible Church consisteth, so irrefragably proved by Mr.*Hudson *in his Treatise of that subject, and his Vindication. Now if whole Nations, yea the whole Universal Visible Church (consisting of discipled Nations) were all Believers, it were a great happiness; the Election would be as large as Vocation, when Christ saith,* Many are called, but few chosen.

§. 46.

R.B.1. TO vindicate my Objections: If it be not sincere Disciples that Christ means in that Text, then no Apostle was bound by that Commission and great Precept to endeavour the making of sincere Disciples (but only counterfeits and half Christians:) But the Antecedent is false, therefore, &c. 2. For your Argument, I grant the Conclusion; and what would you have more? But knew

you

you not that it is not the thing in Question? 3. I grant the Minor, taking the word Disciples equivocally, as a Corps is called a man; and I confess it usual so to take the word: but otherwise I deny the Minor. To be Chrifts Difciple (as to the aged) is to be one that hath unfeignedly taken Chrift for his Mafter, to Teach him and Rule him, renouncing the contrary guidance of the Flefh, the World, and Devil: and it implyeth that he hath already learnt his neceffity of Chrifts Guidance, and who Chrift is, and what a Mafter, & to what End it is that we muft learn of him; and what are the great conditions on which he receiveth his Difciples. And I think they that do this fincerely, are juftified: and they that do not, are but feeming Difciples; but if you will call fuch Difciples (as we muft becaufe they feem fo) then you may fay, They are Really fuch (feeming) Difciples. 4. To your confirmation, I deny the Minor: and I fay, that it is fo new Doctrine to affirm that whole Nations are not capable of being found Believers, that it deferved one word of proof. Much lefs fhould you have hid your Minor, and turned it into a *Negatio exiftentiæ*, when it fhould have been but a *Negatio Capacitatis*. Doth it follow that a Nation is not capable of found faith, becaufe they have it not? or will not have it? 5. Do you think Preachers yet be not bound to endeavour the faving Converfion of whole Nations? If you fay, No: you take them off the work that their mafter hath fet them on. If you fay, Yea, then you think they muft endeavor to perfwade men to that which they have not a capacity of. 6. If there be any Nation uncapable of Faith, then God cannot make them Believers. But that is not true, therefore, &c. 7. You fay not well that the whole Univerfal Vifible Church confifteth of Difcipled Nations, if you mean [only] as you feem. For then poor fcattered Chriftians in a Heathen Nation, fhould be no part of the Univerfal-Vifible Church. 8. Vocation uneffectual, is common to Pagans. Vocation throughly effectual, is of the fame extent as juftification, and (I think) Election. Vocation which is effectual only to bring men to an outward Profeffion of faving Faith, is larger then Election, and makes men fuch whom we are bound to Baptize.

§. 47.

Mr. Bl. *Object.* 2. When he faith, He that Believeth and is baptized fhall be faved, here Faith goes before Baptifm; and that not a common, but a faving Faith; for here is but one Faith fpoken of, and that is before Baptifm. Anfw. 1. *This is the weakeft of all Arguments, to reafon for a precedency of one before another, from the order in which they are placed in Scripture.* So we may fay, John Baptized *before he preached the Baptifm of repentance, for his baptizing is mentioned before preaching of Baptifm*, Mar. 1. 4. So we may fay, *we muft have glory firft, and Vertue after;. for-fo they are placed by the Apoftle*, 2 Pet. 1. 3. *All that can be collected, is, that we muft in Gods ordinary way of conferring falvation, have both Faith and Baptifm; though there be not the like abfolute neceffity of Baptifm as of Faith: Baptifm being neceffary,* neceffitate præcepti, *Jefus Chrift having Inftituted and commanded it; but Faith neceffary both* neceffitate medii & præcepti, *feeing Chrift not onely commanded it, but falvation can at no hand be obtained (by men in capaicty of it) without it: And it hath been well obferved, that in the words following, the like ftrefs is not laid on Baptifm as on Faith: not* [he that is not baptized] *but* [he that believeth not] *fhall be damned.*

§.47.

§. 47.

R. B. IF affirmations be good proof of the weakness of Arguments, then this is sufficiently confuted. But to the rest : 1. I confess there may be a *Hysteron Proteron* in the Scripture: and in such a case we may not gather the reall precedency of that which is first named. But otherwise, I know not whence we should better gather the natural order then from Scripture order in expression. If I may by the order of your speeches gather the order of things in your conception and intentions, then may I observe the Holy Ghosts order also to the like ends : for I suppose you speak not more orderly then the Holy Ghost. But I may sure to that end observe the order of your expressions, therefore. Moreover, this is not one Text going against the order expressed in most others : but contrarily, the same order is usually observed in other Texts that speak of Faith and Baptism, putting Faith first. Furthermore, this is not a meer Historical Narration, or circumstantial by-passage, but it is the very sum of the Law of Grace, solemnly delivered by Christ to his Apostles (with their grand Commission) before his Ascention: and where may we expect if not here ; where in so few words is expressed the substance of the Covenant ? Moreover, it is not doctrinally and in general precepts onely, that this order is held, but in particular precepts, directing in present matter of execution. ¿The Eunuch must Believe with all his heart, and so others commonly must profess belief, before they must be Baptized : and the Scripture gives no hint that this is one kinde of Faith, and that another, *Mar.* 1. 4. shews first in General what *John* did in the wildernesss, *viz.* Baptize : and 2. in what order he did it, *viz.* first preaching that Baptism of Repentance to them. That 2 *Pet.* 1. 3. is spoken in perfect Logical order : It speaks not of Christs order of Execution, and our order of Assecution, but of Gods and our order of Intention. If it had been said that *he giveth us glory and vertue*, it had been a *Hysteron Proteron* : but it is only, *he called us to glory and vertue.* : And of ends the Ultimate is the first in Intention, and all ends are so before their means ; and therefore may well be so in expression.

2. I think as Baptism is truly *Medium ad salutem*, so it may be said to be necessary, *necessitate medii*, as well as *necessitate precepti* : only with a distinction of necessitie, according to its Degrees ; Faith is absolutely necessarie; as *sine qua non*, and Baptism is of an inferior less necessitie, sometime but *ad bene esse, & solemnitatem.* Lastly, the command foregoing, *Disciple me all Nations, Baptizing them* : setteth Faith (in present or persons at age themselves) before Baptism, as included in Discipling : And if this text which contains the Commission, put not Faith before Baptism, its like others do not, and then why may not any Heathens that will, be baptized : and the text speaks but of one faith, for ought I can finde.

§. 48.

Mr. Bl. 2. LEt Peter *where he speaks of salvation by baptism*, interpret these words, Baptism doth now also (saith he) save us by the resurrection of Jesus Christ, 1 Pet. 3.21. *and then explains himself. Not the putting away the filth of the flesh, but the answer of a good conscience towards God ; this answer or restipulation to the outward administration of Baptism, is that which follows upon Baptism, but Justifying Faith is that restipulation (at least a principal branch of it) and therefore there is no necessitie that it go before, but a necessitie that it must follow after baptism. It is true that in men of years, Justifying faith sometimes goes before baptism, as in Abraham it went before Circumcision : but it is not of necessity required to Interest us in a Right, neither of Baptism nor Circumcision.*

---

§. 48.

R. B. I Will not now stand to enquire of the fitness or unfitness of your term, *Restipulation*, as here used. *Varro* useth *Restipulari* as being the same act as *stipulari*: and Civilians use it but rarely. In every stipulation they make two parties, the Stipulator (which is he that asks the question) and the Promiser (which is the answerer, that obligeth himself). Though rarely and unusually also, the Promiser be called Stipulator. But I suppose it is *Responsio Promissoris*, that you mean by Restipulation, and not another Interogation whereby a double stipulation is made; supposing this your meaning I Reply :
1. Why did you not give us one word for proof ; that this Restipulation is a thing following Baptism ? This is too dilute and easie disputing. I took the contrary for an unquestionable truth. The best Interpreters judge, that *Peter* means here; the Answer whereby the Promiser in Baptism did solemnly oblige himself : which was to two Questions. *Credis in Patrem, filium & spiritum sanctum? Credo. Abrenuncias Diabolum, mundum & Carnem? Abrenuncio.* And who knoweth not that these went before the application of the water ? (of which more anon.) Doth not mutual consent expressed go before the sealing of the Covenant? Doth Christ bid us Baptize men into the name of the Father, Son, and Holy-Ghost ; and would you have us do this before they profess their consent? shall we Baptize them first, and ask them whether they believe and consent after ?

2. I gratefully accept your Concession, that *Justifying Faith is that Restipulation*. Which is your minor : (that is, Justifying Faith, professed). And thence I conclude, that then Justifying faith is Essential to the mutual Covenant, and so without it, God is not thus in Covenant with men: For who knows not, that ever read Civil Law, that there is no stipulation *sine Promissione*, which you call (and so do other Divines) Restipulation ? and that this Restipulation is an essential part of the contract, called stipulation ? This being past doubt, it follows, that Justifying Faith being our Restipulation, is an Essential part of the contract or Baptismal Covenant. And it is apparant that *Peter* meant not any other contract which was to be entered between God and man, after the Baptismal Contract, and different from it : for then he would not have said *Baptism saveth us*; and have interpreted it, *de fidei responsione vel promissione, & non de nuda lotione*.

3. The Concession which you were forced to, about men of years, how it doth cut the throat of your cause, I shall shew you anon.

Mr. Bl.

§. 49.

Mr. Bl. *Obj. 3.* That faith to which the promise of Remission and Justification is made, it must also be sealed to, (or that faith which is the condition of the Promise, is the condition *in foro Dei* of the Title to the Seal). But it is only solid true faith which is the Condition of the Promise (of Remission). Therefore it is that only that gives Right *in foro Dei*, to the Seal. *Answ.* Here is an argument first proposed; 2. in a parenthesis paraphrased: For the proposition, I say, Faith is not sealed to, but Remission of sins, or salvation upon condition of Faith. A professor of Faith that goes no further, may engage himself to a lively working Faith, and upon those terms, God engages for, and puts his Seal for Remission and salvation. For the parenthesis, That faith which is the condition of the Promise, is the condition *in foro Dei* of Title to that Seal; I judge the contrary to be undeniable, that Faith which is the condition of the Promise, is not the condition in foro Dei, of Title to the Seal. An acknowledgment of the Necessity of such faith, with engagement to it, is sufficient for a Title to the Seal, and the performance of the condition of like necessity to attain the thing sealed. To promise service and fidelitie in war, is enough to get listed, as to do service is of necessity to be rewarded.

---

§. 49.

R. B. 1. Both Sacraments rightly used, are a mutual Sealing to the mutual Covenant. As in the Lords Supper; Taking and eating, is our Sealing, professing action; so in Baptism, receiving the water applied, is our Seal and professing Passion: (For we are more Passive in our new birth, then in our feeding for growth). So is the presenting our persons, or our children, of our delivering them up to Christ, as his Disciples. It is therefore our part, as well as Gods, that is Sealed to.

2. Where you say, *A professor of Faith may engage to a lively working Faith*; you mean, either *a Professor of that lively faith*, or *a Professor of a dead, not working Faith*. If the first, it is a contradiction to say, *He professeth to have a lively Faith*; and *He only engageth so to believe hereafter*. For if he profess to have it already, then he can engage only to the Continuation, and not the Inception of it. If you mean the latter, then I shall shew you anon, that a man professing a Dead, not-working Faith, is not in Scripture called to Covenant with God in Baptism, to believe lively for the future, (*incepive*) and to believe for the future with a working Faith. In the mean time, this should be proved, which yet I never saw. You suppose then, such a professor as this, coming to Baptism, saying, *Lord I believe that Thou art God alone, and Christ the only Redeemer, and the Holy-Ghost, the Guide and Sanctifier of thy people; and that the World, Flesh, and Devil is to be renounced for thee: but at present these are so dear to me, that I will not forsake them for thee; I will not take Thee for my God, to Rule me, or be my Happiness, nor will I take Christ to Govern me, and Save me in His way, nor will I be Guided or Sanctified by the Holy-Ghost; but hereafter I will, & therefore I come to be Baptized.*

3. That which you judge undeniable, you see I deny. It is not therefore *de facto* undeniable. When you and I can each of us attain to such a height of

confidence, of the Verity of our several Contradictory Propositions, in a matter of such moment, and about the Principles of the Doctrine of Christ, which the Apostle reckoneth as the milk of Babes, who are unskilful in the word of Righteousness (*Heb.* 5, 12, 13, 14. and 6, 1, 2.) it encreaseth my conviction of the great necessity of toleration of some great errors, even in Preachers of the Gospel; For either yours or mine seem such. I finde no proof of your undenyable Proposition. 1. The Seal is but an affix to the Promise: therefore that which is the condition of the Promise, is the condition of the Seal. 2. The use of the Seal is to confirm the Promise to him to whom it is Sealed: Therefore the condition of the Promise is the condition of the Seal. 3. If the Promise and Seal have two distinct conditions, then there are two distinct Covenants (for from the conditions, most commonly are contracts specified; and therefore *Wesenbechius* and such like Logical Civilians, call it the form of the contract, or stipulation to be either *Dura vel in diem, vel sub conditione,* and those sub-conditions are specified oft from their various conditions). But there is not two Covenants, therefore; but of this more anon.

4. Is it not against the nature and common use of Sealing, that it should be in order before the Promise or Covenant? and that men should have first right to that Seal on one condition, before they have right to the Promise; and then have right to the Promise after on another condition? 5. If it be so undenyable, that *that Faith which is the condition of the Promise, is not the condition in foro Dei of Title to the Seal*; as you affirm: why do you then build so much against *Mr. Tombes,* on that argument from Act. 2. *The Promise is to you and your children*; arguing a Right to the Seal, from an Interest in the Promise?

6. Where you say, that *An acknowledgement of the necessity of such faith, with engagement to it, is sufficient for a Title to the Seal.* I Reply, then those that at present renounce Christ, so it be against their knowledge and conscience, and will engage to own him sincerely for the future, have right to Baptism. A convinced persecutor may acknowledge this necessity, and engage, that before he dies he will be a true Believer, and yet resolve to be no Christian till then, no not so much as in profession.

7. Your instance of service & fidelitie in war, runs upon the great mistake which I have so often told you of. The formal Reason and denomination of a condition, is from the Donors constitution or imposition, giving his benefits only on the terms by himself assigned; and not from our Promise to perform them. And therefore our Promise it self, is the chief condition of Gods Promise, and (to speak as your self did). Our Justifing faith being our Restipulation, that Restipulation is not only part of our condition, but the whole as to our first Right to Christ, Justification and Salvation; though that Right shall not be continued, nor we actually glorified, but on condition both of continuing that faith, and of adding (if there be opportunitie) sincere obedience, in perseverance to the death.

---

§. 50.

Mr. Bl. 4. **A**S *for the argument* ad hominem, *framed against those who make initial or common faith, sufficient to entitle to Baptism; and yet affix Remission of sins to all Baptism, even so received without any performance of further engagement; I leave to them to defend, who maintain such Doctrine, and to speak to the Absurdities that follow upon it.* §. 50.

§. 50.

R. B. THough you avoid the dint of this argument, by forsaking Dr. *Ward* here, yet it may perhaps appear that your own way is clogged with more Absurdities then a few.

§. 51.

Mr. Bl. 5. THat of *Philip* to the *Eunuch*, seems to carry most colour; The *Eunuch* must believe with all his heart, before he must be baptized; and I have known it trouble some, that are fully convinced, that a *Dogmatical faith* gives title to baptism, satisfying themselves with this answer, that howsoever Philip called for such a faith which leads to salvation, yet did not express himself so far, that no faith short of this gives title to baptism.

It may be answered, that a *Dogmatical faith is true faith*, suo genere, as well as that which *Justifieth*; therefore I know not why men should give it the term of *false Faith*, seeing Scripture calls it Faith, and such as those Believers, and the heart in such a Faith (as to an entire assent) is required. If we look into the *Eunuchs* answer, in which *Philip* did rest satisfied, and proceeded upon it to baptism, it will take away all scruple: his answer is, *I believe that Jesus Christ is the Son of God*: There is no more in that then a common Faith: this is believed by men not justified: yet this Faith entitles to baptism, and upon this confession of Faith the *Eunuch* is baptized.

§. 51.

R. B. THat will not trouble you, which troubleth others. To your answer I Reply, 1. When we do, with the Scriptures, enquire after Faith in *Christ crucified*, we may well call that a false Faith which pretends to be this, and is not this, however true in *suo genere*. Faith in *Jupiter, Sol, Mahomet*, is true in *suo genere*: and so is humane Faith: yet I would call it a false Faith, if this should be pretended to be Faith in Christ. To believe in Christ as man only, or as God only, or as a Guide to Heaven only, and not as a Redeemer by ransom, or as one that is to justifie us, but not to Sanctifie or Rule us; each of these is true in *suo genere*, but false if they pretend to be that which Scripture calls Faith in Christ; and which denominateth Believers. So is it to believe with the understanding speculatively and superficially, and yet to Dissent with the will. I think, if a man say, *This is the Son, the heir, come let us kill him, and the inheritance shall be ours; we will not have this man Reign over us:* that these are not true Believers, nor have right to Baptism, though their belief that he is the heir, be a Dogmatical Faith, true in its kinde.

2. As *Amesius Medulla* li. 1. cap. 3. §. 20. *Quamvis in Scripturis aliquando Assensus veritati quæ est de Deo & Christo, Joh. 1. 50. habetur pro vera fide, includitur tamen semper specialis fiducia; atque adeo omnibus in locis ubi sermo est de salutari fide, vel præsupponitur fiducia in Messiam, & indicatur tantum determinatio vel applicatio ejus ad personam Jesu Christi, vel per assensum illum designatur, tanquam es-*

Bb 3 *sectum*

fectum per suam causam. And as words of Knowledge and Assent, do in Scripture oft imply affection and consent, so on the contrary, words of consent and affection do alwaies imply Knowledge and Assent. And therefore Faith is sometime denominated from the Intellectual act *Believing*, and sometime from the Wills act *Receiving.*

3. Do you not know how ordinarily even saving Faith it self is denominated from the Intellectual Act alone ? when yet you'l confess the Will is necessarily an Agent in this ? many texts might quickly be cited to that end. Those that *Amesius* citeth may suffice : *Joh.* 11. 25, 26, 27. *He that believeth in me shall live. Believest thou this ? yea Lord, I believe that thou art that Christ the Son of God, that was to come into the world.* Such was *Nathaniels* faith. *Joh.* 1. 49, 50. 1 *Joh.* 4. 15. *Whosoever shall confess that Jesus is the Son of God, God dwelleth in him, and he in God.* And 1 *Joh.* 5. 1. *Whosoever believeth that Jesus is the Christ, is born of God.* Here is more then Right to Baptism. The great doubt was then whether Christ were the true *Messiah*, and therefore this was the greatest and most difficult part of Faith, to Assent to this ; and therefore the whole is denominated from it, it being supposed, when they believed him to be the only sufficient and faithful Physitian, that they were willing to be healed by him in his way.

4. If you think, as you seem by your answer to do, that a man may Assent to the Truth of the Gospel with all his heart, and yet be void of Justifying Faith, you do not lightly err. Though an unregenerate man may believe as many truths as the Regenerate, yet not with all his heart; Christ saith *Math.* 13. *The word hath not rooting in him.* Doubtless, whether or no the Practical understanding do unavoidably determine the Will, yet God doth not sanctifie the understanding truly, and leave the Will unsanctified : which must be said, if the Dogmatical Faith, that is the Intellectual Assent of a wicked man, be as strong as that of a true Believer. Dr. *Downam* in his Treatise of Justification, and against Mr. *Pemble* hath said enough of this, to which I refer you. I take that answer as equal to silence, which yet Mr. *Bl.* so highly values, as to say, It will take away all scruple.

---

§. 52.

HAving Replyed to your Answer, I shall be bold to trouble you with some more Arguments to this point. Mr. *Blake* affirmeth, that Justifying Faith Is the great Condition to which Baptism engageth, and therefore not prerequisite to Baptism ; and that an acknowledgment of the Necessity of such Faith with engagement to it, Is sufficient for a title to the Seal : and so it is a Dogmatical Faith which entitles to Baptism, in which Baptism we must engage to believe with a lively and working Faith hereafter : Against this Doctrine I argue. 1. From Authority (beginning with the lowest Argument). The Reverend Assembly in their Advice for Church Government, Printed after the Directory, pag. 58. of the Church say thus, *Particular Churches in the Primitive times were made up of Visible Saints.* viz. *of such as being of Age, professed faith in*

Rivet in Animad. in Annotat. Grotii in Cassandr. in art. 4. p. 13. fol. *Fides quæ non parit obedientiæ propositum, non est vera fides. Hæc cum primum ingeneratur cum pœnitentia conjuncta est, quæ non potest esse sine obedientiæ proposito. Fidei formatæ & informis apud Veteres Catholicos ne Vestigium quidem reperitur, si de fide Justificante & salvifica, &c.*

[95.]

in Christ, and obedience unto Christ, according to the Rule of Faith and Life, taught by Christ and his Apostles; and of their children: and they cite *Act.* 2. 38, 41, last : compared with *Act.* 5. 14. 1 *Cor.* 1. 2. compared with 2 *Cor.* 9. 13. Now if the Profession of this Saint-ship in Faith and obedience according to the Rule, were necessary, then the profession of Justifying Faith was necessary : For this is justifying Faith without doubt. And if so, then it is not a Faith short of this which is the condition of Church member-ship ; for then the profession of that other imperfect Faith might suffice ; of which more anon. See also the Assemblies Confession. cap. 28. §. 1. 6. and the two Catechisms of Baptism, where 1. observe the ends of Baptism, that it Sealeth Remission, Regeneration, Adoption, &c. 2. the subject, that none are to be Baptized at age till they profess their Faith in Christ and Obedience to him. Which if they do sincerely, no doubt that Faith is no less then justifying. See also what that truly Judicious, Learned, Reverend Divine, Mr. *Gataker* hath Replyed to Dr. *Ward*, (*viz.* against those words which I confuted, not knowing that it was Mr. *Gataker* that the Doctor dealt with) in Mr. *Gatakers Desceptatio de Baptismatis Infantilis vi & efficacia*, pag. 71. where he also cites *Luther, Calvin, Bucer, Whitaker*, &c. and therefore I will cite no more, (Mr. *Marshal* in his late Sermon for Unity, I mentioned before.) A hundred might easily and truly be cited to this purpose.

Argu. 2. My Second Argument shall be from the Testimony and Practice of the purest Antiquity. 1. *Justin Martyr* in his second Apologie, relating the Churches custom in Baptizing, saith , *As many as being perswaded do believe these things to be true which we teach, and do promise to live according to them, they first learn by prayer and fasting to beg pardon of God for their former sins, our selves also joyning our prayer and fasting : Then they are brought to the water and born again, in the same way as we our selves were born again :* So for the other Sacrament he addeth , *This food we call the Eucharist, to which no man is admitted , but he that believeth the Truth of our Doctrine, being washed in the Laver of Regeneration, for Remission of sin, and that so liveth as Christ hath taught.*

2. *Irenæus* l. 4. c. 13. shews that *Abrahams* Faith by which he was justified, is the same with the Christian Faith, yea with that whereby we *begin to be saved.* And cap. 76. having reference to the Baptismal Covenant, wherein men deliver up themselves to Christ, he saith, *Si igitur tradideris ei quod tuum est, id est , fidem in eum & subjectionem, percipies ejus artem, & eris perfectum Dei opus : si autem non credideris ei, & fugeris manus ejus, erit Causa in te,* &c. *Ille enim misit qui vocarent ad Nuptias ; qui autem non obedierunt ei semetipsos privarunt regia cæna.*

3. *Athenagoras in Legat. pro Christianis* p. 3. ὁ ἧς γὰρ χριςιανὸς πονηρὸς εἰ μὴ ὑποκρίνε᾽) τὸν λόγον. *Nullus enim Christianus malus est, nisi hanc professionem simulaverit.* He therefore that only professeth, is but a counterfeit Christian ; and he that professeth any thing lower then Holyness or an obediential Faith, doth profess somewhat short of Christianity, and not Christianity it self.

4. *Tertullian Apolog.* cap. 44. Speaking how the Heathens were fain to punish one another in Prisons and houses of Corrections, addes, *Nemo illic Christianus, nisi plane tantum Christianus, aut si & aliud, jam non Christianus* ; No Christian comes there unless meerly because he is a Christian : or if otherwise (*i. e.* as a wicked liver) then he is no Christian. And *de Baptismo,* he faith, (cap. 6.) *Ita & angelus baptismi arbiter superventuro spiritui sancto vias dirigit ablutione delictorum quam fides impetrat, obsignata in Patre & Filio & spiritu sancto.* Many places might be cited in him, that shew, they took the Baptized for justified Believers.

5. *Cyprian Epist.* 23. *Nam cum Dominus dixerit in nomine Patris , Filii & Spiritus*

sancti gentes tingi, & in Baptismo, præterita peccata dimitti, &c. And *Epist.* 2. §. 2. *Sed postquam unde genitalis auxilii superioris ævi labe deterſa, in expiatum pectus ac purum desuper se lumen infudit, postquam cælitus spiritu hausto in novum me hominem Nativitas Secunda reparavit,* &c. But it is so well known a Case, that Antiquity runs wholly this way, that I think I may spare the labor of transcribing any more. I had at hand the full testimonies of *Clemens Alexand. Origen, Epiphanius, Athanaſius, Lactantius, Nazianzen, Nyſſen, Baſil, Cyril* of *Alexandria, Cyril* of *Jerusalem, Syneſius, Hierom, Macarius, Eusebius,* with divers others, which I now cast by as tedious and unnecessary, but shall produce quickly, if I once finde it of any use. Yet two or three brief ones I will add, which shew that it is the Covenanting or Profeſſing of true Obedience, and consequently of a lively working Faith that is required, and not the profeſſion of an unsound faith only.

6. *Nazianzen Orat.* 40. p. 641. vol. 1. (*Edit. Morel.*) saith, *For to summe up all in a word, we ought to judge, that the force and faculty of Baptism, is nothing else but a Covenant entered with God, for (or a Promise made to God of) a Second Life, (or a new Life) and a more pure courſe of living* : *And therefore that we shall all exceedingly fear, and with all diligence keep our Souls, leſt we be found to have violated this Covenant.* And doubtless to enter such a Covenant sincerely, is the work of a Faith not short of juſtifying: and therefore it is juſtifying Faith which in Baptiſm is profeſſed, and thereto required.

7. *Baſil. Amph.* c. 9. *As we believe in the Father, Son and Holy Ghoſt, so are we Baptized into the name of the Father, Son and Holy Ghoſt. And Confeſſion as Captain leads the way to salvation*: *and Baptiſm sealing up our Promiſe (or Covenant) followeth.* (It is then a Seal of our Promiſe, as well as of Gods.)

8. *Chryſoſtom, Tom.* 5. *Homil. ad Neoph. Would we did answerably go on, and those Symbols and Covenants wherewith we are bound, did ſtick in our hearts*; *we have confeſſed Chriſts Government*; *we have renounced the Devils Tyrannie*; *This Handwriting, this Covenant, this Symbol we are taught is conſcribed*: *See that we be not again found Debtors to this hand-writing.*

9. *Hierom, Dial. adverſ. Lucif.* saith again and again that *Baptiſma non eſt (& nullum eſt) ſine ſpiritu ſancto*: which saying, though I approve not, yet that and many more paſſages in that Dialogue fully shew his judgement in this point.

10. *Salvian de Gubern.* l. 4. initio, saith, *Nam cum hoc ſit hominis Chriſtiani fides, fideliter Chriſti mandata servare, ſit abſque dubio ut nec fidem habeat qui infidelis eſt, nec Chriſtum credat qui Chriſti mandata conculcat. Ac per hoc totum in id revolvitur, ut qui Chriſtiani nominis opus non agit, Chriſtianus non eſſe videatur. Nomen enim ſine actu atque officio ſuo nihil eſt.* Et lib. 3. p. 66. *Quid eſt igitur Credulitas vel fides? opinor fideliter hominem Chriſto credere, id eſt, fidelem Deo eſſe, hoc eſt, fideliter Dei mandata servare.* pag. 67. *Infidelis ſit neceſſe eſt, qui fidei commiſſa non ſervat.*

Argu. 3. If it be required in Baptiſm that men do sincerely promise for the future to Believe savingly, and to obey Chriſt sincerely, then Iuſtifying Faith is required in Baptiſm. But the Antecedent is acknowledged by Mr. *Bl.* (except the word sincerely.) He yieldeth that men muſt in Baptiſm engage to do this hereafter. Now I would know of him, whether God require them to make this engagement seriously, sincerely, *& firmato animo,* or not? If not, then God calls them but to Diſſemble, which is not true. If yea; then I say, This is juſtifying Faith it self, or at leaſt comes from it, if it be a Promise to do this presently without delay. For he that will heartily engage himself to obey Chriſt as his Sovéraign, and reſt on him for salvation, muſt needs be resolved so to do. But he that is so resolved, is a true

Believer:

Believer: For his will is sanctified; or else he could not be thus resolved. But if it be only for so long time hence, that a man promiseth to believe and obey sincerely, with a reserve and resolution to live wickedly till then, I hope few will believe that this is the condition of Baptism, or the true Baptismal Covenant.

Argu. 4. They that are to Renounce the World, Flesh, and Devil, are to be true believers (to justification); but they that are to be baptized, are then to Renounce the World, Flesh and Devil: therefore &c. The major is evident, in that renouncing these, is a renounceing them as Rulers that would command us before God, or as worldly, fleshly pleasures or profits, might seem our chief good, to be preferred before God. Now it is none but the sincere believer that can so renounce these. All others are servants to them, and make them their end. The Minor is proved thus. 1. There can be no *motus* to the *Terminus ad quem*, but there must also be a *Terminus à quo*. The World, Flesh and Devil, are the *Terminus à quo*; without which we cannot be said to take God for our God, or Christ for our Lord-Redeemer. 2. *De facto*, this Abrenunciation hath been used in the Churches Baptism, ever since the Apostles days; as far as we have any History to guide us. *Tertullian, Cyprian,* and all Antiquity *uno ore* that write of these things, put that past question. And I dare not think that Christs Church hath ever required that as necessary in Baptism, which was not requisite till afterward. And if Mr. B¹. say, that they did but promise for the future, not to follow the World, Flesh and Devil before Christ: *I Reply*, They renounced them at present, and thereby shewed the present conversion and Resolution of their hearts, that it was afterward that this was to be manifested in action.

Argu. 5. They that are required to believe sincerely in the Father, Son and Holy Ghost, are required to believe to Justification. But such are all that come to baptism. Therefore. For the major, it requires no more proof, but to explain what it is to believe in the Father, Son and Holy-Ghost. And our Divines against the Papists have enough proved, that the phrase of *Believing in,* comprehendeth the act of the will as well as of the understanding. To believe in God, is to take him for our God: to take him for our God, is to take him for our Soveraign, Ruler and Chief good. This none but a sound believer can truly do. Mr. *Bl.* confesseth elsewhere, that this is the summe of the Covenant, to take God for our God, & give up our selves to be his people.

For the Minor: They that are to be baptized into the name of the Father, Son, and Holy-Ghost, are to believe in the Father, Son, and Holy-Ghost. But all that are baptized, are to be baptized into the name of the Father, Son and Holy-Ghost; therefore.

Were it necessary, many Texts might be cited that prove it is not only Assent, but a believing in Christ, that is requisite. The very Creed shews it, which hath *Credo in Deum,* &c. which Creed, for the main Articles of it, the Church hath ever required all to profess, that would be baptized, before the application of the water. And then that this is required to be done *sincerely,* needs no proof with them that will not believe that God commands or loves dissembling. So that I conclude, This sincere Faith is required in and before baptism, and not only to be promised that we will perform it hereafter.

Argu. 6. They that are required to repent sincerely are required to believe to justification at the same time. But all that come to baptism (at age), are required to repent sincerely; therefore.

The major is evident, 1. In that sincere Repentance and true Faith are inseparable. 2. In that Remission is promised to all that truly Repent, as well as to them that believe. The Minor is proved from several plain Scriptures. *Act.* 2, 38. Repent

pent, and be Baptized every one of you in the Name of Jesus Christ for the Remission of sins: And it was no half or common Repentance that he calls them to, for Remission of sins was to be its Consequent. If Mr. *Bl.* say here also, That it is the weakest of all Arguments, to argue from the order expressed in Scripture: I shall say I will not believe him; because I suppose Scripture in such Practical directions, speaks not more confusedly or preposterously then he or I would do. *Act.* 11. 18. It is called Repentance unto life, which the Gentils had before and in their Baptism: yea they had first the Holy Ghost, *Act.* 10. 47. And *Heb.* 6. 1. *Repentance from dead works is a Principle.* Paul, the Jaylor, and all that we read of that were Baptized, did repent or seemed so to do, and were required to do it before Baptism. If Mr. *Bl.* say, It is a Repentance short of that which is saving, that is here required; I would he would describe it to us, and tell us wherein it is short? 1. Objectively, I hope he will not deny but it is every sin, that men should repent of. 2. Subjectively, it is doubtless, sincere, and not counterfeit, that is required. I conclude therefore, that seeing saving Repentance is prerequisite to Baptism, by Gods appointment, and not only to be promised to be afterward performed, we must say the same of saving Faith.

Argu. 7. If saving Grace be not required in Christs Baptism, then it requireth less then *Johns* Baptism did. But the Consequent is false: therefore so is the Antecedent.

The Consequence of the major is all that requires proof. Which I prove from many Texts, *Mat.* 3. 2, 6, 8. He first preacheth Repentance, and causeth them to confess their sins, and reprehendeth the *Pharises,* that came in Hypocrisie, or with unsound Repentance. And it was true Repentance; for Remission of sins was annext, *Mar.* 1. 4. And it may not only be required after Baptism, but before; and it is called the Baptism of Repentance, because in it they professed Repentance. So *Act.* 13. 24 and 19. 4.

Argu. 8. If Faith-Justifying be required before Remission of sin, then is it required of God before we come to Baptism (or in us before we bring our Infants), But such Faith is prerequisite to Remission of sin; therefore.

The consequence is proved thus. Remission is the end and immediate consequent of Baptism, where men come as God hath required them. Therefore, if sincere Faith be prerequisite to Remission, it is prerequisite also to right to Baptism.

I prove the Antecedent: *Act.* 22. 16. *Ananias* saith to *Paul, Why tarryest thou? arise and be baptized, and wash away thy sins.* This was a present Remission, and not a future only. So *Act.* 2. 38. *Be baptized every one of you, in the name of Jesus Christ for the Remission of sins.* And it is a Faith which hath the Promise of Remission which *Peter* requires of the Gentils before he baptize them. *Act.* 10. 43. *Act.* 13. 39. the Apostle tells them, *All that believe are Justified;* when he is perswading them to believe. It is therefore a believing to Justification, which he was perswading them to. *Rom.* 6. 3, 4. *Know ye not, that as many as were Baptized into Jesus Christ, were baptized into his death? therefore we are buryed with him, by baptism into death, that like as Christ was raised up from the dead, &c.* It is therefore in the act of Baptism, that we are buried and rise Sacramentally, to signifie the present change of our state from the Grave of sin. So *Col.* 2. 11, 12, 13. and 1 *Pet.* 3. 21. Baptism is said to save us, but not the external washing, without the answer of a good conscience; which affordeth two arguments. One In that Baptism saveth, and therefore leaves not man (when rightly used) a childe of of wrath afterward. 2. In that the Answer of a good conscience is required to concurr with Baptism: for so the Apostle plainly intimates, and the best Expositors understand it, and not of a thing to follow, as Mr. *Bl.* doth. *Eph.* 5. 25, 26. *Christ loved the Church, and gave himself for it, that he might sanctifie and cleanse it with the washing of water by the word.* Wherefore *Paul* supposeth them cleansed that are Baptized: 1 *Cor.* 6. 11. *Such were some of you, but ye are washed, but ye are sanctified, but ye are Justified in the name of the Lord Jesus,* &c. And Expositors judge that the Holy-Ghost refers to the sign as well as the thing signified, to the Sacrament as well as Substance, when he makes washing so necessary, and speaks of washing us from our sins in the blood of Christ, *Rev.* 1. 5. Though he make them not equal in necessity. *Joh.* 3. 5. *Except a man be born of water,* &c. *Heb.* 10. 22. *Let us draw neer with a true heart, in full assurance of faith, having our hearts sprinkled from an evil conscience, and our bodyes washed with pure water.* If it be the end of Baptism, to wash our hearts from an evil conscience, (*i. e.* à *Conscientia mali*) then it is the end of Baptism, to Seal the present Remission of sin: But &c. therefore, *Tit.* 3. 5. *He saved us by the washing of Regeneration*: It is a saving work that Baptism is appointed to do. By Regeneration I understand, our new Relative state, at least principally. He that is in Christ is a new creature; old things are passed away; behold all things are become new. He hath a new head, is a member of a new societie, the old guilt of sin is done away, the old enmity between God and us; we have a new Father, new brethren, new right to farther blessings, as well as a new heart. Regeneration is too narrowly taken for a Renovation of the heart alone. So that I think Remission and Reconciliation and Adoption, are meant by Regeneration, in *Tit.* 3. 5. and *Col.* 2. 11, 12. The speaking of Baptism, and the heart-circumcision therein received or professed, saith, they *put off the body of the sins of the flesh, by the circumcision of Christ, being buryed with him in Baptism,* &c. So in 2 *Pet.* 1. 9. The Apostle saith, *He that lacketh these things is blinde, and cannot see far off, and hath forgotten that he was purged from his old sins*: that is Sacramentally, and as far as the Church could go in purifying him: which shews that the end of Baptism is (by obsignation and solemnization) to purge men from their old sins; or as *Paul* speaks, The sins that are past, through the forbearance of God, &c. *Rom.* 5. So that Remission of sins at present, being the end of Baptism rightly received, it must needs follow that Justifying faith is prerequisite to the right receiving it, and that it is not some other Faith, nor is it enough to promise Justifying Faith for hereafter.

Argu. 9. If the Apostles use to communicate the proper Titles of the Justified to all that are Baptized, (till they see them prove apostates or hypocrites) then they did take all the Baptized to be probably justified (though they might know that there were hypocrites among them, yet either they knew them not, or might not denominate the body from a few that they did know) But the Antecedent is true; therefore.

I need not cite Scriptures to prove that the baptized are called by the Apostles, Believers, Saints, Disciples, Christians: Mr. *Blake* hath done it already, *chap.* 28. Now who knows not that salvation is made the Portion of Believers, Saints, Disciples? But what, is it another sort of them? or doth Scripture use to divide Saints, as the Genus into two Species? Not that I know of; It is but as an *æquivocum in sua æquivocata*: The Apostles naming men according to their appearance and Profession, and calling them such as they probably might be.

Why else should they call them such; had not they seemed to be such, and professed it? The names therefore do not primarily agree to these as a true Species, of Believers, Saints, Disciples, Christians; but secondarily, as the name of a man to a Corps, or as the name of a Habit to a disposition, by translation, or Analogie.

But to put the matter beyond doubt, I wish Mr. *Bl.* to consider, that its not only these forementioned titles, but even the rest which he will acknowledge proper to the Regenerate, which are given by the Apostles generally to the baptized. Adoption is ascribed to them, *Gal.* 3. 26, 27. *For yee are all the children of God by Faith in Christ Jesus: For as many of you as have been baptized into Christ, have put on Christ.* 2. The same is extascribed to them Union with Christ; *yee have put on Christ.* 3. And Union with his body, *ye are all one in Christ Jesus.* 4. Yea the next verse addes, *And if ye be Christs, ye are Abrahams seed, and heirs, according to the Promise.* What more proper to the truly sanctified? So the Apostle saith to all the Churches of *Coloss* in general. 5. *That they had put off the body of sin; being buryed with Christ in Baptism, wherein also they were raised with him, through the Faith of the operation of God*; *Col.* 2. 11, 12. 6. Yea in 1 *Cor.* 6. 11. He tells the Corinthians, *they were washed, sanctified, and justified in the name of the Lord Jesus*; so that Justification it self is ascribed to them. 1 *Col.* 2. 13. The Apostle tells them, God had *quickned them with Christ, having forgiven them all trespasses.* 7. Yea the like he saith of their salvation, 1 *Cor.* 15. 2. *Eph.* 2. 5, 6, 7, 8. yea he tells them verse 19: *Now therefore ye are no more strangers and forreiners, but fellow-Citizens with the Saints and of the houshold of God*; and lest any should think that *Saints* and *Citizens, and the houshold of God,* do here signifie but common Priviledges of the visible Church, he addes, *And are built upon the foundation of the Apostles and Prophets, Jesus Christ himself being the chief corner-Stone, in whom all the building fitly framed together, groweth to an holy Temple in the Lord*; *in whom you also are builded together for an habitation of God through the Spirit.* Where most planly the Church is manifested to be but one, and that one to have saving Priviledges, and consequently, those that have not these, to be but equivocally Christians.

Many more texts might be produced, where the most particular Priviledges of the Saints are given to whole Churches in common: which shews that the name is by Analogy or equivocally given from the sincere, to the rest, because we are to judge and denominate on probabilities.

Argu. 10. If the profession of Justifying Faith be requisite in Baptism, then the Faith so professed is requisite to the right receiving of it (and not only to be performed hereafter.) But such profession is requisite; therefore.

The major is as true, as that God requireth no man to lye and dissemble, and to profess that with his mouth which is not in his heart: nor doth he make lying the condition of his Covenant, (let them call it an outward Covenant, or what they will: if it be Gods Covenant, this can be none of the condition.) For it must first in order be a Dutie, before it be made Conditional. And no lye is a Dutie. Professing is a Dutie to them that have the thing they profess: but to others; immediately and in *sensu composito*, it is a hainous sin, and no duty: though it be their duty still to get Faith first, and then to profess it.

The minor is proved already, in the foregoing arguments; and more shall be anon. It is no less then justifying Faith that Christs Church hath ever to this day required the Baptized to profess before the application of the water. To believe

believe in God the Father, Son and Holy-Ghost, and profess Repentance for all sins, and to renounce the world, the flesh and Devil, &c. And when Mr. *Bl.* maketh profession enough to give Right to baptism, I would know whether he mean the profession of Justifying-Faith, or not. If yea, then Justifying Faith is prerequisite, or else the profession of it could not. If not, then the profession of true Christianity is not requisite; but of some part of it. For, as I have shewed, it is not the true Christian Faith, but some part of it only, if it be short of that Faith which is justifying. And let men say no more, that profession is it that entitles to Baptism, without the thing professed, when they take even profession it self of true Christianitie to be consequential, and not prerequisite.

Argu. 11. If Baptism be the solemnizing of the mystical marriage between Christ and the baptized, then true justifying Faith is of God required thereto: but the Antecedent is true; therefore.

Therefore is it said that we are baptized *into Christ*, and *into one body*. And the Church hath ever held the Antecedent to be true. The consequence is evident; in that no man but the sound believer, can truly take Christ as a Husband and Head; for so to do, is justifying Faith. It is Christ himself first in order, and then his benefits that are offered in the Sacraments. The main business of them is to exhibite Christ himself to be received by a marriage Covenanting. The signs are but means and instruments, as a twig and turfe and Key in giving possession; When the minister in Christs name saith, Take, Eat, &c. it is not only bread that he bids men take, but first and principally Christ by Faith. *Joachimus Vadnanus* (*Aphorism. de Eucharist. li.* 3. *pag.* 82.) much commendeth a saying of *Chrysostoms*, viz: *If thou hadst no body, then Christ would have delivered thee all these gifts nakedly* (or immediately): *but because thy Soul is conjoyned with a body, he hath delivered them in and with these sensible things.* It is one of the greatest errors that can be committed in the Sacraments, to overlook Christ himself who is offered, and to look only either to the signs or to his other gifts. We receive him first as our Saviour, our Soveraign, Redeemer, our Head, our Husband, our Captain and Guide. He therefore that comes to these ordinances, doth pretend thus to receive Christ: and doubtless to receive him thus sincerely, is true justifying saving Faith: and therefore it is saving Faith that is called for to the due Receiving of the Sacraments. And doubtless God means a sincere, and not a seeming, dissembled, nominal Faith, in his command.

Argu. 12. If there be no such Covenant mentioned in the Scripture, (specially to be sealed with baptism) wherein men engage themselves to perform hereafter their first act of true Repentance and justifying Faith, then Mr. *Blakes* Doctrine is unsound: but there is no such Covenant; therefore.

Men are oft in Scripture called to Repent and Believe; but nowhere (that I know of) to Covenant with God that they will hereafter begin to do it sincerely; much less is there such a Covenant sealed with Baptism. They that affirm such a thing, let them prove it, if they can.

Argu. 13. If, according to Mr. *Blakes* Doctrine no true sound Believer, or Penitent person, can regularly be baptized; then his Doctrine is unsound. But the Antecedent is true; therefore.

The consequence is proved before. The Antecedent is proved thus: According to his Doctrine, saving Faith, accepting Christ to Justification, is the great condition to which Baptism engageth, and is not prerequisite therein.

Therefore

Therefore he that already performeth that condition, is past such engageing to do it initially hereafter: and so hath no use for baptism as to that engagement, to the great condition: so that if such a person be baptized, it must be to other ends then the Ordinance is appointed for, and so not Regularly. The like may be said of Gods part? for to such a Believer God should Seal Remission past or present; whereas according to Mr. *Bl.* the Ordinance is instituted to seal Remission future.

Argu. 14. If the Doctrine opposed be true, then the Gospel preached before baptism, was not instituted, nor is to be used, as a means (at least an ordinary means) of saving conversion (*i. e.* of producing saving Faith and Repentance). But the consequent is false; therefore so is the Antecedent.

It would be tedious and needless to the Intelligent, to heap up Scripture proof of the minor, *viz.* that the Gospel preached before baptism, is appointed for an ordinary means of working true conversion. We see it was ordinarily done, else Preachers could not endeavor it, or hope or pray for it. The consequence is manifest, in that Mr. *Bl.* makes this true justifying Faith, and consequently true Repentance, to be not prerequisite to baptism, but to be engaged for as to the future performance. And therefore regularly it must be only the word after Baptism that must truly Convert, or not at all.

Argu. 15. If Mr. *Blakes* Doctrine be true, then regularly it must be supposed that all persons are in a state of damnation immediately on their baptism; and if they then dyed, should perish. But the consequent is false; therefore so is the Antecedent.

For the Consequence; if Mr. *Blake* mean, that it is any space of time after baptism that we engage to begin our justifying Faith in, then the consequence is undenyable: for till then, the person is unjustified. But if he mean that in baptism they must engage to believe to Justification in the same instant of time, then this is to make such Faith necessary in the instant of baptism; and this is but an evident vanity, to suppose a man not believing to justification, who yet can and must promise to do it in the same instant, or the next.

Argu. 16. If it be only true justifying Faith that gives men right *coram Deo* (by vertue of his Covenant) to the Sacrament of the Lords Supper, and so be prerequisite to that Sacrament, and not only to be promised for the future; then the same may be said of baptism. But the Antecedent is true; therefore.

The consequence is proved, 1. In that the Sacraments are both Seals of the same Covenant. 2. It is right to Church-priviledges in general that Mr. *Bl.* ascribes to his Dogmatical Faith, and therefore to one Sacrament as well as the other. For the Antecedent, I think our brethren that would so fain keep the Church and Ordinances pure, would hardly admit a man to the Lords Table, that they were sure did not take Christ for his Lord, or that would say, I believe all the Creed and Word of God, but I will not have Christ Reign over me at the present, but I promise that hereafter. I will see Doctor *Drake* against Mr. *Humfrey,* whether they would admit such. *Hierom* argues thus, from Baptism, to the Administration of the Lords Supper: therefore I may do it as to the receiving. *Quamobrem ovo te ut aut sacrificandi ei licentiam tribuas cujus baptisma probas, aut reprobes ejus baptisma, quem non existimas sacerdotem. Neque enim fieri potest, ut qui in baptismate sanctus est, sit apud altare peccator.* Hier. *Dialog. adv. Luciferian.*

Argu. 17.

Argu. 17. That Doctrine which feigneth an un-sealed Covenant for giving right to the Seal of the Covenant of Grace, is unsound: But such is Mr. *Blakes*; therefore.

No Scripture can be brought to prove such an outward Covenant of Gods: And it is against the common reason and custom of men, that a second Covenant should be drawn to convey right to the Seal of the first Covenant, seeing right to Covenant and Seal go together: and if there must be another Covenant to give right to that, then by the same reason there must be another to give right to that, and another to that, and so *in infinitum*.

To the Antecedent, it is apparent that Mr. *Bl.* distinguisheth *ex parte Dei*, between the outward and the inward Covenant. (It is probable that he thus distributes them from the blessings promised, whereof some are inward, and some outward: for though he explain not himself fully, yet I know no other sense that it will bear. It is evident that his outward Covenant hath no Seal. For it is a Covenant *de sigillis conferendis*: If therefore it have a Seal, it is either the same which is promised, or some other. Other I never heard of: they no where tell us what is the Seal of their outward Covenant. The same it cannot be: for the same thing cannot be the *materia foederis* or, the Legacy it self, or the benefit given, and the Seal too of that Covenant whereby it is given.

Argu. 18. That Doctrine which makes it the regular way in Baptism for all men to promise that which they can neither sincerely promise nor perform, is unsound: but such is Mr. *Blakes*; therefore.

The disabilitie which I here speak of, is not such as is in a Godly man, to do any good without Christ and the Spirit; as is in the second cause to act without the first: or in a partial cause, to act without its compartial: but such as is in an unregenerate man to do the work of the Regenerate; or in any broken instrument, or disabled agent, to do its own part of the work till it be altered, and made another thing, as it were. For the consequence, it is evident in that,
1. No man should ever perform Gods command concerning covenanting.
2. And no mans word were fit to be taken concerning the performance of his own Covenant. 1. Whether God may or do command some men, or all men, that which they have not abilitie to perform, is nothing to the point. For yet he gives some of them abilitie, and causeth them to perform it, when he makes it necessarie to salvation. But in this case God should enable no man (regularly) to that Baptismal Covenant which he commandeth, nor should any obey his command. For he commandeth them sincerely to take him for their God, and promise to Love, Believe, and Obey him hereafter. (For to dissemble, he commands none). But this no unrenewed Soul can do, or ever did to this day. They cannot resolve it; therefore they cannot sincerely promise it; and if justifying Faith must regularly begin after baptism (as being the great condition to which it engages, and not prerequisite) then it is only unregenerate men that are the regular subjects of baptism. 2. And its plain that he who cannot sincerely promise, (and therefore doth it dissemblingly, or with a half heart) nor is able to perform his promise, is not to be credited. God himself never enableth an unregenerate man, to believe and repent savingly, while he is such, *in sensu composito*: and therefore is it likely that it is ordinarily and regularly such dead men that must Covenant to Repent and Believe to justification? Renewing Grace must intercede, which is not in their hand: how then can they promise to do

the

the works of the truly Gracious. God may invite and command the dead to live, yea and to do the works of the living, because he gave them life, and gives them means for revival. But I know not where he calls such men to promise to do it: much less is the constant Baptismal Covenant such.

Argu. 19. If the Distribution of the Church into visible and invisible, be but of the subject by divers Adjuncts, and not of a *Genus* into its *Species*, then that part, or those members which are meerly visible, are indeed no part or members of the Church so distributed, (but are only equivocally called a Church, Christians, Church-Members, &c.) But the Antecedent is true; therefore.

The Antecedent is not only the common Doctrine of the Reformed Divines against the Papists, but is expressly affirmed by Mr. *Blake* in this his Book. The consequence is undeniable; in that Adjuncts are no part of the Essence, much less the Form, or the whole Essence; and therefore cannot denominate, (but equivocally) instead of the Essence. Note, that *visibile* is not the same with *visum*.

Argu. 20. If the man without the wedding Garment, had *coram Deo* Right to be there, then would not the Lord have challenged him therein with a *friend, how camest thou in hither, not having on a wedding Garment?* If you will help him that was speechless to an answer, and say for him, *Lord, he was compelled to come in at thy command*; I Reply, He that compelled him by invitation, did not only bid him *come*, but to *come*, not only to *come in*, but to *come in as a Guest should*, to honor and not disgrace the Feast. At lest it should have been known as implyed. It was no unrevealed thing.

Argu. 21. If Circumcision were the Seal of the Righteousness of Faith, even a Justifying Faith already in being; then so is Baptism; but the former is certain, *Rom.* 4. 11, 12. *He received the sign of Circumcision, a Seal of the Righteousness of the Faith, which he had yet being uncircumcised: that he might be the Father of all them that believe, though they be not circumcised, that Righteousness might be imputed to them also.* The last words confirm the consequence also.

Argu. 22. Many texts of Scripture shew that it was Justifying Faith that was by God required in the aged in baptism: which I will cite together, and not stand to fetch an argument from each alone. *Act.* 2. 38, 39. was before cited, verse 41. It was they that gladly received the word that were Baptized. *Act.* 8. 37. also, is before spoke to; *It must be believing with all the heart. Mar.* 16. 15, 16. is very plain; first Christ commands them to preach the Gospel: then he enacteth that on this preaching, *He that believeth and is baptized, shall be saved.* It is then a saving Faith. It is plain that Christ purposely putteth it before baptism, as its due place, even as that preaching to which Faith is here related Is put, before; and in that he gives us here the exact compendium of his new Law. And if it be not this saving Faith that goes before baptism, then Christ doth not so much as mention it. And to imagine that in this summe of his Covenant, he doth both leave wholly unmentioned that Faith which is the prerequisite condition of Baptism, and also put in its place another Faith, which is consequential, this is to suppose Christ to clogg the most essential parts, and clearest, compendiums of his Law, with such insuperable obscurities that it cannot be understood. And say the like by all other Scripture, and you will make it more dark then the Papists accuse it to be. *Act.* 16. 31, 32, 33. The Jaylor asks what he shall

shall do to be saved; *Paul* answers him, *Believe in the Lord Jesus Christ, and thou shalt be saved and thy house*; to which end, *they spake to him the word of the Lord, and to all that were in his house*; and so, *He was Baptized, believing in God with all his house.* The Faith that *Paul* here commends to him, was a saving Faith expresly: He that is said to believe upon that command and instruction, is supposed to believe with the same faith that was so required of him, *Act.* 10. 47, 48. The Gentiles there were not only true Believers, but had the Holy-Ghost before baptism, *Act.* 16. 15. The Lord opened *Lydias* heart (which seems to signifie a special operation of the Spirit) before she was baptized. *Act.* 18. 8. *Crispus and all his house believed on the Lord,* which signifieth more then an Historical Faith. So *Act.* 19. 4, 5. It was believing on Christ, and in his name, that was the Antecedent to their baptism. *Mat.* 28. 19. *Go, Disciple all Nations, baptizing them*; that Discipling which is here commanded, is in order to go before baptism: but it is making men sincere Disciples that is here commanded; therefore. It is presupposed, what ever Discipling it be, that it is not the Event, but the Endeavor that is here made their dutie. And if it be only common Discipleship, then the Apostles and other Preachers of the Gospel, are not commanded to endeavor to make men true sound Believers and Disciples, till they had first baptized them, which is untrue. Moreover the Baptismal Faith, must be a Faith in Christs blood; for the application of the water signifieth the application of Christs blood; and therefore their reception of the one, signifieth the other: But Faith in Christs blood, is Justifying Faith, *Rom.* 3. 25, 26. *The Righteousness of God which is by the Faith of Jesus Christ, is unto all and upon all them that believe*; *Rom.* 3. 22. It is therefore but equivocally called believing in Christ, as being but some part of that belief, which attaineth not this Righteousness. How many times over and over, do Christ and his Apostles promise pardon and salvation to all that believe in Christ, without distinction of believing? whence it seems evident, that it is but improperly and equivocally called *Believing in Christ*, which is not Justifying and saving. See *Joh.* 3. 15, 16, 18. and 11. 25, 26. and 7. 38. and 12. 46, 44. and 5. 24. and 6. 35, 40, 47. and 14. 12. 1 *Joh.* 5. 1, 5, 10. 1 *Pet.* 2. 6. *Rom.* 9. 33. and 4. 5. and 10. 11. *Act.* 13. 48. Moreover, how easie is it to bring many Texts that prove that it was true saving Faith it self that Christ and his Apostles preached to men, and endeavored to bring them to before baptism? Nay finde any one of them that ever did otherwise; whereas according to Mr, *Blakes* Doctrine, they should have perswaded them to a Dogmatical Faith only before baptism (I mean, to be before performed) and a justifying Faith after. But I will adde no more of this.

Argu. 23. The Church hath ever supposed baptized persons to be saved; unless they afterward did violate that Covenant. Therefore they supposed them to have the condition of salvation, Faith and Repentance.

Hence those high elogies of baptism in most of the Fathers, wherein they are now mis-interpreted by many, as if they ascribed it to the external ordinance, whereas they presuppose, as the blood and Covenant of Christ, so the right qualifications of the partie baptized; upon which supposition (which we are bound to entertain of all that make a probable profession) they did so predicate the glorious effects of Baptism, as well they might.

Argu. 24. Mr. *Blakes* Doctrine of Baptismal Faith, leaves us in utter obscuritie, so that no man according to it, can tell whom to Baptize. He hath not

D d (that

(that I can finde) given us any description of that Faith which entitles to baptism; and I verily think is not able to tell us what he would have himself to be taken for it. If it were a meer Dogmatical Faith, then those should be baptized that were utterly unwilling, or at least unwilling to take God for their God, or Christ for their Lord and Saviour, and the Holy-Ghost for their Sanctifier; and should openly profess, *I will not have this man reign over me, for I cannot yet spare the pleasure of my sin.* If Mr. *Bl.* mean that there is requisite somewhat of the will and consent, though not so much as to justifie; why did he not tell us what acts of the Will they be that are necessary? Is it only a consent to have God called their God, and themselves named his people? I will not be so uncharitable as to think that is his meaning; Is it only a consent to be baptized, and to hear the Word, and receive the Sacraments? then might it stand with the foresaid disclaiming of the Government of God and the Redeemer, and so of obedience. I think by that time Mr. *Bl.* hath but adventured to give us an exact definition or description of that Faith which he makes prerequisite and sufficient to baptism (which I hereby intreat him to do) he will have set us up so fair a mark to shoot at, that with a very little skill it may be smitten to the dust.

Argu. 25. 1 *Joh.* 2. 19. *They went out from us, but they were not of us: for if they had been of us, they would no doubt have continued with us: but they went out, that it might be made manifest that they were not all of us.* They were not therefore truly Christians, Disciples, Church-Members, but equivocally.

Argu. 26. I will end as I begun, with humane testimony. 1. Our Divines against the Papists, do generally plead that hypocrites are not true members of the universal Church, but as a woodden leg is to the body. I am loth to turn over books and transcribe without need, but I shall soon do it, if it be denied. 2. Our Divines against the Arminians, do suppose the first act of believing to be the first time that God is as it were engaged to man in the Covenant of Grace; and that it is dangerous to make God to be in actual Covenant with men, in the state of nature, though the conditional covenant may be made to them, and though he have revealed his decree for the sanctifying his elect: but he is supposed to dispence his mercies to the unregenerate freely, as *Dominus absolutus*, or as *Rector supra leges*, and not by giving them a Legal or Covenant-right. And indeed, in my opinion, the Transition is very easie from Mr. *Blakes* opinion to Arminianism, if not unavoidable, save by a retreat, or by not seeing the connexion of the Consequents to the Antecedent. For grant once that common Faith doth *coram Deo* give right to baptism, and it is very easie to prove that it gives right to the end of baptism, God having not instituted it to be an emptie sign to those that have true Right to it. And it will be no hard matter to prove that it is some special Grace that is the end of Baptism, at left Remission of sin. And so upon the good use of common Grace, God should be in Covenant obliged to give them special Grace: which is taken for Pelagianism.

---

§. 53.

WHen I had Replyed thus far to Mr. *Blake*, I was much moved in my minde to have Replyed to his answer to Mr. *Firmin* on the like subject: and also to to have then proved that the children have no Right to baptifm, except the immediate Parent be a believer, for the fake of any of his Anceftors : and that the children of Apoftates and wilfull obftinate wicked livers, fhould not be baptized, (as theirs): and to have anfwered what Mr. *Bl.* hath faid to the contrary : and this meerly in love to the Truth, left the reputation of man fhould cloud it : and in love to the Church and the luftre of the Chriftian name, left this fearful gap fhould let in that pollution that may make Chriftianitie feem no better then the other Religions of the world. For I fear this loofe Doctrine of Baptifm will do more to the pollution of the Church, then others loofe Doctrine of the Lords Supper ; or as much. But I am very loth to go any further in Controverfie, then I fhall be neceffitated : And if Mr. *Firmin* be living, I conjecture by his writings, that he is able eafily to vindicate his own words : Not that I have low thoughts of the abilities and worth of my dear and Reverend friend Mr. *Blake*, but that I take his anfwers on thofe fubjects to be very dilute, *fi pace tanti viri ita dicam* : fo great a difadvantage is an ill caufe to the moft learned man. Mr. *Firmin* I know not any further then by his Book againft Separation. But in that Book I fee fo much Candor, Ingenuitie, Moderation, Love to Peace, and fome convenient terms for Peace difcovered, that I am heartily forrie that there are no more to fecond him, and that his incitements to accommodation are no more laid to heart. But the Peace-makers fhall be bleffed in the Kingdom of Peace, how little foever they may fucceed in this tumultuous world. For as where envy and ftrife is (contentious zeal) there is confufion and every evil work ; fo the fruit of Righteoufnefs is fown in Peace of them that make Peace.

---

§ 54.

I Had thought alfo at the firft view, that it would have been neceffary to have confuted Mr. *Blakes* 31. Chapt. when I found this Title : *A man in covenant with God, and received into the Univerfal Church Vifible, needs no more to give him accefs to, and intereft in particular Vifible Churches.* But I know not whether he mean the accefs and intereft of a ftranger in paffage or a Traufient Member, or of a fixed Member. If of the latter, I fhould have proved moreover that there is Neceffary, both his Cohabitation, and his Confent to be a Member of that Church ; and his confent to fubmit to the particular Paftors of that Church as his Teachers and Spiritual Guides in the Lord. But I finde in the following pages, Mr. *Blake* doth acknowledge all this himfelf.

I fhall therefore pafs on to fome other fubject ; only remembering Mr. *Bl.* that as it is not Number of Arguments but Weight that will carrie the Caufe, fo it is not Number that I truft to : and therefore if any one of thofe 26 Arguments foregoing be good, though 25 be bad, I muft needs think the Caufe bad which I argue againft.

§. 55.

Whether Faith and Repentance be Gods Works.

Mr Bl. CHap. 15. *So Mr.* Baxters *Questionist* qu. How do you make Faith and Repentance to be Conditions of the Covenant on our part, seeing the bestowing of them is part of the condition on Gods part? Can they be our Conditions and Gods too? *Answer,* &c. *And I shall not stand to distinguish of an Absolute and Conditional Covenant, and so making the whole in the Absolute Covenant to be Gods, and in the Conditional this part to be ours* (which I know not whether exactly understood, the Scripture will bear) *but in plain terms deny that they are Gods conditions, and affirm them to be ours. I know what God speaks in his Word, concerning these works; that He will write his Law in our hearts, and put it into our inward parts; that he will take away the heart of stone, and give an heart of flesh: which implyes this work of which we speak. I know likewise what in particular is affirmed of Christ, that he is the Author and Finisher of our Faith,* &c. *Yet all this rises not up higher to make them formally Gods acts, and not ours. Whose acts they be, his Conditions they are; this is evident. But they are our acts; we Believe and Repent; it is not God that Believes, it is not God that Repents,* &c. *Faith and Repentance are mans works, not Gods works; which man in Covenant does; respective to salvation in the Covenant tendered. But the Apostle (some may say) in the next words tells us, That it is God that works the Will and the Deed. There he seems to take them from us, and ascribes the formality of them to God. In this Cooperation of Gods, whether they be formally our works, or Gods, let* Isaiah *determine,* Isa. 26. 12. *Thou hast wrought all our works in us. When God hath wrought it, the work is ours; we have the reward,* &c.

§. 55

R: B: MR *Blakes* businefs here, is to confute the anfwer that I gave to that objection. A brief Reply may eafily fatisfie this confutation. 1. I did explain in what fenfe thefe were called *Covenants,* fhewing that that which is called the Abfolute Covenant, is in fome refpect no part of Gods Legiflative Will, and fo doth not *jus conferre,* but only part of his Decretive Will revealed: but that in other refpects it belongs to the Legiflative Will, and may be called an abfolute promife. And fo the word *Conditions,* applyed to God, is taken for *the thing promifed,* improperly called a condition; but applyed to us, it is ftrictly taken: nor had I ufed the term *Condition* as to God, but as it was neceffary to fatisfie the Objector, who fo called it, intimating the improprietie of it. Alfo I did plainly fhew that the thing called Gods Condition, was not precifely the fame with that called ours: Ours was Believing and Repenting; Gods is the *beftowing of thefe,* as the Queftion expreffed; or *the giving us new and foft hearts, that we may do it our felves, and do it readily and willingly,* &c. as I expreffed, *pag.* 46. becaufe I was not willing to meddle (affirmatively or negatively) with the queftion of Gods immediate Phyfical Efficiencie of our own act; yet I doubt not but God doth truly, powerfully and effectually (to the removing or overcoming all refiftance) move the Soul to the act it felf; and

therefore

therefore it may truly be said, that not only Gods own Action, but also our action of Believing, is the thing promised, (called his Condition by the Querist; and though improperly, yet in a language very common in Mr. *Blakes* Treatise). This much being premised, I Reply more particularly. 1. I will yet say that God hath such an absolute Promise, as well as a Conditional, till you give me better Reasons of your denyal, or your Questioning whether Scripture will bear it. And I shall yet say, that the giving of our Faith and Repentance, is the matter of that absolute promise. For your Argument to the contrarie, hath little in it, to compell me to a change. Your Maior is, *Whose acts they are, his conditions they are*; instead of proof; you say, *This is evident*. I Reply, 1. Negatively, it had been evident *de Actione qua talis*, that it is no ones Condition but his that performs it; as the condition is said to be his that performeth, and not his that imposeth it. But Affirmatively the proposition holds not universally. Nor Negatively, speaking *de Actione qua est quid donandum*. To your Minor, I could better answer if I could have found it. I expected it should have been this, *But our Faith and Repentance are not Gods acts*. But I know not whether I may be so bold as say, you will own that. Before you say, *This rises not to make them formally Gods acts, and not ours:* where 1. you cautelously speak the two Propositions copulatively; and 2. you put in the word *formally*, which may do much to help you out. For the former, it is enough according to your own Rule to prove them Gods Conditions and ours, if they be Gods Actions and ours: for you say, *whose actions they are, his Conditions they are; that is evident*. It is not therefore necessary that I prove them *Gods and not ours*. 2. It is hard to know whether your *formally* respect a natural, or moral form. If the former action is the form it self, it is harder to finde out its matter. Accidents have not properly matter and form; but the subject is called its matter; but Action hath scarce so proper a subject as other Accidents have, seeing it is rather *Agentis*, then *in agente inhæsivè*: Of transients, its beyond doubt; and I think so of Immanents, unles we may with *Scotus*, take them for Qualities; If you speak of Moral formality, were it sinful Action, I should deny God to be the Author; but of Faith and Repentance I dare not do so; I think God is the Author of them formally as well as materially. But in your following words you say, *But they are our acts, &c.* God believes not, *&c.* Reply; 1. To believe is our act; but to give us Faith, or to move us effectually to Believe, as a superior Cause, this is not our work, but Gods. 2. Let it be so; to believe is our work, and our condition; It follows not, that it is not Gods. 3. There are sufficient reasons why God is not said to Believe, though he cause us to believe If you go on the Predeterminants grounds, I suppose you know their reasons, who take notice of the Arminians making this objection. If you enquire of the Jesuits and Arminians, that go the way of determined concourse, or of partial Causality, they think they have yet more to say, of which I suppose you not ignorant. *Durandus* his followers think they have most of all to say, both why God should be said to believe, and why he is not the Author of our sin, in that they suppose that he causeth not the act immediately. And yet all these acknowledge God to be the cause of our acts.

But you adventure a step further, and say, *Faith and Repentance are mans works, not Gods works*. Reply; 1. What mean you then to yield afterward that *God worketh all our works in us*. (those which he worketh are sure his works) And that, *It is God that worketh in us the Will and the Deed*.

2. I never met with any orthodox Divine, but would yield that Faith is a work of Gods Spirit. And the Spirits work is doubtless Gods work.

3. If you go the common way of the Predeterminants, you must acknowldge that God is the Physical, Efficient, Predetermining, Principal, Immediate cause of every act of every creature: and therefore doubtless of our Faith; and that both *Immediatione Virtutis & Suppositi*, so that it is more properly his act then ours. For my part, I confess my self: of Bishop *Davenants* minde who saith, (against *Hoard* p. 116) *As for the predetermination of mens wills, it is a Controversie between the Dominicans and Jesuites, with whose Metaphysical speculations our Protestant Divines love not to torture their brains*; Or, at lest they should not. I take it to be a point beyond the knowledge of any man, which way Gods works on the Will in these respects. Though if I must encline to any one way, it would be rather to *Durandus* (for stronger reasons then I finde in *Ludov. à Dola*, who yet hath more then I have seen well answered), and lest of all to the Predeterminants, for all the numerous arguments of the Dominicans, and the seeming strength that Dr. *Twisse*, *Heereboord*, *Rutherford*, and others of our own, do adde to their cause. But yet I am far from denying our Faith and Repentance to be Gods Works; for I doubt not but he causeth them *ut causa Universalis*, by his general Providence, as they are natural Actions; and also by his special effectual Grace, *contra omnem Resistentiam*, infallibly causeth them as they are the special gifts of the Spirit. So that I marvail that you should say they are not Gods Works.

In the conclusion you adde, *Our dexteritie in holy duties is from the frame into which Grace puts us: so still the work is ours, though power for action is vouchsafed of God.* Reply; Both *Velle & Perficere* is the gift of God, and not only *Posse Velle & perficere*. Why should I trouble the Reader to say any more to that point, when Dr. *Twisse* and others against the Remonstrants have said so much; and *Austin* so much before them all? And yet I never read a Remonstrant that would say that the work is so ours, as that it is only the power that is vouchsafed us by God. I conclude therefore that you have not confuted my answer; 1. In that you have not disproved the absolute Promise of the first special Grace. 2. You have not disproved God to be the Author of our Faith, so as that it is his work. 3. If you had, yet Believing which is our work, is not the same thing with giving Faith, or moving us to believe, which I say is Gods Work.

---

§. 56.

Of the Life Promised, and Death threatned to Adam in the first Law.

Mr. Bl. *I Finde no material difference in the Conditions on Gods part in these Covenants; Life is promised in both in Case of Covenant-keeping: and Death is threatned in both in case of Covenant-breaking. Some indeed have endeavored to finde a great difference in the Life Promised in the Covenant of Works, and the Life that is promised in the Covenant of Grace; as also in the Death that is threatned in the one and in the other; and thereupon move many, and indeed inextricable difficulties, What Life man should have enjoyed in case Adam had not fallen? and what Death man should have dyed, in case Christ had not been promised? From which two, endlesly more by way of Consectary may be drawn, by those that want neither wit nor leisure to debate them. In which the best way of satisfaction, and avoi-*

dance

dance of such puzzeling mazes, is to enquire what Scripture means by Life, which is the good in the Covenant promised, and what by Death, which is the evil threatned. Now for the first, Life contains all whatsoever conduces to true Happiness, to make man blessed in Soul and body. All good that Christ purchases and Heaven enjoyes, is comprised under it in Gospel expressions, &c. On the contrary, under death is comprised all that is injurious to man or mankinde, that tends to his misery in Soul and body; The damnation of Hell, being called death (the uttermost of evils being the separation of Soul and body from God, Joh. 8. 51. 1 Joh. 3. 14.) Sin which leads to it, and is the cause of it, is called death in like manner, Eph. 2. 1. And the separation of Soul from the body being called Death, sickness, plagues, are so called in like manner, Exod. 10. 17. Now happiness being promised to man in Covenant, only indefinitely, under that notion of Life, without limit to this or that way of happiness, in this or that place; God is still at liberty, so that he make man happy, where or however to continue happiness to him, and is not tyed up in his engagement either for earth or heaven. And therefore, though learned Camero in his Tract. de triplici foedere. Thes. 9. make this difference between the Covenant of works and the Covenant of Grace; In the Covenant of Works (which he calls nature) Life was promised, and a most blessed Life, but an animal life in Paradise; in the Covenant of Grace, a life in Heaven and Spiritual. And Mr. Baxter in his Aphor. of Justification, p. 5. saith, That this Life promised was only the continuance of that state that Adam was then in, in Paradise, is the opinion of most Divines; Yet with submission to better Judgements, I see not grounds for it: seeing Scripture no way determines the way and kinde, &c. And indeed there are strong probabilities, Heaven being set out by the name of Paradise, in Christs speech to the theif on the Cross, and in Pauls vision, &c.

---

§. 96.

R. B. 1. Your opinion in this point is moderate, and (I think) sound. I have nothing therefore to say to you, but about our different expressions, and therefore excuse me if I be short; for I love not that work. I think your judgement and mine are the same. 2. Only remember, that it is Mr. Blake also that hath these words, pag. 74. *The Conditions on mans part in the Covenant of Works, were for mans preservation in statu quo; in that condition in which he was created; to hold him in Communion with God, which was his happiness; he expected not to be bettered by his obedience, either respective to happiness (no more is promised then in present he had) nor yet in his Qualifications respective to his conformitie to God in Righteousness and true holiness. What improvement he might have made of the Habit infused, by the exercise of obedience, I shall not determine; but no change in Qualifications was looked after or given in Promise*; so far Mr. Blake.

If the Reader cannot reconcile Mr. Blake and me, let him reconcile Mr. Blake with himself, and the work is done.

3. But I confess that upon more serious consideration of several passages in the New Testament, naming and describing the work of Redemption, I am ready to think it far more probable that Adam was not created *in Patria*, but *in Via*; not in the highest perfection which he should expect, but in the way to it. But whether God would have given it him in the same place that he was in, or in some

some other (called Heaven) upon a remove, I take as Mr. Bl. doth; to be unrevealed, and undetermined in the Promise. So that I could finde in my heart to fall a confuting the same opinion in Mr. Blake, expressed in these last words, which he confuteth in me; but that his former save me the labor.

4. I confess also that I spoke rashly in saying that *it was the opinion of most Divines*; seeing it is so hard a matter to know, which way most go in the point. I also confess that the judgement of *Camero*, Mr. *Ball*, Mr. *Gataker*, &c. swayed much with me; but the silence of the text in *Gen.* much more: but I had not so well weighed several Texts in the New Testament, as I ought, which describing Redemption, give some more light into the point. The same I say concerning the qualitie of the Death threatned.

5. I agree to Mr. *Blakes* first conclusion, that the thing is indeterminate; or at least, hard for us to know; but I cannot reconcile his premises with that conclusion; much less with this his latter speech p. 74. For if (as he saies) the Life promised was *all whatsoever conduces to true happiness, to make men blessed in soul and body*; (by *conducing to*, I suppose he meant *constituting of*) then either the Cælestial Degree of Grace and Glory *conduces not to* that happiness (and then not to ours, who have no greater natural capacitie); or else I see not how it can be said that this greater blessedness was not Promised. Doubtless *Adam* had not in present possession so great a measure of holiness, so confirmed a state of Holiness or Glory, nor so great and full a fruition of God, as Christ hath given us a sure hope of in the Gospel. And therefore, though he say, God is at liberty for the *place* and *way*, yet that is nothing to the *kinde* and *measure*.

6. Observe that the words of mine, which Mr. Bl. opposeth, are but *that Divines are of that judgement*.

---

§. 57.

Mr. Bl. *And what I have said of the Life promised, I say of Death threatned, &c. My Learned friend Mr. Baxter, enquiring into this Death, that was here threatened, saith, that the same Damnation that followed the breach of the second Covenant, it could not be. Aph. p. 15. When I suppose, it rather should be said, that in substance and kinde it can be no other. Infidels that were never under any other Covenant, &c.*

---

§. 57.

R. B. 1. What also I have answered to the former, may suffice to this for the main. 2. One would think that you intended directly to contradict me: but whether you do so indeed, I cannot well tell. I know not what you mean by *substance and kinde*, Pain and Loss have no substance, but a subject: I never doubted but that it is the Loss of the same God, and Blessedness (formally considered) but I am yet very uncertain whether the Blessedness promised by Christ, be not far greater in Degree, then that to *Adam*, and consequently whether the *Pœna Damni* threatned in the Gospel be not far greater. Also I know as to the mediate Blessings, Relative, they are not the same: To be deprived by Unbelief, of Remission, Reconciliation, Adoption, the everlasting praising of

him

him, that Redeemed us by his blood, &c. these are true punishments on unbelievers, that reject the mercies offered to them: but these were none of *Adams* punishments. That was a Negation only to him, that is a Privation to them.

I profess also that I ever took the pain of Sense to be of the same nature, which is due to *Adams* Soul, and which is due to unbelievers. Only I then did and still do doubt, whether any Scripture speak of the everlasting Torments of *Adams* body; or whether it were not only his Soul that should eternally suffer, his body being turned to dust and so suffering the penaltie of loss: Nay, whether the New Testament do not make Resurrection the proper fruit of Christs death and Resurrection? But of this I am not fully resolved my self, much less will I contend for it.

But I must needs say, that I took not a gradual difference in punishments to be inconsiderable. Nay I know that moral specifications are grounded in natural gradual differences. And Rewards and Punishments being moral things formally, they may and oft must be said to differ *specie*, and not to be the same, when naturally they differ but in degree. Yea, whether in naturals themselves, we may not sometimes finde a specification in meer degrees, is not so clear as rashly to be denyed. There is but a gradual difference between the smallest prick with a pin, and to be thrust throow with daggers in 20 places; yet I will not say that it is the same punishment.

§. 58.

Mr. Bl. NEither can I assent to that speech, To say that *Adam* should have gon quick to Hell, if Christ had not been promised, or sin pardoned, is to contradict the Scriptures that make death temporal the wages of Sin. *It were I confess to presume above Scripture, but I cannot see it a contradiction of Scripture. A burning Feaver, Consumption, Leprosie, Pestilence, &c. are in Scripture made the wages of sin. Yet many go to hell through those diseases, &c.*

§. 58.

R. B. I Willingly leave every man to his own judgement in this: But I think it most probable, that the separation of Soul and body was particularly intended in the threatning, *Thou shalt dye the death*. Reas. 1. Because this is it that is *in prima significatione* called Death, and the miseries of Life, but Tropically, much more this or that particular miserie: which answers your objection about sicknesses. 2. This is it that Christ was necessarily to suffer for us: and if it had not been necessary for man to dye thus, by the Commination of that Law, then it would not thence have been necessary for Christ to dye this Death. For it was not the following sentence (which you call *Leges post latas*) which Christ came to satisfie or bear, but the curse of the Law. *Gal.* 3. 13. *he being made a curse for us. Phil.* 2. 8. *Col.* 1. 22. *Heb.* 9. 15. by means of death he was to Redeem the transgressors of the first Law; without Blood there is no Remission. The death of the creatures in sacrificings signified the necessity of this

E e Death

Death of Christ. I have met with none but Mr. *John Goodwin* that faith, Chrifts readynefs or willingnefs to have dyed, might have ferved the turn, though the Jews had not put him to death. *Col.* 1. 20. 14. *Eph.* 1. 7. *Rom.* 3. 25. Its true, the Apoftle fpeaking of the neceffitie of Blood, in *Heb.* hath reference to the Conftitutions of *Mofes* Law : but then it muft be confeffed that that Law did in its Curfe much explicate the former, and direct us to fee what was threatned, and what muft by the Meffiah be fuffered for us. *Heb.* 2. 14. Chrift was to deftroy by death, him that had the power of death, that is the Devil : but it feems, that the Law gave him his power, at the Will and Sentence of the Iudge, for execution. 1 *Cor.* 15. 26. 54. Death is the laft enemy to be overcome. *O Death, where is thy fling? O Grave, where is thy victory?* This is no doubt, the death now in queftion ; It is the evils befallen mankinde in execution of the violated Law, that are called enemies. Though we dye, it feems, there was a neceffitie of Chrifts dying to loofe the bonds of our Death, and procure us a Refurrection. *Rom.* 5. 17. *As by one mans offence death reigned by one, &c.* That one man muft dye for the people, *Caiaphas* prophefied, *Joh.* 18. 14.

3. The fentence ufeth to contain what is threatned in the Law, and though part may be remitted, yet the other part is the fame threatned. But Gods Sentence on *Adam*, contained the penaltie of a temporal Death. Though he mentioned not the Eternal, becaufe he would provide a remedy, yet the temporal, as one part meant in the threatning he laid on man himfelf : *Duft thou art, and to duft fhalt thou return* ; This is not as you imagine, *Lex poft lata* ; but *fententia Judicis Legis violatæ comminationem exequentis*. When it is faid, 1 *Cor.* 15. 22. *In Adam all dye* ; it is, in *Adams* finning all became guilty of it, and in *Adam* then fentenced, all were adjudged to it. Which is intimated alfo *Rom.* 5. 12. *Sin entered into the world, and death by fin, and fo death paffed on all men, for that all have finned.*

So that the fentence expreffing this Death particularly, and Chrift bearing it neceffarily, and (adde moreover) all mankinde, for the generality, bearing it certainly, and alfo *Death* fignifying primarily the feparation of Soul and Body, it feems to me moft probable, that this Death was in fpecial meant in the threatning.

But you fay, *He takes the fame way where his Juftice hath fatisfaction ; thofe that are priviledged from death as the wages of fin, thus Dye.* Reply. I do not believe you that any are Priviledged from death as the wages of fin, who dye. This is the part of, the penalty which the fentence paffed on the offendor himfelf, for all the promifed fatisfaction by a Redeemer : Nor did the Redeemer fatisfie to that end, to prevent our death, or to caufe that it fhould not be the wages of fin, but to deliver us from under the power of it. Where you fay, that this way of God *with unbelievers is voluntary, not neceffitated* : I Reply ; So, it may be, neverthelefs, becaufe it was meant in the threatning. It is dangerous to imagine that God is ever the lefs free, or more neceffitated, fo as that his actions fhould be lefs voluntary, becaufe of his determinations. He doth as voluntarily do what he hath predetermined to do, and foretold he will do, as if he had done neither. God changeth not, and therefore he is as voluntary in the execution, as he was in the determination.

§. 59.

§. 59.

Of the Law as made to Christ.

Mr. Bl. CHap. 6. p. 25. *And though Mr. Baxter doubts whether it be any part of Gods Legiflative Will, as it referrs to Chrift, but only as it belongs to us as a Prophefie what God would do in the advancing of Chrift and his Kingdom, and fo of us* ; Append. p. 39. *Yet me thinks it is plain, feeing Chrift acknowledges a command from his Father, in laying down his life,* Joh. 10. 18. *and the Apoftle fpeaking of the work, faith,* He was obedient in it, &c.

§. 59.

R. B. ONe that had not read what I write, would think by your Anfwer, that I had made a doubt whether there be any Law made to Chrift at all or not? Whereas I fpake only of that called the Covenant between the Father and the Son made from Eternity : or the promifes expreffed by the Prophets as to Chrift in his meer Divine nature, not yet incarnate : For I conceive that Chrift before the incarnation, may not be faid to be a fubject.; and that God is not properly faid to command himfelf, or covenant with himfelf, or make promifes by Prophets to himfelf. But I deny not but that Chrift as man was under a Law, yea and a Law peculiar to himfelf, whereto no other creature is fubject ; even the Law of Mediation, which deferves in the body of Theologie a peculiar place, and the handling of it, as diftinct from all the Laws made with us men, is of fpecial ufe, and if well done, would do much to remove the ftumbling blocks which the Antinomians fall upon.

§. 60.

Whether the Sacraments feal the conditional Promife abfolutely ? or the conclufion conditionally, when only one of the Premifes is of Divine Revelation ? And whether this conclufion be de fide, *I am* Juftified *and fhall be faved.*

Mr. Bl. p. 58. *But that which I may not pafs, is fomewhat of concernment both to my felf and the prefent caufe in hand,* &c.

§. 60.

R. B. I Need not tranfcribe thefe words, being of another, and not fpoke to me. But I will pafs my conjecture to his queftions. 1. I conjecture that the Querift by *Evading*, meant *Owning and Juftifying the fact*, and fo evading the blame. 2. To the fecond I conjecture the Querift had been lately converfant versant in Mr. *Blakes* book, and so it was in his memorie: and whether he knew what those whom you mention do hold I cannot tell. 3. To the third; If by *Sacramental sealing*, you mean *Conditional sealing*, I conjecture his conceit might be this, that as the Promise may be conditionally tendred to Infidels, Murderers, or any other, so might the Seal, if it were but Conditional as the Promise. As we may say to the worst; *If thou wilt believe, thou shalt be saved*; so might we conditionally seal salvation to him. But I take this to be a great mistake.

---

§. 61.

Mr. Bl. p. 40. MR Baxter (*who is put to it, to stoop too low in the answer of such trifles*) *in his answer to this now in hand, hath taken much pains to finde out the way of the Sacraments sealing; and in the result, he and I shall not be found much to differ; yet seeing providence made me the occasion of starting the question, I shall take leave to take some view of what is said.* Mr. Baxter *saith, It is in vain to enquire, whether the Sacraments do seal Absolutely or Conditionally, till you first know what is that they do seal; and in order to the finding this out, he layes down the way that a Christian doth gather the assurance of his Justification and Salvation; which is thus,* He that believeth is Justified, and shall be saved.: but I believe, therefore I am Justified and shall be saved; *I confess if I had been put upon a discovery of that which is sealed in the Sacraments, this Syllogism (I think) would scarce have come into my thoughts, seeing the Seal is Gods (as* Mr. Baxter *observes*) *I should have rather looked for one from him, then to have supposed a believer to have been upon the frame of one.*

---

§. 61.

R. B. THis dispute is so confused, and so much about words that I would not have meddled with it, (let men have made what use of yours they pleased) but only for some matters of greater moment that fall in upon the by, in your handling it. I think your meaning and mine is the same. 1. I not only said, (as you express) that the Seal is Gods, but gave my Reasons to prove a mutual Sealing as well as a mutual Covenanting. 2. What reason have you why I might not illustrate the matter by this Syllogism, as well as another. 3. If you will have a Syllogism of Gods making, why did you not tell us when or where you found it? and let us see as well as you, whence you had it, that we may know God made it. God doth not *netters Syllogismos* for himself, nor *actu immanente*: if he do it, it is only for us *per actum transeuntem*: and then it may be found in his word. But more of that anon. 4. I should think (though for illustration I judged it not unuseful) that it is of no necessitie for you or me to talk of any Syllogism at all, in the enquiry after the sealed proposition. If it be but one proposition, we may express it alone: If more, we may distinctly express them; rather then that shall breed any difference, I care not whether my Syllogism be mentioned any more: Let us see what yours is.

§. 62.

§. 62.

Mr. Bl. ANd such a one I should have looked to have gathered up from the Institution, and thus (I conceive) framed; He to whom I give Christ, to him I give Justification and Salvation: But here I give thee Christ; therefore to thee I give Justification and Salvation.

§. 63.

R. B. 1. WHat mean you by *gathering it* ? Do you mean that you will read it there ready formed ? If so, shew us the Chapter and Verse ? But that must not be expected; for you say anon, that it is something not written that is sealed. Or do you mean that in the Institution, God gives you the materials, and you form it your selves ?. If so, why blamed you mine, which is of mans forming, but yet as you suppose, the materials so far of Gods, that the conclusion is *de fide*. To give you the materials of a Syllogism, is not to give you a Syllogism; for the form *denominates*. I must therefore suppose a Believer yet to be upon the frame of one (as you speak). For I take you to be a Believer; and I finde you here at it very seriously. 2. I confess, (though I have no minde to quarrel with your Syllogism) that I am never the better for the substitution of this in the room of the humane one. I know not the meaning of the first word, (but I will not stand on that, as being I know but a verbal slip) I do not apprehend what use there can be for this Syllogism in this business. 1. It is supposed that every Christian knows that Christ and Remission are given together; and when they know it, what use for syllogizing towards the explication of the use of that Seal ? 2. Nay doth not your arguing intimate that the believer is more assured that Christ is given to him, then that pardon is given him ? Or else if the former were not *quid notius*, how could it be a fit *medium* ? you suppose his doubt to be of pardon and salvation, and the former brought to prove that, whereas I think, few doubt of one, but they doubt of the other : and I think the Sacrament sealeth the gift of Christ, as well as of pardon, as you confess. I see not but you might have laid down as conveniently in this one proposition, all that you say is sealed, *I give thee Christ and Justification and Salvation*. But this is of small moment.

§. 64.

Mr. Bl. THe major here is not sealed; for the Sacraments seal to the truth of no general Propositions, but they seal with application to particular persons to whom the Elements are dispensed, as Protestant Writers have defended against Papists, and put into the definition of a Sacrament, it seals then that which supplies the place of the minor in this tender, which is Gods gift of Christ. In the Sacrament Christ saith, *This is my body*; he saith *this is my blood*; and this is said to all that communicate. Now whether this gift of the body and blood of Christ be Absolutely or Conditionally sealed, will be easily resolved. The outward Elements are given on this

condition

condition that *we receive them, that we eate and drink them*. We have not Christ Sacramentally, till we have taken and eaten and drunk the Elements. We have not Christ in the Sacrament before our Soul's hold faith that which answers to this eating and drinking. That which all do not partake of that receive the Sacrament, is not Absolutely but Conditionally sealed in the Sacrament. None can misse of that which God absolutely grants and absolutely sealeth. - But all do not partake of Christ in the Sacrament; therefore he is not Absolutely but Conditionally sealed in the Sacrament.

§. 64.

R. B. 1. Confusion maketh Controversies endlesse, and gives advantage to mistakes to prevail with the weak Reader. I shall first tell you what I mean by *sealing*, before we further dispute what is sealed, and how. Some sober men, no way inclined to Anabaptism, do think that we ought not to call the Sacraments *Seals*, as being a thing not to be proved from the word; (for all Rom. 4.) But I am not of their minde. Yet I think it is a Metaphore; and to make it the subject of tedious disputations, and lay too great stresse upon a Metaphorical notion, is the way not to edifie, but to lose our selves. I am not so well skilled in Law as to be very confident, or to pretend to any great exactnesse in these matters; but I conceive that in general, a Seal is an Appropriative sign, when it is set upon things, as Goods, Cattels, &c. it signifies them to be ours: when they are applyed to Instruments in writing, they have 1. the common end of a Seal. 2. a special end. 1. The common end is to signifie by a special sign our owning of that writing or Instrument to which it is annexed. 2. The special end is according to the nature and use of the Instruments *viz*. 1. Some Instruments directed to a Communitie, or indefinitly to any whom it may concern. 2. Some to particular persons, or some few Individuals. Both of them are, 1. either *Narratives de re*. 2. Or obligatory Constitutions or acknowledgments *de Debito*. The former are either 1. Doctrinal, and so a man may give it under his hand and seal that he owns such or such a Doctrine, or confession of Faith, or form prescribed by him as Teacher to his Schollers or Hearers, &c. 2. Or Historical; and so a man may give it under his hand and Seal, that such a person is thus or thus qualified; or did this or that act, or suffered losses, pain, &c. 2. The Constitutions *de Debito*, are 1. *De Debito officii*, the Constitution of Dutie. 1. By equals upon voluntary obligation by contract (which concerneth not our businesse). 2. By Superiors to their Subjects or Inferiors, which is either a Law to any or to some Communitie: Or else a Precept to some particulars. And so Soveraigns may give out Laws, aud Proclamations under their hand and Seal; and Justices and Inferior Magistrates may seal their Precepts and Warrants, and Orders, &c. 2. Or they are *de Debito Beneficii*; Constituted 1. by a Legislator or Rector as such. 2. by a Proprietary or Owner or Lord, as such. 1. The former is either Absolute, as the Collation of some honors may be, and some acts of pardon, and the Divisions of Inheritances, as among the Israelites at their first possessing *Canaan*: Or they are Conditional; And the Condition is either pure Acceptance (which is so naturally requisite, that it is usually supposed, and not expressed, and such Collations go commonly under the name of Absolute and Pure Donations, though indeed they are not). Or else some requisite service or moral action, which may properly make the Benefit to be *Præmium*, *a* Reward. All these being sealed, the Seal doth oblige the Benefactor, or Donor, because the Instrument is obligatory, if it be for future conveyance. If a present Collation, then the Seal doth confirm the Receivers Right, against any that may hereafter question it. The like may be said of Acknowledgments, as of Constitutions: The Subject may acknowledge his subjection and Seal it; the Stipulator may cause the Promisor to acknowledge Duty or Debt, and to Seal it: So for Acknowledgments of Debts discharged, Rewards received, Conditions performed, &c. 3. The like may be said *de Debito Pœnæ*, when Penal Laws are sealed: and of Commissions and Warrants for execution; but this less concerns our case.

So that the use of a Seal as such, is but to testifie in a special manner that the Thing or Instrument is really ours, or that we own it: and so as *Amesius* saith, to be *Testimonium Secundarium*, added to the Primary Testimonie of the Covenant or other Instrument. But the special end of the Seal ariseth from the nature and use of the Instrument sealed, and not from the nature of a Seal as such.

My opinion now upon the present Controversies, I give you in these Conclusions.

Concl. 1. Taking the word as strictly as we use to do in English, the Sacraments are not properly Seals, but Metaphorically. But taking the word *Seal* more largely, as it signifieth any instituted sign for testimony of ones owning the Instrument, Revealing, Promising, Exhibiting, &c. so - they may be called Seals.

2. The Sacraments are not to be applyed to universal or indefinite subjects, but to particulars: Indeed they cannot be entire Sacraments, without particular Application; that is, either to that particular Congregation, or a particular person: and still the Receptive Application must be personal.

3. Therefore not meer universal, or particular, or indefinite Enunciations are to be used by the Administer, but singulars also.

4. Yet I conceive that as the Universal Enunciation is first to be expressed; so it is that universal that is sealed, though with application to singular persons; it being not a Collective, but a Distributive Universal; and not Distributive only in *Genera singulorum*, but in *singula Generum*: and therefore may be applyed *ad singula Generum*.

5. I conceive that God may be said to Seal first the truth of the History of Christs death and bloodshed: and also the Truth of the Doctrine of the Gospel, that this Blood was shed as a Ransom for sinners, and that it was for our sins that he dyed.

6. And this *quoad institutionem Sacramentorum*, may be said to be intended to his universal Church; but *quoad exercitium, & actualem applicationem*, it is directly still to singulars.

7. I conceive also that in the Ministerial act of offering, and saying, Take, Eat, Drink, Christ may be said to Seal his Precept, whereby he hath made it the dutie of man, to Take- or Accept an offered Saviour with his benefits, on the Offerers terms.

8. Thus far there is no question but he sealeth to Hypocrites, as well as to true Believers.

9. Concerning the Promise or Testament, we must yet distinctly consider, 1. the Promise it self which goes first. 2. the sealing of this Promise, which is

next.

next. 3. the Delivery or Application by offer which is next. 4. the Reception or Acceptance of the thing offered, which is next. 5. the actual efficacie of the Promise in Constituting the Right of the Receiver in the Benefit, which is next. 6. the mutual obligation of each Partie to fulfill the remainder of the Covenant for the future, which is the last.

10. That Seal which properly confirms the Gospel to be true, is miracles and other gifts of the Holy Ghost; but the Sacraments, though they may do much also to that, as they are a continued publick Commemoration, and so an excellent way of Tradition, yet are they especially Applicatory signs for renewing clear apprehensions, helping memorie, assisting in our Application of the gene\ral Promise, resolving our Wills, exciting our affections to a more lively sense of Christs Love, and our sin and Duty, &c. and actually to help us in the Praises of the Redeemer by so solemn and sensible a Commemoration of his Redemption of us.

11. Ministers are Christs Officers in Explication and Application of his Laws and Covenants.

12. Their Application or Explication is no Addition to the sense, nor any making of a new Law or Covenant. Therefore when God saith, *whosoever will Believe, shall have Christ and Life*; and the Minister saith, *If thou A. B. wilt Believe, thou shalt have Christ and Life*; The Minister addeth not to the Promise, but applyeth it according to its proper sense; seeing a universal Enunciation absolutely so called, may be distributed *in singula generum*, though a Universal *secundum quid* may be only distributed into *Species* or *genera singulorum*.

13. And therefore to seal to that singular Enunciation, is no more then to seal to the Universal, but much less, if it were to that alone.

14. It is Gods Legal Deed of Gift, or Promise written in Scripture, or otherwise expressed, to which the Sacrament is a Seal, and consequently to that singular enunciation, which is but part of the same Promise, and that as it is contained in the universal; but not as it is a thing distinct from the universal Promise, or as supposed to adde to it, or contain more, for sense, in it; nor to the Application of the Minister, as such.

15. But for the right understanding of this, we must explain this word, *to Seal to*, which is of several significations: 1. It is one thing to *seal to* a thing as the *Testimonium primarium*, to which the Seal is the *Testimonium secundarium*. So the Instrument is *sealed to*. 2. It is another thing to *seal to* a thing as the *subjectum materiale obsignatum*: so the matter contained in that Instrument is *sealed to*. 3. It is another thing to *seal to* a thing as the *finis cujus ultimatus*: so the good which the partie ultimately receives from that Donation, Contract, &c. as its end, is *sealed to*. 4. And its another thing to *seal to* a thing as the *finis cujus proximus, vel propior*: and so to our Right to Christ, our Remission, Justification, Adoption, &c. are *sealed to*. 5. And its yet another thing to *seal to* a person as the *finis cui*: and so God *sealeth to* us, the forementioned Covenant, &c. I mean that according to its several respects to these things, the words *seal to* hath several significations. Now the application, the Right delivered, &c. may be said to be *sealed to*, as the *finis proximus cujus*: for it is sealed that it may be delivered and applyed for conveying Right: but these are not sealed to as the *subjectum obsignatum*; that is the Promise or Grant it self, whereby Right is conveyed.

16. The

16. The Sacraments are not only Seals to the Grant or Promise, but furthermore are Exhibiting or Conferring signs, in subserviencie to the Promise; as Instruments to solemnize the Collation of Christ and his Benefits. And this seems to be a far more remarkable end of them, then proper sealing: For Sacraments are such kind of signs, as those in the solemnization of marriage, in giving hands, putting on a ring, expressing Consent, &c. Or as the Crowning of a King, or the lifting a Souldier: or as a twig, a turf, or a Key in giving possession. So that the main use followeth the meer sealing.

17. As Gods Universal Grant of Christ and pardon is but Conditional (in form or sense) to which the Sacrament sealeth; so the minister that distributeth the Universal to singulars, must do it but Conditionally, *If thou A. B. wilt Believe, thou shalt have Christ and Life*: So that still it is no absolute but a Conditional Promise or Grant that is sealed.

18. This Conditional Promise is sealed Absolutely and actually; for were it sealed only Conditionally, then it were not Actually sealed at all, till the Condition is fulfilled: but the sense would run thus, *This Action shall be my Seal, when you believe, or perform some other Condition*. But I conceive God sealeth Actually, and therefore Absolutely, before men truly or really believe, when a Minister on his Command and by his Commission doth it.

19. Yet though God Seal the Conditional Promise Absolutely to such as profess to receive it; that is, though he hereby attest that he owns that Promise as his 'Act' or Deed; yet doth he not either Exhibite or Convey Right to Christ and his Benefits, nor yet oblige himself for the future, Absolutely, but Conditionally only. For in this Conveyance and Obligation the Grant or Covenant is the principal Instrument, and the sign the less principal; and both to the same use: and therefore the latter cannot Absolutely Convey, or Oblige the Promiser, unless the first do it absolutely too.

20. God may therefore seal his Promise, and thereupon offer Christ and Life to men that pretended a willingness to Receive it, and yet not actually convey Right to Christ and Life, nor Actually oblige himself to pardon or save the sinner, because the partie may refuse the offer, either refusing Sacrament and all, or only Refusing in heart the benefit offered, at least as such and on the terms that its offered on, and on which only it may be had. And so when the sealing use is past, the Sacrament may lose its Conveying and obliging force (so far as we may say God obligeth himself) for want of true Reception: and thus it doth with all unsound Believers.

I desire the Reader, according to this explanation to understand that which I wrote against Mr. *Tombes* in my book of Baptism, about the Sacraments sealing to the ungodly.

Having said thus much for the opening of my opinion, and the avoiding of Confusion, I return to Mr. *Blakes* words. And 1. where he saith, *The maior is not sealed; for the Sacraments seal not to the truth of any general propositions, but they seal with application to particular persons*: I Reply, They seal no doubt with respect to particular persons; but that they may not seal both the general Promise and the singular as comprized in it, to that particular person, I hear not yet proved, viz. q. d. *Having promised Christ and Life to every one that will Accept him, lest thou shouldst stagger at this my Promise, I own it by this seal*. 2. Where he saith, *It seals that which supplies the place of the minor*; viz. *I give thee Christ*: I Reply, 1. Its true; because this is no addition to the general Grant, but part of its proper sense : For he that saith, *I give it to all Believers*, saith in sense, *I give it to thee if thou be a Believer.* Otherwise God sealeth not to what he promiseth not : and were not the singular Enunciation comprehended in the sense of the Universal, you could never prove that the singular is sealed. 2. But what is the meaning of your Minor, which you say is sealed ? Is it an Absolute and simple Proposition or Enunciation, as you express it ? Or is it a Conditional one ? Do you mean, *I will give thee Christ on Condition that thou Accept him as offered* : or, *I will give him Absolutely* : And by *giving*, do you mean proper effectual giving which conveys Right ? or only an offer which conveys not Right till it be Accepted on the terms on which its offered ? If you mean by gift, a meer offer, then it may be sealed Absolutely ; for God doth Absolutely offer, where he doth but Conditionally Give. He doth not say, *I will offer you Christ, on condition you will take him* ; for he offereth him whether men Accept him or not. If you mean a full gift, and mean the Enunciation to be Absolute, then that man shall certainly have Christ and Life, whether he accept him or not ; or at least, accepting is no Condition. And then all that God so sealeth to, shall be saved. Nor will it help you to say, that he seals this Absolute Promise but Conditionally : for however, the man must needs be saved by such a Gift or Promise it self, though it were never sealed at all. If you mean (as I suppose you do) *I give thee Christ to be thine, on condition that thou Accept him as offered*; then 1. Why did you express a Conditional Gift, in Absolute terms, leaving out the Condition ? 2. Why then are you so loth to yield that this Conditional Grant is Absolutely sealed, that is, owned by an express sign ; As long as the Grant is but Conditional, yea and the sign it self doth Exhibit or Convey but Conditionally, what danger to say that it sealeth Absolutely ? Is there not more inconvenience in saying that both the Grant is Conditional, and yet also that it is but Conditionally sealed ?

3. You adde, *The outward Elements are given on this Condition, that we receive them, that we eat and drink them* : Reply, I never gave them but on a higher Condition, viz. *If you will take Christ offered, take this which signifieth, &c.* And I think Christ never gave them but on condition, that men Accept him as well as the sign ; though when they performed not what they pretend to do, he doth not suspend his act of Tradition : And in such a case it is a Delivering, but not a proper Giving. And I do not think that you use your selves to give the Sacramental signs meerly on condition that men will Take, and Eat, and Drink them : As you charge a further Condition on them, so I conjecture that if they should profess no more, then so to Take the signs, you would not deliver them.

Next you argue thus, *That which all do not partake of that receive the Sacrament, is not Absolutely, but Conditionally sealed in the Sacrament. But all do not partake of Christ in the Sacrament; therefore he is not Absolutely, but Conditionally sealed* : Reply, 1. What if I should grant all this ? what is it to our present question ? to *Seal Christ*, is somewhat an uncouth phrase. It is either the Grant or Promise of Christ that you mean, which Gives Christ : or it is the *Jus* so Given : (For Christ himself in substance is not Given by the Covenant, otherwise then by giving us Right to him.) If you mean it of Right to Christ, then this is the *Terminus proximus exhibitionis*, and the more remote end of sealing ; whereas our Question was of the subject sealed, and not of the end of sealing. And therefore you should not have thought that you conclude the Question,

when

when you speak only to another question. But if by *sealing Christ*, you mean only *sealing the Promise or Grant of Christ and Life in him*; then 2. I deny your major proposition. If you had said only, *That which all do not partake of that receive the Sacrament, is not absolutely Given*; I should easily have granted it : for it is Given on condition of Receiving : and even a sealed Grant may be uneffectual to Conveyance, through the interposition of the Dissent and Rejection of him that should receive. But you adde for the confirmation of the major, *None can miss of that which God Absolutely Granteth, and Absolutely sealeth*; Reply, 1. But what is this to your major? was there any mention of *Absolute Granting?* This is somewhat a large Addition. 2. And what is this to the question between you and me? You know and acknowledge, that I say, It is the Conditional Grant that is Absolutely sealed : why then do you dispute against Absolute Granting and Sealing? This is loss of time to the best of your Readers; and for the worst, it may make them think my opinion is clean contrary to my own profession.

§. 65.

Mr. Bl. OR in case the Soul frame any Argumentation, I suppose it is to be conceived to this purpose; If God give me Christ, he will give me Justification and Salvation by Christ; but God gives me Christ; therefore he will give me Justification and Salvation. *The major is supposed not sealed : the minor is there sealed : The Elements being tendred by the Minister in Gods stead, and received with my hand, I am confirmed that God gives Christ to my Faith : And the minor being sealed, the Conclusion eo nomine is sealed. The proof of any proposition in a Syllogism, is in order to the proof of the Conclusion; and so the sealing of any proposition is in order to the sealing of the Conclusion; which indeed Mr.* Baxter *grants; where he sayes that the Proposition that God sealeth to runs thus,* If thou do believe, I do pardon thee, and will save thee : *Yet several passages in that Discourse, are I confess beyond my weak apprehension.*

§. 65.

R. B. 1. TO your Argument there needs no more to be said then is said to the former. When God hath in one Deed of Gift bestowed on us Christ and Life, Remission, Justification, Adoption, &c. (1 *Joh.* 5.10,11,12. *Joh.* 1. 11, 12.) it must be in case of great ignorance that the person that knows that God giveth him Christ, must yet be constrained by after arguings to acknowledge that he giveth him Justification. And how this argument tends to explain the nature of Sacramental sealing, I neither know, nor see any thing here to help me to know. If you will suppose such an Argument as this used for Application, I would not stick to yield it useful; *What God doth by his Testament give to all men, on condition they will Accept it, that he gives to me on condition I will Accept it. But he gives Christ and Life in him, to all men if they will Accept it; therefore to me, :* (*Or if you will say, to all that hear the Gospel.*) Though the use of such an Argument is more for lively Application, then confirmation of the Truth of the Grant.

2. Your suppofition that your minor is fealed, and not your major, hath enough faid to it.

3. The Sacraments may confirme your faith in Chrift as given to you, otherwife then by fealing, viz. as they are figns for Remembrance, Excitation to fenfe and lively apprehenfions of Gods Donation, and as they are figns inftrumental in fole Conveyance of the benefit Given, as a twig and a turfe, and a Key in giving poffeffion, and the words and actions of matrimonial folemnization or Contract.

4. It is new Logick to my underftanding, that *the minor being fealed, the Conclufion co nomine is fealed* : The minor of many an Argument may be true, and the conclufion falfe. And therefore when the cafe fo falls out, that both minor and conclufion are true, or fealed, it is not *co nomine*, becaufe the minor is true, that the Conclufion is fo, (or is fealed, *co nomine* becaufe the minor is fo) but becaufe both major and minor, are fo, and not then neither, but upon fuppofition that the Syllogifm be found.

5. But to prove this, you fay, *the proof any Propofition in a Syllogifm, is in order to the proof of the Conclufion : and fo the fealing of any Propofition is in order to the fealing of the Conclufion* : Reply; The firft is true. 1. But what is this to the matter? Is it all one to *prove it* and to *be in order to prove it*, to *feal it* and to *be in order to the fealing of it*? Is the Conclufion proved on the proof of one Propofition? No : therefore according to your own arguing, neither is it fealed by the fealing of one Propofition. 2. That the fealing of one Propofition is in order to the fealing of the Conclufion, I deny. 1. It may be a fingle Propofition that is fealed, not ftanding as part of a Syllogifm : as this, *I Give Chrift and Life, in him to you all that will Accept him*. 2. If it be fuppofed part of a Syllogifm, it is enough fometime that the Conclufion be cleared or confirmed, or we enabled igfallibly to gather it, by the fealing of one Propofition: but it is not neceffary that it be the very fealing of the Conclufion, to which the fealing of that Propofition doth tend. When a Landlord hath fealed a Leafe to his Tenant, he hath fealed this Propofition, *If A. B. well and truly pay fuch Rents, he fhall quietly enjoy fuch Lands* : fuppofe the minor to be, *But A. B. doth or will well and truly pay fuch Rents* : fuppofe this minor Propofition either falfe or uncertain, will you fay then that the fealing of the major was in order to the fealing of the Conclufion? No: the Conclufion is abfolute, therefore A. B. fhall enjoy fuch Lands : but the Propofition fealed is Conditional. It is enough that it fecure his Right, if he pay his Rent, and that it enable him infallibly fo to conclude, while he performs the conditions, though it tend not at all to feal the Conclufion. We feldom ufe feals to Syllogifms, and not to Conclufions as fuch, or *co noimne*, becaufe a major or minor Propofition is proved : though the thing fealed may be to other ufes made part of a Syllogifm.

Yet I grant that where the Syllogifm is fuch as that one of the Propofitions doth morally contain the Conclufion in fenfe, though not in terms, there the conclufion is fealed when that one Propofition is fealed : becaufe it is the fenfe, and not meer terms that are fealed; and undoubted naturals are prefuppofed in moralitie, and therefore the fealing of one is the fealing of both : For example, if you argue either from a Synonimal term, or from the thing as Defined to the thing as named, or from the *Genus* to the *Species*, or from the Species to the Individual; thus, *fuccinum corroborat cerebrum : At Ambarum, vel electrum eft fuccinum :* therefore *Ambarum vel electrum corroborat cerebrum :* or thus, *Privatio vifus visus est naturæ malum. Cæcitas est Privatio visus:* therefore, *Cæcitas est naturæ malum.* Or thus, God made every creature: Man is a creature: therefore God made man. Or thus, All men on earth are sinners. I am a man on earth: therefore I am a sinner. In all these, if you seal the major proposition, or affirm it true, you do indeed, though not in terms, affirm or seal the conclusion morally. The confession that you say I make, reacheth no higher. But observe that its only morally that I say you may be said to say or seal the conclusion; because unquestionable naturals are presupposed in Morals and Legals.

§. 66.

Mr. Bl. HE that Believeth is Justified and shall be saved; is his major Proposition: This he saith is sealed unquestionably: when indeed I have ever thought, and yet think, that it is not at all sealed. Sacraments seal not to the truth of any general Proposition, but with particular application as they are dispensed, so they seal; but they are applyed particularly, Take, Eat, &c. This Mr. Baxter seeth pag. 69. and therefore in that absolute universal Proposition, he finds a particular Conditional Promise, to which he saith God sealeth : If thou believe, I do pardon thee and will save thee.

§. 66.

R. B. ALL this is answered sufficiently already. Only observe that by *shall be saved*, and *I will save thee,* I mean but *shall have, or I will give thee present Right to salvation*; For the continuance of that Right, hath more then Faith for its condition.

§. 67.

Mr. Bl. THat it sealeth not to the truth of the minor Proposition, But I believe, (he says) is beyond dispute, giving in his reasons. It should seal then to that which is not written; for no scripture saith, that I do believe; so certainly Sacraments do seal; they seal to that which is not directly written, they seal with particular application; but the man to whom they are apply'ed hath not his name in scripture written; they seal to an individual person, upon the Warrants of a general Promise: though I do not say that Proposition is sealed, yet me thinks this reason is scarce cogent.

§. 67.

R. B. YOu deny not my assertion, but argue against the reason of it; as before by telling us what you thought, so here by affirming the contrary certain, you attempt the confutation of mine. To your instance I give these two returns 1. It is equivocation, when our question is of sealing to a thing as the *subjectum obsignatum,* for to instance in sealing to a person as the *finis cui.*

The

The seal, that is to application as an end, not to application as the subject sealed.
2. But if you respect not the person as the end of application, but as the party expressed in the Promise which is sealed, then I say, If you can prove that the universal Proposition doth not in sense contain the singulars, so that this singular, *If thou believe, thou shalt be saved*, be not in Moral Law sense contained in this universal, *All that believe shall be saved*, (the Law supposing them all to be men and sinners) then I will prove, that God doth not properly seal to the singulars; But till then I suspend.

---

§. 68.

Mr. Bl. MR Baxter *sayes, The great question is, whether they seal to the Conclusion, as they do to the major Proposition? To which he answers,* No, *directly and properly it doth not. If the Proposition seems directly to prove the Conclusion, then that which directly confirms any Proposition in a rightly formed Syllogism, confirms the Conclusion. If the Conclusion be not sealed, then no Proposition is sealed, or else the Syllogism is ill-framed.*

---

§. 68.

R. B. This is too new Doctrine to be received without one word of proof. Doth he that sealeth the major of this following Syllogism, seal the Conclusion? *All that truly Receive Christ, are the Sons of God, and shall be saved. Judas did truly receive Christ; therefore Judas was the Son of God, and shall be saved.* I think both Premises must be true, before the Conclusion will thence be proved true. And it is not sealed by God, when it is false.

---

§. 69.

Mr. Bl. REasons are given. *This Conclusion is nowhere written in Scripture, and therefore is not properly the object of Faith; whereas the seals are for the confirmation of our Faith;* To which I say, *It is written* Virtually, *though not expresly. That I shall rise in Judgement is nowhere written, yet it is of Faith that I shall rise; and when I have concluded Faith in my heart, as well as Reason in my Soul, knowing my self to be a Believer as I know my self to be a man, I may as well conclude that I shall rise to Life, as that I shall rise to Judgement.*

---

§. 69.

R. B. 1. WHen you oppose *Virtually* to *Expresly*, you seem by Virtually to mean *in sense*, though not in terms! If so, then your Syllogism is tautological. But take it in what sense you will in any propriety, and I deny that it is Virtually written in Scripture, that you or I do Believe; or yet that you or I are Justified and shall be saved. Yet I confess that some Conclusions may be said to be *Interpretative vel secundum loquutionem moralem* in Scripture, when but one of the premises is

there

there: but that is when the other is presupposed as being as certain: but of this more anon, where you speak of this subject more largely.

2. To your instance, I say, It is by Faith and natural knowledg mixt that you conclude you shall rise again. The Conclusion participateth of both Premises, as to the ground of its certainty. That it doth *sequi*, is a right gathered Conclusion, is known only by Reason, and not by Faith: that it is true, is known partly by Reason, and partly by Faith, when the Premises belong to both. Yet though in strict sense, it be thus mixt, in our ordinary discourse we must denominate it from one of the Premises, and usually from the more notable, alwaies from the more Debile. Scripture faith, *All men shall rise*; Reason faith, you are a man. Though the Conclusion here partake of both, yet it is most fitly said to be *de fide*, both because Scripture intended each particular man in the Universal; and because it is supposed as known to all, that they are men; and therefore the other part is it that resolveth the doubt, and is the notable and more debile part.

Its I know undoubted with you, that *Conclusio sequitur partem debiliorem*. Now though Gods Word in it self is most infallible, yet in respect of the evidence to us, it is generally acknowledged that it is far short of natural principles, and objects of sense, in so much that men have taken it for granted, that the objects of faith are not evident (of which I will not now stand to speak what I think, but touch it anon). Therefore it being more evident that you are a man, then it is, that all men shall rise, it is fittest to say the Conclusion is *de fide* as the more debile part. But can we say so of the present Conclusion in question? Have you a fuller evidence that you are a sincere Believer, then you have that, All sincere Believers are Justified? I have not for my part: But it seems by your following words that you have, or suppose others to have; to which I say 3. If you have as evidently concluded that Faith is in your heart, (saving Faith) as that Reason is in your Soul, & know your self to be a Believer as evidently as you know your self to be a man, then your Conclusion may be denominated to be *de fide*, as a *parte debiliore*. But if this be not your case, it is most fit (for all the mixt interest of the Premises) to say that it is not *de fide*, but from the knowledge of your sincerity in the Faith, as a *parte debiliore*. And if it be your case indeed, you are the happiest man that ever I yet spake with. But I know that no man ordinarily can have such evidence of his sincerity; yet because I will not speak of you or others by my self, nor judge others hearts to be as bad as my own, or as all those that I have conversed with, we will if you please thus comprimize the difference: All those whose evidence of sinceritie is as cleer as the evidence of their Reason and manhood, yea or more then Scripture evidence, so that Gods Testimony is *pars debilior* in the Syllogifm; these shall take the Conclusion, *that they are Justified*, to be *de fide*: and all the rest shall take the Conclusion to be not *de fide*, but from the knowledge of themselves: and then let the issue shew whether more will be of your mind or of mine. I think this a fair Agreement.

§. 70.

Mr. Bl. OTherwise (faith he) every man rightly Receiving the Seals, must needs certainly be Justified and saved. *I see no danger in yielding this Conclusion; every man rightly receiving and improving the seals, must be saved and*

and Justified. He that rightly receives the seals, receives Christ in the seals, and receiving Christ, he receives salvation. So he that rightly hears. Hear and your Souls shall live. Isa. 55. So he that rightly prayes. Whosoever calls on the name of the Lord shall be saved. Rom. 10.

§. 70.

R. B. 1. BY *Rightly,* I mean t, *having Right to it,* and that only in *foro Ecclesiæ,* and not *Rectè.* But I confess I should have plainlyer exprest my meaning. 2. Whether you here contradict not your Doctrine of Baptismal Faith, where you suppose Justifying Faith to be the thing promised by us in Baptism, and therefore not prerequisite in it, I leave you to judge, and resolve as by your explication.

§. 71.

Mr. Bl. ANd no man can groundedly administer the Sacrament to any but himself, because he can be certain of no mans Justification and Salvation ; *Upon the same terms that he knows any man may be saved, upon the same he may give him the Sacrament sealing this salvation.* This argument as we heard before, is Bellarmines, and concludes indeed against *Absolute* seals in the Sacrament, but not against Conditional sealing , *as is confessed by Protestant Divines.*

§. 71.

R. B. 1. I know it not to be true of any man that he shall be saved : therefore I may not seal it to any, by your Concession. God Seals to no falshood ; I know not whether it be true or false that *A. B. shall be saved.* Yet it is on some of the Opposers principles that I now argue.
2. I desire you not to answer it as *Bellarmines* argument, but as mine , seeing you choose me to deal with. 3. The Argument makes as much against my asserting the Truth of your Conclusion , as the sealing it : so that let your sealing be Conditional or none at all, I may not so much as affirm to any man whose heart I know not, the Conclusion which you say I must seal. The Conclusion is Absolute, *Thou A. B. art Justified and shalt be saved*; though the Major Proposition, or or Universal Grant be conditional. Now if you will Seal this Absolute Conclusion conditionally, then 1. you will sin in the bare affirming it a true Conclusion, before you seal it , if you go but so far. 2. What is the Condition that you mean ? I suppose true Faith. But if so, then where there is not true Faith , there you do not Actually seal : For a Conditional sealing, is not Actual sealing till the condition be performed ; for the condition not performed suspends the act. And then you have mistaken in thinking that the Covenant is sealed actually to the unregenerate or ungodly. But if you mean any thing short of true Faith, how can you on that condition seal to any man , *that he is Justified, and shall be saved.* I do therefore rather choose to say , *If thou Believe thou shalt*

be

be saved: and thus, as contained in the general Grant, I absolutely seal; then to say, Thou shalt be saved, and this I seal if thou Believe. Though I say again, I make a small matter of this, and suppose your meaning and mine is the same, for all these words.

4. Where you say, *It concludes an Absolute sealing*; I say, No, if it be but to a Conditional Grant, and if Absolute Exhibition or Collation be not added to absolute sealing.

§. 72.

Mr. Bl. MR Baxter *adds*, I am sorry to see what advantage many of our most learned Divines have given the Papists here, as one error draws on many, and leadeth a man into a Labyrinth of Absurdities; being first mistaken in the nature of Justifying Faith, thinking it consists in a belief of the pardon of my own sins (which is the Conclusion) have therefore thought that this is it which the Sacrament sealeth. And when the Papists alledge that it is nowhere written, that such or such a man is Justified; we answer them that it being written, that He that Believeth is justified, this is equivalent. *But Mr. Baxter doubtless knows that many Divines who are out of that error concerning the nature of Justifying Faith, and have learned to distinguish between Faith in the Essence of it and Assurance; yet are confidently perswaded that the Sacrament seals this Conclusion, knowing that the Sacrament sealeth what the Covenant promiseth to the persons in Covenant, and upon the same terms as the Covenant doth promise it. Now the Covenant promiseth forgiveness of sins* (as Mr. Baxter confesses) *conditionally, and this to all in Covenant, and this the Sacrament sealeth.*

§. 72.

R. B. 1. IF there be any that mistake but in one of those points, when others mistake in them all, those are not the men meant that I speak of. I intended not every man that held your opinion, but only those that held it on the ground and with the worser consequent or defence which I expressed. 2. I shall know whom you mean, when I see the Authors and place in them cited. 3. I think most of our great transmarine Divines who write of it against the Papists, do own that which you acknowledge an error; and what advantage that will give the Papists, who are so ready to take a Confutation of one Doctrine of the Protestants for a Confutation of all, you may easily conjecture. 4. This Conclusion many confess sealed, *If thou A. B. do believe, thou shalt be saved*: but not this Conclusion, *Thou A. B. shalt be saved.* 5. I have shewed you that it is one thing to seal to the Promise for form and matter, and another thing to seal to the persons Right to the thing promised. This actual Right is but the end, which is not obtained, till Delivered or offered; Reception and actual Collation go before; and then is not the *subjectum obsignatum*. Your argument I conceive doth nothing for your cause, yea is wholly for mine. Your Conclusion is, *therefore this the Sacrament sealeth*; what is this? why *Forgiveness of sins Conditionally, and this to all in Covenant*. Here 1. you seem to yield that it is not the Absolute but Conditional Promise which is sealed, which is the main thing that I stood on: 2. You seem to apply the word *Conditionally* to forgiveness, and not to *sealing* : and so to confess that the sealing is actual; and if actual, then not meerly conditional. For to say *I conditionally seal*, is to say, *It shall be no seal, till the performance of the Condition*. But you seem to confess it a seal before of Conditional forgiveness. 3. You seem to acknowledge the general Promise sealed, though with application to particular persons.

§. 73.

Mr. Bl. *And as it is an error to hold that to believe my sins are forgiven, is of the nature or essence of Faith, as though none did believe but those that had attained such assurance, (true Faith hath assurance in pursuit only, sometimes, and not alwaies in possession.) So on the other hand it is a mistake to say, that it is no work of Faith. The Apostle calls it the full assurance of Faith*, Heb. 10. 22. *and describeth Faith to be the substance of things hoped for; Faith realizeth salvation which we have in hope to the Soul. A Description of Faith (saith Dr.* Amesius *out of a Schoolman) by one of the most eminent acts that it produceth; therefore I take that to be a good answer that is here charged with error, that when it is written,* He that Believeth is Justified, *it is equivalent, as though it were such or such a man is Justified, in case with assured grounds and infallible Demonstrations he can make it good to his own self that he believeth.*

§. 73.

R. B. 1. IF assurance be not of the nature or Essence of Faith, then it is not Faith: for nothing is Faith, but what is of the nature and Essence of Faith: But according to Mr. *Bl.* assurance is not of the nature or Essence of Faith (for he saith, its an error to hold it); therefore according to Mr. *Bl.* assurance is not Faith. But I suspect by the following words, that by nature and essence, he means the *minimum quod sic*.

2. That which is but either Pursued or Possessed by Faith, is not Faith it self, (for nothing is the Pursuer and Pursued, the Possessor and Possessed; as to the same part: nor will Mr. *Bl.* I conjecture, say, that a less degree of Faith possesseth a greater) but according to Mr. *Bl.* assurance is but pursued or possessed by Faith; therefore is not Faith.

3. I know none that denyeth Assurance to be a Work of Faith, which Mr. *Bl.* here saith is a mistake to say, Love and Obedience are works of Faith, but not Faith it self.

4. I must have better proof before I can believe that it is *Assurance of our own sinceritie, or actual Justification*, which the Apostle calls The full assurance of Faith, Heb. 10. 22. Though how far this may concurr, I now enquire not.

5. And as hardly can I discern assurance of our sinceritie, in the description of Faith, Heb. 11. 1. Unless you mean that hope is part of Faith, and assurance the same with hope; both which need more proof. Hope may be without assurance: and when it is joyned with it, yet it is not the same thing. Only such assurance is a singular help to the exercise of Hope.

6. Its true that Faith may be said, as you speak, to Realize salvation to the Soul; that is, when the Soul doubteth whether there be indeed such a Glory, and

nd Salvation to be expected and enjoyed by Believers, as Christ hath promised; here Faith apprehendeth it as Real or Certain, and so resolves the doubt. But when the doubt is only whether I be a true Believer, Faith resolves it not: and when the doubt is, whether this certain Glory and Salvation shall be mine, Faith only cooperateth to the resolve of it, by affording us one of the Propositions, but not both, and not wholly the Conclusion.

7. I am of Dr. *Ames* minde that it is one of Faiths most eminent acts, by which it is there described: But so think not they that tell us that is none of the Instrumental Justifying act which is there described.

8. This which you took to be a good answer, is that great mistake which hath so hardned the Papists against us; and were it not for this point, I should not have desired much to have said any thing to you of the rest, (about Conditional sealing) as being confident that we mean the same thing in the main.

9. You forsake them that use to give this answer, when you confine it to those only that *with assured grounds and infallible demonstrations can make it good to themselves that they Believe*, i. e. savingly. I doubt that answer then will hold but to very few, if you mean by *Assured grounds, &c.* such as they are actually assured are good and demonstrative.

10. Demonstrations may be infallible, and yet not known to be such to the person: but I suppose that by the word *Demonstration*, you intend that the partie discerns it to be an infallible Demonstration: which sure intimates a very high kinde of certainty.

11. Yet even in that case, I deny that the general Premise, in the major, is equivalent to the Conclusion, *I am Justified and shall be saved*; though I should acknowledge that the Conclusion may be said to be *de fide*, in that the Major hath the predominant Interest in the Conclusion, if so be that the man have better evidence of his sinceritie, then of the Truth of the Promise.

§. 74.

Mr. Bl. But this is said to be a gross mistake, and thus proved, as though the Major Proposition alone were equivalent to the Conclusion: *But here being in our Syllogism, both a Major and a Minor, there is added further*, or as if the Conclusion must or can be meerly *Credenda*, a proper object of Faith, when but one of the Propositions is of Faith, the other of sense and knowledge: *Here the Major is confest to be of Faith; but the Minor, I sincerely Believe, is affirmed to be known by inward sense and self-reflexion. Here I must enter my dissent, that a Conclusion may be* Credenda, *an object of Faith, when but one of the Propositions is of Faith, and the other of sense and knowledge: yea that it will hold in matters of Faith both fundamental and superstructive.*

§. 74.

R. B. 1. It was not *this* according to your limitations that was said to be a gross mistake; but as applyed to ordinary Believers, though my reasons make against both.

Gg 2   2. You

2. You deal more easily to your self, then fairly with me, in your entred Diſſent. 1. I ſaid *meerly Credenda*, as confeſſing it is partly of Faith, and partly of knowledge, as the Premiſes are : and you leave out *meerly*, and put in *Credenda* alone, as if I denyed it to participate of Faith. 2. I denyed it therefore to be *a proper object of Faith*; that is, a meer *Credendum* or Divine Teſtimony ; acknowledging that it may be *participative* and partially, and leſs properly called an Object of Faith ; and you leave out *properly*, and only affirm it *an Object of Faith*, of what ſort ſoever, in general.

3. I have anſwered this ſufficiently, in telling you my opinion : *i. e.* The Concluſion ſtill partakes of the nature of both Premiſes : and therefore when one is *de fide*, and the other *naturaliter revelatum vel cognitum*, there the Concluſion, is not purely either ſupernatural or natural, *de fide*, or *ex cognitione naturali* ; but mixt of both. That its truly a Concluſion, following thoſe Premiſes, is known only by Rational diſcourſe, and is not *de fide* : but that it is a true Propoſition, is known partly naturally, partly by ſupernatural Revelation (which is that we mean, when we ſay it is *de fide*). But becauſe it is fitteſt in our common ſpeech to give this Concluſion a ſimple and not a compound Denomination (for brevitie ſake) therefore we may well denominate it from one of the Propoſitions, and that muſt alwaies be *à parte debiliore* : And therefore when it is *principia naturaliter nota* that make one propoſition or ſenſible things, or what ever that is more evident then the truth of the Propoſition which is of Divine Teſtimony, there it is fitteſt to ſay, The Concluſion is *de fide*, or of ſupernatural Revelation ; As when the one Propoſition is that *there is a God*, or *I am a man*, or *God is Great*, or *Good*, or *True*. But when the other Propoſition is leſs evident then that which is of Divine Revelation, then it is fitteſt to ſay, that the Concluſion is ſuch as that Propoſition is, and not properly *de fide*. For the Concluſion being the joynt iſſue of both Premiſes as its parents or true Cauſes, it cannot be more noble then the more ignoble of them. This explication of my opinion is it that I referr you to as the ſubſtance of my anſwer to all that follows.

§: 75.

Mr. Bl. WHen Fiſher the *Jeſuite* told *Dr.* Featley that it was ſolid Divinity, that a *Concluſion* de fide *muſt neceſſarily by inferred out of two Propoſitions* de fide, *Dr.* Goad (*being preſent as Dr. Featleys Aſſiſtant*) *interpoſed in theſe words*, I will maintain the contrary againſt you or any other. : That a Concluſion may be *de fide*, although both Propoſitions be not *de fide*, but one of them otherwiſe evidently and infallibly true by the light of Reaſon or experience ; *giving inſtance in this Concluſion*, Chriſtus eſt riſibilis, *which he ſaid and truly, was* de fide, *though both Propoſitions whence it is inferred be not* de fide. Omnis homo eſt riſibilis, *is not a Propoſition* de fide, *or ſupernaturally revealed in Scripture* ; *yet thence the Concluſion follows in this Syllogiſm.* Omnis homo eſt riſibilis : Chriſtus eſt homo : *therefore* Chriſtus eſt riſibilis, *which is a Concluſion* de fide, *affirming that* Melchior Canus *had judiciouſly handled and proved this tenent, which he ſaid he could otherwiſe demonſtrate to be infallible: To whom Dr.* Featley aſſents, *ſecond Daies diſpute*, pag. 85. *It were eaſie to frame many ſuch Syllogiſms. If an Heretick ſhould affirm that Chriſt had only a phantaſtick body in appearance only, how would you prove the contrary but with this Syllogiſm*, He that is truly man, hath a true body, and not a phantaſtick body only. *This is a Poſition in reaſon*, Chriſt is is truly a man : *this is a Position de fide in Scripture, whence follows the Conclusion de fide, that* Christ hath not a phantastick body ; *If one should deny that Christ had a reasonable soul, affirming that his body was informed by the Dietie instead of a Soul, must it not be thus proved ?* Every true man hath a reasonable Soul : Christ is a true man, and therefore Christ hath a reasonable Soul. The Citie that ruleth over the Nations of the earth, and is seated on seven hills, is the seat of the Beast. *This is a Scripture Proposition : But that Rome then ruled over the Nations of the Earth, and was seated on 7 hills, we know by History and Geography : Whence the Conclusion follows, that* Rome is the seat of the Beast. *Abundance of these may be framed, where the Proposition opposite to the Conclusion, is either an Heresie or at least an error in Faith. The Conclusion is of Faith Disputing against the Ubiquitarians and Transubstantiation ; to hold up the Orthodox Faith, we are necessitated to make use of maximes of known reason. If they were denyed us, the new Crew now start up, that deny all consequences from Scripture, and will have none but Scripture words, had here a notable advantage. This Argument well followed, would put Mr.* Baxter *himself to a great loss in some of his Arguments (for which yet I give him thanks) to prove that the Scripture is the word of God.*

§. 75.

R. B. THis is fully answered before, even in my last Section. 1. Dr. Goad saith but the same that I say : only I distinguish 1. Between that which is purely *de fide*, and that which is only denominated *de fide* as the more debile of the Premises. In the latter sense the Doctors conclusions are *de fide*, in the former not. 2. When a Conclusion is denyed to be *de fide*, it may be meant either as a Diminution of its evidence, or as magnifying its evidence above that which is purely *de fide*, or as equaling it thereto. When I say this Conclusion is not *de fide*, *A. B. is Justified and shall be saved*, I speak it by way of Diminution of its evidence and authority. And I confidently speak it, and doubt not to maintain it. But when I deny this Conclusion to be simply or purely *de fide*, *I R. B. shall rise again*, I distinguish nothing of the evidence or necessity of it. And when I thus argue, *Omne quod sentit & ratiocinatur, est Animal. Ego* R. B. *sentio & ratiocinor* : therefore *ego sum Animal*; though I say that here the Conclusion is not *de fide*, yet I intend thereby to extoll it for evidence above that which is *de fide*. And when I affirm this Conclusion to be *de fide*, *I R. B. shall rise again*, as denominated *à parte debiliore*, I do speak it in Diminution of its evidence, in comparison of that which is more evident in nature : The Premises are these, *All men shall rise again : I am a man; therefore I shall rise again* (supposing we speak of men that dye). If the Major which is *de fide*, were as evident as the Minor, which is not, the Conclusion would be more evident then it is : and if neither were *de fide*, but both known naturally as the Minor is, the Conclusion would not be *de fide*, but would be more evident. This I speak that you may not think that I deny the Certainty, Evidence or Necessity of every Conclusion, which I deny to be *de fide*, either purely, or by prevalent participation.

3. For the Papists, though ofttimes they take the term *de fide*, as you and I do, for that which is by supernatural Revelation Divine, yet sometimes they take it for any point which is necessary to salvation to be held, without respect to the supernaturality of the Revelation. How *Fisher* used it, I know not.

4. I think your Conclusion, that *Christ hath a true body*, is purely *de fide*, and may be proved by meer Scripture Testimony, without your *medium*.

5. The advantage that you say the new Crew would have upon denyal of the use of Maximes of known reason, I know not who gives them (except *Veronius* and his followers, against whom its long since I read and consented to *Vedelius* in the main). But once again, and once for all, let me tell you, that if the other of your Premises be less evident or proveable then the very Word of God, and be more to be doubted of, then your Conclusion is not *de fide*. For nothing that is truly *de fide*, is less evident then the truth of Gods Word, and that part of the word in particular. But yet though in such a case we tell them that the Conclusion is not *de fide*, yet it follows not that it is untrue, yea or not evident : nor do we therefore deny the use of Reasoning from *mediums* of lower evidence then Scripture; much less of clearer evidence. But many consequences may be true, and yet not *de fide* when one of the Premises is *de fide*.

Note also for the understanding of what I have said concerning the evidence of the objects of Faith, that whereas we do usually so compare Science, Opinion and Divine Faith, as to conclude that Science is an assent both firme, certain and evident ; Divine Faith is an assent, firme and certain, but not evident ; Opinion is sometime firme, but never certain or evident ; I do not speak in the language of these Divines and Philosophers, when I ascribe an Evidence to Divine Faith : But then you must understand that the difference is not (as I conceive) *de re*, but *de nomine* ; For I take not the term *evident*, in so restrained a sense as they do : As to instance in *Rob. Baronius* (that second *Camero*) who saith, *Assensus evidens est cum quis per se, hoc est, vi sui sensus aut rationis, absque alterius informatione & testificatione percipit eam propositionem, cui assentitur, esse veram* : and he makes that an inevident Assent, *cum quis Assentitur propositioni, non quod sensus, aut solida ratio eam veram esse Demonstret : sed vel quod levis & inefficax ratio illud suadeat, vel quod alius testetur eam esse veram* ; *Philos. Theol. an.* p. 148. But I think the term *evident*, is here too much restrained ; and that with great inconvenience, and some wrong to the Christian Faith. I take that to be properly evident, which is to the understanding truly Apparent, or Discernable ; which hath divers degrees : And the Negative addition (that it must be *absque alterius testificatione*) is not only superfluous, but unsound ; And may appear even from the Authors words ; 1. where he opposeth these two, in describing inevident Assent ; *non quod sensus aut solida Ratio eam veram esse demonstret*, and *sed quod alius testetur eam esse veram*. Where he grants that whatsoever solid reason demonstrateth to be true, that is evident. Now I say, that he should not have opposed all Testimony to this. For solid reason doth demonstrate Gods Testimony to be true, and this to be his Testimony. 2. He ascribeth Certainty to Divine Faith, which he describeth to be an Assent, *qui nititur certo aliquo aut solido fundamento, non vero levi aut fallaci ratione* ; and he noteth diligently, that *ad certitudinem assensus requiri, ut fundamentum quo mens nititur dum assensum præbet, non solum ut sit in se certum, sed etiam ut assentienti tale videatur ; nisi enim ille sciat rationem qua nititur esse certam, ejus assensus nullo modo erit certus & stabilis*. Now he confesseth that the object of Science must be evident : and here he saith *nisi sciat rationem esse certam*. If he must *scire certitudinem*, then he must *scire evidentiam*, if all objects of science are evident. And what is it to know, but to discern or understand a discernable, cognoscible, or evident object ? How then can we *scire certitudinem, nisi sciendo aliquam certitudinis Evidentiam* ? I conceive

therefore

therefore that it is true proper evidence which is allowed to Divine Faith, under this name of Certainty, even by them that say it is not evident: I know what a ſtir the School-men make about this point. The Queſtion is not only *de Evidentia fidei*, but *de Evidenti Theologie* alſo, which they diſtinguiſh from *fides*, as *habitus primorum principiorum, & ſcientia Concluſionum* are diſtinct. Though the moſt of the School-men go the other way, yet ſome (as *Henricus Quodlib.* 12. *q.* 2. and *Beza Archiepiſc. Hiſpalenſ. qu.* 1. *prolog. art.* 3. *not.* 3. 4.) do affirm our Theology to have Evidence. *Aquinas* and his followers maintain it to be a Science; but that is, becauſe they ſuppoſe it to be ſubalternate to the Science of God and the Gloryfied. And therefore *Aquin.* 22. *qu.* 1. *art.* 5. *c.* denyeth thoſe things to be *ſcita quæ communiter & ſimpliciter ſub fide continentur,* and that becauſe *omnis ſcientia habetur per aliqua principia per ſe nota, & per conſequens viſa.* But I think that *per conſequens viſa,* will not hold without exceptions and limitations; and I ſuppoſe it to be *ex principiis per ſe notis* originally: Yet in the foregoing Article, *Aquinas* grants that though *quæ ſubſunt fidei Conſiderata in ſpeciali non poſſunt eſſe ſimul viſa & Credita, tamen in generali ſub communi ratione Credibilis ſic viſa ſunt ab eo qui Credit. Non enim Crederet niſi videret ea eſſe Credenda, vel propter Evidentiam ſignorum vel propter aliquid hujuſmodi.* And I eaſily confeſs that matters of meer ſupernatural Revelation are not in themſelves evident, nor *ab Evidentia ipſius rei* muſt we prove it; But that we have Evidence of the Veritie of the Concluſions, by the Evidence of the great Principles and the Conexion, I take yet for ſound Doctrine. The Scotiſts in oppoſition to the Thomiſts make much a doe on the queſtion *Utrum Theologia ſit Scientia*: And if properly Scientia, it ſeems it muſt be evident. *Scotus* lays down four things neceſſary to Science ſtrictly and properly ſo called; 1. *Quod ſit Cognitio certa, i. e. ſine deceptione.* 2. *Quod ſit de objecto neceſſario,& non contingente.* 3. *Debet eſſe Cauſata à Cauſa Evidenti intellectui, id eſt, à principiis evidenter notis intellectui;* by which he ſaith Science is diſtinguiſhed from Faith which is *cognitio obſcura, ænigmatica, & inevidens.* 4. *Quod hujuſmodi principia ſeu cauſa ex terminis evidens intellectui debet applicari per diſcurſum Syllogiſticum bonum & legitimum ad inferendam concluſionem*: and ſo Science is defined *Notitia intellectualis,certa & Evidens alicujus veri, neceſſarii, evidenter deducti ex principiis neceſsariis pr us Evidenter notis.* Yet *Rada* ſaith, the fourth of theſe is accidental. And I ſee not but we have even ſuch a rigid ſtrict Science of the objects of Faith. 1. It may be *Notitia Intellectualis certa,* as all confeſs. 2. And *de objecto neceſſario.* Only let me add, that when we make uſe of infallible Tradition *de facto,* in proving the ſoundneſs of our Records, that this was *Contingens à priori*, yet is it neceſſary *à poſteriore neceſſitate exiſtentiæ;* and that as to the verity, though it be contingent, whether this or that particular man ſpeak truth, yet conſidering but the force of objects and common natural inclinations in determining the Will, it may certainly be concluded that as to a whole Nation, or World, ſome voluntary actions are ſo Contingent, as that yet they are of a moſt certainly diſcernable event: Even men before hand may infallibly know that they will come to paſs, (ſuppoſing the world to continue Rational): As that all this Nation, or all Europe will not famiſh themſelves willfully, and will not hang themſelves, &c. is a thing that may as certainly be foreknown, as if it were not Contingent: much more may the Verity of ſuch paſt actions be known. 3. And that it may have evident principles, ſhall be ſhown anon. 4. And then that it is diſcourſive, is clear. Though *Credere* it ſelf as it is the quieting and repoſe or confidence of the minde upon the authority or apprehended Veracity of the Revealer, is an effect of this diſcourſe, ſeeing *fiducia* is not purely or chiefly, an Intellectual act, nor *fidem alicui habere* as it ſignifieth this repoſe: Yet the

the Truth received on the Speakers Trust or Credit, is received by the Intellect in a discoursive way.

Rada granteth these Conclusions, 1. *Theologia secundum se est verè & propriè scientia.* 2. *Theologia Dei respectu eorum quæ sunt necessaria secundum se, est verè & propriè scient a.* 3. *Theologia in beatis est propriè & verè scientia quoad omnes.* 4. *Conditiones scientiæ.* Yet this eighth Conclusion is that *Theologia prout est in nobis viatoribus non est propriè & strictè scientia.* And the great Argument to prove it is, *prout est in nobis est inevidens, quia principia nostræ Theologiæ sunt tantum Credita,* so that all the weight is laid on this inevidence Briefly, my reasons for the Evidence of the Object of Divine Faith, are these. 1. If it be evident that *Deus est Verax, & Deus hæc testatur,* that God is true of his Word, and that this is his Word or Revelation, then Faith hath evident principles. But the Antecedent is true; therefore. Into these principles we resolve all points of Faith : Whatsoever God witnesseth is true ; but the Doctrine of the Resurrection, judgment, &c. God witnesseth or revealeth; therefore ; That God is true, we have the same Evidence as that he is perfectly good, and that is, that he is God : and that there is a God, I take to be as evident a Truth as any in Nature to Reason, though God himself be so far above our comprehension. That this is a Divine Revelation, hath also its evidence , in evident miracles sealing it to the first witnesses ; and in Evidently Infallible Tradition delivering down to us the Records with the seals. I doubt not to affirm that some humane Testimony affordeth such a Certainty as is unquestionable, because of the Evidence of that Certainty : as that King *James* was King of *England*, &c. and of the matter in question we have as great, and in it self far greater. But of this elsewhere. 2. If Divine Faith give us a Certainty without objective Evidence, then it is miraculous or contrary to nature, or at least above it (not only as rectifying disabled nature, which I grant, but) as moving man not as man, or the Intellect not as an Intellect , which knows naturally no other Action but upon fit objects, and what is wrought by them : It knoweth no apprehension of truth, but as it is apparent or evidenced truth. To understand this Axiom to be true, *All men shall be Judged,* and to see no Evidence of its truth , are contradictions. 3. At left it cannot be concluded in general, that the objects of Faith are not evident to *any*, in that they were evident not only to the Prophets and Apostles themselves, but to all the Churches in that age where they wrought their miracles. For as the *formale fidei objectum,* viz. *Veracitas Revelantis,* is evident to Nature, and so to all that have not lost reason ; so that God himself was the Author or Revealer, was evident to all them whose eyes and ears were witnesses of the frequent Miracles, Languages and Gifts of the Spirit, whereby the truth was then sealed by God. 4. That which hath no Evidence, cannot be Rationally preached to the world: But the Doctrine of Faith may be Rationally preached to the world ; therefore Preaching hath a natural tendency to mens Conversion. It is a shewing men the Evidence of Gospel Truth, and the goodness of Gospel objects, and so thereby perswading men to Believe the one, and Love and Accept the other. He that doth not *prædicare Evidentiam veritatis Evangelicæ,* doth not preach the Gospel, in the first respect, as he that preacheth not the goodness of Christ and his benefits, doth not preach it in the other. Preaching is not like Christs laying on clay and spittle, which hath no natural tendency to open the eyes : For the effect of Preaching, as such, is not miraculous , no nor supernaturally otherwise then as the Doctrine preached being of supernatural Revelation, may be said to be a supernatural Cause, and so relatively the effect called supernatural : though the same effect as proceeding from the Spirit which is a Concause, or superior Cause, may be truly called supernatural. 5. That which may

may be discerned to be certain Truth, without special or extraordinary Grace, even by wicked men and Divels, hath some evidence which causeth this discerning or belief: But such is the Doctrine of Faith; therefore. I know some Divines to the no small wrong of the Chiistian Faith, say, None can really believe it, but the Regenerate. But the Jews believe the supernatural Revelations of the Old Testament, and the Divels and many a thousand wicked men believe, both old and new; experience tells us so: Christ tells us so, that many believe who fall away in persecution. *James* tells such men, that they do well in believing, but the Divel doth so too: else men could not reject or persecute the known Truth. To conclude it is commonly said that infused Habits, *infunduntur ad modum acquisitorum*; and therefore the habit of Faith in the Intellect must be caused by an Impress of evidence: Though the Spirits supernatural act be moreover necessary, yet that makes not other causes unnecessary.

Rada, who concludes, that *Theologia nostra non est evidens*, gives but these two poor reasons (and I should as soon look for strong ones from him, as almost any man of his Religion or party) 1. *Principia Conclusionum nostræ Theologiæ non sunt nobis Evidentia, sed Condita*: therefore *nec Conclusiones*, &c. I deny the Antecedent, which he proves not; *Veracitas Divina est formale objectum fidei*, and that is evident, so is the Revelation, as is said. 2. He saith, *Si conclusiones nostræ Theologiæ essent Evidentes, possemus convincere Infideles, ut fidem nostram susciperent, quia Evidentia convincit Intellectum*. I answer, 1. The greatest Evidence supposeth other necessary concurrents for conviction, as a Will to understand, and divers other things which the wicked want. As it is not for want of Evidence of present Objects, but for want of good eyes that a blinde man seeth not; so it is here. 2. Many Infidels do Believe without special Grace: though not so deeply and clearly as to prevail with their Wills for a through conversion; yea the Divels themselves believe. And whereas he adds *Pauls* words, 2 *Cor.* 5. *We walk by Faith, not by sight*; it speaks not of Rational Evidence, but of sensitive, and that we confess is wanting. Faith is the Evidence of things not seen, *Heb.* 11. 1. Were it not for digressing too far, I would examine the 9. *Qu'st. Mater.* 14. *de fide* of. *Aquinas de Veritate*, and shew how ill he answers the nine Arguments, which he undertakes to answer, and how weak his own Arguments are for the proving that *fides non potest esse de rebus scitis*. And I should shew that Faith is a kinde of Science; or if we will distinguish it from Science, it must not be so widely as is usual, nor upon the reason that it wanteth Evidence. But I suppose he that will impartially read *Aquinas ubi sup.* will without any help see the weakness of his answers, and how he seemed to stagger himself.

Yet let me add this caution or two; 1. I do not mean that every man who hath true Faith, doth discern the great and chiefest Evidence of the Truth of the Doctrine of Faith. 2. Where there is the same Evidence in the thing, there may be such different apprehensions of it, through the diversity of Intellectual capacities and preparations, as that one may have a firme Belief, and certain, and another but a probable opinion, and another none at all. 3. Though I take the Evidence of the Doctrine of Faith to be as full as I have mentioned, yet not so obvious and easily discerned as sensitive evidence; and therefore (as one cause) there are fewer believe, 4. Also the distance of the objects of Faith makes them work less on the affections, and the presence and other advantages of sensual Objects for a facile moving the Spirits, makes them carrie men away so potently, by making greater Commotions in the passions; so that no wonder if senfe do prevail with moft. I confefs alfo that men have need of good acquaintance with Antiquity and other Hiftory, and the Seal of the Church in moft parts of the world, to fee the ftrong Evidence that there is of the Infallible Tradition of the Scriptures down to us: and to fome obfcure men, this may be inevident; as it may be to one brought up in a fecret Cloifter, whether ever we had a King or Parliament or Laws in *England*. But the thing is not therefore inevident to the induftrious; No though it depend on that verity of Report, which as proceeding from each particular perfon is contingent.; feeing there is Evidence of Infallible Verity even in the Circumftances of thefe Contingent reports. And as *Rada*, when he concludes boldly that *Cognitio Dei respectu Contingentium non est proprie & scientia, &c.* yet feems to grant that God may *scire Contingentia ut necessaria, & si non ut Contingentia*: fo it may be faid in our prefent Cafe: the fame Reports which are Contingent, are yet in other refpects of Evident Verity, and fo we know them.

But I finde I have been drawn beyond my intent to digrefs far on this point: but it is becaufe it tends to clear the main point in queftion. To return therefore to Mr. *Blake*, I do not know the meaning of his next words, where he faith, that *This Argument well followed, would put me to a great loss in some of my Arguments for Scripture, &c.* Doth he think that I argue to prove the Divinity of Scriptures, from themfelves alone as the Teftifier thereof to our Faith? or that, I take it to be meerly or primarily *de fide*, that Scripture is Gods Revelation? when I have profeffedly publifhed the contrary, before thofe Arguments? where I have alfo added thefe words of Mr. *Rich. Hooker*, wherewith I will conclude this Section. *Truly it is not a thing impossible, nor greatly hard, even by such kinde of proofs so to manifest and clear that point, that no man living shall be able to deny it, without denying some apparent principles, such as all men acknowledge to be true. Again, Scripture teacheth us that saving Truth which God hath discovered to the world by Revelation; but it presumeth us taught otherwise, that it self is Divine and Sacred. Again, These things we believe, knowing by Reason that Scripture is the Word of God. Again, It is not required, nor can be exacted at our hands, that we should yield it any other Assent then such as doth answer the Evidence. Again, How bold and confident soever we may be in words; when it comes to the tryal, such as the Evidence is which the Truth hath, such is the Assent; nor can it be stronger if grounded as it should be;* fo far Mr. *Hooker* cited once more; *Ecclef. pol.* p. 102, 103, &c.

§. 76.

Mr. Bl. *TO winde up all, though there be some difference in the way between me and my learned friend, yet there is little in the thing it self.* Mr. Baxter *faies that the Proposition to which God sealeth, runs thus,* If thou believe, I do pardon thee and will fave thee. The foul muft affume the Minor. But I believe; from whence the Conclufion will follow, I fhall be pardoned and faved. *And I infer, the Major being sealed, the Conclusion that rightly issues out of it, having its strength from it, is sealed likewise; sealed to him that can make good that Assumption,* But I Believe, *and upon these terms that he be a believer.*

§. 76.

§. 76.

R. B. 1. The difference is so small that were it not for some scattered by-passages, I should scarce have replyed to you. 2. All the quarrel ariseth from the divers understanding of the term *sealed*. I suppose that you include the confirming of the Receiver, and the conferring of Right to the Benefit, both which I have said are done Conditionally, as being to follow the Delivery and Reception; whereas I take it for the *Testimonium secundarium*, or that Obsignation whereby the Instrument is owned: the following effects belonging to it in a further respect. I ever granted that by the sealing of the Conditional Promise, the Believer hath a singular help to raise the Conclusion, and be confirmed in it; but not a help sufficient, without the discerning of his own Faith, which is the Assumption. So that if you will, *participaliter* and *consequenter*, the Conclusion may be said to be sealed to him that hath the Condition (whether he see it, or not). But *totaliter & directè* only the Conditional grant is sealed. 3. The Conclusion issues from, and hath its strength from both Premises jointly, and no more from one alone, then if it were none at all: and therefore where only one of the Premises is sealed, and the other unsealed, there the Conclusion can be but as I said, *participaliter & consequenter* sealed: And though I grant thus much to you for reconciliation, yet I conceive it unfit to say at all, as in proper speech, that the Conclusion is sealed: which I make good by this Argument. *Conclusio sequitur partem debiliorem, vel deteriorem. At Propositio non obsignata est pars debilior vel deterior*: therefore *Conclusio sequitur Propositionem non obsignatam*. And so it is on the same grounds to be denominated, *not sealed*; as a Conclusion is to be denominated Contingent, when one of the Premises is Contingent and the other Necessary; or to be *Negative*, when one of the Premises is Negative and the other Affirmative; or to be *Particular*, when one of the Premises is Particular and the other Universal; And therefore I still say, that it is fittest for you and me to say, that this Conclusion, *Thou A. B. art Justified, and hast Right to Salvation*, is an unsealed Conclusion: till you can prove the Minor sealed, *Thou A. B. art a sincere Believer*. For my part, I know not what objection can be made against either part of the fore-recited Argument, (the major being a Common Canon or Rule that holds in all Figures, and the Minor being yielded by your self) else I would answer to it.

§. 77.

Mr. Bl. MR. Baxters *fourth and fifth Positions in the closing up of his Discourse should be considered*, The Sacrament sealeth to Gods part of the Conditional Covenant, and sealeth this Conditional Promise, not Conditionally but absolutely, as of an undoubted Truth. *To which an easie answer may be given, in order to a fair Reconciliation. When the Covenant tyes to the condition, and the Sacraments seal upon the same terms that the Covenant tyes, the seal is properly Conditional, in case there is any such thing in the world as a Conditional seal. Neither is this Conditional Promise any absolute undoubted Truth, but upon supposal of the Condition put, and so both Promise and Seal absolutely bind.*

Hh 2 §. 77.

[140]

§. 77.

R. B. 1. I Never heard of, nor knew a Conditional sealing in the world: though I have oft heard of the effects of Obligation and Collation of Right to be Conditional, which are not only separable from the *Terminus proximus* of sealing, but also are directly the effects of the Covenant, Promise, Testament, &c. only, and but remotely of the Seals, inasmuch as that Seal is a full owning of the Instrument of Conveyance. Yet such a thing as a Conditional sealing may be imagined, seeing sealing is a Moral Civil action, and so dependeth *quoad formam* on the will of the Agent after the matter is put; the Agent may if he please put the matter now, and introduce the form upon a future Condition (or a present, or a past) as if he should set the wax and material seal to a Deed of Gift, with this addition, *I hereby seal to this, or own it as my deed, if such a man be now living in* France; *or if such a Ship be safe arrived: or if such a man shall do such a thing; otherwise this shall be no seal.* But such exceptions or conditions being alwaies added to the Instrument or Principal obligation or conveyance, and being of no use as to the seals only, I never heard of such, nor I think ever shall do. For if all these or any of these Conditions be in the Deed or Obligation, the Seal doth but confirm that Conditional Obligation, though it be absolutely and actually a Seal: and therefore doth not oblige the Author actually, but conditionally: and therefore to feign a Conditional sealing, besides the conditional Covenanting or Granting, seems very useless and vain, to say no more.

2. I confess that neither Promise nor Seal binde absolutely, till the Condition be performed (which I pray you remember hereafter, if you be tempted to think any person in Covenant with God (the mutual Covenant where both stand obliged) before they perform the Condition of the first benefits or right). But when you say that *the Conditional Promise is not any absolute undoubted Truth, but upon supposal of the Condition put*, you make me see still the necessity of mutual forbearance, and that all our writings must have an allowance, as it were, in respect to some inconsiderateness; and the Authors not to be charged with withholding all the Doctrines which they write. I dare not say it is Mr. *Blakes* judgment, that Gods conditional Promises be not absolute undoubted Truth, till men perform the condition. 1. Though they are not Absolute Promises, yet they are Absolutely and not Conditionally true: Otherwise either it must be said, that till the condition be performed, they are Actually false, and Conditionally true, or else that they are neither capable of Truth or Falshood. The former I will not dare to suppose from you; nor yet the latter. For whether you put it in this form, *Whosoever will Believe, shall be Justified*: or in this, *If thou wilt Believe, thou shalt be Justified*: there is no question that both must be either true or false; and not like an Interrogation that is capable of neither.

2. And then as it is an Absolute Truth, so it is an undoubted Truth: For *Veracitas Divina est formale objectum fidei*: and if Gods Truth be not undoubted, then our Faith hath an uncertain Foundation, and Christianity is not undoubtedly a true Religion. But I charge none of these on you, as not doubting but it is an oversight.

§. 78.

§. 78.

Mr. Bl. *When* Caleb *had engaged himself,* He that smiteth Kiriath-Sepher *and taketh it, to him will I give* Achsah *my daughter to wife :* Othniel *the Son of* Kenaz *taking it, there was an absolute tye upon him for performance,* Josh. 15, 16, 17. *When* Saul *promised his Daughter to* David *on this condition, that he would bring him an hundred of the foreskins of the* Philistins, 1 Sam. 18. 25, David *having made it good with advantage, now there is an absolute tye upon him.*

§. 78.

R. B. This is nothing but what is granted. I yield that God is not as it were obliged till men performe the Condition. But the Question is whether he Absolutely sealeth before, and not whether that Seal oblige before.

§ 79.

Mr. Bl. *Even the* Arminians *Conditional incompleate Election, upon Condition of Faith and perseverance, they confess is absolute and compleat, upon supposal of Faith and perseverance. This I take to be Mr.* Baxters *meaning, that upon supposal of Faith it Absolutely sealeth, which I willingly grant : but it is administred to many who never put in that Condition, nor come up to the terms of God, that believing they may be saved, and so in our sense it sealeth Conditionally.*

§. 79.

R. B. 1. I Have better expressed my own meaning. It is pitty that the Reader should be troubled with so much, about so low a question, which of us two doth best express our meaning ? but that I hope he may gather some things more useful on the by. In your sense, if it be according to your terms, God doth not actually Seal at all to any but the Godly, which is my maine Argument against you. A Conditional seal, is not a seal till the Condition be performed.

§. 80.

Mr. Bl. And I can make nothing else of Mr. Tombes *his Aptitudinal and Actual seal, but that the Sacrament hath an Aptitude to seal in an Absolute way to all that communicate : it doth Actually seal to Believers and Penitent ones.*

H h 3   §. 80.

§. 80.

R. B. 1. I Perceive Mr. *Tombes* and you are more of a minde then I was aware of. 2. *Sealing of*, must not be confounded with *sealing to*, as respecting the end : nor the next end, which is Essential to the Seal, (as the *Terminus* to the Relation) with more separable ends. It is in regard of the first only that I spake against Mr. *Tombes*, and affirmed it to be Actual and not only Aptitudinal, but not in regard of the Obligation (as we may speak) on God, or the actual conveyance of Right, which follow the condition, which I desire Mr. *Tombes* to take notice of, according to my foregoing explication, if he mean to Reply to that.

§. 81.

Mr. Bl. NEither let any think that here I seek a starting hole to recede from any thing that heretofore I have published on this subject. In my answer to Mr. Tombes, pag. 99. I explain my self no otherwise, having quoted Dr. Ames and Mr. Rutherford, in the words now recited, I there add, The Conditional seal of the Sacraments is made Absolute, by our putting in the Condition of believing, &c. In case my answer had been in Mr. Baxters hand when his Appendix came out, as he saies it was not, that he might have seen how I explained my self, I suppose he would have seen that in the result of the whole I little differ from him, so that I can scarce see, that when the matter is brought home, that I have any adversary.

§. 81.

R. B. 1. IT is so rare a thing for men to manifest so much ingenuity and self denyal and impartial love to the Truth, as freely to recant what they have once asserted when they finde it a mistake, that if this had been your case, I would not have been one that should have blamed you for it, or charged you with unconstancy or levity. To err, is common to all men : but freely to recant it, is not so. I never write, but with a supposition that I shall manifest the weakness of my Intellect, and do that which needs reformation. 2. I did not so much as pretend you to be my Adversary ; I did defend you, and not argue against you : and therefore you have little need to perswade me to have lower thoughts of our differences then I did express, or that you and I were no adversaries.

But though I make light of our seeming difference about sealing, I must intreat you to remember, that I not only maintain my former Assertion, *that the Conclusion, I A. B. am Justified, is not* de fide, but that I account it a matter of far greater moment.

It hath been too common Doctrine among the most renowned Divines, that it is not only *de fide*, but every mans duty also, yea a part of the Creed, and so a fundamental, for to Believe that our sins are remitted, (for so they expound the Article of Remission of sins). I will not name the Authors, because I honor them,

them, and would not seem to disparage them; and the Learned know them already: yea they earnestly press men to Believe the pardon of their own sins in particular, and tell them that they have but the Faith of Devils else. By which dangerous Doctrine, 1. most men are perswaded to believe a falshood: for most are not forgiven. 2. The careless world is driven on faster to presumption, to which they are so prone of themselves. 3. Painful Ministers are hindred, and their labors frustrated, whose business is first to break mens false hopes and peace; which they finde so hard a work, that they need not resistance. The ungodly that I deal with, are so confident that their sin is forgiven, and God will not damn them for it, that all that I can say is too little to shake their confidence, which is the nurse of their sin. 4. Gods word, yea the Articles of our Creed, must be abused to do Satan this service, and mens Souls this wrong. All the world cannot finde so strong a prop to the Kingdom of the Devil, nor so powerful an encouragement to presumption or any sin, as mistaken Scripture (either misinterpreted or misapplyed). 5. When wicked men, that have but the Faith of Devils, are immediately required to believe the pardon of their own particular sins, and this made to be *de fide*, God is dishonored with the charge of such untruths, as if falshoods were *de fide*, and God commanded men to believe them.

And for the Godly themselves, it hath in a lower degree many of the same inconveniences. If there be any one that hath as good Evidence of his soundness in Faith, Love and Repentance, as that the Word of God is true, and all sound Believers are Justified; what is such a man to many a thousand that have no such Evidence? yea and for that man, it is impossible that his Evidence should be as constant, as Scripture Evidence, though it were as full; Scripture Evidence varieth not, as the Evidence of Grace doth in our mutable unconstant Souls: But for my part I never yet saw the face of that sober man (to my knowledge) who durst say, That he was as sure or as confident of his own sincerity, as of the Truth of Gods Word, and particularly of that Promise, *He that Believeth shall not perish, but have Everlasting life*. And as I have oft said already, The Conclusion may not be said to be *de fide*, unless the other Proposition be as evident as that which is *de fide*: because *Conclusio sequitur partem deteriorem*. Yea let me be bold to grow a little higher, and to tell you that it seems to me impossible and a contradiction that any man should be more certain that he Believeth sincerely, then he is that Gods Word is true, or that the Promise is Gods Word, which he doth Believe. For the truth of God in his Word, is the formal object of Faith, without which there can be no Faith. No man therefore can be more certain that he believes truly, then he is that Gods Word is true: For to Believe, is to apprehend the certain Truth of the Word. And none can be more certain that he apprehends the word as certain, then he is that the word is certain. If you say, I am certain that I believe the certainty of the word, but weakly: I answer, At least then the saving sincerity of your Faith will be as uncertain to you, as the word is, if not the being of that Faith. And then there is no more certainty, I think, rationally and ordinarily, then there is Evidence.

So much for that Controversie, and so of all; so far as I have observed, which Mr. *Blake* hath with me, for hath called me to give an account of my judgement.

Whether

Whether the Covenant of Grace require perfection, and accept sincerity.

THough I have done with what Mr. *Blake* saith to me, and have no desire to do any thing unnecessary in a way of Controversie: yet because it is of the like nature with a subject formerly handled, or tends to clear up some things about it, I will very briefly touch on his Arguments § *pag.* 107. 108. upon this Question.

§. 82.

Mr. Bl. A Second opinion is, that the Covenant of Grace requires perfection in the exactest way, without help of these mens distinctions, in an equal degree with the Covenant of Works, but with this difference; in the Covenant of Works, there is no indulgence or dispensation in case of failing, but the penalty takes hold, the Curse follows upon it: But the Covenant of Grace, though it call for perfection, such is the exactness of it, yet it accepts of sincerity, such is the qualification of it through Grace, or the mercy in it. If I should take up any opinion in the world for the Authors sake, or those that have appeared as Patrons of it, then I should embrace this: The Reverence deservedly due to him that I suppose first manifested himself in it, hath caused it to finde great entertainment. But upon more then twenty years thoughts about it, I finde it labouring under manifold inconveniences.

§. 82.

R. B. 1. IT may seem audaciousness in a young Divine to question that which you shall now so considerately deliver, after more then twenty years thoughts. But no prejudice must hinder us from a further enquiry after the Truth.

2. I began to conjecture that the Reverend person that you mean is Mr. *Ball*; and yet methinks, you should not suppose him the Author: It is therefore sure some one much elder.

3. For the thing it self, if I may shoot my bolt, upon a shorter deliberation, I conceive, that all your difference with the men of that Judgement, is occasioned by the Ambiguity and various acception of the word *Covenant of Grace*, which in my judgement, you ought to have removed, by distinguishing, before you had argued against their opinion. The term *Covenant of Grace*, is sometime taken strictly for the Contract alone; either 1. for the full Contract, which is mutual or by both parties, which is most properly called a Covenant: Or 2. for the engagement of one part only: 1. either for Gods Promise. 2. or mans. Herein the Condition is implyed, not as commanded, but as tendred. Now it is certain that taking the *Covenant* in this restrained sense, it doth not command Perfection of obedience, for it commands nothing at all: nor doth it propound it as the Condition, for then we were undone. But then it must be known

that

that this is too restrained a sense for us ordinarily to use the word *Covenant* in; God hath made no such Covenant with us, which is not a Law in one respect, as well as a Covenant in another: He layes not by his Sovereignty in Covenanting. Nay they are all more properly called Laws then Covenants: Even the Promise it self is most properly *Lex Gratiæ Remedians*, Like an act of Oblivion or Pardon to a Nation of Rebels. Yet comparatively, the Law of Grace is far more fitly called a Covenant then the Law of Nature (which perhaps is never so called in Scripture), because the Promissory part is the predominant part in the Law of Grace, the precept being but subservient to that; but the preceptive part is most predominant in the Law of nature; the Promise being not so much as expressed by *Moses*, and obscure in nature it self, so that it will hold great dispute, whether God were obliged at all to Reward man with heavenly Glory, yea or any proper Reward (besides non-punishment which is Improperly a Reward). The Lutherans are the leaders of that evil custom and conceit of denying the Gospel to be a Law. 2. In the next place therefore the word *Covenant of Grace* is taken for the New Law, containing Precept, Prohibition, Promise and Threatning. And here it is taken 1. so narrowly as to comprize only the Precept of Believing, with the Promise and Threatning annext, as being indeed the principal parts. 2. Sometime more largely, as containing also the Precepts that Christ hath given the Church since his coming, that were not before given: Principally that of Believing Jesus to be the Christ, and also those of Ministery, Ordinances, Church-Assemblies, &c. together with the Doctrines or Articles of Faith which he since revealed. 3. Sometime it is more largely taken for that whole Systeme of Doctrines, Histories and Laws (Precepts, Promises, and Threats) which directly concern the Recovery of faln mankinde. 4. Sometime for as much of these as was delivered before Christs coming, in Promises, Prophesies and Types, &c. 5. Sometime for as much of these as yet remains in force, whether delivered to the Church before the Incarnation or since, (for many Covenants or Evangelical Promises and Precepts, are ceased now that were in force before: as that Christ should be born, and they should accept his birth, &c.) This last sense, containeth the Doctrine of Redemption by Christ, and the History of his birth, life and Death and Resurrection (as Narrations of the occasion, end and matter are usual appurtenances of a Law) as also the Precepts of Repenting and Believing; Loving God for our Redemption, and Christ as Redeemer; Loving men as Redeemed ones, and as Members of Christ; Ministry, Sacraments, Church-assemblies, proper to the Gospel, with the means to be used for getting, keeping or improving this Grace as such; the command of Hope, or looking for Christs second coming, &c. and of sincere obedience. I conceive the first (as containing the summe of all) and specially this last (as containing the whole Systeme of the Doctrine and Laws of our Redemption and Restauration) are the fittest senses for us ordinarily to use the word *Covenant of Grace* in (*vide* Grotii *dissertationem de nomine* Διαθήκη *ante Annotat. in Novum Testam.*) Now if the question be whether in any of these senses the New Covenant doth command perfect obedience; I answer, All the doubt is of the 3 latter: But I rather think negatively, that in none of these Acceptions can the New Covenant be said to require perfect obedience. 6. But then some take the New Law or Covenant for the whole Law that now stands unrepealed, and obligeth the Subjects of the Mediator, supposing the Moral Law to be now the Law or Covenant of Grace, *i. e.* the matter of it, as it was formerly the matter of the Law of Works: and that the Covenant of Works being totally and absolutely Abrogated, the Moral Law must be the material part of the Covenant or Law of Grace, or of none: and of some it must be: For God gives no precepts but upon some terms, or with some sanction of Reward or Punishment: And hereupon they say, that it is now the Moral Law which is the matter of the new Covenant, which commandeth perfect obedience. This is maintained by an acquaintance and friend of Mr. *Blakes*, a man of extraordinary Learning and Judgement, especially as throughly studyed in these things as any that ever I was acquainted with. For my part, (though I think, the difference is most in notions and terms, yet) I still judge, that the Law of Works, that is, the Precept and Threatning, are not abrogated, though the Promise of that Law be Ceased, and so it is not so fitly now called a Covenant; and some particular Precepts are abrogate or ceased; and so I think it is this remaining Law of nature which Commandeth perfect obedience, and still pronounceth Death, the due punishment of our disobedience. But I acknowledge even this Law of Nature to be now the Law of Christ, who, as Redeemer of all mankinde, hath Nature and its Law and all things else delivered unto him, to dispose of to the advantage of his Redemption Ends: But still I suppose this Law of Nature to be so far from being the same with the Law of Grace, that it is this which the Law of Grace Relaxeth, and whose obligation it dissolveth, when our sins are forgiven. So that the difference is but in the Notion of Unity or Diversity, whether (seeing all is Now the Redeemers Law) it be fittet to say, It is one Law; or that, They are two distinct Laws. For in the matter we are agreed, *viz*. that the Promise of the first Law is ceased; (because God cannot be obliged to a subject made uncapable) and some particular Precepts are ceased *Cessante materia*, and *Moses* Jewish Law is partly ceased, and partly abrogate; and that there is now in force as the Redeemers Law, the Precept of perfect obedience, and the Threatning of Death to every sin, with a Grant of Remission and salvation to all that sincerely Repent and Believe, and a threatning of far sorer punishment to the Impenitent and Unbelievers. Thus far the Agreement. The disagreement is but this; I think that though these are both the Redeemers Laws, yet they are to be taken as two; One in this forme, *Perfect Obedience is thy Duty (or obey perfectly): Death is thy Due for every sin.* The other in this forme, *Repent and Believe, and thou shalt be saved (from the former curse): Or else damned.* Others thinks that it is fitter to say that these two are but one Law, *quoad formam*, running thus, *I command to thee saln mon, perfect obedience, and oblige thee to Punishment for every sin; Yet not remedilesly; but so as that if thou Believe and Repent, this Obligation shall be dissolved, and thou saved; else not.* To this purpose the foresaid Learned, Judicious, and much honored Brother, explains his opinion to me. Now as long as we agree that the former Law, or part of the Law, (call it which you will) doth Actually oblige to perfect obedience, or future Death; and the latter Law, or part of the Law, doth upon the performance of the Condition, dissolve his Obligation, and give us *Jus ad impunitatem & salutem*; what great matter is it, whether we call it One Law or Two? For we are agreed against them that look on the Moral Law as to the meer preceptive part, as standing by it self, being not the matter of any Covenant, or connexed to any sanction to specifie it.

To apply this now to Mr. *Blakes* Question; It is most likely that those Divines that affirm that the Covenant of Grace doth require perfect obedience, and Accept sincere, do take that Covenant in this last and largest sense; and as containing the Moral Law as part of its matter; and so no doubt it is true, if you understand it of perfection for the future, as speaking to a creature already made Imperfect. Now seeing the

the whole difference is but about the Restriction or Extension of the terme *Covenant*, I conceive; after twentie years study, Mr. *Bl.* should not make it so material, nor charge it so heavily. And though I am not of that partie and opinion my self which he chargeth, yet seeing it may tend to reconciliation, and set those men more right in his thoughts, to whom he professeth such exceeding reverence, I will briefly examine his Reasons *ab absurdis* which he here bringeth in against them.

§. 83.

Mr. Bl. 1. IT *establisheth the former opinion opposed by Protestants, and but now refused as to the Obedience and the Degree of it called for in Covenant: and if I should be indulgent to my affections, to cause my Judgement to stoop, dislike of the one would make me as averse from it, as an opinion of the other would make me prone to receive it. Judgement therefore must lead, and Affections be waved.*

§. 83.

R. B. IF you interpret the Papists, as meaning that the Law requires true Perfection, but Accepts of sincere; then if it be spoken of the Law of Works or Nature, it is false, and not the same with theirs whom you oppose, who suppose it is the Covenant of Grace that so accepts of sincerity. If you take them (as no doubt you do) as meaning it of the Law of Christ (as the Trent Council express themselves) then, no doubt, but they take the Law of Christ in the same extended sense as was before expressed; and then they differ from us, but in the forementioned Notion: But then I suppose you wrong them by making them righter then they are: For the very passages which you before expressed out of some of the chief of their writers, do intimate that they do not indeed take the Covenant or Law it self to command true Perfection: but that which they call Perfection, is but (as you say) *No other then the Grace of Sanctification in the very sense as the Orthodox hold it out*; But it is true perfection that those mean whom you now write against. So that I see not the least ground for this first charge.

§. 84.

Mr. Bl. 2. IF *this opinion stand, then God Accepts of Covenant-breakers; of those that deal falsly in it; whereas Scripture charges it upon the wicked, those of whom God complains as Rebellious,* Deut. 29. 25. Josh. 7. 15. Jer. 11. 10. and 22. 8. 9. *Yea it may be charged upon the best, the most holy in the world lying under the guilt of it.*

I i §.

§. 84.

R. B. This charge proceedeth meerly from the confounding of the Duty as such, and the Condition as such. A Covenant which is also a Law as well as a Covenant, may by the preceptive part Constitute much more Duty, then shall be made the Condition of the Promises. Properly it is only the non-performance of the Condition that is Covenant-breaking; and so the Divines whom you oppose are not chargeable with your Consequent : For they say not that *The Covenant of Grace doth make perfect Obedience the Condition of its Promise, and Accept Imperfect.* That were a flat contradiction : for the Condition is *Causa sine qua non, & cum qua* : But only they say, It Requireth or Commandeth perfect obedience, and Accepteth imperfect. And if you will speak so largely, as to say, that all who break the preceptive part of the Covenant, are Covenant-breakers, then no doubt but God Accepteth of many such, and of none but such. And as the word *Covenant* is not taken for the mutual contract, but for Gods new Law, called his Covenant, his Testament, his Disposition, Constitution, Ordination, &c. so no doubt, we all are Covenant-breakers. For whether we say that the new Law commandeth perfect obedience, or not; yet unless you take it exceeding restrainedly, it must be acknowledged that the Precept is of larger extent then the Condition, having appointed some Duties which it hath not made *sine qua non* to salvation : If you send your childe a mile of an errand, and say *I charge you play not by the way, but make haste, and do not go in the dirt, &c. and if you come back by such an houre, I will give you such a Reward*; if not, *you shall be whipt*; He that playes by the way and dirties himself, and yet comes back by the hour appointed, doth break the preceptive part, but not the condition. Or if you suppose a re-engagement by Promise to do both these : he breaketh his own Covenant in the first respect (which was not the condition of Reward or Punishment) but not in the second. And so do true Christians both break the preceptive part of the Covenant, and also some of their own particular covenants with God : as when a man promiseth, I will commit this sin no more, or I will perform such a duty such a day. But these are not the Conditions of the Covenant of Grace, which God hath made the *Causa sine qua non* of Justification or Salvation. So that I conceive this charge unjust, to say no more.

§. 85.

Mr. Bl. 3. Then it will follow that *as none can say that they have so answered the Command of the Law that they have never failed, they have not (if put to answer in the greatest rigor) once transgressed ; so neither can they with the Church make appeal to God, That they have not dealt falsly in the Covenant, nor wickedly departed from their God.* Psal. 44. 17. *Every sin* (*according to this opinion*) *being a breach of it, and a dealing falsly in it.*

§. 85.

§. 85.

K. B. This charge is as unjust as the former; and the absurdity supposed to follow, doth not; but is supposed so to do, upon the forementioned confusion of two acts of the Covenant, or New Law; the one Determining what shall be mans Duty; the other, what shall be *Conditio sine qua non* of Justification and Salvation.

§. 86.

Mr. Bl. 4. Then *the great Promise of mercy from everlasting to everlasting upon them that fear him, and his Righteousness unto childrens children to such as keep his Covenant, and to those that remember his Commandements to do them,* Psal. 103. 17, 18. *only appertains to those that so keep the Law that they sin not at all against it.*

§. 86.

R. B. It follows not. If they sincerely keep the Law, they fulfill the Conditions of the Covenant, though not the Precept. And they keep the Precept in an improper but usual sense, as Keeping is taken for such a less degree of breaking as on Gospel grounds is Accepted. This still runs upon the foresaid Confusion.

§. 87.

Mr. Bl. 5. Then *our Baptism-Vow is never to sin against God; and as often as we renew our Covenant, we do not only humble our selves that we have sinned, but we afresh binde our selves never more to admit the least infirmity, and so live and dye in the breach of it.*

§. 87.

R. B. We do not promise in Baptism to do all that the Precept of the Covenant requireth, but all that is made the Condition of Life, and to Endeavor the rest. Much less as the Covenant is taken in the largest sense, as those seem to do whom you oppose, may it be said that we promise to keep all his Precepts.

§. 88.

Mr. Bl. 6. Then the distinction between those that entred Covenant and brake it, as Jer. 31, 32, 33. and those that have the Law written in their hearts, and put into their inward parts to observe it, falls, all standing equally Guilty of the breach of it, no help of Grace being of power to enable to keep Covenant.

§. 88.

R. B. When sincere obedience and perfect obedience are all one, and when the Precept and the Condition of the Covenant are proved to be of equal extent, then there will be ground for the charging of this Consequence. In the first Covenant of Nature the Precept and the Condition were of equal extent; for perfect obedience was the Condition; but it is not so in the Covenant of Grace.

§. 89.

Mr. Bl. 7. Then it follows that sinceritie is never called for as a Duty, or required as a Grace; but only dispensed with as a failing, indulged as a want. It is not so much a Christians honor or Character, as his blemish or failing; rather his defect then praise. But we finde the contrary in Noah, Job, Asa, Hezekiah, Zachary and Elizabeth, Nathaniel an Israelite indeed that entred Covenant and kept Covenant.

§. 89.

R. B. I Will not say it is past the wit of man to finde the Ground of this charge, i. e. to see how this should follow; but I dare say, it is past my wit. If it had been said, *The Covenant commandeth perfection and not sincerity*; Or *The Covenant accepteth sincerity, but not commandeth it*, there had been some reason for this charge. But do you think that sincerity is no part of Perfection! Can the Covenant require perfection, and not require sincerity, when sincerity is contained in perfection? If you take *sincerity, exclusive* only, as excluding perfection, and not at all *formaliter*; then its true that it is not commanded, nor is a duty, but a failing: For I hope the Gospel doth not command Imperfection, but tender us a Remedy for it. You might with more colour have argued, that *then Repentance is no Duty, because inconsistent with commanded-perfection*. But that will not hold neither: For they suppose, Repentance commanded by the same Law, in case (and upon certain supposal) of Imperfection, or sin.

§. 90.

§. 90.

Mr. Bl. And therefore I conclude that as in the Law there was pure Justice, as well in the command Given, as punishment threatned, without any condescension or indulgence : So in the Covenant there is mercy and condescension, as well in the Condition required, as in the Penalty that is annexed to it. The Covenant requires no more then it accepts.

§. 90.

R. B. ALL this will be easily granted you by those of the contrary part, as nothing to the purpose. It follows not, that because there is condescension in the Condition, that therefore there is such an abatement in the Precept, or that the Covenant hath no Precept but *de præstanda Conditione.* 2. It were strange if the Covenant should require more then it accepts. Did ever sober man (much less such as your Reverened adversaries) imagine a thing so Impious! as if God would not Accept that which himself commandeth. But if you would have said, as your arguing requires, that the Covenant accepteth no less then the whole which it commandeth or requireth, then not only your Antagonists, but my self and many another will deny it, and demand your proof. But here I take this as granted by you, that you take not the word *Covenant* at least so restrainedly as excluding all Precept; for I suppose you mean *Commanding*, in the terms *requiring, and calling for as duty*.

§. 91.

Mr. Bl. THe alone Argument, so far as ever I could learn, that hath brought some of Reverend esteem into this opinion, is, That if the Covenant requires not exact perfection in the same height as the Law calls for it, then a Christian may fall short of the Law in his Obedience, and not sin ; perfection being not called for from him, nor any more called for from him then through Grace he doth perform ; he rises as high as his Rule, and sins not through any Imperfection ; therefore to make it out that a Believers Imperfections are his sins, it must needs be that the Covenant requires perfection ; as to make good that he may be saved in his Imperfections, it must be maintained that he accepts sincerity. But this Argument is not of weight: Christ entring a Gospel-Covenant with man, findes him under the command of the Law, which command the Law still holds, the Gospel being a confirmation, not a destruction of it. All Imperfection then is a sin upon that account, that it is a Transgression of the Law, though (being done against heart, and laboured against) it is no breach of Covenant: wee are under the Law as men ; we are taken into Covenant as Christians : retaining the humane nature, the Law still commands us ; though the covenant in Christ through the abundant Grace of it, upon the terms that it requires and accepts, frees us from the sentence of it.

§. 91.

§. 91.

R. B. 1. I Was at first doubtful, left by *the Law* you had meant (as the *Lutherans*) a Law of God in general, as opposed to the Gospel as being no Law: and that you had meant by the Law, only the Moral Precepts, which is but the matter of the Law of Nature or of Works, or of the Law of Grace (in some respect). But I perceive that you mean the entire Law, both Precept and Sanction, by your mentioning *the Sentence* of it. If therefore you do by *the Law* mean but one Species, *viz.* the Law of Nature, acknowledging the new Law of Grace (commonly called the New Covenant, from the Promise which is the most eminent part) to be a Law too, then I agree with you in this solution as to the matter of Perfection; or else not. And yet I dare not hold that the New Law commandeth no more then its Condition. But for them that use the word *Covenant* for nothing but the bare Promise, I must tell them, that it is but a piece of Gods Law or Instrument, separated from the body which they fasten a Name upon: and if they will signifie so much, that it is but part of the Redeemers Law of Grace, which they call a Covenant, and will give another name to the whole, that so we may understand them, I would not willingly quarrel with them about words. But if it be the thing as well as the name that they err in, affirming that the Gospel is a meer Promise, and that God hath no Law but one, and that one the Law of Works; or else that all his Precepts Natural and Positive, are one Law by themselves as distinct from the Sanctions, when Precepts are but part of Gods Laws, which by their Sanctions are specified and distinguished (as most think into two sorts, of Nature and of Grace; but as *Camero* thinks into three sorts, of Nature, & of Jewish works, & of Grace) then *I* not only profess my dissent, but do esteem the former error very dangerous and intolerable; and the later, such as tendeth to great confusion in the body of Theologie.

2. This very Argument which you recite and answer, doth undenyably prove, that the Divines whom you oppose, do by *the Covenant of Grace*, understand all the Law that is now in force under the Government of the Redeemer. Otherwise they would never imagine that there is no sin but what is against the Covenant of Grace; and that there is no other Rule but this Covenant for a Christians obedience. It is therefore out of doubt, that this difference is but about words, (or little more) they taking *that Covenant of Grace* in a larger sense then you and I think meet to take it.

If you should reply, that it is an unreasonable thing of them to take it so largely: I say that I do not think meet to imitate them in it, but I could shew you so much said that way by the forementioned Reverend, Learned man, your friend and mine, as would convince you that they have more to say for what they do, then every one that is against them is able to answer.

§. 92.

The Conclusion.

HAving thus taken the boldness to examine your Exceptions, and deliver my Reasons against some of your opinions, I do crave your favorable acceptance

tance of what I have done, and your friendly interpretation or remission of any unsavory words that I have let fall : And I must desire you not to suppose that I judge of all the rest of your Book, as I do of this which I have here Replyed to. I value the Wheat, while I help you to weed out the Tares. Pardon my confident Concluding you in the error, and my self in the Truth : whether it be from the convincing self-revealing nature of Light ; or from the common unhappy fate of the deluded ; I must leave you and others to judge by the Evidence that is in my arguments, whatever further evidence I may have my self within ; doubtless the various state of Intellects, doth cause a strange variety of apprehensions, of those objects which are in themselves the same. And words be but defective signs : There is something in Sensation and Intellection, which words cannot fully shew to another. It is but the Species and not the thing it self which you see in this Glass. My most exquisite description of my own Tast, and the sweetness of what I tast, will not cause another to tast that sweetness. And there is somewhat like this in Intellection it self ; for though I confess my self ignorant what manner of thing our Intellection will be, when we are out of the flesh ; yet now me thinks I perceive that it doth in some sort participate of sense, and that vid. August. de Trinit. li. 5. c. 1. initio. Sentio me Intelligere, is a speech not wholly void of Truth. I confess also that I should have little modesty or humility, if I should not think more highly of the understanding of your self and so many Reverend and Learned Brethren who dissent from me in several points here debated, then of mine own. But yet we must prove all things, and not so trust to other mens eyes as to shut our own, or refuse to give credit to our sight. They may far excell me in many other things, though they mistake in this. I remember *Pauls*, *If we or an Angel from heaven*, &c. And I remember *Tertullians*, *Non ex personis probamus fidem, sed ex fide personas* (li. Præscript. adv. hær. c. 3.) And *Irenæus* his, *Presbyteris adhærere oportet qui & Apostolorum doctrinam custodiunt, & cum Presbyterii Ordine sermonem sanum custodiunt* &c. (li. 4. c. 44.) And *Cyprians*, *Quæ ista obstinatio est, quæ præsumptio, humanam traditionem Divinæ dispositioni anteponere? nec animadvertere, indignari & irasci Deum, quoties Divina præcepta solvit & præterit humana traditio.* Epist. 74. ad Jubaian. p. 229. And many a one of *Austins* yet plainer then these, to the same purpose are commonly known. *Paul* himself could do nothing against the Truth, but for the Truth, as having no Authority given him to destruction but to Edification. I am willing to stoop to the judgment of my betters as far as is Reasonable, Conscionable and Possible, and if no further, I hope I may be excused : when I see plain Reason against them, it is *unreasonable* to subscribe to the opinions of the most learned : when Scripture is against them, it were dishonest and unconscionable: And when they are one against another, to assent to all is impossible. In such a case, I must needs bear the Accusations of one party, who think me Arrogant, Proud and Self conceited, as supposing my self to be wiser then they. But I have long been studying and Preaching, (and I think practising) that necessary and excellent Duty, of being so contented with Gods sole approbation, as those that know they stand or fall at his bar : and therefore must esteem it a very small thing to be judged by man. I have long valued and believed that saying of *Austin* (commonly cited, and found, lib. 3. de Trinit. cap. 6. the very last words) *Contra Rationem nemo sobrius ; Contra Scripturas nemo Christianus ; Contra Ecclesiam nemo pacificus.* In the point of Faiths Instrumentality, and the nature of the Justifying act, which I differ from you in, I am constrained upon all these three grounds to my dissent. 1 Lest by renouncing my Reason, I should cease to be sober. (Though yet I think sober men may be contrary minded, not seeing these Reasons). 2. Lest by forsaking the Scripture, I should cease

cease to be a Christian, (Though Christians that observe not, or understand not that the Scripture is against you in this, may judge as you). 3. Lest by contradicting the Church, I should cease to be peaceable ('Though men otherwise peaceable may be drawn to it through prejudice). If you will bring one sound Reason, one word of Scripture, or one approved writer of the Church (yea or one Heretick, or any man whatsoever) for many hundred years after Christ (I think I may say 1300 at least) to prove that Christ as Lord or King is not the object of the Justifying act of Faith, or that Faith Justifieth properly as an Instrument, I am contented so far to lose the Reputation of my Reason, Understanding, Reading, and Memory. For though I have not read all that hath been written for so many hundred years, yet I have read most of the Writers of great note, (except the most Voluminous, which I took but part of) and by that much, I see so far into the sense and language of those times, that I dare stand to the hazard of this adventure. I speak this because you tell me, that there was scarce a dissenting voice among our Divines that are against me about the Instrumentality of Faith. And if there cannot be brought one man that consenteth with them for 1200, or 1400 years after Christ, I pray you tell me whom a humble, modest, peaceable man should follow, were he never so much ready to deny his own understanding? Because a word or an opinion that is unsound, hath got possession of a little corner of the world for about 150 years; therefore I am suspected as singular and as a Novilist, for forsaking it. Whereas it is to avoid singularity, and notorious Novelty, that I assent not to your way. The same I say about the Interest of mans Obedience, in his Justification as continued and consummate in Judgement. If either *Clemens Roman. Polycarp. Ignatius, Justin Martyr, Irenæus, Tertullian, Origen, Athenagoras, Tatianus, Clem. Alexand. Minutius Felix, Arnobius, Lactantius, Cyprian, Athanasius, Eusebius, Greg. Nazianzen, Epiphanius, Cyrill. Hierosol. Synesius, Cyrill Alexandr. Macarius, Hierome, Salvian, Vincentius Lirin. Vigilius,* or any Councel were of your minde in any one of these points, and against mine; then I will confess, at least my supine negligence in reading, or my very faulty memory in retaining their words. And for *Austin, Chrysost.* and others, of whom I have read but the lesser part, I do strongly conjecture by that part, at their sense, and that they concurr with the rest. If you say that the Fathers had their errors, and all this is but humane judgement, and all men are fallible, I confess all this to be true : But as I still say, that *Contra Ecclesiam nemo pacificus,* so I desire leave to Judge those Brethren that oppose me, as fallible, and subject to error, as all the Primitive Fathers were : and therefore that I may be no more blamed or thought singular for contradicting them, then they are for contradicting the Primitive Church; I know as *Austin* saith *de Civitate Dei, li. 22. c. 30. Servandi gradus erant Divini muneris ; ut primum daretur liberum arbitrium, quo non-peccare posset homo ; novissimum, quo peccare non posset; atque illud ad comparandum meritum ; hoc ad recipiendum præmium pertineret.* And the case of the Intellect being the same, we must stay til this time of Reward be come, before we shall receive our *non-posse errare.* I know no Brother that opposeth me, doth pretend to Infallibility. All that I desire by my far greater advantage of humane Testimony, is but to expugn prejudice, that I may stand on even ground with them that contend with me : And could I but prevail for this, that the cause might be decided by meer Scripture-reason, and humane Authority wholly stand by, and the Reader could but impartially consider things, without being byassed to any *side* or *party,* as if he knew not what any man else doth

doth judge of it, I should then make little doubt of the good issue of the Controversie. The most that I meet with, that explain against my judgement, are they that confess that they know not what it is, or else apprehend it to be what it is not: but whatever it is, some that they value are against it, and that is it that satisfieth them that I am in an error. I do unfeignedly desire that in dark Controversies beyond their reach, the unlearned people would more regard the generality of sober Godly Divines, then any single and singular Teacher; yea though it fall out that he be in the Truth, as long as the Evidence of that Truth is out of their reach. But this may not encourage any to shut their eyes, or to neglect to search after the Evidence which they might discern, much less may it excuse such unfaithfulness in Divines themselves; nor yet may it encourage any to captivate their judgement to a party, against the general judgement of the Church: For if I were on one side, and all the Divines in *England* on the other, there is yet the same reason to prefer all the first Churches, before all them, as there is to prefer all them before me. In a word, I shall ever think him more culpably singular, who differeth from Christ, and his Apostles, and all his Church for 1200 or 1400 years, then he that differeth from any party now living, and differeth not from them forementioned. And how the case stands in this between me, and those Reverend Divines that oppose me, in the foresaid points of difference, I am heartily content to refer to any sober, impartial Reader, that takes not things on trust from others, nor judgeth of the Doctrine of antient writers, by any imperfect dismembred parcels.

Georgius Calixtus, *Epitom. Theolog. Moral.* pag. 463.

INterrogati quae fides nostra, quae doctrina, respondemus eam esse fidem & doctrinam nostram, quam Complectitur symbolum Apostolicum, symbolum Nicaenum, Constantinopolitanum, & Athanasianum, Anathematismi Ephesini: Confessio Chalcedonensis: Quae Nestorianorum & Eutichianorum reliquiis, quinta & sexta synodi opposuerunt: Quae item Pelagianis Africana plenaria, sive ut vocari solet milevitana synodus & Arausicana secunda synodus opposuerunt. Haec symbola haec confessiones & declarationes continent, non modo quae Credere, sine quibus fidem & assensum praebere hominem Christianum oportet, & sine quibus creditis atque cognitis salvari nequit; sed illis, etiam qui haec ipsa docendo tractant, & aliis exponunt ὑποτύπωσιν ὑγιαινόντων λόγων quam teneant praescribunt. Quae autem hisce symbolis confessionibus & declarationibus comprehenduntur è Sacra Scriptura hausta sunt: quippe in iis quae aperte in Scriptura posita sunt inveniuntur illa omnia quae continent fidem moresque vivendi, &c. Denique exercemus nos ad conscientiam habendam sine offensa apud Deum & homines semper.

Lutherus, *referente Hopffnero Saxon. Evangel.* p. 110.

Nihil pestilentius in Ecclesia doceri potest, quam si ea quae necessaria non sunt, necessaria fiant. Hac enim tyrannide conscientiae illaqueantur, & Libertas fidei extinguitur; mendacium pro veritate, Idolum pro Deo, Abominatio pro sanctitate colitur.

I conclude with that of *Rup. Meldenius* elsewhere, once before cited, Paraenes. (citante C. Bergio) F. 2.

Verbo dicam: si nos servaremus, in Necessariis Unitatem; in Non-necessariis Libertatem, in Utriisque charitatem, optimo certe loco essent res nostrae. Ita fiat. Amen.

FINIS.

THE REDUCTION OF A DIGRESSOR:

OR

Rich. Baxter's

REPLY

TO

Mr *George Kendall's*

DIGRESSION

in his BOOK againſt

Mr *GOODWIN.*

Job 42.3. *Who is he that hideth Counſel without Knowledge? Therefore have I uttered that I underſtood not, things too wonderfull for me, which I knew not.*

Rom. 11.33. *O the depth of the riches both of the wiſdom and knowledge of God! how unſearchable are his judgements, and his waies paſt finding out!*

Nam quomodo intellectu Deum capit homo, qui ipium intellectum ſuum, quo Eum vult capere, nondum capit? *Auguſtin. de Trinitate, l. 5. c. 1.*

LONDON,

Printed by *A. M.* for *Thomas Underhill*, at the Anchor and Bible in *Pauls* Church-yard near the little North-door, and *Francis Tyton*, at the three Daggers in Fleetſtreet near *Dunſtans* Church. 1654.

REDUCTION
OF A
DIGRESSOR:
OR
Rich. Baxter's
REPLY
TO
Mr George Kendalls
DIGRESSION
in his Books against
Mr GOODWIN, &c.

Nazianzen. *Orat.* 29. *pag.* 493. Edit. Morelli.

Ἐι δὲ πολυπραγμονεῖς ὃσ γέννησιν καὶ πνεύματος πρόοδον, &c.

Quod si in filii generatione & Spiritus processione pervestiganda curiosum te præbes, ego quoq; pari curiositate tuam animæ corporisq; conjunctionem & temperamentum inquiram: Quomodo pulvis es, & Dei Imago? Quid est quod te moveat? aut quid quod moveatur? Quomodo idem movet & movetur? Quomodo sensus in eodem manet, & externa attrahit? Quomodo mens in te manet, & in alia mente sermonem gignit? Quo modo cogitatio per sermonem impertitur? Nondum majora profero; Quæ cæli conversio? quis syderum motus, & ordo? aut modus? quæ conjunctio aut distantia? qui maris termini? unde venti profluant? unde partim anni revolutiones, aut pluviarum effusiones? Si nihil horum intellectu percepisti, ô homo, (percipies autem fortasse aliquando cum perfectionem consecutus fueris & ut conjicere possimus ea quæ nunc cernimus, non veritatem ipsam esse, sed quædam duntaxat veritatis simulachra) si teipsum non nosti, quisquis es qui de his rebus disputas, si hæc nondum intellectu comprehendisti, quorum sensus ipse testis est, quo tandem modo Quid, & Quantus sit Deus, te certò tenere ac scire arbitraris? Magnæ profectò id stultitiæ est. Quocirca siquid mihi obtemperas, hoc est Theologo minimè audaci, ut nonnulla jam percepisti, ita ea quæ sumanent percipias, roga, precibusq; contende. Ea parte quæ in te manet contentus esto: reliqua in supernis thesauris recondita maneat. Per vitæ probitatem ascende: per purgationem, eum qui purus est adipiscere. Vis Theologus aliquando fieri, ac divinitate dignus? Mandata serva: per Dei precepta incede (actio enim gradus est ad contemplationem) ex corpore operam animæ nava. An quisquam est mortalium qui ad eam sublimitatem efferri possit, ut ad Pauli mensuram perveniat? At ille tamen videre se per speculum & ænigma dicit, tempusque affore, quo facie ad faciem visurus sit; sis tu licet aliis in Disputando sublimior: at Deo haud dubie inferior es. Sis licet aliis fortasse acutior & perspicacior: at certe veritate tanto posterior es, quanto essentia Dei essentiam tuam antecellit] See the rest to the end.

Idem

Idem Naz. *Orat.* 34. *pag.* 538, 539.

Θεὸν νοῆσαι μὲν χαλεπὸν φράσαι δὲ ἀδύνατον, &c. *Deum intellectu percipere difficile est, eloqui autem impossibile, ut prophanorum Theologorum* * *quidam docuit, meo quidem judicio non incallidè; nempe ut ex eo quod intellectu difficilem affirmat, opinionem hominibus afferat, se eum cognitione percepisse. Ex eo autem quod nullis verbis eum explicari posse ait, hoc agat ne inscitia sua prodi atque convinci queat. Ego vero ita potius dicendum censeo* [*Dei naturam nullis quidem verbis explicari posse; animo autem atque intellectu comprehendi multo minus posse, Nam quod quis animo atque ratione complexus fuerit, id quoque fortasse sermone declarare queat, si non satis dilucide atque perspicue, at saltem obscure, modò auditorem nactus sit non omnino surdum, tardiq; & stupidi ingenij. At rem tantam animo comprehendere omnino impossibile est, non modo ignavis & languidis, deorsumque vergentibus, sed magnis etiam & excelsis viris, Deique amore præditis, ac mortalibus peraque omnibus, quibus ad veri cognitionem, caligo hæc & carnis crassities tenebras offundit. Atque haud scio an hoc quoque sublimioribus illis & intelligentibus naturis negatum sit, quæ quia Deo propius junctæ sunt, ac toto suo splendore collucent, cernere utiq; fortasse queant, si non prorsus, at certe pleniùs quam nos & solidius, atq; aliæ aliis, pro cujusq; ordine, vel uberius, vel parcius.*

* *Plato* is the man he means. Note that proud Heathens confess a difficulty, but humble Christians an impossibility.

Nec vero hæc verba ita accipi velim, quasi percipi non posse dicam, Quod sit Deus: sed Quid & Quale sit. Neq; enim inanis est prædicatio nostra, nec vana fides nostra; nec id est quod astruimus (ne rursus id quod probè candidèque diximus, in impietatis & calumniæ argumentum trahas, ac nobis ut ignorantiam confitentibus, arroganter insultes.) Plurimum namq; interest, certò tibi persuadeas, aliquid esse, an Quid tandem illud sit compertum habeas. Etenim Quod Deus sit, ac Princeps quædam causa, quæ res omnes procreavit, atq; conservet, tum oculi ipsi, tum Lex naturalis docet, &c. *Ac nimis profectò hebes ac stolidus est, quisquis non hucusq; sponte sua progreditur, naturaliumq; demonstrationum vestigiis insistit, atq; adeo hoc sibi persuadet, Ne id quidem Deum esse, quod vel imagine quadam animi concepimus, vel informavimus, vel orationis penicillo utcunq; descripsimus. Quod siquis unquam cogitatione Deum quoquo modo comprehendit, quonam obsecro argumento id probabit?* &c.

Pag.

Pag. 548. *Quid tandem Deus natura sua & essentia sit, nec hominum quisquam unquam invenit, nec invenire potest. An verò aliquando sit inventurus, quærat hoc, qui volet, ac perscrutetur.*

Pag. 556. Having heaped up many intricacies and insuperable difficulties about the creatures, he addes [*Possuntne hoc expedire Physici, atq; inanis eruditionis laude celebres, ac vere cyatho mare, hoc est, res tantas ingenio suo metientes?*]

I intreat the capable Reader to peruse the rest of that excellent Oration in the Author.

I cite these passages 1. If it were possible to perswade poor mortals that we are no Gods, nor should aspire as did the father of sinners; and therefore that we have less knowledge of Gods Essence and nature, then the vain Disputers called Schoolmen have long pretended to. 2. That hereby the matter of the Churches contentions being removed, our wounds may close again. For who knoweth not, how many curious and vain, though much applauded Volumes, are all built upon the sands of some presumptuous supposition of the Nature of God ? If they did not take it for granted that God doth properly *Understand* and *Will*, and properly *Intendere finem*, with many the like, what matter could they have for their Voluminous contentions ? If but only those two suppositions were known to be (at least) uncertain, what should we do with all those Learned Writings that so subtilly Dispute of the order and number of Gods Decrees ? and how should we esteem them ? He that will reade the *Augustane* Confession, may see what thoughts the first Protestants had of the Controversies about Predestination, and how little of that doctrine did enter their Religion.

Vide Eusebium *Præparat. Evangelic. lib. undecimo, cap.* 12.
Where he affirms that *Moses* and all the Prophets teach that Gods Nature cannot be explicated by words, and that his Name is ineffable, and how *Plato* agreeth with them.

As also *cap.* 9. where he makes the very Name *Ens* proper to God, and alledgeth *Plato*'s consent, and *cap.* 10. the consent of *Numenius*, and *cap.* 11. the consent of *Plutarch*.

Also *lib.* 8. *cap.* 8. *pag.* (*mihi*) 365. out of *Josephus* he citeth this, [That God is the *Beginning*, the *Middle*, the *End* of all things, and as he is in Works and Benefits conspicuous, yea of all things by far the most notable (or known) so is he both in Nature and Greatness most obscure: Nothing that is like him (or no likeness of him) can be seen of us, or imagined by us; nay it is not lawfull so much as lightly to frame it (such a resemblance) in our mindes.]

Novatianus (*nondum lapsus*) lib. 1. *de Trinitate inter opera* Tertulliani, *cap.* 7.

Sed tamen & ipse (Christus) sic adhuc de Deo loquitur hominibus quomodo possunt adhuc audire, vel capere: licet in agnitionem Dei religiosam jam facere incrementa nitatur: Invenimus enim scriptum esse quod Deus charitas dictus sit; nec ex hoc tamen Dei substantia charitas expressa est. Et quod Lux dictus est, nec tamen in hoc substantia Dei est; Sed totum hoc de Deo dictum est quantum dici potest; ut merito & quando spiritus dictus est, non omne id quod est dictus est, sed ut dum mens hominum intelligendo usq; ad ipsum proficit spiritum, conversa jam ipsa in spiritu aliud quid amplius per spiritum conjicere, Deum esse possit. Id enim quod est, secundum id quod est, nec humano sermone edici, nec humanis auribus percipi, nec humanis sensibus colligi potest. *Nam si qua praparavit Deus his qui diligunt illum, nec oculus vidit, nec auris audivit, nec cor hominis, aut mens ipsa percepit, qualis & quantus est ille ipse, qui hac repromittit, ad qua intelligenda & mens hominis & natura defecit.*

This is one note by which it is known not to be *Tertullian*'s writing, because *Tertullian* grosly erred in making God too like the creature, as is well known.

The like passages you may reade, *in* Ruffini *Exposit. in Symbolum Apostolor, Sect.* 4, 5, 6, 8. with several difficulties proposed in things about our selves, to convince us of our ignorance.

Author de Cardinalibus operibus Christi inter opera Cypriani *Prolog.* §. 3. p. 482.

Nec patitur ad liquidum se videri Divinitas, quam utiq; investigatio, fidelis aliquo modo adorat vel sentit: sed puram ejus essentiam nec conspicit, nec comprehendit: Affirmatio quippe de Dei essentia in promptu haberi non potest; neq; enim disinibilis est Divinitas; sed
verius

verius sinceriusq; remotio indicat, negando quid non sit, quam Afferendo quid sit. Quoniam quicquid sensui subjacet, illud esse non potest quod omnem superat intellectum. Quicquid audiri, vel videri vel sciri potest, non convenit majestati; hebes est in hac consideratione omnis acies sensuum & caligat aspectus.—— p. 483. §. 8. Et utinam me ipsum cognoscam & sciam! Quod si anima mea quæ corporis mei obtinet principatum, nec originem scio, nec metior quantitatem, nec qualis sit intueri sufficio, si ignota est mihi ratio quare ipsa delectetur in corpore persecutore suo, &c. patienter me ferre oportet si operatorem universitatis non intelligo, qui in minimis operationum suarum particulis meam profiteor cæcitatem.

Reade the rest of that Prologue excellently, shewing how far God is known, and how far not.

Synesius *de Regno*, pag. 8, 9. *Edit.* Petavianæ.

Nullum unquam nomen inventum est quod Dei naturam assequeretur, sed cum ab ea exprimenda homines aberrarent, per ea quæ ab illo fiebant, ipsum attingere conati sunt; sive ergo Patrem, conditorem, sive aliud quidpiam dixeris, sive Principium, sive causam, hæc omnia respectus quidam sunt, & ad ea quæ ob illo oriuntur comparationes. Eodem modo Regem si apelles ab iis quorum Rex est, non a propria persona naturam illius apprehendere conaberis. Venio jam ad reliqua ejus nomina, &c. Bonum utiq; Deum omnes, tam sapientes quam imperiti homines ubiq; celebrant, &c. Nondum tamen hoc ipsum Bonum *quantumvis extra contextionem positum, Dei in natura sua stabilitatem declarat: ex iis vero quæ posteriora sunt corrogatur. Nec enim* Boni *nomen, absolutum quidauribus sonat, sed illud* Bonum *quorum efficax est, quiq; eo fini possunt, &c. Vide reliq. ib.*

Cyrillus, *Hierosol. Catechef.* 6. pag. 46, 47, 48. is large on this.

Dicimus non quæ oportet de Deo; nam ei soli hac nota sunt: Sed quæ pro suo modulo capere natura humana potest, & quæ imbecillitas nostra ferre valet. Non enim Quid sit Deus exponimus: Nam candide nos accuratam de eo cognitionem non habere confitemur. Quam ignorantiam agnoscentes, magnam de Deo cognitionem profitemur.—— At dicet quispiam, Si comprehendi nequit essentia Divina, quid est quod tu de his enarras? &c. Laude Dominum decorare, non exprimere verbis aggredior, &c. Quid igitur, dicet aliquis, nonne scriptum est quod Angeli

Angeli cælorum vident semper faciem patris mei qui in cælis est? At vident Angeli non sicut Deus est, sed quatenus ipsi capere possunt, &c. Cum igitur Angeli nesciant, nullus homo suam erubescat inscitiam, & ignorantiam confiteri, tum ego qui nunc loquor, tum omnes omnium temporum homines. Quin etiam quomodo enunciare non possumus: Nam quomodo possem eum verbis exprimere, qui ipse dedit ut verba promam? Ego qui Animam habeo nec ejus formam lineamentave possum exprimere, quomodo conservatorem animæ enunciare potero?

Cyrillus Alexandr. *To.1.Thesaur.li.*11.*c.*1. Especially near the end, is full for the same as the former cited Authors, as he doth in divers other places. And in Commentary on *John* among *Cyrill's* Works, but indeed *Clictoveus*, it is frequent. As *li.*1.*c.*13. *Nam quemadmodum quamvis nullus novit quidnam secundum naturam Deus sit, Justificatur tamen per fidem quum credat præmia illum redditurum quærentibus eum: sic etsi operum ejus rationem ignorat, quum tamen fide omnia illum posse non dubitet, non contemnenda tamen probitatis hujus præmia consequetur.*

And *li.*9.*c.*34. *Sed nullus naturæ Deitatis capax intellectus est. Ac ideo furiosus est qui audet temeraria scrutatione rimari quidnam Deus secundum naturam est. Umbris tamen & ænigmatibus ut in speculo,* &c.

Augustin. *de Trinitat.* reproves three sorts of Errours about God, in the entrance, *lib.*1.*cap.*1. 1. Those that judge of spiritual things by corporeal. The second is those *Qui secundum humani animi naturam vel affectum de Deo sentiunt, siquid sentiunt.* 3, Those that do indeed endeavour to transcend the mutable creature that they may raise their intention to God, *sed mortalitatis onere prægravati, eum & videri volunt scire quod nesciunt, & quod volunt scire non possum, præsumptiosis opinionum suarum audacius affirmando, intercludunt sibimet intelligentiæ vias, magis eligentes sententiam suam non corrigere perversam, quam mutare defensam,* &c. *Quæ vero proprie de Deo dicuntur, quanquam in nulla creatura inveniuntur, raro ponit Scriptura Divina,* &c.

Clemens

Clemens Alexandr. *Stromat. li. 5.* commends *Plato* for saying that God cannot be expressed by words, as agreeing with Scripture; and himself addeth that he is neither *Genus, Species, differentia, individuum, numerus, accidens, nec cui aliquid accidit, totum, pars,* &c. *Et ideo est figura expers, & quod nominari non potest. Et si aliquando eum nominemus,* non proprie *vocantes aut Unum, aut Bonum, aut Mentem, aut ipsum id quod est, aut Patrem, aut Deum, aut Creatorem, aut Dominum: non id dicimus tanquam nomen ejus proferentes, sed propter ejus potestatem pulchris utimur nominibus, ut in aliis non aberrans, his inniti possit cogitatio,* &c. I use *Hervetus* translation.

Irenæus *li.* 2. *cap.* 16.
Est autem & super hæc & propter hæc inenarrabilis: sensus enim capax omnium bene & recte dicetur, sed non similis hominum sensui: Et lumen rectissime dicetur; sed nihil simile ei, quod est secundum nos lumini. Si autem est in reliquis hominibus, nulli similis erit omnium pater hominum pusillitati: & dicitur quidem secundum hæc propter dilectionem, sentitur autem super hæc secundum magnitudinem.

Justin Martyr *Serm. ad Gent. exhort.*
Intellexit (Plato) *Deum non indicasse illi* (Mosi) *nomen suum proprium. Nullum enim potest Deo convenire proprie.*
Idem *Apolog.* 1. *Pro Christian. Universorum Pater nullum nomen habet inditum: Pater enim, Deus, Creator, Dominus, Herus, non nomina sunt, sed a beneficentia desumpta vocabula,* &c. *Sicut &* Dei *vocabulum non tam nomen est, quam inenarrabilis rei hominibus innata opinio.*
Idem *Apol.* 2. *Quis enim potest dicere quodnam sit nomen ineffabile? quod nemo nisi deplorate insanus proferre tentaret.*

I conclude from all this, that either it is certain that *Intelligere, Velle, Amare, Intendere,* &c. are not spoken of God Properly, or by Analogy of Attribution (as they speak) or at least, that it is utterly uncertain to us, whether it be so or not: But that we must use

use both these and lower notions of God, from the glass of mans nature and actions, still confessing the Impropriety in all, and that we have no positive formall certain apprehension of the thing expressed (*viz.* God and his acts) but only a general apprehension that it is somewhat which is best represented to us in the glass of these metaphorical Notions, which contain as great a likeness to the thing it self as we are now capable of reaching; and upon these considerations we must stick close to the Scripture phrase which condescendeth so low in speaking of God; and not hearken to the unproved fancies of Schoolmen, that tell us *This act* is properly in God, as implying no imperfection, and *That is* not seeing all humane acts do contain imperfection in their very formall nature.

As *Salvian de Provid. li.*3. *p.*62,63. saith, so, *à fortiore*, do I: *Nescio secretum, & consilium Divinitatis ignoro. Sufficit mihi ad causa hujus probationem dicti cælestis oraculum. Si scire vis quid tenendum sit, habes literas sacras: perfecta ratio est hoc tenere quod legeris. Qua causa autem Deus hæc de quibus loquimur, ita faciat, nolo a me requiras. Homo sum, non intelligo secreta Dei; investigare non audeo, & ideo etiam attentare formido: quia & hoc ipsum genus quasi sacrilegæ temeritatis est, si plus scire cupias, quam sinaris,* &c. *Sicut enim plus est Deus quam omnis ratio humana, sic plus mihi debet esse quam ratio, quod a Deo agi cuncta cognosco.*

Οὐτε γὰρ φύσεως τῆς θεότητ{Θ}· ἐςιν ἡ ψυχὴ, &c. saith *Macarius* Homil.1. *Neq; enim Natura Divina est Anima*(therefore Intellection and Volition are not the Divine Nature) *neq; Natura tenebrarum malitiæ; sed est quid creatum, sensibile, visibile, insigne & admirandum, atque elegans similitudo & Imago Dei.*] Intellection and Volition are in their natures comprehensible, but that which in God we call Intellection and Volition is incomprehensible, and not to be formally understood. *Quis enim potest capere quantus sit Deus?* (saith *Theophylact* in *Luc.*12.) *& manifestum est ex Seraphin, qui se obtegunt propter excellentiam Divini luminis.* Which is as true of Gods Essence as his Greatness: and as true is it of formall proper intellection, as *Minutius Fælix* saith of Vision, *Deum oculis carnalibus vis videre, cum ipsam animam tuam quâ vivificaris & loqueris, nec aspicere possis, nec tueri?*

Epipha-

Epiphanius disputing against those honest Hereticks, called the *Audians* (cast out of the Church by the Bishops for their honesty, and at last banished.) *Hæref.* 70. *pag.* 815, 816. speaking against those that placed the Image of God in the Soul only (as the *Audians* did place it in the Body) because, say they, the soul is Invisible, and hath the Power of Acting, Moving, Understanding, Reasoning, and therefore contains the Image of God, he Answereth, That [If therefore the soul be said to be made to (Gods) Image, it cannot be said to be made after his Image at all: ὁ γὰρ Θεὸς ἐπέκεινα μυει- ευταπλάσιον, &c. *Deus enim Infinitis præ animâ partibus eoq; amplius, comprehensionem omnem ac cogitationem effugit*, &c. *Ipse enim cum omnia comprehendit, tum a nullo comprehenditur.*] And after [*Spiritus enim Deus est qui omnem spiritum exuperat, & lux luce omni præstantior. Quicquid enim ab ipso conditum est, infra illius decus & gloriam est. Sola vero Trinitas comprehendi non potest, & infinitam quandam gloriam obtinet, quæ nec conjecturâ capitur, nec Intelligentiâ percipitur.*

   I conclude with the words of *Colvius in Beverovic. de Termino Vitæ*, pag. 160, 163, 164. [*Non Intelligitis quomodo Intelligatis, centum Syllogismos facitis & nescitis quomodo: & vultis Intelligere quomodo ille Intelligit qui est supra omnem intellectum?* &c.] [*Quod si exigua hæc & contemptibilia naturæ penetrare non potest humani ingenii acies, annon est extremæ impudentiæ nos velle pertingere ad ipsam Divinam essentiam? Quæ est* ἀπερίληπτος, ἀόειστος, ἀτελής *in seipsa, nobis vero* ἀκατάληπτος, ἄγνωστος, ᾗ ὑπεράγνωστος, &c. *Non terminatur visu, non tenetur tactu, non sentitur incessu, non comprehenditur Intellectu; Major omni corde, major omni laude.*——*Novi homines, bulla nascentes & evanescentes*, &c. *exhaurire vultis mare vasculo? terram metiri palmo?* &c. *Furor est cogitare homuncionem videre Dei fines, qui suos non videt, Deum velle metiri qui suam mensuram ignorat, ut capiat Divinitatis terminos quos non capit ipse mundus; cujus vix Imago est spiritus, cujus umbra mundus, judicia abyssus.*——*Deum laudare omnes possumus & debemus, definire nemo potest: Non potest Deus quæri nimis; inveniri nunquam potest, digne ipsum æstimamus cum inæstimabilem confitemur: digne laudamus cum præstupore animi in silentio ipsum adoramus; apprehendi potest voluntate, comprehendi non potest intel-*

intellectu. Major est ipsius Incomprehensibilitas quam comprehendere possumus: Non ita capit eum arguta scientia, quam illum sentit & gustat munda conscientia: Melius nos docet eum Unctio quam eruditio. Hoc est illud manna absconditum, quod ipse dat timentibus ipsum, non autem iis qui in arcana illius temere involant. Et idcirco veniunt indocti & qui Deum summa cum reverentia colunt, & rapiunt regnum cælorum; interim acutissima & superbissima ingenia evanescunt, in propriis subtilitatibus, & merguntur in infernum: loqui volentes de profundis mersi sunt in profundis.-----Quocirca optime bonas horas collocant, qui veritatem summo studio quærunt: Sed pessime judicant qui se illam invenisse putant.-----Desino, & dico cum Hilario, quod non per difficiles quæstiones ad vitam beatam nos ducat Deus.

The Lord repair by Love, Humility and Holy Obedience, the ruines that have long been made in his Church, by Contention, Pride, and unsanctified-presumptuous-ignorant-Learning, and reduce men to the Scripture simplicity of Doctrine, and convince them that their *overmuch* Wisdom is but Folly, and all their *over-doing* but *undoing*.

THE

THE CONTENTS.

§. 1.
The Prologue to M[r] K. — Pag. 1.

§. 2.
M[r] K's stumbling at the threshold. — 3

§. 2.
Whether it be true that D[r] Twiss means not that the Immanent act may be stiled Justification. — 4

§. 2.
M[r] Pemble's words of Justification at Christs death. — 6

§. 3.
M[r] K. confesseth that I affirm not the novelty of Immanent acts in God, and yet chooseth me to Dispute against on the Point. — 6

§. 3.
A free and full Discovery of my own Opinion in that Point. — 7, 8

§. 4.
The Reasons of my mentioning D[r] Twiss as I did: and whether I be guilty of sleighting him: or M[r] K. rather of sleighting the Assembly. — 11, 12

§. 5.
M[r] K's great Argument against new Immanent acts in God, examined. Whether it be certain to us that God hath no Immanent act but of Understanding or Will? A recitall of some Reasons of those that hold new Immanent acts of Understanding in God: with my thoughts of them. Also about the acts of Will. More of their Reasons recited to prove the newness of Immanent acts, or at least the Necessity or Conveniency of Denominating them as New, from the newness of the object. It is as consistent with Gods Eternity and Immutability to have New acts, as with his simplicity to have divers acts: yet must we conceive of his Willing and Nilling and Understanding as divers, or at least so denominate them. — 15, 29

§. 6. & 7.
An Examination of Mr K's Doctrine of Analogy.   30, 36
§. 7. & 8.
Whether Intellection and Volition be ascribed to God by Analogy of Attribution, as Mr K. affirms?   37, 39
§. 9.
The true Analysis and sense of my words which Mr K. opposeth.   40, 41
§. 10, 11, 12.
Whether an Act be properly an Effect?   42, 43
§. 13.
Whether Mr K. speak truly, when he saith [Neither doth it (action) carry that stile (of an effect) in any of these Learned Sophies, &c.]   44, 45
§. 15.
Gods acts no Accidents. Acts inhere not in a subject.   47
§. 16.
Whether Gods Immanent acts have any other Terms then their objects.   48
§. 17.
Whether the difference assigned by Mr K. between Gods Immanent and Transient acts, be as clear as between heaven and earth. And whom I meant in that Question Whether Immanent acts be any more Eternal then Transient?.   49
§. 17.
An Answer to Mr K's 150. 154. pages against Mr Goodwin.   50, 51, 52
§. 18, 19.
The Answers that some make to Mr K's Arguments against the newness of Immanent acts.   53, 54, 55
§. 19.
Whether the ground of such new acts as ascribed be in God or the creature.   55, 57
§. 20.
How ungroundedly Mr K. chargeth me with contending with Dr Twiss and all sober Divines that ever were worthy to speak to a School Point.   58
§. 21.
Whether it be not from the respect to the object that Gods Essence is called Knowledge, or the Knowledge of this or that.   59

Whether

§. 22.
Whether it be all one to know the futurity and the existence of things. 60

§. 23.
M^r K's unworthy fastening on me Words of his divising. 61

§. 24.
An example shewing that Immanent and Transient acts, are of the same nature. 62

§. 25.
M^r K's Answer to the instance of the Sunnes not being changed by objects, is partly Lusory, partly yieldeth the Cause, and partly Erroneous. 63

§. 26.
M^r K's Exceptions about the similitude of a Glasse, refelled. 64,65,66

§. 27.
A Recapitulation of what I have said on this Subject. 67

§. 27.
The great incapacity of man to comprehend the nature and acts of God. 68,69

§. 27.
Rob. Baronius Testimony about Mutation of Immanent acts. And some Scripture Testimony. 72,73

§. 29.
M^r K's second undertaking to little purpose: contrary to the former: and how ill performed. 77

§. 29.
Justification or Remission, not from Eternity. 78,79

§. 29.
M^r K's Reasons to prove Gods Decree to have somewhat like Justification, do as much prove it to have somewhat like Sanctification and Glorification. 80,84

§. 29.
M^r K's Antinomian doctrine, false, that [being justified in Gods sight, is when he makes us to see, or makes it evident to our sight that we are justified.] 85

§. 29.
The boldness and falsness of Mr K. affirmation, that [to Will to Will, was never heard of.] 86

Seven

§. 29.
Seven Arguments proving that the Elicite acts of the Will, may be the object of the Will.   87

§. 29.
Six several cases wherein I finde that I Will the acts of my own Will.   88

§. 29.
Its untrue, that [he that Wils to Will, Wils no more then he doth already.]   ib.

§. 30.
Mr K's doctrine, that [the Decree to Remit sin, carries in it a Remission of them tantamount] is tantamount downright Antinomianism.   89

§. 30.
Ten mischievous consequents of this Doctrine (and so of Justification from Eternity.)   90

§. 30.
Sin may be charged on us before we believe, for all Gods Decree to pardon it.   90, 91

§. 30.
Mr K's Antinomian doctrine, that [there is no danger of suffering for sin, where God decreeth to Remit it] confuted by many arguments: It maketh Christs blood, to have saved us from no danger, and God never to have freed us from danger, &c.   92

§. 30.
Chastisement a species of Punishment.   ib.

§. 31.
What is the Acceptance, which Mr K. makes the object of Gods Decree.   93

§. 34.
Pardon distinguished and defined.   96

§. 34.
Mr K's desperate language, calling the act of the Law of grace or promise [An odde empty, moral, action] and that [by the promulgation of it, God doth as improperly give us Christ, or disable the Law to condemn us.]   98

§. 35.
Mr K's admirable doctrine that [the Covenant justifieth by such an act as Quantitas hath faciendo Quantum, or Paternitas faciendo patrem, viz. informing.   100

His

§. 35.
His profound Notion, that the Covenant justifieth but Aptitudinaliter.
101

§. 35.
The Covenant pardoneth immediately, our faith being but a condition, and not a cause.
ib.

§. 36.
M^r K's horned Argument answered [*God justifies by the Covenant All, or Some*, &c.]
103

§. 37.
M^r K's desperate Conclusion, that [*thus a man wisely justifies himself by beleeving, and more a great deal then the Covenant by promising, or God by promulgating it.*]
104

§. 38.
His further desperate Doctrine [*Just so (as* Adam *brought death into the world rather then God) in the new Covenant, Believe and be justified. Who Justifies the Believer, God or himself?*]
106

§. 39, 40, 41, 42.
Much more to the same purpose, vainly intended to prove that I make man his own justifier.
107

§. 42.
Mr K. saith, the Judge who pronounceth the sentence, or the Law, do not so properly condemn a malefactour as himself: Therefore so the Believer justifieth himself.
108

§. 43.
Whether M^r K's Client be ingeniously instructed, who being saved from the Gallows by his Book, saith, [Grammercy *to my Reading more then to the courtesie of the Law.*]
109

§. 44.
The falsehood of M^r K's Consequence, that [*he that performs the condition makes the grant become Absolute,*] *if it become so on his performance.*
110

§. 45, 46.
He unworthily intimates that I deny faith to be a real effect of God on the soul: saying, he will prove it against me, and pretending to force me to confess it.
111

§. 46.
He falsly affirms that I deny Habits distinct from the soul.
112

§. 47.
About the instrumentality of faith: the untruth of his first Answer,
b
and

and non-sense or worse of the second.) ib.
§. 48.
Mr K. saith, §. 47. [*I shall make it appear to be both Gods instrument and mans in some sense*] and §. 48. he saith [*I do not say it is (Gods Instrument) properly.*] 113

§. 49.
Mr K. untruly saith, [*Faith is as much Gods Instrument as the new Covenant*] *and gives an ill description of faith, as his reason.* ib.

§. 50.
His next Reason nothing to the purpose. 114

§. 51.
His ill explication of Gods Justification by faith, viz. [*declaring hereby the righteousness of Christ to be his own.*] 115

§. 51.
He strangely affirms, that [*man is the Subject, not the Authour of his own act of believing.*] ib.

§. 52, 53.
He makes man his own justifier. 116

§. 53.
He odly saith [*Faith hath a proper causality upon our Justification passively taken, that is, upon our receiving the Righteousness of Christ.*] 117

§. 54.
He confesseth that [*it is needless to say, Faith is a passive Instrument.*] 118

§. 54.
He dangerously saith [*Faith doth help the action of the principal agent, that is, God in our Justification.*] ib.

§. 54.
More of his false Accusation refelled. 119

§. 56.
He makes justifying faith to be an Action which is Virtually a Passion, and that is, A suffering our selves to be led by the Spirit of God, and his authority, against the suggestions of our own reason. 120

§. 56.
But proves the Instrumentality by silence. ib.

§. 57.
His instrument of Receiving no proper Instrument, as being no efficient. 121

Moral

§. 58.
Moral instruments have a Moral action. ib.

§. 59.
How ill Mr K. makes a jest of the Instrumentality of Christs Covenant or Testament. 122

§. 60.
Mr K's unanswerable arguing wherein he vanquisheth me. 123

§. 61.
When I am proving that [the act of faith is not the Instrument of Justification] He confutes me by saying, Faith is a Habit. 124

§. 61.
The reason why I will not contend with them that only call faith, the instrument of Receiving Christ. ib.

§. 62.
Divines affirming commonly, that It is the act of faith, and not the Habit that justifieth, do thereby overthrow their own doctrine of faiths proper Instrumentality in justifying. 125

§. 62.
Mr K. first feigns me to call the Habit of faith a sanctified faculty, and then very gravely Schools me for it. 126

§. 62.
About the Real Identity of the soul, its faculties, holiness. ib.

§. 63.
The Unreasonableness of Mr K's impatiency. 128

§. 64.
How Mr K. can call [Faith a Habit, equivalent to a new faculty.] 129

§. 64.
Dr Twisse's Arguments to prove that faith or other grace is no new power. 130

§. 64.
Faith is truly A moral power, that is, A Habit or Disposition, without which we shall not be true believers. 131

§. 64.
Mr K's dead doctrine, that [Without faith a man can no more do ought towards receiving Christ, then a dead man can walk or speak.] ib.

§. 64.
The vanity of his arguing for faiths instrumental justifying, from its [Giving life to the soul in all spiritual operations.] 132

§. 65.
More of the weakness of his arguings about receiving Christ, manifested.   133

§. 66.
The end of Mr K's undertaking, considered. Whether I unworthily handled Dr Twiss and Mr Pemble? An acknowledgement of all that Deficiency that Mr K. doth tanto molimine *prove me guilty of.*   134

§. 67.
Mr K. concludeth before he hath done his main task, which so oft promised, viz. To tell us what is the Transient-justifying-act of God.   137

§. 67.
A conjecture at his sense. He destroyeth his Cause unawares: Strangely mistakes the nature of a Condition.   138

§. 67.
Justification by faith, in Scripture sense, is not in foro conscientiæ.   139

§. 67.
Gods giving faith is not his immediate justifying act, proved.   141

§. 67.
Arguments proving that it is in Law-sense (commonly called Sententia Legis) *that we are first justified by Faith, and so the Moral act of the Law is Gods immediate justifying act.*   141, 142

§. 68.
The Conclusion.   143

The

The Prologue to M[r] K.

Sir,

Though I would not have you restrained from revealing Truth, yet if I had been worthy to have been of your counsell, I should have advised you to have avoided this quarrelsom way. Our world hath *Contention* enough already; and it comes not from so good a root (*Prov.*13.10.) nor is it so good a symptom, nor doth it produce such lovely effects (*Prov.*22.10. & 17.19, & 19.21.) nor doth it bring to good a name (*Prov.* 21.24.) as may make it seem desirable in my eyes. Had you consulted *Solomon* himself, he would have bid you [*Strive not with a man without a cause, if he have done thee no harm,* Prov.3.30.] and [*Go not forth hastily to strive, lest thou know not what to do in the end thereof, when thy neighbour hath put thee to shame,* 25.8.] for [*The beginning of strife is as when one letteth out water: therefore leave off contention before it be medled with,* 17.14.] It seems a strange thing to me, that you could finde no man to deal with in the main Controversie here chosen out, that was indeed against you, but that you must make to your self, an adversary of one that you confess doth not once deny your Conclusion. Unless it be, because you are likely with such a one to have the easiest conflict. But then you should have remembred, that the Victory will be as small, I pretend not to such a piercing knowledge, nor to such acquaintance in the invisible regions, as to determine infallibly of what Province or Degree, of what quality, *albus an ater*, that spirit was that raised the storm of your Passions, or to know exactly his name and firname, that animated these your lines: But seeing you are pleased to choose me for your adversary, I must desire you to bear with me if I speak sometime less pleasingly; and to use what patience you have left, as knowing you have drawn this trouble upon your self. And whereas you put me on a double imployment: one to defend the Truth; and the other to defend my self; so I perform the first successfully, I hope I may be excused if I be more negligent in the later; yea if I give you the day, and freely confess as much ignorance as you charge me with. It's true that I have not the Titles or Robes of Honour, and as little deserve them, as you here express. But might I be sure that I have right

C to

to that farre better Title (of piety) which you are pleased to bestow on me, I could easily allow you the other. I remember the description of the old Christians by *Minutius Falix*, [*Nos qui non habitu sapientiam, sed mente præferimus; non eloquimur magna, sed vivimus: gloriamur nos consecutos quod illi summa contentione quæsiverunt, nec invenire potuerunt.*] And that of *Mirandula* [*Fælicitatem philosophia quærit, Theologia invenit, Religio possidet.*] And to contend for the reputation of being Learned, I shall scarce think is worth my labour, till I have higher thoughts of the prize. Mens thoughts and words are a poor felicity. Applause is such an aery nourishment, that I see few thrive by! (though I must confess that in me, as well as in others, the unreasonable sin of pride is daily stirring, and convincing me by experience that it is mortified but in part.) O that I may have the honour of being a member of Christ, and then I can spare the vain glory of the world! *Vera ibi gloria erit, ubi laudantis nec errore quisquam, nec adulatione laudabitur: Verus honor qui nulli negabitur digno; nulli deferetur indigno: sed nec ad eum ambiget ullus indignus, ubi nullus permittetur esse nisi dignus:* saith *Austin, de Civit. Dei, li ult. cap. ult.* Only I must crave this of the Reader, that my confessed weakness be no prejudice to Gods truth: and that he will not judge of the cause by the person, nor take the name or person for a fault; which is the thing that the ancient Christians did so deprecate of the Pagans, and therefore I hope every Christian will grant. And I must also desire that want of smooth and pleasing words may not be judged the want of truth. *Enimvero dissoluti est pectoris in rebus seriis quærere voluptatem, & cum tibi sit ratio cum male se habentibus atque ægris, sonos auribus infundere dulciores, non medicinam vulneribus admovere:* inquit *Arnobius li. 1. adv. Gent. p. 49.* I confess I do deeply compassionate ordinary Christians, when I think what a hard thing it is for them to discern the truth, among all the smooth words and plausible arguments of Learned contenders. Usually they think every mans tale good, till they hear the other; and then they think it bad: and at last when they see what fair glosses a Learned man can put on the worst cause, they are ready to run into the other extream, and to believe or regard nothing that they say. As *Minutius Falix* saith, [*Altius movcor de toto genere disputandi: quod plerumque pro differentium viribus & eloquentiæ potestate, etiam perspicua veritatis conditio mutetur: Id accidere pernotum est auditorum facilitate, qui dum verborum lenocinio a rerum intentionibus avocantur, sine delectu assentiuntur dictis omnibus, nec a rectis falsa secernunt, nescientes inesse & in incredibili verum, & in verisimili mendacium. Itaque quo sapius asseverationibus credunt, eo frequentius a peritioribus arguuntur: sic assidue temeritate decepti, culpam judicii transferunt ad incerti querelam, ut damnatis omnibus malint universa suspendere, quam de fallacibus judicare.*] But let such at least hold fast the Foundation, and remember, that we are all agreed in that!

The Reader that I expect should profit by these Writings, must neither be utterly unlearned, nor so learned as your self. For the former are not yet capable of it; and the later are beyond it, and will hardly learn from any but the more learned. It is the younger sort of Students whose edification I intend: who are neither quite above, nor below my instructions; nor so engaged to a Party or Opinion, but that their mindes lye open to any evidence of Truth. *Præventus enim falsæ opinionis errore humanus auditus, ad veri rationem percipiendam, durus & perdifficilis invenitur, quantiscunque testibus urgeatur. Mavult enim pravi dogmatis sententiam, qua semel infectus est, perversus vindicare, quam hanc eandem tantis divinarum humanarumq; legum authoritatibus refutatam salubrius immutare:* inquit Vigilius *contra Eutich. li. 1. initio.*

Lastly,

Lastly, If you should be in the right and I in the wrong in any one Philosophical Controversie, I must expect that the Reader do not thence conclude, that you are right in your Theology. And I could wish that you had so mean thoughts of your Philosophy, as that you might not build your Theology on it too much; nor think much the better of your Writings, or of your self. For doubtless when the Canon of a Council forbad the reading of Heathens Books, these things were not so highly valued as now. I approve not of that extream neither : but shall conclude with that serious exclamation of *Athenagoras* (*Legat. per Christian.* p. 13, 14.) Τίνες ἢ τῶν τοὺς συλλογισμοὺς ἀναλυόντων καὶ τὰς ἀμφιβολίας διαλυόντων, καὶ τὰς ἐτυμολογίας σαφηνιζόντων, ἢ τῶν τὰ ὁμώνυμα καὶ συνώνυμα ᾗ κατηγορήματα καὶ ἀξιώματα, καὶ τί τὸ ὑποκείμενον, καὶ τί τὸ κατηγορούμενον, εὐδαίμονας ἀποτελεῖν, διὰ τούτων καὶ τῶν τοιούτων λόγων ὑπισχνοῦνται τοὺς ζῶντας οὕτως ἐκκεκαθαρμένοι εἰσὶ τὰς ψυχὰς, ὡς ἀντὶ τοῦ μισεῖν τοὺς ἐχθροὺς ἀγαπᾶν, &c.

§. 2.
Pag. 133. Mr K.

For the fuller opening of this particular, I will be content to make some Digression from your Book, and to shew 1. That there can be no new immanent act in God, against Mr Baxter. 2. That there is somewhat like Justification in that immanent act of God, whereby he decrees from eternity to justifie and condemn men. And 3. that yet that immanent act cannot be stiled Justification; nor is it meant so by Dr. Twisse or Mr. Pemble that I know; and so that Justification is not from eternity : and then I shall return to you, &c.

§. 2.
R. B. YOur Digression, methinks, is very sudden, and the occasion to a stranger hardly discernable : Its like it was the uncouth apparition of some ruling wight of another Orb, which made upon your intellect that strange impression, which caused you to reel thus out of your way, and lead you unhappily into this private path, or rather bewildred you in this Maze where we now finde you. But whoever led you in, charity commands me to do my part to help you out, or at least to warn others that they do not follow you.

1. As to your first undertaking, I confess it was very ingenuously done, to say, You will do it [against Mr. *Baxter*] and not [against his doctrine or opinion,] acknowledging afterwards that I deny not your Conclusion. But I am used to Dispute against Doctrines, and not Persons : and therefore will give you the better in this.

2. Your second undertaking is more admirable then the first. For I have met with some besides you that dare adventure on the former, but never man that durst attempt the later. Is it not enough for you to prove Gods Decree of justifying to have somewhat like Justification ? but you must also prove, that the Decree both to justifie and *condemn*, hath somewhat like Justification ? If the Decree to condemn a man have somewhat like justifying him, then the Decree to torment him in hell hath somewhat like glorifying him : and the Decree to kill, hath something in it like quickening him. You must fly to some general point of similitude, or to the Lord *Brookes* doctrine, that all things are One, to make this good. But if it were but your oversight, then I hope hereafter you will be more
com-

compassionate to your Brethren, and no more; so solemnly call men to [see the hand of heaven, in the pompous display of their folly, to appear most ridiculous; and to adore the hand of God in infatuating their parts, &c.] as you do by Mr. *Goodwin* for a smaller mistake then yours. Alas what man so Learned and accurate, as to be free from all oversights.

3. But indeed Sir I cannot so easily excuse your next errour, annexed to the third part of your undertaken-task; where you say [Nor is it so meant by Dr. *Twiß* or Mr. *Pemble* that I know.] What is it that is not so meant by them? Why that this Immanent act can be stiled Justification. You have boldly ventured to write thus: and I will be bold to try how well. Either its true, or not true that they so meant: If true, and undeniably apparent in the Writings of one of them, if not both, and oft repeated by him, and yet Mr. K. knoweth it not, why then he doth not only write before he knows, and Vindicate men before he understand whether they are guilty or innocent, but makes it the great motive of his undertaking, as [not having the patience to see so worthy Divines so unworthily handled.] If in the midst of his impatience he knew not this, then it seems I am not alone ignorant of the businefs that I meddle with. But I will lay it open to the Judgement of the Reader, whether the thing be true, or false? and whether you might not with less learning have known this if you would? and ought not to have known the cause before so zealous a Vindication.

Dr *Twiß Vind.Grat.li.*1. part 2. §.25. p. (*vol.min*) 272, 273. Sic scribit. [*Omnis actualis justificatio est justificatio, & omnis justificatio simpliciter dicta congruenter exponenda est de justificatione actuali. Nam Analogum per se positum stat pro famosiori significato.*] [*Sed libet his pauliſper immorari. Quænam erit illa peccatorum Remissio quæ fidem consequetur; & quam oporteat Spiritus sancto acceptam referre? Remissio enim peccatorum, si quidditatem inspicias, nihil aliud est quam aut Punitionis Negatio, aut Volitionis puniendi negatio. Sit ergo peccata Remittere, nihil aliud quam nolle punire. At hoc nolle punire, ut actus immanens in Deo, fuit ab æterno, nec fidem consequitur,&c. Quod vero operatione Spiritus sancti nobis ex hac parte, per fidem contingit, aliud esse non potest quam sensus gratiæ Dei,* &c. *Quare si quid morte sua*

* Are not Christs *nobis impetrat Christus, quod ad peccatorum nostrorum Remissionem attinet, sensum* * *istum amoris Divini peccata nostra remittentis, nobis impetret necesse est. Et pag.*279. c.1. [*Nam justitia Christi dicitur nobis imputari, & merita ipsius nobis applicari per fidem, non coram Deo, sed apud conscientias nostras: quatenus per fidem generatur in cordibus nostris sensus & agnitio hujus salutaris applicationis ex amore Dei quem ex fide gustamus; & spiritualiter sentimus nos justificantem, & in filios suos adoptantem, ex quo nascitur pax conscientiæ. Quare ante fidem hæc Christi justitia nostra fuit, quatenus ex intentione Dei patris & Christi mediatoris pro nobis præstita,* &c. *Sed adveniente fide quam in cordibus nostris Sp sanctus accendit, tum demum agnoscitur & percipitur hic amor Dei erga nos in Christo Jesu. Unde dicitur justitia Christi imputari nobis per fidem, quia non nisi per fidem dignoscitur a Deo nobis imputari: & tum demum justificari dicimur ejus generis justificatione, atq; absolutione a peccatis nostris, quæ pacem ingenerat conscientiis nostris. Hoc autem duobus argumentis confirmo.* 1. *Quia per ju-stitiam Christi non modo aßequimur remissionem peccatorum, sed & fidem ipsam, atq; resipiscentiam, hoc est, cordis circumcisionem, Eph.*1.3. *ergo etiam ante fidem & resipiscentiam applicatur nobis justitia Christi, utpote propter quam gratiam aßequimur efficacem ad credendum in Christum & agendum pænitentiam. Alterum est, quia justificatio & absolutio, prout significant actum divinæ voluntatis immanentem, sunt ab æterno. Unius*
Merits and the Spirits gifts here highly honoured?

Hujus autem voluntatis notificatio externa, per modum absolutionis cujusdam judicialis & forensis, quæ fit per verbum & spiritum, pro tribunali conscientiæ uniuscujusq;, hæc est illa justitiæ Christi imputatio, itemq; justificatio & remissio atque absolutio quæ fidem consequitur.] Et cont. præfat. p.18.b. Extra controversiam est remissionem peccatorum prout est actus in Deo immanens antecedere nostram fidem & resipiscentiam: Nobis vero non nisi per fidem innotescit, cujus etiam fiducia multo adhuc confirmatior evadit per resipiscentiam.]

Lib.1. Part.2. p.272. [Justificationem vero & Reconciliationem pro eodem haberi ab Arminio (quod & verum est) &c. And he oft maintaineth the eternity of Reconciliation.

Lib.2. P.2. pag.434. [Ergo etiam ante fidem Deus nobis reconciliatus est: neque enim nisi jam reconciliatus & propitius gratificatur nobis fidem. Quid quod remissio peccatorum & acceptatio nostri, Non nisi actus internos & immanentes in Deo notant: cujus generis actiones non suboriuntur Deo de novo.] Lege ult. & postea [Juxta ista distinguere poterimus de reconciliatione dupliciter dicta: Nam & Deus reconciliavit nos sibi in Christo quoad rei veritatem: & in ministris suis posuit verbum reconciliationis, quoad ejusdem pretiosæ veritatis evidentiam & manifestationem. Sic cum inimici essemus dicimur reconciliati fuisse Deo quoad rei veritatem: quod tamen non nisi per Evangelii prædicationem fit quoad ejusdem veritatis patefactionem & salutarem communicationem.] Et p.433. [At Arminius applicationem remissionis peccatorum, ita interpretari videtur, ut per applicationem fiat, & jam quasi de novo esse incipiat: quasi vero non requiratur, ut jam antea existat quod applicandum est Nobis vero sic instituendum videtur. Christus morte sua nobis procuravit redemtionem a peccatis, cum Deo reconciliationem, & peccatorum omnium remissionem; quæ quidem per prædicationem Evangelii & per fidem, nobis applicantur, non ut sint, sed ut nobis innotescant. Nam rationem omnem superat quomodo applicari possit illud quod nondum est, &c.] Pag. 434. Nostra vero interpretatio sic procedit: Christus nobis acquisivit morte sua redemptionem efficacem & actualem, id est, actualem peccatorum remissionem, & reconciliationem cum Deo. Applicantur autem ista per prædicationem Evangelii, non ut de novo fiant, sed ut nobis innotescant, &c. At inquies, actualis Remissio peccatorum est ipsa Justificatio: Justificatio sequatur fidem: nam fide justificamur: ergo nemini peccata remittuntur antequam credat. Respondeo, Cum docet Apostolus nos fide justificari; nihil aliud ex instituto docet, quam nos justificari per sanguinem Christi, sive propter Christum crucifixum.] And in the Index he owns it, that *Remissio actualis est Justificatio:* and therefore we may take what he saith of remission as meant of Justification.

The like *Lib.3. pag.18. & lib.1. p.2. pag. 272.* which we before cited part of [*Nec sane occurrit species aliqua rationis, cur reconciliatio legatur in ordinem cum impetratione remissionis, Justificationis & redemptionis, potius quam cum actuali Remissione, Justificatione & Redemptione.*] So that he puts actual Justification with Remission and Reconciliation.

So *contra Cervinum pag. 48. Et quid quaso Adoptio est quam consequimur per fidem? Dicis esse Acceptationem Dei. Quid autem est Acceptatio? An non actus in Deo immanens? An vero actus Deo immanens supervenit de novo?]*

Its undeniable in this that *Twisse* doth not only affirm Remission and Reconciliation and Adoption to be before we are born, immediatly on Christs death; but also to be immanent Acts, and from Eternity: and though he be more seldom in thus using the word [Justification] yet he affirms Reconciliation and Remission (which he saith are from Eternity) to be the same thing with Justification: yea he expresly entitleth that eternal immanent act [Justification.]

And

And did he only affirm Remission and Adoption and Reconciliation and Acceptation to be immanent acts and from eternity, I beleeve few sober men will think it any better, then to affirm the same of Justification. Yea he plainly intimates a distinction of Justification: one from eternity or from Christs death, and the other upon our believing: And therefore when he speaks of Justification by faith, he cals it [that sort of Justification] intimating the other sort.

Now for Mr. *Pemble*, as he expresly maintains Justification *in foro Dei* to be long before we are born, even on Christs dying, so that is all one to our purpose, as if he maintained it to be from eternity. And it were meet that some of you should have shewed before now, what Transient act it is by which particular sinners not yet born (and therefore not yet sinners) are justified at Christs death * ? If it were (as Mr. *Pemble* intimates, I think) Gods accepting the Price, its worth the while to shew that to be Temporal and Transient, when Dr. *Twiss* will have his accepting of man in Adoption to be immanent and eternal: But if you maintain Gods justifying act at Christs death (whether undertaken or suffered) to be an immanent act, then it must be before Christs death, even eternal too. Mr. *Pembles* words are, *Vind. Grat.* p.21. [But with a distinction of Justification. 1. *In foro Divino*, in Gods sight; and this goeth before all our sanctification. For even whilst the Elect are unconverted, they are then actually justified and freed from all sinne by the death of Christ: and God so esteems of them as free, and having accepted of that satisfaction, is actually reconciled to them. By this Justification we are freed from the guilt of our sinnes: and because that is done away, God in due time proceeds to give us the grace of sanctification to free us from sinnes corruption, still inherent in our persons. 2. *In foro conscientiæ*, in our own sense: which is but the Revelation and certain Declaration of Gods former secret act of accepting Christs Righteousness to our Justification.] So *pag.*23. he speaks again of the same Justification *in foro Dei*, and saith, that all the sinnes of the Elect are actually pardoned, the Debt-Book crossed, the hand-writing cancelled, &c. and that this grand transaction between God and the Mediator Jesus Christ was concluded on and dispatcht in heaven long before we had any being either in nature or grace.] This phrase of [dispatching it in heaven] makes me conjecture that it will prove some immanent act which they call Justification at Christs death. Lay all this together, and judge whether it be true that neither Dr. *Twiss* nor Mr. *Pemble*, do mean that the immanent act can be stiled Justification. Or if it were true, whether Justification before we are born, is not an errour fit to be resisted. Indeed it is true that Mr. K. saith, that neither Dr. *Twiss* nor Mr. *Pemble* did ever mean, that [the Decree of God from eternity to justifie and condemn men, is to be called Justification:] For the Decree to condemn men cannot well be called Justification: But I believe this being but Mr. K. oversight, he will not make use of it to justifie his third Proposition.

* *I pray you Sir remember to do this in your next.*

---

§. 3.
Mr. K. Digression. P. 1.

WHether there may be a new immanent Act in God?] *To the first, By an immanent act, we mean such as is terminated in the Agent; and not in any thing without it. Now that there can be any new immanent act in God,* M. Baxter *doth not adven-*

adventure to affirm. *Only he is pleased to say this;* [*That all immanent acts in God are eternall, he thinks is quite beyond our understanding to know.* Aphor. pag. 174.] *and ho casteth out somewhat to render it suspected*, p. 173. *which I shall examine by and by*.

§. 3.

R. B. THey say of those that are bred souldiers and used to bloodshed and Victory, that the state must make them fresh work and finde them constant imployment, or else they will make work and finde imployment for themselves. A Polemical Divine much used to Disputations, and thereby to the glory and Triumph of Victory, is, as it seems by this Learned man, in the same case. Mr. *Goodwin* found him not work enough, and rather then he would want more, he makes to himself an adversary (for he saith, it is against Mr. *Baxter*) which here in the beginning he confesseth, makes not himself one, so much as by a denial of his Proposition, or an affirming the contrary. Could you finde never a man in the world to deal with, that affirmed that there may be new immanent acts in God ? If you could, they had been fitter for you to take in hand: For its like, they would purposely have maintained that assertion with some shew of reason: If you could not; then your doctrine is so universally received, that I should think it should not need your Arguments now to support it : And then you may well conclude, as you do, that you have done little by this Dispute ; if you have but laboriously maintained that which no man denies. But it seems to me it was some reasons *ab homine*, from the person of your chosen-feigned adversary, rather then from the cause that allured or impelled you to this encounter.

As you well begin with some explication of your sense, so will I also : and the rather seeing I have little else to do. I desire the Reader therefore to understand this much of my thoughts about the subject in hand, before I proceed further.

1. *In generall*, I am very strongly perswaded that it is one of the greatest sins that a great part of Pious Learned Divines are guilty of, that they audaciously adventure to dispute and determine unrevealed things ; and above all others, about the Nature and Actions of the Incomprehensible God. And that this is *The* very thing that hath divided, weakned and ruined the Church, more then any one thing, except plain contempt of God : And that it is under the wounds of these overwise mens Learning, that the poor Church hath lain bleeding many hundred years. Our Contentions, Envyings, Heart-burnings, by perverse zeal, and much of all our warres and calamities, are long of this sinne in these men : That as the Romish Clergy are justly esteemed the greatest Schismaticks on earth; for their audacious and unmercifull additions to the Creed, making such a number of new Keys which heaven must be opened and shut by, which God never made : So are those zealous Learned men, the cruel dividers of the Church, by occasioning our contentions, that will with boldness pry into things unrevealed, and with confidence and peremptoriness determine them, and then with long and subtil and fervent arguings maintain them, and make them seem necessary to the peace of the Church, or the soundness of our faith. Scarce any one thing hath more fully discovered to me the frailty and fearfull pravity of man, then this : To think, that so silly a worm should be no more acquainted with his own weakness, and the infinite distance between God and man ; and should so confidently think that he knows

what

what he doth not know! yea and what he cannot know? yea and be angry with all the world that will not say, It's true; and will not believe that he knows what he pretends to know! If a man should perswade me that I know how many Angels are in heaven, or how many daies it will be till Chrifts coming to Judgement, one would think it were no hard matter for me to know that I do not know any such thing. But if I should perswade my self that I know it, and should expect that all others should believe that I know it, and would write Volumes to prove it, and count all those ignorant or erroneous that will not believe me, or that will not say they know it when they do not, as well as I, whether this were the part of a man awake and in his wits, let others judge. How much more beyond our reach is the unsearchable nature of God, further then he hath revealed himself in his Works and Word, which, alas, affordeth us but a glimpse of his backparts. Yea the wonder is yet greater that these same Learned Divines, when they are at a *nonplus* in their arguing, will plead mans ignorance and incapacity to put off their adversary, and blame others for too bold enquiries and intrusions into Gods secrets: and most of our Reformers do speak hardly of the Schoolmen for it (and very deservedly) and yet will not see the guilt in themselves. No man speaks more against his own natural inclination in this then I do: I feel as great a desire to Know, and to pry into any thing that others have disputed, and as much natural delight in the reading of the most audacious subtil Disputers, as others do. I was wont to say, I could get more out of *Aquinas, Scotus, Durandus*, and such like in a day, then out of many Ancient Fathers, and later Treatisers, in a moneth. But I finde that as desire to know was the beginning of our misery, so is it the continuance. Why do men fear themselves no more, in that which Innocent *Adam* was undone by? I finde that this bait of knowing things unrevealed, doth but entice men into vain hopes, and labours, and self-deluding promises, and flatter men into a pleasant loss of time (and worse:) and in the end faileth all their expectations: and the Learned Disputers come off as *Adam* did, with Gods acknowledgement that he was like God in knowing good and evil (Ironically, as some Divines think; or expressing his unhappiness plainly, as others.) Those leaves of *Bradwardine* and *Twiß Vind.* and *de scient. Med.* &c. which I was wont to reade with longing and delight, I confess I look on now with fear; and many Learned Schoolmen (specially on the first Book of the *Sentences*) I read, as I hear men swear or take Gods name lightly in their common talk; even seldom, unwillingly (looking for other matter) and with horrour. Yet how oft doth Dr. *Twisse* tell *Arminius* and Dr. *Jackson* of the sinfulness, unsafeness and uncertainty of departing from the Scriptures in these high things, about the Nature and Decrees of God? And what *Bradwardine* excellently saith, I desire the Reader to see in him, *de Causi Dei, l.1.c.1. corol.3 2.* But especially I desire the Reader to peruse that excellent Epistle of *Colvius* in *Beverovicius de Termino Vita*; which contains what I have a minde further to have said of this: with *Gibieuf's* first Chapt. *de Libertate Dei* (*lib.2. de lib.*) which shews how far God is above all our highest names and notions: and that *Deus ab illis Liber est*: with much more against the Doctrine that I oppose. See also *Card. Contarenius de officio Episcopi*, *operum* p.410, 411. and what he citeth out of *Lionyfius*. And I intreat you to reade seriously that notable passage, 1 *Tim.*6. 3,4,5. where pride is shewed to be the root, and supposed knowledge said to be but Doting, and they are said to know nothing, that thought they knew most, and the sad effects of all are manifested.

a. I do

2. I do think that most of our profound Disputes, wherewith the Dominicans and Jesuites, the Arminians and Antiarminians have Learnedly troubled the world, are guilty in part, of this hainous sinne before mentioned; and that these great Doctors do dispute for the most part of they know not what. I confess its usual with men that know little themselves, to think that others know as little, and to measure the knowledge of other men by their own: and so its possible I may undervalue the Learning of these men, because having none my self, I cannot understand the largeness of their capacities, and sublimity of their speculations. However I am sure I am wiser and righter in one point then I was: For when I steeped my thoughts in their speculations, and was my self of the same express opinion with one of the parties, I thought that I begun to grow somewhat wise my self; but now I know I was deceived, and it was my folly, and that I knew not what I thought I knew. And though I will be bolder to befool such a one as my self, then men of such sublime incomprehensible knowledge; yet its my opinion that they are but men; and what a man is though I do not yet fully know, yet I am daily both studying and trying: and experience which is the teacher of fools, hath taught me this much of him; that he is no Deity; nor one of the Intelligences that moveth or comprehendeth the orbs; that the wisest are not so wise as they would seem, or as they imagine themselves; that all their conceptions which they judge so comprehensive are comprehended in the compass of a narrow skull, and there lodged in a puddle of such brains, and humours, that a little knock if it hit right may make the wisest man an Ideot, and drive out all that profound Learning which Mr K. thinks is so near kin to the knowledge of God. I confess of late I have accustomed my self to such mean thoughts of man and his imaginations, and such high thoughts of God, that I reade many of the profoundest School Divines (whom yet in some respects I honour) as I hear children discoursing of State matters, or Theology; or as if I heard two disputing in their sleep. The Serpent hath beguiled us as he did *Eve*, by drawing us from the simplicity that is in Christ. Vain Philosophy hath been the bait to deceive the Church: And so we are judiciously broken in pieces and ruined; and have learned to our cost to know good and evil. I think there is no hope of the Churches recovery but by returning to the primitive Christian simplicity; and using *Aristotle* as a help in Naturals, but not preferring him before Christ in the teaching of the highest speculations of Theology, as if we must go learn Gods nature of *Aristotle*, where Christ leaveth us at a loss. When those Learned men, who professing themselves wise became ―― shall become fools that they may be wise, and come quite back again to their *cognosce teipsum*, then they may know more of God then they yet do, and yet perceive that they know less then they thought they had known: and then their knowledge will edifie which now puffeth up.

3. I think that man can have no positive proper conception of God, at least besides *ens* (which the Scotists think proper) and that there is no word in humane language that can express Gods nature in strict propriety, but all our notions of him are so exceeding imperfect, that they express more of our ignorance then of our knowledge. *White* is bold to say (*Instcut. Peripatet. l. 4. lect. 9, 10.*) that none of the Names that we attribute to God, hath a notion which hath in God a formall object: and that that science is of all other the most sublime and proper, which inquireth into the impropriety of the names that are spoken of God, and denieth them all as to him.

4. I think

4. I think that there is no such thing in God as Understanding, Knowledge, Will, Intention, Decree, Election, Love, &c. as these are by men conceived of, and expressed: And that man knows not what it is in God formally which these terms are used by him to express. And that it is a farre less improper speech to say, that the Firmament is a nutshell, or the sun is a glow-worm, or to denominate the reason of men from the apprehensions of a fly or a worm, then to attribute Understanding, Will, &c. to God. What the impropriety is, we shall speak to more anon.

5. Therefore all those reasonings concerning Gods Nature or Acts, which are drawn meerly from the nature and acts of man, as concluding from a supposed Analogy of attribution (much more a formal Identity), is a vain deceitfull reasoning.

6. Yet as Scripture speaks of God in terms improper, according to mans capacity, and fetcht from mans nature and acts, so must we both conceive and speak: that is, not believing that these are proper expressions or conceptions of God, but that there is that in God which we cannot now more fitly conceive of then under these notions, or fitlier express then in these terms. God hath nothing properly cal'ed Knowledge or Will: but he hath or is that which man cannot fitlier express or conceive of then under the notion of Knowledge and Will: But what it is, God knows. We must say, God knows, and God willeth; and God must say so to us: For else man could not hear or speak of God, if God condescended not to the language and capacity of man. *Camero* saith, even of our most perfect state of glory, that *Frui Deo nil aliud est quam potentiæ, sapientiæ, bonitatis divinæ fructum percipere, quem creaturæ modus & ratio ferre potest,* &c. *Et videtur Deus experiundo quis sit* (1. Jo. 3.) *Et qualem se erga nos præstet, cæterum (quicquid dictitent scholastici, homines acuti quidem, sed in hoc argumento nimis acuti, invisibilis est vel Angelis, quibus ad Dei conspectum nulla peccati labes, sola naturæ imbecillitas (creaturæ enim sunt) aditum interclusit. Prælect. de Verb. Dei. Glasg.* c. 7. p. 455. I am more certain that even the eye of our understanding hath no direct and proper sight of God, while we are in the flesh.

7. Yet these attributions of Knowledge and Will, to God, are not falshoods, for there is really somewhat in God which these are made the improper expressions of. Equivocals, and Analogies, are not *eo nomine* false expressions.

8. I am so farre from thinking that it is by Analogy of Attribution (as the Schoolmen call it) that Knowledge, Will, &c. are attributed to God and the creature; that I think these ascribed to God by an exceeding farre fetcht metaphor, further then (as I said) if I should call Heaven a nutshell; there being a thousand fold more likeness between these, then between Gods Knowledge and Will, and mans: For between finite and Infinite there is no proportion. Yea I will not undertake to prove that the *Ratio homonymiæ* is not in Us, only, and not at all in the Things.

9. Yet no doubt, the thing meant by Knowledge and Will when attributed to God, is not only, as many say, most eminently in God; but is solely in God; that which is called knowledge and will in man being not the same thing, but *toto genere diversum*. But yet the conception that we have of Gods Knowledge and Will is but improper derived from the supposed *simile, viz.* our own understanding and will, which representeth it with exceeding imperfection. So that the terms of Knowledge, Will, Decree, &c. are spoken first and properly
of

of the creature, and thence improperly of God.

10. Yet I acknowledge that though all these terms of Attribution, as to God, are exceeding improper, yet there are degrees of impropriety; some being more improper then others are: And so I doubt not but that the terms that are taken from humane passions and imperfections are more Improperly applied to God, then these forementioned of Understanding and Will, &c.

And thus I have told you some of my thoughts, that Mr K. may know on what terms to deal with me, and not contend with one whose minde he understandeth not.

And as to his description of Immanent Acts, I deny that there is any such thing as an Act in God terminated in himself, supposing that you speak not of a meer objective termination (as I know you do not; For else you would call many of these transient acts, as having an extrinsick object.) As I acknowledge no certainty of a proper Act in God, so I acknowledge no positive termination of that which in him we call an Act; and we call it immanent but in that negative sense which the later clause of your description doth express. We are like to make a good dispute of it, when I am forced to deny the subject, as being a *Chymara*.

---

§. 4.

Mr.K. IN the mean time, out of the respect I bear to the memory of Dr. Twisse, I cannot forbear to say, that Mr. Baxter had better consulted his own honour if he had said nothing to the disparagement of that Reverend and Renowned Doctor: of whom he speaks very sleightingly more then once in his otherwise excellent Treatise of Infant-Baptism, and in all his other Books: In which I could wish there were not somewhat of the Doctrinal part not answering that of the Devotional. What Dr. Twisse hath said of Justification from eternity, upon this ground, that there can be no new immanent act in God, and how much some in the Synod said against him, and how little he replied for himself matters not: he was now grown old,

Et videas fessos Rhadamanthon & Æacon annis,
Et Minoa queri———

Like enough, Multum mutatus ab illo
Hectore qui redit exuvias indutus Achillis.

When he beat Arminius, Corvinus, Tilenus, Penottus, Bellarmine, Dr. Jackson, and I know not how many more out of the field; & solus vacua dominatus arena left them all bleeding, as Mr. Goodwin would have said, at the feet of his Writings. It may be he was now at last, but magni nominis umbra, but whose very name really did most of the service, and I am sure was that formidable thing to the learned Adversary: But as old as he was, I question not but he could have easily made this good, There is no new Immanent act in God] against all that opposed him in the Synod, and Mr. Baxter to boot: and I would fain hear any of them all that opposed him, to give a satisfactory answer but to this one Argument.

§. 4.

R. B. 1. You need not argue me to a higher respect to Dr. *Twisse* then I have ever manifested, except you would have me say, He was a God, or an Angel, or an Infallible man.

2. If you cannot forbear, as you say, its pity you should be hindered: Men and women must speak when their list is so great. Who can hold that which will away?

3. I confess, that I did not much consult mine Honour in that writing. Else you had not found your self work as you have done in these leaves. If you mean the Honour of my Honesty, your proof must do more to the determination then your assertion: If you mean the Honour of my Learning, do not you know well enough, how little I have to consult? He that hath nothing, hath nothing to lose.

4. [Sleightingly] is a word that will stretch, and therefore I will not charge you with untruth. In one mans sense, (he sleights a man that cals him [that famous excellent Divine:] but in another mans, sleighting signifieth the esteeming of a man below his worth, and expressing so much, or setting light by a man. I am miserably troubled with those kinde of people that cannot endure [sleighting] as they call it, above all folks in the world. (I use to call them plainly, Proud people, here in the Countrey; but if I were to talk to Learned men I would use more manners:) They think I sleight them, if I do not applaud them, or complement with them, or if I commend them not with so loud a voice as they expect (and they are a people that are never low in their expectations:) or if I do but praise another above them, or speak to another before them, or be short with them (when I am busie) when they look for a longer more respectfull discourse; yea if my Hat should be over mine eyes that I see them not, or my memory so fail me as that I forget them; these and abundance more I am guilty of sleighting every day, that I am now grown accustomed to the vice, and shameless in hearing it charged upon me. But I suspect that my sleighting Dr. *Twisse* consisteth in my supposing him to erre, and telling the world so: that is, in taking him to be a man: for *humanum est errare:* and for saying he knew but in part, that is, that he was not glorified on earth by perfection. If you could have charged me with any more then this, would you not have done it? I say, would you not? when the Vindication of this Reverend man was the end of your encountring me? and it boyled so hot on your stomack, that [you could not forbear: you had not the patience to see so Worthy men so unworthily handled.] Yea your self affirm that which is his doctrine to be untrue, and yet I sleight him for saying so! Lay this with the commanded Adoration of the footsteps, and it seems, it is high matters indeed that you expect. I doubt, by this, that you will say, I slight *you* before I have done, either because I praise you not enough, or because I take you not for infallible and indefectible, or because I value Dr. *Twisse* or Mr. *Pemble* so very, very, very farre before you; when yet I am accused of slighting them. Sir, these Reverend men, I doubt not, are perfected Saints in heaven, and hate pride so much, that if they know it, they will give little thanks to him that will contend for the honour of their Infallibility, yea or for the guilding over any of their errours; much less, if their honour should be made a snare to the entangling of the godly, and a means to the promoting the

King-

Kingdom of darknefs, and oppofing that Truth which they love better then their Honours, and the difhonouring of that God whofe glory is their felicity.

Yea let me tell you that I take my felf bound in confcience to fay more then ever I have yet faid, and that is this [All young Students that will deigne to take advice from fo mean a man as I, as ever you would preferve your graces and converfations, preferve your Judgements; and as ever you would maintain the Doctrine of Chrift, take heed of the Errors of the Antinomians: and as ever you would efcape the fnare of Antinomianifm, take heed of thefe principal Articles of it following:- [That Chrifts fatisfaction is ours *quâ præftita*, before the Application; and that fo far, as that we are actually Pardoned, Juftified, Reconciled and Adopted by it before we were born, much more before we believe: yea that Adoption and Remiffion of fin are immanent acts in God, and fo are from eternity, even before any death of Chrift, or efficacy of it: That pardon of fin is nothing but *Velle non Punire*: That Juftification by faith is nothing but Juftification *in foro confcientiæ*, or the fenfe of that in our hearts, which was really ours from eternity, or from Chrifts death, or both: That juftifying faith is the feeling or apprehenfion of Gods eternal Love, Remiffion and Adoption.] I fay, take heed of thefe mafter-Points of Antinomianifm: And as ever you would avoid thefe, take heed how you receive them on the reputation and plaufible words of any Writer: and efpecially of Dr *Twiß*, who is full of fuch paffages, and being of greater learning and efteem then others is liker to miflead you. For you know, if you receive thefe then you muft receive the reft, if you difcern the concatenation. For if all your fins were pardoned as foon as Chrift died, then what need you pray for pardon, or Repent or Believe or be Baptized for pardon? then God loved you as well when you were his enemies, as fince; and then how can you be reftrained from fin by fear? *&c.* And that you may know I fpeak not this in flighting of the Doctor, as M^r. K. chargeth me. 1. I profefs to do it mainly for Gods glory and Truth, and for the love of fouls. 2. I take my felf the rather bound to it, becaufe I was once drawn my felf to fome of thefe opinions by the meer high eftimation of Mr. *Pemble* and Dr. *Twiße*. 3. I profefs ftill moft highly to love and reverence the names of thefe two bleffed excellent men, as formerly I never honoured any two men more. For Dr. *Twiß*, I am more beholden to his Writings for that little knowledge I have then almoft any one mans, befides: and for Mr. *Pemble*, for ought I can fee in his Book of Juftification, he revoked this fame errour which in his *Vindic. Grat.* he hath delivered: fure I am, no two mens Writings have been more in my hands, and few mens names are yet fo highly honoured in my heart.

This much I take my felf bound to publifh for a common warning. And I would further advife all to take heed how they entertain Dr. *Twiß*'s doctrine about the caufe of fin; of which I fhall be ready to give my reafon when I have a call; but will not now digrefs fo far.

5. For your good wifh [that my Books had not fomething in the Doctrinal part not anfwering the devotional] I thank you: But, alas, ignorance and errour will not be healed with a wifh: Many a year have I ftudied and praied againft them, and yet they ftick by me ftill. But had I erred in the Foundation, it would have fpoiled my Devotion: for *non recte vivitur, ubi de Deo non bene creditur:* And I had rather be defective in leffer doctrinals, then in Devotion. And though I am as confident that you erre in fome of your Doctrinals (as I fhall anon mani-

D 3 (feft)

fest.) as you are of my erring, yet I heartily wish your Devotion be as good as your Judgement in Doctrine; and I think I wish you a greater blessing then iyou wished me.

6. I do not well relish your exceeding coldness in Gods cause, who are so hot for man: When it is for the honour of your Learned Brethren, [you have not patience, you cannot forbear.] But what Dr. *Twiffe* hath said for Justification from Eternity, on the ground that there is no new immanent act in God, this you say, *Matters not*: Is it a phrase beseeming a Preacher of Christs Truth to say, [*It matters not?*] When that Truth is contradicted in so high a Point ? and the souls of men, and the peace of the Church so much endangered ? A *Gallio* might better have spoke thus. *England* hath not sped so well by the Antinomians of late, as that any knowing friend of it, should say, It matters not, when such great Divines promote their cause.

7. And where you also say, that [it matters not what some in the Synod said against him, and how little he said for himself.] I am not of your minde. 1. Is it only the *vestigia Doctoris Twissi & M. K.* that are to be adored ? You shall give me leave to honour you much, and the Doctor more, but the Assembly more then either of you. 2. I do not think the Doctor was so weak, or at least a good cause so friendless in the Assembly, but that himself or some other would have done something considerable to the justification of his cause, if it had been justifiable. 3. I will be bold to ask you, the next time I see you, whether all your heat and impatience for unworthy handling or slighting the Doctor be not meant against the Assembly as well as me ? or if not, Whether it be not respect of persons that made the difference ? or rather the securing of your reputation, which you might think would be elevated by a Victory over others, or at least lose nothing, though the person were so contemptible, as not to adde to your glory; but by an opposition to the Assembly it might have been dasht in pieces ? Or if the Antinomians being questioned by the Assembly shall alleadge Dr. *Twiss*'s words (frequently and plainly uttered) for their Defence; and the Doctors cause being hereupon questioned shall fall without any justification; I pray you tell me, Whether there may not be the same necessity for *us* to take notice of his Errours as the Assembly? and whether after them we may not do it (while we honour his worth as much as I still do) without slighting or wronging him. It is more dishonour to be Questioned by an Assembly and come off unjustified, then to be judged to mistake by so contemptible a person as I.

8. Where you speak of [his very Name doing most of the service.] I do not understand what service you mean. I know you mean not the service done in his Writings: And sure you dare not mean [the service done by the Assembly:] for that were to make them a contemptible Assembly indeed, if a mans Name, yea *magni nominis umbra*, did most of their service: And it were to think as basely of their service as the worst Sectary doth, that I have met with. It were not worth so much cost, and so many years pains, nor worthy the Acceptation of Parliament or People, if it were but the offspring of Dr. *Twiffe*'s Name. But Sir we have received fruits that shew they came from another cause then a name or the shadow of a name. I confess I value their least Catechism for children above all Mr. *Kendall*'s learned Labours, were they twenty times more of the same quality. I never heard but one Learned man speak contemptuously of the Assembly, and his friends say it was because he was not thought Worthy to be one of them (I except those that were against them in the Warre; where heat of opposition might
occasion

occasion diseſteem: But if this were Mr. K's caſe, yet methinks when he changed his Cauſe and Party, he ſhould withall have changed his eſteem of the Aſſembly.) But its likely that Mr. K. means that it was the Doctors Name that did moſt of the ſervice of a Moderator; moſt of his own part in the Aſſembly: It may be ſo: But if he had nothing to work by but his Name, yet had his cauſe been good, it would in that Aſſembly have found ſome friends. But what you mean then by the following words, I do not well know, that his Name you are ſure [was that formidable thing to the Learned adverſary.] Perhaps you mean your ſelf, by the Learned adverſary, of whoſe fears I confeſs you might be ſure, and ſo might know the Name or Word that did affright you: elſe I cannot imagine who you mean, except it were the Kings party or the Epiſcopal Divines together: But for Epiſcopacy, I know of no Diſputes that ever the Aſſembly had upon it, and ſo had no adverſaries in a diſputing way; at leaſt during Dr. Twiſſ's time. And for diſputing the Kings Cauſe, I think they did as little in it. Some choſen men in the Treaties indeed diſputed againſt Epiſcopacy, but with other weapons then Dr. Twiſſe's Name. If you ſhould mean that it was Dr. Twiſſe's Name that made the Learned Epiſcopal Divines have Reverend thoughts of the Aſſembly, I muſt tell you that there were in that Aſſembly no ſmall number of Divines of that excellency for Learning, Piety and Miniſterial Ability, which might command Reverence from the Learnedeſt adverſaries of you all.

9. But though his Name did all the ſervice; yet you [queſtion not but he could have eaſily made it good; That there is no new immanent act in God, againſt, &c.] It ſeems by this that you think this the eaſier to prove of the two: And indeed I am acquainted with none that are minded to oppoſe it.

10. Nor is it reaſonable for you to ſay, that you [would fain have any of them all that oppoſed him, to give a ſatisfactory anſwer to your Argument,] when you know it was not in that Point that they oppoſed him. Would you make more your adverſaries againſt their will as well as me? or do you long for more honourable Antagoniſts to cope with? And whats your Argument?

---

§. 5.

Mr. K. IF there be any new immanent Act in God, it muſt be either of his Underſtanding or his Will: Of his Underſtanding there can be none: elſe muſt he know ſomewhat a new, which inferres he was not Omniſcient, knew not all before this new act of Knowledge: If of his Will, then either this new act is for the better or worſe or indifferent: If for the better, he was not abſolutely perfect before, as, being capable of bettering: If for the worſe; he is not ſo perfect ſince this act as he was before; which is to make him leſs perfect by his new act: If neither, then is this act ſuch as might as well have been out as in: and then it is an imperfection to act ſo impertinently. This ſame Argument as I take it made uſe of by Mr. Goodwin himſelf in a like caſe, and therefore he will not be offended how highly ſoever I value it as an irrefragable Demonſtration.

§. 5.

§. 5.

R. B. Remember that I say not that your Doctrine is *Untrue*, but *Uncertain*. It may be possibly as you say; but whether you can tell that it is so, or prove it to be so, I doubt. To your great Argument, I expect better proof of your *major* Proposition, which indeed hath none at all. Two things I expected you should have proved: 1. That God hath an Understanding and Will which act; properly so called: or that you know what it is that is improperly called Gods Understanding and Will? 2. That God hath no immanent Act but of his Understanding or Will. To begin with the last: I will not say, *datur tertium*. For I dare not say properly *dantur duo*: But I will desire you to prove your *major*: and I think that in the same sense as God is said to have an Understanding and Will, for ought you know he may have other acts, which those two notions will not express. For 1. You are uncertain whether Angels may not have other faculties or acts-immanent, besides Understanding and Will: (If you say, you are sure they have not, prove it:) and so others may be ascribed to God by Analogy from them, as these be by Analogy from man. You know perhaps how many senses you have your self: but how can you prove that no other creature hath a sixth sense, which you are uncapable of knowing the name or nature of? So how know you but Angels may have powers or immanent acts beside Understanding and Willing, which you know nothing of for name or nature? Must all Gods superiour creatures be needs measured by poor man? How much more noble creatures hath God, then these below that dwell in dust! 2. But if you were acquainted with all the Angels in heaven, and were at a certainty about the number or nature of their powers or acts, how prove you that God hath no other act then what Understanding and Willing doth express? That one unconceivable perfect act in God, which *Eminenter* (by an unconceivable transcendent eminence) is *Understanding and Willing*, (yet but Analogically so called) but properly and formally is neither, but somewhat more excellent; is in all likelihood very restrainedly or defectively expressed by these two words; even as to the objective extent. How know we but that in some of Gods creatures, or at least in God himself there may be something found besides Entity, Verity, Goodness; or any thing that is the object of Intellection or Volition, whereof no man had ever any conception. However, is it not unlikely, yea a dangerous imagination, That the powers or acts of such wretched worms as we, should be so farre commensurable with the Infinite Majesty, that as we have no immanent act but of Understanding, or Will (or subordinate to these) so God hath no other; or none but what are expressed in these two notions! Alas, that silly worms should so unreverently presume! and pretend to that knowledge of God which they have not! and might so easily know that they have not!

And for the former, How farre God hath an Understanding or Will, I will peruse your words to Master *Goodwin* when I have done with this Section.

This were enough to your Argument and Challenge: but I proceed to the confirmation of your implied *minor*. And 1. I easily grant you, that it is certain there is no Addition to, or mutation of Gods Essence. 2. I think all the Acts ascribed to God are his Essence, and are one in themselves considered. Pardon that I do but say [I think:] For though principles of reason and Metaphysical Axioms

seem

[17]

seem to lead plainly to this Conclusion; yet I am afraid of pretending to any greater Certainty then I have; or of building too much on the doubtfull conclusions of mans slippery Reasonings, about the nature of the Invisible Incomprehensible God. I think it most sutable to Gods Unity and Simplicity, that all his immanent acts (so called by us) are Himself and are One. But I dare not say I am certain that God cannot be Simple and Perfect, except this be true: both because He is beyond my knowledge, and because the doctrine of the Trinity assureth us that there is in God a true diversity consisting with Unity, Simplicity and Perfection of Essence. 3. You know not what the subject of your Proposition is, (Gods acts of Understanding and Will:) and therefore you are uncapable of such peremptory concluding *de Modis*, knowingly and certainly, as here you pretend to. 4. You cannot prove that there's any such thing in God as an Immanent Act, or an Understanding or a Will in proper sense: but something there is which we cannot fitlier or more profitably conceive or express then under such notions, drawn Analogically from mans acts of Understanding and Willing. Now if we will speak of Gods Incomprehensible nature by such Analogy, and put the names of Understanding and Willing on God, as borrowed from mans understanding and willing, then must we accordingly conceive of Gods understanding and willing, as like to mans in the form of these acts (for we can reach to no higher conceptions, though these be utterly improper.) Now mans actual intellection doth connote and suppose an intelligible object, and his Will doth connote and suppose an appetible object: and consequently it cannot be expected according to the utmost imaginable natural perfection of them, that either should go beyond the extent of their objects, or be such acts without their proper objects: * These things thus premised, some will perhaps think you sufficiently answered (when you say, it inferres that God was not Omniscient, knew not all, *&c.*) by telling you 1. That as Omnisciency signifies a Power of Knowing all things, Analogically ascribed to God *ad captum humanum* as distinct from the act of knowing; so God was yet Omniscient. 2. As Omnisciency signifieth the actual Knowledge of all intelligible objects, so God was Omniscient And no more is requisite to the perfection of his Knowledge. 3. But an Object may have not only its real but its * intelligible Being *de Novo* which it had not before; and therefore as Omnisciency signifieth the Knowledge of all things that *will* be intelligible, as well as those that now *are* intelligible, so (say they) it belongs not to Gods perfection to be Omniscient; for it is unnaturally and improperly called Science (and so Omniscience) which hath not an Object. Their foundation (which may seem absurd to you) *viz.* That some things may *de novo* become the objects of Knowledge, they declare thus: 1. They suppose, that though God be Indivisible, and so his Eternity be Indivisible, and have neither in it, *Præteritum* nor *Futurum*, nor *Nunc* neither, as we understand it, as expressing a present instant of time: yet as God knoweth not Himself only, but the creature also, so he knoweth not Eternity only but Time: He knows how things are ordered and take place in mans Divisible measure of motions: and therefore he knows things as Past, Present and Future, *quoad hominem & tempus*, which are so past, present and future. And he doth not know a thing Past to be Present (*quoad tempus & hominem*) nor a thing Future to be

* *Even as Gods Omnipotency is but dicta ad possibilia, Vid. Aquin. 1. q. 25 a. 3. c.*

* *See Buridane of that question in his Ethicks so far as to shew the great difficulty.*

E

be Paſt : but knows things truly as they be. 2. This being premiſed, they will then aſſume, that *Peter* and *Paul* did not actually exiſt from eternity : Chriſt did not actually ſuffer from eternity : and ſo the actual exiſtence of *Peter* in *nunc temporis*, was not an intelligible object from Eternity : and therefore they think they may conclude, that it could not be known from Eternity. They will urge their reaſon thus : 1. There was no Time from Eternity (that is, before time :) therefore it could not be intelligible, that *Peter* did actually then exiſt in Time. 2. Elſe you will confound Futurition and Preſent exiſtence : God did know from Eternity, that *Peter* would exiſt in Time, *i. e. futuritionem Petri:* therefore it was not *Peter's* preſent actual exiſtence that he knew. 3. The nature of *foreknowledge* is to know things as future, and therefore muſt not be confounded with knowledge of things as exiſtent. 4. This propoſition before the creation was not true [*Peter* doth actually exiſt :] therefore God could not know it to be then true. But after *Peter's* birth it did *de novo* become a true propoſition : and therefore muſt be *de novo* known to be then true. Before that, it was only true that [*Hæc Propoſitio vera futura eſt*] but not [*vera eſt :*] therefore no more but the futurition of the Truth could be known, and not the actual preſent exiſtence (as referring to time :) It is not all one to ſay [*Petrus erit*] and [*Petrus eſt*] nor all one to know it. 5. The contradictory Propoſition was then true [*Peter* doth not exiſt :] But both contradictory Propoſitions could not be known to be true together, that is from Eternity. Therefore God did then know the Negative Propoſition as then true [*Petrus non exiſtit :*] and the Affirmative *de futuro* to be true [*Petrus futurus eſt, vel exiſtet :*] but he did not know the Affirmative *de exiſtentia præſenti* to be true from Eternity [*Petrus in nunc temporis exiſtit*] no nor [*Petrus in nunc Æternitatis exiſtit :*] for they were then falſe Propoſitions : nor yet was it then true that [*Tempus actu exiſtit.*] If you ſay, That there were no Propoſitions from Eternity, and therefore they could not be true or falſe : this alters not the caſe : for 1. We ſpeak on ſuppoſition that there had been creatures to have framed theſe Propoſitions. 2. If we conceive not of Gods Underſtanding as knowing the truth of Propoſitions, concerning things, we ſhall ſcarce have any conception of it as an Underſtanding at all. 3. The Schools commonly ſpeak of the Eternal truth of Propoſitions, *e. g. de futuris contingentibus.* 4. There are Propoſitions in Time, and theſe God knows : and thats all one to the preſent caſe. At *Noahs* flood God knew not this Propoſition to be then true [*Petrus exiſtit :*] for it was not then true. Nor did he know then that [it *is* true *in nunc temporis quo exiſtit Petrus*] but only, that it *will* be true : For *Futura* and not things preſently exiſtent are the objects of Foreknowledge : and that [*Nunc temporis*] it ſelf did not then exiſt. 6. Otherwiſe it would be true that All things do coexiſt with God from Eternity : (which is diſclaimed by thoſe that are now oppoſed :) and ſo that they do exiſt from Eternity. For if this Propoſition were known to be true from Eternity [*Petrus exiſtit, vel Deo coexiſtit,*] then the thing expreſſed is true, *Peter* did ſo exiſt and coexiſt. For that which is falſe cannot be known to be at the ſame time true. If it be granted therefore that *Peter* did not exiſt from Eternity, and conſequently that that Propoſition was not then true, nor intelligible as then true, but only as of future Verity, then when God in time knows it to be of preſent exiſtent Verity, he knows more then when he knows it to be only of future Verity and of preſent falſhood : And ſo about the creatures, When he knows that they do exiſt and knows them as exiſting, he knows more then when he knew them only to be future and as future. For if it be

not-

[19]

not more to know a thing as existent then as future, and so knowledge be not diversified from the object, then it is no more to know something then nothing: For the reason is the same: and future is a term of diminution as to existent. And then it will be all one to know [*Judas* is damned] and [*Peter* is saved:] [*Jacob* is loved] and [*Esau* is hated.] Yea then it would be all one if (*per possibile vel impossibile*) it were known [*Peter* is damned] and [*Judas* is saved] or [*Peter* is saved and damned:] and so it would be all one to know falshood and truth.

Many such reasonings as these will be used against you. Of which if you would know my own opinion, I think they are *de ignotis*, dreams, fightings in the dark, yet much like your own. And though I know severall things that you may say against this reasoning, so do I know much that may be said against yours: and, I think, both sides would do better to profess that ignorance which they can neither overcome nor hide. How constantly do the Schools distinguish between Gods Abstractive and Intuitive Knowledge? *Scientiam simplicis intelligentiæ & puræ Visionis*? and tell us that the former in order of nature goes before the other? If this be so, then God hath a *Prius* and *Posterius* in the acts of his knowledge. The like we may say between Gods Knowledge of Himself and the creature. If they think it not absurd that *etiam in mente Divina* there should be a transition of things *è numero possibilium in numerum futurorum*, and this *sine mutatione*; why may they not admit a knowledge of things as existent only when they are existent, and of things as future when they are future? and this *sine mutatione* too? For the distinction *quoad momenta temporis*, will make but a gradual difference, in point of mutation, from that *quoad ordinem naturæ, vel momenta Rationis*. All distinction, that hath real ground, denotes imperfection, according to our highest speculators, and so must all be denied of God. I refuse not to say (if I must say any thing) of both as Mr. *Barlow* doth *Exercit.* 5. (think him not pedantick, because he is bound with *Schibler*:) *Mutatio illa est solum in objecto cognito, non in cognoscente, seu cognitione; cum cognitio divina ab objecto non dependet, nec ad mutationem objecti mutationem ullam patitur*, &c. *Cum ideo admittit Alvarez res primo esse possibiles solum in ordine ad potentiam & futuras in ordine ad voluntatem, necesse est ut prius cognoscat cognitione abstractiva (quia ut possibiles ea solum cognitione cognosci possunt) & postea cum per voluntatem fiunt futuræ, & etiam actu existentes, illas cognitione intuitiva cognoscet Deus. At hinc nulla in Deo mutatio sequetur, sed solum in objecto (ut fateatur necesse est) Et per consequens hoc dato, quod scientia Dei ab abstractiva in intuitivam mutaretur, tamen non sequetur Deum esse mutabilem, vel cognitionem suam ex parte rei: sed solum quod objecto variato, intellectum noster, varias ei denominationes attribuit: ut quod sit intuitiva, quod abstractiva, quæ solum sunt denominationes variæ cognitioni divinæ ab intellectu nostro impositæ, pro diverso respectu ad creaturam, cum in se sit omnino simplex & invariata*.]

But then I would fain know whether there be not the same necessity that the difference between objects [only future] and [presently existent] should cause our understandings to put the forementioned various denominations on Gods Knowledge, as the difference *inter Possibilia & Futura*, doth so cause us to put on it? And also whether in the same impropriety and imperfection, the very notions of [Understanding, Willing, Acting, Immanently, &c.] be not *Denominationes ab intellectu nostro impositæ*, or assumed by God in condescension to humane weakness, expressing but some little, very little, of that Divine ———— I know not what. For that same thing which man hath a true formall conception of under the notion of [Knowing, Willing] is varied according to the variety of

E 2 objects

objects: But if it be not so with God (as I must think and say, It is not, if I presume to think and say any thing of it,) that is because Knowledge and Willing in Him are not the things that we by those terms use to express; nor yet any thing that we can have formall proper conceptions of: And by the same necessity and warrant as we do bring down the Divine nature so low, as to apply to it the notions of Acting, Understanding, Willing; may we also apply to it the notions of Acting, Knowing and Willing *de novo*; confessing a further addition to the impropriety of speech. And therefore as God himself doth in Scripture accomodate himself to our capacity, by assuming the terms and notions of Understanding and Willing, so doth he also of loving where he before hated; with divers the like, which in man would imply an innocent mutation.

I have here given you some reason of several passages of mine, which your following Pages carp at, before you discerned my meaning, as I shall shew you further anon.

So much to your proof that there is no new immanent act in Gods Understanding. One word to what follows about his Will.

Where you argue thus: [*If of his Will, then this new act is either for the Better, or Worse, or Indifferent,* &c.] *Ans.* In strict propriety, it is taken as unproved, that he hath Will, or Immanent acts. But *ad captum humanum* as we are necessitated to ascribe Willing and Acting to him, so they that think they may on the same grounds ascribe New acts of Will to him (as the Scripture undoubtedly doth,) will think that your Argument is sufficiently answered thus:

1. This arguing supposeth mans silly intellect capable of comprehending the Reasons of the Acts of the Almighty; as if it cannot be, except we can apprehend the reason of it, and whether it be for the better or worse or indifferent; or what it produceth, or to what end it is: which is a most bold arrogant presumption in such moles as we are. As I said before, you know not whether there may not be more Affections or *Modi entium* open to the Divine Intellect and Will, or Nature, then we have any name for or conception of: And though mans will look only at the goodness or appetibility or conveniency of objects, yet you know not what Gods will is; and therefore know not what is its adequate object. Many other reasons also of the obscurity of this might be given.

2. It will be answered you, that the said New act of Gods will, is for the Better: But then they will distinguish of [*Better.*] 1. They will say, It is Better *quoad rerum ordinem*: and it is Better to the creature: (as for God to love him that before he hated: or approve of him, whom before he disapproved.) 2. They distinguish also between that which may be said to be Better to God himself: Either Really, by a real addition to his perfection; and so nothing can be Better to God: Or 2. Relatively and Reputatively; as God is said to be Blessed, Glorified, Honoured, Well pleased, Exalted, Magnified, *&c.* And thus it may be Better to God, though he receive no real addition of felicity; and so not Vain or Indifferent.

3. They will desire you to Answer your own Argument as to transient Acts, and they think it may serve as to immanent acts. (Remembring that they suppose that there be new acts in God without mutation; because they suppose that those very things that we call immanent Acts in him are but denominations of his simple Essence, according to the various aspects or respects of the objects, which make no more mutation then relations do.) Was Gods act of Creation, of rai-

sing

fing Christ from death, &c. for the Better, or Worse; or Indifferent? I think you will say as before, that it was not Better as to God in the adding of any real felicity to him: But to God Reputatively and Relatively, and to the creature really, it was Better. So will they say about immanent acts, which may perfect the whole (as the Honour of the Prince is the good of the Commonwealth) and may be necessary to the Good of particular persons; and the reputative Good of God himself. Its said, God made All things for himself, Was it for Better to himself, or Worse, or Indifferent?

4. Is it Better or Worse for a looking Glass that it receive a hundred various *species de novo*? You will perhaps say, It is no disparagement to the Glass to be receptive of new *species* without being made Better or Worse: as also that its reception is passive, and so is not Gods Understanding or Willing. I know not what it is: but I confess it must needs be a very improper conception to conceive of God as passive in knowing. And yet man hath no true apprehension of a knowledge which is wholly *sine passione*: But how prove you that God cannot, if he please, by his active Knowledge, Know *de novo*, without becoming Better or Worse? or doing it in vain? Are you sure that every new act of intellection (even in a dream) doth make mans understanding better or worse? or else is vain? I confess more may be here said.

5. Having done with your Argument, they will further tell you, that, If God may have new relations without any real change, then, for ought you know, he may have new immanent acts without a real change: But the Antecedent is unquestionably true: (God was not a Creator before he had creatures: nor is he our Father before we are his children; nor our King, Master, &c. before we are his subjects, servants, &c. except *de jure* only.) The Consequence they prove thus: Relations have as true an Entity, as, for ought you know, these which we call Immanent Acts in God, may have: Therefore the Novation of them will make as great a change. Here they suppose that *Actio* and *Relatio* are both accidents: (taken properly) and neither of them meer *Entia Rationis* (for in so thinking they go in the more beaten road) much less nothing: Or if you will say, that *Relatio* is but *Modus entis*, they will say so of action too: Or however they tell you, that it may be so for ought you know, with that which we call an Act in God. And here they suppose that his Acts are not his Essence absolutely and in it self considered; and that it signifies not all one to say, God is God, and to say, God willeth the existence of this worm: And therefore they will say, that these which we call Acts, may be, if not Relations, yet some of *Scotus* his formalities, or something to us unknown, which have either no more Being then Relations, or at least not so much as to make a real change in God. And that there is in his simple, indivisible Essence, a Trinity of persons, without any imperfection: so there may be in his Essence, distinct formalities (or somewhat that we cannot name or conceive of) of a lower nature, then Personality, without any inconvenience: and as these may be superadded to the meer absolute Essence of God (as *Agere, Intelligere, Velle*, are added) without dividing, or multiplying it: so may they on the same grounds be New, or renewed, without any Mutation of Gods Essence; but only of the formality of intellection or Volition, which is added to his Essence.

6. They further think that the nature of transient acts, doth prove that immanent acts may be renewed: But this will be more spoke to anon, when we come to your doctrine of transient Acts. They say, A transient act is not a meer Re-

E 3

lation.

lation or Paſſion or Effect : But there is in it that which may be called action *ab agente*, as well as paſſion *à patiente*. Now if *actio* be *efficientis actio* here, and God in creating the world did *verè agere*, then either the world was created from eternity, or elſe God did create it from Eternity, and yet it was created only in Time, and the Cauſation or Cauſing creating Act was infinitely before the Effect; or elſe there was a new act really performed by God in Time. The firſt none will maintain, that I deal with. The ſecond, ſay they, is againſt common reaſon: For Gods act is the *Cauſa proxima creaturæ*; and *omnis cauſa proxima reciprocatur cum ſuo effectu*: i. e. *Poſita cauſa proxima in actu, neceſſe eſt effectum poni*: If it be *cauſa totalis*, yea and requireth nothing elſe to the effect ſo much as by preparation, or diſpoſition, no nor a ſubject matter, then the act of creation muſt needs immediatly produce the creature; and the *Creare* and *Creari* muſt needs be inſeparable: Its anſwered that Gods creating act was from eternity, but the effect, or creature, was not till its Time. But it will be replied, That either God did more for the creatures production or creation at the time of its paſſive creation, then he did from Eternity, or he did no more: If more, then he did ſomething *de novo*: If no more, then either the creature would have had its Being from Eternity, *quia poſita cauſa ponitur effectus*; or elſe if you ask whats the reaſon that the creature was not in Being ſooner or later, no cauſe can be aſſigned: and ſo God ſhould not be the cauſe. This holds equally (ſay they) whether you make the creating act to be only Gods *Velle*, or a ſuperadded execution of that will, as being the effect of power. For either God willed the creatures preſent exiſtence from eternity, as much as at the time of its creation, or as at this day; or he did not. If he did not, then he willeth *de novo*: If he did, then the creature would have exiſted, as ſoon as it was willed. To ſay, that God willed from Eternity that the creature ſhould be in Time, is true: But is it as much to Will that it *ſhall be*, as to Will its preſent exiſtence? If it be anſwered, That there is no *Paſt* or *Future* with God; I anſwer 1. That this was prevented before; when it was ſaid, that God underſtandeth Time, and propoſitions concerning time, though time be only mans meaſure, and propoſitions mans inſtruments. 2. The men that I ſpeak to, maintain that all things coexiſt not with God from Eternity (though indeed the term [*from*] as here uſed, contradicteth Eternity:) and they diſtinguiſh between Gods willing *rerum futuritionem & exiſtentiam præſentem*: and therefore this ſeemeth to make againſt their anſwer. (But indeed none of all this arguing is ſolid, becauſe of the different manner of producing effects *per voluntatem, & per potentiam exequentem voluntati ſuperadditam*.) Perhaps it will be ſaid, that if all this be granted, yet it followeth not that immanent acts may be *de novo* without a change in God, becauſe the Creating act, or any tranſient act is ſo: For the former is God himſelf, but the later is not. To which it may be replied, 1. We ſpeak not now of a product or effect, called the Creation, but of the creating act, and then why ſhould not that be God himſelf, as well as an immanent act? If you ſay it is a Being, then it is God or diſtinct from God: If diſtinct from God, it is a ſubſtance or accident, or ſome *modus*, or who knows what? Accidents God hath none: Subſtance it cannot be; except it be God. If you ſay it is any *modus*, you know what School contradiction you muſt expect: Or if you ſay it is a Reality or a Formality, thoſe that you deal with will tell you, that they can as well prove the immanent acts to be formalities, or ſuch like, as you can the tranſient. For 2. they ſay (with others) that theſe acts are not called Immanent, Poſitively, as if they had any effect or *terminus* in God himſelf;

but

but Negatively, becaufe they have no effect, *ad extra* ; and do *nihil ponere in objecto*. So that as to the nature of the act it felf, they fay, it is the fame, or at leaft, the later as much effential to God, as the former (though not their effects.) And I have paper converfe with a Divine, if I miftake not, full as Learned as Mr K. (to fpeak fparingly) who maintains, that thofe which you call immanent acts (*viz*. Gods Knowing and Willing other things befides himfelf) are tranfient, and fo to be called ; as having as much an extrinfick object, as thofe that you and I call Tranfient ; though they make no real change on them : but that thofe only are to be called Gods immanent acts, whofe object is himfelf. 3. Moreover you will acknowledge that Gods *Velle* is an immanent act : But how many and how great are they that maintain that Gods Creating act, was but his *Velle* that things fhould be ! I need not tell you of Schoolmen that are for this : but when you (doubtlefs) know that Dr *Twiffe* himfelf affirms it, in his *Vindic.* you muft either be of his minde, or *handle him unworthily* by your Diffent, as I did in another cafe. Now if the act by which God produced the creatures be but his *Velle*, then it is an act which you call immanent. And you well know how commonly it is maintained that *Deus operatur per effentiam :* and that there is no act but his effence it felf, requifite to any effect, which he produceth, as it is the effect of the firft Caufe. But this is but *ad hominem ;* for thefe are not their principles whofe arguings I now recite. They fuppofe that creation and other tranfient acts, are not meer Volitions, but acts of power, in execution of Gods will. To which purpofe how largely many famous Schoolmen have argued, is obvious to them that are converfant in them. *Aureolus* hath fifteen Arguments to this end. *Gregor. Arminienfis* hath many Arguments to prove that how ever Creation or Confervation be taken, neither of them is God himfelf. *Capreolus* I know and other Thomifts anfwer thefe Arguments : and much may be replied and is, to thofe anfwers : fo that in fo dark and unfearchable a Controverfie, ftrong wits may finde fomething to fay, againft each other; longer then the patience of the wifeft of their Readers will hold out to know the iffue of their difputes. *Ægidius, Thom. de Argent. Occam,* and others plead alfo for a neceffity of an executive act of power, diftinct from the meer act of willing, or that Creation is not God. So do *Jacob. Martini, Suarez, Scibler,* and other later Authors. And if (as *Aquinas* faith) tranfient acts be *formaliter in agente,* as well as immanent, then the inception of new immanent acts feems to have no other inconveniences, then the inception of tranfient acts as to the form. But indeed the Thomifts fay the fame of both, that they are only Gods effence, and that God hath no tranfient act at all, but only that his Effence or Will or Underftanding may be fo denominated for the rational Relation of the Object thereto. And therefore *Aquinas* (1.q 25. a. 1.) maintaining that there is in God *Potentia activa* (though not *paffiva*) withall maintains it to be the fame thing, as the action, and as his Will and Underftanding. (And yet fometime he calleth Gods actions tranfient : but in this he fpeaks unconftantly or doubtfully, as *Suarez* noteth *Met. difp.* 20. §. 5.) And the fubftance of all *Capreolus* anfwer to *Aureolus* fifteen Arguments is this fame diftinction, between Gods act of Creation it felf (which is his Will and Effence, immanent and eternal) and the *Relatio rationis* between God and the object ; from which Gods will is denominated a tranfient act. But yet in this tranfient act, it is only the relation, and not the act it felf (which is God himfelf) which may be diverfified or renewed. Now if this meer *relatio rationis* be fufficient ground for our denomination of Gods act to be [Tranfient] and thefe tranfient acts to

be

be new, then it may seem that the relation of the same act to some extrinsick terminative objects (as of Gods knowledge to the present existence of things *in nunc temporis*) doth give the same ground to call those acts new, though not so properly transient. For if one may be denominated from its respect to its object, why not the other: Nay why the same *relatio rationis* may not as well denominate those acts transient also, which we now call immanent, is not easie to discern: For both have respect to an extrinsick object, if that suffice. Nay doth not that act which is called immanent, produce or effect? seeing it is only *Volendo* without any other executive action that God effecteth all things that are effected: and this *Velle* from eternity is. (say they) *causa in actu* of those things that are produced in time. And therefore many say, that God hath no Will as to extrinsicks, but what is effective: and so that his Will hath no extrinsick object properly so called, but only products or effects. That *omne velle Dei est operativum & efficax eorum quæ vult*, and that therefore he may not be said to will any thing but what he doth effect. See *Gibieuf de Libert. li. 2. c. 24. & 1.*

So that in Conclusion, according to the Doctrine of the most Learned Thomists, there is in God neither immanent nor transient act in Mr K's sense. (Except those that are terminated, as they call it, in himself as the object.) Not immanent; for they are not terminated in the Agent, as Mr K. saith, such are; nay they have respect to things extrinsick; nav, say many, they are productive of these extrinsick things. Not transient; for Gods essence doth not *transire in objectum extraneum*, but only cause it without any other executive action; and so respecteth it. In the same sense therefore, and on the same grounds as you will maintain the transient act to be in time, and not eternal, will these men think to prove it also of the immanent. For even the transient acts of God (so called) are not in the creature, but only respect and effect them. As *Capreolus* saith *(li. 2. dist. 1. q. 2. art. 3.)* *Talis actio prædicamentalis & quæ est motus, est subjective in passo: Divina autem actio non est motus, nec mutatio, licet causet motum & mutationem.*

7. But they much insist on that before intimated, that if it be no wrong to Gods simplicity to have diversity or multiplicity of immanent acts ascribed to him, then it is not any wrong to his immutability to have such acts ascribed to him *de novo*: For the reason will prove alike. But that it is no wrong to God to have diversity of immanent acts ascribed to him, is evident by 1. The use of Scripture. 2. The use of all Divines. 3. And the necessity of the thing. 1. I need not tell any man that hath read the Bible, that Scripture distinguisheth of Gods attributes: that it ascribeth to him Understanding, Will, Memory, &c. that it speaketh not of his Love and Hatred, his Approbation and Disallowance, his Justice and Mercy, as being one, not to be distinguished. 2. And what Divines speak otherwise? even of them that make the boldest enquiries into Gods nature, and pass of it the most confident conclusions, as if they had seen the invisible Majesty: I mean the Schoolmen of all sorts: To how little purpose were many a Volume in 1m *Sent.* for the most part, if it were enough to apprehend in God undivisible Unity? How easily on these grounds might we answer all *Bradwardines*, all *Twisses* sublime disputes, about Gods willing sin, his order of intention, and of his Decrees, his Election and Reprobation, whether absolute or conditional, definite or indefinite, and *de rerum possibilitate & futuritione ab æterno*, with many the like? Its easie to say, that all these are one and the same thing: and the same is not before or after it self, &c. Yet this is not taken for a satisfactory

way

way of disputing.' 3. Yea is it not apparent, that there is a necessity of such distinguishing language? How many souls would you be likely to convert, and save? how many sins to prevent, by telling your Auditory, that in deed and truth it is all one thing in God to Decree a man to salvation, or to decree him to damnation?! Its all one to Will that you shall sin, and that you shall not sin : that you shall die this day, and that your Neighbour shall live fourty years longer: Its the same thing, without any true difference, for God to Love you now you believe, and to Hate you while you were a worker of Iniquity; to be pleased and displeased, to Approve and dislike; His Love to *Peter*, to *Jacob*, and his Hatred to *Judas*, to *Esau* was the same thing, only the effects are not the same. I say, how savoury and profitable would this doctrine be?

:. And are there not the same Reasons for our ascribing to God, the beginning and ending of Immanent Acts, as the Diversity of them? Is not one as consistent with his Immutability, as the other with his simplicity? Doth not Scripture ascribe to God the Inception and ending of Immanent Acts, as well as the Diversity of them? And is there not as great a necessity of our using that language as the other? How many souls were you like to save by telling them [God Loved you as well before you believed, yea before Christ died for you, as he doth since! God doth Hate you now as much as he did when you were a worker of iniquity, and is as much offended with you since you believed as he was when you were a childe of wrath! He had the same thoughts of you when you were blaspheming, murdering and committing adultery, as when you repent and pray. God is now decreeing to create the world; he is now decreeing to give the Law by *Moses*, to save *Noah* by the Ark, *Lot* out of *Sodom*: he is now Decreeing that Christ shall suffer for us; he now knows all these as future : he is no more Reconciled to the world by Christ, or Pleased in or by his Sufferings and Merits then he was before: God knows now that [Christ is now on the Cross] or [Christ is not Risen] is a true Proposition, because he did once know that it is a true Proposition : and he ceaseth not to know it :] would this kinde of doctrine seem sound and edifying? Do you use to preach thus?

But you'le say, That Gods Knowledge, Will, Power, Goodness, Justice, Infiniteness, his Willing the End and the Means, the futurition of things, and their present existence, mens salvation or damnation are all diversified onely as to *extrinsick denomination*, and not really : from the variety of objects it is, that one act of God is variously denominated.

Answ. 1. But *Scotus* with his followers, *Sirectus*, *Basolis*, *Trombeta le Roy*, *Gothutius*, *Mayro*, *Faventinus*, and the like, tell us of more then extrinsick denominations: And if there be in God a Diversity of Formalities; it may as well be said, that there is an inception and ending of these Formalities in him. This doth no more derogate from the Immutability of God, then the other from his simplicity.

2. Have these extrinsick Denominations any true Ground in the things denominated, or not? If not, it seems they are all false, and therefore not to be used. If they have, then what is it? The difference of names should suppose an equal difference in the Things. A meer Relative difference, some are loth to grant. If they should, as they plead for a diversity of Relations, others may as well plead for an Inception and Cessation of Relations : (Could they prove Immanent acts to be but Relations.) If they say they are *Modi* or *Entia rationis*, or what ever title rash adventurous wits may impose on them, still others will say as much for their

F   Beginnig

Beginning and Ending, as they do for their Diversity, and that one implies no more a Change in God, then the other denieth his simplicity. The describers of Extrinsick Denomination that place it between *Ens* and *Nihil*, make it to signifie the order of a thing to the subject which yet it is not in. But then it is a meer Relation which is Denominated; or if any more, it should be *ex parte objecti* only in our case.

3. But suppose that it be but a meer extrinsick Denomination, and have no Reall Ground in the thing denominated; see what follows: But this much: That Gods Knowledge, and Will, and Power, and Justice, and Mercy, his Knowing me to be Godly or ungodly, his decreeing *Peter* to life, and *Judas* to death; his loving *Jacob* and hating *Esau*, are all one; his knowing one thing to be future, and another not future, is all one: But yet because of the Diversity of objects it is meet and needfull, that we Denominate extrinsecally Gods acts to be divers: and so to distinguish his Intention of the End, from his Election of the Means; his Election from his Reprobation, his Approbation from his dislike, *&c*. Even so, these acts in God have in themselves no Beginning or End: God did never Begin to Love, to Will this or that, to Know *&c*. But yet because of the Beginning and Ending of objects, it is meet and needfull to Denominate Gods acts extrinsecally as Beginning and Ending, as the objects do, and changing with them. For here the case is the same as to Gods Immutability, as in the other to his simplicity. And if this hold, then those men that should write Voluminous Disputes, about the Beginning and Ending of Immanent acts, would do as warrantably as Dr *Twiss* and others do in writing so of their diversity, priority and posteriority in nature. Nay is it not much more Justifiable then many of their Volumes? For from Eternity there was no reall diversity of objects to denominate Gods Immanent acts from. For that *esse cognitum vel volitum*, which they'le flie to, could be no where, but *in mente & voluntate Divina*: and if there were no Diversity *in mente Divina* at all, then what ground can be imagined of the extrinsick Denominations? For example, *Possibilia & futura* being nothing, could not in themselves differ from eternity: Yet how great a fabrick doth Dr *Twiss* build upon this Proposition, that [the transition of things future *è numero possibilium in numerum futurorum*, being from Eternity, it must needs have an eternal Cause which can be no other then Gods Will.] Now if there were no such transition, but *in mente divina*, and if there were no such notion from Eternity any where else, as is [Future and Possible] and so it must be imagined to be an *Ens rationis Divinæ*, then it plainly follows that there was no such thing as Future, distinct from Possible: for in God is no distinct Immanent acts, (as knowing Possibles, and Knowing things future;) and in the things was no distinction, for they are nothing.

It seems therefore that upon your own Grounds it is as Justifiable and necessary, to Denominate extrinsecally Gods Immanent acts, as having Beginning and End, when the objects have so, as it is to Denominate them divers from the diversity of the object: and that if we made this our ordinary speech in voluminous Disputes, you could no more blame us for it, then all the exactest School-Divines are to be blamed for the other.

Moreover, some may think, that you do teach Infidels to destroy the Christian Faith, or teach a man to prove or disprove what he will, because Contradictories may consist, *e.g.* If they would prove that [Christ is not Risen] thus: That which God knoweth to be true, is true: But God Knoweth this Proposition to be true [Christ is not Risen] Therefore. The *minor* they prove thus: God did
once

once know this Proposition to be true: Therefore he doth so still: for there is no Ending of any Immanent act of God. It will be answered, That this onely shews a difference in the object, that it was once true, which now is not: but Gods act is the same by which he knoweth these mutable objects. Be it so: (yet whether it be certain and can be proved still, is by them doubted:) but is it fit for us to speak of this act as one only? It seems then, it is all one, in God to know a Proposition to be True, and to know it to be false. For the fore-said Proposition [Christ is not Risen] was True one day, and False the next; and God knew both. You'le say, It is all one in God to Know that to be True which is True, and that to be False which is False: but in both he knows *Verè, etsi non verum*. But then you must tell us further, what it is for God to Know [*Truly:*] Is it the Congruency of his Knowledge to the Object, which we call the Truth of it? I think you will say so: And if so, then it is not obvious to shew how there was such a Congruence from Eternity, when there was Nothing but God; and so no other object for his knowledge to agree to: For in God they were all but one, either in *esse cognito*, or *esse volito*; for in him is no reall diversity: and out of him, or in themselves they were not at all: and therefore if God knew all things as many or divers, when they were not at all, and as existent, when they did not exist, where is the Congruence of the act with the object? But all this arguing is but light.

But they further argue thus: Gods Immanent acts, which we are speaking of, are not Himself: and therefore as they may be either diversified or multiplied without his Division or Composition, so they may begin or end without his Mutation. The antecedent they prove by that common Argument: These Immanent acts about the Creature, are Free; God Freely Willeth the existence of this worm or pile of grass: he so Willed it that he could have not willed it, or nilled it. But his own Being is necessary, and cannot but be: Therefore, &c. It seems hard to say, that God did as necessarily Will the pardoning of your sins, as he is necessarily God: Or that he could no more have Willed one pile of grass more or lesse on the earth, or one sand more or lesse on the Sea-shore, or one day more or lesse to any mans life, then he could cease to be God. This is a short way of answering *Beverovicius* question, and of answering the presumptuous enquiry, Whether God could have made any thing better, and a thousand more? *Itane etiam ipsum Numen fato constringitur?* Is it a good Argument? *Deus est; ergo necesse est Creaturas esse, nec plures, nec pauciores, nec priùs, nec posteriùs,* &c? One of my Rabbi's (by whose name I have acquainted Mr. K. with my ignorance) answereth that Gods Decrees are Free, *Solum per terminationem ad extraneum, seu in quantum Volitio Dei, circa objectum aliquod extrinsecum practicè est.* But this is as much as to say, No Immanent act is Free: For Immanent acts (at least if Mr. K. know) are not terminated in any thing without: Or if a man should say, that those that have an extrinsick object, are objectively terminated in something extrinsick; yet this seems none of the Authours sense (as the word *practicè* shews:) and if it were (as perhaps it is) his words would run thus: [Gods Decrees are free, onely as they are such and such Decrees about such objects:] which would but yield the cause, that as such Decrees they are not the same formally with the divine Essence. And were it not for the Connotation of the Object, it were no Decree, nor to be called, but simply Gods Essence. I am sure Dr. *Twisse* will be fully and earnestly enough for those that maintain the liberty of the Divine Decrees which we now mention: and therefore I suppose Mr. K. will be of the same minde.

And

And that there is not such clear Evidence in this case, as to embolden men to such confident Conclusions, or to build so much on them, as some do, let *Suarez* perplexed Dispute *Metaph. Disp. 30. Sect. 9.* testifie, *Quomodo cum divina libertate stet Immutabilitas?* Where after the producing of many opinions, and the Arguments and Answers, he concludes, *Ex his quæ circa has opiniones dicta sunt, satis (ut opinor) declaratum est quanta sit hujus opinionis difficultas; faciliusque esso quamlibet ejus partem impugnare, quam aliquam probe defendere, aut explicare. Quapropter non vereor Confiteri nihil me invenire quod mihi satisfaciat, nisi hoc solum, in hujusmodi rebus id de Deo esse credendum, quod ineffabili ejus perfectioni magis sit consentaneum, quodque ab omni imperfectione alienum sit,* &c.] And how uncertain are men, that some of those things may not consist with the Divine Perfection, which yet they confidently affirm to be inconsistent with it? If it be a point that is so farre past the reach of *Suarez* and many other such subtil Disputers, I think Mr. K. should not pretend to so full an insight into it, which may raise him to that confidence which is here expressed; much lesse should he think it so obvious to the understandings of his inferiours.

How light so ever Dr. *Twiss* make of them, certainly they are accounted no children among the most learned of their side, who do teach, That there may be so far a Beginning and Ceasing of Gods Immanent acts, which have a mutable object, without any change in God himself, as that they may have a new transition to the object, and so God may Will that which before he Willed not, though yet it be all by one simple act. Of this minde is *Penottus, Lychetus, Fr. a Sancta Clara:* And the said *Sancta Clara* citeth others, as countenancing his Doctrine. But though there are but few for this opinion, yet for the formal distinction of Gods Immanent acts (which as is said, seems to be as inconsistent with his simplicity, as this with his Immutability) there are many and that of the most Learned: Vid. quæ habet *Scotus in sent. l. 1. dist. 8. Qu. 3. & dist. 2. Qu. 4. & 7. & dist. 34. & passim.* And *Rada* saith, that *Scoti sententiam ab ejus diebus universa Parienfis Schola semper amplexata fuerit, necnon & Lovaniensis atque Bononiensis Academia; Et in universa Italia apud omnes vivos doctos est celebris & famosa: In Contr 4.* And their Reasons are not contemptible, which may be seen in their several Writers: Specially in those that have wrote whole books of the Formalities. Or *Rada* (a man of a clear understanding and expression) will afford you many in that one *Contr.* 4. which are worthy consideration. And if *Th. Faber Faventinus* his reconciling Interpretation of their Distinction *Rationis Ratiocinatæ*, will prove their sense, then many of the *Thomists* are also of the same minde. *Vid.* Faventin. *Tract de formalitat. cap. 3.*

I do not mean by this Argument to conclude that there *must* be (or in all cases *may* be) an Inception or Cessation of those Acts which admit of a formal Distinction: But only thus, that if a formal Distinction be consistent with the Divine simplicity, then an Inception and Cessation of some such formalities (or acts, *quoad formales differentias*) may seem consistent with Gods Immutability: (And I know no other Argument of moment then left, if that be solved.) What these formalities are, I do not wonder, if they give but a dark account: Yet that they are different objective conceptions they agree. And as *Rada* saith, *ad Distinctionem formalem duo requiruntur. Alterum est, quod utrumque distinctionis extremum dicat aliquid Positivum in re, seclusa operatione Intellectus: Alterum est, quod utrumque extremum dicat propriam formalitatem, secuudum quam sit in rerum natura extra suam causam.* And *Scotus* himself saith of this as applied to God; *Quod Forma in creaturis turæ habet aliquid imperfectionis, scilicet quod est Forma informans aliquid, & Pars compositi: aliquid etiam habet quod non est imperfectionis, sed consequitur eam secundum suam rationem essentialem sive formalem, scilicet, quod ipsa fit quo aliquid est tale, c. g. sapientia in nobis est Accidens, hoc est imperfectionis: sed quod ipsa sit quo aliquid est sapiens, hoc non est imperfectionis, sed essentialis rationis sapientiæ. In divinis autem nihil est forma, secundum illam duplicem rationem imperfectionis, quia nec Informans, nec pars: est tamen ibi sapientia in quantum est quo illud in quo ipsa est, est sapiens, & hoc non per aliquam compositionem, &c. Sent. 1. dist. 8. Q. 3.*

Some think yet clearer Arguments might be fetcht from the Hypostatical Union, from the Acts of generation and spiration, or Love, whereby the Son is begotten of the Father, and the holy Ghost proceedeth from the Father and the Son, and from the distinction of Persons in the Trinity. But I will stop here (as having run further then I intended) lest you should mis-interpret me, and think, that I own all these Arguments that I touch upon. I know what D.*Twiß* against *Pennotus* hath said to one or two of them, and what the Schoolmen commonly say to the same. I mention these only to shew that a full or clear solution of these doubts is not also facile and obvious, as you seem to imagine.

I must again intreat you, and every ingenious Reader, to fasten no opinion on me, but what I own, at least none which I disclaim. If I must be of one side in this Controversie, I will be of Mr.*Kendals* side, and say, that God hath but one act immanent, and that is Eternal. But my thoughts are, that we know not what we talk of when we speak thus, and therefore I will not be of any side in this.

I think, 1. That God hath no Act at all in proper speech: but both Acting, and Understanding, and Willing are by a very, very, very low remote Analogy ascribed to him.

2. Yet I am ready to think, that as we are fain for our own understanding, to speak of God as Acting, Understanding, Willing, Loving, &c. and also for our own understanding to distinguish his Perfections, Properties, Acts, &c. which are but one, so may and must we as much speak of some of his Acts, as beginning and ending (which yet perhaps do not in themselves:) For the Reason and Necessity seems to be the same. For because the word [Knowledge or Understanding] is first used and applied to mans act of Knowledge, and signifieth first only such a Knowledge as is diversified by objects; yea and man can have no proper positive Conception of a Knowledge which is not diversified by the diversity of Objects (but onely a Negative Conception;) therefore it is that we are forced to speak of Gods Knowledge (and so of his Will and other Acts) as divers or distinct: as Divines generally do. And on the same Grounds, as man hath no positive Conception of any Knowledge or Will, about mutable objects, which is not varied with these objects, as to the Being, Beginning and Ending, therefore we must as necessarily denominate Gods acts about such objects, as Beginning and Ending, as we must denominate them Divers. And so we may well say, God willed from Eternity the futurition of the worlds Creation, and Christs Death, &c. But now he doth not will their futurition, but their preterition: and that he Loveth now (as believers in Christ) those whom he before Hated as Workers of Iniquity; and that he is satisfied and well-pleased in his Son, and his Sacrifice, who was not so before. Methinks Mr. K. should think this language as fit for the mouths and pens of Divines, as the former, and not to be blamed or accused as erroneous,

erroneous, because improper, as long as we must speak improperly of God; or not at all. And I am sure that Scripture speaks of God in this language, ascribing to him Immanent acts, as new or as ceasing, and as moved by exteriour causes: Therefore this way of speaking is not unfit or intolerable.

The Summe of all that I say therefore is but this, That we cannot conceive of Gods Immanent acts, as in themselves they are (nor are they truely the same things that we conceive of, when we apply the several denominations to them:) and therefore we must conceive of them by Resemblance to the Acts of Man so denominated, still acknowledging the Impropriety of the terms, and disclaiming all those Imperfections which in man they do express.

But because Mr. K. hath spoken so much to this point already, its like he will take it ill if I take no notice of it. I will therefore a little insist on the consideration of what he saith on it, to Mr. *Goodwin*, pag. 93, 94. (but briefly, as being not to me.)

---

§. 6.

Mr. K. *THis is such a Reason as most of your Disciples needed your favour to reade a Logick Lecture to them, that they might be in a Capacity to give their Judgements on it: You not having been pleased to do it, I will for once gratifie them with a Cast of my old Office; and now supposing my self again in my Deans Chair, I gravely begin thus. That* Univocum *is that which is attributed to several things according to the same Name, and Nature signified by that name; as Animal to a Man and an Asse, to which are opposed on the one hand* Æquivocum, *which is attributed according to the same Name, but not signifying the same Nature, as* Canis *which is said of a Starre, a Beast, and a Fish: either hath the same name* Canis, *but their natures are as different as Heaven, Earth and Water. On the other hand* Analogum, *which is attributed according to the same Name, and as signifying the same Nature; but not in the like manner. Now this same* Analogum *is of two sorts; The terms are promiscuously jumbled together by the Logickmongers, but let that be,* 1. Proportionis; *when the same Name is given to things of the Like, but not the same Nature: as Laughing, &c.* 2. Attributionis: *where the same Name is given to divers things, according to the same Nature: but this same Nature doth not agree to them alike; but to the one first, to the other afterwards,* (secundum priùs & posteriùs: *yea to the later dependantly on the first: as Substance and Accident are each of them* Ens, *a thing, &c.*

---

§. 6.

R. B. HOld a little. 1. The first part of your task, you have competently performed, *viz.* to acquaint us of the lower Orbs of your ancient Dignity: Our distance is so great from the Superiour Planets, that we might never have heard of your Deans Chair, had you not happily here informed us: But I hope you had a more noble Imploiment in your Deans Chair, then this poor, common, Inferiour work, to tell men of *Univocum æquivocum & Analogum*, and to distinguish *Analogum Proportionis & Attributionis*: But though I had not the happiness to be educated at your feet, yet in this your Learned, Elaborate, Polemical writing, I may, no doubt, expect the best of your Judgement; and may conjecture what you were wont to reade to your Pupils by that which you here so *gravely* read to Mr. *Goodwin*. First, you will not, it seems [jumble the terms so promiscuously mifcuoufly as the Logickmongers do:] But, when thefe words had raifed my expectations of fome more exquifite diftribution then ordinary, or at leaft of more apt terms, I am put off with the old diftinction, not only common in the Schoolmen, but in the multitudes of Logick and Metaphyfick Writers, which I had thought you had difdained: Not the fmalleft *Senguerdius* but hath it ; (onely he, with many others term it, but Barbarous ; whereas *Keckerman* terms it *Infipid*, and *Burgerfdicius inept*:) And *Rutgerfius* faith, that *Analogorum nomine folum ea dicuntur quæ fecundum proportionem apud Ariftotelem vocantur, prout notant interpretes ex cap.* 16. *poft c.* 15. *maxime verò ex c.* 6. '1. *Ethic.* &c. *Ufus tamen Latinæ Scholæ & Philofophorum obtinuit, ut etiam ea quæ fecundum attributionem vocantur analogorum nomine cenfeantur.*

But though your Diftinction be very ordinary, I confeffe there is more then ordinary in your Explication of the members: But it is of fuch a nature, as makes me begin to abate the apprehenfions of my infelicity, in that I had never the happinefs to be your Auditor, and to have Learned Logick at your feet. Your *Analogum in genere*, is that [which is attributed according to the fame name, and as fignifying the *fame Nature*, but not in the like manner.] Your *Analogum proportionis*, is [when the fame name is given to things of the *like, but not the fame nature*.] *Analogum in Genere*, is of the *fame* nature, as well as Name. *Analogum Proportionis*, is not the *fame Nature*, but the *Like*. And fo the nature of the *Genus* is not in the *Species*: Nay they are contrary one to the other: and onely the later member (*Analogum Attributionis*) remains an *Analogum*, and each *Species* receives not the definition of the *Genus*. If this be the Doctrine which you fo [Gravely deliver from your Deans Chair, I will fay as you do [I cannot perfwade my felf to leave my old Doctors to follow You.] I will even turn to poor *Keckerman, Burgerfdicius, Suarez* again ; yea to a *Rutgerfius, Facchæus, Gorlæus, Serguerdius, Alftedius*, or any body that's near me of this generation, before I will fwallow what I cannot digeft.

§. 7.

Mr. K. NOw if *Subftance and Accident* be Analoga, *becaufe of the dependance of Accidents on the Subject, then what ever is predicated of God and the Creature, muft be predicated Analogically, becaufe the creature hath it not but by dependance on God, but God independently from the Creature: And as the Being of the Creature, is derived from God in* fieri, *and depends on him in* facto effe *; fo queftionlefs the Knowledge of the Creature, is but a beam from the fountain of light, which is in God, and cannot longer fubfift, then he vouchfafeth to preferve it by a continued irradiation,* &c.

§. 7.

R. B. 1. I Would rather fay that Subftance and Accident are *Analogata*, then *Analoga* ; but you may ufe your Liberty, and call the *Analoga*, *Analegata*. 2. I fhould think that it is not directly and ftrictly [Becaufe of the dependance of Accidents on the Subject, that Subftance and Accident are *Analogata*: but becaufe of the Imperfect Entity which through this dependance the Accidents have in the more perfect Entity of the Subject. 3. It is not that moft General nerall *Analogum*, [*Ens*] as appliable to God and the Creature, that we are now in question of. But it is those inferiour of [Fore-knowledge, Knowledge, Will, Election, &c.] 1. Your [Because] is unsound, and I conceive your Consequence is false, *viz.* [then whatsoever is predicated of God and the Creature must be predicated Analogically] Do you think that nothing may be spoken equivocally of God and the Creature? If you do, you are a singular man. 5. I hope you do not think that our knowledge depends on God, as Accidents on the Subject: If you do, then God hath many Accidents indeed, were that true: I had rather say plainly, that God effecteth our knowledge (by way of natural Causation in some respect, and by moral Causation in other respects) as that which had no Being before, then to talk of Emanation as a Beam from the fountain of Light; considering what ill use many in these times have made of the doctrine of Emanation. 6. It seems by your former Conclusion [whatsoever is predicated of God and the Creature, must be predicated Analogically] and by your present predication of [The fountain of Light which is in God] that you judge [Light] or [the fountain of Light] to be predicated Analogically of God too. Which if you do, and this also must be by Analogy of Attribution, then it seems Heat, Cold, Gravity, Levity, Density, Rarity, Composition, or what ever is in the Creature may be thus attributed to God. 7. As to the point it self in question, 1. I will not meddle with that old Controversie, Whether *Ens* be spoken of God and the Creature Univocally, Æquivocally or Analogically. I have seen what *Scotus* saith for his opinion in *Sent.2.dist.12.& alibi. & 1.dist.3.q.1.& 3.* And what *Anth.Andreæ 4.Metaph.q.1.* Meurisse *Metaph.Scot. l 1. Qu.8. p.108,&c.* And *Phil.Faber.Faventin. Phys.Scot.Theorem.95.pag.654, &c. Reda,* and others say for it: And what *Occham in 1.Sent. dist. 2. q. 8.* And *Guil. Rubio,* say for the Nominals opinion: And what *Cajetan* saith against the Scotists. (By which Scotists the sense of Univocation, Æquivocation, and Analogy, is a little more subtilly opened, then Mr K. doth out of his Deans Chair.) But the Question that I speak to, is onely how farre *Intelligere, Velle* and *Agere,* may be Attributed to God. 2. And for the distribution of *Analoga,* and the sense of Analogy, I think, it will be long ere the Chair-men are agreed. *Meurisse* out of *Rubio* saith, *Univocum opponi soli æquivoco, non verò Analogo, & denominativo: quia Univocum se habet ad æquivocum sicut Unum ad Multa: Unum autem propriè solum multis opponitur: se habet autem ad Analogum & denominativum, tanquam veluti superius ad sua inferiora: Quia Univocum aliud est purum, aliud est non purum: Non purum est aut Analogum, aut Denominativum. Nullum superius autem opponitur suis inferioribus: Itaque Univocum non opponitur Analogo & Denominativo; sed ab Analogo distinguitur tanquam Univocum purum, & à Denominativo Univocum quidditativum, seu illud quod est & prædicatum Univocum & Univocè prædicatur* Others innumerate *Analoga* with the *Homonyma,* distinct from *Synonima.*

Goclenius (who speaks largely of it) gives this distribution, *Lexic.Philos.p.100.* I think in fitter terms then Mr.*Kendal.*

Analoga sunt Proportione { *Propriâ: ut Ens, bonum, principium, natura, motus, &c.* *Impropriâ* { *Attributione tantum: ut sanum ad animal & medicamentum.* *Translata proportione: Risus, comparatione hominis & prati.*

But

But I think poor contemptible *Keckerman* and *Burgerfdicius* have better explained and diftributed *Homonyma* and *Analoga*, then all that ever I had the hap to be acquainted with, not excepting the fubtilleft Scotifts. 3. As for the application hereof to our Queftion, I ftill affirm, That the thing which the word [Knowledge] is fpoken of, in God, is not only more eminently and perfectly in him then the Creature, but is only in him, and not in the creature at all: And the thing which the word Knowledge is fpoken of, or doth fignifie in man, is not at all *formaliter* in God, but there is in him fomething of an Infinite, tranfcendent Excellency above it, which makes it ufelefs; and in God it would be Imperfection: And therefore it may be faid to be in God *eminenter non formaliter*: The word [Knowledge] is firft ufed to fignifie the knowledge of man: It is tranflated to prefs to us that Incomprehenfible perfection of God, which we cannot otherwife conceive of or exprefs. Yet when ever we make ufe of the term, we cannot by it our felves attain to a conception, pofitive and true, of any higher thing then fuch knowledge as our own, with fome negative additions, for removal of the Imperfections; as that it is Infinite, *&c*. fo that man can have no true pofitive Conception of the Nature of that which in God we call Knowledge: Only he apprehendeth it to be fomewhat like that which in man is called Knowledge. But Like is not the fame. As *Goclenius* out of *Ariftot*. ὅμοια τῇ ἀναλογία non funt ὁμογενῆ. *fimilia Analogia non funt ejufdem generis: non funt eadem genere*. It is therefore a proper fpeech to fay [Knowledge is not in God] and proper to fay, it is in man: But yet it is a neceffary fpeech to fay [God knows] becaufe we have no fitter expreffion for that perfection of God, which we fo call. *Aquin. de Veritate Mater.* 2ᵈᵃ *Qu*. 1. faith, *Et quia nulla Ratio fignificata per ipfum nomen definit ipfum Deum, nullum nomen à nobis impofitum eft propriè nomen ejus; fed eft propriè creaturæ quæ definitur ratione fignificata per nomen: Et tamen ifta nomina quæ funt Creaturarum nomina Deo attribuuntur fecundum quod in Creaturis aliqua fimilitudo ejus repræfentatur.* The third Opinion which he there rejecteth is, That Knowledge is attributed to God Metaphorically, as Anger is; againft which he oppofeth his fourth, *Et ideo aliter dicendum eft, quod fcientia Deo attributa fignificat aliquid quod in Deo eft*.] As if thefe might not well confift! Even a Metaphorical expreffion doth expreffe fomething that is in God, though it expreffe it but Metaphorically. And in *Qu. undecimis*, he hath no better anfwer to the fifth Objection, which is drawn from [the greater diftance between God and us, then between *Ens Creatum & non Ens*] then this, *Ad 5ᵐ dicendum, quod Enti & non Enti aliquid fecundum analogiam convenit: quod ipfum non ens analogicè dicitur Ens: ut dicitur in 4ᵒ Metaph. Unde nec diftantia quæ eft inter creaturam & Deum communitatem analogicè impedire poteft*. If the Analogy between Gods Acts, Knowledge, Will, and ours, be no nearer then between *Ens & non ens*, fure it is not fuch as you imagine, and here exprefs. And *contra Gentil*. l. 1. c. 31. he confeffeth, that *in omni nomine à nobis dicto, quantum ad modum fignandi imperfectio invenitur quæ Deo non competit, quam is res fignata aliquo modo exiftenti Deo conveniat*. Now *fcire, velle, agere*, are terms properly fitted only to mans imperfect Mode of Knowing, Willing, Acting, and do afford us no pofitive Conception of any other: fo that if we could devife fome *genus* which did comprehend Gods acts perfect and mans *imperfect*, as *Ens* doth fubftance and Accident, yet that muft not be Knowledge or Will: For thefe are the proper names of the *Genus imperfectum*: As if you fhould fay, *Subftantia eft Accidens*, A certain kinde of Comprehenfion of the Creature God hath, whofe Nature being to us unknown, the proper name is unknown too, and therefore we are fain to call it by the proper name of mans comprehen-

G   fion,

tion, *i. e.* Intellection and Science. And all Divines confess, that as to the order of knowing, and so as to the name we must first begin with the creature, to whom the name is first applicable. So *Aquinas contra Gentil. l.* 1. *c* 35. *Quia ex rebus aliis in Dei cognitionem pervenimus, res nominatim de Deo & aliis rebus dictorum, per prius est in Deo secundum suum modum; sed ratio nominis per posterius: unde & nominari dicitur à suis causatis.* So *Goclenius Lexic. Philosoph. de Analog. Duo sunt distinguenda; nimirum res ipsæ per nomina significatæ, & nominum impositio. Ad res ipsas quod attinet, prius ea de Deo prædicantur, quam de creaturis. Atque hic propriè ordo est & convenientia, quam habent creaturæ ad Deum; cujus ordinis causa dicuntur nomina Analogicè de Deo & de Creaturis. prædicari. Quod vero attinet ad nominum Rationem & Impositionem prius iis nominibus appellatæ fuerunt res creatæ quam Deus. Quare quod dicimus analogicè prædicari nomina de Deo & de Creaturis, quia prius de Deo quam de Creaturis: de Analogia reali seu secundum rem, non autem secundum nominis rationem intelligendum est.* Zanchy hath the same words, whose they are first I know not. How fit a speech this is, *de Analogia reali,* I leave to others to judge: but all grant that the Name is first applied to the Creature, and thence to God. Now all this holds of meer Metaphorical expressions.

To use *Burgersdicius* distribution, I yield that these names applied to God and the Creature, are not *Homonyma à casu,* (such as *Aquinas cont Gentil. ubi sup.* expresseth his meer æquivocals to be) but *à consilio.* But whether the *Ratio Homonymiæ* be *in Rebus,* or *in nobis,* is not easie certainly to determine. *Keckerman* saith, *Ambigua ex similitudine conceptus est, cum rebus toto genere diversis, ut Deo & Creaturis,* idem nomen tribuitur ex cognatione quam mens format. Nimirum intellectus noster ut essentia & operatione finitus est, ita infinitæ Dei naturæ & attributis concipiendis non est proportionatus; atque idcirco in Deo nihil concipit directè, sed obliquè ex similitudine quadam, & imagine rei finitæ tanquam objecti sibi congruentis. Hinc a nobis Deo & attributis ejus voces certæ, propriæ ac directæ imponi nequiverunt, sed indirectæ tantum, homonymæ, & ex similitudine ea qua Deus nobis repræsentatur in creaturis tanquam effectis, quæ repræsentatio valde imperfecta est.* Nomen Jehova, *i.e existentis, sibi ipsi imposuit Deus, at nos ne id quidem directè concipimus: reliqua autem quæ Deo tribuimus, ut misericordiam, Justitiam,* &c. *ejusmodi vocibus exprimimus quæ directè impositæ sunt virtutibus hominum significandis, indirectè autem ad Deum pertinent, quatenus nos tales in Deo virtutes similitudine earum quæ in hominibus sunt virtutum concipimus. Unde non minus pie quam scitè Cyrillus,* in his quæ de Deo dicuntur, Maxima scientia est Ignorantiam confiteri: & *Augustinus, Deus, inquit, magnus est, sed sine quantitate, Bonus, sed sine qualitate: ut verò à nobis magnum sine quantitate, bonum sine qualitate directè & plenè concipi, est impossibile,* &c. Et Julius Scaliger, *Nullis, ait, vocibus tam plenè Deum significamus, quam iis quæ Ignorantiam nostram prætendunt.*

But suppose it be granted, that the *Ratio Homonymiæ* is not only *in nobis, sed in rebus,* the question will remain, Whether it be *ob inæqualem generis attributionem,* or only *ob similitudinem, vel mutuam rerum ad se invicem habitudinem?* and so be Tropical? Mr. K. asserteth the former (under the name of Analogy of Attribution.) The Scotists have long defended their Doctors Assertion, that *Deus non est in genere. Vid. Fab. Faventin. Phys. Scot. Theorem.* 96. his Vindication against *Greg. Ariminensis* and *Bacconius:* and many others of them have done this at large. So doth *Wickleff.* in his Trialog.

And if this hold, then nothing can be attributed to God and the Creature by this Analogy, *per inæqualem generis attributionem.* Yea *Aquinas* himself oft saith,

Deus

Deus non est in genere (as *Sarnanus* notes) in 1.p.q.3.a.5. & 1.d.8.q.4.a.2.3ᵐ. & 1.cont.Gent.c.25. though after in *q.de Potentia*.q.7.a.3. *ad ult. Concedit Deum esse Genere substantiæ reductivè :* which *Scotus* refuteth. So *Estius* in 1ᵐ Sent. d. 8. §. 10. denieth God to be *in ullo genere*. And *Sarnanus* hath no more to say for it in his Conciliation (*pag.* 15) then this, *Esse in genere stat dupliciter : primo modo ut pars subjectiva contenta in illo genere : Et sic negatur Deum esse in genere. Secundo modo, ut principium Continens ipsum Genus : Et hoc modo Deus per appropriationem est in Genere substantiæ. Vid.* Gab. Biel. 1. Sent. dist. 8. q. 1. But this is not for God to be *in genere*, but for that *Genus* to be in God.

As *Burgersdicius* faith, *Omnium longissimè à Synonymis absunt homonyma a Casu, quæq; causam homonymiæ habent in nobis: proprius ad synonymorum naturam accedunt Tropica, ac imprimis Analoga: at omnium proximè quæ ambigua sunt ob inæqualem attributionem.* That these words are not spoken of God and the creature *univocè* all of us agree, and the Schoolmen have fully evinced. Also that they are not spoken *purè æquivocè*, we are also agreed, and the said Schoolmen have evinced (as particularly *Aquin. in sum. de Verit. ubi sup.* by many Reasons : And *Zanchius de Natura Dei* borrows many of them.) But which of the other kindes of homonymy they belong to, is the doubt. Mr. K. thinks that which of all other is the nearest to synonymy : I think not so : but rather to the Tropical or Analogical, strictly so called, that is, *vel propter similitudinem simplicem, vel proportionem* (if not some of them, to those that have the *Rationem homonymiæ in nobis*) *Jacchæus* faith (*Metaph. l. 1. c. 6.*) *Ego verò mallem istam Analogiam referre ad proportionalitatis Analogiam, non Metaphoricam illam* (*quomodo videre attribuitur oculo & menti*) *sed propriam, quomodo principium dicitur de corde, & fundamento domus.* So he disclaims Mr. K's Analogy of Attribution : If the thing be not utterly uncertain to us, who know so little of Gods nature. But that we may venture on a conjecture, I should rather set the Creature at a greater distance from God then they do : and think that these Attributes are all Tropical, somewhat Metonymical, but mostly Metaphorical. I never saw (in *Aquinas* or any other Schoolman that spoke for it) any cogent Reason to prove, that *Intelligere, Velle, Agere, Amare*, are attributed to God in any other kinde then *Reminisci, Gaudere, Odio habere, Irasci*, &c. Only a gradual difference, I easily acknowledge, *viz.* That *Intelligere & Velle* having lesse Imperfection, have therefore lesse impropriety. And who knows not that there is a wide difference of this sort among Metaphors, some being very near, and some so farre fetcht, as to be Catachrestical. *Durandus* faith (in 1. sent dist. 34. q. 4) *Nullum nomen attribuimus Deo nisi ex Creaturis : non enim ponimus nomen nisi rei quam intelligimus ; & quia non intelligimus ! eum, nisi ex creaturis, & tantum quantum concludimus ex creaturis, ideo nullum nomen imponimus Deo nisi ex creaturis, & quantum ad illa, quæ concludimus convenire Deo ex creaturis : constat autem quod non omnia nomina quæ attribuimus Deo dicuntur de eo translativè & metaphoricè,* &c. *Solum autem illa nomina dicuntur de Deo translativè & metaphoricè quæ significant speciales quidditates rerum creatarum : vel perfectiones secundum modum creaturis convenientem, ut Leo, Agnus, Sentire,* &c. *Quia res significata per hæc nomina non est in Deo, sed aliqua ejus similitudo, ut fortitudo, mansuetudo, & cognitio singularium, quæ in nobis pertinet ad sensum.* But I would fain see it proved, That *Intelligere, Velle, Agere*, do not as properly signifie *perfectiones secundum modum Creaturis convenientem*, as *sentire* doth ? And when we say *segetes fluctuant*, fluctuation is no more proper to the motion of the waters, then *Intelligere, Velle, Agere*, are to the perfections and action of man, or other rational creatures. And whereas they say that the terms are applied to

G 2   God

God, with a Remotion of the Imperfections which they imply in us, I answer, So they may say of those lower terms, which they confesse to be Metaphorical; only allowing a gradual difference of impropriety. Nor doth it follow therefore that there is no truth in these expressions of God, or that they are no helps to our knowledge of him, or means of demonstration. For Metaphors are not as pure equivocals: There's some common reason in the similitude, though in the first and proper sense the name be proper to one. When we say, *Segetes fluctuant*, we expresse not only Motion, wherein both agree, but a motion of the Corn like that of the Water. I think, as I said before, that it is no more proper to call God *Scientem, Volentem, Agentem,* then to call the Firmament a Nut-shell, because both seem to have a convexity or concavity, or contain something else within, *&c.* Or to call the Sunne *Reptile,* or a creeping thing, because it moves, and so do creeping things: or then it is proper to call Knowledge, Light, or to put *Video* for *Intelligo* (as Mr. K. cals God the fountain of Light before.) The Scripture saith, *God is Light:* yet I think this will be easily confessed a Metaphor: and I think it is but *Metaphora propinquior,* to say, *Deus Intelligit, Vult, Agit,* &c. And this I judge after long consideration of what *Aquinas* hath said, 1.q.14.a.1. *& q.*19.a.1. *& alibi:* and many other Schoolmen to the like purpose.

Shall I adde one Argument for the Negative (that it is not by Analogy of Attribution, that Knowledge, Will, Power, *&c.* are attributed to God and the Creature; as *Ens* is to Substance and Accident) *ad hominem* specially? That Knowledge which is the same thing with Will and Power, cannot be the one of the Analogates with our Knowledge which is not the same; in this kinde of Analogy *ob inæqualem generis distributionem:* (supposing Knowledge to be the *Genus Analogum.*) But Gods Knowledge is maintained by those that I dispute with, to be the same with his Will and Power) many say, they differ but *denominatione extrinsecâ;*) Therefore, *&c.* For the proof of the *major,* consider: Else on the same grounds [Power] might be thus analogically spoken of Gods Knowledge and mans Power: For where there is no difference in the Thing, there needs to be none in the Name, as requisite from the Nature of the Thing (but only from some extrinsick respect or use) But Power may not Analogically be spoken *de Potestate humanâ, & scientia divinâ,* Ergo, &c. Common reason and use of speech confirms the *minor.* It seems therefore to be evident truth, that as it is from similitude, or some Tropical respect, that Gods Immanent acts, have divers names, rather then one alone: so is it from the same reason that they have these particular names, rather then other: And consequently that these names are not *Analoga inæqualis Attributionis naturæ communis;* but *Analoga Proportionis,* or Tropical. *Durandus* (in sent. 1.dist. 2. q. 2.) saith, *Alia est opinio quæ mihi videtur verior,* viz. *quod distinctio attributorum, secundum rationem non potest sumi, nisi per comparationem ad aliquam realem diversitatem actu existentem in creaturis, vel possibilem. Quod prob.*1.*sic.Differentia Rationis, nisi sit falsa & vana, licet sit completiva ab intellectu, oportet tamen quod habeat fundamentum in re: sed differentia attributorum secundum rationem non potest habere sufficiens fundamentum in natura divinâ absolutè acceptâ; nisi comparetur ad realem diversitatem quæ in creaturis est, vel esse potest, ergo differentia attributorum divinorum secundum rationem, non potest verè sumi nisi per comparationem ad creaturas. Major patet: ratio enim, quam intellectus format, nisi fundetur aliqualiter in re, ficta est & vana,* &c. *Vide reliq.*

I will only adde the words of *Burgersdicius Metaphys. l.* 2. *c.* 8. §. 1. *sequuntur ea* (*attributa*) *quæ creaturis communicari posse diximus, saltem* καὶ ἀναλογίαν: *quæ tamen*

tamen analogia non in ipsis Dei attributis, sed in ipsorum effectis sive operationibus quærenda est. Nam cum attributa infinita sint, æque atque ipsa Dei essentia, & attributa-incommunicabilia, nullam habent cum creaturis ἀναλογίαν, nisi in suis operationibus circa objecta Creata & finita. Apply this to Immanent Acts.

---

§. 8.

Mr. K. pag. 94. IF Fore-knowledge in God and the Creature be not univocally the same, as surely they are not, then is this Fore-knowledge attributed to God and the Creature, either Equivocally or Analogically: If Equivocally, then hath the Fore-knowledge of God and the Creature only the same Name: But that is not so; for God, I hope, fore-knows as truly as the Creature, and the Creature may sometimes truly fore-know. So that here is more then a nominal agreement between Gods and the Creatures fore-knowledge. It remains therefore that this fore knowledge be attributed to God and the Creature Analogically: but is this Analogie either of Proportion or Attribution? If of Proportion, then either God or the Creature is said to fore-know, but either Metaphorically or Metonymically. If only Metaphorically; I pray which of them is but Metaphorically said to fore-know? Not the Creature, &c. And surely much less may God be only Metaphorically said to fore-know these, and all other things that shall come to pass in all Ages. If only Metonymically, as some things are said to be healthy, because they have the signs of sanity in them, (I am bold to use the Boyes instance in this case) Is either God or the Creature only Metonymically said to fore-know? Not the Creature, &c. Not God, for he is the Author of our fore-knowledge: and therefore though his essence be not the subject of his fore-knowledge, nor his fore-knowledge an Accident of his Nature, yet is he said to fore-know without being beholden to any such poor Trope for it. It rests therefore that fore-knowledge is attributed to God by more then this Analogie of Proportion, and consequently by that of Attribution Now I demand which is the famosius Analogatum? Gods fore-knowledge, or the Creatures? Questionless Gods: there being infinitely greater Cause to set the Crown on Gods fore-knowledge, then on that of the Greatures, then there is to set it on substance rather then accident. If so, &c. then onward, as Analogatum per se positum stat pro famosiori Analogato, so true fore-knowledge mentioned by it self, must alwayes be construed of the fore knowledge of God: and therefore fore-knowledge is most properly attributable to God. And thus being now willing to resign my place, Hæc sufficiant pro nunc.

---

§. 8.

R. B. IF I had once done with you, I would take heed of dealing with a Chairman again in haste, for your sake: for I finde I run upon a great disadvantage. For the credit of such mens understandings is so great with themselves at least, that they need no Argument, but their bare affirmation to carry the Cause. Your sole Argument [*sic dico*] doth put me harder to it, then if you had many: For what to say to this, I do not well know. Dispute against it, I cannot: and to set my Negation against your affirmation, will not do, till we stand on even ground.

1. *Aquinas de verit.* and many another Schoolman (and *Zanchy* out of them) might have helpt you to more cogent Arguments, against meer æquivocal denomination. When you speak of Gods fore-knowing, as [truly] that word [truly]

is either opposed to *feigned* and *false*, or to *improperly;* that in God which the term [fore-knowledge] doth denote, is *Truly* in him, and him alone, but that which the word [fore-knowledge] doth properly and primarily signifie, is not in God.

2. Our *Rabbi*s (as you call them *ab alto* with a smile) do seem to us punies, to make a fuller distribution then you ; as I have before shewed : and therefore we take yours to be defective, and consequently your reasoning void : I have told you of divers that please me better.

3. How greedily did I reade on, and follow you at the heels, to see how you proved that it is not spoken of God Metaphorically ? and when I come to the businesse, What's the proof ? Why you say [surely much lesse may God be onely metaphorically said to fore-know.] You passe your word on it : And this is the knotty Argument that I cannot answer, because I am not of your standing in the University : A little more of the University would have done me no harm (as you say) when I am to deal with this kinde of Argument.

4. Our Tutor *Burgersdieius* told us, I remember, that *in cæteris tropis non minus est homonymiæ locus, quam in Metaphora*. And therefore Metaphorical and Metonymical, are not a sufficient enumeration.

5. Do not think ever the worse of your self for using the Boyes instance : for (as you have partly salved your credit by intimating that you are above it, so) *Aquinas, Scotus*, and most of the Schoolmen that I have read, besides *Zanchius*, and many another of our great Divines, do make use of the same instance : And to play with this bigger sort of Boyes, is no such disgrace to you.

6. Here I meet with a thing that runs in the form of a Reason : [for he is the Author of our fore-knowledge] therefore he fore-knoweth not onely Metonymically. I confesse the Conclusion is true ; but I see not the reason of the consequence. As I remember a Metonymy of the effect is, when the efficient is signified by the name of the effect, either by a Verb, as *pallet pro metuit*, or an Adjective, as *mors pallida*; or a Substantive, as *scelus pro scelesto* (I purposely choose the Boyes examples, as best beseeming me.) And I have heard men often call Mr. *Nath. Ward, Discolliminium*, and the simple Cobler : And the Author of that Comedy, by the name of *Ignoramus*. I confesse it is a good Argument [He is the Author of our fore-knowledge, therefore he hath fore-knowledge *eminenter*, or somewhat that is more excellent then fore-knowledge.) But I dare not say, that God hath formally in himself whatsoever he is the Author of. For he is the Author of Nutrition, Augmentation, Composition, of Sorrow, of Fear, of Hell, of Worms, Toads and Vipers. But it was the former (the Metaphorical Denomination, and also that of strict proportion, which some distinguish from the Metaphorical) which I had hoped you would have disproved. But I must take what will be had.

7. You think you plead for the Glory of the Divine Majesty, when you tell us he need not be beholden to a poor Trope. As if we should dispute, whether the Sunne do creep as *reptilia* do ? and I say, Yes, Metaphorically : and you will stand up for the honour of the Sun, and say, we debase it ; and that it doth creep without being beholden to a poor Trope for it : Or if the Question were, Whether the Sunne be a Vegetative, or sensitive creature ? and I say, Yes, Metonymically : for it causeth Vegetation and sense. And you will say, It is Vegetative without being beholden to a Trope. What a Patron is he of the honour of mankinde, that will prove that he is a Worm, a Beast, Nothing, and his life a shadow,

dow, a dream, a Weavers shuttle, without being beholden to a poor Trope! Yet are these unspeakably nearer, then the names of man and his acts, to God: for *inter finitum & infinitum nulla est proportio.*

8. You conclude that the *famosius Analogatum*, is Gods fore-knowledge, your proof is [Questionless it is so :] As strong as the rest. But, when I look further I finde somewhat like a Reason : [there being Infinitely greater cause to set the Crown on Gods fore-knowledge, &c.] My dread of Gods most sacred Majesty, forbiddeth me to set on him such a Crown of Vanity. As if the Sun must be the *famosius Analogatum inter Reptilia*, because the Crown of [Creeping] must be set on its head! What if we should yield to you, that the term [Knowledge, Will, Action, &c.] being first Metaphorically applied to God, that yet it is partly Analogical *quoad inæqualem Generis attributionem*, the term expressing (though improperly as to one) a Nature common to both? It would not yet follow, that here the more noble sort, even Divine Knowledge, &c. were the *famosius Analogatum*: For though it be most excellent and unexpressibly glorious in it self, yet the term agreeing first with the lower, even humane Knowledge, therefore that is the *famosius Analogatum*, as being the thing most famously and notoriously meant by that term. If you ask, Whether the Sunne do glisten (as Glow-worms, or rotten wood) or do *Rutilare* or *Candere*? If you say, Yea; yet I think the Sunne here is not the *famosius Analogatum*, though the light which this word intendeth be more eminently in the Sun, then in the other things.

You conclude, that [true fore knowledge mentioned by it self, must alwayes be understood of the fore-knowledge of God.] Is that so indeed?

1. Why then do the Schoolmen generally acknowledge, that the names are all first applicable to the Creature, though the thing be most excellently in God?

2. Then, it seems, it is not a strictly proper speech to say [Man knows, or fore-knows, or Wils, or acteth :] for none of the *Homonyma*, are spoken of both, in strict propriety. But if you would undertake to prove, that God may in as strict propriety be said to Know, Will or Act, as man is, there are many that would undertake to prove the terms Univocal : which in most Divines Judgement, would be to prove, that man is God : an opinion, which our new world in the Moon *(in Anglia lunatica)* have very confidently imbraced of late years.

In a word, Sir, my thoughts of man, and his Acts, Knowing, Willing, are so low, and my thoughts of the Infinite God, so high, or at a losse, when I go about to have any positive, true apprehensions of his Nature, that I conceive you and I can no more tell what that is in God which we call Knowing, Willing, Acting, then my Horse can tell what Reasoning or Discourse is in me, or thereabouts. And yet I believe that the Knowledge of God is eternal Life too, *viz.* Now (as to the beginning) to know that there is a God, and that there is somewhat in Him which mans Knowledge, Will, Goodness, Justice, &c. have some exceeding, low, distant resemblance of, and which we cannot better apprehend or express then under such notions, and by such terms; it being yet in it self of more unconceivable excellency. And though I know the Schoolmen are confident (without proof) that *Scire, Velle*, &c. do express no Imperfection, but only Modal, and therefore may be applied to God (which I conjecture will also be your Argument) yet I do not believe that Assertion. Comparatively to lower or equal Creatures, it may be said, that it is not Imperfection, which they express. But absolutely,

absolutely or comparatively as to God; it is Imperfection: Not only some accident or *Modus*, but the very thing exprest by these terms, is Imperfect: Else the Creature shall have something equal to God, and so be God. And if it were but a Modal Imperfection; yet when the term doth strictly and properly expresse that Imperfect *Modus* it self, as well as the Thing, then that term cannot be applied to God any nearlier then Tropically. Knowledge, Will, Action, and all the terms fitted to man, are so strictly fitted to expres the humane Mode, as well as that which you separate in your Intellect, and call perfect, that it cannot be applied to one without the other, but abusively or tropically; No more then [creeping] is applicable to the swift motion of the Sun, when the term doth intimately signifie the slowness and Mode of the motion, with the motion it self.

God forbid that I should doubt, whether that in God be Perfect, which we call Knowledge, Will, Action: But what it is that under these names of infinitely remote similitude we do expras, what earthly man can tell? Because I believe Gods Immanent acts to be perfect, therefore I believe them not to be the same thing that man apprehendeth under these terms.

Oh that frail man were more acquainted with his Nothingness! then would he not dare so to lift up himself in comparison with his Maker! Then would not the Christian world for so many hundred years have been filled with quarrels about unsearchable Mysteries; and the great Divines of the Church, be the great Dividers of the Church by voluminous contentions, and censorious, uncharitable, zealous emulations about Gods secrets: They would not have fastened upon utter uncertainties, and things unrevealed, and then have stiled their fancies [the Orthodox Doctrine] and reproached or quarrelled with those that were dissenters. The world would not have been altogether by the ears about things that they know no more then a beast knows what is the soul of man; such as many of the Schoolmens writings are, and most of those points in which the Controversies between the Arminians and anti-Arminians, the Jesuites and Dominicans, are ultimately resolved: Yea, and your Academical Chairs would have been better imployed: and then God would not have been so provoked against them: Nor should I have needed to fear that your Chair is coming down, while I reade here that you are coming down; nor have cause to salute you so sadly at your descent, as fearing a future vacancy of your resigned place.

---

§. 9.

Mr. K. Pag. I *Shall now see what Mr. Baxter saith, though not to answer this Argument, or any other, yet to detract somewhat from the Reputation of the Conclusion, that there can be no new Immanent act in God, but all are Eternal.*

§. 9.

R. B. TO feign a wrong end to a mans speeches, is usually the way to fasten on them a false and alien sense. I therefore who am better acquainted with my own End and meaning then M. K. is (as well as he knows me, by looking through his Prospective Glass from *Cornwell* to *Kidderminster*) shall better acquaint others what was my meaning in the words, which he fastens on. And this is the true and plain Analysis of my words.

Having affirmed Justification to be a transient act, and that (therefore the Inception

ception of it argueth no mutation in God, I was forc't to meet with the opinion of Dr *Twiss*, who takes it to be an Immanent Act, and therefore if it should begin *de novo*, it would argue a change in God. (Not speaking of that *in foro Conscientiæ*.)

These two Conclusions therefore I took as certain, and necessary to be held of every knowing Christian.
1. That God doth not change.
2. That God doth not pardon or justifie men from Eternity; (no nor from the time of Christs death) and therefore that he doth in time justifie and forgive men, even when they believe. These two Conclusions being Certain and necessary, I take the later as assaulted by D. *Twiss*; who thereby would make them seem inconsistent.

His Argument is, Justification and Remission are Immanent Acts, therefore from Eternity. To this I answer, 1. By denying the Antecedent: For I had before shewed, that they are Transient acts, and what Transient acts they are. 2, Having premised, that no acts are Immanent in God Positively but onely Negatively (as *Schibler* speaks;) I answered, That many doubt whether Immanent acts are any further Eternal then Transient acts (which I will open anon when we come to it:) and therefore that this is not a matter of such Certainty as the Proposition opposed is: and therefore Uncertainties must be reduced to Certainties, and not Certainties to Uncertainties: *q. d.* I am sure God doth not pardon and Justifie from Eternity from plain Texts of Scripture: But you are not sure that all Immanent acts are Eternal any more then Transient are; Therefore if these two Propositions were as inconsistent as you imagine, yet I would rather hold the former, and let go the later, then hold the latter and let go the former. Here I supposed it objected, that it is not to be endured that any should argue God of mutability: but the foresaid Doctrine doth so: Therefore, &c. To which I answered, that there is no change in God: and they that do hold this opinion, do yet hold it is consistent with Gods Immutability: and I gave two or three short touches of their reasoning: If you ask me, whom I mean, I answer, I mean *Lychetus*, *Pennottus*, *Franciscus a Sancta Clara*, and in part *Suarez* and *Burgersdicius*, in the words which I shall anon cite in his Metaphysicks. And mark that I do not say, that these plead for the Inception or Cessation of Immanent acts: but that Immanent acts are new as Transient are; that is, not *quoad substantiam actus*, but *transitionem in objectum extraneum*. For here it is supposed, that it is not those Immanent acts, whose object is God himself, which is spoke of, but only those that are about the Creature; Note also, that I never thought of owning this opinion; but had ever owned the opinion of the Eternity of all Immanent acts; and so farre as the matter is discernable, do hold to it still: but I take the point in Question to be past our reach; and therefore not of such Certainty, as to encourage us to reject a plainly revealed truth, upon supposition of their inconsistency.

After this I returned to my first Position, and made it my full, final Answer, that Remission and Justification are Transient acts, and not Immanent, and that in this I had most Divines on my side, though they did not ordinarily explain the Nature of this Transient Act: which thereupon I more fully explain'd.

Thus, Reader, I have given the true Analysis of all these words about Immanent acts, which Mr. K. makes the occasion of his quarrel with me: and which

H   he

[42]

he layeth such a heavy charge on. And, I think, if I had said no more to him, but onely given you this true Analysis, it had been enough to satisfie the impartial, and Judicious, and to free my words from that sandy incoherence and senslesness, which (not understanding them) he doth fasten on them in his charge; and to vindicate my self from those corrupt intentions and errours which he intimates.

§. 10.

Mr. K. First, saith he, *Acts have not the respect of the Adjunct to its Subject, but an effect to its cause: Therefore new Immanent Acts will not inferre an alteration in God: Therefore, &c.*

To this antecedent, I answer, that no Act is properly an effect, or relates as such to the Cause: the Act is rather the Causality then the effect, as Mr. Baxter *may please to learn from his great Doctors in the Metaphysicks, whom I think enough to name in general, though he useth to quote them so exactly, as it were the Chapter and verse.*

§. 10.

R. B. IF I have learning enough to understand your meaning, you endeavour in these words to prove two Conclusions. The first and principal (and I think, the whole scope of your writing) is, that I am Ignorant and unlearned. The second and subordinate is, that Immanent Acts are certainly Eternal, or that the change of them will inferre a change in God. The first you prove by my Pedantick citing of *Schibler* and *Burgersdicius*, the Boyes companions, and that as if they were Doctors in the Metaphysicks, and that so exactly, *&c.* which you think it enough to name. To this I answer, 1. Your Argument labours of two diseases, 1. Obscurity: which may make some, that know you not, conjecture that your design was scarce honest, which you so carry under hand by intimations, when yet it seems the great Cause of this your undertaking: For my part, I think you would never have mentioned my name here, but to this end. 2. Of Needlesness: If you had stooped so low as to consult me in this business, and opened to me your design, I could by three lines have saved you the writing of these leaves: but that's too late: But yet I may prevent your voluminous labour perhaps for the future, if I do it yet. Be it known therefore to all men by these presents that I R. B. do confess my self ignorant and unlearned, especially compared with such as Mr. K. and his *Genius*. *Habetis confitentem reum.* What need you any more Witnesses? I hope now you may save the main labour of your next writing.

Yet, let me tell you the reason of my crime, a little more fully. I take the common good to be the best. I have about thirty Tractates of Metaphysicks by me (an ill workman, that needs so many tools) and I value these two or three Common ones which I cited before, all the rest: and I think so do the Schools that use them most commonly. Nor do I see any great reason hitherto to take Mr. K. for a more learned, authentick, unquestionable Doctor in the Metaphysicks, then *Suarez, Schibler* or *Burgersdicius*, as highly as I value him above my self. Nor indeed did I ever before this, hear of his name (to my remembrance;) much lesse of his Metaphysical writings. But as soon as ever Mr. K's Metaphysicks come to my hands, if I do not bow to them, *& vestigia tanti Philosophi adorare*, then let him call me an unreverent fellow.

Now to your second business: Where, 1. I might better have been understood, if you had not left out the fore-going words; [by Immanent, they must needs mean Negatively, not Positively.] For by this they that see all might have understood that, 2. It is Gods acts that I speak of, 3. And you do out of your own brain, affix the *Ergo*, as if it were mine, making that an Argument, which I there take as presupposed. The rest we will come to anon.

---

§. 11.

Mr. K. THus when the fire warms my hands, the heating is not the effect; but the Heat produced in my hand by the fire. This heat now is considerable three manner of wayes. I shall not honour my Papers with the name of Suarez for this, but referre my Reader, if he be a young Scholar, and not satisfied in it, to his Smith and Brerewood.

---

§. 11.

R. B. YEt again! You will make men believe that I am grown to some Reputation of Learning, when you think it necessary to use so many words, to prove me a freshman. Is not one word of your mouth enough to blast the reputation of such a puny?

---

§. 12.

Mr. K. EIther, 1. As it encreaseth, and in order to the highest degree of heat, and so it is called Motion, which is nothing else but the Terminus in fieri. Or 2. As tis received into the subject, and so it is called Passion, heating like beating being as well taken in a Passive sense as an active. Or, 3. As it is derived from the Agent, and so it is called action: but this action again is considerable two manner of wayes; Either Physically or Logically. Physically, and so the Patient is the subject of it: the heat which undergoes these several denominations, being in my hand, as was supposed. 2. Logically, and so this action is but an extrinsecal denomination, and the Agent is the subject of it: Now take it how you will, Action is an adjunct, as denominating the agent, no way an effect as an action, &c.

---

§. 12.

R. B. 1. THe word [Effect] is sometime taken for every thing that hath a Being and a Cause, and so every Action is an Effect, as having a Being dependant on its Cause: sometime it is taken more restrainedly, for that only which is permanent after the Action, or is Effected by it, and so Action is not an Effect. 2. The use of your distribution or distinctions to our business seems to me so small, as that I know not well to what end you bring them forth. 3. The order of your distinguishing I have no great minde to learn. I should rather have distinguished Logical and Physical Action, in the first place, had there been any use for it. 4. But your Logical action we have nothing to say to: Nor did I speak *de subjecto praedicationis*. 5. Yet I have no great desire of imitating

H 2 you,

you, in calling the Agent, the subject of the extrinsecal denomination [*viz.* Action.] It is your Physical Action, which is so denominated: Though of the verbal predication [*agit*] I would willingly say, that the Agent is the subject. 6. But it is your Physical Action which we have now to do with: and that not as it is *in Patiente*, for so it is Passion, and not formally Action. Whether *Scotus* opinion of a Real difference be true or not (which yet may have more said for it then some superficial answerers do take notice of) yet formally its like it will be granted, that they are not the same: And therefore you should speak of Action as Action, *Ut dicit egressionem & dependentiam ab agente*, and not as it signifieth Passion, that is, Reception of Action, and the effect of it: and so the Patient is not the subject of Action; Nor do I believe it a fit speech to say, that Calefaction is in your hand, though *Calor* be. But we must hear you further; to how great purpose we shall see.

§. 13.

Mr K. 1. Now take it how you will, *Action is an adjunct, as denominating the Agent, no way an Effect, as an Action.* 2. *Nor doth it carry that stile in any of these learned* Sophies, *commonly quoted by Mr.* Baxter *with so much reverence.*

§. 13.

R.B. 1. Say you so! is it an adjunct as denominating the Agent, take it how I will? What if I take it, [as it is received into the Subject, and called Passion] which is your second sense? Why said you that your Logical Action was an extrinsecal denomination of the Agent, if your Physical Action be so too? When you seemed by this to difference them? 2. I marvel that my Reverence to these *Sophies* should be the matter of so many of your lines, and you should think it necessary to rehearse it so oft: Sure you are jealous that your Reader will be very unobservant of your weighty observations. But, Sir, is not Reverence a sign of Lowliness? Why then are you offended at it? You should rather applaud me, and say, If *R.B.* do so much Reverence a *Suarez*, a *Schibler*, a *Burgersdicius*, if he knew me, how much more would he reverence me! But, to deal more plainly with you, the further I go in perusal of your learned Labours, the more I perceive my Reverence to abate. Let any man except your self judge by the next passage, whether you deserve more reverence then these Rabbies and Sophies (as you have honourably be-Titled them.) You boldly and flatly affirm, That Action [is no way an Effect, as an action, nor doth it carry that stile in any of these learned Sophies, *&c.*] Either this Assertion is True or False. If True, Mr. K. hath got little: but I am false, if this be true. If it be false, either Mr. K. knew it to be so, or he did not. If he did, and yet spoke it, and that so confidently, then he must pardon me for Reverencing these childish Authors before him. If it be false and he knew it not, then, 1. He is one that will speak boldly what he knows not, and accordingly to be believed. 2. And then it seems he knows not what he supposeth his Boyes to know, and he looks at as his *A.B.C.* I will finde out a *Tertium* to salve his credit as soon as I can. If there be no other, I'le lay it on a defect of memory, conjunct with a certain audacity, to tell the world in print, that those things are not written which he read when he was a boy, and hath since forgotten.

Let.

Let us try the truth of his Assertion. I must not tell him of some Schoolmen or any other Philosophical Writers; that call [action] an effect, for then he will say, Those are not the Sophies in Question: It must therefore be the very same men. Let *Schibler* speak first *Met.l.2.c.10.Tit.3 Punc.2.p.54.* *Quod ad actionem immanentem attinet; dicitur ea Immanens ab immanendo, quod scilicet in agente maneat, Existimo tamen eam non esse intelligendam Positivè, sed Negativè. Nam actio Immanens quâ talis est, est in Agente, hoc sensu, quia non transit ad Patiens. In ipso autem agente non est per modum Adjuncti, sed simpliciter ad ipsum comparatur ut ad Causam. Unde hæc Propositio, Homo intelligit, vel disputat, non est ut adjuncti de subjecto, sed ut Effecti de Causa: Et patet: Nam Actio transiens nullum habet subjectum, ne quidem ipsum patiens, ut visum est. Ergo etiam actio Immanens à fortiori non postulat subjectum. Consequentia firma est, quia actio transiens magis est ex subjecto, & magis postulat subjectum, quam actio Immanens. Sed actio Transiens in esse Actionis, nullum habuit subjectum, &c. Ergo & confirmatur, quod Actio ut sic, non dicit nisi egressum à virtute activa alicujus agentis. Egressus autem opponitur τῷ esse in. Et hinc relinquitur generatim loquendo de actione ut sic, eam non postulare subjectum. Neq; enim Genus debet habere Naturam repugnantem suis speciebus, &c.*

Yet more, that you may be past doubt of Mr. *K*'s Veracity and Ingenuity, *lib. 1. cap. 22. Tit. 28. Art. 1. Cæterum vox effecti ambigua est,* &c. *Primò Propriè & Adæquatè significat causatum specialiter, nempe cum connotato respectu ad causam efficientem,* &c. *Deinde effectum sumitur generalius & per Synecdochem speciei pro genere, quomodo dicitur æquipollenter ad Causatum, quomodo jam Cicero loquebatur,* &c. *Jam præterea 3° effectum (sicut & Causatum) aliquando specialiter accipiuntur; prout significant esse stans & permanens post actionem: In quo distinguuntur contra effectionem vel actionem, vel motum: atque ita aliqui aiunt Actionem non esse effectum: sed id quo producitur effectus. Hic tamen communius Effectum & Causatum sumuntur, Diciturque id omne Causatum quod habet esse per dependentiam ab aliqua Causa sive sit Actio, sive Res per Actionem facta.* Atque ita etiam Ramus in *Logic.l.1.c.9.* Huc, inquit, *in doctrina Effecti,* pertinet motus & res motu facta, &c. *Vid.ult.11. Et Art. 3. De effecto specialiter dicto. Nihil autem occurrit hic explicandum præter specialia nomina effectorum; qualia sunt* ἐνέργεια, ἐνέργημα, ἀποτέλεσμα, πρᾶξις & ποίησις. *Igitur* ἐνέργεια *hoc loco nihil aliud est quam ipsa Actio, Damasc.lib.3.de Orthod. fid. c.15. eam definit, quod sit efficax & substantialis naturæ motus. De hoc effectus genere, hoc est, de Actione, intelligendus est iste Canon, Cessante causa cessat effectus: Effectus inquam qui est* ἐνέργεια: *(Cessante Patre cessat, (non Filius sed) Generatio Filii: Cessante Architecto cessit (non domus sed) ædificatio.* ἐνέργημα *autem opus est post actionem manens,* &c. πρᾶξις *quandoq; generatim significat operationem, sicut & Latina vox Actionis,* &c. *Vid reliq.*

So in his *Compend. Philos. de Logic.l.1.§.1.c.5.p.17. Ad effectum tanquam exemplum ejus pertinet motus, & res motu facta.*

And *Metaph.l.2.c.3. Tit.17.n.630.* he saith, *Resp. Esse ambiguitatem in voce creati entis: Creatum enim Ens quandoque dicitur id solum quod per Actionem creativam incipit esse, quodque est quasi Creationis terminus: Et sic Creatio non est aliquid creatum: Quandoque vero Creatum Ens dicitur omne illud quod dependenter est ab Ente increato, sive id sit per modum Actionis, sive per modum rei factæ per actionem. Et hoc modo Creatio est quid Creatum. Simile quid est in voce Effecti vel Effectus: Dicitur enim quandoque effectum pro eo quod est quasi Actionis Terminus, quomodo domus,* v.g. *est effectum. Aliquando* *Calliovius* Metaphys. Divin. *sub.p.524. In genere causatum est operatio,* & ἐνέργεια, vel opus & ἐνέργημα. verò *vero sumitur communiùs ut dicatur effectum quicquid à Causa est, sive id sit per modum Actionis seu motus, sive per motum rei per motum factæ; Et sic etiam ipsæ Actiones dicuntur effecta,* &c. *Atque ita sicut nostræ Actiones sunt effecta, ipsæ tamen non postulant, ut per alias actiones fiant,* &c.

So *lib.2.cap.10. Tit.3. Art.3.n.31,32. Nam & ipsæ Actiones dicentur effectus præcise, & in se, quia habent esse dependens aliunde,* &c. So *n.* 41, 42. *& n.* 49, 50, 51. *Et confirmatur per* Aristot. *l.3. Phys. T. 20. Ubi ait, eundem Actum esse Agentis tanquam à quo, & patientis tanquam in quo, hoc est, ibi habet respectum effecti, hic verò habet respectum adjuncti.*

Again, *l.2 c.3. Tit.*14.*n.*418. *Potentia ad suum Actum comparatur ut effectum illius, Unde Intellectio, v.g. esset effectus potentiæ intellectivæ,* &c.

Now let Mr. K's auditors consider the next time he ascendeth his Chair, how farre their great Master is to be credited, and with what Cautions his most confident Assertions must be received. Let a man speak never so many Doctrinal untruths, we may modestly and handsomly confute them without offensive language: but when men speak such palpable untruths in matter of fact, I love not to dispute with them, seeing a man hath no answer for them, beseeming their errour, but a plain *desideratur veritas*, which seems so unhandsome language that it 'is usually ill taken what ever be the cause.

But let us hear another of the Sophies, *viz.* Suarez. *Metaph. disp.*18. *Sect.*10. *n.* 8. *Quod si nomine Effectus comprehendamus non solum rem productam, sed quicquid à virtute agentis manat, sic concedimus actionem esse aliquo modo effectum agentis, cum sit dependens vel potius ipsamet dependentia ab illo: Esse autem Effectum hoc lato modo, non repugnat causalitati: quin potius in omnibus causis quas hactenus tractavimus, Causalitas est effectus causæ,* &c.

It were no hard matter to produce more Reverend Sophies for Mr. K. who use the same language and call Actions Effects; but being about *Vid. Alting.* Problem. Theolog. so small a matter, I think it is not worth the labour. In this part.1.p.55. much the Reader may perceive to what a loss of time he may be lead in reading such Controversies, where men leave the Things, and fall upon Persons and Words, out of an earnest desire to finde out some way to cast Contempt upon their Brethren.

---

§. 14.

Mr. K. WHat was wont to be more common in horse-fair then An Actio sit in Agente, which with the knack of this hackney distinction, every dull Jade could turn at their pleasure, and hold sometimes affirmatively, sometimes negatively. So then thus farre little is said to the prejudice of that truth, that there is no new Immanent act in God?

---

§. 14.

R. B. YOur horse-fair, and hackney distinction, and dull Jade, are passages so profound that I must pass them as unanswerable by any that hath not attained to your Degrees. But doubtless you knew also how common it is to maintain the Negative on other grounds, and to say, that *Actio est Agentis, non in Agente*: and this is the language that I have hitherto thought fittest: and your contrary judgement alone will scarce move me to change. As for the safety of your

Conclusion,

Conclusion, I must tell you, it is no such glorious Atchievement for you to vindicate it against one that never opposed or denied it.

§. 15.

Mr. K. *But* 2. *Though this should be granted to Mr. Baxter to be true in acts transient, yet an immanent act is questionless an Adjunct, and not onely denominate the Agent, but where in it. For I ask, Is Knowing or Willing a Substance or Accident? an Accident questionlesse. If an Accident; In what Subject? Out of the Agent, you will finde no place where it may set the sole of its foot. Therefore it is in the Agent, and so an Adjunct: and if so, sure Immanent acts in God must needs infer an alteration. For*

§. 15.

R. B. I Confess your first on-set (so sudden, so causless against a feigned Adversary) made me suspect you to be some *pugnacissimum animal* (as Dr. *Twiß* cals his Adversary) but your prosecution puts me out of doubt. 1. Had you confined these speeches of yours only to the Creatures Acts, you had said but as many others have done before you: But it is Gods acts that you speak of, as you ascertain us in your application [and if so, sure Immanent acts in God must needs inferre an alteration.] But indeed do you believe that God is compounded of Substance and Accident? Yea doth the contentious disposition so potently carry you on, that you dare speak in such confident language, as to say that it is [an accident questionless] which you attribute to God? What could *Vorstius* have said more? I thought you had concurred in opinion with your Brethren, that use to call Gods Immanent acts, as diversified and as distinct from his Essence, only Extrinsick Denominations: But it seems you think otherwise (for a little time, while your haste doth hurry you that way *per modum naturæ*.) 2. If you say, That you meant onely this much [Immanent acts are Accidents inherent in man: Therefore they inferre an alteration in God] You might so easily foreknow that I would deny your Consequence, that me thinks so great a Disputant should not so drily have passed over the proof. I do not stick on the strangeness of the Conclusion it self, that [Immanent acts in God must needs inferre an alteration;] which is against your self and all Divines, who maintain that there are Immanent acts in God. For I doubt not but your haste which the disputing itch provoked you to, caused you to put [Immanent acts] for new Immanent acts.] 3. But its strange, that you could bethink you of no answer that might be made to your Question [If an Accident, in what Subject?] when you know it is so common to deny that Inhesion is necessary to every Accident; And when you know that in this case an *esse ab*, or a dependant *Egresse*, is affirmed sufficient by so many. I cited the words of *Schibler* to that sense even now, where he purposely opposeth that which you asserted, lib. 2. cap. 10. Tit. 3. n. 54, 55. I will not trouble you to rehearse them, it being a Book so farre below you. Now to your Proof.

§. 16. Mr. K.

§. 16.

Mr. K. **F**or, 3. *Though Action as Action logically considered, be but an extrinsecal Denomination, and so only denominate the Agent, not inhere in it, as much of Reality as there is in all Transient Actions being in the Patient, even Physically, or rather Metaphysically considered; yet these Immanent actions have their Terms too, say the said Sages, and those in the Agent; he that hath a minde to look it, may soon finde it in* Suarez, *or his* Scapula Schibler, *in the predicament of Action. Thus then the first bolt hath done little execution against this truth, that there can be no new Immanent Acts in God.*

§. 16.

R. B. IS this all the proof that we have waited for [Immanent actions have their terms too?] 1. Either you mean it of all Immanent acts, or but of some, if but of some, then it is a learned Argument: [some Immanent acts have their terms: Therefore there can be no new Immanent acts in God.] But I suppose you mean it of All: But then by [terms] do you mean [objects] which sometime are called *termini*? Or do you mean, the form to which the action tendeth, and which by it is produced or induced? If the first, then the *Terminus* of these Divine acts which we are speaking of, is oft *Without*, (as we use to say;) as when God knoweth, Approveth, Willeth, Loveth, the Creature. And therefore some few will not call these Immanent acts, but onely those whose object is God himself. But I suppose you mean the later, and then, 3. You might easily foresee, that though I had yielded all that you say of the Creatures acts, yet I would deny it of Gods: And blame me not for it, if I be lesse bold then you: and if I dare not imagine that there is in God either *Motus* or *Terminus ad quem,* or effect, or form acquired, when he Knows, Willeth, Approveth or Loveth the Creature, I am in hope that you believe no such thing your self, when the disputing itch is a little allayed. But however, could you possibly think it so obvious and easie a point as to need no proof? Why have we never a word here to that end, who need so many? I love not these Happy Disputers that can prove that by silence, which neither themselves nor any other can prove by Argument. If you will flie to your Analogy, and say [There are *Termini actionum Immanentium* in man: Therefore there are so in God] I should tell you that you may as wisely say [There are Accidents, Effects and Mutations in man: Therefore there are such in God.] At least I should importune you for the proof of your consequence. 4. But for the Terms of Immanent Actions you say [The said Sages say it] and [he that hath a minde to look it, may soon finde it in *Suarez,* and his *Scapula Schibler*] Truly, Sir, I have hitherto hinted your faults in Ironies: but I think it fit to ask you now (seeing it is not once or twice, nor a slip of your pen) how you dare put such things in print, and set so light by honest Truth-telling, and leave such things on record against your self? You that do *tanto fastu* referre us to *Schibler* as our *Scapula,* sure know his Doctrine: or at least, if you know it not, you should not take on you to know it, and say, we may soon finde that in him, which he so largely and purposely disputes against. He saith indeed, that some Immanent acts have terms, as Syllogizing: but that cannot be your meaning: for you well know it will do nothing to inferre your Conclusion: But doth not *Schibler* (*l.* 2. *c.* 10. *Tit.* 3. *art.* 3. *punct.*

[49]

punct.1,2.) largely dispute it, that many Immanent acts have no terms, no not Vision or Intellection: and answer the Objections against him, and conclude that *Actio ut sic non dicit respectum ad terminum?* And if Intellection have no Term, then Decree, and the rest that we were mentioning in the beginning, can have none *in agente.* 5. Nay what a great part of the great Philosophers and School-Divines do deny, that Immanent acts are true acts? *Scotus* takes them to be qualities, and not in the predicament of Action. *Soncinus, Ferrariensis* (and saith *Schibler Thomistæ frequenter ita docent*) deny them to be true acts. And if so, then sure they have not the *terminos* of true acts.

And I before told you at the beginning of your Discourse, that we do not all agree with you in your Description of an Immanent act, if you mean that it is such as is not only negatively, but Positively terminated in the Agent, as your words import: You may see *Schibler* denying it (when you shall condescend to look it in him) *in Met.l.2.c.10.Tit.3.n.54.& Tit.5.art.1.n.64.* But let this be how it will in man, I do very confidently deny that there is any such act in God, either of Knowledge or Will, as is either in the predicament of Action, or hath any *Terminus* in himself, further then as himself is the object of any act. And therefore you should first prove, that such Acts are in God at all, before you dispute whether they may be in him *de novo.*

§. 17.

Mr.K. Consider we what follows: [*Whether all such Immanent acts are any more eternal then transient acts, is much questioned*] saith *Mr.*Baxter. *By whom I pray? A clear difference between them as between heaven and earth: transient acts as I told you but now, being in the Patient, Immanent in the Agent.*

§. 17.

R.B. 1. O Happy, too happy wit! that hath not onely with *Moses* seen the back parts of God, but hath taken so full a Survey of his Nature, that it can discern as clear a difference between his several acts, as between heaven and earth! I dare not attempt the like survey: but I may receive instruction from you that have survey'd it. And what is the difference? Why [transient acts are in the Patient, and Immanent in the Agent.] What's the proof? Why it is this [I told you so but even now.] This may be a Demonstration to those that are capable of it: but *recipitur ad modum recipientis:* with me you have lost your Authority, so farre, that I need another kinde of proof. I will rather call it Passion then Action when it is *in Patiente*. *Forma dat nomen:* and Passion and Action are not the same *formaliter,* whatsoever they may be materially. Use the names promiscuously, if there be no difference in the things.

You know the subtil *Scotists* say, That Action and Passion are not the same, and that Action is in the Agent. And I have yet seen no reason to preferre you before *Scotus.* But I rather say, that Transient Acts are *ab agente*, but neither *in agente nec patiente*; as having a Cause but no Subject, as I have before expressed. And you may finde in my *Scapula, Met.l.2 c.10. Tit.3.n.51. That Omne accidens est in alio sensu Negativo,* &c. *alias loquendo de generali essentia accidentis, non est ea in Inhærendo, si rigorose loquamur, sed in eo quod id quod accidens est afficit subjectum extra essentialiter, sive extra essentiam, aut rationem ejus existendo. Proinde etsi actio*

I *rigorose*

rigorose loquendo non inhæreat, tamen satis habet de ratione accidentis, quia substantiam afficit & denominat extra essentialiter. Unde porrò resp. ad assump. prosyllog. admittendo quod Actio Transiens non sit in Patiente, loquendo de actione ut sic, & subesse Actionis. Quod igitur Actio transiens dicitur esse in patiente, id non est Intelligendum formaliter, sed materialiter: nempe illa res quæ est Actio est in Patiente: non tamen sub formali Actionis, sed sub formali passionis: Eadem enim res quæ Actio est, est etiam Passio. Now I hope you are more accurate in your speeches then to use to denominate from the matter, rather then the form: and therefore I hope hereafter you will forbear saying, that *Actio est in Patiente*, how common soever it may be. At least remember that you humbled your self but even now, to use a Hackney distinction, with which every dull Jade could maintain the Negative at their pleasure. And what if I adventured to use one Argument, *Actio est efficientis causalitas: At efficientis Causalitas non est in Patiente: Ergò, Actio non est in Patiente.* The *major* I prove by Infallible Authority, viz. Mr. K's, pag. 136. For the *minor*, If the Causality of the Agent were in the Patient, then we might fitly call it *Patientis Causalitas*. (For the name should be fitted to the thing) But that were absurd, Therefore, &c. Further, That which is in the Patient is a *Causatum*, or effect of the Agent *per Actionem vel Causalitatem*. But Causality or Action is not a *Causatum* or effect of the Agent *per actionem vel causalitatem*: Therefore that which is in the Patient is not Action or Causality. The *major* needs no proof; and its meant of every received form. The *minor* hath a full demonstration, viz. Mr. K's Authority; who denieth Action to be an effect. And those that be not moved with his authority, may observe that I here take the word [effect] in the more restrained sense as it excludeth Causality or Action; and therefore that I say [it is not an Effect *per Actionem*] and that is proved fully, in that otherwise, there must be another Action to effect this Action, and so *in infinitum*. But I did not think to have said any thing on this. All that Mr. K. can expect we should grant him is, that *Actio qua Passio est in Patiente*: but still *Actio transiens qua Actio non est in Patiente*, no more then is an Immanent action. Or if it were, yet the Authority of so many learned gain-sayers, makes the difference seem scarce so clear as that between heaven and earth.

Moreover, that which in God we call a Transient Act, is by the Schoolmen in greatest credit, affirmed to be Gods Essence only connoting the creature-*Relatio* to it: so that besides the creature it self (which though *Scotus* cals Creation, yet is sure the effect and not the act) and besides the Relation (which can be no proper act) there remains nothing but Gods essence, to be the substance of the Act which we call both Immanent and Transient. *Capreolus* saith, *Nulla Divina operatio aut actio qua formaliter agit aut operatur, est transiens in passum, sic quod in passo formaliter recipiatur, cum ejus agere sit ejus Velle & Intelligere, quæ sunt actiones Immanentes. Sed concedi potest quod divina actio dicitur quandoque transiens propter respectum rationis ad realem effectum in Creatura, ut Creatio, Conservatio,* &c. *l.2.dist.1.q.2.art.3.* And the Thomists (saith *Suarez, Met. disp. 20. §.5.*) say, That *Non solum Creatio, verum neque ulla actio respectu illius potest esse Transiens*. Where then is Mr. K's clear difference as between heaven and earth?

And though I am loth to put my finger into the fire, by medling with Mr. K. any further then he invites me, yet perhaps he may expect I should somewhat take notice what he saith of this point to Mr. *Goodwin*, pag. 150, 154.

1. When he saith, [There are so many Immutations in Gods Essence] if transient operations be the same with his Essence, &c. I deny the consequence: because

because the *Terminus* or effect is not the same with his Essence, though the act be. The Effect only is Many; the Act but one. 2. To his solution of the first Question, where he saith, It is a myltery passing all understanding, that God should incline the heart to believe and not act anew, *&c.*] I say, I believe him for the mysteriousness. But as all multiplicity comes from Unity, so do all temporals from that act which is Eternal. To all Mr. K's Instances the Schoolmen say, It is the effect only that is New: In giving the spirit, faith, raising Christ,*&c.* God had no new act: Yet God did it by *Velle*, which is his eternal act and essence. To his answer to the second Question, I Reply, M.K's Questions are insipid and fallacious. [Did he Plant faith by making Plants? Did he make me to differ by making the world?] For though it was by the same act, yet that act hath divers denominations from its respect to divers objects. To [make the world] connoteth a particular object, viz. the world: and therefore the act which causeth you to believe, cannot be called [Creating the world] not because the act is not the same, but because it respecteth not the same object. The third Question belongs not to me. To the fourth I say as before: the act is Gods *Velle*: his *Velle* is his Essence: Therefore Eternal. His Questions [Whether the world were drowned by the same Act by which it was made? *&c.*] are answered as before: It was by the same Act, viz. *Velle Divinum*; but to be denominated variously according to the Variety of objects which it doth respect and connote. Even as it is the same Act which is Immanent and Eternal, which in Time is denominated Transient from its respect to the effect.

But, *Pag.* 154. I finde him citing Mr. *G*. as saying [Learned men Generally acknowledge, that (the act) is really and formally one and the same thing with his Essence.] And Mr. K. saith contrary, that [No man ever asserted Transient acts to be the same with the Agent] and that [all Transient acts be the same with the term, say all men that meddle with Metaphysicks] and he appeals to any Reader that hath but tasted the first principles of Logick. Truly these two Divines are very contrary: and have bewrayed both of them that which they might have concealed with much more credit to their Reading. Yet Mr. *G.* may interpret [Generally] with such limitations as may bring him off in part: but Mr. K's presumption and boldness is intolerable. When a man of so small Reading as I am, know so well, that the Metaphysical Doctors do some speak one way, and some another: as I undertake by quotations now to manifest when I shall understand it worth any time and labour. I remember Mr K's words in his third Epistle of the sufficiency of [a pair of Sheers and a met-yard.] But it is not so farre sufficient without more Reading, as to encourage a tender conscienc't man, to averre untruths so confidently, that [*No man ever asserted*, &c.] And where he saith [The Question is not of the acts of his *Will*, but of his *Power*, &c.] Knoweth he not that Dr. *Twiß* and the highly honoured Thomists do make God to work *per essentiam*, and say, that his Power is but his Will, called Power in respect to the effect which it doth produce? *Vid.* Aquin. 1.q.15.art.1.4^m. Truly me thinks that Mr. K. doth even to the meanly learned expose himself to great disgrace, to say so boldly, that [all men that meddle with Metaphysicks say, that all Transient acts be the same with the term.] Did he never at least reade *Scotus* so oft asserting and arguing for the contrary? Nor any one of his followers, nor one of all the other parties that deny this? If he had not, yet he should have blushed so peremptorily to affirm what he did not know. At least he should have known that *Schibler* hath this Conclusion, which he largely argues for [3° *Actiones quæ*

I 2

tendunt

tendunt ad terminum non sunt realiter idem cum termino] and saith, *Calefactionem à Calore specie distingui.* And he there tels you of *Venetus, Aureolus, Suarez & Colleg.Conimbric.* that say as he : At least he that so derides me for citing these puerile Authors, should not have dared to say All men [that meddle with Metaphys.] say as he in this, when both common School-books, and the two most famous Sects of Schoolmen, Scotists and Thomists are against him (as *Suarez* will tell him, *disp*.48.*ser*.5.n.2. of *Cajet. Hispalens.Flandr. & communiter Scotist.&c.*] And for the fuller answering of Mr.K's Questions before mentioned, I desire the learned Reader among others to peruse the foresaid Answer of *Capreolus* to *Aureolus* 15. arguments *in l.2.sent.dist*.1.*q.*2. *a.*3. But I must intreat you still to remember that my own opinion is, That action is not properly ascribd to God at all ; nay farre more Improperly then men will easily believe : *Suarez* himself *Metaph. disp*.48. §. 5.n.11. maintaineth Gods Immanent acts, *Intelligere & Velle* are properly not acts, nor to be so called. But of this before.

Reade also *Gibieuf. de Libert.L.*1. *cap.*25. §. 13. shewing that the act whereby God made all things of nothing is Eternal : and *c.*6. *p.*323. And Cardin. *Contzreuus de prædestinatione, pag.* (*operum*) 606. saith , *Simplici & Unica Actione, quà cum ipsius substantia eadem est (si tamen substantiam appellare licet) omnes effectus producit : ita nullo etiam tempore aut temporis aliqua parte, actionem ejus contineri,*&c.] *Vid.*Aquin.*contr.Gent.l* 1,2.*c.*35,36,37. 17,18,19.

And that the Action is not the same with the *Terminus*, see the Arguments of *Ludovic. a Dola de Concursu Part.*1. *cap.*2. §.6. *Aquin.* is cited by *Capreolus in* 2. *sent. dis*.1.*q.*2.*a.*3. as saying thus, *de pot.Dei q.*3.*d.*17.*ad* 12ᵐ. *Dei Actio est æterna, cum sit ejus substantia : dicitur autem incipere agere ratione novi effectus, qui ab æterna actione consequitur dispositionem voluntatis qui intelligitur quasi actionis principium in ordine ad effectum.*]

2. But the other part of the assigned difference goes down with me no better, but much worse, 1. In that he knows, I think, that it is not such a commonly received opinion [that Immanent actions are in the Agent] in a Positive sense, and not meerly negative, as that he should think it needed no more proof then his mentioning. I gave him the opposition of one Sophie, as he cals him, even now. 2. And if it were so in man, I again tell him, that I will not take his bare word, no nor his oath, that it is so in God.

But Mr.K. must needs know who they be that make question of this. What if it were but some private familiars of mine ? Must Mr.K. needs know their names? But I had thought he had been well acquainted with the doctrine of *Lychetus, Pennotus* and *Sancta Clara* in this Point., Who affirm, That though the act in it self be God himself, and so eternal, yet the transition of it to several objects, and so the denomination may be new ; and so that God may to day predestinate him that before was not predestinated, or Love him that before was not Loved, and this without any change in God. Indeed these are the men that I mean. I thought with these men of the higher form you had deigned to be familiar : but because you speak of the matter so strangely, I will come down again to our own form, and rehearse a few words of *Burgersdicius* familiarly known to those at your footstool. Metaph.l.2. §.16. *Est enim in Deo concipiendus unus actus, qui nihil aliud est quam essentia divina. Hic actus respicere potest diversa objecta creata, seu, quod eodem redit, Deus per istum actum tendere potest in diversa objecta, vel etiam non tendere: & cum in illa tendit, reverâ ea vult : Dixi in objecta creata : Nam semetipsum Deus non potest non amare. Decreta ergo Dei duo involvunt, actum scilicet, & illius actus tendentiam*

sine

sine applicatione ad diversa objecta creata. Actus ipse liber non est, non magis quam Dei vel Immensitas, vel Æternitas: sed libera est illius actus applicatio ad objecta: quæ tamen quia nihil Deo addit entis, sed solum denominationem quandam externam, sumptam a connotatione objecti creati, tanquam termini sui, neque compositionem efficere potest, neque mutationem. Quod adeo verum est, ut existimem, si Deus decreta rescindere posset, illud imperfectionem allaturam Deo, non propter mutationem Decretorum, sed propter causam mutationis, quæ aut imprudentia semper est aut impotentia.

Suarez hath such a like passage, which Fr. a Sancta Clara reciting, answers this Objection about Imprudence or Impotency, as Posnaniensis before him: *Problem. quart. pag. 31. sed hac ratio ejus est debilis, ut recte notavit Posnaniensis: Nam imprudentiæ vel inconstantiæ vitium non est, siquis propositis duobus bonis, primo eligat minus bonum & postea majus: nisi forte ex passione vel timore difficultatis, vel alia inordinata affectione id proveniat; ut patet de bono cælibatus & conjugii. Deus autem nullo modo obligatur, nec passionibus laborat, sed ex mera liberalitate hoc non illud eligit: Ergo potest eligere sine nota inconstantiæ. Hæc ille. Unde* August. *Si non es prædestinatus, fac ut prædestineris.* Et Ambrosius *(in c. 1. Luc.) Novit Dominus mutare sententiam, si tu noveris emendare delictum.* Subtilissimus etiam Bradwardinus dicit hanc sententiam suum aliquando pulsasse animum, &c.

Thus I have given you some answer to your incredulous Question [By whom I pray?] But another kinde of answer might be given, concerning another sort of men, who deny the Act it self to be Gods Essence, but somewhat that hath no more Being then a Relation, or a Formality, or *Ens rationis ratiocinatæ*, or at least then a *modus Entis*: and consequently that as this may be without any composition in God (which they prove by the confession of our own Doctors) so may it begin and end without Mutation in God. But I'le not offend Mr. K's ears with the names of these men.

---

§. 18.

Mr. K. *Surely transient Acts there could be none before the Creation, there being no term of such Acts, no subject for them, unless there were either somewhat that was not made, or somewhat made before there was a Creation: but as for Immanent Acts, as Knowing and Willing in God, they were before the foundation of the world was laid.* It is a very crude passage thus to say [It is much questioned whether all such Immanent Acts are any more eternal then transient Acts:] For if the meaning be that any transient Act be eternal, that is a mystery beyond all that hath been heard: then somewhat was made from eternity: If the meaning be, that no Immanent Act is eternal, that's after the same rate. The first made the Creature eternal: the second denies God to be eternal: Did he not know from Eternity, yea fore-know all that hath been since the Creation, is or shall be to the dissolution of the world, he were not perfect, and therefore not God from eternity. So then neither can it be affirmed, that there was any transient act eternal, nor can it be denied but that some Immanent acts are eternal: and if some, then all, or els a change in God must of necessity be granted. So that if the meaning be [Its questioned, Whether some immanent Acts be no more eternal then transient Acts] that is, some immanent Acts be not eternal, the Argument returns with the old charge, that an alteration must be yielded in God, immanent Acts being not to be reckoned with any colour among effects, but adjuncts, and no ground of putting any such new immanent Act in God in time, which I demonstrate further thus.

§. 18.

R. B. THe meaning of my words is not hid, but according to the proper literal sense, and I had some respect to the two sorts of men before-mentioned, but chiefly to one. And what I say in Reply to your words, you must be so just as to take to be according to their grounds, and not mine own: For it is but the unsearchableness of these things that I am all this while maintaining.

And first to your Argumentation against the Eternity of transient acts, it may be replied, that in transient acts you must distinguish between the Act it self, which is called transient, and the Passion or Reception of that act in the subject or the product, or effect of that act. The denomination of *Transient* is given to that act in the later respect as it doth connote the Product, Effect, Passion and Subject: yea is properly taken so from them, as that it signifieth nothing essential to the Act it self as an Act: So that all that same Act which is in Time denominated Transient, because in time it did produce its effect, was really from eternity it self; though the effect were not; and so differs not *quoad rationem formalem actus*, from an Immanent act. Proved, 1. The Act by which God created the world, was his simple *Velle:* But Gods simple *Velle* was from Eternity: Therefore *&c*. The *major* is indeed denied by such Punies as *Schibler*, and many more of his minde: but it needs no proof with Mr. K. for it is the opinion (I am sure the saying) of Dr *Twiss*: And indeed it comes all to one, as to our business, if you go on the others grounds. The *major*, Mr. K. maintains. 2. *Deus operatur per essentiam immediatè: sed essentia divina est æterna: Ergo*, &c. The *major* is spoken exclusively as to all acts which are not Gods Essence; and is so common with many Schoolmen, that I will spare the proof (for I perceive its easier taking it for granted then proving it) The *minor* none denieth that confesseth God. So that it is granted Mr. K. that these acts were not to be called Transient from Eternity, because they were not received, or rather did not produce the effect but in time: But yet the act which in Time received the denomination of Transient, was it self Eternal: God Willed from Eternity that the Creature should Be in time, and produced it in that time by that Will which was Eternal. So much on that side.

Now to your Argumentation for the Eternity of Immanent acts, you would receive two several kindes of Answer from the several men that I before told you of.

One sort of them think that the Thing it self which we call an Act, is nothing but Gods Essence, and so Eternal: but that the transition of this Act to several objects (as *Sancta Clara* cals it) or the Application of it to these objects (as *Burgersdicius* speaks) and so the connotation of, and respect to these objects, is not Eternal, where the object is not Eternal: and withall they think that the denomination specifical of the several Acts, yea and the diversification of them, is taken from these temporal transitions, or applications and respects to the objects; and therefore that they must be used as temporal denominations, and it is fittest to say, God Knew, Loved, *&c*. *Peter* as existing, not from Eternity, but when he did exist: Yea they think the very name of an Act, is most fit to be used in this later sense; rather then applied to the pure Essence of God: however some call him in another sense, a simple Act.

The

The other sort of men do think, that the very Act it self is some *Modus* or formality distinct from Gods Essence, and may begin without his Mutation, as it may be his without his Composition, as I have before said.. Now both these sorts will Reply, that your Charge of [making God not Eternal] and of [making alteration in God] which you oft repeat, are but your bare word without any proof, and therefore not by them to be regarded. That God fore-knew all things that should come to pass they easily grant you: but if he know not that to be existent, which is but future, or that to be future which is wholly past, they say, this makes not God to be imperfect, or not eternal.

But I marvel that you still call Gods Immanent Acts [Adjuncts in God] which before you also called Accidents; not fearing hereby to be guilty of making a Compounded God, while you maintain him Eternal: Or not discerning that you give advantage to your Adversary to maintain, that those Accidents or Adjuncts which may be in God without Composition, may as well Beginne or End notwithstanding his Immutability, if their Object be such as doth Beginne or End. Now to your New Demonstration.

§. 19.

Mr. K. IF there be a ground of putting a New immanent Act in God; Ergo, This ground must be either in God or the Creature. If a Ground in God which was not before, then an alteration in him beyond reply: a ground in the Creature there can be none to put a new immanent Act in God; for that an immanent Act hath nothing to do with any thing without the Agent, it being herein contradistinguished from transient Acts, that transient Acts terminantur in passo, immanent Acts in agente. I confess somewhat without the Agent, is many times, yea commonly the object of immanent Acts: but if ever either the Subject or Term, I will publickly burn my Books, as Mr. Baxter desires his may be, when he goes one note beyond Dr. Twiss. I am confident he needs not fear coming so high: I am sure he fals infinitely short in this Argument, as will appear more fully by what he subjoyns.

§. 19.

R. B. THis is the Demonstration. I shall understand that word, in your mouth, better hereafter. Your horned Argument will be thus answered. The word [Ground] is ambiguous. If you take it largely for any sufficient Reason of the attribution, then there is Ground both in the Creature and in God: But if you take it more strictly for some one sort of Reason, then it may be in one and not in the other. The ground may be in the Creature as the Object, and in God as the efficient: and in one as the relate, and the other as the correlate. But you say [if in God, then an alteration in him, beyond reply:] that's a pretty way to prevent a Reply: But your confident Assertions shall hereafter be annumerated with the weakest of your Arguments, though called Demonstrations.

1. Some will take it for a sufficient Reply to deny your Consequence, and think you had dealt fairlier to have proved it. For they will think that there may be in God an Eternal Ground of a New Immanent Act, as well as there is of a New Transient act: The newness of the Act, will not prove the newness of the Ground. And therefore you easily suppose that it must be [a ground in God which was not before]

before] if the act be such as was not before. But this you should have foreseen would be denied. And if you say, that the newness or change in the effect doth argue something changed or new in the cause; they will deny it; and tell you that then every transient act would argue something new in God.

2. Those (of whom I spoke before) that maintain that immanent acts as acts need no subject, will think they reply sufficiently by telling you, that the novity of immanent acts, having a ground in God, will only prove that *aliquid Dei vel a Deo* is altered, but not that *aliquid in Deo* is altered: because that action speaks but a dependant egress, and not an inhesion. The like they will say as to any form introduced in the subject by immanent acts, who deny to many and most immanent acts, a *terminus*; and particularly to intellection. And if you think that there can be no action without some effect within or without, I refer you for an answer to my *Scapula*, as you conceit him.

3. However many of us will hardly be brought to beleeve that Gods immanent acts have in proper sense a *terminus*: though mans may.

4. Some will think they Reply sufficiently, by telling you that by [alteration in God] you mean, either [an alteration of his essence] and then they deny your consequence: or [an alteration of some *modus*, or relation, or formality;] and such they will grant; and say, as oft before, that it is no more against Gods immutability, then the existence of that *modus*, relation, or formality is against his simplicity.

* *All consent not the Relation is only* ex parte creaturæ *and not mutuall.*

5. If when God created the world, he had a * new relation (of Creatour) which he had not before, and this without change, then he may have a new immanent act without change, for ought you know.

6. For Gods acts are not so well known to such Moles and Bats as you and I are, that we should be able so peremptory to conclude that the novity of them must needs argue himself to be mutable: we know not so well how much Being, or of what kinde, those acts have.

So much for Reply to that which is past Reply. Now to the next horn of your Dilemma.

You say [A ground in the creature there can be none to put a new immanent act in God.] And why? Because [an immanent act hath nothing to do with any thing without the Agent.] 1. How? nothing! neither as an occasion, nor an object? do not you confess within a few lines that something without may be its object? It is ordinarily said, and by some of your friends, that the Attributes and Immanent acts of God are diversified only by extrinsick denomination; as an immoveable rock in the sea that is washt sometime with one wave and sometime with another, without its own change: (It seems they take the passion or reception of these motions of the waves, to be no change.) So do diversity of objects, say they, diversifie Gods acts and attributes *quoad denominationem extrinsecam*. If that be so, then objects specifie those acts *quoad denominationem extrinsecam*, which in themselves are but one: and then the said objects may as well cause a novity as a diversity of immanent acts *quoad denominationem extrinsecam*: And then there is no more impropriety in saying, God doth *de Novo* Will or Nill; then in saying, that it is not all one, for God to Will my salvation, and to Nill it: see what you have brought your cause to. 2. There are men in the world that

that conceive of God, as we do of the sun, that is still shining, but not still shining on this or that creature: it may begin or cease to shine on this place or that, without any change in it self or its actual shining: and so they think it is with God as to some of his acts, which have the creature for their objects: And for your objection, That this is a transient act of the sun, I shall reply to it anon, where you mention it.

But you are again harping on your old string; *viz*. [That immanent acts are terminated in the Agent.] And I again tell you, that Gods acts and mans are not so near kin, as that you may conclude of the termination of his acts from the termination of ours: yea I tell you, that I will not beleeve you that Gods willing or knowing the creature hath any *terminus* in himself (further then as you may say the creature is in himself;) that is no *terminus* strictly ascribed to actions distinct from a meet objective termination. A word of proof. 1. Where there is neither *motus* or mutation there is no *terminus*? But in God acting immanently there is neither *motus vel mutatio*: Therefore, &c. I think I need not confirm either part. 2. Where there is no effect or form acquired or introduced, there is no *terminus* (in the sense in question:) But in God there is no effect or form acquired or introduced (by such immanent acts) Therefore, &c. The *major* is plain from the common definition of a *terminus*. The *minor* is past question.

But here you confess that *the objects of immanent acts may be extrinsick* (Yet I could tell you, that *Viguerius Institut*. and others conclude, that *Voluntas Divina non habet objectum extrinsecum*:) *but if subject or term you will burn your Books*, &c. But hold your hand a little. Before I dare be guilty of that, I would fain know what Books they are. But you speak cautelously: for you tell us not who shall be Judge in this business: and if I should shew you never so many that are against you, you may keep your word by saying they all mistake, and by being the Judge your self. But, alas Sir, what cause have you thus to threaten your Books? Who can riddle the occasion of it? I tell you, that as good Philosophers (for ought I yet finde by you) as you, do think that such acts have no subject nor term: and you say, that if any thing extrinsick be the subject or term you will burn your Books! which if you do, let all bear witness that I was no occasion of it: If they have no subject or term at all, then they can have none without. Sure if you were not very quarrelsome you would not in such high words feign him to be your adversary, that saith more against the opposed Point, then your self.

As for that out-leap wherewith you recreate your self, of my coming so high as Dr. *Twiss*, in the sense I spoke I yet desire it not; in the sense you speak (lusorily) I expect it not: nor do I know any man so simple as to compare me with him, or that needed this learned Digression. Yet I confess I thought my self somewhat neerer both Dr. *Twiss* and your self then you suppose me to be: For though I was ready to obey your conclusive command, of adoring the footsteps of such, yet I thought not that I had come *infinitely short*, as you here inform me, I do. I thought only God had infinitely excelled the meanest creature. Nay then, if you will be needs our Gods, *Numina Academica*, I am afraid you will shortly be lower then men; and lest I shall hear that news which I equally fear and abhorre, that you and such like will ere long be cast out of that Academical Paradise. But let that go: I suppose [infinitely] was but a high word, by a high spirit, *quasi ab alto*, from a high place. I have stood my self ere now on a mountain, and every thing in the valley seemed small to me.

K   But

But I forgot to tell you one thing: that (though I suppose I know what kinde of termination you mean, yet) you should have spoken more cautelously, and distinguished, and told your Reader more plainly what you deny; and not have resolved to burn your Books, if we prove things without the Agent to be a term in general. For you know that we distinguish of Objects into Motive and Terminative; and ordinarily say that the creatures are terminative objects of Gods Will, though not moving objects. *Meurisse* saith (*Metaphys. Scot. li.* 1: *Q.* 1 c. pag. 127.) *Objectum secundarium non potest movere intellectum divinum ad cognitionem sui, licet possit illum terminare, ut docent Theologi.* And *Schibler li.* 2. *c.* 3. *tit.* 15. *n.* 507. *Non quasi putemus esse aliquid quod actuet quasi voluntatem divinam,* (*quod officium alias solet esse objectorum, in ordine ad habitus & potentias,*) *sed quia apprehendimus voluntatem Divinam Terminari ad aliquid quod hactenus habet rationem objecti. Est enim ad rationem objecti satis, si terminet actum aliquem.* And *Punct.* 2. *n.* 510. the assertion is, *Dei voluntas terminatur etiam ad res creatas*. But enough of that. Now lets see the proof of our infinite distance.

---

§. 20.

Mr. K. [*A*S for God to know that the world doth now exist: that such a man is sanctified, just, &c. Gods foreknowledge is not a knowing that such a thing is which is not, but that such a thing will be which is not: yet doth this make no change in God, no more then the sun is changed by the variety of creatures which it doth enlighten and warm; or the glasse by the variety of faces which it representeth, or the eye by the variety of colours which it beholdeth: (For, whatsoever some say, I do not think that every variation of the object makes a reall change in the eye, or that the beholding of ten distinct colours at one view doth make ten distinct acts of the sight, or alterations on it; *Apb.* p. 173, 174.] I cannot tell what to make of this rope, but find it is, and nothing else, as shall strait appear; and how ill a match this Authour was, thus to descend in arenam with Twisse, Pemble, and I dare say all the sober Divines that ever were worthy to speak to a School Point.

---

§. 20.

R. B. *S*Anguinolent men do dream of fighting and killing: It seems you have accustomed your minde so to contending, that through the errour of your phantasie, all words seem chidings, and all actions seem fightings to you: 'And so you dreamed not only that I was in *arena*, but 2. that Dr. *Twisse* and Mr. *P.* were there with me. 3. Yea and all Divines worthy to speak to a School Point. 4. And that we were there coping for masteries: and in the end of your dream you rise up as Judge and give them the better, and proclaim me an ill match. But 1. he that reades my Book will finde that I argue not as from my self, but only shew how other mens argumentations do manifest such a difficulty in the Point, that we should not lay too great a stress on it; as I have shewed you before in the explication of my own words. Nay I do not once deny the Point (that immanent acts are eternal) but only say, It is much questioned (by others) whether they are any more eternal then transient acts: and annex a touch of some mens arguings for it: concluding only in a parenthesis, that the Point is, as I think, beyond our reach. So much to the first fiction. 2. And if I contended not with any then not with Dr. *Twiss* and Mr. *P.* on this Point: it being plain that it is

on.

on another Point that I deal with them. Thats for the second fiction. 3. The third is mounted with great confidence; you [dare say:] What dare you say? Why that I [thus descend in *arenam* with all the sober Divines that ever were worthy to speak to a School Point.] You are a daring man, that dare say this. But I have tasted so much of your temper before, that I perceive your veracity is oft least where your audacity is greatest: I thought I had contended with no man in those words; and you dare say, I contend with all men, worthy to speak to a School Point. What if it had been true that I had been here contending, and that against a Point which all these hold? doth it indeed follow that I do in *arenam descendere* with them all? and seek to match them? And what reason have we that know you not, to take you for Judge of all the Divines in the world, who shall be accounted sober, and who not; and who is worthy to speak to a School Point, and who not? Or why should I think you more worthy then the Learned men that I have before named, *Lychetus*, *Pennottus*, *Burgersdicius*, &c?

§. 21.

Mr. K. TO *know, that the world doth now exist when once it did not, and that such a man now is sanctified which before he was not, makes no change in God, but only shews a change in the object: but to know now that the world doth exist which before God did not know, or to know now that such a man is sanctified, who before was not, which before God did not know, makes a change in God, as well as the object.*

§. 21.

R. B. WHo would look for such answers from you, that had heard you judge of School Divines with such Authority? The first part of your Answer is not against any thing that I said: The second is a meer begging of the Question. Some think that *quoad substantiam actus* Gods knowledge is the same whatever the object be; but yet because [Knowing this or that] connoteth the object with the act, therefore the eternal essence of God simply in it self considered is not to be called [Knowledge] much less [the knowledge of this or that creature;] and that without the object it neither is Knowledge, nor ought to be so called; and so as from the object we distinguish Gods Knowing and Willing, so must we the several acts of his knowledge; and though the act *quoad substantiam*, which we call [Knowledge] in God be but one, yet the *ratio formalis* which must give the denomination, being in the respect of that one act to its objects, it is most fit to say that Gods knowledge of *Peters* salvation and *Judas* damnation, is not the same knowledge, though it be the same substantial act: the like is said of his Will: And as this must be said without wrong to his simplicity, so the like must be said of his beginning or ceasing to Know, without wrong to his immutability: and that as it is not all one for God to know the Futurity and the present existence of a thing, so we must say, that he began to know the present existence when the thing began to exist, and that God did not know before the creation, that this proposition was true, *Petrus existit:* and that he ceaseth to know the Futuri ion of a thing that ceaseth to be future; and that God doth not now know, that Christ will be born and dye and rise: and that therefore immanent acts in God are not

K 2

to

to be said to be all eternal; but only those that have an eternal object; because the act is to be denominated from its respect to the object: and therefore it being Gods Knowing and Willing which we call immanent acts here, where it is unmeet to say that act of Knowledge or Will is eternall, then it is unmeet to say, Gods immanent acts are eternal: but when you will express Gods immutability, it is fitter to say [God is unchangeable, or Gods essence or nature is eternall,] then to say, his knowledge, will, or immanent acts (in this sense) are so: because when we connote not the object, we are to call it Gods Essence, and not Gods Knowledge, Will, or such acts: so that here is no real change in God himself, but only a respective, or modal, or formal (as the *Scotists* speak) or such as we cannot now apprehend, affording new objective conceptions; all the change being in the creature.

Now how doth Mr. K. prove that this doctrine must [make a change in God as well as the object?] why he learnedly affirmeth it. He that can finde a word more, let him make his best of it. But in this case, all the proof lieth on the affirmer; which we might well have expected from him.

§. 22.

Mr. K. *ANd therefore all sober Divines use to be wary in their expressions in this kinde; acknowledging no difference between Gods knowledge and foreknowledge, but this, that his foreknowledge is in order to the object only, and not of any act of Gods: so that it is not opposed to post-science, but it signifieth only a futurity of the object, as was shewed at large in the third Chapter. God knows that that is to day which was not yesterday; but God as perfectly knew it yesterday as to day, and knew at once, all the various successions in time; or did he otherwise, a chauge cannot possibly be avoided, notwithstanding all Master Baxter alleadgeth to the contrary.*

§. 22.

R. B. 1. IF your first sentence be true, I must lament the paucity of sober Divines; for sure I am, that of those which have written on these Points, too few have been wary in their expressions: and no wonder when they are no more wary in their conceptions; and when men dare maintain themselves to have that capacity which they have not, and to know certainly that which they do not, and might easily know they do not: When even such learned men as you will not be perswaded that these things are above your reach, but do with such haughty contention oppose one poor sentence in a Parenthesis (which is all my sentence) wherein I say, it is beyond our reach.

2. You lift up your self too high, in taking on you to judge all those Divines to be unsober, that are not in this of your opinion.

3. If the word [prescience] signifie only a futurity of the object, then these are equipollent expressions [*Deus hoc præscit*] and [*Hoc est futurum;*] but that is not true.

4. The same humane frailty and distance from God, which makes it necessary to us to ascribe Acting, Knowing and Willing to God, and to conceive of him under these notions, doth equally necessitate us to conceive of his Knowledge and Will, as distinct, and not altogether the same: else we should ascribe a meer name, without

without any conception of the thing named: For we cannot conceive of any such Knowledge as is the same with Willing, nor of any such Willing which is the same with Nilling; and yet we beleeve the simplicity of God. And the same necessity that compelleth us to conceive of Gods Knowing, Willing and Nilling, as divers, *ab objectorum diversitate*, doth compell us to conceive of his Knowledge of things as Future, and his Knowledge of things existent, as divers; yet still we deny a Mutation of God himself; only we conceive as the Scotists, that there is a diversity of the objective conceptions, and that our various denominations have *fundamentum in re*: but what it is, let him tell that knows.

5. Against all this that which you oppose is but your naked assertion, which I regard less then perhaps you expected. I affirm the uncertainty, and you the certainty; and therefore it is you that should prove that certainty which you affirm to have: For no man hath a certainty without some evidence or other to force assent; and therefore that evidence should be produced, if you are indeed a man of as Angelicall intellectuals as you seem to conceit your self.

6. God did yesterday know that the sun is not risen to day, *i. e.* that to day is not come: You will say, he did at the same time yesterday know that to day is come and the sun is risen? some will think to make this true, you must verifie contradictories, and say, [It is] and [It is not] at once, may both be absolutely true (and then farewell our first Metaphysicall certainty in composition.) Or else you must assert the coexistence of all things with God in eternity; which how loath you will be to admit, I conjecture partly from the tendency of your tenets, and partly from your adhesion to Dr. *Twisse*, and others of his minde.

7. For your third Chapter I have said as much to it already as I finde either need or list, being loath you should cast on me Master *Goodwins* task.

§. 23.

Mr. K. *ANd to the first illustration the case is strangely different; yet I confess, if it did hold, it would prove the point a fortiori:* Thus the sun, *saith he,* enlightens and warms variety of creatures, yet is not changed: therefore nor need God be said to be changed, though he know to day a variation in the creature: *I yield all the conclusion: but all that is nothing to the purpose: for the question is not whether to know a variation in the creature prove a change in God? but whether a variation of the acts of his knowledge, according to the variation in the creatures do not prove a change in him? now the putting of a new immanent act, as a new knowing, is a putting of variation upon him.*

§. 23.

R.B. 1. WEre my advice of any weight with you, I should perswade you never to expect any illustration of Gods immanent acts by the creature, without a great difference in the case; and therefore that you would no more take such difference as so *strange*. 2. Your concession that it will prove the point *a fortiori*, if it hold, is as much as I could desire or expect. 3. A man would think, that the argument you here lay down as mine, were mine indeed, who findes so Learned a Divine saying so, that should abhorre falshood: when you put the words in a distinct character, with a [saith he,] as if they had been my express terms: but I desire the Reader not to judge of all your Writings by such passages as this: He may speak true at one time, that yet takes liberty to speak falsly at another. You did take the easiest course imaginable, to fain a conclusion which you could grant, and then to grant it and say it is nothing to the businefs. 4. I will not consent to your stating the question in new terms of your own, in the midst of a dispute. Do not feign me to dispute any question which you make many years after my Writing, and which is not to be found in my Writing in terms. 5. The word [Act] may signifie 1. the Divine essence; and so he that feigns a new act feigns a new God: 2. Or that mode, formality, respect (or whatever else it is to be called,) of God, arising from the nature or state of extrinsick objects; which *Burgersdicius* cals, the Application to the Object. The question is only of this now, which some think may most fitly be called, Gods acts. Your naked repeated affirmation that a variation is put on God, when you prove it not, I take no more for a Demonstration.

§. 24.

Mr.K. SEcondly, *When we are speaking of immanent acts, what have we to do with the suns enlightening or warming? I had thought those had been transient acts, and so not proper in this case! Yet*

§. 24.

R. B. REmember you not the *crude* question that we were on? [Whether such immanent acts are any more eternall then transient acts?] The Questionists mean it *quoad formalem naturam actus*; for they take the dominations of [immanent] and [transient] to be but from the effect or *terminus*: And that you may see what they imagined, when they mention the similitude of the sun, let me intreat you to suppose for disputation sake (*per possibile vel impossibile*) that God had made at first no creature but the sun: I would fain know whether that sun in shining and casting out its rayes and emanation, did act immanently or transiently? I conceive not transiently: because there were no subjects existing into which its act should pass, or which should as its extrinsick *terminus* receive from it any new form. It seems then it must be immanently: but that is but *in sensu Negativo*, because it is not transient: suppose next that the rest of the creatures were afterwards made, and placed as they are under the influence of this sun, and so were the receptive subjects of its action: Is it not the same sort of Action, without any change in it self, which before was immanent, and now is become transient?

But I need say no more to this; for you are pleased to confess.

§. 25.

Mr.K. YEt thirdly, *Did it hold, I yield it were* Argumentum a majori ad minus: *If the sun be not changed notwithstanding all its warmth and lightening, then neither were God. But sure the sun is changed, and changeth perpetually, and could not act as a Universall cause upon the great variety of creatures in the world; did it not rejoice like*

like a *Gyant* to run its course; did it stand still but one year together at one point, yea or but walk within one Hemisphere for a year, What should we do for that variety of seasons we need? All Summer would be as bad as all Winter. In opposition to this change of the Sun, is the Father of Lights said to be without shadow of turning. He hath no such Solstices or Tropicks; no motions, but a perpetual permanency. There is a great difference between *Immanent acts* and *transient*: that supposing the Sun to stand still as in Joshua's time, and to act without motion; here were no alteration to be acknowledged in the Sun, notwithstanding all the variety of objects, yea and variety of operations upon those objects, all which might proceed from the same Act as to the Sun, the difference being meerly in the Patient: As for instance, the same live-coal doth at once by its heat melt the wax, and harden the clay; here are different transient acts, but no change or difference at all in the fire; but only in the disposition of the matter on which it works. But in *Immanent acts* the Case is contrary; for they being in the subject, the variation of them makes an alteration in that, and not the object: as the same man unchanged may be the object sometimes of mens Love, sometimes of their hatred: the variety of these acts makes a difference in the *Agent*, doth not alwayes suppose any in the Object; and so here, Gods knowing now that this is, Gods not knowing yesterday, that it is now, makes a change in God, but indeed God cannot be said now to know that such a thing is; but to know that now such a thing is [which was not before] and this he did know, what ever is now even from all eternity, his prescience being a Knowledge in præsenti to him, though not de præsenti, as to the object; against whose being in eternity more shall be said hereafter against Mr Goodwin, but now I attend Mr Baxter, who proceeds.

§. 25.

R.B. 1. You seem rather to answer in jest then in earnest, when you tell us of the Suns local motion, when our Question was, Whether [the Sun be changed by the variety of Creatures which it doth enlighten and warm] that is, Whether it self receive any change from the *terminus* or objects of its acts? Do you intend the information of your Reader, or the discovery of Truth, when you shuffle in such an alien Answer? 2. All that its good for, that I know of, is to acquaint us, that you have some full Demonstration against *Copernicus*, which hath given you a Certainty that he erres; And if one should hear it, perhaps it would prove like your Ordinary Demonstrations: for that which is hinted in your words, seems of kin to them. 3. You yield all that I say concerning the Sun, acknowledging that it is not changed by the variety of Objects: And in the first words you say [Did it hold, I yield it were *Argumentum à majori ad minus.*] Lay both these together, and judge whether you yield not the whole Cause which you opposed. 4. You still harp on the old string, affirming, Immanent Acts to be in the Subject, and that their variation alters it; when as good Philosophers say they have no Subject, and that Vision, Intellection, &c. have no *Termini*: Your naked affirmations so oft repeated, rather weary then convince. 5. However you cannot from mans Immanent Acts, argue to Gods, unless they were more like. 6. I am unsatisfied whether a Transient Act (though not *qua* Transient) make not as much alteration on the Agent as an Immanent? Whether a Transient act be not the same with the Immanent, containing in it all that it contains, with the superaddition of its Reception in, and effect upon a Passive Subject? As in the fore-mentioned instance: If the Sun had been created first alone, its action whereby it now lighteth and heateth, would have been immanent;

nent; and yet when the same action shall afterwards become transient by the addition of other creatures to be its Objects, who will imagine that it is ever the less in the Subject (as you say) or that the alteration of it would make ever the less change of the Agent? I confess, I conceive not yet why there should in this point of changing the Agent be any difference between Immanent acts and Transient: though I easily conceive that one only doth change the object. 7. Your friend Mr *Jeanes*, pag. 231. useth the similitude of [a Rock in a River standing immovable, notwithstanding the succession in the waters that glide by it;] which I think is as defective a similitude, as these here used: yet its plain, that you cannot truly say, This Rock toucheth the water that is an hundred miles from it. Suppose the Sun were an eye, and could see all the world at once, and that *pura activitate sine receptione specierum ab objectis*: Suppose one man be born, or one flower spring up this day, which was not in being or visible yesterday: This Sun would see that to day which it did not see yesterday without any mutation in it self: And yet *seeing* is an Immanent act. Now I would know, whether it be fit to say, This Sun sees that as in *being* which is not in being: Or, Whether it be not fittest to say [It begins to day to see that Creature which begun this day to *exist*], though by so beginning it be not changed? Its true, God *fore-knows* all things that shall be: but that is not to *know that they be*, but that *they shall be*. 8. Mr *Jeans* ibid. saith [Yet this is no hinderance but that there may be and is a change in the extrinsecal Denominations of Gods knowledge from the variation of the objects hereof, &c.] so others commonly: And may I not hence conclude, 1 1. That then I may denominate Gods knowledge of the present existence of things, as Beginning with its object: and his knowledge of the existence or futurity of things, as Ending with its object; that is, when the thing ceaseth to be future or to exist? 2. And may I not conclude, that this Denomination is fittest, and so those that thus speak, do speak more fitly then they that speak otherwise? 3. And that there is some *fundamentum in re* for such a denomination: or else it were an unfit denomination, seeing names and words should be fitted to the things signified as neer as may be? 9. Do not you imply as much your self, when you say his Prescience is a Knowledge *in praesenti* to him, though not *de praesenti*? You confess then that God doth not know *de praesenti*, the things that now are not: but when they exist he knoweth them *de praesenti*; I confess the doctrine of the coexistence of all things with God in Eternity, would salve many of these things: but that you here disclaim. 10. Where you say, that [Indeed God cannot be said Now to know that such a thing is, but to know that now such a thing is (which was not before, as in the *Errat.* you adde)] it is a saying which I understand not, and conjecture it is still maimed of some necessary limb which should make it speak your sense: For I hope you do not believe what ever you say, That Indeed God cannot be said Now to know that those things are, which are Indeed: If he know it not Now, when will he know it?

§. 26.

Mr. K. AS the glass by the variety of faces which it represents, *hoc est, as the glass without any change in it represents various faces*, now one, now another; so doth God know various objects, now one, now another, yet without change. The Antecedent is manifestly false; for that each of these several faces cast a new species on the glass, and those several species make several changes. For this purpose Mr. Baxter
might

might have remembred what his great Logick and Metaphysick Masters say, concerning *Ens* intentionale, that it is opposed to reale and materiale: The species in the glass is indeed Ens intentionale, in opposition to Materiale, it is not so in opposition to Reale: But their putting and non-putting, or the presence and absence of the species, makes a real change, though not a material one in the glass; so real a one as that it may be seen, though not a material one that the childe that catcheth at is ever like to take hold of it; Plainly thus, That is a Real Accident which is in the Subject really, and so is that species, for we see it in the glass; that is a Material Accident which is so in the subject as to depend on it alone for its support, without influence of the efficient; heat or cold have such dependance on the subject, as that that alone can maintain them; as the heat will stick a while in the water, though taken off from the fire, and cold in my hand, though taken out of the water: But these Intentional Accidents though really in the subject, yet are so little supported by it, as that if the efficient do not continue its influence, they immediately perish as light in the air, these species, whether in my glass or my eye; who hath so much Logick and Metaphysicks to spill upon all occasions as Mr. Baxter, would have betrayed, I will not say ignorance, but incogitancy in so trivial a punctillio? Onwards, the case is the same for the species in the eye and the glass, and a change is made by the presence or absence of the species.

---

§. 26.

R. B. *Disputatore nimium fœlici, nihil infœlicius; & nimium sapiente quis minus sapiens?* If I spill as much Logick upon all occasions, as you do words, sure I am a voluminous Logician, and make up in number what I want in weight. You wanted an opportunity to multiply words, for ought I know to no purpose, unless to acquaint the unobservant world with your well-furnished Intellect, that they may be assured, that you have all those things at your fingers end, as trivial punctillio's; which I am so ignorant of; and these few words of mine have occasioned the opening of your pack, and the expansion of your wares.

But, 1. You are fain to use the old artifice of putting my words but as the ground of your paraphrase, and then dealing with that paraphrase of your own. This is not so innocent as common a trick. I speak of a change [*of the glass*] and you put [*a change in it:*] Had not you newly risen up as the final decider, I should have said, it is yet *sub Judice*, whether the Intentional or Spiritual Being, in question, be indeed *Res* or not? And so whether it make any Real change in the glass. I confess you easily dispatch the business, which makes me think of *Gorlæus* words, *Exercit. Philos.* 7. §. 2. p. 108. *Quid species sint visibiles inquirendum est: Tam enim earum natura intellectui est ignota, quam ea sensibus notæ. Peripateticis tamen & hic, sicut & alibi facilis expeditio. Qualitates aiunt esse spirituales, & corporis esse objectivum, quod habet in speculo vel simili corpori. Nobis hoc non est satis: qui quærimus porro; quid qualitas spiritalis, aut quomodo corpus objective possit esse in speculo? Nam hæ videntur contradictionem quandam implicare, corporis dari qualitatem spiritalem, & rem extra speculum existentem esse in speculo,* &c.

2. But see what unreverent thoughts such Ignorants as I, are apt to have of learned men! I am confidently perswaded, that you, who are so fully acquainted with Gods Nature and Immanent Acts, as to be at a certainty where I am at a loss, for all that do not know what that is that you see with your eyes; nor whether it be in the glass or not! And therefore the Lecture that you have read me of *Ens intentionale* hath been lost labour as to me!

L   3. And

[66]

3. And you had done but your part if you had observed that I speak, not of the meer Reception of the agents action, but of the Representation to us of the *species*; which should not be confounded.

4. Are you sure that it is from the object, that the glass receives that variation that you imagine? If it be, Rocks and stones are more active creatures then some dull souls will easily believe; when at the same time the same Rock or mountain may perform 100000 actions upon so many eyes or glasses. Yea if in the midst of the Action of this stone or Rock, you do but give your glass a knock, and break it into a hundred pieces, it will multiply the action of the Rock an hundred fold; and that without touching or coming near the Agent. Is it not pretty sport to see the activity of these nimble Rocks and Mountains? I am one of those Hereticks, that think these works of God must be the matter of our admiration, but cannot be comprehended by us here: and that it is no good consequence, that because you and your fellows nakedly affirm the contrary (yea notwithstanding all your proofs) therefore *Des Cartes*, Sr *K. Digby*, *White*, *Hobbes*, besides all the old Adversaries, are certainly in errour. I shall acknowledge more action of the Light, or air on the glass, then of the object, which seems but *sive qua non*. But withall I suspect, that the same Light or air doth perform the same action in the glass when you stand not before it, or when the object is absent; and yet no *species* is then seen; no nor visible. And I think that there is the same action on every glass-window, yea on every wall, or stone, or other body, as is on your *speculum*; and yet you see nothing on them as you do on it. And *Hobbes* saith, That it is in the eye and not in the glass, which you think you see in the glass (his reproaching of our Doctrine of visible *species*, I pretermit:) and if so, then there is not so much alteration in the glass, as you imagine. And indeed, you say little to prove it. If your Argument from sight would prove any thing, it would prove that the face is a foot or a yard (or more if you draw back) behinde the glass, and not in the glass: And yet if you go behinde you, shall see nothing: Will you believe your eyes that things change into such various colours, and shapes, and quantities as some glasses by small mutations of posture do represent them? Will you believe your eyes that a strait staff is crooked in the water? I can tell you by my observation when I was a Boy, that if you will kill a Fish in a River with a Gun, you must allow much to the fallacy of your *medium*. If then either it be the action of the light or air, or something else, and not the object, then it is nothing to me, who spoke only against a change by variation of objects: Or if the foresaid action being supposed to be the same on the glass, when several objects, or no objects are before it, that which is superadded from the object is *nihil reale*, this is nothing against me: Or if the *species* which seems a foot behinde the glass be not in the glass, but in the eye or some where else, and so the glass be more truly an Agent by Reflection, then a Recipient of that *species* which I see, still this is nothing against what I said. So that laying aside all that Reception of the action of light, or any thing else, which the glass receives when there is no object present, and laying aside all that which is Received into the eye and air, and not in the glass, and whereof the glass is but a *Causa sine qua non*; then call the rest an *Ens intentionale* or *spirituale*, or what you will; but prove it to be *quid reale* altering the glass, and do not nakedly affirm it.

You say, that my great Logick and Metaphysick Masters say, That *Ens intentionale*, is opposed to *Reale & Materiale*: and yet you say that the *species* in the glass is not opposed to *Ens reale*. It is, and it is not, seem reconcilable to you then without

a dia distinction. Indeed as Real is opposed to [feigned] I doubt not it is Real; but as it is opposed to Modes and Relations, and such like, that some place between *Ens* and *Nihil*, it must better be known what it is, then the name of *Ens intentionale* or *spirituale* will acquaint us; before we can conclude for certain that it is Real.

As for your Material Accident, it will require more ado to prove, that there is any such thing in the world, as an Accident depending on the Subject alone for support, especially a quality, as you instance in : Sure you intend not the withdrawing of the influence of every efficient, but of some lower or instrumental: I think, at least, Gods efficiency is necessary to be continued, for the Continuation of the being of every Accident, and ordinarily some lower efficiency too.

As for the Logick and Metaphysicks which on all occasions I spill, I take the charge as unfit to be answered, as not coming from your head or heart, but from your Naturals, your spleen and gal.

My Ignorance in comparison of you, I am so easily brought to acknowledge; that I wonder you should think so many words necessary to evince it : (yet you should have done it in intelligible language, and not abrupt expressions, defective of sense, almost such as *Hierom* describeth in his *lib. 1. cont. Jovin. initio.*) But how did you prove my Ignorance or Incogitancy of *Ens intentionale* ? Deep silence! Because I did not mention it, or else who knows why ? By that reason I am ignorant that Mr K. is an honest man, because I do not mention it ; But by what is said, you may see its possible to have heard talk of *Ens intentionale*, and yet to think this similitude tolerable.

And what if you obtain all that you contend for *viz.* That the similitude is faulty ! Alas, I shall easily grant it of any similitude whereby we illustrate the Nature or Acts of God. Suppose then that this glass did make the same Representations *fine receptione specierum* : Or because these inanimates are more remote,)use the similitude of the *Oculus Universalis*, which I mentioned even now. I am troubled that you force me to weary the poor Reader with so many words on so poor and unprofitable a business : But there's no remedy.

§. 27.

Mr. K. NOw whereas *Mr.* Baxter addes, *That whatsoever some say, he doth not think, that the beholding of ten distinct colours at one view, doth make ten distinct acts of the sight, or alterations on it ;* I do not think that ever rational man said they do, for it were strange there should be but one view, and yet ten distinct acts of sight ; but the question is, Whether the change of one of these objects doth not change the species in the eye, and so occasion another view or sight ? Or rather it is beyond all question that they do : and yet whether they do or no need not be questioned neither ; the point that lies before us, is, Whether distinct or new acts do not Cause an alteration? Which is that that we have just Cause to affirm with confidence, can have no place in God ; and consequently no new Immanent Act ; so then there being nothing produced by Mr. Baxter which may suggest a supposition that there may now Immanent Acts be admitted in God, or any but such as are Eternal, Come we to the ———

§. 27.

R. B. YOu are minded to play with the ambiguity of the word [View] which I take for all that Reception in the eye, or activity of it which it performeth

formeth in one Instant; and so for that natural Act whereby I fix my eye on one place at once, seeing as many things as at once I am capable of seeing: You take it, it seems for your intentional Action, or also the act which the visive power performeth, as in reception of that alone. I think the sense I use it in, is more common. And I say again, that it is none of our question, what light, air, &c. do on the eye: for they do no more when I behold one Rock, then when I behold the sands on the shore: But the Question is, What the objects do over and above on the eye? And whether if I see many millions of millions of sands at one instant, there be so many Real Actions of my eye at that instant? And whether every distinct sand that is added or taken away, there be one Act added or taken away, and so a real alteration in my eye? The rest which you adde is over and over answered before, and therefore being ashamed that I have said so much on so unprofitable a point (though constrained) I surcease: Onely adding this brief rehearsal of what is said before.

1. Remember that we speak not of those Immanent acts whose object is Eternal: but of those that have a temporary object, as the actual existence of things, &c.

2. These kinde of Immanent Acts may be called Transient after a sort, in that they do *quoad Terminationem objectivam*, pass to an extrinsick object.

3. *Agere*, in the sense now taken, when applied to God, signifieth something more then meerly *Esse*.

4. The whole Generical Essence of Action is found in the *species* of Action.

5. *Intelligere, Velle, Amare*, relate to some Objects: *Qui Intelligit, aliquid Intelligit: qui Amat, aliquid Amat.* These terms therefore do alwayes (when affirmed, as being in God) connote their Objects.

6. There is a necessity therefore that the acts be variously denominated from the diversity of objects. It is no way fit to say, That God doth Nill Good, or Will sin, or that his *Velle & Nolle* is all one: Or that his *Intelligere & Velle* is all one. For, as it is said, the Act connotes the Object: and therefore we are not so much as to ascribe the act to God when there is not an object for it; or as to an aliene Object. Else we might say, *Dei Intelligere & Velle sunt idem : Deus Intelligit Peccata : Ergo Deus Vult peccata :* And that God Nilleth Good, because he Willeth Good, seeing in God *Velle* and *Nolle* are all one.

7. This necessity of various extrinsecal denominations is ordinarily confessed by the most rigid Divines. I shall cite one more anon.

8. This Denomination hath *fundamentum in re*, or else it were delusory and abusive; these being the fittest names that most agree to the Things (of which see *Meuriss. Metaph. Scoti, li. 2. c. 3. Conclus. 3. & Durand. l. 1. diff. 19. q. 5. §. 13, 14. & Aquin. de Veritate, Mater. 7. q. 1, 2, &c.*) Notions and Names are true or false, as they agree or disagree to the things.

9. On the same ground as God may thus be said to Understand, Will, Nill, Love, &c. and these may be said to be not the same, he may also be said to have divers acts of Intellection, Willing, Nilling, and these not to be the same: e.g. That it is not all one to elect *Peter*, and to elect *John*.

10. Whatsoever this diversity of names implieth, as its foundation in God, (whether a bare Relative diversity, or also a Modal, or what ever the like) it is certain that it implieth no Composition in him, but it is onely what is consistent with his simplicity.

11. Some of the objects of Gods Knowledge and Love, are not from Eternity.

The

The Existence is more then the meer *Esse Volitum*, or Will that they shall exist: And it is not all one to know the Thing it self in it self, and to know it in its Cause. 1 Though God therefore did from Eternity intuitively know the *Esse Volitum*, and know the Creature in himself its Cause, and know its futurity, and so fore-know all things: yet it follows not that he intuitively knew the Creature in it self, as existing, (Unlesse we assert the co-existence of all things in Eternity with God.

12. There is therefore the same reason to Denominate Gods Intellection, Love, &c. as beginning and Ending with its Objects, as there is to denominate them as divers from the diversity of objects. And therefore this is a fit and necessary way of speech. It is not fit to say, God is now Creating the world *quoad actionis formalitatem*, though you over-look the effect: it is not fit to say, That God now knows that the world will be Created (unlesse you respect some new Creation) or that *Abraham*, *Moses*, *David*, shall Die, or that Christ shall rise again, &c.

13. This Denomination of Gods acts as beginning and ending, hath as much foundation in the thing, and is as true as the Denomination of his acts as various. And this may as well consist with Gods Immutability, as the other with his Simplicity. The reason is evidently the same.

Now for the one, hear what others say. Schibler *Met. l.2. c. 3. Tit. 6. n. 247, 248. Quæstio est de Accidentibus quæ in Deo sint. Hæc enim solum possunt compositionem in Deo facere;* &c. *Unde specialiter relinquitur, quod in Deo non fiat compositio ex subjecto & accidente, si maximè ei conveniat* Agere, *tali actione quæ prædicamentalis dici possit. Nam actiones non comparantur ad agens, per modum essendi in, sed solum per modum essendi ab alio, ut infra,* &c. *Atque ita actiones tantum apprehenduntur ut egredientes ab essentia rei. Quod autem egreditur ab essentia rei, hoc, eo ipso, non potest cum essentia facere compositionem, quæ extremorum unionem requirit.* And *n.* 97. *Nam Actiones Divinæ transeuntes, non sunt subjectivè in Deo, sed solum a Deo procedunt; unde nullam compositionem cum Deo faciunt,* &c. *Quanquam id etiam (verum) est de actionibus Immanentibus: Hæ enim non dicuntur Immanentes positivè, quasi in agente rigide loquendo subjectentur, sed Negativè solum, quia in externam materiam non transfiunt. Unde ad rationem actionis simpliciter & Immanentis & transeuntis, non requiritur esse in, sed solum esse ab: Ideoque neutrum facit cum agente Compositionem. Et sic anima nostra, si incipiat intelligere aut Velle, non tamen componitur, tum ex suo esse & Intellectione & Volitione quà tales sunt: sed in utroque statu æque est Anima simplex. Dixi, quà tales sunt, Quia ad intellectionem potest consequi aliqua compositio, si sit per speciem Intelligibilem.]*

Keckerman *in Systim. Theolog. l.1. t.3.* maintaineth, that the Persons in the Trinity, differ from the Divine Essence; as *Modus à re*, and from each other as *Modus à Modo*, and that *Ens* and *Modus* make no Composition. Much more may it be so said of Relations to things external.

Altingius, *Problem. Theolog. Par. 1. pag. 55.* distinguisheth Gods actions, 1. *Sunt actus intrinsici & Immanentes qui non transeunt in objectum externum & nullum prorsus respectum aut σχέσιν ad τὰ ἔξω. Tales sunt actus personales quos Scholastici* notionales vocant, gignere, *spirare,* &c. *Horum absoluta est necessitas absque potentia ad oppositum, & sunt æterni.* 2. *Sunt actus extrinsici qui non sunt in Deo; sed à Deo; sive qui a Deo sunt effective, in Creaturis autem subjectivè: sicut creare, gubernare, redimere,* &c. *Deus enim extrinsecus solum ab iis denominatur.* 3. *Sunt Actus Intrinseci quidem in Deo, sed Connotantes respectum ac χέσιν ad extra, ut scire, velle. Scit enim Deus*

Deus non solum se, sed etiam omnino quicquid est scibile, sive ut possibile, sive ut futurum. Vult etiam non solum se, sed etiam alia extra se, &c. *Hujusmodi actus sunt Decreta, relativi nimirum ad extra, & præter voluntatem χοσιν statuunt rerum externarum. Compositio autem hinc male infertur,* &c. Mark also, that he names the first sort onely Immanent acts.

And for the fitnesse and necessity of the Denominations, hear what *Estius* confesseth *in Sent. l. 1. dist. 39. §. 3. De hac igitur scientia Dei* (viz. *ad enunciabilia*) *quamvis & ipsa sine dubio sit in se invariabilis, varie tamen loqui nos oportet, prout variantur propositiones secundum tempora. Cum enim nullam propositionem scire quis dicatur, hoc sciendi modo, nisi veram, eademque propositio propter mutationem rerum ac temporum, modo vera sit, modo falsa; consequens erit, Deum nunc scire propositionem aliquam quam postea nesciat, & contra. Quod per singulas temporum differentias facile est declarare. Nam propositionem veram de præterito, ut, Christus natus est, ante bis mille annos non sciebat, sed Christo nato scire cœpit; eademtamen nunquam scire desinet, sicut nec ullam aliam quæ sit præteriti temporis, quia propositio de præterito vera, semper erit vera. Quod intellige de præterito in genere: Nam si certum tempus designes, ut Heri natus est Christus, scire eam desijt, & de futuro simpliciter, ut, Post biduum pascha fiet. Rursum propositionem de futuro veram, ut Omnes resurgemus, scivit quidem ab æterno, nec fieri potest ut talem aliquando incipiat scire, quia propositio de futuro vera,semper fuit vera, loquendo similiter de futuro in genere. Sed eam aliquando scire desinet; nempe post resurrectionem factam, quia tum vera esse desinet ipsa propositio. Denique propositionem de præsenti veram, scit tantisper dum ea vera manet, velut istam, Ecclesia militat. Ac talem incipit aliquando scire, & aliquando scire desinit; nisi forte veritas propositionis sit perpetua,* &c. *Porro omnis hæc loquendi varietas non inde nascitur, quod circa Dei scientiam accidat aliqua Mutatio, sed quia mutantur res subjectæ. Unde necesse est & ipsas mutari propositiones,* &c. *Manifestum est autem rebus mutatis non necessario scientiam mutari, ne creatam quidem, nisi quid aliud concurrat, velut Compositio aut divisio, aut certitudo major per experientiam rei præsentis accepta. Quæ in Deo locum non habent. Sicut ergo scientia Medici invariata permanet dum eidem homini ob variam ejus affectionem, modo hæc pharmaca, modo alia diversa præscribit,* &c.]

14. Lastly, I again desire the Reader to remember, that if I seem in all this to speak sceptically, it is no wonder, when all that I intend is but to convince these self-conceited Learned men, that these things are indeed beyond their reach, and that they know not what they think they know: it being my own opinion, That Action, Intellection and Will, are but Metaphorically ascribed to God, and that we cannot know what that is in propriety, which these expressions do shadow out in God. *Tho. White* saith, *Institut. Sacrar. li. 2. Lect. 1.* pag. 136, 137. *Quare dicimus abstrahendo a nostris conceptibus, esse Deum unum simplicitatem simplicissimam, qua neque sit Deus, neque eus, neque aliud formaliter quod nos cogitare possimus; sed nostras cogitationes eam inadequate repræsentare; non quasi accipientes aliquod unum ex pluribus quæ ibi actu sint, sed accipiendo participationes quasdam inferiores eo quod ipse est, & dissimiliores quam saliva vel pediculus est respectu hominis.* Whether this hold or not of the notions, *Deus & Ens;* I doubt not but it holds of Intellection and Volition: or at least that women are uncertain what these are in God. And the strange confidence of men in this, that they know that which no man knows indeed, hath made them unreverently vent their conceits, and fill the Church with perplexing controversies about things that none can determine. As Mr *Burgess* saith of Justific. Lect. 20. [Only you must take notice that we are

in

[71]

in meer darkness, and not able to comprehend how God is said to act or work, &c. Therefore it is a sure truth, *De Deo etiam vera dicere periculosum est, & tunc dignè Deum æstimamus, cum inæstimabilem dicimus;* [then do we rightly esteem of him, when we Judge him above our thoughts or esteem.] *Matth. Paris* speaking of the Dominicans teaching, which caused that great dissention and confusion in the University of *Paris*, writes thus (ad annum Dom. 1243. as he is cited by the Prefacer to *Guiliel. de Sancto Amore*) *Incipiebant disputare & disserere subtilius & celsius quam decuit aut expedivit: Qui non verentes tangere montes a gloria Dei opprimendi nitebantur secreta Dei investigabilia temere perscrutari, & Judicia Dei quæ sunt abyssus multa, nimis præsumptuosè indagare. Deo enim plus placet firmæ fidei simplicitas, quam nimis transcendens in Theologia subtilitas.*] : Dr. *Twiss Vindic. Grat. l. 2. Crim. 3. §. 15.* '*Sed quid fiet si hæc humana ratio non ferat? An nihil credendum nobis incumbit nisi quod quomodo fiat; humana ratione explicare possit? Mysterium hoc forsitan adorandum potius quam scrutandum,* &c.: *Et li. 2. Crim. 3. §. 20. pag. (ibi) 405. Etiam non erubesco fateri, licet nunquam dubitarem de sancta Dei natura, tanquam de omni sceleris reatu alienissima, hoc tamen diu me suspensum tenuisse (forte etiam hodie non paucos suspensos tenet) quænam scilicet sit illa vera ratio, qui modus operationis Divinæ quo fiat ut se in omni actione tanquam Causa efficacissima immisceat, extra tamen omnem vitii contagionem; citra justam culpæ suspicionem: Et an hodie per omnia satis explicatum habeamus, Deus novit,* &c. *Significat etiam* Calvinus, *multis hunc nodum visum esse inexplicabilem,* &c. *Hoc modo tutius consulendum censuit nostræ pietati, si fateamur hebitudinem sensus nostri mysterium hoc non capere.*] "And why should not the same Confession extend to the present case also? Though we do not use to confess our Ignorance till we are utterly at a loss (and then we say as *Cajetan* when he was stall'd, It doth not *quietare intellectum*) yet we have oft as great cause to confess it where we are confident sometimes; as perhaps *Ariba* that blames *Cajetan* for his Confession of Ignorance, might know as little as *Alvarez* that commends it for a most holy and pious speech.

See Mr K's own confession, how little we can conceive or express of God, in the end of his Epist. Dedicat.

I had thought to have said no more to this point, but finding a most Learned, * Orthodox, Judicious Divine Robert *Baronius* (Camero *secundus, vel* Cameroni *secundus*) to speak so fully in this point, in his excellent Treatise *de Peccato Mortali & Veniali*, I have adventured to transcribe the whole Chapter, it being not long, both that the Reader may see the Reasons of the like passages in my fore-going Replies more clearly, and that Mr. K. may be yet better satisfied that I am not so singular in these things, as he seems to think me.

* *I know Mr.* Rutherford *hath some jarring with him; and I do not undertake to justifie all that any man hath said, when I call them Orthodox; but I confess I think that for solidity in*

the controverted points that they meddle with, Davenant, Camero *and* Baronius *are the glory of* Britain, *as having happily hit on that mean, which many others have mist of, which I would not have understood as disparaging any others: for even in this, they have many excellent Companions, and others have their excellencies, that were not in this so happy as they. Our Renowned B.* Usher, *D.* Preston, *D.* Field, *and many another famous light in* England, *have not only deserved the honour of eminent Learning and Piety, but even in this judicious Discovery of the truth, between the extreams which others have run into, they have helped to reduce the violent to Moderation, and to shew men a surer way to overcome the adversary, then their disadvantagious extreams.*

Disp.

Disp. Parte 1ª sect.6. Deum posse eos amare quos prius odit, & odisse eos quos prius amavit, absq; ulla vel physica, vel morali voluntatis suæ mutatione, obiter Declaratur.

*E*x doctrina præcedenti sectione tradita de justificatorum ad certum tempus exclusione ab eo favoris Divini gradu, quo prius diligebantur, nequaquam sequitur Deum, aut voluntatem Dei in se mutabilem esse, sive loquamur de mutabilitate physica, sive de mutabilitate morali.

Nam quod ad divinum amorem executionis attinet, Deum non amare justificatos peccati mortalis reatu involutos amore executionis, nihil aliud est, quàm eum non conferre in illos ea bona spiritualia, seu media salutis, quæ prius in eos conferebat nulla igitur est bic mutatio quoad actus immanentes, qui in ipso Deo existunt, sed tantum quoad actus transeuntes, qui sunt extra Deum & in hominibus recipiuntur. Et proinde iis mutatis non mutatur Deus, sed illi in quibus bi actus, & eorum effecta recipiuntur. Dicet aliquis: Deus non solùm non confert illa beneficia in eos, sed etiam durante eo statu non vult ea conferre: prius autem voluit ea conferre: & proinde mutatus est. Resp. Voluit prius illa beneficia communicare iis existentibus in alio statu. Sed iis existentibus in hoc statu impietatis, & impænitentiæ, neq; jam vult, neq; unquam voluit, imo ab æterno noluit hæc beneficia communicare. Quamvis igitur durante hoc statu benevolentia Dei quasi ligata & impedita sit; ut supra monui, hinc tamen non sequitur eam in se mutatam esse: sed tantum mutatum esse ejus objectum, quia viz. objectum ejus, hoc est, homines electi, prius erant capaces istorum beneficiorum nunc vero eorum capaces non sunt.

13. Major & gravior difficultas est de amore complacentiæ, & odio displicentiæ ei opposito. Cum enim bi actus sint immanentes, hoc est, in ipso Deo existentes, iis mutatis videtur ipse Deus in se mutari. Responderi solet primo, non mutari hos actus realiter, & à parte rei; quia uterq; hic actus in Deo fuit ab æterno, & in æternum in eo durabit, cum respectu ad diversos istius hominis status, quorum alter alteri in tempore successit. Ita respondet Fonseca tom.3.Metaph.lib.7.cap.8.quæst.5. sect.7. Quod si (inquit) quis objiciat eundem posse prius odio haberi a Deo, si sit injustus, posteà verò diligi, si sit justus, & vice versa, sine ulla divinæ voluntatis mutatione, ergo nihil repugnare quo minus divina voluntas nullo modo mutata transeat à nolitione in volitionem rei ejusdem, ex dictis patet solutio. Deus enim non eundem odio habet, ac diligit pro eodem tempore, sed pro diversis. Adde, quod etsi in eodem homine justitia succedit peccato, aut peccatum justitiæ, tamen odio, quo Deus illum prosequitur ut peccatorem, non succedit amor, quo illum diligit ut justum, aut contra; sed uterq; affectus divinus æternus est respiciens diversos hominis status, quorum alter alteri succedit in tempore.

4. Secundò respondeo: quamvis concederemus esse aliquam mutationem & successionem in actibus immanentibus amoris & odii divini formaliter consideratis, quatenus per rationem distinguuntur ab essentia divina & inter se, hoc est, quamvis diceremus actum amoris complacentiæ erga electum in hoc casu non amplius esse in Deo, eiq; succedere actum odii displicentiæ, non tamen inde sequeretur esse mutationem aliquam realem in ipso Deo. Nam actus Dei liberi nihil superaddunt voluntati aut essentiæ divinæ, præter respectum seu relationem rationis, aut extrinsecam aliquam connotationem, quæ tamen ad realem eorum entitatem non pertinent: nam tota eorum entitas realis est ipsa Dei essentia, nihilq; intrinsecè includunt præter eam. Quamvis igitur

igitur *Deus defineret amare eos quos prius amabat, non mutaretur mutatione reali, quia nihil reale amitteret, siq́; inciperet eos amare quos prius odit, non mutaretur, quia nihil reale ei accederet; mutatio autem realis non fit, sine aliqua additione aut ablatione reali.*

5. *Non necesse est ut hic probem actus illos nullam realem entitatem (sive ea vocetur perfectio, sive extensio actus divini ad objecta) superaddere essentiæ divinæ. Nam Evangelici omnes hoc unanimiter tenent: & quod ad Pontificios attinet, quamvis* Cojetanus *in 1.ᵐ partem Thomæ quæst. 19. art. 2 & 3* Fonseca *tom. 3. Metaph. lib. 7. cap. 8. quæst. 5. sect. 4. &* Salas *1a.2æ. quæst. 6. art. 3. tract. 3. disp. 3. sect. 8. doceant actus liberos Dei, seu decreta ejus, superaddere essentiæ divinæ realem quandam entitatem, quæ ab æterno potuit non esse in Deo, quæq́; revera in eo non fuisset, si ab æterno aliter decrevisset, & hos actus non habuisset, major tamen & melior eorum pars in contraria est sententia viz.* Suarez. *tom. 2. Metaph. disp. 30. sect. 9. &* Vasquez. *in 1.ᵐ partem Thomæ, disput. 80. cap. 1. & 2.* Valent. *tom. 1. disput. 1. quæst. 19. punct. 4.* Arrubal *in primam partem Thomæ, disput. 54. cap. 2. & se sequentibus.* Becanus *in summa, Parte 1. Tract. 1. cap. 11. quæst. 4.* Trigosus *in summa Theologica Bonaventuræ quæst. 13. art. 2. dub 3. conclus. 1.* Franciscus Cumel *variarum disput. tom. 1. in disp de præscientia Dei dub. 3 p. 57, &c. Horum sententia proculdubio est verior illa altera, quia si in Deo est realis aliqua entitas, quæ ab æterno potuit in eo non esse, atq́; adeo potuit non omnino esse, seu esse merum nihil, necessario sequitur aliquid esse in Deo quod non est Deus.*

6. *Dicet aliquis: si mutatis actibus liberis Deus realiter non mutatur, poterit salva sua immutabilitate, mutare decreta sua de rebus futuris, & proinde poterit incipere velle quod nunquam antea voluit, vel desinere velle quod prius voluit. Nam talis mutatio decretorum divinorum fit sine aliqua additione, aut ablatione reali. Resp. Duplicem esse mutationem, viz. Physicam & Moralem. Physica, seu realis mutatio fit per additionem, aut ablationem alicujus entitatis realis. Moralis mutatio est propositi & voluntatis, aut etiam cognitionis & scientiæ mutatio; ut si quis quod antea putabat verum, deinde falsum judicet; & quod antea facere decreverat postea nolit; quod sane magnam imperfectionem in eo qui sic mutatur arguit. Vide* Vasquezium *in 1.ᵐ partem Thomæ super quæst. 9. art. 4. Cum igitur Deus dicitur absolute immutabilis id non minus intelligitur de morali quam de Physica immutabilitate, nam mutatio propositi & consilii quæ moralis vocatur, arguit inconstantiam, imprudentiam, & cognitionis imperfectionem, quæ non minus summæ & absolutæ Dei perfectioni repugnant, quam Physica, seu realis mutatio, ut bene observat* Suarez. *tom. 2. Metaph. disp. 30. sect. 9. num. 58.*

7. *Ex his patet Deum, cum odio displicentiæ prosequitur electum, quem prius amabat amore complacentiæ, non mutari; quamvis fortasse nunc minime sit in eo actus complacentiæ, consideratus ut respectum rationis ad tale objectum divinæ essentiæ superaddit: Primò enim ablato tali actu, Deus physicè & realiter non mutatur, quia nihil ei decedit præter merum respectum rationis ut irrefragabilibus argumentis demonstrant* Suarez. *&* Vasquez, *locis citatis. Secundò, neque mutatur moraliter, quia non mutat propositum, sed contra, permanet in suo proposito, aut potius in naturali sua inclinatione, qua ab æterno fuit, nunc est, & semper erit, propensus ad amandam virtutem, & ad detestanda vitia, seu peccata. Permanet etiam in suo proposito perducendi eos quos elegit & justificavit ad æternam gloriam, nam solidum stat Dei fundamentum, habens sigillum hoc, Novit Dominus eos qui sunt sui,* 2 Tim. 2. 19.

M

Mark

Mark here that the reason which *Baronius, Burgersdicius* and others give against Gods change of his Decrees, *viz*. he should be morally mutable, holds not of the immanent acts which presuppose their objects, and whose objects are really mutable: as *Baronius* here manifesteth. It is certain that things are sometime future, sometime present or existent, and sometime past: and that they are so is of God, but without moral mutation: therefore his Knowing them so, and his Willing and Approving them so, is without moral mutation too. So the same man is good or holy to day that was bad and unholy yesterday: therefore God may love him to day with complacency and approbation, whom he disliked before; and may know him to be as he is, which before he did not, because he was not as he is. 2. Note the reason why God cannot change his Decrees: Both because they do effect or produce their own objects (as commonly called) viz. *Rerum futuritionem*, when as Gods Approbation, his Knowledge *puræ visionis*, his Complacency, &c. do presuppose their objects. 2. And it would be a contradiction for the same event, to be future and not future, *e. g.* mans salvation: therefore if God absolutely Decree that *Peter* shall be saved, and after Decree the contrary, the first Decree must be changed causlesly, and for want of power not be executed; and also as it is *verbum mentis*, it must be false: which cannot be.

I Had thought to have said nothing of particular Scriptures that speak of Gods acts which we call Immanent as Beginning or Ending, because they are so commonly known: But lest any should think I slight Scripture Argument, which I principally esteem, or lest they take it for granted that there is none such, because none are produced, I will adde some texts in confirmation of the *minor* of this following Argument.

If God himself in his Word do ordinarily speak of his own Acts, which we call Immanent, as Beginning or Ending, then is it not unfit for us to do so to. (God knows best how to express his own Acts.)

But God himself in his Word doth ordinarily speak of his own Acts, which we call Immanent, as Beginning or Ending:

Therefore.

Luk. 2. 52. *Jesus increased in favour with God and man:*] Gods [favouring] Christ is an Immanent act: and yet Christ increased in Gods favour: Increase signifieth mutation, by an inception of further degrees.

Rom. 9. 25. *I will call them my People which were not my people, and her Beloved which was not beloved.*] Love is an Immanent act.

Joh. 16. 27. *The Father himself loveth you, because ye have loved me and beleeved, &c.*] Therefore it was when they beleeved and loved Christ, that the Father in this sense began to love them.

Joh. 14. 21, 23. *He that loveth me shall be loved of my Father, and I will love him, &c. And my Father will love him, and we will come unto him, &c.*]

Pro. 8. 17. *I love them that love me, &c.*] Therefore with this same love, they were not before beloved, though with another sort of love they were.

Joh. 10. 17. *Therefore doth the Father love me, because I lay down my life, &c.*

Hof. 11. 1. *When Israel was a childe then I loved him.*

Deut.

Deut.7.12,13. *If ye hearken,&c. the Lord thy God will keep unto thee the Covenant, &c. And he will love thee,&c.*

Hof.9.15. *I will love them no more: All their Princes are revolters.*

Pſal.5.5. *Thou hateſt all the workers of iniquity.*] Such are the Elect before conversion.

Gen.4.7. *If thou do well ſhalt thou not be Accepted, &c?*

So all thoſe texts that ſpeak of Gods being reconciled, which properly ſignifies an Immanent act.

Act.10.35. *He that feareth God and worketh righteouſneſs is Accepted of him.*

Mat.3.17. *This is my Beloved Son in whom I am well pleaſed.*

Heb.13.16. *With ſuch ſacrifice God is well pleaſed.*

Heb.11.5. *He had this teſtimony that he pleaſed God.*

1 King.3.10. *And the ſpeech pleaſed the Lord that Solomon asked, &c.*

Heb.11.6. *Without faith it is impoſſible to pleaſe God.*

1 Theſſ.4.1. *How ye ought to walk and pleaſe God.*

1 Cor.7.32. *He that is unmarried careth, &c. how he may pleaſe the Lord.*

Rom.8.8. *They that are in the fleſh cannot pleaſe God.*

Prov.15.8. *The prayer of the upright is his delight.*

2 Sam.15.26. *If be thus ſay, I have no delight in thee,&c.*

Jer.9.24. *For in theſe things do I delight ſaith the Lord.*

Zeph.3.17. *He will rejoyce over thee with joy, he will reſt in his love; he will joy over thee,&c.*

Deut.28.63. *And it ſhall come to paſſe, as the Lord rejoyced over you to do you good, &c. ſo the Lord will rejoyce over you to deſtroy you,&c.*

Deut.30.9. *For the Lord will again rejoyce over thee for good.*

Pſal.104.31. *The Lord ſhall rejoyce in his works.*

Iſa.62.5. *As the bridegroom Rejoyceth over the bride, ſo ſhall thy God Rejoyce over thee.*

2 Tim.2.15. *Study to ſhew thy ſelf approved unto God.*

Deut.32.19. *When the Lord ſaw it, he abhorred them.*

Gen.1.4,10,13,31. *God ſaw the light that it was good.*

Iſa.59.15,16. *And the Lord ſaw it, and it diſpleaſed him, that there was no judgement: And he ſaw that there was no man, and wondred,&c.*

Gen.29.31. *When the Lord ſaw that Leah was hated, he, &c.*

Jer.26.2,3. *Diminiſh not a word. If ſo be they will hearken and turn every man from his evil way, that I may repent me of the evil, which I purpoſe to do unto them, becauſe of the evil of their doings.*

Jer.36.3. *It may be the houſe of Judah will hear all the evil which I purpoſe to do unto them, that they may return every man from his evil way, that I may forgive, &c.*

Gen.6.6. *It repented the Lord that he had made man.*] So the 7th verſe.

Exod.32.14. *And the Lord repented of the evil which he thought to do unto his people.*

1 Sam.15.35. *The Lord Repented he had made Saul King*] So the eleventh verſe.

2 Sam.24.16. *The Lord Repented him of the evil, and ſaid to the Angel,&c.*

Pſal.106.46. *He remembred for them his Covenant, and Repented according to the multitude of his mercies.*

Jer.26.19. *And the Lord Repented him of the evil,&c.*

Amos 7. 3. *The Lord Repented for this: It shall not be saith the Lord.*] So verse 6.

Jonah 4. 2. *I knew that thou art a gracious God, and mercifull, slow to anger and of great kindness, and Repentest thee of the evil.*

Jon. 3. 10. *And God saw their works that they turned from their evil way, and God Repented of the evil that he had said he would do unto them, and did it not.*

Joel 2. 13. *He is gracious, &c. slow to anger, and Repenteth him of the evil.*

Jer. 15. 6. *I am weary with Repenting.*

Hos. 11. 8. *My heart is turned within me: my repentings are kindled together.*

Psal. 30. 5. *For his Anger endureth but for a moment.*

Psal. 103. 8, 9. *The Lord is mercifull and gracious, slow to Anger, &c. Neither will he keep his Anger for ever.*

Isa. 63. 10. *Therefore he was Turned to be their enemy, &c.*

Psal. 85. 3. *Thou hast taken away all thy wrath, thou hast turned thy self from the fiercenesse of thy anger.*

2 Chron. 12. 12. *And when he humbled himself the wrath of the Lord turned from him that he would not destroy him.*

Josh. 7. 26. *So the Lord turned from the fiercenesse of his wrath.*

So 2 Chron. 29. 10. & 30. 8, 9. & Psal. 106. 23. Jer. 18. 20. and so frequently. Also very many places that mention the kindling or arising of Gods wrath.

Psal. 78. 38. *Many a time turned he his anger away and did not stirre up all his wrath.*

Prov. 24. 18. *Lest the Lord see it, and it displease him, and turn away his wrath from him.* There are three several immanent acts mentioned together.

So all those Texts where Remembring and Forgetting are spoken of God,

So many more Texts that mention Gods being displeased, *Gen.* 38. 10. *Num.* 11. 1. 1 *Chron.* 21. 7. *Ps.* 60. 1. *Zech.* 1. 2. 15.

So many Texts that speak of Gods *seeing*, as *Gen* 18. 21, &c.

Psal. 34. 17. *The righteous cry and the Lord heareth and delivereth*, &c.

Psal. 69. 33. *For the Lord heareth the poor and despiseth not his prisoners.*

With many more places that speak of Gods Hearing and Hearkening.

So many Texts that mention his Regarding, and his Considering, and Pondering.

And many that mention his Abhorring, and his despising.

And many Texts that speak of Gods Pity and Compassion to the miserable.

And many that speak of his Favour as beginning or ending, and mans finding favour in his eyes.

And many that speak of his Grace when it signifieth favour, and is expressed as beginning or changing. With many more to the same purpose.

Judg. 10. 13. 16. *Ye have forsaken me and served other Gods; Wherefore I will deliver you no more.* Vers. 16. *They put away the strange Gods and served the Lord, and his soul was grieved for the misery of Israel*, &c.] And he did deliver them by *Jephtah.* Yet here God seemeth to revoke a peremptory sentence.

If any shall say, that all these later are but figurative speeches applied to God from the manner of men: I as easily grant it as any man: But withall remember these two things. 1. That I suppose it is as true of Gods Knowing and Willing, his Electing, Decreeing, Purposing, *&c.* only differing in the degree of impropriety: Till the contrary be better proved then I have seen it, I think this will be

my

my opinion. 2. It is onely the fitnesse or unfitnesse of these wayes of speech concerning God, that I am now enquiring into; and not of the propriety. If it be the Scripture-way so ordinarily to speak of Gods Immanent acts as New, as Beginning or Ceasing, then is it not unlawfull or unfit for us so to speak, in imitation of the holy Ghost: still acknowledging the unavoidable Impropriety of our expressions, and the Incomprehensiblenels of that in God, which by such expressions is hinted out unto us.

I remember what *Zanchius* saith *in Epist.* Joh. Cratoni, in the third Vol. of his Works, pag. (*mihi*) 135. *Quod ait, Precibus moveri Deum ἀνθρωποπάθεια est, quam si tollamus è Scripturis, quæ impietates & quot pugnantia non è Scripturis colligentur?*

The Second Point.

§. 28.

Mr. K. Second; THat there is somewhat like to *Justification* in the Eternal *Decrees* of *God* to *Justifie* men.

§. 28.

R. B. IF this also be intended against me, then, Whether this Learned man did not want Work, when he undertook this, I leave the indifferent Reader to judge. The former Question which he propounded to dispute, he knew and confessed that I denied not: (Yet he hath forced me to spend many words on it, and to say more then I thought to have done.) This which he makes his second Labour, he will not say that I was ever his adversary in; or that ever I debated the Proposition, much less denied it: And yet all this seems intended against me, and by name anon he brings me in. If this man had not somewhat *ab homine* more forcible then any thing in the matter disputed, which instigated his pugnacious soul to this conflict, then must I confess my self quite mistaken in the Motives of his undertaking. The former part of his Dispute hath convinced me of this. I remember we had such sparks among us when I was a School-boy, that were wont (for maintaining the reputation of their valour) to appoint fighting matches, and to the field they must go, before ever they thought what should be the matter of quarrel, and when they came to the place, they must be dared by a third, to spit in anothers face to make the quarrel; and he that refused was the Coward, and he that spit first, and struck first, had the first glory, though sometime not the last.

What I should do with all these following words of Mr. K's that concern me not, I do not well know. I hope none will expect that I should engage my self against him to prove, that [there is nothing like to Justification in the Eternal Decrees of God to Justifie] nor that I should answer to all that he brings to prove it it. Yet becauſe I take his Diſcourſe to be very feeble, and to ſmall purpoſe, I ſhall take a brief notice of it in the way, whether it were intended againſt me Directly, or but Collaterally.

§. 29.

Mr. K. *And I make it good, not from this, that by reaſon of this Decree, God is ſaid to have Juſtified whom he predeſtinated,* Rom. 8. For indeed he is ſaid to have glorified them alſo; though glorifying of many of them be not till the end of the world, yea that full glorifying of none of them be till then, and the Decree to glorifie all whom he will glorifie at the end of the world, was before the beginning of the world: and yet this expreſſion ſhews the Certainty of their Juſtification and Glorifying, who are predeſtinated; the Preter tenſe being uſed only to expreſs the Certainty of the future. But this I will not inſiſt on; but run another courſe, and that is this: Juſtification is by the Conſent of all men (I mean Proteſtants) a Remiſſion of our ſins, and Accepting of us as Righteous: Now this is either a meer immanent, or a meer tranſient Act, or both. I know no man will ſay it is a meer tranſient Act: there being no tranſient Act of God which doth not ſuppoſe an Immanent one; for that he acts nothing upon the Creature, but what he firſt purpoſed in himſelf to act: ſo then an Immanent act there muſt be confeſt, if there be a tranſient one; and a tranſient one I ſhall acknowledge as well as an Immanent, and what it is will enquire by and by: But firſt I contend that immanent Act there can be no other then the Decree of God to paſs this tranſient Act, and that this Decree of God to paſs the tranſient Act of Juſtifying, carries in it as much as concerns Gods Remiſſion of ſins, and Acceptance of us as Righteous; and therefore hath much in it like to Juſtification; and may be ſtiled ſo without Blaſphemy, as Mr. Goodwin is pleaſed to brand it in his Rhetorick. And that this Decree to Juſtifie us, carries as much as concerns Remiſſion of ſins, and accepting of us as righteous, I prove thus: If it do not, then the Remiſſion of ſins, and Accepting of us as Righteous, are other immanent Acts. But that cannot be, for then, either in the Underſtanding or Will: but neither can be ſaid with ſobriety, for ſure God cannot be ſaid to Decree to know any thing, or to decree to Will any thing: not to know any thing: for though he know things in his Decree, yet doth he not decree to know, his Knowledge being neceſſary, his Decree arbitrary: and if he did decree to know any thing, we muſt conclude he might have not known it; for decrees are only of things which may be or not be: Therefore whatſoever it be, it is no ſuch diſtinct immanent Act in Gods Underſtanding; and though we uſe to ſay, Now a man is Juſtified in Gods ſight, yet doth not this put any new Act of Knowledge in God, but ſignifies only a Teſtimony given by God, whereby he makes us know that we are Juſtified before God, or in his ſight; and I am ſure that Mr. Baxter, who quoteth Suarez, Schibler and Keckerman at every bout, cannot be ignorant that the word of ſight, though it be for the form Active, is for the ſubſtance of it rather Paſſive, and therefore is not attributable to God as it is to us; but in him it ſignifies a making of us to ſee, and we are ſaid to be Juſtified in his ſight, when he makes it as it were evident to our ſight that we are Juſtified: as when God is ſaid to know what was in Hezekiahs heart, the meaning is, he made known to Hezekiah what was in his heart.

2. To Decree to Will God cannot be ſaid; for that is as much as to Will to Will, which was never heard of, the object of the Will being at beſt but the imperate Act, not his own elicite Act; for what need of Willing to will a thing, when one Willing is enough? And he that wils to will, wils no more then he doth already, which is to will, one of theſe Acts muſt needs be ſuperfluous; and there is no ground to put any ſuch in God, yea or man.

I ac-

I acknowledge a man in some cases may be said to Will to be more willing, as when the flesh interposeth and draws him off from willing fully, or at least from executing his will: but this is rather to will a freedom from a disturbance of the sensitive appetite, then to will the exercise of the rational will; now such an incumbrance of the will of God, there can be none, and consequently no ground whereon to raise such an assertion as this, that he may be said to Will, or decree to Will, which is equivalent. And thus it appears in general, that there is no new immanent Act in God required, yea possible, to the Justifying of a man, besides his decree to Justifie m.

§. 29.

R.B. I Confess I had farre rather be imployed in debating the point of Justification, then of Gods Immanent acts, which you before insisted on. But to deal freely with you, I never read from a Learned, Orthodox man, a more superficial, unprofitable Discourse on that Subject, or that less expresseth a competent understanding of the point, if my Judgement fail not, as probably it may.

1. To what purpose you tell us what Arguments you will not use (*viz*. from *Rom*. 8. 30.) I know not.

2. Though I little know to what good use it would be, to acquaint us *what is like Justification*, yet, me thinks, were it useful, it should have been better proved. And first me thinks your Memory fails you (which you had need to take extraordinary care of:) The last Discourse was much spent in shewing that [there is a *great* difference between Immanent Acts and Transient] and that [there is a clear difference between them as between heaven and earth: Transient Acts being in the Patient, and Immanent in the Agent] So that to equal them in Eternity [is either to make the Creature eternal, or to deny God to be Eternal.] And now the second Discourse must be to prove them to be like: For the Decree which is an Immanent Act hath somewhat like Justification, which you confess a Transient Act. But yet I doubt not but your Learning can make this good: For you that can prove that Gods Immanent Acts which are his Essence, do differ no more from poor mans, then as you have expressed, may well prove, that Gods Immanent Acts are like Transient Acts; much more that Heaven and Earth are like. And doubtless your undertaking is very feasible: For you may well prove, that there is a similitude between Gods Immanent acts, and a stone, or a tree, or a worm, or any thing in the world: For you will say, that Gods Immanent acts are God himself, and that these Creatures are all Good: and then all things that are Good, are somewhat Like to God: Therefore every thing in the world (having some Good) is somewhat Like God: Also they have a Being, and therefore have some likenesse to the first Being. But then what Likenesse this is, or in what Degree, you have more Wit then to undertake to tell.

4. The Reason that you give for your not arguing from *Rom*. 8. 30. is because [indeed he is said to have Glorified them also.] But how fell it out that you observed not, that on the same Reason, you should have rejected the Argument which you here use? Because indeed it saith as much (for ought I knew) to prove Gods Decree to be like Glorification, as to be like Justification.

5. Should you not have told us in what sense you take Justification before you

Define

define it? Who knows whether you mean Justification Constitutive, or Sententiall &c (not to speak of the many other distinctions of Justification.)

6. Why would you tell the world what *all Protestants* take Justification to be? as if you knew them all?

7. At least, how comes it to pass that so Learned a man hath read so little, and would bewray it so easily? as to say that [All Protestants consent that Justification is the Remission of sin, and Accepting of us as Righteous.?]. Would you be believed in such notorious untruths which you fear not to utter even in a matter of fact, where there is so much visible evidence against you? How many of our English Divines (besides all others) affirm Remission of sin to be a fruit or consequent, and no part of Justification? had you read but Mr. *Bradshaw* and Mr. *Gataker*, you would have known some. How many on the other side make Remission of sin antecedent to Justification in order of nature? and Justification to be its immediate consequent? How many take Remission of sin to be the whole of our Justification? yea what full Disputes and Treatises are written only or principally, or at least very much to prove this? and what famous Divines are they that maintain it? How many be there that take Justification to consist partly in Remission of sin, and partly in the imputation of Christs own Righteousnels? and these with the former say, that Accepting us as Righteous is a consequent of Justification: Sin must first be remitted, say the former, and Christs Righteousnels imputed ours, say the later, before God can Accept any man as Righteous: For man must first be Righteous, before he can be accepted as such. Yea Mr. *Arthur Dent* in his Catechism, defines justification to be, A cleansing and renewing of our nature by the Spirit of God.

The number that are of these several opinions are so great, and the men so eminent, and well known to Divines that have been much verst in this Controversie, or are of any considerable reading in our Modern Writers, that I shall think it needlesse to cite any of them. Hath Mr. K. read none of all these? or will he blot out their Names from the number of Protestants?

8. Yet more grossely doth he affirm, that he [knows no man that will say it is a meer transient act.] I think then you have either read little of this Controversie, or little remember what you have read: at least, are an unfit man to tell us what All men hold, or all Protestants, when you profess to know so little. You might have seen this in some plain English books, that are in the hands of the multitude of those below you. Mr. *Tho. Hooker* maintains it, That Justification is, not an Immanent but a Transient act. But what need I name any, when it is known to to be the common Judgement of our Divines, and those few that have maintained Justification to be an Immanent act (and consequently eternal) have been taken for Erroneous therein, and as militating so farre for the Antinomians. See Mr. *Burgess* of Justification, Lect. 20. p. 167, 168, 169.

9. If Justification be a Transient act, and yet not a meer Transient act, then is it both an Immanent and a Transient act. And if so, then either it is two acts, or else the Immanent and Transient act are one. If Justification (Active) be two acts, then it seems it is divisible; yea and one part of it is Eternal, and the other in Time only: And then we must not enquire, What the justifying act is? but What each of these justifying acts are? Of this if I knew your minde, perhaps I might say more. If the Immanent and Transient act be but one, diversly considered (1. As in the meer form of an Act, having not yet effected any thing; 2. And as the same act is received into the subject Passive, and so is the Passion)

then

then the same act is no more immanent, when it is once transient; and then we must say, that the act of Justification was eternal, but the passion or effect in time only. But this sense seems so much to contradict, both your foregoing discourse of the difference of Immanent and Transient acts, and your after hint of the Transient act which justifyeth, that I will not imagine it to be the sense you intend.

10. But your reason why no man will say it is a meer transient act, is very darkly discovered: It is because [there is no transient act of God, which doth not suppose an immanent one.] But doth it follow that therefore Justification is not a meer transient act, because it supposeth an immanent act? Why did you not tell us whether it suppose it as an antecedent, or as a part of Justification, or as what else? But you know that all that is supposed is not therefore a part. Or if it were never so necessary a foregoing cause, yet it follows not that the neerer cause may not be *causa totalis in suo genere*, and so be denominated. May not you on these grounds as well say, that there is nothing in the world is a meer transient act, because it supposeth an immanent? The building of a house I think is a transient act; and yet it supposeth divers immanent acts in the builder, and an immanent act of God that willed it.

11. But what is this immanent act? You adde [For that he acts nothing upon the creature, but what he first purposed in himself to act.] I doubt not but you easily see, that if this reason prove any thing, it will as well prove that Creation, Redemption, Sanctification, Resurrection, Glorification, are none of them meer transient acts: For God acts these in Time: and therefore he first purposed to act them. Yea it will do as much to prove that God never did, nor can perform a meer transient act: because he can do nothing but what he purposeth. What need you then apply this to Justification any more then to any thing else? as if Justification had any peculiar participation in this honour, above some other acts! By your reason, the dividing the red sea, the sending of Manna and Quails, the writing of the ten Commandments, were none of them meer transient acts.

12. Immanent acts pass not into the extrinsick objects and make no change on them, and therefore are not causall: and therefore cannot well as causals be denominated from their effects: therefore no immanent act of God can be called Justification, or part of Justification, or a justifying act: For it must be so denominated from the effect of justifying: But it is the transient act only that effecteth Justification (Passive:) therefore it is the transient act only that is to be called Justification.

13. I have oft times asked the Antinomians, what text of Scripture they could shew that calleth any Immanent Eternal act of God by the name of Justification, or of part of Justification? and I could never yet see any that they produced: and I suppose that you are also unable to shew any such; or else you would its like, have done it.

14. When you say [God decreed to Justifie] do not you plainly make [Decreeing] and [Justifying] two things? and denominate only the transient act which is in time [Justification?] So of other acts; as when we say [God decreed to create:] you do not say, His Decreeing was Creating.

15. You conclude that [an Immanent act must be confest if there be a Transient one.] *Ans.* It is easily confest that an Immanent act (so called, for our understanding) there is from Eternity concerning every thing that is in Time pro-

produced: but that proves not that the producing act in Time, is not meerly transient.' I all this while suppose that you mean by denying Justification to be [a meer transient act] to include some other act justifying, or as part of Justification, and not only to prove an antecedency or concomitancy of such an Immanent act. Else your reasoning would be absurd or against your self.

16. Having thus proved that there must be an Immanent act, you next say, that [There can be no other then the Decree of God to pass this transient act.] Your contention for this is bold, your proof of it weak. As Gods immanent acts are the same with his Essence, so he hath but One, that is, he is but One: Understanding, Willing, Nilling, is all One; and so there is but one Immanent act in Justification, Condemnation, or what you will else, because there is but One God: Or rather God hath nothing properly called an Act, because he is God. But as we ascribe One act to God Analogically speaking of him according to our capacity, so must we on the same necessity ascribe to him more then One, and that is by denominating them from the variety of objects which they respect and connote. And so as truly as you can distinguish between the Divine Intellection and Volition, so truly may we distinguish the Volitions of God, according to the divers state of the objects. And so if we could yield to you that there is any Immanent act a part of Justification, or that carrieth in it as much as concerneth acceptance of us as Righteous, we might fairly say as much, at least, for another act, as you can do for the Decree: For the Decree that you speak of, is only [a Decree to pass a transient act] and so hath for its object something future: But the Will of God *de præsenti*, by which he willeth the relation of the justified person, is yet neerer the effect. So is his mentall approbation, and his acceptance of the person as Righteous (Willingly and Approvingly judging him Just;) some call his estimation of us to be Just *sententiam conceptam* as distinct from *sententia lata*, but neerer to it then the Immanent Decree to pass an act *de futuro*.

17. You adde [That this Decree of God to pass the transient act of justifying, carries in it as much as concerns Gods remission of sins, and acceptance of us as Righteous.] By which words you may mean almost what your list; but how any man should understand your meaning that knows not your minde by some better discovery, I do not know. 1. Whether do you mean by [as much as concerns] an essential constitutive concernment, *q. d.* [as much as constituteth?] But if so, then you should exclude your transient act, and the immanent alone should not be [somewhat like Justification] but Justification it self. For if this immanent be as much as constituteth remission of sin, and acceptance of us as Righteous, and Justification consisteth of these two only, then the immanent act is the whole of Justification. Or if you mean [as much as concerneth it antecedently *ex parte Dei*] that were manifestly false: For the giving of Christ, the accepting his Satisfaction and Intercession, and many other acts concerning Remission and Acceptance, are antecedent to Justification. Or if you should mean it in the full latitude, as your words import, *viz.* That nothing concerneth our Remission and Acceptance but only Gods Decree, then it is yet more palpably false: but this is so gross that I may not suppose you guilty of it, though your unlimited words do seem to express it. Or do you mean [as much of Gods immanent action as concerns Remission and Acceptance is found in this Decree to pass the transient act,] supposing this to be part of our Justification, and the transient act the

other

other part? But 1. your next words before and after seem to contradict that. For you say it is [a Decree to justifie]: which therefore cannot be part of the thing Decreed. d 2. And what mean you then, to plead that it is [somewhat Like Justification] if it be a part, and such a part. Is it worthy a Divine laboriously to prove that a mans soul is Like a man? Or that [laying the Foundation] is somewhat Like to Building? The truth is, your terms perswade me either that you hold that Antinomian eternal Justification, which you are ashamed plainly to reveal, or else that you know not what you hold your self.

18. Yet do you repeat these ambiguous words again, as those, it seems, which best fit your design: and you prove them thus: [If it do not, then the Remission of sins, and Accepting of us as Righteous, are other immanent acts: but that cannot be:] Here you seem to explain your meaning of the former words, that it is [a constitutive concernment] that you spoke of: (but whether as the whole or as a part only I cannot tell.). For you say, that else these [are other immanent acts] viz. [Remission and Acceptance are either Gods Decree, or other immanent acts.] But 1. why then do you make it your design to prove Gods immanent act to be somewhat like Justification? Remission and acceptance of us as Righteous, are more then like it. Did not you say before [Justification is, by the consent of all Protestants, a Remission of sin and an acceptance of us as Righteous? 2. Why did you before lay your proof no higher then this, [that every transient act *supposeth* an immanent, viz. Gods Decree.] 3. It seems to me here that you assert eternal Justification in the definition, while you disclaim it as to name. 4. At least, you seem (if I can understand you) to maintain that Remission of sin and Acceptation of us as Righteous are from eternity. For you here import that these [are] Gods Decree, and you elsewhere say enough for the eternity of the Decrees. But you knew, its like, that this is such gross Antinomianism, as that it was not for your credit openly to own it in the plainest terms. You give me not sufficient occasion here to stay long in confutation of this Error: yet briefly this I shall oppose. 1. He that was not a sinner from eternity, was not a pardoned sinner from eternity: (or, he that had no sin, had none remitted.) But you were not a sinner from eternity: Therefore, &c. For the *minor*: He that *was* not from eternity, was not a sinner from eternity: but you were not from eternity: Therefore, &c. If you say to the *major*, that it is enough to make us capable of Remission, that we were sinners *in esse cognito*: I answer, either you speak *de esse futuritionis*, or *de esse existentiæ ut cognito*: If of the former, the assertion is false: for [Future] is a term of Diminution, as to any true Being. An innocet man is not a subject capable of Remission of sin, *eo nomine*, because he will sin hereafter. If of the later, I say, God knows no man to be a sinner *quoad existentiam præsentem*, that is not a sinner: Else he should know untruly. 2. Where there is no obligation to punishment there is no remission of sin. But on you or me there was no obligation to punishment from eternity: Therefore, &c. The *major* is proved from the definition of Remission: which is A dissolution of an obligation to punishment. Where there's no obligation, there's none to be dissolved. The *minor* is proved thus: He that is not a sinner is not obliged to punishment: But you were not a sinner from eternity: Therefore, &c. Also *Qui non Est, non est obligatus ad pænam: At tu ab æterno non fuisti*: Therefore, &c. 3. That which is undone in Time was not done from Eternity. But sin is unpardoned in Time, (viz. till we be united to Christ by faith, as Scripture abundantly witnesseth:) Therefore it was not pardoned from Eternity. 4. God ac-

cepteth

cepteth no man as Righteous that is not Righteous (yea that is not) (for he accepteth men as they are, and not as they are not.) But no man was Righteous from Eternity: Therefore God accepted none as Righteous from Eternity. But enough of that, till you speak more openly.

19. Your proof, (that Remission and Acceptance are no other acts immanent but the Decree) is this: [For, then either in the Understanding or the Will: but neither, &c.] *Anf.* 1. I easily yield that Remission is no other immanent act; because it is none at all. 2. But your proof seems none to me. You say, [Surely God cannot be said to Decree to know any thing, or to Decree to will any thing.] Your argument I think lies thus: [If God cannot be said to Decree to know or will, any thing, then he hath no other immanent act but his Decree: But, &c. Therefore, &c.] But here's no proof of the Consequence; which needs proof. God cannot be said to Decree to know himself (according to you; for I profess I am ignorant of these high mysteries:) Doth it follow that therefore he doth not know himself? I think not. Nor doth it follow that the knowledge of himself is only his Decree, as I hope you will easily confess. Moreover, (according to you) God cannot be said to Decree to know things to be Past: (For you say he cannot be said to Decree to know.) Yet I think God doth know, as his own Eternity, so our Time, and the Futurition, Presence, and Preterition of things in our Time: and therefore it doth not follow that he hath no knowledge of things, but his Decree. For this Decree (as now taken) is *de futuris*: but besides that God hath 1. a knowledge *de Præteritis*, and 2. *de Præsentibus*. You argue, from the Necessity of Gods knowledge and the Arbitrariness of his Decree: and many words you use which shew that confidence which I admire at: that you should pretend to be so far acquainted with the Divine Nature, as not only to ascribe to God the acts of man so far as you do, but to determine which acts are necessary, and which arbitrary; and that he cannot Decree to Know or to Will. I confess I am ready to tremble instead of replying, to think into what Mysteries you lead me so boldly. But I resolve no further to follow you, then to manifest your presumption; and to shew you that they are things unsearchable which you vainly pretend so well to know. Gods Knowledge is commonly distinguished into *simplicis Intelligentiæ, & Puræ Visionis:* The former is said to be in order before the Decree, and the later in order after it: therefore neither of them are taken for the Decree it self: and will you overthrow both by reducing all to the Decree? The knowledge of Vision is taken not to be necessary simply, but only on supposition of the Decree, which anteceding in order of nature doth cause the Intelligible objects. For, say they, it is by this Decree that things pass from the number of Possibles, into the number of things Future: and they cannot be known as future, till they are future; and they are made future Freely and not Necessarily: therefore in the knowledge of Futures there is a freedom *radicaliter & participativè.* And so it is no such hard or absurd concession, to say, God might not have known what he knows: as long as he might not have made it an intelligible object.

20. You next proceed to an objection, which you cast in your own way: and though I conceive you would not have made your self any work, but what you were confident you could honourably and easily dispatch, yet here I think it fals out otherwise. The objection is from our use of saying [Now we are justified in Gods sight.] Here 1. you say [This puts not a new act of knowledge in God] of which I have said enough before. 2. You tell us the sense of it: *viz.* that

that [It signifies only a Testimony given by God, whereby he makes us know that we are justified before God] and you say [Sight in God signifies a making us to see: and we are said to be justified in his sight, when he makes it, as it were, evident to our sight that we are justified.] This interpretation is to me something strange, and not easily received, both because of its Errour, and because you say so little to cover that Errour, but thrust so gross a conceit upon us upon your own authority. I rather think that the ascribing of such New acts to God, is 1. From the Moral Act of his Law, God being said to do that which his Law doth: and so he is said to judge us Righteous, when his Law of grace doth so judge us: and we are said to be Righteous *in æstimatione Divina*, when we are so *in sensu Legis*. 2. From the change of the object: For as the variety of objects denominateth Gods acts as divers, so on the same reason the Novity of the objects must denominate them as new, though they be immanent acts. 3. And by an Anthropopathie, Sight is oft put for Gods Remembrance or Observation.

But you thrust upon us pure Antinomian fancies. 1. If your conceits be true, then none is to be accounted [Justified in Gods sight] that do not see themselves to be justified; for you think [Sight in God, signifies a making us see.] Then wo to all those honest souls that see not themselves justified, nay rather think themselves condemned: But yet if I discourse with such, I will venture to give them better encouragement, for all your doctrine; and to tell them [You may be justified in Gods sight, when you are condemned in your own.] 2. Shall we peruse the Scriptures that use that phrase, and see whether all or any one of them can be understood as Mr. K. expoundeth them in the Antinomian way of *Manifestation*. Psal. 143.2. *For in thy sight shall no man be justified.* Doth it mean, no man shall see himself justified? Jer. 18.23. *Forgive not their iniquity, neither blot out their sin from thy sight.* Is that only meant of hiding the remission from their sight? or letting them know the *non-forgiveness*? Where the Scripture speaks so oft of *doing that which is good in the sight of God,* or *that which is evil in his sight,* Doth it mean Gods making us to see that it is good or evil? What is so good in the sight of sinners as that which is evil in the sight of God? Job 15. 15. *The heavens are not clean in his sight.* Job 25.5. *The starres are not pure in his sight.* Is this sight of God a making the creature see? Heb. 13.21. *Working in you that which is well pleasing in his sight.* Is this making us see? It were too long to recite all; if the Reader will peruse the rest, 1 Joh 3.22. Exod. 15.26. 2 Sam. 12.9. 1 Chron. 19.13. Psal. 72.14. Hos. 6.2. Rom 3.20. Mat. 11.26. Luk. 10.21. & 15.21. Psal. 19.14. & 51.4. & 9.19. & 5.5 Gen. 18.3. & 19.19. or any other where this phrase is used concerning God, I leave it to his own judgement whether any one of them be taken in Mr. K's sense: That of 2 *Chron.* 32.31. which he brings, is neither the same phrase, nor hath the same sense, and therefore is nothing to the matter. Yet is not Mr. K's exposition of that satisfactory neither: For he cannot prove that it is meant meerly of discovering *Hezekiah's* heart to himself. It may be as much the discovery of it by the effects to others for their warning, and so shew the frailty of man: But the plain sense of the text referres that knowledge to God himself and not to any man; even by such an Anthropopathie which is ordinary in Scripture, as in *Ezek.* 12.3. *It may be they will consider, though they are a rebellious house,* as if God had been in an uncertain hope of it. So *Luk.* 10.13. *Jer.* 36.3. So where God is said to repent. If God speak of himself to man, after the manner of his own infirmity, must we therefore say, he means [our knowledge] when he mentioneth his own?

21. That

21. That I may know whom he speaks to, he addeth [I am sure Mr. Baxter who quoteth Suarez, Schibler and Keckerman at every bout cannot be ignorant, &c.] The matter which he mentioneth is nothing to his Cause. But see what an overcharged stomack this Learned man hath? How many casts hath he had already in vomiting up the choler of his scorn? And yet it comes up still as fresh and as bitter as if he felt no *levamen* by all that evacuation. Truly his oft scornfull repeating my quotation of these childish Authours, caused me at last to turn over all my Book to see how oft it is that I quote them. And I can finde *Suarez* but once named, and no place of him cited. *Keckerman* but once cited, and there twice named; and *Schibler* thrice. Yet doth this man tell the world I quote them at every turn; so well may we believe his confident Assertions about the unsearchable nature and mysteries of God, who hath the face to speak thus in a visible matter of fact, where any man that will but try it may finde him —— Nay, see the modesty of the man! I cited two of them once, and the third thrice in a whole Book: and in these five or six leaves he tels me of it, or scorns me for it twelve times!

22. He next addeth. [To Decree to Will, cannot be said: for that is as much as to Will to Will, which was never heard of; the object of the Will being at best, but her imperate act, not her own elicite act.] *Reply*, 1. I still abhor your presumptuous pretence of knowing more of God then you do know, and of so measuring him by man. 2. Still *desiderantur modestia & veritas*. Who would think that a man pretending so much to Learning, should never have met with Schoolman, or Philosopher that speaks that which he here saith [was never heard of] or having read it (yea or not having read it) durst so boldly speak thus? At least he might have seen it in the most ordinary and obvious Writings of our own Divines. In *Amesius* his Cases of Consc. li. 1. cap. 7. these are the last words: *Hinc verè dicimus & ex omnium gentium consensu, Velle Velle*. Believe which thou wilt, Reader; but I am sure there's a wide difference between these two men: when one saith, *Dicimus omnium gentium consensu*; and the other saith [*It was never heard of*.] Yea *Ferrius in Scholastic. Orthodox. cap. 19.* (a Chapter worth the reading *de prædeterminatione & causa peccati*) affirms it of God himself [*Ideo videtur quod cum Deus permittit lapsum, non se habet mere Negative, sed cum aliquo actu positivo: & ideo non solum non vult, sed etiam vult non Velle, i. e. Voluntas reflectitur supra se non volentem: Dum scilicet non Vult Adamum peccare, suspendendo actum Volutionis mera negatione, sed etiam Vult se non Velle: & hæc est actualis & positiva permissio. Ita tamen ut in primo signo sit Negatio pura, &c. Proinde cum Deus Voluerit ab æterno non Velle lapsum, habuit actum reflexivum super negationem, &c. At Determinavit fore inquies. Minime: absit hoc,*] This is approved by Churches of France. And yet this Learned man dare tell the world in print, that it was never heard of: which, that he might have safely done, he had need of more ears then two. And it seems this Learned man hath read little of the contentions of the Jesuites and Dominicans about the nature of free-will, where he might have seen many of them touch this Question, as *Petavius* doth against *Vincentius Lenis*, aliàs, *Fromondus*, and others frequently. Nay it seems he is a stranger to the Schoolmen too: Perhaps in stead of reading them, he contemns them, as he doth *Schibler*, *Suarez* and *Keckerman*. *Scotus in 4. sent. dist. 49. q. 3. fol. (mihi) 266. B.* saith, *Finis extra est simpliciter optimum & summe volendum: Ergo inter ea quæ sunt ad finem quod est sibi immediatius est magis volendum: sed Velle est sibi immediatius, quia immediate tendit in ipsum ut in finem ultimum, cum finis ultimus ut hujusmodi sit proprium objectum ipsius Velle. Probo majorem: Illud est magis Volendum voluntate libera*

libera quod appetitui naturali naturaliter est magis appetendum: hujusmodi est quod propinquius est ultimo, quod simpliciter maxime appetitur naturaliter. Praeterea *Voluntas potest Velle suum actum, sicut Intellectus Intelligit suum actum: aut ergo Vult suum Velle propter Intelligere, aut è converso, aut neutrum propter alterum: & loquor de Velle ordinato.*

Nicol. d' Orbellis saith, *in sent. l. 2. dist. 25. dub. 2.* [*Omne quod Vult, appetit ad sui ipsius imperium: quia sic Vult aliquid ut Velit se Velle illud: Et ideo in actu Volendi seipsum movet, & sibi dominatur, & pro tanto dicitur liberum (arbitrium) quamvis immutabiliter ordinetur ad illud.*] And *Gibieuf* shews, that God hath *Actum voluntatis positivum circa suam permissionem li. 2. de Libert. cap 24. & cap. 22. § 7, 8, &c.* And why not as well then about his act. And Gods Will is his Essence: Therefore he willeth it. For that *Deus vult seipsum* hath hitherto been unquestioned, for ought I know (so farre as he may be said, at all to Will.) *Aquinas* 2. 1ae. q. 25. a. 2. c. saith, *Quia enim Voluntatis objectum est Bonum Universale, quicquid sub ratione boni continetur, potest cadere sub actu Voluntatis. Et quia ipsum Velle est quoddam Bonum, potest Velle se Velle, sicut & Intellectus cujus objectum est Verum, Intelligit se Intelligere, quia hoc etiam est quoddam Verum.*] *Vid & 1. q. 87. 3. 2.*ᵐ. If I thought it necessary, it were easie to heap up many more that are of the same minde. But I shall only in brotherly duty admonish Mr. K. to make more Conscience hereafter of false speaking: and seeing he hath read so very little, or lost it again, rather humbly to acknowledge his Imperfection (as we that are guilty of the like must also do) then to make a confident vain-glorious ostentation of that which it seems by this, and many the like passages, he hath nor.

Let us adde some Reasons, that the Elicite acts may be the objects of other Elicite acts of the Will, and not the Imperate only, as Mr. K. saith.

1. As *Scotus* argueth before from the proportion with the Intellect. A man may understand that he doth understand, by a reflect act: Therefore he may Will that he Will.

2. That which is an apprehended Good may be Willed: But an Elicite Act of the Will may be an apprehended Good: Therefore, &c.

3. A man may Will his everlasting Happiness: (For if the End may not be Willed, what may?) But his everlasting Happiness consisteth partly in the Elicite Acts of his own Will, everlastingly to be exercised on God: [God being Objectively our Happiness) Therefore, &c. *Velle, Amare, Frui,* are acts that must be perpetuated, and either may be Willed, or no man may will his own happiness.

4. Whatsoever is apprehended to be a fit means to this End or Happiness, may be Willed: But the Elicit acts of the Will may be apprehended a fit means hereto: Therefore, &c. They are commanded, and they are made Conditions of Happiness: and therefore are a means.

5. The Effects of Gods special saving Grace on the soul may be Willed: But the Elicite Acts of the sanctified Will, are the Effects (and principal effects) of Gods special saving Grace on the soul: Therefore, &c.

6. That which a Christian may pray for, that he may and must Will: But he may pray for the Elicite Acts of a sanctified Will: Therefore, &c. As he may pray, Lord, I Believe, help my Unbelief: So he may pray [Lord I am Willing, make me more Willing, and hereafter Willing, &c.

7. Experience is in stead of a thousand arguments, I feel that my Willingness is the object of my unwillingness; and that in these several wayes. 1. I feel that

upon

upon the review of my past Willingness, and the sight of my present Willingness (in any Good) my Will hath a Complacency in it, which is a true *Velle*, yea the first and principal Elicite Act of the Will.   2. I finde that by a less perfect and intense Act, I do Will a more perfect Act. I am somewhat Willing, but I would fain be more Willing.   Nay to procure the Amendment of my own heart by this increase of my Willingness (which is indeed the Increase of most of my Graces) is the main business of my life, committed to me by God, and to be intended by my self. And if I should cast off this great business, and neither desire more Willingness or Grace, nor pray for more, nor labour for more, because Mr. K. out of his subtilty tels me, that the Elicite Act is not the Wils object, I should be befool'd out of my Christianity and Salvation by a trivial trick of vain Philosophy.   3. I finde that by a present Act of Will, I do Will a future Act. I do Will now that I may also Will to morrow, and to my lives end, and for ever in glory, and that better then now I do.   4. I feel that I do Will a more sincere Willingness. I do Will Salvation with too much respect to my self in it, and too little to Gods honour. Now I would fain Will this more for God then I do. 5. I would fain Nill many things which through my corruption I now Will. 6. I would fain oft suspend a vicious act of my Will, at least. In all these respects, the Elicite Act of my Will is the object of my Will.

But Mr. K. will be Learned in despight of Natural and Gracious Experience (for I hope, for all his Learning, that he Would Love God more, as Love is taken for an act of the Rational part, and that he Wils a greater and a persevering, yea a perpetual Willingness of God and obedience; and a fruition of God, and *frui* is an act of the Will:) He will therefore prove what he once saith, and that's thus. [For what need of Willing to Will a thing, when one Willing is enough? And he that Wils to Will, Wils no more then he doth already, which is to Will: one of these acts must needs be superfluous, &c.] To which I Reply; You may see in the several Instances which I gave before, that it is needfull, and that it is not superfluous, as you say, and that it is more then he did before; A more perfect act, a future act, a perpetuated act, are more then he did before. Yea its a doubt, Whether a very gracelesse man may not *Velle intendere Deum, vel frui Deo* yea strictly Will to Will God as his happiness, or to Will Holiness before Voluptuousness, who yet doth it not already. And me thinks so acute a man might see that this is not the same act which he performeth already, for it hath not the same object. The man is Willing to be saved from Hell, but Unwilling to be Holy : He is convinced that he shall not be saved, unlesse he become Willing to be Holy : Therefore he wisheth he were Willing to be Holy. If this were but with a Velleity, it is yet an Elicite Act of the Will; but it may be called a Volition, though uneffectual, because there is a stronger contrary Will : So that it is *Volitio quoad actum Absolutum*, but *quoad actum Comparatum*, he is unwilling. The Object of that Will which he hath, is his *Velle sanctitatem :* the Object of that Will which he would have, is Holinels it self. If that *Velle & sanctitas* be not all one, then these two Acts be not all one.

But Mr. K confesseth at last that a man may be said to Will to be more Willing, but he saith [this is rather to Will a freedom from a disturbance of the sensitive appetite, then to Will the exercise of the rational Will.] But why is it that this man would not be disturbed by the sensitive appetite? Is it not because he would Will freely? Doth not he that Willeth the means, much more Will the End?

And

And is not the Removal of the Impediment, a Means to your freer and more Intense Willing? And do not you your self Will the increase of your Willingness upon the quieting of that Appetite? Besides, I hope you do not think that the disturbance of the sensitive Appetite, is the onely Cause of our Imperfection in actual Willing: Or that our own Habitual Corruption and distemper of the Will it self, is not a greater Cause.

' After all this you conclude, that [it appears there is no new Immanent act in God required yea possible to the justifying of a man, besides his Decree to justifie.] To which I say, Though it little appear to me from any of your arguing, yet I easily yield to the Negative part of your Conclusion; and I say, that the Decree it self is no part of Justification, but an Antecedent.

Again, Let it be observed, that all this arguing will as much prove that Gods Immanent act is like to Creation, Sanctification, Glorification, Damnation, or any thing that ever God did, as to Justification: For of all his Works it is as true, that he doth nothing but what he decreed to do. And so it may as well be said that our Glorification is an Immanent act from Eternity, as our Justification.

§. 30.

Mr. K. *More particularly, it will be as Evident that his Decreeing to Remit our sins, carries a Remission of them tantamount: For who shall charge them on us, where God decreeth to remit them? The Conscience I confess may; so may the Devil joyning with our conscience, but all this while their charge is of no great danger to us, when God hath decreed to remit them to us: and though they may trouble us they cannot damn us, for that their charge is to be brought in Gods Name, as for sins committed against his Crown and Dignity: Now where he hath decreed to remit those sins, there is no danger of suffering for them, let what ever accusers manage the Evidence against us, all that they can do is but this, to bring us to cry Guilty, and thereupon to appeal to God for Mercy; who upon our appeal to him for Mercy, he is graciously pleased to pronounce pardon to us. God himself I acknowledge also may charge them on us; and proceed in severity against us for a while; but this charge is not any way obstructive to his Decree to remit sin, but rather subservient to it, and to bring us to see and confess our sins, and cast our selves wholly on his Mercy in Christ, in which respect I might better say, that God doth shew love even in punishing unregenerate men that are Elect, then you did erewhiles; that he may be said to hate Godly men, when he punisheth or rather correcteth them: Punishment ayming chiefly at the satisfaction of Justice, Correction at the amendment of the offender. So then his Decree of Remitting carries in it as much as is required for any immanent Act in him to our Remission, and so much as necessarily procures the transient Act in the time that he hath appointed for it. His Decrees are like Mount Zion, and stand fast for ever: The Counsel of the Lord standeth for ever, the thoughts of his heart to all generations,* Psal. 33. 11.

§. 30.

R. B. Your [tantomount] is a word made for your use; Causes that dare not see the light, use to go covered with such terms as will stretch. But if you mean plainly, that the Decree doth amount to as much as a remission of sin,] then I must needs say, that your Doctrine is tantamount Antinomianism. Let the conscientious Reader that loves Gods truth and his own Peace, consider by these few particulars following, what a Theology, nay what a Christianity this Learned man would introduce.

1. Doth not this lead men to slight Christ and his sufferings, and to look on his Death as that which did them no great good? For when all our sins were tantamount forgiven from Eternity, there was little left for Christ to do by his Death, Merit, Intercession, &c. as to our Remission.

2. How small a matter is left for the Regenerate to receive upon their Repenting and Believing in Christ, as to Remission of sins, when they are tantamount (I must use Mr K's School-term) remitted already? Is this the Repenting and Believing for Remission of sin which Scripture mentioneth?

3. How small a matter is left for Baptism to seal and exhibit, as to Remission, when all sin was tantamount Remitted from Eternity?

4. Where is the Excellency and Glory of the Gospel, either as to the Narrative, Preceptive, or Promissory part? For the Narrative, it makes a large Declaration how Christ was Promised, Incarnate, Born, how he Obeyed, Suffered, Satisfied, Merited, Rose, Intercedeth to procure a Remission which was tantamount done already even from Eternity. For the Preceptive, it prescribeth man a way to obtain Remission by coming to Christ, and to maintain that Remission by abiding in Christ, when our sins were tantamount remitted from Eternity. The Promise seemeth to hold forth an excellent benefit, and all men are invited to Receive it; and when all's done, it offereth and promiseth to do that which is done tantamount already from Eternity. If you say, that yet Christ and the Gospel have their Excellency as they respect other benefits, viz. our Sanctification and Glorification: I answer according to Mr. K's grounds, it must be said that these also were done tantamount from Eternity, in that they were Decreed.

5. How small a matter have Christians daily to pray for, in that Petition [*Forgive us our trespasses*] when they were tantamount forgiven from Eternity? And what a spur is this to prayer?

6. How small a matter have they to Give Thanks for, as received through Christ from the promise, upon prayer, &c.

7. How small a matter as to Remission of sin, do we receive in the Lords Supper, when it was done tantamount before?

8. How great a help doth this Doctrine give to Obedience, when men are told that all their sins are tantamount forgiven from Eternity?

9. How small a Difference between the state of the Regenerate and unregenerate, supposing them Elect? The sins of one are forgiven, and the other tantamount.

10. How unsoundly do we perswade wicked men of their misery, and tell them that God hateth all the workers of iniquity, and that they are by nature children of wrath, &c. when for ought we know all their sins were tantamount forgiven from Eternity? And how hard to convince them of any such misery, when they have this Reply? Lay all this together, and see how much of our Religion and Christianity is left!

But he proves all this by a Question [Who shall charge them on us where God decreeth to remit them?] I Reply, The same persons, and as many as might have charg'd them on us, if God had not decreed it. His Decree takes off no charge, nor disables any from charging us. It were not an Immanent Act, if it did *ponere aliquid in objecto*. 1. We are as much under the Charge, Curse, or

Condemnation

Condemnation of the Law, till we believe; as if no such Decree had passed. 2. What the Law doth, God doth by it; for it is his Instrument. 3. Satan may charge us. 4. And so may conscience. 5. And men. But you confess your self that Conscience, Satan, and God may charge us: But you say [there is no danger] Reply. 1. What if you were to lie all your life in torment with the stone or gout, and yet were sure that you should die never the sooner, and so there were no danger? Would you think your self tantamount a sound man? Is it so small a matter in your eyes for an elect man to lie under the guilt of sin, and as an enemy to God till near his death, so be it he be not in danger of damnation? 2. If you mean that their damnation is *non futura*, I confess it: And so it would be if God should but fore-know it, and not decree it (supposing it might be the object of such a fore-knowledge.) 3. But yet I think it is not fit language to say [there is no danger of suffering for sins that God hath decreed to remit.] I see still whither Antinomianism tends. 1. If Christ did die to deliver us from danger of suffering, then we were in danger of suffering: But Christ did die to deliver us from it: Therefore, &c. Would you make us believe that Christ saved us from no danger by his death? 2. The actual Conversion and Justification of the Elect, is a saving them from danger: Therefore they were in danger. 3. If the Elect unconverted are in no danger, then you must preach no danger to them, nor perswade them to avoid any, nor to repent the incurring of any: or if, because you know not the Elect, you speak to all of danger, you must tell them that you mean it not of the Elect: But what success such preaching would have, is easie to conjecture. 4. Where men are bound to Fear and Apprehend danger, there is danger: But God bindeth the Elect (even after Conversion, much more before) to Fear and Apprehend danger: Therefore, &c. There can be no Fear, where there is no Apprehension of danger; no more then there can be Love without the Apprehension of Good to be beloved. Christ bids his Disciples, *Fear him that is able to destroy both body and soul in hell fire:* And so Heb. 4. 1. *Fear lest a promise being left of entring into his rest, any of you should come short of it.* God bids us fear: Mr. K. tantamount bids us, Fear not, by telling us there is no danger. 5. Where men are bound to labour, run, strive, and use much means to escape danger, there is danger: But so God hath bound the Elect: Therefore, &c. How many Texts might be cited that binde us to save our selves, and seek our deliverance, and that speak of our escaping, our deliverance and salvation, which all imply a danger from which we escape, are saved and delivered? 6. *Matth.* 5. 21, 22. *He that calleth his brother Fool, is in danger of hell fire:* But an Elect man hath called his brother fool: Therefore, &c. 7. Nay if this be true, then God never saved his people from any Danger. For he that never was in danger cannot be saved out of it. And he that was from Eternity Decreed to be pardoned, according to your Doctrine, was never in danger. 8. And then we ought to give no thanks to God the Father, or to Christ the Redeemer, or to the holy Ghost the Sanctifier, nor to any Preacher or other Instrument, for saving us from any danger of punishment. I think these are not matters to be made light of: nor that Doctrine of Libertinism to be cherished, which plainly leadeth to such unhappy fruits.

But let us peruse your Reasons: You say [the charge is to be brought in Gods name.] Reply. So it may be nevertheless for the Decree; for that takes off none of the charge. You adde [All they can do is but this, to bring us to cry Guilty, and thereupon appeal to God for Mercy, &c.] Reply. 1. Must they cry Guilty, and look for Mercy and Remission, that were tantamount forgiven from Eternity? 2. Either you speak of an unconverted elect person, in this life; or else as supposing he were at Judgement in that estate. If the later be your meaning, then their Accusation might and would, do more then you speak of, and would tend to condemnation (if such a case might be supposed.) If the former be your meaning, then these Elect persons do [Cry Guilty, and appeal to Mercy] with true Faith, or without it. If with Faith, then their sins are remitted further then by Decree, and these are not the persons now in Question. If without faith then they are not Forgiven for all this.] As long as the Elect remain unregenerate, though that Law, and Satan, and Conscience accuse them, yet they do not Believingly seek mercy: and if they were in that state at Judgement, it were too late to seek Mercy.

Next you [acknowledge that God himself also may charge sin on us, and proceed in severity against us for a while; but this charge is not any way obstructive to his Decree to Remit sin, &c.]. Reply. God may be said to charge sinne on the Elect before faith. 1. By obliging them by his Law to punishment. 2. By inflicting some small part of the punishment on them. You seem to me to take notice notice only of the later. But every Christian must acknowledge that for all Gods Decree, we are all *Obligati ad pœnam sempiternam*, till we are united to Christ by faith. To say this is not obstructive to Gods Decree, is nothing to the question. The worlds being uncreated from Eternity, did not obstruct Gods Decree of making it, and the Elect's being unsanctified or unglorified doth not obstruct Gods Decree of Sanctifying and Glorifying them: and yet this proves not persecuting *Saul* was tantamount sanctified and Glorified. And what if God make the knowledge of our Damnable state, or our *non-remission*, a means to Remission? That doth not prove that we are before remitted in whole or in part, or tantamount.

Whether you speak to Mr. *Goodwin* or me, about the phrase of [hating the Godly] I know not: but if to me, I do not believe that ever I so spoke.

Your distinction of Punishment from chastisement, is perverse: so learned a man should know, that Punishment is the *Genus* and Chastisement is a *Species* of it. All Punishment is for the Demonstration of Justice; but not all for the satisfaction of Justice, Correction is as well for a Demonstration of Justice, as for Amending the Offendor: Else it were meer Affliction, and no Correction.

Your Conclusion next laid down, much differs from the divers formerly laid down, and which you should have proved; and yet I have shewed, for part of this, how ill you have proved it: though, for my part, I know no Cause that I am engaged in that will be any whit prejudiced by yielding you all; as I easily yield you, that the Transient Act will certainly follow.

§. 31.

Mr. K. NExt his *Decree to Accept us, carrieth as much too; and there needs nothing but a Transient Act to prove his Acceptance, and evidence it to us: for to decree to look upon us as righteous, is not to look upon us as righteous in our selves, but his Son; and to this looking on us, there needs no new immanent Act, beyond his electing us to faith in his Son, and perseverance in that faith: Thus he may be said to give us to his Son before.*

before, and so then there is no new immanent act. Gods Remitting our sins, and accepting us as Righteous, though they sound like Immanet acts, are to be sensed as Transient, and how shall be shewed next: in the interim this which hath been said is sufficient to shew, That in the Decree of God to justifie us, there is somewhat that looks like Justification; and no other immanent act in God is required to our Justification; besides his Decree from Eternity to justifie us in time.

§. 31.

R. B. I Shall never think the highest pretenders to exact explications to be the best performers, for your sake. You treat of Acceptance; but who can finde by all that you say, what you mean by [Acceptance.] You say, [Though it sound like an Immanent act it is to be sensed as Transient,] but what that Transient act is, for all your promises, I can hardly finde you discovering. Surely [to Accept] in our ordinary speech signifieth an Immanent act of the Will; but so you take it not; else must you yield that Immanent acts may be Decreed. Besides this, it may signifie the Moral action of the Law of Grace, which virtually judgeth the person Righteous, and its action is Gods action. But this you can less digest: and therefore what your [Acceptance] means, let him tell that knows. All that I can finde is, either that it is [the Giving of faith] or [the Making us know our Acceptance] of which more anon.

You say [There needs nothing but a Transient act to prove his Acceptance, and evidence it to us.] *Rep.* Here is then but two Acts needfull: the one is [Decreeing to Accept us as Righteous:] This is not Accepting, as the word and your own confession witness: The other is [a Transient act to prove and evidence his Acceptance.] This cannot be acceptance neither: For what man will say, that the evidence and proof is formally the same with the thing proved and evidenced? Is it all one [to Accept] and [to evidence and prove Acceptance?] What a maze do you run your self into under pretence of discovering the truth? You have fairly disputed [Acceptance] into Nothing.

You adde [For to Decree to look upon us as Righteous, is not to look upon us as Righteous in our selves but in his Son.] *Rep.* To Decree to look, is not to Look: else you may say, it is a Decree to Decree. Your phrases of [in our selves] and [in his Son] may be so interpreted as to make your sense true; but if you mean that it is Christ only and not we, who is the subject of that relative Righteousness, which formally makes us Just, then it is false.

You say [And to this looking on us, there needs no new Immanent act besides electing to Faith and Perseverance.] *Rep.* I pray you then tell us what you mean by [Looking on us:] an Immanent act, it is not, you think: And is Gods [Looking on us as Just] a transient act? What act then is it? Did you say, That God is said to Look on us as Just, when his Law call us Just, I should not disagree with you: but you disclaim that. But I forgot that you did expound your meaning before upon [Gods seeing:] as Gods seeing is a making us to see, so its like you mean [Gods Decree to look on us as Just] is a Decree to make us Look on our selves as Just: and so the person is changed. But if this be your meaning, I had as lieve you said nothing.

But I will tell you again, that if you will take [an Immanent act] *formaliter* for Gods essence, so there is none new, nor is there any more then one; Knowing, Willing and Nilling, Love and Hatred are all one. But if you will condescend to us of the simpler sort, and speak of Immanent acts as applied to God after the manner of men, and as his acts are *formaliter*, or *modaliter*, or *relativè*, or *denominativè*; or however else (in a way unknown to us) distinct from his essence, so as they may be diversified among themselves without disparagement to Gods simplicity, they may also begin and end without disparagement to his Immutability, for any thing that you have yet said to the contrary. And so, as they are diversified or said to begin *denominativè ex connotatione objecti*, they may as well be said to be the objects of Gods eternal Decree. And thus I conceive, Decree respecting the future, and [Accepting and Approving] being acts that connote a present object, and so may not be said [to be such acts] till the object exist, therefore God may well be said to Decree to Accept us, and Approve us, and Love us, and Delight in us, &c. though all be Immanent acts. And so my conclusion shall be contrary to yours, that you have not proved that there is no other Immanent act in God required to our Justification, besides his Decree; and if you had, yet you had done little to the business: And that you have no more proved [that in the Decree is something that looks like Justification] then that it looks like Creation, Salvation, Damnation; And had you proved it never so strongly, I know not to what purpose it is. It is somewhat like God that is called his Image in his Saints: and yet he that cals the Saints, God, may blaspheme for all that.

§. 32.

Mr. K. 3. THat this Immanent act cannot be called *Justification*, appears hence, that no Immanent act makes a real change in the subject, as *Justification doth*: That a Will to justifie us, is as Mr. Baxter rightly saith, terminus diminuens, and cannot be the act whereby we are justified, That *Justification is on all hands confessed to be pronouncing or declaring of us Righteous*, which cannot be done by an Immanent act alone: What then is the Transient act? Before I can speak punctually to this, it is fit to set down that Remission of sins, and estating us in the condition and priviledges of Righteous, are the two main parts distinguished ratione ratiocinata at least, all grant, I must needs say, I think Really. Remission of sins being the first, and which of course draws the other after it, enquire we 1. Whether there be a Transient act of God whereby he remits our our sins? 2. What this is?

§ 32.

R. B. I Am loath to speak against you where you are pleased to plead my cause; yet I must give you these brief Animadversions. 1. That Justification makes on the subject a real change, as opposed to Feigned, Nominal, Potential, &c. I yield: but not as opposite to Relative: Wherefore our Divines ordinarily call Sanctification a Real change, as opposite to the Relative change of Justification. 2. It is but one sort of Justification which is [on all hands confessed to be a pronouncing or declaring us Righteous:] your self do afterwards speak of Justification in a sense that will not agree with this. Who doth not yield that Constitutive Justification goes before Sentential? Doth not God make us Just before he judge and pronounce us so? Yet in this confusion do you go on still; and such a stirre do you make with [Immanent and Transient] as if you would wear these words thredbare, or never have done with them? So Immanent are these

these Notions in your Phantasie, that when they will be Transient I cannot tell.

So often do you promise us over and over to enquire what is the Transient act in Justification, and talk of [speaking punctually to it] that you raised my expectation to such a height, that I looked for much more then ordinary: But when I had read to the end, and could scarce perceive certainly, whether ever you spake to the Point at all, or at least in so few syllables and so obscurely, that I am uncertain whether I understand what you mean, I confess you left me between admiration and indignation! that after all your prologues and promises, and our greatest hopes, you should drop asleep when you should come to the work, or cease before you remembred the performance, made me resolve to set lighter by such promises hereafter.

§. 33.

Mr. K. [TO *prove that there is a Transient act, they tell us no more* (saith Mr. Baxter) *but this, that it doth transfere in subjectum extraneum, by making a morall change on our Relations, though not a real upon our persons.*] I confess every transitio, to use that word, in subjectum extraneum making a Morall change, is not necessarily a Transient act: For if it be only as upon an Object, whereto is given but an extrinsecall denomination, not as upon the subject of a Reall change, made by the act, the act hath no title to Transient: for knowledge doth this much: but whereever is a Moral or a Legal change made, there is of necessity a Transient act: for that the Laws of men take no notice of Immanent acts; and the Law of God takes no notice of any change made in the object of bare Immanent acts: A man by lusting after a woman commits Adultery punishable by the Law of God; the woman is nothing the more defiled: So a man that covets his neighbours goods, is lookt on by God as a thief; the goods notwithstanding remain in the same place, and possession of the Owner, nor doth God challenge them as Felons goods; no change made on them; Wherever then there is a Morall, i. e. a Legall change, there is a Transient act, and this being in Justification a Transient act is necessarily required to this change. Now I yield Mr. Baxter that [no Transient act is immediatly termined in a Relation, and the immediate effect of Gods Justification or Remission of sins, must be somewhat Really wrought, either upon the sinner, or somewhat else for him.

§. 33.

R. B. I Will not stand to open any weaknesses or impertinencies in this Section, as long as the scope is sound, lest I shew my self as quarrelsome as you.

§. 34.

Mr. K. THe second Question is, What is this? and so what the Transient act is? Mr. Baxter saith, [1. That the passing the grant of the New Covenant, or the promulgation of it, is a Transient act. 2. So may the continuance of it also be. 3. This Law or Grant hath a Moral improper action, whereby it may be said to pardon or justifie, which properly is but virtuall justifying. 4. By this grant 1. God doth give us the Righteousness of Christ to be ours when we believe. 2. And disableth the Law to

oblige

oblige us to punishment or Condemnation. 3. *Which Real foundations being thus laid, our Relations of Justified and Pardoned in Title of Law do necessarily follow.*]

I cannot perswade my self to leave my old Doctors to follow Mr. Baxter, for any thing be hath said in all this. Let the promulgation of the New Covenant first and still be a transient act; this Covenant hath an odde empty Moral action in justifying us when we believe; and by the promulgation of this Covenant God doth as improperly give us the Righteousness of Christ, and disable the Law to condemn us, as shall appear by considering that all here spoken of actions, is but of actions improperly so called, and such as cannot suffice to make a Reall effect.

---

§. 34.

R. B. WHo your old Doctors are is utterly unknown to me; for I remember not that I have ever read any Doctor before you that goeth your way (if I know it) and am in hope that I never shall reade any such hereafter. For your not following me, as I have not been very eager to obtrude my opinions on any, so if it be no more for your own advantage then mine, I am not so desirous of your company, but that I can be without it. Now to the matter.

I am very glad that I am come to a Controversie more easie and more usefull then that which you made and stuck in so long before. As for my opinion about the nature of Remission of sin, I have had occasion to view and review it since the writing of my Aphorismes, and have received Animadversions on this very Point of another nature then are these of Mr. K's, both for Learning, Sobriety, and Exactness of Judgement; and upon my most faithfull and impartial perusal of all, I must needs profess my self much more satisfied in my first opinion, and confident of its verity, then I was before: And some Learned men (as most *England* hath) do fully consent to it, and confirm it in their Animadversions; and I remember none of the rest (save the first intimated Reverend Learned Brother) that doth contradict it, of all those Judicious excellent men that have vouchsafed me their private Animadversions. And even he doth confess all that action of the Law and change made by it, which I mention, as being a known truth beyond Controversie; only he thinketh that the name of Justification is to be given to no act but a Judicial Sentence, which I call, the most perfect sort of Justification. Indeed I am ashamed that I spake so strangely of so easie and familiar a Truth, as if it had been some new discovery, when all that are verst in Politicks and Laws may discern it to be so obvious: but the reason was, that I had not read any thing of it in Divines as to our present case.

Before I come to Mr. K. let me tell the Reader my thoughts of Remission more fully. Pardon actively taken is an act of God. Passive pardon is the *terminus* or effect of that act. Pardon Active, is 1. Mentall, in a more imperfect, diminute, and less-proper sense called Pardon: As when a Prince doth pardon a traytour secretly in his own thoughts and resolution only. This is applied to God speaking after the manner of men (in which manner we are necessitated to speak of God:) and it is not (as Mr. K. imagineth) to be conceived of by us as being the same with his Decree *de futuro* (so far as we may conceive of Gods Immanent acts as divers:) though it be but the same act that receiveth these divers denomi-

nations

nations from the diversity of the objects. 2. The second Active Pardon is Signal, Legal and Constitutive; which by signifying Gods Will, doth Legally constitute us pardoned, by causing our *Jus ad Impunitatem vel Liberationem, i. e.* by dissolving the Obligation to punishment, or by taking away guilt. The action or causation of this pardon, is but such as is that of every *Fundamentum* in causing its Relation. 3. Pardon taken actively also may signifie the very Grant of the act of Pardon (whether particular or general, absolute or conditional) that is, the act of Legislation (in our case) whereby the Law of Grace is formed, as the remitting Instrument. This goes before that forementioned; as being the causing of that *Fundamentum*, which in time causeth the Relation aforesaid. 4. The Promulgation or Proclamation of this Law of Grace, or Act of Oblivion, may also be called Pardon. This Legal pardon is an Act of God as *Rector supra Leges* in respect to the old Law whose Obligation it dissolveth; and it is the Act of God as Legislator in respect of the Law of Grace which dissolveth the Obligation of the Law of Works.

Accordingly Pardon in a Passive sense, is taken as many waies. 1. With men for the effects of mentall pardon in the heart and minde. 2. For the *Jus ad Impunitatem*, or the Dissolution of the Obligation to punishment, caused by the second act. 3. For the Law of Grace, or the promise it self. And so the pardoning Instrument of a King, is commonly called a Pardon. 4. For the hopefull Relation or state that he is in that hath pardon offered him on very easie and reasonable terms (as for the Acceptance with thanks.) I think all these senses the word is used in the Scriptures; I am sure in Writers and common speech it is so. Now it is easie to discern that all the rest are but imperfect pardons, and so called in a diminute sense, except only the second, which is the full and proper pardon. 2. All this I speak of Pardon in Law sense, the same with that which I call Justification constitutive (or but notionally differing:) But besides all this there is Pardon and Justification *per sententiam Judicis*, which these are but the means to, and which is the most perfect of all. But note that as the word Justification is most proper to [the sentence:] So the word [*Pardon*] is most proper to the Civil or Legal act that goes before Judgement. 3. And as God pardoneth, 1. as *Rector supra Leges* by Donation and a new Law, 2. and as Judge by sentence: so 3. also as the executor of Law and sentence or his Will: And so pardoning is but Not-punishing. Where note 1. That this sometime may be before and without the first, by meer providence: and so wicked men are pardoned without a promise, in such measure as God abateth and forbeareth punishing them. 2. That in our case this executive pardon *quoad initium* presupposeth the first Legal pardon, and *quoad complementum* it presupposeth the sentential absolution. 3. Note that this sort of pardon hath divers degrees, according to the degrees of any due penalty which is remitted: and so may alter. So that in a word, all pardon is of one of these three sorts. 1. By God as Author of the New Covenant, giving Right to Impunity. 2. By God as Judge absolving. 3. By God as executing.

All this being premised our question is, which of these it is that Scripture ascribeth to Faith, and is called Remission, or Believing, or Justification by Faith? Some say, It is only Gods mental pardon: Some say, It is none of these, but a Declaration to the Angels in heaven, who is Just. Some say, It is none of these, but a Manifestation to our consciences (as some speak) or a sentence of God in our hearts (as others speak.) Some say, It is *ipsa Impunitas*, or *non Punire* (as

P   *Twisse*

Twisse sometime, or *nolle Punire*, as other times.) I think it is the Dissolving of the obligation to punishment, or the giving us a *Jus ad liberationem vel ad impunitatem*, or Gods remitting his *Jus puniendi*: Where the immediate *terminus* is the Dissolution of the obligation, or our *Debitum liberationis, vel jus ad impunitatem*: and the remote *terminus* (which is yet connoted in the term Pardon, as essentially necessary) is Impunity it self, or actual liberation from punishment, or *non-punire*. And withall, as in man a mentall Remission goes before the actual Signal, Legal Remission, so there is in God, a *Nolle punire*, and after the manner of men, it may be ascribed to God, as then beginning when the Law remitteth, and the sinner is a capable subject, because it cannot be denominated Remission, but by connotation of the object, and that must be, when there is an object fit: And so after the manner of men, we attribute it to God, as an act which in time he is moved to by an Impulsive cause, *viz.* the Satisfaction and Merits of Christ: though strictly we use to say, there is nothing *ab extra* can be an impulsive cause to God: Much more then this I have said for explication of this Point in private Papers to some Learned Friends; but this may suffice for the right understanding of what here passeth between Mr. K. and me. And now I proceed to his words.

1. He acknowledgeth the Promulgation of the New Covenant to be a Transient act: It is the same Instrument of God that is called his Covenant and his Law here. And as it is a Law, the term [Promulgation] doth most fitly agree to it. And I doubt not but either Mr. K. implieth Legislation, (perhaps he mistakes the terms for equipollent) or at least he will as freely acknowledge that a Transient act. But he saith, 1. That [this Covenant hath an odde empty morall action.] Let any man, that reades these words of this Learned man, judge whether I be not excusable for that censure in the Preface to the Appendix of my Book of Baptism! A School Divine, and a Chair man, and know no more the nature of a Law, Covenant, or any Legal Instrument! A Divine, and an *Aristarchus*, and yet dare to speak such words of all the holy Laws and Covenants of God! Why what doth this man study and preach, that thinks so basely of Gods Laws? The Moral action of the Law of Grace, or Testament of Christ he calleth, [an odde empty Moral action:] Yet its like he knows that Commonwealths are chiefly upheld and ordered by Laws, Contracts, Conveyances, &c. and consequently by actions of the same nature. The whole body of the Commonwealth, and each member of it, do hold their Estates, Liberties and Lives by such odde empty actions. Take away the odde empty Moral action of Laws, Testaments, Obligations, Deeds of Sale, Leases, &c. and what is a Commonwealth, and what a Rector, and what security have you of any thing you possess? or what orderly commerce among men? His next assertion is as desperate as the former, that [by the promulgation of this Covenant, God doth as improperly give us the Righteousness of Christ, or disable the Law to condemn us.] Could any words (not certainly destructive to Christianity it self) have fallen from this Learned man more unworthy a Divine? Doth not the Testament of the Lord Jesus properly convey the Legacy? Doth not Gods Deed of gift of Christ and his Righteousness to us, properly convey? and doth not God properly Give thereby? Why how can a more proper way of Giving be imaginable? 1. If a man do properly give, by a Testament or Deed of Gift, then so doth God: But a man doth, &c. Therefore, &c. 2. Where there is a plain signification of the Will of the Donor to confer thereby the benefit on the Receiver, there is a proper Giving: But

But in the Gospel-promise or Testament of Christ there is such a signification of the Donors Will: Therefore,&c. Doth not an Act of Oblivion or Pardon properly give pardon to all that it pardoneth? Doth not any Act of Grace give the favours expressed?

2. And where he saith, that [God doth hereby as improperly disable the Law to condemn us.] I Reply. 1. Nothing in the world can more properly disable the Law from effectual condemning us, that is, so as to procure sentence and execution, then a general Act of pardon, or then the new Law doth, which is in its very nature *Lex Remedians, & obligationem ad pœnam prioris dissolvens.* Though still the Law as to its sense is the same, and therefore doth virtually condemn till the said dissolution. How can the Law of the Land be more disabled from effectual condemning all Traytors, for what is past, then by an Act of Oblivion, or a particular pardon under the Soveraigns Hand and Seal? 2. Yea this Learned man disputes against the very formall nature and definition of a pardon: which is to be *an Act of the Rector freeing the guilty from punishment by dissolving the obligation.* And certainly as the obligation it self is one of these [odde, empty Moral actions,] so must the dissolution of it needs be. Indeed *Theologus est Jurisconsultus Christianus,* a Christian Lawyer: and what a Lawyer he is that knows not the nature, use and force of Laws, is easie to be judged. I could wish men would lay by their over-bold enquiries into Gods Decrees and other Immanent acts, or at least, their vain pretendings to a knowledge which they never had of them, and study this intelligible and necessary part of Theology a little more.

But Mr. K. tels us that he will make all this strange doctrine [appear:] and how? Why [by considering that all here spoken of actions, is but of actions improperly so called, and such as cannot suffice to make a real effect.] *Rep.* Do you oppose [Real] to [feigned or nominal] or to [Relative?] If the former, it is such doctrine as I dare say, no Divine will believe, no Lawyer, no understanding member of a Commonwealth, and I think, no Christian, that understandeth what you say. Think not the words rash, for I think him not fit to be accounted a Divine, no nor a Christian (supposing him to understand the matter) that will or dare maintain, That neither the curse of the Law, or threatning of the new Law, whereby so many are adjudged to Hell, nor yet the Testament, Covenant, Promise of the Gospel, whereby Christ and his Benefits, Justification, Adoption, Salvation (*quoad Jus*) are given, do any of them make a true change? But if you oppose [Real] to [Relative,] then I must tell you, that [Remission and Justification Passive] are no Real effects, but Relative; which I had thought you need not have been told. The act of Legislation and Promulgation makes a real effect; but the *Fundamentum* once laid, causeth but a relation. Do not you know that the very formal nature of all morality is Relative? What else is *Æquum, Justum, Meritum, Debitum, Jus,* yea *bonum morale, & malum,* &c?

Again I must tell you, that you do not well to mention *Promulgation* alone, when I spoke of Enacting, or Granting, or Legislation, before Promulgation. I hope you take not both these for one. Nay indeed Promulgation is proper to a Law as it is obligatory to the subject, and so is necessary after Legislation, *ad actualem obligationem:* but a Law of Grace which doth conferre benefits, and whereby the Legislator doth, as it were, oblige himself, may be in force in some degree, without a Promulgation: because a man may be made capable of Right to Benefit without his knowledge, though he cannot be obliged to duty without his knowledge, except when he is Ignorant through his own fault.

P 2   Mr. K.

§ 35.

Mr. K. *For first, The Covenant Justifies us, not by any act, but meerly by the tenour of it, as a Law, not Agent, and many things in this kinde are said to do, when there, I wis, is no action at all:* Quantitas facit quantum; *I hope no Action, it doth it* formaliter, *not* efficienter : Paternitas facit patrem; *I know no Action that ever was ascribed to Relation, it doth it* formaliter, *not* efficienter : *and so doth the Covenant not Justifie a Believer by any Act,* let Mr. Baxter *mince it as he will,* a moral improper Action, *but as his* great Metaphysical Rabbies *would speak* aptitudinaliter, *and this but* extrinsecè *too*; *for* fœdus non facit Justum *of it self, but it must be beholden to many intervenient Causes.*

---

§. 35.

R. B. 1. THanks to Inadvertency (as I suppose) it is here acknowledged that the Covenant doth Justifie, and that as a Law, which if it do, we shall see anon whether it can be any other way then that which I affirm. 2. But little thanks is due to this Authour from the friends of Truth, for his discovery of the way of the Covenants Justifying. [It is (saith he) by the Tenour of it, as a Law :] True: How else should it be? [but not Agent] Not by a Physical proper Action : that's true : But have Laws, Testaments, Covenants, Grants, Pardons, &c. no Moral Action ? Or is this Moral so contemptible a matter, that a Learned Divine should make Nothing of it ? When all mens estates and lives depend on it here, and all mens Salvation or Damnation hereafter. But how is it then that the New Covenant Justifies ? why he thus proceeds [*Quantitas facit quantum* ;. I hope no Action : it doth it *formaliter*, not *efficienter* : *Paternitas facit patrem*, I know no Action that ever was ascribed to Relation, it doth it *formaliter*, not *efficienter*.] Reply. 1. I thought that [*facere*] had been as improperly applied to a formal Causation, as [*Agere*] and that I may, at least; as fairly do the later, as you the former. 2. If this Learned man do indeed think that the Covenant doth *formaliter* Justifie, as *Quantitas facit quantum, & paternitas patrem*, I shall the less repent that I was not his Pupil: And if I knew who be his old Doctors that he here speaks of, I would never read them, if they be no better in the rest: nay, I would take heed of looking into them, lest they had a power of fascination : What is the *Matter* that the Covenant doth Inform ? Gods Act, or mans Quality, Act, or what ? What matter doth it concurre with to constitute the *Compositum?* Is not *Justitia* that which formally maketh Just ? Is the Covenant the Relation of *Just* in the Abstract ? Why then doth not the denomination follow the form ? Is it the Covenant *quod explicat, quid sit Justificatus?* Or by which *Justus est id quod est?* But let us make the best construction imaginable of M^r K's words, and suppose that he would only prove the Negative [what way it is by which the Covenant justifieth not, viz. not *efficienter*] and not [what way it doth Justifie, viz. *formaliter*] yet I should demand, 1. What is then the use or purpose of his Instances, or fore-going words ? 2. What the better are we for his discourse, if he tell us not what way it is ? 3. What Cause will he make it if not an efficient ? Will he say it is either Material or Final ? I think not. But he saith, that [the Covenant doth not Justifie a Believer by any Act, let Mr. B. mince it as he will, a Moral Improper Action, but as his great Metaphysical Rabbies would speak, *aptitudinaliter*, and this but *extrinsecè* too.] Reply. What Reader is much the wiser for

for this anfwer? Would you know whether *Fœdus facit Juſtum, ut forma, vel ut efficiens?* Why Mr. K. telleth you, it doth it but *aptitudinaliter.* If ſo, then certainly, not *ut forma:* for *forma aptitudinalis faciens informatum,* is a ſtrange creature. It muſt then be matter or efficient. I would not think ſo hardly of Mr. K. as to imagine that he takes it for a Material Cauſe; much leſs that he takes it for *Materia aptitudinalis Juſtificationis actualis.* I hope ſuch doctrine never dropt from his Chair. What is left then, but that it be an efficient. And if ſo, is not all efficiency by Action of one ſort or other? And moreover, how comes *Efficiens tantum Aptitudinalis,* to be *Efficiens Actualis?* And if not *Actualis,* how comes the Effect to be produced, *viz.* The Believer to be Juſtified? But I dare not impute this *non*-ſenſe to Mr. K. Perhaps he takes the Covenant to be no Cauſe at all of Juſtification? But that will not hold neither? For he plainly ſaith, that [the Covenant juſtifieth] twice here together. And ſure *Juſtifying* ſignifieth ſome Cauſation.

Yet he amuſeth me more by adding [and this but *extrinſecè* too.] Why, who is it that hath found out another Juſtifying efficient, But onely the extrinſecal? By this I ſee he takes it not for Matter or Form; for they are not extrinſecal. But is not the Law, the Jury, the Advocate, the Judge, each of them an extrinſecal efficient in juſtifying every man that is juſtified *in foro humano?* It may be Mr. K. hath reſpect to the juſtification of Conſcience: But doth he think that there are not extrinſick efficients, that do more properly and more nobly juſtifie then our conſciences do? Then let man be his own pardoner and juſtifier, and be preferred before the bloud of Chriſt, the Law, the Advocate, and the Judge of Believers. I think it is no diſparagement to our Glorious Judge, that he will juſtifie us extrinſecally. Conſcience which juſtifieth (in ſome ſenſe) intrinſecally, doth it by ſo low an Act, by ſo ſmall Authority, that it is very doubtfull whether it be fit to call that Act either Conſtitutive or ſentential Juſtifying, ſo great is the Impropriety: (Of which I have ſpoke more fully elſwhere.)

If Mr. K. had named ſome of thoſe Metaphyſical Rabbies, and been guilty of naming as it were the Chapter and Verſe (of which crime he accuſeth me) I ſhould the better have known whether he ſay true or falſe, when he tels us that they would ſay the Covenant juſtifieth *aptitudinaliter,* and not by any act. Its true that the Covenant juſtifieth, *Ut ſignum voluntatis Divinæ per hoc Peccata remittentis:* And had he ſaid that it is *ſignum Aptitudinale* to men before they believe, and *Signum Actuale* after, there had been ſome ſenſe in his words, though yet they had been defective of Truth or Fitneſs: For they are *ſignum actuale* to millions of the unjuſtified, though not *ſignum actualiter Juſtificans.* But it is Believers that are actually juſtified, of whom he ſpeaks expreſly: and therefore he hath ſome other meaning, what ever it is.

Yet if Mr K. had denied to the Covenant in juſtifying, a proper Phyſical act only, we were agreed; But he denieth [an improper moral action] as he tels me, I mince it: which if I ſhould do, I ſhould expect to be told, that I were a very ſingular man indeed: For I doubt not but this Learned man hath read many a large Volume of Politicks, and particularly *de Legibus,* and there read their Diſcourſes *de Legum actionibus,* viz. *præcipere, prohibere, præmiare, punire:* I doubt not but he hath read many a large Volume of the Civil Law in ſpecial, and therein of the Nature of Obligations of all ſorts: (For I would not ſuppoſe him defective in his reading of any thing.) And after all this for ſo Orthodox a man to deny [a Moral improper action] to Gods Laws, and ſo to all Laws, and

P 3 therein

therein differ from all the Lawyers and Divines that ever the world knew (so farre as I can learn) 'is singularity indeed! Yea and never yet to write one Volume of his Reasons against all the world, that we might be undeceived? Seriously I wonder what he thinks of Gods Laws, Covenants, Promises, Testament, and how he preacheth them, yea or believeth them, or what work they have on his soul, who takes them to have no Moral improper Action? I should think such a *merus Physicus* were a strange man to make a Divine. But let us hear his reason: [For *Fœdus non facit justum* of it self, but it must be beholden to many intervenient Causes] Reply. 1. It seems to be here granted that *Fœdus facit justum intervenientibus alijs Causis*: And if so, it is an efficient; and if so it hath some kinde of Action. 2. *Negatur sequela*: What if the Covenant justifie not *nisi intervenientibus aliis quibusdam Causis*? Doth it thence follow that it hath no moral Action? And we must speak *non* sense to say, that it justifieth but *Aptitudinaliter*? 3. I deny that there is any other Cause doth intervene between the Covenant, and the Effect. A Condition on mans part must be performed before the Law or Covenant of Grace will *Actu Causare*, i. e. *Justificare*. And this Condition hath its Causes: But Remission and Justification have no intervening Causes.

I have in Answer to other Reverend Brethren so fully and distinctly laid down my own thoughts of this whole business, viz. of the several sorts of Righteousness, and of the nature of each, and the Causes, that I will suppose I may be excused that I do it not here. Only I may tell Mr. K. that I take Righteousness as now in Question, to be a Relation (whether predicamental or Transcendental, we will not now dispute; but I suppose it is the later.) And as Relation is so small or low a Being, that it is by some reckoned between *Ens & Nihil*, so the way of its production must be answerable; and must be by as low a kinde of Action. Yet if it have any kinde of Being at all, it must have some Cause, and that must have some Action. And therefore Rabbi *Keckerman* saith, *Fundamentum idem significat quod Efficiens; Terminus idem quod finis*. I suppose Mr. K. will acknowledge the Causation of procatarctick Causes, *objectum, occasio, meritum*: and yet will finde these efficients to have but an improper Action (at least some of them) as well the *Fundamentum* hath in causing a Relation. Besides all this, it is found no easie matter to reduce all Politicall Notions to the Notions of Logick or Metaphysicks; and some think that when we speak of Politicks, we must speak in the terms of Politicks, and that it is an unfit or impossible attempt to speak there in the strict language of Logicians, though I am not of their minde in the later.

But suppose that I had granted all that Mr. K. hath hitherto said: What is it to that which he shou'd prove? He undertakes to prove, 1. That the Covenants Action (as I call it) is [an odde, empty, Moral Action] and so cannot make this Effect: But he hath not yet proved, that the Relation of our Righteousness may not Result from the Covenant as its *Fundamentum*, though without a proper Action; as soon as the Condition is performed on our parts to make us fit Subjects. 2. He undertakes to prove, that [by the Promulgation of this Covenant God doth as improperly give us the Righteousness of Christ, and disable the Law to condemn us, because all here spoken of Actions, is but of Actions improperly so called] But doth he indeed think that Legislation, or Promulgation, or Covenant making is but Improperly called Action? If he do, I will not waste time in such a work as the Confuting him is.

Lastly,

Lastly, If his Argument be good [We are not properly justified by an Action improperly called Action: But the Action of the Covenant is Improperly called Action: Therefore, &c.] then it will follow that we are not properly Justified by any Action of God. For it is generally held, that [Action] is not properly applied to God, but Analogically, and after the manner of the creature. I think this first Argument of Mr. K. deserves no more answer.

§. 36.

Mr. K. 2. GOd is not properly said to Justifie us by this transient Act of the Covenant: For either he Justifies all, or only some. Not all: for all I hope are not justified: not some more then others; for the New Covenant makes no difference of it self: and so God justifieth none by it.

§. 36.

R. B. 1. EIther you mean, that [it is not by the Transient act Alone that God Justifies] or [not by it at all.] If the former, I confesse it, because the Moral Act which followeth doth intervene to the production of the Effect. It is not by the transient Act of Generation *alone*, that *Pater causat filiationem.* But it seems you take it in the later sense, and so it is false. Though the *Fundamentum* do *suo modo Causare Relationem, idque immediatè,* yet that Act which Causeth the *Fundamentum*, doth properly Cause the Relation too.

2. I seriously professe that it seems to me a very sad Case, that any man that is called a Divine, or a Christian should argue, and that so weakly, and so wilfully against all the efficacy of Gods Testament, Law or Covenant in conveying to us the saving Relative benefits of Christ! If it were only (as some Divines that I deal with) that he acknowledged the thing, and denied onely the fitness of the Name of Justifying to the Act of the Covenant, it were a smaller matter: But it is Remission of sin it self; the giving us Christs Righteousness, the disabling the Law to condemn us, that he speaks of, as you may see before: and so he here dares to conclude, That God justifies none by it. To this lamentable *Dilemma* here brought for proof, I say, 1. *Conditionally* God Justifieth *All* by his Covenant, at least All to whom it is Revealed. *Actually* he Justifieth only them that have the Condition. I oppose *Actually* to *Conditionally*, because that while it is but *Conditional*, it is not *Actual* in Law sense, that is, Effectual, though it is in *Actu*; so farre done as it is: And indeed it is not in strict sense that a man is called, Justified, while it is but Conditional: though yet it is a common phrase, because the Agent hath done it *quantum in se*, when the Condition is but Acceptance. 2. God doth Justifie some more then others by his Covenant, *viz.* Believers more then Unbelievers: This me thinks a Divine should not have denied. But he hath reason for his denial: and what's that? Why, he saith [for the New Covenant makes no difference of it self.] A strong Reason: It doth it not of it self: Therefore it doth it not at all. But I Reply: There is a two-fold difference made between men in these spiritual changes, The first is Real, when one that was an Infidel is made a Believer: and this is done by the Spirit and Word ordinarily; and it is but to prepare men to be fit objects for the justifying Act: The second is Relative, when we are Pardoned, Justified, Adopted, and have a Right

given

given us to other Benefits: This difference the Covenant makes of it self, the former preparatory difference being before made. To say, the Covenant makes not the first Real difference; Therefore it makes no difference, is ill arguing.

I would desire the Reader to try how Mr. K's argument will fit the Laws or Conveyances of men. If a Parent bequeath to each of his children an hundred pound on Condition they marry, to become due at the day of Marriage; according to Mr. K. you may argue thus: Either this Testament Giveth the Legacy to All, or to None: Not to All, if All marry not: Not to some above others: for the Testament of it self, makes no difference: Therefore it Giveth it to none. Or if a King give out a Pardon, or passe an Act of Pardon or Oblivion for all Traitors that are up in arms against him, on Condition that they lay down arms, and Accept the pardon: Mr. K. would argue; it seems thus: Either this Act pardoneth All, or Some: Not All: for All will not lay down Armes, and Accept it: Not Some onely; for the act makes no difference of it self: Therefore it pardoneth none. See what an Interpreters hand the Gospel is fallen into at *Blisland!*

§. 37.

Mr. K. 3. *MAn shall properly be said to Justifie himself (a thing which Mr. Baxter looks on, as well he may, as* Monstrum horendum) *For where there is a promise of a reward made to All, upon a Condition of performing such a service, he that obtains the reward, gets it by his own service; without which the promise would have brought him never the nearer to the reward: and thus a man wisely Justifies himself by Believing, and more a great deal then God doth Justifie him by his Promulgation of the New Covenant, which would have left him in his old Condition had he not better provided for himself by Believing, then the Covenant did by Promising.*

§. 37.

R. B. O How much have I been too blame, in my indignation against poor ignorant Christians, for taking up the absurdest Antinomian fancies so easily! When even such Divines as this shall use such reasoning as I here finde!

1. I deny the Consequence, as being *verba somniantis.*

2. I think, I shall anon shew, that himself is undeniably guilty of this Consequence, which here is called *Monstrum horrendum.*

3. For his reason, 1. Its pity that he cannot distinguish between a Cause and a meer Condition: Where he saith [he that obtains the reward gets it by his service] I say, it is here By it, as by a Condition *sine qua non*, but not By it, as by a Cause. 2. And its pity that any Divine should not distinguish between service and service. There is a service which is *operari*, or some way profitable to him that we perform it to; which therefore may oblige by commutative Justice to reward us: and here the Reward is not of Grace, but Debt; and the Work is a Meritorious Cause, properly so called. There is a Work which is a Means of Moral-natural Necessity (on terms of Reason and common honesty) to our orderly participation of a Benefit freely Given: As if a Traitor shall have a pardon

don on Condition he will Accept it, and come in: Or as if a Woman-Traitor should not only have pardon and life, but also be Princess, on condition she will marry the Kings son, that hath Ransomed her. Here the act may improperly be called service, because Commanded: but properly and in its principal Consideration, it is a necessary reasonable means, to her own happiness: And this act is but a meer Condition *sine qua non*, of her Pardon and Dignity, and no proper Meritorious, or efficient Cause.

4. What a dangerous reasoning is this, to teach men proudly to thank themselves for their pardon and happiness, and deny God the thanks! To say [Gods promise would have brought me never the nearer the reward, had not I believed: and I did a great deal more to Justifie my self by Believing then God did by his Covenant.]

5. Nay, I would desire the Reader to observe, what shift Mr. K. hath left for himself to disclaim this wicked Conclusion: Is there any of the Premises which he doth not own? 1. I hope he will not deny but the Promise of pardon and salvation is made to all that hear it, on Condition, they will Repent and Believe: 2. If he regard not better proof, I hope he will believe Dr. *Twiss* (so oft repeating it) that salvation is given *per modum præmii*. 3. I hope he believes, that without believing, the Covenant would not have brought him to salvation. Must not this man then conclude on his own principles, that [he wisely justifies himself by believing? and more a great deal then God doth justifie him by his promulgation of the new Covenant, which would have left him in his old Condition, had he not better provided for himself by Believing, then the Covenant did by promising.] I am loth to give these words so bad an Epithete as is their due. Why may not any Traitor say the like that Receives a free pardon? Or a beggar that Receives a free alms, when Receiving or Accepting is the Condition *sive qua non* of their attaining and possessing it?

6. The Gospel hath a promise of Faith it self to some: and this Faith is Caused by the holy Ghost: Therefore it is still God that provideth for the Elect, better then they provide for themselves, howsoever such disputers may talk. But we must not therefore confound the nature of Gods Gifts, nor their Causes, or way of production. The Spirit gives us Faith first, which is our Condition, and makes us capable objects or subjects of Justification: which being done, the new Law of Grace doth immediately Pardon, Justifie and Adopt us: which way then doth Mr K's desperate consequence follow? Or what shew of ground hath it? It seems if this man had forfeited his life, if a pardon were offered him but on Condition that he would Take it, and say, I thank you; he would say, he did a great deal more to his own pardon by Thanks and Acceptance, then the King that granted it, did by his Grant; because the Grant would have left him in the old Condition, had he not better provided for himself by Thankfull Acceptance, then the King did by his Pardon.] Yea and in our Case the Acceptance is Given too, though another way. I confess my detestation of this disputing, is beyond my expression.

Zanchy in 1 Joh. 1. *loc. de Remiss. p.* 41, 42. saith, Baptism is not perpetually a visible Instrument by which Remission is offered [*Verbum autem perpetuò est tale Instrumentum. Verbum ergo non Baptismus, est illud proprium & perpetuum instrumentum per quod perpetuo peccatorum remissio nobis offertur & donatur* (so multitudes more) And in *compend. Theol. p.* 764. *Per Evangelium Deus gratis Justificat*.

§. 38.

§. 38.

Mr. K. *It's clear in this case of the New Covenant, as in that of the Old: The Covenant ran, In the day thou eatest thereof, thou shalt die: This was Gods Threat: I pray who brought death into the world, God or Adam? Just so in the New Covenant, Believe and be Justified: Who justifies the Believer, God or himself?*
Turpe est doctori cum culpa redarguit ipsum.

§. 38.

R. B. NEver let any cause be thought so bad, but that it may have the greatest confidence to credit it with the world. [Its clear] saith Mr. K. in the beginning, and with his proverbiall Poetry, he triumphantly concludes. But if ever man met with weaker grounds of such triumph and confidence, in a man of such learning; he is of larger experience then I am.

1. To his first Question, I Reply: *Adam* brought death into the world as the Deserver, God as the Legislator, making it Due to him, if he sinned, and as the Judge, sentencing him to it for sin; and as the principal Cause of the Execution. But *Adam* was the culpable Cause.

2. To his second Question, I say, God justifieth the Believer, as Legislator, and as Judge, and as Rector *supra Leges*, and as Donor or Benefactor. And the Believer is not so much as the Meriter of his own Justification, as *Adam* was of his Condemnation. Did I think that any Learned Protestant had not known this? That he hath his Condemnation by his Merit, and his Justification without his Merit, upon the performance of that Condition which is the Acceptance of Christ that hath Merited it for us? That Death is the wages of sinne, and Eternal Life the Gift of God through Jesus Christ.

3. But again, I admire what the man means! Whether he own the wicked Conclusion [Man justifieth himself] or not? For he makes it to be the Consequence of this tenour of the Covenant [Believe and be Justified] And dare he say, that the Covenant doth not say, Believe and be Justified? Yea neverthelesss, though it also give faith.

§. 39.

Mr. K. *THat first born of Abominations in Mr. Goodwins phrase is unluckily laid at Mr. Baxters own door; and it may appear it is not wrongfully fathered upon him, by that very argument which he undertakes to answer, and doth well enough for so much as is exprest, but there is more implied in it.*

§. 39.

R. B. 1. [UNluckily] must be interpreted [by false accusation] I expect to have such unlucky hands lay more such abominations at my door.
2. Mr. K. confesseth, that I well enough answer the Argument for so much as is

is expreſt: And let the Reader well obſerve what the implied addition is that he makes.

§. 40.

Mr. K. THat the Promulgation of the New Covenant was from the beginning: Many men ſhall not be Juſtified till towards the end of the World: No man till a long time after the Promulgation: Therefore not ſo much by Gods Promulgation of the Covenant, as the man covenanter his performing the Condition, which is the Immediate Cauſe of it, and therefore he juſtifies himſelf, and that more then God in the New Covenant.

---

§. 40.

R. B. 1. VVHat is here added as implied to that which he confeſſeth, that I well enough anſwered? Let him tell that can.

2. How can he prove that *Adam* was not juſtified till a long time after the Promulgation of the New Covenant? A bold aſſertion, me thinks.

3. The Conſequence is a putid *non-ſequitur*: What ſhew doth the man bring to make any man believe his Conſequence, but the bare Credit of his own word?

4. What a ſtrait doth this Diſputer bring himſelf into? He muſt either ſay, that the Goſpel or New Covenant doth not promiſe Pardon and Juſtification on Condition of Believing. (And is he fit to preach the Goſpel that would deny ſo great a part of it.) Or elſe he muſt hold his wicked Concluſion, That man juſtifieth himſelf, and that more then God in the Covenant. And for ought I can underſtand by him he means to own one of theſe.

5. The ground of all this rotten doctrine, is another notorious errour here expreſſed, viz. That [mans performing the Condition is the Immediate Cauſe of his Juſtification:] when it is properly no Cauſe at all. A Condition may ſometime be alſo a Moral Cauſe, *i e.* when there is ſomewhat in the excellency or nature of the thing Conditioned, to move the principal Cauſer: But ſuch a Condition as is purpoſely choſen for the abaſing of man, and the honour of free Grace, and conſiſteth but either in Accepting a free Gift, or in not rejecting it again, or not ſpitting in the face of the Giver, this is no Cauſe, but *ſine qua non.* It ſeems, this Learned man hath too arrogant thoughts of his own faith, as if it were the Immediate Cauſe of his Juſtification, and ſo he juſtified himſelf more then God by his Covenant.

---

§. 41.

Mr.K. AS for inſtance: There was a Law made in Queen Elizabeths time, That every Engliſh man having taken Orders in the Romiſh Church, coming into England, ſhall ſuffer as a Traitor: That Engliſh man, which having taken Orders in the Romiſh Church, comes now into England, and is condemned, hath not ſo much reaſon to charge his condemnation on the Queen, as himſelf.

§. 41.

R. B. THat is becaufe he is the culpable meriting Caufe. Are we the Deferver s of pardon?

§. 42.

Mr. K. THe Law condemns him; but fhe doth not who made the Law, who died many years fince: yea the Judge who pronounceth the fentence doth not fo properly do it as the Seminary himfelf: No nor the Law, as the Prieft himfelf; who had he been minded to have fecured himfelf, might have done it at his pleafure, ftayed at Rheines or Doway, and condemned the Law of Tyranny; yea and avoucht all thofe that fuffered by it as Traytors to be really Martyrs. The cafe is the fame, though in a different matter.

§. 42.

R. B. 1. YOu confefs here that the Law condemneth: and then no doubt it juftifieth too.

2. Where you fay, [Shee doth not that made the Law] I fay, that is becaufe the Law doth operate or caufe, as it is a fign of the Will of the Rector, to conftitute that *Jus* which he had power to conftitute. Now when the Queen and Parliament were dead, they had no power to oblige them that fhould live after them, much lefs if contrary to the Will of their fucceffors: Nor yet had they power while they were alive, fo to binde pofterity. The Laws therefore were divolved into other hands, and now bindes as *fignum voluntatis Rectoris jam exiftentis:* For it is his will that it fhould continue; and that will animates it: Yet where any hath power, the figns of their will may be effectual when they are dead: Or elfe Teftaments were little worth, and Legataries were in an ill cafe. But whats this to our cafe? God dieth not, and the Laws of his Kingdom lofe not their force, nor change their Mafter, by the change of Governours. But if you had dealt ingenuoufly, you fhould rather have enquired, whether the prefent Rector and Mafter of the Law, may be faid to condemn him that the Law condemns. And that methinks you fhould not deny. Yea, and it may be faid that dead *Lycurgus* was a caufe of the condemnation of furviving offendors, for all your bare deniall.

3. Where you fay that [the Judge who pronounceth the fentence doth not fo properly condemn him, as the Seminary himfelf.] Seeing you yield that both condemn him, the Judge Sententially, and himfelf Meritoriously, and the queftion is but of the greater or lefs propriety in the word [Condemn] I think it not worth the contending about. Yet *Appello Jurifconfultos:* and if they fay not that it is a more proper fpeech to fay [The Judge condemneth him] then to fay [He condemned himfelf by breaking the Law] then I am content the next time its acted to take *Ignoramus* his part, and confefs that I know little of the Lawyers language. Indeed I ftill fay it is the offendour that is the culpable caufe. Where you fay that the cafe is here the fame: I anfwer, then it feems you think you deferve a Pardon, as a thief deferves the Gallows. I durft not have called thefe cafes the fame.

§. 43. Mr. K.

§. 43.

Mr. K. *IN a like matter take it thus. A man is found guilty of a felony; the Law saith, He shall be saved if he shall reade: he reads and is saved: Gramercy, saith he, to my Reading more then to the courtesie of the Law: and though he acknowledge pro forma that it is the courtesie and grace of the State to him, yet as the bad English man, God bless her Father and Mother that taught her to reade, else the Law would have been severe enough; he may be said to have saved himself.*

---

§. 43.

R. B. 1. You say, [It is a like matter.] But you say so much and prove so little, that you lose much of your labour, as to me. It is not a like matter. The Law for saving him that reads *ut Clericus*, was made partly to spare Learned men, because the Prince or Commonwealth hath need of them, and sustaineth a greater loss in the death of such then of the unlearned; and partly in a respect to the worth of their Learning, if not with some special indulgence to the Clergy for their Office, and to please the Pope. But Gods Law of Grace pardoning a penitent, gracefull Believer, hath no such intent: God needs not us, as the Commonwealth needs the Learned. Besides the Law hath laid the condition of escape in intellectual Abilities, without any Moral respect to the virtue of the party: but God hath laid it more in the meer consent of the Will.

2. But if you will interpret the Law of the Land otherwise, as if it were an act of purest grace, then I say, your Client with his *Gramercy* is an ungratefull fellow, and your bad Englishman, is the picture of a bad Christian, indeed no Christian: But by your speeches I perceive that about these matters experience is a great advantage to the right understanding of the Truth; by the means whereof many an unlearned Christian knows more then some Learned Disputers. He that hath felt what it is to be condemned by the Law, and afterward pardoned by the Gospel; and put into a state of salvation by Christ, doth not say as Mr. K. that he is more beholden to his believing then to Gods promise, but heartily ascribeth all to God. Faith is the act of an humbled soul accepting of Christ as he is offered in the Gospel. And can any humbled soul give thanks to his own Acceptance, more then to Gods Gift? yea when the power and act of Accepting is his Gift also? If Mr. K. have an imagination that in every conditional Donation, there is more thanks due to the performer of the condition then to the giver, I dare say, he is an ungratefull person to God and men. If his father leave him all his Estate on condition he give a younger Brother 6d out of it, or that he give 6d to the poor; it seems he will more thank himself then his father. If he had forfeited his life, and a pardon were given him, on condition he would Accept it thankfully and humbly on his knees, and that he would not spit in the face of him that giveth it, nor seek his death, he would give the chiefest thanks to himself. As for the phrase of [saving himself] he knows it is the Scripture phrase, 1 Tim. 4. last. though pardoning our selves be not.

§. 44.

Mr. K. YEs Mr. Baxter expresseth somewhat in his answer which makes up full measure of evidence against him. He saith, The condition being performed, the Conditionall grant becomes absolute. Ergo, say I, He that performs the Condition, makes the grant to be absolute, and so doth more to his Justification then God, who made only a Conditionall grant, and which notwithstanding he might have perisht, yea must without his own act of believing. And truly whoever makes faith the Condition of the New Covenant in such a sense as full obedience was the Condition of the Old, cannot avoid it, but that man is justified chiefly by himself, his own acts, not so much by Gods grace in imputing Christs Righteousness, but more by his own faith, which I hope is his own act, though Gods work.

§. 44.

R. B. 1. All's clear against me, if you be Judge; but the whole charge depends but on the credit of your bare word. That [*Ergo*, say I] is the strong proof. Your consequence is none, but a meer fiction. By [Absolute] I mean, it actually conferres without any further Condition, when all the Condition is performed. Its a hard case that a man so Learned in his own eyes should be ignorant what a Condition is, *in sensu Civili, vel Legali*. Were you not so, you would not still make it a cause; when (unless somewhat beyond the meer nature of a Condition be added) it is no cause at all. It is false therefore that the performer in our case makes the grant to be Absolute, if by *making*, you mean *causing*, as you before express your self, it is only a performing that, *sine qua Donatio non erit Actualis vel Absoluta*. It is the Donor (yea though he were dead before) that makes the Conditional grant become Actual or Absolute when the Condition is performed. And if it still stick in your stomack, that he performeth no new act to do this; I answer, it needs not: the first act of making his Testament, Deed of gift, Contract, Law, &c. doth all this. The Law or other instrument, is but the signifier of his Will, and therefore conveyeth when and on what terms he will (in a case within his power.) If it be his will that this Instrument shall *Jus* conferre presently and absolutely, it doth it: If but *in diem* and absolutely, it doth it: If *sub conditione*, it doth it: and in both the last cases, its his will that the Instrument shall give no Actual Right till the day come, or till the Condition be performed: so that a Condition is no true cause of the effect: the *non*-performance of it suspendeth the act of the grant, but the performance doth not cause it; unless you mean it of a *causa fatua*, which doth but *removere impedimentum*; so that if the Day be twenty years after the Testators death, that the Legacy becomes due, or if the Condition be so long after performed, it is the will of the Donor that maketh that Instrument then convey Right, which did not before; because it works only *significando voluntatem Donatoris*, [and so when and how he expressed his will it should work. Would one think such trivial obvious points should be unknown to Mr. K.?

2. Where you talk of [faith being a condition of the New Covenant in the same sense as full Obedience of the Old.] I say your words [in the same sense] are ambiguous: *Quoad rationem formalem Conditionis in genere*, it is in the same sense a Condition. But it is not a Condition of the same *species*. It differs in the

matter;

matter; one being the humble thankfull Acceptance of Christ and Life freely restored and given; the other being a perfect fulfilling of a perfect Law: the ends are different: One is to obtain part in Life purchased by Christ, when we were undone by sin: the other to maintain continued interest in the felicity first given by the Creator: One is to abase the sinner by self-deniall, and to extoll Free-grace; the other was to obtain the Reward in a way as honourable to man, as he was capable of. More differences might easily be added.

3. Let the Reader mark what our Question was [Whether God Pardon or Justifie us by the Covenant grant?] and whether Mr. K. hath now carried it? It was all this while maintained, that the performer of the Condition, is not Justified so much by the Covenant as by himself: Now it is come to these terms: [Not so much by Gods Grace in Imputing Christs Righteousnesse, but more by his own faith.] He seems to me to yield, that we are as sure-ly Justified by the Covenant, as by Gods Grace imputing Christs Righte-ousnesse.

§. 45.

Mr. K. YEs say I against Mr. Baxter 2. That faith is the Reall effect which God works, by a Transient act on a person whom he justifies.

§. 45.

R. B. YOu are resolved, it seems, it shall be against Mr. *Baxter* whatever you say. But what Rational Animal besides your self can tell how this is against me? If it be against me, its either Directly or Consequentially. If Directly, then I have somewhere denied it, or spoke the contrary: Shew where and shame me. If Consequentially, why is there no hint given us which way it makes against me? or against what opinion or words of mine? It seems it was intentionally against me, not against my Doctrine but Me: Your minde may be against me, but Truth is not against me.

§. 46.

Mr. K. THat faith is a Reall effect, others will admit without proving: Mr. Baxter who denies faculties and habits distinct from the soul, may be forced to yield it by this Argument. If faith be not a Reall effect on the soul, then neither is any other grace, for all flow from faith, and consequently no reall alteration wrought in Sanctification, and consequently no sanctified soul Really differs from her self when unsanctified, no nor more then numero from unsanctified worldlings; they are all alike. Taking it then that faith is a Real effect: 2. It is acknowledged it is wrought by God, and that not of our selves, it is the gift of God. And 3. that it is wrought by a transient act, as being a Reall effect by God in subjecto extraneo. Let us see now how by this transient act whereby God works faith, he may truly be said to justifie us in time as he decreed from eternity?

§. 46.

§. 46.

R. B. 1. THe man would have his Reader believe that I must be forced by his Arguments to confess faith to be a real effect. 2. Till he prove it, I will take it for a meer slander, that I deny Faculties and Habits distinct from the soul. 1. I said I thought [it would not be proved,] but I rose not to the confidence of a flat deniall; as knowing what is said on both sides. 2. What was it that I said would not be proved? That the faculties were not *Really distinct* from the soul or one another: but not that they were not *distinct*, as Mr. K. saith. They may be distinct modally or formally, though not *ut Res & Res*. 3. When did I say this of Habits, as Mr. K. affirmeth? But I will hereafter expect no more truth from him, even in matters of fact, then according to the proportion of the foregoing dispute. 4. To the point it self I say, we must distinguish of Reality: If you oppose Real either to Feigned, or Privative, or Negative, or Potential, or to an extrinsecall denomination, or to meerly Relative, so it's out of doubt that faith and all graces in the act and habit are Real effects. But if by Real you mean more then a distinction formall, or *Ratione Ratiocinati*, or Modal, I will neither affirm nor deny it, till I better understand it: You that know so well the nature of the Immanent acts of God, may a thousand times more easily know the nature of the Immanent acts and habits of man: but I confess exceeding great ignorance of both: and to tell you my opinions of these things would be but vain and unseasonable. 5. Your last words contain the mystery, that by [that transient act whereby God worketh faith, he may be said to Justifie;] we shall have good stuff, I think, when this mystery comes to be opened.

Whether Faith Justifie as an Instrument.

§. 47.

Mr. K. *Mr Baxter objects against faiths being an instrument of our Justification: and that it is neither mans nor Gods instrument. I shall make it appear to be both Gods and mans in some sense, though in different respects, notwithstanding all he hath said to the contrary. Saith he, If faith be an Instrument of our Justification, It is the Instrument of God or man: not of man; for man is not the principall efficient, he doth not justifie himself. I Answer* 1. *According to his doctrine, man doth justifie himself, ut supra.* 2. *That man is not the principall efficient of his faith, more then of his Justification; it is God who must have that honour.* 3. *That man doth receive his Justification by faith as an Instrument, as shall be shewed hereafter.*

§. 47.

R. B. THis quarrelsome man wanting work, had a minde to take in this Controversie also, about faiths Instrumentality in Justifying: but what an unhandsome Transition he makes to draw it in, may be easily discerned. Let the Reader remember, that the thing which I deny is, that faith is an Instrument

in

in the strict Logical sense, that is, an Instrumental efficient cause of our Justification: and that I expresly disclaim contending *de nomine,* or contradicting any that only use the word Instrument in an improper larger sense, as Mechanicks and Rhetoricians do: so that the Question is *de re,* whether it efficiently cause our Justification as an Instrument? This I deny. And to his triple Answer I Reply. 1. The first is of the old stamp; a gross untruth, needing no other reply then a deniall. 2. The second if it be sense, implieth the deniall of this maxime, that [*Instrumentum est efficientis principalis Instrumentum,*] and thence inferreth, that [as man may be his own Instrument in effecting faith, though he be not the principall cause, so may he be in Justification of himself.] If this be not the sense of it (if contradictions may be called sense) then I cannot understand it. But the denied maxime needs no proof: that man is his own Instrument in effecting his faith, needs no more then a deniall to disprove it (speaking thus *de homine*, and not *de parte aliqua hominis organicâ.*) That man is not *causa principalis* in beleeving, is untrue; though God be *Causa prima:* May none but the *Causa prima* be called *Causa principalis?* then no creature is capable of using an Instrument. 3. His third must be considered when we come to the fuller proof which he referres us to.

§. 48.

Mr. K. *But when he saith, Faith is not Gods Instrument,* 1. *I do not say it is properly, but it is his work, and by giving us faith he justifies us, as shall be shewed anon, he giving us that which is our Instrument, whereby we receive the Righteousness of Christ.*

§. 48.

R. B. 1. Even now he undertook to prove it Gods Instrument, but now, he doth not say it is properly: and I will not contend against an improper term, when the thing is disclaimed. 2. Here is another touch upon the mystery, that [by giving us faith he justifies us] but we shall be shewed it anon: therefore I must not overhastily anticipate it.

§. 49.

Mr. K. 2. *But it is as much his Instrument as the new Covenant is: for faith working in my heart, is that whereby God pronounceth the New Covenant to be of benefit to me for my Justification.*

§. 49.

R. B. 1. If the New Covenant be properly Gods Instrument, and faith be not, then faith is not as much his Instrument as the New Covenant: But the Antecedent is true: Therefore, &c. The second member of the Antecedent Mr. K. now yielded. For the first I will appeal to all Lawyers and Politicians, or any that understands what an Instrument is, what Civil commerce is, and what a Law or any Contract is, whether a Deed of gift, a Testament, or a Law be not as proper Instruments *conferendi Jus, constituendi Debitum,* as is imaginable,

R

or

or as the nature of the thing conftituted or conferred (*Debitum*) is capable of. In the mean time, I leave Mr. K. to examine it, by the common Canons and properties of an Inftrument. 2. Faith is not [Gods pronouncing,] but your belief of what he pronounceth, and Acceptance of what he offers: Will you confound faith with its object? Divine Teftimony is the object of faith, and you make it faith it felf. 3. I know the Antinomians take faith to be [the belief of our Juftification: or the perfwafion or apprehenfion of Gods love to me in fpecial,] but fo do not our modern Proteftants. 4. If this be true doctrine, then wo to poor Chriftians that have no Affurance of their Juftification: and then, how few have faith? For I think it is comparatively but a fmall number that have felt God pronouncing in their hearts, that the Covenant is of benefit to their own particular Juftification: except by the term [of benefit] be meant, a conditional Juftification, or a tendency or means towards their Juftification; and fo even ungodly men may know that it's [of benefit] to them for Juftification (as Mr. K. phrafeth it.) 5. Doth not Mr. K. fhew here that the Truth fticks in his minde, and that he is fain to hide it in ambiguous terms. What can he mean by this faying [God pronounceth the New Covenant to be of benefit to me for my Juftification] but this [That the New Covenant juftifieth me?] He would not openly tell us which way it benefiteth him to Juftification, and yet be no efficient inftrumentall caufe of it.

§. 50.

Mr. K. ANd 3. *it may be Gods Inftrument notwithftanding his Argument: whereof the firft is* [*for it is not God that believeth*] *nor needs it, fay I: it is enough that God maketh me believe, and fo receive the Righteoufnefs of Chrift: yea God by making me believe gives me an hand wherewith to receive, opens my hand whereby I receive it: I alone receive, but thefe are Gods acts, and though God be not faid to believe, he truly may be faid to be the Authour of my belief; my belief is an immanent act in me, and fo denominates me the believer, a tranfient act, as from God, and denominates him only the Authour of my believing: in me it is an adjunct, it hath to him only the relation of an effect. For example, I throw a bowl: the motion of this bowl is more from me then the bowl, and I accordingly am faid to have bowled well or ill: but the motion doth not denominate me otherwife then in the Agent, not the fubject; and though I be faid to bowl well, the bowl in this cafe is only faid to run, not I. So the chief Authour of my Believing is God, and he muft have the glory of turning and framing and upholding and working all in my heart, as being the Authour, Preferver and Finifher of my faith; yet I alone am faid to believe, not God; though my faith be more properly Gods work, then it is my own: had not he begun it in me, I had no more believed in Chrift, then the bowl would have run to the mark of it felf; all the progrefs of my faith is from him, and to him be all the glory.*

§. 50.

R. B. 1. NOne of all this is brought againft my Conclufion, for he yieldeth that; (that our faith is not properly Gods Inftrument in juftifying) but it is to fhew the ftrength of his wit againft my *mediums*. If he yield it to be the truth which I maintain, the matter is the lefs if I fail in proving it: Or if one *medium* be defective, it is little matter, if the reft, or any one fuffice. 2. What hath

hath he said in all these words, more then what I said in those few words which he opposeth, viz. [It is not God that Believeth, though its true he is the first Cause of all Actions:] Is not this the full substance of his speech? 3. All his words seem to tend but to prove that God may be said to be the principal Cause of our faith, and it to be his act: but what's that to its instrumentality in justifying. 4. I intended this first Proposition, chiefly as preparatory to the rest, rather then as a full proof of the Conclusion by it self. Perhaps we may give him some plainer Argument anon, when he hath done with these.

§. 51.

Mr. K. *Mr. Baxters second Argument to prove it, not Gods Instrument that man is Causa secunda between God and the Action, and so still said to justifie himself.* I answer, 1. Man is indeed Causa secunda, but not between God and the Action, for God doth immediately concurre to it, and man is in regard of the habit of faith purely passive, not active at all, for that though other habits may be acquired, faith is infused both for the essence and degree. 2. Man may not be said by his believing to justifie himself, but to Believe to his Justification, and to receive Justification by believing, for that by faith, as it is Gods work, God doth justifie him, viz. declares hereby the Righteousnesse of Christ to be his own; he doth apprehend or receive the Righteousness of Christ by believing, as it is his own act, whereof still he is the Subject, not the Author, as the Bowl is of it running.

§. 51.

R. B. 1. Whether God concurre Immediately to all humane actions, I have no minde to dispute: If Mr. K. want work on that subject, he may answer *Ludov. à Dola*. But it sufficeth me that man also is an Immediate Cause of his Believing. 2. Whether man be Passive or not in receiving the habit, is nothing, that I know of, to the matter; as long as the act which justifieth is immediately by him. 3. It is a great uncertainty which you affirm so confidently. You know not but that the Spirit of God by the Word, may excite an act of faith before he infuse a habit, and by that act (or more) produce a habit. 4. And so the habit may be said to be Infused as from God, and acquired by man too: and it is commonly granted, that Infused habits are attained *secundum modum acquisitorum*.

To the second Answer, I say, 1. For your Receiving Instrument, we shall speak to it anon. 2. *Si fides efficit Justificationem, tum Credens per fidem efficit Justificationem: At fides si modò Instrumentum Justificationis est, Justificationem efficit: Ergo*, &c. The *major* is evident, in that man is the immediate proper Cause of the act, therefore if the act doth it, the Agent by that act doth it. The Instrument is his that immediately and properly useth it. The *minor* is undeniable, speaking of a true instrumental Cause: For there is no instrumental Cause in any kinde, but of efficients.

2. A hint I perceive more here of your opinion, what is Gods justifying act, viz. Working faith in us: but I will wait till this opinion dare come into the light.

3. I perceive also here what you take Justification to be, viz. [declaring Christs

Righteousness to be his own] Right Antinomianism. 1. Will you tell us whether [Declaring Christs Righteousness to be mine] do not suppose it to be first mine? Else it is the Declaring of an untruth. And if it were mine before, was not I just before? and so *constitutivè* justified? 2. Why did you not tell us when and how that was done? And what was the act whereby God did constitute me just? Which is first to be known, and which you knew that I was speaking of. 3. Where, and to whom is it that [God declares this] you speak of? Onely in Conscience, and not to others, no doubt. But I doubt not fully to shame (in due place) this Antinomian fancy, that Justification by faith (in Scripture sense) is but Justification in Conscience. 4. Many a soul hath justifying faith (of Assent and Consent) who yet doth not believe that Christs Righteousness is their own. 5. May not other Graces declare Christs Righteousness to be ours? (I know not whether it be *sano sensu* that you speak of Christs Righteousness being made ours, but I will not digresse to enquire further into it now.) 6. You do strangely affirm, that man is not the author of his own act (whether he be the subject, I referre to what is said:). If by the Author, you mean, not the perswader, but the Agent, the vital, voluntary self-determiner, then he is the Author; or else I could tell you of such unavoidable consequents, as you will be ashamed to own. If you be indeed one of those that think man a free Agent, is no more the author of his own acts, then your Bowl is, I shall fear, lest you will think your self very excusable for all the evil you do, and therefore little care what you do: I shall be loath to trust a man of such principles, if his carnal interest carry him to do me a mischief. How many Philosophers or Divines are of your minde in this, that man is but the Subject and not the Authnr of his own act of Believing?

§. 52.

Mr. K. TO his third Argument, that the Action of the principal Cause, and of the Instrument is the same, *is true, and when he asks,* Who dare say that faith is so Gods Instrument? *I understand not any great danger in affirming, that God giving me faith, the habit and thereby the act of believing, concurs with my faith, which he hath given in enabling me to receive Christ; he gives me an hand, stretcheth it out, and opens it, and puts Christs Righteousnesse into it: Why is not my hand here his Instrument whereby he conveys Christs Righteousness to me, as well or more then my own whereby I apprehend it?*

§. 52.

R. B. 1. IF it be true, that the Action of the Principal and Instrumental Cause be the same, then it unavoidably follows, that man justifieth and pardoneth himself, when God doth it. For then when God effecteth our Justification, Faith, which is his Instrument doth effect it too: When God forgiveth us *effectivè*, faith forgiveth us *effectivè*: and consequently the immediate agent man, doth it too. 2. Again, I tell you, the place to examine your Receiving Instrumentality is anon where your self hath designed it: I may not anticipate you.

§. 53.

§. 53.

Mr. K. ANd whereas he faith, Fourthly, *The Instrument hath an Influx on the effect, by a proper Causality, which who dare say of faith? I answer,* 1. That it hath a proper Causality upon our *Justification passively taken, that is, upon our Receiving the Righteousness of Christ. And no more need: for we make it an Instrument not to work, but to receive.* But secondly, according to him it hath more then the Influx of an Instrumental, that of the principal efficient upon our *Justification, as being that which makes this Conditional Grant in the Covenant to become Absolute: And all the benefit we receive by the Covenant is more to be ascribed to our faith, then Gods grace in the Covenant, which would have been of no advantage to us at all, had it not been that our faith came in and rendred it of use to us. Thus then we do not deprive God of his Glory in justifying us by faith, though we ascribe Justification to faith; for we ascribe our faith to God, and make our believing his work, which as it comes from him is an active declaration, as in us a Passive resenting of his favour to us in Christ, of which we alwayes may though we not actually assure our selves.*

---

§. 53.

R. B. 1. REceiving is either Properly, which is alwayes Passive: Or improperly, morally, imputatively, which is the Consent of the will when a thing is offered, and it is active, called Receiving, because it is necessary to the Passive proper Receiving.

In the former sense, to Receive pardon and Justification is nothing but to be pardoned and justified: it is a meer Relative Reception. In the later sense, faith it self is our [Receiving] If Mr. K. mean the former, when he faith, that [faith hath a proper Causality upon it] I say, His words are scarce sense. To have [Causality upon] implieth a subject upon which there may be such Causality: But the Reception of a Relation is no such capable Subject. If he mean only [a Causality of that Reception] I say, There is no natural proper Cause of the Reception of a Relation, but that which causeth the Relation it self, by Causing its foundation: though there may be other Causes of the fitness of the Subject, yet that fitness effecteth not the Reception. Moral Causes there may be besides; but this is not pleaded such. An efficient Instrument of the Reception of a Relation, (that is, *Justitiæ, vel juris ad impunitatem*) we shall believe it to be when we first finde sense, and then truth in that assertion. 2. And for the second kinde of *Receiving* Christs Righteousnesse, it is Faith it self. And to say, that faith hath a proper Causality on it self, is a hard saying.

Your second Answer is the meer repetition of a notorious slander, not onely unproved, but bewraying the grosse mistake of the Nature of a Legal Condition; as I have sufficiently shewed, and will not waste time to recite.

I conclude therefore contrary to your Conclusion, that if you make faith the proper Instrument of justifying, you make man his own pardoner, and rob God of his Soveraignty. Your reason to the contrary is such as the Papists bring to excuse their doctrine of Merit: they say, Christ hath Merited for them a power of Meriting, and so the glory redounds to him: so you say, [We ascribe our faith to God, though we ascribe Justification to faith.] But you must needs ascribe it also immediatly to your self, if you be the man that believes.

R 3   Again,

Again, you touch the way of Gods justifying darkly: [As it comes from him (you say) it is an active declaration, as in us a Passive resenting his favour to us in Christ.] But, 1. do you mean, it is a Declaration Enunciative? Or meerly signal? If the former, it is very false. To speak a Truth, and to Cause one to believe it, are not all one. If the later, then it seems you think God justifies a man, every time he giveth him any Evidence of his Grace. And if so, then other Graces justifie as well as faith; and then Justification is increased upon every increase of every Grace: But more of this when you come to it of purpose.

And Passive Resenting Gods Love or Favour is an ill description of justifying faith, and not a little dangerous.

§. 54.

Mr. K. Mr. Baxter proceeds to take off an Objection. [But some would evade it thus: Faith, say they, is a Passive Instrument, not an Active] I know not who say it, nor matters it much, yea it is needless to say so: But *Mr.* Baxters answer to this I conceive to be very unsatisfactory: For where he saith [1. Even Passive instruments are said to help the Action of the principal Agent, Kecker.log. p.131. and he that saith faith doth so, in my judgement gives too much to it] I answer, That without offence it may be said, that Faith doth help the Action of the principal Agent, i. e. God in our Justification, God doing nothing in it without faith; I speak of such as are adulti, or of years. 2. That Mr. Baxter must say so, for that according to him faith makes Gods Conditional Grant in the New Covenant to become absolute, and therefore doth the main of Gods work.

§. 54.

R. B. 1. Let it be observed that Mr. K. takes it for needless, to say, Faith is a Passive Instrument: and therefore he must maintain it to be an Active Instrument, or none.

2. I doubt Mr. K. would have thought me near to a Blasphemer (supposing the interest of his Cause to have carried him another way) if I had said and maintained that mans Faith doth help the Action of God: 1. If Gods Action were taken to be *Causa partialis* (which I think Mr. K. doth not believe it to be) yet mans Action would help to produce the Effect, only by concurring with Gods Action, but not properly, help Gods Action; for it would have no influx into it. 2. If Gods Action be *Causa totalis in suo genere*, and mans Action subordinate to it, much lesse can mans Action be said properly to help Gods action. 3. But the truth is in pardoning sin, and justifying us, Mans action of believing is no Cause at all, and therefore no proper Help to Gods action. God hath no need of our help to pardon our sin. The performing of our Condition by Thankfull Accepting Christ and Life, is no Helping Gods Action. But its strange to see how Mr. K. reels too and fro! Sometime he dare say it over and over, that if the New Covenant say [Believe and be Justified] and make our faith the Condition of our Justification, then a man justifies himself by believing, and more a great deal then God doth by the promulgation of his Covenant, and that he is justified chiefly by himself and his own acts, and not so much by Gods Grace in imputing Christs Righteousness, but by his own faith.] And yet now he

dare

dare say, that mans Believing doth help God in Pardoning or Justifying him.

3. And what's his proof? Why [God doth nothing without faith.] A strange proof! So every Matter, Object, *Dispositio Materiæ*, or Condition *sine qua non*, should help the Action of the Efficient. Sure Helping is acting, and therefore Effecting. So he may as well say, that the preparation of the soul for Receiving Regenerating, Sanctifying Grace, doth help the Spirits Action of infusing it.

4. As for his second Answer, that [I must say so too, for that according to me, faith makes Gods Conditional Grant to become absolute] I Reply, that this is an oft repeated slander of a hard fore-head, without shew of proof. If this be mine, it is either directly or consequentially. If directly, let him produce my words. If consequentially, let him prove it if he can. If he attempt it, it must be by this Syllogism, [He that saith, Upon the performance of the Condition, the Covenant becomes absolute, doth say in sense, that the performance of the Condition, makes the Covenant become Absolutely, *i.e.* effects it: But M.B. saith the former: Therefore, &c.] Let him that knows no difference between an efficient Cause, and a meer Condition *sine qua non*, believe the major. I know so much difference, that I dare say, it is false.

§. 55.

Mr. K. WHereas he saith [2. It is past my Capacity to conceive of a Passive Moral Instrument.] I answer, whatever Mr. Baxter may conceive, nothing is more obvious then that many men at least are used by others meerly for blindes, to bring about their designes, and so do very much towards them, by doing nothing but standing still.

§ 55.

R. B. I Knew before I heard of your name, that the same thing which *in sensu Physico* is a Passion or Privation, may *in sensu Morali*, i.e. *reputativè*, be Action or an Instrument. But I ever supposed that as it is *Moraliter vel reputativè Instrumentum*, so hath it *Moralem vel reputativam actionem*. 2. That [some men are used by others meerly for blinds about their designs] this blinde work of Mr. K. doth partly perswade me.

§. 56.

Mr. K. WHen he saith [how can the act of believing (which hath no other being, but to be an Act) be possibly a Passive Instrument? Doth this act effect by suffering? Or can wise men have a grosser conceit then this?] I answer that this Act is equivalent to suffering, as consisting chiefly in a reliance on Christs righteousnesse, without exalting our thoughts against it, captivating our thoughts to it, renouncing all thoughts of our own righteousnesse, yea all thoughts that are too apt to rise against it from the consideration of our own righteousnesse; howbeit for the form it be an action, yet virtually this action is a suffering our selves to be led by the Spirit of God, and by his Authority against the suggestions of our own reason.

§. 56

§. 56.

R. B. 1. TWo things you have here to prove : 1. That the Act of faith is a suffering. 2. That by suffering it effecteth our pardon or Justification as an Instrumental Cause. For the former, you say [It is equivalent to suffering.] Reply 1. It seems then it is but equivalent. 2. Wherein it is equivalent? 1. As to its nature? That were a strange act. 2. Or in excellency: so it is more then equivalent to suffering. 3. Or is it as to its use and end? I easily grant you that the use of this Action is to make us capable subjects of pardon, or fit objects for Gods act, and disposed matter to receive Justification; as Mr. *Benjamin Woodbridge* hath plainly and truly, though briefly taught you in his Sermon of Justification (think not much to learn of him in that, and other points there touched.) If you have a minde to call this *Passio Reputativa vel Moralis*, I will not contend with you : it being *Conditio actus ad Receptionem propriam requisita.* Doubtless the Reliance and Renunciation which you mention, are actions. 3. And where you say, that it is [*Virtually* a suffering our selves to be led by the Spirit, though it be an action for the form] I never heard before of an Action immanent which was *virtually* suffering : and that from such a Cause as Authority is : Sure it is somewhat more then such a suffering ; and therefore it is new Logick to say, that it is *Virtually* suffering. Though as I said, if you have a minde to call it a Moral or Reputative Passion, I will not contend. 4. But then what a suffering is that you imagine it? I thought you would have come nearer the matter, and have said that it is *Receptio Christi, vel Justitiæ donatæ :* but you say, It is a suffering our selves to be led by Gods Spirit and authority.

2. But now I come to the great business, I finde you as mute as a fish : You had another Assertion to prove, [that this Act doth by suffering Effect our pardon :] On this lay all the controversie : and of this I finde not a word. I pray you remember by the next to satisfie your Reader, that [this Act which is Virtually a suffering our selves to be led by Gods Spirit, and by his Authority against the suggestion of our own Reason, doth by that suffering effect our pardon or Justification.] Nay, I thought if you had made it but a Receiving instrument; as you phrase it, that it had been the Receiving Christ or Righteousness, and not the suffering our selves to be led by Gods Spirit and Authority against the suggestions of reason, which (*qua talis*) would have been affirmed the instrument of our Justification? But you saw not what Roman doctrine this implieth.

§. 57.

Mr. K. WHereas he adds [4. *And lastly, I believe with* Schibler, *that there is no such thing as a Passive Instrument*] I believe he hath seen a man often hold up a fire-shovel to receive coles, which fire-shovel is an Instrument, but in that case meerly passive, and he hath seen questionless boyes at trap hold up their hats to receive the ball ; here their hats are Instruments, but meerly Passive. What examples Burgersdicius or Keckerman give, is not considerable ; What if they mistook in their instances of Passive Instruments ? Follows it there are none ?

[§. 57.

§. 57.

R.B. 1. THe Smith may call his fire-shovel, a Passive Instrument, and so your boy may do his hat. I will allow them both that name among Mechanicks, Rhetoricians, &c. but I shall not believe that Logicians should so call them, or that either of them is an instrumental, efficient Cause, or do effect by suffering, till you have better proved it, then this put-off comes to. 2. I have found no reason yet in all the reading of your labours, to judge your Logick more considerable then *Burgersdicius* and *Keckermans*; or that you are likely to finde out fit instances, where they could finde none. 3. *Callovius* and many more are of the same opinion as *Scibler* in this.

§. 58.

Mr.K. BUt say you [the Instrument is an Efficient Cause: all efficiency is by action: and that which doth not act, doth not effect:] *You have forgotten that the great Instruments of the Roman State, did all by doing Nothing.* Unus homo nobis cunctando restituit rem. *Their strength, saith the Prophet, is to sit still.*

§. 58.

R.B. 1. SUch a thing I now perceive may be: for I think when you have here done all, you had done more if you had done nothing.
2. I answered enough to this before. What if the Consequents of doing nothing prove better, then if there had been Action, and thereupon you do call [doing nothing] by the name of [Action?] Is it therefore Action indeed? Or if you therefore ascribe a Causality to it, is it therefore a Cause indeed? I say again, as such are *Moraliter vel Reputative instrumenta,* i. e. *Causæ efficientes instrumentales, cum Physicè & reverâ non sunt*; so morally and reputatively they are Agents, and therefore not to be called Passive instruments.
3. Let it be observed what a superficial kinde of answers Mr. K's Chair doth vouchsafe us? He durst neither plainly deny, that an instrument is an efficient Cause; nor yet that all efficiency is by Action: and yet satisfies himself with the touch of an alien instance, implying the denial of the later.

§. 59.

Mr.K. [INdeed (saith Mr. Baxter in the close) as some extend the use of the word, Instrument, you may call almost any thing an Instrument, which is any way conducible to the production of the effect under the first Cause, and so you may call faith an Instrument.] Belike it is Instrumentum quoddam vocatum, what you will in the Lawyers Latine, and you must be beholden to that to make the *New Covenant* Gods Instrument in *Justification.* Instrumentum Novum for Testamentum Novum, say the Criticks.

§. 59.

R.B. 1. These words I spoke, to signifie my resolution, not to contend about words; and if any man will use the term [Instrument] improperly, and tell us his meaning, and not make it the efficient Cause of our pardon and Justification, much less make the Papists believe, that in that notion lieth the very kernel of the Protestant doctrine about Justification by faith alone, I am content such a man speak as he thinks meet, allowing others the like liberty. To this Mr. K. gives this learned answer: [Belike its *Instrumentum quoddam vocatum*, what you will in the Lawyers Latine] Out of which words, or any yet spoken by him, if the Reader can pick an argument to prove faith the instrumental Cause of forgiveness or Justification, let him make his best of it. A jest is readier then a good Argument.

2. It ill becomes any Preacher of it, to deny or jest at the instrumentality of Gods Law, Covenant or Testament, It bewrayes that which you might with more credit have concealed. If Gods Deed of Gift of Christ, Life, Pardon, &c. be any Cause of our Right to Christ, Life, Pardon, &c then is it an instrumental efficient Cause, constituting that Right: (Let Mr. K. tell me what other cause it is, if not this.) But some Cause it is: Therefore, &c. Onely as Relations have an imperfect Being, so the Causing of them is answerable to it. If Gods Deed of Gift, Law, Covenant, Testament, be no proper instrument, then there is no such thing as a proper Instrument known in Laws, Politicks, Morality, for the conveying of any Right. As *Sayrus* saith, *Clav. Regiâ li. 6. cap. 6. n. 23. p. 330. Natura instituit voces & signa tanquam Instrumenta & media sine quibus unus homo alteri non possit obligari.* Not only are they certain Instruments when used, but is commonly held that they are so necessary instruments, that by a meer mental Conception without words a man is not obliged to another. So saith *Almain. in 4. d. 15. q. 2. Jos. Angles in flor. 4. sent. q. de voto art. 2. diffic. 4. Armil. verb. promissio. Petr. de Arragon. 2. 2. q. 88. art. 3. dub. 4. Mich. Salon. in 22. 10. 1 q. 5. de domino art. 2. dub. 1. Lud. Lopez p. 2. instr. conf. cap. 30. Emanuel Rodriquez part. 2. Sum c. 17. Concl.* And its certain that conceptions give no Right to men, though the conceiver of a promise may *coram Deo* be obliged.

§. 60.

Mr. K. *This were not worth the insisting on, but to shew with what tools Mr. Baxter endeavours to break the works of so many eminent Master-builders, and with what formidable weapons he valiantly sets himself against those great Champions,*

——— Sic dama Leonem
Insequitur, audetque Viro concurrere Virgo———

O the miserable fate of poor Divinity! that must be put to School to Burgersdicius and Keckermans Logick! and be so beaten for greasie Jack Seaton! Had not Mr. Baxter been as they say he was ἀυτοδίδακτος, he had not set so high a price on these beggarly elements, as to let them make utramque paginam *in this noble controversie.*

§. 60.

§. 60.

R. B. WHether this merry Rhetorical Triumph were grounded on such a reall victory as the man dreams of, or whether premises and Conclusion be any other then a meer Rapsody of windy oftentation, I must leave to the judgement of the impartial, understanding Reader. I confess they shew that he is not only unreasonable; for *ridere* is proper to a Reasonable Creature. I had thought to have given a particular answer to each passage in this Paragraph, but upon review I finde that the Replying to such like, hath occasioned more ironies and sharp passages then I dare approve; and therefore I think it best to say nothing to it, only to reminde him of these few things:

1. That I will be none of his adversary, where he argues only to prove me ignorant. It never came into my head to make it the Question, whether Mr. K. or I were the more wise or learned man? I have much more ignorance then he is aware of.

2. That yet I dare contend with him in point of veracity, if he use to do, with others; as he doth with me, particularly to talk of [making *utramque paginam*] and to scorn at it no less then twelve times in five or six leaves, for my citing these Authours once or twice, and *Schibler* thrice in a whole book.

3. That all is not Divinity that such Theologues maintain: For I think he is not Theology in the Abstract: and therefore its possible to finde an errour in such a man as Mr. K. without Schooling or beating Divinity: Nor do I think that sound Theology would feel it, though he had a knock or two more.

4. That he proves out of *Keckerman*, or others such like, that two and two is four, doth not much abuse Divinity by it: Nor he that cites them to shew that all efficiency is by Action, though as learned a man as Mr. K. deny it. Nor do I finde Mr. K. having recourse to the Bible to prove the contrary, *viz.* that there is efficiency without Action. And I think the Scripture Texts may be soon numbred by which he attempts to prove Faith to be the instrumental Cause of Justification.

§. 61.

Mr. K. HE hath one *Question* more [*But though Faith be not the Instrument of Justification, may it not be called the Instrument of Receiving Christ who Justifies us? I do not* (saith he) *stick so much at this speech as at the former* (we are beholden to you: *some indulgence yet in this particular*) *Yet is it no proper or fit expression neither. For,* 1. *the Act of Faith which is it that justifieth is our Actual Receiving of Christ, and therefore cannot be the Instrument of Receiving. To say our Receiving is the Instrument of our Receiving, is a hard saying.*] Be the act of Faith the actual Receiving of Christ: Why I wonder may not faith be said to be the Instrument of Receiving Christ? Is faith only an Act? I had thought it had been an Habit? And though the Receiving be not the Instrument of Receiving Christ, as being the actual receiving of him; yet faith may very well be so called: as though my receiving of a book be not the Instrument of receiving it, yet the hand may without any great absurdity be allowed that name.

§. 61.

R. B. 1. I Argued, that if faith be the Instrument of Receiving Christ, then either the Act of faith, or the Habit: but neither the Act nor Habit: Therefore, &c. To prove that the act of faith is not the instrument of Receiving Christ, I used the words that he here cites. What doth this Learned man but confute this by saying, that the Habit is the Instrument? [I had thought (saith he) faith had been a Habit.] Thus he confutes me, who argue that the Act is not the Instrument, by saying that the Habit is. I think he that is *αὐτοδίδακτος* need not much lament that he lost the benefit of such a disputants tutorage, if he be never in a more waking mood then here.

2. His Rhetorick is the best part of his answer. But when will he prove that the Habit of faith so farre differs from the act, and both from the soul, as that the Habit may as truly or fitly be called the instrument of Believing or Receiving, as the Hand is of its Act or the effect? If his similitude would prove any thing it would rather be that the Faculty is the Instrument, then that the Habit is: which yet I finde him not here attempt: I think that the Habit of faith, and the act are not of so different natures as is the Hand and its act.

3. Let it still be remembred, that I do not much regard how this Question is determined (for which Mr. *K.* doth so humbly tell me, he is beholden,) it being much different from the former Question. For in the former, the term [Instrument] is taken properly for an instrumental efficient Cause, in which sense I deny that faith justifieth: But here it is taken Metaphorically or Vulgarly, and not properly: For that which effecteth not is not an instrumental efficient Cause. And that which they call an Instrument of Receiving, is in Naturals but *Dispositio materiæ*, and in Morals, but *Dispositio Moralis, vel Reputativa, vel Actus ad Receptionem passivam, propriam, veram necessarius*; and in our present case, strictly nothing but a Condition. Now if any will be pleased to speak so vulgarly and improperly, as to call such a Condition, or Aptitude Moral or Natural [an Instrument of Receiving] so he do not build any unsound Doctrine upon it, I do again professe that I will not contend with him. But the Reasons why I thought it necessary for all that, to contradict the common Doctrine of faiths being the Instrument of Justification, I have fully manifested in answer to other Brethren.

§. 62.

Mr. K. But secondly, saith Mr. Baxter [*The seed or Habit of faith cannot fitly be called an Instrument,* 1. *The sanctified faculty it self cannot be the Instrument, it being the soul it self, and not any thing really distinct from it, as* Scotus, D'O. bellis, Scaliger, &c. Dr. Jackson, Mr. Pemble *think, and* Mr. Ball *questions.* 2. *The Holinesse of the faculties, is not their Instrument: For,* 1. *it is nothing but themselves rectified, and not a Being so distinct as may be called their Instrument.* 2. *Who ever called Habits or Dispositions the souls Instruments? The Aptitude of a Cause to produce its effect, cannot be called, The Instrument of it. You may as well call a mans Life the Instrument of Acting, or the sharpnesse of the knife, the knives Instrument, as to call our Holinesse or Habitual faith, the Instrument of Receiving Christ.*] I answer, you proceed by certain steps, and to deny the Habit of faith to be the Instrument of Receiving
Christ,

Chrift, you fay, 1. *The fanctified faculty it felf cannot be the Inftrument. And* 2. *What if it cannot? Who reckons the Habit of faith for a fanctified faculty? This is that which fanctifies the faculties: The faculty is of one Species of quality, potentia naturalis; faith which fanctifies of another, habitus: You are, it feems, now and then out in your Logick, as much as you trouble us with it, and had need review your Burgerfdicius and Keckerman.* 2. *How prove you that the fanctified faculty is the foul it felf, In-ftead of the few Names you mufter up, I may bring you thoufands that are againft it: and yet a few Reafons weigh more then all thefe great Names. If the faculty be the fame with the foul, then the Holineffe of the faculty cannot be really diftinct from the foul, for that this Holineß is to be received into the faculties; and if no faculty be really diftinct from the foul, then is there no receiving into it any thing really diftinct from the foul, and if Holineffe be not Really diftinct from the foul, a holy foul, and an unholy one, are not Really diftinct; and fo you feem to imply in your fecond, when you fay* ——

§. 62.

R. B. 1. Mr. K. yieldeth, if I am able to underftand him, that the Act of faith is not the Inftrument of Receiving Chrift: and he layes it on the Habit. Before we proceed here obferve,

1. That the Generality of Divines that plead for faiths inftrumentality, fay, that it is not the Habit, but the Act of faith that juftifieth: (I faid fo too when I wrote my Aphorifms, taking it on truft, but I now recant it.) If that be fo, then they cannot (as they do) argue thus: [Faith is the Inftrument of Receiving Chrift and his Righteoufneſs: Therefore faith juſtifieth as an Inftrument] becaufe they fpeak of the Habit in the Antecedent, and of the act in the Confequent; and fo by [faith] mean not in both the fame thing: and fo there are *quatuor termini.*

2. Obferve, that it is commonly granted, that the Habit of faith is not alwayes in act: as in fleep, and when we are wholly taken up with thoughts of an aliene fubject, and all the time of Infancy (according to them that think Infants have the Habit of faith.) This being fo, it muſt needs follow, that faith is not alwayes the Inftrument of Receiving Chrift, and of Juftifying: (nay perhaps, but feldome comparatively) For the Caufality of the Inftrument is in Action, and faith is not alwayes acting. If therefore faith juftifie as an Inftrument, and we are alway juftified, and yet faith be not alway an Inftrument, then either we are not juftified by faith, but fome other way, at thofe times when faith acteth not, or elſe *ceſſante Causâ non ceſſat effectus*: which though in fome cafes it may be true, yet here it cannot: becaufe the effect being but a *Jus ad rem*, a tranfcendental Relation, it hath no neareft Caufe, but its Foundation and Subject: and when thofe ceafe the Relation ceafeth: And none affirmeth that faith is a Remote caufe of Receiving Chrift, that is, Right to Chrift (with his benefits.) And if it were, yet the *Fundamentum Relationis* muſt have the fuftentation of a continned Caufe. But in the way that I affirm faith to juftifie, as a moral Condition only (having no Caufality), all thefe inconveniences, or rather contradictions are avoided: For it being the meer will of the Donor, that createth the neareft neceſſity of the Condition, and fo requires the Condition to fuch an end, he may make either act or Habit the Condition, and may make the act the Condition of Beginning our Right to Chrift and Life, and the Habit continued, to be the Condition of continuing that Right, even when the act is intermitted:

S 3 and

and yet the effect may still continue, because the Will of the Donor, and the Law or Covenant which is his Instrument, do both continue; and it is they that are the efficient Causes.

3. Observe also, that both the man for whom Mr. K. is here so zealous, viz. Mr. Pemble, and many more, do make the Habit of faith to be nothing else, but our New Life, our Holiness of the renewed faculties, the Spirit of God in us, and that all Graces are in the Habit and seed but one; and so accordingly it follows, that it is our internal Sanctification or Holiness that is the Instrument of our Justification: A Doctrine that I think these men will scarce own upon consideration.

4. Observe also, that hence it will follow, that it is other graces that justifie instrumentally as well as faith: because they say, it is the Habit that is the Instrument: and this Habit is but one: not one Habit of faith, and another of Love, Hope, &c. but all one: and this one Habit justifies, even when men are Infants, or asleep, and do not act.

5. That which is now commonly called, the Habit of Grace, is in Scripture called, [the Spirit in us:] and so the holy Ghost is made our Instrument of Justification.

Now to Mr. K's words here. In the words of mine which he cites, I do both indirectly, or *in transitu* confute a third opinion, viz. that the sanctified faculties are the Instrument, though the sanctity of the faculties be not: and directly I argue *à fortiore*, that if the sanctified Faculties themselves may not properly be called the Instrument of Receiving Christ, much less can the sanctity of the faculties be so called: But, &c. Therefore, &c. Hereupon this too learned man feigns me to think, or say, or imply, the Habit of faith to be a sanctified faculty; and with seeming seriousness fals a schooling me, and tels me, that [the faculty is of one *species* of quality, and faith of another;] yea proceeds in his dream as confidently as if he were waking, to tell me, that I [am now and then out in my Logick, and had need to review my *Burgersdicius* and *Keckerman.*] But would he a little rub his eyes, I would desire him to tell his Reader, where I did directly or indirectly say, that Faith is a sanctified faculty? And I would know of him, whether a man should not understand a matter before he make an answer to it!

Next, it seems, he expected I should have proved, that the faculty is the soul it self: And would not that have been as wise a Digression, and as Necessary, as is this of his? The Scope of my words was but this, q. d. [It is a controverted, doubtful point, Whether the Faculties are distinct from the soul, as *Res & Res*, and therefore not fit to bear such a weight as those that I oppose do lay upon the affirmative] (and my own opinion inclineth to the Negative: yet so as I dare not be so presumptuous as confidently to interpose among so many learned men, and maintain my own opinion as certain truth.) As wise a man as Mr. K. (and in my opinion an eight at least above him) thought the like answer to be good in another case. *Davenant. Determ. Qu. 37. pag. 166. Quod philosophantur voluntatem & intellectum esse duas potentias reipsa distinctas, dogma Philosophicum est, ab omnibus haud receptum, & Theologicis dogmatibus firmandis aut infirmandis, fundamentum minime idoneum.* And he knows, that the two Questions, 1. Whether the faculties be *realiter inter se distinctae*? And, 2. Whether they be *realiter ab anima distinctae*? use to stand and fall together in the Determination.

For the few names that he tels me I mutter up, its like he may know that it were
easie

easie to give him a farre larger muster-roll, especially of the Scotists. And as for the thousands that he saith he may bring against it (no doubt he means Writers) I confess plainly, that he hath so farre lost his credit with me, that I do not believe him. For though I know they are many, yet I do not think he hath read many thousands on all sides of that Subject. But if he have indeed read so many thousand books of that one point, alas, how many hath he read in all? No wonder if poor *Burgersdicius, Schibler* or *Suarez* be despised by him. It may be that's the reason that both the margin and Text of his book are so naked of quotations; he having read so many thousands that he knew not which to preferre, or where to beginne; or else would have few mens names to his Works but his own (except as Adversaries) left they should share of the honour. Nay, if he should have said or meant, that there are thousands that so write, which others have read though he have not, I doubt he cannot prove it true.

For his great weighing Reasons, I will honour them as soon as I can see them, but he had little Reason to expect me to Reason that Case. If this that he next addes be one of his few Reasons, that weigh so much, I must tell him, Every man to his minde. I doubt he overvalues his own Reasons: For my part, one thousand great Names, yea one, will weigh as much with me, as this his Reason. For, 1. I deny his Consequence, and say, that the Holiness may be Really distinct from the soul, though the faculties are not; and that Holiness may immediately inhere in the soul without the mediation of faculties really distinct from it. It had been easie to have seen the necessity of giving some answer to this denyall. As wise a man as most we have (if I conjecture not amiss) and a publick Professour in *Oxford*, and now resident where Mr. K. had his Chair, I mean Mr. *Wallis*; saith thus: [And so, however it may be true, that a faculty or natural Power may be so far the same with the soul, as that it differ only *ratione ratiocinatâ*, yet in a Habit we must of necessity grant a distinction *ex parte rei*: For where there may be a real separation, and not only mental, there must needs be granted a distinction *in re*.]

But what if I grant Mr. K's hardest Conclusion that Holiness is not Really distinct from the soul, nor a holy soul from an unholy as [Really] is taken for a distinction *inter Rem & Rem*. We shall see anon what danger would be in it. But then Mr. K. must be so honest, as not to perswade any that I therefore deny a Real distinction, as [Real] is opposed to feigned, mental, called *Rationis*, Relative, or Denominative.

§. 63.

Mr. K. You say [*The Holiness of the faculties is not their Instrument, for it is nothing but themselves rectified, and not a Being so distinct as may be called their Instrument.*] But is it nothing but themselves rectified? I had thought it had been the Rectifying of them, which potest adesse & abesse sine subjecti interitu? and consequently it is not the faculties themselves. As well you may say, that the rightnesse of a stick is nothing but the stick made right; and the whitenesse of the wall, nothing but the wall made white. Quis tulerit Gracchos sive Graculos!

§. 63.

R.B. 1. ALl that I assert is, that Holiness differs not from the faculties, as *Res & Res*, but as *Res & modus*. 2. I think the abstract hath no existence, but as in the Concrete, but is a meer Notion. Seeing therefore that it is so, I think the properest denomination, as most agreeable to the thing denominated, is to speak of it as *in Concreto*. 3. You did therefore too suddenly start up into your wondering interrogation, as if there were any contradiction between those two sayings! As if he that saith [a Rectified faculty: a white wall] did not as truly expresse the Rectitude, and the whiteness, as you that expres them *in Concreto*! It is too grosse a fiction, if (as you seem) you would make men believe that I intend to prove the Rectitude to be *Formaliter* the same with the Faculty or soul! My meaning is plainly, that Holiness is nothing but the souls Rectitude, and though I expressed it in the Concrete, I say not, that it is the Faculty as a Faculty, but as Rectified; shewing in the next words what it is that I exclude, viz. [A Being so distinct, &c.] 4. May not a Relation or *Modus* be present or absent *fine subjecti interitu*? though it be not a distinct Thing?

For your *Quis tulerit*? I Reply: Pride makes men impatient. Did you think no more highly of your own Note, then some wise observers do, you would, instead of your impatient *Quis tulerit*, have compassionated your self, and me, and sit down by me, with a *Nos Græculi*. However, why should you be so impatient with one so farre below you? Will you set your wit to the wit of a *Græculus*?

But I will make bold to try your Patience further. Will you hear the voice of the afore-said Learned and Judicious man Mr *Wallis*, who is now in the same Nest that you were bred in? See his *Truth Tried*, chap. 8. pag. 44, 45. [A Habit therefore whether Infused or Acquired, being but a facilitation of the faculty, cannot be a Thing distinct from that faculty, but only a *Modus* of it, which hath not in it self a Positive Absolute Being of its own, but is a Modification of another Being: And its Physical Being, *Existentia Rei*, must be the same with the Being of that which is thus Modificated: For it is not *ipsum existens*, but *Modus existendi*: And this Manner of Existing, hath not an Existence of its own, distinct from the Existence of that which doth Exist in this Manner. Yet its Formal and Metaphysical Being is distinct. Yea and its Physical Existence, such as it is capable of, that is, *Existentia modi*; for not being *Res*, but *Modus Rei*, we must not expect that it should have any Existence of its own, besides the Existence of a *Modus*: and this *Existentia modi* is the actual modificating of the Thing Existing after this Manner: The which Existence, though it be not *Existentia Rei*, yet is it a real Existence (*Existentia in re*) and not Mental: For the thing Existent is not only supposed to exist in this manner, but indeed doth so, thus ordered, thus modificated: And therefore that *Modus* doth actually and really modificate, and is not only supposed so to do. But if you will not admit with *Scotus*, &c. And thus it is true which his Lordship speaks, that Habitual Knowledge is Nothing but Light more or lesse Glorious. It is Reason cleared: It's only *Facultas facilitata*, or *Facultatis facilitas*: And to this Faculty or Readiness to operate, I cannot allow a Physical Existence of its own, *as neither to any Habit whatsoever, as being but* Modi, *and not* Entia: It's not a Being, but a Manner of Being: Not

Ens,

Ens, but *Aliquid Entis.* And I should easily be perswaded to grant the same concerning all accidents whatsoever, which have long since been called *Entis entia:* And however an Accident hath been accounted to be *Res,* and so to have *existentiam Rei,* yet not *subsistentiam Rei.*] So far Mr *Wallis.*

---

§. 64.

Mr. K. SAy you [*Who ever called Habits or Dispositions the souls Instruments? The Aptitude of a Cause to produce its effect, cannot be called its Instrument.*] I *Answer* and yield you, that ordinarily it is not so: In all Acquired Habits, there is meerly an Aptitude gotten: but by faith which is an infused Habit, there is an Ability gotten; this being indeed a Habit, but a Habit equivalent to a new Faculty; and so we hear of a new heart and new spirit, and without faith a man can no more receive Christ nor do ought towards it, then a dead man can walk or speak, and so it gives life to the soul in regard of all spiritual operations: and though life cannot be said to be an Instrument, yet I hope that which gives life may; as doth faith, which is as the soul to the soul in all its holy and heavenly thoughts and desires: Life cannot be said to be an Instrument: for Life as Life is no cause at all, but an Union of those causes which are required to the making up of the* Animatum.

---

§. 64.

R. B. 1. IF Habits were never so properly to be called the souls instruments, yet this reacheth not the Question, whether they may properly be called (*Logicè loquendo*) instruments of Receiving when they are not instruments Effecting. I did therefore give them too much advantage in this arguing.

2. If you grant that acquired Habits are not to be called the souls instruments, and yet maintain that infused are, you must give some good reason from the difference.

Your reason is that [*This is a Habit, but equivalent to a new faculty.*] To which I Reply, 1. What reason is this? When I even now said, That [the sanctified faculty it self cannot be the Instrument] you never did gainsay it: therefore if faith were a faculty or *Potentia,* it were not therefore the Instrument of Reception.

2. The term [equivalent] is so ambiguous, that you may yet make your words true or false by an interpretation. 1. If you mean that infused Habits are of the same nature, and of the same *species* of quality, as the *Potentia naturalis* is, that should have been well proved, and not nakedly asserted. 2. If you mean that it performeth the same kinde of operations, and *quoad usum* is equivalent, though not of the same nature or kinde; that also needs great proof, seeing it contradicteth common principles: The operation of things is such as the Being. 3. If you mean but that it is of equal necessity to the Act, thats nothing to the purpose; for the necessity proves it not an instrument.

But I conceive the first of the three is your sense, or else I cannot make sense of it; for the two later do no way tend to prove it an Instrument; and your words do most plainly import that sense. But, if so 1. Sure you forgot your own words but a little before, where you were pleased so farre to School me, as to tell me that [the faculty is of one *species* of quality, *Potentia naturalis,* faith which sanctifies of another, *habitus.*] And you gravely told me, I was now and then out in

T my

my Logick, and demanded of me, Who reckons the Habit of faith for a sanctified Faculty? 2. How can you say still that it is a Habit? For if it be truly a Habit, it must be of the same *species* of quality, as Habit; and admit the definition of a Habit, and therefore not admit the definition of *Potentia* or *Facultas*, nor be of that *species*: and I suppose you will not say it is of both, and be but one Quality: And I suppose also that you will not say, it is *Potentia supernaturalis*, and therefore may be of another *species* then *Potentia naturalis*, seeing it is not the way of efficiency, but the nature of the Effect or Thing produced, which diversifieth the *species* of Quality.

But because I have great reason to think, that you will Honour the same thing from Dr *Twisse*, which you contemn from me, will you be pleased to hear him speak to you a few words: *Contra Corvinum* pag. 361. [*Sed quia deventum est ad genus disputationis Philosophicum, agendum secundum principia Philosophiæ, sive naturalis, sive moralis, sive mixtæ, cum doctoribus illis congrediamur. Itaque juxta Philosophiam quid aliud est voluntas, quam Potentia volendi? rursus quid aliud est objectum quam bonum? unicuiq; verò quod apparet; non* Sybillæ *folium recitè, sed Aristotelis magni illius naturæ mystæ. Ergo non modo secundum Augustinum, sed & secundum Aristotelem, natura est hominum posse Velle quod ei appareat esse bonum, posse autem Velle quod vere bonum sit, ne Corvinus quidem hoc loco attribuit gratiæ suæ communi. Ego vero ultra feror, & ex Augustino disputo, etiam posse credere, posse Deum amare, naturæ esse hominum, juxta argumentationem superiorem: quod & hoc argumento contendo. Si potentia credendi, vel quidvis boni faciendi, nobis accederet ex gratia, tum potentia subjectum esset potentiæ; naturalis gratiosæ, quod quidem hactenus prorsus est inauditum; nempe ut potentia volendi subjectum esset potentiæ volendi. Voluntas fateor est subjectum habituum; etiam omnis potentia rationalis, tam intellectus quam voluntas capax est habituum, sive naturalium, quibus magis idonea fiat ad res naturales, tam intelligendas, quam agendas; sive supernaturalium, quibus elevetur ad objecta supernaturalia: At ut potentia aliqua capax sit potentiarum novarum, ne fando quidem hactenus accepi, priusquam mysteria sua mundo communicarunt Arminiani.*] Many more places to the same purpose might be cited out of Dr *Twisse*. *Boethius* de *Trinit.* saith, *Forma simplex subjectum esse nequit*: I leave you to gather the consequent. What if I adde a Novelist or two (they shall not be unlearned) that Mr K. may see that a *Graculus* is not so solitary as a *Phænix*?

Thom. White in his *Institut. Sacr.* l. 1. lect. 13. p. 90. saith, [*Sed & Habitum non esse aliud quam ipsum actum debilius manentem, omnino constat, ex eo quod impressio facta in subjectum, absq; aliquo contrario destruente, interire non potest: quia est modus ipsius subjecti; & quod alio modo imbui requirit novam actionem. Permanet itaq; actus donec a contrario destruatur. In anima vero non est alia contrarietas quam contradictionis. Donec itaque retractetur, ex necessitate semper manet actus, & dicitur Habitus. Objicies, esse contra manifestam experientiam quod actus maneant,* &c. *Respondetur, manifestum esse post actum intellectus vel phantasiæ, potentiam manere in actu illius objecti quod cognovit. Experientia enim docet, eam posse iterum cognoscere quod vult; quod ante primam cognitionem non potuit,* &c. *Manet itaque impressio; id est actus substantia, quatenus ens, & non tantum motio est: Unde cum in anima non possit esse motus, ibi adæquate manet impressio; id est actus. Quod autem non appareat manere, est quia anima in corpore non agit ex sese; sed præcisè quatenus movetur a corpore, seu per corpus; & per consequens non facit sensum sui, nisi in effectu corporeo. Et hinc fit ut cum rursus agimus, sentiamus actum faciliorem, vel fortiorem, vel directum & modificatum ab anima, ratione prioris actus; quod arguit impressionem manere: Sed modum ipsius impressionis,*

in.

in sese, videre non possumus; & ideo credimus ipsum actu non mansisse.] And pag. 94. [*Ex quibus satis clarum est, non esse habitus supernaturales, suis primis actibus prærequisitos; neque esse per modum potentiarum, sed omnino sicut habitus naturales; nisi quod circa alia objecta versentur; & discurrendum esse prorsus de iis, ad modum quo philosophamur de naturalibus, observatis specialibus differentiis.*]

Yea there are some that think, Habits are in the body. *Taurellus in Philosoph. Triumph. pag. 52.* saith, [*Vere tamen rem si quis intueatur, nil habitus aliud sunt, quam acquisita quædam intelligendi, vel alicujus expetendi promptitudo, non animæ, sed corpori adscribenda, cum per se anima nec impediatur, nec aptior fieri possit, ad exercendas actiones, sed quoniam corpore, ceu instrumento utitur, fit ut ejus respectu, vel habiliores, vel ineptiores ad aliquid efficiendum simus.*] This he afterward thus correcteth, [*Non corpori solum, sed animæ etiam, videntur esse ascribendi (habitus) Eundem intellectum & agentem esse dicimus & patientem: Per se quidem actionum causa est, nec pati, nec impediri dicitur; sed respectu ejus cui conjungitur corpori patitur, atque impeditur quo minus probe possit intelligere. Hac habitus accidentis ratione, non menti, sed corpori primo possunt attribui; veluti vice versa menti primo actiones, sed corpori secundario adscribuntur. Eadem voluntatis est ratio.*]

I cite not these, as owning them; but to shew Mr. K. that as learned men as he, have not the same thoughts of Habits, and therefore he should not be too hastily confident: And I confess, as highly as I think of Mr. K's learning, I do not think he truly and clearly knows what a Habit of the soul is, nor wherein it is distinct from the soul, the faculties, and the act, and the intelligible *species*: no nor a wiser man then himself neither. Every man knows not so much as he boasteth of, or thinks he knoweth. (And how likely then he is to know so much of God as he here pretendeth to, we may easily judge.) It was as wise a man as he that said [*Nam quomodo intellectu Deum capit homo, qui ipsum intellectum suum, quo eum vult capere, nondum capit?* August. *de Trinitat. li. 5. cap. 1.*]

3. I easily acknowledge that grace giveth such a *power* as is commonly called Moral, distinct from the natural faculties, as our corrupt estate contains an opposite impotency. But this is but an applying of the terms [Can] and [Cannot] [Power] and [Impotency] to Dispositions and Undisposedness, to Habits and their Privations.

4. A new heart and spirit, I easily confess necessary. But those words do commonly signifie in Scripture, only new Inclinations, Dispositions, Qualifications. It is a new heart; though only the old faculties and substance. I hope you will not follow *Illyricus.*

5. Where you say that [without faith a man can no more Receive Christ, nor do ought towards it, then a dead man can walk or speak.] I Reply 1. That proves not faith to be equivalent to a *Potentia vel facultas*, any otherwise then that it is of as absolute necessity, but not that it is of the same nature. If you shew an illiterate man a Greek or Hebrew book, he can no more reade in it then a dead man, that is, both are truly *in sensu composito* impossible: But yet it is but a habit that is wanting to one, and a power or faculty natural, to the other. And so it may truly be said that a sinner cannot do well that hath accustomed to do evil, no more then a Leopard can change his spots, or a Blackmoore his skin. Yet if you mean that such are equally distant from an actual change as a dead man, it is but a dead comparison. A dead man wants both natural faculties, and an inclination or moral power. An unbeliever wants but one.

2. That [without faith, such can no more do ought towards the receiving of

T 2 Christ,

Christ, then a dead man can walk or speak] is a dead doctrine, like the rest of Antinomianism, tending to licentiousness, and to subvert the precepts of the Gospel, and the salvation of men, and unfit for any man that shall use the Name of Christ, much more unfit for a Divine. The Ranting sect hath got the word too: and when they are reproved for wickedness, or perswaded to duty, they say, [*What can the creature do?*] To go out of an Alehouse or Whorehouse, and to go to hear the Gospel preached, is somewhat *towards* receiving Christ: for faith comes by hearing; and can no man do this without faith? Cannot the Eunuch reade a Chapter and ask help of an Interpreter without faith? Cannot men Fast and Pray, if not as *Cornelius*, yet as *Ahab*, without faith? Is there not a common Grace of the Spirit, drawing men *towards Christ* that were farre from him, which goes before the special Grace (at least sometimes) whereby they are drawn *to Christ*? This that you maintain is not the doctrine of Mr. *Tho. Hooker*, Mr. *Joh. Rogers*, Mr. *Bolton*, *Perkins*, or any of our experimental practical Divines; no nor of any Protestants that I know; I am sure not of the Syned of *Dort*; but of the Libertines and Antinomists. To what end do you preach to any unbelievers? Do you perswade to any means or duty towards the getting of faith? or do you not? If not, its like you Preach as you Dispute; and then I doubt whether you live at *Blisland*: If you do, sure that duty tends to faith, and may be performed before faith.

3. I think you do more boldly assert, then you can solidly prove that [without faith a man can no more receive Christ, then a dead man walk] if you mean it of the Habit of faith, as, no doubt, you do. If you should mean it of the Act, it were a merry arguing: *q.d.* [We cannot Receive Christ without Receiving him: therefore Receiving him is a Power, and so an Instrument] Actual faith, is actual moral Receiving Christ. But I suppose you mean it of the Habit, in conformity to your former Dispute; And then you suppose that God cannot cause the Act of faith by his Spirit, before the Habit, and by the first act cause a habit (as *Camero* taught, and his followers do still teach.) I suppose if the question were put but *de facto*, Whether God do ordinarily thus cause faith? it is past Mr. K's power to prove the Negative: Much more if the question be *de potentia divina*, whether God *can* do it.

4. Where you say [It gives life to the soul in regard of all spiritual operations.] I Reply, 1. How industriously doth Mr. *Pemble* prove that faith is not the Mother grace? not properly the root of all other graces, nor the first degree of our sanctification and spiritual life, either in the Habit or the Act: *Vindic. Grat.* pag. 12, 13, 14. Yet Mr. K. that is so zealous in defending him, sticks not to gainsay it.

2 Knowledge and Love may be said to give life to the soul, if the exciting and assisting other graces, be giving life.

3. It is in effecting or receiving a relation (*Jus ad Christum, impunitatem, salutem*) that we are enquiring after faiths Instrumentality. And you do turn the business to [giving Life to the soul in regard of spiritual operations;] whereby you seem to mean that faith is no otherwise an Instrument of receiving Christ, then as it is an Instrument of every other operation which it performeth; and as every other habit of grace (Love, Fear, *&c.*) are instruments of their acts.

4. You play with the ambiguity of the term [Life.] You take it for the Union of Causes. You know how commonly it is used for the *Forma Viventis*.

5. And

5. And so faith is, as *Pemble* saith, part of the souls new life, that is; new spirituall Rectitude; or as others, the whole *semen vel principium*. But this is only a formall, and not an efficient quickening, or giving life. And if you speak of faith exciting other graces: 1. That it doth by the Act, which you yet affirm not to be an Instrument. 2. So do all graces in their places help the rest.

Lastly, If you did prove that Habits are fitly called the souls instruments in producing the Acts, yet it is all nothing to our businefs. For we are enquiring how farre it is the Instrument of the effect, or of reception. And I still say, that where the Act is no efficient cause, there the Habit by causing the act, is no instrument of the effect. But in our Justification, the act of faith is no efficient cause (Justification is the immediate effect of God by the Act of grace now, and by his Sentence hereafter.) Therefore, &c. And for reception, I say it hath no instrument, but as the instrument of the effect, may be called its instrument; except you will speak as a Mechanick, a Rhetorician, or *Vulgariter*, and not Logically. And when Mr. K. gives me cogent Reasons against this, I hope I shall regard them.

---

§. 65.

Mr. K. Whereas *you adde lastly,* [*The sharpneß of the knife cannot be called the knives Instrument.*] *I must without disparagement to your confest acumen in other things, tell you, that this is but a dull instance: for faith is not as the sharpneß, but as the knife; and faith admits sometime a greater sharpneß, sometimes a leß, which qualifies it in its acting better or worse, more or leß. And* 2. *The sharpneß of the knife, may be called an instrument in a larger sense, as first qualities in the elements. The fire is said to act by its heat: the water by its cold; by the heat instrumentaliter, by its form* principaliter. *And thus* 3. *may the soul be said to act by its faith in receiving Christ, without which it were as impossible to receive benefit by Christ, as to return service to him.*

---

§. 65.

R. B. 1. I Acknowledge the instance of little use to the main Question, because it pertains but to the Act of faith, and not the following passion or effect.

2. The sharpneß of your Answer, serves but to cut your own fingers. That faith is as the knife, is feigned, and not proved. The knife is the substance, and the keenneß is the accident or *modus*. Faith is not a substance; but a *modus* or acccident of the soul.

3. In your large sense, you may say *quid vis fere de quovis*, and so I told you I did not contradict you.

4. I am so censorious as to imagine that you speak more by rote, then on true knowledge in your Physicks, about fire; but thats no matter.

5. Who doubts but the soul may, in the sense you mention, be said [to act by faith in receiving?] But once more distinguish of receiving: which is 1. The act of consenting to, or accepting of the offer of Christ and Life; which is *Receptio Ethica*, metaphorically called Reception. 2. The true passive reception of Right to Christ and Life; which follows on the former. The first is but the

Condition, and not the Cause of the later, and is in Morality to the later, as in Naturals the *Dispositio materiæ* is to the Reception of the form: but the efficient Cause of the later Reception is Gods Will, signified by his Law; and his Law signifying his Will, and Constituting the Duness. Now if you will say, that Faith in the Habit is the instrumental efficient Cause of the first Receiving Christ, that is no more then to say, the Habit is the instrumental Cause of the Act, *viz*. its own Assent and Consent: as Love may be said of its Act. And whether this Speech be proper or improper, I leave it to your self, I will not meddle with it. But for all Faith, might be called the instrument of Believing (supposing it may) and that Believing is tropically called Receiving, yet I deny that it can therefore be properly called the Instrument of consequent, proper, Passive Reception of Right to Christ. (The Passion is such as Relations in their Reception are capable of.) Yet improperly, vulgarly, as an Instrument is not taken for an Efficient Cause, I did profess and still do, that I will contend with none that will call Faith the Instrument of Receiving (or any Consent of the Will, call it Love, or what you will; as well as Belief in Christ, may so be call'd an Instrument.) But that Faith is no true Instrumental Cause of forgiving our sins, or Justifying us, I shall yet maintain till I see stronger Reasons then M.K. hath here produced; and to that I am moved upon Reasons of great weight, which I have elsewhere manifested.

Lastly, M.K. speaks too unlimitedly [of the Impossibility of Receiving Benefit by Christ without Faith.] I dare say, that many a thousand (if not all men) have received Benefit by Christ before faith. What say you by the Gospel? What say you by Faith it self? I hope it is not the Instrument of our Receiving it self? Yea, and it is more then Mr. K. can prove, That God could not if he would, have given pardon it self to some without faith, upon Christs meer Satisfaction. But what need I talk of this, to a man that thinks we have so much of, or towards Remission, Justification, Acceptation before faith, as he before disputed for, *i.e.* to be tantamount Justified? Though he takes them to be from Eternity, and so no fruits of Christs Death, yet he cannot deny, but as to us, we are as capable of Receiving such Benefits, without faith, from Christ, as without Christ.

§. 66.

Mr. K. ANd I acknowledge I have done very little by this *Dispute*; only I had not the patience to see so worthy Divines so unworthily bundled, as if they had need to be taught a *Logick* lesson by Mr. Baxter, who (as I have heard to the disparagement of both Universities) was scarce bred in either, but as much as I esteem his excellent parts, and I doubt not singular piety, yet may I be bold to say, somewhat more of the University would have done him no harm: And I conclude all with this Item to my self, though Mr. Baxter need not take notice of it,

———Ne tu Divinam Iliada tentes,
Sed longe sequere, & Vestigia semper adora.

§. 66.

R.B. 1. I Think your first Conclusion (that you have done little by this Dispute) hath as cogent Evidence, as most that you have maintained in these six leaves. But it had been more wisdom to have foreseen your loss of time, and to have prevented it, rather then to confess it to your disgrace.

2. Where you say, you [had not patience] I say, If you cannot forbear, there's no remedy: who can hold that which will away? The tongue is an unruly member. Perhaps your case is as his *Discollimin.* p. 54.

3. I dare not excuse, much lesse justifie my tongue or Pen, from too sharp and unmannerly speeches of my betters: Even where I discern no fault, I do suspect some, as knowing so much evil in that heart which is the fountain: And I hope all those pious Brethren whom I shall injure by my rashness, will heartily forgive it; which I earnestly request, and by Gods assistance, shall do the like by others. But yet I must needs say, that my Conscience doth not accuse me of [handling unworthily] Dr *Twiss* or Mr *P.* of any men. For as I have excessively honoured them, so do I very highly honour them still; and their mistakes I had not mentioned, but 1. That I had been by them ensnared in some of them, and thought my self bound to warn others of the danger. 2. The name of such worthy men may do more in propagating an errour, then a thousand unlearned Antinomians can do, and therefore should their mistakes be more diligently disclosed. 3. It is pity Gods gifts and Saints should be a Defensative to errour, and a snare to the Church. 4. I am confident the souls of these two Saints of God, if they know these things below, will give Mr. *K.* no thanks for his Vindication, nor be offended with me for disclosing their mistakes, which they now do farre more detest then I. 5. It was no such Crime in the late Reverend Assembly to question one of them for these mistakes, or in Learned Bishop *Downame* to write a hundred times more then I against the other: And why then is it a Crime in me? 6. Reverend Mr. *Owen*, who approves your book, doth say farre more against Dr. *Twiss* then ever I did, in his late excellent, learned *Diatrib. de Just. Vindicat.* and yet I hear none accuse him for unworthy handling him: Yea he ingeniously confesseth his own former errour, and writes against it; and why then may not a man for Truths sake be allowed to do by another, what he doth by himself? Had I been my self the Authour of Dr. *Twisses* Works (pardon the presumption of the supposition) I should say ten times more against several things in them, then I ever yet did. 7. Mr. *K.* himself here confesseth the opinions that I mention of theirs to be erroneous: And is not that as unworthy handling them as mine? 8. I intreat the impartial Reader to peruse my words themselves, and then let him judge as he seeth Cause. They are but these [A great Question it is, Whether Remission and Justification be Immanent or Transient acts of God: The mistake of this one point was it that led those two most excellent famous Divines Dr. *Twiss* and Mr. *Pemble* to that errour and Pillar of Antinomianism, *viz.* Justification from Eternity. For saith Dr. *Twiss* often, All Acts immanent in God are from Eternity: But Justification and Remission of sins are immanent Acts: Therefore.] Is this such unworthy handling? Mr. *K.* durst not once say that I falsly accused them; or that it was not their errour. And could I give them a higher Elogy, then to call them [most Excellent, Famous Divines.] I am confident the greatest Archbishops or Cardinals, yea the Pope himself would think such Titles no

way

way injurious to them. The Lord General will be content with lower Titles then [most Excellent and Famous] Do not such as Mr.K. go about to confirm the vile reproaches of the times, as if Ministers were the most intollerably proud men on earth, when this is taken for unworthy handling! And when they that expect that their hearers should bear their sharpest and frequent reproofs, cannot bear such an honourable mention of their mistakes?

4. Whether there be one true word in Mr.K's particular accusation [as if they had need to be taught a Logick lesson of Mr.*Baxter*] I am content my very enemies should Judge. Did I ever contend about any point of Logick with them? It was not, what an immanent Act is? But onely, Whether Justification be an Immanent Act, and so Eternal, that I enquired, and in which I opposed them? I do therefore take it as my duty to Admonish my learned Brother of his great sin, who hath not once, twice, or thrice, but so oft in six leaves spoken such palpable untruths in matter of fact, and made so little Conscience of the ninth Commandment.

5. If in this Paragraph Mr.K. do discover the very end of his undertaking, not to be so much the Vindicating of any truth of God, but of Worthy Divines, and Academicall Honour (of which I leave the Reader to Judge) then may we hence conjecture at the Reason of severall Passages through the whole: for the Means may not be better then the End; and no wonder if they be suited to it.

6. As for all that follows concerning my [being scarce bred in either University, &c.] I have nothing to say. Did Mr.K. ever hear me contend, for the Reputation of being Learned? He easily carries the Cause here, having no contradiction.

7. And where he saith, that [somewhat more of the University would have done me no harm] I do not believe him: For though I have been as sensible of my want of such happy opportunities, and my defects thereupon, as ever Mr.K. was, at least; yet I believe that all things work together for Good to them that love God; and that by that three-fold Cord (on my Friends, Body, and scrupulous Conscience) by which God restrained me from such advantages, and confined me to a more private course of studies, he did also restrain me from some evil that I might else have run upon, or prevent some that he saw would befall me: (and indeed he hath satisfied me now of the particulars.)

8. What men or other creatures those were that Mr.K. did [hear boast of me to the disparagement of both Universities] I cannot conjecture. But this I will promise Mr.K. that how little soever I have received from the Universities, they shall have my frequent and earnest prayers to God, and my best endeavours with men, for their Prosperity. The Lord purge them from Pride, Sensuality, Manpleasing and Self-seeking, and cause them humbly to study Christ above all, and zealously to lay out themselves for his Glory, and with considerate, resolved Self-denial and Unreservedness, wholly to resign themselves to his service, and make it their main business to win souls to that true felicity which they have first tasted of themselves; and then I should not so much fear any policy or power of their Enemies.

9. And for Mr.K's concluding Poetical injunction; I heartily confess my utter unworthiness to be annumerated to the Ambassadours of the Lord Jesus, or ever to have been permitted to speak in his Name; much more with any such success and encouragement as he hath vouchsafed me: And the Lord forbid that ever

I should

I should be so arrogant, as to equal my self with the Worthies of the Church, much lesse to envy the honour of their preheminence. Yet in regard of the Churches present necessities, I dare not give over, for all my imperfections. Though I have ever been of a spirit too easily discouraged, and have many a time been under *Jonas*'s temptation, and ready to say as *Jeremy*, *I will speak no more in his Name*; yet God hath so suited his providences to my infirmities and necessities, as not only to cure my backwardnesse and despondency, but also to convince me of the pleasantness of his work. I am assured that it was the Lord that sent me into his Vineyard, and without him none shall force me out. He that gave me fewer Talents then others, will expect but an answerable improvement at my hands: but be they never so small, I dare not hide them. He that calleth for two mites will accept them: He despiseth not the day of small things. He sometime revealeth that to babes which he hideth from the wise and prudent: For the wisdome of the world is foolishness with God, and the foolishness of God is wiser then men: and no flesh shall Glory in his sight. How many learned men have lost the main end of their Learning, and engaged God so farre against them, as to lay both them and their honour in the dust, because they would not devote it more faithfully to his service! The Lord grant that I may so use the small abilities that I have, that I be not condemned as an unprofitable and unfaithfull servant; and then I do not fear being condemned for their smalness. There are many learneder men then Mr. K. in hell, and many more unlearned then I in heaven.

But should I deny my self to be Vile against the Accusations of Mr. K. when I daily confess my self Vile to God, I should but prove the hypocrisie of my prayers. And therefore Dispute for Reputation that will for me. When I am tempted to such a work by Accusers, or by my own heart, I desire God to save me from the Temptation. He that works principally for himself, must be his own Paymaster.

§. 67.

Mr. K. The summe of all that hath been hitherto said in this *Paragraph, is this, That to Justification there is required a transient act of Gods, or the working of Faith in our heart: which shews, That albeit Gods Decree to Justifie us have much in it that looks so well like Justification, that it may be called so without Blasphemy, yet that indeed Justification is in time, not from Eternity: And it appears further thus: That Justification being the Absolving us from our sins, and the Accepting us as righteous, albeit God the Father Decreed it, the Son Purchased it, a Grant of it were made, and under Seal; yet till it be pleaded there is no Pardoning; as appears by comparing Gods pardon with that of Princes, which is not of Value till Pleaded, and not pleaded till after the Jury hath found the Offendor Guilty: so this Justification which begins at our Believing* in foro Conscientiæ, *a more private Sessions is again made more Publick in Heaven at our death, and this at Gods Bar before Angels and Saints deceased; and yet more publick before all the world at the General Judgement. This pardon was Purchased, Resolved, or Issued out, Sealed, Received, Pleaded at first: but as new sins are committed we plead it again, and so may be said to be particularly Justified from particular sins,* toties quoties, *but alwayes by virtue of our General Pardon.*

§. 67.

R.B. WE are now paſt the End, and yet new to begin. If in this Recollection he had not ſtumbled on a word or two, that come from the Core of his Errour, I ſhould ſcarce have underſtood any of his minde about the Controverſie in hand, ſave only Negatively, and that he is againſt Me. And yet it is not much that I can diſcern of it. Among all the Diſſerters of all Sects that ever I had to do with, that pretended to Learning, I have ſeldome met with the like ſlippery dealing, as in Mr. K. who pretending to make ſome notable diſcovery of the Truth, did ſo loſe himſelf in the eager purſute of a contemptible Adverſary, that he ſeems to have quite forgot his undertaking, and leave his errand behinde him. But to deal truly, it is my opinion, that though the man were drawn to engage himſelf, yet when he had emptied his bilious ſtomack, he found his work done, and therefore was willing to drop aſleep when he ſhould have performed his Promiſe. He doth over and over again promiſe us to open to us *what is the Tranſient Juſtifying Act*, yea, pag. 139. to *ſpeak Punctually to it*; and when all's done, the buſineſs is ſo farre undone, that for my part, I cannot certainly tell yet whether he once name it, or what his opinion about it is. *Pag.* 141. He ſaith [by Giving us faith, he Juſtifies us, as ſhall be ſhewed anon, he giving us that which is our Inſtrument, whereby we receive the Righteouſneſs of Chriſt.] That [anon] is not yet come; for I finde no fuller diſcovery of his minde, but only a little glance in this Recollection, wherewith he doth conclude. In thoſe former words he ſeems to make the Immediate Juſtifying act to be the Giving of Faith; and yet contradicts it in the next words; for that Faith he makes to be Given, that it may be our Inſtrument of Receiving. Now

1. We are enquiring after Gods act, and not mans Inſtrument.
2. We are enquiring after the Immediate effecting Act, and not a Receiving, which is no effecting.

Let us ſee whether theſe words under conſideration will any better diſcover his ſenſe.

1. He ſaith [that to Juſtification there is required a Tranſient Act of Gods; or the working of faith in our heart] This is all the tranſient Act I can learn he intends from firſt to laſt. But though before he ſaid [by Giving us faith, he Juſtifies us], yet here he thought it ſafer to ſpeak more ambiguouſly, and onely ſaith, that [this is required to Juſtification.] But there are many things required to it, beſides that Act which doth immediately Effect it: Antecedents, Conditions, the Cauſes of thoſe Conditions, are all Required to it; when yet none of them is *the* juſtifying Act. But if indeed he do mean that *Fidem dare*, is *Juſtificare*, I will ſpeak to that anon. Next he ſaith, that [Gods Decree to juſtifie, looks well like Juſtification] but that is not it. Next he ſaith, that [Juſtification is the Abſolving us from our ſins, and Accepting us as Righteous] that he may come to ſhew us what is not, and what is, the Abſolving and Accepting Act. And firſt again he excludes *Decreeing* from being the Act enquired after: then he excludes Chriſts Purchaſe; then he excludes the Grant made and ſealed; then he ſaith [Till it be pleaded there is no pardoning, as appears by comparing Gods pardon with that of Princes.] Perhaps then he means that [Pleading] is Pardoning, or the juſtifying Act. No, not ſo neither: For he only ſaith, that till it be Pleaded, there is no Pardoning] which plainly expreſſeth, That Pleading

ing is but a prerequisite Condition, the want whereof suspendeth the act of Pardon, but is not the Pardoning act it self. In the Conclusion he gives us a little more light to see part of his meaning, where he saith [so this Justification which begins at our Believing *in foro Conscientiæ*, a more private Sessions, is again made more publick in Heaven at our death, and this at Gods Bar before Angels, &c.] Here he tels us more then yet I could gather from him, *in quo foro justificamur fide*, that it is but *in foro Conscientiæ*, a more private Sessions, so that we are left to search for the justifying Act; which though he vouchsafe not expresly to mention, yet we may possibly conjecture at by this last passage. If the Reader would see the whole mystery which is thus darkly lapt up, as being somewhat afraid of the light, as far as I can gather, it is this.

Mr. K. being of the Antinomian faith, That Remission and Justification are Immanent Acts, and from Eternity (and consequently not purchased by Chrifts bloud) and that Justification by faith; which the Scripture speaks of, is only Justification *in foro Conscientiæ*, or the apprehension of the former; he thought, in these times, when Antinomianism hath an ill savour with the best, that it is the wisest way to appropriate the name of Remission and Justification by faith (in this life) to this Justification *in foro Conscientiæ*, and to give to the Immanent Eternal Act, the description without the name. And therefore he thought it fittest to say, that [Gods decreeing to Remit our sins, carries in it a Remission of them tantamount; for who shall charge them on us, where God decrees to Remit them?] *Pag.* 138. That [Gods Decree to passe the transient Act of justifying, carries in it as much as concerns Gods Remission of sins, and Acceptance of us as Righteous.] But the change that is made in time by the transient Act, is in our Feeling or Knowledge, and therefore he saith, that when we say [Now a man is justified in Gods sight] it [signifies only a testimony given by God, whereby he makes us know that we are justified before God, or in his sight] and that [in God it signifies, A making us to see: and we are said to be justified in his sight, when he makes it, as it were evident to our sight, that we are justified] *p.* 138. (Here before he was aware, he gives it the name of justification before we see it.) Now being Resolved to appropriate the name of Remission and Justification (in this life) to that which is *in foro Conscientiæ*, he is hard put to it, to deliver his meaning of the transient justifying Act, without opening the shame of his opinion. And therefore sometimes he saith, It is the Giving of faith to be our Instrument: Sometime that this faith is necessary to it: but concludes, that it is *in foro Conscientiæ*, a private Sessions, that we are justified before death: So that the Summe is this: That Iustification, and Remission, and Acceptation do consist in our Conscience's apprehension or feeling of that which God did from Eternity (which must not be called Remission, but Tantamount Remission·) and because Conscience cannot know or feel this, but by Believing, and because we cannot Believe till God give us the Grace of faith, therefore God justifies or pardons us by Giving us that Grace: that is, We by Believing or being Conscious of our Eternal Acceptance, do immediately justifie and forgive our selves; but mediately God forgiveth and justifieth us by Causing us to Believe, and Causing our Consciences to justifie us immediately.

I will not say, that I am certain I have hit of Mr. K's minde in this explication: for who can be certain in such a mist? And therefore I leave every Reader that thinks I mistake it, to gather it better, if he can.

What ever it is, I am sure he oft contradicts himself. He that here tels us it is *in foro*

foro Conscientiæ, and talkt before of evidencing it to our selves, doth say *Pag.* 139. l.*ult.* [Where ever there is a Moral, *i. e.* a Legal change, there is a transient act, and this being in justification, a transient act is necessarily required to this change] Now a meer Legal change is *de jure*, and not in the feeling of Conscience: and it is *in foro nullo actualiter, sed virtualiter in foro divino*, it being *actus illius Legis quæ est Norma Judicii:* and therefore not *in foro Conscientiæ, vel aliquo privato.* And if it be confest to be a Moral, *i e.* a Legal change, what man sees not that it must be a change *per Legem?* i.e. *novam, remediantem*, or *per actum moralem?* Nay, mark how in the very words of this Conclusion, he yields the Cause and doth not see it. He confesseth that we are pardoned as Offendors are by a Prince's pardon, which is not of Value till pleaded. Now let any man of understanding judge, whether the Princes Pardon Granted and Sealed, be not the immediate, efficient Cause of this Delinquents absolution or passive pardon, when he doth plead it: And whether it be not first a *Jus impunitatis* that is hereby Given him, which (whatever is here said) is of Value upon the Accepting, before the pleading, though the pleading is also necessary to stop judgement, or prevent Execution, and so to have the full benefit. And what though the Pardon Granted and Sealed be not Effectual till Accepted or Pleaded? Doth it follow, that it is not the immediate Cause afterwards? Let it not seem unmannerly if I speak my thoughts; that all this proceeds from this Learned mans great mistake or inconsiderateness of the Nature of Laws and their Actions, and of the nature and use of Conditions, whose non-performance doth suspend the action of the Law or Grant, (because the Will of the Legislator or Donor was, that it should so be) but the performance doth not cause its action, much less immediatly cause the Effect; unless there be something in it that may work as a procatarcktick efficient Cause, by way of Merit, or the like, over and above its meer Office of a Condition. If a man by his Testament leave his Son a thousand pound *per annum* on Condition that he do voluntaily Register his Thankful Acceptance of it: It is not the performance of this Condition that doth at all causally constitute the *Jus ad rem legatam*, or *conferre Debitum*, or *Donare*; though the *non*-performance may suspend the Collation of Right: but it is the Testament that doth immediately constitute this Right, when the suspension is removed, which before it did not, because the Testator would not have it so. Grotius in *Cass and. art.* 4. *p.* 280. *Promissi enim ea Vis ut Conditionem implenti Jus conferat. Vid. de Jur. Belli. L.* 1.*c.* 1. §.4.& *l.* 1.*c.* 11. §.1,&c. If then it were true, as M.K. here affirmeth, that it is at this private Sessions *in foro Conscientiæ*, that we are first justified on our Believing, then the immediate justifying Act (which Mr.K. hath talked so oft of) can be no other then either our own Apprehension, or belief that we are Pardoned and Righteous, or some such like Apprehension or Conclusion of our own hearts. For if it be *in foro Conscientiæ*, it must be By Conscience as the Agent, that is, By the understandings Concluding us to be what we are. But this both supposeth us to be Pardoned and Righteous before (for the Being of a thing goeth before the true Knowledge that it is in Being: None can be truly Conscious of a Righteousness or Pardon which he hath not:) and also it makes us to pardon and justifie our selves; and the transient justifying Act of God, so long enquired after, should be only Gods cooperating with us in our Believing, or Causing us to Believe. Yea rather, the Act of justifying faith (which is the Acceptance of an offered Christ and Life, 1 *Joh.* 5. 11, 12.) goes before this Act now mentioned, and this is but Assurance or a Consciousness of the State that by Believing we are in. Let any man that is willing to know the truth, but examine every Text of Scripture that speak of Justification by faith, and he may easily see that they do not (no not one of them) speak of Justification in *foro Conscienciæ*, or of any consciousness of our Righteousness, but of Justification before God.

And that Gods giving faith is not the immediate justifying act, appears 1. From the very name. [To give faith] is one thing, and [to justifie] is another. 2. From the real difference. Faith is given by a Physical act immediatly: Righteousness, immediatly by a Legal or Moral act. Faith is a real Quality (in the habit) or Act: Righteousness is a Relation, and is immediatly by a meer Resultancy. Nay the very matter or meritorious cause of the Righteousness now in question, is not faith, but Christs satisfaction and merits. The *terminus* therefore of the justifying act ( ) speak now of our constitutive Justification) is Righteousness, a Relation: but the *terminus* of Gods act in giving Faith, is the Faith so given. The Object also of the justifying act, and the Subject of Justification, is *credens*, a man already Believing: but the object of that act which giveth faith, is an Unbeliever. 3. Is not this flat Popery? to make Justification to lye in a real change, and not a relative? and so to make it the same with Vocation, Conversion, Regeneration, or Sanctification? Whereas the holy Ghost saith, [*Whom he called them he justified*, Rom. 8. 30.] For to give faith is Vocation (as those Divines say, that make faith to go before other graces in habit and act:) or it is Vocation, Regeneration and Sanctification; as Mr. Pemble thinks, who supposeth all infused *in uno semine*. So that if *Fidem dare*, and *Justificare* be all one, then to Justifie and to Call or Sanctifie is all one.

I had once thought to have heaped up divers Arguments here in the conclusion on these two last points. 1. To prove that our first Justification by faith, which Scripture speaks of, is not *in foro conscienciæ*. 2. To prove that [to give faith] is not the proper or immediate justifying act of God. But I shall forbear 1. Because Mr. K. gives me so little invitation to it, seeing he gives but a few dark hints of his own minde. 2. In that I finde upon review that almost all this paper is unavoidably taken up with a meer defence of my words against his injury, and he hath not given me occasion for many further profitable explications or disputes: and therefore I will reserve these for a fitter place. 3. Because I have larglier already Argued against both these in private answers to the Animadversions of learned Friends: and though those are not for publique view, yet I have a backwardness to the doing of one thing so oft. 4. Because this little that I have here said, seems enough, and proportionable to his brevity which doth occasion it.

This one thing seems necessary, in the Conclusion, that I adde a few Reasons to prove that it is in Law-sense that we are first justified by faith, and so that the Moral Act of the Law is the immediate justifying act (and consequently the enacting of that Law of grace, or granting that Deed of gift, is the next foregoing efficient act.) There are Reasons enough in my Aphorismes, but Mr. K. thought it easiest to take no notice of them.

Arg. 1. *A termino.*

The thing that is given by Remission is *Jus ad Impunitatem*: But it is only by Laws, Contracts, Deeds of gift, or the like Moral acts, that Right is immediatly conveyed: Therefore it is by these immediatly that we are forgiven: (and so Justified *Constitutivè*.)

I suppose it will not be denied that Remission is a Giving? *Qui condonat, Donat.* So Lawyers generally say of Remitting a wrong; and it will hold in case of crimes, especially in our case, against God. *Fragosus de Regimine Reipub. Christ. part. 7. li. 6.*

*li.*6. *Disp.* 17. *n.*95. *p.* 844. faith, *Remittere injuriam est Donare, & Donare est jactare suum.*

Arg. 2. *A malo remoto, contrario, & Termino a quo.*

The Diffolution of a Legal obligation, muſt be by a Moral act of the Rector, of the ſame kinde with the obliging act. But Remiſſion of ſin is a Diſſolution of ſuch an Obligation. Therefore, &c.

The *major* is proved by that common maxime, *Eodem modo dissolvitur obligatio, quo contrahitur.* The *minor* is proved by the true definition of Pardon: Which is in criminals, The Act of a Rector diſſolving an Obligation to puniſhment. *Remiſſio est proximè Reatus Remiſſio; remotius Pœna : Reatus est Obligatio ad Pœnam.*

Arg. 3. *Ab officio Legis.*

If it be the uſe of the Law to be *Norma Judicii*, then he that is juſtified *per sententiam Judicis*, muſt be firſt juſtified in Law : But the Antecedent is true : Therefore, &c.

When I ſay [Juſtified in Law] I do not mean [by the Law] ſtrictly taken as moſt do, for one only *Species* of Law : But I mean [by Law] in general, as it is truly defined to be, *Conſtitutiva Determinatio Rectoris de Debito. Vel ſignum Voluntatis Rectoris Debitum Conſtituens.* For many Lawyers do call only written and ſtanding Laws, by the name of Laws, and do exclude verball precepts of a Rector : In this limited ſenſe, as it is taken for [Law by an Excellency] I do not now uſe it.

Arg. 4. *A naturâ Sententiæ.*

Declarative ſentential, Juſtification or Pardon, preſuppoſeth Juſtification Conſtitutive. Therefore Juſtification Conſtitutive goes before ſentential Juſtification.

Here I ſuppoſe 1. That Conſtitutive is *per Legem*, and not *per Sententiam*, which is paſt diſpute. 2. That it is by faith (as the condition) that we are juſtified *Conſtitutivè*, it being only Believers that are Morally qualified to be fit ſubjects for this Juſtification, and whom alone the new Law pronounceth Righteous, and to whom alone it effectually giveth Chriſt and Life. The Antecedent is plain, in that the Judge muſt ſentence a man to be as he is, and according to his Cauſe. A man muſt be juſt, before he juſtly be pronounced Juſt. He that condemneth the Righteous, and he that juſtifieth the wicked, they both are abomination to the Lord, *Prov.* 17.15. *He that ſaith to the wicked, Thou art Righteous, him ſhall Nations curſe, people ſhall abhorre him*, Prov. 24.24. So that whether the ſentence be in conſcience or Heaven, it muſt preſuppoſe Juſtification Conſtitutive.

Arg. 5. *A naturâ fidei Juſtificantis.*

If the nature of that act of faith which juſtifieth, be only ſuch as may be the condition of the Laws conſtitutive Juſtification, and not ſuch as may be the Inſtrument of ſentencing us Juſt, then Juſtification by faith (which Scripture mentioneth ſo oft) is Juſtification in Law ſenſe, and not Sentential : But the Antecedent is true, as is proved from the Act, which I have elſewhere proved to be [the Accepting of an offered Chriſt and Life] (including Aſſent) and not the Antinomian, ſpecial Belief that we are pardoned, or a perſwaſion of Gods ſpecial Love to us, or a conſciouſneſs of our Righteouſneſs, or Aſſurance of it, which are ſaid to juſtifie ſententially *in foro Conſcientiæ.*

Arg. 6. *A communi conſenſu, & uſu loquendi.*

It is the common judgement of men to think, and common cuſtom to ſay, that

that [A King pardoneth by his written, or verbal Pardon, as his Instrument] and to distinguish [*Justificationem Legis*] a *Justificatione Judicis*, the former being presupposed: therefore we must do so here, unless any special reason can be brought against it: For Gods Law hath the common nature of a Law, and his Judgement the common nature of judgement.

To prove the Antecedent I need but to appeal to the common use of men acquainted with Legal and Judicial affairs. Yea even Mr. K. himself cannot forbear acknowledging it: Yea besides the forementioned acknowledgements, he is strangely guided to conclude with it, as the very last word of his Digression, against me [We may be said to be particularly justified from particular sins *toties quoties*, but alwaies by vertue of our general pardon.] This general pardon is that which God issued out and sealed as he saith, which becoming effectual when received and pleaded, doth by its virtue justifie us from particular sins: that is, by its moral or civil action.

Arg. 7. When the Scripture so oft denieth Justification by the Law, it plainly implieth that there is such a thing *in rerum natura*, as Justification by a Law, and that it is no improper unfit speech: For else God would not use it, *Gal.* 5. 4. & 3. 11. Yea it opposeth Justification by grace in Christ, to Justification by the Law, *Act.* 13. 39. *By him all that believe are justified from all things from which they could not be justified by the Law of Moses*: Where note the opposition that [by Christ and Grace] is opposed to [by works] and so [by the Law of Christ and Grace] is opposed to [by the Law of *Moses* and Works.] That therefore is affirmed of the Law of Grace, which is denied of the Law of Works: *viz.* to justifie. And the reason why the Law of Works could not justifie, was for that it was weak through the flesh, and not that it was an action or effect disagreeable to the nature of a Law.

Many other actions of Law to the same purpose, I recited out of several Scriptures, in my Aphorismes, *pag.* 178, 179. which I will not trouble the Reader to repeat.

---

§. 68.

ANd thus I have done that ungratefull work which Mr. K. was pleased by Digressing to put me upon: which I confess appears not lovely to me on the review. For I finde though I have easily born the charges of this Learned man, yet it is no very usefull work to the Reader that he hath here called me to; and I thought it not fitte to go beyond my call. In the first part I have little to do, but to obtrude his confidence, and to shew that he meerly feigned me his adversary, forgetting that of *Seneca, Victoriæ sine adversario brevis est laus*: In the rest I have not much to do, but to open the vanity and fallacy of many words, and to shew what a windy Triumph it is which followeth such a windy Opposition, and what his Reader oweth him, who doth *importare verba & sonum pro meritis*: And what can the Reader gain also by such a discovery. I finde also, that though I resolved to forbear all harsh language when I begun, that I have not satisfied my self in the performance. For when I came to his most injurious words, I could not tell how to answer them but by shewing plainly what they are, and calling a Spade, a Spade; which cannot be done in smooth and pleasing words; and I finde that I have used more Ironies then I dare approve of. My resolution therefore is, to stifle this work till I have a call to publish it, and then to commit it to

some

some moderate hand, to correct all that shall seem too unmannerly. For though I think I have spoken nothing but what Mr. K. ought to hear, yet I doubt whether it be not more then was fit for me to speak. It is my purpose therefore to deal with him no more, left I be drawn again to the same inconvenience. For I finde I cannot Reply to such a man in such termes as I do to the Moderate and Candide. Till his breath be sweeter or sounder I think it safest to stand further from him. When he disgorgeth his stomack on me, I have not the skill of shaking it off so mannerly, and cleansing my self without his disgrace, as I could wish I had. And if a man stirre them not very tenderly; *Plus fætent stercora mota.* I finde also that it is a very hard thing against the guilty to speak both truly and pleasingly: For *nemini blanditur Veritas:* and I have a natural inclination to speak nakedly and plainly; which being seconded with some degree of opinion, that *qui loquitur planè, loquitur sanè,* may quickly occasion me to step too farre. But the principal cause is, that I am truly aweary of the Warres of Divines: Many an opportunity and importunity have I put by, as finding here also, that *Impendii belli sunt præmiis majora:* and especially in this civil uncivil Warre of Brethren, the gainer usually loseth: unless men could be brought to deal more with the *Matter,* and less with *Words* and *Men.* Contentions are both the Daughter and the Mother of Pride. They are (as soot) the fuel of that flame that caused them. If the contender be overcome, he glorieth not as a Christian in the Victory of Truth, but repineth as a man at his own overthrow; and *pro plumeis noxis plumbeas iras gerit:* If he seem to conquer *supercilia erigit,* and it doth puff him up, and so increase his vice, and hasten his ruine: for

Vindicat elatos justa ruina gradus.

However it sets men usually on two eager a studying for their own Reputation; which is the way that god resolveth shall ruine it: For he that will be great must be the servant of all, and he that will be wise must become a fool, and he that will save his honour must lose it: *qui propagat nomen, perdit nomen.* My soul tasteth an admirable sweetness in Peace: The Churches Peace, the Concord of Brethren is my daily study, prayer and endeavour; which O that I were able any right way to promote! What I do that way, I do with pleasure: my greatest zeal doth carry me to it. But what I do in way of Controversie, yea even when necessitated, so that I dare not forbear, least I should betray or wrong the Truth, yet is it grievous and ungratefull to me: I have little pleasure in it. I am resolved therefore to draw back from this work, as much as I finde consistent with my Fidelity to the Truth of Christ; and to do nothing in it till I am satisfied of a Call that must not be resisted. And when I follow God, I may safely commit to him my Way and Labours: for I have found that he draweth forth nothing, which he knows not how to use for good. And the more any Brother is perswaded that I transgress my bounds in writing too sharply, I intreat him the more to pray for the pardon of my fault, and the more watchfully to shun the like himself; and to joyn with me, and all the Churches friends, in daily and importunate requests to God, that he would guide our feet into the way of Truth and Peace; even of that Truth, which lying between extreams, is the only way to stedfast Peace; and of that Peace, which is the Means and End of Truth. *Amen.*

Kederminster, August 1º 1653º.

POSTSCRIPT.

Christian **]** Have been willing to hope that my work of this kinde, and
Reader, with this kinde of men, was almoſt at an end, and that God
would in mercy grant me ſome little vacancy for more profitable labors (of practicall Theology) which I have long affected, and earneſtly
deſired an opportunity to perform: But the unceſſant aſſaults of contentious men do make me begin to lay aſide ſuch hopes; The enemy of
truth is too ſubtle for me; It's like he doth conjecture at the ſhortneſs
of my time, and therefore contriveth to force me upon other works
till my glaſſe is run. I have long foreſeen his plot, and yet I am not
able to diſappoint him: To quiet the ſpirits of the contentious is beyond my power; To bear in ſilence their Reproaches of my ſelf, and
to ſpend but little time or none in vindicating of any Intereſt of mine
own, this I have purpoſed and promiſed to my Brethren. But when I
ſee apparently that it is an intereſt higher then mine that is aſſaulted,
and that Gods Truth and the ſouls of men do command my endeavours for their defence, I have no power to forbear. Since the Printing of this Book, there is come to my hands a ſecond Volume of
Mr *G. Kendals* againſt Mr *John Goodwin* on the point of perſeverance;
wherein he hath aſſaulted my *Directions for Peace of Conſcience* in a
large Preface; and my Book of *Reſt*, in a Digreſſion: Had he fallen
on my *Aphoriſmes* again, I think I ſhould have ſilently yeelded them
up as a ſacrifice to his ſcorn; But thoſe other Practicall Writings, I ſuppoſe it my duty juſtly to defend. 1. Becauſe I know it is the Serpents
malicious deſign to make my Labours unprofitable to the Church:
And ſeeing God in great mercy hath ſatisfied me by experience, that
how weak ſoever, they have been hitherto ſucceſsfull, I take it for no
proud over-valuing them, but for a judgement upon experience, to
conclude that it will be ſome wrong to the Church of God and ſouls
of men if I ſilently give way to this ſerpentine deſign. 2. I have heard
ſuch Jealouſies and terrible accuſations ſpread abroad by this ſort of
Divines againſt my Writings, and eſpecially my *Directions for Peace*,
as cauſed me much to admire what the cauſe of the offence ſhould be.
Never could I hear but one particular accuſation of it, which is the
ſhameleſſe falſhood, that I was againſt the doctrine of the *Saints Perſeverance*; to which I annexed an Apology to the ſecond Edition. But
I found it was further buz'd into the heads of the people, that there
were many other dangerous errors in it; But all was in generals, and I
could never learn any of the particulars till now: Nay the people
that were deterred from reading it, knew none of the particulars themſelves, but took on truſt from jealous fame that ſuch there were. And
I learned, that there is among ſome Brethren of this ſtrain, a Combination,

tion, by raifing fuch reports to deterre the people from the reading of my writings. I confefs, upon all this I was not much forry for the event, that Mr *K.* had in this book brought forth his accufations, that at laft I might know my errors that I could never hear of before, & that I was at laft put into a capacity of making my defence; when if it had not been for this man I might have ftill been judged erroneous, & neither I nor thofe that believed and reported it, could with all our diligence have learned *wherein*; I underftand that the fame fpirit doth fometime carry this learned man into the Pulpit, and there inftigate him to the like emploiment, wherewith he once tickled or netled the ears of the Auditory at *Aldermanbury.* Truly I never thought my name, or defcription, worthy to be brought into a Pulpit, though in a way of oppofition. I thought none had thus over-honoured me but Mr *Tombs,* nor durft I think my name capable of being the matter of fo honorable a triumph to Mr *K.* as by the diligence he ufeth for a victory he feemeth to expect. But feeing he hath fo much advantage of the ground (and fomtime the winde, though not the Sun) when he manfully preacheth againft me at a hundred miles diftance; I muft give him the better there, and take him when he comes within my reach. And though I fhall be as be as brief as I can, yet fo much I intend, if God vouchfafe me time and ability, as fhall fhew you reafon to pity this Learned man, that ever his corruptions fhould lay him open to the prevalency of thofe temptations which have ingaged him in fo unhappy a defign as to ferve the enemy of truth in employing his excellent parts in falfe accufing and unjuft defaming his brother that would fain live in peace, endeavouring to deprive mens fouls of the benefit of his labors, and that in his mercenary ferving the lufts of another, for a little vain-glory of applaufe he fhould fo wound his Reputation with the fober and godly, and make fuch work for an accufing confcience, as he hath once and again done; yea, that he fhould ftill fo much neglect the 9th Command. as to become Mr *Eyres* fecond, and Mr *Crandons* third. And for thofe Reverend Brethren, who have (from feveral parts) folicited me to forbear further Controverfal debates, left I be deprived of opportunity for more profitable works (whereto they importune me) I profefs to them that I take it for the greateft affliction of my life, that I am neceffitated to this defenfive controverfal way of writing, & moft gladly would I be at peace, if men would give me leave; and if they will but convince me, that I may lawfully be filent where the Truth of God, the fuccefs of all my former labors, and the good of men is fo nearly concerned, I fhall refolve on filence; (For my own intereft I hope I can fubject it to Chrifts;) But till then I muft crave their pardon, yea, and their compaffion of me, who am to my great trouble detained from a more pleafing kinde of work.

May. 23. 1654.

REader, *To prevent the mistake of my sense, I desire thee to correct these faults before thou readest; many smaller there are which may be easily discerned.*

Errata in the Epistle to C. G. *Whaly.*

PAge 4. line 23. reade *To which end.* l. penult. r. *your self.* p. 5. l. 19. for *their* r. *your* p. 6. l. 7. for *undeservedly* r. *unreservedly.*

Against *Blake.*

Pag. 1. l. 32. for *1.* r. *i.e.* l. 5. for *Cor.* r. *Sen.* p. 6. l. 45. for *our faith* r. *one faith.* p. 7. l. 30. for *former* r. *formall.* p. 25. l. 33. for *recipiatur* r. *recipitur.* l. 38. r. *so receiveth.* p. 38. l. 22. r. *non contingat.* p. 46. l. 11. for *su.* r. *so.* p. 62. l. 15. for *man* r. *an unregenerate man.* p. 85. l. 5. for *Justification* r. *Imposition* or *Institution.* p. 89. l. 15. r, *expect order.* p. 91. l. 33. r. *inceptive.* p. 92. l. 14. for *dura* r. *pura.* and for *subconditions* r. *sub conditione.* p. 97. l. 22. r. *though it was.* p. 99. l. 25. r. *The Apostle speaking.* p. 100. l. 32. for *particular* r. *peculiar.* p. 104. l. 22. r. *but so come.* p. 117. r. *your self.* p. 118. l. 36. r. *to many.* p. 120. l. 41. blot out *to.* p. 133. l. 30. for *distinguish* r. *diminish.* p. 134. l. 41. blot out *that.* p. 136. l. 5. for *4.* r. *quatuor.* l. 6. for *this* r. *his.* p. 138. l. 2. for *seal* r. *state.* p. 145. l. 11. r. *by Moses* Gen. 2.

Against Mr *K.*

Pag. 4. l. 25. r. *spiritui.* p. 5. l. 3 t. r. *nemini.* p. 29. l. antepenult. r. *be so called.* p. 28. l. 30. for *vivos* r. *viros.* p. 31. l. 42. for *the* r. *them.* p. 51. l. 34. for *now* r. *enough.* p. 97. l. 45. r. *on beleeving.* p. 109. l. 17. for *gracefull* r. *gratefull.* p. 110. l. 31. r. *in diem.* p. 111. l. 9. r. *whither.* p. 121. l. 25. r. *efficientes.* p. 123. l. 6. for *only* r. *wholly.* l. 24. r. *he that proves.* p. 143. l. 37. for *obtrude* r. *obtunde.*

In the Epistle before that against *L. Colvin.*

Pag. 3. l. 24. for *fear.* r. *bear.* ibid Præf. Apol. p. 3. l. 18. for *meer* r. *neer.* p. 4. l. 13. r. *reversus.* In the Contents p. 3. l. 6. for *Decree* r. *Degree.*

Against *L. C.*

P. 194. l. 3. r. *before both.* p. 224 l. 2. r. *work?* and *Dispositio.* p. 229. l. 28. r. *neerly.* p. 237. l. 21. for *after you* r. *ofter than.* p. 250. l. 14. for *because* r. *besides.* p. 255. l. 38. for *sins* r. *sons.* p. 257. l. 35. for *formerly* r. *formally.* p. 282. l. 23. for *Cavell* r. *Ravell.* p. 294. l. 23. for *Relative* r. *declarative.* p. 301. l. 6. r. *in tantum.* p. 309. l. antepen. for *Now* r. *Note.* p. 310. l. ult. for *sive de merito* r. *sine demerito.* p. 324. l. 14. r. *an instrument.* p. 326. l. ult. r. *salvo.*

Against *Crandon.*

Pag. 12. l. 36. for *parties* r. *partes.* p. 15. l. 28. for *endlesse* r. *ended.* p. 28 l. 2. for *Now* r. *Nor.* p. 35. l. 6. for *wherein* r. *without.* p. 37. l. 14 for *solid* r. *sol'd.* p. 55. l. 8. for *that* r. *the.* l. 14. r. *obtrude.*

WHatsoever hath escaped me in these Writings that is against Meeknesse, Peace, and Brotherly Love, let it be all unsaid, and hereby revoked, and I desire the pardon of it from God and Man.

RICHARD BAXTER.

FINIS.

Richard Baxter's
CONFVTATION
OF A
DISSERTATION
For the Justification of Infidels:
VVritten by *Ludiomæus Colvinus*,
aliàs *Ludovicus Molinæus*, Dr. of Physick
and History-Professor in *Oxford*,
against his Brother *Cyrus Molinæus*.

Heb. 11.6.
But without Faith it is impossible to please God.
Joh. 3. 16, 17, 18.
For God so loved the world that he gave his only begotten Son, that whosoever believeth in him, should not perish but have Everlasting Life.
For God sent not his Son into the world, to condemn the world, but that the world through him might be saved. He that believeth on him is not condemned; but he that believeth not is condemned already, because he hath not believed in the name of the only begotten Son of God.

LONDON,
Printed, by R. W. Anno Dom. 1654.

Concil. Milevitan. Can. 7. & 8. Contr. Pelagianos.

C. 7. Item. Placuit ut quicunque dixerit in Oratione Dominica ideo dicere sanctos Dimitte nobis Debita nostra ; ut non pro seipsis hoc dicant, quia non est eis jam necessaria ista Petitio, sed pro aliis, qui sunt in suo populo peccatores, & ideo non dicere unumquemque Sanctorum ; Dimitte mihi debita mea ; sed, Dimitte nobis debita nostra, ut hoc pro aliis potius quam pro se Justus petere intelligatur, Anathema sit.

C. 8. Item placuit ut quicunque Verba ipsa Dominicæ Orationis, ubi dicimus, Dimitte nobis debita nostra, ista volunt à Sanctis dici ut humiliter, non veraciter hoc dicatur, Anathema sit. Quis enim ferat orantem, & non hominibus sed ipsi Domino mentientem, qui labiis sibi dicit dimitti velle, & Corde dicit, quæ sibi dimittantur Debita non habere ?

POSTSCRIPT.

HAving perceived by a friend that perused these Papers since the Printing of them, that the n. 5th §. 11. p. 25. against Mr. Blake, is through too great brevity like to be misunderstood, I thought meet to adde this Explication.

I distinguish between the Real Operations and Mutations on mans soul, by Objects; and the Conveyance of Right to several Benefits by the Covenant of God. It is not the former that I speak of in that place. I confess that as the Apprehension of one of Gods Attributes, makes one effect on the soul, and the apprehension of another makes another effect, so the apprehension of Christs Kingdome; Righteousness, Death, Obedience, Intercession, Judgement, &c. do make also their several Impressions according to the Nature of the thing apprehended. But I utterly deny that it is so in Conveying Right to these, as much as I deny that Justification is Sanctification, or a Real Change of our Qualities as it is. This therefore is my Argument: If the Apprehension of Christs Righteousness, and no other Act, should strictly be the Justifying Act of Faith, and that eo nomine, because it is the object of that apprehension which is the matter of our Justification, then it would follow, 1. That the Apprehension of nothing else is the Justifying Act. 2. And that we have Right to every other particular Mercy eo nomine, because we apprehend that Mercy, and so our Right to every particular Benefit of Christ, were Received by a distinct Act of Faith, But the Consequent is false. Therefore so is the Antecedent.

The minor only requires proof: which is proved by the tenour of the Covenant of Grace, which Giveth us Christ, and with him all things: He that hath the Son hath Life: He that believeth on him shall not perish, nor come into Condemnation. As many as Received him, to them gave he power to become the sons of God. So that one entire faith, which is the Receiving of Christ as he is offered, that is, as our Saviour and King, is the Condition of our Right to all particular Benefits. Godliness hath the promise of this life, and that to come. *It is a womans taking such a man for her Husband that Gives her first Interest in him, and then in all that he hath: It is not accepting this house, and that Land, and that Servant, &c. that gives her a distinct right in them. There is not a marrying to all these, and a particular Acceptance of every of his Goods and Chattel requisite to a right in them, though there be to a use of them.* 2. *And the Opinion being utterly unproved, is sufficiently confuted.* In what Book that ever was written have these nice distinguishers proved their Doctrine by Scripture or sound reason? Lex non distinguit, ergo, &c. 3. *And it discovers its own absurdity:* For if this be true, then to apprehend Christs death is the only act that gives right to that, and to apprehend his obedience to that; and to apprehend Adoption is the only act that gives right to that, and so of all other benefits: So that there should be one act of Faith giving right to Christ himself, and another giving right to pardon; another to sentential Justification, another to Adoption, another to the Spirit and Sanctification, another to Perseverance; another to Glory: Yea one to every particular gift or part of Sanctification; and one to the pardon of every particular known sin that is pardoned: One to the Gospel written, another to the Ministry, one to health, another to life, and one to every blessing. And so that act of faith which Receives Adoption should not Justifie, nor that which Receives Christ himself neither directly: but only that which receiveth Justification. Whereas it is one Reception, or Act of faith morally taken (Apprehending the entire object) that God hath made the Condition of his Promise. So that to apprehend Christ as the Do-

nor

nor of Glory, *doth as much towards our* Justification, *as apprehending him as* Justifier : *And to Believe in him as our Sanctifier and King, doth as Really conduce to our* Justification, *and as much, as the apprehending him as one that will pardon our sins.* He that believeth shall be saved, *is the simple Scripture doctrine.*
4. *And if all this were not so, yet it is the apprehending of* Christ *as* King *according to them, then, that must be the Pardoning and Justifying act, more then as a Sacrifice: For as Satisfier and a Ransome, he only meriteth our Pardon and Justification. But to pardon by Grant, is unquestionably an act of Soveraignty as such: It being not the pardon of a private injury, but a publick Crime that we have to speak of. And to Justifie by Plea is* Christs *act as an Advocate, and not as a Sacrifice. And to Justifie by sentence is* Christs *act as Judge: So that if their own Doctrine did hold (of the diversifying of our Right by the diversity of the formal reason of the object apprehended) then would it but infallibly prove against them, that it is the Receiving of* Christ *as* King *and* Judge *that is the Act of Pardoning and Justifying faith, more then the Receiving him as a Sacrifice or Ransome.*

FINIS.

To my dearly Beloved, and much Honored and valued friend, Colonel *Sylvanus Taylor*.

Dear Friend,

THough Providence hath long kept me from the sight of your face, yet hath it maintained in me that unfeigned Love to you, which many years ago it kindled. Our Union in *Christ*, and similitude of Spirit continuing; Local distance is no Division. As iniquity in these latter days hath abounded, so hath the love of many waxed cold; And when they grow strange, and cold to *Christ* the Center of Union, no wonder if they do so one to another. Yet as there is in true Saints a Perseverance of all other Graces, so is there of Love to the Brethren. That I am yet no Apostate as to my due affections to your self, I would willingly acquaint you in part by this Compellation, and by directing to you, and to the world with your name, this writing. That I speak to you so openly in the hearing of the world, Custom and Affection are my best excuse. And that yet you may know I do not forget you, I remember about 16 or 17. years ago, as you were wont to express your great dislike of the people called *Antinomians*; (in London and New-England then making head) so you were wont to profess for your self, that you could not hearken or incline to those opinions which

L l   take

The Epistle Dedicatory

take men off from Duty to God, or which open a Gap to Licentiousness. And indeed you may be sure that cannot be of God which is against God : and that which is against Duty is against the Law ; and that which is against the Law, is against the King and Law-giver. Take down Law and Obedience, and you take down God from his Government of the World ; as much as in man lyes. But though Obedience is none where it is denyed, yet those men will find that Law is Law still for all their denyal : and though they can hinder the fulfilling of the precept, because Obedience is Voluntary or none ; yet can they not hinder the fulfilling of the Threatning, because the Penalty is suffered involuntarily. The name of this party was first taken up from their opposition to the Law ; but in my judgement they do more dangerously oppose the Gospel or Law of Grace, then the pure Moral Law. For it is but a few of the wilder and more ignorant sort that do deny all Law, even as to the Regenerate : For that is, as I said, plainly to deny God to be our Governor, that is, to be our God ; and is so bruitish a conceit against the Light of nature, that we need not much fear the prevalency of it very far, while men keep in their wits : But it is only the Law of Moses, or the Law of Works, or the Moral Law, as given to Adam or by Moses, which the more sober sort denyed : but the same Moral Law, as the Law of Christ, they do allow. And this our most Learned opposers of them, think tollerable. For indeed though the Law of nature be still Gods Law, and Christ destroyed it not, but confirmed it, yet it stands not to the same ends, nor on the same terms altogether now as at first it did; that first Promise ceasing upon our first sin, and the remaining threatning (annexed to the Precept) being no longer Remediless, when by the Promise of Grace a Remedy was provided. And it is no great danger to say, that even the Moral Law was abrogated as it was part of the matter of Moses Law, (the parts falling with the whole, and the matter with the form ; not in themselves and absolutely, but As parts, and As that Matter,)

The Epistle Dedicatory.

as long as the same Law is confessed to be still in force, as part of the Redeemers Law. I doubt another opinion of theirs, wherein many better men have by incautelous speeches encouraged them, will do more then this against the Law; I mean, the root, the heart of all Antinomianism, from whence all the rest doth unavoidably follow: and that is the misunderstanding of the nature and use of Chrifts *Death and Obedience, and thinking that* Christ *obeyed or satisfied by suffering, or both, as in our Persons, so that the Law takes it, to all ends and uses, as done by us our selves, as when a man payeth a debt by his Delegate. This opinion, if I understand it, blots out Law and Gospel at one dash. The Gospel, for it is the use of that to be* Gods *instrument of conveying Pardon and Grace in Christ, and bringing us into a Right to the benefits of his suffering, and so to the possession. But if in Law sense it was we our selves, that either fully satisfied or obeyed in Christ, then there needs none of all this, nor is it possible: For the benefit was all ours* ipso facto, *upon the payment. What* Justice *can require more then the* Idem in obligatione, *the very Debt; or can refuse to give a present Acquittance, upon such a payment? It overthrows the Law too; for if we have perfectly fulfilled it already in Christ, it cannot possibly oblige us still to one act of obedience,* pro eo tempore, *for that time which we are supposed to have fulfilled it for; and that is to the end of this life. Nay, if we did but perfectly bear the penalty of the Law in Christ, as some suppose, and that for all the sins of our lives absolutely without exception, then the Law cannot possibly oblige us in this life to Duty, any more then to Punishment: because it doth naturally oblige but disjunctively, either to Obedience or to Punishment, and not to both, for the same time: Nay it would be a contradiction so to fulfill the Penalty of the Law before the Violation, unless that fulfilling be taken in its* esse morale *to come after each particular sin, as it is the penalty of that sin; and if so, we must not be supposed to have done it before. Its the bottom of all our Peace that the*

Ll 2   Lord

The Epistle Dedicatory.

Lord Jesus suffered for our sins, yea in our stead, as a ransom by sacrifice, and hath made satisfaction to Gods Justice: But the misunderstanding of the nature and effects of that satisfaction, hath been the breeder of this unhappy Sect, and almost all the Monsters that they have hatched. The best things corrupted, or abused, are oft worst. Hence is this opinion which I oppose in this Book, that We are Justified before we believe, nay before we sin, nay before we are born, nay that it is an Immanent act in God, (and therefore eternal) and that Infidels are Justified as Infidels. *I hope you need not much argumentation against such opinions as these, the very nature of saving Grace being so flat against them, that a practical experienced Christian doth hear the very mention of them, as nature seeth a dead Corps, or tasteth Gall, or smelleth a stink. The Spirit of Sanctification helpeth more against such unholy Doctrines, then much Learning without it would do. Yet how necessary a clear judgement is in conjunction with Sanctification, and how far some men have been carryed this way, that once were the wonder of the world for their Zeal and Diligence; the sad examples of some of our old friends, now leading men in the Propagation of these Anti-Gospel-fancies, do too fully witness.* England *hath seen within these few last years, the Antinomian Doctrine as effectually brought into practise, and that which seemed but a tollerable speculation, bring forth as real doleful effects, as most ever Nation did on earth: It hath appeared among us, what a power the judgement hath on the Heart and Life, and that bad opinions are not so innocent as some men suppose them: when it bringeth men, and such men, even to be Ranters, Shakers, and I think, possessed with Devils. It was misbelief that made the Papists attempt the blowing up of the Parliament, and that made the Jews kill the Lord of Glory. And indeed our Nations sins are legible Judgements; God hath given in his Testimony against the Pride and Error of Professors in Old* England *as well as New, and that so visibly, that he that runs may read it. For my part I profess the hand of God is so con-*
spicuous

The Epistle Dedicatory.

spicious in both, that it much strengthens my Faith in the main cause of Christianity, by revealing the workings of a special Governing Providence thereabout. I think the Ages to come will be as ready to doubt of the Truth of our Reports of the Monsters in New England, and the multitude of Professors turned Ranters here, and of their carriages and lives, their Extasies and unnatural shakings and other motions of the body, the plain effects of a Diabolical Power, to which they are given up, as men are now ready to doubt of the former Miracles of Christ and his Disciples: And though the beginning of these mens misery, be usually Pride of their supposed Graces, leading them first to separation from their Brethren, and Contempt of their Guides, and next to Anabaptistry, (and even these have been sadly given up to miscarriages) yet seldom are men thus evidently given over to a spirit of madness, till they turn Antinomians and Libertines. When men will so horribly abuse the Son of God, as to make him a friend to sin, that hath done and suffered so much to destroy it, and to make his blood to be the chiefest defensative of transgression, and the price of a Lawless and Licentious life, which was shed to demonstrate Gods hatred of sin, and to purge the souls of men from its Power and Pollution; when men do make those Sacraments which should seal up our Abrenunciation of sin, and our strongest engagement to the Lord in a Covenant of new Obedience, to be Seals of an indulgence, more freely to transgress: when they make the Spirit of holiness to be an unclean Spirit, to take men off from Humiliation, Confession, Praying for Pardon, Laboring for Salvation, &c. In a word, when they turn Gods Grace into meer wantonness and wickedness, and put God in the Likeness of Satan, the Spirit of disobedience and uncleanness; Its no wonder then if God bear no longer, but do appear against them from Heaven; excommunicate them, and deliver them up to Satan, the Spirit of Delusion.

Though the Lord Brooke's book of the Union of the Soul and Truth, contained the spawn of the worst of these abomina-

The Epistle Dedicatory.

tions, yet he hath left it on Record in his Book against Episcopacy, pag. 88, 89, 90, 91. *that that hateful people prophesied of,* 1 Tim. 3..1,2,3,4,5,6. *are not Papists, Socinians, Arminians, or the like, but saith he,* But if I be not much mistaken, somewhat beyond and within all these, that I suppose which *seems to them to be the Spirit,* This I conceive is the Basis of all their Vanity, Pride and Insolence. They have the Spirit, and so know more then all the Learned, Pious, Godly men in the World. They have the Spirit, they cannot sin, they cannot err : They will not pray but when that Spirit moves. Adultery is but an act of the flesh, but they are all Spirit and no flesh; what should these men do with *Natural Affections,* they are all Spirit : In this case, if they be Traytors, High-minded, Heady, &c. who will wonder? what may they not be carryed up to by the imagination of the Spirit? But let them take heed if they have any thing of God in them : let them be wise in this their day, for the time may come when it will be too late. In the mean time, I will say as *Peter* did to *Simon, Pray that (if it be possible) this wickedness of heart may be forgiven.* If we look on the other part of their character, *Having a form of Godliness, but denying the power thereof, creeping into the houses of silly women laden with divers lusts, &c.* How can these be spoken of Arminians, Socinians, or our Prelates? &c: It seems very probable to me, that the Holy-Ghost in this text points out some such as the Family of Love, the Antinomians, and Grindletonians are, if (at least) they are not much belyed. And to these I think every piece of this Character will most properly belong : Yea, and the close of it also, or the issue of that Sect ; They shall proceed no further, for their folly shall be made manifest to all men, which can hardly be understood of Arminianism, or Prelacy, since that in several names, this in several dresses hath been in the world above 1000 years. *So far the Lord* Brook, *who*

saith

The Epistle Dedicatory.

faith pag. 88. *that* This one Heresie the Scripture foretelleth of, which is not yet (perhaps) come; it may be it is now in the birth; sure it is not far off.

Dear Sir, As I bless God that hath confirmed you in his Truth, and kept you fast in these shaking times, and manifested you approved when Heresies did arise; so I must confess my self your debtor for the utmost of my endeavors, for your stability and progress; and if these Papers may be any helps to it, I shall be glad. But see that it be your daily business to live upon that Truth which you have owned: Many thousands are of the true Religion, that are not true to that Religion. Orthodoxness is one of the deluders of hypocrites: As if God would save men meerly because they know their masters will! They must receive the Love of the Truth that would be saved, 2 Thes. 2. 10, 11. *For want of this we have seen so many given up to strong delusions. They that will not let Truth into the Heart, do soonest lose it out of the Head: it likes not a Lodging in the Porch. The great and glorious things of Eternal life, deserve better entertainment then they find with the best. Truth enlighteneth in the Head: but in the heart only doth it enliven, comfort and confirm. To be Religious no further then the brain and tongue, is but to look on the Light, and play with it, which God set them up to work by, and to guide them unto Glory. I am but commending to you that which I have long loved and honored in you, A working Faith, A Practical Religiousness, and a Detestation of those Errors that are destructive to this. That God that hath brought you into this way, and upheld you therein, I doubt not will establish you and preserve you to the end: which is the prayer of him who is,*

*An unfeigned friend to you,
if to any man,*

Kederminster,
March 8. 1653.

Rich. Baxter.

REader, when my Animadversions were in the Press, I received this following Letter, which I therefore annex, though my Papers being gone out of my hand, I cannot review them, to see whether this require any alteration or addition.

R. B.

Reverend Sir,

BEing told to the *Author of the tract* de fidei partibus in Justificatione, *that you were pleased to take notice of it, he wisht earnestly that you would likewise take notice of some errors committed in the Printing, and of one notable omission by the Author.*

The errors are pag. 28. line 16. Leg. promittitur Christum venturum, p. 64. lin. 2. leg. cognitionis, p. 71. lin. 12. & 13. dele quemadmodum in prima reconciliatione, p. 76. lin. 17. leg. ut ut.

The omission is pag. 90. line 5. *after* desertorem, *add this Clause*;
Quinimo Arminianorum dogma Deus elegit credentes *magis rationi consonat, quam illud, quod vulgo orthodoxum existimatur* Deus Justificat fideles: *namque rationi congruit ut ex pluribus promiscuè in medio positis optima quæque eligantur: ac absonum videtur ut qui jam justus est* Justitiâ Christi, *justificetur, & operiatur veste; qui jam à calce ad caput communitus & convestitus est; nam eo quod quis est fidelis jam est justificatus.*

Tis from your humble Servant,

London, March 6. 1654/5.

L. Col.

The Apologetical-Preface.

IF any fuspect me as addicted to Contending, becaufe I have confuted this Learned mans Differtation, who medled not with me; or becaufe I have ufed a language fomewhat fharp, and unpleafant to the guilty, I give them this true account of my doings, both for the work, and for the manner. 1. I muft not write for my felf, but for Chrift and his Truth, and therefore muft do more for their vindication, then if it had been for my own. 2. I fhould hope it will be rather taken the better, becaufe it is no perfonal quarrel that doth inftigate me, and no honor of my own is concerned in the thing. 3. I had newly written a Reply to Mr. *G. Kendal*; by whom the Juftification of Infidels *tantamount* (as he fpeaks) is maintained; and about the very day that I had finifhed it, this Differtation was fent me; which coming in fuch a feafon, and with equal Confidence and Learning, endeavoring the promotion of the fame Caufe that I had been refuting, and carrying it in fome points higher then Mr. *Kendall* had done, I thought it not unneceffary for me to annex a brief Confutation of this alfo. And indeed my thoughts were impelled to prefent action, and I fuddenly fet upon it, with an intent of doing no more, but only to cull out the ftrength of his chief arguments, and let pafs the reft. Whereupon I did at firft pafs over the beginning of his book, and began about the difcovery of his judgement in the main point. But when I had begun, I perceived that it would not be convenient to leave out any part of it: for he might poffibly fay, I left out his ftrength, or that which was neceffary to the clearing of the reft: Whereupon I refolved to take him word by word. 4. My apprehenfions of the danger of that Doctrine, commonly known by the name of *Antinomian*, or *Libertine*, are fuch as will not fuffer me to make light of it, or patiently to fit ftill in filence whileft the Gofpel is fubverted by it, and the fouls of poor people enticed to perdition. I confidently think that the main fubftance of the Gofpel

[11]   is

is by too neceſſary conſquence overthrown by their miſtakes, and that our difference with moſt of them about the Law, is but the ſmaller part. 5. We were never ſo much called out to contradict this way as now. Formerly it was only a few giddy ignorant ſouls that went this way, that had ſcarce parts or intereſt, or plauſible pretence to do any great harm: and moſt of their lives were a ſhame to their Doctrine. The Pelagian and Semi-Pelagian faction did get many learned abettors; but the main body of this party conſiſted of the illiterate: But now (to the grief of the ſober and Godly) men are riſen up to defend this way of darkneſs, who have ſomething more of Learning and Piety to Credit and Countenance the Cauſe that they engage in: And too far hath it already taken with many well-meaning leſs judicious men. 6. This Cauſe hath ever tended to worſe, and led men into ſuch wayes, as have made them the grief of their friends, and the great ſcourge of the Church of God: New *England* can give you a ſad Teſtimony of this; See Mr. *Welds* Book of the riſe and fall of Antinomianiſm in New *England*. 7. In which Book, (and by full Teſtimony from men of Godlineſs, Credit, and Authority in that Land) I underſtand ſo much of Gods ſtrange Judgements from heaven againſt that Party, that I dare not over-look or forget it; nor make light of thoſe Errors which God makes not light of. My wit and learning may be much leſs then ſome of theirs; and therefore men may ſay, Why ſhould we not ſooner believe them then you? But as they diſpute againſt the Sun, even the moſt expreſs Word of God; ſo when the God of Heaven ſhall ſet in and determine the Cauſe by ſuch a miraculous Teſtimony, or do ſo much towards the determination as there was done, it muſt be a *Pharaoh* that muſt ſhut his eyes and go on. No wonder if the ſtrain of the New-*England* Preachers, (as *Hooker, Shephard*, &c.) be ſo contrary to the Antinomian ſtrain, when the hand of heaven hath ſo interpoſed in their Controverſie! But of this I have ſpoken in my Book of Baptiſm, as noting Gods Judgements on both theſe Sects: But for the dangerous tendency of their Doctrine, there is no compariſon between them: (I mean ſuch as only deny the Baptiſm of Infants, and theſe:) I ſpeak not all this, as putting the Title of Libertine or Antinomian on this Learned man: For ſeeing it is but ſome of their Doctrine which he maintaineth here, for ought I know he may not ſee the Concatenation, and ſo may be innocent in all the reſt: But this part is of the nature of the reſt.

The Apologetical-Preface.

rest. 8. I hope this Learned man cannot be offended with my writing for the thing, confidering that I do no more againſt him, then he hath firſt done againſt his own Brother. If Brother write againſt Brother, a ſtranger may interpoſe, with leſs appearance of any defect or breach of Chriſtian Moderation or Love. 9. Yea he confuted his Brothers Private Letters, and I confute but his Publick writings, which endanger the ſafety of the Church and Truth: I confeſs, if I had been of his minde, I would rather have made ſome writing already publick (of which he might have had enough) the ſubject of my confutation, then the private Letters of my own brother. 10. Yea, he knew that it was his brothers; but I knew not that this was his. 11. Yea, I hope this Learned man will rather give me thanks, then be offended: For I wrote for him intentionally, when I wrote againſt him actually. Little did I know that *Ludiomæus Colvinus*, was *Ludovicus Molinæus*. The very name of *Cyrus Molinæus*, as being the Son of that man (*Peter Molinæus*) whoſe name muſt ſtill be venerable to us all, did inſtigate me to his Vindication. Beſides his meer relation to the late learned *Rivet*: The names of theſe two men will be honorable while Chriſt hath a Reformed Church in Europe. 12. Laſtly, I ſaw more ſaid for the Juſtification of unbelievers, and againſt Juſtification by Faith, in this Book which I confute, then I had before ſeen in ſuch order, and in ſo narrow a room; and therefore I thought that the confutation of it might not be unuſeful, but might ſerve inſtead of the confutation of many, eſpecially it being written in ſuch modeſt language, which would occaſion no wordy altercations or contentions. Thus I have given you my Apology for this undertaking.

Next for the manner of it, I have two queſtions to ſatisfie: 1. Why I anſwered not more tenderly. 2. Why I anſwered a Latine Book in Engliſh. 1. For the former, the very truth is, in theſe two anſwers, 1. I apprehend great evil and dangerous tendency in the Doctrine which I reſiſt; and therefore durſt not ſpeak of it too eaſily or favorably. 2. As I have ſaid, I knew not the Author till it was too late: but rather by my zeal, for the name of *Molinæus*, was more ſharpened againſt any adverſary of that name. An Engliſhman, I quickly perceived he was not; and I ſuſpected *Colvinus* was a counterfeit name: but this was fitter matter to raiſe jealouſies of a ſtranger then Reverence;

[11 2] eſpecially

The Apologetical-Preface.

especially in these times. No reason therefore can accuse my sharpest passages as guilty of any disrespect to the learned Author of this Dissertation, when I knew not who he was. And indeed I have yet no such certainty, as flatly to conclude that he is the undoubted Author: but lest any think I feign it, and so wrong him, I shall only give them my (too late) Intelligence, which was in two Letters. The one was in these words, *Dum Londini itinerans diversabar, occurrit mihi obviam* Ludiomæus Colvinus, *simulque Oedipus adstitit qui nomen illud Anagrammaticôs obscuratum luce donavit, ac me certiorem fecit in propriam formam resolvendo literas,* Ludovicum Molinæum *in re Hystoricâ apud Oxoniensis professorem significare. Nec sine causa certe nomini suo consultum iri studuit, à tam fœdi Erroris Maculâ: hodie domum, cum Deo, reversas raptim perlegi: Et quantum mihi sapit palatum, plus Veritatis & Theologiæ sanioris sentio, in* Molinæi *fragmentis, quàm inter omnes* Colvini *apparatus.* The other was in these words, Ludiomæus Colvinus *is only (transversis Literis)* Ludovicus Molinæus, *who is the very Author*——— I think I need not add, that he is a Frenchman, Petri Molinæi *filius, &c.* the rest contained a Commendation of the Author, and his former writings against Episcopacy (against Bishop *Hall*) and that this *de Justificatione* was against his own Brother *Cyrus Molinæus,* living in *York-shire.* And I think he that wrote this, did well know it to be true.

The second thing *de modo,* that some may demand, is why I confute him in English? The true answer is this: I verily thought when I begun to have written but two or three sheets against him, and annexed them to that against Mr. *Kendal* then going to the Press; and it being to be bound with an English Book, it would not have been tollerable to do it in Latin: Besides, it is the benefit of Englishmen that I intend; and I hear not of any part of the world so much tainted with the Doctrines which I gainsay, as *England* is. That none may blame me for unfaithfulness in Translating him, I desire them that understand the Latin tongue, to take his own words in his book, and then they need not trust to my translation: Yet, though I did it very hastily, I suppose I have not done it unfaithfully. I have translated it all, except the Epistle to Mr. *Sadler.*

I intended to have added in the end, several Arguments more then he answereth here, against the Justification of Unbelievers, and as many to prove that it is not *in foro Conscientiæ* that we are said so oft in Scripture to be Justified by Faith: but being called to another writing,

where

The Apologetical-Preface.

where I must perform that, I will omit it here. I desire the Reader also to understand, that the difference betwixt us, and those that are for Justification before Faith, doth not lye about Gods Decrees, or Immanent acts: but we prove that Justification is none such. We do maintain as well as they that God Decreed from eternity to Call, Justifie, Sanctifie and Save all his Chosen: and thus far he loved them before they believed: Had he not loved them before, he had not given Christ for them, nor given them Faith. But as there is very great difference between this Love, and that wherewith he Loveth them, when they are in Christ by Faith, so this is not Iustification, but a Purpose of Justifying hereafter, which plainly intimates that men were not then Justified. As the world was not created really, when it was but created in Gods Decree, nor is it actually now burnt with fire, because it is burnt in Gods Decree: for to be *Created*, or *burnt* in *Decree*, is but this much: God hath Decreed to create, or *burn* the world; and so it is the object of that Decree, but not of the act decreed: but contrarily it is a certain argument that the thing Decreed is not yet done; so is it in the present case. It is certain that man is neither Pardoned, Justified, Sanctified or Glorified, who is but yet Decreed to be so; for how can God be said to Decree to do that hereafter, which is done already? It is not therefore Gods *Nolle Punire* simply that we enquire after, but his actual pardon or discharge as Legislator and Judge. This much I thought meet to add, because some that are against us, do bear their Reader in hand, as if we denyed Gods Eternal Decrees and Love to his Elect; and as if there were no mean between their way, and the way of the Pelagians.

Reader, though I meddle with no Controversie but with great reluctancy and distaste, and am so weary of it, that I was once resolving never to meddle in that way more, yet I am forced to suspend such Resolutions, and so I suppose thou wilt approve my thoughts upon these two Considerations. 1. As mans Intellect naturally abhorreth error, and a sanctified man doth doubly abhor error in things Divine, so doth he most of all abhor the Corruption of the Vitals. and those errors which have a potent influence upon the heart and Life, as these which I oppose most evidently have. Mistakes we all have, and shall have: but the more they stop the motions of heart and hand, the more dangerous are they. 2. As I have been long grieved at the great Error of almost all the Churches, in extending too far those necessary Doctrines in which all Believers may have brotherly Communion and Concord,

[ll 3]

Concord, and making controverted points of lower moment to seem undoubted Truths, of so great necessity, that we must defame and cast off those that own them not, and so every one must needs reduce all others to his opinion, as if his judgement were the infallible standard of verity, and so we have proved too proud and uncharitable, while we would be *Orthodox Overmuch*; so I am much afraid we are now like to fall into the other extream (perhaps God intends it for the cure of the former); and that the gap of Liberty will be for a while (and but a while) too wide: And I doubt the suppression of error will be so far cast upon the Ministers alone, as if it did not belong to the Magistrate, that it will be necessary for us to do the more. And if it so fall out, I hope the Lord will raise up Divines of accurate judgement, and able to defend his Truth against all gainsayers, and will give them Resolution with boldness and diligence to go through the work: Especially, I advise my Brethren, to prepare their weapons against the Papists, and Socinians, and Antinomians, above all other Sects: and to Associate speedily, and carry on all their work in Unity, if ever they will succeed. But the great thing that I foresee and lament, is this: while necessity compels Ministers to study, preach and write against errors, the practical part will be neglected; and let them do what they can, experience will soon tell them, that Controversie will lamentably cool their better zeal, and hinder the exercise of Faith and Love, and keep their hearts much out of Heaven, and from the study of themselves; and such preaching wil starve up the power of Godliness in their hearers: and then ungodliness will again draw in errors, while we were laboring to keep them out. The Lord teach us therefore to take his Work together, and so to do the lesser, as never to neglect the greater; but still to regard the Heart and Life.

The

The Contents.

Chap. 1. *The Epistle of* Cyrus Molinæus.
§. 1. L. Colvinus *charge against Papists, Arminians, Amyraldus and the Fathers, and our Divines, that make Faith a necessary cause of Justification. The necessity of Faith is not from any insufficiency of Christs merits.* L. Colvinus *judgement laid down; after* Molinæus *his judgement. My own judgement about this matter of Justification at large in 20 Conclusions.* —— *Wherein is shewed the several sorts of Justification, and of Remission, with the causes: the difference between Remission and Justification: the nature and sorts of Imputation. How Christs satisfaction is ours. Of our twofold Righteousness. Of the office of Faith in each sort of Justification. Which is the Justification by Faith which Scripture means.*

§. 3. *If to be Justified by Faith, were but to be manifested Justified, then we might be said to be Elected or Redeemed by Faith, because we are manifested by it to be Elected and redeemed.* 2 Thes. 2. 13. *abused by the Dissertor. Redemption and Election have divers significations.*

§. 4. *Faith how put for* Christ *the object:* Calvin *vindicated.*
§. 5. *Our Divines call not Faith* Justification.
§. 6. *They confound not Gods Act with the Patefaction to conscience.*
§. 7. *We are as properly pardoned by Faith, as Justified by Faith.*
§. 8. *Whether Faith enter the definition of Justification?*
§. 9. *Faith necessary to our participation of Christs righteousness.*
§. 10. *Faith and Obedience, conditions and means of salvation, and not only signs. The dangerous tendency of the contrary Doctrine.*
§. 11. *To be made Sons, is not only to know that we were Sons before.*
§. 12. 2 Thes. 2. 13. *Vindicated.*
§. 13. 1 Pet. 1. 2. 1 Thes. 1. 3. *Vindicated.*
§. 15. *Regeneration what, and in what order wrought. Works what?*
§. 16. *The avoiding of Arminianism, no sufficient reason to deny Justification by faith. How many wayes faith is no work. Of a twofold righteousness. How far faith it self is imputed for righteousness. The Habit of faith, how far Justifying.*
§. 17. *Works what, and how excluded by* Paul. *Imperfections of sincere Obedience no cause of despair.*
§. 18. *The formal reason of Faiths interest in Justification.*
§. 19. 2 Pet. 1. 3. *Vindicated.*
§. 20. Christs *death makes not means of our participation for pardon needless.*
Chap. 2. §. 1. *Its necessary to our first Assent, that* Christ *dyed for us in particular, that his satisfaction be for all as to the sufficiency. Faith not meerly Passive.*
§. 2. *Of his second act of faith.*
§ 3. *Several misinterpreted texts vindicated.*
§. 4. *Faith pertains to remission: Works attest it.*
§. 5. *All Grace given through* Christ, *supposeth not Justification. Gods Love, Hatred, Reconciliation, what?*
§. 6. *What Promise is fulfilled in the giving of faith.*
Chap. 3. §. 1. *The Dissertor will give the sense of Scripture, but not be an Interpreter.*

§. 2.

The Contents.

§. 2. Rom. 3. 22. *Vindicated*.

§. 3. Rom. 3. 24. *Vindicated*. §. 4. Verse 25. *Vindicated*. §. 5. Verse 27. 31.

§. 6. Verse 26. *Vindicated*; what *Justifying the ungodly* is.

§. 7. Rom. 5. 18. *Vindicated*. *Christs formal Justification not ours*. None *actually sinners* or *Just before they exist*. Calvins *Exposition* of Rom. 5. 18. for *common Grace*.

§. 8. *Christ satisfied not Legally in our person, nor have we right to his righteousness before Faith*.

§. 9. Rom. 5. 1. *vindicated*.

§. 10. Gal. 2. 6. *vindicated*.

§. 11. Phil. 3. 9. *with* Calvins *Exposition vindicated*.

§. 12. Act. 13. 3, 8. *vindicated*. The *Dissertors gross abuse of Scripture*.

§. 13. and 14. *More of his abuse opened*.

§. 15. *The Dissertors false and immodest defence of Popery*.

§. 16. Iam. 2. God hath chosen the rich in Faith, *proves not Election upon foreseen Faith*.

Chap. 4. §. 1. *Imputation, Remission, Justification, how far one*.

§. 2. *Christs righteousness but the cause of ours*.

§. 3. *Whether Remission be the whole of our Justification ? whether Christ give us any greater filicity then was promised to Adam ? whether a further merit of Christ, beside satisfaction, were necessary to purchase us Justification or Salvation?*

§. 4. *Whether all Justified by one act ? and when*.

§. 5. *How far God was reconciled immediately on Christs satisfaction : and how far to all men?*

§. 6. and 7. 2 Cor. 5. 21. and Heb. 10. 10. *vindicated*.

§. 8. Col. 2. 13, 14. 2 Cor. 5. 18. *vindicated. More of immediate Reconciliation on Christs death : and whether pardon have degrees*.

§. 9. *The Dissertor proved not perfectly blessed. Pardon not perfect in this life, fully proved. Judgement is more then bare Declaration*.

§. 10. *Of* Rom. 5. 19. *All men not guilty at the time of* Adams *sin*.

§. 11. *Of* Ioh. 3. 18.

§. 12. *Of* Ioshuahs *changed raiment*, Zach. 3.

§. 13. Amesius *vindicated*.

§. 14. Piscator *vindicated*.

§. 15. Rollock *vindicated*.

§. 16. *The Dissertors self-contradictions*.

§. 17. Twiss *for the Dissertor*.

§. 18. *Christ took not sin from the sinner, meerly by taking them on himself*.

§. 19. *Justification not an Immanent act. The Dissertors contradictions*.

§. 20. *Pardon what, and of how many sorts ?* Nolle Punire, *not Justification by Faith*.

§. 22. *If Union with Christ went before faith, it proves not that Justification doth so. Union with Christ of divers sorts, Union with Christ is not before Faith, proved by 8 anguments. All Grace is not from Christ, as from the Head to Members, but some to make them members. How our life is in Christ. Our life of Holyness did never exist in Christ. The Holy-Ghost, how given us; and how dwels in us.* Ioh. 15. 5. Gal. 5. 22. *vindicated*.

§. 23. *Of Infants*.

§. 24. *How far other Graces, as well as Faith, go before Union with Christ*.

§. 25.

The Contents.

§. 25. *Justification of Infidels, an ill way to confute Arminians.* The Dissertor wrongs Christ in his Kingly, Prophetical office, and Priestly Intercession, by pretending to honor his sufferings: yea wrongeth his death, if he deny that it procured sin to be Remissible. Full satisfaction pardoneth not immediately. The Dissertor it makes Justification by Faith to be Arminianism.

§ 26. *Giving Faith is a Decree of executive Remission, but not the full proper Gospel Remission.* Luk. 1. 77. abused by the Dissertor. Whether David were pardoned before Repentance.

§ 27. *The false Doctrine, that all true Repentance proceeds from the knowledge of Remission, concludes all those impenitent that want this knowledge, and leaves their comfort by ordinary rational means Impossible.* Luk. 7. 38. 1 Ioh. 4. 9. vindicated.

§. 28. *Absolute Justification not proved by Absolute Vocation.* The Dissertor maintains that God Justifieth the ungodly, qua tales, and consequently All the ungodly, and only the ungodly. His great abuse of Gal. 3. 8. to prove that God Justifieth Heathens. His abuse of Rom. 5. 6. Col. 1. 21. *Justification in Scripture is used more restrainedly then reconciliation or remission.*

§. 29. *The Dissertor makes dying for sinners, an Immanent act of God.* Proved that Christ dyed to purchase us pardon and reconciliation, and not only conversion, that we may feel that we were before pardoned or reconciled. *None reconciled before they fall out.*

Chap. 5. **§. 1.** *Reconciliation of God to man, and man to God, opened: some texts vindicated.*

§ 2. *Whether the Holy-Ghost and Sanctification, go before Faith? Our concord and discord in this.*

The Dissertor saith we are Sons by grace, given in Christ before the world began.

§. 4. Of Ioh. 3. 16. 1 Ioh. 4. 10.

§. 6. *Of Justification in conscience.*

§. 7. *Religion lyeth not all in Comfort.*

§. 8. *The necessity of Faith and Obedience.* How much their description of a Christian state who place almost all in comfort and feeling, doth differ from the Scripture description.

§. 10. 12. *How sanctification is put before Justification.*

§. 11. *What kinde of Condition Faith is.*

§. 14. *Repentance a Condition of pardon as well as Faith.*

§. 15. *His mistake about Conditions.*

§. 16. *Remission neverthelesse from Faith, because from Union with Christ.*

§. 17. *The reward never the more of debt because Faith is the Condition, then if the gift had been Absolute.*

§. 19. *No ground of Assurance of pardon can by any man be produced, but on the performance of the Condition: No ground for the first act of Faith in the Dissertors way.*

Chap. 6. **§. 1.** *Faith enters the definition of Justification.*

§. 2. *Faith a Legal, not natural Condition.*

§. 3. *Dr. Hammond vindicated from the Dissertors mistakes: The desparate consequent of his Doctrine, that a wicked man and Infidel, qua talis, is Justified.*

§. 4. *The Dissertors unhappy reconciliation of Paul and Iames: Neither Paul nor Iames do treat of meer Justification in conscience or before men, proved.*

§. 6. *A plain and brief explication of the reason of Faiths interest in Justification.*

Mm §. 7. 8. 9.

The Contents.

§. 7. 8. 9. His reasons against the common Doctrine of Faiths Justifying.
§. 11. The conveniency of the Covenants Conditions.
§. 13. Bucanus, Keckerman, Ursin vindicated.
Chap. 7. §. 1. The Dissertors vain confidence.
§. 2. Rom. 8. 30. His exposition makes all to be damned that have not had Assurance that they are righteous.
§. 3. That Rom. 8. 30. neglecteth not the order of grace. 1 Cor. 6. 11. 2 Thes. 2. 13. 1 Tim. 1. 9. 2 Pet. 1. 10 explained.
§. 4. The text threatning non remissien in this life, or that to come, how meant, and how against the Dissertor.
§. 5. Many truths destructive to Antinomian sin, here confessed by the Dissertor.
§. 6. A nen ens no subject of Justification. Six acts of Gods understanding and will mentioned, none of which seems to be it that the Dissertor calls Justification. How far our sin was imputed to Christ before his Incarnation. How far Christ was guilty of our sin, and by what obligation.
§. 7. He undertakes the confutation of Scharpius Arguments against the Papists for Justification by Faith alone.
§. 8. 9. 10. 11. Scharpius arguments defended.
§. 12. Calvin and Rivet vindicated.
§. 13. 14. 15. More of Scharpius arguments briefly defended.
§. 16. Christ intercedeth for pardon and right to Life. None properly Heirs while Infidels or unborn, proved. Christs Intercession vindicated.
Chap. 8. §. 1. Zanchy vindicated, as being against the Justification of Infidels.
§. 2. 3. Alstedius and Tossanus vindicated.
§. 4. Twiss and Maccovius confessed to be for the Justification of Infidels. Their great Argument answered, Except God were reconciled to us, and had pardoned us, he would not give us Faith.
§ 5. Pemble proved in his Treat. of Justification, to be against the Justification of unbelievers, though before in his Vind. grat. he was for it.
§. 6. Mr. Walkers testimony for Justification of unbelievers, backed with weak reason. Polanus, Chamier, &c. confessed to speak sometime the same way.

The

The Fragment of an Epistle, which was the cause of this Dissertation.

I Had not as yet heard of this new Controversie about the nature of Justification: I may freely say, that it is not of so great moment, that for it your Churches ought to be dashed one against another: For if it be more neerly examined, it consisteth more in words then in Doctrine: some say, that Faith goes before Justification. Others on the contrary assert that Justification goes before Faith: In my judgement it is easie to agree the Dissenters; for as there are divers acts and motions of faith, some go before, and some follow Justification. For the act of Faith which accompanyeth Repentance, and whereby we implore the mercy of God and the Remission of sins, and fly to the death and righteousness of Christ, doth without doubt, go before Justification: But that act of Faith, whereby we acquiesce in the perswasion of forgiveness, doth follow Justification, and is an effect of the Holy Ghost, which sealeth up to the Believer the promises of the Gospel, and beareth witness that he is the Son of God, and that through Christ, his sins are pardoned to him; whence ariseth Peace and Tranquility of conscience, *Rom.* 5. *Being Justified by Faith, we have peace with God.* Moreover, that this controversie between you, may be composed, it were necessary to determine what is meant by Justification. Our Divines acknowledge that this name of Justification, is forensick, and that in this question, it signifieth an act of God the Judge, whereby he pronounceth Righteous, and Absolveth from sin, one that is ungodly and a sinner in himself, and obnoxious to his wrath, of his meer grace, for the perfect obedience of Christ, received by Faith. This I think is a true definition of Justification, as I have almost in the same words taken it out of *Rom.* 3. 22. &c. And this Justification is fitly considered in three distinct seasons: 1. In Gods Decree: 2. When God doth actually pardon the believer: 3. In the life to come, when the sentence of Justification shall be pronounced in the last Judgement. *God be merciful to him in that day,* 2 *Tim.* 1. 18. and *Act.* 3. 19. *Repent and be converted, that your sins may be blotted out when the times of refreshing shall come from the presence of the Lord, and he shall send Jesus Christ, who before was preached to you.* Of the first and third season, there can be no doubt, but that Justification in decree doth go before actual Faith, and Justification at the last day, follow it. But if you consider Justification as it is

actually

actually bestowed on the believing sinner, somewhat (as I said) of Faith goes before Justification, and somewhat follows after it.

But as far as I can gather by your words, you do, with Dr. *Twiss*, seem to acknowledge no other justification; then that in Decree ; to wit, that free love of God, whereby he embraced us in Christ from eternity, and whereby he decreed to absolve us from sin, for his death and obedience ; and you seem to disallow of the common distinction of *the Decree, and the execution of the Decree*. But to me this distinction seemeth very good, and speaking properly. The Decree of justifying is not justification ; no more then the Decree of Calling is Vocation ; and the free Love of God whereby he loved us in Christ before the foundations of the world, doth differ from Justification and Vocation, as the cause from the effects, the spring head from the streams : and when the Scripture doth so expresly distinguish them, *Rom.* 8. *Whom he foreknew*, &c. (*virf.* 29, 30.) in that Golden Chain, it seems to me, they ought not to be confounded : And as oft as the Scripture speaks of actual Remission of sins, wherein, as you confess, consisteth our justification, it referreth only to two seasons, to this life, and to that to come; *Mat.* 12. *It shall not be forgiven in this world, nor in the world to come*. And reason confirmeth this : for properly, sins are forgiven, when they may be punished, and the Penalty is Relaxed to him: but only in this life and that to come may they be punished : therefore only in these two seasons may they be remitted. But if sins must be considered only as *forgiven*, and not as *to be forgiven*, and Faith, as you say, should justifie us only * relatively, and by revealing to us that our sins are forgiven, then in vain should Christ and his Apostles exhort us so frequently, to seek of God forgiveness of sin ; and a believer who hath once had a true sense of his Reconciliation and Justification, should no more have need for the time to come to implore Gods mercy even for his most grievous sins. Do you think that *David* before his adultery and murder was not justified, and had the true sense of Gods Love ? To what purpose then after those new sins, were so many groans and tears ? If any man then had been tainted with *Twisses* Doctrine, might he not deservedly have suggested to him, *Why groanest thou fool ? Why beggest thou for mercy and the washing away of thy sins ? Knowest thou not that all thy sins were blotted out long ago ?* And if your opinion were true, Repentance which follows Faith, that sorrow according to God, that trembling and fear, with which the Apostle *Phil.* 2. would have us to work out our salvation, should not be Dispositions to salvation,

* *I conjecture it is false Printed for* revelative.

tion, saving, and acceptable to God, but rather the sins of Faith, weaknesses, foolish doubtings of Gods Love and our salvation. And if the Remission of sin were only the feeling of sin as remitted, why doth the Scripture never exhort us to ask this feeling, but to ask Remission? Certainly when *Peter* said to *Simon Magus*, (not despairing of his salvation) *Repent of that thy wickedness, and pray God, if perhaps the thought of thy heart may be forgiven thee*; he did not speak of Justification as past, but as future.

I think therefore that we must believe, that God doth indeed and properly Justifie a believer and forgive him his sins, as often as after true Repentance and Faith in Christs merit, he giveth to his conscience assurance that such and such a sin is remitted, saying to him as Christ did to the Paralitick man, '*Be of good cheer, Son, thy sins are forgiven thee*; and that the act of justification is reiterated, as oft as the merciful God by his Spirit pronounceth this judgement to the conscience. For seeing, as we said, Iustification is properly the judgement of God whereby he pronounceth righteous him that believeth in Christ, through Christs righteousness, why are you unwilling to call this private sentence of absolution, which God pronounceth to every believer, by the name of Justification? and when we have also the Devil and our consciences for Accusers, and Christ for our Advocate, is it not also necessary that we have God for our Iudge, to absolve us from those accusations? as the Apostle saith, Rom. 8. *Who shall lay any thing to the charge, &c. it is God that Justifieth*; seeing therefore the Scripture speaketh of Iustification as of a thing present; and which is still given us, and that God justifieth us at present, why abhor we the stile of Scripture?

You will say, that our sins were forgiven formerly in Christs death, and that God was reconciled to us in Christ-dying, and accepted his sacrifice for the payment of our debts. But the answer is easie: For we must not confound the Impetration of salvation and remission of sins, with the Application of it: And although we do not with the Arminians extend the Impetration to more then the application, yet is it certain that they are things different both in time and nature: The Impetration was made by Christ-dying sixteen hundred years ago, the application is made daily by the Holy-Ghost: the Impetration was made on the Cross; the Application in the heart of the Believer. And as the sacrifice was one thing, and the sprinkling of the blood another, under the Law; so under the Gospel, Christs sacrifice whereby he obtained for us Reconciliation and Iustification, is one thing, and actual Iustification whereby God by his Spirit refresheth (or sprinkleth) the consciences by Christs blood, is another thing. Moreover, if in Christs death our sins had been actually forgiven, and we actually Iustified, what should Christs intercession, and the presentation of his sacrifice now profit us? Is it only, that we might have the sense? the giving of the Spirit would have been sufficient (for that): But the Scripture speaks more excellently and efficaciously of Christs Intercession, and refers it not only to *feeling*, but to true and actual Iustification, saying, that Christs blood speaketh better things then the blood of *Abel*; and that this blood is still fresh and living; and that because Christ alway liveth and intercedeth for the faithful, he can therefore perfectly save all that come to God by him.

This difference of Impetration, from Application, and Iustification, appeareth by the Scriptures diversity of speech: for when it speaks of Christs death, it saith, that Christ dyed for enemies and sinners; but when (it speaks) of Iustification, which is the Application of that death, it saith that God forgiveth sins to the penitent and Believer: Nor did I ever yet finde any place in Scripture, where it is said that any mans sins were forgiven before he believe, and that a sinner that is yet impenitent is Iustified. *Paul* saith indeed, *Rom.* 4. that God Iustifieth the ungodly; but in the same verse, he tels us who the ungodly one is, that is, *He that believeth in him that Iustifieth the ungodly*; [* *That is, unjustifiable.*] that is, one * ungodly in himself, but righteous through Christs obedience, accepted by Faith. The Apostle also saith, *Rom.* 5. *That when we were enemies, we were reconciled*: but in the same place he manifestly distinguisheth the Reconciliation which we obtained in the death of Christ, from *saving from his wrath*; whence it appeareth that the Apostle by *Iustification and Reconciliation* doth mean the Impetration and Acquisition of Remission of sins. For *to be saved from wrath*, and *to be absolved from sin*, is altogether the same thing. *If when we were enemies, we were reconciled to God by the death of his Son, much more being reconciled, shall we be saved by his life.*

Hence it appeareth how infirm Dr. *Twisses* Objection is, *Faith is Gods Gift, and proceedeth from God as propitious and appeased by Christ: therefore we were Iustified before Faith.* For after the same manner might it be objected, *Saving Vocation is the gift of God appeased by Christ, therefore we were Iustified before we were called*: which yet the Apostle denyeth, *Rom.* 8. *Whom he called, them he justified.* But the answer is very easie: for God being appeased in Christ-dying, doth bestow on his Elect the effects of that Reconciliation, after many Ages, calling them, and Iustifying them in his own time.

This order therefore do I conceive in the Oeconomie of salvation, which the Apostle teacheth, *Rom.* 8. *Whom he foreknew, &c.* For God

from

The Fragment of an Epistle, &c.

from eternity, of his meer good pleasure, did choose certain persons to himself whom he would save; for them he sent Christ into the world: to them, being reconciled by the death of Christ, that he might bestow on them the salvation which decreed, in time he called them, touching their hearts with true Repentance; the penitent sinner flyeth to Christ by faith; he imploreth Gods mercy: Christ intercedeth for the sinner: he offereth the price of his sacrifice: God the Father heareth: he accepteth his Sons Intercession: and on the beholding of * him, he pardoneth the sins of the Penitent and Believer: and this Remission he sealeth to the heart by the Spirit, whence comes the Peace and Joy of Faith. *Or, it.*

These things being thus determined, as it seemeth to me, according to Scripture, I cannot consent to your positions, that Justification absolutely goes before Faith; and that Faith is of not the definition of justification, and that Faith doth only Justifie us, by revealing: for though we think not that we are Iustified by Faith formally and meritoriously, as if by its own Virtue it did Iustifie us before God, or merit absolution, or, as the Arminians teach that God did accept Faith, as an Evangelical and Imperfect obedience, for that rigorous and exact obedience of the Law: Yet doth it Iustifie us, as the Evangelical Condition, without which we should not be Justified, and as an Instrument whereby we apply to our selves the death of Christ, by the vertue and merit whereof we are Justified. And that Faith and Repentance are prerequisite Conditions to Justification and Remission of sins, is most certain from Scripture: *Act.* 10. *To him give all the Prophets Witness, that Whosoever believeth, &c. Act.* 13. *Be it known to you, that by him who ever believeth is Justified from all things, from which,* &c. *Rom.* 10. as he maketh this the Condition of the Law, *He that doth these things shall live in them*; on the other side he placeth this as the Condition of the Gospel, *If thou believe, thou shalt be saved.* Therefore even as man had been Justified, if he had fulfilled the former Condition, so also is it necessary that the Condition of the Gospel being fulfilled, the man be Justified; though not by the Vertue or Merit of that fulfilling. This being so determined, it is past doubt that Faith goes before Justification: for in every Covenant the Conditions must be performed, before the things promised in the Covenant be bestowed. Moreover, there is no true Repentance without Faith. But Repentance goes before Justification, and is a necessary Condition of the pardon of sins. *Act.* 3. *Repent and be converted, that your sins may be blotted out.* Moreover, Faith doth necessarily accompany saving Vocation: but Vocation doth at least, in order of nature, go before Justification. *Whom he called, them he justified,* Rom. 8. therefore Faith, &c. Besides, the Apostle *Rom.* 3. doth expresly teach, that a believing man is the object of Justification: *verse* 20.

Justifying

The Fragment of an Epistle, &c.

Justifying him that believeth in Jesus. And therefore the Righteousness by which we are Justified, is called, verse 22. *The Righteousness by the Faith of Jesus Christ unto all, and upon all them that believe.* Whence it is plain, that you err from the truth, when you say that Faith is not of the Definition of Justification. I will say more: Though the Decree of Justifying do go before actual Justification, yet in the Decree, the Consideration of Faith goes first: because God hath decreed to pardon sin only to the penitent and believer: this the Apostle teacheth verse 25. saying, *That God set forth Christ a propitiation through Faith.* For God in the same order Decreeth to execute things, in which he afterwrad executeth them: but according to the Apostle, he calleth before he Justifieth, *Rom.* 8. therefore in the Decree he first considered man as called and believing, before, as Justified. Add to this, that if Justification did go before Faith and Repentance, God should forgive sin to the unbeliever and impenitent, contrary to Scripture, *He that believeth on the Son, hath everlasting life; he that believeth not in the Son, shall not see Life, but the wrath of God abideth on him:* But the matter following so easily, carryeth me away too far.

R. B. I Thought it necessary to translate this Epistle, and put it in the beginning. (though the answerer puts it in the end.) 1. That the Answerers words may be the better understood. 2. For the much excellent usefull matter which it containeth. And indeed it sufficiently confuteth Justification from eternity (though it is so Antichristian a Doctrine, that much more may deservedly be said against it.) But yet, I must desire the Reader, not to suppose, that I approve every word in it. 1. I think he speaks in the beginning (its like with a reconciling intent) too gently and favourably of this monstrous Doctrine, and makes the difference less then it is. 2. His great oversight, in my Judgement is, that he only takes notice of Sentential Justification, which is the act of God, as Judge, (besides the decree, which is no Justification,) and not at all of Legal or Testamentary Justification, which is the act of God as Legislator, and Covenanter, and free Donor. It is true, that sentential Justification is most strictly and fully so called: but its as true that Legal or Covenant Justification, is true Justification also, yea and always goes before the former, and is that which the Scripture most commonly means, when it speaks of Justification by faith. Divines call it, Constitutive Justification. 3. And hence this learned man is driven to place Justification in the Spirits pronouncing a sentence in our Consciences, which I have elsewhere proved largely to be a great mistake, and of ill tendency. 4. He takes notice of the Application of the impetrated benefits, by the Spirit, but not of that Application, whereby the Gospel, as Gods deed of gift, or Christs Testament, doth confer right to the Believer; which is the Application by which Relative mercies are given. Yet after he distinguisheth between pardon, and the sense and sealing of it, which follows. 5. I conjecture that he is of the same mind as I, about faiths interest in our Justification. For though he call it an Instrument, it seems he means by Instrument, but a fit receiving means or act; It being ord a ry with Divines to use that term, many continue it, but in a Metaphorical or improper sence. For this learned man doth first place its conditional office, and then the instrumental, seeming to make that but the material aptitude to the former: some other following expressions also intimate as much. 6. I consent not to what he addeth about Gods decreeing things in the order that he executeth them, unless the meaning had been only this, He decreeth to execute them, in the order in which he doth execute them. But in the main the Epistle is such as shews the Author Judicious and Orthodox, and saith more then all the Libertines and Antinomians living will ever well answer. L.C.

L. C. Of the Part of Faith in Justification*.

*That is, None, as to true Justification.

Chap. I.
The cause of erring in this matter.

§. 1.

Seeing the Doctrine of Justification is the summe of our salvation, and the chief Consolation of our Souls; Satan hath bent his care with all his strength, to substitute instead of Christs righteousness, another that is loose and unstable, that cannot stand before the tribunal of God; such as the Papists have forged; and moreover to finde out or make such as to the wrong of Gods Righteousness do give so much to Faith, in Justification, as to make it, both to be before Election, as the Arminians do, and assert it to be antecedent to Christs satisfaction and death, as that Interpolator of Arminianism, Amyraldus, teacheth. And so easie is it to slip into error in this point, that even some of the holy Fathers by occasion of the words Faith Justifieth, misunderstood, did give too much to Faith, and inherent righteousness: Yea and a great part of Godly and Learned men, at this day of right judgement in the other Articles of the Doctrine of Faith, do seem by writing and word, to joyn to Christs Righteousness another efficient Cause, though less principal; to wit, Faith; as though Christs Righteousness alone were not sufficient to justifie a man at the Tribunal of God, unless Faith also come in to help it.

Among these is the most famous man Cyrus Molinæus, whose sense may be gathered by the fragment of an Epistle, which he wrote to his Brother, a Professor in the University of Oxford; which controversie he yet calls a meer fighting of shaddows, or rather a strife about words, and not a matter of such moment as that common Christians should be troubled for it. Truly though it were a far greater controversie, it were meet that a Christian man should so judge of his brother in Christ, as that in the mean time he should pray to God, and hope to find him at last of the same minde, as St. Paul promiseth himself of the Philippians; and so to deal with him, as with his dearest natural brother, differing from his in Judgement and opinion, whom he endeavoreth with all moderation of minde and words to draw to himself.

But the whole controversie throughly weighed, and examined by the touchstone of the holy Scripture, I could not perswade my self that the controversie is meerly in words, but in Things, and of so great moment, that I think the Doctrine of Justification by Faith, such as the Author of the Epistle holdeth, doth either furnish the Papists and Arminians with weapons, or, if not so, and if it be not against sound Doctrine; at least it darkneth a chief Article of our Faith, and labors of sayings not consonant to right reason and congruous speech.

The Author of the Epistle contendeth, that a man is said properly and without a Trope, to be Justified by Faith, and that Faith is of the definition of Justification, and so that man hath Faith before he is Justified.

But I do constantly assert, that When to Justifie, is the same as to Absolve; to Impute Christs Righteousness, to make Righteous, and to forgive sins; to declare or pronounce just without mans barr: and whensoever Scripture speaks of that righteousness by which at Gods Bar, and by God we are made and acknowledged just and heirs of Eternal Life, then a man can in no wise be said to be justified by Faith: According whereto we judge, that a man is justified before he have Faith, and that a man faithful or believing is not the adequate object of justification, and that Faith hath no part (or place) in the Definition of justification, or of Remission of sins.

But when to justifie, signifieth to reveal Christs Righteousness, to shew it, to make it known, to bring it to the knowledge of the understanding and conscience, then I grant that by Faith, and through Faith a man is justified, in as much as by Faith it is known to a man, that Christs Righteousness belongs to him.

---

§. 1.

R. B. THe Author of this Dissertation, freely confesseth in his title page, that the opinion which he opposeth, and D. *Molinæus* in this Epistle defendeth, is commonly accounted Orthodox: and I shall shew that it is not without very great reason; and that he should have been tender of departing from the part which is commonly judged Orthodox in so great a point, without stronger reasons to move him, then any he produceth.

Pag. 1. 2. I willingly with him detest the substitution of any Righteousness of our own, or any others instead of the Righteousness of Christ, though I know we must have a personal Gospel-Righteousness, subordinate to that of Christ; which yet Christ also must give us. I as freely reject the Arminians making Faith (whether in it self or Gods consideration) to go before Election: And I believe that we are elected *ad fidem*, as well as *ad salutem per fidem*.

And if his Accusation against *Amyraldus* be true, that *he maketh Faith antecedaneous to Christs satisfaction and death*, I as much dislike that at least as the former. I cannot say, he slanders him, because I have not read every word that ever *Amyraldus* wrote. But I must say that I not only confidently believe that he slanders him, but take it for my duty so to believe: and I leave my reasons to the censure of the equal. 1. I am bound to believe the best of my Brother, till worse be made appear, and not to receive an accusation without proof *. 2. *Amyraldus* doth not only frequently confess that Faith is the fruit of Christs death, (when yet *Camero* in *Ep. ad. L. C.* looked on it as flowing immediately from Election, as the gift of Christ himself to the world, did from Gods Love) but also he doth in an Elaborate search disclose to the world the difference between Christs procuring Faith, and his procuring Remission and Salvation: which point well understood would do more to the opening of many difficulties, and the composing of those controversies, then most consider. Its pitty that one point is not more diligently enquired into.

* *And he brings no proof.*

It is not well that * this dealing is the beginning of this Differtation: to charge a man in print with that which he writes againft, and that so diligently. And I think with no lefs Verity, (though with far more shew of Verity) doth he call *Amyraldus* an Interpolator of Arminianifm. He is as little and lefs a friend to any error, who avoids the contrary extream, then he that runs into it. Were all our Britifh Divines in the Synod of *Dort* Interpolators of Arminianifm? as also the *Bream* Divines? who in the main points went the fame way? For my part I diffent from *Amyraldus* in his Expofition of *Rom.* 7. and in many other points: But I think that Mr. Hoord doth take neither him nor *Davenant* for his moft contemptible adverfaries: Nor do I think any Arminian hath been more judiciously and ftrongly anfwered (though not with such triumphing words) then he hath been by them two. And *Tilenus* thought *Camero* no friend to Arminianifm. The middle terms that thefe men go on, doth give a man such exceeding advantage againft the Arminians, that I think no

* *Vid. specim. Animadverf. Gener. part. 1. pag. 39. 40. 41. He makes Chrifts Death to procure us Faith, as a finall caufe, and faith that Chrifts death is the caufe of Faith, and that, Chriftus fidem à Deo nobis certe impetravit. And how he can make Faith then which he calls the means, antecedent to Chrifts death which he calls the procuring end, I know not. I confefs I think that point may be yet far clearlyer opened then he hath done; but I suppofe that endeavor not vain, though fhort.*

man elfe can folidly confute them. Pardon my confidence: I am sure I fee the vanity of my own arguings when I was in the other extream.

After the Papifts, Arminians and *Amyraldus*, his next charge is againft *some of the Fathers, for giving too much to Faith and inherent Righteoufnefs*. If he had faid fo of almoft all the Fathers, I would not have contradicted him, at leaft, meaning it of their unmeet phrafes. But I should think that thofe who give it too little, and run into the other extream, should be the lefs paffionate for their way, when they read what was the judgement of all former ages of the Church: at leaft they should the lefs cenfure their Brethren, who go not so far as the Fathers went.

His fifth charge is againft *A great part this day of the Godly and Learned, who judge aright in the reft of the Articles of the Doctrine of Faith, that feem by writing and by voice to joyn to Chrifts Righteoufnefs, another efficient caufe, though lefs principal, that is, Faith: as if Chrifts Righteoufnefs alone were not sufficient to juftifie a man at Gods Tribunal, unlefs Faith be called in to help it.* I confefs I am of the opinion which your words exprefs, I mean, I do as well as you diflike the making Faith an efficient, *i. e.* inftrumental caufe of Juftification: and I fay, as you, Chrifts Righteoufnefs needeth no help from it. But though Chrifts Righteoufnefs be fufficient in *suo genere* to do its own part, yet not in *omni genere*, and to do every thing that belongs to Juftification. And you know *Molineus* the Author of the Epiftle proves Faith to be the condition of juftification; and I suppofe you will grant that a condition, as such, is no efficient caufe; nor doth it in the leaft derogate from the honor of the purchafer or donor: I pray you anfwer me thefe few Queftions. 1. Whether, if a King fay to a Traytor, I will give thee free pardon and honor withall, if thou wilt thankfully accept it and repent of thy Treafon; yea, if his Son did purchafe this grant of his Father for the Traytor; is it now any diminution to the honor of the Kings pardon, or the Princes purchafe, if we fay, that without the Traytors acceptance it shall not be effectual?

Nn 2

[180]

effectual? Or would you say, that we call his acceptance in to help the King to pardon him, or the Prince to merit it? I put these Questions, because though you in terms argue against Faiths efficiency or instrumental causation only, yet you after shew that you intend it against the necessity of Faith, as a Condition, *sine qua non*: and you odly drive against *Molinæus* assertion, and yet silence the main part of it, here. Indeed he mentioneth Faiths Instrumentality too: but it is after its office of a Condition, intimating, that by an Instrument he intends but that Receptive nature of Faith, whereby it is naturally apt to be the Condition of the freest gift; and so takes the word Instrument, improperly or vulgarly, and not Logically for an efficient cause; and takes the conditionality to be the *Ratio proxima* of Faiths interest in Justification.

2. I further demand of you, whether if you be accused at Judgement of final Impenitency or Infidelity, it be a sufficient answer to say, *Christs Righteousness is sufficient for me, without the help of my own Faith*. Or if the Accuser say, Its true, Christs Righteousness is sufficient for those that have part in it; but thou hast no part in it, will you be justified against this charge, by recurring to the sufficiency? that will not be *ad rem;* when the question is of your interest in it. For if all may make that answer, then all may be Justified. If onely some, they must have some reason for it more then All; and they must shew their Title.

3. Doth not a rational justification at the bar of your own conscience now require the same method?

4. Do not your reproachful accusations fall as much on God and his Gospel, as on the Reformed Doctrine, or on *Molinæus*? For its God that saith, *He that Believeth and is baptized shall be saved, and he that believeth not shall be damned:* Mar. 16. 16. *And all they shall be damned that obeyed not the truth, but had pleasure in unrighteousness.* 2 Thes. 2. 12. *And except ye Repent ye shall all likewise perish.* Luke 13. 3, 5. Will you now reply to Christ, *Lord, is not Thy Righteousness sufficient, unless my Believing and Repenting be called in to help it?*

Pag. 4. 5. Page 4. I do yield it to you, as an undoubted Truth, that the difference is not small, nor only in words. And where you say, that *Molinæus* (that is, the Protestant, yea the Christian) Doctrine doth arm the Papists and Arminians. I reply, 1. Not against our selves, save onely, as it is an occasion, which any wicked man may raise his abuse on; and as the world do make Christ himself and the Gospel, and as you do in this Dissertation make Christs Righteousness the occasion of your Licentious Doctrine: But I confess against you, and against all Jews, Turks and Infidels, our Doctrine doth *arm the Papists and Arminians.* For what you adde, that *at least it doth darken a chief Article of Faith:* I say, it is but of the Libertines Faith: *and that it labors of speeches not consonant to reason,* I say, whether that Reason be sound and Reason indeed, we shall see by the proof of what you affirm.

Pag. 5. 6. Page 5. You do not much fail in Reciting *Molinæus* Doctrine, *That man is said properly and without a Trope, to be Justified by Faith, and that Faith is of the definition of Justification, as a Believing man is the adequate object of Justification, and so that man hath Faith before he is Justified.* Only remember that you must distinguish between infants and adult, and between the persons Faith, and the parents Faith; and that as to personal Faith, this is affirmed only of the adult; but as to parents Faith, of Infants also.

Your own Doctrine (for that is the best title I can give it) you lay down thus,

But

But I do constantly assert, that when to justifie, *signifies the same*, as to absolve, to impute the Righteousness of Christ, to forgive sin, to declare or pronounce just *without the Bar of man; and whensoever Scripture speaks of that Righteousness by which we are by God at his Tribunal, constituted and acknowledged just, and Sons, and heirs of Eternal Life; then man can in no sort be said to be Justified by Faith : According to these we judge that a man is Justified before he have Faith, and that a man faithful or believing is not the adæquate object of Justification, and that Faith hath no parts in the definition of Justification, or Remission of sin. But when to Justifie, signifieth to reveal Christs righteousness, to shew it, to make it known, to bring it to the knowledge of the understanding and conscience; Then I grant that by Faith, and through Faith a man is Justified, as by Faith it is known to a man that Christs Righteousness belongs to him.* Adde to this your larger explication afterward, wherein you assert justification to be an immanent act, and we shall see more of the face of this Antichristian Doctrine.

  * *Extra.*

 It is not seasonable for me to fall upon your opinion here, while you do but barely name it, seeing I shall be called to it when you come to confirm it. I will next tell you also somewhat of my opinion, as you have laid down the Authors and your own, that the Reader may have all three together.

 Iustification active, is first Constitutive, which is a making just. 2. Iudicial, which is either principal or subservient. The principal is by the sentence of the Iudge, and that is 1. Improper, *per sententiam conceptam*; or 2. Properly so called: *viz. Per sententiam prolatam.* The subservient Iustification, is 1. Assertive, as by the witnesses. 2. Apologetical, which is 1. by denying false Accusations, either *de facto*, or *de jure*. 2. By Demonstrating, 1. the true Righteousness of the Cause first, and so of the person. 2. that therefore the person is to be sentenced just, or absolved by the Iudge. These few senses of the term Iustification, which are most pertinent to our business, I have taken from among many more. And now so much of my opinion as is of necessity to be discovered for the understanding of what follows, take in these Conclusions.

 Concl. 1. Constitutive Iustification goes before judicial; and is the first Justification by Faith, yea the first of all that Scripture mentioneth.

 Concl. 2. The Principal efficient cause of this iustification is God : the instrumental is the Promise or Grant of the new Law or Covenant, conveying Right to us, as Gods Deed of Gift, or Christs Testament. 2. The satisfaction of Christ is the meritorious cause, and as it were, the material. 3. The Condition *sine qua non*, is 1. The sole Faith of the sinner, that is, his Belief of the Gospel, and thankful, loving acceptance of Christ as he is there offered (in which Repentance is comprized); for the inception of his justification. 2. The continuance of this Faith; with the addition of external sincere obedience, is necessary to the confirmation and continuation of this justification in this life. 4. The form of it, is to make just by Donation, or Condonation.

 Concl. 3. It is the same act of God that is called Constitutive Justification, and pardon of sin; so far as Justification is taken as comprehending only the restoring of us to the happiness that we fell from: (but if you take it for the superadding of any degree or sort of blessing which we never lost, nor was given in the first Covenant, then Iustification containeth so much more then Remission). Yet do they notionally or respectively differ, though not Really.

 Concl. 4. Remission is taken in very many senses as well as Justification, as sometime for meer not-punishing, sometime for meer forbearance for a time; some-

sometime for remission of part of the penalty only: sometime for admitting to a treaty for full pardon, and delaying execution that while: sometime for a *nolle punire*, in him that before did intend to punish, or a meer mental Remission. In a word, all Rectoral pardon (distinct from that of equals) is 1. the Rectors Civil, or Legal, or supralegal Remission, whereby he giveth *Jus ad Impunitatem*, viz. *vel totalem, vel partialem; vel Conditionaliter, vel Absolute, vel de præsenti, vel in diem.* 2. The sentential pardon of the Iudge, by which our Right to Impunity is not onely declared, as some imagine, but Decisively determined, and thereby fully confirmed, as no more to be controverted. 3. *Remissio executiva*, whereby (before or after sentence) the penalty is remitted in whole or part. This is also called pardon in Scripture. But the first is that which is the full proper Remission of sin, viz. that Scripture mentioneth most. *An Act of God as Rector by his Gospel Grant dissolving the Obligation to punishment (or giving right to impunity) to a Believing sinner, for the sake of Christs satisfaction.* The principal efficient cause is God; not as Absolute Proprietory directly, but as Rector. And by his derived power, Christ as man as well as God, doth forgive sins. 2. The Instrument is the Testament, Promise, or Gospel-Grant, which is really Gods Act of Grace or Oblivion, and a pardoning Law. 1. By an act of Law are we obliged to punishment, and by an act of Law (in the large sense) must we be disobliged. For *eodem modo dissolvitur obligatio quo contrahitur*. 2. Legal, or Civil acts are the proper means of conveying Right, as such; Legal only, when it is from a Rector, as such; and Donatory, when from a Benefactor, as such. And God doth it as both, as *rector benefaciens*. 3. We find an act of Grace and Conditional pardon in the Gospel *de facto*, and therefore cannot doubt of it, when we read it there.

3. The object is a believing sinner: that is, being presupposed a sinner, Faith is the Condition, as in naturals the *Dispositio materiæ*: if it be one at age, it must be his own Faith, if an infant, his parents, which reputatively and legally is his own: and therefore it is not absurd to call infants *fideles*, faithful, reputatively, no more then to call them Christians, or to call the Infidels children, Infidels, which we may well do. 4. The formal act of Remission is *Dissolving* the obligation: or *Relaxing it*, or *Giving* Right to impunity: which are civil actions. 5. The *Terminus Proximus* of this act of Dissolving, is *Obligatio ad Pœnam*, that is, Guilt: or, as it is a Donation, the *Terminus proximus* is *Jus ad impunitatem*; For to Dissolve the obligation to punishment; and to give a right to impunity to a sinner, is all one act, containing two notions; 6. The remote *Terminus* is *Pœna remissa*, which we were obliged to, or the impunity given. For these are not as many dream, the neerest term. And therefore Dr. *Twisse* and you speak unsoundly when you say that Remission of sin is but *non punire*: Yea, or but *nolle punire*, if you speak it of Gods immanent Will of Purpose, and not of his Will *de Debito* expressed in his Covenant, or his Legislative Will, which Dr. *Twisse* took special notice of as in *præcepto*, and its pitty he had not observed it as well in the Promise and Threatning, which constitute the *Debitum prœmii & pœnæ*, as the Precept doth the *Debitum officii*.

This therefore being the proper act of pardon, which hath the *Obligatio ad pœnam*, or the *Jus ad impunitatem*, for its neerest *Terminus*, it is evident, that the name of a pardon is given to the other forementioned acts, less properly, for their participation in the nature of this proper pardon: especially from their respect to the penalty it self: which is here the ultimate term, and so *non punire*,

and

and *nolle punire*, may be, and are called pardon, imperfect or participative, as containing part of the nature of full pardon in them.

Concl. 5. Though Remission and Justification be thus far one, yet the word Remission is more principally and emphatically spoken in respect to the penalty remitted, and less of its immediate term, *viz.* the obligation: but contrarily, Justification doth more notably express the respect to the obligation and right, and less the Penalty, or Impunity it self, yet each term expresseth or signifieth both.

Concl. 6. Also the term Justification is most properly used of the sentential Absolution at judgement, and somewhat less properly, of the justification in Law sense, or by present Imputation or Donation. (yet fitly of both) But contrarily Pardon is most strictly and properly applyed to Gods present act by the Law of Grace or Promise; and somewhat less properly, to the judicial sentential absolution (though fitly too of both, and Scripture useth them both waies.)

Concl. 7. The sentence as conceived in Gods own brest, that is his esteeming the sinner now just, or his willing him now just, is less properly called justifying.

Concl. 8. If it were this act that were meant in Scripture, yet must it be differenced from his Decree, to justifie, which was from eternity: and it must be denominated as beginning in time: For though Gods own essence, commonly called the substance of this act, be eternal, yet the superadded respect to a new object, gives it the Denomination. And therefore it must receive that Denomination *de novo*, when the object begins. For it is absurd, if you ask *what is Gods Essence*, to say, It is an Approbation, Acceptance, Love to Justification of a sinner, Though *sanctus futurus, & in esse volito & cognito*, might be said to be loved of God from eternity, yet not in *esse existenti*: But in time he is first hated *in esse existenti*, and afterward loved in *esse existenti*, as a Saint: he is first esteemed by God unjust, and after esteemed just, and accepted accordingly, and all this without any change in God: but the change of the object necessitateth us to denominate Gods acts as new and various.   * *Psalm* 5. 4, 5.

Conclu. 9. As Justification *per sententiam Judicis* is the most perfect proper Justification, so we know of no such act of God (properly) but at the particular Judgement after death, and the last General Judgement.

Conclu. 10. When it is usually said that our Justification is *the imputation of Christs Righteousness to us*; we must distinguish of both terms, of act and object. 1. Christs Righteousness is taken either materially for that obedience, or satisfaction, wherein his Righteousness might partly be said to consist: or else for the form of Righteousness it self, which is relative. 2. Also the matter, Christs satisfaction and merit is said to be Imputed or Given us, either immediately in it self, or else in its effect. 3. Imputation signifies either 1. Donation, 2. or Adjudication, and that *mente vel sententia prolata*. Hereupon I conclude as followeth, 1. Christs Righteousness formally is incommunicable to any other. Our Union with Christ makes us not the same person with him, to be the same subject of the same Accident, *Righteousness*. 2. God doth not untruly suppose or Judge us to be what we are not, or to have done what we did not, as to have satisfied, or perfectly obeyed, or both, in or by Christ. 3. Christs satisfaction and merit was given or tendred in it self to the Father, and not to us. 4. Remission and

and Righteousness merited by Christs satisfaction is given to us, and adjudged to us, and we judged righteous hereby. 5. This is the Righteousness of God, and of Christ, as given and as merited, as it is ours as the subjects of it. 6. Christs own Righteousness materially may well be said to be given us, and adjudged to us, though not in it self immediately, yet because it is for our use and sake. As a father that gives 1000 l. to buy land for his Son, may be said to give him 1000 l. though it were in land, and not immediately in money: or as one that giveth 1000 l. to redeem a Captive, may be said to give him 1000 l. in that he gave it for him; though the thing immediately given him be liberty. 7. So that both by Donation, and Adjudication, Christs Righteousness is imputed to us, in the forementioned sense. Of which see *Bradshaw de Justific.*

Conclu. 11. Christ Iustifieth us Apologetically, as our Advocate, now and hereafter, but sententially as our Iudge only.

Conclu. 12. Apologetically, a man may iustifie himself, though yet he need a better Advocate.

Conclu. 13. The Iustification of conscience or any other *per modum Testis,* is not that which is ordinarily called Gods Iustification, but a means to it.

Conclu. 14. The Iustification of conscience in this Life, as an internal Iudge, is improper, low, fallible oft-times, and is not that which Scripture means by Iustification by Faith, or before God.

Conclu. 15. There is no known way of Gods passing a sentence within us, but by causing our own understanding or conscience to know and judge that we are iust or iustified: and this is not the Iustification neither which Scripture treates of, as Gods Iustification of a sinner.

Conclu. 16. The righteousness of his cause is the reason why the person is Iustified in iudgment: and therefore in order goes first.

Conclu. 17. As God hath made two Covenants or Laws, and both are *Regula actionum & Judicii,* and the New Law of Grace is but *Lex particularis,* and the Law of nature is *Lex universalis,* and the Law of Grace is but subservient to the Law of Nature, being *Lex Remedians,* purposely ordained for the dissolving of its obligation to punishment; so also we have a twofold cause to make good at judgement against the Accuser: the one is, that though we are sinners, yet not to be condemned by the Law, because through Christs satisfaction and the Gospels free Promise or Grant, the obligation of it is dissolved. To prove this as Christs blood and the Testaments Donation, must be produced and pleaded on one hand, so must our peculiar interest in this Grant be pleaded also, as the Condition. And here comes in the second Cause which is first to be determined, *viz.* seeing the Gospel gives pardon and Life to none but true Believers, whether we be such or not? (yea sincere obedience for the continuation, and final absolution, is part of the condition to be enquired after) And here in this cause, it is only the producing of our Faith, and Obedience, *i. e.* of our performance of the Conditions of the New Covenant, that will serve to justifie us.

Conclu. 18. Now to review all these, and shew what part Faith hath in our justification, I say, 1. Faith is strictly and properly a Condition, as the word is used in a civil sense, of our Constitutive justification by Gods written pardon, or Gospel Grant. 2. As to Gods internal Acceptation, or esteeming, or approving as just, Faith is a necessary qualification of the object, without which no Act of Gods, (*i. e.* his Essence indeed) cannot have these denominations, because they

are

are denominated *ex connotatione objecti*. So that here also Faith is *Conditio sine quâ non in sensu naturali*, but not *Civili*. 3. Faith primarily, and obedience secondarily, are proper Conditions without which God will not save us, nor justifie us by sentence in publick judgement. 4. Sincere Faith, Repentance and Obedience (all that God hath made the Condition of our Justification at Judgement and salvation) is the very matter of consciences, or Gods Justification *ad modum Testis*, asserting *de facto*, that we did perform the Condition. 5. When we are accused before God, or Conscience, of meer sin, as sin simply; or that the Law of works doth oblige us to punishment; we must plead the Gospel pardon in and for the blood of Christ: and this is our *Justitia Causæ* here. But when we are accused of final non-performance of the Conditions of the New Covenant, and so of final Impenitency, Infidelity and Rebellion against the Redeemer, here we must be justified by producing our performance of the Conditions, and denying the truth of the accusation: and not by pleading that Christ dyed for our final non-performance of these Conditions. So that here Faith and sincere Obedience is it self the very matter of our righteousness, to be pleaded. 6. At the inferior improper bar of conscience here in this life, Faith hath several parts in our Justification. In some respect it is a part of the efficient Cause: In some respect it is the Evidence: In some respect it is the matter of our Justification. So that these I think, are the offices of Faith.

Yet note, that when Faith or Obedience is said to be sometime our material righteousness it self, on which we must be Justified, that is not the least derogation to Christs satisfaction or righteousness: For our personal performance is not our *Justitia Universalis*, nor any part of that by which the Law must be answered, which condemneth all that perfectly obey not. But it is onely our *Justitia particularis*, and that subordinate and subservient to Christ who is our *Justitia Universalis*; and first to be produced that our Title to Christ and Universal Righteousness may be made good. If men or Devils accuse me of killing a man in *India*, whom I never thought of; I may justifie my self against that false Accusation by denying it; and when this is the cause under tryal, my own innocency is my righteousness: yet none will say that this is a wrong to the righteousness of Christ. Christs righteousness pardoneth my sins, and not my innocency or duty as such; nor will he pardon the final non-performance of the Conditions of the New Covenant in any, nor died for that end. Note also that though a wicked man may have *Justitiam particularem in foro Divino*, that is, may be falsly accused; yet that will not save him, for it is this only thing which the Gospel makes the Condition of Life, which is it that will be the great cause of the day, to be enquired after, and which Absolution or Condemnation will follow upon.

Conclu. 19. Among all these, it is principally Constitutive Legal Justification, or Remission, and sentential Justification at judgement, which is meant in Scripture, where it is ascribed to Faith and Christs blood: though Apologetical by Christ as our Advocate may be also implyed.

That Justification by the Covenant-Grant is first in order, is evident; and that it is by Faith as the Condition is as evident. Also that Justification which is said to be by faith ordinarily in Scripture, is the same with Remission of sin. But that it is most properly it which is by the Covenant: therefore, &c. The major shall be proved hereafter, where I finde this Author denying it.

Conclu. 20. Gods meer Decree to pardon or justifie, is no where in Scripture called

O o

called Pardon or Justification, nor in reason so to be called: much less is it that Pardon or Justification which Scripture ordinarily treats of. Nor is any act of God upon Christs death, called our Justification, or pardon: but only that the general Grant of pardon to all that will Believe, may well be said to be a general Conditional pardon and justification. But while it is but conditional, and the condition not performed, it is not actual. Nor doth the Scripture call any man Justified in any one place, before upon the condition of his own or his parents Faith, he be Justified. (I put in the latter, to put by their cavil about infants.)

And thus I have given my sence before I confute yours, and the rather, because in other Writers, I like not a meer destructive arguing, though it be easiest, and may save much labor to the opponent, yet it is not the best to Edification: and because I hold nothing that I am ashamed should see the light; and with my brethren that dissent from me, I am so far from hiding my opinion, that I most fear, least I should not fully enough reveal it.

---

§. 2.

Pag. 7. L. C. For in the former sense I conceive not how by Faith a man may be made righteous, or pronounced righteous at Gods Tribunal, and his sins pardoned: but in the second sense it is easie and of obvious understanding to say, that by Faith, sins are not remitted, but made known to be remitted.

---

§. 2.

R. B. I Have now told you that which you say you conceive not, how it may be, nay more, it is an easier intelligible Truth, how Faith should be the Condition of Gospel pardon, and sentential Justification, then how it should reveal them. For though it help to reveal them, yet the knowledge of Justification is that which we call Assurance, and not, as the Libertines conceive, Justifying-Faith.

---

§. 3.

L. C. 1. IF under other Divine Actions there lay the same ambiguity and homonymie, (as are Praedestination, Election, Creation, Redemption, Adoption, &c.) as is in the action of Justification, it might as properly be said that we are Elected by Faith, or the world created by Faith, because by Faith we know our selves to be Elect, or by Faith we know that God created the world; for the Apostle also saith, 2 Thes. 2. 13. That we are Elect through belief of the Truth. And yet from that place the Author of the Epistle would not assert that Faith is of the definition of Election, or that Election is by Faith. Therefore though to Justifie did every where retain the same signification as to Create, Elect, Adopt, do not vary theirs; I see not, that when Paul saith, A man is Justified by Faith, thereby Faith is any more set before Justification or Remission of sins, then Faith is by him made the cause of Election, or that he had less unfitly said that our sins are pardoned by Faith, then that we are elected by Faith.

§. 3.

§. 3.

R. B. Here you had the wit to foresee an argument that would be used against you, but had not a cause that made you capable of a tolerable Answer. We argue thus; If it were but the knowledge of Remission and Justification that is ascribed to Faith, then we might as fitly be said to be elected by Faith, Redeemed by Faith, Created by Faith, as Justified by Faith: But the consequent is false: therefore so is the Antecedent.

The argument is unanswerable; But let us see the shifts of this Author to evade it. 1. That Election, Redemption, &c. vary not their sense, and are not used in divers senses, is a falshood very notorious! How oft is Election taken for the Actual choosing some out of the world in time, by vocation? and at other times (*Grotius* thinks only *Eph.* 1. but amiss) for the Eternal Decree? How oft is Redemption taken for the paying of the price of our deliverance? yet how oft also for actual Liberation? and that sometime as begun in this Life; sometime in perfection hereafter. *Wilson, Martinius, Illericus, Ravanellus*, and all that open Scripture terms, will contradict this Dissertor. 3. If he object, But Election and Redemption are never, or not usually taken for the knowledge of Election and Redemption, as Justification is usually taken for the knowledge of Justification: I answer, the later is easier begged then proved or granted, that ever Justification or Remission is so taken, much less usually.

4. What reason is there why the knowledge of election or redemption may not be called election and redemption, as well as the knowledge of Justification may be called Justification. 5. Yea it would in us be somewhat more Justifiable to use that language then this latter. Because election and redemption are truly pre-existent to our knowledge of them; and therefore we should borrow a name from somewhat that truly is. But Justification pre-existent to our Faith, (in men at age) is a *Chymæra*, a Fiction, and therefore you borrow a name from that which never was. Scripture speaks of election and redemption before Faith; but never once of Justification before Faith. 6. Your arguing from 2 *Thes.* 2. 13. is so notorious an abuse of the text, as shews either great weakness or immodesty, to speak easily of it. Suppose that ἐν ἁγιασμῷ πνεύματος ᾳ πίστει ἀληθείας must be translated *per sanctificationem spiritus & fidem veritatis.* yet you know it is not simply *elected through Faith*, but *elected to salvation through sanctification of the Spirit, and belief of the Truth*. You should not have left out εἰς σωτηρίαν. By signifieth the nature of a means in order to some end. God hath elected us to be saved by the means of Faith. Here salvation is the end of Faith, but so is not Election. You might well have gathered hence that we are saved by faith, but what shew of a Conclusion that we are elected by Faith, as if Faith were a means to Election, which is plainly in the text made the Consequent of it? But when it is said we are Justified by Faith, the word *Justified*, plainly expressed the end to which Faith is a means. If you do indeed think that in this speech *Justified* stands in the same place as *Elected* did in the former, then *Justified* must signifie no Effect or Consequent of Faith at all, but a Cause or Antecedent; for so *Elected* doth: and then I pray you what doth *by faith* signifie, you will make utter non-sense of it. Lastly, dare you interpret 2 *Thes.* 2. 13. *Elected to salvation through sanctification, &c. i. e.* We know our own Election through Sanctification. I confess *Grotius* and some Arminians will say that the text signifieth a temporal Election following Faith; (yet never dream of your sense) But

But I hope you will not so interpret *ἀπ' ἀρχῆς*, as if the Apostle meant, *from the beginning God hath made you know your Election*. If you do, I shall doubt you will next so interpret *from or before the foundations of the world*, which is joyned with Election in other Texts of Scripture.

§. 4.

L. C. 2. THe cause of the error is not only in the homonymie of the word Iustifying, but also of the word Faith, which is oft taken either for the Doctrine of the Gospel, or for the object of faith : So when the Scripture saith Abraham was Justified by faith, it is plain that it means, Abraham was Iustified by Christ the object of Faith, as Calvin and Rivet interpret it.

§. 4.

R. B. A Deep discovery you make of the cause of our error. Who knows not that Faith is sometime put for the Doctrine or object of faith ? But would you have us believe that it is so taken in the text you cite, or in all texts that speak of Iustification by Faith ? then must we first renounce our reason, *& contra Rationem nemo sobrius*; and we must renounce the plain evident sense of Scripture, *& contra Scripturam nemo Christianus*; and we must renounce the exposition of the Church in all ages ; *Et contra Ecclesiam nemo pacificus*. We well know that others as well as *Calvin* and *Rivet*, suppose that Christ the object of Faith is implyed in the word Faith, yea principally intended in the Apostles dispute. But do they think therefore that either Faith is not included, or that by Faith is meant not Faith, but Christ ? nothing less. If the question be whether such a poor woman became rich and honorable by her own labor, or by marriage (supposing she marry a man of honor and riches) *If I say not by her Labor or work, but by marriage* : I do principally mean by her husband ; but that is but as it is implyed in the word Marriage ? Sure I do not exclude marriage it self, nor put the word *marriage* simply for a husband : but by connotation only. So doth Faith connote Christ believed in, but doth not directly signifie Christ. Do you think that when *James* disputes whether Faith only Iustifie, that he means whether Christ only Iustifie ? Peruse his arguments, and think so if you can. Divines use to say, by Faith alone he means a dead Faith, and by Works, a working Faith. Do you think he means *a dead Christ and a working Christ*. And would the mentioning of *Abrahams* Iustification by Christ only, have done any thing to prove his conclusion ? I pray peruse *Rom.* 4. and see what sense your Exposition puts upon it, *vers.* 3. Abraham *believed God, and it was counted*, &c. Is *Believed* put for *Christ* here ? then how is it an act ? Christ is no act: then how is God made the object ? *vers.* 5. *To him that worketh not, but believeth on him that Iustifieth the ungodly*, &c. If *believeth*, here signifie Christ, then what is meant by *on him* : Is Christ the object and act both ? So *vers.* 11, 12, 13, 14, 16, 17, 18. Against hope he believed in hope. Is *believing* here put for Christ, and not for Faith it self ? So 19, 20, 21. I am ashamed to argue any more in so palpable a case, further then to intreat the Reader that is not satisfied, to peruse the Texts, and also the History in *Genesis*, and if he can believe after

this,

[189]

this, that it is Christ onely and not Faith that is meant by Faith, he is none of those that I write for, *vers.* 23, 24. the Apostle applyes all thus. It was not written for his sake alone that it was imputed to him: but for us also to whom it shall be imputed, if we believe on him that raised up Jesus, &c. All things are here as plain against you as can be imagined. The Object Christ is here expressed: Believing is mans act, and therefore not Christ: Believing is it that is imputed. Believing is plainly made a Condition on mans part: imputing is a thing to be done after Faith, and not done before; *It shall be imputed, if we believe.* And do you think those texts that promise Remission and Justification to men if they will believe, and that whosoever believeth in him shall receive remission of sins, and be Justified from all things, &c. do mean *Christ* only by believing? Believing is 1. an act then. 2. a duty of mans. 3. his condition, Christ is not so. I refer you for this, to what is already written by Mr. *Wotton*, and Mr. *Goodwin* of Justification: which I would not have you think you have answered, by charging him with error in other things; which are nothing to the question. Nay observe the ingenuity of this Dissertor, who mentioneth *Calvin*, as intimating him to expound this text as he: when as *Calvin* on *Rom.* 4. 3. where the text is, hath not a word for him, (nay how little for the connotation of the object which I before allowed, directly and expresly in comparison of what he saith for the act) but on the contrary much. He saith, *Locus qui citatur ex Gen. 15. 6. sumptus est. Ubi Verbum Credendi, non ad particulare aliquod dictum restringi debet, sed ad totum: salutis foedus, & adoptionis gratiam quam dicitur* Abraham *fide apprehendisse. Quare* Abraham *Credendo nihil quam oblatam sibi gratiam amplectitur, ne irrita sit. Si hoc illi imputatur, in Justitiam, sequitur non aliter esse Justum, nisi quia Dei bonitate Confisus; omnia ab ipso sperare audet. Hanc promissionis & fidei relationem necessarium est ad statuendam Justitiam, intelligere: quoniam eadem est hic inter Deum & nos ratio, quæ apud jurisconsultos, inter Datorem & donatarium. Neque enim Justitiam aliter consequimur, nisi quia sicuti, Evangelii, Promissione nobis defertur, ita ejus possessionem fide quasi Cernimus.*

But perhaps he means on *Gen.* 15. 6. that *Calvin* saith as he intimates. Not a word there neither, but much against him. Let these words witness, *Denique non minoris stuporis quam impudentiæ est, quum hoc illi imputatum fuisse dicitur, in justitiam, alium sensum Comminisci quam fidem Abrahæ fuisse pro Justitia apud Deum, &c. Nec sane alia de Causa nos Justificat fides, nisi quia nos Deo reconciliat; neque id suo merito; sed dum gratiam nobis in promissionibus oblatam Recipimus, &c.* Nay he saith more then I dare by much. *Quum dicit Moses imputatam fuisse Abræ fidem pro Justitia, non significat istam fidem primam fuisse Justitiæ Causam, quæ efficiens dicitur, sed* formalam *duntaxat.*

§. 5.

L. C. 3. A*Nother cause of the Error is, that they promiscuously make those to be* * *homonyma, which indeed are very divers: so when Justification is an individual action, without us, which pronounceth us just for the sake of Christ, absolveth and pardoneth sins, and is the imputation of Righteousness; Nevertheless, they also call by the name of* Justification *that internal act of man, whereby he believeth in God, and trusteth that Christs obedience is imputed to him, and given him of God.*

* The same words signifying divers things.

§. 5.

R. B. 1. Will you do so much as fit your own Doctrine to this your own description of Iustification, and to tell us by the next, what this extrinsick Pronunciation is? You say, that Iustification is an immanent act: And is *pronouncing us just* an immanent act? I never heard of such a one till now. And seeing it must needs be a Transient act, will you describe that act whereby at Christs death, or from Eternity, God did pronounce you just? The first that I know of, is the Covenant-Grant, which is a Conditional general Iustification or pardon.

2. And will you do so much by the next, as give us a Catalogue of some of those men that call their believing, by the name of Iustification. I never saw any such passage but one slip in a popular Sermon by a Learned Dr. that knew better. *I know that Confessions and Authors of all Countries speak otherwise. I mean, of those men who maintain the Doctrine which you oppose; and call Faith the Condition of Iustification, and an instrument of Iustification (that is, as I interpret the more judicious of them); A Receiving act, metaphorically called an instrument of receiving, not of effecting. Or till you have cited them, will you give us leave to take this for an injurious dealing against the Ninth Commandment.

Except in those of your own way, or the Papists.

§. 6.

Pag. 10. L. C. So *when Iustification is a gracious sentence of the Judge, absolving one obnoxious to wrath and guilty of eternal death; yet do they confound the patefaction of that gracious sentence made to the conscience of the guilty person by faith, with the Action of God performed without him; at lest they refer it to Iustification taken in the first sense.*

§. 6.

R. B. 1. AGain, describe that immanent act, or any act from eternity, or from Christs death, which may be called, A gracious sentence of the Judge absolving one guilty of eternal death, &c. 2. Some do indeed give the same name of *Iustification* to that patefaction which you mention, and so do you, over and over. But who, or how many take it for the same thing? But that sure you mean not to charge them with when you say, *They make those homonyma which are diversissima;* I know not therefore what you charge them with, but what you do your self.

3. We do, and iustly do refer Faith to Iustification before God. But I pray you observe these 3 things, 1. that by *Iustification* we mean not any eternal act of God, or any done before Faith. 2. that by Faith, we mean not any manifestation to our consciences that we are iustified: that is the Antinomian Description of Faith, though it cannot be denyed but many of our

our Divines formerly have been carried too far to such like expressions, in their opposition to Popish doubting. But by Faith we mean *The Assent to the Truth of the Gospel, and the accepting of an offered Christ.* 3. observe in what sense we refer this Faith to Iustification before God. 1. *Proximè & quoad rationem formalem,* as a Condition of that Iustification, which is but *Causa sine qua non*: and remotely, as apt to this office, being in its nature the acceptance of a free Gift, which is commonly called its Instrumentality. Do not confute us before you understand us.

§. 7.

Pag. 10. L. C. *And it is worthy the noting, that Scripture saith indeed, that we are Iustified by Faith, and it never affirmeth that sins are forgiven by Faith, which yet might as well be, if to justifie, and to forgive sins, did alway stand in equal signification. But seeing that one may be said properly, and the other but improperly, it is plain that to justifie by Faith (when to Iustifie is the same as to forgive sins) is as improperly said as to forgive sins by Faith. And therefore that the speech to Iustifie by Faith, that it may be properly spoken, must signifie something else then to remit sins by Faith; to wit, by the Grace of Faith, to make known to the sinner that by Chrifts Righteousness he is Iustified, and so his sin forgiven.*

§. 7.

R. B. 1. THis is a notable argument, where the Consequent contradicteth the Antecedent; *If these two speeches to Iustifie by Faith, and to remit sin by Faith, be one of them used properly, and the other improperly (one being in Scripture and the other not) and yet to Iustifie and Remit sin be all one; then the one is spoken improperly as well as the other: But the Antecedent is true; therefore.* I think this is your argument, which I will not laugh at, as remembring what case such arguers have brought the Church into: nor will I confute it further, lest I offend my Reader, and lose time. 2. But do not you read of *Remitting sins, if we believe?* and to do it on condition we believe, and to do it *by Believing as a Condition* is all one. Rom. 4. 6, 7. the Apostle makes Iustification by Faith, before mentioned, to be the same with forgiveness of sin. Act. 26. 18. *That they may receive forgiveness of sins, &c. through Faith that is in me.* Here is receiving remission (not the bare knowledge of Remission) through Faith, Act. 13. 38, 39. *Through this man is preached to you the forgiveness of sins; and by him all that believe are Iustified from all things from which ye could not be Iustified by the Law of Moses.* Here they are made all one. Act. 3. 38. *Repent and be baptized for the Remission of sin;* and doubtless Faith is principally intended in both these, baptism being the solemn profession of Faith on our parts, and unbelief being the sin that he perswades them to Repent of. Act. 10. 43. *Through his name, whoever Believeth in him shall receive remission of sins.* Here is as much as we affirm. If you say, It saith not *by believing,* I say, when we say we are Iustified *by Faith,* we mean no more then this, nor doth Paul mean more, but that *whoever believeth is Iustified.* Rom. 3. 25. *Whom God hath*

hath set forth to be a propitiation through Faith in his blood, to declare his Righteousness, for the remission of sins that are past, &c. Gal. 3. 22. But the Scripture hath concluded all under sin, that the Promise by Faith of Jesus Christ might be given to them that believe. By promise here, no doubt, is meant the good Promised, and that is Remission of sin, as being opposed to *Concluding under sin*, and this is given *by Faith*: And all are before concluded under sin; and therefore not justified or forgiven.

3. We maintain that it is a proper speech to say, *We are forgiven by or through Faith*, as well as that *We are Justified by Faith*. And if you had never read in Scripture of *Receiving Remission of sin by faith, Act.* 26. 18. or forgiving by faith; It doth not follow that it is therefore any less proper, then Iustifying by Faith. Nor can your self give any reason after your own way, why one is not as proper as the other.

4. What if we were forced to confess an impropriety in the words, *Justified by faith*? Must it therefore needs be taken in your sense for manifestation? Nothing less. If it were less proper to say *by faith*, as seeming to express a Cause, yet we truly say; It means as by a Condition: Though indeed it is not improper.

---

§. 8.

Pag. 11. L. C. ANother cause of the error is, that they would have the acts of Remitting sins, and of Apprehending the Remission of sins, to be done together, and perpetually to cohere: but those things that do alway cohere, are neither the same, nor is one alwayes of the definition of the other: for the same men would have Justification and Sanctification alway Companions, when they plainly differ in the definition, yea they no way agree in the parts of the definition: But it shall after appear that the Actions of God Remitting sins, and of the Beleiver apprehending Remission of sins, are not alwayes Concomitant.

---

§. 8.

R. B. 1. IF you will deal fairly, distinguish of *Apprehending*. We will easily prove that Apprehension, as it signifies but Assent and Consent, or Acceptance, alwayes goes with, that is, before actual Remission (in the adult.) But apprehension as it signifieth the knowledge that sin is already remitted, follows after it; God knows how long, sometime longer, sometime shorter time. 2. Who ever argued (as you seem to accuse them) from *constant coherence*, to a *necessity of entring the definition*; It is rather from *the necessity of faith to Iustification*, whereto it so cohereth; and that as the immediate Condition qualifying the matter. 3. Your Controversie, *whether it should enter the definition of Justification* is of small moment: It must, or must not, according as you take the word *Justification*: If you intend to define *ut Physicus*, only the Iustifying act, no doubt Faith must not come in. If you intend so restrained a definition as shall contain nothing but Causes, Faith is none such: But if you intend a more full definition, *ut Jurisconsultus Christianus*, which may fully delineate to the understanding of your reader, the nature of the Iustifying act, (which is, *Donatio Conditionalis, & non Absoluta*, before

before the Condition be performed ; and is *quasi Absoluta* only on the performance of that Condition) then it is fit you should put Faith into your Definition. I would you would mark whether Scripture use to leave it out of its descriptions.

4. The separability of Justification from Faith (in the adult) we shall believe you will indeed make appear, 1. Either when you have proved the justification of Infidels. 2. Or when by fascination, you have put on our noses your spectacles, which cause this strange apparition to your self.

---

§. 9.

Pag. 12. 13. L. C. THis also is *a cause of the error, that The cause why Christs Righteousness is made known to us and applyed, is made an efficient cause of Justification, at lest, Instrumental and less principal. What? is the Application of Christs Righteousness imputed to us, and of Remission of sins, a cause of Remission of sins and of Christs satisfaction, when Faith is not so much as required, that Christ may satisfie for us? Nor matters it that Faith is required that that satisfaction may be known to us. If a Prince absolve a condemned Malefactor by his written-pardon, shall that pardon be the less valid, because when it was written, the Malefactor knew nothing of it? Or is it requisite to the validity of the sentence of the Judge, that the Defendant do Believe the Judge?*

---

§. 9.

R. B. 1. IT cannot be denyed but some, and too many have made the Doctrine of Justification a stumbling block, and given advantage to the Adversaries, by making Faith the proper instrumental cause of Justification. I defend them not, having sufficiently offended them. But yet remember, that for ought I can understand, you have no great reason to charge *C. Molinæus* with that, nor many more of our Divines who use the word *Instrument* ; because they mean but this much, that *Faith Justifieth not by Deserving, but Receiving a free Gift*, and so I consent to them, supposing that it includeth the *rationem Conditionis* as its neerest interest. And so they take not the word Instrument properly, for an Instrumental Cause.

2. You still give us your own erroneous description of Faith, as ours, as if it were the making known, or the knowing of Christs Righteousness, (to be ours: for so no doubt you mean : for I confess it is one act of Faith, to assent to the Testimony of God concerning Christs Righteousness) indeed we call faith *the Application of that Righteousness*: but that is not for the meer knowledge that *its ours*, but first that it *may be ours* ; It is a Receptive Application of a Gift, and not a Discovering of what we have already. Nay, how vainly do you take it for granted, and go away with it as undoubted, that, the Faith which we treat of, is *The Application of Christs Righteousness imputed, viz.* already? When you know, (if you know almost any thing of this kinde), that we make Faith *An Application*, i. e. Acceptation *of that Righteousness, that it may be imputed, i. e.* by Donation actual, and by adjudication. For that Imputation we make to be the same with Justification ; *viz.* Imputation by the Gospel Donation, is Justification Constitutive,

tutive, or makes us first Righteous: and Imputation by adjudication, doth Judicially abſolve us, or determine us to be Righteous. And you know we make faith to go both before theſe acts of juſtifying.

3. But what an injurious intimation is it to joyn together Remiſſion and Chriſts ſatisfaction, and to intimate that we make faith, or the Application of Chriſts righteouſneſs, a Cauſe of Chriſts ſatisfaction? who is the Proteſtant Divine that hath done ſo? In what book and page do you find it? Tell us punctually if you can. We believe that Chriſts ſatisfaction is the meritorious Cauſe of our Remiſſion, and not Remiſſion it ſelf, but long before it.

4. For your intimation, as if we made it the uſe of faith, that Remiſſion or ſatisfaction may be known to us: I anſw. 1. It is not that Remiſſion may be known, but that the conditional remiſſion granted in the Act of Oblivion or Grace, which is known, may become actual to us in particular by Acceptance: and ſo that it may be ours. 2. And for ſatisfaction, faith believeth the truth of it, and accepteth the fruit of it, with him that performed it.

5. How lame is your ſimilitude, fitted to your own maimed apprehenſions of the nature of the Goſpel? the Princes pardon that you mention is either Abſolute or Conditional: If abſolute, I confeſs to you, it is valid before it be known or believed. But if you would have ſpoke as one that underſtandeth the Goſpel, you ſhould have ſuppoſed your Princes pardon to be conditional, and the Condition to be the Acceptance of the Prince himſelf, as your Redeemer and Lord, and pardon but with him; and then you would eaſily ſee that you could not have right either to him or his pardon, but upon your Acceptance.

6. I confeſs your arguing may prove that God might, if he had pleaſed, have pardoned men that never knew of it. (Though ſome Divines that I argue with maintain the contrary) and ſo that faith is not of abſolute natural neceſſity to all that ſhould be pardoned. But then when God hath once made it

That among men, a Promiſe gives not Right, till accepted uſually. See Sayrus Clau.Reg. lib.c.6.p.329, 330. n. 22, 23.

the Condition of his Gift, his Ordination hath made it neceſſary And where the Goſpel is revealed, and Chriſt offered, it is of natural moral neceſſity that he be accepted; ſo far as that you may eaſily diſcern it fit that no man ſhould be pardoned by Chriſt while he deſpiſeth him, and the means of pardon: no more then a Phyſitian ſhould heal a man (well in his wits) that will not believe but that he is a deceiver, and that will not truſt him, nor take him for his Phyſitian.

7. For your other ſimilitude, it ſhews your miſtake: You ſuppoſe it is believing our ſentential juſtification by the Judge to be true, that is made the juſtifying act of faith. But thats falſe; It is the believing the Act of Grace, the Remedying Law; And accepting the Redeemer and his benefits, which is the Condition of final Abſolution, as well as of conſtitutive Juſtification. For the Law is *Norma Judicii*: and therefore that which makes a man juſt in Law, will cauſe the Iudge to pronounce him Iuſt. For the Iudge doth therefore pronounce him Iuſt; becauſe he is Iuſt in Law-ſence firſt.

§. 10.

L. C. Pa.13. Nor do they leſs err, in taking amiſs very many places of Scripture, and which as well favour the Papiſts and Arminians conceits; not unlike thoſe which the Author of the Epiſtle did lay before his foundation: ſuch as are thoſe

1. With

1. Without faith no man can please God, *and so no man can be Justified without Faith, which is a prerequisite Condition of Justification. With that weapon do the Arminians assault us, to prove election to be of foreseen faith : with the same strength as the words* Gal. 2. 26. *are cited,* We are the sons of God by faith, *therefore we are Justified by faith* : Forsooth six hundred such places may be produced, *in which seemingly Faith, yea and Holiness of life, and Repentance seem to be made something antecedaneous to, and a cause of Election, Adoption, Justification and Salvation : when yet faith is only the Manifestation and patefaction, that we are the sons of God, that we are elect, and shall obtain salvation.*

---

§. 10.

R. B. 1. NOne readier to cry out of Error, then the most desperately seduced and seducers. I shall never more take that for a note of the Orthodox, for the sake of many in this age. 2. That these texts as well favour the Papists and Arminians, as those that put faith before Justification, is spoken more boldly then truly. Election is not Gods Love of complacency in the person as a present real object of Love ; And therefore though men be elect, it follows not that they please God ; much less *quoad actiones*. Neither Papists, Arminians, nor you therefore can gather the least advantage from that text.

3. Let it be observed that this Dissertor doth confess, that six hundred such places may be produced : and if he can give any tolerable answer to any one of them, I am contented to forfeit the reputation of my Reason.

4. It is false that ever Holiness of life is made in Scripture antecedent to Adoption or Justification constitutive, as begun : but it is true that they are secondary Conditions of our Justification and Adoption, as continued and consummate at Judgement ; or as *Conrad. Bergius* and *L. Crocius* say, they are Conditions *of our not losing the Justification once freely given* : And this *Iames* means in part, by Justification by Works, I think.

5. Election is taken in Scripture in many senses : But when it is taken for Gods Decree, yea or for his temporal choosing his people out of the world by Vocation, let this Dissertor shew me if he can one text of Scripture that makes holiness, faith or repentance to be Causes of it, yea or antecedent at all ; Till then I shall take this for another irregular practice, conform to the tendency of their doctrine. One would think that the man did under hand seek credit to the Popish Cause, which he seems to oppose by the contrary extream. For truly here is such evident prevarication, that may make one a little jealous ; but that I will not suspect a stranger without great cause.

6. His last Conclusion hath two infirmities : the one is, that it is against the scope and manifest words of the Gospel. The other is, that it hath nothing but his word to prove it. 1. That faith and obedience are not only *a patefaction and manifestation that we shall obtain salvation,* but a Means, that is, a Condition the whole Church hath held till the Flaccians and Libertines did question it : and methinks no sober Christians should deny : And I came but lately from citing so many texts to prove it, that it irks me to do it again. Only these few I desire the Reader to peruse, if he be so blind as to doubt of it. *Mat.* 25. throughout. *Gal.* 6, 7, 8, 9. *Rom.* 6. 22. *James* 3. 18. and 4. 7, 8. 2 *Cor.* 9. 6, 7, 8, 9, 10. *Heb.* 6. 10. 2 *Tim.* 4. 8. and 4. 1. *Rom.* 8. 13. *Mat.* 5. 20. *Rom.* 2, 5, 6, 7, 10. *Acts* 10. 35. 1 *Tim* 4. 16; 1 *Ioh.* 3. 7.

Eph. 6. 8. *Mat.* 7. 21, 22, 23, 24. *Job.* 16. 27. 2 *Cor.* 5. 10. 1 *Pet.* I. 16, 17. *Phil.* 4 17. 1. *Tim.* 6. 18, 19. 1 *Cor.* 9. 25, 26, 27. *Mat.* 11. 12. *Luke* 13. 24. *Phil.* 2. 12. *Heb.* 11. 26. and 10. 35. *Mat.* 10. 41, 42. 1 *Cor.* 3 8, 14. and 9. 17. *Col.* 3. 23, 24. 1 *Joh.* 3. 22, 23. 2 *Chron.* 34. 21. *Gen* 22. 16. *Pfal.* 91. 9, 14. *Rev.* 2. 14. Reader, I thought it would be tedious to thee as well as me to transcribe the words but of thefe many texts, much more to form arguments; but if thou wilt be at the pains to read them, if thou find not that Repentance and Obedience (much more evidently faith) do more to our falvation then to manifeft it, then either thou or I are notoriously deluded. And if thou wilt but perufe thofe texts, where Chrift promifeth falvation to men, if they will believe, and reprehendeth them for unbelief, and faith, *Ye will not come to me that ye may have life*, Joh. 5. 40. Yea, condemns them to Hell for not believing; If yet thou canft think that it is but a manifefting fign that Chrift fo commandeth and cals men to, and promifeth life upon, and condemneth men for want of, I muft ftill profefs that either thou or I are deplorately Ignorant : and that the Scripture to me is an unintelligible writing, if this mans doctrine be true.

7. I defire the Reader alfo to weigh with me the tendency and natural iffue of this Antinomian doctrine : and then be offended with me, if thou canft, for being fo much againft them. I am as tender of cenfuring diffenters in tolerable differences as another, but I am not indifferent to truth and falfhood, the Gofpel, and the fubverters of it. You find by this Differtor, that he wonders at men for thinking that Gods pardon is not valid, unlefs we know or believe it! And he may as well fay, that a man may have right to falvation though he know it not : and its true; for not knowing our right deftroys it not. I pray thee, Reader, then tell me how this man is like to live, that thinks his faith doth only manifeft his falvation, or right to it ? doubtlefs he will not give more to Love or Works : fo that if he be an Infidel, if he be an Adulterer, Drunkard, or what is worft, it is but his knowledge of his falvation that is diminifhed, but his Right is never the lefs; fo that to get or keep fuch right, he hath no means to ufe, but figns to get. He hath nothing to do for falvation ! If I know a man of thefe principles, I profefs, I will neither truft my purfe, my credit, my wife (if I had her) nor my throat to him, further then I muft whether I will or not. It may be he will pretend, that though he have nothing to do as a means to his falvation, yet he hath a new nature that will not fuffer him to do evil. But he that knows what mans foul and humane actions are, is more fober then to think that a right efficient may fuffice without the end, knowing that they are educed and fpecified by the end. If he fay, that Gods Glory is his end : I anfwer, Gods Glory hath as little need of his faith, as his own falvation hath. And he that knows 1. How neer man is to himfelf, and how infeparable the principle of felf-prefervation, and the love of himfelf, and what is *fibi bonum*, is from him, and 2. How Chrift himfelf in redeeming us, and God in all his merciful workings, refpected our falvation. 3. And what directions he hath given man in working out his falvation, and what precepts to ftrive for it, fight for it, and feek it with violence; yea, that this is the main drift of all the Scriptures, I fay he that knows but thefe, I warrant him will never more think of making Gods Glory his end, fo as to exclude his falvation; or that one without the other is fufficient to make fuch imperfect men as we to live as Chriftians.

2. And Adoption it felf is not only manifefted by faith, but given on condition of faith, *Joh.* 1. 11, 12. *As many as received him, to them gave he power to become the fons of God, even to them that believe in his Name.* It is an interpretation of

too much liberty, to say that by *Power to become his sons*, is meant Manifestation that we are already sons. Pardon me Reader, If I be a little warm against these mortal doctrines. I dare say, It is for God and thee; and not above the Cause.

---

§. 11.

Pag. 14. L. C. *For I pray you, what meaneth this phrase, We are the Sons of God by faith, but by faith we are certain of our Adoption to be sons?*

---

§. 11.

R. B. 1. IT meaneth as it speaketh. Is it all one to be *Sons by faith*, and to be *sure by faith that we are sons*? He gives us Power on our Believing, which is the Condition, to become sons: Is becoming sons, nothing but being sure that we were sons before? so here: The man would make us Believe that *to be sons by faith*, and *to be sure we were sons before faith*, signifie one thing. I know not what Countreyman he is; and therefore what this phrase may signifie in his language, I know not: but sure I am, in all languages that I understand, *to be*, or *become*, doth not signifie *to be sure that we were before*.

2. Note also that it is a notorious falshood that he intimates, as if believing were to *be certain we were sons*, whereas Assurance is a fruit of faith, and such a fruit as many a thousand Christians know not in this life; much less as soon as they are believers. He feigns also Paul to say to the *Galathians* (of whom he had before spoken so sharply and doubtfully) *Ye are all the sons of God*, that is, you all know certainly that ye are the sons of God by faith in Christ Jesus, whereas he will never prove either that they were all certain, or that faith is such a Certainty.

3. I desire the Reader to note how slily and silently he passeth over the first text, which he mentioneth as objected against him, *Heb.* 11. 6. *without faith it is impossible to please God*; To which he hath nothing to say, but that Papists and Arminians use it against us.

---

§. 12.

Pag. 14, 15. L. C. *And when the Apostle 2 Thes. 2. 13. saith, that We are elected through sanctification of the Spirit and belief of the Truth, what else can be the meaning of the Holy man, then that the Regeneration and Illumination by which we believe the Gospel, are certain signs of our Election?*

---

§. 12.

R. B. 1. SEE how he again is not afraid to leave out εἰς σωτηρίαν, as if it were simply *elected through sanctification and faith*, and not *elect to salvation, through sanctification and faith*. 2. The meaning is as plain as humane language can utter it, that, God hath chosen us to obtain salvation by the means of sanctification and faith. From which, its true, we may consequently conclude that we are elected, when we possess the fruits.

P p 3   §. 13.

§. 13.

I. C. As when Pet.1. Ep. 1, 2. *faith, that the faithful in* Pontus, Galatia, *&c. were elected through the sanctification of the Spirit* ; *what elle doth he intimate, but that which Saint* Paul *doth ? And when the same* Paul 1 Thef. 1. 3. *faith, that he was certain of the Election of the* Thessalonians, *because their faith & charity were manifest to him: how much rather* * *had the* Thessalonians *themselves pronounced of themselves that they were elected by faith; because they were conscious of the work of faith and charity kindled in their hearts ? and in like manner that by faith, their sins were forgiven, because their own faith gave them testimony of the Remission of their sins ?*

* or might have

---

§. 13.

R. B. 1. AGain he useth another text as ill as the former : as if *Peter* had said simply, *they were elect through sanctification of the Spirit*, and so election had been the end, and sanctification the means, when he faith, *elect according to the foreknowledge of God the Father, through sanctification of the Spirit, unto obedience and sprinkling of the blood of Iesus Christ* ; plainly making election the *Principium* and Spring of all that follows, and that it was to obedience and Remission, through the Spirits sanctification that they were elected : or In sanctification : or To sanctification : ἐν ἁγιασμῷ πνεύματος. Whether you do, as some, take Foreknowledge for the eternal Decree, and election for temporal Actual Choosing by effectual Vocation ; Or else take it for the eternal election, it varyeth not our present Case in debate.

2. Nay see how fully this text destroys his Cause ! which plainly faith we are elect by, or through, or in sanctification of the Spirit to Obedience and sprinkling of the blood of Christ. Where sprinkling of Christs blood, means Remission, Justification, or Purifying from Guilt by Christs blood applyed. (Though *Grotius* would have it otherwise understood, lest it should prove that the Holy Ghost is given in order before Remission.) Now if this be so, then not only election, but the first sanctification of the Spirit, goes before Justification ; And then it is neither from eternity, nor from Christs death.

3. Whether you take election 1 Thef. 1. 4. for temporal or eternal election, your Argument is irregular ; you might well have argued, that if *Paul* knew their election by their faith and charity, that they might have known it themselves also by their faith and charity. But to argue thus, *Paul* knew by their faith that they were elected ; therefore they might know that they are elected by faith, making faith in the Antecedent only the means of knowing, and in the Consequent, the means of election ; this is absurd. And if this be not your meaning (at least to prove an appearance of such a thing, where indeed is none) then you say nothing to the purpose ; we deny not but it may be said, that a man by faith may know his election. But doth *Paul* give you the least shew of any more ?

§. 14.

§. 14,

Pag. 16. L. C. *Lastly, as* Paul *saying, faith is of the elect, meant not that faith is the Cause of Election, or that a Believer is the adequate object of election; so must we accordngly iudge of faith in respect to Justification.*

---

§. 14.

R. B. AS if there were the least Appearance of likelihood in the several speeches! Is it all one to say *the faith of the elect,* and to say *we are elected by faith,* as it is said we are justified by faith! When do you read in Scripture, *God so loved the world that he gave his only son, that whoever believeth in him shall be elected?* as we read, *whoever believeth shall not perish?* Or where read you, that whoever believeth shall not be reprobate, as we read, that *they shall not come into Condemnation,* we read of many promises of Remission if we will believe; you read no promise of election if you will believe. We are said to receive Remission of sins through faith ; but not to receive election through faith. I seriously profess the evidence of Scripture is so full, that faith is a means to Justification, Remission and Salvation, and not only a manifestation of what is done already, that he that impartially peruseth it, and doth not believe this truth, I think he may do well to search whether he believe that Christ is God, or that the Gospel is true; if he be a man of competent intellectuals. And confident I am a learned man could not be so blinded, but his will must be deeply guilty of it.

---

§. 15.

Pag. 17. L. C. *But the chief Cause of the Error is, that they make the faith which they call Justifying to be something different from Regeneration; when yet the faith of the elect is not only conjunct with holiness in one and the same subject, but is formally our Holiness; not indeed the whole, but a part; even as Hope and Charity which are equally the fruits of the Spirit,* Gal. 5. 22. 2. *Part of the Commandments.* 3. *which have increases and decreases, as it falls out with every good work. By this part of the Error Regeneration is made to go before Justification; For if Faith in Christ go before Justification, it follows that Regeneration, whereof faith is the chief part, doth also go before Justification. On the contrary, this error being well discerned, faith will only hold the first place in the rank of the three graces, in which Company we must not think that justification goes before good works and follows faith: For seeing faith hope and charity are inseparable, and Iustification goes before good works, it follows that Iustification must go before faith.*

§. 15;

§. 15.

R. B. WHen a man is in the dark, no wonder if he grope and yet be loft: so is this Differtor even when he pretendeth to difcover *the chief caufe of our error*. All this difcourfe needs but thefe two eafie diftinctions to difcover its infirmity. 1. Of Regeneration. 2. Of good Works. Regeneration is taken fometime for the whole new ftate of a Believer, which he enters upon in his firft change, *viz*. His new nature, new relations to his Head, Husband, Lord: When he that is in Chrift is a new Creature, old things are paffed away; behold all things are become new. In this large fenfe, Iuftification, and Remiffion, and Adoption are part of our Regeneration. I think in Scripture and in Fathers, the word is not feldom (comparatively to the other) taken in this fenfe. Sometime Regeneration fignifieth the work of the Spirit, working in the Soul the firft fpecial Grace. Concerning this, Divines are of three different judgements; 1. Moft of ours fay that Faith (or Repentance only with it) are firft given in the feed, which is a begun habit: then in the act, then we are united to Chrift: then we are juftified: then other habits of Hope, Love, &c. are given. See Bifhop *Downam* againft *Pemble*. The firft they call Vocation, the laft Sanctification: and fome give the name of Regeneration to the firft, and fome to the laft, yet making all thefe go together. 2. Mr. *Pemble* (from whom I received it, and held it faft till lately) doth think, that the feed or habit of all Grace equally is given firft at once, and the acts only go one before another. 3. *Camero* thinks that the Holy-Ghoft by the object (fet home more powerfully then man could do) and fo by the word, doth firft caufe the act and habit of Faith, but in order of nature the act firft, and by that act a habit, and hereby other facred acts and habits in order; and Iuftification follows immediately on our believing, by force of the foederal Donation. I think for my part, the precife order and manner of Gods Work on the Soul is unfearchable: (though this laft feem moft congruous to the nature of mans Soul). The firft and laft way anfwer your objection; that although Faith, Hope and Charity be infeparable, in time, yet not in order of nature: If you go *Pembles* way, I fay, that they are all *in femine* before Iuftification: but the queftion is of the act. Yea for my part, I grant it as undoubted Truth, that fomething of Love to Chrift and Hope in him, are not only concomitant with juftifying Faith, but the modification, or parts of it: it is no one act that is called juftifying-Faith, as it is not in one fingle confideration that the object is prefented and to be received. This Faith is, as an Affent to the Truth of the Gofpel, fo a Thankful Loving Acceptance of Chrift as offered.: *Calvin* makes *fperare* the act of juftifying-Faith: in the place I cited a few leaves before. When *Paul* fpeaks of Faith as faving or juftifying, he ever implyeth Hope and Love as to the fame object, Chrift and Life. But why it is named from the act of believing, I have elfewhere already given the reafon: When he diftinguifheth Faith, Hope and Love, he taketh Faith in a more reftrained fenfe: as *James* doth alfo where he makes it feparable from juftification and good Works.

And in this fenfe Regeneration doth ftill go before juftification (in the adult.) 2. You muft diftinguifh of good Works. As working is taken in the fenfe rejected by *Paul, Rom*. 4. 4. for works of proper merit, which make the reward to be of Debt and not of Grace, so we must not once dream that there is such a thing in the world. But as *Works* are taken for good actions, so they are either Inward or Outward. Faith, Hope and Love, are inward Good Works: and these do go before Justification. But neither Scripture nor Fathers use the word *Good Works* in that sense, at least often; but only for outward Works of obedience. And so Good Works *sequuntur Justificatum, non precedunt Justificandum*, as *Austin* saith, they follow Justification. Yea you must distinguish more exactly of Inward Works. As in every Army or Common-wealth, the first fundamental act of him that will be a Member, is, To consent to the Relation, and take such a man for his General or Soveraign; and then after he must Love, Honor and Obey him as such. The first is not formally Obedience, but the consenting to his Soveraignty that he may obey him, so is it here: The Faith that first justifieth us as a Condition, is the Taking Christ for our Saviour and Lord-Redeemer: and Justification followeth on this before any act of formal obedience to him as such, internal or external: So that the Love to Christ Accepted, which is a real part of that Acceptance (for Good cannot as Good be Accepted without Love), goes before Justification: but the Love that followeth that Acceptance, followeth our first Justification also: yet is it necessary as the Condition of the Continuance of that Justification.

As for your saying, *It is part of the Commandments*, that is no reason why it may not be the Condition of Justification. For it must be *officium*, Duty, in order of nature before it be a Condition.

And its as little to the business that Faith hath increases and decreases: seeing it is not the further Degrees, but the meer sincerity, (or such a Degree as makes it sincere) which is the Condition of justification.

---

§. 16.

Pag. 17, 18. L. C. **H**E that thus judgeth of Faith, shall more easily shift himself out of the hands of the Arminians; shall give more glory to the Justice of God, taking that from Faith, which he may give to the glorious Grace and the Gracious Glory of God. For I will willingly grant the Arminians, that Faith is a work, and part of our Obedience; yea and that by that Faith we are Justified; but declaratively, and as Faith is a Messenger to conscience, of Peace, and Remission of sins: but not that Faith is formally imputed to us for righteousness, or that we are Justified by the habit or inherent quality; which venome and ulcer of the Arminians we touch not, but avoid as much as any.

---

§. 16.

R. B. **A** Careless Reader would not think what notorious great errors are in these smooth words. 1. To your first commodity I answer, *sic vitant, &c.* We have somewhat else to think of, then only to fly from Arminianism. Truth borders close to error, and therefore close to Arminianism. To be neer to error is a sign of Truth. If you will fly further, and go to Antinomianism, to avoid Arminianism, you will go out of the ashes into the fire. The next way to decide all controversies about Scriptures, between us and the Papists, were with the Infidels, to deny their Verity: But is that therefore the best way, because it avoids Popery? 2. You are quite mistaken in your own supposition too. Going on false principles, disables any man to deal with his adversary: and the discovering of our erroneous extreams, hardens them in theirs. I am confident some few such mistakes in some Divines, hath multiplyed Arminians, or hardned them: and that if our disputers had gone no higher against them, then *Davenant*, *Camero*, *Lud. Crocius*, or then the Synod of *Dort* hath done, we had more effectually confuted them.

3. To your second Commodity I say, when men will devise ways of their own to honor Gods Grace and Justice, contrary to Gods way and Word, it is a goodly honor they give him; even the greatest dishonor. God best knows what is honorable to himself. If taking all from Faith and Works, and giving it to God, had been the way, none of all those texts which I before heaped up, had spoke as they do. What an honor were it to God to say, that our Faith Accepts not Christ and Life, but Christ doth all himself? It were but conform to this conceit, to say, that it is best say, that Infidels, Pagans, Murderers, Adulterers, Lyers, Perjured, that live and dye such, are the object of Justification and Salvation, for then nothing is given to man, but all to God.

4. But how prove you that it will Glorifie his Justice? when man is no object of justice? if he have not some Conditions of Life or Death propounded to him.

You dangerously err in making Faith a part of our obedience, if you mean it of Christian obedience, of our first Faith, as you must. For it is the Taking Christ for our Lord and Saviour, that for the future we may obey him: and so is an engagement to Obedience. All obedience is obedience to a Rector, so taken to be. He must therefore be so taken, before he can be obeyed. Though how much of obedience to God as Creator, the Taking him as Redeemer may have in it, I will not now stand to enquire: but sure it is no act of Christian obedience to God-Redeemer, but the seed of all obedience following. And therefore you will overshoot your self in granting this to the Arminians.

6. It hath troubled our Divines to shew how Faith is no Work, and yet Justifyeth. Some say, that it is a meer Passion, because it is improperly or morally at best called a Reception; this is fond. Some say, it is a work, but Justifies only as an Instrument. This is as vain: for that which they call its instrumentality, is its Acceptance, and that is an act: and every proper Instrument effecteth: and all efficiency is by Action. So that to say, It is the Instrument, is most plainly to say, It justifieth by working or Acting, which is *efficientis causalitas*. So that this opinion of Faiths Instrumentality leads men into the same Conclusion which they use it to avoid: which is no new thing with ill chosen means. I say, Faith is no work in any of these 5. senses. 1. as working is taken for perfect obeying, for salvation, according to the tenor of the Law of Nature, so Faith is no work. 2. As working is taken for performing the Ceremonial task of the abrogated Law of *Moses*, so Faith is not working. 3. As working is taken for works deserving a Reward by Commutative justice, as benefiting God, and so making the reward of Debt and not of Grace: so Faith is no work. But in none of these senses are our new obedience works neither. 4. But that which I further note is this, that works are often put for obediential works to God our Redeemer; and not in meer Physical sense for an Act; or for an act meerly good to our selves, or good because of the nature and the object, or in obedience to God as Creator only. Now our first Faith is no such work. It is commanded,

ed, but we do it not *eo nomine*, because commanded by God as Redeemer: for it is the first acknowledgement of his Authority and Consent to it, and our first consent to be subjects: and the Relation must be tyed before any office of Relation can be performed. As if you speak to a perfect Atheist (if there be such a thing) and perswade him to believe in God: his first belief is no act of obedience, but the Assent to Gods soveraignty, and consent to obey hereafter. So is it with our first Faith in the Redeemer, as to Christian obedience. But now all after good actions are acts of obedience. 5. Also sometime the term *Works* signifyeth those Actions which are done, as our Duty (or on other accounts) to the good of some other principally; and so it is distinguished, from receiving that good that is freely given to our selves: in this sense also Faith is Receiving, and not Working; For it is but the Accepting Christ and Life with him, as offered to us in the Gospel. And though this Acceptance must be fitted to the object, and so Christ must be received in his most honorable titles, and on honorable terms, yet the work thus modifyed, is but the accepting of an offered Saviour, as that good which we most need for the healing and preventing of our misery. So much to acquaint you how far you may yield that Faith is a work, and how far not.

7. That Faith is the condition of our constitutive and sentencial Iustification before God, and not only of the Declaration to conscience, I mean to prove yet more fully before I leave you.

8. When you say, Faith is *not formally imputed to us for Righteousness*, I do not understand you. Righteousness is two-fold, according to the two Covenants or Laws of God. The Righteousness of the first materially is Perfect Obedience. This we have not; nor doth God take our Faith to be such: But the satisfaction and merit of Christ is to us instead of it, as dissolving the obligation to punishment (*quoad meritum*) which we for want of that Righteousness had contracted; and so is, as I may call it, our *Justitia pro legalis*. But because it pleased not God to give us this Righteousness immediately or absolutely, but by the means of another Covenant, as the instrument of conveyance; and that Covenant makes our Acceptance, its condition; therefore that Acceptance is our material particular subordinate Righteousness, so called by this new Covenant or Law of Grace: Though Christs Righteousness may also be called the Righteousness of the New Covenant in another respect, *viz*. as the means of conveying and discovering it. So that as the performance of the condition of the New Covenant, may be called the Righteousness of that Covenant, so Faith is imputed, that is, truly esteemed and judged to be our Righteousness. But if you ask whether this Faith be now instead of the perfect obedience of the Law of nature? I answer, that obedience was considerable as a meritorious work, and *quoad rei valorem*, or else as our own personal Act. In the former respect, only Christs satisfaction and merit is instead of our perfect obedience; as being only of value to Justifie us for itself. But because God will not make men partakers of that Righteousness of Christ, without some Act of his own, as a condition of his Right, therefore Faith hath now the formal nature of a condition in the new Covenant, as perfect obedience had in the old: that is, Faith is the condition of our interest in Christs Righteousness freely given us, as perfect obedience was then the condition of continuing mans right in paradice, and of any further Reward that God would supperadd. And as God then required that perfect obedience, so he now requires of the sinner himself, only the performance of the conditions of the

the new Covenant: (which also he enableth his elect to perform). And thus far Faith is instead of perfect obedience, and no further: and this is the true Doctrine of imputing Faith for Righteousness.

9. For what you say of the *Habit and Inherent quality*; I say, (though I once wrote otherwise upon trust) that, if not first, yet at least after, for our continued Justification, the Habit of Faith is sufficient to be the condition of our Justification, when the act is not performed (as when we sleep): yet not as an Habit and quality (nor the act as an act) but as the condition *formally*, and as a Habitual Reception or Acceptance of Christ and Life, *Aptitudinally*. And this is the common Doctrine of Protestants (of whom many think infants so justified), and no venemous ulcer of Arminianism.

---

§. 17.

Pag. 18. L. C. *And that Scripture opposeth Faith to Good Works, and layeth them by in the business of Justification, is no wonder; in as much as among good Works, Faith only bringeth to our conscience the glad tydings of our Reconciliation; 2. Applyeth the benefits procured by Christ; 3. Only resteth in Gods Love; 4. Is the root of Good Works. Also because Faith is often taken for the Gospel it self, or the object of Faith; no wonder, however Faith and Justification be taken, if Faith be included in Justification; and Good Works shut out. Moreover, though Faith it self be a good Work; yet Faith and other good Works are divided by contrary effects: for it raiseth the sinner into hope of Remission: but good Works, even the most exact, do cast the sinner into terror, when he revieweth himself and his works; for then he despaireth of himself and them: it increaseth the opposition that Faith doth give nothing to God, but Receive: but Good Works are as it were Eucharistical sacrifices.*

---

§. 17.

R. B. 1. I Shewed in the former Section, how far Faith is distinct from Good Works. But I conceive that the Apostle in his frequent exclusion of Works, compared with Faith, doth mainly intend 1. The Works of *Moses* Law: 2. Specially as the Pharises and other Jews dreamed of Appeasing God by them for sin committed; 3. And that the perfect obedience of the Law of nature, is consequentially only excluded, as being in sinners a *non-ens*, there is no such thing: and imperfect obedience is damning according to that Law: But it is not a Justification, consisting in perfect innocency, that the Apostle disputes against, for the Jews never dreamt of that: But a Justification consisting in Remission of sin, which they thought the bare sacrifices and other Works of the Law would procure. But that the Apostle excludeth obedience to the Redeemer in subordination to his Righteousness, from being the Condition of our Justification constitutive as continued, or of our sentential Justification at judgement, is utterly false. It is most evident in the whole scope of his arguing, that it is works as opposed to Christ, or Coordinate with Christs Righteousness, that he disputeth against; but not directly against the works that stand in a necessary subordination to Christ, as such, and keeping that station.

2. The

[205]

2. The reason that you first give, is no reason, but an absurdity, unless you mean, the offer and conditional Grant of Reconciliation in the Gospel, through Christs blood : for Faith cannot bring the report of Actual Reconciliation before it is: and it is not before Faith, as shall be fully proved. Besides many a thousand are reconciled that yet have not the knowledge of it in conscience, yet have they Faith in Christ, which is requisite to that reconciliation. Justifying Faith is another thing then the Assurance of Reconciliation, or Justification in conscience.

3. Love and Hope apply Christs benefits in part, and yet you exclude them; therefore your second reason needs some limitation.

4. The like may be said to your third reason. Love is the Souls Complacency in God, and therefore resteth in him. So doth Hope, and Trust.

5. Is Love no Root of Good Works? Or is it necessary that Faith Justifie us in conscience, and not Good Works, because Faith is the root of Good Works? Rather as the fruits are more discernable then the root; so Good Works should Justifie us more then (or as much as) Faith, if it were only in conscience that Faith justified. You will never give a solid reason, why Love, Hope, Repentance, and any true part of sanctification should not Justifie us in as proper a sense as Faith, if it were only in conscience that Faith Justified us.

6. Your next reason, *because Faith is oft taken for the Gospel and object*, is no answer as to all those common texts where Faith is not taken for the Gospel or object.

7. For your next reason, that *Faith raiseth the sinner into hope of Remission, but Good Works cast into terror and despair, &c.* I answer, why may not sincere obedience as well as Faith, by way of manifestation, as signs, give us hope of Remission? sure the Apostle saith, *we know we are translated from death to life, because ye love the Brethren. And if ye by the Spirit do mortifie the deeds of the body ye shall live.*

8. Let the Reader but observe whether this Doctrine tendeth. How well are those men like to obey Christ, that think works of obedience, even the best, do cast us into terror and despair? who then will not avoid them, that would avoid despair and terror? Its true, if a man had no Christ to look to, nor any remedying-Covenant of Grace, but stood on the meer terms of the Law of Works, then his works would drive him to despair: He that hath no Saviour nor Promise to look at, may well despair by his imperfection and the sinfulness of his works: And so he might in his Faith too, because of its imperfection, if he looked at his Faith to be instead of Christ its object: But he that looks at his works in subordination to Christ only; and as accepted with God, who is well pleased with such sacrifices, *Heb.* 13.10. and having all the imperfections pardoned in Christ, and as being Gods Love-tokens, and the conditions of our salvation, I think, need not be cast by them into terror or despair, but may exceedingly rejoyce in them, though he must be humbled for their imperfections. *Paul* could say, *This is our rejoycing, the Testimony of our consciences, that in simplicity and Godly sincerity we have had our conversation among you.*

9. Even now you put *Hope* among Good Works that follow remission: and here you make it an act or effect of Faith, to *Hope* for Remission.

10. I pray you tell us which of your two sorts of remission is this? not the Eternal,

Eternal, or from Chrifts dying: for that cannot be hoped for; not that in confcience upon our firft believing; for that is already known; if juftifying Faith be the knowledge of our Iuftification, then every one that hath that Faith, doth know that he is Iuftified: And if fo, how can Faith *raife him into hope of that which he hath already*; when the object of Hope is alway future? And I think, this contradicteth your former and after defcriptions of Faith: For to know our paft Iuftification, and to hope for it, do much differ. Yea if it be but that knowledge it felf of it, which you mean we hope for: The act and the object are not the fame thing.

---

§. 18.

Pag. 20. L. C. *HEnce it is that Divines will not have the firft act of Faith, whereby it receiveth Chrift, to Juftifie as it is a Work, Action, or Vertue, becaufe in that act, Faith * is as a Patient or Recipient: But what is that (*ratio entis*) reafon of being by which Faith is faid to Juftifie and to Remit fin; is not yet manifeft.*

* Se habet ad modum patientis, &c.

---

§. 18.

R. B. FAith is an Action; but you may if you pleafe call it a Patient or Recipient, in that it is fuch an action *ad Receptionem Paffivam neceffaria*, as that it is commonly called *Receiving* it felf in a moral fenfe; becaufe there is no receiving without it, in a Phyfical fenfe. It is the *Difpofitio moralis materiæ*.

2. The reafon of Faiths Iuftifying intereft, is manifeft, and a moft eafie Truth, if vain difputes had not poffeft mens mindes with feducing Notions, to turn them from the Truth. The neereft formal reafon of Faiths intereft in our Iuftification, is, that it is the condition on which God in the Covenant hath given remiffion or Iuftification to us: The meer will of the free Donor hath defigned it to this office, to whom it belongeth to make over to men his benefits on what terms he pleafe. The remote reafon, is Faiths Aptitude to this affigned office. How fhould a Saviour fitlyer convey himfelf and his benefits, then on condition that men will acknowledge him to be their Saviour, and Accept of the Gift? I have purpofely put the Queftion to fome underftanding, Learned Gentlemen, who I knew had never then heard or read of the Controverfie among Divines, (but only had out of Scripture, and ordinary writers and Teachers gathered folid knowledge in the main body of Divinity); and I asked them, In what refpect they thought Faith, rather then any thing elfe, did Iuftifie? And confulting the Scripture and the nature of the thing, having no foreftalling notions one way or other, they ftill anfwered to the fame effect, *viz.* That it was becaufe God was pleafed to give us pardon on thefe terms, and of his own good pleafure to appoint Faith to this dignity.

§. 19.

§. 19.

L. C. Nor is it to be omitted, that Scripture, to excite in us the gift of Grace, doth oft ascribe so much to Good Works, Faith and our saving knowledge, that it makes them Causes, why God maketh us partakers of the Kingdom of Heaven: So when it is said, 2 Pet. 1. 3. that by the knowledge which we have of God, is granted to us, whatsoever pertains to Life and Godliness; its wonder if in that company Remission of sin have not a place: which knowledge of God doth yet no otherwise Remit sins, then Faith Justifieth or remitteth sins: to wit, when by the knowledge of God, or by Faith, Remission of sin is known to us.

§. 19.

R. B. This is not to prove, but still to beg the Question. 1. The knowledge of him that hath called us; in 2 Pet. 1. 3. is Faith it self, which is a true knowledge and acknowledgement of Christ, and God as reconciled by him, so far as to give conditional pardon to others, and the Condition also to his elect, in its season. 2. You can make the Scripture speak what you list, by your violating conceits. God saith, He hath given us all these things by the knowledge of Christ, that is, by Faith. You say, It is but the knowledge of these things, and not the things themselves that he so giveth us. You expound Scripture by contradicting it, at pleasure. And indeed, do you think, that it is but the knowledge of our Good Works, or sanctity of Life, or of our growth in Grace, that is given us by faith, or this knowledge of God in Christ; and not the things themselves? If you dare not say so of them, say not so of Remission.

§. 20.

L. C. Lastly, the Author of the Epistle, that he might avoid one extream, doth run into another; and while he feareth to confound Justification with Election, doth commix Sanctification, of which Faith is a principal part, with Justification. For he will have Application, which properly is an act of Faith, to belong to Justification, as a part to the whole; making, if I mistake not, Impetration to be Justification begun, and Application to be Justification Consummate: But if the reason be rightly considered, that Impetration is coincident with Justification or Reconciliation, which he confesseth Christ obtained for us by the sacrifice of the Cross: If this be so, what need is there of another reason of sparing by Application, when once the pardon of his crime is impetrated for the guilty?

§. 20.

§. 20.

R. B. IT is a fine world when men of such Doctrines cry out of extreams. But 1. Remember that here you confess the confounding Justification with Election is one extream. Why then do you make it to be an immanent act? and Dr. *Twiss*, to be eternal?

2. The word *Sanctification*, or Sanctimony, is most commonly used in Scripture, for the holyness of our lives, or some progressive holyness of heart, following our first Faith. Whether you mistake the Author of the Epistle or no, I will leave to the Reader to enquire and judge; but sure I am, the reformed Churches generally, who maintain the Doctrine of Justification by Faith, which you oppose, do not make Faith any part of Justification, (that were a ridiculous fancy) but a prerequisite thereto.

3. I doubt not but you mistake *Molin.* in supposing him to make Impetration to be begun Justification. It is indeed a *Principium*, that is, a meritorious cause of Justification. But the meritorious Cause is not the effect begun.

4. What though he confess that Christs sacrifice on the Cross, obtained our Reconciliation or Justification? doth it follow either that obtaining and the thing obtained, is all one? or that there needs no more? I answer therefore, to your last unworthy question: Though Christ did Impetrate then our Justification, yet not then presently, nor absolutely after to be conferred: but to be given first, afterward in its season: 2. But conditionally in the tenor of the Deed of Gift: though God decreed, and the dying-redeemer willed, that all the Elect should be enabled (and caused) to perform the Condition. So that there was need afterward, that God should cause us to perform it; and that we should accordingly do it, that so we might be pardoned and justified in Gods way and order, according to the terms of his Covenant or Law of Liberty or Grace, which we must be judged and justified by. It is utterly unbeseeming not only a Divine, but any sober knowing Christian, that hath ever considered the scope of the Gospel, to put such a question as this, *what need is there of another* ratio parcendi *by application, when once the pardon of sin is Impetrated?* If God should let loose but horrors of conscience on you, yea or sickness of body, I hope your prayers would intimate, that there is another *ratio parcendi* necessary. Hath a persecuting *Saul*, a hater of God and goodness, a wicked wretch that is a stranger to the Covenant of Promise, without God in the world, and a childe of wrath, supposing this man elect, hath he no need of further remission or reconciliation or Justification, but only to know it? nor should he pray for any more? This is so unlike the Doctrine of Christ, that I dare boldly call it Antichristian Doctrine.

CHAP.

CHAP. II.

Of the Acts of Faith.

§. 1.

Pag. 22. L. C. *But that it may more clearly appear what part faith obtaineth in our Justification, it will not be amiss to rehearse and explicate the acts of a lively faith. There is therefore a threefold act of faith; The first is that whereby by means of the Holy Ghost, the Believer seeth all Righteousness fulfilled in Christ and by Christ; that he dyed for sinners; and that there is no cause why he should exempt himself out of the number of those sinners: And this direct act is active in respect of God, and the Divine influx, or of God giving faith, but Passive in respect of man receiving.*

§. 1.

R. B. This act of Assent to the Truth of the Gospel concerning Christs satisfaction, is indeed the first, and of flat necessity, and part of justifying faith: But let me give you these two or three animadversions, 1. Though we must believe that Christ as Mediatour did fulfil all righteousness, yet we are not to believe that he then justified us actually, or forgave our sins; but contrarily, that he did not: the Scripture making that plain to us, past doubt.

2. It is not enough to believe that Christ so satisfied for sinners, as that I see no Cause to exclude my self. But I must see Cause to include my self, and that upon certain Grounds, which may be a sure support to faith; Otherwise it will only warrant me, *not to believe my self excluded*, or that it may be true for ought I know to the contrary, that I am included; but it will be no warrant to me to believe my self Included, nor for any Action to which this is presupposed. And I think it is no saving faith to think and say, *It may be Christ dyed for me, and it may be he did not; I do not, nor can possibly know at present.* It must therefore be a general satisfaction, sufficient for All, that must warrant this first act of faith.

3. It is strange doctrine to say that our Act of faith is Active as to Gods giving, and passive in respect of man receiving. 1. An active Power I have heard of, and so if an Act be taken for a power, or for a habit, or for the being which is their subject, you may call it active; but if you take it not pro *Actu secundo*, you so equivocate, that few will understand you: and if you do, I think an *Active act* is but a Tautologie at best. 2. But a Passive Act is yet stranger, and that in respect of us, who sure if I mistake not are the Agents. Do we perswade men only to suffer, when we perswade them to believe? Are unbelievers condemned for not suffering only, or at all? I pray you vouchsafe to tell us by the next, what it is that Faith suffers, and from whom? If you had said the person had been passive, I should have believed you; but that the Act should be passive is very new Logick to me. I know Acceptance of a Gift is commonly called *Receiving*, but not *in sensu Physico*, as *Recipere est Pati*:

but

[210]

but Morally and Metonymically, it being an act necessarily Antecedent to Passive Reception. But your doctrine here is conform enough to the rest.

§. 2.

Pag. 23. L. C. THe second act, active and reflex in respect of man, is that whereby a sinner becomes conscious of his sin and misery, and also of so great a benefit offered, and thence by the operation of the same Spirit of Adoption, doth move himself toward Christ, with Love, Affiance and Hope. The third Act is that whereby faith acteth by good works.

§. 2.

R. B. 1. THis second Active Act in my opinion is more then one, two, or three acts. To be conscious of sin, is one act, it may be many hundred, according to the many hundred sins that we are conscious of. To be conscious of misery is another act at least; To be conscious of the greatness of the benefit (If you will call it Consciousness) is another; and to know that It is offered is another. To move toward Christ, you confess comprehends many, viz. Love, Affiance, and Hope. To move toward Christ indeed is a general term; we usually call faith, a coming to Christ; and if meer moving toward him, contain all these, Love, Affiance and Hope, then blame not me, If faith or coming to Christ, be in sense said to comprehend these. Your third is but remotely an act of faith, in that faith causeth the will to command the other faculties to do those good works. But Sir, here is one act which is implied in Love and Affiance, but properly called the Acceptance of an offered Christ and Life, or Consent to the offer and terms of the Covenant, which is the great act of justifying faith, which you seem much to overlook. As many as received him, to them gave he power, &c. Ioh. 1. 11, 12. You seem not to be an Englishman, but if you understand English, If you will read Dr. Prestons works well, he will better acquaint you with the nature of faith; Or In shorter room, If you will but read Mr. Scudders Daily Walk on that subject, you shall see justifying faith most solidly described; and by our late reverend Assembly in their Catechism well defined: as also by Mr. Norton of New-England in his Catechism.

§. 3.

L. C. THe first act of faith you have, Rom. 1. 7. and Gal. 1. 15. Eph. 1. 13, 14. In whom after ye believed (which words are followed with others belonging to the second act) ye were sealed with the holy Spirit of promise. To the same second act belong the words, Ephes. 3. 17. and those Ephes. 3. 12. In whom we have freedom and access with confidence to the faith of him; which place is a Paraphrase of the words, to be justified by faith; To wit, it is the nature of true faith to move it self towards Christ. There is an express place Rom. 8. 16. which expresseth the second act. The Spirit it self witnesseth with our Spirit that we are the Sons of God. Where the Spirit of God acting in our hearts by faith, not only witnesseth that we are Sons of God, but causeth us firmly to adhere to God, to hope in him, delight in him,

him, *rest upon him*, *and trust to him.* Hither pertain the words Gal. 5. 5. and 4. 6. which place aptly exhibiteth both the *second act of faith*, and the *whole reason of Justification by faith*, as if he said, Becaufe God hath adopted you for fons, forgiven your fins, and imputed the righteoufnefs of Chrift, he would make you certain of fo great a benefit, by giving you precious faith, which the Spirit of God hath created in your hearts, by which ye reft in God the Father, and caft your cares on him, as into the bofome of a Father, and have accefs to him with confidence.

The third act is fulfilled, when (Tit. 3.8.) *we confirm our faith by good works, and faith worketh by love*: Gal. 5.6. Of the fame act St. Paul, Rom. 8.11. To wit, when the Spirit of Chrift dwelling in us by faith, promoteth the *work of Regeneration*; quickneth, fanctifieth us, and createth a new life, whose fruits are recited, Gal. 5. 22, 23.

In thefe acts and places true *Juftification by faith is set before our eyes*: Thefe are the acts of juftifying faith, but not of Juftification or Imputation of Chrifts righteoufnefs; yet are thefe acts true effects of juftification, or the action of God whereby he abfolveth the miferable finner, and imputeth to him Chrifts obedience.

---

§. 3.

R. B. ALL this is to little purpofe, and much confufed, and Scriptures confidently expounded, without reafon, and againft it. 1. *Rom.* 1.17. fignifieth more then bare Affent. Proved; The faith that the Juft live by, is more then bare Affent; but the Apoftle there exprefly fpeaks of the faith which the Juft fhall live by, therefore Gal 1.15. *Gods Revealing Chrift in* Paul, alfo fignifieth more then Affent. Eph. 1.13,14. is abufed. The firft words fignifie more then Affent, for *Believing in*, *or on Chrift* is more. Thofe that you fay exprefs the fecond act of faith, do not fpeak at all of faith, any more then other graces; but of the Spirit of promife, that is, the promifed Spirit in general. Eph. 3. 17. doth indeed belong to your fecond act which is many acts. But by what licenfe will you fay, Chrifts dwelling in our hearts, is our knowledge that he dwells there, or that we are juftifyed? That Eph. 3. 12. is a paraphrafe of *Juftification by faith*, is your naked affirmation without any fhew of proof: why are we bound to take your word? I doubt not but they are acts of faith, following juftification by faith. Many a foul is juftified by faith that wants boldnefs and confidence. But if the juftifying act be here, it doth not follow that there is no more; or that thefe words are a paraphrafe of Juftification by faith. Seeing here is no mention of juftification, or any thing of that nature. Yet it is true, that its the nature of faith to move toward Chrift, or rather to come to Chrift, that is, properly to accept him as offered You do but feign of your own brain, that *Rom.* 8.16. expreffeth your fecond juftifying act. The Spirits witneffing objectively, as a teftimony, or efficiently, as fhewing us our ftate, do come after juftifying faith. There is not a word of juftification. You make here hope, delight, &c. Iuftifying acts too. Gal. 5. 5. fpeaks of Hope of the Reward which by faith we are excited to: I will not exclude that act from Iuftification, but you fhould not overlook the main act, *Acceptance of Chrift given, & Life in him,* of which all the reft are but modification, and attendents. That text Gal. 1.6. which you fay exhibits the whole reafon of Iuftification, never fpeaks of it at all. Adoption is a concomitant Relation with Iuftification, received on the fame condition of faith or acceptance, which is not here mentioned in the text, nor by you obferved. The Spirits crying *Abba* father, is no

where

where called justifyng faith; but you still give us your dreams instead of proof, and presume to tell us, that texts speak what you imagine them to speak, without giving us any proof of it. You prove not that the Spirit may not enable us to cry *Abba* Father, without giving us Assurance of our justification: (There may be the knowledge of Gods gracious inclination, and conditional promises, and there may be thence a filial desire, dependance, love, proceeding from justifying faith, and yet no such Assurance of actual Justification.) much less do you prove that this Assurance is justifying faith : and least of all, that it is the sole or first Justifying act.

2. You need not tell us that the acts of Justifying faith are not justification, or Imputation; you do but slander us in intimating that we so teach. We only say that they are the necessary means to Justification (*viz.* Conditions) therefore not Justification it self.

3. That faith, (at least our first faith) is an effect of Justification, is one of your falshoods nakedly affirmed, which you can never prove.

§. 4.

L. C. *For these acts of recurring to Christ, resting on him, reposing all our confidence in him, quieting our selves in his Love, do nothing pertain to the acts of absolving, pardoning sin, or justifying. But plainly these acts, yea all the acts of faith do Justifie, when* Iustifying *signifies the same as to make known, or give Testimony; even the third act Justifieth, where good works are the witnesses of our Faith, both at the bar of conscience, and in the eyes of our neighbours.*

§ 4.

R. B. 1. The first Assertion is false. For faith pertaineth to Gods act of Remitting, as the condition pertaineth to the act or moral efficacy of the Grant, Testament, or Deed of Gift. 2. You seem to equal works with faith in Iustifying. For no doubt, but love, hope, obedience, do by way of sign, directly and certainly discover our justification. But then what reason have you to say, that good works Iustifie as witnesses of our faith? It seems somewhat of the truth sticks latent in your mind, which these words discover. Is it not because Faith is the primary Condition of our right, that is, of our Iustification, and Adoption, that therefore works must witness its sincerity, and prove it to be that current faith which is the condition; and so Iustifie the person by Iustifying the faith ? No doubt but sincere obedience might otherwise in your sense discover remission immediately as a sign, and not only by way of witnessing to the soundness of our faith.

§. 5.

L. C. *Moreover all these acts, such as Incumbency, &c. seeing they are the work of grace, and are bestowed for the sake of Christ, do suppose precedent Reconciliation, and therefore Justification. And that we were received before we had the grace of these acts.*

§. 5.

R. B. A very raw miſtaken Arguing to uphold a pernicious Error! *All works of Grace beſtowed for Chriſt, do ſuppoſe Iuſtification.* But ſuch is this: therefore the major is falſe and unproved. 1. Works of common grace beſtowed for Chriſts merits, do not ſuppoſe Juſtification : ſuch as are, the giving of the Goſpel, and other means; ſanctifying men by the blood of the Covenant, ſo far as Apoſtates were, *Heb.* 10.29. 2. Faith and Repentance are works of ſpecial grace beſtowed for Chriſts ſake; and yet ſuppoſe not antecedent Iuſtification, nor Reconciliation full and actual, but only *in tantum, ſecundum quid*, and conditional. Your ſaying that *we were received* is ambiguous. 1. Its true we were from eternity ſo far loved of God, as that he decreed to give us in time all that good which we afterward receive. 2. Its true, that before faith we are all redeemed from that neceſſity of periſhing for want of an expiatory ſacrifice, which before we lay under, or ſhould have layen under without Chriſt. But what is this to Iuſtification? Nay its true, that a Conditional act of 'Remiſſion was granted to all : but it is as true, that it did not actually remit, till the Condition was performed. So that all this Diſſertors other errours proceed from his meer ignorance of the nature of remiſſion and Iuſtification, and of Iuſtifying faith; and from his confounding the acts of Gods eternal Decree and Purpoſe *de rerum eventu*, with his moral acts of Government, as Rector of the rational creature, conſtituting *Jus vel debitum Beneficii, Præmii, & Pœnæ.* The ſtrength of his argument muſt lye in this, that *God would not give ſo great a mercy if he were not reconciled*, To which I anſwer 1. It only follows, that he would not give it unleſs he loved us : and what is that Love, but his decretive Will to ſave us? Which yet may ſtand with his Hatred. (Not that Hatred which is oppoſite, *viz.* A will and decree to damn us, but he hath a rectoral love and hatred, as well as a decretive : His Love as *Rector, ſecundum Leges*, is his Will, that ſuch and ſuch benefits ſhall be our due according to that Law by which we muſt be Iudged; and ſo he is *quaſi obligatus*, ſo far as God can be obliged to the Creature) to confer them on us, and that by his own Law or Promiſe. His Hatred as Rector, is, when he willeth that ſuch a Puniſhment as Damnation ſhall be our legal Due, according to that Law that we muſt be Iudged by; and is, as it were, obliged as Iudge to execute it, if we be judged in that ſtate. His Reconciliation as Rector, is, when upon the change of the ſinner, by his performance of the Conditions of the Covenant, his relation being changed, and God is now in Law-ſenſe related to him as a father, and is as it were, obliged by his own Law to remit and accept him : yea doth by the act of Grace or Law of Liberty, diſſolve the obligation to puniſhment of the Law of Works, which is remiſſion and Iuſtification, and ſo that wrath or puniſhment ceaſeth to be due which was due before, and that ſalvation is due which before was not. Thus God hath made Laws that can do and undo, bind and looſe, ſave and damn, Condemn and Iuſtifie, as the ſinner changeth, and all this without any change in God. But for this Diſſertor, or any other to dream of a reconciliation of God in reſpect of his decretive will *de eventu*, is intolerable. Even Chriſts Death made no change in Gods decree, but fulfilled them. I muſt deſire this Diſſertor that he will pardon me for preſuming to ſpeak thus in a teaching ſtrain : for he leaves me no other work. To confute his arguings is ſo eaſie and ſhort a work, that it requireth in moſt places but a bare denial of his crude affirmations; but I am loath to leave the

[214]

Reader at a non-plus, but would as well shew him which is the truth, as which is errour. And if this learned man be humble enough to receive the Truth, he may in these few words see so much light as may shew him the vanity of his licentious conceits and arguings, though he may desire much more for the full clearing of the point

§. 6.

L. C. *Lastly, these Acts are the works and effects of our grace, or our Justification. For example, the first act of faith, and so our first Affiance doth not arise from sanctification, nor from such a promise whereby Remission of sin is promised to the Penitent, but from this Promise whereby Christ is promised to come into the world, that he might be propitious to the miserable, and to sinners.*

---

§. 6.

R. B. 1. THat the Acts of faith are the effects of Grace, who but a Pelagian will deny? 2. But that they are all the effects of our Justification, who but they in the contrary extream would affirm? And from such men who can expect proof? when yet there is a double necessity of proof; one from the invalidity of their affirming words, who are become of such suspected credit: the other from the novelty and improbability of the thing affirmed.

3. As sanctification is taken for our progress in grace or sanctity of Life, so faith and affiance arise not (in the first act at least) from sanctification: but as it is taken for the first principle of our new life, or the operation of the Spirit in causing that principle, so our faith ariseth from sanctification, as *Pemble* useth the word.

4. What Reader can find out the force of your example? how your following words do any way conduce to shew that faith is the effect of Justification.

5. Your words are ambiguous about *faiths arising from a promise*. If you mean it objectively, that our first faith is not *our Believing of the promise of Remission, &c. but of Christs coming, &c.* I say, It must believe both, though the latter first in order of nature. But if you mean it *efficienter*, that when God giveth our first faith, it is not in fulfilling this promise, but the other, I must tell you, that you speak confusedly. For you should not contradistinguish the general promise *of Gods giving Christ to be merciful to sinners*, from the particular promise of giving remission only. Understand that the word Promise signifieth; 1. A discovery of Gods gracious Purpose, which yet giveth no man right to the thing promised: 2. A proper Gift or Grant conferring right, either absolutely at present, or absolutely *in diem*, or conditionally. When God only saith, such a thing I will do in the world, or for some men whom I please to choose, this shews, as Prophecies do, that the thing shall come to pass; But no particular man hath any right to the benefit by this promise, nor can claim any. Gods promise of a Saviour to the world to dye for their sins, and to Justifie and Glorifie some in time, gave no man right to Justification or Glory. Yet you may truly say that Faith, Justification, Glorification, and all, are the fulfilling of that general promise. But if you go to a particular promise, I say 1. Its true, that the giving of Faith is not the fulfilling of that Promise, *Believe and be Justified*: but the giving of Justification is. 2. The Promise to the elect in general, of taking the hard heart out of their bodies (as it is commonly interpreted) is fulfilled in Gods giving us faith: yet did that promise give no man right

to

to Faith before hand. 3. God is not in Covenant with any unbelievers, promising to give them Faith on any condition by them to be performed: for that would be plain Pelagianism to affirm. 4. I conclude therefore that God hath given to Christ his Elect in special, that by the Spirit Christ might draw them to Believe, and so be saved: and he hath told us that his Elect shall be thus drawn and saved: and if you please you may call this a Covenant with Christ, giving him right to the Elect, and to do this work upon them, but it giveth no personal right to Faith, to any individual sinner, of which right himself shall be the subject: Nor is God in Covenant with any before they believe, as to be obliged to them to give them the blessing of Faith. So much for the dispelling of the mists that you raise as you go, and to deliver the weaker Readers a little from your confusions and obscurities.

CHAP. III.

An Explication of some places that treat of Justification.

§. I.

L. C. *THat it may the more clearly appear what parts Faith holdeth in Justification, we must run through some places, which make mention of Justification; to which I bring not in my self an Interpreter, but I put that sense to them, which seems to me to be more conform to the Divine Intellect of the Scripture.*

§. I.

R. B. I Know not whether this be contradictory non-sense, or Popery. If you mean that *the part of an Interpreter is to Give a Judicial Decisive Interpretation, whereas you give but a Teaching, Directive Interpretation, telling men your reasons of your sense;* then I undertake to prove against you, that there is no such Interpreter on earth, whether Pope or General Council, or both together. But if you intend not your self any such Interpretation, then you contradict your self, and say in effect, *I will not be an Interpreter, but I will Interpret;* But by your performance, I doubt the sense of your promise is; *I will not give you any good reasons for what I hold, but I will tell you my own opinion;* which indeed is so bad a way of Interpreting, especially for you, that you do not amiss to deny it the name.

§. 2.

L. C. R Om. 3. 22. *The Righteousness of God, by the Faith of Jesus Christ, upon all, and over all them that believe.* The sense is, that the Righteousness of God flowing into Believers of what sort soever, is revealed by the Doctrine of the Gospel, or is known by the gift of Faith, given to every Believer.

§. 3.

§. 2.

R. B. 1. The Apostle had in the former verse said, that Gods Righteousness is manifested: and in this verse he comes to shew what Righteousness it is that is so manifested: and he saith it is, *even the Righteousness of God, which is by the Faith of Jesus Christ, unto all, and upon all them that Believe.* So that the Apostle saith, *It is by Faith on Believers*; and the Dissertor saith, *It is manifested by the Doctrine of the Gospel, or known by the Gift of Faith.* 2. But the man is yet much more overseen: For what if it were manifestation to Believers that is here spoken of, It is only Gods Righteousness, (that is, the way of God for Justifying sinners, with the demonstration of his own Justice and mercy) witnessed by the Law and the Prophets, which is here said to be manifested. But it is not that you or I have part in this Righteousness. Do the Law and the Prophets witness that L. C. is righteous? God manifesteth Christs Righteousness, or his righteousness provided for sinners, or the righteous way of pardoning the guilty, 1. By Christs Life, Death, Resurrection, &c. 2. By his own and his Apostles preaching. 3. By his Spirits effectual internal Demonstration. And this manifesting is the very act whereby God giveth us our first true Faith. But it may be long after this that he will manifest that we have Faith, and are our selves truly righteous: However it is a different work.

§. 3.

L. C. Verse 24. Being Justified freely by his Grace through the redemption that is in Jesus Christ, *To wit, he makes Redemption or Remission of sin to be the formal cause of our Justification.*

§. 3.

R. B. 1. The preposition *διά*, signifieth not a formal Causality, but an efficient, *i. e.* a meritorious. 2. Redemption is taken in Scripture sometime for paying the Price, sometime for our actual Liberation. It is here taken in the former sense, and so it goes before our Justification long, and is not the same with remission, as you faign. 3. In the latter sense you may as well say it is the same with our Glorification, and final absolution after the resurrection: for that is part of our Liberation I think, and oft called by the name of redemption. 4. We yield you, that remission of sin is the formal Cause of our Justification: and what is that to the advantage of your error?

§. 4.

§. 4.

L. C. Verse 25. *Whom God hath set forth to be a propitiation through Faith in his blood, to declare his righteousness for remission of sins that are past*, &c. This place is cleared by this Paraphrase, The Doctrine of the Gospel, or the Gospel righteousness (which is sometime called by the name of Faith) declareth that the blood of Christ, shed for sinners, is the propitiation by which God is reconciled to them : *Or,* Faith doth reveal, declare Iesus Christ to be righteousness, and a propitiation for sins, even those committed before the publication of the Gospel by the Evangelists and Apostles.

§. 4.

R. B. 1. After this manner of expounding you may make Scripture speak what you please. I know not a readyer way to set up Popery, and perswade men of the necessity of a Iudge on earth to decide all differences about the meaning of Scripture, then thus to put on it an alien sense, and make people believe that the plainest passages of it are not to be understood.

2. Would this Dissertor have us receive his exposition, when he doth so ill agree with himself? and knows not himself yet what to Believe? He here gives us three distinct senses of the word Faith, 1. He saith it is *The Doctrine of the Gospel :* 2. Or *the Gospel Righteousness :* (yet he seems to put these two as synonimal : which is strange, as if *Doctrine* and *Righteousness* were all one. 3. And in his next Paraphrase he takes it properly for *Faith it self.*

3. How dark or partial an Expositor is this, (if I may so call him, that disclaimeth being an Interpreter) that when Scripture speaks of *Faith in his Blood,* and that with a preposition before it, which shews it to be a *medium* of a propitiation, doth yet make this to be spoken of Gospel Doctrine or Righteousness. He tells us in a parenthesis, that this is sometime called by the name of *Faith.* But mark, he durst not say, It is called *Faith in his Blood,* which is the phrase in the text. Let him shew us, if he be able, where *Faith in his Blood* is put for *Gospel Doctrine, or Righteousness.*

4. Who knows what he means by Gospel righteousness? If he means *Christs own Righteousness*, that consisteth partly in his bloodshed : and so he would make the sense to be, *the Righteousness of Christs suffering declareth that his suffering is a propitiation.* Doth such expounding need confutation?

5. The text saith, *God hath set forth Christ to be a propitiation through Faith in his blood* : plainly making Faith the means prerequisite to the actual propitiating or reconciling of God to us ; and *for the remission of sins past.* But this Interpreter, (and no Interpreter) transposeth Faith, joyning it with his manifestation as the means of that, when the text joyns it with Propitiation and Remission, as the means to that. Yea he makes it go after remission, contrary to the express Text.

6. We doubt not but the Gospel declareth Christ to be the propitiation, and sacrifice. But will you by the next tell us, where in the Gospel it is declared,

S f that

that *L. Col.* is righteous, or hath any part in Chrift; or doth belong to that number that you suppose Juftified so long ago.

7. May not the Gospel declare *that Chrift is the propitiation* to men that have not Faith in his blood?

8. Seeing you expound *fins paft* of those that were committed before the preaching of the Apoftles, and (I suppose) judge that it was at his death that Chrift did propitiate; will you refolve us, whether no fins were pardoned before Chrifts death, since *Adam* ? and whether you are of the *Roman* Faith, that the Fathers before Chrift were in Limbo?

For I pray mark the next words, '*To declare, I say, at this time his Righteousnefs.*

§. 5.

L. C. IN the following verses its plain that S. Paul by the *Law of Faith*, underftandeth either the object of *Faith*, or that Evangelical Oeconomie, which is opposed to the *Mofaical*: The 27 and 31 verses teach that. The sense of this is plain, Do we make void the true ufe of the Law, when we declare the Gospel? God forbid: but we rather ftablifh it.

§. 5.

R. B. 1. BUt what is this to the purpose? The *Law of Faith*, and *Faith* it self are not all one? what if *the Law of Faith* fignifie that object or Oeconomie? doth it follow that *Faith* doth fo too? But the Law of faith is plain language, and as eafie, at leaft, to be underftood, as *the Law of Works*; fo called, because one makes Faith, and the other Works the condition of Life. And yet it is fcarce a fober Interpretation, to say, that by the Law of works is meant the object of works.

2. You feign *Faith* to be put for *Gospel* in the 31 verse, and say, Its plain. But that is no proof. Its true that the fenfe is the fame, which ever were exprefsed, because one connoteth the other, and both are here intended, q. d. *Do we make void the Law, by making Faith the way of Justification and Life? God forbid.* This is as plain as yours: and then why muft the words of the text be altered without need?

3. But you would have done fomething to purpofe, if you had proved that in verfe 26 and 28 and 30. it is the object of Faith that is meant by *believing* and by *Faith*.

§. 6.

L. C. THe 26 verfe doth no more, *according to the Letter*, *make a Believer to be the object of Justification*, then the fifth verse of the following Chapter (doth make) *the ungodly*.

§. 6.

§. 6.

R. B. Come hither, all that are not willing to be deceived, and see the way of Licentious expounding the Scriptures! when he meets with a Text that speaks so expresly against him, that he hath not a word to say against it, then he hath no way left but to attempt to set the Scripture by the ears (as we say) and say, The Letter of this Text is no plainer on one side, then another is on the other side. Thus do the Romanists to perswade the world of the necessity of a Reconciler of Scriptures.

Beza in loc. ait, Quo respectu impius censeatur, quum de vero coram Deo Justitia quæritur, quisquis vel in minimo legis apice, comparitur legis violatæ reus.

2. But I shall prove the falsness of what he would here insinuate, by comparing both Texts. 1. Note that here is no possibility left him in this Text for evading in his ordinary wayes. 1. He cannot say, that *Faith* is here put for the Gospel, both because *Declaration* is before distinctly expressed as antecedent, and because the Text useth not the term *faith*, but *him that believeth in Jesus*. 2. Nor can he say, that any other Declaration of Gods Righteousness is meant, for the same reasons. 3. Nor can he say that Gods Righteousness it self is meant by our Believing: for that also is distinctly mentioned before it. 4. Nor can he say that it is Christ the object of Faith that is meant by the word believing, otherwise then as connoted: for that object is distinctly expressed also, *that he might be the Justifier of him that Believeth in Jesus*. Doth that man mean to make the word, the rule of his Faith, or his conceits the rule of the meaning of the word, that yet will deny that *he that Believeth in Jesus*, is the object of Justification? 2. Now let us see what the Text that he alledgeth, may say to the contrary; *Rom.* 4: 5. *To him that worketh not, but believeth on him that justifieth the ungodly, his faith is counted for Righteousness.* Note here, 1. If both texts be plain, and both true: then certainly both must be joyned together, and not one set against another. If one Text say, Christ justifieth the ungodly, and the other say, *he is the Justifier of him that Believeth in Jesus*; then we must say, that those whom God justifieth are both ungodly and believers: for both are true: And therefore 2. the ungodliness here meant, is such an ungodliness as is found in true Believers, and not that which is in Infidels. 3. And the Text it self expresly saith so: and shews that by *ungodly* here is meant *one that is unjust or unjustifyable according to the Law of Works*, and such are all the faithful to the death. And that this is the sense, appears, 1. In that it is made equipolent with *him that worketh not*. It is the ungodly that worketh not, that is justified: now it is past doubt, that *by worketh not*, is meant only Legal working for life; 1. Either in perfect obeying; 2. Or Mosaical tasks; 3. Or works conceited meritorious; and not that which Christ saith is the work of God, to believe in him whom the Father hath sent. *Joh.* 6. 29. not that Faith which worketh by Love (*Gal.* 5. 6.) and by good works. *Jam.* 2. 24. 2. Note that the Text expresly saith, that the ungodly man here justified, is one *that Believeth in him that Justifieth the ungodly*; so that it is *an ungodly Believer* only, that is, a Legally-unjust Believer, that is here meant. 3. Note that the Text doth expresly say, *His faith is counted to him for righteousness*: to shew that it is not only undone before

Sf 2

his

his Faith, but Faith it self hath a great hand in it. What is meant by this, and how far it is Faith it self, and how far it is Chrifts righteoufnefs that is imputed, I have fully shewed elsewhere *, and Mr. Gataker againſt Saltmaiſh hath ſhewed the cauſeleſneſs of the quarrel among Divines of late about this. 4. Note alſo, that the Holy-Ghoſt, as if he had foreſeen how the Libertines would abuſe the Scripture, doth ſo expreſs the Iuſtification of the ungodly here, as to leave no room for their evaſions: For as they cannot now ſay, with any modeſty, that it is an unbeliever that is here meant, when God ſaith, 1. It is *he that believeth*, and that *his faith is counted for righteouſneſs*; ſo they cannot now with any modeſty ſay, that this is but Iuſtification in and by conſcience, or in our feeling only, or the knowledge that we were before Iuſtified, that is here meant: For the Text ſaith, *their faith is accounted or imputed to them for righteouſneſs; And ſurely to impute or count for righteouſneſs*, is not meerly to make known, that we were before righteous: and it is God and not our ſelves by feeling and conſcience, that doth count or impute it for righteouſneſs. Nay verſe 2. It expreſſy ſhews that it is Iuſtification *before God*, that is here ſpoken of.

* *And before in this Vol.*

So that you ſee, this one Text which the Diſſertor brings as ſo expreſs for his turn, doth ſay ſo much againſt him, as might put the caſe out of doubt, if there were no other ſpoke to that end.

But yet further conſider, if it were proved that the word *ungodly*, is taken in oppoſition to Goſpel obedience, and not to legal perfect obedience, yet it maketh nothing for his cauſe: for it is undenyable that *ungodly* is either the *Terminus à quo*, or it is taken *in ſenſu diviſo & non compoſito*, and faith implyed in Iuſtification as conjunct. If a Phyſitian cure the ſick, doth it follow that while they are ſick, they are cured? If you heal a wound, is it a wound when it is healed? Chriſt came to be a Phyſitian to the ſick, and to call, not the righteous, but ſinners: but it was from ſin that he called them, and from ſickneſs that he recovered them. He came to ſet at liberty the Captives. Doth it follow that they were Captives when they were ſet at liberty? This arguing is like the cauſe for which it is uſed, very irregular.

§. 7.

L. C. Rom. 5. 18. As by one offence all men were condemned: (*that is as to guilt*) ſo by one Iuſtification all men have received Iuſtification to Life.

Here all things are plain. *Juſtification or the Imputation of Chriſts Righteouſneſs, or that Juſtification by which all are judged juſt, is oppoſed to the Imputation of the offence by which all men are condemned; Abſolution is oppoſed to Condemnation: the ſin of Adam to the Righteouſneſs of Chriſt. The gift or imputation of the Righteouſneſs of Chriſt, is made the cauſe why we are judged righteous before God, and our ſins are forgiven us, for the obtaining of eternal life, as the offence of Adam is made the cauſe why all men are guilty of eternal death. Here is no account of Faith at all: for faith is not the imputation of Chriſts Righteouſneſs; nor is it Remiſſion of ſin, and ſo not Juſtification: Nor is faith Abſolution, nor a cauſe or gift for which we are judged righteous before God. But in the following verſe the moſt formal reaſon of Juſtification is expreſſed without any regard to faith. As by the obedience of one man*

many

many were made sinners, so by the obedience of one are many made Righteous. *In this opposition,* Faith hath *no place* : For *not faith, but the Righteousness of Christ is opposed to the offence :* and as Scripture no where saith that we are made Righteous by faith, but by the obedience of death or blood of Christ ; so when to justifie, is the same as to make just and absolve, neither doth Scripture any where say, that we are *Justified* or *Absolved by faith*, but by *Christs Obedience, Death or Blood.*

---

§. 7.

R. B. 1. WHether you do thus interpret as *Beza* and the Claramontane coppy *Græcolat.* which he mentions on verse 17. or whether you follow the vulgar and almost all other Translators that interpret δἰ ἑνὸς παραπ]ώματος *per unius offensam vel delictum,* rather then *per unam offensam*, the matter is little or nothing to our present business. But you must remember, that though you are pleased to translate both δικαίωμα and δικαίωσις by *Justificatio*, yet the first signifieth only those material performances for which we are justified, and the latter Justification it self. And therefore the vulgar, *Piscator* and most others do rather choose to express the first by *Justitia* then *Justificatio*, as also our English Translators do by the name of Righteousness: And *Beza* that translates it by *Justificatio*, doth it with a wish that he might have leave to call it *Justificamen* or *Justificamentum*; and will by no means admit that it is of the same signification with δικαίωσις in this place, but that δικαίωμα *ipsam Justificationis nostræ materiam hic declarat ab effectu, nempe illam Christi obedientiam cujus Imputatio nos Justos in ipso facit.* If you ask to what purpose is this obvious note? I say, to let you know that though the same obedience and suffering of Christ may be, as it were, the matter both of Christs righteousness and ours, as being the meritorious cause of ours, yet it is not the same δικαίωσις or Justification formally, (whether you take it Actively or Passively) by which Christ and we are Justified : But that material Righteousness, δικαίωμα, by which Christ was Justified because he performed it, doth not *eo nomine* Justifie us because Christ performed it, or *quatenus* performed by Christ, and so accepted as sufficient satisfaction or merit on his part ; but *eo nomine* because it is imputed to us, which is not till our Acceptance : or because for the sake of that satisfaction and merit, we are forgiven and justified when we perform the condition imposed by the free Donor upon us to that end. The ignorance of this one point, then which scarce any one thing is more frequently and expresly delivered in the Scripture, hath undone the Libertines.

2. What honest reason have you to translate εἰς πάντας ἀνθρώπους εἰς δικαίωσιν ζωῆς, *omnes homines acceperunt Justificationem ad vitam ?* Where is the *Acceperunt* in the Text, or any thing that intimates any such thing? Adding to Gods Word, is not proving your opinions. Christs merits may be *in omnes homines ad Justificationem vitæ*, in regard of the tendency, and use of them, as a plaister is for a sore, and an inward medicine for such or such a sickness, before the application : yea further, as God hath absolutely Decreed, that it shall be applyed and effectual to this use in its season, *viz.* when he hath caused us to perform the condition of his gift. And yet it follows not that all men have received, yea or all the Elect received this Righteousness or Iustification already.

4. Nay,

3. Nay, will you pleafe to note, that the words in the next verfe, which moft exprefly fets forth the comparifon, are δίκαιοι καταςαθήςονται οἱ πολλοὶ: in the future tenfe, *Jufti conftituentur illi multi:* not *conftituti funt.* So that Chrifts righteoufnefs is the matter or meritorious caufe, by and for which the Elect *fhall be* all Iuftified in their feafon, but not by which they are Iuftified upon the bare performance, or before they believe.

4. This being fo, what honeft reafon had you to tranflate it *Conftituuntur* for *Conftituentur*? I know that moft Interpreters judge that the future-tenfe is put for a continued prefent tenfe, as *Grotius* fpeaks: but that is an expofition, not a tranflation; they dare not therefore put the prefent tenfe for the future, as as you do; and befides it is but a conjecture. It feems plainly to exprefs, that though Chrift be juftified by his righteoufnefs on the petformance, yet fo are not all his Elect; but it is only faid, *They fhall be*, in their feafon. *Beza* faith, that he read καταςαθήςονται in the future tenfe, *in omnibus codicibus*.

5. You that imagine all fo plain for you in this Text, why cannot you fhew us one word that doth exprefs or intimate that it was at the time of Chrift obeying or fuffering, or any time before our Faith, that we are Iuftified by his Righteoufnefs? fhew us if you can a word for this! The text tells us, to our unfpeakable comfort, that *by one mans obedience, many fhall be made Righteous:* but what is that to prove that they are fo already? It compares the caufes of death and life, but it mentioneth not obfervably the feafon as a part of the comparifon, yet intimates it to be future, as to moft after Chrifts coming.

6. Or if you will needs have the comparifon extend to the time alfo, why do you not obferve that it utterly deftroys your caufe? Was ever I, or any Reprobate Son of *Adam* actually guilty or condemned at the time of *Adams* finning? doubtlefs no: *Qui non eft, non eft Reus, vel Condemnatus* (unlefs you dream of a guilt and condemnation which adjectively is *Terminus diminuens*) Guilt is an Accident, and the fubject muft fubfift, and therefore it muft exift, and therefore it muft be *extra caufas*. But all Reprobates were not *extra caufas* when *Adam* finned: therefore they were not actually guilty. May it not be enough, that as the caufe of themfelves was then in *Adam*, fo the caufe of their future guilt was in him? and fuch a caufe as would infallibly make them guilty as foon as they did exift? feeing none can bring a clean thing out of an unclean. I argue therefore hence againft your felf. As Guilt was derived from *Adam*, fo is Righteoufnefs from Chrift, (as to the feafon); But guilt was derived from *Adam*, to none of his pofterity actually, till they did exift from him. Therefore Righteoufnefs is derived from Chrift to none of his Elect, till they do exift in him.

7. For ought I know you muft on your terms, not only affert univerfal Redemption, but univerfal actual Iuftification and Salvation. For you interpret it, *All men have received Juftification to Life*; why then do not all men live, as being Iuftified to life? If you fay that by All, is meant All the Elect onely; I do not believe it: both becaufe the exprefs words, and the force of the comparifon reach further; and in the 19. *verfe* the article added fhews it (οἱ πολλοὶ.) which therefore *Beza* and others ordinary tranflate, *Illi multi,* that is, *qui peccatores conftituti funt, de quibus ante*. I conceive therefore, that the fenfe is this; As Adams firft fin was the matter or caufe of the guilt of all mankinde, fuppofing that they receive their nature from his loins, in the ordinary way of propogation, (which

Chrift

Chriſt did not) ſo is Chriſts ſatisfaction and merit, the matter or cauſe of the Righteouſ-neſs of all mankinde, if they will be united unto him. Only here is the difference, that for the conveying of *Adams* ſin, there was no more requiſite but a conveyance of that nature, which muſt be the ſubject of our guilt: and ſo our being propagated by him, is but *conditio naturalis*: But Iuſtification comes by way of Grace; and therefore our Faith is *Conditio arbitraria, & moralis.* And ſo it may well be ſaid that Chriſt dyed for the Iuſtifying of all men Conditionally: which indeed is ſo far out of doubt, that we have under his hand, an Act of Grace, which is a conditional pardon or Iuſtification of all. If any mans zeal for his novel opinion againſt this univerſal ſatisfaction, do make him angry with me, I intreate him to give me leave to be of *Calvins* opinion in the expoſition of this text, whoſe words are theſe, *Communem omnium Gratiam facit, quia omnibus expoſita eſt; non quod ad omnes extendatur reipſa* (that is, as to the actually poſſeſſion of Remiſſion or ſalvation) *nam etſi paſſus eſt Chriſtus pro peccatis totius mundi, atque omnibus indifferenter Dei benignitate offertur, non tamen omnes apprehendunt.* i. e. He makes Grace common to all, becauſe it is expoſed to all: not that it is extended to all in the thing it ſelf: For though Chriſt did ſuffer for the ſins of the whole world, and is, by the benignity of God, offered to all men indifferently, yet all men do not apprehend (or receive) him. Mark, that *Calvin* takes not *all men*, and *the whole world* here, for the Elect only.

8. When you have told us that all is plain, in the points that we do not deny, *viz.* that *Adams* offence and Chriſts Righteouſneſs, are oppoſed; that Abſolution and Iuſtification are oppoſed; you next come to your cauſe, and tell us that *Here is no mention of Faith.* But I give you theſe anſwers to that, 1. Is it excluded becauſe not mentioned? that is wild arguing. 2. I can ſhew you many a a text where our Iuſtification by Faith is mentioned, without any expreſs mention of Chriſt, Doth it follow therefore that Chriſt is there excluded? I trow not. 3. Faith connotes Chriſt where ever we are ſaid to be Iuſtified by Faith; and Chriſt connotes Faith, where ever we are ſaid to be Iuſtified by Chriſt. He that ſaith, I am fed *by eating*, means by *my meat* alſo: and he that ſaith, I am fed *by my meat*, means *by my meat eaten*, and not lying by. Though I know in our caſe the neceſſity of Faith is *ex ordinatione divina poſitiva*, and the neceſſity of eating is *ex ordinatione naturali*. 4. Here is no mention in the Text of our Propagation from *Adam*: and yet it is plainly implyed as the natural condition, without which we ſhall not derive guilt from him (as Chriſt did not). So is faith in Chriſt implyed as the moral condition, without which we ſhall not receive Iuſtification from Chriſt. 5. But yet for all this, I do not believe you, that believing is not mentioned or regarded in the Text. Do you not finde the very next words, in the end of the 17. *verſe* to be theſe, Τῆς δωρεᾶς τῆς δικαιωσύνης λαμ.Cάνοντες, &c. *qui donum Gratiæ Recipiunt*? And we take receiving the gift to be believing, as we are taught *Job.* 1. 11, 12. For though Phyſical proper Reception is Paſſion and not Action, yet λαμβάνω ſignifieth firſt and properly that Active conſent to the offered gift; which morally we call receiving, and ſo implyeth Paſſive Reception as its conſequent: as *Grotius* truly expounds the word here, λαμβάνοντες, id eſt, *Qui Voluerunt accipere, & ſic acceperunt, re ipſi.*

9. What need you tell the world that *Faith is not imputation of Chriſts Righteouſneſs, nor Remiſſion of ſin, nor Abſolution?* who ſaith it is. Nor yet a cauſe (ſpeaking Logically) or gift for which (as the meritorious cauſe) we are judged righteous?

righteous? would you thence gather, that therefore Faith hath no place in the works? It is the condition *sine qua non*, which is as the *Depositio materiæ*: is that no place? Yea and when the question is at Gods Tribunal, whether we were true Believers or no? the sincerity of our Faith will be the very *Justitia Causæ* materially, upon which the person must be Justified against that accusation: which, as it seems by the descriptions of the Judgement in Scripture, will be the great enquiry of that day.

10. When you again say, that *the next verse giveth us the formal reason of Justification, without any mention of Faith*; I answer, Nor doth it mention our propagation from *Adam*, as having any place in our Guilt or Condemnation, and yet implyes it certainly as the cause without which we shall not be guilty. But the thing I justly blame you for, is, that seeming a Learned man, and therefore knowing (or should have known) that our Divines do ordinarily give this answer, that yet it pleased you not so much as to take notice of it; but go on as smoothly as if none had ever answered your objections.

11. When you say last, that *when to Justifie, signifieth to make Just or Absolve, Scripture doth no where say that we are Justified by Faith*; I answer, 1. This is a meer begging the question. 2. Our Divines against the Papists have so fully proved that justifying is taken for remitting sin and absolving, where we are said to be Justified by Faith, that it is needless for me to do that work again. Yet something I may perhaps do before I conclude, on a fit occasion: but in the mean time, let the Reader observe, how slily this confident Assertor, did even now over-pass *Rom.* 3. 28. 30. when he was purposely speaking of the sense of the next verses, and in the general of those. And let the more unprejudiced thence judge, whether his assertion here be true or false? *v.* 28. *Therefore we conclude, that a man is Justified by Faith, without the deeds of the Law.* 3. *It is one God which shall Justifie the circumcision by Faith, and the uncircumcision through Faith*: One would think these words should be plain enough to satisfie.

---

§. 8.

L. C. *Lastly, Chrifts obedience is our Justification, which consisteth in this, Not that we believe in Christ, but that Christ was made sin (or a sacrifice for sin) in our stead.*

---

§. 8.

R. B. This is the very root and master vein of all Antinomianism, *viz.* that Christ did so obey or suffer in our stead, as that *in sensu Legali vel Civili*, it was our selves that did it by him; as if he had done it as our Delegate, and not as Mediator, and so the benefit of it were ours, because the obedience *qua præstita* is ours. Too many of our own Divines have spoke less cautelously of this point then was meet. I shall now say but this. I have more fully in other papers proved that this Doctrine overthrows the very Christian Religion, and is of more pernicious consequence, then most ever were introduced by any Hereticks into the Church. In particular, it leaves no room for any pardon of sin at all, seeing no Law can require more then the debt, or the very penalty threatned.

If therefore we have paid the same debt, or suffered the same penalty, though not in *sensu physico*, yet in *sensu Civili*, no more can be required of us, nor is there any room for pardon. Be it known to you therefore, that Christ did obey and suffer in the person of a Mediator, and not *in persona delinquentis*, though for the sins of the delinquent, (being obliged to suffer by his voluntary undertaking) : and therefore his sufferings or obedience are none of ours, as performed by him : but God was pleased to make him our King on this Redemption Title, and by a new Act or Law of Grace, to convey right to Christ and his sufferings or merits, that is, as to the fruits of them, on certain conditions, *i. e.* Of grateful, penitent Acceptance ; and of obediential Retention. The Gospel offers us Christ for our head and husband : and till we have Legal Right to him, on our Acceptance, we have none to Iustification or Life.

§. 9.

L. C. Rom. 5. 1. Being Iustified by Faith (or of Faith) we have peace with God. *The sense is, either* After that it was known to us that Christs Righteousness belonged to us, Peace of conscience did thence arise ; *Or,* The Doctrine of the Gospel, or Christ himself by the Doctrine of the Gospel, which is oft called in Scripture by the name of Faith, doth absolve us from all guilt : whence ariseth peace of conscience and tranquility of minde, and affiance whereby we rest upon him. *Or is the meaning rather,* Being Iustified, we have Peace with God ; that is, we are reconciled to God, *as* Twiss *thinketh*.

§. 9.

R. B. THis Interpreter, who saith, he will be no Interpreter, doth interpret as if he interpreted not. 1. How many senses will he devise to make Light consist with Darkness, and to obscure, if possible, words as plain as we could wish. What hard words are these, *Being Justified by Faith, we have Peace with God,* that need all these devices to explain them ? or rather, what clear expressions are these for Iustification by Faith, that this Learned man hath so much ado to draw a curtain over them, or to shut his eyes to keep out their light ? Here are three several wayes that he attempteth to make them fit his turn, and all to little purpose. For the first, the text saith, *Being Justified by Faith,* and he saith, it means, *When we knew that we were justified, or that Christs Righteousness was ours.* As if *doing a thing,* and *making us know that it is done already,* were all one ; or as if God had given him a Commission to change his word at his pleasure ! Let him if he can, or any men living, shew us but one Text, where Iustification is taken meerly for the making known to our selves that we were Iustified before : I say, let him shew it, and prove it, if he can.

2. I suppose it is in vain to tell him, that *Calvin, Beza,* with the generality of Interpreters, are against his exposition ; It is like he knows that already.

3. What a strange thing is it, that he doth not see that both his two latter expositions do destroy his own cause. For the second, If it be the Doctrine of the

T t Gospel,

Gospel; or Christ by that Doctrine that doth Justifie us, then his Righteousness is not ours *qua præstita*, but as given us by the Gospel: And then it must be on the Gospel terms; and let him shew, if he be able, where the Gospel Justifieth any Infidel? If it be by the Doctrine of the Gospel that Christ doth Absolve us from all guilt, then it is not an immanent act in God, nor done before the Gospel is published, or established at least: Nor can any say, that he here means a Justification by meer manifestation that we were Justified for he expresseth himself to mean it of *Absolving us from all guilt*: The Doctrine that I maintain, is no other then this, That Christ by the Gospel doth pardon us on condition of our Faith, and so when we believe (which also is his. Work).

And for his third Exposition which he ascribeth to Dr. *Twiss*, what can be more express against both Dr. *Twiss* and himself? For if it be *Reconciliation with God*, that is meant by *Peace with God*, then it is not only the manifestation of our Reconciliation: Nor can it be then said, that we are reconciled from Eternity, as *Twiss* oft saith we are, seeing the text saith, *Being Justified by Faith, we have Peace with God*? And if they should mean, that God was before-Reconciled to us, but we were not Reconciled to him till we believe; I answer, 1. If they mean it of our Passive Relative Reconciliation, it is a contradiction: For, God to Love me, and yet I not to be Loved of him; and so to be appeased or reconciled to me, and yet I not to be one to whom he is reconciled, are contradictions. 2. If they mean it of our Active and Qualitative Reconciliation, that is the habit and act of Love, Faith, &c. to God, then they cross the text, which speaks of Reconciliation with God: *vid. Bezam & Calvin. in loc.* And then, they make Justification by faith to go before faith, which is contradictory. For the Souls Reconciliation to God, in this sense, (as wrought on us by the Spirit) doth consist in Faith as well as Love: And the Justification her spoken of, is Justification by Faith: And so their sense would be this, *Being Justified by Faith, our Souls are inclined to God by Faith and Love.* God is more merciful in plain expressing his minde to us, then some men would have him be.

§. 10.

L. C. Gal. 2. 16. We know that man is not Justified by the Works of the Law, but by the Faith of Jesus Christ; we I say have believed in Jesus Christ, that we might be Justified by the Faith of Christ, and not by the Works of the Law, because that by the works of the Law shall no flesh be Justified. *I do not think that any thing else is meant in this place, then that it is the neerest and chiefest fruit of Faith, that Christ may be known to us, with all his benefits; and that he is not revealed to our consciences by the Good Works of a new life, how exact*
Internuntium. soever, but only by the gift of Faith, by which as a Messenger between *, *we are certain of Reconciliation, and of Remission of sin.*
Or is the Gospel meant by Faith, that it may be opposed to the works of the Law and Ceremonies, which the false Apostles did require to be joyned with the Faith of Christ, or the Gospel?

§. 10.

§. 10.

R. B. IF it were againſt the moſt dangerous errors that I were diſputing, it would be unſavory to ſome if I ſhould give the fitteſt Epithets to ſuch arguings. I ſhall therefore leave the Reader to give what Epithets he pleaſe, to ſuch dealing with Gods ſacred Word, as he here finds. 1. You ſee ſtill the man is to ſeek himſelf, what may be the meaning of the text: but any thing will ſerve except the truth. 2. It hath pleaſed the Holy-Ghoſt no leſs then three times in this one verſe, to uſe the word *Juſtified*; beſides the next verſe again. Yet doth this Diſſertor make nothing of all, but that we are by Faith certain of Reconciliation and Remiſſion; what language ſhould God uſe to convince ſuch men as theſe of his meaning?

3. I would intreat the Reader to note how much theſe men differ from the Jews in the point of Juſtification by Faith, or by Works? It is but meerly in manifeſting that we are Juſtified, that they give Faith the precedency: when no mans ſalvation lyeth on that. If a man be Juſtified, though he cannot have the comfort of it till he know it, yet he may nevertheleſs be ſaved.

4. Yea, is it not falſe, that Works of a holy life reveal not our Juſtification by Chriſt? and did not himſelf confeſs as much before?

5. Its very true that the Work of Faith is, that *Chriſt be known to us with his benefits*; For to believe, is ſo to know Chriſt upon Gods Revelation, as to accept him; But its one thing to know Chriſt and what he hath procured, and offereth to us, and ſo to Accept him that he may be Juſtified by him: and another thing to know that he hath forgiven and Juſtified us already.

6. Obſerve what Libertiniſm is in the laſt ſhift (for I muſt remember, it muſt not be called an Interpretation): Three times doth the Holy Ghoſt uſe the word, *Faith of Jeſus Chriſt, and believing in Chriſt*, in the beginning of this one verſe: Yet doth he queſtion, Is it not the Goſpel that is meant by Faith? If it be, this is the Paraphraſe, *Knowing that as man is not Juſtified by the Works of the Law, but by the Goſpel, even we have ——— (what ſhall I ſay?) Goſpel, or Goſpelled, in Jeſus Chriſt, that we might be Juſtified by the Goſpel.* But, (if it be worth the while to uſe reaſoning with this ſort of men,) 1. I intreat him by the next, to prove to me out of Scripture, that the word *Faith of Jeſus*, is ever taken for the Goſpel? ſpecially when Iuſtifying is made the conſequent, as here it is? 2. If it were the Goſpel that were meant by Faith, it would connote the act of our Faith: For therefore it is that the Goſpel is called Faith, becauſe it is believed, and the name is transferred from the act to the object. 3. Doth this Diſſertor in conſcience really think, that the Faith which here we are ſaid to be juſtified by, is not an act of mans? at leaſt that theſe words, *Even we have believed in Jeſus Chriſt*, doth not ſignifie our act, but the Goſpel? If he do, let him think ſo ſtill for me: for words ſignifie nothing to him, but what he impoſeth on them. 4. If he yield that *believing in Jeſus Chriſt*, doth ſignifie our Faith, and not the Goſpel, then he muſt confeſs that our Iuſtification by Faith here mentioned, follows our believing, ſeeing we therefore believe in Chriſt, that we might be juſtified by the Faith of Chriſt?

§. 11.

§. 11.

L. C. Phil. 3. 9. That I may be found in him, not having my own Righteousness which is of the Law, but that which is by the Faith of Iesus Christ, even the Righteousness which is of God by Faith. *S. Paul seemeth in this place, in shew, to assert that the act of believing is of Gospel Righteousness. But Calvin on the place saith, that the minde of the Apostle is to compare the two Righteousnesses together;* One proper to man; the other which is of God, and is obtained by Faith; *And a little after, that he asserteth the Righteousness of Faith to be of God, is not only because Faith is Gods gift, but because God justifieth us of his own goodness, or because by Faith we receive the Righteousness given us of God. To wit, both the Righteousness of God, and Faith, are equally Gods gifts; the one, which makes us Righteous, the other, by which we know that this Righteousness belongs to us.*

§. 11.

R. B. 1. When I see the man name *Calvin*, I should hope he hath some regard to his judgement, but he confuteth quickly such thoughts; but is it not strange that it the man could finde no words of *calvin* but what make against him, that he would not rather silence then cite them? You see here are two clauses of *Calvin* cited: in the first he saith, that the Righteousness which is of God, *is obtained by Faith*; (not made known to be already obtained by us) In the second he saith, *it is given of God, and received by Faith*, what more true and plain can be spoken? or what more pertinent against the Libertines that plead for the Iustification of Infidels?

2. Yet doth this man adde in the conclusion, that by Faith we do but *know that this Righteousness belongs to us*; and he seems to intimate as if *Calvin* and the text so meant. As if *Obtaining* and *Receiving*, were but to know that we have obtained and received.

3. Nay mark how he left out the end of *Calvins* first sentence, (as faithfully as he deals with the Text). *Calvins* words are these, *Insignis locus siquis certam Justitiæ fidei definitionem habere cupiat, & tenere veram ejus naturam:* And so he speaks what here is cited, saying of the latter sort of Righteousness, *alteram ex Deo esse tradit, & per fidem obtineri* (this much he citeth) *ac in fide Christi repositam* (this he left out).

4. Mark also how plainly the Text is against his Doctrine: It saith, that *Righteousness is by the Faith of Jesus Christ*. The Dissertor saith, no: It is but the knowledge of Righteousness that is by Faith: Let him, if he can, prove that ever Righteousness is put for the meer knowledge of Righteousness, as he would pretend that Iustification is put for the knowledge or manifestation of Iustification. Nay twice doth this Text immediately together tell us, that this Righteousness is by Faith.

§. 12.

§. 12.

L. C. Act. 13. 38. Be it known to you, that by him all that believe are justified from all things, from which ye could not be Justified by the Law of *Moses*; He seems to make Faith a condition prerequisite to Justification: but what the sense of the place is, Calvin *on the place teacheth*; Paul declareth how men obtain the Righteousness of Christ, even when they Receive it by Faith.

§. 12.

R. B. I Thought verily the man had been contradicting us, and he is pleading for us, and yieldeth all. Doth he not confess that *Calvin* teacheth us *Pauls* sense? and doth not he cite *Calvin*, saying the same as we, that Chrifts Righteousness is obtained by Faith? I hope he doth not think that by *Potiantur*, *Calvin* means, that they may know they have obtained while they were Infidels, yea while they were not at all: Nay, *Calvin* on this text exprefly faith, *They remain under guilt who do not fly to Christ and seek expiation from sins in his death;* and that till God pardon us we are all enemies to him by sin, and are all driven from the Kingdom of God, and addicted to eternal death; and that *this is the Righteousness of faith, when God takes us for Righteous, in not imputing our sin to us*; Yea the next words to those which he citeth, are, *quod autem impetrat fides, &c.* So that Faith, in his judgement obtaineth Righteousness, and not only knoweth that we had it before; would this man be of *Calvins* minde, our Controversie with him were at an end.

Reader, I love as little as another to turn my speech to the moving of affections, from meer argumentation: yet do I think it my duty to tell thee, that as Gods Word is holy, and is part of his name, so he will not hold him guiltless that takes it in vain, and unreverently abuseth it: that the business of a sinners Justification and Salvation is of greater moment then to Jest about; and that it meerly concerneth thee to take heed upon what reasonings thou buildest thy hopes. This man would perswade thee that God Justifies Infidels. I say, God justifieth none at age and of discretion, but Believers (for ought is revealed to any man in his Word). I would not have thee taken with any arguings of mine or his: but lay by both a while, and in the fear of God, with prayer, humility and impartiality, do but read these very texts that he himself hath here cited: and judge as in conscience thou seest cause, whether they deny not the Justification of Infidels? And when thou haft done, read his Comments, and judge but rationally, whether he say any thing to purpose, or do not talk like a dreamer, or much worse? I profess for my part, I never met with Papist that had neer such shameless expositions of Scripture, and so many together, and that if I could bring my conscience to such a liberty of expounding, I should be never the more of a Religion because of Scripture; but might for all the plainest passages of it, be as free to choose my Religion, as if there were no such word: Nay, I should take my self for one that believed not Gods Word to be true: For he that can believe that it is a word that will bend and yield to such handling as this, and bear

T t 3   any

any sense, though contrary to its plainest importance, I should think doth scarce heartily believe it to be the the Word of God: Judge of this Differtor, but by this one text expounded by him.

§. 13.

L. C. THis place and such like, doth the Author of the Epistle alledge, to prove that Faith; yea Repentance and a holy Life do go before Justification, and that a believer is the object of Justification: such are Act. 10. 43. To him give all the Prophets witness, that through his death (*Name it should be*) whosoever believeth in him, shall receive remission of sins: *And such as these,* Repent and be converted, that your sins may be blotted out; and, the Iustifier of him, that is of the Faith of Iesus, Rom. 3. 26. But that force of Arguments drawn from these places, by which he thinks to binde us, we shall easily decline anon; as also what appertaineth to the object of Justification, which they would have to be a Believer.

§. 13.

R. B. 1. THat Faith and Repentance go before Iustification, we affirm: but that a Holy Life goeth before it, we deny, and I remember not that *Cyr. Molineus* hath any such word, for all your saying it: Indeed to our Iustification as continued, and as consummate at the judgement, Good Works are antecedent, if there be time to do them.

2. Reader, mark the texts that are here made so light of; whether thou couldest wish God to speak plainer, in asserting Faith to go before Remission, and to be the condition of it?

3. I believe you will *easily decline* all these, who have got that unhappy declining art. But take heed of declining too much against Light, and remember another day, that you were warned. You do it with more *ease* then *honesty*.

§. 14.

L. C. FOr in these places is denoted the quality of them whose sins are forgiven.

§. 14.

R. B. IS this your best declining? 1. The Scripture makes Remission consequential to Faith, saying, *Believers shall receive Remission*; and *be converted that your sins may be forgiven, &c.* And this man easily declines all these, by saying, that by *shall*, and *may be*, is meant *are already forgiven*, q. d. by saying the word is false. Is not this with more ease then honesty? Nay the Scripture saith, *That whoever believeth not, is condemned already, and the wrath of God abideth on him,* &c.

2. Who would think by his words here, but he did at left yield that all men that

that are already forgiven, are presently qualified with Faith ? But its no such matter. How can you say Faith is the quality of the Justified, when, if your Doctrine be true, they may be many a year without Faith after Justification. Nay, when you say, that God justifieth alwayes before Faith; and therefore you should rather say, Infidelity is the quality of those that are forgiven. Nay when you hold that we are all justified, when we had no existence: and can Faith be the quality of that which is not; what a conscience have you that can put by such plain and frequent Scripture testimony, with such shifts as these ?

§. 15.

L. C. WIth six hundred such *Paralogisms and Parallel places as these*, do the *Papists maintain the merit of Works, and Arminians Election from foreseen Faith.*

§. 15.

R. B. MY conscience forbids me raising jealousies without clear ground of any man: But what man would not be jealous that this man were a Papist under an Antinomian Vizor, finding him under a strange name, in these dayes in *England* ? Yea did I know that he had formerly been an enemy to Popery, did I know him, I would watch him ; lest he were since perverted. Let any sober Reader judge, whether that man (being of good intellectuals) who verily thinks the Papists have six hundred texts for merits (which is not once named in the Scripture) such as these are for Faith going before Justification, can choose but think the Papists in the right, if he believe the Scripture ? And what he saith of the Arminians, (of Election on foreseen Faith) is a point of Popery too.

2. I am confident that this his assertion is so notorious a falshood, and of so hard a forehead, that few modest Papists will dare to own it themselves: What man ! six hundred such text for merits ; and Scripture never once mention it ? Either this practise is Antinomian, as is your Doctrine, or else there is no Law for⸺.

§. 16.

L. C. *THere is no less strength in the words, Iam. 2. God hath chosen Believers; to prove that Faith is prerequisite to Election, then in the words,* Believers receive Remission of sins ; *to prove that Faith goes before Remission of sins.*

§. 16.

R. B. ANother very immodest falshood. 1. Who knows not how frequently the word *Elect* is taken for Gods Temporal Election by the act of Vocation, by which he doth, as Christ saith of another temporal Election, Take one and forsake another in the same house, of the same blood, and bed, and imployment. And so God is said by *James* 2.5. *To have chosen (that is, by actual vocation) the poor of the world (to be) rich in Faith, and heirs of the Kingdom promised,* &c. not as you unfaithfully read it, *God hath chosen Believers* ; as if there were no mention to what he had chosen them, or what manner of Election it is.

2. Suppose it be granted you, that it is the eternal Election that is here meant: what shew of truth doth it put on your words, if you speak of the whole work of Election ? Though Gods Decree be but one in it self, as to the act ; which is himself ; yet seeing it is denominated from the object which it respects, and to our capacity must be conceived of and expressed as several acts, so therefore Divines use to distinguish between the Decree of glorifying, and the Decree of Giving Faith and Renewing Grace : and they tell you that the first, *viz.* the Decree of glorifying hath for its object, *a Believer persevering*, that is, God Decreeth to glorifie none but such, and those Individuals that he will gloryfie are such, and rewarded as such.: But the object of the former act, *is an unbeliever* ; Or else how could God be said to Decree to give him Faith. But this doth not intimate that foreseen Faith is the cause of the Decree of glorifying, but that Faith is Decreed to be the condition of glorification. So that Gods Decree of glorifying is about a Believer, *i. e.* to glorifie Believers : but his Decree of giving Faith, is about unbelievers. Now these being diversified but for our apprehension, and being in it self one Decree, when you speak of the Decree of Election, without such distinction, you cannot say, that it is *ex fide previsa*, because it is *ad fidem*, as well as *ad salutem*. And so much to your unreverent abuse of Gods Word.

CHAP. IIII.

Of the Acts of God Justifying.

§. 1.

L. C. OF these we must see what they are, when and whether they be done together and at once ? Most of the sincerer Divines will have these acts to be two, Imputation of Christs Righteousness, and Remission of sin ; and that they are divers parts of Justification : Yet some will have them distinct in word only,

only, and not in being; so that either of them taken alone may express the nature of Justification; which they say is manifest in Rom. 4. 6, 7. Where the Apostle professedly handling this Argument, useth remitting sin and Imputing Christs righteousness, as equipollent; and that the distinction respecteth not the Integrant parts of Justification; but the two terms à quo & ad quem : which they thus illustrate, as by one and the same act the darkness is driven out of the air, and the light introduced into the air ; so an ungodly man is by one and the same act of Iustification absolved from guilt, and pronounced Iust.

§. 1.

R. B. 1. First goes one and the same act of the Law of grace, which pardoneth the sin, and constituteth us righteous ; for all is but to make us *non obligatos ad pœnam*: And then followeth the act that you mention, Absolving from guilt, viz. by sentence and pronouncing Iust : for what is it to pronounce Iust, but to pronounce not guilty *quoad pœnam*? 2. That Remission and Iustification are one thing, though under notions a little differing, taken from several respects, is so largely proved by *Parœus* and many other Divines, that I shall say nothing to it. Those judicious Divines that do argue for a difference, do either prove but such a notional difference (one name more directly respecting the punishment, the other the Accusation and Obligation, as the *Terminus à quo*;) or else they take remission for the legal discharge or disobliging; and Iustification for the sentential : whereas these are two sorts of Remission and Justification both.

§. 2.

L. C. I Confess that I rather slide into the opinion of the former, yea am drawn into it, though unwilling, (or whether I will or no) seeing in the business of salvation, it is safer to admit those things which may be believed without wrong to Gods truth, then to seem any whit to detract from it : and the method which the Author of the Epistle giveth in his Catechism, doth most please me : for there he so conjoyneth the righteousness of Christ with the remission of sin, as that this should be the effect of the former, or of the perfect obedience which Christ performed to the Father, and which he chiefly testified in dying, offering himself a sacrifice propitiatory for the sins of men.

§. 2.

R. B. 1. VNder pretence of giving more to this or that part of divine truth or operations, many recede from the truth, and breaking Gods sacred frame of doctrine, they let in many errors which they never dreamt of. 2. I never saw the Authors Catechism: but I like the order expressed as well as you can do: & wish that one truth were but well received, that *Christs suffering and obedience is but the cause of our remission*, and so of our formal righteousness, & not remission or our formal righteousness it self, (though our material it may be called) : and this is enough to overthrow your whole frame : as *Alstedius* saith, *Christs righteousness is our righteousness causally,*

V u *not*

not formally. But as this is the meritorious Cause, so the Immediate efficient must intervene between the impulsive meritorious Cause and the Effect, and therefore Chrifts righteousness doth not *co nomine* Iustifie us actually, because it is the meritorious Cause; or doth not presently Iustifie us as soon as performed.

§. 3.

L. C. B*ut* * *without this method, it is not to be denyed; besides that, Scripture placeth our Righteousness as to the most part, in remission of sins, that also the Divines who embrace two Parts of Justification, are inconsiderately drawn to lean more to one of them.*

*extra.

In the Tractate of the true reason of Christian Pacification ascribed to John Calvin, c. 2. de Justif. p. 9. Who doubteth but the whole Righteousness of man, to which he must trust, is contained in the free remission of sins? *and a little after*, Deservedly doth Paul include the righteousness of faith, simply in remission of sins, saying, that it is described by David, when he pronounced the man blessed to whom sin is not imputed: and certainly the blessedness that David mentioneth, flows from righteousness. It follows therefore that we are therefore just, because our sins are not imputed to us.

Rivet Dialysi, p. 88. *speaking of the twofold Grace we receive from Christ*, saith, These we have from Christ, who is made to us righteousness through the remission of sin, and sanctification, by the working of his Spirit in us.

The same Rivet prayseth Cassanders words p. 90. It is said, and it is past controversie, that the righteousness by which we are justified consisteth in remission of sins: that is, when for the merit of Christs suffering which he underwent for our sake, our sins are not imputed to us: which is nothing else then the very merit of Christ to be imputed to us to the remission of sins.

The same man in his Animadvers. on Grot. annot. p. 31. saith, that Melancthon constantly taught, that Iustification signifieth Remission of sins, or the Acceptation of the person to everlasting life.

The sixteenth Article of the Confession of the French Churches is express, We believe that our whole righteousness is founded in remission of sins; in which also our felicity consisteth, as David saith: Excellently Bernard serm. 23. in Cantic. Mans righteousness is Gods indulgence: *The same man*, 'Gods righteousness is not to sin, the righteousness of man is, for Righteousness * not to be imputed.

*It should be sin sure.

And indeed the holy Scripture doth for the most part, not only place our Righteousness and Blessedness in the Remission of sin; but also fetcheth most exhortations to sanctity from the consideration of Christs death; when yet the Righteousness of Christ in fulfilling the Law might seem a far sharper spur to the study of a holy and new Life, which our Lord did perfectly accomplish. It is not light which St Paul, saith, Rom. 6. 7. *that he that is dead is Iustified (or freed) from sin; as if he would teach us these two most weighty things.* 1. *That Christs suffering and dying doth justifie and free us from the guilt of sin.* 2. *That we being dead in Christ and crucified with him, are so freed from sin, that it shall not reign in us: which two benefits in which all our righteousness doth consist, do flow from the one death of Christ.*

§. 3.

§ 3.

R. B. 1. As to the question, whether Remission be the whole of our Justification? briefly and plainly, this seems to me the truth. First it must be known whether Christ give us any other or higher felicity then *Adam* had in possession or in pomise, upon Condition of perseverance in perfect obedience? If this question be determined Negatively, then Justification is wholly comprehended in remission of sin: For seeing Remission freeth us from the Penalty of loss, as well as of sense, it restoreth us to the same condition, not only as we *were in* (for it is not only Original sin that is forgiven) but as we *should have been in* if we had persevered in our first Integrity, that is, if we had not sinned. But if the question be determined affirmatively, that Christ did procure us a higher felicity then the first Covenant promised, then we must further consider this much: *viz.* That the word Justification is taken for *Legal* or *Sentential* Justification: and in both it is taken either more strictly, or more comprehensively. Justification in Law sense, or constitutive in the strictest sense, is only the making us righteous of unrighteous; and that is only the remission of our sin or guilt, and so putting us in the state we should be in if we had never sinned. Justification constitutive in the more comprehensive sense, contains the addition of all those higher benefits purchased by Christ; (supposing there are such,) that is, It is the putting us into a right to all that felicity which God will bestow on the just in Christ. So Justification at judgement is strictly taken, The Absolution of a sinner from the Accusation of Guilt, that is, Obligation to punishment of loss and sense; But largely taken, It is also the adjudging him to a greater Glory, or the absolving him from the false accusation of having no right to that greater Glory. If you ask my opinion of this, I am loath to determine so doubtful a Case; But it seems most probable to me, that the felicity that *Adam* should have had, and that which Christ will give us, are of the same nature; because the Nature and Capacity of man is the same. But what gradual or Accidental difference there is, God knows, for I do not. But I suppose that the term *Justification* in Scripture, is commonly taken in the former stricter sense, for meer remission of sin, or making us relatively righteous of unrighteous; yet so as to connote, or imply the concurrence of some special Gospel-priviledges; which when particularly intended, are rather expressed by *Adoption, Membership of Christ*, &c. then by Justification.

By this also it may be discerned, whether there were any meritorious obedience of Christ necessary, besides that which was for satisfaction of Justice, and restoring us into the state that we should have been in, if we had not sinned. To our strict Justification and Restauration, no more but satisfaction was necessary: But if there be any degree of felicity superadded which the first Covenant gave not, then the question is yet more difficult, as to that part. But then first it must be known that God being well pleased with Christs very satisfaction, as Glorifying him more then the sinners own sufferings would have done, might give power to his Son to glorifie his Members with a higher then the first Glory, even for that his satisfaction: There is nothing to hinder God from a larger shewing of mercy, when his Justice is once satisfied. We must not feign God to be so backward to do good, as if he would or could do nothing for us, but what is bought with a price; when once the bar or impediment is removed. 2. And we must remember that it could not be the Law of Works that made Christs further (supposed) merit, beyond that of satisfaction, necessary

V u 2

cessary for our Glorification. For meer remission, through the merit of meer satisfaction (which is by obeying to the death) was sufficient to restore us to our right of felicity which the Law could give: And if Christ give us any more, it being not the Law that gives it, or ever gave it, so the Law is not it that requireth a new purchase of it to be made. 3. And therefore it is not by way of Legal Righteousness to be imputed to us that Christs further obeying in our stead could be necessary, when the work of satisfaction was once performed: For what Law required such a righteousness? But these things deserve more punctual explication in season. I thought not to say this much, but I hope the judicious Reader will not think it in vain.

2. For your collections from *Rom.* 6. 7. 1. If you mean that Christ freed us from guilt at the time of his death, it is your groundless fancy. It was his will that the liberation then purchased, should be made ours by a new Law on certain conditions. 2. If sin shall not reign in us who are dead in Christ, then why make you those to be Iustified by Christ in whom sin raigneth? Are they justified by him, and yet not dead with him? 3. How falls it from your Pen that the not-raigning of sin in us, is one of those two benefits of Christs death, in which all our righteousness doth consist? sure thats a righteousness that we had not while we were Infidels or unregenerate? much less from the time of Christs death? (otherwise then negatively, as sin raigneth not in a *non-ens*.) But Error is oblivious; and oblivion self-contradicting.

§. 4.

L. C. WHen *these acts are done, let us see, whether when we are elected? or then when we believe? or as soon as Christ was promised to be Mediatour, which more agreeth to the verity of faith.*

But whensoever these acts be done, if they be done in one act, it is thence sufficiently evinced, that the act of Iustification precedeth faith in Christ; Otherwise we must suppose that the act of Iustification is reiterated, and that Iustification as well as faith, hath its increasings and declinings, (or intermissions.)

§. 4.

R. B. 1. WHat hopes was I in, when I first saw this question started, that we should have had his opinion, and the proof of it in the answer: But the man seems indifferent what opinion he be of, so he be not of that which is commonly accounted orthodox. Let the time of Iustification be either when we are elected (that is, before time), or when Christ was promised, so it be not when we believe, he is content. I pray the Reader not to forget hereafter, 1. That here he doth not make the time to be at Christs death, but the first promise. 2. That he doth not mean by this promise Gods decree of giving Christ, which was from eternity; for he distinguisheth it from the time of Election. It is therefore at the promise after *Adams* fall, that he supposeth we were actually pardoned and Iustified. 3. But then is not this a new way, and disliked by his own party, to make this to be an immanent act? As if immanent acts were no elder then since *Adams* fall? which his Dr. *Twiss* would have taught him are from eternity? But of this more anon.

2. To your saying they are done *uno actu*, in one act, I say, that the conditional general

general pardon was indeed one act, and at the same season enacted as you imagine; when God made that act of grace. But this pardoneth and justifieth not Actually, till the Condition be performed; why did you say never a word to prove it one act, but nakedly affirm it? But do you mean that all men are Justified by one Act? or only each particular man? If the former, I acknowledge it, as to one Physical Act of Legislation, which doth but conditionally Justifie: But it is not by one Civil or Moral Act: For this one Law performeth many thousand Legal acts, and produceth effects, according to the will of the Legislator.

3. Faith goes before Justification; and what shew of strength is there in your reason to the contrary? You say, *Then Justification must be reiterated, and increase, and decrease.* I answer, If you mean that one man will be justified to day, and another to morrow, what inconvenience follows that? If you mean it of the same man, you must distinguish between justifying a man from a state of sin and wrath, and justifying him from the guilt of a particular sin only. The former is done but once when he believeth; The later is done daily; and what doubt of this? or what inconvenience follows it? yet will it not follow that Justification increaseth and decreaseth as faith doth. For our Justification consisteth in our right to Impunity: And the Testament gives us this right upon the sincerity of our faith, and not upon the degree; and therefore the decrease of it alters not our right as long as it is so much as to be sincere. Indeed the Antinomian Justification by faith in meer manifestation doth rise and fall, and I think after you we, rise and lye down again, more or less; at least, with many.

§. 5.

L. C. THe words of St. Paul are plain: *Col.* 1. 20. It pleased the Father to reconcile all things to himself, both things in Earth, and things in Heaven, having made Peace by the blood of his Cross: *Then are the Elect Justified together and at once, when Reconciled: and then Reconciled when he made peace by the blood of the Cross.*

§. 5.

R. B. 1. HEres no talk in the Text of Justifying; and that we are then Justified when Reconciled, you should have proved, and not nakedly affirmed; For without distinguishing of reconciliation, it is false. 2. Though God is never said to Justifie us from Christs death, yet it may be well said, that he then reconciled all things to himself. For 1. The Price of Reconciliation was given and taken, and so *quantum ad pretium*, it was done. 2. God was so far actuallly reconciled, as to deliver all men from the Legal necessity of perishing they were in before, so that they are not under a remediless Obligation for want of an expiatory sacrifice; and he hath put them that were helpless, on the use of means for recovery. 3. Yea he hath actually granted a full free conditional pardon to all; and the Condition is but acceptance of his gift (Christ and Life); which is so reasonable, that among men such gifts do pass as absolute, supposing the Legatary, or delinquent will not be so mad as to refuse it. And thus Christ may be said to have reconciled all the world to God, in that he hath done it, 1. *Quan-*

tum ad pretium : 2. *Quantum in se*, as Satisfier ; 3. And God hath granted it *quantum in se* as Legiflator of the new Law. But mark my limitations. 1. I fay not that Chrift hath done it *quantum in se* as Redeemer abfolutely. For the work of Redemption comprizeth alfo his fpecial intent in dying for the infallible falvation of his chofen. 2. Nor do I fay, that God hath done it *quantum in se* abfolutely, but only as Legiflator, or Donor of remiffion by the Teftament or Deed of gift to all that will accept it. For he doth more for his chofen ; but in another refpect ; even as the eternal elector of them, and as intending the work of redemption to the infallible accomplifhment of this election-ends. So that you fee, God having as Covenant-Donor or Legiflator, and as fending his Son to fatisfie, and Chrift alfo as meer fatisfier, done *quantum in se* to the work of Reconciliation, and Remiffion, and Juftification, and fo much as in reafon there fhould be no ftop left (in our Acceptance), It is not unufual, nor unfit language, to call this by the name of reconciliation ; yea or remiffion : And I know men of fingular Learning and Judgement that fay, This is the meaning of *Eph.* 1. 7. and other like texts ; and that this is truly *Remiffio inchoata*, in that fin is made remiffible as to perfect pardon, and fo much done towards it, as Chrift hath done.

2. But ftill it muft be acknowledged, that it is not actual reconciliation or remiffion yet for all this, till the Condition be performed. This is a known cafe among men, If a company of Rebels be fallen under the cenfure of the Law and Condemned for Traytors, and the Prince undergo fome publike fhame, for Iuftice fake, for their redemption, upon confideration whereof, the King grants them a general Act of Oblivion, pardoning all that will return to their Allegiance, and accept of his pardon, and the Princes favour. It is here no unmeet fpeech, nor unufual to fay, The King hath pardoned them all : or the King is reconciled to them, becaufe it is conditionally done, and *quantum in se*, in that regard. But yet no man is actually pardoned or reconciled till he perform the Condition. So if you will call the paying of the Price, and the general act of pardon, a reconciling or pardoning, I will not contend with you, on condition 1. That you acknowledge this is yet no Actual pardon, nor reconciliation (except *in tantum & fecundum quid*) 2. And that this is common to the unbelieving and non-elect that perifh : and 3. That this is not the Iuftification by faith, which Scripture mentioneth ; yet of this is meant that 2 *Cor.* 5. 19, 20. And fo *Heb.* 1. 3. And fo what if I fhould yield that this Text is *Col.* 1. 20. I eafily confefs that Chrifts death and univerfal fatisfaction, and alfo the general Conditional act of grace or pardon, do go before faith : but fo doth not actual pardon.

2. But though this anfwer be enough, yet indeed there is nothing in the text that urgeth me to this much : For the text faith not, that either Peace was made, or reconciliation juft at the time of Chrifts death : but only mentioneth the caufes of peace and reconciliation whenever attained ; Chrift may do it by the blood of his Crofs, as the meritorious Caufe, though the effect follow not of long after.

3. But indeed, the former claufe (having made peace) feemeth to intimate an immediate effect (*viz.* having paid the Price, and brought God into a Covenant of grace with man, which is a degree of peace and reconciliation) But the latter Claufe feems to intimate a diftant effect, *viz.* reconciliation upon actual application and reception of the benefits.

3. Many Expofitors think, that it is but the bringing the Gentile world into the Church, or making peace between them and the Jews, and clofing them in one body, that is here meant.

I have been the larger in explaining this text, especially in opening the doctrine of that degree of Reconciliation, which is the immediate and general fruit of Christs death, because I mean not to repeat it oft, but to referr you hither when other texts of the like nature are discussed. And remember that here is no mention of Justification or Remission.

§. 6.

L. C. THe words are plain also, 2 Cor. 5. 21. He made him sin for us, who knew no sin, that we might be made the righteousness of God in him.

§. 6.

R. B. DO these words make any mention of our being Justified when Christ suffered? It only tels us to what end he was made sin for us: but not when the end is attained. He dyed to Glorifie us, as well as Justifie us: and yet we are not glorified when he dyed.

§. 7.

L. C. TO wit, he was made sin when he bore our diseases, Isa. 53. and then we were Justifyed together and at once, the sins of the Elect being cast upon him, and the oblation being performed, Heb. 10. 10. For one Sacrifice being offered for sins for ever, and so they being perfected; in like manner, for ever, whom he sanctified, he is set at the right hand of God. v. 12, 13, 14.

§. 7.

R. B. 1. THat we were then Justified together, you do but affirm, and not prove. 2. Isa. 53. hath not a word to that end; the laying our sins on him, is not the taking them off from us; as Dr. Crisp vainly imagined. 3. Heb. 10. 10. makes against you, and not for you. It is *through* Christs death that we are sanctified; but whether at his death, nay many thousand years before, is the question. The 14. tell us 1. That Christ perfected them for ever by his offering; but not at the time of that offering, or presently *after* Adams fall. 2. Nay it saith, It is them that are sanctified, that he perfected; Therefore not the unsanctified, nor till they are sanctified. Or if the sanctification here spoken of be a common sanctification, so named from the Legal Purifications; then the sense can be but this, *Christ hath by once dying made a sufficient expiation for sin, whereby the world are so far cleansed as to be brought neerer to God, and under a new Covenant of Grace: and the expiation that he hath thus made is sufficient, and hath perfectly done for them the work of expiation, and there needeth no more.* But if sanctifying and perfecting be meant either of justifying or renewing, then they may be by *Christs Sacrifice* in their seasons, but not *At the time of that sacrifice.* You know we are not perfected till Glory, (at least not while we are Infidels or unborn); and yet you suppose us then perfected, if you suppose the effects mentioned in this Text, to be immediately concomitant or consequent to Christs Sacrifice.

§. 8.

§. 8.

L. C. Moreover it is proved, because the Scripture frequently speaking of Remission of sin, saith that they are pardoned to us together and at once. See Col. 13, 14. and 2 Cor. 5:18. where he saith not that we are Reconciled in Christ, but that we were Reconciled in Christ heretofore. The next words are clear, God was in Christ reconciling the world to himself, not imputing to them their sins.

§. 8.

R. B. 1. Your Assertion is like the rest, bold as well as false. To say that *Scripture frequently saith this*, when it never once saith it, is not well done. Indeed it saith that our past sins and present are at once forgiven, and that is all that then is sin : but where is there one word of God that saith, that God pardoneth sin before it is committed? much less all future sins at once? which I know is your meaning.

2. Col. 2. 13. saith, God had *forgiven them all trespasses*; But doth it say, He had forgiven them what were no trespasses, as being not committed? There is no mention of forgiving all that *will be a Trespass*, but only all that is a Trespass.

3. 2 Cor. 5. 18. I have expounded before, 1. It is past all doubt, manifested in the very text, that it is not actual full reconciliation and remission that is here mentioned; the Apostle expresly affirming that the message of Reconciliation was committed to them, and that they were Embassadours in Christs stead to beseech men to be reconciled; shewing that yet it was not done. 2. It is plain therefore that its Reconciliation *ex parte Dei*, on supposition of their Acceptance; that it is Gods providing and accepting the price of Reconciliation, and giving a free pardon to All upon Condition of accepting the Gift (Christ and Life) this is the reconciling and not imputing sin : And though this be not actual reconciliation and remission, plenary and proper, yet I shewed you before that it is not unfitly so called : what man will think a Kings Pardon to a Traytor on Condition of Acceptance, and Returning to his Allegiance, to be unworthy the name of a Pardon? would not any man say the King hath pardoned him? And yet it is not an actual effectual pardon till accepted, and the Condition performed. Yea had there been no Condition expressed; yet Acceptance is naturally implyed among men, and the Refuser supposed to have violated a Condition so naturally reasonable; that he forfeits his hopes of the benefit.

Though Pardon in Law sense fully discharging us from Guilt, and giving us right to Impunity, be in its own kind compleat at once, as to all past sins; yet there are many steps towards that full Pardon, which may be well called Pardon too, which yet are common to the ungodly and non-elect. God may well be said not to impute sin to the world, when he is paying so dear a Price for their sin, & using such a means for reconciliation, and giving pardon on so free and reasonable terms. Besides, there is, as Gods Legal pardoning, and his sentential pardoning, so a third sort, even his executive pardoning, which is but not punishing or remitting the Punishment, (though not the Obligation to punishment) This is very variable, and hath divers degrees; and thus God may punish one day, and forgive the next, that is not punish and punish the next

again;

again; yea and punish one sin more, or less: But especially when God takes off, or remitteth the punishment as a means to Reconciliation, and holdeth still the rod, while he offers us full pardon, even his so doing is a degree of actual pardon; Though it be not the full legal pardon, which dissolveth the obligation to punishment, yet is it a true actual executive pardon, in some degree. The plain truth is, it hath done the Church much wrong, that Divines have not rightly understood the nature of pardon, (though an Article of the Creed); And have too crudely asserted that it hath no Degrees; and have laid the grounds of those fancies which the Antinomians have built up. Even that Legal pardon which I called plenary and compleat in its kind, is yet imperfect in regard to what follows, nor is it a fit speech without explication, to say that our pardon in this life is perfect.

§. 9.

L. C. *And when David saith, that He is blessed whose sins are forgiven; it is certain that he speaks of a perfect Blessedness; that is, when all sins are Remitted.*

§. 9.

R. B. 1. Sure this man lives in some Paradise, where ever it is, that thinks he hath perfect blessedness already. If he lived my life, he would not think so, though I bless the Lord of my Comforts, I am not without some tasts of his Love: I had hoped he had not been so far tainted. But I am confident, (let a man but keep his senses, and in his wit) and it is as curable an error as most he could have faln upon: Nor do I think, if he be sober, that he will think he is perfectly blessed one seven years together; Except (which I almost forgot) he should be so unhappy as to think, that there is no Blessedness after this Life. But I will not suspect him of that Infidelity.

2. If you are perfectly Blessed, shew it by your perfect holiness, and perfect knowledge; or else they are more credulous then I that will believe you. Such darkness and falshoods as this book is stuffed with, do convince me that you are not perfectly blessed.

3. Nor did it ever come into *Davids* minde, to imagine men perfectly blessed on earth. Cannot a man be called blessed, because of a Right to perfect Blessedness, (which yet is but a conditional Right, and in it self Losable, though God will see that we lose it not), but you must fondly thence gather, that he is perfectly blessed. Let the bunch of Grapes suffice, without dreaming of Heaven upon Earth.

4. No, nor is it perfect Remission that *David* speaks of, nor that any man enjoys in this life. For 1. Many sins are yet to be pardoned; which are not committed. 2. Our present pardon by Donation in Law sense, is but conditional; as to the continuance and perfection of it: There are *Conditiones non amittendi*, conditions of not losing what we have: and conditions of actual pardon for particular sins when committed, that are yet to be performed. We must

to that end believe still Habitually, and again actually, and Repent, and Confess, and Pray for pardon. And doubtless a conditional pardon is not of so perfect a kinde, as an absolute one. 3. Our pardon which gives us right to impunity, is as to some parts of the punishment, but *in diem*, for the future, and not *de praesenti*. God never by any pardon did discharge us from all punishment in this life, nor give Right to immediate perfect Impunity, but only to immediate Impunity, as to the destroying punishment, and, to the sanctification and fruits of Castigatory punishments, and to a perfect impunity, in the life to come. This is true, and plain in Scripture, as can be desired, however prejudiced men may reject it: As Scripture calleth wicked mens punishments. Chastisements, and Godly mens sufferings Punishments, so that which we commonly call Paternal Chastisement, is a Species of Punishment. 4. Our executive pardon (which I so call, because God gives it as Exicutioner of Justice, remitting that Execution) is not perfect in this life, for much punishment is yet to be suffered, and the last enemy Death, must yet do execution on us; and our very lying in the dust till the Resurrection, is a punishment; and the sin it self that adhereth to us, is maintained to be a punishment of former sin, by many Divines that are not partial for me, in this case. 5. The final Absolution which we shall have at the great judgement, is the most perfect pardon of all: and this is yet behind. And whereas some say, that this is properly no pardon nor justification; but a Declaring that we were pardoned and Justified before, I answer, 1. They contradict the Scripture, that calls it both blotting out sin, and justification. *Act. 3. 19. That your sins may be blotted out, when the time of refreshing comes, &c. Rom. 3. 4. Mat. 12. 37. By thy words shalt thou be Justified.* 2. And though such a Declaration, may be called Justification, yet what ignorance do these men shew of the nature of judgement, to think it doth but barely declare? Determining, is more then Declaring. By Law, i. e. the remedying Act of Grace we have our *Jus ad Impunitatem & ad Gloriam ut Donatum &c. Constitutum*: our constituted Right: and by Judgement Absolving us, we have our *Jus judicatum, & Determinatione stabilitum.* Our right put out of all question and controversie for the future, notwithstanding the malice of all Accusers.

I do not heap up Scriptures to prove the Imperfection of Pardon in this life, when these five notorious defects may put it out of doubt with the impartial Reader; and when every man may turn to his Concordance and finde enough. Mark but that 2 *King.* 24. 4. which yet mentioneth another imperfect Pardon, viz. when God will save the sinner, and yet retain some of the punishment to be inflicted even on Posterity, as he did by *Manasseh*; *Surely at the Commandment of the Lord, came this upon Iudah, to remove them out of his sight, for the sins of Manasseh, according to all that he did, and also for the innocent blood that he shed (for he filled Jerusalem with innocent blood) which the Lord would not pardon*: and mark another kinde of imperfect Pardon *in tantum* only, and not in totum, *Num.* 14. 19, 20, 21, 22, 33. *Pardon I beseech thee, the iniquity of this people, &c.* and the Lord said, *I have pardoned according to thy word: But as truly as I live, all the earth shall be filled with the Glory of the Lord.* Because all those men which have seen my Glory and my Miracles, which I did in Egypt, and in the Wilderness, and have tempted me, now these ten times, and have not harkned to my Voice, surely they shall not see the Land which I sware unto their Fathers, neither shall any of them that provoked me see it. Such plainly was *Davids* case, 2 *Sam* 12. 10, 11, 12, 13, 14. God forgiving the present death due to himself, and the eternal punishment, but not all the temporal punishment. However some in opposition to the Papists, have run into the contrary extream in denying this, yet plain Scripture and experience will make men believe, when prejudice and partiality, which hot disputes have bred, is cured or allayed.

§. 10.

L. C. *There is no small weight in the words*, Rom. 5. 19. As by the contumacy of one man many are made sinners, so by the obedience of one, many are made righteous. *As if he should say*; As by the sin of *Adam* many are condemned, so by the obedience of Christ only, many are Justified; *that it may be spoke of forensick and judicial acts, in both cases, past and performed in one act; as the opposition teacheth between the Justified by Christs obedience; and the guilty of damnation for the sin of* Adam: *for as the sin of* Adam *doth by one act involve posterity in the same guilt, so the Righteousness of Christ hath by one act Justified the sinners, for whom he dyed.*

§. 10.

R. B. ALL this I have answered already; what a fancy is it for this man to think, that all *Adams* posterity are guilty at once, even before they are his posterity or subjects capable of Guilt? They are all guilty of one act; but not all constituted so *By one act* of application. So are we all righteous through one satisfaction of Christ, (which yet was more then one act), but not all by one applicatory act. Cannot you distinguish both in Guilt and Remission the meritorious or material Cause, from the immediate Efficient? The former is one to us all, and at once caused in it self. The latter is as divers as the persons. Nor is there a word in the text to intimate your conceits. Yea again you boldly put *Constituuntur peccatores*, for *Constituuntur*, and when you have done, tell us it speaks of acts past. If ever you deal in this kinde more, either speak to none but your Disciples that will take your word, be it true or false; or else affirm less, and prove more.

§. 11.

L. C. BY *the like opposition as* Joh. 3. 18. *the believer is in like manner taken to be Justified already, as the unbeliever is expresly said, for that reason, because he believeth not to be condemned already: For as he that believeth not is already condemned, so he that believeth is already Justified: but if we believe the Author of the Epistle, then is a man first Justified when he believeth in Christ.*

§. 11.

R. B. This *Job.* 3. speaks of the Time of Reception of Justification: but that *Rom.* 5. doth speak of the meritorious Cause directly, and but imply the time of our participation.

2. Are not this mans eyes strangely shut, that he can neither see himself, nor the text so expresly speaking against himself? How can he believingly recite a text that saith, *He that believeth not is condemned already.*, and yet maintain that thousands that beleve not, are Justified already? Yea and see that Justification and Condemnation are contraries? yea and gather hence that a man is justified already that believeth? yea and gather hence that men are condemned *eo ipso quod non credant*? But if he mean only, that he is condemned in conscience, as he means falsly, seeing many a wicked mans blinded conscience condemneth him not (ye are they that Justifie your selves, &c.) So poor unbelievers will finde to their cost, that it is another kinde of Condemnation then that of conscience, that they are obnoxious to, and lye under: for the wrath of God abideth on them: and the Dissertor expresseth it by *jam perditioni adjudicatus*. But Oh what difference is there between the Libertines and the Gospel? the Gospel calls the unbelievers, men condemned already, Children of wrath, strangers to the Covenant of Promise, without hope, without God in the world, &c. And this man saith a little before, not only that they are pardoned, and justified, but Blessed; yea, have *perfect Blessedness*: If all the wicked that are elect, are perfectly Blessed, even in heaven, while they are whoring, perjured, killing the Saints, &c. how much have we been mistaken in the unhappiness of an unregenerate estate? and in perswading men out of it, or to be so humbled for it afterward? I cannot perceive by *Pauls* description of his former state, that he thought himself perfectly Blessed in it? nor were the Godly of my old acquaintance wont to think or speak so of their former state: whatever our Religious profane Libertines may now do. Bear with my sharpness, for I dare not repent it, so far short is it of the Cause.

§. 12.

L. C. Nor is there less strength in the vision that is Zach. 3. *where the act of Justification is skilfully expressed*: The Angel answering, spoke to them that stood before him, saying, Take away the filthy Garments from him: and to him he said, Behold I have caused thine iniquity to pass from thee, and I will cloath thee with changed rayment: *Here in one act are taken away the filthy Garments, and clean rayment is put on.*

§. 12.

§. 12.

R. B. Though I believe not that it is *Joshuahs* first Iustification that is here expressed, much less an act done, when *Adam* was yet in Paradise, yet I marvail what the man means to talk of such strength in this text for him, and make such a flourish with it, when he could fasten no sense on it himself, (who yet goes as far that way as most) but what we grant as freely as he. Who denyeth that at once (whether at one act or no) our filthy garments are taken away, and clean garments put on? But doth this prove that we shall never more fall in the dirt, nor catch a spot, nor need Christs blood any more to purge us from our sins?

You have seen how the Dissertor did *Ludionem agere*, with the sacred Scripture, I think as bad as if he had made a Stage-play of it; we must next see how he dealeth with Divines. I confess he may finde more footing for an error in mens words then Gods; and men may well bear abuse from him, that dare abuse God himself.

§. 13.

L. C. Sound Divines accord with Scripture. Amesius de Iustif. Thes. 5. Iustification admits of no degrees, but is perfect in one act, together and at once, although as to the manifestaaion, sense and effects it hath divers degrees. *Again* Thes. 23. *Not only the past sins of the Justified are forgiven, but also in some sort the future.* Num. 23. 25. He beholdeth not iniquity in *Jacob*, nor transgression in *Israel*. *Again*, Thes. 25. *The Justified daily beg forgiveness of sin, that the sense and manifestation of it may be more and more perceived, as particular sins require.*

§. 13.

R. B. 1. Some unhappy men pick up all the infirmities and mistakes of excellent Divines, and make a Religion of them, or rather make them a pretence to their errors: Our late Divines against the Antinomians, have particularly dealt with these passages of Doctor *Ames*, and have shewed the unfitness of his expressions.

2. But what is this to prove the Iustification of Infidels? You know *Amesius* saith, and many a time saith, that we are not actually Iustified till we Believe. If therefore he do make Iustification done at once, it is not before we believe.

3. *Amesius* in the first passage speaks of Iustification from a sinful state, not from a sinful act; and saith it is perfect, as to all past sins; but if he mean as to future, he erreth.

4. Nay he shews that he doth not: for he only saith of future sins, that they are *aliquo modo*, remitted, and so say I too, as before at large. *Aliquo modo*, is a large word. This shews that he took them not to be *eodem modo*, as fully forgiven

given as past sins were; and therefore that Remission was not perfect as to all sin. He saith, *Futura peccata virtualiter tantum, & in subjecto,* not *Formaliter & in sese, remittentur.*

5. You deal as you use with the 25. *Thes.* mentioning one reason only of our asking pardon, as if that were all that *Amesius* mentioned, when he hath two more.

6. If you will learn of him, I pray you learn the 14. 16. 20. 12. *Thes. Est autem hæc Justificatio propter Christum, non absolute consideratum, quo sensu Christus etiam est causa ipsius Vocationis: sed propter Christum fide apprehensum, quæ fides vocationem sequitur tanquam effectum: unde & Justitia dicitur esse ex fide,* Rom. 9. 30. 10. 6. *& Justificatio per fidem,* Rom. 3. 28. Thes. 16. *Neque est (propriè loquendo) specialis fiducia, qua Remissionem peccatorum & ipsam Justificationem apprehendimus: Fides enim Justificans præcedit Justificationem ipsam,* * *ut Causa suum effectum: sed fides Justificationem apprehendens, necessario præsupponit ac sequitur Justificationem, ut actus objectum.*

* That is too much, it is but *Conditio.*

And I pray learn of him, *Thes.* 20. what pardon is, and then you will see that he includeth not perfect Remission of all temporal punishment in it, *Justificatio absolvit à peccato & morte, non immediate tollendo culpam, aut maculam, aut omnia effecta peccati; sed obligationem & Reatum ad mortem æternam subeundam,* Rom. 8. 1, 33, 34. And I could wish those that think Christs Righteousness *in formali sua ratione,* is made ours by Imputation, would learn the *Thes.* 12. *Christi Justitia in Justificatione fidelibus Imputatur, quatenus ejus merito Justi coram Deo reputantur.* Phil. 3. 9. So much for *Amesius.*

---

§. 14.

L. C. *Piscator in Cap. 6. mat. in Orat. Domin.* Hic potissimum petimus ut cordibus nostris per spiritum sanctum persuadeat quod nobis remiserit peccata nostra propter Christum. *Here we specially ask that he would by the Holy Ghost perswade our hearts that he hath forgiven our sins through Christ.*

---

§. 14.

R. B. *Piscator* is as fairly dealt with as the former. These words which are put alone by you, as if they contained *Piscators* full sense, are but an addition to his former part of the explication, which is this, *Remitte: id est, Condona: noli postulare à nobis per solutionem aut satisfactionem: denique noli nos propter peccata nostra punire;* And in the Analysis, *Agitur in penultima (petitione) de peccatorum præteritorum, & à nobis admissorum abolitione.* What a friend *Piscator* is to the justification of Infidels, among a hundred places, I will shew you out of one in *Rom.* 3. 22, 23, &c. *Observanda hic sunt Causæ Justificationis, sive Justitiæ illius cujus respectu coram Deo Justificamur. Causa efficiens principalis & agens est Deus. Causa efficiens ad agendum impellens interna est Gratia & Justitia seu veritas Dei. Causa efficiens ad agendum impellens externa (quæ etiam vocari potest Causa Instrumentalis extra nos) est Redemptio facta per Christum, vir, per sanguinem illius. Hæc à nonnullis vocatur Justitiæ nostræ materia, &c. Causa Instrumentalis in nobis est fides qua Redemptionem illam seu satisfactionem Christi apprehendimus.*

hendimus. Forma est Remissio Peccatorum. Finis est Declaratio Justitiæ Dei. So much for *Piscator*.

§. 15.

L. C. Rollock Tract. de Iustif. *When we ask Remission of sin, we do not ask the benefit it self, as not yet given, but we ask the increase of our confidence, and the application of the benefit which is by Faith, and the increase of Faith.*

§. 15.

R. B. I Have not that piece of *Rollock* at hand, to see how he is used. but certain I am, that no Divine of name, that ever wrote, was a greater adversary to this mans Doctrine, of the Iustification of Infidels, then *Rollock* was: he being one of the principal leaders for that method of putting Faith after Vocation, before Justification and Regeneration, or Sanctification, as *Twiss* observes, e. g. in *Colos.* 1. 14. *Jam per efficacem, vocationem, translati in regnum filii dei, & ipsi inserti per fidem; redimimur à peccato & morte; sed proprius accedimus ad Regem nostrum Christum eique inserimur per fidem & incorporamur: Inserti autem & incorporati in eo, haurimus ex eo tanquam Capite nostro omnem gratiam.* The same he repeats again, shewing that Remission and Justification flow from our Union with Christ; which is by Faith: and the like most frequently in other places.

§. 16.

L. C. *God doth forgive* Believers *their sins, as a Father doth to his beloved son; A Father even offended is a Father: and a son, though certain of his Fathers good will, doth not cease to ask him the forgiveness of his faults: but if it were absurd for him whom God hath forgiven his sin, to ask forgiveness of sin of God, it would likewise seem as absurd for one that hath Faith to ask the gift of Faith, as one that is wholly destitute of it. But when a Believer asketh that which he hath already, he asketh the sense of the Grace of Gods presence, which God doth give more illustriously to the penitent. Certainly he that asketh Remission of sin, even thereby hath the marks of sin, being already forgiven; and yet ought not thereby to be the more remiss in seeking both Remission and Faith. And seeing it were in vain asked, which may not be expected, we must needs think that that is deservedly granted which we may lawfully ask; and that the Promises to the penitent and believers are not in vain, as* Act. 3. 19. *and such as the Author of the Epistle urgeth, to prove that the act of faith goeth before Remission of sins.*

§. 16.

R. B. 1. THe mans mouth condemns himself against his will. He saith, *God doth forgive Believers, as a Father, &c.* when he is proving that God forgiveth Infidels, or no-Believers, yea no men now but only men-*future.*

2. For my part I ask not only for the sense of that Faith and Grace which I have; but also 1. the increase of it, 2. the continuance and perseverance, 3. And the exercise of it. What kinde of prayers doth this man make, that asketh only the feeling of Grace! Did not I tell you, that an Antinomian Faith will cause Antinomian Piety and practise?

3. I thought it had been past doubt that it is absurd for him that knows he hath Faith, to ask for it, as one that is *plainly destitute of it.* And so it is in case of pardon. I will ask for both, but not as one plainly destitute. I ask for the continuance of former Iustification, and for the addition of actual pardon for each particular following sin; but not as one that was never pardoned before.

4. He doth still *Ludionem agere*; and here most vainly: to tell us that a man should be never the more remiss in begging pardon and Grace, because he asketh but the feeling of that which he hath already: *q. d. You must not ask for pardon, yet you must ask for it never the more Remisly.* Perhaps he means, *you must use the word Pardon, as much and as loud as if you did mean, Pardon indeed, as you speak;* and so of Faith. Or else he means, *you must ask the feeling of Grace and Pardon, as earnestly as if you were asking Grace and pardon it self.* But who can do so? to ask as earnestly for a smaller mercy as for a greater?

§. 17.

L. C. TWiss *de Erratis, Sect.* 9. In our Justification we receive of God, not only the Remission of sins past, but of future: that is, we are ascertained of the Remission of them. For the Internal act of God, whereby he willeth to remit sin, nor the act of remitting, that is, not Imputing, cannot be renovated in God: Nor is it probable that Justification is oft renewed afresh: otherwise how shall that be true, *Whom he Justified, he Glorified?* I judge it most certain, that to whomsoever God once remitteth sin, he forgiveth him alwayes his sins, of what sort and how great soever; the pronunciation of which absolution, is oft repeated from Gods Word to the penitent, and the feeling of this Divine favor is not ever alike strong in Believers, but is obscured and debilitated by reason of emergent sins, or is strengthened and revived again, as repentance is again renewed. *And if the act of Justification be not renewed; it is not credible, when we ask pardon of sins, that we ask, or are commanded to ask the reiteration of the act of Remission of sin, or reiterated Justification.*

The same man, *ad Perk. Vindicias, Pref.* It is beyond controversie that Remission of sin, as it is an immanent act in God, goeth before both our Faith and Repentance: but to us it is not known but by Faith; the confidence also whereof is further much confirmed by repentance.

§. 17.

§. 17.

R. B. I Will not do as you do, pretend those to be for me, who are against me: I confess Dr. *Twiss* is on your side in this point: and his reasons no better then yours. 2. I say as well as you, that Iustification from a state of guilt, is not reiterated; but particular Remission, and Iustification from the guilt of particular sins, is frequently performed.

§. 18.

L. C. REason consenteth with *Testimony*.
1. *Christ was Mediator, as soon as he was promised to be Mediator. If Mediator, then a Surety: if a Surety, then did he take on himself the sins of all for whom he was a pledge.*

§. 18.

R. B. YOur Reason proceedeth from a sad ignorance of the very nature of Christs suretyship and undertaking. This one point is (as I said before) the master vein of all Antinomianism. Christs sufferings were for the sins of all for whom he was Surety; and so far he took their sins on him, as to bear a voluntary penalty to demonstrate Gods Justice for those sins. But he took them not off the sinner, by the act of taking them on himself: but suffered for them with this intent and resolution, that they should have no actual pardon by it, till they should believe in him, that is, Assent to his word, and accept him for their Lord and Saviour: and on these terms was his satisfaction accepted by his Father. Disprove this Doctrine, and I will quickly and plainly prove that all men shall be saved? which is as false as yours. *Ex intentione Dei & Christi pro nobis simpliciter & absolute præstita est satisfactio antequam credamus: at ea non Imputatur nobis ut fructum inde consequamur priusquam credamus: Hinc fidei Conditio ad Remissionem peccatorum & vitam æternam prærequiritur.* Essenius de satisfact. l. 1. Sect. 5. c. 3. p. 341.

§. 19.

L. C. 2. IUstification *is an immanent act of God, done in an instant, which puts nothing in the Justified, though in the adult it necessarily createth Faith, as Faith doth Good Works: For Remission of sins is an effect of Christs death, as Faith is of Remission of sin.*

§. 19.

R. B. IS this arguing? and shall such words be called Reasons? what abundance of strange passages are here huddled up together? 1. That Justification is an immanent act. 2. And yet done in an instant. 3. That it puts nothing in the Justified. 4. Yet it createth Faith in the adult, and Faith is an effect of Remission of sin. All notoriously false, and of very dangerous consequence. Let us peruse them in order.

1. If Justification be an immanent act, then your Dr. *Twiss* will tell you, it must needs be from eternity, and have no beginning. And if so, I would know of you at present, but these two things: 1. Why you say it is done when the Promise was first made? was the Promise made from eternity? 2. Whether you do not exclude the Death and all the merits and intercession of Christ, as well as Faith? surely Christs death and merits were in time; and that which is in time, cannot be the cause of that which was from eternity? Because they tell us, that Gods immanent acts are his Essence, even God himself. And I think, Christs merits were not the cause of Gods Essence. Will you not be angry if I desire the Reader but to consider well, whether this be not consequentially infidelity it self? and whether Antinomians may not much fitter be called Anti-Christians, or Anti-Gospellers? Can he be a Christian that denyeth all Christs merits of obedience or suffering, and his Resurrection, Ascension, and Intercession, to be any causes of our Remission, or Justification, but only of our feeling of it? And can he take Christs death or merits to be any cause, who takes Justification to be an immanent act from eternity? These are no jesting matters.

2. But what a strange immanent act is that which is done in an instant? But it may be you call eternity one instant, as some do.

3. It is most false that Justification put nothing in the Justified. It puts in him a right to Impunity, and to the blessings that belong to it: It puts on him a new Relation: It disobligeth him as to punishment.

4. And what a strange immanent act is that which createth Faith? an immanent creating act? Yea expresly it is said, that it putteth nothing in the Justified: and yet it createth Faith. Belike Faith is taken to be nothing; and then it is suitable to the Justification which they suppose it to know or make known; as that Justification is suitable to the sins by it remitted. Sin which is no sin, pardoned by a pardon which is no pardon, made known or perceived by a Faith which is nothing.

2. But that Faith is the effect (yea or the consequent either) of Remission of sin, is so fully contrary to the common language of the Gospel, that me thinks, this Dissertor should not have judged his bare word a sufficient proof of it.

§. 20.

L. C. I *Said it is an immanent Action: For Remission of sin, if you respect the quiddity, is nothing else then a Negation of punishment: So therefore to remit sin, is nothing else but to Nill to Punish: which act was immanent in God, and*

and followeth not Faith, nor is found to terminate in us the operation of the Holy-Ghost: but that which by the operation of the Holy-Ghost doth come to us, is nothing but Faith or the feeling of Gods favor.

§. 20.

R. B. NO wonder if all your discourse of the season and way of Remission, be vain and erroneous, when you know not what Remission of sin is. I shall be bold therefore 1. to tell you better what it is, and 2. to shew you the error of your speeches. 1. The former having done before, I need only to repeat what is there said. God doth Remit sin, 1. As Rector, by his signal pardon, *viz.* The Law of Grace, or the Promise, *per modum Donationis.* 2. As Judge, by his Sentence. 3. As Executioner, which is by not punishing. The first act doth dissolve the obligation to Punishment, and give us Right to Impunity. The 2. act doth determine finally our controverted Right, and put it past all further controversie : The third act doth take off, or keep off the punishment it self : which hath various degrees, according to the variety of punishments. Not one of these is an immanent act, but all three Rectoral. Faith is the Condition *sine qua non*, of the first and second, and of the third as to the Eternal destroying punishment, but not as to all punishment. God may give many mercies to Infidels, and so remit proportionably much penalty to them, in this third sense. Yea what ever mercy he gives them proportionably, doth he truly remit penalty : and so in giving them Faith it self and the Spirit, he doth really remit the penalty of infidelity and privation of the Spirit, which were the penalty of former sins. In this sense, Remission is not a meer Relative change, but a real: but in the two first senses, it is only Relative. So much in few words of the true nature of pardon. Only I adde that the pardon spoken so much of in the Gospel, proper to Believers, and the immediate consequent of Faith, is the first, *viz.* the giving *Jus ad impunitatem*, dissolving the obligation to punishment, and the executive Liberation from destructive and eternal punishment, annext thereto, though a suspension went before it. To which is added the publick sentencee in its season at judgement, which is the perfection of our Relative pardon, and our most proper plenary Justification; and lastly is added our actual Liberation by Glorification, in execution of that sentence, which putting an end to all the lesser degrees of penalty, (death, rottenness, sin, &c.) which were not till then fully remitted to Believers, is it self our most perfect final executive Remission. And so our sins shall be perfectly blotted out, when that blessed day of refreshing comes.

2. Now to your definitions. 1. You make nothing of contradicting your self even in definitions. 1. You tell us that the quiddity of pardon, is nothing but *a Negation of punishment.* 2. You tell us in the very next words, that to remit sin, is nothing but *Nolle punire.* But do you think that *Non punire*, and *Nolle punire* is all one ? I know Dr. *Twiss* talks thus before you, so unhappy a thing is it for that man to have a mistaken guide, that is necessitated or disposed only to follow; and cannot see his own way. I suppose it drew Dr. *Twiss* into many other mistakes about Justification, that he knew not the nature of it, or of pardon of sin.

But let us consider them severally. 1. *Non punire*, not to punish, is but the

Yy 2 Exc-

Executive pardon, and the other two are more principally called **pardon**: and the 2. *Non punire*, is such a pardon as Reprobates have in some degree for some season, past all doubt. The wicked should be pardoned the torments of hell, as well as the Godly, as long as they live in prosperity on earth. But who will question whether there be not a further pardon besides *Non-punire*, that finds it written in Gods Word. Will not sight put it out of doubt? And that there is a sentential Absolution yet remaining, I hope for all this you shall know by experience.

2. Now to your second definition. I have shewed you already that there are two sorts of pardon besides *Non-punire*, and three besides *Nolle-punire*. I shall now further shew you that *Nolle-punire*, is no pardon at all: and that thus, 1. pardon hath either guilt, punishment, or the guilty, for its object. There is a *Nolle-punire* that hath none of these for its object. Therefore there is a *Nolle-punire* which is not pardon of sin. The minor is proved, of Gods eternal *Nolle-punire*, when there was neither sin, guilt, nor sinner, nor punishment.

2. Argument, Pardon is not an eternal act; *Nolle-punire* is an eternal act; therefore *Nolle-punire* is not pardon.

3. Argument, Pardon is the fruit of Christs blood. *Nolle-punire* (being eternal) is not the fruit of Christs blood, therefore.

4. Argument, Pardon is not the same with Election, Predestination, the Decree of saving or not punishing. *Nolle-punire* is the same with this Decree; therefore *Nolle punire* is not pardon.

And if no pardon at all, then judge how ingeniously the Dissertor saith that *Pardon is nothing else*.

Yet as I have said this much on grounds commonly owned; so let me concede somewhat on a further ground. My opinion is, that Gods Essence should neither be named an Action (in our present sense) *in genere*, nor *Velle* or *Nolle in Specie*, but respectively to some object. Take *Nolle punire* then for *Nolle infligere pœnam jam debitam*, and so the object (*pœna debita*) being *quoad esse reale*, in Time, so Gods *Velle* or *Nolle* which do respect it in *esse reali*, are to be denominated as in time, or as beginning: and thus his *Velle* or *Nolle* may be called a sort of Remission also, and a consequent of Christs death and mans Faith: Though the Essence of God which we so denominate, is eternal.

2. But in the next passage you have one of the most monstrous suppositions in chase, that ever I heard from the mouth of a Christian, *viz.* that this immanent act of God *doth not Terminate in us the operation of the Holy-Ghost*; Did ever any of your adversaries say it did? or doth it follow any of their Doctrines? that man that should say, that the Holy-Ghost by his operation on us doth produce an immanent act of God, as his *Terminus*, would be thought to be besides himself (if he be taken for learned) by all that should hear and understand his words, I confess you have an easie dispute of this.

3. That Faith (Justifying) is the feeling of Gods favor (if you mean his special favor to the Believer himself) is but your conceit, and easier said then proved.

§. 21.

L. C. Hither pertaineth, that that action much differs from transient actions, which put a real mutation in the object, as are Conversion, Vivification, &c. which are effected within us: but by the act of Believing, Remission of sin is not effected, but received: not so of Vivification, and Sanctification, which by Faith are effected in us. But Justification is not done by Faith, but by Faith is revealed and known.

§. 21.

R. B. The last is a crude false assertion, oft repeated. The rest is true, but nothing to your advantage. For though Faith do not effect Justification, yet is it the Condition, *sine qua non à Deo per Legem Gratiæ efficitur*. God pardoneth no man (adult) by the Gospel act of donation, or condonation, till they first believe.

§. 22.

L. C. 3. The reason of our Union with Christ, requireth that we be Justified before we do Believe, at left in priority of nature and order, if not of time. All Graces flow from the Union of the Members of Christ with Christ the head: and therefore Faith, Joh. 15. 5. *Without me ye can do nothing:* It is as if he had said; Unless ye are first united and ingraffed into me, ye cannot believe. For he that is not graffed into Christ, can perform no act or work: Hence it is that Faith, Gal. 5. 22. *floweth from that Union.* Nor do I conceive how the graft and the tree should grow into one *life; and bring   *Vitam forte pro vitem. forth leaves and fruits conjunct by a common life, unless they are first joyned together by insition. *He that hath the Son, hath life;* 1 Joh. 5. 12.

§. 22.

R. B. 1. All this makes against your self. For if it were so that Union with Christ went before Faith; yet if they that have the Son have life; and the graft when it is in the tree hath the life of the tree, how then can they remain in the slavery of the Divel, whom you suppose to have been Justified in Christ since *Adams* being in *Paradise*? And if you would yield that the difference is not in time but nature, your error were not so dangerous: as long as Justification and Faith begin in an instant together, you cannot plead for the Justification of Infidels so long before.

2. If we granted you that Union with Christ goeth before Faith, how do you thence prove that Faith goes not before Justification? Forsooth; because all life

flows from Union with Chrift ; what is that to the queftion ? If we yield that Faith and juftification do both flow from Union with Chrift, may not yet Faith be in order of nature the firft ? why fhould you run away with fuch an unproved Conclufion, as if Iuftification muft needs be firft, becaufe both flow from one root, Union with Chrift.

3. I utterly deny that Union goes before Faith. As you may know the ftream of Proteftant Divines goes againft you, fo doth Scripture plainly ; and then I lefs value mans contradicting reafons. The greateft task here is to expound what Union with Chrift is. There is a manifold Union that we have with Chrift. 1. The firft is a Relative Union, he being our Head, Husband, King, and we being his incorporate Members, his Spoufe and Subjects : and fo both make one Myftical perfon, that is, one Corporation, Family, Common-wealth. 2. A Union intentional, fuch as is between every object and the intellect, or will of man that is exercifed about it, by knowing, willing, &c. 3. A Union of fimilitude, (largely not properly called Union) : fo Chrift being holy, and his people like him, may be faid to be one with him. 4. A Union of Concord : when Chrift and we do agree in judgement, and affection, and action. This is but imperfect here. Thus the Primitive Chriftians were of one heart and Soul, and had one Table, one Purfe. This doth Chrift very much intend in his prayer, *Joh.* 17. *That they may be one, &c. and one in me*: that is, may agree in one and the fame Doctrine that I have taught them (though this is not all) : and fo may have one heart, that what one Loveth the other Loveth, and what one hateth the other hateth : when Chrift and man are at peace, and of one minde, they may be faid to be all one. 5. A Union of Friendfhip or Internal affection : fo we are faid to be one with thofe that we ftrongly love, and they are faid to dwell in our minds by cogitation, and in our hearts by Love and Delight : So Chrift dwels in our hearts, *Anima eft ubi amat.* 6. A Union of Familiarity, or as to the effects of Friendfhip : when men are ftill together, and communicate to one another, they are faid to be one, becaufe they fhew the effects of that Internal Friendfhip before mentioned : fo Chrift and we are one. 7. A Union (in a large fenfe) through communication of the excellencies of his fpiritual nature ; giving us the Holy-Ghoft : and fo animating us with his own Life. Yet this makes us not one Perfon natural with Chrift, nor one Divine Nature and Effence. The Father is a Conveyer of the fame nature to his Son, and all creatures to their young, and yet are not the fame perfon, or fuppofite. Yet we are not fo neer : for Chrift doth not poffefs us in ftrict fenfe with Gods Effence or Nature ; but 1. with a Nature called Divine, becaufe it is eminently of God, and inclined to Divine things, and fitted for them. 2. With Right to Chrift, who hath the Divine nature. The Sun doth generate all inferior Animates, and yet not make them Suns.

This laft Union, by communication of Spirit, is not properly fpoken of all that have the Works of that Spirit, in any kinde or meafure, no nor of all the faving Work. The Spirit hath three operations : The firft to convince and draw men neerer towards Chrift who are far from him : This is a common Work, and thus many are made partakers of the Holy-Ghoft, as alfo by miraculous Gifts, who yet may not fitly be faid to be united to Chrift. The fecond is the drawing men to Chrift ; and caufing them to Accept him ; and this is giving them Faith : It is not the language of Scripture, to call this a ftate of

Union

Union with Christ, or to say that men before Believing in order of nature are one with Christ. The third is the Spirits indwelling, being given to the Believer as his Sanctyfier and Guide, by relation and residence or operation: This is it that Scripture calls the giving us the Holy-Ghost; but whether it be the neerest reason why we are called one with Christ, I dare not determine. If there be any neerer Union yet then I have mentioned, (as I dare not say flatly there is none, so I must say) I know it not. Only I abhor that proud and blasphemous fancy of them that say, we are real beams, sparks, parts of the God-head, or of the Essence of God, or personally one with Christ.

Now of all these sorts of Union, I suppose the first is that which is chiefly hinted in Scripture; including the rest as consequents and effects of it. And this Union is after Faith, and so are all the rest, except the second (which is little to our business) and the last in the two first branches of it, or communications of Spirit; which are not fitly called Union. If any will needs say, that the Spirits working Faith in us, is a Union of the Soul to Christ; then 1. I shall yield, that is before Faith: 2. But I shall not agree with them of the fitness of the term Union applyed to that state, nor do I know that ever Scripture so useth it: 3. Much less that this is the Union which Scripture so frequently hinteth to us. I come now to prove that Union is after Faith.

Argument 1. We are United to Christ as to our Husband in marriage Covenant. But it is by Faith that we are so United, and not before it, therefore: Faith is but our Consent, which is part of the marriage-Union, *Eph.* 5. 30, 31, 32. 28, 29. *We are members of his body, of his flesh, and of his bones. They two shall be one flesh. I speak of Christ and the Church.* Now Marriage before mutual Consent here is none. *I have espoused you,* saith Paul, *to one Husband;* that is, by drawing them to Believe in Christ.

2. That which causeth the Dwelling of Christ in our hearts, causeth our Uniting to him; and that which goes before one, goes before the other: (for Christs dwelling in us is a term to express our Union by): But Christ doth dwell in our hearts by Faith. *Eph.* 3. 17. therefore we are united to him by Faith.

3. If the Life of Christ in us be by Faith, then so is our Union with him: But the former is true, *Phil.* 2. 9. *Gal.* 2. 20. *Christ liveth in me: and the life which I now live in the flesh, I live by the Faith of the Son of God.*

4. If Faith be before our Adoption, then it is before our Union with Christ; (for being United to him who is the Son, we have by an immediate resultancy the relation of sins and Coheirs): but Faith is before our Adoption, therefore; *Joh.* 1. 12. *As many as received him, to them gave he power to become the Sons of God, even to them that believe in his name. Gal.* 3. 26. *Ye are all the Sons of God by Faith in Christ Jesus.*

5. If Faith follow not our receiving Christ, then it follows not our Union with him: But Faith (the beginning of it) is not after our receiving Christ, therefore; The major is plain, in that we receive Christ into Union, and Marriage-Covenant: and Scripture never speaks of Union before. The minor is plain, in that Faith is our Active Receiving it self, prerequisite to our Passive, that is, to our Right in him, as our Husband and Head, *Joh.* 1. 12. *Col.* 2. 6. *As ye have Received Christ Jesus the Lord, so walk ye in him.*

6. Faith doth not follow our Coming to Christ that we may have life (for it is that Coming it self) therefore it followeth not our Union with

with him. *Joh.* 5. verſ. 40. *Ye will not come to me that ye may have life.* *Joh.* 6. 44, 45. *No man can come to me (that is, believe) except the Father that hath ſent me draw him;* viz. by the Spirit; therefore the Spirits drawing is in order before our coming to Chriſt; and we are not in Scripture-ſenſe united to him, before we come to him.

7. We are not united to Chriſt till we eat him as the bread of Life (for that ſignifieth the Incorporation and Union) But it is by faith that we eat him, or feed on him. *Joh.* 6. 48, 49, 50, 51, 53. *Except ye eat the fleſh of the ſon of man, and drink his blood, ye have no life in you.* 56, 57. *He that eateth my fleſh and drinketh my blood, dwelleth in me, and I in him. As the living Father hath ſent me, and I live by the Father, ſo he that eateth me, even he ſhall live by me.* So verſ. 34, 35, 36, 37, 40. By faith we joyn our ſelves to Chriſt and his Church, and ſo are members of his body, 1 Cor. 12. 27. and being joyned to him, are one Spirit. 1 Cor. 6. 17. If we are not joyned or united to the Church before Faith, then not to Chriſt (for we are made members of the body and head at one act.) But we are not united to the Church nor made members of it before faith; therefore. The Minor is eaſie to be proved by very many Scriptures. And Chriſt is head of none but the body, the Church; *Col.* 1. 18. and 2. 19. *Eph.* 1. 22. and 4. 15, 16. and 5. 23.

Much more might be ſaid to prove that faith goes before all that union with Chriſt which Scripture doth ever mention. And it is enough, that no one text can be cited to prove that any man is united to Chriſt before faith: and therefore it ought not to be affirmed. But I come at length to your reaſons.

1. You ſay *All Graces flow from Union of the Members with the Head, therefore faith*; I deny your Antecedent, and therefore your conſequent. 1. The Grace of Predeſtination flowed not from Chriſt as Head. 2. Nor the Grace of Redemption. 3. Nor the Goſpel it ſelf, nor the preaching of it. 4. Nor any of thoſe common Graces of the Spirit by which men are brought near Chriſt; ſome are made partakers of the Holy Ghoſt, and are inlightened, and taſt of the Heavenly Gift, and the Powers of the world to come, and are ſanctified by the blood of the Covenant, and yet are not united to Chriſt: *Heb.* 6. and 10. and ſome eſcape the pollutions of the world through the knowledge of Chriſt, and yet are not united to him, as *Peter* tell us. And faith it ſelf is not that life that flows into us as Members (I mean ſtill our firſt faith) proved: That which makes us members, is not given us as already members, but as to be made ſuch: But faith make us members; Therefore. If you deny the Minor, I ask you as *Paul, what communion hath light with darkneſs, or Chriſt with an Infidel?* I ſtill confeſs that faith is a Grace of Chriſt, and a ſpecial Grace: but not given to his Members, but to make them Members.

Nay I will convince you on your own principles. Tell me whether the Spirit which Chriſt gives to work the firſt faith, be given as from the Head to Members, or not? If it be, then men are united to him, not only before faith, but before the Spirit be given to work faith; which I hope is againſt your own doctrine. If not, then the Spirit to work faith is a gift that flows not from Chriſt as Head unto Members. And if Chriſt can give the Spirit to men that are not yet his Members, why may he not as well give faith to them? The truth is, as in the natural body, ſo in the myſtical, the noble parts (the head and heart) being firſt formed, do then form the reſt: Chriſt is our head and heart, our principle of being; and he makes his own members by ſending forth his Word and Spirit, and drawing and joyning them to himſelf. Now that act whereby he makes members, is not from him as the head to members already made, but as the head drawing to him and forming his own members: we are then *in fieri*, not *in facto eſſe*, members.

Nor:

Nor is this any depressing of the nobility of faith: we do not say that any can come to Christ except the Father draw him: we acknowledge that all Grace is from Christ, but not all given to members; but 1. Some given to prepare men to be members. 2. And some to make them members. 3. And then the rest to them as members for continuance, growth and exercise. If it be said, as Mr. *Pemble* doth, that Faith is not the act of a dead soul, but of a living. I answer, 1. Faith is as *Amesius* saith, *Primum actus vitæ spiritualis*: But there is a Life flows from Christ to draw men to him, and so naturally goes before Union with him. As there goes force from the Load-stone to the Iron, first to draw it to it self, and then to detain it there: so that the Iron receives of the forcible attractive operation of the Stone before it is joyned with the Stone; so doth the soul receive life from Christ to come to him for union, and then to be continued and nourished in him. 2. Faith is a vital act, but whether first from a habit of new life in our selves which may denominate us habitually living, no man living can tell, I think. Whether the Spirit do without infusing a habit first excite and cause a potent act of faith, and by that act, a habit (as *Camero* thinks), himself being in stead of a habit to the first act; or whether he do give at once the habit and act, or the habit first, will never be known till the nature of habits and acts, and of the soul it self be better known, and the way of the Spirit be fullyer revealed, which now is as the wind, *blowing where it list, but we know not whence it cometh, or whither it goeth,* that is, its way of motion: *so is every one that is born of the Spirit.* Joh. 3.

If any say as Mr. *Pemble*, that there is a twofold union: one of the Spirit on Christs part, and the other of faith on our part, and that the first is before faith, and the second is by faith; I answer, we agree with those men that say so in the matter, but we differ only in the word *union*. We agree that the work of the Spirit causing faith is before faith; but we think that it is not the phrase of Scripture to call that a union on Christs part. The union that Scripture mentions, is a moral and mystical union, caused by mutual consent, such as is between man and wife, and the members and head of a Body Politick: and a real natural Communication of Spirit and Life there is also: yet I dare not say, such as is from a natural head to the members; For 1. Scripture metaphors must not be stretched beyond the intended points of similitude, left we run into dangerous conceptions and expressions.

2. Though the holy Ghost be given to men to work life, and to be the preserver of it, yet those sacred habits and acts which are our real spiritual life, or the souls Rectitude, are such as never were formerly existing in Christ himself, as the spirits were in the natural body that are communicated from the heart and brain to the members: I know here are two weighty questions under hand, how our Life is in Christ? and how the Holy Ghost is said to be given to us? For the first, our Life is in Christ, 1. Causally, as the effect in the Cause of it, Being and Conservation. 2. Objectively, seeing that our Life is exercised on him, and the welfare of it consisteth in the enjoyment of God in him. And so our life is hid with Christ in God both as the Cause (which is latent oft when the effect appeareth) and as the Glorious fruition of the blessed Object is yet unrevealed to us, that Glory being yet with Christ in God, but beyond our reach. And Christ is here said to live in us, 1. Causally, in that his Spirit causeth our new Life, and so is said also to live in us; 2. Objectively, as we do by Faith and Love embrace him, 3. *Civiliter*, as a man possesseth a house at a distance by his goods and servants, which is in Law-sense to dwell in it. But I dare not say, that this very habitual or actual Grace or Life, which I now have was once existent in Christ; For if so, it was either his humane nature or his

Divine:

Divine: but our Grace was neither God nor man before it came to us. As the soul was in God, but Causally, and not formally existing before it was in us (whatever many in these daies say, that think they are eternal, and Gods), so was our Life of Grace in Christ; For Grace in us, is a created quality or act, and therefore was not the Creator, nor a Creature before it was created. It had no being, but causal, before it was in us, and therefore was not first in Christ; Though there is in him a Life specifically (in a larger sense) the same; but not numerically.

And for the second Question, in a word, I conceive that the manner of the Holy Ghosts dwelling as well as his working in us, is incomprehensible to us now; Only this much we may conceive, 1. That the Holy Ghost is said to be given to us, when he is given to be the Cause of our first faith, and to draw our hearts to Christ; but I doubt whether in Scripture this be ever called the giving of the Holy Ghost. 2. The Holy Ghost is given us, when he is given in Relation to us, to be our Guide and Sanctifier, as a Guardian or Tutor is given to a Child, and may be said to be their Tutor or Guardian, even when he is not teaching or doing any thing to him; so even when we feel not the Spirit work (yea should it cease to work, as it doth not wholly) yet by this Relation might the Holy Ghost be said to be given us, and we to have him; He hath taken charge of us as Christs members, to guide, sanctifie, preserve and excite us. Thus the Angels under the Holy Ghost also, take charge of us. Thus Dr. *Orbellis* and some other Schoolmen expound the giving of the Holy Ghost. 2. The Holy Ghost is given us, when the effects of him are given us, *viz.* such effects as follow our engrafting into Christ. And so the Graces of the Spirit are oft called the Spirit. But I think the Spirit is commonly in Scripture said to be given us in the second sense, connoting the first, and especially the third. And so the Spirit is usually distinguished from the Gifts of the Spirit, especially in the matter of sanctification. But I digress too far.

2. You next alledge *Joh* 15. 5. to which I answer, we grant that without Christ we can do nothing: but it follows not that without union with him we can do nothing. 2. If those words are to be expounded (as some do, and as I think they ought) of continued union with Christ, yet mark that Christ speaks it only to those that were in him already, and the full sense of the words is but this, If ye depart, or be cut off from me, ye are dead and can do nothing, as the branch is when it is broken off from the tree. But yet this is no denyal, that they that were never in him can by his Spirit come to him. They must come to him that they may have life, *Joh.* 5. 40. They do come to Christ that are drawn by the Father, *Joh.* 6. 44, 45. The father draws them, and graffs them into Christ; though of themselves they cannot do that.

3. Therefore your paraphrase is unsound, *unless ye are first united and engraffed into me, ye cannot believe.*

4. And too crudely do you say, that such can perform no act; what not go, or speak, yea or believe for a time, and receive the word with Ioy, and taste the powers of the world to come, and forsake and escape the pollutions of the world through lust, &c. these are acts. But if you speak of the special Grace, yet I have disproved it in the sense you intend.

5. *Gal.* 5. 22. saith not faith is a fruit of union with Christ, but a fruit of the Spirit; Now the Spirit first draws men to Christ, and then animates them as his members. 2. Nor is it said, that our first act of Believing is the faith meant in that Text; but the habitual fidelity of the soul to Christ. But we readily grant that all faith is the fruit of the Spirit (whether meant in that text or not): but not all,

all, a fruit of our union with Chrift : the firſt act uniteth us to Chriſt, the reſt flow from union.

6. To your fimilitude I fay; Infition by your confeffion goes before growth; and Faith is the fouls ingraffing into Chriſt. Mr. Tho. Hooker ſpeaks all this at large.

7. 1 *Joh.* 5. 11, 12. Is a moſt full place againſt your ſelf. For the text ſhews that God doth by a deed of Gift, give Chriſt and eternal life in him, to the world; and that they that believe not, that is, receive not this Gift, make God a Lyar : and ſo they that have the Son (that is, that do believe, and ſo come to Chriſt when the reſt would not) have Life, *viz.* 1. Habitually. 2. Right to eternal life; ſo that it is not the firſt act of coming to Chriſt by faith that is here called Life, but the following Life, which in the context is plainly diſtinct from that. I have ſtood the longer on this, becauſe all the appearance of your ſtrength lyes in it, and it is of moment. Yet again remember, 1. That if all were granted, (that union is before faith) it is no proof that Iuſtification is before faith. 2. If both were granted, it only proves that they differ in order of nature, being both in the ſame inſtant of time; and what is this to your Cauſe, of the Iuſtification of men before they were born?

---

§. 23.

L. C. THat I ſpeak not of that *Union which appeareth in elect Infants, which are members of Chriſt, and therefore united to Chriſt by the Spirit of Chriſt, though not yet fruitful in faith and good works.*

---

§. 23.

R. B. THe faith of the parent is the Condition of the Infants relative union to Chriſt as a member of him, and the Church his body. 2. Whether you are certain of any further union in Infants, I ſhall better know when I ſee your proofs. In the mean time, I have told you my thoughts in my Epiſtle Accomodatory to Mr. *Bedford*, in the end of the third Edition of my book of Baptiſm, whither I refer you.

---

§. 24.

L. C. MOreover faith cannot be called the Inſtrument of that *Union, unleſs it be put before Union : and ſeeing faith cannot be inſtrumental unleſs it draw with it into the ſociety of the work, the other Graces, it muſt be ſaid that union with Chriſt is not only after faith, but after good works : For Good works cannot be ſeparated from faith, and therefore all graces are called by the name of the ſanctification of the Spirit,* 1 Pet. 1. 2. *as being in one inſtant together, and at once infuſed into the ſoul.*

§. 24.

R. B. I Anſwered this fully once before. Neither Faith nor any Grace go before the giving of the Spirit to work them. But faith modified with Love and Gratitude, and whatever act is neceſſary to the Reception of the Object, *Chriſt and Life* according to its nature, do go before our union with Chriſt Relative, and in Scripture-ſenſe ſo called. For faith in the Goſpel, when Juſtification is aſcribed to it, and when Chriſt himſelf is made the object, doth comprehend ſome act of Love. For Chriſt muſt be received as Chriſt, or he is not received to Iuſtification; And therefore as the Object hath its neceſſary Qualifications, ſo muſt the act. *e. g.* if Chriſt be not received as Good, he is not truly received at all : But the ſoul cannot receive Good as Good, without Love. But then you do ill to call theſe Good works, if you intend to ſpeak in the ſenſe as Scripture doth, when it diſtinguiſheth Faith from good works. For Faith and Love in their firſt Reception of Chriſt are not ſo much as acts of Chriſtian Obedience : but only the Acceptance of a Chriſt to be obeyed ; as Marriage Conſent in the woman is not an act of a wife, or of matrimonial fidelity or obedience ; but the Contract which obligeth to that for the future. It is the Spirits working by the advantage of our ſelf love, deſire of felicity, fear of miſery, and diſcovery of ſufficiency in Chriſt for our ſalvation, that firſt brings us to faith , but not by the Authority of Chriſt commanding it ; for we are but now acknowledging him our Commander, and conſenting to his Government.

When you ſay, Good works cannot be ſeparated from Faith, I ſay, in Scripture-ſenſe they may for want of opportunity, as when one is aſleep ; however they are in order of nature after it. Laſtly, all Grace may be called the ſanctification of the Spirit, though all be not wrought at once. Or if all be *in uno ſemine* called a Habit, yet Mr. *Pemble* himſelf will confeſs, they act not all at once ; ſo that the acts of other Graces may follow whatever the ſeed do. And moſt Expoſitors take ſanctification, even in 1 *Pet.* 1, 2. as well as in other Scriptures, for the work of the Spirit following faith, and diſtinct from Vocation, and that in the *Theſs.* once, where ſanctification is put firſt, it is but a tranſpoſition of the words, but of that more anon. And in that place of *Peter*, it ſeems to be put after obedience and ſprinkling of Chriſts blood. And *Beza* judgeth that by Foreknowledge there is meant Predeſtination, by *Election* is meant Vocation, which is actual Election ; and by ſanctification is meant, the ſeparation of Believers from the reſt of the (periſhing) world.

§. 25.

L. C. 4. WE muſt needs admit *Remiſſion of ſins before faith :* ' *nor with a keener ſword do we cut the throat of the Arminians, aſſerting both Reconcilableneſs and not Reconciliation by Chriſts death, and potential Remiſſion in Chriſts death, and not Actual. For Chriſt dyed not to make Remiſſion of ſins poſſible ; nor only to impetrate Remiſſion, but actually to remit the ſins of the elect, and confer Remiſſion of ſins : Did not our Lord Jeſus when he dyed, at leaſt ſatiſfie for all the elect, paying a full price for the ſins of all the elect? Did he only obtain in his death, that the elect ſhall attain remiſſion of ſins when they ſhould believe hereafter in Chriſt? what if they never come to age, ſhall their ſalvation and remiſſion be ſuſpended on faith which they ſhall never*

never have? Forsooth when John Baptist *said,* Behold the Lamb of God that taketh away the sins of the world; *he should have said,* Who will take them away if the world will believe: *Or when our Saviour himself said,* This is my blood which is shed for the Remission of sins; *In stead of sins, he shou'd have substituted,* of believers. *Verily they that thus explicate these sayings, do voluntarily pass into the tents of the Arminians, with whom* Actual Remission, and Justification, and Redemption do befall none but Believers, and such as have the Spirit of Christ.

§. 25.

R. B. Sic vitant vitia────── 1. If you had nothing else to do but cut the throats of Arminians, the next way were to deny Christ, his death, and grace altogether: and the subject being denied, their predications do vanish.

2. Reconciliation and Remission *secundum quid* and conditional, as I have told you, go before faith: Besides, moral and natural Possibility and Impossibility must be distinguished. Our Remission was always possible in the later sense (or else it could not be future) but not in the former. A moral Impossibility *pro tempore, rebus sic stantibus,* Christ removed by his death: Now what if the Arminians say, this is all? must we needs either say that this was none of the effect of Christs death, or that there is as much to be ascribed to his death immediately as you do? sin was pardonable before Christs death, and might be pardoned upon supposition of satisfaction to Justice: Now Justice is satisfied, so far as to pardon it to all that will believe. It is now pardonable *in sensu proximo,* which before was so but *in sensu remotiore.* Nay now it is pardoned conditionally, and the Condition is nothing but the Acceptance of the full gift. The Arminians give too little to Christs death, as well as they do to Gods decree, while they make both the elected, and the redeemed to infallible pardon and salvation, to be no Individuals, but Believers in general, affirming that Christs death may have its full end, though none were saved by it: (thus our Divines report them, and some say so) we affirm that as God in electing, so Christ in dying did intend the infallible pardoning and saving of all that are pardoned and saved; but yet that as he did not therefore pardon or save them at the time of his election, (I mean from eternity) so neither doth he pardon or glorifie them at the time of Christs death. It may be procured as a thing infallibly to be enjoyed in its season, that is sufficient against the Arminians, and yet it was not done at the death of Christ, that is your error on the other extreme. You think you honour Christ much by your doctrine; but indeed you much dishonour him; For what you ascribe to his death, you take from his Intercession, and from the continued exercise of his Kingly, Priestly and Prophetical office. The Scripture saith, he is now able to save to the utmost all that come to God by him; and makes it the great work of his office actually to save them. You will have all this done by Christs death (I think all or more then Scripture speaks of), and nothing left for him to do now in the exercise of these offices, but manifestation. How can Christs death any other way procure our pardon then by way of satisfaction and merit? And we acknowledge as much this way, as can be desired, that is, that Christs satisfaction and merit is full and perfect, and have done all their part to the remission of sin. It seems then you give no more to Christs merit then we, but only give all that which we ascribe to his intercession, as to no cause, or else to Gods will alone; which yet will

will not hit right, in that we ascribe also to Gods Will a perfection of Causation in its kind. It is Christs office as King to grant upon his death, the act of Grace (obscurely upon his death undertaken, plainly upon his suffering and resurrection), and thereby to pardon men first conditionally, and then actually, and to be petitioned for Pardon from day to day; It is his office as Prophet, to teach us the way and means of obtaining pardon and salvation. It is his office as Priest, to make continual intercession, and to appear before God for us; and as our advocate, he Justifieth us apologetically against all Accusation; And at the last Judgement he will fully absolve us. Is it any honour to Christ, if you will pretend to give him the greater honour of his death, and rob him of almost all the rest? Nay you wrong his very sufferings, when you say, *Christ dyed not to make Remission of sin possible*, though not to make it absolutely possible, (for so it was before) yet to make it remissible in a neerer sense, Christ did dye; though this was not all, will you say this was none of the ends of his death? If there were not some Impediment of Remission, (*viz.* unsatisfied Justice,) which Christs death did remove, it will be hard for you to tell us how it was necessary at all, or how it should pardon us.

2. You deal not ingenuously nor honestly, to make that to be Arminianism, which the generality of the Antiarminians, except Antinomians, do hold as well as they; and which the Synod of *Dort* that condemned the Arminians doth profess, and with them the national or Church-confessions of all the reformed : *viz.* that sin is not pardoned, nor man Justified before faith. This dealing doth but disable and indispose men to believe you hereafter.

3. To your Questions I say, Christ hath made full satisfaction : But it is 1. Satisfaction strictly so called, which is but *solutio tantidem*, and not *solutio ipsius debiti*; or to speak properly, *supplicium ipsius delinquentis* : and therefore it was *solutio Recusabilis*, a refusable payment or satisfaction; and therefore doth not *ipso facto* discharge us, but on what terms the Rector please. 2. And it was never the will of the Redeemer or the offended Rector, that by this satisfaction any should be actually pardoned or justified, (being at age) till they do believe. And beyond their wills the satisfaction cannot effect any thing. The not understanding of Christs satisfaction, its nature and effects, leadeth men into the Antinomian doctrines above any thing. The conceit that satisfaction as such, must needs absolve the sinner *ipso facto* upon the payment, is a desperate error, which you may see confuted in our Divines against the Socinians at large; *Essenius* in his defence of *Grotius*, *Johan. Junius* and others. But *Grotius de satisfact.* alone, well studyed, without prejudice, might profit some Divines more then many years study of many large volumes hath hitherto done. (It was written before his defection.)

4. To your question of *dying in Infancy*, I answer, 1. The parents faith is the condition of the Infants interest in Christ. 2. If God had made personal faith necessary to all, he would have saved all Elect Infants from death, till they come to age and believe.

5 Your paraphrase on *John Baptists* words which you suppose unsound or absurd, is very common in many other Scriptures : Did you never read the like from Christ himself, that whoever believeth in him shall not perish, shall be saved, shall receive remission of sins? &c. For the sense of the Text, I suppose it speaks of taking away sin only, *quantum ad pretium*, Christ having done all that belonged to him as satisfier, for taking it away. But if you will needs understand it of actual proper remission, yet I may tell you that the text saith, not when Christ takes away the sins of the world,

world, but only that he takes them away. Now our question is, when, and whether absolutely, or on a condition.

6. As to the other text you cite, I answer, It is a vain thing to suppose that we are to substitute *believers* for *sins*, as if believers had no sins. And must every text that tels us why and for what Christ suffered, needs tell us the qualification of the persons that shall have the benefit? and the condition on which the effect is attained? Is it not enough that an hundred other texts tell it us?

7. And its very hard dealing to make as plain a Truth as any is in Gods word to be Arminianism, *viz.* that Christ shed his blood for the remission of the sins of Believers, and that none but believers (at age) have Remission and Justification. Had I a design to credit Arminianism, I know not how to do it better then as you do, if men had so little wit as to believe me. Could you make the world believe once, that the doctrine of Justification by faith, or Remission of the sins of believers, is Arminianism or Popery, and that your doctrine of the Actual Justification of Infidels, or of men that are no men, is the Protestant Doctrine, what man would not turn Papist or Arminian, and abhor the contrary, that ever well studyed the Scripture?

---

§. 26.

L. C. WHich Opinion if we must receive, we must place Remission of sins, both before and after faith, and the giving of the holy Ghost: For seeing faith and the giving of the holy Ghost are effects of Remission of sin, and the righteousness of Christ imputed to us, we must make another act of Remission of sins to be after faith, and the giving of the holy Ghost: and so Justification and Remission of sins shall not be done together and at once. It is a wonder therefore what moved the Author of the Epistle to pronounce, That God decreed to pardon sins only to the believer and penitent. I thought hitherto that a man doth believe and repent, because God hath pardoned him through and for Christ. Zachary, Luke 1. 77. maketh the knowledge of salvation, and so Faith and Repentance, to be the effect of Remission of sins: for therefore doth he undergo Repentance, because his sins were forgiven him: Davids Grand Crime of Adultery and Murther, was first-forgiven, before he repented of the fact.

---

§. 26.

R. B. 1. I have fully told you already what Remission goes before faith. If you will call unbelief, a Punishment, and will call the bare removal of that unbelief, a Remitting of that particular punishment, such an executive, improper, particular Remission we confess not going before faith, but being the very same thing with the giving of faith. But if you speak of a proper Remission by Covenant-Grant, in the Gospel sense, whereby God disobligeth the sinner from the suffering of eternal death, and the sinne hath actual right to Impunity (as to that suffering), this follows faith; and you will never while you breath, prove that faith is the effect of this Remission.

2. This

2. This great Remission of a state of sin, is done together and at once; but Remission of particular following sins, doth follow this, and the great sentential Remission follows both. Nor is it any dangerous or needless thing to contradict your *Justification, simul & semel*, if you otherwise understand it, and express it unlimitedly.

2. And (that we may wonder together) I do wonder, that you do not wonder as much at Scripture and Christianity it self, as at the Author of the Epistle, for the passage you mention. And the best proof that I finde of your contrary assertion, is, that you hitherto thought it.

3. You do sadly abuse *Luke* 1. 77. as you do other Scripture, as much as most that ever I read. You say, *Zachary makes the knowledge of Salvation, and so of Faith and Repentance, to be the effect of Remission of sins*: not a true word. 1. It is not the knowledge of *Salvation*, but *Salvation* it self; which is there made the effect or end of Remission; *To give knowledge of Salvation to his people by the Remission of their sin*: that is, To reveal to them, that God by Christ will save them by Remitting their sins: and not *to make them know by forgiving them, that God will save them.* As *Beza in loc.* faith, Remission of sin is the very manner by which God the Father saveth us in his Son, as Paul teacheth, Rom. 4. 7. 2. Nor is Faith or Repentance the same thing with *the knowledge of Salvation*: if by it you mean of our own being actually saved, or that we shall be saved: though Faith is the knowledge of Christ who doth save us, and of what he hath done towards it; which may be both called Salvation.

4. *Davids* case affords your opinion as little countenance. For 1. *David* was a Believer before, and repented of sin in general; and this was not his first faith or repentance: He totally lost not his Habitual Faith and Repentance by his sin. 2. Yet do you rashly and without any proof say even of his particular pardon, that it went before his Repentance of the fact. For 1. you are not sure that he repented not, till *Nathan* spoke to him: I make no question but he did, because it is the nature of true Habitual Repentance, to act more or less when the sin is known, and this could not be unknown to him: But its plain that his Repentance was not so great and evident as after, nor his heart so humbled as it was meet for such a sin. 2. When *Nathan* did speak to him, the never pronounced his forgiveness, till *David* first cryed out, *I have sinned against the Lord*, 2 Sam 12. 13. And how eminently that pardon respected the temporal punishment of *David* by death, is not obscure; so that the just season of the Remission of the eternal punishment, is not mentioned in that text: but must needs be upon the performance of the condition.

§. 27.

L. C. True Repentance ariseth from the conscience of Gods mercy, forgiving many sins to the sinner; such as was the mournful condition of the woman, Luc. 7. 38. who loved much, repented, wept much, because *Jesus Christ* had forgiven much. Our Love to God which we most manifest when we repent, doth fetch its original from the sense of Gods Love to us, as John teacheth, 1 Epist. 4. 9.

§. 27.

§. 27.

R. B. 1. Either you mean, All true repentance, or only some. The first is false; the latter nothing to the purpose. No doubt the sense of actual pardon may increase Repentance: But the first Gospel Repentance according to Gods order, is from the knowledge of Gods Love and Mercy in giving Christ to be a sufficient sacrifice for sins, and in giving pardon through Christ to him (as to all) on condition of Acceptance. This great, but general mercy mentioned *Joh.* 3. 16. is the rise of the first Evangelical Repentance, if it proceed as it ought: with which is conjoyned the sense of misery, and fear of Gods wrath: When will you prove that all these, together with Conviction of the evil of sin, the worth and necessity of holyness, and the desirableness of Celestial happiness above sensual things, may not (by the Spirits help) produce a true change of minde and sorrow for sin, without the sense of the actual Remission of my own sins?

2. How contrary go you to Scripture, which bids us Repent and be Baptized for Remission of sin, and promiseth Remission, if we repent: and you say, repentance must arise from the knowledge of remission; as if we could not truly repent till God have forgiven us, and we know it?

3. Both you and all that go your way, are sad Comforters to the most poor distressed consciences: For whereas most or many of them have not the feeling or knowledge of the pardon of their sins, you will conclude them all impenitent, and so to lye under all the curses that belong to the Impenitent. But it will be long before all the Libertines living will prove all those poor Christians Impenitent that have not the knowledge that their sins are forgiven.

4. You teach men to go the wrong way to Assurance, and consequently to be without it. For whereas God teacheth them to judge of their pardon by their repentance, telling them that the sins of the penitent are forgiven, you contrarily teach them to judge of their Repentance by the knowledge of pardon: and this is a thing that cannot be known by ordinary means, before Repentance be known; both because it is an act of God, which can be no otherwise known to us, then he revealeth it, and because he hath revealed it to be the consequent of repentance, having given it in his Word on the Condition of repentance, and to no Impenitent ones. So that according to your method, no man shall ever have Assurance that his sins are pardoned, till God will reveal it to him from heaven by extraordinary Revelation: for he must know his Remission without any signs of it, (whereof Repentance and Faith are the first) and that is by no natural or ordinary means. It would puzzle you to give a sensible interpretation of those Scriptures that call people to the tryal of their states, to examine whether Christ be in them, or whether they be Reprobates, if this be the way of tryal? for though I can try and examine my own heart, to discover the acts of Repentance and Faith, and the knowledge of remission, yet I know not how to search or try immediately, whether God hath forgiven me, that I may know it, otherwise then in the word, which forgiveth me but on Condition of my Faith and repentance. Else I must examine God, and not my self. All tryal is by some evidence: where the thing is such as is not the object of sense it self, or knowledge immediately, (*& prius in sensu quam in intellectu.*) it must be discerned

Aaa by

by somewhat that is known. Our pardon and righteousness are relations, and therefore not discernable immediately in themselves. Indeed it is evident, that the knowledge of pardon which you make to be necessary before true Repentance, is not a knowledge that comes by tryal, examination, or any rational way of discovery, but by direct extraordinary Revelation from heaven.

5. And then see the fruits of this Doctrine. One part of the Godly (that have not Assurance) must remain in distress of minde; and must not have Assurance, *eo nomine*, because they have it not already: Others will be looking for these revelations of pardon, and so deluded with every conceit and fancy of their own, or by those common suggestions of Satan, whereby he perswades the most of the world that they are forgiven. And all will be taken off the duty of examination, and the use of Gods means for a rational way of Assurance: how directly tendeth this Doctrine to Confusion, Delusion, and Perdition of Souls?

6. The woman *Luk.* 7. Loved and wept much, because much was forgiven: Doth it follow therefore she never repented truly till she knew much was forgiven? what shew of such a consequence?

7. *1 Joh.* 4. 9. hath not a word to your purpose. 1. The Text speaks only of Gods general Love in giving his Son, mentioned *Joh.* 3. 16. and not at all of our actual forgiveness. 2 Much less of our knowledge of that forgiveness. 3. The next verse indeed saith, *Herein is Love, not that we loved God, but that he loved us*; but 1. It is only the Love of sending his Son to be the propitiation for our sins, that is mentioned, and not the actual pardon of them. 2. Though a further Love went before ours, *viz.* his Love of Election, and intent to give us Faith, and so Remission and Salvation, yet that is not known to us when we first repent, nor doth the text intimate any such thing. That general Love of God, in giving his Son to be the Saviour of the world, which some elevate and make nothing of, hath enough in it, if well considered, to fill the heart with Repentance and Love: yea and is appointed to be the great means to that end, and therefore is not so vain as they make it.

§. 28.

L. C 5. But the act of Believing is so far from going before the act of Remitting sins, that in the very acts of calling, sanctifying, quickning, &c. which are thought to make a real mutation in the Called, Sanctified, &c. God doth not act, but on a subject destitute; and Gods actions are conversant about an object void of a Condition or Vertue prerequisite. The Kingdom of God is received of Infants, innocent by the sole ignorance of evil, not by the knowledge of good, before they grow up to manhood. God raiseth and quickneth the dead: he communicateth the Spirit to unbelievers, that they may believe: And as Vocation is an act of Gods mercy exercised on the miserable, so he calleth the stupid and sluggish, who think of nothing less then going to Christ: he translateth them from the Kingdom of Satan, and from darkness to light: There is at least the like reason; though much more strong in the act of Justification. God Justifieth the ungodly as ungodly, not in a divided, but a compound sense. Rom. 4. 5. For he cannot be called ungodly that hath Faith in the Lord Jesus.

Jesus. *He also Justifieth Ethnicks*, Gal. 3. 8. Without strength; and ungodly, Rom. 5. 6. As yet sinners: *verf.* 8. Enemies,: *verf.* 10. For then were we reconciled, when we were enemies, sinners, strangers and open enemies. *Col.* 1. 21. *For what can be more absurdly spoken then to Reconcile friends. God by remitting sin, declareth to the sinner, that himself is just, and he unjust : But of the object of Justification* in Specie, we shall deal afterwards.

§.28.

R. B. 1. There is no truth, nor likelyhood of truth in your consequence, that *there is the same Reason, and stronger, of Justification, as of Vocation*; being without a prerequisite Condition. The deciding of this must be from the tenor of the Promise; Vocation is not given by a Conditional Promise (only means prescribed men to be used for it), but it flows from Election and Redemption, as joyned with Election, revealed in an absolute Prediction or Promise, *I will take the hard heart out of their bodies, and give them hearts of flesh, a new heart, &c.* Contrarily Remission is promised only on Condition of Faith and Repentance. And therefore to say the reason is like, when God hath made it so unlike in the tenor of his Covenant, is to exalt your fancies above the Law. God gives the first (though not alwayes, nor usually without preparations of the heart, which are qualifications to fit the subject): yet without any prerequisite Condition (properly so called in Law-sense) on our part; But doth it follow that he gives the second Grace so too? Justification is not the first Grace.

2. You say, *God Justifieth Impios quâ Impios*; the ungodly as such. If you mean but *dum Impii*, while such, you say true, taking the word *ungodly*, as the text doth, for unjust or sinners: but you say more: and a most ungodly Doctrine it is that you deliver, as ever came, I think, from the mouth of a Christian: To justifie the ungodly as such, *quâ tales*, is to justifie all that are ungodly: for doubtless a *quatenus ad omne valet Consequentia*. And if God Justifie all the ungodly, then he will save all the ungodly. A fair Doctrine to preach to the world! Nay add but the sense in which you take the word *ungodly*, viz. for one unregenerate, and that hath not the true fear of God, and it will appear more monstrous; that God Justifieth all the ungodly, as such: And so the world must be taught, that as long as they are ungodly, there is no danger nor possibility of their damnation; for God Justifieth them *quâ impii*, as ungodly: but if they turn Godly, what will become of them, when it is *as ungodly* only that God Justifieth men.

3. Where you say, *it is not in a divided, but compound sense*: I answer, Its true, because by *ungodly*, is meant *unjust*, or sinners: But prove that by *ungodly*, is meant *unsanctified*, and I will prove it to be *in sensu diviso*.

4. Where you say, *He cannot be called ungodly, that hath Faith*; I answer, Not in our common Evangelical sense, but in a legal sense, in which the Apostle there speaks, (according to the Law of works) he may, and is: ungodly being there, but a sinner and unjust. Besides, *quoad actiones vitæ externas proximè precedentes*, as to his conversation next foregoing, he is ungodly in your sense when first Justified; but not as to his heart, nor present life: (for while he repenteth, he suspendeth his former exercise of such evils, though he must have time to pra-

Aaa 2

[268]

rise good). For all your naked denyal, he is called ungodly, as a sinner, who is yet Evangelically Godly, and a Believer. And how grosly deal you with God, to say *he cannot be so called*, when God calls him so in the text cited? Are not the words, *He that Believeth in him that Justifieth the ungodly*? It is then an ungodly Believer, that is there mentioned, that is, one unjustifiable according to the Law of Works.

5. In gross abusing the text *Gal. 3. 8.* you disclose more of the meaning of your Doctrine. You say, *God Justifieth Heathens*: you mean *while Heathens*, plainly. A comfortable Doctrine for Heathens, if the Author could prove it: But they shall have a Judge that is of another minde: and then it is not a Libertine Doctor that can save them, when God condemns them. What a vain thing make you all the Gospel to be, which calleth men to Faith and Repentance that they may be justified? and what a small matter make you of Christianity it self? when God Justifieth Heathens: yea, and in this (as you said before) they are blessed with a perfect blessedness? Oh what difference between the Scripture language and yours? May you not as soberly say from *Mat. 21. 31.* That Publicans and Harlots shall enter into the Kingdom of Heaven? when its plain by the parable foregoing, that Christ means those that then were, or before had been Publicans and Harlots, but after repented and were converted. I know you not, nor know I of what Country or language you are, nor what world you inhabite; but if you live in this world, let them that know you, observe you but a few years, and I conjecture they shall finde you either recanting these conceits, or else forsaking the Scriptures as true or sufficient, so palpably are your Doctrines contrary to it.

2. But as to this text, could you be ignorant that it speaks *in sensu diviso*? 1. It saith not that God doth Justifie the Heathens; but *the Scripture foreseeing that God would Justifie* them: that is, the heathen part of the world distinct from the Iews: 2. Why left you out that part of the sentence that confoundeth your interpretation? *That God would Justifie the Heathen through Faith.* If Faith be the means through which he will Justifie them, then they are Believers when he Justifieth them. Do you not love the Truth, that you will thus hide and wink at the express words of the text?

6. As bad almost do you use *Rom. 5. 6.* to speak an open untruth of the text, as if it said, that God Justifieth *the ungodly without strength*, when it only saith, *When we were yet without strength, in due time Christ dyed for the ungodly*. As if Christs dying for them, and Justifying them were all one, or done at once. And perhaps *ungodly*, is there also taken for *sinners*.

7. And so it is expounded *verse 8.* which you unworthily again apply to Justification, when the Text speaks it only of Christs dying for them. Yet we doubt not but all are sinners that are Justified: what therefore is that to your advantage?

8. For *Col. 1. 21.* (and so 2 *Cor. 5. 18.*) I have spoken enough before; how far we were reconciled before Faith.

9. Its easily granted you, that it is absurd to talk of Reconciling friends (so far as they are friends): Did ever any of us say or dream that men are friends to God, before they are reconciled or made friends? But what is this to prove that Believing, that is, Accepting the Reconciler and Reconciliation offered, is not the Condition, in order going before Reconciliation? To reconcile a Believer, is not so absurd a phrase, as to reconcile a friend. For though every Be-

liever

hever be a friend, yet that is, becaufe believing is made, the Condition of Reconciliation, and fo friendfhip relative refults upon it, from the gift to the receiver.

10. Let me here on the by tell you once for all, (that you run not on a miftake) that Iuftification in the Scripture ufe of the word, is a ftricter term then remiffion or reconciliation : reconciliation is fometime taken for fo much as Chrift did on the Crofs, though it be not full actual reconciliation ; But fo is Iuftification never taken : remiffion is fometime taken, as is faid, for partial executive remiffion, going before Iuftification ; but Iuftification is never fo taken. Yet remiffion is moft ufually taken for the Legal Condonation or Remiffion of the guilt of eternal punifhment; and fo it is the fame thing (notionally differing in fome fmall refpect) as Iuftification. But there is a remiffion in Scripture fenfe, that goes before Faith, yea, which thofe may have that perifh, (or elfe they could have no mercy: for every mercy remitteth fome degree of their punifhment). But Conftitutive Iuftification is proper to Believers.

§. 29.

L. C. *But the immanent acts of God, performed together and at once, as to Elect, to Iuftifie, to dye for finners, are carried to their object in a divers refpect. So Chrift dyed as well for his friends as his enemies : for his friends, becaufe God already loved them, and had already Juftified them : but he dyed for his enemies, becaufe they loved not God, nor were yet converted to the Faith, that they might have the fenfe of that Love. But in what refpect foever the acts of Remiffion of fin, yea Vocation, Sanctification, &c. are done, they are carried to an object deftitute of a prerequifite Condition, that the action may promote it felf into act.*

§. 29.

R. B. WOe to the Church or Soul that practically entertains this Doctrine. 1. It is untrue and Antichriftian, that Iuftification is an immanent act of God : For then it is from eternity, and then Chrifts death is no caufe of it, nor any other work of Chrifts Mediatorfhip whatfoever. Is not this good Chriftianity ?

2. Did ever the ear of man before this time, hear, that *to die for finners* is an immanent act of God ? If God dye, and dying be an act (both which may have a good fenfe) yet let it not be an immanent act.

3. He faith, *God already loved, and had Juftified them* : before Chrift dyed for them, and therefore they were his friends. If he mean it of Chrifts undertaking to die for them, and when he was promifed in the Garden to *Adam*, viz. that before this they were fo Iuftified, then you may fee how much he fets by Chrifts death, while he pretends to extoll it to the detriment of the honor of all the reft of his mediatory actions that follow for the conferring of this fruit of his death. And by faying, It is an immanent act, he feems fo to mean. And then I would know of him, whether this be not down-right Socinianifm ? But if he mean it of Chrifts actual dying, then its true that he dyed for fome that were reconciled by virtue of that death, as undertaken. But yet *in ordine Civili*,

Chrifts death goes before their reconciliation, and he dyed for none but enemies.

4. But his next words leave me no hopes of this latter being his fenfe. For all the enmity that he acknowledged in thofe that Chrift dyed for, is this, that *They Loved not God, nor were yet converted to the Faith, that they might have the fenfe of that Love.* See here all you that have favorable thoughts of the Antinomian Doctrine, and think verily that it extolleth Chrift and Grace, what the true face of it is, and whether you are lead. Here is your honoring of the Mediatorfhip of Chrift: All that you leave Chrift to do, in coming into the world, Obeying, Dying, Rifing, Interceding, Giving out the Spirit, &c. is not to reconcile God to us, nor to procure our Juftification, for we had thefe before, but only to caufe us to Love God, and be converted, that we may have the fenfe of that Love. Whether this Religion may be called Chriftianity or not, I will not now determine; but I would defire the owners of it, to anfwer me thefe two or three queftions.

1. How it can with any truth be faid that Chrift dyed for our fins, and fuffered for us, and was a facrifice for us, and for our fins, and an attonement and propitiation for our fins, and bore our fins in his body on the tree, and was a ranfom for us, with many the like, if he dyed not to procure us Reconciliation or Iuftification, but only the fenfe of what was done before? 2. What reafon can you give why Chrift fhould dye for us, if it were only to procure us to Love God, and feel his Love? Is it not the work of the Holy-Ghoft to caufe thefe in us? If there be no need of Chrifts death for fatisfaction, reconciliation of God to man, or Iuftification, what need is there of it for fanctification and comfort (on that fuppofition)? why might not God have as well caufed us to love him, and feel his Love, without Chrifts death, as with it? 3. Do you not feign God to be cruel and blood thirfty, that when Juftice doth not at all require it for remiffion, will yet require the blood of the innocent, yea his own Son? 4. Yea do you not feign God to be lother to reveal his Love, then to Love us, and to reveal Juftification, then to Juftifie us; when he will Juftifie us for nothing, but will not reveal it, unlefs his Son will purchafe it with his innocent blood? 5. Is it not a Popifh or far more ridiculous contradiction, to feign us to be pardoned or juftified before, and yet to have none of the punifhment removed; but to lye under all the unholynefs of our nature (which is in fome refpect a punifhment, as left on us) and under the fenfe of Gods wrath? what is Hell but a ftate of fin, and the fenfe of Gods wrath? would it be any comfort to any of the damned to have fuch a Iuftification, as fhall not remove fin or mifery in the fenfe of Gods wrath? What is it that hindreth man from the full fenfe of Love, and continueth fufferings on him, and keeps him fo long out of heaven, if he were abfolutely and perfectly pardoned from eternity? 6. What expofition give you of all thofe texts that defcribe the mifery of an unregenerate eftate? and exprefs the necefsity of holynefs? But I will add no more of this now. A love of Election we acknowledge from eternity, but not of reconciliation, and Iuftification. It is as ftrange a thing for a man to be reconciled before ever he fell out with him, as you faid it was to reconcile friends.

To your laft claufe I anfwered before. The firft Grace of Vocation hath a prerequifite condition, though oft preparations, and alwayes fome means which the perfon is obliged to ufe for it: But Iuftification and right to Salvation are not the firft Grace, but are given on condition of Faith and repentance.

CHAP.

CHAP. V.

Of the Concurse of the Acts.

§. 1.

L. C. This *Concurse* a twofold Reconciliation doth illustrate. The first, by which God is reconciled to us: The second, by which we are reconciled to God. Of the first Reconciliation, Paul speaks, when he saith, that we were reconciled when we were enemies, Rom. 5. 10. Col. 1. 21. 2 Cor. 5. 18, 19. but of the second he speaketh in the next verse, We beseech you, that ye will be reconciled to God; which is done when we apprehend the first Reconciliation, and know God Benevolent to us. By and for Christs obedience God is reconciled to us, but by Faith are we reconciled to God. He that believeth on the Son, hath Life, yea, seeth Life, Joh. 3. 36. and can cry Abba Father: he, that is so reconciled hath peace with God. Rom. 5. 1.

§. 1.

R. B. Reconciliation is a returning to friendship from enmity, or falling out: enmity is (as *scientia ad scibile*) either a disposition, and so a quality of the minde, or an act therefrom; or else it imports the Relation to the object. Reconciliation is first the removal of the act and disposition of the minde contrary to friendship; and 2. the removal hereupon of the relation from the object: when a man ceaseth to hate me, and be my enemy, I cease to be hated by him, and to be his enemy relatively and objectively. And then if I have a hatred or actual enmity to him, this requireth the like change.

The enmity that God hath to man and his reconciliation from this enmity, are not as in man, dispositions and mutations. But 1. There is somewhat in God, which we cannot better conceive of or express, then under these notions, though improper. 2. Gods Essence hath various and mutable Denominations from the various and mutable respect of objects thereto. So that as mans nature is Lovely or Hateful, God is Denominated as Loving or Hating him. 3. But principally, God as Rector, is said to be at enmity and to hate, where he is by his Law, and vindictive Justice, as it were, obliged or engaged to use that man as an enemy, if he so continue; or may, at least, use him as an enemy at present, according to his Laws; or to speak more properly, when in Law such dealing is due to man from God, as men use to receive from enemies. Contrarily, Gods reconciliation is, the change of relations, and Legal obligations, viz. when that punishment is no longer Due to us, according to the tenor of Gods Law, the obligation being dissolved, and when such dealing is our due by the Law of Grace, as is to be expected from friends. Thus much to shew you a little more of the nature of reconciliation, then your defective distinction, which is worn thred-bare by the Antinomians, doth shew.

To apply this, God is not reconciled to us by a mutation in himself, but by a

mu-

mutation in us, the objects, and by the new Law-ſtate, that we ſtand in towards him: whence you may eaſily ſee, if you love the truth. 1. That God is not reconciled to us from eternity; nor from the firſt Promiſe, nor from Chriſts death actually: but only when we are by Faith, under the Promiſe, and not before. 2. That the great reconciliation of man to God, which Scripture ſpeaks of, is objective and relative; and is the ſame thing, and done by the ſame act, as is Gods reconciliation to us, only reſpectively differing: that act that cauſeth you to ceaſe hating me, cauſeth me to ceaſe to be hated by you. — Our great reconciliation with God, purchaſed by Chriſt, and given in the promiſe, is our being hated by him no more, or ceaſing to be paſſively and objectively his enemies. 3. Our reconciliation Active and Qualitative, whereby our own minds are reconciled to God, conteineth the whole work of Sanctification on the heart, from our new birth to our death. 4. The firſt part or degree of our mental reconciliation to God goes in order of nature, but not of time, before Gods reconciliation to us, and our objective, paſſive relative reconciliation with God. For indeed our mental reconciliation in its ſincere beginning, is nothing but our Faith and repentance, which are the condition of the other. And Gods reconciliation to us, is the ſame thing with our forgiveneſs and Juſtification, all under diſtinct notions. And our great relative reconciliation to God, is our being pardoned and juſtified. 5. Yet the reconciliation *quoad pretium, & ſecundum quid*, which is heretofore deſcribed, is long before all this: even from Chriſts death undertaken, and the enacting of the Law of Grace. But that is to us but Conditional, not Actual reconciliation. Having told you my minde, I will take an account of yours.

1. *Paul* in *Rom.* 5. 10. ſeems to me to ſpeak of actual reconciliation of God to us, and us to him, following Faith: though he ſay, we were reconciled *By* Chriſts death, he ſaith not *At* Chriſts death. If you will needs have it otherwiſe, then is it but the conditional reconciliation foredeſcribed, *Col.* 1. 21. and 2 *Cor.* 5. 18. I have ſpoke to twice before. For the 20. *verſe*, I ſuppoſe *Paul* beſeecheth them firſt in order of nature to believe, and ſo be mentally reconciled, but principally intending in the word *Reconciled*, their relative paſſive Reconciliation. *q. d.* Seeing God hath ſo far laid down his diſpleaſure, *as not to leave your Souls remedileſs, but to provide himſelf a Saviour for you, and ſo hath received a ſufficient ſacrifice and ſatisfaction to his Juſtice for you, and hath given you a conditional pardon in his Goſpel, and ſo is on his part fully reconciled to you, ſo you will but Accept Chriſt and Reconciliation offered, and hath commiſſioned us to beſeech you to this Acceptance, we do as his Embaſſadors, beſeech you to yield to theſe reaſonable terms, that ſo you may be pardoned and reconciled to him, and he may take you actually and fully for his friends.*

2. What you talk of doing it, *when we apprehend Reconciliation, and God benevolent to us,* if you mean it of actual full Reconciliation apprehended, I have oft enough confuted: If of conditional reconciliation it is true.

3. When you ſay, *By and for Chriſts obedience God is reconciled to us.* 1. Why then ſaid you before, It was an immanent act? and that the thing which Chriſts death doth, is to cure that enmity which conſiſts in *our not Loving God, and not feeling his Love.* 2. God is not actually reconciled by Chriſts death till we believe.

4. Our Faith is the Antecedent and Condition of Gods reconciliation to us, and the formal reaſon of our mental reconciliation to him (as is our Love alſo) ſo that we are not mentally reconciled by Faith, as the efficient of our firſt mental reconciliation, but formally; and as efficient of what follows.

5. *Joh.* 3. 36.

5. Joh. 3.36. Is not meant of the bare sense of love: but *he that believeth on the son hath Life.* 1. He hath Christ the fountain and cause of Life: 2. He hath a new spiritual Life of inherent grace. 3. But principally, (as to the text) he hath the Relative Life of Justification, and right to eternal life, in seeing and enjoying God. But for your fourth, It is an unsound and uncomfortable addition; to drive thousands of poor Christians to conclude they have no faith, because they have not the peace and sense of Love which you vainly make the nature or inseparable effect of true faith.

6. I have lately explained that of the Spirit of Adoption, crying *Abba* Father, in another book.

7. *Rom.* 5.1. seems to me to speak of objective Relative Peace with God, and not mental peace, as if a potent adversary cease war with us, we are said to have peace with them.

§ 2.

L. C. *The first Reconciliation is the Cause of the second: For that we are the sons of God is the Cause that he gives us the Spirit.* Gal. 4.6. *Because ye are sons, God hath sent forth the Spirit of his son into your hearts, to cry Abba Father, to wit, ye are sons by that Grace given in Christ before the world did begin.*

§ 2.

R. B. 1. The Spirit in Scripture is said to be given us after our first believing, and so after our Justification and Adoption. That we may know how far we agree or differ in this point, I will tell you first how far we consent about the Matter, and then that we have a further controversie about the words. 1. We grant that the common works of Grace upon unbelievers or unsound believers, bringing them nigh to the Kingdom of God, and making them almost Christians, and giving them some Illumination, and tast of the heavenly Gift, and of the good word of God, and the powers of the world to come, and to receive the word with Joy, and believe for a time, all these are the works of the Holy Ghost: and so far the Holy Ghost may be said to be given them, and they are said to be partakers of the holy Ghost, *Heb.* 6.4. 2. We grant that the Gift of working miracles, casting out Devils, &c. which many unsound believers had, was the work of the Holy Ghost, and so they are partakers of him. 3. We grant that it is the Holy Ghost that causeth us to believe to Justification, and worketh in us the first Grace; and thus we may say, the Holy Ghost is given us savingly before our Justification. 4. We further affirm, that after our believing, the holy Ghost is given to us in a more eminent manner then ever before, 1. Relatively, as undertaking to be our guide and sanctifier, and to possess us for Christ, and secure his Interest in us. 2. And Really to do these works; sanctifying us in a more eminent sort then in the first act of Believing; and helping us in duties, and against temptations, and striving in us against the flesh. 5. We affirm that this last giving of the Holy Ghost is after our believing in order of nature, and faith is the Condition upon which it is promised: 6. As also that the forementioned Gift of Miracles is usually if not ever in Scripture found to be consequential to faith, either found or unsound. Thus much for the thing. Now for the name, 1. I suppose that the common sense of this phrase in Scripture, *of giving the holy Ghost*, is of such a giving as follows faith:

Bbb   And

And that the Spirits working the firſt Grace, is not uſually (nor at all that I know of) called the Gift of the Holy Ghoſt. So that when you read of Gods giving us his Spirit, it is meant of one of the former works, viz. the ſanctifying work, or the work of miracles, both following faith : (the one in unſound Profeſſors following only an unſound faith) Thus the Holy Ghoſt is ſaid to dwell in our hearts, and work in us, &c. whereas in working us to believe the Spirit, is not ſaid to dwell in us, nor to be given us ; but only to open our hearts, to draw us to Chriſt, as ſignifying, as Mr. Tho. Hooker ſaith, the Spirits making its way into our hearts, or his opening the door, as it were, that he may come in and dwell in us. Or may the reaſon be according to Camero's Iudgement ; that the Spirit at firſt exciteth an act of faith without a foregoing Habit, and by that act, forcibly, but congruouſly cauſed, he doth cauſe a Habit : and therefore it being acts more directly then Habits that we are commanded and exhorted to, and God working on man in a way agreeable to his nature (Infuſed Habits being cauſed *ad modum acquiſitorum*, as is commonly ſaid), it ſeemeth beſt to God to deal with us as free rational agents, and to command us to believe, and exhort us to it, while we are yet without any habit of faith ; and withall to make it the Condition of his promiſe, on which we ſhall receive, as Juſtification, ſo habitual Grace ; and ſo by the precept and promiſe without, and by his Spirit powerfully working within, to cauſe the firſt act in his elect, and thereby the habit : and ſo it is only upon the receiving of this habit, that the Holy Ghoſt is ſaid in Scripture to be given us, and to dwell in us. And this opinion ſeems beſt to ſuite with the common Doctrine of the reformed Churches, who generally make Vocation to be the effecting of faith and repentance, (or faith alone ſay ſome) and Remiſſion and Juſtification to be next, and Sanctification, diſtinct from Vocation, to be next : ſo that when Mr. Pemble begun another way of conceiving and expreſſing this work, Biſhop Downam wrote againſt it as an innovation. I was long a zealous follower of Mr. Pemble in this point, as appears in the firſt part of my book of Reſt, In the third Edition whereof I have partly revoked it : not as now reſolved of the rightneſs of any other way, but as apprehending the thing either unrevealed, or at leaſt uncertain to me. But this is paſt doubt, that the term *ſanctification* is uſually taken in Scripture, not for the giving of the firſt Grace of faith, but for ſome following ſort or degree of change in our hearts and lives : (and perhaps much reſpecting the actual Covenant of Dedication, and the Relation of being dedicate or ſeparated to God.) And it is as certain that the ordinary meaning of Scripture, when it ſpeaks of our receiving the Spirit, is not of the Spirit to work faith at firſt, but of ſome eminent habitual change and gift following faith, as its Condition.

This I will now prove from ſome Scriptures, Eph. 1. 13. *In whom alſo after ye believed, ye were ſealed with the holy Spirit of promiſe* (that is, the promiſed Spirit) Gal. 3. 14. *That the bleſſing of Abraham might come on the Gentiles through Jeſus Chriſt : that we might receive the promiſe of the Spirit* (i.e. the promiſed Spirit) *through faith*. Prov. 1. 23. *Turn you at my reproof ; behold I will pour out my Spirit unto you*, &c. Act. 19. 2. *Have ye received the Holy Ghoſt ſince ye believed ?* &c. verſ. 6. Joh. 7. 39. *This he ſpake of the Spirit, which they that believe on him ſhould receive ; for the Holy Ghoſt was not yet given, becauſe that Jeſus was not yet glorified ;* verſ. 38. *He that believeth on me, as the Scripture hath ſaid, out of his belly ſhall flow rivers of living water.* By this time you may ſee the ſenſe of the Text alledged by the Diſſertor, Gal. 4. 6: *And becauſe ye are Sons, God hath ſent forth the Spirit of his Son into your hearts, crying* Abba, Father ; This therefore moſt evidently ſpeaks of *a giving of the Spirit*, after faith, and not before it, as he would unreaſonably perſwade us.

For

For that Adoption is consequential to faith, is as true as Gods word. Gal. 3. 26. *Ye are all the Children of God by faith in Chrift Jefus.* Joh. 1. 12. *As many as received him, to them gave he power to become the Sons of God, even to them that believe in his name.*

3. There is yet one claufe to be anfwered, that is fo monftrous, that I know not well what to make of it. He faith ye *are Sons by that Grace, given in Chrift Jefus before the world did begin;* as making this the paraphrafe of *Gal.* 3 6. Here it appears, 1. That he takes us to be fons before the world began. 2. That he takes us to have received Grace in Chrift before the world began. The former is confuted by all that is, and will be faid againft Juftification from eternity; For Iuftification and Adoption go infeparably together. The fecond is a myfterie beyond my conceiving: How we fhould have Grace given us from eternity? or how it is given in Chrift from eternity? I believe that we are elected from eternity; and that we are elected in Chrift, that is, elected to be lovely, wel-pleafing to God, juftified and faved in Chrift.: but not in the Arminian fenfe, that God confidereth us as in Chrift before he electeth us, or that men confidered in Chrift are the only object of Election: for I fuppofe that they are *elected to be in Chrift*, and to believe, and this is the difcriminating Election principally. (See Dr. *Twifs Vind Digrefs.* of this fpeech; *elected in Chrift.*) But though we are elected in Chrift, as is faid, yet how can Grace, even Adoption, be then given us in Chrift? when Chrift was not mediator, nor we fubjects to receive it? Decreeing to give it, is not giving: And decreeing from eternity that *David* fhould be Gods fon, did no more adopt him or make him a fon from eternity, then decreeing that he fhould be King of *Ifrael*, made him king from eternity. 3. By this we fee what hold there is of this mans words; Before he thought it moft agreeable to the Scripture; to fay that it was from the firft giving of the promife that we are Iuftified: and now he faith, It is before the world began, that the Grace of Adoption was given us in Chrift. It may be he will fay that the firft promife was given before the world began too, and reduce all our Theologie to one act, *viz.* Gods Decree. 4. And when I compare this with his former fpeech, when he cals *Chrifts dying for finners*, an Immanent act, I begin to fufpect that he thinks Chrift dyed before the world begun too, even as he thinks we were adopted and received Grace in him! But the truth is, a delufory, vertiginous doctrine muft be accordingly delivered: When men are fo far once out of their way, they are moithred and loft.

§. 3.

L. C. BVt the place Gal. 3. 26. Ye are all the fons of God by faith *belongeth to the effect of the firft Reconciliation; for there he fpeaks of our Reconciliation, or the Manifeftation of the firft Reconciliation.*

§. 3.

R. B. I have explained the fenfe. There is no Adoption mentioned in Scripture which is from eternity.

§. 4.

L. C. THe firſt Reconciliation may be called Original; of which Ioh. 3. 16. and 1 Ioh. 4. 10. The ſecond Actual, which is performed in our Conſciences.

§ 4.

R. B. 1. ANd in this your darkneſs, you do not ſee the true actual Scripture-Reconciliation and Iuſtification by faith, either as at firſt in Lawſenſe, or as at laſt in ſentence, which is neither of theſe (Though the firſt only is called Reconciliation, the latter is the fulleſt Iuſtification) 2. Mark that he ſeems to yield that his Immanent Original Reconciliation is not Actual: And if ſo, it is but potential and improper. 3. What ſaith *Joh.* 3. 16. of Reconciliation? not a word. But of ſo loving the world as to give his ſon, *that whoever believeth ſhould not periſh.* 4. 1 *Ioh.* 4. 10. ſaith but thus, *Herein is Love: not that we loved God, but that he loved us, and ſent his ſon to be the propitiation for our ſins*; Is here any thing of Reconciliation? I deſire the Diſſertor to be informed, 1. That God did from Eternity ſend his ſon to be a propitiation for ſin, but in the fulneſs of time: 2. That if he had, yet we are not Actually but Conditionally Reconciled or Iuſtified, as ſoon as Chriſt was ſent a propitiation. 3. That Gods eternal Love is not his being reconciled or juſtifying us. 4. That he doth but dream, when he thinks of reconciliation before any falling out.

§. 5.

L. C. BOth Reconciliations doth Twiſs *thus exhibit to us,* Vindic, p. 196. So God reconciled us to himſelf in Chriſt as to the truth of the thing; but in his Miniſters hath he put the word of reconciliation, as to the manifeſtation of the ſame precious truth ; ſo when we were enemies are we ſaid to be reconciled to God as to the truth of the thing; which yet is not done but by the preaching of the Goſpel, as to the patefaction and ſaving communication of the ſame truth.

§. 5.

R. B. THe ſame Anſwers confute Dr. *Twiſs,* that confute you: For ſuch paſſages as theſe was he queſtioned in the Aſſembly. He was ſo taken up with the doctrine of the Decrees and Divine knowledge, and other School-points, that I more then ſuſpect he was very little ſeen in this part of Theologie, about ſatisfaction, remiſſion, juſtification, as evidently appears in his writings.

§. 6.

§. 6.

L. C. *After the examplar of the Concurse of these acts in reconciliation, we easily suffer the acts of Iustification to be exscribed; yea we think that it clearly exhibits the whole formal reason of Iustification. That is, in the first reconciliation, Chrifts righteousnefs was ours, both in the intention and purpose of God, and in the performance of the Mediator: The Righteousnefs of Chrift is imputed to us, yea applyed to us, even before faith and repentance; but in the second reconciliation, upon the coming of faith, at length we acknowledge and perceive the Love of God towards us in Chrift Iefus: whence the righteousnefs of Chrift is said to be imputed to us by faith, because it is by faith only known to be imputed to us of God; and then are we said to be Iustified by that kind of justification and absolution from our sins, which breedeth peace in our Confciences; For God hath set up a tribunal in our Confciences, in which after a sort is done Condemnation, Remission of sin, Justification and Absolution; which then followeth faith: and according to this sense Iustification is by faith: for in that tribunal of Confcience, God doth according to his Law charge us as guilty, caft us down, torment us; at length by the mercy of God, and the Holy Ghoft operating, by kindling faith in our hearts, the conscience erected and secure in the satisfaction of Chrift in which it refteth, pronounceth that his sins are forgiven for Chrift; but this Iustification is not a decretory absolution; but only a pronunciation that its known to him that his sins are remitted for Chrift.*

---

§. 6.

R. B. ALL this is but a rehearsal of what is before, and commonly by the Antinomians long ago delivered, to which I have already sufficiently answered; and am loth to tire the Reader with needless things. Only briefly I add, 1. That Gods purpose and intention, and Chrifts sacrifice, did lay the ground on which his righteousnefs should be ours in season; but did not make it ours till then, nor give us any actual right to it. You may as well seize on your fathers Lands before he is dead, and say, God purposed it should be mine when you are dead, and therefore it is mine before: Nor is it only knowledge in Confcience that is wanting, as this Differtor dreams, but first there is wanting a true right in sense of Law, and the dissolution of the obligation to punishment which from the violated Law was on us. 2. All this Iustification in Confcience I have manifefted, and God willing, shall fullyer do, to be none of that which Scripture cals Iustification by faith; but a thing far separable, and of incomparably less concernment as to our salvation.

---

§. 7.

L. C. *But in that Iustification by faith, or second Reconciliation, faith and repentance is not required that Chrift may satisfie for us, as in the first Reconciliation; but that that satisfaction of Chrift already performed may be known to us, and by the tafte and experience of its sweetnefs, our confciences may be recreated and pro-*

voked to thankfulness to God and the study of good works. But God who blesseth us with all spiritual blessings in Christ, never gives one Grace without another, at least in the adult, in whose consciences he begetteth faith, and giveth them a spiritual feeling, whereby they know themselves justified, and therefore seriously rejoice.

§. 7.

R. B. THis is but the same song. 1. Faith is not given that Christ may satisfie for us, nor yet that we may feel that we are justified, first or principally, but that Christ and his benefits may be ours, that we may have life in him. 2. God giveth Christ and Justification to those that are not sure they are justified many a year after, and perhaps never while they live here. 3. This man is of a jocund religion, that supposeth almost all to consist in rejoycing; But the spiritual practical Christian feels more need of other Graces then of Joy.

§. 8.

L. C. G*Od could have redeemed, Justified and saved his elect by Christ, without giving them this feeling of favour, as it fals out to Infants and the deaf; but such is the goodness and the greatness of Gods mercies to the adult, that he accounts it not enough to justifie them by Christ, unless he also give them sure arguments, assuring them of their Election and Justification. The argument which far most strongly perswades them, is Faith, or that inward Testimony, of which* 1 Joh. 5. 10. *by which we know that have eternal life.* v. 13.

§. 8.

R. B. 1. GOd both could, and doth save many a thousand without giving them in this life the feeling and assurance of their being Justified: but whatever he can do; he will save none (for ought we can know by his word) either Infants or Adult, without giving such a personal Interest in Christ and Justification which they had not by Election or Christs death alone or before that time. 2. God could have made him that is man now, to have been another creature: but making him Man, he makes him a Creature necessarily to be ruled, and to be ruled by a Law, and that Law must *præcipere, præmiare & punire,* if it be suited to mans state; and God must needs be his supreme Rector. This being so, God can do nothing inconvenient, nor contrary to good order; nor can he, being Rector, rule imperfectly or amiss: much less be unjust. And therefore God having made a Law for rewarding the faithful, and punishing the unfaithful, it is a presumptuous thing (to speak easily) to imagine that God can (punish the faithful, or) reward the unfaithful: Nay, a Reward it cannot be, if he save them: that is a contradiction. For the reward relateth to the Duty. But Gods Law giveth salvation *per modum præmii,* as a reward, as Dr. *Twiss* tels you often, and Scripture more oft, therefore he cannot so give it to the unfaithful. I hope it is agreed on by all that take Gods word to be true, that he will not, and in a moral sense cannot reward final Infidels with salvation; If you say, He might have made other Laws, I answ. 1. These things are much above us, to determine

determine of too boldly. 2. But it seems he hath fitted his Laws to our nature and condition ; and that the Law of Grace is as exactly fitted to the nature and state of faln lost mankind, as the Law of Nature was to the state of perfect man. And therefore an alteration must presuppose an alteration of our nature and condition. However, Gods will may satisfie the sober, without disputing his Power.

3. But let me tell you, though a man might be brought to Heaven without the Feeling and Assurance you mention, (and multitudes are so whatever you say) yet it is a contradiction for an unsanctified man to be saved in Heaven. For what is salvation and felicity, but the blessed fruition of God by Love and Ioy, and praysing him for ever ? And how can the haters of God do this ? It is therefore of absolute necessity *ex natura rei*, that in order of nature at least, men be holy and lovers of God, before they can be saved and happy.

4. You shew great ingratitude for Gods mercy in your Iustification by faith, Sanctification, and your Union and Communion with Christ, to reduce all these into the narrow compass of meer feeling and assurance of Gods favour : which you say, God might have saved us without : And yet you pretend to extoll this his mercy ; But I pray you more impartially lay all together ! suppose an elect man, living as *Solomon*, in all worldly contents, having whatsoever his lustful greedy flesh can desire to feed its raging Appetite ; and for God and his soul he never thinks of them, and perhaps believes not that there is any life after this, or if he do, is confident that he shall be saved. Suppose another elect man lyeth in *Jobs* sores, or *Lazarus* his poverty, or *Pauls* labors or sufferings, or spends his daies in pain, scorn, disgrace, or imprisonment ! Is it such an observable mercy as you describe it, for the former elect man to be converted, and brought into the state of the latter, meerly for the comfort of it ? I confess it is, if God give the latter much spiritual comfort, yea but a little. But then consider, 1. I doubt whether you will make the world believe it ? and whether this way of preaching would ever save a soul, to tell them, *Sirs, while you are whoremongers, drunkards, murderers, haters of God, you may be truly Iustified, and as much beloved of God, as if you were weaned from the world, and mortified the flesh ; but you cannot feel your own Happiness.* 2. Yea, I will be bold to say, to the comfort or support of the drooping souls of many true believers, that there are many in a state of saving Grace, that have more fears and terrors from God then comforts, and many saved, that have not assurance of Salvation, yea that dye in horror : and I had rather be in the case of some that have so died, then of any Libertine that ever I yet knew. Lastly, observe how unlike your description of the sanctified is to that of Gods word ! I know the Gospel is of it self the way to fill the soul with Ioy and Peace in believing, and that many Believers rejoyce with Ioy unspeakable and full of Glory : but the great difference between the sanctified and unsanctified, is so far from being principally placed in their comforts and feelings of mercy to themselves in special, that they often think on God and are troubled, their spirits are full of anguish, they cry and God seemeth not to regard, but to shut out their complaints, their moisture is as the drought of Summer ; all the night long they water their couch with tears ; their bones consume by their daily complaining ; they are forced to cry out, My God, why hast thou forsaken me ! hast thou forgotten to be merciful, and shut up thy loving kindness in displeasure ! All this was *Davids* case ; God seemeth to be their Enemy, and to write bitter things against them, and to seal up their iniquities, and to set them as a mark to shoot at, as he did by *Job*. They are distressed, afflicted, persecuted, tormented, as *Paul*, and those *Heb.* 11. and this was not expresly for present comfort, but for a better resurrection, and their respect to the recompence

compence of Reward: They endured the afflictions of this present life, as not worthy to be compared with the Joy that shall be revealed hereafter. *Lazarus* is at the door in sores, when the rich man fares deliciously. Was Christ of your mind? did he think the main difference in their present condition (besides that without them, which the elect have before Conversion) was in their Comfort? *Remember son, faith Abraham, that thou in thy life time receivedst pleasure, but Lazarus pain; but now contrariwise thou art tormented, and he is comforted; now he is comforted. Ye shall weep and lament, and the world shall rejoyce* (faith Christ) *but your sorrow shall be turned into Ioy. Blessed are ye that weep, for ye shall laugh: Blessed are ye that mourn, for you shall be comforted;* at least, when the times of refreshing is come from the presence of the Lord; but till then the bridegroom is taken from us, and therefore we shall mourn. They that sow in tears, reap in Ioy; and God will then wipe away all tears from their eyes. For my part, I think the life of a Christian, as prescribed by God, is the joyfullest life on earth; but I am so far from making all or most of Gods mercy to me, in and since Conversion to consist in comfortable feelings, that if he would help me to love him more, and give up my self more faithfully to him, and mortifie my corruptions, and make me more truly obedient and serviceable to him, and more to addict my self to his Glory, and put me in a state of safety for everlasting, methinks I could value it highly, though I had no great comfort! or methinks I would now choose that condition, though I should have no certainty or feeling of my own felicity, before a state of less Grace, and more feeling. However I am sure safety without feeling of Comfort, is an unspeakable mercy.

§. 9.

L. C. *FUrthermore as our remission of sins is not suspended on faith (which yet it would be if by faith sins were forgiven), so neither do the faithful say that they are more or less Iustified by the sense of Gods favours; they judge nothing to be imputed to them for righteousness, but that which is most perfect; such as the righteousness of Christ, wherewith being covered,* 1. *They are set righteous before the Tribunal of God.* 2. *They take not themselves to be Iust by their own righteousness, but anothers.* 3. *And that eternal.* 4. *Which God doth not command, but decree, and to which he doth not exhort men. Now when faith hath none of these; is imperfect, is ours, and not anothers, and that for a time only, having its accesses and recesses; and is commanded, and God exhorts us to it: no wonder if in the Righteousness by which we are Iustified with God, the sinner do lean on Christs Righteousness alone; according to the saying of* Cassander, *alledged and praised by* Rivet, Dialys. p. 92. *The faithful soul doth not lean on this righteousness, but to the sole righteousness of Christ given to us. Whence it follows, that only that righteousness doth justifie us, on which we must rest. Its wonder if* Elihu Job 33. *from ver.* 19 *to the* 28. *do not give us an illustrious idea of a sinner and miserable man Iustified by faith; to wit, when Consciences are recreated by confidence of Spiritual savity, and remission of sins which the Sequester* ✻ *of Peace hath obtained for him, and signified to him.*

* He into whose hands it is put.

§. 9.

§. 9.

R. B. 1. Your Iustification in feeling (which is your second) cannot be denyed to rise and fall every day, as feeling doth. 2. No man is righteous at Gods bar, by Chrifts death, till he believe or be brought into Covenant with him, nor hath any right to Chrift till then, (not Infants, but on the Condition of their parents Faith). 3. All this is nothing to the purpofe. For who denyeth that it is only the righteoufnefs of Chrift given us, that we muft reft on, and that can juftifie us againft the accufation of the Law? But our queftion is, whether this be not offered to men to be accepted by Faith? and whether any man have it actually given him, fo as to have right in it in Law-fenfe, before he believe? or could plead it at Gods bar? Chrifts righteoufnefs only is the meritorious caufe or matter of our Iuftification againft the Laws accufation: but yet Faith is the condition *fine qua non* of our right to it.

4. And underftand that, when the queftion is whether we have performed this condition or no? (which is like to be the turning point) then Faith it felf is the righteoufnefs by which only we can be juftified, (with repentance, fincere obedience and perfeverance, which are the full condition of final abfolution) againft any that accufe us of non-performance. But this is not a fort of righteoufnefs co-ordinate with Chrifts, to fupply its defects; but an inferior particular Righteoufnefs, fubordinate to Chrifts, that it may be firft made, and then proved to be ours. And thus far as a condition of our Right in Chrift, we may reft on it: but not otherwife.

§. 10.

L. C. And here I must admire, that they who do (*defervedly*) place *Juftification* before *Sanctification*, if not in time, yet in nature, and alwayes teach that a man is *Juftified before he is Sanctified*, yet they, when they couple the acts of God remitting fins, and of Faith apprehending remiffion of fins, that *Juftification may be performed*, do make not only the act of Faith, but repentance alfo to go before the act of remitting fins. They are the words of the Author of the Epiftle, Repentance goes before Iuftification, and is a neceffary Condition of Remiffion of fins.

§. 10.

R. B. I have faid enough before to fhew you the reafon of this. They do with the Scripture, take fanctification, not for the firft faith and repentance, but that Habitual, or ftated Holinefs of heart, and that of Life, which follows Iuftification, in order. But when they take Sanctification for the firft fpecial Grace, (of Faith and repentance) they make it to go before Iuftification.

2. Repentance and Faith do not only go together, but are in fome refpects, and the chiefeft, the fame thing in feveral notions. Repentance is the change of the minde:

minde : Changing the minde from infidelity to Faith is believing. And if it were not so, yet you know that Scripture puts repentance as well as Faith, before remission and Iustification : yea and repentance is oft placed before Faith : Did you never read, *Ye Repented not, that ye might Believe.*

---

§. 11.

L. C. *NO doubt, by the same consequence, as when a Prince giveth the dignity of a Senator only, to one that hath money, it follows that money is the condition antecedent of obtaining the Senators dignity.*

---

§. 11.

R. B. NO doubt, your words are false. Your Senators money is not, as you put the case, *Conditio civilis,* but Faith is: It is not *Conditio potestativa, id est, Voluntaria vel moralis :* but Faith is. I will tell you trulyer how it is, if you will hear me. It is as a Prince that hath ransomed a condemned woman, doth offer her himself to be her husband, and her life to be saved (it being put into his hands upon the ransom) upon condition that she will take him for her husband and redeemer, and repent of her Treason for which she was condemned, and ask the King mercy: else she shall perish, if she refuse this offer, (which yet Christ will cause his chosen to accept.)

---

§. 12.

L. C. *THus they cavel (or undo) what they had begun ; not only putting Repentance before Justification, but Sanctification also, which comprehendeth almost Repentance alone ; thus troubling the order of the rings of the golden Chain ; Rom. 8. 30. where Justifying is put before Sanctifying.*

---

§. 12.

R. B. 1. THe first part of the charge is answered already. 2. The word *Sanctifying* is not mentioned at all in the Golden Chain, *Rom.* 8. 30. And if you mean the thing and not the word ; 1. You give us but your bare word, and we take it not to be so credible as to perswade us without reason. 3. You contradict your leader Mr. *Pemble*, who makes Sanctification there to be comprized in Vocation, and put before Iustification. 4. The truth is, the word *Sanctifie* is large, and may comprehend all three, Vocation, Iustification, and Newness of life, (with stability of Grace): and so the Apostle did not express it there by name; as comprehended in the other acts. As it signifies our first change, it is the same with Vocation; as it signifieth our new relations, it is at least partly, in Iustification : But the common Scripture use of the word is for our Devotions to God, holyness of heart and life, following Faith, and so some Divines take it, (with the Papists) to be in Iustification, but most to be there com-

comprized in glorification; and some to be omitted: which words so ever you take it to be expressed in, the difference is but about the name: for the Thing and Order, Divines are almost all agreed (till Mr. *Pemble*), and therefore do not disorder that Chain.

§. 13.

L. C. *But it is the greatest Paralogism of the Author of the Epistle, to infer that Justification cannot be defined, but Faith must be concluded in it, because the act of Christ Remitting sin, and Faith apprehending Remission of sins, are done together (if they be so): For Justification hath a definition different from Sanctification, though they are so connexed, that one cannot be conceived without the other. In like manner Christian Virtues, as Goodness, Patience, Humility, though in deed, and in kinde unlike, do yet so mutually help each other, and are so connexed, that they cannot be separated in a Believer: so Faith cannot be separated from good Works, which yet are in their definition differenced among themselves, and from Faith.*

§. 13.

R. B. 1. Nothing but mistakes still! It is not because Faith and Justification go together, that Faith is put in the Definition, but because Justification is performed by a conditional promise, and Faith is the condition. 2. How far Faith must, or must not enter the definition of Justification, I shewed in the beginning; even as the word definition is taken.

§. 14.

L. C. *Furthermore when the Author of the Epistle saith, that Faith is a Condition prerequisite to the forgiveness of sins, it is mervail that he maketh not the rest of the graces of the Sanctifying Spirit, as well Conditions to forgiveness of sins; seeing all are equally the Condition of the New-Covenant; not indeed the Condition of merit, but, as they speak of qualification.*

§. 14.

R. B. 1. Did he not make Repentance a part of the prerequisite Condition too? and did not you complain of it, and say that Sanctification conteined almost nothing but repentance? And yet now you stand wondering that he brings not in the rest. 2. Faith, as it is the Assent to the Verity of the Word, and as it is a belief sufficient to the working of miracles, is in Scripture distinct from Hope and Love. But Faith as it is the Accepting of Christ and Life in him as offered in the Gospel, and so is the Condition of Justification, is taken in a moral or political sense, as the word *Marriage* is, or as *Taking* a man to be my Physitian, or my Soveraign, or my Tutor, or the like: and so it com-

comprehendeth Love to Chriſt ſo Taken, and Hope of the Glory for which we Take him. This is true, though ſome carping wits quarrel with it, who give up their underſtandings more to their Party and Leading men, then to the Scripture: Yea this is a truth of great neceſſity, for the expediting of many difficulties in Theologie.

3. The Covenant promiſeth ſeveral bleſſings: Faith (in the foreſaid ſenſe) and repentance are its Conditions of our begun Juſtification. Obedience actual is the condition of its continuance, or *non amittendæ* annexed to the continuance of Faith: As a wife hath right in her husbands eſtate at firſt upon marriage conſent; but to the continuance of it, ſhe muſt alſo perform her marriage Covenant, of fidelity.

§. 15.

L. C. For the Mediator of the *New Covenant* took upon him to create *Faith, Repentance, Fear, Humility, ſincere Obedience,* and the reſt of the acts of *Regeneration*, in them whom he brings in the ſociety of the Covenant to God. We muſt not therefore think that Faith alone is the Condition of the New Covenant, ſeeing that contradicteth the Scripture: For Deut. 6. 5. *to love God with all our heart, and with all our ſtrength, is the Condition of the Covenant*; and Jer. 32. 40. *I will make an everlaſting Covenant with them, to do them good, and I will put my fear in their hearts*; So Gen. 17. 1. *Sanctity and integrity of life are made the Condition of the Covenant.*

§. 15.

R. B. THis learned man either knows not what a Condition is *in ſenſu legali vel civili*, or elſe he diſſembles it (which is unlikely): He takes the condition of the Covenant to be whatſoever Chriſt hath undertaken to work in us, and God promiſed to give (if his words ſhew his minde): But thoſe are Gods Conditions and not ours, which we are ſpeaking of; our condition is that which God hath impoſed on us to be done, as that without which we ſhall not have the thing promiſed, and ſo ſuſpendeth the efficacy of the promiſe till we have performed it.

§. 16.

L. C. BUt it is ſo far from being true, that *Remiſſion* of ſins is given on condition of *Faith* or *Repentance*, that God is not ſo much as a helper to the penitent and thirſty, under *a Law or Condition, or for a Condition*, either of Repentance, or deſire of Grace and any gracious gift, *which is created*; but for the *Union of the faithful Soul with Chriſt*, Gal. 3. 26.

§. 16.

§. 16.

R. B. HEre is nothing but crude unproved assertions, fitter to tire a Reader, then to convince him: 1. Did you never read such promises as these, *Isa.* 55. 1, 2. *Ho every one that thirsteth, come to the waters, &c. Rev.* 22. *Whoever will, let him take of the waters of Life freely, &c. To him that hath shall be given* with many the like, which I would stand to produce if I thought it worth the labor.

2. If real changes were not given on condition, it would not follow that Relative are not.

3. I know not what you meant to cite *Gal.* 3. 26. unless to contradict and disprove your own opinion, *Ye are all the Children of God by Faith in Christ Jesus*; therefore Remission or Divine help is not given on condition of Faith. A gallant inference.

4. You oppose things that are conjunct. Our Union with Christ, is the Virtual Donation of the blessing it self. All being Virtually or Causally in him: as the wife hath all her honor and riches in and with her husband (she being before a beggar); and yet her own marriage consent, or taking that man for her husband, is the condition on her part of enjoyning him and all that he hath. So is it in our case. It is therefore as putid and senseless an assertion, to say it is not by Faith, but by Union with Christ, as to say in the former case; It is not by her marrying him, or taking him for her husband, but by marriage-Union with him, that a woman hath Right to the Dignities and Riches of her husband. But this way of setting Gods truths by the ears, and opposing the several links of his Chain, one against another, and saying, *It is not This, but This*; when it is both, is the Antinomian way of illuminating the world.

---

§. 17.

L. C. ELse the thing promised should be of *Debt*, and not of *Grace*: For that which is promised under a certain condition and Law, afterward when the condition is fulfilled, hath the force of a debt.

---

§. 17.

R. B. WOrse and worse! 1. A thing is said to be of debt, either when its due, because freely given: or when due, because deserved by the worth of something given for it. *Paul* denyeth the reward to be of debt only in the latter sense, and not in the former. It is not so of debt, as not to be of grace. But if this Dissertor would have us believe that the reward *non Debetur*, is not due to us at all, by Promise and gift, then 1. he makes it no reward: 2. Then he must deny that there is such a thing as any Promise or Gift of God: For it is a strange gift that makes not the thing due, by giving. 3. Then what hath the man talked all this while, of our Justification in Christ, and our part in his Righteousness before Faith, if no such thing be due at all? 4. Then God cannot in Justice pardon

pardon or save any man; because it is justice to give every man his right or due: And if no man have right to Christ, and to the reward as his due, (by gift) then God cannot adjudge that to him, which is not due to him. Whereas Scripture saith, that God giveth us Heaven as a Reward, and that as a Righteous Iudge, and that he is not unjust to forget our work and labor of love, with many the like.

'- 2. He tells us that that which is promised on a condition, hath the force of a Debt, when the condition is fulfilled. What an intollerable inclination is here! Either he speaks of Duties in general, or of debt as opposed to grace. If the former, is it possible that so learned a man should think, that a conditional gift doth any more make the thing given, to be due or debt, then an Absolute! would it not have been debt or due, if God had said, *I do pardon the sins of all men*; without any condition ? If he mean it of Debt merited by the value of the work, and so opposed to grace, I answer him ; When the condition is a meritorious work, by its value deserving the reward, then his Doctrine is true. But when the Condition is no such work at all, but the accepting of the free gift according to its nature, and that you shall not throw it away, or tread the pearl under your feet, nor spit in the face of him that gives it, doth this make the debt to be not of Grace ? Let Scripture language decide the case. It makes me pitty the poor unstudyed Christians in many parts of *England*, to see with what silly cavils they are deluded.

§. 18.

L. C. *The gifts of God, such as Gods continual help, the increase of Faith and Grace, consolation in the heart of the contrite, yea eternal salvation it self; which follow upon the precedent collation of Faith and Repentance, are not conferred on us, as to the given Conditions of Faith, repentance, humili-*
* Compotes. *ty, &c. but because we are united to Christ : for we are not by these gifts made the more * possessors of the Promise, but by them we are made so much more certain of the gift of the thing promised; so, not because I thirst, therefore do I challenge to my self the promise ; but thirst doth impell me the more ardently to quench my thirst ; and I must Desire, that with Desire, not for Desire of grace; my conscience may perswade me that God will be propitious to me.*

§. 18.

R. B. 1. GOds gifts or our acts, are no reasons moving him to give more, who being immutable cannot be moved : but they are not only preparations to following gifts, but conditions on which God in his Law of Grace hath promised the following gifts : which he hath done to excite and engage us the more to the performance. 2. We are therefore upon the performance of the Condition, not only (nor alway) made certain of the thing promised, but alway put into a Right, and into possession of Justification, which consisteth but in a Right.

3. The word *For*, is equivocal. I expect not Gods favor or pardon, for my Faith or desire as the meritorious cause : But I expect it upon, and so for them, as meer Conditions of a free gift. You trifle with unexplained words.

§. 19.

§. 19.

L. C. IN *like manner, not for any degrees of Faith, humility, self-denyal, hope, &c. do I expect the thing promised; but with these I ardently request (or desire) that the thing given or promised may be more clearly known to me, and that I am a Member of Christ, and that the fruits of the mystical Union shall also redound to me. God who hath made the Covenant of Grace with his own, moved by no consideration, loveth his own, but for himself: he uniteth them to Christ, he maketh them by a new life conformable to Christs death: and createth and confirmeth in the hearts of Believers the gifts of Grace.* Isa. 59. 21, 22. *that as he hath given us the summ of the matter, even Christ, together also in Christ he may give us the rest of his gifts for an overplus; of which gifts the profit and fruits are very great; for though they be not a cause or argument, on which resting, I promise my self Salvation, yet do they compell me to Christ the fountain, that from him I may drink with open mouth: and may place my hope of Salvation, not in any condition of Faith or Repentance; but in Christ as dead for sinners, with whom I reckon my self the chief; denying all Righteousness howsoever called, besides Christs Righteousness; and also denying all unrighteousness, when I fly to the altar of Salvation.*

---

§. 19.

R. B. MOst of this is fully answered, and I will have some compassion on the Reader.

1. It is not Scripture-sense or language to say, all gifts are given with Christ as overplus: indeed, outward things are said to be so given: *Mat.* 6. 33. but if pardon, sanctification and salvation be but an overplus, how came Christ to dye for the procuring them, and to propound himself still in the Gospel to be received as a means to these? The end is not given with the means by way of overplus. I know that in some respect Christ also is the end of them.

3. We place no hope of salvation in any works as meritorious, or co-ordinate with Christ, but only as subordinate to him, and as such means as himself hath been pleased to constitute them.

4. I dare provoke this man, whoever he be, on his principles, to produce any rational ground of this expectation of Salvation, or assurance of his pardon, if he fetch it not from his performance of the condition of the promise. He will, I am certain, be presently driven to non-sense, or to bottom his assurance upon Enthusiasms, or inward perswasions, which have no reason to support them, or prove them solid. If any word of God be the ground of your assurance, it is either an Absolute promise or a Conditional. If a Conditional, you can have no more assurance of your right in the thing promised, then you have first assurance that you perform the Condition. As if it be on this promise, *Whoever believeth is Justified from all things, &c.* or *shall not perish, but have everlasting life.* You can hence have no more assurance of being Justified or saved, then you have first assurance that you believe in the sense as those texts require it. If it be an absolute promise that assureth you, either it is general to all, or special to you. If to all,

all, then all shall be saved as well as you, (and their ignorance of it will not hinder it). If it be a special promise to you, then either you are named in it, (which is not in my Bible, that I know of) or you are but described. If described either by a common character (and that will not distinguish you from others) or by a special; and then either that special character is some condition performed (and then we are where we were) or some inherent qualifying mark; but that you will not affirm, for then you must equally try by that, and so far rest on that. If you say, It is as one of the Elect, or one that Christ dyed for more then others, the question recurrs how you know your self to be Elect, or one that Christ so dyed for. The shift which I conjecture you will fly to, is this, You will believe first that it is true, and then if you can do so, it is certain it was true: for God will not enable any to believe themselves in Christ, Justified or Elect, that are not. But 1. Thousands believe it falsly, and all our preaching will not cure this presumption in them. 2. Then the first act of your belief was false or groundless, and not a rational belief. For the object, as such, is before the act: and it is not a true act that is not fitted to the object. If at first you believe it to be true, without any reason of that beliefe, or any evidence of truth in the object, then it is an irrational act: nay indeed you cannot do it: you must apprehend some truth in the object, and see some shew of reason to make you believe it, or you cannot believe it. Besides, all the wicked about you are commanded to believe as well as you: and it is certainly a truth which God commandeth them to believe. God commandeth no man to believe falshoods. And it is the same thing which they and you are commanded to believe: therefore it is certain that it is not that you are Elect, or that you are Justified and shall be saved: for this is false of many. It is therefore to believe the Truth of the Gospel, and Accept Christ and Life offered in it, as offered; by so doing you perform the Condition of the gift or promise: and so have right to Christ and Life: upon the review of this performance you may know groundedly and rationally that you are Justified: No other way can you know it: Men will be reasonable while they are men; Grace makes them not bruits, but more rational: Do not therefore lay mens duty and comfort in such a Faith as hath no bottom, nor you can give no reason for, but say I do believe, because I will believe; or I believe it true, because I would have it to be true: and so lead men to meer dreams, or make extraordinary revelations the way of ordinary comfort, and so leave the generality of humble souls in distress, that have no such revelations. These vain Doctrines will not hold long. And if they be right, our common prophane people, that generally believe they are pardoned by Christ, because they would have it so, are in a better Condition then I took them to be in. I seriously profess, to my best observation it appears to me, that the Antinomian Doctrine is the very same in almost every point, which I finde naturally fastned in the hearts of the common prophane multitudes, and that in all my discourses with them I find, that though the ignorant cannot mouth it so plausibly, nor talk not so much of free Grace, yet have they the same tenets, and all men are naturally of the Antinomian Religion; and that very work of Preachers (when Christs death and the Promise of pardon and Life is once revealed) is principally the cure of natural Antinomianism; and this is that we call the work of conversion. I do not wonder therefore if these men would have the Ministry down, when their very daily work is to root out their Religion from the Souls of men.

CHAP.

CHAP. VI.

That a sinner and ungodly man, and not the faithfull and believer, is the adequate Object of Justification.

§. 1.

L. C. But let us in the mean time act their part, who will have Faith, Repentance, a New-life, and all the acts of Regeneration to go before, not only the acts of Justification, but also of Election, in Nature, Order, and Time: I contend that it agreeth not so much as with that opinion, that a believing man be the Object of Justification, or faith be the instrumental cause of Justification, or of Remission of sins; or that it enter the definition of Justification; And that this is abhorrent from right reason and Aristotelical Discipline: For if I would be of their opinion, I would easily grant that it rightly follows, that Faith, Repentance, &c. are a cause sine qua non, and prerequisite conditions, and which are supposed to be in them that are Justified: But I would deny that it thence follows, that Justification respecteth a man believing and penitent, as the adequate object of Justification, whose adequate object rather is a sinner, an ungodly man, yea an incredulous man, and an Infidel (though otherwise faithfull and of an unblameable life) in as much as in the best, the seeds of incredulity lye hid. Mar. 9. 24. and sin is the off-spring of Infidelity: For every action both Natural and Moral is carried to the object according to the formal Reason: so a Physitian considereth a man not in respect of Rationability or Risibility, but of Sanability: In like manner the action of Remitting sin is carried to its object, after the formal reason of the object, to wit, to a sinner capable of Remission, and not as endowed with faith and Repentance.

§. 1.

R. B. 1. All this a do to bring forth a poor *petitio principii*, or a contradiction. You confess as much as we desire, that the formal reason of the Object is: *A sinner capable of Remission*: We doubt not but you mean an Immediate capacity: And we say, that you beg the question in the next words, which contradict the former: *and not as endowed with faith and Repentance*. When will you once prove that an Impenitent Infidel is a sinner immediately capable of Justification. You have but one way to attempt it, and that is by proving the Scripture not to be true, which so frequently says otherwise. No man is immediately capable of the benefit given by a conditional Donation or act of Grace, but he that hath performed the condition. But Justification and Remission is a benefit given by a conditional Donation or act of Grace (and faith is the condition) therefore, &c.

2. I have spoke already to the question, whether faith must enter the Definition of Justification: It enters not the Definition of Justification in General, nor of any other species, but of this species, even Evangelical Justification, consist-

ing in Remission of sin, or sentential Absolution, it doth enter the Definition. *Adam* and the Angels might be Iustified without faith in Christ, and so was Christ himself (in the sence that we now speak of) but man cannot; and it being the condition of the gift, must enter the Definition.

§. 2.

L. C. *Nor matters it that Faith and Repentance are supposed to be first in the Subject before he be Justified. Suppose a Prince choose none into his Counsel but a monyed man; I do not think it thence follows that money and the mans riches are the formal cause, the Impulsive, Inductive, Intrinsick, or Extrinsick, for which he is chosen among the Counsellors, when the Prince, as when he chose Titius into the Senate, had respect to the mans Judgement exercised by much experience, and his Prudence meet to handle the great business of the Common wealth: but the mans riches were no more the cause that Titius was admitted, then that he liveth, is of a sound body, nor is either blind or lame, to hinder him from being in the Senate: which conditions found or supposed in* Titius, *could not be the object to which the Prince applied himself when he chose him Counsellor.*

§. 2.

R. B. I Was troubled once already with your monied man, let who will be troubled with him again for me: and for *Titius*, as I ken not the man, so I have nothing to do with him, nor he, for any thing I can percieve, with our business. Do but distinguish between a natural condition, which is a qualification of the matter, and a Legal or Civil condition properly so called, which morally qualifieth *ex ordinatione donantis vel legislatoris*, and you have answer enough. Our condition is expressed in the Law or Testament, and so was not *Titius* his money, nor his life, health, or limbs. Morals suppose naturals, and constitute them not.

§. 3.

L. C. THat most famous man, and every way most learned, Dr. Hammond: but who seems to me more addicted to the conceits of the Arminians, saw this: Yet nevertheless in his Catechism, though he make Faith, Repentance; Yea all the acts of Sanctification to go before Justification or Remission of sin as Conditions, Qualities, and Qualifications, as he speaks, necessary and prerequisite in the subject to be Justified; Yet doth he exclude faith or a believer from the definition of Justification, and denieth faith to be an Instrument or cause of Justification: For he will have Justification to be an act of God which is done * without us: but let
* Extra nos.   us here him speak, though not in his countrey language wherein he wrote his Catechism.

What is Justification? R. It is Gods accepting our persons, and not imputing our sins, his covering or pardoning our iniquities, his being so reconciled unto sinners that he determines not to punish us eternally.

What is the cause of Justification? R. Gods free mercy to us in Christ revealed in the New Covenant.

What

what the Instrumental cause? R. As an Instrument is logically and properly taken, and signifies an inferior less principal efficient cause, so nothing in us can have any thing to do (*i.e.* any kind of physical efficiency) in this work; neither is it imaginable it should, it being a work of Gods upon us, without us, concerning us, but not within us at all. And if you mark Justification being in plain terms but the accepting our persons, and pardoning of sins, it would be very improper and harsh to affirm, that our works or any thing, even our faith it self, should accept our persons, or pardon our sins, though in never so inferior a Notion; which yet they must, if they were Instrumental in our Justification. Tis true indeed, those necessary qualifications which the Gospel requires in us are conditions, or moral Instruments, without which we shall not be Justified; but those are not properly called instruments or causes.

What are those qualifications?

R. Faith, Repentance, Firm purpose of a new life, and the rest of those Graces upon which in the Gospel pardon is promised the Christian; all comprizable in the new Creature, Conversion, Regeneration, &c.

Truly according to this opinion, if any man were more exact in his forepast life then Paul or Iob was, yet would I stifly maintain (as it is humane to slip) that God doth not Justifie him as a believer, but as ungodly and a sinner, yea as an Infidel: For a Prince doth not free from punishment, a good man, but a guilty (or Delinquent:) So God in remitting sin considereth not man as a believer or penitent, but obnoxious: to conclude, it seems as unfit a speech to say that God forgiveth sin to a believer and to the faithfull, as to affirm, that a father pardoneth a Son, not as erring, but as obedient; or that the adequate object of the Father chastising his Son, is a Son as obedient, and not as forsaking his duty.

§. 3.

R. B. 1. IT is the same Doctrine for the substance that these words of Dr. *Hammonds* do express, which I maintain against you. Let those that assert a proper Instrumentality and efficiency of faith to Justification, see to themselves.

2. You do not well to say that Dr. *Hammond* excludeth faith from the Definition of justification. For you may easily see that he never intended those words for a Definition of justification, much less in the most comprehensive sence, but a discovery of the nature of the mear act of justifying in it self considered.

3. Let us agree of the order, nature and office of faith in justification, and we will freely give you leave to put it in your Definition, or leave it out, as you please: This is but a small and frivolous business.

4. You do with great resolution profess to maintain, that which you perform with lamentable infirmity, nor doth your performance any whit answer your undertaking, to prove that God justifies a man as an infidel: and for all your talk of Aristotelical Discipline, you do utterly fail our expectations of the fruits of it, in your proof. Here's not a word of Argument that I can find, for what you will so stifly maintain.

1. You must distinguish between a man as he needs pardon: and as a man as he shall receive pardon. The guilty, as guilty, need pardon, and not as Believers: the penitent and believers as they are the persons to whom the promise is made, shall receive pardon, and not any other guilty persons.

2. You must distinguish between the object of Punishment, of Obliga-

tion to punishment, and of condemnation, and the object of Impunity, Remission and Justification. The object of punishment is the guilty, the object of Obligation to punishment, or subject of guilt, is a sinner, as having offended a penal Law: The object of Impunity, Remission, Justification, is a guilty sinner too; but thats not all, nor enough to make him an object immediatly capable of these acts. The subject of Impunity, (as we now take it) is a pardoned sinner (call him Subject or Object; we must allow some impropriety from the imperfection of the thing.) The Object of Remission and constitutive Justification, is a believing sinner. Can you prove it, enough to make a man an Adequate object of Remission, that he hath in him the matter to be remitted? If you consider him before Gods act of Grace was passed, and so it is true, it is enough that he is a guilty sinner, for whom Christ died (for I must tell you that must go in to a full Definition too:) But if you speak not of an object of the conditional pardon in the Law or promise, but of the actual pardon by that promise becoming effectual, as no doubt you do, then it is a believing sinner that is the Adequate object. There is the *materia removenda*, the *Terminus à quo* in him, as he is guilty: But there will not be the actual removal, the *motus ab hoc termino ad liberationem, Justitiam, Jus ad Impunitatem*, till the condition of faith be performed, and this condition being not a meer naturally-prerequisite qualification, but a proper condition in Law-sence, expressed fully in the words of the Covenant or Law, it follows that by so doing the Law hath made it of that moral necessity, that a sinner is no adequate object of Justification without it.

But you say, *A Prince doth not free from punishment a good man, but a guilty.* I answer, If your Princes pardon be absolute, he freeth a nicer offendor: but thats not our case: But if he pardon a Traytor on condition he come in and thankfully accept a pardon, and return to his allegiance, then there are two things considerable in him whom he pardons to make him a fit object. That he need it, and therefore be guilty; and that he be in the nearest capacity of receiving it, and so that he perform the condition. So God considereth us both as guilty and so needing pardon, and as believers in Christ, and so fit, for it on the terms on which he was pleased to confer it in his Law.

Where you say what an unfit or unreasonable speech it is to say, that *God pardoneth sins to Believers*: Consider whether you accuse not the Holy Ghost, who knew better how to speak then you can teach him.

To your further similitude I say, It is no fit speech to say, that God forgiveth us our obedience or our faith, or forgiveth a believer for believing: Nor for to say a father forgiveth his sons obedience. But if that father say, kneel down and ask me forgiveness, and I will forgive thee: It is no unfit speech to say that the father forgiveth an offending submissive child, that is, forgiveth his offence upon his submission.

Your last speech discovers more infirmity then wisdom would have had you manifest. Is it as unreasonable a speech to say: *God pardoneth sin to a believer*, as to say, that the adequate object of the fathers Chastising his son, is a son as obedient, and not as faulty? Whither will not partiality carry men? Besides that all this strikes at the face of Scripture, what an unworthy trick of a learned disputant is it; to take so gross a point for granted, and run away with it so easily, as if pardoning required no more in the object to make it adequate, then chastising doth. Is it usual even with men to chastise and pardon in the same respect? Do men pardon their children, or Princes their trayterous Subjects, mearly as offendors?

offendors? They punish them as offendors; but they will have a further reason of pardoning them; sure I am, God pardoneth not men as sinners, but as redeemed believing sinners.

And if you still say that he *pardoneth* us *As* Infidels (telling us before of the formal reason herein) then I again desire you to tell us why all sinners, or all Infidels are not pardoned? I know the word *qui* or *quatenus* may be so taken largely, as that the consequence, *ad omne* shall not hold: but as you expresly say: *it is according to the formal reason, as the act is carried to the object*: so a *quatenus ad omne valet consequentia*; and so all Infidels must be Justified. Nay, infidelity must be the reason of the predicate, and so we must therefore call them Justified, because infidels. For as *Goclenius* saith, *Lexic. Philos. pag. 906. Reduplicatio exigit, ut reduplicatum sit causa cur praedicatum primo & aequate insit subjecto.*

Quatenus or *qua* (as *Goclen. ibid.*) is used to express. 1. *Subjectum passionis primum* (and so the object of action) so we must say, *Peccator redemptus fidelis, vel fide Christo conjunctus*, is the Object and Subject of Justification. 2. *Qui significat causam praedicati à parte subjecti*: And so we must say that, *Fidelis qui fidelis, vel Peccator-redemptus-fidelis quâ fidelis Justificatur.* For though faith be no proper cause of Justification, yet being *conditio donationis*, it may be the *causa praedicandi Subjectum Justificatum.* 3. *Quâ*, signifieth the formal reason of considering. 4. And the condition. The *Objectum materiale* is man offending: the *objectum formale* is *miser-redemptus-credens.* For all these concur *ad atonem objecti formalem*, but not all on the same reason are appointed hereto: Gods immanent acts have no *objectum formale*, as ours have (without him) as really specifying them, and being the reason of them: But his legal moral actions have that in the object which may be called, *ratio formalis* (as have his immanent acts *quoad denominationem extrinsecam* also, *& respective.*) Redemption is a meritorious cause, and faith but a condition: Christ and Remission being given to the Redeemed on that condition, it doth therefore enter the formal reason of the object; as *sine quâ non*, *& cum quâ.*

Note also that we speak not of the *Objectum quod*, for that is, just, but of the *objectum cui*, and that is as expressed. From all this it appears what an Antichristian Doctrine it is to say that an Infidel, as such, is the adequate object of Justification: For then every infidel, because an infidel, must be said to be Justified. Note also, that all this is spoken of Constitutive Justification or pardon: For the formal object of sentential Justification is *Justus*. God so Justifieth not any but the righteous, and curseth those that do otherwise.

§. 4.

L. C. BY what is said, it appeareth with what *inconveniences* the *usual Doctrine of Justification by faith is urged: and contrariwise how apt that is which we exhibite, especially in that it reconcileth* Paul *with* James, *whose sentences seemingly differing, have hitherto tormented commentators: For what intricaty will there be, if we say that both Faith and Good-works do Justifie, in that faith witnesseth our Reconciliation, and works witness to our faith, either in our Consciences or before men? Or what need is there to labour so anxiously to prove against the Papists that faith alone Justifieth, when that Good-works do almost (or in a manner) equally Justifie, if in both parts, to Justifie, signifie to Witness, Reveal, Judge? But if on both parts to Justifie, be the same as to Remit sin, and impute Christs Righteousness, then neither faith alone, nor good-works do Justifie, unless faith be taken for the object of faith.*

§. 4.

R. B. EVery man is naturally pleased with his own inventions and Notions, and so are you, it seems, to the very great overvaluing of them: I confess the Doctrine of Iustification is so inconveniently explained in some parts by too many that might possibly give you and many others so much offence as might occasion your error: but you are so far from escaping those inconveniences as you imagine, that you are run from the Sands into the Gulf, from the Ashes into the Fire, into incomparably greater evils then they, seeking to cure an inconvenience with a mischief. For my part I see no great appearance of any contradiction between *Paul* and *James*, as I have elsewhere declared. But your way, I am past all doubt, contradicteth them both, while you think to reconcile them; yea, you quite reject the very subject of their disputes; not speaking of, yea expresly exploding the Iustification that they treat of; You say, *Works witness to faith:* And why do not they in your way as well witness directly to Iustification, as faith doth? Nay, you profess that for your declarative Iustification, they do Iustifie *propemodum ex æquo.* But did *Paul* think so? or is this any such clear Reconciling *Paul* and *James*? You do not fully tell us, whether they speak of your Immanent, or your Relative Iustification: and yet you reconcile them? You say, If we speak of the former, they Iustifie almost equally? Is that any satisfactory interpreting of *Paul,* that saith, *If of works, then not of Grace? and that a man is Justified by Faith without the works of the Law.* But you do indeed seem to determine that its your declarative Iustification that they speak of; For you add: *If we say that both faith and works Justifie, &c. in our Consciences or before men:* But it is put past all doubt in the Text, that it is not meer Iustification in Conscience or before men, that either *Paul* or *James* speak of. I have so often manifested that to others in divers private writings, that I am loth to take this slight occasion to do it again. Only in a word 1. for *Paul,* he saith, *Rom.* 3. 19. 20. *Whatsoever the Law saith, it saith to them that are under the Law, that every mouth may be stopped, and all the world may become guilty before God:* Here you see that the guilt is, 1. Before God. 2. By legal obligation. *Therefore by the deeds of the Law shall no flesh be Justified in his sight, for by the Law is the knowledge of sin:* Here you see also that first it is before God. 2. And by a civil kind of act, that we are Iustified; or as it is *ver.* 27. By the Law of Faith: And *ver.* 28. when he had said: *A man is Justified by faith without the works of that Law:* he adds: *Is he the God of the Jews only, &c.* And 3. *It is one God that shall Justifie the Circumcision by faith, and the Uncircumcision through faith:* So that you see it is Iustification by God, and in Gods sight that *Paul* mentioneth: And therefore *Chap.* 4. 3, 5, 6, &c. it is called *imputing Righteousness, Justifying the ungodly, forgiving sin, &c.* See also *ver.* 16. 24.

And for *James,* 1. He speaks of such a Iustifying as is equivalent to *saving,* or of the same nature, *ver.* 14. *cap.* 2. *Can Faith save him?* It is not only in our Consciences, and before men, that faith or works save. 2. He speaks of *Abraham*

Abrahams Iustification, which was before God, and not only in Conscience, and before men? specially for such an act as men would condemn him for, and was done in private. 3. He speaks of imputing to Righteousness, ver. 23. and that is before God, for it is he that imputeth. 4. He makes it equivalent to being *the friend of God*: and that is a change of Relation. Much more might be added.

Yea you might easily see, if you are willing, that it is no such low poor business, as Iustification in Conscience or before men, that the Scripture talks of; but of that which our Salvation lyeth on. We are not thereby Iustified, as *Paul* saith, though we know nothing by our selves, that is, Conscience is not the decider of the controversie, whether we are just or unjust; or shall live or dye: We have one that judgeth us, even the Lord. It is his prerogative: and it is his high and honorable judgement, that Scripture commonly speaks of; Yea always when it directeth us what to do to be justified, or tells us of Iustification by faith. And for men; it is also a small thing to us to be Iudged by man, or at mans day or Iudgement, See 2 Cor. 4. 3, 4, 5. While therefore you pretend to reconcile *Paul* and *James*, you speak of a Iustification that neither of them meddle with, nor honor with that name.

In reconciling us with the Papists you deal as slipperily. I am thought by some to say too much for Works my self: But I must make another kind of difference both between Faith and Works, and between Protestants and Papists herein, then you do, or then your *Propemodum ex æquo* do intimate.

Well, it is undoubtedly certain that Iustification in Scripture signifieth, to remit Sin, and to constitute Righteous, and to judge righteous by sentence. How then will you reconcile us and the Papists? Why, 1. For *Judging*, it is one of the sences wherein you say, Faith and Works do Iustifie *propemodum ex æquo*: And doubtless this is the highest and noblest Iustification, but I am not of your mind, if you take Works as *Paul* doth.

2. But *if to Justifie, signifie, to Remit sin, or impute Righteousness (you say) neither faith alone, nor Works Justifie*: A fair Reconciliation, either of *Paul* and *James*, or of Protestant and Papists; whats this but to say plainly: *Both* Paul *and* Iames, *both Protestants and Papists, are out? You both speak falsly*: on faith it is only Faith, and the other, it is also Works, when indeed it is neither. This is the way to reconcile Lyars and Quarrellers, to chide them and say, you are both Knaves; But this is not an honest way of Reconciling Gods word, where the difference is only in our misapprehension.

Yet let me remember you of one thing, that for my part I rather use the Phrase, *Justified by faith*: then that, *faith Justifieth*. 1. Because the Scripture still useth the former, but never, that I know, the later. 2. Because the one seemeth more to intend an efficiency in faith (which I deny) and the other but a conditionally, which I maintain. For we may be said to be Iustified by the condition, as well as by the efficient. And therefore whenever I use the Phrase, *faith Justifieth*: I do it in imitation of others, but take it in the latter sence.

Sess.

§. 5.

L. C. Astly, then this Method of teaching Justification by faith, nothing more sound and more clear; there is nothing that useth violence with the Intellect, or contradicteth right reason: as that saying doth, faith forgiveth sins, or Justifieth objectively: to the understanding whereof, as well as to the dissolving of that peripatetical (saying) the form is educed è potentia materiæ: there is need of the wit of an Oedipus. For it is not possible to discern the falsity or verity of a proposition, whose terms you can neither understand apart nor together, and in which the definition is more obscure then the thing defined.

§. 5.

R. B. I Will not Justifie or excuse the Phrases which you accuse: and I think it as unfit as you can do, for men to make themselves a Religion of words not intelligible, and to be angry with the World for questioning that which themselves did never understand: But for your own extolled Method; I think seriously, that it is the most false and dissonant from Gods word, and from the very nature of Justification, that ever was yet to my knowledge published by sober Christians; and far more unsound and dangerous then either *Osianders* or the *Papists*: though I was in my youth inclining to your opinion. As for your snatch at the Peripatetick Doctrine of the education of the form *è potentia materiæ*, I can better forbear you in Philosophical Novelties then in Theological.

§. 6.

L. C. 1. Doth faith make us righteous either for the Virtue and dignity of the object, or by Participation of the Virtue which the object communicateth with faith? I conceive not that faith doth either way Justifie: For a created thing cannot have force to produce an effect, such as Remission of sin is, which agreeth only to an eternal and increated object, which force yet they will have it to have, neither from it self, nor from the Object. Neither doth faith Justifie or forgive sin by participation of Virtue which the object communicateth with faith; for then faith should formally Justifie.

§. 6.

R. B. CHrist was not the guilty person, nor did he so bear the very person of any man in suffering, as that in Law-sence we are said to suffer or satisfie in him: But in the third person of a Mediator, taking on him the punishment of our sins, he made by sacrifice satisfaction to Justice, to this end, and thus far, that the sinners might be delivered into his hands as their redeemer, and that by a new Law of Grace the benefits of his sufferings might be made

over

over to them. It is therefore only by this Law that any man hath right to Chrift and his righteoufnefs: It pleafed the Father and the Redeemer to make this Law conditionall; but with a condition fitted to the honoring of free-grace, *viz.* that men fhall accept the gift as it is offered, and glorifie God in the penitent confeffion of their fins, and praying for pardon. Though Chrift will caufe all his Elect to perform this condition, yet the Law is general, impofing the condition, and promifing the benefit thereupon to all: it being fecret internal grace flowing from Election, and from Chrifts death, as concatenated with Election, that makes the firft difference: But the Grace given by Chrift as Legiflator makes not that difference, nor any at all, till it find this difference made by temporal Election, (that is, internal vocation) the fruit of eternal. It being therefore Gods will that Chrift fhould be given, and life in him, only by a New-Law, which hath a condition, and not abfolutely, it thence follows from the meer will of the free donor, that Faith and Repentance have the Intereft of a condition in our Juftification, and this is the formal reafon of its Juftifying us (to fpeak vulgarly) or of our being juftified by it (to fpeak with Scripture.)

And for thofe fencelefs men that think it derogatory from Free-grace, that Juftification be given on fuch a condition, it is as much as to fay, *It derogateth from Gods grace to require you to glorifie his Grace, to proclaim it free, to confefs you deferve not, and fo condemn your felves, to ask it as free Grace; in a word, If God give you Grace in the Covenant, on condition you will accept it, and honor the freenefs of it, hereby it is difhonored.* Is not this a fenfelefs conceit? God meant fo to pardon finners, as principally in the gift to look to his honor, and impofe on them conditions both honorable to the giver, and fitted to the neceffity and mifery of the receiver, and fo to deliver the guilty, as not to make him Mafterlefs or Lawlefs. Thus I have fhewed you my judgement, why and in what refpect we are Juftified by faith.

2. Your laft words, *then faith fhould formally Juftifie,* fhew you to hold another error, that Chrifts righteoufnefs doth formally Juftifie. The righteoufnefs given by Chrift doth, that is, Remiffion of fin: but for Chrifts own righteoufnefs, it is but the meritorious caufe of that Remiffion, or *Jus ad impunitatem & ad Regnum,* which is our Righteoufnefs formally. This you feemed once to profefs, when you faid you confented to the Author in his Catechife: But when men underftand not themfelves, there is no hold of them.

---

§. 7.

L.C. 2. Will they fay, Faith Juftifieth as it apprehendeth Chrift? But when the chief benefit in Chrift which we apprehend is Remiffion of fin it felf, it will follow, that faith Juftifieth or remitteth fin, becaufe it apprehendeth Remiffion of fin.

---

§. 7.

R.B. I Confefs that is the common Doctrine: which I like not, as commonly expreffed: but you fay little againft it. Plainly, and truly, faith is appointed to this office, becaufe of its fitnefs for it, in the nature of the act, as being the acceptance of Chrift firft, and life in him freely given: But the neareft formal

mal reason of its interest in our Iustification, is this, that it is a condition of the gift, so made by the will of the Donor.

§. 8.

L. C. 3. *PErhaps that τὸ apprehendere doth make Just, and remit sin: which seeing it is an act or action of faith moving it self to Christ the object, and this act is not the first and direct from Christ to the soul, but the reflexed and second from the soul to Christ, by which act it relyeth on Christ, and resteth in his love; what can that apprehension be, beside the virtue, action or work which are in, or are done in the believer, unless to apprehend be the same as to believe? On both sides it will follow, either that a quality, action or work that are in men, do forgive sins; or (if to apprehend, be to believe) that faith justifies because it is faith in Christ; which is as absurd.*

§. 8.

R. B. NO doubt the last is their sence, whom you dispute against, that faith, as Faith in Christ Iustifies: And if they expounded it only of its Aptitude to the office, it were true: but seeing they do go further, I leave them to defend themselves, for I cannot.

§. 9.

L. C. 4. *Doth any virtue flow into faith from Christs Righteousness, which virtue doth imprint in faith a power of Justifying or forgiving sins? but the Papists put the like power into their works.*

§. 9.

R. B. A Good cause is a great advantage. I confess you may say much against this common mistake.

§. 10.

L. C. 5. *IF they say, faith is the internal Instrument of Application, it is that which I would have; For that Application is faith it self, at least a second act of true faith, and the principal formal reason of faith: yet is not a man justified or made just by it, but only trusteth that he is Just: I understand application in respect of man; For in respect of God Application is the same with imputation of Righteousness.*

§. 10.

§. 10.

R. B. ALL this is true: only understand, that the main act of Faith is to accept an offered Christ, first Believing him to be the Christ; and not to trust that we are justified.

§. 11.

L. C. 6. Lastly, Faith is not the Instrument of Remission of sins, unless it be made the efficient cause, though less principal, why God forgiveth sins; doth an eternal cause need a temporary and transient Instrument to produce an eternal effect? But its wonder that God should need this Instrument to remit sin, when even an earthly Prince hath no need of the faith of a condemned man, to whom by his pardon he granteth life: though to his vital life it is necessary that he know the truth of the written pardon: but this is nothing to the act of the Prince, the act of whose pardon is not suspended on any mans belief: nor hath he need to the giving of pardon, that any condition be found in him: Much less doth the most great God pre-require faith, or use it as an instrument to forgive sin.

§. 11.

R. B. YOur reasons have force enough. 1. Against the Instrumental efficiency of faith. 2. And against its having interest in Remission *proximè ex natura actus, & non ex voluntate ordinantis*: But further against faith being the assigned condition, you say nothing, but a crude affirmation in the end. God hath no need of our faith to forgive us; But God doth all things in wisdom, and he saw it fittest to draw men to Repent and Believe by giving them Remission upon these conditions, that so the reward might allure them to the duty. God works on man as man; Even where omnipotency worketh Grace, it is by rational means. Besides, do you think it honorable to the Redeemer to say to the world: *I will Justifie and save you, though you will not believe in me, but take me for a deceiver; and though you despise me, spit in my face; You cannot have life but in and with me; and you shall have me whether you will or no.* These be not terms honorable to God, nor fit for man.

Note also that you do most erroneously call Justification *an eternal effect*: This utterly denieth Christ as Mediator to be any cause of it; and so what is it, but to deny Christ! even the Lord that bought you. This is a matter of greater moment then the ordering of our Notions about faiths interest in Justifying.

§. 12.

L. C. YEt this difference there is between God and the Prince, that the Princes pardon is not always followed with repentance; but God, in that he remitteth sin, doth thereby give Faith and a new heart. But the example that I have in hand doth well express the nature of Justification by faith. Suppose the miserable man detained

tained in the Dungeon, expecting daily the execution of the horrible sentence to be thundred on his head; and in a few days delay comes from the Prince, a good Messenger bringing a Pardon, (or act) of Grace: will he therefore think he was abjolved and freed from punishment, because he gave credit to the Prince? Or who will believe that the Prince did absolve the Delinquent by that faith whereby he believed that the Pardon was not invalid.

§. 12.

R. B. Let those that you charge, defend themselves as they can: Only I must tell you, that in your similitude you far mistake the case: You suppose your Princes pardon to be absolute, and then believing can do nothing but comfort the man: But the Gospel pardoning Act is Conditional. Rather should you put the case as I did before. A woman is condemned for Treason: The Kings son loveth her, though a Traitor and Beggar, and pays her Ransome, and sendeth a Messenger with a Pardon, on these terms: *If thou wilt thankfully and lovingly acknowledge the favour I have shewed in Redeeming thee, and wilt accept me both for thy Husband and Lord, and return to thy allegiance, I will pardon and save thee: If not, thou shalt dye a far soarer death for thy Ingratitude:* This is nearer our case.

§. 13.

L. C. Into this Method also do the Assertors of the vulgar opinion incogitantly slide. Bucanus Loc. 31. de Iustif. Qu. 20. *Maketh the Subject of Justification to be the Elect before the Constitution of the World;* And Qu. 17. the matter not prepared, to wit, ungodly and sinners. See Ursin Catechef. Qu. 60. Where he makes a double Application. 1. The Imputation of Christs Righteousness in respect of God. 2. The act it self of believing in respect of us, whereby we certainly trust, that Christs obedience is Imputed and given to us of God. Idem Qu. 61. faith, We are Iustified by Faith alone, because we are Iustified by the Object of Faith alone: *A little after*, Faith is Correlatively taken: by Faith alone; that is, by Christs merit alone, we are Iustified. *What? That many, though of the same opinion with* Ursin, *among these* Keckerman, *do make two Justifications, and Righteousnesses; one Active, the other Passive; which is improperly called Righteousness, seeing it is only the feeling of the Active, and its Reception.*

§. 13.

R. B. You seem to me, either not to understand the Authors you alledge, or wilfully wrong at least two of them. 1. Bucanus faith, *Soli electi ante constitutionem mundi Justificantur?* But whats that for you? He never said, that they were only considered as elect, or that it was the elect, as elect, that were the formal or adequate object of Justification: or that meer Election before faith made them the object: much less that before the world was made, they were justified. For your

second

second saying of *Bucanus*, I know not whether he mean to number o. ly the two distinct considerations of the Subject of Justification, or also to distinguish of the time, and of two Justifications received, one by ungodly, the other by Believers. If the former be his sence, it is Justifiable, if the later, I excuse it not.

Ursin doth only less fitly in those words express the nature of faith in justification, which yet presently he better explaineth: But he taketh not Gods Application to be from Eternity, nor at all before our faith actually, but only conditionally, and after it actually: his words are these: *Utramque applicationem necesse est concurrere. Deus enim hac lege nobis applicat Justitiam Christi per imputationem, ut nos ipsi quoque eam nobis applicemus per fidem. Etiamsi enim aliquis alteri offerat beneficium, tamen si is cui offertur id non Accipiat, non ipsi applicatur, nec fit ejus beneficium. Sine nostra igitur applicatione, Divina applicatio non est, & tamen nostra etiam est à Deo.* This is sound Doctrine. Its true, in the next words he saith, Gods Application of Christs satisfaction to us is before ours: and so it is, 1. *It tantum*: so far as to give us Grace to believe, which is a fruit of Christs merits. 2. And to give us a conditional Pardon and Grant of justification and life. 3. But not to give actual pardon and justification, till after our believing.

The second passage cited by you out of *Ursin* is true: But fair dealing would have confessed that it is but part of *Ursins* Explication: And so, no doubt when we are said to be justified by faith alone, it is Christs merits connoted that are principally intended; but not only; For faith *quoad conditionem* is intended as of necessity, to our right to Christ, but Christ only is intended as the satisfactory Meritorious cause. And therefore *Ursin* adds. 2. *Quia proprius actus fidei est apprehendere & sibi applicare Justitiam Christi: Immo fides nihil est aliud, quam Acceptio & apprehensio Justitiae alienae, seu meriti Christi in Evangelii promissione nobis oblati, &c.* And he gives the reason why we say *fide sola.* 1. To *express that it is gratis, &c.* 2. *Ut omnia opera & merita nostra, vel aliena? Causa Justificationis excludantur, &c.* 3 *Ut non modo omne nostrum meritum, sed etiam ipsa fides excludatur ab eo quod fide accipitur; & sit sensus, sola fide, id est, non merendo sed tantum accipiendo, Justificamur, &c.* 4. *Ut intelligatur Necessitas fidei ad Justificationem; Et sciatur, non quidem Merito fidei, sed tamen non nisi fide Accipiente Justitiam Christi, nos Justificari; quia fidei alius proprius est, Justitiam eam Accipere.*

To all this I subscribe (supposing it the principal act of Faith to accept Christ himself.) And if this will satisfie those that quarrel with me for ascribing too much to works, or for Levelling Faith and works, I again say, I willingly subscribe to it.

For what you speak of two sorts of Justification, Active and Passive, it seems you understand not those you carp at. Divines ordinarily mean by it no more then this, that Justification signifieth either the act or the *Terminus*, and effect, the *Justificare*, or *Justificari*. Can you quarrel at this? Doth God Justifie a man (*Active*) and yet he is not Justified (*Passive*)? I confess *Maccovius*, a leader of your fraternity, makes another kind of difference, and will have Active Justification to go many a hundred years before Passive: and much more such wilde stuff he hath in his Antinomian *Theses* of Justification, (which I had once thought to have confuted, but that I considered it is but the same matter that I have here confuted in you, and that other Divines have already confuted,

confuted, as Mr. *Burgess*, Mr. *Woodbridge*, Mr. *Gere* against *Crispe*, Mr. *Bedford* against the *Antinomians*, Mr. *Gataker* against *Salimarsh*, and many more.) As for *Keckerman*, you quarrel with him to your dishonor, his words are unquestionable, in the sence I mentioned. 1. *Vox Justificationis interdum Active, interdum Passivè significat. Activè significat Absolutionem, sive actum ejus qui Absolvit: Passivè verò significat Absolutionem qua aliquis absolvitur, sive receptionem ut sic dicam Absolutionis. Pleraque ejusmodi vocabula Activè simul & Passivè Significant. Ut Redemptio, &c.* You may see that by reception, *Keckerman* doth not mean, Faith, which is *Receptio Moralis Activa improprie sic dicta*: But our *Justificari*, which is *Receptio Naturalis Passiva propriè sic dicta*.

As for their common distinction of righteousness into Active and Passive, that is another business, and is taken from the different matter in which Righteousness consisteth, and is commonlly used about Christs righteousness; which I need not say any more about, upon so slight an occasion.

But it is your very great mistake to think that our Divines mean, by Passive Iustification, that which you call, *the sence of Justification*. Till you better understand them, if you will take my Counsel, contradict them no more. Yet I will not undertake to vindicate all: For as others err as well as you, so some that write for the Truth, do write before they well understand the matter, as well as you; and all of us know but in part, and therefore shall unavoidably err in part.

CHAP. VII.

Objections are Answered.

---

§. 1.

L. C. THe only sight of those things that we have brought, might dissipate all Objections: Yet lest we omit any thing that should Illustrate so weighty a question, I am willing concisely to answer them also.

---

§. 1.

R. B. EIther you much overvalue your own reasonings, or else I much undervalue them: which if I do, it is not through an unwillingness to see the truth, but from an utter disability to discern any such convincing evidence in your words. Nay I do not think you can more admire that we are not convinced by you, then I do admire how any tender conscienc't man, that ever soberly read the Bible, and believeth it to be true, can be of your mind! And yet the great experience of my own and others frailty, the darkness of mans Intellect, the power of prejudice and self-conceitedness, and the too great paucity of judicious discerning men, doth much abate my admiration: And should I hear even learned men, and such as once seemed Religious, as confident against the Deity of Christ, the truth of Scripture, the Immortality of the soul, and the obedience to God in the use of ordinances, as you are confident of the justification of Infidels *qua* Infidels, experience hath taught me that the wonder is not so great as I once took it to be. Though you think that the sight of what you have said should be so potent, having viewed all as impartially as I could, I find much smoak, enough to draw tears from a tender eye, to think what toyes can delude the Godly, but little light to acquaint us with the Truth. Your whole discourse seems to me to speak with *Demosrates* lungs, that do *multum spirare, & parum valere.*

---

§. 2.

L. C. 1. IT is Objected, that Justification is put after Vocation, Rom. 8. 30.

Answ. *Deservedly is it done, if Justification there signifie the declaration or manifestation that we are Just. For there is no doubt but God doth work the work of Conversion in us, and translateth us from darkness to light, and from the power of Satan to the Kingdom of God, before that he do fully, and with full assurance insinuate and instil into our hearts that the Righteousness of Christ belongeth to us, and that we are indeed in the Kingdom of God.*

---

§. 2.

R. B. YOu say but *if* this be the sense; but what *if* it be not? It is a matter of nothing with you to make a Scripture, or contradict it, in stead of expounding it; and when God saith it is Justification, for you to say, It is the assurance of our Justification. Will you be content with this one Reason against your exposition?

If your exposition be true, then all that live and dye without Assurance of their own Justification are certainly damned. But all that so live and dye are not certainly damned: Therefore your exposition is false.

The Consequence of the major I prove thus. All those that live and dye without the Justification mentioned in that Text, are certainly damned; Therefore if the Justification there mentioned be the Assurance of Justification, as you expound it, Then all that dye without that Assurance are certainly damned. The Antecedent I prove thus. All that dye without Vocation, and that are not predestinated, are certainly damned; But all that live and dye without the Justification there meant, do dye without Vocation, and were not predestinate; Therefore they are certainly damned. The Major you will grant, except you hold that Infidels are saved, while such, as well as Justified as such; yea though you do so hold, yet I conjecture that you will not hold that the non-predestinate are saved. The Minor is past doubt in the text. *Whom he predestinated them he Called, whom he Called them he Justified.*

---

§. 3.

L. C. 2. BVt though to Justifie here did signifie to impute Christs Righteousness, and to remit sins; it would not hinder that Calling is here before Justifying: For the Apostles in reciting Gods works do not always observe the order of nature, or of time; so 1 Cor. 6. 11. *Sanctification goes before Justification*; and 2 Thes. 2. 13. Sanctification of the Spirit is put before the Belief of the Truth: *what? that*
1 Tim,

1 Tim. 1. 9. *Vocation follows the giving of Salvation*, and 2 Pet. 1. 10. *Vocation is put before Election.*

---

§. 3.

R. B. t. IT seems then, if the Holy Ghost speak not of things in the same order as they are wrought once or twice, or more, you will never believe that he hath any regard to order at all; and then we must go look for some other School-master to teach us the order of Gods works. There may be great Reason sometime to mention that first, which is wrought last, and sometime to disregard the order; but yet doubtless the Holy Ghost doth teach us that order, or it is not known.

2. And for this text, you call it your self before, the golden chain; and it is evident that it is the full intent of the Holy Ghost in it, to shew the order and concatenation of these several works; and I think you cannot find another text in Scripture, where it is more exactly and of purpose done. If therefore we may not here expect a certain observation of the Order, I think you cannot tell where we may expect it. Would you not think him blinded by partiality that should deny, that from this text we may prove that Predestination goes before Vocation? or that Vocation and Justification goes before Glorification? what then may we think of you, that deny that it can be proved from this text, that Vocation goes before Justification, when the evidence is the very same for the one as for the other.

Moreover I pray you mark one thing, That in this text the person is expresly noted by every one of the precedent acts to be qualified for the subsequent, and so the object of the following act is one that hath received the precedent. Who doth God call? Why the predestinated. Whom doth he Justifie? The Called. Whom doth he glorifie? The Justified. To my understanding this text is so plain against you, that were there no more, I could not be of your opinion, without stronger arguments then you bring.

And withal consider, that this text doth but second the current of the precedent parts of Scripture, which expresly make vocation and faith to be Means to our justification and forgiveness of sin.

Though this much may well serve, yet to the particular texts cited by you, I add this: 1. That in 1 *Cor.* 6. 11. *Calvin* saith, expresseth but one thing in the three terms; that is, it was but the Apostles intent to tell them God had delivered them from that sinful state; and therefore there was no need of noting the order of working.

2. I am perswaded that your self do think, that Sanctification there is taken for the first work of special Grace, in giving the seed of the new Life; And if that be so, then the order observed is exact; for we maintain that Justification follows such a Sanctification.

3. A man that disclaims the popish sense of the word *Justifying* ordinarily, may yet possibly think that this text takes it for a progress in real holiness, and say as Grotius in loc. *Baptizati estis & deinde accepistis Spiritum sanctum, & majores quotidie in Justitia progressus fecistis. Nam ita illud ἐδικαιώθητε hoc loco sumi suadet ordo, & idem sensus in* Apoc. 22. 11.

As for 2 *Thes.* 2. 13. I answer, 1. If Sanctification be taken for the first work of saving Grace, then the order is such as you would desire. Doubtless the Spirit causeth our faith, and therefore its causing work is in order of nature before the effect. 2. But for

my

my part, I suppose sanctification is taken as usually in Scripture, either for that change which follows faith, or else for the whole change of heart and life, whereof faith is but the very enterance or first act, and so are distinguished as the Door and the House. And I say that the Apostle here spoke in exact order: for he spoke not of the order of execution, but of intention. *God hath from the beginning chosen you to salvation, through sanctification of the Spirit and belief of the truth*, i. e. He hath chosen you to be *saved or glorified by sanctification, and to be sanctified by faith*; when Scripture speaks *de ordine ut decreto*, as here, when it speaks of election, it observeth oft the order of Intention.

That in 2 *Tim.* 1. 9. is in perfect order: For by saving is meant so much of salvation as they had before and in Vocation, whereof the latter part is the same as Vocation. q. d. *who hath saved us by Christs satisfaction from being Remedilesly miserable, and hath also saved us from the sins of the world in which we lived, by calling us to Holiness*. Or if you will take salvation for Glorification (which they yet had not) yet the reason of the Apostles order may be this; teaching them in using Gods mercies as motives to Gratitude, to begin at the end which is the greatest, and so proceed to the means, which cannot be fully seen, but in the end first seen.

And for that in 2 *Pet.* 1. 10. the order is most exact as can be wished. The Apostle is not speaking which was wrought first, but which was to be made sure first: And how should he then speak in better order, then to say, *Give all diligence to make your Calling and Election sure*; i. e. make your Calling sure first, and thereby your Election. For none can know his election before or without the knowledge of his Calling.

§. 4.

L. C. 2. THat of Mat. is objected. This kind of sin shall not be forgiven, neither in this life, nor in that to come.

Answ. That either the Holy Ghost doth speak and deal of mercy here performed, and in the world to come to be declared, as Famous Reignolds doth interpret it, praelect. 172. 173. Or which is more probable, the sense of the place is, that he that blasphemeth against the Holy Ghost shall be punished, not only in this present life, but also at the day of Judgement, and to everlasting: to wit, sin is taken for the punishment of sin, as elsewhere, sin for a sacrifice for sin; and it shall not be forgiven him for ever, is the same, as he shall be eternally punished. Now he that is punished everlastingly, was before adjudged to that same destruction, the wrath of God did rest upon him, and so his sins were before retained; in the like sort, as the Glorification of the faithful is a certain sign that his sins were before forgiven, and that God was reconciled to him before he enjoyed the celestial Glory. For as it may come to pass that the blasphemer may for a time be unpunished, to whom yet at that time God had not forgiven his sins; so may it fall out, that at what time God punisheth him, yet then Gods anger resteth not on him, but long before, his sins were * not remitted.

* I think it should be, *were Remitted*.

Fff §. 4.

§ 4.

R. B. 1. You take no notice at all of the force of the Argument, from the text expounded. The text makes not only Remission after this life, but Remission in this life to be future. *It shall not be forgiven in this life,* having before said of other sins, *they shall be forgiven,* and not, *they are forgiven.* Now let it be only *Remissio executiva,* that is, *non punire,* or let it be Iudicial Remission by sentence that is meant in the life to come; yet that it is Remission by Legal dissolution of the obligation to punishment, which is in this life, I have proved, and shall do further, God willing; so that you have said nothing at all to the Argument. 2. Yet in that which you have said there is a full acknowledgement, that *non punire,* is not the sole or great Remission of sin, contrary to what you seemed to hold but even now, (for you hold that either *non punire,* or *nolle punire,* is the only remission.) pag. 56.
3. Dr. *Reignolds* in the *prelect.* cited, labours to prove against *Bellarmine,* that neither *in this life, nor that to come,* means *never* without intimating any future remission. Your exposition, *he shall be punished in this life, and that to come,* is good for the latter part, but scarce sound for the former, For though all men living are punished in this life; yet the text seems to speak of some more then ordinary punishment for that Blasphemy: which yet is somewhat doubtful, whether God be obliged still to execute in this life, or do execute on such. I suppose the meaning is according to the plain letter of the text. There is as I have said, a threefold Remission: the first, by the Act of Grace, is in this life: The second by the sentence of the Iudge (the full Iustification) is after this life. The third, *viz.* not executing the Punishment deserved, is partly in this life, but Principally in that to come. Now Christ saith, He that Blasphemeth the Holy Ghost shall not have either the Legal pardon in this Life, nor the sentential or executive pardon in the Life to come; though whether he have any of the executive Remission in this life, I determine not. Thus it appears how you have quite overlooked the Argument from this text.

§ 5.

L. C. And indeed by the solution of this Objection, the support in like manner fals, which are fetcht from so many places of *Scripture, in which they think it proved, that the acts of remitting sins are reiterated; and that God doth pardon sin all our life time, even after a man is endowed with true faith, so that there is no need to fly to the explication before brought, to wit, that God doth daily pardon sin, in that he vouchsafeth us the feeling of pardon; or that when we daily ask of God the forgiveness of sin, we only ask the confidence of Remission, and the application of the benefit which is done by faith, and the increase of faith For seeing almost every where in holy Scripture,* to remit sin, *and* to punish*, are opposite: it is plain, that* to remit sin, and not to punish; *and* to punish, and not to remit sin, *are parallels; and therefore it may well be said that God doth through a mans whole life forgive him his sins, in as much as he doth not punish him; and that we do no less piously and properly ask daily of God remission of sin, because by that Petition we ask that we may not be punished, and that God would not inflict on us, how faithful soever, the stripes which we deserve. But if at*

any

any time to remit sin, and to punish *are not opposite, as it fals. out when* to punish *is not meant of eternal punishment, but of temporal punishment for a particular sin, such as* Davids *in the matter of* Uriah, *then* to remit sin, *is not the same as* not to punish; *but it signifieth, to declare God to be propitious and benevolent, and that he will not exact eternal punishment. The history of* David *shews this, to whom, when* David *had declared that God had pardoned his enormous sin; thereby he would have understood, that* David *was not fallen from the Kingdom, as* Saul, *nor from the favour of God, nor that God would require of him eternal punishment: But not that God remitted his sin in that sense, as that he should not be punished for sin in this life. In what sence soever, there was Reason for* David *to beg remission of sin with cryes and lamentation, whether he prayed that God would give him the sense of his favour, or not to be eternally punished, or else begged of God the removal of the temporary Punishment.*

§. 5.

R. B. 1. IF the solution of an objection not solved can do so much, its strange.
2. What you here add, doth say nothing at all, (nor that before neither) against a new act of pardon, resulting from the Law of Grace, upon every new act of sin repented of. When God makes a Law or standing Grant, that *every believer confessing his sin, and asking pardon through Christ, shall be forgiven.* This same Law doth by a new moral action remit every sin after it is committed, on these terms performed.

3. You do in part in this discourse say the same with those that you oppose. And indeed there is more solidity, Judgement and sobriety in this Section, then I have yet found in all your book: For though you do not take notice of the Legal Remission, which is the main, and oft renewed, and which we daily beg in prayer, because prayer is one part of the Condition of our full obtaining it; yet these several truths are well acknowledged in this Section. 1. That besides the Decree of pardon (from eternity, which is no pardon) and the sense of pardon (which is no pardon, further then as it is the removing the contrary sense, which is a punishment, and giving that mercy, whose privation is a punishment), there is also a pardoning in this life by not executing deserved punishment. And indeed every mercy that we receive, is such a pardoning as this. 2. That God may thus renew pardon again and again, as oft as he forbeareth, to punish upon our provocations, This is plainly intimated. 3. That we may beg for this renewed pardon, consisting in impunity; which is much more then to pray for meer feeling of pardon. 4. It is implyed that God may thus pardon sin more or less in the same pardon, yea the same sin, as he remitteth more or less of the punishment. 5. It is implyed that a Reprobate may be pardoned, so far as any punishment in this life is remitted to him: though this be a small degree of pardon comparatively. 6. You confess that God may remit the eternal punishment, and yet not remit all the temporal. This is true, but not only the Antinomians, but some of our own Divines will be angry with you for it. 7. You confess, that our chastisements in this life, such as David suffered are indeed punishments. 8 Yea and consider I pray you one consequence of your doctrine here. If *David* may be punished for sin (as you say) notwithstanding Christs suretyship and satisfaction; then 1 Christ did not so take the punishment of our sins on him, as thereby to take it totally off from us; 2. Yea then all Remission is not ours *eo nomine*, only because Christ dyed for us, without any further act for giving it to us;

Fff 2 else

else why do we pray for it? 3. Much less can it truly be said in Law-sense that we obeyed or satisfied in Christ, or that it is equally ours, as if we had done it: For if we had perfectly either obeyed or satisfied, God could not in Justice have punished us, (as *Twiss* oft confesseth): though he might have tormented us, yet it would have been no punishment. 4. And if it stand well with Gods Justice to punish a *David* for the sin that Christ hath satisfied for, then as its no sound arguing, *Christ hath satisfied: therefore the sin he satisfied for is remitted*, much less *it is eo nomine, and at that time remitted*, so it may on the same grounds stand with Gods Justice; to delay any actual Remission at all, (which giveth Legal right to Impunity, to the Delinquent) till the Condition of his Covenant be performed. These consequences (destructive to the foundation of Antinomianism) are unavoidable from your own concessions. And indeed this one Section gives me hope that you have yet so much light and Capacity of Truth, as that upon Consideration, you will see your former mistakes.

§. 6.

L. C. 3. IT is Objected, that it is absurd for a man to be Justified before he exist. Answ. Gods actions and acts are conversant even about objects, that yet are not, but are future, and have an esse cognitum * in Gods understanding,
* Or in respect of God. to whom all his works are known from eternity, Act. 15. 18. and therefore men: for example; God imputed to Christ the sins of all the elect, who were, are, and are to come, as soon as he was promised to be Mediator; though when the promise was made, he was not yet man: In like manner God imputed Christs satisfaction to all, whose sins he transferred upon Christ, whether they were born, or not yet born; and he freed (or discharged) them from imputation of sin, and indued them with Christs Righteousness.

§. 6.

R. B. THis Section is as unlike the former, as if they had not come from the same man. Either you mean, that all or some of Gods Actions have objects not existent. If all; then nothing more false: Preservation, Deliverance from afflictions, Vocation, Sanctification, Glorification, Afflicting, with multitudes more, are sure about objects that do exist. If you mean it but of *some* of Gods actions, It is nothing to the point, unless you would have shewed us that Justification is one of them, which you say nothing to prove. Gods works are all foreknown: but only as foreknown they are not the object of all his actions. Gods actions are Immanent or Transient. The former are either most strictly so called, which do not *Transire ne quidem objective*, of which God himself is the object: these belong not to our purpose: or else they are more largely and imperfectly such: when they are *objective transeuntes; & effective, (vel quoad effectum) Immanentes, i. e. in sensu negativo*. These are either the acts of Gods Knowledge, or his Will (so far as we can conceive of them) Though we must not affirm a real diversity; yet to our conceiving they are distinct, and so denominated from the objects which respect them. Divines are bold to distinguish these thus. (1.) The first of these acts of Gods, (to our understanding) is his *scientia simplicis Intelligentiæ*, whereby he knows

knows what is possible, convenient, and what would be upon supposition of such or such causes put: Thus God knew the Possibility of our Justification, and its conveniency as a means to his Glory, before he decreed it (In the order that Divines have laid the frame.) I suppose this is not the act that you call Justification. (2) Next to this, is Gods will that these or those things shall be, in such a time, and order, and manner. Me thinks you should not mean this act. 1. Because the object of this act is not so much as *cognitum ut futurum* (for, say Divines it must be made future first by Volition, before it can be known as such), but only *cognitum ut possibile*; and out of the infinite number of Possibles, it is but a finite number that are willed to be future. 2. Because *Futurum* is *terminus diminuens quoad esse reale*; and therefore to will the Futurition of our Justification, is not to Justifie. (3) Next is placed Gods Knowledge *puræ visionis*: which though one in it self (as are his knowledge and will) yet must needs be distinguished to our understanding, from the state of the objects respecting it: And therefore the knowledge of things future, as such, is made the next act. This cannot make for your opinion; both because it is an act of the Intellect, and Justification (as seems to me) in your sense, is an act of the will; and because the object of it is but *futurum*; and doubtless to know that we shall be Justified, is inclusively to know that we are not Justified.

The next act (the fourth,) is the Will of God *de præsenti rerum existentia prima*, which is *effective* first, and is it which we call creation or the production of any thing, and so ascribe it to omnipotency, in that Gods very Will is omnipotent. This is said to be the same act with his first will *de rerum futuritione*; only *denominatione extrinsecâ* differenced to our apprehension (and so we might as well say of the rest.) As *futurum & existens* are not all one, so we denominate these acts as not all one. And the three former acts are eternal, but this last we denominate as being in time. I should conjecture that this is not it that you mean by Justification. 1. Because it is not ordinary to mention this with any distinction from the former; most divines calling all immanent acts eternal. 2. Because this hath not for its object a meer *esse cognitum*, but an *esse reale*; Gods Will being productive of its object; and it being first the effect, before it is properly the object. This therefore cannot be it that you here mean by Justification in this answer. 3. And indeed this concurs in time with the existence of the thing willed, as *Creatio & Creatura* are *eodem momento*. The fifth act of God is his *scientia visionis circa objectum jam existens*, most strictly called his *intuitive knowledge*; which though it be in substance the same with his *scientia futurorum* (and so are all his Immanent acts) yet as *futura & existentia* differ, so must we extrinsically denominate these acts as different. By this God knoweth all things to be, that are, (and by the like act, all things to be past, that are past.) This I suppose is not the Justification you intend, both because it is an intellectual act, and because it follows the existence of our justification. When the act that you mention, hath only an *esse cognitum* for its object. The sixth Act of God in order is, the act of his will about objects already existent. This *denominatione extrinsecâ* is differenced necessarily from the former; and is Gods Complacency in the goodness of his own works, and his Displacency at the evil of sin. This act makes not its own object as the former, though some School Divines say, *omne Dei velle est effectivum*; but is that described after the Creation, that *God Rested, &c.* in other places where God is said to be *wel-pleased*. Now here that Gods will may be said to have on object. 1. Immediate or neerest; as is the Quality of Holiness in the soul, when God either produceth it or loveth it. 2. Remote, such is the soul in which God is producing or implanting that Quality.

As for Gods creating or causing accidents, I include it in the fourth act, as well as his causing substances. Now I suppose this last is not your meaning neither; for this followeth our first Iustification. What therefore you mean by that Iustification whose object is but *esse Cognitum*, I do not know.

You see it is only immanent acts that are about objects as *in esse cognito*, and not all those neither: and this is no immanent act. And for transient acts, as you deny Iustification to be such, so I suppose you will assign them an existent object, either *in fieri*, or *in facto esse*. The truth is, Iustification is Gods act by his Law of Grace (as is oft said), which conteineth in it these several acts; 1. The neerest to the effect is the moral Act of the Law, as a Law or Deed of Gift. 2. The concomitant is the fourth act before mentioned, as applyed to this effect. For though it be called by some an inmanent act, because it is Gods *Velle*, yet by most a transient act, in that it doth produce an effect *ad extra*. And so *denominatione extrinseca*, we say that God, by the Law of Grace, as his Instrument, doth *Volendo* produce our Iustification at that time when it is produced. 3. To this may be added, Gods willing that Law which is his Instrument, and his making it: that is, his Legislation: which yet is in time before its effect, and effecteth not til the condition be performed.

4. And Gods approbation or estimative justification immediately follows our being first Iustified.

Now to your example about imputation of sin to Christ; see how you prove nothing, yea mar your cause by it. 1. It is no Scripture phrase, that sin was imputed to Christ: and though I admit in the sence as our Divines ordinarily use it, yet that sense is not the same in which the Scripture useth the word Imputation. 2. I know he was made sin for us. but that was in time; even when he suffered: for as you before say, sin is put for a sacrifice for sin. I know also that he bore our iniquities; that is, the punishment of them; but that was not before his Incarnation.

3. I perceive it is Christs humane nature not yet existent, which you say God imputed sin to. And then whatever you mean by Imputation, it is plain, you cannot mean it, that Christ was made really guilty in his humane nature; For *omne accidens est subjecti accidens. Reatus est Accidens*. Therefore Guilt could not exist in a subject not existent, nor yet without a subject. All therefore that you can reasonably mean is but this, That *the second person in the Trinity, in the Divine nature, having from eternity willed to be in time the Redeemer of the world; did partly from the state of faln man, and partly by Gods promise, from that time (and not before) stand related as one that was engaged to assume mans nature in the fulness of time, and in it to be a sacrifice for the expiation of sin, upon the foreconsideration of which sacrifice to be made, God then made a Covenant of Grace with mankind, pardoning them for the sake of that future satisfaction, as having an* esse *morale by Vertue of the undertakers Consent, and the Fathers Acceptance*. This is the truth, and all that you can well mean. And in all this there is no guilt on the humane nature not yet existing, nor any thing like it; If any obligation is to be supposed before the Incarnation, it is only on the Divine nature, and not on the humane.

4. But let us make the best of your Answer (seeing it is your best,) and suppose you argued thus. *If Christ might be Guilty of, or punished for sin not yet existent, then so may we be justified from a Guilt not existing: But*, &c. *Therefore, &c.* To which I reply. As you must distinguish between the *esse cognitum*, and the *esse reale*, so of the latter you must distinguish between the *esse naturale existens*, and the *esse morale existens*. 2. You must distinguish between proper guilt *ex obligatione Legis, & ex merito peccati*, and improper Guilt *ex obligatione sponsionis propriæ, sive de merito*. And

so

so I say, 1. Christ was never properly and truly guilty. 2. Nor did God judge him so to be. 3. Nor did the Law ever oblige him to punishment. 4. It was therefore *ex sponsione propria* only that Christ was obliged to suffer, even to suffer what we had deserved, to free us from it. 5 Nor was it the same punishment formally that we should have suffered, *in sensu naturali vel morali*; but only the same materially (and that but in some part), and the *Tantundem vel Æquivalens* morally. 6. This being so, it appears that it was not the same formal guilt which lay on Christ, that lieth or should have layn on any of the elect: much less on each man, as you seem to suppose. 7. If you deny all this, and would suppose that Christ had taken upon him the very Demerit and Guilt of our sin, and not the punishment only, yet consider that his contract or consent to undertake it, might give it an *esse morale* as to him, and to that punishment, and the meer foreknowledge of it might suffice to procure that consent or voluntary undertaking which gave it the moral being so far. But it will not follow that our sin can be punished or pardoned to our selves before it is in being; because we have given no such consent to make us guilty, as Christ gave in his undertaking: and without Guilt there can be no Remission; for *Remissio est Reatus Remissio*. I do therefore deny both the Antecedent and consequence of the forementioned argument.

Further note here, that you make our Guilt and Justification before we were to have no more reality then Christs guilt (or the effect of that which you call Imputation of our sin to him) had in his humane nature before it had a being: But that was none at all, properly and really.

Note also that you make this Imputation to be but from the first promise, and yet before you make it an Immanent act, and to be before the world was made.

But the great answer that I give you is this: that your consequence is not sound; Though all you say of Gods imputing sin to Christ were true, yet its not true, that in like manner God did then impute Christs satisfaction to us, nor gave us any discharge from guilt. It was the will of the father and son himself that Christ should then suffer for us; and it was their will that we should not be discharged, nor Justified thereby till we were in Christ by faith. And the efficacy of Christs satisfaction can go no further then his own and his fathers will. I shall say more to this argument anon.

§. 7.

L. C. Sharplu's *Arguments drawn out at length, by which he proves that Faith alone Justifies, though they directly militate against the Papists; yet because they obliquely rather touch us, then strike us, I will bring some of them to examination.*

§. 7.

R. B. IT seems you feel the Arguments touch you; that are brought against the Papists. And though I should think that the Antinomians and they are far enough asunder, even in the two extreams, yet I confess I wondered to find Dr. Baily (of whom I made no doubt then but that he was a Papist, as since he hath declared himself.) in the conference between the late King and the Marquess of *Worcester*, to declare himself in the point of Justification, in the pure Antinomian strain, according to the very scope of this book of yours.

§. 8.

§. 8.

L. C. Arg. 1. THe promise or things promised cannot be received but by faith alone: *Rom.*4.16. *Gal.*3.22. But Remission of sin, Reconciliation, Justification are the promises: Therefore Justification is by faith alone.

Answ. *That argument proves nothing but that Gods promises are known to us by Faith, but not that they are made by Faith. For the promise is not made by Faith.*

§. 8.

R. B. DAtur tertium. It proves (supposing the Divine constitution) that the good promised shall not be ours *de jure*, till we accept Christ as offered.

§. 9.

L. C. Arg. 2. IN the same manner as we obtain Remission of sins, are we all Justified: But only by faith in Christ do we obtain Remission of sins: *He proves the minor*: As we apprehend Christ, so do we obtain Remission of sins: But we apprehend Christ the Mediator by faith alone: therefore by faith alone do we obtain Remission of sins.

Answ. *The Major of the second Syllogism is denied: For we do not obtain Remission of sins in the same manner as we apprehend Christ: For we do not obtain, but apprehend Remission of sins by faith.*

§. 9.

R. B. WEE do accept Christ as Lord and Saviour, which is the condition of our actual pardon. The word *Apprehend*, is too much used by Divines: But they mean not as you, an apprehending that we are already pardoned, but an accepting Christ and pardon as an offered gift.

§. 10.

L. C. Arg. 3. BY that which Christs Righteousness is imputed to us only, by that we are justified: But by faith alone is Christs Righteousness imputed to us, *Rom.*3.22,28.

Answ. *In these places Paul speaks of Gods Righteousness, which by Faith, or by the Doctrine of the Gospel is revealed; But of these places above: Nor doth the Scripture any where say, that Christs Righteousness is imputed by Faith: though by an Acurologie and Synecdoche I would not deny, but it may be said that Christs Righteousness is imputed to us by faith: to wit, as by faith the Holy Ghost gives me a testimony that Christs*

righte-

righteousness belongs to me: For in that sence, *even Salvation is obtained by Faith, and we are elected by Faith.*

§. 10.

R. B. I Have answered all this oft enough. I seriously profess, as much as I am for a toleration of dissenters, if you should live near me, and preach this Doctrine, that you are saved by Faith (much more by obedience) no further then as a testimony to assure you that you shall be saved, and that it had no whit of the nature of a means to the obtaining Salvation it self: Or that we are saved no more by faith then we are elected by Faith (which you seem to intimate) I would avoid you after a first and second admonition, and I would take heed of trusting you, or expecting much good fruits of this Doctrine in your life. But all the hope that I have of the Salvation of many in these times that hold damnable errors, is this : I hope they receive them but speculatively, and that the truth lies nearer their harts, which is received practically: and so live contrary to their desparate opinions.

§. 11.

L. C. Arg. 4. BY what alone we have access to the Father, by that alone are we Justified : But only by Faith in Christ have we access to the Father.

Answ. *That access to the Father is a second act of faith, which after Christ is revealed in us, is carried to God by Faith and Love.*

§. 11.

R. B. THe Text cited by *Scharpius*, is *Rom.* 5.2. which saith that by Faith we were brought into this Grace ; (i. e. state of Gods favour) wherein we now stand. In other places, by access to God, Is meant also the Liberty, Favor, and Priviledge of drawing near him, and is Reconciliation it self. Your answer is nothing to the purpose.

§. 12.

L. C. Arg. 5. BY that only are we Justified, by which *Abraham* the Father of the faithfull was Justified : But *Abraham* was Justified by Faith alone.

Answ. *The rigid assertors of Justification by Faith* (say) *that the words of the Apostle here are to be interpreted Synecdochically, so as that faith is taken for the Gospel, or for Christ himself the object of our Faith* : *but seeing the word,* he believed, *as* Calvin *witnesseth, is not to be restrained to the bare act of believing, but to the whole Covenant of Salvation and Grace of Adoption which* Abraham *did apprehend by*

Ggg *faith,*

faith, I *see not that any thing can be drawn from this place, but that free Adoption was* Abrahams *true Righteousness, that he believed should here mean he was a Covenanter, or he was in Covenant; And* Calvin *on the place teacheth, that we do no otherwise obtain righteousness, then because we do by faith as it were see the possession of it; that is, we obtain Remission by faith, when by faith we see that our sins are remitted by God.* Rivet dialyſ. p. 108. *taketh faith for the object of faith;* and *Apologet.* p. 57. The Apostle saith that we are justified by faith, or that faith is imputed for righteousness, because that is the proper object of faith in the matter of Iustification, whereby we believe, that God having accepted Chriſts satisfaction, doth give us remission of sins, and is reconciled to us.

§. 12.

R. B. THis is answered already. 1. Moſt Interpreters do take *faith* to mean *Chriſt* no otherwise then by Connotation, including and principally intending Chriſt. 2. No man more expreſly againſt you then *Calvin*. I have before shewed your abuſe of him, and seeing you are not ashamed to repeat it, I muſt needs tell you, that you are a moſt partial unworthy handler of Authors. Let the Reader Iudge. In the firſt place, *Calvin* speaking againſt them, that to avoid Iuſtification by faith, would expound that of *Abraham* only of a particular Iuſtification ariſing from a particular act of faith, believing one single word of promiſe about *Iſaac*, he ſaith, that *Verbum credendi non ad particulare aliquod dictum reſtringi debet, ſed ad totum ſalutis fœdus & adoptionis Gratiam, quam dicitur* Abraham *fide apprehendiſſe;* that is, objectively; it ought not to be reſtrained to one ſaying of God, as if it were but that one that *Abraham* is commended for believing, but the whole Covenant. Now what doth this Diſſertor but ſay, that *Calvin* ſaith, the word *Believed* is not to be reſtrained *to the bare act of Believing*, and ſo puts out *ad particulare aliquod dictum*, and puts in *ad nudum actum credendi*. Did ever *Calvin* or any man elſe think that the act can be without an object? Can a man *credere, & tamen nihil credere?*

In the next place, *Calvin* expreſly ſpeaks againſt his doctrine, yet doth he 1. Leave out the former ſentence that fully ſhews it. 2. Leave out the the middle words of the very ſentence which he citeth 3. And miſunderſtand even thoſe he citeth, or draw others to miſunderſtand them. *Calvins* words next before are theſe, *Hanc promiſſionem & fidei Relationem neceſſarium eſt ad ſtatuendam Iuſtitiam intelligere: quoniam eadem eſt hic inter Deum & nos ratio, quæ apud Jurisconſultos inter Datorem & Donatarium:* Then follow the words which he cites, *Neque enim Iuſtitiam aliter conſequimur, niſi quia ſicuti Evangelii promiſſione nobis defertur, ita ejus poſſeſsionem fide quaſi cernimus.* Where note, 1. He leaves out *Sicuti Evangelii promiſsione nobis defertur*, without which the reſt cannot be underſtood, this ſpeaking of the offer, and the reſt of the Acceptance. 2. Puts *niſi quia ejus poſſeſsionem fide quaſi cernimus*, as if *Calvin* by *Cernimus* meant the knowledge of a Poſſeſsion before obtained; and as if this Diſſertor did not know that *Poſſeſionem cernere*, is to enter upon, or take poſſeſsion? and the context expreſly ſhews this to be *Calvins* ſenſe.

Rivets words speak of Chriſt connoted by faith, and principally intended by the Apoſtle, but not as excluding the act of faith: perhaps *Rivet* excludeth it from being any part of the *Iuſtitia imputata*; but he includeth it as a *Conditio ſine quâ qua non*, of the Imputation; and that is expressed in the next words before, which the Dissertor leaves out: He saith, *Non imputantur autem actum non credentibus, sed credentibus.*

---

§. 13.

L. C. *Arg.* 6. THey that are not Justified but by faith in Iesus Christ, are Iustified by faith alone. But none is Iustified but by faith in Iesus Christ, *Gal.* 2. 16. Therefore;

Answ. *Nothing is thence concluded, but that we are Iustified either by faith, or the object of faith, or as Chrifts Righteousnefs is made known to us.*

---

§. 13.

R. B. IT is one thing to have Chrifts Righteousnefs made known to us, and another thing to have our Interest in it made known. I doubt not you mean the later; and then I must needs say, that both these Interpretations are against so clear light of Scripture Evidence, that it shews your will faulty as well as your intellect: as I have sufficiently manifested, and more shall do, God willing.

---

§. 14.

L. C. *Arg.* 7. THat which Christ saith he requires alone on our parts to the receiving of his benefits and Grace, that alone and always Justifieth: But he requireth faith only to receive these, *Mar.* 5. 36. *Luk.* 8. 50. *Mar.* 9. 20.

Answ. *Chrift doth not require faith that we may be Juftified, that is, that Chrifts Righteoufnefs may be imputed to us; but that it may be known to us that Chrifts Righteoufnefs belongeth to us; for that which receives Gods benefits, is not of our righteoufnefs.*

---

§. 14.

R. B. 1. THe answer is an express contradiction of the text: *Rom.* 4. 21, 22, 23, 24. *And therefore it was imputed to him for Righteoufnefs; Now it was not written for his fake only that it was imputed to him; But for us also, to whom it shall be imputed if we believe on him that raifed up our Lord Iefus from the dead.*

2. To your reason I say, Faith is the condition of our universal Righteoufnefs by Chrift; and thereby it self becomes a particular subordinate Righteoufnefs, by which we must stand or fall in judgement.

Ggg 2 §. 15.

§. 15.

L. C. *Arg.* 8. BY what we are the sons of God, and have peace with him, by that only and always are we Iustified; But by faith only have we these. *Answ.* *So far are we said to be the sons of God by faith, as faith dictateth that we are but sons.*

---

§. 15.

R. B. IS' It not in vain to urge such men with Scriptures? May they not as well say, that what Scripture speaketh of the worlds Creation, Christs death and Resurrection, was all meant only of our knowledge of it, or of an appearance to us? God saith, *Ye are all the sons of God by faith*; The Dissertor saith, *Faith only telleth you that you are his sons before*; God saith, *He gave them Power to become the sons of God, even to as many as believe*, &c. The Dissertor saith, *He only makes known that we were sons before.* If this be not to profane Gods word, and use the name of God against God, I know what is.

---

§. 16.

L. C. A Greater Objection is brought from the *Intercession of Christ*; For if Christ daily intercede, then Iustification is not yet finished, nor is done in one act. I answer; Christ doth in Heaven represent his performed sacrifice, expiated sins,
*Ad Jus. and seeketh that believers be admitted to * a right of the Kingdom, (but
regni.* not that they may be made heirs of the Kingdom, or believers) and in the mean time that the force and merit of Christs death be aplyed to us: For continually are the satisfaction of Christ and his obedience, the price of Redemption so before Gods eyes, that God gives us nothing but for the sake thereof; also Christ intercedeth to excite in us Groans that cannot be uttered, Rom. 8. 26. and to offer our prayers and thanksgivings to God; which he doth by making them gratefull and acceptable to him: Lastly, Christ intercedeth to that end, that they who by his satisfaction are righteous, may be conserved in Grace.

---

§. 16.

R. B. IT had been more policy to have silenced this Objection, then to have thus shamed your cause by such an answer. 1. You say Christ seeketh or petitioneth that Believers be admitted *ad Jus regni*; If you will hold to these words in the full proper sense as here without limitation you seem to take them, all is destroyed that you
have

have said, and we are agreed. For if by *Jus Regni* you me an *Jus ad regnum*, Right to the Kingdom, yea, or but include this as part of your meaning, you yield all the cause I desire no more. For to give *Ius ad regnum* is the justifying act, or at least concomitant inseparably. To Iustifie is to give *Ius ad Impunitatem*, or *Iustum constituere*, i. e. *non reum pœnæ*: and then to sentence him accordingly, and then to use him accordingly. The first is Iustification by faith here, or our first actual Iustification. Punishment is of loss and of pain: *Pœna damni* is our loss of Right to, and enjoyment of the Kingdom (so far as *Adam* should have had it on his obedience to the first Law.) To remit our *Pœna damni*, therefore is to give us *Ius ad regnum*, and so this is a part of Iustification: so much as Christ hath superadded to what *Adam* was capable of, is still given with the rest, and never before it; so that it is past doubt, that if Christ do intercede that we may have *Jus regni*, then he intercedeth that we may be Iustified.

2 But if you have made this word but a cover for your deceitful erroneous sense, and will say, that you mean not *Ius ad Regnum*, but *Ius in Regno*, you will but plead against Christs intercession, by which I hope he is pleading for you; And if you dare say (as you seem to drive at it here) that Christ doth not intercede for your Right to the Kingdom, nor for your pardon or Iustification, you will shew how you advance Christ and free Grace; and I hope elsewhere more fully to manifest your error. Besides, as the Kingdom consisteth in Righteousness, the giving of one is the giving of the other.

4. You say Christ seeketh *not that they be made Heirs of the Kingdom*. This is another dishonourable derogation from Christs Intercession, and a falsehood, robbing him of the Glory of his free Grace. You here confess that it is for Christs merits represented to the father, that he gives us all things. All then that is given us after, or at our believing, must be given for those merits represented, and that representation is Intercession, as you say: Now I shall shew you that we were not Heirs before we were born, or before we believe; Though still I acknowledge that we were destinated to reign before the world was made, and our Right purchased into Christs hands to dispose of to us in season; and if this were enough to denominate us heirs, then are we heirs before; But this is not enough; seeing an Heir is one that hath a natural or donative Right *in diem*, an actual right, though not to the present fruition of the inheritance (and though forfeitable) But so have not Infidels: and Scripture doth use the word Heirs as appropriate to Believers at least ordinarily. Gal. 4. 7. *If a Son, then an Heir*, shews that these go together: *But it is by faith that we have power to become the Sons of God*: Joh. 1. 12. Therefore, &c. Heb. 11. 7. Noah *by faith*, &c. *became heir of the Righteousness which is by faith*. Rom. 8. 17. *If Children, then heirs*; Therefore not heirs till Children. Gal. 3. 26, 29. *Ye are all the Children of God by faith in Christ Iesus. And if ye be Christs, then are ye Abrahams seed, and heirs according to the promise*. All Heirs are *Abrahams* seed, and *Abraham* is the Father of the faithful, and not of Infidels. Tit. 3. 5, 6, 7. *He saved us by the washing of Regeneration, and renewing of the Holy Ghost*, &c. *That being Iustified by his Grace, we shou'd be made Heirs, according to the hope of Eternal Life*. To a plain man this seems undoubtedly to speak, that Iustification, and making us Heirs are concomitant or consequent to Regeneration. Jam. 2. 5. The rich in faith are Heirs of the Kingdom. Heb. 1. 14. *Who shall be heirs of salvation*.

3. You say that Christ doth not seek *that they may be made believers*: If you mean,

he doth not intercede that those that are *believers* already be made believers, I know not to what purpose you mention such a contradiction. But if you mean, as is most probable by your words, that Christ doth not intercede for us before we believe, that we may be made believers, then you take faith to be no fruit of Christs Intercession: But then why should you think any other Grace, any more then faith, a fruit of it. If it be a fruit of Christs merits, it must be a fruit of his Intercession; for his Intercession is the pleading for the fruits of his merits. But I hope you will not say Christs merits procured not our faith; nor yet that we believed before we were born, and therefore needed no Intercession for collation of the benefit.

4. You yield that Christ intercedeth *that the force and merit of his death be applyed to us.* And by *merit* you must mean, either the thing merited, and by *applyed*, bestowed: or else you must mean the merit is so far applyed, as that we shall have the good merited. Now doubtless pardon of sin and Justification is the fruit of Christs merit; therefore he intercedeth that we may have these (for that we had them before, is yet unproved.)

5. You say *Christ intercedeth to excite in us unutterable groans.* But 1. May he not intercede for pardon too? 2. What must we groan for according to your doctrine? not pardon and Iustification, for that we had already: And for salvation, if what we do be but signs of our salvation; then our Prayers can be no means: Therefore we may not use prayer as a means to salvation. And for sanctification, if that be but a sign it self, then the means to that sign is of the less use. So that when you take down the matter of our prayer, then you tell us, Christ intercedes for unutterable groans, that is, groans for comfort.

Lastly, where you say, Christ *offers our prayers,* It must not be any prayers for Iustification, no nor pardon of daily sin, but for the feeling of it; only for non-punishing I remember you granted we may pray, not seeing how that contradicted the rest. The sum of your answer I take to be a denyal that Christ intercedeth for our Remission or Iustification, which perhaps I shall say more to prove elsewhere.

CHAP. VIII.

The Testimonies of Divines not of lowest note.

---

§. 1.

L. C. THat our Zanchy is for the same way of delivering (the doctrine of) Iustification by faith, is hence evident, in that he also admitteth a certain sanctification in the elect before they are born: For on Ephesians 2. 5. He admits a double *Vivification;* one, which is once wrought in our Head *Jesus Christ,* and in our name; the other which is continually done in this present life; the words are; Both must be considered, first in Christ, then in us; as to the first, God quickeneth us in the person of Christ, when by the death of Christ our sin being expiated, he freed from the guilt of internal death, and endowed with right of a Celestial and Eternal life, all the elect, as many as were from the Creation of the world, and will be to the end, as members of Christ, considered in them their head.

§. 1.

R. B. WHat is the reason of your citing these Authors? If to make us believe that the ordinary Orthodox Divines go your way, your Title page, and all our knowledge contradicteth you. If to perswade us that at least, *Zanchy, Alstedius* and *Tossanus* were of your mind, the contrary is undeniable, by the larger plainer passages of their writings. If to perswade us that they contradict themselves, that is no great advantage to you?

1. *Zanchy* speaks here in terms not convenient, and which I will not justifie, because they agree not with Scripture.

2. Yet it is plain that *Zanchy* means not actual Iustification, Liberation, Remission; But that which *Amesius* calls Virtual. Now though Scripture speak of no Virtual Justification, yet if any man will use that word, and withall open his meaning, that he intendeth not actual justification, but such a Iustification as is *in Causâ* only, the effect itself not yet existing, I would not much contend about the word, though such new use of words is dangerous.

3. That *Zanchy* meant no more, and was in judgement against you, a hundred places in his writings fully prove. The next words to those cited by you, are these: *In nobis vero ipsis nos Reapse vivificat, hoc primo vivificationis genere, cum donatos fide in Christum, donat etiam Remissione Peccatorum, & Justitiæ Christi imputatione, & ita Justificat. Tunc enim Re ipsa liberamur Reatu mortis æternæ, & donamur jure vitæ cælestis atq; Divinæ:* dicente Christo, Joh. 3.

On the same Chapter ver. 8. he is more full and express, in so much that he saith, Faith receives Grace, and Grace in the adult cannot be without faith.

So on 1 *Joh.* 1. *Loc. de Remiss.* he handleth this yet more fully: And to the fourth Question: To whom sins are remitted, he concludes that, *Quanquam omnibus hominibus offeratur Remissio peccatorum, re vera tamen peccata non remitti, nisi E'e 'Tis, fidelibus, non autem Infidelibus: iis qui sunt in Ecclesia, non autem iis qui sunt extra ecclesiam.* And to the fifth question, By what means sin is Remitted? Having shewed well that all is given in Christ, and none but with him, and that the Gospel is the external Instrument of Donation; and the spirit the internal (as he calls it,) so he makes mans heart the *Instrumentum in quo*, and Hearing, and Believing the *Instrumenta per quæ*, of our reception (Though I suppose he useth the term Instrument improperly, yet it shews his judgement against you fully.) Yea he saith, *sine fide Recipi peccatorum Remissio non potest*: Though I will not dissemble, that he describes justifying faith but too like you, in which more of those times were for you, then are now. To the sixth Question, On what conditions Remission of sins is offered and bestowed? he hath an excellent discourse (which I would those would peruse that think I ascribe more then the reformed Divines do to Works, or other Graces besides Faith)

Therein

Therein he shews that pardon is given on condition. 1. Of true and constant Repentance. 2. Of confession. 3. Of forgiving others. And he very well answers the Objection, that if pardon have all these conditions, then it is not of free Grace. And after *page (mihi) 53.* he saith, *Fides impetrat Remissionem omnium peccatorum*: and saith that Scripture affirmeth absolute, *per fidem peccatorum Remissionem impetrare*.

And in his *Compendium Theolog. page 755. vol. 3.* he saith, *Quantalibet Sanctitate sint Filii Dei: hac tamen conditione semper sunt, quamdiu in Mortali Corpore habitant, ut sine Peccatorum Remissione consistere nequeant coram Deo*; and shews that sins are daily pardoned.

Nay he is so far from thinking that all our Righteousness was received at Christs death, that he affirmeth that our Works themselves are imputed for Righteousness, the sinfulness being pardoned. *Ibid. Loc. undecimo de Justific. p 793.*

And *Loco nono de pœnitent.* page 764. *Tota vita nostra semper labimur & egemus Remissione peccatorum. Remissio autem Peccatorum non contingit nisi pœnitentibus: Ergo, semper pœnitentia nobis opus est si remissionem peccatorum assequi velimus.*

And in his *Christian Relig. Fid.* which he commends as the work of his experienced age, *cap. 27. Thess. 6.* he professeth to believe, that *as in Christ only we have Redemption, Remission, &c.* so only the elect, endowed with true repentance and faith, and graffed into Christ as members to the head, are partakers of it, though remission be declared or offered to all: And *Thess. 2.* He shews what it is to Remit sin, and addeth, *Et nos cum in oratione petimus remitti nobis debita nostra, non solum petimus nos à culpa absolvi, Et iniquitatem nobis non imputari, verum etiam pœnam & condemnationem, nobis propter iniquitatem debitam, condonari, taliq; nos reatu ac debito liberari.* But I have been too long on *Zanchy,* and therefore will be briefer with the rest.

---

§. 2.

L. C. ALstedius *in the supplement added to the end of* Chamiers *works*, p. 204. *when* Bellarmine *impugned the Sanctity of the Doctrine of Protestants, and produced that Doctrine as the greatest Paradox, to wit, that I am Iustified by faith, and yet that Iustifying faith is to Believe that I am just, which,* saith Bellarmine, *is against reason.* Alstedius *among other things answereth, that Christ and the Elect are like one person, and therefore that the Elect are Originally Iustified in Christ before God, and at last by faith are Iustified, seeing Faith is the Instrument by which the righteousness of Christ is received.*

---

§. 2.

R. B. ALstedius *plainly sheweth you that by* Iustification *Originaliter,* he meaneth not actual Iustification, but taketh that *Originaliter,* as *terminus diminuens,* as to actual Iustification: which is as much as to say, that the *Origo vel causa Justificationis jam existit*: As when we say, *We were eternally Justified*

Justified in Gods Decree: the meaning is, *We were eternally Decreed to be Justified*, that is, we were not justified, or else we could not be predestinated to it.

2. I confess others have spoken too mistakingly of Christ and we being one person in his obedience and sufferings, as if he had been our instrument or Delegate, which is the very foundation of the Antinomian frame, and *Alstedius* speaks too like them, and in language not fit, but fully shews he is not of their mind in many places.

3. And that he is not of yours, that and many other places fully shew. As for example, *Distinct. Theolog. cap.* 23. §. 37. *Fides est prior Justificatione non tempore sed natura : Est enim Causa Justificationis organica* : So in his *Definit. Theol. de Remiss. & Justific. & Passim.* Yet I confess he speaks, *de Justificatione ante tempora*, which is but Gods Decree to Iustifie us.

§. 3.

L. C. T*Ossanus Epist. ad Vorstium* : You confound Iustification with the Application: For all the Elect are justified in Christ, if you respect his merit, before they were born ; and so before we believe, we are Iustified and Redeemed in Christ.

§. 3.

R. B. I Have not this of *Tossanus* by me, and therefore cannot examine this Allegation, nor is it any great matter.

For 1. I am sure he ordinarily speaks for justification by faith.

2. It is no wonder to have Divines let fall inconvenient expressions, and strictly irreconcilable; specially about justification by faith.

3. Nor is it any wonder if this Dissertor pervert and abuse the Authors he alledgeth.

But for these words, as cited, they are but an improper use of the word, *Justification*, For it is here a diminutive term, as to actual Iustification. To be justified *quoad meritum*, is to have Christ merit our justification; as to be justified *quoad decretum*, is to have God decree to justifie us: But merit being a Moral cause, may go long before the effect.

Hhh §. 4.

§. 4.

L. C. Twiss is express, and with him Maccovius, *saying almost the same things as he*: For thus Maccovious, disp. 8. de Justific. God endoweth none but the Justified with his holy Spirit and with faith: For unless God had so accepted us in Christ, and for Christ been propitious to us, he would not at all have given us effectual Grace, by which we should believe in Christ; therefore also before faith God was reconciled to us; For he gives us not faith, unless he be first reconciled and propitious. What is spoken gives light to these and other Phrases: A man is not Justified but by faith in Jesus Christ. We believe in Christ that we may be Justified, *Gal*. 2. 16. that we may be Justified by faith, *Gal*. 3. 24. For the sence of these Phrases is, by that thing which faith apprehendeth, that is, his satisfaction for sins, and his merit, we are justified before God; that is, we know and feel by faith that we are righteous before God, who hath forgiven us our sins, and given us right of eternal life, for the bloody satisfaction of Christ, and his imputed righteousness; and by much the more faith increaseth, by so much the more doth the feeling of justification, or larger fruit arise, *Rom*. 1. 17.

You will object. Scripture oft teacheth that we are Justified by Faith, therefore we were not Justified before, but are then Justified when we are endowed with faith.

I Answer from Twiss: *that righteousess of Christ was performed for us before our faith, but was not in possession ours as to sence and the knowledge of so great a benefit: For this knowledge ariseth and proceedeth through faith.*

Idem disp. 10. *A man is Justified before he have faith; and when he is said to be Justified by faith, and by faith to receive remission of sins, and inheritance among the Sanctified, it is nothing else but to know that he is Justified.*

§. 4.

R. B. WE well know that *Maccovius* and Dr. *Twiss* were of the Antinomian faith in this point, and therefore we are not so immodest as to go about to contradict you in that, or perswade the world of the contrary; the same answers that satisfie your arguings, do satisfie theirs.

As for this great Argument of *Maccovius*, I know it is also Dr. *Twisses* Master argument, That God would not have given us faith, unless we were first Pardoned, Justified and Reconciled. And might not the good men have seen easily, that it will as well follow, God would not have given his son Iesus Christ to die for the world, unless they had been first Pardoned, Justified and Reconciled? And thus Christ must die, only to make them know that they were Pardoned and Justified, (which he might have told them as well from the Pulpit as from the Cross,) and not to Merit it, or to satisfie for their sins. And thus Socinianism, if not Infidelity, is the natural issue of Antinomianism. And all this is, because

because men will not hold to Scripture, but set up their vain reasonings against it, yea when they have received a false Model or Platform of Theologie in their brains, and then will stretch all Scriptures to speak their sence, and serve their turns.

§. 5.

L. C. PEmble, *an Englishman, a man exceeding Reverend, and conspicuous in Doctrine, is of the same opinion, in his work of Justification*, page 124. *The Elect not yet converted are actually Justified, and freed from the guilt of sin, by the death of Christ, and so God reputeth and taketh them as discharged, and having accepted of satisfaction, is actually reconciled to them.*

§. 5.

R. B. I Believe there is no such thing in *Pemble* of Justification at all: But in his book called *Vindic. Gratiæ*, he hath such a thing, though not at that page (with me.) But its known Mr. *Pemble* was young when he delivered this, (dying about thirty,) and his Treatise of Justification came from a througher consideration of that point, and in that he wholly lays by (and seems to reclaim) his former conceit. For here he industriously proves that Justification is opposite to Accusation and Condemnation, and defineth it, *pag.* 15. *cap.* 2. *A Gracious act of God whereby he absolves a believing sinner accused at the Tribunal of his Justice, pronouncing him just, and acquitting him of all punishment for Christs sake.* (Though indeed he is constituted just for Christs sake, before he is so pronounced.) And he maintains it, that *The condition required in such as shall be partaker of this Grace of Justification, is true faith, whereunto God hath ordinarily annexed this great Priviledge; that by faith, and faith only a sinner shall be Justified.* pag. 22. And that *the tenor of the Covenant of Grace is, Believe in the Lord Jesus, and thou shalt be saved; the condition of this Covenant is faith; the performance whereof differs from the performance of the condition of the other Covenant.* Do this and live, *is a Compact of pure Justice, wherein wages is given by Debt, &c.* Believe this and live, *is a Compact of freest and purest Mercy, wherein the reward of eternal life is given us* in favour for *(mark for) that which bears not the least proportion of worth with it, so that he which performs the condition, cannot yet demand the wages as due unto him in severity of Justice, but only by the Grace of a freer promise, the fulfilling of which he may humbly sue for.* This is true and sound Doctrine. *pag.* 23. and *pag.* 24. But in that other proposition (*a man is Justified by faith*) we must understand all things *Relatively*, thus: *A sinner is Justified in the sight of God from all sin and punishment, by Faith, that is, by the obedience of Jesus Christ believed on, and embraced by a true faith; which act of the Justification of a sinner, although it be properly the only work of God, for the only merit of Christ, yet is it rightly ascribed to faith, and it alone,* Forasmuch as faith is that main condition of that

New Covenant, which, as we must perform if we will be Justified, so by the performance thereof we are said to obtain Justification and life. For, when God by Grace hath enabled us to perform the condition of believing, then we do begin to enjoy the benefit of the Covenant: So he adds as the second reason: 2. *Faith and no other Grace directly respects the promises of the Gospel, accepting what God offers, &c.* By this you may see both that Iustification is a consequent of faith, and in what sence faith Iustifies, i.e. 1. Directly and formally, as the condition of the Covenant performed. 2. More remotely, as the reason of its Aptitude to that Office, Its accepting Relative nature, that is, that it being the receiving of a free gift, was fittest to be the condition of our right to Christ who is given as a free gift. This last (even the nature of faith as faith) is it that is commonly called the instrumentality of it in Iustifying, which is but the secondary, and not the nearest reason why we are Iustified by it: and so *Pemble* pag. 57. *Faith Iustifies us only as a condition required of us; and one Instrument embracing Christs Righteousness*; that is, an instrument improperly so called, not an efficient Instrumental cause.

So that you see *Pembles* more digested thoughts did reject your opinion, which he first entertained.

---

§. 6.

L. C. GEorge Walker, one of the late delegates from the City of London to the Assembly, a rigid defendor of the Presbyterian Discipline, and a most sharp contender for *Gods righteousness* against *Iohn Goodwin* the Arminian, in his Catechism is express.

Quest. How are the Elect Iustified, and their sins forgiven?

R. They are Justified and their sins forgiven by faith, not as it is an Instrumental cause, and a means by which they are constituted righteous before God; but as faith is the hand of the soul, receiving and applying to themselves Christs righteousness, that thence they may perceive and feel that they are Righteous.

Quest. Can any man be justified before he actually believe?

R. If we take Justification in the proper and most principal sence, as it is the act of God alone communicating the righteousness, and satisfaction of Christ with the Elect, then it must be confessed that man is Justified before he perform any act of believing: as is evident in Infants, and those that are not yet called: or by the example of a Noble mans son, who though he have full right to the Possession, yet knoweth not yet his own goods.

But if we take Justification in a secondary sence, for the act whereby the Elect do mingle works with God, receiving and applying to themselves the free gift of righteousness, and possessing it, then actual believing goeth before Justification as an Instrumentall cause, by which God Justifies them in feeling and internal perception: But if we take Justification in a Judiciary and forensick sence, for Declaration, and proof, and pronunciation, then not only actual faith, but Repentance, and all works of Piety, must go before as Arguments and Testimonies convincing of the Remission of sins.

§. 6.

R. B. I Will not seek to take from you the advantage of Mr. *Walkers* testimony: But as I cannot speak in excuse of it, so I will say but this against it; It is his mistake, as it is yours, and without proof. And for his instance of a Noble mans Son that hath full right to the Possession, I say, it is destructive to Religion, and contrary to the very Scope of Gods word, to affirm that Infidels elect have full right to the possession; Yea, or any proper true right: Though I easily grant that they are predestinated to the right and the Possession, and that Christ hath a right by Redemption, to give them a right in season, and so the price is paid already. And I again say, that even of constituting us just before God, and judging us just sententially, faith is the means and antecedent, that is, the condition: And how far obedience hath a hand, especially in that last, which Mr. *Walker* mentioneth, I have shewed elsewhere.

And thus I have perused your Testimonies, wherein I find, some of our Divines first mentioned, you deal scarce fairly with, and the rest are but three or four that were known to be of your side, as different from the rest. And I confess some great Divines speak mistakingly and inconveniently on these points. If I should say, that the Doctrine of Christs satisfaction, and of Justification, hath been yet scarce clearly delivered by all or most, the differences and controversies among our selves would too evidently prove it. And though I have no mind to credit your bad cause, nor yet to discredit any learned Divines: Yet I must confess, that besides *Twiss*, *Maccovius*, *Pemble*, (at first) and Mr. *Walker*, who are downright for you, I could tell you of more great names that unadvisedly say, Justification is before Faith, on this poor ground, that the Act must needs presuppose the Object: So *Polanus* in *Ezek.* and so *Chamier* himself. *Sam. Maresius Colleg. loc.* 11. §. 58.

Who yet in other * places contradict this and themselves. As if it were Justification that were the object of Justifying faith: when indeed it is Christ himself, whom we receive, that we may be justified. Or if you will call Justification the Object, it is not Justification in being, but as offered, that by acceptance it may exist: As if a Prince offer to pardon a Traytor, it is not an actual pardon, but a conditional, that it may become actual, which he accepteth: Though a written pardon be called a pardon, as a written Prayer is called a Prayer, yet it doth not formally act, or

* *This comes through a misapprehension of the nature of justification, and of Justifying faith. Yet they are far from thinking that we are Justified in time before faith, much less before we are born.*

Tempore vix prior est, cum parum interstitii possit concipi, &c. Tantum abest ut activa nostra Iustificatio Natales nostro precedat, ut nonnulli somniant aut Vocatione nostra prior sit, &c. inquit *Maresius. Ibid. pag.* 287.

pardon, till we believe, being but before a conditional grant, which will be actual upon the performance of the condition. And so, I doubt not, God hath pardoned all, in the tenor of the New Covenant, when yet it is not all that are actually forgiven. *Objectum fidei Justificantis est Christus qui perfecte potest servare*

omnes

omnes per ipsum accedentes ad Deum, atq; adeo Deus per ipsum propitius: Remissio peccatorum & salus ipso a̵ n̅obis applicata, non est Objectum fidei, sed effectus consequens. Andr. Essenius, Defens. Grotii. lib. 1. §. 5. cap. 3. pag. 341.

Cocceius and *Cloppenburgius* give you too much countenance, by their misapprehensions of the Doctrine of the Covenant. For my own part, I am as willing we should lay by the words of men (though the unanimous vote of the Church of Christ till * *Islebius* daies, is not contemptible,) as you are, & to remit all that advantage that we have against you in this kind, so be it we may try the cause by the plain word of God. And I much rejoyce in his mercy, that hath made these things so plain in his word: Were many other controverted points, but neer so plainly delivered as this, I should not doubt but the sad contentions of the Churches would have been less about them, and they would have been as unanimous in them as they are in this; I am confident, at least, that my own Intellect would be much more quieted then it is: For, I bless God, in these matters it is not a little satisfied. And truly, I think, (and its sad to consider) that it may be said of many Scriptures that speak of Iustification, as I have read, not only *Maldonat*, but some Protestant Expositors saying of some Controverted Texts: *This Text had been plain, if none had expounded it*: And as I have heard many a one say of their health: *I had been a sound man in likelyhood, if it had not been for Physitians: the curing of a disease which I had but in conceit, hath brought on me many, which now I have indeed.* I think verily, that those Godly Christians that have by Practical Divinity been brought to saving Grace, and never heard much of these controversies about the place of faith, compared with Repentance and Obedience in matter of Remission, Iustification and Salvation, but what the bare words of Scripture do express, have usually sounder apprehensions of the business then they that have read controversies of it, and thereby have perverted their understandings by adhering to parties, and making use of *aliene* unscriptural Notions. And I think the present disturbed, divided, exasperated Churches, may say as the Emperor *Hadrian* when he was dying: *Turba medicorum me perdidit; si pace Doctorum ita dicam, & semper Salva honore Ministrali.*

* *Who turned round, from a Papist to a Lutheran, and thence to an Antinomian, and thence (as they said, for a Bishoprick) to the interim, and so to a Papist again, and then he was in statu quo: And this is the first Antinomian that ever I read of; His followers may some of them dance the same round, if the Jesuites can but lead them on by the nose as they have begun.*

FINIS.

The Preface.

READER,

I Think it not inconvenient to give thee some advertisement of the occasion of this writing. Having met with a Sermon of Mr. *B. Woodbridge* Pastor of *Newbury*, for Justification by faith, and against the Justification of Infidels, I saw so much worth in a narrow room, which caused me to bless God that his Church had such a man, and especially *Newbury* who had so excellently learned a Pastor before, who had mistaken so much in this very Point; and withall in the Epistle of a small Book that I since printed, to commend it to others: Mr *Eyre* of *Salisbury* was offended it seems at this; and in an Answer to Mr *Woodbridge*, newly published, with an Epistle of Mr *Owens* prefixed, he was pleased to speak of me what thou hast here answered.

In his Epistle against me, he telleth us of one Mr *Crandon* of *Hampshire* that [hath now in the Press a large and full Answer to my Paradoxicall Aphorismes.] The Character that Mr *Eyre* gives of this man is, That he is [a faithfull servant of the Lord Jesus, a workman that needs not to be ashamed,] This is good news if it be true: for then he will not write so many things that deserve shame, as are in this book of Mr *Eyre*'s. But by his wish that others [of more strength and far greater helps] may by him be provoked to shame, I am afraid what the fruit of his Weakness may prove. I confess I have heard neer this twelvemoneth, that this man hath been about this work. The last I heard, informed me, that [he is against the Morality of the Sabboth in Doctrine and Practice notoriously, and one that calls it Legall preaching to Convince men of sinne and misery, and supposed to be of Mr *Eyre*'s Judgment for the justification of Unbelievers; and that he having communicated it to Mr *Eyre*, was

A 2   gon-

gone with him to *London*, to print a large Answer not only to my Aphorismes, but Passages in my other Books; His book about a hundred sheets, and some six Shillings price, having more leaves then Arguments, but most liberally pouring forth the Titles of Papist, Jesuite, &c. which is both the Logick and the Rhetorick of it. Also that he had written to the Eminentest Ministers in severall Counties, whom he took to be most disaffected to my Aphorismes, to desire them for themselves and friends to take off his Books, which way is much by some distasted. I can say nothing of him of my own knowledge, nor of his Book till I see it. But if these two men be Brethren in a party, and Mr *Eyre* so much the more esteemed, as I hear; the Reader then may see what to expect by this. I have purposely hasted the Reply to this, that Mr *Crandon* may before his Book come forth, consider better of some things wherein he shall finde his Brother overshot himself, and correct what may tend to his hurt: for I would prevent his sinne. And I do hereby inform thee, Reader, that as soon as ever Mr *Crandon*'s Book doth come to my hands, seeing the scope of it is to revile me as a Papist, I purpose to print a plain Confession of my Faith, and specially how much I ascribe to Works, and how farre I am from Arminianisme also, which these Brethren do accuse me of, and I shall do it in as little room as I can; and then shall leave it to thy choice, whether thou wilt bestow six Pence to understand my true Belief and Profession, or six Shillings and six weeks reading (at least) to have thy ears charmed with the delicious notes of Papist, Jesuit, Arminian, Socinian, and what not of that kinde? If I finde the Book worth the answering, I know not but I may attempt it at large if ever I have time (which is not like,) But if it be according to my information of it, I shall not trouble my self or thee. It is my lot to be troubled by two sorts of men, commonly called Anabaptists and Antinomians, because I was called by God to Vindicate his truth against them. There came but lately to my hands two of one sort, and the report of a third that are written against me, Mr *Fisher*, Mr *Hagger*, and Mr *Keye*; but when I found them fraught with non-sense, and reviling, I laid them by, and never mean to meddle with them more. Mr *Eyre* and Mr *Crandon* take the next turn: what one hath done I have seen: what the other will do, I know not but by report. But for my own part, I confess I had a hundred times rather encounter with this party then the former: Because I do not apprehend neer so much danger in the opinion of Rebaptizing, or not Baptizing Infants, as in the other. I confess this

also

also hath been strangely followed with spiritual Judgements: But I suppose the main cause is, because it openeth the door to Separations, Contendings, and so Contempt of the Ministry that are against it; but it is hard to see in the nature of the meer Opinions such hainous evils as we have seen attend it. But for the other, in my Judgment they do as dangerously subvert the very tenour of the Gospel as well as the Law (and much more) as any Sect that I have known, that hath such men to countenance it. I confess also that I do apprehend some more duty lie on us now to resist that way, then hath been ever heretofore: For it was formerly a very rare thing to meet with a man of Learning or considerable Judgement, of that way: What men had D*r* *Taylor* to deal with? D*r* *Crisp*, *Eaton*, *Town*, were the chiefest Champions since, whom M*r* *Burgess*, M*r* *Geree*, M*r* *Bedford* have confuted. At last *Den*, *Paul Hobson*, M*r* *Saltmarsh* took the Chair: The later strangely cryed up by many ignorant souls, and his weakness laid open by that Excellent, Learned, Reverend M*r* *Gataker*. But now Libertinism grows into better Reputation. It makes a greater noise in City and Countrey; yea and men of some name for Learning, are the Patrons of no small portion of it. Lately came forth a Latine Dissertation of *Ludiomæus Colvinus*, aliàs, *Ludovicus Molinæus Med.* Doctor and History Professour in *Oxford*, written against his own Brother *Cyrus Molinæus* a Minister. I answered it, before I knew the Authour; and had no sooner finished it, but I received this of M*r* *Eyres*. I profess the desire of my soul is so great for the Unity of Brethren and the Churches Peace, that I could heartily wish both contendings and dividing Titles as much as may be laid aside: And therefore for those Reverend Brethren that hold but the more tolerable part of Antinomianism, I would not have them called by that name. But for the rest, to be tender of the credit of such pernicious errours, and to indulge them by favourable titles, is plainly to betray the Gospel, and mens souls.

For my part, if I should not preach against the opinion of the Libertines, I could not preach against prophaneness: When I look back on the Sermons which I preached many years ago, meerly to work mens hearts to Christ, never thinking of the Libertine Controversies, I finde they were the very same things that I am fain to preach now against these Disputers. I was feign to prove to them their natural misery, and that before believing they were children of wrath, and all their sins were unpardoned, with the necessity of Faith,

Faith, Repentance and Confession, for pardon: and the necessity of faithfull Endeavours for the attaining of Salvation; together with the necessity of Renewing Repentance, and begging pardon through the bloud of Christ, when we fall. Lay by all these and such like which the Libertines dispute against, and what have we almost to preach to those that will not have Christ to Reign over them? Truly I finde as farre as I can discern, that most of the prophane people in every Parish where yet I have liv'd, are Antinomians; They are born and bred such; and it is the very natural Religion of men, that have but the advantage to believe traditionally in Christ: I mean, their corrupt nature carrieth them without any teaching to make this use of Christ and the Gospel. And almost all the successe of my Labours which hath so much comforted me, hath been in bringing men from natural Antinomianism or Libertinism, to true Repentance and saving Faith in Christ. And therefore should I now side with them, I must unsay what I have been long saying from the plain word of God, to the ungodly that I have preached to. Blessed be God that the Church hath such writings for plain men to reade, as *Hookers, Boltons, Perkins, Dods, Rogers, Whateleys, Hildershams, &c.* which are written in a sounder strain: Yea that we have such writings as *Sibbes, Prestons, Baynes,* &c. to shew them, that Consciences may be Pacified without Antinomianism.

I am no Prophet; but I confesse I am so confident that the prevalency of this Sect will be but of short continuance, that I do not much fear them. For though nature be ready enough to befriend it, yet two disadvantages they runne upon, that will infallibly dash them all in pieces, as soon as the storm of Temptation is allayed. First, They contradict the experiences of the souls of Believers; and the very nature of the New-man is against them: The greatest part of the Spirits work on the Soul is against Libertinism, and the rest against Popery and Pelagianism; supposing the prerequisite foundation laid. And surely the workings of the Spirit are unresistable, and shall bear down these natural conceits before it. The contest between the Gospel and Libertinism in the Church, is like the Contest between the Spirit and the flesh within us, and goes much on the same terms: and Christ will be Conquerour and bring forth Judgement unto Victory, in both. Sound-hearted Christians, that be not only tickled with Sermons, but sanctified by the Spirit, will not long be drawn from such apparent Truths, and sweet and needfull Duties, by the bare names of Free-grace: nor will they deny Free-grace,

and

and the glory of Chrifts Interceffion and Kingdom, upon an empty pretence of magnifying his death ? when that very magnifying is but a difhonour. A found-hearted Chriftian I am perfwaded hath something within him that potently ftrives againft Libertinifm and Pelagianifm. For example, In prayer, Let a Libertine tell him, [Your fins were all pardoned before you were born, and therefore you muft not pray for pardon, but for the Feeling of pardon;] He hath a fpirit of prayer within, and a fecret impulfe to bewail his finnes, and make out to God for Remiffion, that will not let him obey thofe delufions. So, if a Pelagian fhould fay [The Power is in thy own Will to pleafe God, and Love and fear him.] The new nature of a Chriftian doth contradict this, and is inclining him ftill to beg grace of God, which is a real confeffion of his own infufficiency. Yea though this Chriftian fhould be tainted with either of thefe Delufions, I am perfwaded even while fpeculatively he holdeth them and talks for them, yet other principles lie deeper in his heart, and are fecretly working him a contrary way, even to pray for pardon, contrary to the Libertine, and for prevailing Grace, contrary to the Pelagian.

Another Rock the Libertines run againft that will fhortly dafh them all to pieces: and that is [the clear light of exprefs Scripture.] So plainly hath God been pleafed to reveal his minde in thefe cafes, that though a few may fhut their eyes by prejudice, moft will fee: and if they are blindfolded a while, it is not like to be long. If all Difputers fail us, as long as plain honeft Chriftians have but recourfe to the Word of God, it will convince them at laft, and fhew them the Error. For example, in this very Difcourfe (by one of the rationaleft men of that way that I have met with) what plain light doth fhine in his face! what palpable abufe is he forced to offer to the Scriptures? So that I dare truft a Reader of any competent judgement and honefty, that is not deeply foreftalled, to confute him by the bare reading and obfervation of the Text. As for inftance, That to be juftified by faith, is to be juftified by Chrift, without faith. So *pag.* 42 he expounds *Gal.* 2. 16. [*That we might be juftified by the faith of Chrift*] i. e. That it might be manifeft that we were juftified before we had faith in Chrift. But that's common: *pag.* 43. That text *Rom.* 8. 30: which moft exactly and purpofely expreffeth the order of Gods works, [*Whom he called them he juftified*] is put off but thus, 1. The order of words in Scripture do not fhew the order and dependance of things, &c. 2. The Apoftle's fcope

here

here is not to shew in what order these benefits are bestowed, &c.
3. I see no inconvenience at all, in saying that the Apostle here speaks of Justification as declared and terminated in conscience, which some Learned men (Mr Owen and Mr Kendall) do make the *formale* of Justification. But more grossely, *pag.* 44. he expounds *Rom.*4.24. [*Righteousness shall be imputed to us if we beleeve.*] 1. He saith, "[The particle [*if*] is not conditional, but declarative, describing "him to whom the benefit belongs.] Yet one would think that it might hence be gathered at least, that This benefit belongs not to Infidels: But to avoid that too, this is his Paraphrase, "[*q.d.*Here-"by we may know and be assured that Christs righteousness is im-"puted to us, &c.] The Apostle saith [*It shall be imputed, if we be-leeve.*] Mr *Eyre* saith [We know by this that it was imputed before.] To put the time past for the time present, and a Declarative for a Conditional, is the way of such bold Interpreters, as make their own faith. But tender-conscienc't Christians will not long suffer you so to make their faith, though you may your own.

Besides such Expositions, the Book contains Conclusions so contrary 1. To plain reason: 2. To known Truths in Divinity: 3. To the new nature or inclination of Beleevers: 4. To his own professions; that though itching ears may be pleased by it, and for the bait of [the name of Free Grace] it may be swallowed down, yet when Judgement, Affection and Practice should digest it, the humble soul will vomit it up again. I will give you but a brief touch of his dealing in the four respects mentioned.

1. Against common reason and use, he affirms that [If it have any condition, it is not free] and takes Mr *Walkers* patronage, *p.*93. and applauds and repeats Mr *Kendals* gross Discourse, which would give much more of the honour and thanks to the Beleever, then the Giver, and repeats his *Welsh* example, [*God bless her father and mother, who taught her to reade.*] Yea this gross conceit is the very soul of his Discourse; by which it may appear how bruitishly it is animated. But I have proved to him, that a thing may be free that is conditional. *Donatio, Absoluta, Pura,* and *Gratuita* be not all one, or equipollent terms.

2. And contrary to all sound Divinity, *pag.*134. he affirms that [Christs death was *solutio ejusdem,* because Christ was held in the same obligation that we were under: *Gal.*4.3,4. *he was made under the Law;* not another, but the very same.] Either he means here [the same obligation to duty] or [the same obligation to punishment.]

ment.] If the former, what a proof is here that Christs suffering is *solutio ejusdem*? When the Law obligeth a man to duty, can you thence prove that it obligeth him to punishment? then *Adam* before his fall, and Christ as an innocent creature, and the Angels in heaven are obliged to punishment. But its like he means the later: And then 1. It is most unsound and dangerous doctrine, to say no more: Christs obligation was *sponsionis propriæ*, the obligation of Contract or Consent, and as a creature of the special command of his Father thereto: Our obligation is *violatæ Legis*. Obligation to punishment is guilt; our guilt was *Reatus culpæ & pænæ propter culpam, ex obligatione legis*: Christs guilt is but *Reatus pænæ propter culpam nostram, ex voluntaria susceptione*. Christ was *obligatus ad eandem pænam* (the same in value) but not, *eadem obligatione*. 2. And how doth *Gal*. 4. 3, 4. prove it? Who can think that it means, Christ was made under the curse of the Law? He was indeed made a curse for us by undergoing the penalty; but not said to be made under the curse, nor under the Law as cursing, but as obliging to duty: though its granted that it was part of his humiliation to undertake that task of ceremonious duty.

So *pag*. 191. he saith, "[Let them consider whether it be more ea-"sie for a man that is dead in sinne, to believe in Christ, to love "God, *&c*. then it was for *Adam* in his innocency, *&c*. to abstain "from the fruit of one tree, when he had a thousand besides as good "as that: there can be no condition imagined more facile and fea-"sable then *Adams* was.] This is against them that say, Evangelical conditions are easier then Legal works. Where he seems plainly to think, that it was not perfect obedience internal or external that was the condition of Life to *Adam*, but only the not eating of that tree, and so he makes it the easiest thing imaginable. Do you not see how admirably he exalteth the Gospel above the Law, and Christs easie yoak and burden, and his commands that are not grievous, above that which *Adam* was under? Is it not admirable to see that these men must needs have the new Covenant to have no condition, lest it be not free, and those must be cried down as enemies to free Grace, and Legal Preachers, that teach the necessity of faith and repentance to remission of sinnes, when yet the more rigorous Law of nature, *Do this and Live*, the condition of *Adam*, is the most easie imaginable? And what thoughts hath he of *Adams* sin, If ye see not the Apostacy from God to the creature, unbelief, and many hainous sins were in it, as well as eating of that Tree?

B 3. Against

3. Against all sound Divinity, and the very sense of a gracious soul, he hath many doctrines which the godly will be ready to tremble at. As *pag.* 122. "[That the Elect *Corinthians* had no more "Right to salvation after their Believing then they had before.] You see in this mans Judgement what we preach for, and what is the state of a natural man, yea of the veriest Rebel, Whoremonger, Murderer, that is Elect : he may have more knowledge of his happiness after, but he hath no more right to salvation then before. Why say our Divines then that such are not in a state of salvation ?

So *pag.* 103. he saith, "[Though men will not impute or charge "sin upon themselves when there is not a Law to convince them of "it, yet it follows not but God did impute sin to men before there "was any Law promulged, or before the sin was actually committed. "For what is Gods hating of a person but his imputing of sin, or his "will to punish him for his sin?] Thus Gods preterition or non-election, called hatred, is confounded with his hatred of Justice and actual displeasure: and God is made to impute sin to the innocent who have no sin, yea to them that are not : When as Imputation of sin is but either the estimation and judging of a sinner to be a sinner, or the adjudication of punishment for that sin, or the execution of that punishment : all which follow the act of sin; and so he makes Gods act of Imputation to be both *untrue* and unjust ; but that indeed he gives the name of Imputation to the eternal Decree, to which God never gave it.

So *pag.* 61. he saith, concerning all that Christ died for, though yet Infidels and Wicked, that "[Divine Justice cannot charge up-"on them any of their sins, nor inflict upon them *the least* of those "punishments which their sins deserve ; but contrarily he beholds "them as persons perfectly righteous, and accordingly deals with "them as such who have no sin at all in his sight.] What humble soul would not tremble to say this of himself now regenerate ; much more of the unregenerate? Must God be unjust if he inflict on us the *least punishment* for sin ? And yet Scripture say so oft that God punisheth his people, in express words ? If it be *pæna propter culpam* it is punishment : and is none of your pain, losses, crosses, such ? Is not the smalness of your knowledge, love, &c. and the remnant of sin, as suffered upon you, a punishment? nor death, nor the bodies remaining in the grave? Are not chastisements a *species* of punishment ? Is not a man punished when he is hang'd for a sin ? yea and that by God as well as man ? What man dare say, [Lord, if thou

hadst

hadst laid the least punishment on my body, before Conversion, even in the height of my sin, thou hadst been unjust? yea or if yet thou do it.] Was there no punishment in the dominion of sin, and the want of the sense of Gods favour, which they make to be the contrary to Remission and Justification? The Lord deliver poor souls from such Doctrines as these! Yea so far as they have grace, so far they are delivered. And I hope M*r* *Eyre* speaks against his own heart, by the conduct of his fancy, and the instigation of his contentious passion.

4. Is it not against his own pretence, that he saith, in his Epistle to the Parliament, "[Though God doth effectually move and per-"swade mens hearts, yet he doth not Necessitate them to believe and "embrace the truth.] Would you think and reade this that the man were so zealous against the Arminians, when I, who am called Papist and Arminian, do think, that God doth so effectually move men to believe, as thereby to necessitate them? Though still he doth cause us to do it *liberè*, though *necessariò*, and so necessitate us, as that the act is still contingent in it self, as from our will.

So *pag.* 117. he hath these words, "[I dare say, a more unsound "Assertion cannot be picked out of the Papists or Arminians, then "this is, that faith (taking it as he doth in a proper sense) hath the "same place in the Covenant of Grace, as works have in the Cove-"nant of Works.] Where mark, that M*r* *Woodbridge* speaks only of the *place* of faith, and not of the worth, nature, dignity, nor full use; as if it properly or fully had the same office as works, but the same order in the Covenant. And then see 1. Whether this man doth not make Papists of the generality of the Protestant Churches, and Writers? 2. Or make the Papists as sound as the Protestants. 3. Of what credit this mans word is, that ushers it in with such confidence, [I dare say it,] and whether the reason why he *dares say* that and so many more such things, may not be because he thinks all's pardoned already, even before he beleeved. 4. He pretendeth M*r* *Pemble* to be of his Judgement; yet see whether he make not M*r* *Pemble* to hold as unsound doctrine, as any can be picked out of the Writings of Papists or Arminians? I may well bear his heavy charge, when M*r* *Pemble* must bear it, who saies, Treat. of *Justif.* pag. 23. [*There are two Covenants that God hath made with man, By one of which, and by no other means in the World, salvation is to be obtained. The one is the Covenant of Works, the tenour whereof is* [Do this and thou shalt live, *&c.*] *The other is the Covenant of Grace, the tenour* *whereof is* [Beleeve in the Lord Jesus, and thou shalt be saved, &c.] *The condition of this Covenant is Faith.*] And so goes on to shew that the performance and nature of Faith and Works differ; but here gives them the same place of a condition in the Covenant. And *pag.* 22. he saith, [*The condition required in such as shall be partakers of this grace of Justification is true faith, whereunto God hath ordinarily annexed this great priviledge, That by faith and faith only a sinner shall be justified.*]

So *pag.*206. he ensnares himself in an objection, which he cannot answer, as I doubt not but Mr *Woodbridge* will fully shew him, when he hath sifted what is the adequate object of that *Assensus intellectus* and *amplexus voluntatis* which Mr *Eyre* acknowledgeth. But I must ask pardon of Mr *Woodbridge* for thus anticipating his work. Reader, do but study God and thy own heart, and keep a tender conscience, and an upright life, and a little knowledge more may preserve thee from being a Libertine.

One thing I forgot, which I now adde, To intreat Mr *Eyre* and his partakers, to tell me, upon their grounds, Whether God do accept of the Works as well as the Person of an Elect Infidel? If they say, No: How then are they in Christ, and God perfectly pleased with them? and all the sinfulnesse of those works forgiven? Doth not God accept of that work in which there is no sin imputed? but all-pardoned? nothing but the sinfulnesse can hinder his Acceptance of it? And where then is their vain distinction (that God is pleased with the person and not the work) by which they answer us when we tell them truly, that *Without faith it is impossible to please God?* Heb.11.6.

THE

THE CONTENTS.

§. 1.

The Defence of my Praises of Mr Woodbridges Sermon. Of my sleighting all Protestant Divines that differ from me, particularly Dr Twiss.

Of my Daring as a Dictator to prescribe what men shall reade.

Whether it be true, that with me an Antinomian and an Anabaptist are all one?

About the name Antinomian.

Whether only sins against the light of nature must be punished by Magistrates?

Whether it be no contradiction to have no sin punished but what's against the light of nature: and yet to have a penalty on them that will call men Antinomians? and not on Mr E. for calling Papist?

Whether all the Reformed Churches hold that which I call Antinomianisme?

Severall slanders of Mr E. refuted, About Merit and ascribing to Works.

Of my saying Christs satisfaction is Causa sine quâ non of Justification.

Gardiners Positions answered, which Mr E. makes like mine.

§. 2.

Of my Censure of Maccovius and others. Mr Eyres testimonies examined: Pemble, Rutherford, &c.

§. 3.

Whether I make all Antinomians that deny Justification by personall Righteousnesse? and whether I be singular therein?

§. 4.

How I deny or hold Christ to be our Materiall Righteousnesse? and imputation to be the form of Justification.

Of making Christ a Causa sine quâ non. More about Merit. Mr Es befriending the Papists.

§. 5.

§. 5.

More about our personall Righteousness. My Judgment about Justification by our personall Righteousness opened in 12. Conclusions.

Mr E^s Arguments against personall Righteousness in Justification answered: Paul excludes not all Works: nor all that Debt which is by free Guift of promise. What Justification by Works Paul speaks against.

Whether Protestants acknowledging an Evangelicall inherent Righteousness, do not eo nomine *acknowledge that We are Justified by it as far as I do?*

Mr E. gives up his Cause, confessing that it is Christ and not We that are the subjects of Justification before We are born: No addition to Christs Righteousness to be Justified by faith or personall Righteousness in subordination to it. Imperfect faith may be the Condition of the pardon of its own Imperfections. How faith is taken for the object, in the matter of Justification.

§. 6.

Whether I include Works in Faith?

§. 7.

All Conditions are not Morall Causes, no nor any qua *Conditions.*

Mr E. denying Christs death to be the Cause of Gods Justifying, makes it as much a sine qua non *as ever I did, and much more. He is desired to expedite, How Christs death can be the Meritorious Cause* rei volitæ, *without Causing the* actum volentis? *All the effects of Electing Love are not given, by, through and for Christ,* viz. *as the Meritorious Cause.*

§. 8.

M^r E^s uncharitable Censure of Mr J. Woodbridge. How our Divines deny Dispositions and preparations to Justification.

§. 9.

His urging the invinciblenesse of Mr Owens Answer, about Reconciliation being an Immediate effect of Christs death.

§. 10.

His citation of Mr Strong. Proved against him (which may serve to the like of Mr Owen) that it is not of necessity that a Condition be quoad eventum *unknown to the promiser; and that God hath Conditionall Promises and Threats though the Condition be foreknown as to the event.*

§. 11.

Mr Eyres proved a notorious slanderer, in saying, that the Papists ascribe no more meritousness to Works then I do,] by the testimony of Bellarmine, Aquinas, and Mr Perkins, as a tast till I come to Mr Crandon. Many grosse passages of his Book are also opened in the Preface.

§. 1.

§. I.

Reverend Brother,

I Lately received a Book of your writing (whereof I had before intelligence by the weekly News book) entituled. [*Justification without Conditions, or The free Justification of a sinner*] against Mr *Woodbridge*, Mr *Cranford* and my self, as Assertors of *Conditional Justification*. Your scope is to prove the Justification of Infidels, or of the Elect before Faith, and before they are men, if I understand you. Methinks, there appears in your lines, much more Piety, Candor and Judgement, then I am wont to meet with in men of your Way; though with mixed discoveries of too much defect, especially in the two last. For my own part, I bless God, I have at last learned to love and honour a Christian as a Christian; and therefore all that are Christians; though they have that withall that is displeasing to Christ, and must be so to me. This Debt I confess I owe you; Christ in you is nevertheless Christ, because of your frailties; and though he delay much of the cure of your distempers, I hope he will in due time accomplish it; and when the remnants of your darkness are removed, you will see that truth which now you see not. I ought not to despise you for these infirmities, when I am daily groaning under them my self; and am in the hands of the same Physition; and am so conscious of a necessity of his tender handling. If Christ would not take me with all my faults, and distinguish betwixt his own and mine, between me and my sins, and put up many a thousand provocations, I were lost. And ought I not to honour Christ in you, and see his amiableness through the clouds of such humane frailties, which you as well as your sinfull Brethren, are yet liable to? Yet as Christ loves my sins never the more (that is, hates them nevertheless) for all his incomprehensible love to me, no more will he allow me to love yours. And as I must not think well of them, so neither must I speak well of them. If I should not mistake that for your sin which is none, I suppose I shall have your free consent to acquaint you with it: And if I mistake not those for your Errours which are none, I suppose you will consent that I warn all those that reade your Book, to take heed of them and reject them. For I suppose you are Virtually contrary to those Opinions which you Actually hold and maintain, and those Practises which Actually you venture to commit. I take it therefore for my duty, as to manifest your Errours with a hatred to them, because they are against Christ; so with Christian charity to your self; because you intended well, and are Virtually for Christ, even when you do

most

most against him. For I perceive you have a zeal for Christ, though it seems to me, not according to knowledge: And though some of your opinions, I much fear, are destructive of Fundamentals, and would not stand with salvation, if they were fully reduced to practice, yet I perceive great reason of hopes in the rest of your Writings, and by that good which I have heard of you, that you hold them but speculatively, and that in the main you live contrary to the natural tendency of your opinions. I remember therefore that I am writing to a Brother that I must live with in Everlasting Glory, where we shall be both of one minde, when we are perfected in Knowledge: I remember that I am Writing against such sins as are pardoned in the blood of Christ; and as will be very shortly renounced by your self, and against which you will be incomparably more zealous then I can now be, and will speak more disgracefully of them then now I must do. If in the mean time you are confident in the dark, and angry with those that would do you good, yea and abuse them who walk not according to your conceits; it is no wonder, considering what man is, even the best of the Saints while they live in the flesh: Being my self liable to the same distempers, I crave your pardon, if I shall any way injure you in these following lines.

The substance of your Book I perceive is against M*r* *Woodbridge*, M*r Cranford* and I are brought in but on the by, but so as that you deal with him but in the beginning, and with me almost throughout. I shall not anticipate M*r Woodbridge*, and therefore intend not the answering of your Book, but to give you a brief account of my thoughts, of so much of it as concerns my self.

Your first onset is in your third Epistle. My title is [*A leading man in these times:*] when I have neither worldly advantages, nor eminency of Abilities, nor yet opportunities, to be much Leading to any but my own charge. I live I believe as retiredly as you, cloistred up in obscurity, daily exercised with the chastisements of my Lord, and waiting for my change, and minding little to be the Leader of any, further then to help them to heaven to the utmost of my power. And for leading of men into any Parties, from the Unity of Christians, my soul is possessed with as deep a detestation of it, as of most sins that the world is guilty of. And I think no man did ever yet come to you, and say, that I once laboured with him to bring him to any private opinion of my own: My Writings contain all my fault of that kinde, that I know of. And for them, I desire you and all men to understand me, not as peremptorily affirming every thing that I speak in difficult Controversies, to be infallible Verities, but only as giving you my own opinion of it, and leaving you and all Readers to accept or reject it, according to the evidence. If what I speak, have evidence of Truth, you cannot darken it by what you say against my person: If it have none, my person hath no advantage, to make my opinion taking with the world.

The matter which you first charge me with is, my commendation of M. *Woodbridge's* Book in the Epistle to my *Directions for Comfort*. And your self are pleased to give M. *Woodbridge* your free commendations for the eminency of his natural and acquired parts, even to be as *Saul* above his Brethren: and that you seem to confine his worth to these, as if in spirituals the matter were otherwise, will make his cause never the worse before his Judge. You adde that " [It is not to be won-
" dred at that M. *B.* hath given this superlative *encomium* to M. *Woodbridge's* Ser-
" mon; he knew well enough that it would rebound upon himself, M.*W.* being a
" son of his own faith, and this notion of his, but a spark from out of M. *Baxter's*
" forge.] *Repl.* 1. Thus do bad causes hang together, and the sentences of the

Oblivious

Oblivious deftroy each other. My great imperfections are commonly known: Mr *W.* you confefs to be as *Saul* above his Brethren: What likelihood then of his receiving thefe things from me? 2. If you speak of the caufe in hand, do you ferioufly think that I am the firft that hath faid, that [*Infidels are not juftified*] or that [*The Elect are not juftified till they have faith.*] Think you that Mr.*W.* need to come to fuch a one as I, to learn that which the Church hath held ever fince it was called Chriftian? 3. Truly I never faw Mr. *Woodbridge*, nor did there ever a meflage or word in writing pafs between us; nay (living here obfcurely out of the obfervation of things remote) I had never to my knowledge heard of him, till I faw his Book. But when I did fee, *ex pede Herculem*, I faw fuch difcoveries in it of a clear underftanding, which caufed me to blefs God for fuch a man, and in fpecial that you had drawn him out into the world; nor am I forry much for this your Anfwer to him, as not doubting but it will draw forth yet more of Gods precious gifts, which he is furnifhed with for his Church: I alfo much rejoyced in that providence of God which had made him fucceffor at *Newbury* to Dr.*Twiffe*, giving that people a man fo found, and fo able to inform them better, in that one point, wherein the Doctor did fo miftake. And indeed Sir, I fhould take it for a great priviledge, were I near him, to be the Auditor and Scholar of fo Judicious a man; and I doubt not you will finde, that he is well able to manifeft your miftakes to the world. And I confefs I honour him yet more then I did, fince you tell me in this Book (which I knew not before) that Mr. *Parker* was his Grandfather; the name of that man for his Labours and Patience (and efpecially that excellent Treatife *de Defcenfu*) being very precious to me. 4. And for your intimation of my felf-feeking in commending his Book; you knew it is our Mafters prerogative to be the Searcher of hearts. Do not you know that an honeft man may value thofe moft that are of his own minde? Nay *muft do, cæteris paribus;* for elfe he cannot value a man for the fake of Gods Truth: For did we not take it to be truth, we could not be of that minde our felves. Doth not this raife your eftimation of the Learned commender of your Book, and of others whom you oft quote? Would you have envied the praifes of Mr. *W.* or his Labours, if he had been of your opinion? Do as you would be done by: Would you have been offended if I had as much commended you and yours?

You adde "[I suppofe Mr. *Baxter*'s praifes or difpraifes are not greatly regar-
" ded by fober-minded Chriftians, who have obferved how highly he magnifies
" *J Goodwin* with others of his notion, and how flightingly he mentions Dr.*Twiffe*
" and all our Proteftant Divines that differ from him.]

Repl. I confefs in refpect of ability of judging of mens Learning, and the worth of fuperlative Divines above my reach, my praife is fmall addition to any mans honour: But whether my confcience be fo fmall that fober-minded Chriftians neither *fhould* nor *do* regard my words, muft be determined by my Judge, to whofe blefled and more equitable fentence I am approaching. And fo farre as I am guilty of Error or partiality, I beg his pardon (for its according to my Judgement fo to do.) For the high magnifying of *Jo.Goodwin* which you mention, I defire the time and the words may be confidered; and then I think he that would then envy him fuch a commendation, is more partial then I am, though I were as contrary to him as you. I thought it had been only unmannerly language to my Brethren that I had been blamed for: but it feems it's praifing them too, if it be againft the intereft of the adverfe party. Have you ever heard me praife him for any evil? If you have, fpeak it out: If not, give me leave to love a Chriftian as

a Chria Chriſtian, and a mans Parts and Labours ſo farre as they deſerve, and to honour ſo much of Chriſt as I ſee in any. But how plainly do you ſtill confute your ſelf? You intimate that my commending men is becauſe I am of the ſame minde: and yet you know or ſhould do, that I do in that very place profeſs my own Judgement to be contrary to that of Mr. *Goodwin* and the reſt there named, and that I only reprehend men for their bitterneſs and contempt of them. Now Sir, if your conſcience will warrant you in ſuch dealing as this, to ſay I commend men as *of my notion*, (if you mean mine) even when I purpoſely expreſs my opinion to be againſt them, and write againſt theirs, it is not of the ſame complexion as mine is, as bad as I am.

And as little truth is there in your words of my ſlighting Dr. *Twiſs*, yea and all our Proteſtant Divines! Which be the words Sir that are guilty of that charge? For Dr. *Twiſs* I have honoured few men living more formerly; and much honour his Name and Labours ſtill; though I rejoyce that I am got out of the ſnare of one or two of his miſtakes. You are no Papiſt I hope; and therefore do not think a man ſlighted that is not taken to be infallible, or perfect. But of this I have ſaid enough to Mr. *Kendall*. The reſt of your Accuſation, (as to all Proteſtant Divines that differ from me) is either a breach of the ninth Commandment, or elſe my Tongue or Pen hath ſome where ſpoken quite contrary to my heart.

I marvell at your next ſpeeches, that " [Mr. *W.* throughout all his Sermon, " never ſo much as hinted, how or in what ſenſe we are juſtified by faith.] Whenas he doth it as ſolidly (in my weak judgement) as ever I read in any Divine? Nay when your ſelf beſtow ſome labour to confute him: Doth he not tell you it juſtifies us by the way of a condition, though Naturally Active, yet morally as it were Paſſive, qualifying us for Gods free Juſtification by his Covenant? To this purpoſe, but more largely, I well remember he ſpeaks: How then durſt you ſay, and publiſh to the world, that he never hinted how or in what ſenſe we are juſtified by faith? Sure Brother, this is not well done.

Next you ſay of me, that " [His advice to all Chriſtians to buy one of theſe " Sermons, argues rather his conceit of himſelf, then his charity to them.] *Repl.* Both theſe ſins, ſelf-conceitedneſs and want of charity, are latent in the heart, and by the Searcher of hearts it is that I muſt be tried, whoſe high prerogative, my opinion is, you ſhould not uſurp. Truly Brother, I have as much reaſon to value Truth, ſo far as I know it, as you or other men: and as little reaſon as many to be byaſſed in my ſeeking it. I dare ſay, I dearly love it, and that the ſearching for it doth coſt me ſomewhat? If I know it not, it is not becauſe I would not know it if I could. It is my hourly ſtudied, and daily prayers, and if I knew any other lawfull poſſible way to attain it, how gladly would I uſe it, though it were to the loſs of all I have in the world, or though the Truth were contrary to my former opinions, or though it would ſubject me to the hatred of my deareſt friends! He that knows my heart, knows that I ſpeak my heart, if I know it my ſelf. Nor do I take this for any high commendations; for mans intellect (as *participative* voluntary) doth Will Truth as its proper natural object. I mean, it would know things as they are (where carnal intereſt and enmity cauſeth not the perverting of the ſoul herein.) And I do not finde in my *fleſh* the leaſt oppoſition to your opinion.

Where you adde your reaſon " [That he dares take upon him the Office of a " Univerſal Dictator to preſcribe not only to his *Kederminſterians*, but to all private
" Chriſtians

" Chriſtians what Books they ſhall reade.] *Repl.* If by [*preſcribing*] you mean [*commanding*] iall men know that I am no Commander, and therefore my commands were more likely to be derided then obeyed. If you mean [*adviſing*] Why may I not dare to do that? Is that the work of a Dictator? If I may adviſe in other points of duty, I know not why I may not do the like in this. I have adviſed to the reading of other Books (as Hat, I think, againſt your opinion) *Bolton, Perkins, Hooker, Preſton,* &c. yet none ever charged me with [daring to preſcribe as a Dictator.] However you know my word will not take much, and therefore you need not be ſo much offended. And for all the diſtinctions which you are pleaſed to take as Herring-bones, I doubt not but to mean Chriſtians, that Book may be profitable: and that may prove happy food to others, which you call *Poiſon.*

You adde " [As for the title of Antinomianiſm which he beſtows upon our " doctrine, it is no great ſlander out of Mr. *Baxter's* mouth, with whom an An-" tinomian and an Antipapiſt are *termini convertibiles.*]

Repl. 1. To begin with your laſt becauſe it is the reaſon of the former: It is written, *Thou ſhalt not hate thy brother in thy heart, but ſhalt in any wiſe rebuke thy neighbour and not ſuffer ſin upon him,* Lev. 19.17. I perceive by your words that you are Paſtor of a Gathered Church (as its call'd) were I one of your neer communion, I ſhould openly deſire ſatisfaction concerning theſe words, not as to my ſelf for the wrong, but as to the Church, that otherwiſe if you prove impenitent, we might avoid you. My reaſons are, becauſe God hath ſaid, *Thou ſhalt not bear falſe witneß againſt thy neighbour.* And Lev. 19.11. *Ye ſhall not ſteal, neither deal falſly, neither lye one to another.* Deut. 19.18, 19. *Behold, if the witneß be a falſe witneß, and hath teſtified falſly againſt his brother; then ſhall ye do unto him as he had thought to have done unto his brother.* And I ſuppoſe you would avoid communion with a Papiſt, and have men ſo to do. Prov. 6.16, 19. *Six things doth the Lord hate, yea ſeven are abomination to him: A proud look, a lying tongue,---a falſe witneß that ſpeaketh lies, and him that ſoweth diſcord among brethren.* Prov. 19.5. *A falſe witneß ſhall not be unpuniſhed, and he that ſpeaketh lies ſhall not eſcape.* So ver. 9. Prov. 14.5. & 12 17. Rev. 22.15. *Without are ---- and whoſoever loveth and maketh a lye.* Pſal. 15.1,2,3. *Lord who ſhall abide in thy Tabernacle? who ſhall dwell in thy holy Hill? He that walketh uprightly and worketh righteouſneß, and ſpeaketh the truth in his heart.* Now as to the fact I prove it thus: If with me an Antipapiſt and an Antinomian be *termini convertibiles,* or all one, then I take all Antipapiſts for Antinomians. But the later is falſe: Therefore ſo is the former. All the Churches of *France, Belgia, Bohemia, Helvetia, Scotland, England,* &c. who ſubſcribed the Harmony of Confeſſions, or owned them: All our Reverend Aſſemblies that made the late Confeſſion of Faith, and Catechiſms, and all that own them: All that ſubſcribed the Synod of *Dort,* I take for Ant papiſts, and yet I take them not for Antinomians, no, nor any man for an Antinomian who beleeveth any one of all theſe: Therefore I take not all Antipapiſts for Antinomians. Again, either you ſpeak of my heart or of my language. For the later, ſhew where, or prove when I ſaid that Papiſts and Antinomians are *termini convertibiles,* expreſly or implicitly, and then call me a ſlanderer and ſpare not. If you ſpeak of my Thoughts, I know them better then you, and I profeſs them to be otherwiſe. Nay in the very particulars wherein I differ or ſeem to differ from my Brethren, I have received large Animadverſions from very many Learned men, and I profeſs to take not one of them all for an Antinomian. So much for your ground-work. Now to your ſtructure.

C 2

As for the term [Antinomian] I confess I think it more fitly applied to the Practice of those whom I have known, of that way, then to their Doctrine: For whereas the name is taken from one of the least of their great Errors, it should have rather been taken from the greater. For my part I heartily wish that among those whose opinions unfit them not for the Communion of Saints, and suffice not to Excommunicate them, all names of Parties or of Reproach were utterly laid aside; and would willingly contribute my best endeavours to that end, and heartily joyn with you in your motion to the Parliament that a Penalty might restrain such Dividing wayes. But yet 1. while men go commonly under such a name, we can scarce tell how to make known whom we speak of, but by the name or a description equipollent. 2. And I take a full Antinomian to be one that is unfit for Christian communion, as subverting the very substance of Christian Religion. But I confess I think it fitter to call them Antigospellers, or Antichristian, or Libertines, then Antinomians: And because it is the old and fit name, hereafter I will use rather the name of *Libertines*. But for sober moderate men, which are but half Antinomians, holding but the less dangerous part of their opinions, and disclaiming the rest, (though they are shrewdly concatenated) and not seeing that the rest do follow them, truly, as I dare not disaffect them, nor would avoid communion with them, so neither would I have them called Antinomians, further then to themselves to convince them of their participation in that sinfull way, as the name may be used in a course of arguing. And of these I hope you are one: and I hope it is no worse with some of your partakers.

But Sir, methinks you have some very strange passages in your Epistle Dedicatory about these things: I would warn you to search your heart whether the latter part of the second page of that Epistle, be not the venting of pure malice, and a trampling upon men that have more to say against you, then you seem to take notice of. But the thing I mean is 1. Your most dangerous doctrine. 2. Your most palpable self-contradiction by word and deed. 1. In the bottom of the third page in your parenthesis " [Nor can I excuse their connivence at any of those " evils that are contrary to the Law of nature.] You seem to teach that the Magistrate should punish no other evils; for these words, following a discourse against force in matter of Religion, can bear no other sense that I know of. But is this your friendship to Christ, that you would have the Magistrate be indifferent to him and Mahomet or Antichrist? What? not command the preaching of Christ? and punish the neglect of it in those that should do it? Nor hinder men from preaching against Christ, or calling him a Deceiver, or blaspheming the holy Ghost? nor for preaching up Mahomet? Is this your friendship to the Parliament as to draw them into such a guilt, which would cause God to curse them and cast them out, and make their names hatefull to the Christian world? Is this your love to the Churches of Christ, that you would have this deluge of guilt and confusion let in upon us? Methinks the very thoughts of such a dolefull state of the Church, should make your heart sad! Is this your love to your native Land, to open upon it such a Floodgate of desolation? And is this your love to the souls of men to prostitute them to all deluders? If you think that truth is so discernable to good and bad, that if all may but speak there is no great danger! do but open your eyes and Judge by the experience which these times afford you! You can scarce get men to receive the truth that hear none contradicting it: How much less when they have ten speaking against it, for one that speaks for it, and that with such subtilty as they cannot resist?

Nay,

Nay, Sir, I had hoped that you who do so let fly at me as a Papist, would not have proved such a friend to Popery. Would you have Popery have Liberty in *England* again in all the Points of it that are not against the Light of Nature? Truly you shew me but what I saw before! that all over-doing is undoing! and that none would sooner let in Popery then those that fly to the contrary extream. But shall I tell you Sir; If once they have full liberty here as you have, I think you will finde, that their numbers and prevalency will cloud your sect, and all the rest of the sects in *England*. And as very a Papist as I am, I would far rather joyn with you to keep them out; and would intreat you for the Peace of your own Conscience that you would unsay this again, and write a recantation of it to the Parliament.

I would have you also to consider your strange Contradictions to your own words.

1. You would have Names of Obloquy, and in particular that of *Antinomians*, restrained by Penalties. But is it against the light of nature for a man that is in Judgment against you, to call you Antinomian? If the Religion or doctrine may be tolerated, why may not the Naming of men accordingly? You will allow men to Do Evil, but not to be called Evil Doers? Where the Light of Nature teacheth not the Thing, me thinks it should not reach the Name! He that should judge you a Heretick, and thinks it his duty to make it known, seeth not by the light of Nature that he may not Call you so.

2. May not the Lord Jesus (for whom you seem zealous) have some of that favour from you, or respect, or tenderness of his Name and Honour, which you would have your self? If the Parliament must lay a Penalty on them that will call you Antinomian, I pray you put in one word with it, that they may lay a Penalty on any that will Call Christ a Deceiver, or reproach his Holy Name, or doctrine, or wayes; or would set up Mahomet or Antichrist against him; whether this be against the light of Nature or no. At least it is against the light of Nature to despise God: and Christ saith, *He that despiseth you* (his Ministers) *despiseth me, and he that despiseth me, despiseth him that sent me.*

3. If all these Names must be restrayned by Penalties, then I doubt the Name of Papist must be restrayned, and Socinian too: And would you indeed have a Law made to punish all that call men Papists or Socinians? and yet seem so zealous against them. Still the *Overdoing* Enemies, are the greatest friends, to Popery and other Errors.

4. But how comes it to pass that I must be so frequently with you a Papist, Socinian, Arminian, and yet it is a sin to be restrayned by Penalties to use Names of obloquy? But you shew us plainly what kinde of Liberty of Conscience it is that men are now for: A Liberty for them and others to abuse Christ, his truth, and their Brethren: but a restraint of speaking against their reputation. It seems though you speak generally, it was the Name of Antinomian or Libertine that you meant. Truly Sir, though Mr *Woodbridge*, Mr. *Cranford* and I, deserve not so much respect at your hands, yet me thinks the Parliament deserved sounder advice, and better and more carefull language of you then this? You should not have bespoken them with such Contradictions and dangerous Intimations.

You proceed with me thus ["Let him shew us any one Church or single per-
"son, accounted Orthodox till this present age, that did not hold some, yea most
"of those Points which he calls Antinomianisme, and I will openly acknowledge
"I have done him wrong: otherwise let him be looked upon as a slanderer and
"reviler

[8]

"reviler of all the Protestant Churches, who under a shew of friendship, hath en-
"deavoured to expose them to the scorn and obloquy of their enemies.

Repl. I willingly stand to your motion: But I must needs say, that the tempter hath much foiled you, when he prevailed with you to write these and the following words! and to add impudency to falshood and slander: for so it is. You should have cited my words which you lay this charge upon, or else I know not what to vindicate; for I know not what you mean. But observe, that the question between us is not, Whether any of the reformed Churches do differ from me in any thing, or, Whether I erre therein? But, Whether they hold any, yea most of those opinions which I call Antinomianisme? Would you make men believe that all the Protestant Churches are of your opinion? This is to put out mens eyes, and bid them renounce both sense and reason. I will call no man an Antinomian that doth hold the doctrines of the most Imperfect Confession in all the Harmony: Nay, I provoke you if you are able to name one man in the first, second, third, fourth or fifth Century, yea or for a thousand if not fourteen hundred years after Christ, that held any two, yea one, of the opinions which I ever call'd Antinomianisme? except it were some that were notorious Hereticks. Till then, I suppose it is not the Accused, but the Accuser that is reputed the Calumniator till he make good his charge.

You proceed, [" *Mr.B.* (the better to engage his Reader) tells him his do-
" ctrine is of a middle strain, as if all the reformed Churches had hitherto been in
" an extream, in this fundamentall point of our Justification.]

Rep. 1. Though Justification be a fundamentall, yet so is not every point that concerneth it.

2. I hope you will not perswade us that all the Protestant Churches are for the Justification of Infidels! unles it be by taking the name of Protestant Churches from all that will not say as you.

3. What Divine of note can you name, but doth in one thing or other, differ from the greater part? I think but few. Yet we do not for that one Point separate him from the rest. And let me add to the former Section, that if it be proved of any one or more of our Divines, that they hold one or two lesser points of Antinomianisme, I think it not fit therefore to call them Antinomians. I will not call *Zanchy* a Papist, because he denied the Pope to be The Antichrist: or because of his so much differencing *Johns* Baptisme and Christs: nor will I call him an Anabaptist, because he thought that those in *Acts* 19. were twice baptized, alledging so many Fathers of his minde. The like I may say of many another.

4. No wonder if any doctrine that avoideth your extream be contemned by you: It hath alway been so with men in extreams. But the day is coming, when moderation and Truth (which lieth between extreams) will be better regarded.

5. As for my [engaging my Reader] which you talk of; I know not whether it discover more of the secrets of your own heart or mine: sure I am you know not mine, but should know your own: And if you speak according to yours, I will speak according to mine, and thats this; that I love Gods Truth, and therefore would propagate it; and I love mens souls, and therefore would do them all the good that I can: but for any advantage that I aime at to my self by *engaging* men to me, besides the doing of my duty, I yet know it not. Nay I must needs reckon upon the loss of mens esteem before I resolve to cross them in their opinions.

You proceed like the rest [" I am sure he gives as much unto Works and less
" unto Christ then the Papists do.]

Rep.

Rep. *A false witness shall not be unpunished, and he that speaketh lies shall not escape,* Prov. 19.5. Review the texts before cited. Truly, Sir, I cannot think you durst sin thus without shame and fear, if you had not been hardened in security, by thinking your sins were forgiven before you were born! What good will all your Arguments do to prove to any man, that your doctrine encourageth not men in sin, while they shall see you run on in it so boldly? What hear we *words* for, when we see contrary *deeds*? As the Papists have done as much against their Religion, by Powder plots, Treasons, lying, as by their very erroneous doctrines, among those that judge by such experiences; so have the men of your sect done, to the wonder of observers. Whether your words here be true or not, I shall refer the Reader to my Reply to Mr. *Crandon*, whither I reserve it.

You add [" He makes Works by Virtue of God's Promises and Covenant, to be " the meritorious Causes of Justification and Salvation, and in no other sense do " the Papists affirm it."]

Rep. *Thou shalt not bear false witness against thy neighbour.* It is a harsh provoking kind of answering, for to give a brother a plain *mentiris*: and therefore I love not to deal with those sayings, that will admit of no other answer in termes or sense. If the ninth Commandement be Law, then this practice of yours is Antinomian. Produce that place; express those words of mine, which may make good this charge. I have ever professed that our best works are not in the least degree meritorious, no not of a bit of bread, much less of Justification and salvation. There never fell from my pen such a word as you charge me with, and yet you dare do it. One would think that common wit should have told you, that when the falshood of such passages *de facto* are discovered, it should redound to your own shame, and consequently to the great prejudice of your Cause. Nay I durst not acknowledge any Causality in faith to our Justification, and therefore in that Point adventured to differ from many Brethren: Yet doth this man say, that I [*make Works by Virtue of Gods Promise and Covenant, meritorious Causes of Justification.* And mark what an occasion he takes of this slander. In the 26. *Thes.* of my *Aphor.* I purposely speak against the doctrine of Merit; shewing that properly no works of ours can be called Meritorious, but in the end did concede that Improperly they may: This I did, because the Fathers for many hundred years after Christ use the word *Merit*, in application to mans works; and because all our Divines that ever I read against the Papists, *nemine contradicente*, do answer that the Fathers used the word *Merit* improperly. But these three things I ever professed in speech and writing on all occasions: 1. That no acts or works of ours are Meritorious Causes of salvation, much less of Justification. 2. That therefore the word Merit cannot be applied to them, but Improperly. 3. That therefore it is not fit to use so much as the word. And though when we read it in the Councils or Fathers, we must interpret it with a due reverence to them, yet is it fit to be excluded among our selves. Yet should I meet with any godly, sober man of a contrary judgment, that thought the name might be used while he interprets it in the same sense which the Reformed Churches hold, I would not approve of that mans opinion of the use of the word, but yet I would not for the bare word pretend that we are of different Religions, or do differ in the Thing which he expresseth by that word. I should think it very unjust if I should report all of my brother, which may be said of him Improperly. If *David* say, *All men are Lyars*, meaning, not able to help in time of need, and therefore not to be trusted in, as being fallacious; may I therefore call every man that I speak with a Lyar? What is there that may not be spoken of you, truly

truly in Impropriety? But suppose you would have made the worst of my words that malice could have done without express falshood, should you not then have taken up with my own words, without the addition of your forgeries? I said that [This is Improperly called Merit,] But I never said that [our works are the Meritorious Causes of Justification or salvation.] For as I have still maintained that they are No Causes at all, so in saying that they are called Merit Improperly, I say, they are no Causes Meritorious: no more then a *Causa sine qua non* is a true Cause, because it is Improperly so called. Nay I never once said, that as to our Justification begun, that works are so much as existent, but alway maintained that we are truly and fully as from all sins past Justified by faith, before Works of externall obedience are in being.

The next words [" and in no other sense do the Papists affirm it,] is another notorious falshood: which if it were in Doctrinals only, I could answer it with a cold *Negatur*; but thus to multiply falshoods one after another, seems a sad practice from a godly man. He might well know, if indeed he know what the Papists hold, that they are of severall parties among themselves differing about this Point, yet all of them except *Waldensis*, or very few more, do maintain the fitness of the word Merit: most assert both Merit of Congruity before Regeneration, and Merit of Condignity after; and *Scotus* and a few more that reduce all to the right by promise are rejected by the rest, who affirm a Merit of value or proportion: And our own Divines generally approve of them that hold only *Meritum ex pacto*, as to the thing, denying only the fitness of the name, and that this is any proper Merit. This all Divines know to be true that have read the Papists writings and ours against them. And yet this man did not fear to say, that [in no other sense do the Papists affirm it,] yea and that I [give as much to Works and less to Christ then the Papists:] I shall purposely delay my particular proof of the contrary till I speak to Mr. *Crandon*.

Nay a little before he saith of me [" Its like he thinks, that the Papists are " much neerer the line of truth then any of them,] *i.e.* of all the Protestant Churches. Here are two sins as evident as his sense, *viz.* false-speaking and uncharitableness.

A little before he said, he [feareth the men of *Kederminster* are fed but with lit- " tle better food,] yet did this man never hear me preach, never see my face, and yet can censure my teaching! Nay had he but enquired of me, he might have learned how little I meddle with Controversie in the Pulpit: Or if I did, and did all erroneously, yet I read the Scripture to them, I publish the doctrine of the Creed and Catechisme, is all this *poison or choaky meat* as he speaks? Judge of the affection and practice of this man by the Apostles marks, 1 *Cor.* 13. 3, 4, 5, 6, 7. and see what Charity he hath: *Charity thinketh no evil:* But how much of his own surmising hath he vented in a few lines? And yet he proceeds as fresh and fearless as before.

For he adds [" I must needs say, I never met with that Papist, which calls " Christ a *sine qua non* (*i.a.* a Cause which effects nothing) of our Justification.]

Rep. Would you not think here that the man did intimate that I say this, and but this of Christ? But mark the Case. In *Thes.* 56. *p.* 215. I speak only of Christs satisfaction, and not of any other work of Christ: And I say that it hath severall wayes of Causing our Justification. 1. That it is the Meritorious Cause, I say, I know few but Socinians will deny. 2. That it is also the Principall Cause *sine qua non*, as Removing Impediments: withall I shew, that I so call it only

only in respect of its Physicall operation, but as to Morall Dignity, I plead for its preheminence. Now what doth this man but lay down this word alone, that I call Christ the *Causa sine qua non*, and leave out that I call his satisfaction the Meritorious Cause, and allow it the preheminence in Morall respect. Nay, mark that himself makes Justification to be from Eternity, and not at all Caused or procured by Christs death *quoad actum volentis*, but only *quoad rem volitam*: And let any man tell me what he can possibly ascribe to Christs satisfaction on those termes more then I do in the place that he carps at. Those things that are but *Causa sine qua non in sensu physico*, are of singular Morall Causality, and so I shewed that Christs death is; but that faith is so a *causa sine qua non*, as to have no Morall Causality at all, as being but the Accepting of a free Gift. These things are so far from Popery, that they accord with the opinions of his own Patrons, as expressed hereabouts, and yet this man saith he never met with Papist that said so.

He next proceeds to compare my doctrine with some Positions of *Gardiners* in *Foxes Martyrology*. I have not the book at this time in my study to examine his dealing, but to his Positions I shall answer particularly, thus. 1. All the effects of Christs Passion have not a Condition: The satisfaction of Justice, the making of the new Covenant, the sealing it with Miracles, the publishing it to the world, and preaching it now to any Nation or Person, and the first Grace of faith and repentance; all these are given absolutely, and not made over upon any Condition on mans part. But Justification, Remission, Adoption and Salvation, are given Conditionally. 2. His second Position hath its answer in the first. 3. The third is false; for faith is the Condition it self, and not somewhat antecedent by which we must know it, unless he speak of any common faith which helpeth a man to perceive the need of saving faith; or unless he speak of the Condition of our Glorification or Justification as consummate, which is sincere obedience, in subserviency to faith and concomitancy with it. 4. To the fourth, I will believe that faith is the Gift of God, if all the Papists living believe it, and that by this Gift, I do well in believing in order of nature, but not of time, before I am Justified. 5. And so that I do well toward the attainment of Justification; But not of Justification in the Popish sense, which comprehendeth sanctification even in the first act, for so I do not well before it, so as any of my actions are Accepted of God in Christ, and their Infirmities pardoned; but only as an unbeliever may comparatively be said to Do well in coming to hear the word, rather then in going to an alehouse. 6. I believe that Faith and Charity thrive together: I am a Papist if this be Popery; that Faith works by Love. I do not think it sound doctrine, that to the Attainment of Justification is required Faith and Charity, without limitations and explication: For though a Love to Christ the Object is essentiall to that Faith that must Accept him (for let men say what they will, Christ must be Accepted as Good, and Good cannot be Accepted without Love,) yet Charity usually signifies that Grace, as extended to all other objects of Love, as well as an offered Christ, and so the Proposition is false, understood of our first being justified, as the word [Attainment] shewes it is. 8. The eighth Proposition is false. If only the beginning be free, then the rest is not free. 9. The ninth is answered in the former. 10. The tenth I never heard Protestant deny in *sensu diviso*; I believe that God gives the grace of Repentance to men in deadly sinne, even to all that have it, and I know not else how they should have it; and that this Repentance is a Condition of Justification, in the Pro-

D testant

testant sense, but not in the Popish sense, that is, of the first renewing of our natures. And now Brother I would I had given you all I have in the world, yea twenty lives, if I had so many to lay down, on condition you could but make it good, that the Papists erre no more then this; yea no more then these words of *Gardiners* in their obvious sense. But if you would be believed in crediting the Papists, you must get you Readers that never read their writings, or that have read none but such as the late *Christian Moderator*, that tells you by Merit they mean nothing but rewardableness. If you will make all the Papists Orthodox to prove me a Papist, youl shew how much your extremities hurt their Cause. For my part, I say again, would I had lost my life so that it were true. I would no more remove from the truth because the Papists own it, then I would deny God because they profess him. And if you can make me believe that the Papists are as Orthodox men as you pretend them to be, you will but exceedingly glad my heart, and not a whit remove me from my own opinion. These be but words to affright such children that receive their faith on the credit of man, and that must know what the Papists hold, that they may be contrary, before they can tell what to hold themselves. These move not men that wait for the Law at the mouth of Christ, and that attend the Spirit for Illumination by the study of the word, and go to the Law and to the Testimony, and call no man Master on earth. The worst you can do by such Toyes of malice, are but to diminish my reputation, with factious men, that follow parties for their faith, and know not what the Unity of the faith means, nor what it is to depend for teaching upon Christ. Though these men may be godly and zealous, and such as I dearly love, yet were it not for being made uncapable of doing them good, and diminishing Gods interest and their benefit, by the diminution of mine, I think you would not much assault me with these weapons, if you knew how little I value their esteem, when I cannot have it with Innocency and Truth. Brother, I am proud and sinfull the Lord knows as well as others: but yet I can truly say, that I have bent my studies and vigilancy against the sin of Pride above most others, for divers years past, and that I have stood so long on the brink of the grave and the door of eternity, that I can with very little trouble bear all the quarrels and contempts of men. How small a matter is it to me to be judged by man, who am daily looking to be called to the barre of God? I am almost out of this wrangling censorious world, and know its Gods Approbation which I must stand by, and then think of me all as you please; if God justifie me, I care not for your condemning me. But you proceed.

[" And for his choice notion of Justification by Works as they are our new Covenant-Righteousness, I finde it was a shift of the Papists long ago, &c."]

Rep. You are very unfit to parallell the Papists and me, who for ought I perceive understand neither of us. I need not tell Divines that read them the Papists opinion: but for my own I say still that we are justified first, without so much as the presence of Works, and finally without their Causality: but yet had rather expound *James*, then deny the truth of his words. Nor do I acknowledge any Universall Righteousness but Christs, consisting in the remission of sins. Only I think not that Christ died to pardon my Faith and Love as such, but to pardon the infirmity of them: to forgive my sins as sins, and not my duty as duty, and therefore that we have a particular Righteousness by which in subordination to Christs as being only the Condition of our Enjoying it, we may be said to be justified. But of these things more fully God willing hereafter.

He adds [" I shall not trace Mr. B. any further,„ there being now in the Press,

as

" as I am informed, a large and full Answer to his Paradoxicall Aphorismes, by a
" faithfull servant of the Lord Jesus Mr *Crandon* of *Fawley* in *Hampshire*, a Work-
" man that need not be ashamed.]

Rep. Of this book I have spoke in the Epistle enough. Why speak you of it as a strange matter [as I am informed ?] Its long since I was informed of your being with him at *London*, as combined together in the same Cause, and promoting each others work; one against Mr. *Woodbridge*, the other against me.

Your next shewes your modesty, in calling such books [" farre more dangerous " then the Ranters Blasphemous Pamphlets] and intimating that they are Popish and Arminian, and how *Reignolds, Whittakers, Davenant, Prideaux* would not have endured them.] Would you make the world believe that these men were of your minde for the Justification of Infidels ? Truly if you will be of the same minde as these men were, though I may differ from you in some point of Method or Words, yet I will never oppose you nor write against you, if you will but give me leave to forbear. My differences with these men are nothing to my differences with you. Nay you might have known if you would, that *Davenant* maintains the Conditionality of sincere obedience to the Continuance of our Justification in the same termes as I do. And so much to your Epistle. Now to your Treatise.

§. 2.

THe first place that I observe you falling on me, is *Pag.* 15. about *Maccovius*, where you say [" Though one of our late writers (Mr. *B. App. p.* 147.) men-
" tions this Doctors opinion with much contempt and oscitancy, calling his As-
" sertions strange, senseless and abhorred (which is the less to be regarded, seeing
" he usually metes out the same measure unto all men else, whose Notions do not
" square with his own mold.]

Rep. Thou shalt not bear false witness against thy neighbour. My words of *Maccovius* doctrine I refer to the consideration of any that are impartiall : for my part I cannot repent of them, any more then for saying that whoredom or drunkenness are to be abhorred. But that I [usually mete out the same measure to all men else whose Notions square not with my mold,] is a gross untruth, which any man that converseth with me, and hath read my writings, may quickly know. But let's hear your proof.

["As Dr *Twiß*,' Mr. *Walker*, and them that hold the Imputation of Christs
" active Righteousness, whom he calls A sort of Ignorant and unstudied
" Divines, &c.

Rep. Divers more gross falshoods in these few words, are added to the rest. I am loath to call you Antinomian, but if the ninth Commandement be Law, I am sure you make as bold to break it, if that be Antinomianisme, as most that I have dealt with. 1. Why did you not quote the place where I [mete out the same measure] to Dr. *Twiß* ? Mr. *Kendall* accuseth me of slighting him indeed ? and what is my language ? why I call him [that most excellent famous Divine.] But I judge him to mistake in saying Remission of sin is from eternity': that is, I judge him not Infallible nor free from error : Thus Protestants abuse all men, and Papists all save the Pope and his Generall Councell. 2. For Mr. *Walker* I confess I spoke undiscreetly, as having no call to meddle with him, and I hereby revoke it, and do repent it, that I intimated him to be *Ignorant*, and that I medled with his *Reviling*:

But

But yet I will take no man for a competent Judge of my fault, that hath not read his Book against Mr. *Goodwin*, and Mr. *Gatakers* Book against him in Defence of Mr. *Wotton*. 3. It is here intimated, that the cause of my speech wa from my mold : that is, as he means my opinions (for indeed the Scripture is my mold : Whereas the reason of my words against Mr. *Walker*, was his exceeding hard language to his Brethren; which as being against love and peace, I so far reprehended, as to say [He strongly reviled and weakly disputed] when in discourse and Pulpit he had done so much for above 20 years, against such learned, choice servants of God, as Mr. *Wotton*, Mr. *Bradshaw*, &c. and when in the Press the terme Heretick, Blasphemer, &c. are so familiar; and he even proceeds to the Curse of Anathema Maran-atha. But what if I spoke unreverently to this Reverend man, in saying he Reviled ? is it just that I be accused of doing so to all men, or any others, when I never was guilty ? 4. Next I am charged with the like, as to [" them that hold the Imputation of Christs active Righteousness.] Another falshood, as thus without limitation expressed : For I there professed to hold it my self, as part of satisfaction, and I hold it as Meritorious of all that higher felicity then the first Covenant gave (if there be any such :) But it was only one sort or sense of Imputation there explained which I spoke against. 5. Another untruth it is, that I [call these, A sort of Ignorant unstudied Divines] The words are these [" The maintainers of it, beside some Able men, are the vulgar sort of un-
" studied Divines, who having not ability or diligence to search deep into so pro-
" found a Controversie, do still hold that opinion which is most common and in
" credit.] Where I divide those that are for this way into two sorts; some Able men, and others the common unstudied Divines that take it on credit : And this is a known truth that too many such there are, that so, receive even much of their Religion : As if you did not think so your self of the most that are against your particular opinion ? Do you not think they go for company against you ? So I do not call all *Ignorant* that go that way, nor any man because he goes that way.

You adde of *Maccovius*. [" I dare say his Arguments in this particular will not
" seem so weak and ridiculous as Mr. *Baxter* makes them, to an indifferent reader
" that shall compare them with the exceptions that he hath shaped unto them. Sharp Censures are but dull Answers.]

Repl. I am not desirous to blast the reputation of that Learned man, if I were of any power to do it. But I confess his Doctrine in the matter of Justification I would have all friends of mine avoid ; and I took it for my duty so to tell them : which I know not why you should be so offended at. I suppose you know how the Synod of *Dort* judged of his harsh language in another case, wherein he opposed *Lubbertus*.

And seeing I am thus brought to take notice of the Witnesses that you produce as for your Cause; give me leave a little to review them.

The first is Mr. *Pemble*: But as Mr. *Pemble* is for you in his *Vind. Grat.* so when he came purposely to treat of that subject, it seems he changed his judgment: For in his *Treat. of Justification*, he saith as much of that as most of your adversaies: I pray you read him *Pag.* 15. c. 2. & p. 22, 23, 24, 57. and then you will sure boast of M. *Pemble* no more :. If he were once of your minde and afterward rejected it, as he seems fully to have done, that is no great credit to it.

Your second is Mr. *Rutherford*, who you say hath said as much as any of you. Will you give the Reader leave to judge how far M. *Rutherford* was for you, by these words of his own, written after a fuller knowledge of the men of your Sect ; In his

Trial

Trial and Triumph of Faith, pag. 55. Serm. 8. he answers these Objections (as against his first words, wherein he asserteth that [The condition of the Covenant is, faith: Holiness and sanctification the Condition of the Covenanters.) *This Do* was the condition of the Covenant of Works; *This Believe* is the condition of this Covenant.]

[*Obj.* 1. But some teach that this Covenant hath no Condition at all, so Dr. *Crispe* and other Libertines.] [*Obj.* 2. *I will put my law in your inward parts*, is no condition to be performed by us, but by God only.] [*Obj.* 4. Believing and obedience is but a consequent of the Covenant, not an Antecedent: so I must believe upon other grounds; but not in way of the condition of the Covenant, for in that tenour I am to do nothing.] [*Obj.* 5. The Covenant is Gods love to man to take him to himself, and that before the children do good or ill, and to him that worketh is the reward not reckoned of grace but of debt.] [*Obj.* 6. Our act of believing is a work, and no work can be a condition of the Covenant of grace: yea Christ alone justifieth: Faith is not Christ, nor any partner with him in the work; yea we are justified before we beleeve, and faith only serveth for the manifestation of Justification to our conscience, for we believe no lie, when we believe we are justified, but a truth; then it must be true, that we are justified before we believe.] These Mr *Rutherford* answers as the Libertines Objections. It would be too tedious to recite his Answers, only some of that to the last I will recite.

He saith, *p.* 59,60,61,62. [Christ alone as the meritorious cause justifieth, and his imputed Righteousness as the formall cause: and this way Christ alone justifieth the Patriarchs, *&c.* and all believers before they be born, but this is but the fountain ready to wash: but believe it Christ washeth not, while we be foul, *&c.* nor is his Name *Our Righteousness* while we be sinners (*i.e.* unrenewed.) 1. Men not born cannot be the object of actual Righteousness; the unborn childe needeth no actual application of Christs eye-salve, gold, righteousness: Now Justification is a real favour applied to us in time, just as Sanctification in the New birth, *&c.* We cannot be justified before we beleeve. 1. We are damned before we beleeve, *Joh.* 3. 2. He that is justified is glorified, *Rom.* 8.30. 3. We are born and by nature the sons of wrath, *Eph.* 2.2,7. *Rom.* 7.5,6. & 6.14. 4. By faith we are only united to Christ, possessed of him, Christ dwelling in us, *&c.* 5. This Justification without faith casteth loose the Covenant, *I will be your God.* But here's a condition, God is not bound and we free: Therefore this is the other part, *Ye shall be my people.* Now it is taught by Libertines, that there can be no closing with Christ in a promise that hath a qualification or condition expressed, and that conditional Promises are Legal, *&c.* (Here he rejecteth Conditions, 1. In the Arminian sense, as they are the work of Free-will not acted by the predetermining grace of Christ. 2. In the Popish sense, as they are meritorious, as work of wages: and so I reject them too.) 6. *Paul* in the Epistles to the *Romans* and *Galatians*, takes it for granted that Justification is a work done in time, transient on us, not an immanent and eternal action, remaining either in God from eternity, or performed by Christ on the Cross before we believe, and so never taketh on him to prove that we are justified before we either do the works of the Law, or believe in Jesus Christ, but that we are justified by faith, *&c.* and faith is not the naked Manifestation of our Justification, so as we are justified before we have faith: Satisfaction is indeed given to Justice by Christ on the Cross, for all our sins before we believe, and before any justified person who lived this 1500 years was born; but, alas, that is not Justification, but only the meritorious cause of it: that is, as if one should say, This wall is white since the Creation of the world, though this very day only it was whited, because whiteness was in the world since the Creation.

And that you may know the true nature of Justification, and Mr *Kendall* and you may see what others say of the nature of the act as well as Mr *Woodbridge* and I, mark the next words [Justification is a Forensical sentence in time pronounced *in the Gospel*, and applied to *me Now*, and never till the instant Now, that I beleeve: Its not formally an act of the understanding to know a truth concerning my self; But its an heart-adherence of the affections to Christ as the Saviour of sinners, at the presence of which a sentence of free absolution is pronounced: Suppose the Prince have it in his minde to pardon twenty malefactors; his grace is the cause why they are pardoned, yet are they never *in Law* pardoned, so as they can *in Law* plead immunity till they can produce their Princes royal sealed pardon.] So Serm. 18. *pag.* 148. [Nay give me leave to say, that Antinomians make Justification and free grace their common place of Divinity, as if they only had seen the visions of the Almighty and no other, but they are utterly ignorant thereof: For they confound and mix what the word distinguisheth, because *Justification is only a Removal of sinne by a Law-way, so that in Law* it cannot actually condemn.] So *pag.* 151. [Justification freeth *us in this life from all Law-guilt and Obligation* to wrath, which is but the second act of sin.] So *pag.* 153. [All which are true in a Law-sense, and in a Legal and Moral freedom from sin, *&c.*], and, [For they are in their actual guilt as touching the *Law-sting*, and power, as no sinnes, *&c.* removed and taken away *quoad actualem reatum eternæ mortis*, in their Law-demerit and guilt, *&c.* This is a Law-removal of sin.] So oft *pag.* 154. *& passim*: & *p.* 161. speaking of Christs sufferings [This threefold taking away of sins I clear from Scripture. 1. Christ taketh away our sins on the Cross *Causatively*, and by way of merit, whileas he suffereth for our sins on the Cross. So *Joh.* 1.29. 1 *Cor.* 5.21. 1 *Pet.* 2.24. *Isa.* 53.10. Now this was the paying of a ransom for us, and a Legal translation of the eternal punishment of our sins, but it is not Justification, nor ever called Justification: there is a sort of imputation of sin to Christ here, and a summe paid for me; but, with leave, No *formall imputation*, no forensicall, and no personal Law-reckoning to me who am not yet born, farre less cited before a Tribunal and absolved from sin: When Christ had compleatly paid this summe, Christ was justified Legally, as a publique person, and all his seed *Fundamentally, Meritoriously, Causatively*, but not in their persons. There is a second removal of sin, when the believer is justified by faith. This which is formally the Justification of the believing sinner, the Believers person is Accepted, Reconciled, Justified, and really translated by a *Law-change*, from one state to another.]

I have been the longer in reciting Mr *Rutherford's* words, 1. Because of themselves they suffice to confute your Opinion. 2. Because you so talk of [the Protestant Divines and Churches,] and yet of those few that you produce for you, it may appear what they judge of your Cause. 3. That your allegations may be understood hereafter by your Reader.

Your third Dr *Twiss*, and also *Maccovius*, I acknowledge are for you in the point now in question.

Mr. *Parker's* words imply no more then *Rutherfords*, viz. That in Christs Justification we were justified *causally*; but that is a term of diminution, as to the formal Justification; for till it be *extra causas* it doth not exist: and it is an improper use of the word Justification.

Cha-

Chamier I have oft noted to have some passages that make for your Opinion: but that he contradicteth them elsewhere, I think is not hard to manifest. I will not deny the truth for the credit of the man.

Calvin is so express and frequent against you as few men more. I came but now from citing some passages to that end against *Ludiomæus Colvinus*, and therefore will not now lose time in doing it again, when all men that will reade his Books may quickly finde that he was no friend to the Justification of Infidels. I marvell rather that you had not cited *Zuinglius*, who indeed is blamed for leaning that way, and called *Seneca* by such a Christian name (unless perhaps he was deceived by *Hierome*, as *Hierome* was by his counterfeit Epistle, and thought *Seneca* a believer indeed.) And you might have alleadged an inclination in *Erasmus* for you, who could scarce forbear saying, *Sancte Socrates ora pro nobis*. *Calvin's* words mean but this much (which you cite) that seeing God offereth Remission and we do but Accept it by faith, therefore God doing his part in offering it, he saith that *respectu Dei Justificatio fidem præcedit*, though we are not actually justified till after. For that offer is common to Infidels. In that very Discourse *Calvin* hath many passages against you: As *pag.* (*mihi fol.*) 390. *Nos autem meminerimus fidei naturam a Christo æstimandam esse: quia quod nobis offert Deus in Christo, non nisi fide recipimus. Proinde quicquid nobis est Christus id ad fidem transfertur, quæ nos compotes & Christi & omnium ejus bonorum facit. Neq; aliter veram esset illud Johannis, fidem nostram esse victoriam, qua mundus vincitur, nisi nos in Christum insereret qui solus est mundi victor.*]

Zanchy in the words cited by you useth inconvenient expressions, but that he is fully against you, is manifest in many places of his Writing. But I have newly Vindicated *Zanchy* from *Ludiomæus Colvinus*, who urgeth the same words as you do.

So I have done *Alstedius* too, and therefore shall say no more of him.

So also have I vindicated *Amesius* against the same *Colvinus*: and as for this testimony which you adde more then he, *viz. ex Antisynodal.* p. 164. his [*aliquo modo*] *in favorem restituti*, by which he there expoundeth reconciliation, is so stretching a word, as may well be yielded true: for it will let in as improper a reconciliation as yours: but yet *Amesius* will not use the word Justification so improperly, at least without discovering the impropriety.

§. 3.

THe next bout that you have with me is *pag.* 25. when you have done with Mr. *Burgess*. And you there fall on to some purpose, thus: " [Mr. *Baxter's* character of an Antinomian will bring all our Protestant Writers under " this censure.]

Repl. Still more falshood! Is the ninth Commandment blotted out of your Decalogue, as the second out of the Papists? Or think you that you are under no Law; or that God sees no iniquity in you, so as to hate it?

But let's hear your proof. " [For with him they are Antinomians who hold " (1.) That our Evangelical Righteousness is without us in Christ, or performed " by him and not by our selves.]

Repl. Here are more untruths then one in these words also. 1. I never said that they who denied this were Antinomians, but that it was a piece of Antino-

mian

mian doctrine, and that the Antinomians did deny it: Nay left any should think that I accounted all Antinomians that are offended at this; [I added [and some that are no Antinomians,&c. p. 109] I call not, all Antinomians, that hold, any one of their doctrines. 2. It is untrue that all our Protestant Writers are against this (as I have fully shewed elsewhere) yea or any one accounted Orthodox that ever I met with, as to the sense of my words: For though some of them will not allow the name of *Righteousness* to our faith and obedience (though the Scripture useth it twenty and twenty times I think) and others commonly will call it Righteousness, but will not say that we are righteous or justified by it. (A strange Righteousness that doth not make righteous *formaliter*, as it is a strange existent whiteness, that makes no man white, and a strange honesty or goodness, or nobility, that makes no man honest, good or noble:) yet do all the Protestants that ever I met with yield to my explicatory Proposition, which I purposely annexed, that none might mistake me and quarrell about words, *viz.* [Though Christ performed the conditions of the Law and satisfied for our *non*-performance, yet it is our selves that must perform the conditions of the Gospel,] *i. e.* by the grace of God. Who deny this but your own Sect, and a few Divines, that in that point joyn with you in making the new Covenant to have no Condition: who are but very few indeed comparatively. Nay, of the very Libertines, the first that I remember that taught men when they doubted of the truth of their faith or repentance, to comfort themselves with this perswasion, that Christ hath beleeved and repented for them, was *Saltmarsh*; against whom Mr. *Gataker* hath told you more truth then I perceive you are willing to learn. 3. Here is added to these open untruths a secret calumny: For you deliver it in general terms, as if I did hold that which Divines commonly call our Evangelical Righteousness to be in our selves and not in Christ. When as I purposely explained my self, to avoid all strife about words, that as Christs Righteousness is called Evangelical, because the Gospel revealeth and giveth it; so our righteousness Evangelical is without us. This you hide, to make the Reader that seeth but your words to think that I hold some monstrous thing. Be it known therefore to you and all men, That I trust on that Righteousness of Christ which is without me Materially, and formally consisteth in *my Right to Impunity and to the Kingdom of Glory*; and that I acknowledge no righteousness within me consisting in faith, repentance or obedience, but only A particular Righteousness required by the new Covenant in meer subordination to Christs Righteousness, as the condition on which it is made ours; which is first in order of nature a meer condition of our full righteousness in Christ, and then secondarily a particular Righteousness it self, when the Cause comes to trial, Whether we did perform that condition or not. If you do not understand these few words, I intreat you either to study them till you do, or else forbear any more to reproach that which you understand not: and do not intimate me to be an Infidel, in denying Christs Righteousness.

You proceed, "[Qu. 2.) that Justification is a free act of God without any "condition on our part for the obtaining of it.]

Rep. This is in sense the same with the former. Here also is more untruths then one intimated or expressed (I confess they fall so thick from you, that I doubt I shall be thought a railer by your party, and too sharp by others, for numbring them to you, and desiring you to repent.) 1. I only said that [the Antinomians think grace cannot be free if there be any condition on our part for enjoying it.] But doth it follow, that because I say, [the Antinomians say so] that therefore I

say

say [they are Antinomians who do say so.] The Papists say, Episcopacy is a superiour order to Presbytery: but [they are not therefore Papists that shall so say, unless there be somewhat else so to denominate them.] 2. Do not all the Learned men into whose hands your Book shall fall, know that it is false, that the Protestants do hold the opinion which I here call Antinomian? Do not the Confessions of the Churches, and the generality of Divines make faith the condition of the Covenant, and yet maintain it to be free? If you will speak untruths hereafter, for your credit sake, do it more modestly and warily, and open not your shame in the sight of the world. It were no great wisdom in me on this occasion to heap up the Testimonies of Churches and Divines, in a case so well known.

You adde, " [Or else (3.) that Justification is an immanent act, and con-
" sequently from eternity, which was the judgement of *Alsted, Pemble, Twiss,*
" *Rutherford,* &c.]

Rep. I think there are at least two untruths and a half here too. 1. Whether it were *Rutherford's* judgement, let the Reader judge by what is written out of him before. 2. Of *Alsted* I speak as afore I said against *Colvinus.* 3. It is half true of *Pemble,* in that he was once of that opinion, and but half true, because in his Treat. of *Justification* he fully asserteth ours. 4. What are these four men to all the Protestant Writers which you affirmed I would bring under this censure?

You adde, " [Or (4.) that we must not perform duty For life and salvation,
" but from life and salvation: or that we must not make the attaining of Justifi-
" cation or salvation the end of our endeavours, but obey in Thankfulness, and be-
" cause we *are* justified and saved, *&c.*]

Rep. 1. In the place quoted *pag.* 14. is no such thing in any of the four Editions of that Book. But I well remember the sense of most of it about p 10. or 11. and that I largely prove it in the Appendix of my *Aphor.* 2. But indeed dare you say, that all (or any) Protestant Writers do hold this Point? Now God forbid! If they did, I profess seriously I would scarce be called a Protestant if they held but that one Errour alone. Did not you know in this Point, that not only Learned men, but the ordinary sort of Christians can disprove you? I appeal to all honest men, women and children of understanding, that use to reade *Dod, Bolton, Perkins, Preston, Hooker, Rogers, Wheatly,* &c. What say you Sirs? Do these Writers teach you that you must use no endeavours for your salvation? that you must do nothing for eternal life? Nay do they teach you that the very unregenerate must do nothing to obtain the life of grace? 3. Truly I hoped well in the beginning that you had not been near so far gone your self, as to own this desperate opinion. The Lord keep you from practising it, or, I think, you are a lost man. 4. Yet let me tell you, that I further believe, 1 That thankfulness and Love should be the chiefest spring of duty. 2. Yea even with the unregenerate, our first labour should be when we have convinced them of sin and misery, and the truth of the Gospel, to possess them with thanks and love for that common redemption which I suppose you deny; I mean there is matter in Christs common love in his satisfaction, for us to plead with sinners for gratitude (before assurance of special love) though they have not hearts to perceive it to purpose, till God open their hearts by his Spirit. 3. The principle of our new spiritual life is it that Christians must act from, in their whole course. Thus far I say we must act from life and love. 4. And also, from Gods love antecedent to ours.

E   You

[20]

You conclude, "[Now let any man who is moderately versed in our Protestant Writers but speak on whom this Arrow fals: I might instance in many others, but I will not put the Reader to so much trouble.]"

Rep. Now let any man who hath read the ninth Commandment, and the words of Christ, *By their fruits ye shall know them*, judge 1. Whether it be not his duty to lament the sinfull state of this Brother, and to pray God to forgive him (though I know not whether he will pray so for himself.) 2. And to pity poor Christians that shall hear and reade the confident words of such men, and have not means to discern their vanity. 3. And judge whether that be not a bad opinion that can entangle even a godly man in such a course of sin: And whether we ought not all to take heed of believing that we were justified before we were born, or that we ought to do nothing for our own salvation; or that pardon is given without any condition, so much as Acceptance. For my part I impute these faults to the Opinion first, and to the man but as from thence. And it may be Gods will to permit him to practice according to the tendency of his Doctrine even in the Book wherein he maintaineth it, that those that cannot understand his errours in themselves, may see them in their effects.

---

§. 4.

THe next bout that you have with me you begin thus, *pag.* 29. "[He may if he will compare his doctrine with Mr *Baxter*'s notions (whom Mr. *W.* follows at the very heels) *Thes.* 56, 26, 73, &c. in his *Aph.* who denies, That Christs obedience is the material, the imputation of his Righteousness the formal cause of our Justification, or that faith is the instrument by which we do receive it.]"

Rep. What an unhappy name is mine to your mouth, that is seldom mentioned without sin! 1. I did not deny Christs obedience to be the material cause in the sense as Divines commonly so called it; and therefore not absolutely and without explication, as you recite it. But 1. As matter is proper to substance, so Justification being an accident hath no matter. Are not you of the same minde? 2. As accidents do inhere in the subject, so the subject is commonly called their matter: In this sense too our Righteousness or Justification passive is not in Christs Righteousness, but in our selves, and so our selves are the matter: for I think it is we that are justified. Nor do I believe yet that it is one act whereby Christ and we are justified. There is then no other proper matter of our Justification (the later being not properly so called it self.) 3. But yet as our Divines commonly call Christs Righteousness of satisfaction the matter of ours, because it is the matter that merited it, so am I well content to do, and so I willingly profess that our righteousness is materially out of us, in Christs satisfaction: and therefore I there said that they speak nearer the matter that call it [the matter of our Righteousness] then they that call it the matter of our active Justification.

2. Your next charge is that I deny Imputation to be the form. 1. I both grant it and deny it, as you understand the words. I did in that place take the word Imputation in one onely sense, for Donation, and so said, it was rather in order of nature before Justification, *i. e.* sentential: and so saith many another. 2. But I would desire you and all men to take notice that those two pages 218, 219.

I have

I have much altered, as finding the expressions unfit, and therefore do revoke them. And I say, 1. That Imputation is taken either for Donation or Adjudication, and that mentall, by meer estimation, or Judicial by sentence. 2. That Justification is Constitutive, or Sentential. And so I judge 1. That Imputation of Christs Righteousness taken for Donation is the form of constitutive Justification (Active Donation of Active Justification, and Passive Donation of Passive Justification.) 2. That sentential adjudication of Christs Righteousness to us, is the form of our sentential Justification. 3. And that after the manner of men, or by extrinsick denomination *à novitate objecti*, it may be said, that God doth impute righteousness to us by mental estimation or acceptation, or approbation, when he looks on us as then Righteous and not before, and therefore may be said then to begin so to esteem, accept or approve us, because before there was no object for an act of such denomination. And this may be called the form of a mentall Justification. So in all three senses I say that Imputation is the form of Justification, but not one sort of Imputation the form of another sort of Justification; which was all that I there meant to deny, but unfitly expressed my minde, as in some other places of that Book, for which I have ever since suppressed it.

3. How far I deny faith to be the instrument, I refer the Reader to my Reply to Mr. *Blake* and Mr. *Kendall*. You a little after could say, You thought I argued rationally in that when it fitted your turn.

You adde, " [He plainly ascribes the same kinde of Causality to Christ and " faith, making them to differ *Only secundum magis & minus*, that Christ is the *fine* " *qua non principalis*, and faith the *fine qua non minus principalis*.]

Rep. 1. More calumny and untruth. 1. I said [*Christs satisfaction*,] you say [Christ:] as if Christ caused no other way but by satisfaction. 2. The word [*Only*] is your notorious forgery. 3. I did in the same place expresly say that Christs satisfaction is the Meritorious Cause, and *fine qua non*, in several respects. 4. It was only in *sensu physico* that I called it *causa fine qua non* (and so do your best friends, in sense) but a moral cause, yea, of highest dignity I asserted it to be. 5. I affirmed that faith was no moral cause at all. And now let the Reader judge of your Veracity, and whether you recite not my words just as, you know who, is commonly said to have cited Scripture to Christ.

You adjoyn in a parenthesis, " [He might have lifted sin in the same rank, " which too, is a *fine qua non* of our Justification.]

Rep. 1. Every thing *sine qua non res existet*, is not *Causa sine qua non*. Though this have no true causality, yet it is a *medium ad finem*, and hath a tendency to the effect, by which it doth so far emulate causality that it receiveth the nature. But who ever called privation *Causam sine qua non*? and yet it is *Principium sine quo non*. Sin in being is the true cause of guilt: and guilt is the *materia removenda*, or the *Terminus a quo* of Justification, it being the very thing that remission doth destroy; even as life doth death, or light darkness. 2. What if you had spoke sense in this? yet what had it been to the strengthening of your accusation? Would you have your Reader believe that I make sin to be the meritorious cause of our Justification, or to have that Dignity in moral causation which I ascribed to the satisfaction of Christ?

Next you say, " [That faith and works in a larger sense are meritorious causes " of life and blessedness.]

Rep. Another false witness: I mentioned merit in a larger improper sense: (as

E 2 all

all Divines that ever I read against the Papists on that Point do), but never called them [a Meritorious cause] that I know of. Why would you print such things, which you knew might be discovered? It may be you will say, It is all one. I answer, 1. You should then have said that I speak to that sense, and not that I speak so: Nay you should have put down my own words, and left the Reader to judge of the sense, and not put your own sense on them, and then say, I speak so. 2. It is not all one. For in denying them to be properly Merit, I deny them to be any way causing by that Merit: therefore you feign me to yield to a further impropriety then I did, or else to false doctrine. 3. But will you go tell the world what is my Judgement, because I take the word *Merit* in the Fathers in a larger, improper sense? Christ called *Peter* Satan, for his carnal counsel: Will you determine thence that Christ judged *Peter* to be the devil? *David* was *a worm and no man* in improper sense: Must he needs be lasht by you for speaking false doctrine in so saying? Will you accuse Christ of Errour for saying, He is the Vine, and his Father the Husbandman? He is the Way, the Door, the Shepherd, &c? The word *Reward* is oft enough used in Scripture, and so is the word [*Worthy*], and yet you conclude they are both used improperly: And will you therefore say, that Christ was a Papist, or Socinian, or Erroneous, for using those words improperly? Having spoken so much to your Head, let me say this to your Heart: Brother, you engaged your self in Baptism to fight against the devil: your life is or should be a continual combat against him: How comes it to pass then that you have so learned his accusing art, when you should have learned of Christ to be *holy* and *to love your brother*, and to *speak the truth*? I do seriously advise you to repent of these waies, and to bethink you whether your opinions encourage you not hereto. If you reject this wholsom advice, take heed that it rise not up against you in Judgement, and if you proceed in such courses impenitently, take heed left those sins prove unpardoned hereafter, which you say were pardoned before you believed or repented or were born. Because I desire it may not be so, therefore do I warn you.

Pag. 30. you say, " [Too many of our Protestants (setting aside the word " Merit, which yet Mr *B.* thinks may be admitted) do tread directly in their steps; " they ascribe as much to works as Papists do.]

Rep. 1. It seems then other Protestants are as much Papists herein as I, in sense, though not in word. 2. Another slander you are guilty of (I say Guilty, for all you say its pardoned before committed.) Did ever I say [The word Merit may be admitted.] Shew where if you can. I said indeed that in that large improper sense, [Works may be called Merits,] thereby intending no *moral admission* of it: but only a *capacity in the term*, to signifie such a thing by improper use. But I never said that it is no sin in them that do use words so improperly, or that [it may be admitted.] For my part, I think the danger is so great, that the very use of the word is to be avoided by us, except in Interpretations of others, or with them that will use it whether we will or not; and so we must speak to men in their own language sometime, or say nothing. 3. Better men then you, or I, have used the word Merit, even the Church of Christ, the Councils and Fathers for 1400 years and more: And *Austin* that most eminently vindicated the glory of free grace, yet never disused this word himself. If I have sinned therefore but as all the Church hath done so long, and in its spring, I hope I am no Papist. 4. I would again have you and all men take notice how these Overdoing men are the greatest Undoers. How could this man credit Popery more almost then he doth? As bad

as

as I am (which is bad, I confess) yet if he could make all my neighbours believe that Papists be such as I, he would do more to make them Papists, then such arguings as this Book contains would undo. And I think some Rulers that now may be in the minde to deny Papists the liberty of their Religion, or at least of preaching to others, would grant them both, if they thought that the Religion of Papists were no worse then mine? So the argument would run thus; R. B. is a Papist: But he should have liberty: Therefore Papists should have liberty. But yet this is not that I aim at: But that he should place Popery in a thing which the Church hath used for so many hundred years, even as high as any Ecclesiastical History or Writing can give us light, is not this the way to make all turn Papists, and say, Hath Christ had no Church but Papists so long? then we will be Papists too: For sure the Head had still a Body. Well, when God will heal his Churches divisions, he will teach men moderation.

§. 5.

THe next assault I meet with, is p. 50, 51. [§. 5. "Some of our late Divines (who "seem to disclaim the doctrine of the Papists and Arminians) say the very "same; who explain themselves to this effect. That faith doth justifie as a Con- "dition, or antecedent qualification, by which we are made capable of being Ju- "stified, according to the order and Constitution of God: The fulfilling of which "Condition say they is our Evangelicall Righteousness, whereby we are justified "in the sight of God. Mr. Baxter is so fond of this notion, that although in one "place he findes fault with the length of our Creeds and Confessions, yet he would "have this made an Article of the Creed, a part of our Childrens Catechismes, "and to be believed by every man that is a Christian, so apt are we to smile upon "our own babes.]

Rep. More of the old language still: 1. Is this [the very same] as the Papists and Arminians hold, which you say it is the *very same* with, viz. [that God for Christs sake accounts our imperfect faith, to be perfect Righteousness? You know *they* take not [perfect Righteousness] for Righteousness only that hath a formall Metaphysicall perfection of Entity as I do. You say [Their opinion is, that God in the Covenant of Grace requires faith which in his gracious Acceptation stands in stead of that obedience to the Morall Law which we ought to perform:] But I say that Christs satisfaction is instead of that obedience, in that it is in stead of our suffering for disobedience. You credit the Papists and Arminians still, if you can prove that their opinion is the very same with this. Do they renounce Merit? and do not our Divines generally make that the point of our difference about Justification by Works? viz. Whether the merit of Good Works justifie? which I heartily and constantly deny.

2. I have told you before, that I say, that we are no otherwise justified by the Evangelicall Righteousness in question, then in necessary subordination to Christs own Righteousness, as the Condition of our Legal title to it, of his own appointing. This you conceal.

3. It is another fiction, that it is this *Notion* that I would have an Article of the Creed (if you mean the *Notiones secundæ*, yea or the *primæ* directly.) For I told you that I spoke of the Matter and not the phrase: It is the substance of the doctrine, viz. That we must *beleeve* our selves, and not think we may be excused, as

E 3 having

having a Saviour that hath beleeved in himself for us.

4. For my part as I am confident it is implied in the Creed, so it shall be my Creed while I breathe, by the grace of God. And I think Christ put it into the Creed if ever he made a Creed: sure it is the summe or principall heads of the Gospell which he sent his Disciples to preach to the world, and I think that is part of the Creed: and what that was is evident, *Mar.*16.16. *He that Beleeveth and is baptized shall be saved, and he that beleeveth not shall be damned.* And it was the Creed that was taught them before baptisme: and that was, *Repent and Beleeve for remission of sins.*

You add [" Though I honour Mr. *Baxter* for his excellent parts, yet I must " suspend my Assent to his new Creed.]

Rep. 1. No newer then the Scripture, nay elder then Scripture, for it is as old as the Covenant of Grace. 2. I had rather be without your Honour, then you should be without the Truth: not that I much care whether you be of my opinion, as such; but that I care for your salvation. But my hope is, that though you take not faith to be a Condition of Salvation, yet you do Beleeve on other Grounds; and if you have that which is the Condition, I doubt not but you may be saved, though you know it not to be the Condition: And if you think you may not Endeavour for salvation, yet if you *do endeavour it,* and *act for it* while you say the contrary that it may not be done, I doubt not of your safety, because you hold that Practically which you deny speculatively. But I must tell you, that he that thinks, though but speculatively, that he *ought not to do it,* is in great danger of being drawn to omit it.

You proceed [" I shall prove anon that faith is not said to justifie as an Ante-
" cedent Condition, which qualifies us for Justification: but at present I shall on-
" ly render him the reasons of my disbelief, why I cannot look upon faith as that
" Evangelicall Righteousnefs, by which we are justified. I shall not insist upon it,
" though it be not altogether unconsiderable, that this notion is Guilty of too
" much confederacy with the forenamed enemies of the Christian faith: For
" though it is no good argument to say, that Papists, Socinians, &c. do hold this
" or that, therefore it is not true; yet it will follow that such and such Tenets have
" been held by Papists, &c. and unanimously opposed by our Protestant writers;
" therefore they ought to be the more suspected, and especially such tenets of theirs,
" as have been the chief points in difference between us and them, as this is.]

Rep. 1. I shall as readily suspect such points as bear your description, as you. 2. It is untrue that this is such, *quoad terminos,* much more *quoad sensum.* All our Divines maintain an Inherent Righteousnefs, and in the same sense as they (so far as I understand them of chief note) do deny them to justifie us, I deny it too.

You add [" Our Brethren that have started this Notion, do take faith as the
" others do, in a proper sense, they attribute as much to the τὸ *credere,* as *Bellar-*
" *mine, Arminius,* or any other. Faith it self (saith Mr. *B.*) is our Righteousnefs:
" There was never any Papist so absurd as to say, that our Faith, Love, &c. are
" perfect legall Righteousnefs; but that God *judicio misericordiæ, non justitiæ,* doth
" account and accept of it instead of perfect righteousnefs. For my part I must
" confess that I can see no difference between them but in expressions. The Pa-
" pists do acknowledge the satisfaction of Christ, and that he is the meritorious
" Cause of our Justification. They say indeed that we are not justified by the
" Righteousnefs of Christ Imputed, but by a Righteousnefs inherent in us, or
" righ-

[25]

righteous actions performed by us. And what do our Brethren say less then this? But I shall follow this parallell no further.

Rep. 1. What do they say less then this, who maintain Imputed Righteousness, *viz.* less then those that deny it ? I'le put another question upon this of yours: Whether a Question can be false ? A Logician will say, It cannot be false; and yet a Divine will say, It may be *mendacium*; and yet both say true : Is not that strange ! 2. I desire the Reader to excuse me from the trouble of enumerating all the untruths in these lines (for I am aweary of that work, and its to little profit,) and to expect my full satisfaction to this Parallell, in my Reply to Mr. *Crandon*(if God will,) where I shall shew him whether I be a Papist or an Arminian : and whether his tongue and his brothers be any slander.

You proceed [§.6. " The Reasons which turn the scales of my judgment " against this Notion, that our faith or faithfull actions, are that Evangelicall " Righteousness,by which we are justified,Are]

Rep. Before I weigh your Reasons, I will do the Reader that favour which you deny him, *viz.* To let him know a little better the state of the Question, and what it is that I maintain.

Understand therefore Reader,that I hold these Conclusions (which I shall fullier open, God willing, in Reply to Mr.*Crandon.*) 1. That Gods Universall Law of Nature requireth of us perfect Obedience, on Pain of eternall death if we perform it not. 2. We all sinned, and so were liable to that Death. 3. Christ became the Mediator, and stept between us and the full execution, and took the penalty upon himself, and became a sacrifice to offended Justice, and a Ransome for the sinners. 4. Upon this he acquired *Novum Jus Dominii & Novum Jus Imperii* over all men ; being now the Soveraign of the world as Redeemer, as superadded to the former Dominion and Soveraignty w'ich the Father, Son and holy Ghost had as Creator. 5. As Christ the Anointed and Soveraign Redeemer, he made *Legem Remediantem*, An Act of Oblivion, A new Law, *viz.* A Law of Grace ; thereby Granting free pardon, Justification, Adoption, and right to Glory to all that will sincerely Repent and Beleeve in him ; and Peremptorily Concluding those to everlasting death that will not. 6. This Repenting and Beleeving is nothing but Assenting so heartily to the Truth of the Gospel, a thereupon to Accept the Lord Jesus Christ and Life in him,as he is offered, *viz.* As a pardoner by Gratefull Consent and Confidence, as Good to us, by Love ; as Soveraign by giving up our selves to him for Guidance, and to take him for the Physition of our souls, to rest on him, and apply his sharpest plaisters and take his bitterest medicines, and which are most ungratefull to flesh and blood (and not to beleeve that the cure is done already :) and, as a *free gift* we must accept this Grace, with confession of our own utter undeserving, and our desert of eternal wrath, and therefore with *Repentance* to the glory of him that *freely* saveth us : and lastly, as he is the Purchaser, Giver, and Conductor to the *unseen* everlasting Glory, which is the great End for which we do receive him ; without respect to which End, faith were no saving faith. 6. Remission and Justification by Christs Satisfaction and Merit, being given us by a New Law, which hath its Precepts and Penalty, we are obliged by this Law to perform these Conditions, and shall be judged by this Law, whether we have performed them or no. In which judgement,he that is accused not to have performed them, *i. e.* to be an unbeliever and Rebel against the Lord Redeemer, must plead his own actual performance, and deny the accusation. And therefore that performance is the *Justitia causa*, the righteousness of

that

that his cause, and of his person so farre. 7. In respect to this personal New Covenant Righteousness, the Scripture doth twenty times, if not twenty more, ca'l men Righteous: yea even in the description of the Judgement; *Mat. 25. last.* 8. As this New Law is but *Lex particularis Remedians,* properly subordinate to the Law of Nature, so this personal Righteousness, is not our *Justitia universalis,* but a particular Righteousness, subordinate to the Righteousness of the Lord Jesus. 9. There being therefore a twofold Justification or Righteousness, principal and subordinate, one which answers the Law of nature, the other which answers the false charge of not performing the condition of the Law of Grace, one in Christs Satisfaction and Merit, the other in our faith and repentance, one consisting in the Pardon of all our sin and the Right to Impunity and the Kingdom; the other in our having the true condition of pardon and right; It follows that when the question is of Justification in the first sense, and of the matter (as we call it) of that Justification, *i.e.* the thing for which we are justified meritoriously, that we must then conclude that it is only Chrifts Righteousness that is our Justification or our Righteousness; and that faith or repentance is not the least part of it: But if the Question be only of the meer subordinate Righteousness and Justification, then we must say that our own faith and repentance, and not Christs Satisfaction is that Righteousness: For it is a debasing of Christs Righteousness, to bring it so low; and it is no other exalting of faith then God hath in his Covenant exalted it, to raise it so high, as to be thus subordinate to Christs Righteousness, that it may become ours. 10. In regard of the first great Justification of a sinner consisting in Remission of sin (*constitutivè*) and sentential absolving him from guilt, Faith or any work of mans is but the condition *sine qua non,* and not the least part of that Righteousness (as is said) But in regard of that subordinate Justification which is but a means to the former, faith and repentance are our Righteousness it self, so that faith is first in order of nature but a condition; but secondarily, when the case at Judgement is, Whether we have performed that condition or not, then consequentially it is our subordinate particular Righteousness. 11. No man can perform this condition without Gods special grace. 12. It was the intent and absolute Will, yea and undertaking of Christ dying, to cause all the Elect of God infallibly to perform this condition. Thus Reader I have anticipated some part of what I intended to say in my Answer to Mr *Crandon,* as being unwilling to delay thy information, or be guilty of the continuance of thy prejudice against the truth. I confess I have lately received Animadversions from Learned men, against the thing here laid down, *viz.* a personal Righteousness; but Gods Word is so plain and mens reasons against it in my eyes so weak, that I am more then ever confirmed in it. I equally hate vain distinction and confusion: But to distinguish between the Law of nature, and the Law of grace, between Christs Righteousness imputed, and the condition of Imputation, and so between our primary Righteousness and our subordinate Righteousness, I think are no vain distinctions. Let's make it plain by a similitude. In a time of Rebellion, upon the Princes intercession and satisfaction, An Act of grace is granted, that whoever will acknowledge the Princes favour and the Kings, and Accept a pardon, shall be forgiven and shall not die. Is it not one thing here to accuse a man as a Traytor, and another thing to accuse him of not accepting the pardon? and are not these two causes referring to two Laws? yet one subordinate to the other, and not coordinate. When he is accused of Treason, he is justified by the Act of Grace: and this is his *Titulus ad Liberationem.* But when

when it is but one Traytor of many that Accepteth the Act of Grace, and he is accused of *non-acceptance*, and the case to be decided fals to be this, Whether the Act of Grace give that man any Right to Impunity? then because it was a conditional act, he must be here justified by pleading that he did perform the condition. And so that Justification which is but subordinate, and in order of dignity but secondary, as a means to the former, is yet in order of Plea at Judgement to go before it, as the means must be before the end.

If thou be unprejudiced, Reader, and lovest the truth, I should think that I need not say much to Mr *Eyre*'s Arguments, having given thee in these Conclusions, so clear a ground of answering them all; But I shall briefly take an account of them, and so return to Mr *Eyre*. Who thus begins.

" [1. If we are not justified by our own works, then our beleeving, &c. is not
" that Evangelical righteousness by which we are justified: But we are not justi-
" fied by our own works: Therefore.]

Rep. Distinguish of works, and distinguish of justifying. 1. That Justification which consisteth in remission of sin, is not in our own faith; but that which consisteth in performing the condition of remission is. 2. Works are taken either as *Paul* doth (which he describeth Rom. 4. 4. *Which make the reward to be not of grace but of debt:* Or as *James* doth, in necessary subordination to Christ. In the former sense I deny your consequence; In the later sense I deny your minor or antecedent. And if you say that *Paul* supposeth that All works do make the reward to be of debt; I answer, 1. Then *James* saith we are justified by impossibility, or by unlawfull waies. The works that *James* mentions are possible and lawfull: works that make the reward to be of debt are impossible, and the attempt of such unlawfull: Therefore there are some works which do not make the reward to be of debt. 2. The same *Paul* that saith we are justified by Christ, saith oft enough that we are justified by faith, and that faith is and shall be imputed to us for Righteousness.

2. *Paul* takes works for Meritorious actions deserving wages. Faith is no such work; therefore on that ground still I deny your consequence.

3. You must distinguish of the word [by] when you say, We are, or are not justified [by] faith. Its one thing to be justified [by] faith, as the matter of our Righteousness. So we deny it, as to our great principal Justification. And its another thing to be justified [by] faith as a meerly subordinate condition *fine qua non*: and so *Paul* still includeth it as plain as a man can speak. Still saying, We are justified by faith. This answers fully the Texts cited by you: and is another answer then that of the Papists to which you here Reply. Yet, to your answers to the last, (that *Others say, It is not works of the Law, but Gospel.*) I must give you these brief Notes (supposing that the words you answer are none of mine till better explained, limited and reformed.)

To your first, I say, *distinguit Lex. Paul* and *James* else will hardly be reconciled: Yea *Paul* himself distinguisheth, by punctual expressing the works of the Law, or telling you he means only works that make *the reward to be not of grace but of debt*; and taking in faith as that by which we are justified.

To your second, you speak very darkly and dangerously: and against you I return. If *Paul* exclude all Debt which follows upon promise, then he excludes all that follows upon an absolute promise, as well as upon a conditional: But the Consequent is false, therefore so is the Antecedent. The reason of the consequence is clear. Either you mean that this is [From the promise as a promise] or

F   else

else [From the promise as conditional.] If the former, then it follows an absolute promise as much as a conditional; and then you must deny all Gods promises, and then you will be against the Gospel indeed. If the later, then I say, That the promise *qua* conditional, gives no right; distinguish of conditions: Some are of such value as to be Meritorious: these cause the debt by Merit: Others have no meriting value (as the acceptance of a free gift:) these are no causes so much as Moral, but meer conditions. And whoever knows what a condition in Law-sense is, knows that as such, it only suspends the act of a Testament or other gift, till it be performed, but doth not cause it, when it is performed.

To your third, it is answered already.

To your fourth, see my answer to Mr *Blake*. Also, The Gospel is a subordinate Law, and the matter of its precept is taken out of the general Law of nature: but informed with a new promise. *Adams* body was earth; but yet to be distinguished from common earth, and worthy of another name, when it was informed with a new form, even his soul. I doubt you will not apprehend well what these short expressions contain, unless you will please to consider and digest them.

To your fifth *Paulus Burgensis*, a Christian Jew, on *Fam. add. ad* Lyrani *Annot.* tels us that his Countreymens opinion was, that God denominated a man righteous or wicked according to the greater part of his works. If he had more good works then bad, he was Righteous: else not. The Jews did not think to be justified by perfect unsinning obedience: for they were to confess sin, and sacrifice for it. But they thought that their sacrifices themselves and their good works might so procure the pardon of their sins, or prevail against their evil works, that they looked not for righteousness to Christ the end of the Law. This is the Justification by works which *Paul* argues against directly; and only consequentially *à fortiore* we may gather it, as of perfect obedience, which is to us impossible, as it may be supposed to justifie us from the charge [of being sinners.] Yet because their obedience was not perfect, *Paul* might well convince them that it could not justifie when they erred in thinking, that imperfect obedience, by the help of sacrifices, might justifie.

2. Your second Argument is this, " [-2. If the righteousness whereby we are " justified be a perfect Righteousnes, then we are not justified by our obedience " to Gospel precepts: But, *&c.* Therefore.]

This is answered in the former, by the same distinctions. The righteousnes whereby we are justified as [by the Matter, or Meritorious cause] is perfect: and therefore faith or obedience is not such. But the righteousness whereby we are justified as a meer condition, and consequentially a righteousnes, subordinate to the former, is not perfect; and therefore of this your consequence fails. All your following words therefore to this, are meerly beside the Point and vain. I never doubted of that, Whether any imperfect thing can be our universal grand Righteousnes? no doubt it cannot: But you should prove that it cannot be a subordinate conditional particular Righteousnes.

You do here confess that our Protestant Divines do call inherent Holiness, Evangelical Righteousness: Very good: I desire no more then those words contain: Yet I pray you confess that the Scripture commonly cals it so before them. 1. Certainly *justum fieri & justificari*, as to constitutive Justification is all one. He therefore that is righteous is doubtless justified *constitutivè*. And doubtless to be sentenced Just, and to be justified by sentence, is all one. And he that is first just by constitution, must needs be justified by sentence. But then all this is but *in tantum:*

so

so far as he is juſt, ſo far he is undoubtedly *juſtificatus conſtitutivè, & juſtificandus per ſententiam*; and (as I ſaid before) is it not as ſtrange a righteouſneſs which makes not a man righteous *in tantum*, (I ſpeak of a formal Making) as a Whiteneſs that makes not white, or a *Paternitas* that makes not *Patrem*? 2. Do not all men know that (as Mr *Bradſhaw* ſaith) a very reprobate may have ſome particular righteouſneſs? If you accuſe *Judas* of killing the man that was ſlain yeſterday, he is righteous as to this cauſe. Why then ſhould you think the name of Righteouſneſs ſo intollerable, when applied to faith and obedience.

O but (ſaith a Learned man to me) then you aſcribe but ſuch a kinde of righteouſneſs to faith and obedience, as a reprobate may have? that's a fair advancement to faith. *Anſ*. 1. Methinks then you ſhould not ſay I am a Papiſt, and give too much to faith? 2. But conſider, though both may have a *juſtitiam particularem*, yet to one it is in a caſe of no advantage to him: but in the other it is A condition of his eternal felicity, and ſo made by the Law of God. When ſalvation lies on one as a condition, and not on the other, I think there is much difference.

Now to your third Argument where you ſay, " [If the righteouſneſs whereby " we are juſtified be the righteouſneſs of God, then we are not juſtified by our " obedience to Goſpel-precepts: But, &c. Therefore.]

Rep. All is of Gods gift. But in your ſenſe I ſay, Our ſubordinate particular conditional Righteouſneſs, is not the Righteouſneſs performed by God without us: The word [by] therefore, and [juſtified] and [Righteouſneſs] muſt be diſtinguiſhed as before. All the reſt of your words on this need no other anſwer, and I deſire not to tire the Reader. The righteouſneſs mentioned *Mat*. 25. was perſonal: ſo was that which *James* ſpeaks of when he ſaith, *We are juſtified by works*: and that which *John* mentions, when he ſaith, *He that doth Righteouſneſs is Righteous*: and fourty more.

Your fourth Argument is this, " [If we are not juſtified by two righteouſneſ-" ſes exiſting in two diſtinct ſubjects, then our obedience to Goſpel-precepts is " not that righteouſneſs whereby we are juſtified: But, &c. Therefore.]

Rep. 1. To the Antecedent I ſay, of two coordinate righteouſneſſes it is true; but of two, whereof one is coordinate and the other ſubordinate, it is falſe, that there is not two. 2. But formally they are both in one ſubject: for it is We that are Righteous by Chriſts Righteouſneſs: that is, by that which is Chriſts materially, and in another numericall form; for ſurely one Accident is not in two ſubjects. But I ſay, Materially one is in Chriſt, and the other in us.

And here I remember an odd paſſage that you have, *pag*. 7. which I ſhall recite, " [It doth not follow that Chriſts Righteouſneſs cannot be imputed to us, before " we have an actual created being, becauſe Accidents cannot ſubſiſt without their " ſubjects: for as much as imputed righteouſneſs is not an accident inherent in us, " and conſequently doth not neceſſarily require our exiſtence. Chriſt is the ſubject " of this Righteouſneſs, and the imputation of it as an act of God.]

Rep. Hear all you that have been ſeduced by Mr *Eyre* to believe that man was juſtified before he was born: Here he explaineth his minde to you. He ſaid [*man*] but he meant [*Chriſt*.] If it be not we but Chriſt that is the ſubject, then doubtleſs it is not *we* but *Chriſt* that hath the Accident, and that is to be denominated by it: And then it is Chriſt that was righteous before we were born, and not we. Or elſe Chriſt makes us righteous, and yet we are not Righteous, or we are righteous and not righteous at once (even when we are not men) and that in reſpect of the ſame righteouſneſs. When I reade ſuch paſſages as theſe, I underſtand the

meaning

meaning of your Patrons, that wonder men should seek to bring Gods Truths down to the reason of man: i.e. we must become bruits that we may become Christians (a horrid thing to speak;) and we must put out the eye of reason, that we may see with faith, which is the only supernatural elevation of reason.

But you have an Argument *pag.* 57. to prove the assumption of your last, *viz.* " [If by Christs righteousness alone we are made perfectly just and righteous in " the sight of God, then there is no other righteousness which concurres with his " to our Justification: For what needs an addition to that which is perfect? But *&c.* Therefore.] All is granted, if you speak of the matter or form of our principal Righteousness; The addition of a condition is through no defect or imperfection in it: but God hath made it necessary to our participation of that which was not done by our selves but by another. It is not true that we are made righteous by Christs Righteousness till the condition be performed: but when it is performed, we are justified perfectly by Christs Righteousness alone, as to the principal general Justification; the condition performed being but a subservient particular Righteousness. I would you would well consider, that Christ died to pardon nothing but our sinnes, and that he that hath nothing but sinne, is not pardoned.

You adde, " [If we be justified partly by Christs Righteousness and partly by " our own, then our faith for Justification must rely partly upon Christs Righte- " ousness and partly upon our selves: But *&c.* Therefore.].

Rep: I deny the Consequence. It is the relying on Christ that is our subordinate righteousness it self; and therefore is such because it is made the condition of our part in Christ: They are not coordinate, nor is faith our principal Righteousness, but of a lower sort. God hath said, that if by faith we receive Christ, we shall be justified, and our faith shall be imputed to us for righteousness: but he hath never said, If we will rest on our own faith, we shall be righteous: For then resting on that faith would be a third sort of righteousness subordinate to faith it self. These be but raw fancies.

Your fifth Argument is, " [That which overthrows the main difference be- " tween the Law and the Gospel, ought not to be admitted: for the confounding " them will open an inlet to innumerable errours; nay by this means the Gospel " it self will become a meer Cypher,*&c.* But the making our obedience to Gospel " precepts the righteousness whereby we are justified, overthrows the main diffe- " rence between the Law and the Gospel: Therefore. For herein stands the chief " agreement and difference between the Law and Gospel: They agree in this, " That to Justification both do require the perfect fulfilling of the Law: but " herein they differ, That the Law requireth to Justification, a righteousness in- " herent in us, and perfect obedience to be performed in our own persons: The " Gospel reveals for our Justification the perfect righteousness of another, even of " Christ, which is accepted in their behalf that do *beleeve* in him,*&c.*]

Rep. These words which you cite out of Bishop *Downham*, say as I say in full sense; and say nothing to confirm your *minor*, which I deny, if you speak but of a subordinate particular righteousness: else I grant all. Do I say that we are justified by perfect obedience, which *Downham* speaks of? yea or by any in coordination with Christ? If you understood the difference your self between the Law and Gospel, you would correct all these errours, and be a wiser man then I think either you or I are now. I pray you do me the favour as to consult but Mr. *Pemble* of Justification, in the place cited even now (seeing you suppose him to be your own,

own, but it seems disclaimed you a little before he went to heaven) and see how he differenceth the Law and the Gospel.

You say; " [A defect in degrees is a sin against the Gospel, &c.]

Rep. It is not a *non*-performance of the Gospel condition, and then it is no hinderance to our Justification by it. Some Learned men have much boasted of that Argument [*Obedience is it self imperfect, and therefore cannot be the condition of our Justification (as consummate at Judgement, or continued) for then what shall pardon the defects of it.*] As if imperfect obedience might not be the condition of the pardon of its own imperfections (subordinate to faith, as is said :) May not an imperfect faith be the condition of the pardon of its own imperfections?

But to Mr. *Eyre,* who having done with me, addes, " [Now briefly my sense " of this Proposition, [*We are justified by faith*] is no other then that which hath " been given by all our ancient Protestant Divines, who take faith herein obje- " ctively, not properly, *&c.*]

Rep. Our Divines take faith objectively, when the matter of our righteousness is spoken of; but how ? Only by connotation of the object; and not by exclusion of faith it self : as if the word [*faith*] signified Christ. Else you would fasten a strange sense on *Paul,* when it is said [*If we believe it shall be imputed to us also,*] doth the word believe stand for the word [*Christ ?*] But this our Divines have so fully confuted, that I will say no more to it but this, That if by [*believing*] be not meant [Believing] but [*Christ*] when it is so many and many times rehearsed, 1. Scripture is made the most useless unintelligible writing in the world, when no man can know the sense by the words a hundred times repeated. For your saying that *Paul* by [faith] means not *faith,* is no evidence to convince me. O how glad are the Papists of such expositions as yours, that may convince men that none can understand the Scripture without a Judge of its sense. 2. And then, why might it not as well be said that a man is justified by seeing Christ, or hearing him, or hearing of him, or any other act, as well as Believing, if it be not Beleeving that is meant; where it is spoken ? But I will not anticipate Mr. *Woodbridge* in his work.

---

§. 6.

THe next assault that I meet with is *pag.* 90. 91. where you say, " [Mr. *B.* " (*Thes.*70.) includes all works of obedience to Evangelical precepts in the " definition of faith, in which sense I presume no Papist will deny that we are " justified by faith alone, taking it as he doth for *fides formata,* or faith animated " with charity and other Good works.]

Rep. Here is at least one untruth expressed, and another implied. 1. There is no mention in those words of mine of obedience to all Evangelical precepts : but only of that sincere obedience which is made by God the condition of salvation. Now obedience may be sincere, and yet not be to all precepts which are in the Gospel : Many a lesser particular duty may be unknown to one that obeys sincerely : Mr. *Eyre* is bound by the Gospel to believe that faith goes before Justification, and yet he knows not this: may he not for all that obey sincerely ? The Gospel requireth Baptism; and I think of Infants; yet it will not follow that no man is sincerely obedient that is unbaptized, as mistaking it to be now no duty, or that is against Infant-Baptism, on the like mistake.

F 3   2. You

2. You intimate that it is our first justifying faith, or faith strictly taken that I here describe; and so adde your parallell of the Papists. But honesty required you to have confessed on the contrary, that I had before spoke of faith in the proper strict sense, as it is the condition upon which every man receiveth the remission of all the sins past of his whole life, and that Justification *quoad statum*, which some call universal Justification, as distinct from particular Justification and Remission following upon every new sin: and that in the words which you cite I only described faith in a more large improper sense, and as it is the condition only of our glorification, and final Justification in the great Judgement. Why should you conceal this, and imply the contrary?

§. 7.

THe next touch that I finde is *pag.* 94. where you tell Mr. *W.* " [2. If faith " were a condition morally disposing us for Justification, we should then be " concurrent causes with the Merits of Christ in procuring our Justification: for " the Merits of Christ are not a Physical but a moral cause, which obtain their " effect by vertue of that Covenant which was made between him and the Father: " now by ascribing unto faith a moral causal influx in our Justification, we do clear-" ly put it *in eodem genere causæ* with the blood of Christ: which I hope Mr. *W.* " will better consider of, before he engage too far in Mr. *Baxters* cause.]

Rep. Because you are pleased to make it my cause, I will be bold to give my Reply. There are very palpable errors delivered with confidence in these words.
1. You confound moral *Disposing*, and moral *Causing*: All *disposing* is not *causing*.
2. You most falsly suppose that we ascribe to faith [a moral causal influx in Justification:] and do nothing to prove it.
3. All is grounded on that gross Error, That [all Civil or Legal conditions, are Moral causes,] which is so farre from truth that the clean contrary is true. [No Civil or Legal condition, *qua talis*, is a moral cause.] 1. A condition only while unperformed suspendeth the act of the Law or Testament, that is, It was the Will of the Legislator or Testator, or Donor, that his Law, Testament,&c. should act, or effect when the condition is performed, and not before: but not that it should be any cause: no more then *quando venit dies* the time is a cause. 2. A condition is but *causa sine qua non*; therefore it is no moral cause. Yet its true that among men, most conditions in another respect are moral causes; but none of them, *as conditions.* Men use to make somewhat a condition (though not alway) which is of worth to themselves, and so hath somewhat in the nature of the thing which is meritorious (when the condition is not casual, but Potestative or mixt:) and this is a moral cause, not as it is a condition, but as meritorious. Would you have the world believe, without better manifestation, that you are so excellent a Lawyer, that we must take your word against common sense, and the common judgement of men that should be wiser in their own profession? You know sure that its common in the Civil Law to have cases of such casual conditions, as cannot be causall? As [if such a Ship come into such a Harbour, such a day] being nothing to the Donors advantage. [If such a son live to such an age, he shall have such Lands.] [If the arrow that is shot up, fall within such a space.] And the like is true in Potestative conditions (as they call them) that is, voluntary: [I give thee a pardon on condition thou wilt accept it: or not refuse it: or not ungratefully

gratefully abuse me when I have given it thee: not spit in my face: not seek my life, ruine, dishonour, &c.] None of these are Meritorious, and therefore none of them causal.

4. Have you never observed that your friend Dr *Twiss* doth not once or twice, but ordinarily, affirm that faith is a condition and *medium* of our Justification, and that Good works are *causa dispositiva*, and *praeparatoria salutis*? I may tell you more of his minde hereafter.

One thing more in this Section I desire your resolution of. You here say, that [the Merits of Christ are not a Physical but a Moral cause:] upon which I would know; 1. Do not you take as much from it as I, and make the Merits of Christ as much a *causa sine qua non in sensu physico*, as I? For what can you do more then say it is no Physical cause at all? And with what justice or modesty then could you before pretend that I am worse in this very point then the Papists themselves, when I am no worse then you? A moral causality I allow it, as well as you.

Nay secondly give me leave to enquire whether in deed and truth you do allow it a moral causality of our Justification at all: In your *pag.* 66. you answer a shrewd Objection, which would prove you near to infidelity, *viz.* " [That " you make void the Death of Christ: for if Justification be an immanent " act in God, it is antecedent not only to faith, but to the Merits of Christ, " which is contrary to many Scriptures, that do ascribe our Justification to his " blood, as to a meritorious cause.] To which you Answer, [That although " Gods will not to punish be antecedent to the death of Christ; yet for all we may " be said to be justified in him, because the whole effect of that Will is by and " for the sake of Christ. As though electing love precede the consideration of " Christ, *Joh.*3.16. yet are we said to be chosen in him, *Eph.*2.4. because all " the effects of that Love, are given by and through and for him. Gods *not* " *punishing* us, is the fruits of his death: yet his Will not to punish, is antece- " dent thereunto.

Rep. This distinction of *Actus volentis*, and *res volita*, we have oft here on such occasions. But 1. Do not you here make our active Justification to be no fruit of Christs Merits at all, but only our passive? Now if you would publish this doctrine nakedly, That *Justificatio justificans*, or Gods active Justification, is not at all procured by Christ, it would be more candid and open dealing, then you use while you pretend so much to exalt Christs Merit, in your denying the parts or interest of faith and obedience.

2. Surely then we must finde out another Active Justification, whereof Christs Merits are the cause, as well as of the passive, if we will be ruled by Scripture; and this your Brethren have done, for which you oppose them.

3. I would commend it to your consideration, Whether it be not a work worth your labour, the next time you set upon these imployments, to open to us like a Philosopher and Divine, how and in what sense and respect it is, that the Merits of Christ can cause the effect and not the act? the *rem Volitam*, and not the *actum Volendi*? And how Christs Merits can be a moral cause, or a meriting cause, and yet not cause the act of God? Merit you know is reckoned among the remote efficients of our pardon and sanctification and salvation. Now if God be the nearer efficient, how can Merit which is the remote, cause these effects, and not cause Gods act? I would intreat you to answer it, as to all these effects, even Sanctification and Glorification as well as pardon. You know also, I suppose, that Merit

is

is accounted one of the Procatarctical less-principal efficients: Now the nature of this cause is to incite the principal cause *ad agendum* extrinsically. And Merit is said to be that which moveth the agent *ad talionem reddendam*. Now if Christs Merits move not God as a Procatarctical cause, then how are they truly meritorious causes? You know also, I doubt not, that A *moral causing* in such cases as ours about voluntary Agents, doth consist in an argumentative, objective, or the like moral moving of the Agent. Now how can Christs Merits be moral causes here, and work nothing upon God the principal Cause? when this moral cause is a remote cause, and a remote cause produceth the effect *media causa propinquiore?* I do not hereby conclude my self that Gods Will was moved by Christs Merits: but there is another wedge then yours by which we must cleave this knotty block; which if I tell you of, its like you will be prejudiced against it, because it is from me; but if you will study to expedite the business your self a little better then here you have done, it may reduce you to a better minde in the main. But if it should prove upon these considerations, that you do contradict your self, and do indeed deny Christ to be any cause, so much as Moral and Meritorious of Justification active or passive, of the *Actus volentis* or *Res volita*, then I think you have been an unhappy exalter of Christ, while your zeal carried you against the interest of faith.

And methinks it should be scarce savoury to a friend of Christ and an exalter of his Merits, to have them made no more a cause of our Justification, then of our Election; that is, of the effects of both which are in time, but of neither of themselves which are from eternity.

And I take it but for private Theology that [all the effects of electing love are given by, through and for Christ.] Whereby you plainly intimate him to be the *meritorious* cause of the *effects*, which you deny of the *Act*. But, 1. the giving of Christ himself is no small effect of electing love, and yet not given for and through himself. Christ was not given to Merit, for the sake of his Merit, as any efficient cause. 2. *Adam* and the Creation I think were not made upon the procurement of Christs Merits. 3. Nor was man endowed then with the Image of God. 4. Nor made Lord of the inferiour creatures. 5. Nor placed in a Paradise. 6. Nor had the promise of immortality and felicity, if he sinned not; upon the procurement of the Merits of Christ. Yet all these were effects of electing love, being all means for the attainment of the ends of election. But many such things as these your Reader must bear with you in, unless he be a less scrupulous man that can swallow all.

---

§. 8.

THe next place that I finde my self snapt at is *pag.* 101. where you say, "[He "gives us a youthfull frolike to shew his gallantry, like Mr. *Baxter's* chal- "lenge, [*Let the Antinomians shew one Scripture which speaks of Justification from* "*eternity.*] The Antinomians, saith he (Mr.*W.*) the Antipapists and Anti- "arminians he means) may reade their eyes out, before they produce us one "Text, for any other Justification in Scripture, which is not by Faith or "Works.]

Rep. This requires small answer. 1. Why could not such a rude challenge as this, once provoke you to open your Bible and transcribe one Text to that sense?

Had

Had not one such Text been as soon cited, as all this Book written? But something is wanting? He that cannot say what he should, must say what he can, rather then yield or say nothing.

2. I perceive it is not only I that am a Papist or Arminian with you, or with whom an Antinomian signifies an Antipapist, and an Antiarminian? Mr. *Woodbridge* fals under the same lash. But, Sir, while the Harmony of Confessions, and the Synod of *Dort*, and the late Confession of our Assembly are visible, the world hath a better caracter to know a Papist and Arminian by, then yours; and will hardly be perswaded that all are Papists and Arminians that hold not the eternity of Justification or Remission, and that it is before the death and purchase of Christ, or that hold not that we are justified before we are men, or pardoned before we have sinned; no nor all those that hold not the Justification of Infidels.

But I perceive you are not sparing of your accusations of those that are not of your party and opinion; when *pag.*84. you do so let fly at his Brother Mr *John Woodbridge*, forsooth " [as no hearty friend to *gathering* and reforming Church-" es, as deserting a Congregation in *New England*, whereof he was Pastor, to " become a Parish-Parson in the *Old*; and not only so, but hath stood to main-" tain that Parishes are true Churches.] And you say, [Its like his Parsonage is " better, *&c.*]

Where 1. you venture to cast your censure upon the hidden thoughts of a mans heart, which is Gods prerogative: *Who art thou that judgest another mans servant?* Do you know that it was a better Parsonage that is the cause of what you mention? You that dare do this, dare do more. 2. If you deny that any Parishes, yea that many hundred Parishes in *England* are true Churches, you do more then judge a particular Brother, and more then you are ever able to make good, and more then the Brethren of *New England* would affirm. But I perceive your errour is not a single one, not only in Doctrinals: Separation will not perform in the conclusion, what the Leading Dividers do promise.

Pag. 89, 90. Though I am not named, yet perhaps concerned, I am sure the truth is, where you say, " [I desire the Reader to observe how much Mr. *W.* is " beholden to a Popish Tenent, opposed (by all our Protestant Writers) to sup-" port his cause, which is [*That faith goes before Justification to dispose us for it.*] " *Bellarmine* undertakes to prove, *&c.* Against whom all our Protestant Divines " which my little Library hath obtained, do unanimously affirm, that faith doth " not dispose or prepare us for Justification.]

Rep. Like Cause, like carriage in maintaining it. 1. I suppose you know that our Divines do speak it of Justification in the Popish sense, which comprizeth sanctification and faith it self. But this you would not see or have your Reader see: This is but *pia fraus*. 2. I suppose you know that our Divines by [Disposition and preparation] do mean by way of condition *sine quâ non*; and so your Brethren teach as well as you, that faith the first grace, is given without any prerequisite condition on our parts, properly so called; the contrary is taught by Pelagians, Jesuites and Arminians; but your pious fraud did hide this too. Is deceiving the best Teaching? for errour it is, but not for truth. Do you not know that the honest women of your Congregation that ever read Mr. *Hookers Souls preparation for Christ*, and *Souls effectual Vocation*, and *Souls Justification*, or Mr. *Jo. Rogers of Faith*, or Mr. *Bolton*, *Perkins*, or the like honest old Practical Divines, could quickly confute your general assertion, and tell you, Sir our Library is larger then yours, for all these Divines do tell us of a preparation necessary to Justi-

G fication,

fication, yea to faith it self; yea and they make this the great necessary doctrine for the breaking of hard hearts, and confuting the presumptions of the prophane. It is worth the observation of every honest Christian, how prophaness and Antinomianism, do run hand in hand, and speak with one tongue, and put our Divines to one and the same labour. So that in this point of preparation for Christ, and many others, we must confute the same conceits of both. 3. Nay sure you know that the generality of these Divines of ours, do make faith a condition, and most of them an instrument of our Justification: and an efficient cause is a little more then a passive preparation in *sensu morali*, by the act of faith.

§. 9.

The next place that I finde my name in is *pag.* 145. (and divers other places in the margin) " [Our reconciliation is an immediate effect of the death of " Christ, as Mr. *Owen* hath invincibly proved in his Answer to *Baxter*, p. 34.] Thus you: and oft that Answer and Mr. *Kendall*'s is cited.

To which I say but this. I so far abhorre contention, and thirst after the Churches Peace, that I did impose it as a penalty on my self, not to answer that Book of Mr. *Owens*, till I saw a clear call proving it my duty, because I had been foolishly drawn to be the beginner of the Controversie: But I would not have you therefore talk of [*Invincible proof*] of such Tenets as these. Were that Reverend man and I to joyn Wit to Wit, and Learning to Learning, and the contest depended on the strength of the Contesters, I should easily yield that he were invincible by such a one as I, and that the congress between him and me would be as unequal, as I too hastily said it would have been between Mr. *Ball* and him. But when I see what an advantage the Truth yields to a weak Defendor, and consider the disadvantage that he hath cast himself upon in that Book, I must profess to you, that I take it for as easie a thing to Answer it sufficiently, almost as to write so much paper as that Answer will take up. You force me by your frequent references to that Book to say this much, which else I would not have said, least I should exasperate. And for Mr. *Kendall* I have told you my thoughts of his Learned Notions more at large.

§. 10.

The next passage that toucheth me that I meet with, is *pag.* 174. where you say, " [A Learned man of the late Assembly in a Sermon before the Parliament " then sitting declared, that *all* the Promises of the New Covenant are Absolute, " not only *citra meritum*, but *citra conditionem*, without any prerequired conditions " of us: amongst many other places he cites this Text (Mr. *Strong* Serm. 1 *Sam.* " 2. 30.) Besides this I might adde abundance more: But I believe Mr. *Baxter* is " *instar omnium* with Mr. *W.*]

Rep. 1. I believe the plain Texts of Gods Word, not to be evaded with modesty, is *instar omnium* with Mr. *Woodbridge*. He that reads his digested Sermon, and your acknowledgement of his supereminent parts, natural and acquired, will not believe that he takes his doctrine on trust from any man, much less from such a man as I. 2. It is great immodesty in you, if you intend hereby to perswade

the

the world, that it is my singular opinion that the New Covenant hath conditions, yea or that the current of the Reformed Divines, and Churches do not expreslely contradict your conceit. For me to prove this, were as needlesss as to heap up testimonies to prove that the Protestant Divines do hold that the Scripture is Gods Word. He that is ignorant of their judgement in this, let him be ignorant still for me. I except here three or four late Writers; especially those three *Fravequerani Maccovius, Coccius* and *Cloppenburgius.* 3. But for Mr. *Strong,* I can say nothing, as having not his Sermon at hand; but what I have heard of the piety, Judgement and Moderation of that Learned man, and what I finde of your boldness in this Book in frequent untruths, I confess doth make me resolve rather to believe you wrong him, till I shall see the words; though not peremptorily to conclude it and charge you with it. I have oft my self maintained that the promise of the first Grace is Absolute; but I shall never beleeve that *all* the promises of the New Covenant are Absolute, as long as I take Gods Word for my Rule, which I hope will be till death. But here I must give you some Animadversions on your descriptions of a Condition, *pag.* 184.

And to the first (out of Dr. *Cawell*) I say, that it be appointed for suspending the efficacy of the act or grant, is indeed essential to a condition: But that it be Uncertain is meetly Accidentall; Uncertain is put for Contingent, because what is contingent is usually among men uncertain; It means an uncertainty in *natura rei,* when it may tend *ad esse vel non esse;* and not that it be *actu incertum, id est, ignotum Donatori.* Contingent things may be certain to God; and yet contingent in themselves still: As D' *Twiss* oft saith, He hath *decreed* not only that contingent things shall come to pass, but *contingentia contingenter eventura.* So doth he *foreknow* that contingent things shall contingently come to pass. Yet while they are contingent they are the fit matter for a condition, though he foreknow them. An unbeliever himself knows not that he shall believe. And if a man had a spirit of Prophesie to foreknow such future events, do you think that makes him uncapable of making a conditional contract? If a Prophet had a House or Land to sett, might he not make a Legal conditional Contract, because he foreknows the Rent will be paid? You may as well say, God should make no Law, because he foreknows it will be fulfilled, or men will do the thing commanded · But may he not therefore oblige them to do it? And if so, by a precept, I see not but the case is the same as to a sanction, and condition which is essential to that sanction.

And I must further tell you that you must not separate what God hath conjoyned. As he foreknows that we will perform the condition, so he foreknows that it will be a condition by his constitution before we perform it. For we cannot perform a condition which is no condition. And God did not foreknow that we should meerly perform the *act* of believing, but that we should perform the *condition* of believing: even as he did not only foreknow that we should perform the *act* of faith, but the *duty* of faith, and therefore that it must first be a duty.

Moreover I would know whether ever God threatned an elect man or not in his Law, yea or the reprobate? If not, 1. How said he to *Adam, In the day thou eatest thou shalt dye?* 2. Then the first Law had no threatning (then which nothing more false) or else *Adam* was not elect. 3. How then are unbelievers condemned already. 4. There are an hundred express threatnings in the Word. 5. The contrary opinion is Antinomianism indeed, to take believers to be not at all threatned by the Law. 6. At least are they not threatned with temporal punishments, or chaſtiſements? 7. And then wicked reprobates are not threatned, which is falſe.

If you grant the threatning to the Elect or others, then it is either a conditional threatning or Abſolute: If Abſolute then they muſt bear it: there is no eſcape; nor are all abſolute to them that muſt bear it. If conditional: then either God knows whether they will commit that ſin which is the condition of the threatning, or he doth not. The later you will diſclaim I doubt not: The former grants that there may be a condition which is yet certainly foreknown to God.

You will finde the Prophet *Jeremy* making a conditional contract by Gods appointment, in a caſe wherein God had before revealed to him the event.

If (as Dr. *Twiſs* hath well proved) the ſame thing may be neceſſary and contingent, then the ſame thing may be neceſſary, foreknown, and yet conditionally given out or threatned in Law.

It is a moſt dangerous courſe of Divines to ſet Gods Decrees, Foreknowledge or Diſpoſal of Events, in oppoſition to his moral Rectorſhip, if the acts of one muſt be inconſiſtent with the acts of the other. Let me ſpeak it out, though to the provocation of the contemptuous and ſelfconceited, that this one grand miſtake, hath introduced moſt of their Errors, and feedeth moſt of your contentions. They cannot reconcile the acts of Gods Abſolute Dominion, with the moral acts of Regiment; nor can they ſee in what a diſtinct ſeries they ſtand.

The like Anſwer ſerves to the ſame word [*incertum*] in the next definition of *Cooke*. Your two later I wholly allow of, interpreting [*by performance*] to mean [*upon performance.*] Your concluſion *pag*. 185. is falſe, that *Omnis conditio antecedens eſt effectiva*. Though I remember *Chamier* hath ſuch a word, but enough to the contrary.

I have ſpoke thus much of this, that you may alſo ſee, that though the Truths, in Mr. *Owens* Book are Invincible, yet the Miſtakes are not; and if you will conſider it well, I think you will finde that the pulling out of this one Pin, hath cauſed his Fabrick to fall in pieces. For my part I profeſs to follow my conſcience, which upon the moſt impartial ſearch of Scripture that I am able to make, doth tell me that the Scripture doth ſo evidently contain conditional threatnings and promiſes to the Elect, that to deny it, would be, to me, to renounce my underſtanding, and proclaim Scripture to be utterly unintelligible, which were to be no Word of God.

§. 11.

YEt you have not done with me: for *pag*. 190. you fall on without fear or ⸺ that the end may be like the beginning. You ſay, "[1. That the Papiſts "aſſert no other works and condition to be neceſſary to our Juſtification and Sal-"vation then what our adverſaries do. 2. Neither Papiſts nor Arminians do "aſcribe any more Meritoriouſneſs to Works then our opponents,&c. And in this "ſenſe Mr. *Baxter* will tell you that the performers of a condition may be ſaid to "merit the Reward. The Papiſts never pleaded for Merit upon any other ac-"count.]

Rep. 1. If this be true our Divines are notorious liars and ſlanderers ſo frequently to charge them with more. Which yet I had rather of the two believe of Mr. *Eyre* then of them, if I muſt needs do one. 2. If this be true, the Papiſts are

notorious

notorious liars and slanderers, to wrong one another so much as they do, by affirming more of one another. 3. If this be true, doth not Mr. *Eyre* speak better of the Papists then we are use to hear? and should not all honest men be glad to hear that so great a part of Christendom, are farre better men then we took them for. 4. Doth not this intimate; Why may not the Papists be encouraged and have liberty in *England* as we, R. *B.* and a hundred Divines that say as much as he? Especially if you compare this passage with what he saith to Mr. *W.* pag. 117. [*I dare say a more unsound Assertion cannot be picked out of the Writings either of Papists or Arminians then this is.*] And why then should not we be respected alike, if we be corrupted alike? Whether he mean that we should be restrained as they, I know not well; but by his Epistle to the Parliament it is liker he means that they should have Liberty as well as we. You that are Mr. *Eyre* his neighbours, wrong him sorely if you think him a friend to Popery, you may see the Papists will endure you to call Mr. *W.* and I and all the Reformed Churches, Papists, if you will but open the door and let them in, and help them in weakning our hands and resisting us in the work of Christ.

You adde, " [Though Mr. *B.* seems to mince the matter, calling his conditi-
" ons but a *sine qua non*, and a Pepper corn, &c. he attributes as much, if not more
" to Works then the Papists, Arminians and Socinians have done. The Papists
" will not say that Works do merit in a strict and proper sense.]

Rep. Pro. 19. 5. *A false witness shall not be unpunished, and he that speaketh lies shall not escape.* Though I delay this businefs purposely till I come to Mr. *Crandon*, yet I will give the Reader one word here beforehand.

1. Out of one of their own; *Bellarmine* (Printed *Ingolst.* 8º 1605.) *pag.* 2567, 2568, &c. *cap.* 17. *l.* 5. *de Justific.* thus determineth this Question, [*Vtrum opera Bona sint Meritoria ex condigno ratione pacti tantum? an ratione operis tantum? an ratione utriusq;?*] *Media sententia nobis videtur probabilior, quæ docet, Opera bona Justorum Meritoria esse vitæ æternæ ex condigno, ratione Pacti & operis simul,* &c.] And p. 2570, 2571. he bringeth seven Arguments to prove that *in opere bono ex Gratia procedente, est quædam proportio & æqualitas ad premium vitæ æternæ.* And *li.* 1. *c.* 21. pag. 2208, 2209. he endeavoureth to prove [*Meritum de congruo fundari in aliqua Dignitate operis potius quam in promissione.*] Judge now Reader, what credit is to be given to Mr. *Eyre's* words? and how dangerous a thing this Antinomian conceit is, that sin is all pardoned before we repent or are born. Durst such a pious man as this else over and over, even here on one page repeat in Print so notorious a falshood? and say, [Neither Papists nor Arminians ascribe any more Meritoriousnefs to Works] then we do? Nay that [I attribute as much, if not more to Works then the Papists.] Was *Bellarmine* no Papist? I deny all Merit to our Faith or Works; unlefs by the word [Merit] you mean somewhat that is not Merit. Doth *Bellarmine* do so? Nay he saith again here [The Papist never pleaded for Merit upon any other Account] then *ex pacto.* The Lord pardon this audacious falshood to you Brother, and humble you for it.

But if *Bellarmine* be no Papist with you, what say you by *Aquinas*? See him 12 *a. q.* 114 *art.* 1. *c. & art.* 3. *c.* [*Si consideretur secundum operis substantiam & secundum quod procedit ex libero arbitrio, sic non potest ibi esse condignitas propter maximam inæqualitatem: Sed est ibi congruitas propter quandam æqualitatem proportionis. Si autem loquamur de opere Meritorio secundum quod procedit ex gratia Spiritus sancti, sic est Meritorium vitæ æternæ ex condigno: sic enim Valor meriti attenditur secundum virtutem Spiritus sancti moventis nos in vitam æternam,* &c.]

3. The world knows that the Papists have commonly maintained (I say not, every man of them) the Merit of congruity, the very nature of which they ordinarily affirm to be from the respect of the work it self, and not from the Pact or Promise.

4. Our Divines commonly charge them with more. *Perkins* Reformed *Cathol. of Merit,Vol.*1.p.574,545.saith, [The Popish Church placeth Merits within man, making two sorts thereof: the Merit of the person, and the Merit of the work: The Merit of the work is a dignity or excellency in the work, whereby it is made fit and enabled to deserve Life Everlasting for the doer: And Works as they teach are meritorious two waies, 1. By covenant, because God hath made a promise of Reward to them. 2. By their own dignity: For Christ hath merited that our Works might merit: And this is the substance of their Doctrine.] So far *Perkins*.

I will adde no more, but leave it to the consideration of Mr. *Eyre*'s Church-members, whether for this publique sinne, they ought not to admonish him, and desire him publiquely to profess his repentance? If not, let them at least see the evil fruits of his Doctrine, and that all his words are not to be beleeved. Its scarce likely that he will make much more conscience of an untruth in the Pulpit, then in the Press; the later being the most publique, and therefore should be most advised and cautelous way of delivering our mindes.

Yet he is at it again before he comes to the end of the same Page, saying, "[But now Mr. *B.* goes a step beyond them, in that he ascribes a Meritoriousness to Works, which the Arminians and Socinians have not dared to do.]

Rep. I am glad this is the last place where I finde my self named. For I love not above all Writings to deal with those which are capable of no other Answer for substance, then that one *Word* by which the fellow confuted all *Bellarmine*. Methinks it fouls my mouth, so much as to tell you what your words are; and it cannot but be unsavoury and unprofitable to the Reader; and therefore I shall say no more to you; but heartily desire the Lord to recover and forgive you, and to that end to make you ask forgiveness beleevingly and penitently, and to that end to convince you that you are guilty, till forgiveness come, and that no Infidels or Impenitent Rebels are forgiven: And I heartily desire that if you preach this to your people, which you publish in this Book, the sad effects of it may never appear in their hearts and lives, but that Gods truth may lye neerer their hearts and prevail, and the face of your doctrine may not be seen in the face of your hearers conversation or your own.

FINIS.

Errata.

PRef.pag.7.lin.penult. for *ye* reade *he.* In the Contents, l.6. for *Anabaptist* r. *Antipapist.* p.5.l.43.for *Papists* r.*Antipapists.*p.21.l.3.for *nature* r.*name.* p.38.l.15.for *if* r. *as if.* p.39.l.6.for *as we* r. *as well as.*

Novemb. 26. 1653.

Reader,

Understand that for all the hot words between us, Mr Eyre and I are agreed, if he be a man to be believed. For pag. 67. he hath these words, [However were the thing it self granted, That there was in God from Everlasting an Absolute, Fixed and Immutable Will never to deal with his people according to their sins, but to deal with them as Righteous persons, this Controversie were ended.]

Supposing that it is in regard of eternal punishment that he speaks, and not of meer Legal Obligations, Convictions or Condemnations by Law, Conscience, or Men (in all which respects God deals not with the unrighteous as with righteous men) I do grant the whole, and here subscribe my concession: and so if Mr E. be a man of his word, The Controversie is Ended.

Rich. Baxter.

POSTSCRIPT.

READER,

BEcause Mr Eyre hath the modesty to alleadge Mr Rutherfords Judgement for his Opinion, I intreat thee to get and reade a full Volume of Mr Rutherfords (which I had forgotten when I cited those words before) called [A Survey of the Spiritual Antichrist: opening the Secrets of Familism and Antinomianism, against Mr Saltmarsh, Mr Dell, Town, Dr Crispe, H. Den, Eaton, &c. in which is revealed the Rise and Spring of Antinomians, Familists, Libertines, &c.]

It is not only as against Mr Eyre's Testimony that I desire this of thee, but especially because it is one of the fullest Books that I know extant, against the Errors of this Sect; and very usefull to the godly in these seducing times.

READER.

Since this Book was Printed I am able to give thee a more certain account of Mr *Crandon*'s Learned Examination of my *Aphorisms*: If thou wouldst know the Contents, I'le tell thee the main substance of his Book in one word, viz. [*That I am a Papist, and one of the worser sort of them too.*] This one dish adorned with the flowers of *Billingsgate* Rhetorick, and sawced with many hundred palpable falshoods, is the precious feast which Mr *Eyre* hath invited thee to. But if thou think that I tell thee this for my own ends, and as envying thee such felicity as the reading of his Volume, take thy course, and believe me when thou hast tried, *Fisher, Haggar, Reyes*, Mr *Eyre*, and all that have opened their mouths against me, are but meal-mouth'd fellows to this Mr *Crandon*. But if it work on thee as it did on me, thou wilt have some mirth at least for thy money: For I confess I was not able to forbear laughter to see the ridiculous monster come forth, and act such a Tragedy before my face: Nor can I yet forbear when I cast my eye on it, and think how seriously the man perswades me that I am a Papist. But then remember that thy mirth must cost thee sorrow, as mine doth, when I consider that I laugh at the signes of a mans misery, and at that which discovereth our common depravedness, and the misery of our poor people that must be both corrupted and distracted by such Teachers as these. But if thou have a minde to learn Mr *Crandon*'s Ethicks, or Theology, take them and make thy best of them; but I pray thee expect not that ever I should particularly Reply to it, till I have so much time that I know not how better to spend, or dare give an account to God of such an expence of it, and till I am more inclined to stirre in such a puddle as that is. If thou be not able to confute Mr *Crandon*'s strong lines without my help, its not long of me, nor can I have while to help thee, though I pity thee: Yet lest thou say I shift it off, I intend God willing, to give thee that which shall be the matter of an Answer, to the exceptions of him and many others, even a plain and full Confession of my Faith, and especially in the

Point

Point in queſtion: How much it is that I aſcribe to man or any of his actions in the work of Juſtification? with ſo much more againſt the main charges of Mr *Cr.* and Mr *Eyre,* as ſhall give thee cauſe enough to lament, that Opinion, Faction, and Paſſion, ſhould make Chriſtians ſo cruel to their own conſciences, as theſe men have been; and ſhall convince thee, that whatever they do by the reſt of the Law, the ninth Commandment is uſed but little better by them, then the ſecond is by the Papiſts. For all theſe crying ſins, I am in hope, by their zealous pretendings to the honour of Free-Grace, that they mean well in the main: And then I deſire thoſe that fear God to conſider, what crooked pieces the beſt of us are, what need we have of daily pardon of ſin, and what great cauſe to bear with abundance of darkneſs even in Teachers themſelves, and to put up many and great injuries from one another, if ever we expect any quietneſs to the Church: and not only to ſee that we forgive them our ſelves, but alſo to pray for them in imitation of our Lord, [*Father, forgive them, for they know not what they do.*] And though Mr *Eyre* hath clawed his Brother with this commendation, that he is [*a faithfull ſervant of Jeſus Chriſt, and a Workman that need not be aſhamed.*] Yet I intreat Mr *Cr.* to ſee that he be not hardened in impenitency by this warrant: For Mr *E.* cannot ſecure him hereby from future ſhame, though he may do ſomewhat to deſtroy the remnants of his preſent modeſty. If ſuch a maſs of Railing Accuſation, that is, Slander and Reviling twiſted together, be the work of [A Workman that need not be aſhamed] I confeſs I know not what men ſhould be aſhamed of: and muſt ſay, that ſuch men are not over-baſhfull. Indeed if there were no Law, and ſo no tranſgreſſion, they might prove that they need not be aſhamed: Or had they well proved that all their ſinne was perfectly pardoned before they were born, I ſhould yield that they need not be aſhamed, ſo far as ſhame is a puniſhment for ſinne: and therefore muſt ceaſe upon a perfect Remiſſion. But Impeniteny and Impudency have no good foundation.

FINIS.

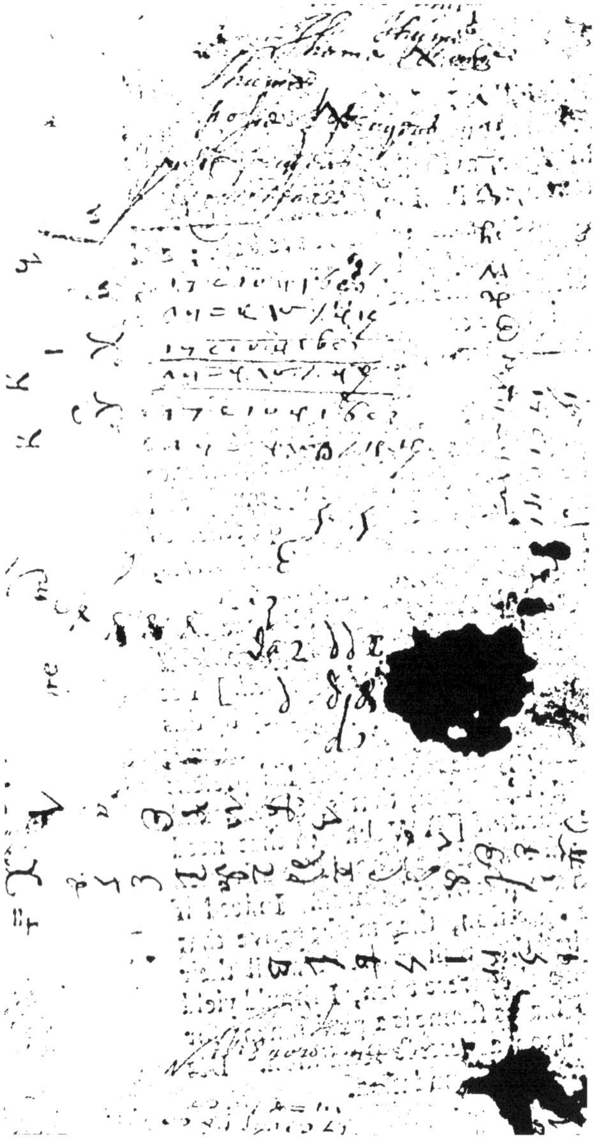

AN Unsavoury Volume

OF

Mr *JO. CRANDON*'S

ANATOMIZED:

OR A

NOSEGAY

OF THE

Choicest Flowers in that GARDEN,

Presented to

Mr *JOSEPH CARYL*

BY

RICH. BAXTER

---

1 COR. 4. 3,4,5.

But with me it is a very small thing that I should be judged of you, or of mans judgement: Yea I judge not my own self. For I know nothing by my self, yet am I not hereby justified: but he that judgeth me, is the Lord. Therefore judge nothing before the time, untill the Lord come, who both will bring to Light the hidden things of darkness, and will make Manifest the counsels of the hearts.

LONDON,

Printed by *A. M.* for *Thomas Underhill* at the Anchor and Bible in *Pauls* Church-yard, and *Francis Tyton* at the three Daggers in *Fleetstreet*, 1654.

AN
Unsavoury Volume
OF
Mr. VOX. GRAND Goose
ANATOMIZED
OR A
POSIGAY
OF THE
Choicest Flowers in his Garden

BY
JOSEPH CORY
AND
RICH. BAXTER

LONDON

TO THE READER.

READER:

I Suppose I owe thee an Account, both of the Reasons which drew forth this following Reply, and why it is transferred hither from its proper place. For the first; I was once purposed never to have written one line by way of particular Reply to M*r* *Crandon*: and I think I should have continued that Resolution, if there had been no more but his own writing to have called me to such a work. The first sight that I had of it, was only of the midst of the book, before the Epistles or the end were annexed: But when I saw M*r* *Caryls* Epistle Commendatory, I apprehended it my duty to endeavour the satisfaction of so Reverend a man, and to let him know that I dissent not from him without, at least, a shew of Reason.

2. I had written much of my Confession, before I saw this Epistle of M*r* *Caryls*; And upon the sight hereof I added 1. Some Conclusions more then I had before done, of my judgement about Justification by faith; and how far I take in or leave out works. 2. Some Conclusions containing my judgement, how far believers are freed or not freed from the Law: Because these are the two great points wherein I perceive I offend M*r* *Caryll*, and the Fundamentals of a Christians Comfort, which he supposeth M*r* *Cr*. to have vindicated.

3. And then I thought it fit to adjoyn my Reasons which forced me to dissent from the judgement of M*r* *Caryll* concerning the substance of the book which he commendeth. All this fell in, in the midst of my Confession, and while I set down things as they came to hand and occasions call'd from them, I presently made a medley work:

I.2 And

And finding upon the review when I had finished my Confession, that this contending piece would disturb the Reader in his course, and was like to be as the carkass of *Amasa* to the pursuing *Israelites*, 2 *Sam.* 20. 12. I thought it best to remove it out of the way, and place it here with the rest of its consorts.

And if the style of this writing seem too harsh to thee, I will not justifie it, but only acquaint thee with these two things for the guidance of thy censure: 1. That I had not skill enough to finde out any gentler termes which would be suitable to the matter. Truth requires that I call things as they are; though modesty require that we use the cleanliest termes we can about an uncleanly businefs; which I think you will say I have not wholly neglected, if you compare impartially his words and mine, and discern aright the occasion of my speeches. 2. That this was all written (and most of my Confession) before I heard of Mr *Crandons* death: and I had some hopes of bringing him to Repentance. But had I been to have written it again when he was dead, I should have studied yet harder for more gentle termes, though they had been less fitted to the quality of the subject. I hope the Lord hath forgiven him the many and great sinnes of his Volume, as the rest of his life; as I daily pray for pardon to my self for the failings of my doctrine, for matter and manner, as well as of my life. The pain and languishing in which I am writing these lines, assure me that I am hasting after him apace; and I hope to finde him in that Kingdome of Peace, where no flanders or Reproaches, or any failings will be owned; and where we shall both partake of that perfect Light, which will cause us to disown our former errours, and when both our Sanctification, and our pardon and Justification will be found more perfect, then when we first believed, even by those that vehemently denied and disclaimed it, and defamed me as a seducer for affirming such a thing. I doubt not but we shall then finde a greater difference between Heaven and earth, between Christs Hospitall, and the Fathers perfect Kingdom, then this passionate self-conceited generation will now believe.

If any think that upon the hearing of Mr *Crandons* death, I should have been at the pains of altering the whole stile of this writing to a gentler strain, I only say, 1. I had not leisure because of extreme weakness, and greater works. 2. I had not much will to it, because when I am gone hence as well as Mr *Crandon*, his writing will remain in the hands of men that knew neither him nor me: And though I perceive that this age which knew us both doth distastfully reject his
opprobrious

opprobrious, calumniating Volume, and make my Reply unneceſſary as to them; Yet when a generation ſhall ariſe that knew neither of us, they may eaſily be drawn to Credit him, if his Falſhood be not plainly laid open to their view. As I hope God hath forgiven him more fully then he was forgiven before he was born, ſo I beſeech the ſame God of mercy to pardon whatſoever I have here or elſewhere committed, againſt his Truth, and the Love of my Brethren, and with the reſt of my ſinnes, to bury them in everlaſting oblivion.

Kederminſter, March 31.
1654.

R. B.

THE CONTENTS.

SECT. I.

MY *first Reason, why I take not Mr Crandons book to be Profitable to the Church of God, and worthy the publike view, as Mr.* Caryll *doth, is from the multitude of falshoods in it, in matter of fact. Instances given of his Calumniations, not only in his speeches against me, but against Mr.* Ball, *the* London *Ministers, and the Assembly, and the Ministers of* England. *The Ministers of* England *Vindicated from the heavy Charge of fraudulent obscuring Christ and Grace, and keeping the Prophane from it. His solemn fiction of my designes and Legates to propagate my opinions.*

SECT.II. *My second Reason, From the Railing, Raging, scornfull language which that book is composed of; so that the matter of Argument cannot easily be found. No need in this Age, to pick Truth out of such excrements, when it may be found in more cleanly Writings.*

SECT.III. *Whether Mr.*Crandon *vindicate Gods Truths, yea fundamentals, as Mr.*Caryll *supposeth? His Assertion of Eternal Justification, perfected in Christs death, and that faith justifieth only in our own apprehension or conscience, examined; Also, that good Works are not the Way to the Kingdom above, but only Christ: that Christ hath not merited from Gods natural but his ordinate Justice, and not in the strict, but the large sense: That Christ merited not the Eternall Justification; nor that in Conscience but Improperly. How Immanent Acts may begin, and Christ may merit them.*

SECT.IV. *His direfull Accusations of the most high God: as that he is unjust if he Impute any sinne to any man (though an Infidell) which was Imputed to Christ, and for which he satisfied. That my doctrine (that our Chastisements are Punishments, and from Gods Wrath, for our sinne as the meritorious Cause) makes all our Salvation, a glorious Priviledge! such as a man may finde at* Billingsgate *for a box on the ear from the worst of men that he meets with,* &c. *Likening God to the devil,*

or

or a divellized man *and prodigy of nature, with much more such fearfull Blasphemy! 27 false reports of my words all together.*

SECT.V. *A Reply to all* Mr. Cr^s *answers to my Arguments, to prove that our sufferings are Punishments, and sinne the meritorious Cause (which he denieth:) Where Mr.* Caryll *may see how he vindicateth Fundamentall Truths.*

SECT.VI. *An Appeal to Scripture in the point, many Texts produced, with twelve Queres; for Mr.* Caryl's *further satisfaction.*

SECT.VII. *My Reasons tendered to Mr.* Caryll, *that Mr.* Cr^s *vindication of Justification by faith without Works (the other Point mentioned by Mr.* Caryll*) is not profitable to the Church of God, nor worthy the publike view. First, Because he granteth the main Point in question after his fiercest contradiction; Proved in many particulars. A Confutation of his fiction of many and great differences between our Divines and me, about the Word* [Conditions.] *His false doctrine, that they that have not the Gospel, are bound to seek Justification and salvation by the works of the Law or Natural Righteousness: With more of the like.*

SECT.VIII. *My next Reason to Mr.* Caryll: *because they are none of my doctrines or words which Mr.* Crandon *doth confute, but the meer forgeries of his own brain. The substance of all his book, herein examined, and found, a meer pack of false Reports. The vanity of his ascribing so much humane learning to me, and his copious Invective against the use of such Learning in Theologie. His self-contradicting. His vain Charge against me, as pleading for an Implicit faith of the People in their Teachers.*

To

To the Reverend
Mr *JOSEPH CARYL,*
Preacher of the
Gospel of CHRIST.

Reverend Sir,

IT is the great respect I bear to your Name, for the good things of the Spirit that I have heard of you, and seen in your Writings, which occasioned me, contrary to my former Resolutions, to say so much to Mr *Crandon,* as here you will finde : Not that I despised the man, but judged the uncleanly matter unfit for Agitation, as being liker more to Annoy then to Edifie. As many Reverend and Godly Brethren have told me, they more wonder at your Epistle, then all M^r *Cr's* Book; so do I feel my self more obliged by a line of yours to be at the pains of tendring you satisfaction, then I did by all his Volume of falshoods and reproaches, of one line in Reply.

Sir, both you and I are short of Heaven, and therefore Imperfect ; and Know but in part, and therefore fallible. Though I will not be so presumptuous as to conclude with confidence that I am in the right, and you in the wrong ; yet to suppose you under a possibility of Erring, I hope is no injury ; nor to make an Enquiry whether it be you or I that actually Erre. I have such eyes upon me as our Master had, that will conclude him a friend of Publicans

and

and sinners; and a wine-bibber, if he come eating and drinking; and him to have a devil that comes not so. If I say, I am in the right, and you and others erre, I am sure to hear the titles of Proud, Arrogant and Self-conceited: If I think that modesty and consciousness of our present darkness and imperfection, require some abatement of my confidence, and in suspition of my self and estimation of your judgement, I should seem but to be dubious, and question the verity of what I deliver, I am sure to be called a Sceptick, and Heretical Questionist, that looks for new light, and remaineth in a fluctuation. Seeing I must unavoidably be one of these sorts, I have resolved to be the later: and to profess to you, that my Intellect lieth open to the force of what evidence you shall be pleased to afford me. If therefore, as you seem to judge me an Opposer of the Fundamentals of a Christians Consolation, you will but put forth your helping hand to deliver me from such Errors, I hope I shall not through obstinacy hinder the success, but shall as well digest your Instructions as my low degree of the Spirit and his Graces will enable me. I have in my Confession enlarged the disclosure of my thoughts for your satisfaction; to which I immediatly subjoyned these Reasons of my dissent from your Judgement about Mr C^{rs} Book; which upon review I removed hither, as unfit for that place. I submit them both to your Consideration, and desire your own Reprehension of their Errours. A page from your self (which doubtless will be with much Clearness, and convincing Evidence and Candor) may do more with me, then the sending forth of many such Volumes, as that is which is honoured with your Name and Commendations. And I cannot doubt but that as the love of Truth could make you the Midwife of a Volume of false Accusations and Reproaches, so will the same Affection cause you to be the Authour of some brief Informations, whereby your straying Brother may be recovered: It being a more desirable work to Reduce, then to befriend any slanders and defamations, though with the modestest seeming to disrelish them: and it being (in my Judgement) an easier task for you, by a few clear Scriptures and Reasons to bring me to a Recantation, then by twenty Commendatory Prefaces, to make such a Book as that, appear to sober unprejudiced men, a Vindication of Fundamental Truths, and profitable to Gods Church. I beseech you interpret not my words as a challenge of Dispute, but as the request of an earnest lover of the Truth, who prayes for it, studieth for it in pain and weakneſs night and day, and would thankfully accept your help to diſcover it; and is confident that you think you have very clear evidence againſt my Doctrine, before you would proceed to do as you have done; and will be ready to communicate that Evidence for my Recovery: Or if you ſhould finde that you have erred (bear with the ſuppoſition) I remain confident that your pious minde will finde no reſt, till you have righted Gods Truth and your Brother as publiquely as you have wronged them, and left as legible a Teſtimony to Poſterity of your Repentance as of your ſinne; as beleeving that *Non Remittitur Peccatum niſi reſtituatur ablatum*. Or if you ſhould think it Popery that ſuch Good Works be judged Conditions of your Remiſſion, yet I doubt not but you will regard them as neceſſary ſignes of the ſincerity of your Repentance, and that of your Faith.

SECT.

SECT. I.

Though all Gods Truths are precious, yet Contention is to me so grievous, that I did many years ago unfeignedly groan forth the complaint of *Summerhardt*, *Quis me miserum tandem liberabit ab ista rixosa Theologia!* and I approved of *Bucholcers* Resolution, and subscribed to his commendation, *Qui cum eximiis a Deo dotibus esset decoratus, in certamen tamen cum Rabiosis illius seculi Theologis descendere noluit: Desit, inquit Disputare, cœpi supputare,* * &c.   * Saints Rest,
Little did I then think that I must   P. 4 pag 94, 95
drink so deep of this bitter Cup, and be necessitated to wast my daies of languishing, in a work which I so detested, and was so fully Resolved against. But he that Made us must Rule us; and he that putteth us in the Vineyard must measure out our Work: I may not with *Jonah* turn my back, because the work may seem ungratefull: If he set me to labour among the thorns, which cannot be taken with hands, but the man that shall touch them must be fenced with iron, and the staff of a Spear (2 *Sam.* 23. 6, 7.) Yea though *the best of them were as a briar, and the most upright sharper then a thorn hedge* (*Mic.* 7. 4.) yet have we a gracious Master, his work is good, his end will satisfie us; we shall then have the Grapes and Figs, which thorns and thistles would not yield us. So great have been my neglects of God and his Spirit, so little is my love to him, and the Life to come, that I am very conscious of my unworthinefs, not only of heaven it self, but of living so near to heaven in my thoughts, and of so much delight in its foretasts, as in more peaceable and practical studies I might have found. I thought seven years ago I had been even entering into the promised Land of Rest: and it seemed good to the Lord, to detain me in the wildernefs, and to exercife me in ungratefull skirmishes on the borders; and that not with enemies, but with Brethren. If *Melancthon* longed for heaven that he might be delivered *a Rabie Theologorum!* If the said *Bucholcer* met with such *Rabiosis Theologis, qui arrepta ex aliquibus voculis calumniandi materia, hæreseos insimulare & traducere optimum virum non erubescerent; Frustra obtestante ipso, dextrè data, dextrè acciperent;* There's great reason that I a worser man, so farre below them in all kinde of worth, should patiently bear as much as they. And though I dare no more resolve to avoid such employments, nor dare runne from my Colours, or sell Gods Truth, for the ease

[2]

of my minde; yet the sharpness of this last assault, and the sensible decayes of my frail flesh, do put me somewhat out of fear of being called out to much more of this unpleasing work: (though I expect some men should do their parts in provocation.)

That which I am now to do is to satisfie Mr *Caryl*, that his Reasons are not sufficient for the emission of such a Volume as a Vindication of Truths Fundamental to our Comfort, and as profitable to the Church of God, and worthy the publike view. For I conceive that the Judgement of so Reverend a man is not by silence to be contemned.

And 1. Methinks the Reasons of his commendation are unsatisfactory. 1. That it is large is no commendation, unless it be Good as well as Great. For of evils the least is to be preferred. 2. That it is Elaborate proves it but a more aggravated sinne, if that labour be bestowed to do evil. But I confess I see nothing but the writing that need to cost much labour: Sinne floweth easily from depraved nature, and is oft born without any great travel or the help of a midwife: and the better part of this book need not cost much study. 3. All the question then is, Whether M^r *Cr.* [do Maintain and Vindicate any Doctrinals of such moment, and so Fundamental in Religion for the comfort of souls, that any Essay tending to the clearing of them, much more this Large and Elaborate Discourse, is profitable to the Church of God, &c.] as Mr. *Caryl* supposeth. And 1. no Fundamentals can be vindicated against me which I did not oppose: And if I opposed any such, it was either in deed and sense, or in words and seeming. Not meerly in words: For 1. it is sense and not meer words which are Fundamentals. 2. I meet with few that will deny my terms to be the terms of Scripture, in the main matters in question. Who denieth that Scripture calleth our sufferings punishments! or that it saith, [*By thy words thou shalt be justified*] and [*A man is justified by works and not by faith only.*] 2. And if it be in sense that I have denied Fundamentals, I shall wait in hope that Mr. *Caryl* will evince it, especially now I have given him my sense more fully: And in the mean time I shall freely acquaint him with some of those Reasons which make me to think otherwise then he doth of Mr. *Cr's* Discourse; and make that labour so unprofitable to me, which Mr. *Car.* judgeth profitable to the Church of God. And in doing this, as I will not purposely bawlk any momentous passages in him; so I will have so much compassion on the Reader and my self, as not to recite or confute the greater part of his Railings and Calumniations; but will choose out those passages where he recapitulateth his Accusations, and where the chiefest strength of his Arguments seem to lye. And the first Reason of my dissent from Mr. *Caryl* is this:

1. Falshoods or books abounding with falshoods, are not profitable to the Church of God, (unless *per accidens*) nor worthy the publique view. But Mr. *Crandons* Book aboundeth and swarmeth with falshoods: Therefore I think it unprofitable to the Church of God, and unworthy the publique view.

I know it is unsavoury language for Ministers to give each other the Lye: But I think it might be as meet to call a *Lye* by its proper name, as Swearing, Drunkenness or Whoredom by theirs, when the case is so gross as that the offendour ought to be openly convinced. And for the *minor*, I do seriously, deliberately, and solemnly profess in the word of a Christian and Minister of the Gospel, that of all the Theological Writings that ever I saw, I did never see any one, to the utmost of my remembrance, either of Papist, Socinian, Anabaptist, or any Protestant,

that

that did neer so much abound with untruths as to matter of fact, as Mr. *Crandons* Book doth. One of the neerest to it that ever I saw was *Harding* the Papist; and *Stapleton, Martyn,* Bishop *Campian,*&c. are not sparing that way; but farre short of Mr. *Crandon,* if I be able to discern : It is not Doctrinal Errours that I call untruths, those are fitter to be confuted by argument then refelled with such language : But it is [untruths about matter of fact :] And whether the man did it with an intention to deceive, I presume not to judge, as not knowing (his face much less) his heart : But that they are palpable untruths in matter of fact, and slanders and calumnies, I averre. I now opened the Book of purpose, and without choice took the page that presented it self to me, and I counted fifteen untruths in matter of fact, by way of slander, in one page. I do remember but very few leaves in all the book that I have observed (and I have run over the greater part) which have not many the like. So that according to the number of the pages, I do confidently conjecture that there can be no less then some thousands in the whole Book. And if any say, that I am an incompetent Judge, as being a party, I answer, 1. I take not on me to be a deciding Judge, but a Discerner. 2. I think I am the ablest on earth to discern it. For his calumnies are most of them of one of these two sorts : Either charging me to write what I never writ, or thought : Or else (which is the most common) searching my heart, and charging me to think what I never thought, and to mean what I never meant, and telling the world my designes and intentions, which my soul was never acquainted with : So that when he meeteth with a passage that he disliketh, in stead of confuting the words and sense of them, he presently fals on an enquiry into my thoughts, and tels the world with down right affirmations, what I think and intend, and that this or that is my design in it, as if it were he that made my heart and must judge it. Yea when he meets with words which he liketh, the difference of his opposition is but small; for he presently tels the world, that I subtilly hide my minde, and mean not as I speak, or I have this or that reserve, so that Popery it must be in the issue howsoever. In a word, one falshood and calumny doth animate the Book from end to end, which is, that I am a Papist, yea and none of the moderate sort of Papists, but of the grossest and worst; and not only that I am of the same opinion with the Papists in the point of Justification, but that I am a flat Papist, and am subtilly endeavouring to bring as many to *Rome* with me as I can; and the Arminians are, as it were, behinde me, and I would draw them on after me to be Papists too. Yea he describeth, according to his confident conjecture, how I was made a Papist, and what Books they were, that turned me to them, and how, in his Preface, in these words : [" But finding him a man of excellent, both natural " and acquired parts, of a very rational brain, delighted more in depths then in " shallows, in the Logical deep and serious, then in the lighter and superficiary " parts of Learning; I conceive him to have been carried out by his own *genius* " to the reading of the deepest Scholastick Writers, with the purpose that *Virgil* " once applied himself to the reading of *Ennius,* though not with the same success. " The purpose of both probably was to fetch out *è stercore gemmam,* a jewel out of " the dunghill : But this man meeting with Learning perfectly agreeing with his " natural *genius,* became impotent to obtain his purpose; for being delighted with " the dunghill, he hath made it his sphere and element : the depth of rationality " which he found in his Authors, hath drawn and captivated him to their most " cursed opinions."] Would you think that this were a man that never saw me, nor knows what my studies have been, nor ever was informed by any one that doth

know ? Nay he often tells his Readers, that I took such and such things out of the Jesuites and other Papists; yea in the main points that he dealeth against, he tells them, I had all from the Papists, and he can tell them where I had it, and undertakes to shew them the very place whence I fetcht it, when he shall be called thereto. Yea when I cite Scriptures, he tells them confidently, I fetcht them not out of the Bible, but out of the Papists and Jesuites, as I found them cited to my hand. What Reply am I capable of making to this man? If I deny all this; his answer is ready, I am not to be believed, I subtilly and dissemblingly hide my Religion, or deny the Truth. Doth he indeed know my thoughts, so much better then I, or the way of my studies? I was bold to mention in the Append. how those things that were excepted against as novelty, were made known to me in my solitude and weakness, when I had no books but my Bible with me, and that in that case studying the Scripture alone, I thought I saw more in one fortnight then of many moneths before : yet left any should think that I hereby would encourage men to cast off studies and read no book but the Bible, and contemn all humane Learning, and writings of Fathers and Modern Divines, and wait only on the Spirit, without such means, I added, that I did not hereby judge books needless, and that I should not my self have been so capable of improving those solitary hours in studying the Scripture, if I had read no other books before : And how doth this man interpret these words? Why, whereas I mentioned my profiting [in a fortnight] he doubteth not to conclude, that I vouchsafed the Scripture but a fortnights study, as if it had been then no longer, and as if I had contemned and not studied it, the rest of my life, as being too low for my studies. And; from the Caution that I put in about former Reading (because we were then where I was, pestered with some Teachers, that perswaded men to read no books but the Bible,) he gathers, that it was Jesuites and Papists, that I had read before, and then brought it out. Hath a man any Plea against such an Accuser of the Heart, which man can justifie by? Or must be not only Appeal to the Judge of hearts. As *Job*, and *Paul* in his Epistles, did by solemne Oathes, Appeal from Accusers and false surmisers, to that Record in Heaven, and that Omniscient Witness, so do I take it to be my duty, in such a case as this is, to Appeal from M.*Cr.* that only pretendeth to know my heart to the All knowing God that is acquainted with it indeed, who made it, and I think possessed it with that Light, for which I suffer these Reproaches; and deliberately and in his fear I do solemnly professe ;
1. That if I were a Papist the world should soon know it; for I hate the dissembling of my Religion : and (as I said) I scorn that Religion that is a just cause of shame, or that will not bring him off on gainfull termes, that shall suffer in the defence of it. And whether I have ever gone that way that shunneth danger and sufferings in the world, and whether my Conscience hath stooped for the securing of my flesh, I desire them to judge that have known me in the course of my Life and Ministry before the wartes, and that have been my associates in the warres.
2. And for the particular in question, I do before the same heart-searching God profess, that these things that the Accuser writes, are false ; and that I did not, to the utmost of my remembrance, learn, or borrow, or transcribe from Jesuites, or any other Papist, one line, or word in that book (but what I have cited them for, which is as I remember, but once the name of *Scotus* and D'*Orbellis*, in a common question of Philosophy, and *Suarez* once or twice in a common point of Metaphysicks or Logick, and one trivial sentence in the Epistle out of *White*;) nor did I transcribe one Text of Scripture out of any of them : Nay that I had read then

but

but very few Jesuites on any subject, and to this day, their books are an exceeding small part of my reading : some Schoolmen I confess I have read (and some few Jesuites,) but the main part of my first time was spent in reading English Protestants, and my next in Latine Protestants, and my later years have been mainly spent in the Fathers and Ancient writers: And I further profess before the same God, that I remember not one Point of Religion wherein the Papists and Protestants differ, wherein the reading of any Schoolman, Jesuite or other Papist, or conferring with any of them, hath changed my judgement from the Protestants to them. And I renew the same profession, that the points, or method, or termes in that book of Aphorismes, which cause the great offence, and are charged by others with Novelty, and by Mr. *Cr.* with Popery, I did not to my utmost remembrance, receive from any Book or Person in the world; but only upon former study, of the Scriptures, some undigested conceptions stuck in my minde, and at the time of my conceiving and entertaining those Notions (about the Nature and Necessity of a twofold Righteousness, and many the like) I was in a strange place, where I had no book but my Bible (and a Concordance, I think, and two or three Physick books were with or near me,) and that in extream weakness, I was preparing my own thoughts for my remove to God, and thereupon began for my own use, to write those things which I have since published in a book entituled *The Saints Rest*; and when I came to that place which is now at *pag.* 68, and 72. in the 4th Edit. I was urged, partly by the occurring difficulty, and partly by a question put to me, to resolve, In what sense it is that men are called Righteous, and publikely Justified at the day of Judgement in reference to the Improvement of their Talents, and the feeding, visiting, cloathing, &c. of Christ? and in what sense Christ gives this as the Reason of the sentence. The expounding of *Matth.* 25. was the task, which I was set upon : which as I seriously set my self to understand, I found so great difficulties as drove me to God again and again ; and thereupon so great light that I could not resist ; so that I solemnly professe that it was partly on my knees, and partly in diligent consideration of the naked Text (when I had not so much as Authours or the thought of them with me) that I received the substance of the fore-mentioned particulars. An over-pewring Light (I thought) did suddenly give me a clear apprehension of those things, which I had oft reached after before in vain. Whereupon I suddenly wrote down the bare Propositions (so many of them as concerns Righteousness and Justification,) and so let them lye by me long after. And then falling into further languishing, and into more confident expectations of death, I revised them, and thrust them out too hastily and undigested, little thinking to have lived so long to have reviewed them ; and so, having none about me, to afford me such assistance or advice as had been meet, and I being unacquainted with the ticklish captious humour of the world, never doubted of mens favourable acceptance, or toleration of its imperfections, thereupon too simply and rashly rushed into the Press, scarce knowing what I did, and I confess, did by oversight and haste incur the guilt of severall harsh expressions, and some unmeet, and that might seem to a suspicious reader, more unsound then they were in my intention, and so did give cause of just offence to pious and judicious men. Yet little thought I but my brethren would have dealt as friendly and compassionately by me and mine infirmities, as I should have done in the like case by theirs : but with some it proved otherwise. Yet, let me add, that where I say I used no Authors, Papists or Protestants, for the forementioned Theses, I say not so for all in the explications : Two I must confess my self much to have

profited

profited by in that doctrine; the one is Mr. *Bradshaw*, the other is *Grotius de satisfactione*, a book written while he remained with the orthodox, and approved much by them, and defended by *Essenius* against *Crellius*: Yet had I almost finished those Aphorismes before ever I read a leaf of *Grotius*, having only heard of him by no encouraging fame; and being at that time in speech with Mr. *Tombes*, upon his high commendations of it, I borrowed it of him to peruse, and found it fully to answer his commendations: and I confess, I learned more out of it, then I did out of any book except the Scriptures, of many a year before.

Little did I think to trouble men with this tedious Narrative: but I have no other Reply left to Mr. *Crandons* unmanly confident affirmations, of my taking it word by word, from the Jesuites and Papists, yea the very Texts of Scripture which I cited.

But suppose Mr. *Cr.* had a Toleration to write a Volume of false Accusations against me, my poor opinion is (which I submit to better judgements) that Mr. *Caryl* should more have disrelished his abuse and slanderous reports of others far more worthy then I, then to judge such a work to be profitable to the Church.

To begin with the lowest (because but a single man) how inhumanely dealeth he with that holy, Learned man of God Mr. *John Ball*? a man so far beyond the reach of slanderous tongues, both for Holiness, Learning, Abilities of all sorts, especially of Disputation, soundness of judgement, and distance from the very appearance of such Matter of Reproach? Yet doth this man once fall on him, *c.24. part.1. pag.298,299.* telling men that ["he heard long since that this Mr. *Ball* "seeing fashionableness and formality tending somewhat to the Popish outside- "ness in Religion was the way to preferment, had before his death somewhat de- "clined:] yet he will here be so charitable when he hath printed this report, not to entertain it, till he see the grounds. But before he endeth, his little modesty is quite spent; and *part 2.pag.207.* he falls on again in these words ["If elsewhere "he contradicts himself I shall oppose *Ball* against *Ball*; yea *Ball* in afflictions, "when he lived by faith, and had nothing else but Christ apprehended by faith "to support his troubled soul, to *Ball* now raised to a prosperous state in the "world, and who seeing the Court infected with Popery, Socinianisme and Ar- "minianisme, and no other bridge to preferment so effectuall as some shew of "bending at least to these wayes, might possibly as far as conscience would per- "mit him, make use of the language there held most authentick; I say, of the "language, for I cannot condemn his doctrine alledged in his three following "Testimonies, if taken in a good sense. But his ambiguity of words, seem to speak "him only to have had a levell to somewhat else besides the supporting of the "Truth, &c.] Unworthy man! to publish such base surmises and slanders of the dead! to talk of his eying a Court infected with Popery, Socinianisme and Arminianisme, for preferment, and making a bridge to that in his writings, that never saw the light till he was dead? He that was known to live (and dye) a Nonconformist, in a poor house, a poor habit, a poor maintenance of about 20^{lb} *per an.* in an obscure Village, and teaching school all the week for a further supply, deserving as high esteem and honour as the best Bishop in *England*, yet looking after no higher things, but living comfortably and prosperously with these. Did this man deserve such Accusations as these to be published

All this was raised of him for writing against the Separatists.

against his precious name, which envy shall never be able to fret and disparage, but shall be honourable in *England* while the English tongue and the Christian faith shall here abide.

abide. I marvell this man had no more wit; if he would needs vent his flanders, that he chose not some forrainers to be the subject of such language, whom the English knew only by fame, and could not therefore so well disprove him. Doth he think that he will get any credit by such tales, in *Staffordshire, Cheshire, London*, or any where that his name was known? especially while those holy, upright, worthy servants of Christ, Mr. *Langley*, Mr. *Ash*, Mr. *Cook*, &c. are yet living to vindicate him, who were his familiar acquaintance, and with him in the worst times maintained their Integrity.

So *Par.* 1. *pag.* 59. he lets fly at some Ministers that have in that point spoke (he saith) almost the same things with me; and adds [" It hath filled my spirit with
" sadness, to hear not only in the pulpits of the Country, but of the City of *London*,
" pronounced by the mouthes of some in great esteem, both for Piety and Learn-
" ing, that *to say God doth not punish his Saints for their sins is flat Antinomianisme*;
" and affirmed that *the Afflictions of believers are punishments for their sinne*. I beseech
" these men to consider whom they here explode as Antinomians? whether be-
" sides the Apostles and Fathers of the Primitive Church, they do not brand all
" the Reformed Churches, and their Champions against the Papists, with this ig-
" nominy? Whether there be any one Article of Christian Religion, that hath
" more stoutly defended by these against the Papists, then this which heat of zeal
" without knowledge (or consideration at least) hath of late called Antinomian?
" Let them produce any besides the Socinian and Arminian Sophisters, that have
" stumbled at this doctrine as offensive.]

Here I offer it to your consideration, 1. Whether he do not expresly make these *London* Ministers of great esteem, to take part with the Papists against Protestants, even in that one Article of Christian Religion which they have so stoutly defended, as none more? 2. Yea against all the Reformed Churches. 3. Yea in a point that none (that they can produce) besides Socinians and Arminians have stumbled at: so that there are great store of Socinians, Arminians and Papists in the world, it seems. 4. Whether he involve them not in all the Curses and Blasphemous, and Popish Consequents, which he there chargeth on me for the same opinion? 5. Whether this man did remember to make use of his Modesty, when he durst publish to the world, 1. That it is the Apostles, 2. Fathers, 3. All the Reformed Churches, that deny believers sufferings to be punishments? When 1. The Apostles have never a word to that end, I dare confidently affirm: nay they have much against it: affirming them to be chastisements, which are a species of punishment; and that they are the effects of sinne, and of the provocation of God to jealousie and anger, and we are judged of the Lord when we are chastened, and that our God being a consuming fire, and a Judger of his People, must be served with fear, and not provoked to anger, &c. 2. Did not the man know, that by this Assertion of the Fathers, he did prostitute the credit of his Reading, or Veracity, or both, to the scorn and pity, of all that ever took notice of the sense of the Fathers herein? Did he think to be believed in such Assertions, by any men that are able to open their books, and try the truth of his sayings? when it is a known case, that the generality of the Fathers are judged by the most eminent Protestants, to go but too farre into the contrary extream. And though I would interpret them as favourably and modestly as I can, yet indeed, their termes at least are not to be excused. As for his judging the zeal of these Divines to be without knowledge or consideration, it is but the mild part of his censure. 6. And is it not sleeping immodesty in him, to talk of all the

L   Reformed

Reformed Churches; and challenging them to produce any besides Socinians and Arminians, &c? Hath the man read all Proteſtant Writers, that he durſt make ſuch a confident challenge? I have now I am writing this, the Teſtimonies of (as I remember,) about 20 or 30, that call believers ſufferings, puniſhments, lying by me, which I collected on other occaſions: And I think it eaſie to have as many more. But to what purpoſe! I confeſs many ancient and ſome later Proteſtants, do ſay that believers ſufferings are not puniſhments, but chaſtiſements, taking the word Puniſhment in a reſtrained ſenſe for meer Vindictive Puniſhment (as it is commonly called.) But what man that ever read Philoſopher, Divines, Lawyers, of the nature of Puniſhment, can be ignorant that Chaſtiſement is a ſpecies of Puniſhment? I dare not challenge Mr *Crandon* to produce any but Libertines that ever denied it, for little do I know how many ſuch books as his own may lurk in the world that I never ſaw, and hope never ſhall ſee; but if he will name a man (whoſe name is not a ſcourge or trouble to the ears of the ſober) that ever gave a Definition of Puniſhment *in Genere*, which did not comprehend Chaſtiſement or Paternal Correction as a ſpecies, I will accept it as a novelty, and thank him for ſhewing me that which I never ſaw before, though I reject the thing as a vanity.

And it is but a cenſorious reproach with a pretence of ſome more modeſty, which the late Reverend Aſſembly receive at his hands in the ſeventh page of his Epiſtle Dedic. in theſe words, [" Beſides I have been told, that ſome of the late Reve-
" rend Synod diſreliſhed the doctrine (that Juſtification is an Immanent act in
" God, and actually compleated in the Redemption which is by Chriſt and in
" Chriſt, both theſe before we believe, as *pag.5*.) but cannot finde that any one
" of them hath publiſhed his Reaſons for ſuch a diſreliſh. And charity will not
" permit me, to harbour the lighteſt imagination, that any one of thoſe grave Di-
" vines called and ſelected out of the whole Nation, for their eminency in Godli-
" neſs and Learning, ſhould without any means uſed for information and convi-
" ction, exerciſe a tyranny over the conſciences of their leſſer Brethren, to force
" them into an implicite faith to believe as themſelves believe ; ſpecially when do-
" ing it, they ſhall put out that, which they think at leaſt to be the light of the
" word in their conſcience, and in conſenting with them without hearing a
" Reaſon, they ſhall diſſent from others (whom their modeſty will confeſſe
" to be of no leſſe deſervings in the Church) who have given their Rea-
" ſons.]

But might they not debate the caſe with Dr. *Twiß*, and give him their reaſons within their own wals, without ſuch tyranny on our conſciences, or giving us thoſe Reaſons? They do tell you what Scripture Juſtification is in their Confeſſion and Catechiſm, and give you their Reaſons for it, if Gods Word may go for Reaſons, and prove that it follows faith : But they never offered violence to your Conſcience, if it lead you to believe that there is another, or two, Juſtifications before this. Or if you think it ſuch a wrong to Conſcience, to aſſert that [Remiſſion of ſinne and Accepting us as Righteous] do follow faith, it is Gods Word, which they produce, that you muſt lay the charge on. Had they reſtrained you from ſaying, that another Juſtification is an Immanent act, its like they would have given you Scripture Reaſon for it.

But all this againſt Mr. *Ball*, the *London* Miniſters, and the Aſſembly, is a ſmal matter to that flood of reproach which he pours out on the moſt of the Miniſters of *England*, in the 11. and 12. *page* of his Preface to the Reader, too long to be all recited.

recited. [" That since the heat of Controversie between us and the Papists about
" it, abated, this Doctrine (of Justification) sounded in few Pulpits, which be-
" fore sounded in all, that the *Pia fraus*, as they termed it, prevailed every where, a
" godly deceit to withhold from the people the knowledge of the liberty which they
" have by Christ, lest they should turn it into licentiousness. That as this pious
" fraud passed from hand to hand among Ministers, many of them while they
" were deceiving, were themselves deceived, and verily thought it the right art of
" profitable preaching to hold out the Law and keep in the Gospel, to wash the
" utter part of the cup and platter, leaving that which is within full of guilt and
" corruption. Hence it came to pass that the Law by many was turned to a twofold
" use, like the sword of *Achilles*, &c. such repentances for sinne, such degrees of
" Contrition and Reformation, prescribed out of the Law, which being practi-
" ced, pardon of sinne and eternal life must needs follow. Thus man was made
" not only his own condemner, but his own Saviour also; his evil works in tranf-
" gressing the Law pursuing him with vengeance, and his returning by repentance
" to good works in strict obedience to the Law, restoring him to life and salvation.
" In mean while Christ was left in a corner to look upon all, but without interpo-
" sition of his operation or Passion. Sometimes indeed much might be heard of
" the riches of Gods grace, of the efficacy of Christs merits to save the chief of
" sinners; so that the people might even see the door of heaven open to them: but
" in conclusion, the Preacher, as if he had been deputed to the office of the Che-
" rubims, *Gen.* 2. *ult.* to keep the way of the tree of Life, with his flaming sword
" turning every way, affrighted the poor souls from all hope of entring, crying,
" *Procul hinc, procul ite prophani*, no prophane or unclean person hath right to med-
" dle with this grace. No: first they must have such heart preparations, purifi-
" cations, and prejacent qualifications, before they draw near to partake of mercy;
" must first cleanse and cure themselves, and then come to Christ afterwards, must
" be cloathed with an inherent Righteousness first, and then expect to be cloathed
" upon with a Righteousness imputed. Such hath been, and still is the doctrine
" delivered in many Congregations within this Nation. I neither fain nor aggra-
" vate. It is that whereof my self not without grief, have been oft an ear witness,
" and that from the mouths of very zealous Ministers And I fear the Lord hath a
" Controversie against the Ministry, and wi l more yet obscure and vilifie many of
" them, for their obscuring of his Grace and his Christ.]

1. And who are these zealous Ministers that must bear all this thunder of reproach and threatning ? It seems it is all saving [a few :] for he excepteth but [a
few Pulpits.] And who may those few be, is not hard to conjecture. I know no
men that he is so likely to mean, as such as Mr. *John Rogers* of *Dedham*, Mr. *Fen-
ner*, Mr. *Tho. Hooker*, Mr. *Tho. Shephard*, Mr. *Bolton*, and the generality of our old
solid soul-searching Preachers, that go the same way: Of whom I will say but
one word to him, and one to others. To him, That he would conscionably observe whether the Labours of these Reverend, Faithfull Servants of Christ, have
not been blessed with another kinde of success, then the Labours of Dr. *Crisp*, Mr.
Den, Mr. *Randall*, Mr. *Saltmarsh*, Mr. *Town*, or any of that strain: unless he will
deal by them and their converts, as by me, and say, that they brought men to the
Pope and the Devil, and not to Christ. As Mr. *Shephard* saith, *God hath given so
full a blessing on this way of Preaching, and the most Godly have so generally approved
it from experiences, that one would think we should never have been put so to plead
for it.*

L 2   2. And

2. And it is observable, that he laies all this Accusation on us of obscuring Christ [since the ceasing of the heat of Controversie.] It seems it is the heat of Controversie that first gave life to his way of revealing Christ, and that must keep life in it: and for want of the heat of Controversie, it will die. Its past doubt then, that he hath done his part to keep life in it. Truly in my best observation, the heat of Controversie drives men to extreams, while it sets even wise and good men a studying, what to say against the adversary, and how to draw all to the strengthening of their cause: and when in happy peace men have leisure soberly to review such arguings, and can patiently hear all sides speak, and are withall put to try their own doctrines on their own and the peoples spirits, and to see them truly reduced to practise, then it is that men come home by repentance to Truth and Moderation, which Controversie lost, and sober Practice findeth again.

2. To others therefore I again give my advice, that they highly value, and diligently reade these practical, searching Authours; and what ever such men as this may judge of such Preachers or Writers, be thankfull for them as the greatest blessing of this age, wherein it excelleth other ages, as this Land doth other Nations. I would not advise Countrey people of Vulgar capacities to trouble their heads with much Controversie, no not against the Antinomists themselves. But as a better preservative I would every family that hath a care of spiritual things, would but keep in their houses, hands and hearts, four or five of our old solid succesfull, practical Divines, and I should not fear the prevalency of Antinomianism: Especially get Mr. *Pinkes* five Sermons, Mr. *Whitfield*, Mr. *Rogers* Doctrine of Faith and Love: Mr. *Boltons* and Mr. *T.Hookers* Works, Mr. *Fenners*, Mr. *Whateleys* New birth, *Dod* on the Commandments, and (as a full Confutation of all their Libertinism in a practical strain) Mr. *Shephard*, especially his *Sound Beleever*, a Book that well answers the Title, in giving the true caracter of such.

3. I know not how large Mr. *Crandons* acquaintance may be in *England* beyond mine: but I have been in many Counties, if not by farre the most; and I shall be bold to leave my contrary observation to posterity, for the Vindication of the Ministry, so farre as my credit will go: And I must profess seriously, that though I have frequently and heartily lamented the great number of weak or worldly, or negligent Ministers in many parts, yet did I never hear, to my best remembrance, any one man, no not of the worst that ever I heard, except the late wandring Sectaries, 1. That ever preached any pardon of sin, but by the Bloodshed and Merits of Jesus Christ, and the free grace of God: 2. Or that ever did tell men that they must merit pardon or life themselves. 3. Or that ever told men they could by their own strength so prepare themselves for pardon, as that pardon must needs follow. 4. Or that ever made any preparations or works a Price for the purchasing of Christ or Grace. 5. Or that ever preached the Law and not the Gospel. 6. Or that ever (so farre as I could discern) did by that which he cals a pious fraud, conceale from the people their Liberty by Christ. 7. Or that taught them only to wash the outside. 8. Or that ever sent men to Works in stead of Christ. 9. Or that ever told them that their Conversion or Reformation, did so much as joyn with Christ in satisfying or meriting. 10. Yea that ever kept poor sinners from the Tree of Life, or the wounded soul from comfort, except those that spoke against their wounding. 11. Or that ever told them they must first cure themselves and then come to Christ. 12. Or that ever obscured Christ and Grace out of design (so farre as I was able to discern,) but only out of weakness,

all

all having not the same measure of ability in preaching the Gospel: Not one man did I ever hear that was guilty of any one of these accusations, so farre as I could possibly perceive. Nay I solemnly profess, that in all my daies, since I understood any thing of these matters, the thing that all the carnal and scandalous and formall Preachers about us, were blamed, and censured for, by all the godly of my acquaintance (till the Wartes) was their too liberal giving out pardon and free grace and hope of salvation to the ungodly, and making the gate wider and the way broader then Christ had made it, and preaching comfort so generally, that all the wicked might take it to themselves: and that the generality of Godly, Conscionable Ministers went the contrary way, searching, differencing, driving to through humiliation, and broakenness of heart, and Reformation of Life, and were very cautelous in all their offers of pardon, left the prophane should snatch it, to whom it belonged not : and that this was the only preaching that godly people then loved (so far as my acquaintenca extended) and that wicked men hated, and for which they reproached the Preachers as Puritans and Precisians, and were use to say, that they would make men mad. This Testimony I leave against Mr. *Crandons* reproach of the *English* Ministry ; who thinks it not enough to get into the seat of the scorners, when God hath with thunderbolts struck them out to the ground before his eyes, but he dareth also from that seat, to denounce [" a Controversie from " the Lord against the Ministry, that he will more yet obscure and vilifie many " of them, for their obscuring of his Grace, and his Christ.] And no wonder if he that dare pass this sentence as from God, dare also execute that which he takes to be Gods will, and so do bend himself to obscure and villifie that Ministry.

4. What Grace is it that these Ministers say, No prophane person hath right to meddle with ? " Wherein they play the part of the Cherubims and keep men " from the Tree of Life ? Is it the grace of sanctification ? No, he dares not yet to say it, that they tell men they must not yet be sanctified because they are prophane ? Is it the grace of faith ? Certainly he never heard the Ministers so commonly say, None of you that are prophane persons must believe in Christ for Remission of sinne. Indeed these two things he might hear, for we must preach them, 1. That no prophane man can accept or believe in an offered Christ to pardon and Justification, till he feel the need of Christ, by feeling the evil of sinne and misery. 2. That no prophane person ought while prophane to believe that his sinne is actually pardoned, and he justified by Christ : And if this be the quarrell, I say, It is presumption and not faith that such keep men from, and it is Satans most potent delusions, and not Gods graces, that we would destroy. But 3. It seems it is the grace of pardon it self that he speaks of : And indeed do Ministers so commonly tell the prophane that they must not take the grace of pardon ? In the Libertine sense they do: for so, *Taking* is but to believe or conceit that they *are pardoned* already : But in the Scripture sense, they do not, but call the prophane to take pardon, that is, to accept it on Gods terms of faith and repentance ; to Take Christ, and whole Christ first, and pardon with him : And hath God a controversie with us, and will make us vile for preaching this doctrine ? Dare any but a Libertine say to all the prophane, Believe that you are all pardoned, and actually justified without exception ? Or would he have the Gospel that we must preach to be only this : Believe that all Gods Elect only are pardoned, whether prophane or not prophane ? This would be as terrible a doctrine, and drive them, as he speaks, from the Tree of Life, as much as ours: for how long would it be before

he could tell them, which are the Elect and which not : And if believing that the Elect shall be saved, would save, without any personal application, why might not the devils be saved, who, no doubt, believe that the Elect shall be saved. For my part, I must profess, I finde it no hard matter to perswade any common prophane people that their sinnes are forgiven by free grace through Christs blood, and that they shall be saved ; but all the difficulty lies in destroying such perswasions, and breaking down their false faith and hope ; and very hardly and heavily doth that work go on: and if Mr. *Crandon* take the contrary course, I am confident his preaching hath more, (I dare not say better) success then mine, and his Converts are more numerous, unless a prophane presumptuous heart, be not the same thing in *Hampshire*, as in other Countries. But I bestow too many words on so plain a case.

To recite all the gross calumnies and shameless forgeries of that Book, would be a weary and ungratefull task to the Writer, and no better to the Reader, and must indeed be a transcribing of no small part of his Book, if not the farre greatest ? What a solemn fiction have we in the third page of his *Epist. Ded.* That I have my [" circumforaneous Legates, which having their Provinces assigned either
' of one or more Counties, are still circling and compassing them ; first to dis-
" perse this his mystery of iniquity with such acuratenesse, that there may be no
" one that hath the repute of a pious Gentleman or Minister, a stranger to it : and
" then by their frequent visitations, to examine how the *Baxterian* faith thrives in
" each person and to hold them fixed to it : These returning once in six or seven
" moneths out of their circuits to their grand Master, may possibly speak in things
" that they know not, what they think may be plausible to him.]

Conform to this are his following words in the same Epist. [" 2. It sprang
" from other mens, yea Ministers, too much admiration and almost adoration of
" him, when from all parts there was such concourse in a way of Pilgrimage to
" him, to bless him, or be blessed by him, and the admirers returned to the de-
" ceiving of others, with no less applause and triumph, then the *Turk* from visit-
" ing the shrine of their *Mahomet*, &c.]

Would any think this man lived at such a distance from me, and knew so little of what he saith ? when he pretendeth to know our very discourses, contrivances, and correspondences ? I stand not on the visible envy that he expresseth ; but what an impudent falshood is the substance of the story ? I confess, with thanks to God and them, that I have sometime the favour of my Brethrens visitations, for an hour, or a night, from several parties ; but it is for the most part, but when they pass this way as travellers ; it being usual with Ministers, so farre to shew love to each other. But I do solemnly profess (for I have no other way to clear my self)
1. That I never sent man, or provoked man to promote that Book, or any singular opinions of mine, or any of those that I am judged to differ in from the common way, any other way then the generality of godly Ministers promote them.
2. That I never asked any man living (to the utmost of my memory, and I am very confident of it, in this) whether Ministers or Gentlemen, or who, or how many, did favour that Book, or any singular opinion of mine, or any so called.
3. That I never asked so much as one man, to my utmost remembrance, that came to me, How he liked that Book, or whether himself were of my minde in the points in Controversie between me and my Brethren. 4. That to this day I do not so much as know the Judgements of those Reverend Brethren, or any one of them, that ever came to me out of that County where Mr. *Cr.* dwels, or any neighbour

bour County, and of very few in *England*, that ever came to me from any part. Except it be those that dissent, and came to give me their exceptions. 5. That Mr. *Crandons* neighbours, whom it seems he raiseth this slander of, are men of another spirit, then to drive a trade of venting new Opinions, or Errours: and that it is not that Book which he deals against, but my other Labours that I have had their thanks for (to the best of my remembrance:) yea that their Conference is upon Practicals, wholly bending another way, then the Accuser of the Brethren dreams of. 6. Yea I will adde further (because it seems Mr. *Crandon* knows them) that I know not one Minister of *Hampshire* or *Wiltshire* who hath been with me, and with whom I have any familiarity (except one, who medled not with me on such things) but they have by their Letters perswaded me from Controversie to Practical Writings, yea and some of them have dealt as freely with me (when by misunderstanding that word in my *Directions for Peace of Consc.* they suspected me to waver in the point of Perseverance) as any other men have done. 7. That I know none of any part in *England* that I have any familiar correspondence with, but men reputed Godly, and none that ever visited me purposely (as Ministers, for familiarity or acquaintance) but meerly on that account; nor do I ever use to have much discourse with any of them about any such Opinions; nor is it Opinionatists that are my familiars. 8. That I use to mention that Book of Aphorismes as sparingly as I can, to any, being truly ashamed of it (and willingly so publish my self) for its indigested passages and imperfections. 9. That when I am forced to speak of it, it is commonly by way of accusation, or confession of my Rashness, and that especially for the distast of some Brethren (which I never dreamt of before hand) I do repent that ever I published it, and so do hereby profess. 10. That this is my course with neighbour Ministers, as well as strangers. Let any man living that can, witness against me, that I set upon him to draw him to any opinion of mine, wherein I differ from the generality of my Brethren, or am supposed so to do. 11. Yea let any man of my own Congregation, witness against me, if they can, that I have bestowed one quarter or half quarter of an hours discourse with them to that end: What I preach publiquely the Town and Country knows. 12. Yea I have hindered very many from the reading of that Book; both of my neighbours and young Schollars in the Universities, that any whit depended on me for advice. 13. And besides all this I have suppressed it, from being again Printed, this five years or thereabout, contrary to the importunity of multitudes of Letters; when there was never but a thousand Printed in all, as the Booksellers told me. Lay all this together, which I solemnly profess to be the truth, and then judge of the truth of this mans long forged story, of Legacies, and Circuits, and Examinations, and the driving on such a laborious enterprise, for propagation of my Opinions, as he adventured to affirm and engage his Credit on! Doth this man know what spirit it is that actuates him? If I have any opinion differing from others, I think he hath seldom known any man, that ever was lesse zealous in propagating such Opinions. Oh that I knew how to further the Unity and Peace of the Church, and to close our wounds, on the condition that Book were burnt that M. *Crandon* is so angry at.

But I will not for five times the price of Mr. *Cr's* Volume, undertake to enumerate one half the gross falshoods in matter of fact, which he confidently affirmeth. This then is my first Reason, which I tender to Mr. *Caryl*, why I think the Church is not like to get any great profit by this Book of his, and that it was not worthy of the publick view.

SECT...

SECT. II.

MY second Reason is this, That book which is so filled from end to end with Railing, scorning and Raving words, that it is hard so much as to finde the very sense of the mans Reasons, in such an age as this is, when men need not pick up Truths out of mens excrements, doth seem to me unprofitable to the Church, and unworthy to be publick: But such is M*r* *Crandons* book: Therefore.

I confess my Conscience would have received more then such a [little Check] as M*r* *Caryl* received, if I had been desired to approve or applaud such a book, though it had been against mine Enemy that it had been written (or else I know nothing of mine own heart:) It would sure have been [a Check] effectuall to the suspending of my Approbation? I have not read all the book (nor ever mean to do,) but I have perused the farre greatest part: and in most places, if not almost all, that seeming reason which he produceth, is so buried in a heap of Raging language, that I must read a great deal, before I can finde it. And so constant is he, and so violent in this language, upon no apparent cause given him, that I truly profess, I cannot but question whether the mans brain be sound or crackt, and the next I meet with that knowes him, I shall enquire better of it.

But I suppose M*r* *Caryl* will say, that for all this his book will be profitable to the Church of God, for the Doctrines sake that it containeth: But is sound Doctrine grown so rare in *England*, that it can be had from no cleanlier a hand then this? Are all our sober Divines turned Hereticks? And are all the old books that delivered sound Doctrine, lost or burnt. Sure when a Christian may gather all the sound Doctrine of this book from 500 more, where it is cleanlier delivered, it is not profitable to Gods Church to have the same delivered, in such infernall language. Are you sure that most or all Readers, will receive no hurt by such a Volume of false and Railing words? and that they who take the truth, will not take the filth and all? Had Mr. *Crandons* great friend desired me so to approve of such a book written against Mr. *Caryl* (supposing him of my judgement and me of his,) I think I should have taken it for a task of no more honour, then to have pind my name upon his close stool, to invite men to it as fit matter for publick food; and to tell them, that though it be matter of ill Resentment, yet it was Good till he concocted it, and perhaps there may be an Apple or two in the bottom if you can finde them. The words may seem unmannerly: but if our Righteousness be as Menstruous raggs, and the Sacrifices of wicked men be Dung, in the language of God, I think this Unrighteous, Impure Fardell, may patiently bear the same denominations.

But perhaps M*r* *Caryl* may say, Though all the sound Doctrine of this book be common, yet it is worthy of the publike view, and profitable to the Church, for the confutation of my Errors, and preserving men from the danger of infection. To which I say, 1. Will not the same sound Doctrine as it lay before in sober mens writings, preserve them better? 2. I do not believe that any one man will be preserved by the Argumentative part of his book: If the Reproaches preserve them not, by firing their affections, they are like to be neverthelefs in danger for this book. 3. But because this is the All that can be said, I will (though contrary to my former purposes) give a tast to Mr. *Caryl* of the force of this Authors *Vindication* of the Truth, and Confutation of the Errors; and it shall be the most substantiall

stantiall part of his book that I will take notice of, in which you may be able to judge of the rest.

SECT. III.

THe first thing that I will do, shall be to give you a tast of that Truth which he Vindicateth; and the second shall be to shew you the strength of his Confutations of my greatest Errors.

1. In his Epistle Dedicatory, his two first Points, which he seeks to vindicate from the Charge of Antinomianisme, are thus expressed [" 1. Justification is an " Immanent act in God; as actually Compleated in the Redemption which is by " Christ, and in Christ, both these before we believe. If he meant that Gods Immanent act is Compleated by Christ, it would according to himself make God himself Incompleat till Christ Compleat him: But, his meaning is, I beleeve, that Justification in Generall, and not that sort or act is Compleated in and by Christ before we believe; and if so, then it is as compleat to Infidels as to Christians: But because he puts in a Reserve afterwards, for caution [As far as I hold it] let us search how far he holds it. And *pag.* 106. he saith [" 4. Faith it " self (much less any other qualification, gift or act) is not a Condition of Ju- " stification *in foro Dei*: there Christ pleaded our discharge by his blood, and still " maketh intercession for us: but a means or Instrument by which we receive " Christ Jesus, and the Righteousness and Justification that is in him to our " selves for consolation and salvation *in foro conscientiæ.*] So then we are saved *in foro conscientiæ* by faith, and *in foro Dei* without it. Yet he forgot that elsewhere he calls it, *forum Dei in conscience,* as being of a better sound. And *pag.* 116. he saith [" That the blood of Christ is sufficient to Compleat our Justification be- " fore God, and that this is its own work: but that there are other Necessaries " to Justifie us in our selves and our own apprehensions, which being supposed " the work is endless. So *pag.* 89. [" Though as to themselves and their own " judgements, and as to the apprehensions of men, they are under the Law, under " wrath, yet in Christ they have done their Law, their Iniquities past, present " and to come are blotted out, their peace made, and they reconciled to God.] *Pag.* 354. He heaps up abusively severall texts of Scripture [as giving testimony of our Justification in Christ before faith entred to purifie our hearts, *&c.*] and annexeth [and all this before we had a being. *&c.*] when yet there is not so much as mention of Justification in any text but one that he citeth, and that one is abused; the words [being now Justified] being made to be [when we were enemies we were Justified;] and were nothing for him, if they had been so, as I have have shewed against *Colvinus:* Many other passages manifest his opinion, that Justification is from Eternity, and compleated before we were born, and that by faith, is but in our own Conscience, to save us there.

From hence it must needs follow, that no elect person, though an Infidell, may Confess any other Guilt or Misery but that which is opposite to Justification in Conscience: and that they must not Pray for any other Justification or pardon, and that they must not be beholden to Christ, nor thank him for any other pardon or Justification received since they believed or were born, but only this in Conscience; with abundance of the like consequents, of which I intend to say more anon.

M But

But these are not all his mistakes. *Part* 2. *pag.* 205. he saith that the saying of *Bernard* [" *Via regni sunt, non Causa regnandi*; some do, and all should thus construe: " not that they are the way to the Kingdom above, Christ alone being this way, " but they are the way of the Saints which are Christs spirituall Kingdome.] As if *Bernard* by *Via Regni*, meant the Kingdom now within us, when he opposeth it to *Causa Regnandi!* But see what an opposition he makes between [the way to the Kingdom above] and [the way of the Saints!] As if it might not, yea must not be both! As if he should say to a traveller [that is not the way to such or such a place, but it is the way of the traveller] The word [*way*] implieth no more then to have the nature of a Means to that End: and this man will have Christ only to be the *way* to the Kingdom above! as if Faith, Love, Obedience, Promises, Sacraments, other Ordinances, were no Means to the Kingdom above, and so that our salvation there were no End of any of these: and as if nothing else can be the way in subordination to Christ because Christ is the only way. These words may be toyes to some, and may please those ears that do by the opinions which they call Orthodox, as others in these times do by the opinions which are novell and heterodox, even place their Religion in holding such opinions: but I desire God to preserve his Church from the practising of them, as small a matter as they may seem to be: He that makes not Heaven his End, and knoweth of no Means to it, but Christ, never knew Christ aright, nor shall never come there. This I say, because I believe God.

Part 1. *pag.* 193. That [" Christ hath not Merited from Gods Naturall, but " his ordinate Justice, not in the *strict*, but in the *large* sense :] and this he makes " the ground of his bold Affirmation, [" That I do equallize the Merits of mans, " with the Merits of Christs Righteousness.] For the first part of his Assertion, I had rather Mr. *Owen* might school him, by his late *Diatrib. de Justitia vindicatrice*, then I dispute it with him: For the later, I know what I should have (justly) heard, if I had said that Christ merited not in the strict, but in the large sense. The large sense which I there express, is when there's no value in the thing, but meetly the promise of the Donor, that can be any Cause of that called Merit; and when it makes not the Reward to be of Debt, but meerly of Grace. And indeed is that man orthodox, and a vindicater of Christ and his Merits against Popery, that affirmeth that Christ hath no otherwise merited then thus? I will not ask, Whether this be consistent with Christianity it self: But I that am, with this man the great enemy of free Grace, do profess to believe, that it was the Value of Christs performance that made it Meritorious, as it was a most excellent Means to the attainment of Gods Ends: and that it made the Reward to be of Debt to Christ, and not of meer Grace; and that it was Merit in the strictest sense, even on the termes of Commutative Justice, considering it as undertaken and dignified by the second Person in Trinity, who was never obliged by subjection but by voluntary sponsion; and that afterward as performed by God-man, under the Law, it was strictly and properly meritorious from Distributive Justice. See then how the Vindicators of free Grace, do Maintain it by Denying it, and the supposed enemies of it acknowledge and maintain it! And whether this Doctrine be Profitable to the Church of God, and worthy of the publick view?

Part 1. *pag* 320, 321. You may see more how he advanceth Christ in the work of our Justification. He tells me that [" He will deny my Assertion [that " Christs satisfaction is the Meritorious Cause of Justification] unless I will " grant him these 4 or 5 suppositions. 1. That so farre as Justification is an act
" Eternall

" Eternall and Immanent in God, Chrifts fatisfaction is not the Meritorious
" Caufe of it. 2. If in fome other refpect it be the Meritorious Caufe, that God
" doth therein merit of himfelf. 3. That this Merit muft in no wife hinder but
" that the entire benefit of Juftification muft come to us freely without money or
" price. 4. That it is but unproperly termed Merit, even then when it refpecteth
" the difcharge which God giveth into a mans confcience, &c. 5. That Chrifts
" fatisfaction is more properly to be called Gods foundation of this our new Re-
" lation of Juftified perfons, upon which he hath inabled himfelf to Juftifie us in
" Mercy, without any feeming diminution of his Juftice and truth.] You fee now
how far Chrift hath merited our Juftification, according to this zealous Patron
of his Merits. 1. The Immanent Juftification, he neither did nor could merit:
as p.321. he faith again, and he faith I will and muft grant it: But I conjecture
(for its a high bufinefs) that Gods effence is but *Denominatione extrinfec.i* called
[Juftifying] or [fuch or fuch an immanent act:] and that this extrinfick Denomination may *oriri de novo*, and not be eternal; becaufe of the newnefs of the
object: it being a denomination from Relation, which is not fubjected properly
in God as Related to the object really, but in the objects Relation to God, from
whence it is only denominatively and rationally given to God: This is the doctrine of *Aquinas, Capreolus*, and the reft of that Tribe, and the other Schoolmen in
greateft credit (Papifts) confefs, but) owned alfo by thofe Proteftants that are
the greateft adverfaries to the Arminian Caufe: This being fo, even the Immanent Juftification, if there be any fo to be called (as the Efteeming and Accepting us as Righteous) is the effect of Chrifts Merits, and the Confequent of faith:
(Though I eafily acknowledge, the Eternall Decree to Juftifie, is not fo.) And
do not our Divines of the Affembly, in the Catechifme and Confeffion, define
Juftification by Remiffion and *Accepting* us as Righteous? And Accepting is
taken for an Immanent Act (and is, unlefs you take it improperly for the Acceptance of the Law it felf, rather then of the Law-giver.) And yet they affirm it to
follow faith, and to be the fruit of Chrifts Merit.

2. But this Juftification Mr. *Crandon* denieth to proceed from Chrifts Merits,
and the fecond here named is but [the difcharge given in to Confcience:] and in
refpect to this he faith, it is but improperly termed merit. Is not Chrifts Merit
then well advanced? Juftification in God he meriteth not at all; Juftification in
Confcience he meriteth but [improperly.]

But perhaps you will fay, He might yet properly Merit a third Juftification not
there mentioned, *viz.* his own as the publick perfon, and ours in him. I anfwer,
1. There is no fuch thing as our Juftification in Chrift, properly fo called; (and
the phrafe that I ufed that way, I have already publifhed my revocation of. 2. He
that knowes no Juftification of us perfonally, but Immanent in God from eternity,
and Tranfient in Confcience, will likely acknowledge no other to Chrift: and fo
the Juftification of Chrift himfelf as the publick perfon, is either Immanent, and
that, fay they, he merited not; or tranfient in the Confcience of Chrift, and that
is but unproperly called Merit. A fair Advancement of Chrifts Merit. Thus over-
doers are the moft fuccefsfull undoers.

But fuppofe that he had acknowledged the moft proper Meriting of Juftification
in Confcience, (both in the Confcience of Chrift, if he will fo fpeak, and of us;)
is this a fair dignifying of the Merit of Chrift? what! to Merit no Juftification
but that in Confcience; I affure Mr. *Caryl*, I that am taken by him for the op-
pofer [of Juftification by Chrifts fatisfaction alone without works] do give in-

M 2   comparably

comparably more then this to his satisfaction alone without works. And should I write such a Volume to maintain that Christ Merited only Justification in Conscience, my conscience would tell me I could not well be justified from the Imputation of either Socinianisme or Judaisme. Woe to him that hath not a more necessary Justification in Law, going before that in Conscience, and a more noble Justification in Gods sentence following after it.

And seeing it is but Justification in Conscience that he ascribeth to faith, how can he exclude other graces from it, when they may evidence Justification to the Conscience as well as faith ? and it is not Justifying faith it self that is the Receiving of this sense of Comfort or Peace, called Justification in Conscience, (though it Receive Christ that gives it,) but it is directly the Internall sense, and self-reflecting Knowledge, that is the Reception of this kinde of Justification. And how much the men of these principles are forced to give to Works, to Justifie in Conscience, may be seen in *Colvinus* and others.

I had thought to have shewed you more of his Doctrines, to try whether they are profitable to the Church of God : but I am weary of thus much: and doubt the Reader will be so to. Yet let me give you a tast of the humility and modesty of his language of the high God.

SECT. IV.

Part 1. *pag.* 301. Against my Conditionall Justification, he thus argueth ; [" 1. Whatsoever sinnes of whatsoever persons were Imputed to Christ, and for " which he hath made full satisfaction to Gods Justice, these are no more Impu- " ted, but for ever remitted in Christ Absolutely and unconditionally to them who " were the committers thereof. But all the sinnes of all the Elect, and of them on- " ly, and not of the world, were Imputed to Christ, and he hath made full satis- " faction, &c Therefore.] The Proposition is a desperate errour, of such consequence, as is fearfull to consider : yet is said by this man [to be clear, unless we will pronounce God to be unjust.] See here a little more of the face of his sound Doctrine ! *Paul* saith, Rom 4. 24. that faith shall be Imputed to us for Righteousness, if we believe,] and till Righteousness is Imputed sinne is Imputed. *Paul* saith, that *God hath shut up all under sinne, that the promise in Jesus Christ might be to them that believe*: Christ saith, *He that believeth not, is condemned already*, [and the *wrath of God abideth on him*. How frequently doth Scripture describe the misery of an unregenerate mans estate, that he is *by nature the childe of wrath*, that such are *strangers to the Covenant of Promise, without Hope, without God in the world* (at least the Gentile part,) and still they Receive Remission, and Justification, and Adoption, when they believe. Yet this man dare say, That no sinne is ever Imputed more to these men, though Infidels, if Elect, because Christ hath satisfied, but they are all Absolutely and unconditionally Remitted to them who were the committers thereof.] So that if this be true, no Elect Infidell, is capable of any pardon of sinne from his youth to his death, all being done in Christ before (except assuring us in Conscience of it :) and so they have no such pardon to pray for, desire, endeavour after, or acknowledge. Do not call this Doctrine Libertinisme, least you wrong it, or be a Papist for so doing.

But there is his proof, That [" God is unjust, if any sinne be Imputed to any " man, which was before Imputed to Christ, and he satisfied for.] He saith
[" For

[" For if he should Impute to the offender any one sinne, which, was Imputed to
" Christ, and for which Christ hath fully satisfied Gods Justice, then should
" God be unjust in taking vengeance twice of the same sinne, &c. contrary to the
" equity of his Iustice, and infallibility of his Truth, &c.] See how high a charge
this Brother of ours, this dust, this earth-worm, dare lay against the Almighty God,
even as high, as of Injustice and untruth, should he but Impute one sinfull word or
thought to an Infidell or Pagan, that is elect.

But yet this is his more humble and meeker language. *Pag 55. Part.1.* He
fals on me as a Papist, for saying that 1. Some part of the curse (that is, the evil
threatned for sinne) is executed on the whole man, soul and body. 2. That till
the resurrection, all the effects of sinne, and Law and wrath will not be removed.
3. That there is no unpardoned sinne in the death of Believers which shall procure further judgement, and so no hatred in it, though there be anger. I recite
the words as he rakes them together in his order: But let this stand at present.
What if I affirm that the death of the Godly is a penal effect of sinne, and the law
and Gods wrath? (still maintaining that this which is of it self a penal evil, is
sanctified by God for their good, he maketh all their chastisements to be their advantage, and the effects of his anger are means to prevent that destruction which
is the effect of his hatred to them that suffer it:) What if I say that their death
may be from Gods anger yet from his love as prevalent, and that there is no unpardoned sinne in that death, to bring further judgement on them? Why you
shall hear what thanks this man would give God for such a mercy as his eternal
salvation, supposing that there be any sinne, law and anger the cause of his death.
He saith [" A glorious priviledge no doubt! such as, according to our usual
" Proverb, a man may finde at *Billingsgate* for a box on the ear, from the worst of
" men that he meets with! When a man hath in revengefull fury persecuted his
" hated neighbour with all the strokes and storms of wrath and mischief, and after
" many years persecution, hath at last slaughtered him, and trampled his dead
" corps into the mire and dust, now at last he ceaseth from hatred, and is but an-
" gry with his poor relicks, forgives him all the rest, when he can do no more
" to him, and forgiveness can do him no good. Such tender mercies of cruelty (as
" the wise man terms them, *Prov.* 12.10.) doth Mr *Baxter* here ascribe unto God,
" in his gracious dealings with believers for Christs sake, viz. to persecute them
" with all the stroaks of his wrath, and all the curses of the Law, all their life
" time, sparing neither their body nor soul, and at last with great indignation to
" destroy them, and trample their bodies into the earth, dust and rottenness, yea
" and their souls whither he list, and under what torments he list, and after this
" (so remarkable is his love) he will hate them no more, but be angry with them
" still. When they are dead and can offend no more, and God hath inflicted up-
" on them all his judgements, that he can inflict no more, now their sins shall be
" so pardoned that they shall suffer no more, no more then all, which they already
" suffer. Who denies this to be the very quintessence of mercy and spirits of love,
" when Mr *Baxter* hath so defined it, and held it forth to us as the most celestial
" comfort that we shall finde in death. There is, saith he, no unpardoned sin in
" the death of Believers that shall procure further judgement.]

The Lord pardon the great hardness of my heart, that trembleth no more at the
most horrid blaspheming of his sacred Name! and that is no more deeply affected with zeal for God, and compassion to the man that durst use this direfull language! If it should prove true, that the chastisements and death of the Saints are

penalties,

Penalties, and though sanctified to their good, are yet in themselves evil, and so far as evil, the effects of Gods displeasure and wrath; dare man therefore vomit out all these horrid reproaches against the God of heaven! Is God as bad as the worst of men for this? Would the worst of men for a box on the ear, bestow everlasting salvation on us, besides all the unspeakable riches of mercy, which (for all these penal chastisements) we receive in this life? Doth God no more then the worst of men would do for nothing, if he give us his Christ to redeem us from the curse that we were fallen under by our sinne, and to become the Physitian of our wounded, defiled souls, and to undertake the perfect cure (though he will not finish it till death) giving us his Spirit, remitting our sins perfectly at the present, as to all the destructive punishment, and making a saving Medicine of all the castigatory punishment which remains? Is it nothing to be delivered from Gods burning jealousie and hatred which he beareth to all the workers of iniquity, and from eternal flames which else we must have undergone? The Lord pity and watch over the hearts of his people! or else whither will they run! O sad case, to hear a Christian zealot speak the language of a *Rabshakeh*. He will say, no doubt, he intends these but against me, as the consequents of my doctrine: But should the dreadfull God be thus desperately charged, in case my supposition were true! And hath he not reason, at least, to take it as disputable, when the Scripture speaks it in most express terms, so frequently as it doth? How commonly doth it call our sufferings, chastisements, and punishments, and express God as angry with his People, and make their sinne the cause! See the texts cited before in my Confession. And beside the fearfull language here given to God, what a multitude of false Accusations, palpable falshoods are here heaped up and charged on me, as if it were my doctrine, (whether directly or consequentially.) 1. The scornfull term of [A glorious priviledge!] implies a falshood, as if heaven were no such thing. 2. That he may have the like of the worst of men for a box on the ear, is as false as horrid. 3. That God persecuteth his people in revengefull fury, or that I ever so taught, is as false. 4. That it is with all the strokes and storms of wrath and mischief : when I still professed that it is but the Remnants of sinne, moderated by Paternal affections of abundant Love. 5. That God having slaughtered us, trampleth our dead corps in the mire and dust; all expressing revengefull enmity. 6. That he ceaseth then from hatred; when the man himself is forced to take notice, that I deny God to do any thing in hatred to his people, but in anger and love as fathers chastise, speaking of the affect from the effect; and so the love still greater then the anger. 7. That he feigns me to make God angry with his reliques : when I never so said; though now I will say, that our bodies being so many years in the dust, when else they should have been in Paradise, is penal, and so farre may be said to be an effect of Gods anger, as it is penal. 8. That God then forgives him the rest, when he can do no more to him, is a scorn of salvation, and a falshood : What! can God do no more to a man when he is dead! Cannot he raise his body to torments, and torment his soul, and shut him everlastingly out of his glory! What desperate words are these! 9. That forgiveness can then do him no good, is as false, unless the Everlasting fruition of God, and the escape of damnation be no good. 10. As false and horrid is it, that such dealing is cruelty, or that I charge Gods tender mercies to be cruelty, as he vilely applies *Prov.* 12.10. to God, which describeth the wicked. 11. He repeats the same falshood again, that I make God to persecute them with all the stroaks of his wrath. 12. And with all the curses of the Law : as if we were delivered

livered from no curse, if our castigations are in any measure penal. 13. As false is it, that I say, He spareth neither their bodies nor souls! when he unconceivably spareth them in his sharpest chastisements! Is there no sparing, if there be any penalty? 14. As false that I say, he doth at last in great indignation, destroy them: Though death destroy the body, I called it not a destroying the man, nor said God did it in great indignation. 15. Nor did I say he tramples their bodies to rottenness. 16. Nor did I ever say, he trampleth their souls whither he list: for his list is to glorifie, and not trample them. 17. Much less said I, that he trampleth them to what torments he list, when I expresly said, they had no further punishments, and elsewhere proved by twenty Arguments against the Socinians, that they go immediatly to blessedness with Christ. 18. After the scorn at Gods love, the next words are as false, that I say, He will hate them no more, as if I said that he hated them till then, or said not the contrary. 19. And as false that I say, He will be angry with them still. 20. Its not true that the dead can offend no more, if they are such as lie under all Gods judgements. 21. Its false that I say, God inflicteth on them All his judgements. 22. Or that he can Inflict no more. 23. Or that they have suffered all already. 24. Or that I ever said directly or consequentially, that this is all the Comfort we shall finde in death. All these are as false, as that the Sunne is meer darkness. Yet the very next words add more of the same nature. 25. He saith, I say not absolutely there is no unpardoned sinne on the Saints after death, but none so unpardoned: when my words were these: [" There is no unpardoned sinne in it, which shall procure " further Iudgement, and so no hatred, though there be anger.] And I think in Scripture sense, no sinne is unpardoned, when the sinner hath Absolute Right to Glory and Impunity, at present for the soul, and *in diem* for the body to be with Christ. 26. Next he addeth, That [" I deny not, but rather imply, their sinnes " to be yet still unpardoned, to the holding on them those Iudgements already in- " flicted: a comfort that the Devils and Reprobates in Hell shall not want after " the very day of Iudgement in the midst of those flames, &c.] 27. He makes me to affirm that the soul shall suffer till the Resurrection: And thus he goes on in falshoods as thick almost as lines, and sometimes more! Contrary to my express words from which he would force them. When I say, that In the death of believers, that is, on dying believers, there is no unpardoned sinne, which shall procure further Iudgement, besides or after death it self; he falsly chargeth me to say, that even the soul suffereth after; when I have many years ago in my book of *Rest* by twenty Arguments (as is said) proved that they go to rest with Christ.

***

But I am fallen before I intended it on the second part of my task, to shew Mr. *Caryl* how this man vindicateth the truth against me. And because I am cast on this point, and this is the first point that Mr. *Caryl* mentions as vindicated against me, I will proceed a little further to try the success of his attempts.

1. That which is Vindicated by most direfull blasphemings of the Name of God, is not well Vindicated: But such is Mr. *Cr*'s supposed Vindication of truth, as I have begun to shew; and if you will reade on, you may finde him proceed in the same rage.

His third charge against this Doctrine (that Believers sufferings are punishments) is this: He saith, [" It is scandalous to the grace and mercy of God, &c. " making flames of fury to break out from the very bowels of his compassion, that
"poor

[22]

"poor souls believing what he saith, will be apt to fly from God as from a Satan, and from his Gospel dispensations, as from death and hell it self. When they hear him to be so bloody, to take delight in cursing, crushing, rending, tearing and tormenting in soul and body, unto death, and after death, his own sons and daughters, and that under a profession of grace and love to them, what difference can they conceive to be between such a God and the Devil? If there be such bitterness in his Love, who will desire the least draughts thereof? If his armes of embracing be such Lions paws, who will not shun all union, all drawing nigh to him, &c.] The next Accusation is this. [4. It is slanderous to the justice of God, 1. By accusing it there to inflict the curse, wrath and judgements, where he imputeth no sinne. 2. By charging it to receive full satisfaction for our debt, from Christ our Surety, and afterward when all is paid to require satisfaction from us too. A piece of injustice so odious to the light of nature it self, that Mr. Baxter would account him a prodigy of Nature, a Devillized man that should so do, yet hath he the face to charge the most righteous God therewith.] Thus he proceedeth, heaping up more of these direfull consequents, as he imagineth, to the number of ten. These words I consider first as they are a charge against God, and secondly, as a charge against me. 1. What will you call that man, that durst lay all this to the charge of God, supposing he did deal with man as hardly as I expressed? Suppose God did lay all the evil that we bear upon us as penal, yet sanctifying this to our advantage, and saving us for ever; shall the creature conclude to the face of God, that he is cruel, bloudy, delighting in tormenting soul and body, and that there's little or no difference between him and the Devil? and his love and union not to be desired, &c? I professe my flesh trembleth at the writing and thinking of these words? What if it were true (for disputation sake he will sure give us leave to suppose it), that after all Christs satisfaction, God should inflict the penalty of a toothach, or of sickness, or of temporal death on our selves, shall dust and ashes stand up, and tell God, that *none but a prodigie of Nature, a Devillized man would do so*, among men! O Christians look to your hearts! you see what fruits the corrupt seed that is there latent would bring forth, if God should leave you to your selves. Did I think that God had had a creature on the earth, that durst have uttered such words, till the Ranters lately arose, and till I now read them in this Book? Did I think there had been a Preacher of the Gospel, zealous for the honour of Gods grace, that durst have spoke thus? O sinfull man, whither art thou fallen? O patient God, what indignities dost thou put up! Open your eyes, whoever of you are of this mans opinion, that there is no penal effects of sinne remaining on us, and see whether you need any further proof, then the legible demonstration of his own hideous reproaches of the Almighty? Is the withdrawing of the Spirit of God, so farre, as that all this sinne should follow no punishment? Is all this horrid sinne the fruit of nothing but Love in God? Is former sin no cause of this? O blinded man that can believe it.

2. As all these are made the doctrine which I deliver, and he saith, I charge the righteous God therewith, I have but one answer, That the Accuser is the most monstrous false speaker that ever I had to do with. Here are almost as many untruths as lines still. Where and when did I ever say, that *God requireth satisfaction of us, or that God was bloody, or took delight in cursing, crushing, rending, tearing, tormenting soul and body unto death and after death, of his own children, and that under a profession of Grace and Love?* Nay where said I that ever he doth, though without

out delight, torment them after death? Nay how expresly have I denied all this here? Besides what I have largelier written of Afflictions and Death, in my Book of Rest, Part 3ᵈ, *Chap.* 12. and *Part* 4. *Chap.*2. which I desire the Reader to see, if he would know whether this mans Accusations be true or false.

My second Reason therefore which I give Mʳ *Caryl* against the profitableness of this Vindication is this. To heap up a multitude of Lies is not a Vindication of Fundamental Truth, profitable to the Church of God: But such is this Vindication of Mr. *Crandons*: Therefore.

I troubled my self and the Reader to number 27 even now in one piece of a leaf, there being more on the same leaf: And how many are in the next? It goes against my minde, and is unsavoury to me, so much as to name the fault of this Volume: but I must profess that I never saw a Theological discourse (to my best remembrance) that might be so sufficiently answered almost from end to end (in the points of difference) with one word, *Mentiris* (as *Bellarmine* was once answered) as this Book of Mr.*Cr*'s.

And because this is the great point of offence, I will go back to his stating the Question, and his arguings and Answers to my Arguments.

SECT. V.

Ag. 31. he poureth out his raving terms for not right stating the Question, and thereupon he will state it better, and deal with me as an opposer of the new Question of his stating, and not of that which I stated my self: I professed only to dissent from them that deny our sufferings to be any sort of punishments, or the moral effects of sinne, or to proceed from Gods anger or threatning. For as I maintain on one hand, that they are but meer chastisements, having more good in them by Accident then evil in themselves, and therefore more of Gods love then his wrath; so I maintain that still as they are evil of themselves, and as farre as they are penal, our sinne and Gods anger and threat are the causes of them.

Yet here I confess two faults that I committed in that Dispute. The first was in wronging the Reformed Divines, by making the opinion which I oppose to be more commonly held by them then indeed it is. But the Reasons of my mistake were 1. That I had not then read so many that speak otherwise as since I have done: 2. I had last been reading two or three of great Name that speak in that language, and I so much fixed on their words, that I enquired not with sufficient diligence into the words of others. This I do now reverse, as finding that it is very common among the Reformed Divines to hold and maintain that our Afflictions are Penal. The second thing which I now disapprove is, that I used the word [Curse] though I expressed that I meant nothing by it, but either any part of the Threatning, or any part of the evil Threatned: and though the Scripture it self do frequently apply the word [Curse] even to chastisements upon Believers, as I have proved before at large: Yet because our common use of the word [Curse] is such as intimateth some Revenging, Destructive Punishment, that may denominate the man Accursed, I think I should have forborn it, and hereafter purpose so to do. Though I ever professed that it is utterly unfit to call Believers Accursed, though their penalty might be called some part of the Curse; because the Person is to be Denominated from that which is Predominant: and

[24]

the Curse or Evil is but comparatively small, and in the way of certain Cure; but the Good of Blessing is so great, that the weakest Christian is a Blessed Man.

But Mr. *Cr.* would perswade us, *pag.* 31. that the Reformed Divines that I opposed in that Point, are of his minde, [" That our Sufferings are Chastisements " and Trials flowing from the same Grace and Love, by which Christ himself, " and the Redemption we have by him, issued, *&c.*] What gross contradictions doth this man hold? *viz.* That our Sufferings are Chastisements, and yet 1. no Punishments, 2. nor for sinne, 3. nor from Gods Wrath? I easily confess that they proceed from Gods Love: Did I not maintain that in the Papers which he writes against? But so farre as they are Evil and Penal they proceed not from his Love; but only so faire as they are Medicinal and Means intended to our further benefit. Did ever man on earth, before this man, know such a thing as chastisement which was not for sinne as the Meritorious Cause? or which was no whit Penal? Its as palpable a contradiction as to say, This Paper hath whitenes, and this Ink hath blacknes, but neither of them hath Colour: or that Mr. *Cr.* is a Man, but not an Animal.

I must desire the Reader therefore well to observe these two things, 1. What is indeed the Judgement of our Divines and Churches in this point. 2. What is Mr. *Crandons* Judgement, and the true state of the Controversie between him and me. 1. The Reformed Churches and Divines do very frequently give the name of Penalty to our Chastifements: But yet *Pet. Martyr* and some more in their Disputings with the Papists, do deny them to be Punishments. But then mark, that the reason is because they did appropriate the name of Punishment to one *species*, which we call Destructive, Vindictive Punishment: so that it was but the Name and not the Thing that they denied: For they still give it the definition of Punishment, and confess it to be a natural evil (usually involuntary) inflicted for a moral evil: and then sinne is its meritorious cause, as it is evil. And it is undeniable that these Divines did very unjustly deny the name of the *genus* to one *species,* and where they give the definition. Whether the heat of Disputation were the cause of this (which Mr. *Cr.* so much ascribeth his opinion of Justification to), or what else, I will not judge; but as herein they contradicted multitudes of their Brethren, so did they contradict all Philosophers and Lawyers, or any other Politicians, that ever I read or heard of, or I think, ever shall do. But still this is but a verbal difference. 2. But it is a Real Difference between us and Mr. *Crandon.* The true state of the Controversie you may gather partly from what is cited out of him before, where he makes it so horrid, prodigious and devillish a thing, to inflict any punishment on us, to satisfie for those sinnes that Christ hath satisfied for, withall (falsly) supposing that all punishment is Satisfactory to Justice: But fully doth he express his minde, *pag.* 41. in these words, [*We grant a Believers sinne to be oft the Occasion, never the proper Cause of his suffering.*

On the contrary, I maintain that sinne is ever the meritorious cause of all his castigatory sufferings, so farre as they are penal, and that penal they are so farre as evil (at least usually) and that evil they are of themselves, notwithstanding the greater accidental good which shall follow them.

Here then is the true state of the Question between Mr. *Cr.* and me: and for my part I undertook to maintain no more in sense, then this: and who can engage me to more against my will, I know not. I again profess, that though my own

opinion

opinion be, that these Chastisements (especially death, sinne (as a consequent of the withdrawing of the Spirit) and loss of Communion with God in so great a measure, and the decaies of grace) are partly the remnants of the (curse, as I then called it, or) threatned and inflicted Penalty of the first Law, as the evil that Christ our Physitian is curing, and by degrees taking off, and partly the effects of the threatning of the Law of Grace, in execution of Paternal Justice; yet I will not contend with any man, *what Law they come from*, whether the Moral Law, or the Law of Grace, so they will but yield that sinne is the Meritorious Cause, and some Law of God is the Cause by its Commination; and Paternal displeasure and Justice in God, is the cause so farre as it is penal and evil. Or if they grant any one of these, I take it as the granting of all.

Now when this is the true state of the Question, see how honestly Mr. *Cr.* stateth it, *pag.* 32,33. 1. He saith [" It is agreed on both sides, that the curse is " the penalty, or the revenging judgement, or an effect of Gods revenging wrath, " by the execution whereof he taketh satisfaction to his Justice upon transgressors, " for the breach of his Law: so Mr. *B.* makes it out, *p* 17.]

The simple Reader, seeing such a man as Mr. *Caryl* commend the Vindication of these points, may easily think, All this is sure true; when there are as many falshoods as lines. My words which he referres you to, as agreeing to all this, are these only, [This Covenant being soon by man violated, the threatning must be fulfilled, and so the penalty suffered] (these words should have been added [unless sufficient satisfaction were made to God.]) 1. I never said that the curse or penalty now in question, is The penalty absolutely considered, or the whole penalty, but a part of that penalty, comparatively exceeding small, managed by the Physitians hands for our cure. 2. Is here ever a word of mine that mentioneth [Revenging Justice?] I maintain that so small a part of the penalty, used by a father as a means to save us from the whole, is not Revenging Justice, (as the word is commonly taken, for that Justice which will have the ruine of the offendour, or that affliction where it is intended to do him more hurt then good) but it is Paternal Justice that now disposeth it. 3. Nor did I there or ever say, It is an effect of Gods Revenging Wrath. 4. Nor did I there or ever agree, that in execution hereof God taketh any satisfaction to his Justice. Compare my words with his, and see if there be ever such a word as any of these.

His next words, as expressing how far we are agreed, are these [" 2. That the " Justice of God is so fully satisfied, by this curse or penalty, as by a compleat full- " filling of all the righteousness which the Law requireth, *p*.48,50.]

To which I Reply, 1. If the Reader will peruse my Book in the pages quoted, he shall finde no such word there. I only speak there of Christs satisfaction, and not of any suffering, or execution at all. I do not think that the sufferings of the damned do satisfie Justice properly; for if Justice were satisfied they should be freed. 2. If I had said the words that he citeth of the whole Penalty, doth he well and truly in applying it to an inconsiderable part turned to good? Will it follow that because I teach that Justice is satisfied when the whole penalty of eternal damnation is born, therefore it is satisfied if God leave on us but the least part, though for our own advantage? 3. He cannot be content to put untruths on me, but he addeth *non* sense to it: when he speaks of the satisfaction of Justice by suffering, he can mean none but punishing justice: And did I ever say that this justice is as fully satisfied by bearing the curse, as by fulfilling all Righteousness which it requireth? This were to imply, that Punient or Vindictive justice is satisfied also by Obedience, or fulfilling Righteousnesse; which was never before heard of. Obedience is the fulfilling of the Precept, and not of the Threat.

His third and fourth agreed Propositions are [That Christ hath satisfied, and that God is satisfied fully.] Which I easily agree to, supposing still that the fulness of Christs satisfaction be judged of from the true ends of it, and not by feigned ends. It was never the end of Christs satisfaction, immediatly to effect our full deliverance, but to bring us into Christs Kingdom of grace first, that in the time of this life he might perform the cure, and so deliver us Perfect into the Fathers Kingdom of Glory. The same God that received satisfaction, received it with this intent and to this end, that we might be delivered by degrees from the penal effects of our sinne, and sinne it self, and might be brought under a lighter burden and easier yoak, even a Law of Grace, which hath its Comminations as well as its Promises, yea some Comminations to Believers for their miscarriages, and the principal penalty of this Law is, more or less, a *non*-liberation from the penalty or misery that we had brought on our selves by violating the Law of Nature, or Works, or the Moral Law (call it which you will.) So that as the *non*-liberation from eternal torments is its penalty executed on the finally impenitent, so the *non*-liberation from some degrees of sinne, of outward and inward temporal penalties, and death it self, is its penalty executed on Believers for their sinnes. So that God never intended in receiving satisfaction, to free them presently from all penalty, even castigatory as well as destructive; nor to leave them Lawless, nor under a Law that had no Commination, or none that should be executed on them. The great ignorance of this one point, and the misunderstanding of the Doctrine of Christs satisfaction is the very Heart of all the Antinomian Errours. I told you before that even the Authour of the *Marrow of Modern Divinity* approved by Mr. *Caryl*, and here Vindicated (in his common way) by Mr. *Cr.* doth confesse our Chastisements to be Penalties of the Law of Christ executed on us for sinne.

Because it is a weighty point, and if Mr. *Cr.* be cured it must be here, from whence all the rest of his mistakes do seem to rise, I will propound to his Consideration these things following, as a few of my reasons against his way.

1. He seemeth to me to confound the Kingdom of Glory and of Grace, or not to understand the difference. God hath three Kingdoms, in *specie*, over mankinde, whereof the first two are on earth and the third in heaven (though in regard of the Identity of the Soveraign, subjects, &c. they may be called all one:) These are grounded on a threefold *Jus Dominii & Imperii*, Right of Propriety and Government: *viz*. His Creation, Redemption, and Raising and Glorifying us. The first was the Kingdom of God over Perfect man, and is never called the Kingdom of the Son, or the Mediatour, or Redeemer: This endured but till the fall of man. The second is the Kingdom of the Son, or Redeemer, which is distinguished from the rest by the Foundation of Right (General Redemption) by its Ends, Laws, State of the subjects, &c. The work and end of this Kingdom, is to effect mans cure and recovery, and to bring the lapsed disobedient creature, to a perfect Conformity and Obedience to God again: so that this whole Kingdom, from first to last, will be imployed in Recovery and Cure, and when that is finished, the Son then shall deliver up the Kingdom to the Father, 1 *Cor.* 15. 24, 25, 27. not laying by his humane Nature, Authority or Honour, but that *species* of Government which was Medicinal, Restorative, and for Reduction of the dis-

obedient

obedient to God that made them; and so as a Conquering General, as a Physitian that hath finished the Cure, so will the Kingdom of Christ then cease, his work being done, and the Restored delivered Spotless to the Father: And then it shall be the Kingdom of the Father, of God, again, in the fullest sense.

Now Mr. *Cr.* supposing that Christs satisfaction hath set us presently on as good terms as if we had never sinned, and perfecteth our state, as to all guilt and punishment, and that upon the very sacrifice offered, doth hereby confound the Kingdom of Grace and Glory (a small mistake!) and while he takes himself to be perfected (in those particulars, though not in holiness) he destroyeth Christs Kingdom, and dreameth that he is in another, that the good man never yet did see. Perfection is reserved to the Kingdom of Perfection. If he have no punishment to suffer, then he is certainly in heaven already: Unlesse to be out of heaven so long, and to be without more Communion with God, and without perfection of holinefs, be no *Pœna damni*: which I will not yet believe.

2. If God may justly Threaten damnation to them for whom Christ hath satisfied, then he may justly execute the penalty of some bodily sufferings and death: But the Antecedent is true: therefore so is the Consequent. [*Except ye Repent, ye shall all likewise perish: If ye live after the flesh ye shall die: If any man draw back, his soul shall have no pleasure in him:* Luk. 13.5. Rom. 8.13. Heb. 10.38. with multitudes of the like, are undeniably conditional Threats to the Redeemed, as well as those supposed to be unredeemed.

3. Nay doth not Mr. *Cr*'s direfull charge against God, if he should punish us for the same sinne that Christ satisfied for, as evidently fall upon God for his very Threatnings? For an unjust Law, is no more justifiable then an unjust execution. And if the least execution of penalty were so unjust and vile a thing as he makes it, must not the Threatning of incomparably more, be so much more injustice in the Law? But I will adde no more of this, but proceed to Mr. *Cr.* enumeration of our Agreements.

5. The fifth is, " That Afflictions are incident to Believers. The sixth is, " That these Afflictions have in them a smart and bitternefs, as they befall the " Saints, so that ofttimes in their apprehension the very wrath and curse seems to " be in them.]

But here's no Agreement, that any of this is for sin, and so is a Chastifement, which is ever Penal.

[" The difference then (faith Mr. *Cr.*) betwixt him and us, consists princi- " pally in these two things. 1. Whether when Christ hath by doing their Law, " paying their debt, and bearing their curse, satisfied the justice of God for " the sinnes of Believers, when God hath accepted the satisfaction given, when " Believers have by faith apprehended and laid hold on it, they do yet re- " main liable to the curse of the Law in whole or in part to be inflicted on " them.]

1. Here he fraudulently would make the Reader believe that it is only the case of Believers that is in Question, when he hath poured forth such direfull Accusations against God, if he punish any man for that which Christ hath satisfied for; whether he be a Believer, or yet an Infidell, varies not the case. 2. He falsly maketh the Question to concern the *whole* curse of the Law, or part, when it only concerneth the smallest part for a small time. 3. He fasteneth upon the term [Curse] thinking the sound will somewhat advantage him, and letteth passe

the

the terms that I more frequently used, as the Threatning, the Anger of God, &c. Now doth he let the Reader know that by the Curse I explained my self to mean some small part of the Threatned evil, sanctified to a greater good. He proceeds.

[" 2. Whether the Afflictions which God inflicteth on believers in this life, are "the effects of Gods Revenging Justice, the Curse which the Law threatneth, "and so consequently, whether after that God hath taken full satisfaction from "Christ, he doth in whole or in part require and take satisfaction from them al- "so. Mr *Baxter* with the Papists and Arminians maintains the affirmative of "both these questions, we the Negative: He saith that 1. After Christ hath born "the Curse of the Law for believers, they are liable to bear it in whole or in part "themselves also. 2. That the afflictions which they suffer are from the Reveng- "ing Justice of God, the effects and Curse of the Law, Vindictive Punishment "of sinne, full of the wrath of God; as in his answer to the third question he de- "clares himself.]

Are we not like to dispute fairly, when in the state of the Question we have such a heap of forgeries? How false is it that ever I said 1. That our Afflictions are the effects of Gods Revenging Iustice? 2. Or Vindictive Punishments. 3. Or full of the Wrath of God. As all these are the fictions of the false Accuser, and never spoken or written by me, so neither do I hold them to be from Vindictive Iustice in any other sense then Paternal Chastisements are.

Upon this Calumniation, called a stating of the Question, he proceeds to his proofs for his opinion, from some Scriptures abused, and others that expresly condemn his cause, calling our sufferings, the Chastisements of Children. And did Mr. *Crandon* ever know a Father chastise his childe for no fault, in meer Love, or without any fault as the meritorious cause but only the occasion? I will not trouble the Readers Patience with his vain Reasonings.

Next he proceedeth to answer my Arguments: *p.38.c.6.* To the first from *Gen.*3.7, to 20. he saith [" He must first prove that they were believers, which a "meer and dark promulgation of a Saviour, *Gen.*3.15.doth not evince (for many "thousands have had the Gospel more fully and clearly preached to them, yet have "continued in unbelief. 2. That the sufferings to which his quotations direct, "were inflicted upon them as a Curse by Gods revenging Justice.] To which I Reply: 1. If his Cause have so ticklish a standing, that it must fall unless *Adam* and *Eve* were Infidels, I suppose it will stand but in the judgement of a very few. 2. I thought according to his doctrine, the very entring of that Covenant of Grace with them, would have proved them elect, and the promising of a Saviour for them. 2. I took it as undeniable, that the sentence *Gen.*3. was not passed upon one man only personally considered, but on mankinde or the whole nature that should be derived from him in the ordinary way of propagation: and that thence it is that women have still pain in childbearing, and the earth bringeth forth briars, and that men return to dust. To the second I Reply, what he foisteth in of Revenging justice, I did not engage my self to prove, and he hath no authority by false Accusations to impose it on me to prove it. 2. That it was Gods sentence on sinfull man, adjudging him to the personall suffering of so much of the Death before that was before threatned to him for his sinne, is a thing that needeth not proof with any that read the text, but such as Mr.*Crandon*. For his answer out of *Austin* and *Salect* somewhere else given, I will not trouble my self to seek for it.

To

To the second he gives no better an answer. He saith ["that the wicked feel "all those sorrows that he mentioneth, and bear the curse and hatred of God in "them, is not denied. But the godly have their part in the same sorrowes, yet "they bear not the curse and hatred of God therein.]

1. Mark here that he granteth all that ever I pleaded for, as to the wicked, and denieth it only of the godly. And are none of the wicked Elect and Redeemed? Doth he not here make himself guilty of all those hideous Accusations of the Almighty which he after chargeth on me? surely Christ satisfied for the sins of wicked men: and if God may yet hate them and punish them, I hope you will no more compare him to [a prodigie of nature, a divellized man] for so doing.

2. He learnedly confuteth me, by saying as I say, That the godly bear not Gods hatred in their sufferings. 3. Once more for all, to put an end to your vain clamours from the word [Curse] I grant that as the Curse signifieth any effect of Gods hatred to the person, or any destructive punishment, that Christ hath taken it all away, and there is none of it in the sufferings of the godly. But as [the Curse] signifieth any part of the penalty threatned, I deny that the whole is so removed. But the question between us should be, Whether our sufferings are penal; and sinne be the cause or only the occasion, as himself expresseth it? all the Railings to the end of that Section I pass.

To the third of mine he answereth, That ["there is nothing in it but a wre-"sting of Scriptures from their proper sense, &c.] And first to 1 Cor 15.21,22. *For since by man came death, so by man came also the resurrection from the dead. For as in Adam All dye, even so in Christ shall All be made alive.* He saith this is wrested, *viz.* by citing the place. The summe of his answer is, That ["here is not any "mention of the Death of believers, much less of the Curse and wrath in their "death, but that the meaning is this, *As in Adam all dye,* i.e. All that live and "die in *Adam* perish hopelesly and everlastingly: *so in Christ all shall be made alive*, "*i.e.* All that are translated out of *Adam* into Christ.] This is his setting right the Text that I wrested, by citing the place to prove that we die in *Adam* a bodily or temporall death. 1. I wrested it, by judging that the words [*All die*] is meant [All die] as it speaketh. He sets all right by saying that by [*All*] is meant [only them that perish everlastingly.] 2. I wrested the Text, by judging that [*All shall be made alive*] meaneth [All] indeed as it speaketh. And he righteth it by saying, that by All is meant none but believers. 3. I wrested the text, by supposing that the Apostle is here expressing the Misery and Death that Christ raiseth us from, to intimate that it being part of our Deliverance, we are to value it accordingly: and so that he meaneth plainly [*Adam* killed us, and Christ Reviveth us.] He righteth the Text, by expounding all this, as not speaking of any Death that Christ doth Recover us from, but that which the damned only must suffer. 4. I wrested the Text, by supposing that when the Apostle mentioneth [All dying, and All Rising] he means the same *All*. He supposeth that he obscurely changeth the subject or persons, and means none of the same. 5. I wrested the Text, by supposing that the Apostle by *Death*, meant the same Death, in both places; and that when he saith, *By man also came Resurrection from death*, he meant a Resurrection from the same Death that he saith came by man in the foregoing words. Mr. *Crand.* vindicateth the Text from my abuse, by supposing that the Apostle equivocateth here, and means one thing by Death in one sentence, and another in the next. 6. I thought that this much had been plainly intimated in the causall ἐπειδὴ γὰρ: [*since* or *because, by man came death, so by man came also the resurrection.* To such a

simple

simple man as I, the causall declareth that its the same death he speaks of; and that else it would not conclude what he intended. 7. I thought the Apostle had been directly proving the Resurrection of them he speaks of, opposed to their death; and but consequentially the Salvation that followeth it. 8. Yea I thought it was the Resurrection in Generall that the seducers and seduced among the *Corinthians* questioned, *that there was no Resurrection,* ver. 12. and not only the Resurrection of the faithfull, as granting a Resurrection to Damnation and none to Salvation. 9. Yet I doubted not but it was finally to the consolation of the faithfull who shall live after the Resurrection in happiness, that the Apostle speaks this; and therefore applieth it still to them: But I supposed that the thing that he was proving directly was the Resurrection of all man, or that there is a Resurrection, (though he speak not *to* all;) that from hence the faithfull might receive their consolation, seeing there must needs then be a Resurrection for them.

To Rom. 6. 23. *The wages of sinne is death,* &c. he answereth, ["Who doubteth "but it is so to them that are under the Guilt and Dominion of sinne? But what "is this to believers?] I confess the Apostle extendeth it also to eternall death where it is suffered, but so as including temporall also, and that even of all that suffer it. For his scope is not to shew how God dealeth with the wicked and how with the godly; only or chiefly: but what are the different fruits of grace and sinne. So that death is the reward of sinne, whose death soever it be. The Apostle doth not say, The wages of sinne is the death of unbelievers only: and I will not limit where I finde not the word limit it self. And you may take Death for the subject and wages of sinne] for the predicate, or *wages* for the *subject,* and death for the predicate; the difference is small. Gen. 3. and other Scriptures that assure us that even the death of the godly is the wages of sinne, do teach us to expound this Text.

3. To the next Text 1 Cor. 11. 30, 31, 32. he saith [is as pat as the two former] *For this cause many are weak and sick among you, and many sleep: For if we would judge our selves, we should not be judged. But when we are judged we are chastened of the Lord, that we should not be condemned with the world.* A simple man would think it impossible to speak plainer, to prove that sinne is the cause of the sickness, death, chastisement and judgement of them that are not condemned with the world. But M[r] *Crandon* saith ["The Apostle writes to a visible Church, in which it appears "there were some true, and some formall temporary believers. Christ is in the "midst of this Church dispensing his Discipline. The true believers by the con- "tagion of the formall professors had somewhat prophaned the Lords Table, by "resorting to it somewhat disorderly. The other had totally violated it by coming "to it drunken (and so were worse then beasts) from their own tables. Here now "had Christ inflicted chastisements of sickness and weakness, for humbling and "amending those that were his; but death and vengeance upon them, that while "they professed faith in him, yet were indeed disposers of him and his Ordinan- "ces: what is this to the curse of the Law upon believers? Therefore I shall add "to Mr. *Baxters* [And if so] my [and if so:] if so that wresting of Scripture will "serve the turn, Mr. *B.* will surely have the water run in his ground, and his fancy "stand, though Gods truth thereby fall to the earth.

This Vindication may be thought profitable to the Church by Mr. *Car.* but not by me, for these Reasons. 1. The Apostle doth as expresly as the tongue of a man can speak, say it of those men that are not condemned with the world, 1. That they are chastened of God (and therefore punished.) 2. That they are judged of

the

the Lord: 3. That self-judging would prevent it (and therefore it is penall.) 4 That the matter of this judgement or chastisement was, sickness and weakness on some, and death on others. 5. That sinne was the cause: *For this cause.* And shall I believe him then that saith sinne is but the occasion and no proper cause?

2. Though there were formalists in the Church, the Apostle doth here as usually elsewhere, bespeak them all as believers. 3. For all the greatness of the sin, here is not a word in the text censuring any of them whom he speaks of as Reprobates: the quality of the sinne doth no more prove them so, then *Davids* and *Lots* and *Solomons* did prove them such. 4. What word in the text intimates that it was the Elect that the sickness was laid on, and the Reprobates that the death was laid on? 5. He is forced to yield that the sickness and weakness was laid on the godly: And is not that as much as the cause needeth that I defend, as long as the Holy Ghost saith, that [*for this cause some are sickly and weak*] and that we are judged of the Lord and chastened, that we might not be condemned with the world. For my part I believe Gods word, and therefore cannot take such palpable contradicting of it, for a profitable Vindication: I desire no more but that any Reader, not willing to erre, do but reade the bare text, and chuse whether he will take notice of any explications of mine: and if he cannot there finde, that sinne is the cause of the godlies chastisements, and that they are judged of God, let him be Mr. *Cr*'s disciple for me. Yet see the confidence of the man, that can conclude such unworthy evasions and perverting of the Text, with such triumphant scornes.

4. To my fourth, where I say [It is manifest that our sufferings are in their own nature evils to us, and the sanctifying of them to us taketh not away their natural evil, but only produceth by it, as by an occasion, a greater good: Doubtless so far as it is the effect of sin, it is evil, and the effect also of the Law.] His answer is twofold.

1. That he knows not what I mean by evil. A judicious answer, worthy the publick view. He knows not what kinde of evil *malum pœnæ* is; when I called it natural evil in the words before him. But he that would not know, cannot understand!

And let the Reader judge, whether the man take notice in his charges against me, of what I here and elsewhere confess, *viz.* That [this evil is sanctified to us, and God produceth by it a greater good.]

2. His next answer is, [" We deny it to be the effect of sinne, as the meritorious cause thereof, so that the suffering of a believer should be the curse or revenging punishment for his sinne.]

Can you tell by this, whether he absolutely deny sinne to be the meritorious cause, or no? His [so that] would seem a restriction; but indeed is but by the sound to divert the odium from himself on me. This his next words shew, before cited [We grant a Believers sinne to be oft the occasion, never the proper cause of a Believers sufferings.] This proper cause denied, is that before named A Meritorious Cause: and thats a cause proper enough of such an effect as the formal nature of punishment is. It seems undeniable then, that this Vindicatour doth not use to confess that his sinnes deserve any of the castigations that God layeth on him, or any other that he taketh for a true Believer: It seems he dare tell God in his sufferings, Lord, no sinnes of mine have deserved any of this at thy hands! I dare not do so. I have lived in the school of Affliction from my youth, and am writing these words in great pain and weakness: and I durst never tell God, I

O deser-

deserved it not: Nor do I think such praying and preaching would be profitable to our Congregations, and therefore I think not that such Books are profitable to the Church of God.

To my fifth he saith, [" We deny not the sufferings of Believers to be oft in "Scripture ascribed to *Gods Anger*: But it is after the manner of men, &c. not " that God hath passions: 2. In respect of the sufferers apprehension, who be- " ing weak in faith, and too much prejudiced by sense, is apt for a season some- " times in great trials to conclude himself cast out of Gods favour, and overwhel- " med with his wrath and fury. Not that it is so really: for God hath forgiven " their sinnes. Therefore after his forgiving to retain wrath and anger, may be " ascribed to malicious men, whom we shall hear saying, I will *forgive*, but never " forget him: But in no wise to the most righteous God, &c.]

This Vindication is like the rest. First he confesseth that Scripture ascribeth our sufferings to Gods wrath: And what, must Scripture be cast by when it fitteth not his turn, as if God knew not how to speak of himself to us? Who would think that this were the same man that heaped up so many leaves against humane Learning, and not sticking to the simplicity of the Scripture!

And (to his first) What though anger be not properly in God? no more is Hatred, Pleasure, Displeasure, Love, or, I think, any humane act! But there is somewhat in God, which he propoundeth to our conceptions under these Notions, till we are capable of higher. 2. Let us, as is usual, say, that denomination is taken from the effect: There is that done by God to his children, which is an effect of wrath in men, that is, punishing them. 3. Why did he not apply this answer of his to all that flood of Accusation, when he anon doth so mouth it, against God, as furious, and pouring out his wrath, &c? Could he not say, God hath no passion? 4. Is it fitter for us to learn to speak of God or of Mr. *Cr*? If the Scripture say, that our sufferings are from Gods wrath; am I a Papist for saying so? I will keep close to the Scripture language as near as I can, for all Mr. *Cr*'s higher conceptions.

To his second I say, The godly too oft think that there is more of Gods Anger and less love in their sufferings then there is: But doth it follow that there is therefore none at all of his anger in them? 2. Who dare think that because deluded men do falsly imagine that Gods chastisements are effects of his anger, therefore God himself will a hundred times over say so too, and fit his speech to the false speeches or conceptions of erring men?

Let Mr. *Cr.* therefore not renounce the judgement of the word, or else not renounce the name of an Antinomian: And then let him soberly (if possible) tell us, Whether God do us Good (as such) in Wrath and Anger? and whether it be not some Penal evil that is ascribed to Gods Wrath? Light will be Light, though there were no creatures in the world but Batts and Owles.

My sixth Reason was, [They are called Punishments in Scripture: therefore we may call them so.] And I cited many Texts. To this he answereth, [" I will " not fall into a λογομαχίαν, a strife about words and names. Let Mr. *B.* agree " with us in the Matter, and we will not stick to close with him in the Name and " Words. Let him deny all Malignity and *Curse* in the sufferings of the godly, " and to do him a pleasure we will call them Punishments as he doth.]

See how milde the man is when there is no remedy! 1. Then, If by Malignity and Curse he mean, any effect of Gods Hatred, or any Destructive Punish-

ment,

ment, I yielded to him before he desired it. I never said there was Malignity in them : I oft say, They are chastisements, sanctified to our Greater good. But if he mean I must deny that they are for sinne as the Meritorious Cause, and from Paternal Justice and Anger, and from the Threatning, or have any Penal evil in them, then this is the summe of his Answer, *q. d.* I confess God cals them Punishments; and let Mr. *B.* grant that they are not Punishments, and then we will (to please him) speak as God doth, and call them that which they are not. 2. But what are Names for, but to signifie Things ? And if God mean not that they are Punishments when he so calleth them, then how shall we know his mind ? 3. What hath Mr. *Cr.* against me but Words ? How else doth he know my mind ? If then my words be Scripture words, for ought he knows I may have the Scripture meaning. 4. At least let him give me leave to speak as God doth, and blame my words no more when they are his: Nor let him say that all these are *Bellarmines* and the Jesuites words, yea Scriptures taken out of them, and thereupon reject them. If God say, They are Punishments, I will believe it, and say so to.

I intreat the Reader to consider, whether such answers as this, be not a yielding of the Cause: and whether after such Concessions, it beseemed him to use such direfull language against God, as afterward he doth, in case he do punish us for sinne: and whether this man adhere as close to Scripture as he doth pretend.

In the seventh, I did by oversight put the word [Affliction] in stead of [Chastisement:] upon which he insulteth, as if I had spoke the most detestable Heresie: and tels us of [a pack of little sense, and much arrogance, a compound of absurdity and presumption.] Blot out *Affliction*, and put in Chastisement, and I hope this horrid evil is cured.

2. Note that yet here he can tell that I mean [evil of Punishment] but even now when he should have answered he knew not what I meant.

3. He addeth that [" If I had said Chastisements are in their own nature so "qualified, we should have born with it: but he shunneth that word as a Rock "upon which he might have dashed the Curse, &c.]

See after and before such hideous outcries, that yet the man and I must be friends. Hee'l bear with me if I say the same of *Chastisements*, and a little wit and charity might have sufficed to assure him, that that was my meaning. 2. How then could I dash the Curse on it, when I mean but *Chastisements* by the *Curse*. 3. How falsly saith he that I shun the word *Chastisements*, when it is Printed in my Book before his eyes, and himself thence recited it ? 4. But are we indeed now agreed, as we seem ? I am content hereafter to forbear the word [Curse] and to use the word [Chastisements] more frequently. But for all this we are agreed but in words, and not in deed: For by Chastisements I mean as I speak, *Chastisements*, which are penalties for sin, to the Amendment of the sinner: but by *Chastisements*, he means contrarily, that they are no *Chastisements*, no penalty for sin as the Meritorious Cause.

That which follows in that Section, needs no other answer then is given, it being nothing but his mouthing the word *Curse*, to a false interpretation of my sense: and an Accusation that [I insinuate, that they deny all *Pain* in the sufferings of believers,] which is but another of his untruths. I contend against those that deny our chastisements to be *Pœnam*, formal Punishment; but I never insinuated that any man denied them to be *pain* or *hurts*. Upon this he annexeth a

O 2   double

double charge: 1. My [" abasing opinion of others in the superlative confidence that I have of my self, and in my self, thinking almost all others to be meer *Terræ filios*, clods of clay in comparison of my self, &c.] And how is all this proved? Why [I shake out my absurdities as Oracles.] If every man that speaks Absurdities be so hainously proud and contemptuous, where will this good man shew his face? But where did I tell him that I took my absurdities for Oracles? The summe of his Argument must be this: He that once by oversight calleth Chastisements by the name of Afflictions, hath an abasing opinion of others in a superlative self-confidence. But so did I: Therefore. *Negatur major Domine.*

The second charge is my [" suspending Conscience, that while I pretend to truth, yet I take the reins by any absurd false tricks to subvert it.] I will leave this and a hundred and hundred more, for him to Answer, who justifieth the Slandered against the Accuser. Let the Reader finde out the ground of his charge if he can.

But the great storm is poured out on me for asking this Question, [What Reason can be given why God should not do us all that good without our sufferings which now he doth by them, if there were not sinne, and wrath, and Law in them? Sure he could better us by easier means.] Let the Accuser know that is not ascending into the Chair of God to judge him: It is but speaking his Revealed will. He hath revealed himself to be Good, and to do Good, and to have no pleasure in mens sufferings and death: Nay he hath oft told us, that our sinne is the cause, and if it were not for that, he would not chasten us. Have not I good ground to conclude then, that if we did judge our selves, we should not be judged of the Lord, in Chastisements? and that he would do us all that good without Castigation, which he now doth by it, if it were not for sinne. Nay the man himself confesseth sinne to be oft the *Occasion*, though he deny it to be the proper Cause.

In the eighth place, I shewed that the Scriptures commonly brought against this, do only prove a predominancy of Love in our Chastisements, but not that there is no Anger or sinne the Cause. To this there is nothing but rage, which I cannot well answer I confess. But for my speaking of Love and Anger mixt in God, &c. he tels me I [" make God to be in a commotion against himself, to carry fire in one hand, and water in the other, to fight with the right hand against the left, sometimes the one and sometimes the other overcoming, &c. an excellent Disputer to have stood alway at *Marcions* elbow, prompting him with arguments to prove this God a Malignant and envious God, the Authour of all evil to mankinde, &c.] So that for God to have Love and Anger to the same person in several respects, it seems laies him open to these more direfull reproaches of a worm! Its well for us that we serve a patient God. This man did but even now confess that our sufferings are said in Scripture to come from Gods wrath, and himself maintaineth that they come from his Love. And must not this man then either lay all these Blasphemies to the charge of Scripture, or take them to himself, or both? Dare he deny that it is the language of the Holy Ghost, that God doth chasten us because he loveth us, and also because he is Angry or displeased? This we must hear, for speaking as the Scripture. Nay is there any Divine that ever wrote of this subject, that is not of the same minde? None but Libertines that ever I knew of.

And for setting God against himself in commotion, let him know that as we speak of God, as Scripture doth after the manner of man, so we still acknowledge

the

the impropriety of all such attributions, and desire to separate from God; so much of them as implieth Imperfection, and yet we will use these notions till we are perfect and capable of better: As also that it is (say Divines) by extrinsecall denomination that these Affections are attributed to God, and so we may well attribute to him various Affections at once, as safely as any at all: He knowes how to love his childe and be angry with him both at once, in severall respects, wherein incurring all this Reproach.

And must God be termed [Malignant and Envious, and the Author of all Evil] if he Punish in Anger, even when Love is predominant ! The Lord, in mercy pardon all this language to this man ! I would intreat the Reader to mark these two things. 1. Are these men fit to tell us that we make God the author of all evil, when we have such indignation for pleading against some of their strain, for the vindication of God, as not being the author of sinne? and when themselves do commonly maintain it with such zeal, that God doth by an Immediate Physicall efficient premotion, predetermine mans will to every act that is sinfull, which he chooseth; and that by unresistible power. 2. Should these men charge us to make God Malignant, Envious, &c. for punishing his children in Anger, though for their Good, with greater Love, when yet we must bear such a flood of Reproach from them, because we will not deny that Christ died, for any but the elect, and will not believe that the rest of men have no more satisfaction made by him for their sinne then the Devils have, when yet the same suffering was sufficient to have been a satisfaction for all ! Yet, God forbid, that I should charge the contrary minded, with such Accusations, though the Cause be incomparably greater.

Here he scorneth at my citing 1 *Cor.* 15. 55, 56. But these words well considered, I think, evince all that I have maintained on this point. *The sting of death is sinne*, i.e. sinne animates it, to do what it doth against us: *the strength of sinne is the Law*: that is, the Threatning of the Law, which I called the Curse! But we may triumph over death as conquerours in Christ, and say, *O death, where is thy sting! O grave where is thy victory!* Not that the full actual conquest over it is past !. but we have it in promise, and faith can foresee it, and make it as present ; for it certainly will be. For the 54 verse saith, *So when this corruptible shall have put on incorruption, and this mortall shall have put on immortality, Then shall be brought to pass the saying that is written, Death is swallowed up in victory.* Mark that the victory is not till then. Yet so farre as unpardoned sinne obliging to eternall punishment, and leaving under enmity to God, is the sting, so farre it is taken out before.

In the 9th I instanced 1. Death. 2. Sinne. The former out of 1 *Cor.* 15. 26. *The last enemy that shall be destroyed is death.* I supposed the meaning to be this [the last of the enemies of the Churches felicity :] Christ being by Office our Redeemer, his work is to rescue us from all the calamity that we had brought on our selves, and against all enemies that would hinder our recovery. Now one and the last part of the work is, by Resurrection to restore us from the dust, and so cure the last penal calamity that we lay under for sinne, and to finish his cure and conquest. Mr. *Crandon* understandeth it thus, that [" when all Christs enemies are " sent to hell, then death it self shall be destroyed, because there is no more use of " it. As if it were no act of Liberation to the Saints by a Resurrection that is here spoken of, but an end of killing the Reprobates : contrary to the scope of the chapter. Whose exposition now is right, Mr. *Crandons* or mine? Certainly his, if you will not judge him past all modesty in his confidence: For he saith [" That " this

"this is the proper meaning of this Text, a blinde man may see (better perhaps "then a seeing man) and consequently see it to be sinfully wrested by M *Baxter*.] I leave my self then to the censure of the blinde, seeing there is no escaping it: and I leave them to follow this confident expositor.

2. To my second Instance, That all our corruption of heart, shall not be cured till death, he saith he hath spoken before: But as I finde not where (and mean not more to search) so I must needs think that somewhat is the matter that made him here so sparing of his words: I finde him not so short winded, and concise elsewhere: and he could not but know that I laid great stress on this Instance. Truly he that thinks Mr. *Crandon* is perfect when he hath read this his Volume, shall freely enjoy his opinion for me: And he that thinketh that the withdrawing of the Spirit, whence followeth scandalous sinnes, decay of Grace, of Love, Faith, Humility, *&c.* and this to the death (which may befall a Saint,) is no penal evill, nor is caused by our sinne, nor by Gods Anger or Grieving the Spirit, but only from Gods Love, this man hath not those thoughts of sinne and Grace as I have; nor I think as he should have.

In the tenth place I brought a General Reason, from the tenour of the word, when it mentioneth the freedom that we have by Christ from temporall punishments: *viz.* that it doth not make him presently to take them all off, but only to manage them for our best advantage (in order to our sanctity and Recovery.) A man would think these words should be pardonable: Yet the charge of Impudency, Blasphemy, *&c.* is heaped upon them in words at length, and not in figures. Nay he pretendeth me to be so wholly destitute of any Scripture for this (when yet I had given so many before, which himself plainly confesseth, to call our sufferings Punishments from Gods wrath, *&c.*) that he saith ["that curse is de-"nounced against my self, *Rev.* 22.18,19. All plagues on him that shall add "any thing, *&c.*] Which of my words are Additions? 1. That Christ takes not presently all penalty for sinne off his people, all the fore-cited texts and a hundred more manifest. 2. That all are in his power or hands, many Scriptures express, that say, *All things are delivered into his hands*, Joh. 13.3. and *All power in Heaven and earth is given him*, and *the Father hath committed all Judgement to him*, and *he is the Lord and King*, &c. 3. That he manageth these penalties for our advantage, I thought Mr. *Crandon* could not deny (if he yeelded but that there are such things.) Yet saith he [no drop of Scripture hath a relish of it.]

For the Texts he citeth, I confess with joy that *Christ hath delivered us from the curse of the Law, being made a curse for us:* that is, *quoad pretium*, he hath done it perfectly in his suffering: *quoad actualem liberationem*, he hath delivered us from the actuall obligation to eternall punishment, and from our present state of enmity to God, then when we first believe: and as to a perfect freedom from all temporall chastisements, as he hath freed us *quoad pretium*, so he hath given us a promise of perfect actuall freedom in a very short time; alas, it is as nothing, till the day of our Redemption come, and we shall sinne and suffer no more: This is I think, a sufficient Redeeming us from the Curse. And *that there is no condemnation to them that are in Christ*, I gladly acknowledge. But my opinion still is, that there may not only be Castigatory Punishments where there is no condemnation, but also that even therefore *are we judged and chastened, that we might not be condemned with the world:* And I think this is Scripture for all these hot words.

Yet doth he here proceed to accuse my arguing ["as tending to the abasing, "annihilating and even unchristing of Christ, as purchasing to himself a Mono-
"poly

"poly of Cursing, &c."] with more of the like. Alas, must our dear Lord hear all this reproach from his poor creatures, unless he deliver them at the very present from all punishment for sinne, though managed to their own advantage, and continued for their own necessary use? Must Christ be no Christ, if we suffer but one lash for sinne! Me thinks his sanctified ones should be more humble and thankfull, and should confess it infinite mercy, if they were in hell but for such a moment as this life, much more to lye under fatherly corrections, and then be advanced to eternall Glory! So much for that Chapter.

In the next Chapter is all that fearfull language against God that I before mentioned, with more the like, which I am aweary of reciting: And multitudes of falshoods do fill up most leaves. These last words of mine (that Afflictions are managed by Christ to our advantage and good, he mentions again *pag.* 54. and addeth ["What means he by this advantage and good? Not our purifying and "bettering, &c. as we hold: for this as we have seen he shakes off as a single solid "supposition with a kinde of *Apage*.] Hath he the face of a Christian and Preacher of the Gospel, that dare heap up such shameless falshoods? Finde but the least word in any writing of mine, where there is any such thing as he accuseth me of, and then believe him and spare not. It is past the power of my imagination, to conjecture whence he should have the least appearance of it.

I dare not for all this say of him as he is bold to do of me, *pag.* 58. ["He seems "to me to be so left of God, destitute of his Spirit, that he can see no further then "a meer naturall man in spirituall things, and so following the letter, and scarce "the letter, without the spirit of the Word, he can think of no other way to Hap-"pinest, but that which the instinct of nature suggesteth, namely a mans own wil-"ling, running and procurements.]

You see a man that knows me not can suppose me a meer Pagan. When I understand that *Willing* to have Christ, and Running to obey him, are inconsistent with his being the Way to my Happiness, then I may be of your Religion and Charity too.

I will conclude this point with these two or three Observations. 1. After all his Accusations, as if I made God —— (I am afraid to recite his words so oft,) yet, for ought I know this man saith not one word less then I do, of the sufferings of the godly, but only denieth sinne to be the cause, and that they proceed from the threat and Gods anger. He cannot deny but we are sick, weak, sinfull, enjoy little of God in comparison of what we shall, &c. Do I name any one thing that we suffer which he denieth? What Mercy doth he proclaim then more then I? Doth he say, it is for our our advantage, having more of Gods Love in his anger, and none of his hatred? so do I. Doth he say, that there is no Anger of God in it? He confesseth the Scripture saith the contrary: Yea but he saith, there is no Curse? If he mean, destructive punishment, or that which tendeth more to our hurt, then our good, I deny it too. If he mean any penall nature, that is, not to make the Mercy greater, but sinne to have no hand in our suffering, laying all on God himself. And doth that man so highly advance free Grace, that saith [God killeth us meetly of his own will without any desert of ours as the cause,] more then he that saith, he doth it for our own sinne? And for any Good that God intendeth us, and effecteth by affliction, I do not yet finde where he ascribeth any more to it then I do. So that all these hideous outcries, are not of the *misery*, which both alike, I think, confess; but of the Cause of it: whether God do it because of our sin as the Meritorious Cause, or without any desert of our selves.

1. You

2. You may see *pag. 59.* (as is said) that he powreth out all these Accusations consequentially, against the *London* Divines as against me; who, as he saith [speak almost the same thing with me]' and say [that to say God doth not punish his Saints for their sinnes, is flat Antinomianisme.]

SECT. VI.

TO conclude, As I have said all this (more then I intended) to satisfie Mr *Caryl*, that this book, no not for its vindication of this point, is not profitable to the Church of God, or worthy of publick view; so besides all that is said; I will recite here some more of the words of God, and leave you to judge of the worth of this Vindication.

And 1. Let us see whether sinne be the Cause of our castigations or punishments, as I say, or only the Occasion, as the Vindicator saith; premising this much, that it is no great credit to us, the Guides and Teachers of the flocks of Christ, to put one another upon such tasks as these, to prove that *Pæna est peccati pæna*, that all punishment or chastisement is for some fault, when it is the very *formalis ratio pænæ*: and I hope there is no silly woman in our Congregations but knowes it, except the diligence of seducers have put out the Light of Nature in them: and if I must either put out the Light of Nature or be a Papist, the case seems hard.

2 Sam. 12. 9, 10, 11, 12, 13, 14. *Wherefore hast thou despised the Commandement of the Lord to do evil in his sight? thou hast killed Uriah the Hittite with the sword,* &c. *Now therefore the sword shall never depart from thine house, because thou hast despised me, and hast taken the wife,* &c. *Thus saith the Lord, I will raise up evil against thee out of thine own house, and I will take thy wives before thine eyes,* &c. Vers 13, 14. *The Lord also hath put away thy sinne, thou shalt not die. Howbeit, because by this deed thou hast given great occasion to the enemies of the Lord to blaspheme, the childe also that is born unto thee shall surely die.*

The case of *Manasseh* and the *Israelites*, Numb. 14. I mentioned before.

Numb. 12. 10, 11, 12. *Aaron looked upon Miriam, and behold she was leprous. And Aaron said to Moses, Alas my Lord! I beseech thee lay not the sinne upon us, wherein we have done foolishly,* &c.

Numb. 27. 3. *Our Father died in the wildernes, and he was not in the company of them that gathered themselves together against the Lord in the company of Corah, but died in his own sinne and had no sonnes.*

1 King. 8. 33, 34, 35, 38. *When thy people Israel be smitten down before the enemy, because they have sinned against thee, and shall turn again,* &c. *then hear thou in Heaven and forgive the sinne of thy people Israel, and bring again unto the land,* &c. *When Heaven is shut up, and there is no rain because they have sinned against thee; if they pray towards this place and confess thy Name, and turn from their sinne when thou afflictest them: Then hear thou in Heaven, and forgive the sinne of thy servant, and of thy people Israel, that thou teach them the good way,* &c.

Lam. 4. 6. *For the punishment of the iniquity of the daughter of people, is greater then the punishment of the sinne of Sodome,* &c. Lam. 3. 34. *Wherefore doth a living man complain? a man for the punishment of his sinne. Let us search and try our wayes,* &c. v. 42. *We have transgressed, and have rebelled, thou hast not pardoned.*

Psal. 38. 1, 2, 3. *There is no soundness in my flesh because of thine anger, neither is there*

yet

any rest in my bones because of my sinne. For mine iniquities are gone over my head,&c. verf.18. For I will declare mine iniquity, I will be sorry for my sin.

Psal.32.4,5. For day and night thy hand was heavy upon me, &c. I acknowledged my sinne unto thee, and mine iniquity have I not hid. I said I will confess my transgressions unto the Lord, and thou forgavest the iniquity of my sin.

Read Psal.51.1. Dan.9.5. We have sinned and committed iniquity,&c. verf.7. Whither thou hast driven them because of their trespass which they have trespassed against thee. O Lord to us belongeth confusion of face, to our Kings, to our Princes, to our Fathers, because we have sinned against thee. Verf.11. Therefore the curse is poured upon us, &c. because we have sinned against him. Verf.14. Therefore hath the Lord watched upon the evil, and brought it upon us: for the Lord our God is righteous in all his works which he doth, for we obeyed not his voice. So verf.16.

Exod.32.34. Nevertheless in the day when I visit, I will visit their sin upon them.

Numb.32.23. Be sure your sin will finde you out.

1 King.11.11. The Lord said to Solomon, Forasmuch as this is done of thee, and thou hast not kept my Covenant and my statutes which I commanded thee, I will surely rend the Kingdom from thee, &c. Read the Chapter.

Joh.5.14. Behold thou art made whole: sinne no more lest a worst thing come unto thee.

1 Joh.5.16. If any man see his brother sin a sin which is not unto death, he shall ask, and he shall give him life for them that sin not unto death.

Jam.5.15,16. And the prayer of faith shall save the sick, and the Lord shall raise him up, and if he have committed sins, they shall be forgiven him. Confess your faults one to another, and pray one for another that ye may be healed.

Heb.3.17. But with whom was he grieved forty years? was it not with them that had sinned, whose carkasses fell in the wilderness?

Rom.5.12. Wherefore as by one man sin entred into the world, and death by sinne, and so death passed upon all men for that all have sinned.

See 2 Sam.24. Job 33.27,28,&c.

Micah.7.9. I will bear the indignation of the Lord, because I have sinned against him.

Ezra 9.13. And after all that is come upon us for our evil deeds, and for our great trespass, seeing that thou our God hast punished us, less then our iniquities do deserve, &c.

See Neh.1.6,8,9. Jer.5.25. Your iniquities have turned away these things, and your sins have withholden good things from you.

Josh.24.19. He is an holy God: he is a jealous God, he will not forgive your transgressions nor your sins.

Exod.23.21. Beware of him, and obey his voice, provoke him not: for he will not pardon your transgressions, for my name is in him.

Lev.26.18,24,28. I will punish you yet seven times more for your sins.

1 Cor.5.5. To deliver such a one to Satan for the destruction of the flesh, that the spirit may be saved in the day of the Lord Jesus.

Isa.40.1,2. Comfort ye, comfort ye my people, saith your God, &c. Her iniquity is pardoned; for she hath received of the Lords hand double for all her sins.

Jer.30.11,14,15. For I am with thee saith the Lord to save thee: though I make a full end of all nations, whither I have scattered thee, yet will I not make a full end of thee: but I will correct thee in measure, and will not leave thee altogether unpunished. Verf.14. For I have wounded thee with the wound of an enemy, with the chastisement of a cruel one, for the multitude of thine iniquity, because thy sins were encreased. Verf.15. Why cryest thou for thine Affliction? thy sorrow is incurable for the multitude of thine iniquity, because

[40]

because thy sins were increased, I have done these things to thee.
Mic.1.5. *For the transgression of Jacob is all this, and for the sins of the house of Israel.*
Lev.26.41,42. *If then their uncircumcised hearts be humbled, and they then accept the punishment of their iniquity, then will I remember my Covenant with Jacob, and also my Covenant with Isaac, and also my Covenant with Abraham,&c.*
Psal.39.10,11. *Remove thy stroak away from me; I am consumed by the blow of thine hand. When thou with rebukes doest correct man for iniquity, thou makest his beauty to consume,&c.*
Psal.89.30,31,32. *If his children forsake my Law, and walk not in my judgements: if they break my statutes and keep not my Commandements; then will I visit their transgression with the rod, and their iniquity with stripes.*

If this be not enough to prove sin the Cause of our Punishment, and that we are really punished for sin, I undertake to bring forty and forty more texts, when I see it necessary.

2. Next let us see whether this Punishment come from Gods Anger or wrath.
Numb.12.9,10. *And the Anger of the Lord was kindled against them* (Aaron and Miriam) *and behold Miriam became leprous, as snow.*
1 King.11.9,11. *And the Lord was angry with Solomon, because his heart was turned from the Lord God of Israel,&c.*
Psal.30.5. *His anger endureth but for a moment.*
Psal.38.3. *There is no soundness in my flesh because of thine anger.*
Psal.74.1. *Why doth thine anger smoak against the sheep of thy pasture?*
Psal.78.49. *He cast upon them the fierceness of his anger, wrath, and indignation, and trouble, by sending evil Angels among them. He made a way to his anger, he spared not their soul from death, but gave their life over to the pestilence.*
Psal.85.2,3,4,5. *Thou hast forgiven the iniquity of thy people, thou hast covered all their sin. Thou hast taken away all thy wrath, thou hast turned thy self from the fierceness of thine anger. Turn us O God of our salvation, and cause thine anger toward us to cease. Wilt thou be angry with us for ever? wilt thou draw out thine anger to all generations?*
Psal.6.1. *O Lord rebuke me not in thine anger, neither chasten me in thy hot displeasure.*
Psal.90.7,8,11. *For we are consumed by thine anger, and by thy wrath are we troubled. Thou hast set our iniquities before thee, our secret sins in the light of thy countenance. Who knoweth the power of thine anger,&c.*
Psal.103.8,9,10. *Slow to anger and plenteous in mercy. He will not always chide, neither will he keep his anger for ever. He hath not dealt with us after our sins,&c.*
Isa.5.25. and 42.25. *He poured out on him the fury of his anger,&c.* Jer.25.38. and 36.6. and 42.18. Lam.2.1,6,21,22. and 3.43. *Thou hast covered with anger, and persecuted us,&c.* and 4.11. *The Lord hath accomplished his fury, and poured out his fierce anger,&c.* Jon.3.9.
Exod.4.14. *The anger of the Lord was kindled against Moses,&c.*
2 Sam.6.7. *The anger of the Lord kindled against Uzzah,&c.* 1 Chron.13.10.
Deut.1.37. and 4.21. *The Lord was angry with me for your sakes,&c.* Deut.9.20. *And the Lord was very angry with Aaron to have destroyed him,&c.*
Ezra 9.14. *Should we again break thy Commandements,&c. wouldst thou not be angry with us, till thou hast consumed us,&c.*
Psal.88.16. *Thy fierce wrath goeth over me, thy terrors have cut me off.*

Vers.7.

Verſ. 7. *Thy wrath lyeth hard upon me, and thou haſt afflicted me with all thy waves.* Pſal. 102. 9, 10. *For I have eaten aſhes like bread, and mingled my drink with weeping, becauſe of thine indignation and thy wrath*, &c.

Multitudes more there be of the like to theſe in Scripture; but this Mr *Grandon* denieth not.

3. Yea Gods Jealouſie, fury, indignation, are made in Scripture the Cauſe of our ſufferings.

Pſal. 79. 5. *Shall thy jealouſie burn like fire*, &c? 1 Cor. 10. 22. *Do we provoke the Lord to jealouſie? are we ſtronger then he?* Joſh. 24. 19. Dan. 9. 16. *Let thy fury be turned away*, &c. Lam. 2. 4. *He poured out his fury like fire*, &c. and 4. 11. Mich. 7. 9. *Ile bear the indignation of the Lord, becauſe I have ſinned againſt him.* Pſal. 102. 10. with many more like places.

4. Our ſufferings are called Gods Judgements. 1 Cor. 11. 32. *When we are judged, we are chaſtened of the Lord*, &c. Pſal. 119. 120. *I am afraid of thy judgements.* 1 Pet. 4. 17. *The time is come that judgement muſt begin at the houſe of God*, &c. (Some interpret this, as performed in this life, ſome of the laſt judgement.

5. Our ſufferings are called Plagues in Scripture.

Pſal. 73. 5, 14. *They are not plagued like other men*, &c. *All the day long have I been plagued, and chaſtened every morning.*

6. Yea, ſee whether or no, God himſelf will teach us to call our ſufferings Curſes, or not: and think as ill of this phraſe as Mr. *Cr.* doth.

Dan. 9. 11. *Yea all Iſrael hath tranſgreſſed,* &c. *therefore the curſe is poured upon us, &c.* Gen. 27. 12, 13. Joſh. 6. 18. *Keep your ſelves from the accurſed thing, leſt ye make your ſelves accuſed when ye take of the accurſed thing, and make the Camp of Iſrael a curſe, and trouble it.* Iſa. 43. 27, 28. *Thy firſt father hath ſinned, and thy teachers have tranſgreſſed againſt me, therefore I have profaned the Princes of the ſanctuary, and have given Jacob to the curſe and Iſrael to reproaches.* Jer. 24. 9. and 25. 18. Zach. 8. 13. *As ye were a curſe among the heathen, O houſe of Judah, and houſe of Iſrael, ſo will I ſave you and ye ſhall be a bleſſing.* Mal. 3. 9. *Ye are curſed with a curſe, for ye have robbed me, even this whole nation:* (Doubtleſs among theſe people, had God his choſen (or no where) though involved too far in the ſins of the times.) Mal. 2. 2. *I will ſend a curſe upon you, and will curſe your bleſſings, yea I have curſed them already,* &c. (It is not certain or probable that all theſe Prieſts were reprobates.) Nay it is the laſt word in the old Teſtament, *Leſt I come and ſmite the earth with a curſe.*

And remarkable is that *Rev.* 22. 3. *And there ſhall be no more curſe, but the Throne of God and the Lamb ſhall be in it:* To ſhew when the curſe ſhall wholly ceaſe.

Joſh. 9. 23. *Now therefore ye are curſed, and there ſhall none of you be freed from being bondmen, and hewers of wood,* &c. (yet might they be freed from damnation.) *Joſh.* 7. 12. *The children of Iſrael turned their backs before their enemies, becauſe they were accurſed.*

And ſee what the Scripture ſaith of ſome other termes as offenſive to Mr. *Crandon* as this.

Lev. 26. 25. *I will ſend a ſword upon you, which ſhall avenge the quarrell of my Covenant.* 1. Theſ. 4. 6. *That no man go beyond and defraud his brother in any matter, becauſe that the Lord is the avenger of all ſuch, as we alſo have forewarned you and teſtified.* (And a godly man may be drawn to defraud. Rom. 3. 4. *He is the Miniſter of God, a revenger to execute wrath upon him that doth evil.*

Pſal. 99. 8. *Thou anſweredſt them O Lord our God: thou waſt a God that forgaveſt them, though thou tookeſt vengeance on their inventions.*

I will

I will not weary the Reader with adding more, but conclude with these two or three Queries following.

Qu. 1. Whether just Governours be not Gods Ministers, acting by his Commission, and that which they do justly, he doth by them, as the Soveraigne by his Minister?

Qu. 2. Whether just Laws be not Gods Laws, and Justice in execution be not Gods Justice, who hath said, Vengeance is mine: the Righteous Lord loveth Righteousness?

Qu. 3. Whether godly men ought not to be punished, even with death or excommunication if they deserve it? and may not possibly deserve such punishment?

Qu. 4. Whether then to teach that Christs satisfaction hath freed us from all punishment and execution of justice (Gods justice by his Ministers,) be not destructive to the being of Christian Magistrates and their Government, and Christian Ministers and their Government?

Qu. 5. Whether then it be not destructive to the being of all Christian societies, either Churches or Commonwealths? as long as government and penalties are of such necessity to their being?

Qu. 6. Whether this doctrine do not make it the work of Christs satisfaction, to take men from under Gods government, and so to be masterless rebels, or gods to our selves? seeing government here is by Law: and the generall nature of a Law is to oblige to obedience or punishment in case of disobedience? And if God be disabled from making or executing any penall Law, on his subjects, at all, how is he their governour? while man is sinfull and imperfect, needing a government by penall Laws. Nay its considerable, whether the doctrine of these men do not disable God from making a meer precept, though without execution of a penalty; seeing the Law obligeth but *aut ad obedientiam, aut ad penam; aut hoc agere, aut hoc pati*, and not both to obey and suffer too, (as to the same time, and the same Numericall act:) yet I know that satisfaction as maintained by the Orthodox, that understand its nature and order, hath no such consequence.

Qu. 7. Whether the foresaid doctrine, do not make Christs satisfaction, destructive of, or inconsistent with his Kingdom and Lordship, on the foresaid grounds?

Qu. 8. Whether they that affirm that God inflicteth on us, all the sufferings which we undergo, without any deserving cause on our part; or they that say, he inflicteth them for our sin (withall making them medicinall for our cure,) do more honour Gods free grace, wisedom and justice? Both agreeing as to the matter of suffering.

Qu. 9. Whether the maintainers of the foresaid doctrine, go not against the light of nature? and the full stream of many hundred plain Scripture texts? And then Whether they indeed make Scripture the judge as they pretend to do?

Qu. 10. Whether (considering all the forecited Scriptures) it be fit to say, without any restriction or limitation, that pardon of sinne is absolutely perfect before death? while there are yet more sinnes to be pardoned, and penalties to be suffered?

Qu. 11. Whether (upon all the forementioned considerations) 'it 'appear not, that they who teach that we did legally obey or satisfie perfectly in Christ,' or that Christ hath so satisfied for all our sins, 'as that God cannot (nor Christ himself,) inflict the least penalty on the Redeemed, without injustice (as requiring satisfaction twice for our sin,) I say whether these turn not the grace of God into licentiousness, and the doctrine of Redemption into a doctrine of Rebellion,

subverting

subverting all government of God and man ? and making him the greatest friend to sin, that died to destroy it ?

Qu. 12. Whether this aforesaid be not one of the doctrines which our late Charter of this Commonwealth, *Art.* 38. hath excepted from liberty and protection, under the terme [Licentiousness?]

M*r Crandons* two following Chapters about the force of the Law, have nothing in them worthy a Reply, which is not before confuted in my Conclusions. Only that he feigneth me to feign, that some teach the Law of Works to be abrogate to Believers, and others to all the world, and he insultingly scorns me for such lying insinuations: when as the former saying is common in English Writers, and for the later, as Learned, Judicious Animadversions on my Aphorismes as ever I received, do almost wholly maintain, that the Covenant or Law of Works is properly Abrogated to all the world. And as the name is given to the whole from the promisory part, I my self do now maintain, that there is no such thing as a Covenant of Works now in being to any on earth.

The Texts that Mr. *Crandon* cites *Cap.* 8. speak of the Mosaical Law. And so much for that Point.

SECT. VII.

I Have given Mr. *Caryl* some of my Reasons why I judge not Mr. *Crandons* Vindication of our freedom from the curse of the Law to be profitable to the Church of God, and worthy the publique view. I shall give some few Reasons also why I judge so of his Vindication of our Justification by faith without works, which is the other point for which Mr. *Caryl* esteemeth and commendeth it.

And the summe of my Reasons are these 1. Because he granteth the main points in question, or which I assert. 2. He makes my assertions to be what they are not, and heapeth up such a multitude of false Accusations, and then bestoweth his labour in confuting his own forgeries, and that with copious scorn and railing, that I appeal to any sober Reader, who will be at the pains to examine his book by mine, whether his Volume can have any Title so proper as *Liber Mendaciorum & convitiorum*. 3. Yea he often contradicteth his own Confutations.

1. The first of these Reasons (that he granteth what I seek) I thus manifest. That our Gospel-obedience is frequently in Scripture called our Righteousness, and the performers in respect to it called Righteous, he cannot, he doth not deny. For he yet confesseth the Scripture to be true.

2. The thing then that he denieth is, that we are justified by that Righteousness. Here the Question must be either 1. Of our Universal Justification at Judgement against all Accusations: 2. Or of a particular Justification at Judgement (or in this life) against the particular Accusation of being Infidels, and Impenitent Rebels. 3. Of that Justification at our first believing, which wholly consisteth in (or only signifieth) Remission of sinne, and Accepting us as pardoned. 4. For the constituting of us Righteous Inherently, or personally in *tantum*; so farre as indeed we are, by that personal Righteousness, which the Scripture ascribeth to us.

For the first of these, as it is not that which he usually speaks of, so I affirm that

P 3

that our *Non Reatus mortis* and *Jus ad Præmium* is our Righteousnefs formally: and our Title is the Covenant Grant; and the Condition of that Title is our faith, repentance, fincere obedience and perfeverance (as to the Judicial abfolution and poffeffion of the Kingdom;) and the Righteousnefs of Chrift is the fole Meritorious Caufe.

2. As to the fecond, I affirm that when the Queftion is, Whether we have truly performed the Condition? and that is the point to be decided, then our own performance is fo farre our Righteousnefs: fo that the fame performance which as to our main final Juftification, is but a condition of our Juftification, and not our Juftice it felf: Yet in this fubfervient preparatory Juftification, which is but *Juftificatio particularis*, it comes to be the *Juftitia Caufæ* materially it felf (whether any fuch act be, I have fpoke before, and its evident in *Mat.*25. & *Mat.*12. 37, *&c*.).

3. For the third, it is that fenfe in which Mr. *Cr.* takes Juftification, as perfected in Confcience on our believing, which was perfected *in foro Dei* before we were born. Now here I grant him as much or more then he defireth: *viz.* That obedience to Chrift doth not fo juftifie us; nay that it is not then in Being, but follows that Juftification. Indeed I affirm that when we are juftified before and without fuch obedience, yet it is a *Caufa fine qua non*, fubordinate to faith, of our continuance in a juftified ftate, or of not-lofing our Juftification; but here I affirm it to be but a Condition, and no Caufe, much lefs the Matter or Meritorious Caufe of our Righteousnefs.

4. As to the fourth I know not any fober man that will deny it, but that if to conftitute Juft, may be called juftifying, then that Inherent Righteousnefs which conftituteth us Righteous fo farre, doth fo farre juftifie us as our Righteousnefs. But this is a Righteousnefs that is fo farre from juftifying us at Gods Barre againft the Accufation of Guilt of death, that it will not merit the pardon of one finne, and ferveth but to intitle us to Chrift, by whofe Merits we are fo juftified.

So that in fumme the Queftion between Mr. *Cr.* and me can be no more then this, Whether Obedience to the Redeemer, be a condition of continuing or not-lofing our Juftification, given before it? and a condition of our Juftification at Judgement or not? Now let us fee what he faith to this.

And firft for the foundation of the whole bufinefs, whereas I argued from the true nature of Chrifts Satisfaction, that God might notwithftanding Chrifts fuffering for us, give us the benefits of it, but upon a condition appointed by himfelf. Mr. *Cr. Part* 1. *pag.* 117. grants it in thefe words [Becaufe our Juftification is an act proceeding from the meer and free will of God and of Chrift, it was therefore in their power after payment made by Chrift and accepted by the Father in our behalf, to Covenant and accomplifh our difcharge, either forthwith or a long time after, either fimply or upon Conditions.] This Mr. *Cr.* not denying doth falfly accufe me of arguing a *poffe ad effe*, and cals it A mad Argumentation. I only by this argued for the *Poffe*, which I think was with good fuccefs, when it hath forced that mans Pen to concede it, who before durft liken God to [a prodigle of nature, a devillized man] if he fhould by any punifhment on us require (as he cals it) fatisfaction for the fame finnes that Chrift hath already fatisfied for. As for the actual conveyance of the gift of Juftification *fub conditione*, by way of condition, I proved that otherwaies, by a multitude of Scriptures, and if I did not prove it indeed, let Mr. *Cr.* call me a mad Arguer, and

and spare not. But remember that here the *Posse* is granted, *viz.* that for all the payment made by Christ and Accepted by the Father, it was neverthelefs in the power of God and his Christ, to discharge us simply or on condition, suddenly or long after.

2. Well: Let us next see what he saith of the condition it self, and whether Justification be granted Conditionally in the tenour of the Covenant or not.

Pag. 349. he saith, [" Yea in this point I should be totally silent, because
" Mr. *B*. in words speaks no more here, then what some of our most sound and
" godly Divines have spoken before him, that faith is the Condition of Justifi-
" cation, were it that Mr. *B*. meaneth as they mean. For though in the best
" meaning of the best men, the propriety of the terms or phrase may be much que-
" stioned, and give occasion of much dispute, yet traversing Controversies about
" words, when there is agreement in the substance to which both parties drive,
" is in my apprehension a business so farre tending to distraction and breach of
" union among the Saints, that it is the last and least trade, I am confident, that
" ever will betall me to drive.] '*Ex ore tuo*, &c. O modesty! who would easily have believed that a man in his wits could possibly have been so ignorant of his own heart, and write such a Volume as this, and know no more what he hath done? But perhaps the word [Saints] will be some salve to his credit; for he hath before pronounced me forsaken of God, and destitute of the Spirit, as a meer natural man, &c. But here you see that my words are justified by the Accuser himself so farre as to be the same with the words of the soundest and godliest Divines: and he addes [" But in this point though Mr. *B*. here speaks in words
" what some of ours have said, and do say still, and that without any detriment,
" that I can see, to the Gospel; yet his meaning and theirs are in no less antipa-
" thy then a Hawk and a Heron, and that as in other lesser so principally in these
" particulars of moment.] Lets hear now the principal difference. [1. By faith
" they mean our Application, or faith as it is our Instrument of applying Christ,
" and the grace of God in Christ to our Justification. He by faith means not
" only the *το credere* as a part of our inherent Righteousness; But as a generall and
" common word, that comprizeth within it self all good qualifications and good
" works whatsoever, as elsewhere, and specially in and under his 70, & 71. *Thesis*
" he declareth himself; so that he makes, and under the word *faith* understandeth
" all these as equal conditions with faith, of our Justification.]

Here's the first principal difference. More plainly this: M*r* Cr. speaks truly and charitably of the words of our Divines, but falsly and maliciously of mine. A wide difference! But 1. What's all this to the point of Conditionality? It seems then we differ not in that, whether the Covenant be conditional? or whether faith be the Condition? and so whether Justification be conditionally granted? but only what that faith is which is the condition? At least, here he mentioneth no other difference; but *de Materia*.

2. Do they, by *faith*, mean [our Application?] so do I, if the Acceptance of a free gift be Application. And are we not yet agreed?

3. But they mean faith [as it is our instrument of applying Christ, &c.] Its pity a man that so abhorreth contending about words, should lay so great a stress on the word [Instrument.] But seeing the man himself here cals it not the instrument of Justification, but only of applying Christ, why should we differ, when I openly professed *pag* 221, 222. that I do not so much
stick

stick at this speech, though I judge it not proper. I will contend with no man for calling it our *Instrument* of receiving Christ, largely, vulgarly, or metaphorically so called: My question was Whether it justifie *as* an instrument? Is not all that our Divines mean by the word Instrument comprized in the nature of the act of faith, as exercised on its object? and is not this act confessed to be the Acceptance of Christ freely given? All this I confess as much as any of them. And are we not then agreed in the Matter? By [Instrument] they mean a *Receiving* of the thing Given: and I confess faith is such a Receiving.

4. Well, but what is it that I mean, if Mr. *Cr.* speak true? 1. [I mean the τὸ credere.] And do not those that he mentioneth mean it too?; I thought it had been the act of faith which they call Application, Apprehension, and an Instrument? If it be the Habit; I will agree with them too: If neither act nor habit, what is it? and why do they call it faith?

5. But if Mr *Cr.* would intimate that I make the τὸ credere to justifie formally as such, *sub hâc ratione*, I do as constantly deny it, as he is constant in false accusing. Nay consider whether they that make faith *qua instrumentum* to justifie, do not make the τὸ credere in *Christum* to justifie as such? For action is the causality of the instrument in effecting, and this is the action: It is τὸ credere in *Christum* which they call instrumentality. I say still τὸ credere, that is, Faith is the matter of the condition, but justifies not as such, but as a condition appointed to this office in the instrument of conveyance by the free giver.

6. The same answer serves to the next charge [as a part of our inherent Righteousness.] Had he left out [as] and meant that *fides quæ*, faith which is a part of our inherent Righteousness, is also a condition of our Justification, I should own it, and think all our Divines will do so too: If not, I would gladly know what faith it is that they mean: For if it be no part of our inherent righteousness, it is absolutely a sinne: And I confess thats none of my sense, that God justifieth us by a forbidden act.

But he puts in his *quatenus* to shew you that he forgetteth not his old trade; as if I made faith to justifie, or to be the condition of our Justification, qua *Justitia inherens*; whereas clean contrarily, I take it to be our inherent Righteousness in a peculiar sense, *a posteriore*, because it is our fulfilling of the condition? and that it justifieth (in our Remission, and Acceptation with God) not as Righteousness but *as* the Condition. (I said no more then this in my Book: but now I adde, that if any Accuse us of being Infidels, against that particular Accusation, faith must justifie us, as the particular Righteousness of our cause.) So that here is a meer false accusation of Mr. *Cr's* and no opinion of mine: Nor could the man shew a line or word of mine that contained any such thing.

Two gross falshoods more follow, as if they were my sense of the point. 1. That I take faith in a general sense here as comprizing all good qualifications and good works whatsoever. 2. And these as equal conditions with faith of our Justification.] 1. I maintained indeed that justifying faith hath more acts natural, then one, *viz.* both the assent of the intellect and consent of the will, as is afore explained: but I made it contain none but what are a Reception of Christ as offered in the Gospel. I comprized love in it indeed; not all love that is a grace; but that it must be a *Velle*, a loving acceptance of Christ, of which I am ready to give a fuller account then I shall now stand to do. But that I comprehended all

good

good works, is M*r* *Cr's* own. I still contradistinguished justifying faith from obedience to Christ, and made obedience a fruit of faith. Its true, I made subjection essential to faith: For to take Christ as King, is subjecting our selves to him: But I ever maintain, that to engage my self as a subject, is in order before my obeying as a subject, and is the cause of it.

I confess also, that I mentioned several acts, (as Repenting, begging pardon, &c.) which though they are not faith, are yet implied as attendants, when we are said to be justified by faith: but as I made not these to be faith, so I never said so much as that of all obedience, or any obedience to Christ, at least, as such.

I also confess that I said that faith is sometime taken yet in a larger sense, as containing all Gospel-proper obedience: but I do not say that ever faith is so taken when we are said to be justified by it. So that Mr. *Crandons* fictions are more naked, then to seem credible to any that will examine before they believe.

And his last is as false: for though I say that Repentance is a Condition as well as faith, (which yet I never said of all good works) yet I never said it was [an equal condition with faith.] Nay I did purposely attempt to open how those other Acts, stood in subordination to faith, which are made conditions with it in the Gospel; and therefore fitted to be conditions, because they necessarily appertain to faith, it being the *acceptance* of Christ, and they making it a right reception, as to the Moral Modifications.

So that for all M*r Crandons* false accusations, I am not here manifested to differ from the Divines in question, so much as about the matter of the Condition; much less the form; or Whether Justification be given on Condition or not. His next difference is this.

[2. " By [Condition] they mean that which being once attained and once " fixed upon Christ, speaks us absolutely justified for ever. So that in calling " faith a Condition of Justification, they mean, we cannot be justified without " it, but having once by faith apprehended Christ, we are by it united and joined " to Christ, and by force of our union with him, are thenceforth absolutely and " irrevocably pardoned and accepted as Righteous in Gods sight.]

Now he comes to the formal difference between me and others, about the nature of a Condition, having spoken before only of a feigned difference in the nature of Faith. And what difference doth he here shew? not a word that I can finde, as if we did at all differ *de formali ratione conditionis*. What my sense is of the word Condition, I have shewed in my Reply to Mr. *Blake*. I take it in *sensu Civili*, as a Moral condition, agreeable to the nature of the subject, and not for a meer natural qualification called a condition by some, as the driness of the wood, and its proximity to the fire is its condition of burning. The difference that he here feigneth between me and others, is only of the sufficiency of this condition to the perpetuating of the effect of the Donor in Justification, and not of the formal nature of a Condition. Remember therefore that for all Mr. *Crandon* can say, I take the word Condition in the same sense, as Reformed Divines ordinarily do.

And for the difference that he feigneth, who knows his meaning? either he means only that a man once justified, shall never lose his Faith and Justification; and if so, he plaies but the old game of false accusing, in feigning me to deny it. Or else he means, that the tenour of the Covenant is such, as giveth a perpetual

Q pardon

pardon of all sinnes past, present and to come, on condition only of that first act of faith ? If so, 1. I'le tell him my dissent. 2. Why I think our Divines do not so judge as he feigneth them to do.

1. My opinion is, that the Reason why Believers lose not Justification, is from Gods immutable Decree of Election, and the special purpose of Christ in his sacrifice, to effect infallibly the salvation of all such, as are chosen and given him by the Father to be so saved: as also from some discoveries of this Will or Decree of God, in the Word, which may be called promises: But withall I believe that the Law of Grace, or the promise, which doth convey our Justification is one and the same, and not changed by our believing, and therefore continueth to justifie only Believers : and should we cease believing that promise would cease justifying : and that we do not cease believing is from the forementioned causes, and not from that promise. So that the same God that decreed to maintain the faith of his chosen people to the death (that is, of all Believers in sincerity) did yet think meet for the right government of the world, and for the suiting of his dealings to the condition of man, to make over the right to this benefit by a conditional general act of pardon, or Law of Grace, which would condemn and not justifie them if they should turn unbelievers : Though by his secret grace he will keep them from such Apostacy, yet Threatnings and conditional Promises are his moral means thereto, which he sees meet to use : And if the special work of the spirit excluded, or included not moral means; then would it exclude, or not include the Word, Sacraments, and all other as well as this. So that the conditionality of the promise is nothing against the Certainty of perseverance : And Mr. *Crandons* zeal in making the doctrine of Conditions to be damning (as he elsewhere doth) doth but make the plain Doctrine and Gospel of Christ to be damning.

2. The Reasons why I conceive our Divines mean as I in this, are these :

1. Because it is evidently the Truth of God (which I will not believe them to deny till I needs must.) And that it is truth, I prove now by these three Arguments only. 1. In that the Scripture promise of salvation is still Conditional ; yea Overcoming and Continuing to the end are made its Conditions. And he that should lose his right to Salvation would lose his Justification : if Right to Salvation (*i. e.* Glorification) be not part of Justification it self: yea praying for pardon, forgiving others, repenting, are made conditions frequently of renewed pardon. 2. If Justification were given in the promise to be perpetual on condition of our first beleeving only, then all after-acts, or habits of faith should not be justifying faith, nor should any man have justifying faith after the first minute of his first beleeving: which let him beleeve that can for me. 3. If Justification were Absolutely given as perpetual, or God gave us a pardon of all sin past, present and to come, at our first beleeving, then his threatning us with damnation, if we should Apostatize, would be a Threatning to break his own promise, or to reverse that which he gave us an irreversible Right to. But thats not true : Therefore I take it for granted that Mr. *Crandon* is not yet so farre gone as to deny that God any where threatneth his people, if they Apostatize ; (though he will preserve them from it, making the threatning his moral means of preservation :) If he should, I would dispute no more with him out of the Bible; but from some principles which he will acknowledge. I know God may Decree to give us perseverance, and reveal that Decree, which Revelation, (or Pollicitation if you will) declare to us that if he should not accomplish it, he were mutable; and yet

he.

he may give us Right to our final Absolution and Salvation, but on condition: and in these there is no contradiction; because Purposes and Pollicitations (which are distinct *a promissionibus*) give no Right: besides other reasons that are at hand. But to say, [I now give thee absolute final irreversible Justification from all sinne past, present and to come] and at the same time to make a Law which faith to the same man [If thou draw back my soul shall have no pleasure in thee,] seems to be a contradiction (though he should resolve to maintain him in the faith:) because in the later, he threatens on a condition to take away that which is supposed to have been given him absolutely and irreversibly: For to be in Law under a conditional threat of losing it, shews that in Law the continuance of our possession is but conditional.

The second Reason that perswades me that our Divines do not think that our first beleeving doth give us in Law sense, an irreversible Title to final Justification, nor an absolute pardon of all sins to come, or absolute Justification as to the continuance, is this: Because they commonly teach that no sin is pardoned before it is committed: *In potentia vel virtute Causæ*, some (as *Ames*.) say they are: but not Actually.

A third Reason is, Because the same Divines commonly affirm renewed repentance, faith, prayer for pardon, &c. to be conditions of the renewed pardon of known (especially gross) sins.

A fourth Reason is, Because they do commonly affirm that faith justifieth, not only in the first act, but to our lives end; and that we must go to Christ by faith for daily pardon.

A fifth Reason is, Because many of our most Learned Divines do maintain that Justification is a continued act, and not so *simul & semel* as to be ended *quoad actum Justificantem* as soon as begun. See Bishop *Downame* of Justification, proving this at large. And Mr. *Crandon* himself durst not deny it. So that I think it is manifest, that not only *de formali ratione Conditionis* our Divines say the same as I, and I as they, but also *de sufficientia primi actus fidei ad continuandam Justificationem*, which is the thing wherein he feigns a difference. Now let us see what he makes to be my opinion, when I have owned theirs.

He addes [" He cals it so a condition, as that it continues still a condition, " justifying us only conditionally and not absolutely: so that it leaves our estate " still one and the same; no more justified and pardoned when Beleevers, then " when unbelievers. For by the satisfaction of Christ, we are before faith com- " eth conditionally justified if we beleeve, and when faith is come we remain still " but conditionally justified if we believe, our safety being as loose and uncer- " tain then as before, depending still upon the residence and abode of faith in us, " as before it did upon the possibility of its future ingeneration into us and acting " in us, and that we are no longer justified then when we beleeve and obey: so " that by beleeving and unbeleeving, obeying and rebelling, we may be justified " and unjustified again a thousand times before we die; and how often after, " himself expresses not. I need not mention more: these two differences are " enough to declare, that though here he speak in the same tone with some of " our Divines, yet his Judgement no more agrees with theirs, then the Pope with " *Luther* and *Calvin*, *Elymas* with *Paul*, *Simon Magus* with *Peter*, or the Scribes " and Pharisees with Christ.]

Here is little but what one denial doth honestly and sufficiently answer, it being so false.

1. Its

1. Its false, where he makes me to deny that we are absolutely justified, and assert only a conditional Justification. For though I once said that the discharge or justifying Law remains conditional still, yet I ever expressed my self to hold that we are actually and absolutely in a justified state as soon as we believe, and did we die in that moment should be saved: only, I say, that in the tenour of the Law, the future continuance is conditional if we continue here.

2. It is spoken in Mr. *Crandons* Dialect, in antipathy to the ninth Commandment, that I [" leave our estate one and the same, no more justified and par-" doned. when Believers then when unbelievers.] Let any *animal Rationale* be judge, whether a pardoned Traytor be in no better case then an unpardoned, because if he turn Traytor again he shall die for all his former pardon. If a Prince offer himself in marriage to one poor condemned woman, and she refuse him and deliverence offered with him; and he offereth the same to another, and she accepteth the offer and is married to him; Is this last in no better a case who is made a Princess, then the former that lies in Jail, looking for the Assizes to be executed, because that if she be unfaithfull, and seek her husbands life, or play the Adulteress, she shall be divorced again? A Landlord offereth two poor men, that if they will but Accept his curtesie, and once a year in stead of Rent, put off their hats and thank him, they shall have a Lease of a large Revenew. The one refuseth the offer, and thereupon hath neither Lease, House nor Land: The other accepteth it, and is put in possession, and his Lease sealed: Is this man in the very same case as he was, and as the other is, and no more a Tenant, because he holdeth his Lease upon the Condition of an act of Homage? (I'le name the Pepper corn no more, for *Doeg* overheard me the last time.)

3. His reason is reasonless: [Both before and after, he saith, it is Conditional.] But Sir, before the whole Right and possession is only conditional, and not actual at all: but after the Right and Possession for the present is actual, and only the continuance is Conditional: Is that all one?

4. Where he talks of [our safety being as loose and uncertain as before.] 1. He feigneth me to make it uncertain, when I affirm that it is certain in it self and to God, then and before, upon the foundation of Gods Decree. 2. Doth not himself make it as uncertain as before? that is, as certain before as then?

5. The like fiction of his venturous brain is that following, that I make this Certainty to depend on our faith, which I ever judged to depend on Gods Decree.

6. And worse is the next, that I say [we are no longer justified then we believe and obey,] which the man never found a word for in my Writings: else sleeping men should be unjustified. Nay that was one reason still that I had against instrumentality being the formal reason of faiths interest in Justification, and conditionality is that Interest: because the former being a meer Physical interest, we can be no longer justified then we are believing, and faith no longer an instrument, and consequently no longer justifying then it acteth: but the later being a Moral Legal Interest, may suffice to the effect *propter beneplacitum Donatoris* even when the act is intermitted: for it reputatively continueth while the Habit continueth. But if Mr. *Crandon* think that in case he should turn Infidel again, he should continue justified, I will not believe him as credible a man as he is.

7. Another forgery of his it is, that I teach that we may by believing and unbelieving be justified and unjustified again a thousand times before we die.] When

I still

I still affirm that God will preserve us from turning unbelievers, notwithstanding the conditionality of this promise, yea by the means of this conditionality to excite us to vigilancy and care for perseverance.

8. What he saith about being unpardoned in the life to come, is but the intimation of ridiculous malice, which cannot lie latent for a few lines, even where it confesseth it wanteth matter to work on.

All this laid together, I should not doubt to convince Mr. *Crandon*, were his black choller but a while allayed, that the Pope, and *Elimas*, and *Simon Magus*, and the Pharisees, shall all be saved, if they differ no more from Christ, from *Peter* and *Paul*, from *Calvin* and *Luther*, then I do from the Reformed Divines about the conditionality of the promise of Justification, or the meaning of the word Condition.

Further hear him make his own Confession, *pag.* 356. ["We have granted "before the promulgation and offer of Justification by the Gospel to be condi-"tional: but the gift and being of it to be Absolute, &c."] *Concedo totum*: You and I are agreed: I plead for no more but that the Tenour of the Gospel-promise, (which is the offer, and the gift in an active sense) is conditional: and so Justification actual none at all till we believe: but when we believe, the gift in a Passive sense is absolute, and in an Active sense absolute or equivalent; as I did before explain my thoughts. You see then what is like to become of Mr. *Crandon*, who holdeth this doctrine of Conditions, which he saith will condition me to damnation.

P. 104. The next place where I finde him undertaking a fuller discovery of the difference between the Protestant Divines, and me a Papist, in this Point, and how farre they make Works to be Conditions, he putteth down their Judgement (as he takes it) in these Propositions. [" 1. They grant that the promulgation " of Righteousness and Life is to be made Universally and Conditionally to all: " God knoweth who are his: but the Heralds of his Grace know not. Therefore " by the command of Christ they are to testifie this Word of Life to all without " exception, promising upon condition of believing, in the Name and by the " Word of Christ, Righteousness and Salvation. In the mean time they maintain, " Christ hath satisfied only for those that the Father hath given him, so effectual-" ly as that by vertue of Christs purchase they shall receive power from above to " believe unto salvation."]

Repl. Is it not strange that even in the Point of Universal Redemption, and Conditional pardoning of all, the Papists and Protestants should so fully accord? Shall they both be damned? or both be saved? and the Accuser prove false? I profess my self wholly to agree to all this, as being according to my Judgement. The second is

[" 2. They are wont oft to use the word *Salvation* (as the Scripture also " doth) for Glorification hereafter: and so take it as a distinct thing from " Justification, and involve into the Salvation more then into the condition of " Justification.

Hitherto I am a Protestant still: For even so do I; understanding not Justification at Judgement, which hath the same conditions with Glorification, but as they do, our Justification upon our first believing, by which we receive actually the pardon of all our sins, Reconciliation with God, and Title to Glorification. Let us hear the rest.

[" 3. By the word *Condition* they understand oft all the necessary Antecedents, " and

" and sometimes also the necessary Consequents of Justification and salvation. But
" so, as they terme such Antecedents the Conditions, without which going before,
" these ends cannot be attained ; and those Consequents, the Conditions without
" which following we cannot attain the certain knowledge that we are justified
" and intighted to glory.]

I doubt the Protestants anon will be made two-fold more the children of damnation then I. For it seems they hold two sorts of Conditions, and I but one : and if my one sort, will condition me to condemnation, as he speaks; what will that and more do ? I am wholly a Protestant in holding Antecedents Condition, but Consequent I know none. But who would have thought that I had come short of Mr. *Crandon* and the Protestants, where he makes me to go beyond them as farre as the Jesuites ? I confess *Chamier* makes a distinction of Conditions into Antecedent and Consequent, but confessing (justly) the unfitness of the termes, and using them in a farre other sense then here Mr *Crandon* doth (of which more in the testimonies in the end.) Nay Mr. *Crandon* makes his own conditions Antecedent, while he names them Consequent : for when he calls them [Conditions without which we know not our Justification] They are plainly made Antecedent Conditions of that Knowledge, but no Conditions at all of Justification it self. I confess also that there are (in *Chamiers* sense) Conditions following the Benefit, but they are not Conditions as Consequent, nor of the Benefit as past, but of the continuance of that Benefit, which continuance is still future. Also let Mr. *Crandon* know that I speak *de moralibus*, and therefore of Conditions in a morall or Law sense, and not *ut merus Physicus*, of naturall, necessary qualifications as such : (as its a condition of my Believing that I have my hearing or other senses, and the use of reason, &c.) that were but a ridiculous transition from one Genus or subject to another. And thus it seems I am hitherto a Protestant, at the worst.

The fourth followeth [" 4. That as oft as they speak of the Conditions of Ju-
" stification, they mean the Justification of the new Covenant, not the Justifi-
" cation immanent in God, or that which Mr. *B.* calleth, Chrifts own Justification
" as the publick person.]

Rep. So do I : yea I acknowledge no such thing as a justification of any man properly so called, either eternall, or in Chrifts Justification : though I used that last terme once, speaking as in their language to whom I spake. Hitherto yet I am a Protestant, and differ not from others here mentioned.

The fifth of Mr *Crandons* Propositions is this [" 5. They utterly deny Morall
" obedience and Good-works to be in any other sense a Condition of Justifica-
" tion, but as it is a Consequent thereof to evidence it.]

Rep. 1. I will anon, God willing, prove this to be false as so generally delivered, past all doubt : For this is expresly to deny it to be any Condition of Justification at all, and to make it only a Condition of our discerning that we are justified. And a sign as such is not a morall Condition. 2. But yet taking Justification only for Gods putting us into a justified, pardoned state at the first, and not as extensive to the continuance of that Justification, or to our justification at the judgement, so I confess more then Mr. *Crandon* here desireth, *viz.* that Morall obedience, and good works, are no conditions of that Justification at all, but meer consequents and signes of it. And because I am confident that Mr. *Crandon* and many Protestant Divines do so understand the word Justification, in this dispute, therefore I think I may take my self of their minde in the thing, and so farre yet no Papist.

The

The sixth Proposition followeth: Saith Mr. *Crandon* " They deny all Causality of Good works to salvation.

Rep. 1. Taking salvation generally as comprehending sanctification and consolation, this is not true. 2. But taking it for the Right to Glorification (as I doubt not but Mr. *Crandon* doth) and I as confidently deny it as they: which if Mr. *Crandon* will not know when he readeth it, thats not my fault. So that hitherto yet I am no Papist.

The seventh Proposition is this, " Much more a concausality in the same kinde " with faith and the satisfaction of Christ.

Rep. This would intimate as if I give to works what Protestants are here said to deny. But its untrue. 1. For faith, I deny it to have any proper causality as to our justification or right to salvation: and how can I then give works a concausality? But you stumble not at such straws as this.

2. I affirm Christ to be the meritorious cause, and works to be no cause, nor any condition of our justification at first, and but conditions subordinate to faith, of our justification at judgement, and the non-amission of it in this life: and this not as works in *Pauls* sense, but in *James*'s sense.

But I know the thing that the man looks at (with little ingenuity) is that I once said, that Christs satisfaction was as a meritorious cause, so a *fine qua non*: But that was in severall respects, and I wish themselves give any more to it at all: But did I not then and still maintain that satisfaction to be also the meritorious cause? But of this I have said enough to Mr. *Eyre*. Yet then I am no Papist.

The eighth Proposition is this [" Most of all, that they in any rationall sense merit it."]

Rep. Little matter from without will serve a Spider to make a net. I have ever disclaimed Merit. I have said fourty times more for it in this book, only to moderate the over-zealous against the phrase in Fathers and Protestants, then ever I said in any book or Sermon before. Nor did I ever say that it may be used in a rationall sense: but said when I was pleading against Merit, that yet in a large improper sense, our performance of the condition may be called worthiness and Merit: Not that it may lawfully be so called, but that the word improperly used may signifie such a thing. What Mr. *Crandon* will call a rationall sense, little do I know: only I know that I use not much Ratiocination in finding out the meaning of the words, more then to finde how they have been used. Custom helps me more then Reasoning from any thing in the word, to know the meaning of it. I take words to be arbitrary signes, and not naturall signes: And if custom will but change, and call [bread] a stone, and a stone bread, I will not censure it as irrationall, much less, as Popery: And for the irrationall Fathers and Churches that used the word Merit for so many hundred years, and the irrationall Protestants that used it in the Augustine Confession, and the irrationall *Calvin*, *Bucer*, &c. as well as *Luther*, *Melancthon*, &c. that did subscribe it, and all the irrationall Protestant Churches that adhere to it to this day, I say for all these I am more willing to excuse them, and consult with Charity then spleenish Zeal, for the understanding of them, then to imitate them, or approve their use of the word. Thus far therefore I see not that I am a Papist.

The ninth Proposition followeth [" Or that as they make up the Inherent " Rightness of man to be a collaterall with the sacrifice of, or righteousness which " is by Christ to salvation; so that we are saved by works, for works; as by Christ, " and for Christ. All this dirt they leave to Mr. *B.* to lick off from the nails of " the

"the Jesuites, bidding defiance against it, as a cursed doctrine.

Never did it once enter into my thoughts, or fall from my mouth or pen, that our Inherent Righteousness is collaterall with Chrifts sacrifice and Righteousness, to salvation: or that we are saved by and for works, as by and for Chrift! If I must be affirmed to hold this or any thing that this man will say I hold, and made a Papist whether I will or no, what remedy.

These are all the Propositions wherein he expresseth the judgement of Protestant Divines as differing from me; and now I leave it to any sober Christian to compare them together, and judge of the difference: only supposing that my own profession of my belief is more to be credited then Mr. *Crandons* recitall of it, according to his own invention. And I desire Mr. *Crandon* to consider, whether the fear of the Lord were operative in his spirit, when he durst insinuate or plainly affirm that I hold all these things which he faith [they bid defiance to as a cursed doctrine?] when he said [they leave all this dirt to me, &c.] Did he remember the ninth Commandement and the day of Judgement, when he wrote this, and such a Volume of the like?

He addeth next [" What they understand then of Works as a condition of salvation is in this comprized, that to salvation already attained, they have the relation of an adjunct, consequent and effect: But to the salvation hereafter to be attained, the relation of an adjunct, antecedent and disponent, as also of an argument confirming the hope and assurance thereof.]

Rep. This is my very sense also; and yet must I be a Papist whether I will or no? Only I must tell Mr. *Crandon*, 1. That he doth not in these words give us any thing of the nature of the Condition, but only the reasons why it is made a Condition; and our Divines do call it a condition, and without doubt did know what a Condition is, better then any man can learn from these words of his. 2. That I use not to call Works [a Condition of salvation already obtained,] nor do I know any such Condition, but know it is a contradiction. Yet I say as he, that they are an Adjunct, Consequent and Effect. 3. But I add, that they are part of that salvation it self. I think our love to God, our hatred of sinne, our new obedience, are parts of our begun Recovery, Health or Salvation, and not only Adjuncts, Consequents and Effects. 4. To be an Adjunct, antecedent and disponent to future salvation, is full as much as ever I gave to any acts of man: (though these words are but an ill favoured definition of a Condition.

And now I here appeal to any moderate man, whether Mr. *Crandon* make not all Protestant Divines and himself as much Papist as me? I profess to ascribe no more to works, then to be, as he speaks, to be [Antecedent, Disponent Adjuncts to future salvation] or to Dispose the person thereto: This much he maketh all Protestants to hold as well as I: Doth he not then damn them and himself as much as me? I confess my self blinde and ignorant of the English tongue if he do not.

If you say [You make them Conditions disponent to Justification, and so doth not he,] I answer, Not to the Receiving of a state of Justification; nor never did: but only to the Continuing or not losing that state, and to our particular remission of and justification from particular sins when they are committed. And all this is future: especially the justification at judgement. *Obj.* But Mr. *Crandon* doth take Justification to be perfect at first, and so to have no need of these Conditions. *Ans.* It is a perfect Remission of all sinne that then is sinne: but if Mr. *Crandon* dare think or say, 1. That we need not Chrift or Grace, nor are beholden

to

to God to continue that Justification, 2. Or to Remit particular sinnes when we commit them, 3. Or to justifie us at judgement, 4. Or that these are not parts of our future salvation; I am sure our Protestant Divines will renounce him, and dare not or do not say any such thing, but the clean contrary.

He next adds [" They express themselves usually in the phrase of that Father " (though possibly misunderstood by some) *via Regni sunt, non causa regnandi:* " which some do, all should thus construe; not that they are the way to the King- " dom above, Christ alone being this way; but, they are that way of the Saints " which are Christs spirituall Kingdom.]

Rep. 1. That good works are *via Regni*, is as much as ever I held. A *way* hath the nature of a Means to the end, and I know no lower means then meer conditions. 2. If our Divines mean as this man saith, that [Works are not the way to the Kingdom above, but of the Saints who are Christs Kingdom,] then I professe my self unable to understand them: in the mean time I dare ayer that this man doth unworthily abuse them, and doth abtrude upon us a ridiculous piece of non-sense, which I opened before. 3. Doth he not here contradict what he said in the foregoing words? There he saith that [Works are Disponent Adjuncts to future salvation,] Here he saith [They are not the way to the Kingdom above.] Is not the Kingdom above, our salvation which yet remains to be attained? and doth [a way] signifie here any more then [an Antecedent, Disponent, Condition?]

Will you hear now how this man concludes his parallell? in these words ["Let " now the vast difference and contrariety in so many particulars, between Mr. *Bax-* " *ters* and these Divines opinions, about this question be considered, and then let " it be judged whether Mr. *Baxter* had not taken his leave of all bashfullness, when " he would impose on his Readers an opinion that he delivers upon this argument " nothing but what they had taught before him.]

To which I only add; 1. Let the words be shewed where I sought to impose that opinion. 2. If I had, let the differences indeed be weighed as he desires, and let the forehead of this man be judged of as it shall be found. I think I have shewed that he here granteth as much as I desire in this point of the Conditionality of Works; and makes the Protestants to do the like.

Let us follow him yet further. *Part* 2. *pag.* 142, 143, 144. you shall finde him in four Propositions granting as much to mans actions for life and salvation (though with self-contradictions intermixt) as that for which I am charged with Popery. I will not weary the Reader with the rehersall of the words; he that will, may read them in his book. Nay he granteth more then I desire, or indeed then is true and safe. His first Proposition begins thus [" We grant that they which are wholly " under the old Covenant, having never the Gospel revealed to them, are Bound " to seek Justification and salvation by the works of the Law or naturall Righte- " ousness still.

Rep. A vile and false assertion, and of desperate consequence. I prove the contrary thus:

1 He that is bound to acknowledge that he hath lost all possibility of justification and salvation, without some supernaturall remedy, is not bound to seek justification and salvation by the works of the Law: But those that have not the Gospel, are bound to acknowledge that they have lost all possibility of justification and salvation, without some supernaturall remedy. Therefore.

2. By the light of nature they may see that they are sinners, and that sinne deserveth

R   death

death, and that justice must be done (See M*r* *Owen de Justit. Vindicat.*) and this light of nature they are bound to improve.

2. No man is bound to a naturall impossibility: For a sinner to be justified and saved by the Law, or naturall righteousness, is a naturall impossibility (it being a contradiction, to be a sinner, and to be justified by that Law that condemneth all sinners:) Therefore.

Though men may be bound to morall impossibilities, when they have made a Duty impossible by disabling themselves, yet not to naturall impossibilities, nor to believe contradictions. He that is bound to believe it impossible for the Law of nature to justifie him, is not bound to seek Justification by that Law :: But all sinners are so bound: Therefore.

3. No man is bound to rob God of his honour, and overlook the righteous sentence of his judgement: For a condemned sinner to seek yet to be justified by the Law that condemned him, is to rob God of his honor, and to overlook the righteous sentence of his judgement: Therefore.

Such men being under condemnation already, are bound to acknowledge their misery, and give God the glory of his justice, and to despair of ever being justified by that Law which condemned them.

4. No man is bound to go the way clean contrary to his salvation: For a sinner condemned already, to seek justification by that Law, is to go the way clean contrary to to his salvation. Therefore.

Such seeking would carry him further from God, and fasten him under a greater guilt. He is at that time bound, as to confess his sinne and misery, so to enquire far and neer after any discoveries of Gods way of Mercy, and to hearken after Light, to see if it be possible to finde out the way of Grace, and in the mean time, to be led to Repentance by the mercies and long-suffering of God, and not to seek Justification and salvation, where he is bound to despair of ever finding it. Let none call this man an Antinomian, in this point, where he preacheth the Law in so destructive a sense, as would be the everlasting ruine of those that obey him.

Part 2. *pag.* 132. He granteth [" 1. That the whole world that hath not heard of " Christ shall be judged according to their works to life or death. 2. The whole bulk " of professed Christians shall be judged according to their works, *&c.* 3. That the " very Saints as compared one with another shall be judged according to their " works, *i.e.* sha'l be adjudged to glory in severall measures above, according to " the severall measures of their services and sufferings here, *&c.*] See the rest. One would think this man were a Papist as gross as I am. But what's the difference? Why 1. He saith, this is [the sentence of judgement, but not the justifying sentence!] If he have found out a sentence of judgement, which doth neither justifie nor condemn, he hath done like himself, *Mat.* 12. 36, 37.

2. He saith [It is not according to Works as a Condition.] As what then? If the word [According to] be taken *secundum subjecti naturam*, i.e. *in sensu forensi*, I appeal to any man that hath eyes in his head, whether it can signifie any thing lower then a Condition? And here he blattereth out a deal of his language of darkness; that evil works cannot be the condition of justification, and therefore we are not justified by works at judgement as by a Condition, as I affirmed; with more such stuff which I am aweary of reading over, and will not add the trouble of reciting.

Part 1. *pag.* 370. When I had shewed that I did confess faiths Receptive nature (as having Christ for the object.) to be the remote reason of its Interest in our

Justification,

Justification, as being its Aptitude to that office; but maintained that the neerest or formall Reason of its Interest is, its being the condition of the promise, freely by God designed to this office; See how he confuteth me, [" The question con- " troverted between us and the Papists first, and in these later times the Armi- " nians also, is not Whether Gods Instituting of faith in Christ, or else the acting " of faith so Instituted, be one the formall, and the other the Remote reason why " it justifieth? but whether so Instituted of God to be the mean or Instrument of " Justification, it doth justifie by virtue received from Christ its object; or else by " its own virtue as it is a good work, or as it is an act of righteousness performed " in obedience to Gods Commandments. That which they maintain is, that faith " justifieth by virtue of its object Christ, denying the Papists work, and the Ar- " minians act. If Mr. *B.* did labour more for truth then for victory, we should not " finde in him so much fraud, and so little of sincerity. It is not Christs, but An- " tichrists kingdom, that is maintained by the pillarage of shifts and sophismes. " Let him not astonish the poor Saints of Christ with words that they cannot un- " derstand, obscuring the truth with needless terms of Art.] And so he proceeds in his accustomed Rhetorick.

Let the Judicious here be judge, 1. Whether he do not grant all that I desire; and that is indeed, the main point opposed by most in my book, *viz.* That faiths apprehension, *i.e.* faith as faith, or as faith in Christ, is not the formall Reason of its Interest in Justification, but only the Remote, and Gods Instituting it to the office of justifying, is the formall or neerest reason. If I understand him he grant- eth this; or denieth it not: and I desire no more. 2, When he hath proclaimed me a Papist, he vomits out his reproaches against me, because I will not maintain the Popish or Arminian Cause; telling us that this is not the Question between the Papists and us, and so I am guilty of [much fraud, little sincerity, upholding Antichrists Kingdom by the pillarage of shifts,] with much of the like, because I will not maintain the Papists doctrine, nor state the question as they do. 3. When I do solemnly profess, that I do now disclaim and detest, and have still disclaim- ed and detested, the doctrine of the Papists and Arminians, as himself here layes it down (whether it be theirs or no, I leave to him.) I never thought that faith Ju- stifieth [by its own virtue as it is a good work, or as it is an act of Righteous- ness performed in obedience to Gods commands;] but as it is by the free donor made the condition of our Justification. And thus I fully wrote in that book which he opposeth; and yet doth this man load me with Reproaches, for not maintaining the opinions which I wrote against, *i.e.* for not being a Papist in do- ctrine, when he hath told the world that I am one. If ever man in the Church of Christ, before me, had such an adversary as this, I confess, his name and sirname is to me unknown.

As for what he adds, of [faiths justifying by virtue received from Christ its object,] I will believe it when I see Scripture for it, or sense in it. I beleeve that Christ justifieth, but I believe not that as he is faiths object, he coveyeth virtue into it, to justifie. It seems the man is of the Papists opinion himself, for ought I see by him, after all this noise against me, for not owning it: If faith receive virtue from Christ to justifie, then faith hath in it self (so received) a virtue to justifie: But this man affirmeth it to be the Protestant doctrine, that faith doth justifie by virtue received from Christ its object: Therefore,

If faith receive such virtue, doubtless it hath the virtue in it self which it hath re- ceived.

R 2   2. If

2. If faith juſtifie by a received virtue, it ſeems its made a Cauſe of our Juſtification, (for virtue is exerciſed by way of cauſality, to produce the effect,) But faith is not the Cauſe of Juſtification: Therefore.

3. If faith receive this virtue from Chriſt its object as its object, then faith as faith, that is, as this faith, doth juſtifie : (for it is eſſential to the act *in ſpecie* to have ſuch or ſuch an object :) But the Antecedent is falſe : therefore ſo is the Conſequent.

See now how well Mr *Crandons* doctrine takes down man in the work of Juſtification, and freeth it ſelf from the miſchiefs which it pretendeth to oppoſe ! Even as errors uſe to do.

For my part, I ſay not that faith receives virtue from Chriſt to juſtifie, becauſe it is no Scripture phraſe, and leſt I intimate in it a Cauſall Intereſt of our Juſtification : much leſs do I ſay that it receives it from Chriſt as its object, that is, that it is in faith, as faith : But I ſay, that the place or Intereſt which faith hath in Juſtification is two-fold : One remote and Aptitudinall : this it receives from God as the New Creator, or Author of our faith. The other is its neereſt or formall Intereſt, and that is, its being the Condition of the promiſe (as the former was its Receptive nature,) And this it receives from God, as Promiſer, Donor, or Legiſlator of the Law of Grace, or act of obedience and pardon.

Part 2. pag. 26, 27, 28. He firſt chargeth me with dealing worſe then *Bellarmine*: What's the crime ? In not manifeſting what I mean by Repentance. Then he ſaith [" All the Scriptures which have the leaſt ſhew or ſound of ſpeaking for me, " I have them, in part from *Bellarmine*, whom I here follow, and in part from other " Jeſuites and Friars that controverſally handle the Popiſh Juſtification againſt " us."] In all which if there be one true word, let me be ſtigmatized for the moſt Impudent Lyer, that ever dared to write of holy things. Yea if ever I took one text or word out of *Bellarmine*, or any Papiſt, or any but the Bible, of all that he here mentioneth.

Then he proceedeth to tell us [" what the Scriptures mean by Repentance, when " they hold forth the Promiſe of Life upon Condition of Repentance to ſinners,] (A Condition it ſeems it is then, how damnable ſoever it is in me to ſay ſo.) And firſt he tells you, that theſe texts ſpeak ſometime of a Legall, and ſometime of an Evangelicall Repentance. And of the Legal he ſaith thus [A Legal, conſiſting " meetly in a feeling of humiliation and contrition for, hatred againſt, departing " from ſinne, and applying of the endeavours to all morall virtue and obedience. " This is a meetly morall Repentance, derivable from the ſtrength of na-" turall conſcience, illuminated by the Law and common knowledge of Gods will " and nature. In this ſenſe is the word taken in moſt of the Scriptures quoted " from the old Teſtament, and ſome alſo of thoſe poſſibly that are quoted out of " the new.

Rep. O holy doctrine, and far from Arminianiſme ! Naturall ſtrength can do all this : O that it could but do one thing more ; even perſwade men that they are Juſtified and ſhall be ſaved, and then what need of Grace ? But according to this Character I muſt change my judgement of moſt of my neighbours: For moſt of the vicious ignorant people, will believe that they are juſtified and ſhall be ſaved, let me ſay what I can : but thoſe that Mr *Crandon* here deſcribeth [that are humbled, and hate ſinne, and depart from it, and apply their endeavours to all morall virtue and obedience] are much more rare, and ſuch as I had better thoughts of. If hatred of ſinne, and endeavours of univerſall obedience may come from nature, I

confeſs

confess Nature is not so bad as I supposed it, nor Free will so much captivated and corrupted, as we Papists and Arminians did imagine. At least he might have yielded to the necessity of a common Grace for this much, if not a special: and such a common grace as shall work upon the will, and not only give that Light which he mentioneth to natural Conscience.

But he addes, that [" the Life by these Scriptures promised, is not the life of " Justification or of spiritual and supernatural blessedness, but that which the ad- " ministration under the Law is wont to call Life, viz. 1. The fruition of the " Land of *Canaan* which prefigured the life and rest both of Grace and Glory. " 2. Of the blessings of health, honour, peace, plenty, safety and other temporal " benefits promised to the obedient in the Land of *Canaan*.]

Rep. I will not enter the Controversie, what the Life was that was promised by *Moses* Law, as such: But as I doubt not, but it was Eternal Life that was promised in the first Law, so I doubt not but the old Testament aboundeth with Gospel promises of eternal Life: and that these are such, at least many of them, which make Repentance the Condition of Life, as the Gospel it self also doth. Will Mr. *Cr.* blot out all the Gospel part of the old Testament at a dash, which promiseth life to the penitent, yea and tell us the like of some places in the New.

Consider also what a mean kinde of Repentance this man feigneth God to require in the Old Testament, even such as natural strength may perform: or else what strength of nature and freedome of will men had then, that could Repent without supernatural Grace: and what an easie Law that was, which *Paul* accounted such an intollerable yoak of bondage, which required but such a repentance, which natural strength may perform!

But I forget my task, which is not now to rake in the channel of Mr. *Crandons* Errours, but to discover his concessions of as much as I need. The main Errour that I am supposed guilty of, is bringing other acts under the name of faith, to be with it the conditions of Justification or Salvation, though but in a subordination to it: Let the Reader that regards the business, mark these following words of Mr. *Cr.* pag. 28, 29, 30. and see whether he prove not my defendour. [" 2. Those " Scriptures which he quotes that. offer Life upon condition of Evangelical Re- " pentance, do not make for him, any more then the former: For Gospel Re- " pentance is taken either in a large or in a strict sense. In the more large sense " it is the same with *Conversion* or *Regeneration,* and ofttimes equipollent and the " same thing with faith, though some little consider it to be so: And this is as " oft as Repentance is put for the One and Whole thing required on our part " to put us into the actual and sensible possession of the Grace and Life of the " Gospel: as *Matth.* 3. 2. *Mark* 6. 12. *Repent for the Kingdom of God is at hand.* " The summe of their preaching was, *Repent:* So *Luke* 13. 3. 5. *Except ye Re- " pent, ye shall all likewise perish:* and 24. 47. and many other of the Scriptures which " he quoteth.]

Here we see Repentance that is the condition of, Life is the same thing with *Conversion, Regeneration* and *Faith.* Hear him go on.

[" In all these places Repentance containeth *primarily* the change of our Rela- " tion, and but *secondarily* of our qualifications and manners.]

It was not for nothing that the man did make so long an Oration against humane Learning used in these Divines things: he would, he must I mean, have liberty to speak contradictions. Here is a strange precept of God, that requires men [Primarily to change their Relations, and but Secondarily their Qualifica-

tions

tions and Manners.] An imaginary impoſſible change, like the Libertines faith that is made the cauſe of it. Was there ever a Relation Primarily required, before that act which is its Foundation; or ever a Relation without ſome Foundation firſt laid? or did ever any Law require the change of Relation, before the change of acts or qualities? I know not what ſuch a Relation is. If he ſay, As in Marriage it is firſt required of the woman that ſhe take the Relation of ſuch a mans Wife, ſo of men coming to Chriſt it is firſt required that they be Related to him, as his Members: I anſwer, It was never heard that either of them was primarily required. It is Marriage Conſent and Covenanting that is firſt required as the *Fundamentum* of the Marriage Relation: And it is the Conſent and Covenant to be the Diſciples of Chriſt, that is firſt required, before the Relation of Diſciples. Shall we feign God, or any wiſe man to teach and command a natural Impoſſibility, ſuch as is a Relation before that in which it is founded, or the *ratio fundandi*? Our acts muſt be changed before we are juſtified or related as Members of Chriſt, whatever theſe men ſay: We muſt have the act of Faith and Repentance, and ſo farre the old and hard heart taken out of us, and a heart of fleſh and a new heart given us: elſe that will prove a conditional promiſe. But he proceeds thus, [" It is a *quidam motus* in which *acti agimus*, being moved by Gods Spirit we move] Is not this a ſtrange Relation that is a *quidam motus* in which *acti agimus*? It ſhall never have my Vote to ſtand in the old predicament of Relation: nor any of the ten: but ſhall have the honour of making an eleventh predicament, or elſe be Tranſcendental. He goes on, [" The *Terminus à quo* in this motion is ſelf, our
" ſelf-righteouſneſs and ſelf-confidences from which we turn no leſs then from
" our polluted ſelf, ſinfull ſelf, and ſinfull waies. The *Terminus ad quem* is God,
" the grace of God inviting us. The *Medium per quod* is the Lord Chriſt, through
" whom we have acceſs to the Father, for Remiſſion firſt, and then for Sanctifi-
" cation alſo.] And after [What will ye call this obedience to the faith, this
" cloſing of his heart with Chriſt in ſtead of further daſhing againſt him?
" Was it not his *Converſion*? his Repentance? Or is the promiſe of Life, I mean,
" the Life of Juſtification, made to any other Repentance beſides this? In this
" ſenſe therefore Repentance is not a *quid diſtinctum*, a thing diſtinct from, but
" one and the ſame with juſtifying faith; or if it be objected that it is ſomewhat
" larger then juſtifying faith, I ſhall not contend, but acknowledge that it com-
" prehends Whole faith, both *qua Juſtificat* and *qua Sanctificat*. Yet this hin-
" ders not but that theſe two phraſes, Repentance to Life and Remiſſion of ſins,
" and Faith to Life and Remiſſion of ſins, are in the language of the holy Ghoſt
" one and the ſame.]

You ſee then that juſtifying faith in Mr. *Crandons* ſenſe, is Converſion of the heart from Self and ſelf-confidence to Chriſt, and the ſame with Repentance, and he will not deny but that Repentance contains more then juſtifying faith, even Whole faith. What faith this man leſs then I here? but only that I maintain that it is only *Whole faith* that is the Condition of Juſtification: and that faith as faith doth neither juſtifie nor ſanctifie, though both follow it. Yet hear him further, [" Where Repentance is taken in a ſtricter ſenſe, and ſome of the Scri-
" pture which he quotes ſeem to promiſe Remiſſion of ſin, or Life to it, we muſt
" neceſſarily underſtand of every ſuch Scriptures that it ſpeaketh of the Repen-
" tance which is actuated in our firſt Converſion, Calling, or after it. That
" which is in our firſt Converſion or Calling, when it is taken in a ſtrict ſenſe,
" is not as in the former ſenſe put as the whole thing required on our parts, but
" ſeems

"seems in words a coordinate with faith to interest us in the Righteousness and
"Life which are by Christ. Such are these Scriptures, *Repent and believe the
"Gospel: Repentance towards God and faith towards the Lord Jesus Christ,* Mar. 1.
"15. *Act.* 20. 21. and many other. But in these Repentance and Faith together,
"make up no more then in other Scriptures, either Faith alone or Repentance
"alone in their larger sense import: and so Repentance is taken for self-denial,
"self-abhorring, self-subduing, and Faith for embracing Christ: both these are
"repentance or faith in their larger sense, *&c.* And Repentance here is no di-
"stinct thing from Faith, nor Faith from Repentance; and so in naming these
"two the holy Ghost nameth not two gifts of Grace, but two acts of the same gift
"of Grace in us.]

You see here Mr. *Crandon* confesseth that Repentance is in Scripture so made the Condition of Justification, that it seems in words a coordinate with faith, that it is indeed faith it self: that it is a self-denying, self-abhorring, and self-subduing; and so these acts are the conditions of Justification. How easily, were he like other men, could I prove to him, that in this Conversion, it is not only self, as opposite to Christs Righteousness, that this Repentance turns us from? When himself makes Christ but the *Medium*, and God the *Terminus ad quem* of the change, no doubt then it is from *Self* as opposite to this *Terminus ad quem*; and that is, as we are our own Idols, and esteemed, honoured, loved, pleased, before God: and this essentially contains a turning from all those things (worldly pleasures, profits and honours) by which this *Self* doth please it self above God: and so the cleaving to God as our only happiness and ultimate End, as well as to Christ as the Way. See now what a deal is here taken in, and whether his own concession lead him not into that damnable Popery which he takes me to be in.

But let us see the very bottom of the whole business: Doth he indeed make this Conversion, this self-denying, self-abhorring, self-subduing, all justifying acts, and that equal with faith it self? Just as far as I do, if I can understand him! That is, that faith is the only apprehending act, and is the principal part of the Condition, and Repentance, self-denial, self-subduing, are required or made conditional, but as requisite to our right believing: Only he gives more to faith in appearance, then I do: Hear his words [" Though these two acts must
"needs cooperate together, *viz.* the casting out of *Self*, and the receiving of
"Christ, yet it is the later alone that doth properly and instrumentally justifie,
"by receiving the Justifier and his Righteousness. The former act doth but *disso-*
"*nere materiam* (as one saith not too catechrestically) doth but put a man, as it
"were, into a justifiable posture and capacity; doth but *obicem tollere,* pluck out
"and cast away the barre that might fasten the door against Christs entrance; and
"this it doth not as a distinct virtue from faith, but as a subservient act of faith
"to its receiving of Christ.]

Is it not pity that this man and I must be of two Religions, when we hold the same thing in the great point of difference? We differ in being of one minde. He saith the same that I more largely explicate and maintain. Here is not a faith of one single act, but of many. Here is as much given to Repentance as ever I gave to it or any act of man, that is, to dispose the matter and remove the barre. And yet must I be a Papist and he a Protestant? But here's the difference, I deny faith to be the Instrument of Justification, and so give less to it then he: But if I do, I give so much the less to man, when I give to the lower act no more then he gives to the highest. State the case right then, and let the difference lie where it is: M*r* *Crandon* and I are agreed that the subservient act doth but *disponere materiam* and *tollere obicem*: we are agreed that Faith is a receiving of Christ for Life: but he saith that one act is an instrument of justifying, and this I deny. Nay but stay a while: Though I differ from others I am reconciled with Mr. *Crandon* in this also: For Justification with him, is but Justification in sense, and *in foro Conscientiæ*: and I confess that Faith may be called an Instrument, or some efficient cause of that kinde of Justification. Is there yet any remaining difference? Doth not Mr. *Crandon* make one act subordinate, and the other superiour, when I make them coordinate (Faith and Repentance?) No: I say as he for that: It is receiving Christ that is the Principal act: it is in subordination to this that Repentance, self-denial, self-abhorring, self-subduing are required and made the condition: Only give me leave to add also, The aversion of the soul from sin, or worldly Idols, and conversion to God, as our chiefest good, must finde a place in Repentance or Faith, or both.

Can you bethink you of any thing else wherein you would wish Mr. *Crandon* and me agreed? Yes, that one point before named. He makes Justification by faith (to say nothing of his other two before faith) to be *in foro Conscientiæ*, and in our sense of former Justification, and I make it to be, a state or right in Law, (whether we feel it or not;) by which we have the obligation to punishment actually dissolved, or right to impunity given us. Stay a little, and see whether Mr. *Cr.* and I be not friends whether he will or no. Reade *Part.* 1. *pag.* 324. these words having recited many Texts of the Evangelists, that call Justification by the name of Life, he addeth [In all which and many other Texts of this Evangelist none can deny but by Life is to be understood chiefly, if not *Only, Life in Law, the Life of Justification.*]

What say you to this? are we not yet agreed? No: Mr. *Crandon* doth up and down, made his Life in Law to consist in the sense of pardon in Conscience. A wonderfull Law title, which consisteth in the sense of Conscience! A strange Relation that is the same thing with an internal Passion or Action! But we must bear now and then with a contradiction in an Authour that is at such mortal odds with Philosophy. Here then is the difference. Mr. *Crandon* confesseth all that I desire, that Justification by faith is chiefly if not only that in Law: but he super-addeth elsewhere, that even this same is the feeling of pardon in conscience: whereas I take this to be as palpable a contradiction, as to say, *Paternitas, filiatio, Jus, Debitum,* &c. are Passions or Actions in Conscience. I take them to be two things, both separable and frequently separated, and that the same man that is pardoned and justified in Law, is yet ofttimes unsensible and ignorant of that benefit.

And now I leave it to sober consideration, Whether this Book of Mr. *Crandons* which granteth what it opposeth, and yet poureth out upon me such a storm of reproach, for that which he openly owneth himself, be a profitable piece for the Church of God, and worthy the publike view, or a just Vindication of the Fundamentals of a Christians Comfort. I have said as much as I mean to do on that Reason to the contrary, drawn from his Concessions. I now come to the next, which is drawn from his false Accusations, and making that to be my Doctrine which never entered into my thoughts, nor ever fell from my Mouth or Pen.

SECT.

SECT. VIII.

IF it be none of my Doctrines, but his own forgeries, about which Mr. *Crandon* bestoweth most (if not almost all) of his labour in Confutation, then his Book is not profitable to the Church of God, nor worthy the publike view : And whether the Antecedent be true, or no, though I resolve not to trouble my self and the Reader with so large a trial, as the recital of most of his Book would be, yet I shall give you a taste of the substance of what he chargeth on me ; and this for Mr. *Caryl's* satisfaction.

You have seen no small part of his dealing with me this way, in what hath been said already : The best way to see the rest with least trouble is, to take it from those places where he summes up my Errors, and speaks more directly to the point, for in other places you will scarce quickly finde the matter it is so buried in heaps of personal Reproach.

Part 1. *pag.* 78. he heapeth up many of my supposed Errours : The first he scornfully reports thus. [" 1. That they (the Elect Saints) have so large a dis- " charge from the rigour of the Law as any of the worst Reprobates.]

Repl. If he intend an equality, how proves he that this is any Doctrine of mine ? Because I say the Law of Works is not to them Abrogated. Doth not the Assembly say as much in the place before cited ? As for the term [Covenant of Works] I have shewed in what sense I take that to be ceased, or continued, which we call by that name: Are all Reprobates actually pardoned, as Believers are ? Is this man a Divine, and doth not know that if the Law were not in force to oblige to punishment there could be no pardon ? For how can an obligation be dissolved that is no obligation ? But he thinks we are pardoned from Eternity.

His next is [" 2. That they have no more discharge from the Laws curse then " the worst of Reprobates.] *Repl.* Would you think any Christian durst speak such Accusations without any truth ? There is not a true word in any of his charge. Hear the proof, which he ushers in with this scorn. [" Must we not " account him a Saint that hath a fastidious stomack, or sore mouth that cannot " relish these dainties ? The former Conclusion he reacheth to us in these words, " so farre is the Law dispensed with to all, as to suspend the rigorous execution of " it for a time, and a liberation and discharge conditional procured and granted " them. *Jam sumus ergo pares:* In this the Sons of God are in as good a case as " the reprobates, and somewhat before the devils.]

Repl. Its true that the Saints in heaven are in as good a case as Reprobates : but to what purpose speaks he this, but to intimate that I make them to be in no better a case ? Is it not pity that any man that preacheth the Gospel, should be yet ignorant of the truth of those two assertions of mine which he here brings in ? 1. Should a Preacher of the Gospel dare to say, that reprobates are dealt with at present according to the utmost rigour of the Law ? and to tell them that God never shewed them any mercy since the Fall ? and therefore they owe him no thanks for any mercy, nor is their sinne aggravated by any mercy, nor should his mercy and longsuffering leade them to repentance ? Would this Preacher honour Free Grace, or edifie souls ? 2. How can that man preach the Gospel that knoweth not that it containeth a General Conditional Discharge ? even on the condi-

S   tion

tion of Repenting and Believing? He addeth ["The later Conclusion in these words, But an Absolute discharge is granted to no man in this life: *Jam sumus ergo pares.* Yet have we as large cause of exulting and joy in the holy Ghost, as the reprobates, that (as far as we can discern) we are no neerer to hell then the children of hell, whose inheritance is in hell for ever."]

Repl. I have before shewed, that by [an Absolute Discharge] in the words that he carps at, I meant not *Liberationem Passivam, sed activam*; not pardon as it is ours, but the grant of pardon in the word: and so I say still, that the word containeth a Conditional pardon to all, and no Absolute pardon to any, that is, no act of pardon that is in Absolute terms, from which any receive an actual Remission. And in regard of Passive pardon or discharge, I maintain this also, that till death the continuance of it is still conditional. But I ever plainly affirmed, that all Believers are Actually and so Absolutely pardoned as to all their sinne, (for that to come is yet no sinne:) though the pardoning act remain still the same in the Gospel in Conditional terms, yet when we perform the condition by believing; the effect is actual and so farre absolute. And can he prove that Reprobates are in Gods favour, and have all their sins pardoned, yea and shall be kept by grace from falling away, which I affirm of the Elect? You see the truth and ground then of these Accusations.

He proceeds thus ["To prove the later Assertion, that none are, that Believers are not Absolutely discharged from the Law as a Covenant of Works in this life, he borroweth matter from Pelagians, Papists, Socinians, Arminians, and the whole rabble of professed enemies to the grace of God in Christ."]

Repl. Not a true word.

After some railing lines, he next addes, ["The Popish Errors which he brings as an addition to confirm, that Believers are during life under the Law, are these: 1: That they which are in Christ have not their sins fully pardoned, neither are themselves wholly justified in this world."]

Repl. Very false: shew any such words of mine. I still affirm that they which are in Christ have their sinnes fully pardoned, that is, all sinne past, and present fully pardoned as to eternal punishment: though castigatory punishment may remain, and though future sinnes are not yet pardoned. And I affirm that we are wholly justified in this world, as Justification is taken for Remission of sinne, or Right to impunity and to life: But I confess it is my opinion that the great day of Judgement shall not be till you and I are dead; and that the Justification which we shall there have, is our most full and compleat Justification: And therefore I said, that in its kinde Justification here is perfect, but it is not the most perfect kinde of Justification. And therefore it is not fit to say without explication, that any mans present pardon or Justification is perfect. An easie truth, the Lord knows, if men were not blinded with prejudice: when we are taught to pray for daily pardon.

He next addeth [" 2. That whosoever shall be justified in the world to come, must procure it by his own willing, running and persevering in this world."]
Repl. Shew any such words of mine. If [Procuring] signifie [Causing] it is false, and ever by me disclaimed: but if it signifie no more but that our willing, running and persevering are Conditions without which none shall be then justified, I say, Its pity any Preacher of the Gospel should be ignorant of it.

His

His third follows [" 3. That they which are in Chrıſt may fall away and be " damned.] *Repl.* A moſt immodeſt falſhood: when I ever maintained the contrary, yea in that very Book.

[" 4. That no man while he lives can be certain of ſalvation.] *Repl.* Shew where I ever ſaid ſo, or bear the name of a ſhameleſs ſlanderer. I have largely proved the contrary in my Book of Reſt.

[" 5. To this he addeth one worſe, then any Popiſh or Socinian hereſie, as " proper to himſelf and from himſelf alone: *viz*. That all believers, notwithſtand-" ing Chriſts ſatisfaction for them, notwithſtanding their perſevering faith " in him, yet muſt be at laſt damned for ever.] *Repl.* Go on: for I am a-weary and aſhamed of mentioning your faults. We ſhall now hear the proof.

[" The firſt he expreſly affirmeth, *&c*.] *Repl.* As is before explained only.

[" So that in this life there is no diſcharge, but a conditional promiſe that " poſſibly we may in the world to come be diſcharged.] *Repl.* Very falſe: We are actually diſcharged as to all ſin paſt:, but conditionally for the future: and our Juſtification in the life to come, as you ſpeak, is not only Poſſible but Certain: How ill beſeems it you, to make ſo light, and ſuch a ſcorn of Juſtification in the life to come? You will value it more one day.

The ſecond he proves, becauſe I ſay, We muſt continue to perform the conditions, and addes, [" And ſo it is by our own ſtrong and laſting endeavours, that " after the world is ended our ſinnes may be poſſibly forgiven, and we ſaved.] *Repl.* It is no otherwiſe by our endeavours then as by conditions of Gods making: Himſelf conteſſeth Faith and Repentance to be conditions: and muſt not we continue Believers and penitent, if we will be ſaved? He that will reade *Mat.* 25. *Rev.* 2, & 3. may anſwer this without my help.

[" 3. That they that are in Chriſt may fall away, and be damned, if they " continue in their apoſtacy, or may after their many apoſtacies, oft renew again " their union with Chriſt, and ſo at laſt be juſtified, he ſpeaks out fully, in tel-" ling us, [It is not one Inſtantaneous act of believing, but a continued " faith, that ſhall quite diſcharge us: that no longer are we diſcharged then " we are Believers; and when we ceaſe to believe, the Law is ſtill in force and con-" demneth.],

Repl. 1. The laſt words of mine he falſifieth: I ſay, *If we ſhould ceaſe to believe, the Law is in force, and would condemn us*; and ſay withall, that God will cauſe his people to perſevere. He faineth me to ſay, [*When we ceaſe to believe, &c.*] 2. Whether my words contain any ſuch thing as he ſaith I ſpeak out fully, or whether all be meer forgery, I leave to any man that can reade Engliſh and underſtand it. If God threaten his own people, if they draw back, his ſoul ſhall have no pleaſure in them, and this as a means to preſerve them from Apoſtacy, will this man ſay that God *ſpeaks out fully*, that they fall away? Cannot God make a conditional grant, as certainly to be accompliſhed as an abſolute? One would think that this man judged us to be from under all Law and Government.

He next ſaith, [" If I argue from impoſſibilities, it makes not for my pur-" poſe] and concludeth, [But he argueth as from a poſſible and uſual caſe.] *Repl.* Still falſe: It is poſſible in the nature of the thing in it ſelf conſidered, but it never comes to paſs; and the threatning and Conditionality of the Promiſe,

[66]

is one means of God to hinder it from coming to pass.

The fourth, ["That none can in this life be certain of salvation"] he saith "[depends on the former: for if we cannot be certain of our Perseverance, we "cannot be certain of Eternal Happiness.]" *Repl.* A conscionable way of Accusation! to make one falshood of your own feigning to be mine, and then gather more out of it. Produce a word where ever I said, that none can be certain of Perseverance or Salvation! or else confess your self to be, what this Volume proclaims you.

His fifth slander (that all Believers shall be damned) he will needs have me affirm in saying they are under a Covenant of Works: of which I have opened my minde before so fully, that I will not with such a raving Disputer say any more.

He undertakes here also to declare the grounds of these my Errours, which he "saith [are principally these two 1. That faith as an infused gift of grace, "and a part of our inherent Righteousness, doth justifie, &c.] *Repl.* Never such a thing came into my thoughts, to own it, or believe it. I have still thought, that the same faith which is a gift of grace, and part of our inherent Righteousness justifieth, that is, It is the condition of our pardon: but never did I think it was *as such* a gift of grace, but only as a condition of Gods free constitution.

The second follows [" 2. That faith and all those its concomitants, with "their fruits and effects depend upon our free will, to gain and retain, refuse "and lose them, at the pleasure and lust of our corrupt free will.] *Repl.* How dare this man heap up such things as these and believe there is a God that hateth falshood! I believe that corrupt free will refuseth Christ, but only sanctified free will accepteth him; and that sanctification of it is from Gods special grace, on whom free will and all things depend. Yet I believe that none have Christ, or pardon, or heaven against their wils, that is, continuing unwilling. Nor do I know that ever in any writing I gave the man any occasion of these false reports, nor doth he once tell us whence he fetcheth them; but only boldly saith, It is so.

But the principal place where I finde him gather together my Errours, is *Part* 2. *pag.* 272, 273, 274. When I had expresly professed that I take not any act of mans to justifie us, [1. Not as works simply considered. 2. Not as Legal works. 3. Not as Meritorious works. 4. Not as good works which God is pleased with. 5. But as conditions to which the free Lawgiver hath promised Justification and Life: and that I dare not give so much to any act of man, as is usually given to faith, to say that it justifieth *as* it apprehendeth Christ, which is its intrinsecal Nature, and Essence, and so faith as faith should justifie, whereas I give all the honour to the free Donor who hath constituted this the condition of his gift.] Mr. *Crandon* gives this following answer hereto.

["All this hath been oft and fully examined before in its place also, and how lit-"tle truth there is in any part or parcel thereof discovered. It would be weari-"ness to the flesh and vexation to the Spirit, but to look so often upon his "great Goddesse, his Queen of Heaven, *CONDITION*, as he blesseth her. "O that his Conscience had been so well acquainted with Christ, as his fancy "is with this Idol! he would not then have pestered the Church with such an "imaginary Deity, nor prostituted all that is called God, at the feet of such a "*Proserpina.*]

Repl.

Repl. If Mr. *Caryl* think this a Vindication of Gods Truth, and profitable to the Church, he is not of my Judgement: Nor have I any Answer for it now, but to minde the Reader, that the generality of Reformed Divines do say the same of this *Conditionality* as I do, and that the mouth that so reproacheth it, doth acknowledge their use of the word in the same sense as I use it.

He proceeds, [" I am weary any more to attend to him, making the Will of " God, *i. e.* God willing, Conditional; and so the Immutable God, a Conditi-" onal God, the salvation of Christ Conditional, and so Christ a conditional " Saviour; or the witness and seal of Christ a conditional seal and witness, and " so the holy Ghost a conditional Spirit of Adoption; or the Gospel of Righ-" teousness, Forgiveness and Life, a conditional Gospel, and consequently " nulling all these, and pronouncing them no God, no Christ, no holy Ghost, " no Gospel.]

It is a most sad consideration that the worst of the sons of men should be given up to such a spirit as animateth these lines: Was there ever a man called a Protestant Divine that durst say, that there was no conditional Promises or Threats in the Word of God? Nay, do not the Antinomians themselves confess some, even when they cavil against Conditions? as Mr. *Gataker* hath manifested even in *Saltmarsh* himself. Doth that man know what the Bible is that knoweth no conditional Promises or Threats in it? And do every one of these in Scripture make God a conditional God, and Christ a conditional Christ, &c. and Null God, Christ, the holy Ghost, and Gospel? I profess I admire that Mr. *Caryl* durst think such a Book worthy the Publick view that laies this highest Blasphemy to the charge of all Christian Divines in the world, (unless the Libertines are such:) Mr. *Caryl* knows that all our Divines affirm God to have Conditional promises and threats; and knows that there are such things indeed in the Scripture: and yet could he finde in his heart to be the Midwife of that Book that shall proclaim all these Divines, yea and Scripture it self to Null God, Christ, the holy Ghost, and the Gospel? and pronounce them no God, no Christ, &c. sure he will not say, It fals only on me: For if I pronounce God to be no God, because he hath a Conditional promise or threatning, then so doth every Divine, so doth Scripture that saith the same. And he that dare stand out and say, There is no conditional promise or threatning in Scripture, let him send me his Name and his Reasons, and if I manifest him not unworthy to be a Preacher of the Gospel, let me be the common scorn of Divines. Had I said that Gods Will *de rerum eventu* had been Conditional, and that so as that there are conditions of the act of his Will on which he willeth or not willeth, and not only conditions *rei volitæ*, of the thing willed, then this mouth might have been opened thus, with more shew of reason, and less impudency: but when it is only a Conditional Promise and Threatning that I speak of, what answer should one make to such a man. Did not I tell him where even Dr. *Twiss* hath these words following? [" *Ger. Vossius* " interpreteth the Will of God touching the salvation of all, of a Conditional " Will, thus: God will have all to be saved, to wit, in case they believe: which " Conditional Will, in this sense, neither *Austin* did, nor do we deny. *Confid.* " *Synod. Dort* and *Arles reduct.* to pract. pag. 61.] And pag. 143, 144 [" I wil-" lingly profess that Christ died for All in respect of procuring the benefit (of " pardon and salvation) Conditionally, on condition of their faith.] And against Mr. *Cotton*, pag. 71. [" Still you prove that which no man denieth (*mark* " *No man*) *viz.* That God purposed Life to the world upon Condition of obedience

"dience and Repentance, provided that you underſtand it right, viz. that Obe-
"dience and Repentance is ordained of God as a Condition of Life, not of Gods
"purpoſe.] And againſt *Armin. Vindic. Grat. l. 2. part. 2. Crim. 3. §. 6. pag. vol.
minor. 441. ["I confeſs Salvation, and ſo pardon and Adoption are offered to
"All and ſingular men, on Condition they believe, &c. And ſo I deny not that
"Redemption is ſo farre obtained for *all* and every man.] Theſe with eight more
places I cited and referd to Dr *Twiſſ* in the book which he oppoſeth. I would not
mention any Divines words in ſuch a common thing, but that I know this ſort of
men do more then ordinarily reverence Dr *Twiſſ*, for his favouring them in two or
three opinions.

He next proceeds to ["mind the Reader of two things. 1. That both the
"whole and every leaſt fragment of all that is here collected, whether we look to
"the ſubſtance or Artifice uſed about it, is not his, but borrowed partly from
"the Papiſts, partly from the Socinians, and their Apes the Arminians, as hath
"been before ſhewed: and if I ſhall be called thereto, I am ready more fully to
"ſhew, by quoting the Authors out of whom he hath tranſcribed All, almoſt word
"for word, to his uſe.]

Rep. If there be one true word in theſe lines; if ever I tranſcribed or borrowed
a word of what he mentions from Papiſt, Socinian or Arminian, let me never more
be known by any other name, then, *The moſt impudent Lyar.* If all be falſe ———

Next, after a torrent of gumble ſtoole oratory, perſwading his Reader not to
believe me, when I profeſs my own belief, ſeeing my words are [falſe fallacious
flatteries,] he heaps up theſe following Accuſations, to prove that I am not to be
believed.

["I. He maketh our Righteouſneſs of works, and Chriſts ſatisfactory Righ-
"teouſneſs, coordinate and collaterall in the procurement of our Juſtification: the
"one as abſolutely neceſſary as the other to the attainment of this end: the one to
"purchaſe a poſſibility of Juſtification; the other to render that which was but
"in poſſibility, actuall and effectuall to us: Both ſatisfactory: the one as a ſuffi-
"cient fine and payment, the other as ſatisfactory Rent and homage. *Aph. Theſ.* 17,
18, 19. p. 129.

Repl. A heap of inventions of his own brain, which he well uſhereth in with a
Nulla fides verbis. 1. Never were my thoughts or pen guilty of making, that is,
judging and aſſerting, either our works to be any proper cauſes of our Juſtification at all, or (much leſs) coordinate and collaterall with Chriſts Righteouſneſs.
Finde ſuch a word, and burn the book at the market-Croſs. 2. I take faith and
obedience to be Abſolutely neceſſary to their ends, and Chriſts Righteouſneſs to
its end: but never thought that they had the ſame office towards the attainment of
that end, or that they had at all the ſame neereſt ends. It ſhould ſeem the man is
offended that I make faith and obedience of Abſolute neceſſity: that is, that Infidels and Rebels may not be ſaved. Such a Volume as he hath written, doth well
ſuit with the opinion, that Infidels are juſtified, and neither faith of Abſolute neceſſity to our firſt ſtate of juſtification, nor obedience to that at judgement. Yet
do I make a great difference between the Reaſons of the Neceſſity of Chriſts ſatisfaction, and the Neceſſity of our faith and obedience: But ſtill I ſuppoſe both
Abſolutely Neceſſary on ſuppoſition of Gods Ordination. Should I ſay otherwiſe
to pleaſe the Antinomians who would have elect Infidels be juſtified, I ſhould by
others be thought an Arminian, as pleading for the poſſibility of the juſtification
of thoſe Infidels, that never heard the Goſpel. Its hard pleaſing all this kind of
men.

men. 3. I never said either that our Justification was but in Possibility before our faith, nor that Christ purchased but a Possibility: These are still his fearless forgeries. *Datur tertium*. Though our Justification were not Actuall before faith, yet it was more then Possible, for it was Infallibly and Immutably Future. That's all that I know of it (and that it was *in causâ*;) he that knowes more, let him reveal it. 4. I never thought that [our Righteousnels of works did render that Justification actuall and effectuall to us, which was but Possible.] For 1. This Rendring effectuall plainly speaks a causality, which I still denied to any act of ours as to Justification. 2. I maintained that our Justification is actuall and effectuall upon the Condition of our faith alone, before works of obedience; and that they are but the Conditions of our not-losing it, and of that at judgement. 5. Never did I think or say that our faith or works were satisfactory for any sinne committed, as Christs sufferings were. 6. There is not a word in the places that he cites for any of these his forgeries. 7. Yea in the 129 *page* which he citeth, raising an *odium* from the word [Rent] I purposely explained my thoughts to be these; that our faith and obedience was required as homage in acknowledgment of the free Grace of the Deliverer; But have not the least *rationem pretij*: and lest any should think otherwise because I used the word [Rent] when I mentioned the similitude of a Pepper-corn, I did (as distinguishing between a Rent that had in it *rationem pretij*, and a Rent that had nothing but meer Acknowledgement) express my minde in these words, which he refers to, which I am not ashamed to recite, that the Reader may see whether they contain that which he boldly avers they do. [Two things are considerable in this Debt of Righteousness: The Value, and the personall performance or Interest. The *Value* of Christs satisfaction is Imputed to us in stead of the Value of a perfect obedience of our own performing; and the *Value* of our faith is not so Imputed: But because there must be some personall performance of homage, therefore the personall performance of faith shall be imputed to us, for a sufficient personall payment, as if we had paid the full Rent, because Christ whom we believe in, hath paid it, and he will take this for satisfactory homage : so it is in point of personall performance, and not of Value, that faith is Imputed.] Can you finde in these words that which he accuseth them of? Only he eagerly fastens on the word [Satisfactory homage], desiring to make the Reader believe, that I make this homage satisfactory in the same sense as I do Christs sufferings? whenas one is a proper satisfaction to vindictive Justice, *A Redditio æquivalentis aliàs indebiti*, as the Schoolmen and Dr. *Ames* define satisfaction. The other is but *Desiderium in tantum implere :* to be *satisfactory*, was with me, but to be *Acceptable*, and hereafter I will be more cautelous, when I consider what snarlers I must converse with.

He proceeds in the next words thus [" 2. He puts both in the same order and "kind of Causes, making our Righteousness and Christs satisfaction to be both "the *Causa sine qua non*, Thes. 56. For although he names faith there, yet himself "declares himself under faith, to mean and comprehend obedience also. This "Civility Alone he vouchsafeth to Christ, that he names Christs satisfaction be-"fore our faith or obedience, because it seems, that is the elder. But in or-"der, Power and Authority to the producing of this effect, Christ hath *no* prehe-"minence given him above men.]

Repl. The Lord pardon this audacious, fearless speaking of untruths; and shew you the sinfullness of it, that it may be pardoned. 1. I did expresly in the same place affirm, that Christs satisfaction is the meritorious Cause of our pardon, and

and that faith is not; yet this preacher of the Gospel dare before the Lord, [write and publish to the world, that [in order, Power and Authority to the producing of this effect, Christ hath no preheminence given him above man] and that I [vouchsafe Christ this Civility Alone] to be first named, &c. Lord! what will men become, if thou leave them to themselves?

2. I do not finde that ever the man doth once dare to accuse this saying of falshood (that Chrifts satisfaction is in one respect a *Causa sine qua non,*) for all the reproach he poureth out upon it. It removeth impediments: Every superior contains its inferior: had I said, It was no more then so, or not assigned more to it, well might he have spoken to my Reproach.

3. Nay, for ought I see, he and his patty give no more to it, then as to a *Causa sine qua non,* as I have shewed elsewhere.

4. Yea how can they that say Justification is an Immanent act of God from Eternity, give so much to Christs death, for the attaining it, as to a *Causa sine qua non?*

His next words are these [" 3. He affirms mans Righteousnefs to be as Perfect " as Chrifts Righteousness in order to Juftification : viz. both perfect [*in suo gere-* " *nere*] Chrifts Righteousness perfect to do its work, and mans to its work : or " (as he explains himself) both perfect, in the perfection of sufficiency in order " to its end. So that here also is a parity : no efficiency in Chrifts Righteousness " without mans, nor in mans without Chrifts to juftifie : But when the two per-" fections meet, if neither lose its perfection, they may after the world is ended, " perfect our Juftification, *Thef* 24 p. 132. In the mean while, till our works be " added to Chrifts satisfaction, what he saith of faith, that he every where impli-" eth of the satisfaction of Chrift, that it is dead being alone, as to the use and " purpose of Juftifying : and so as works make faith alive, so they make Chrifts " satisfaction alive, as to the attainment of its end, Juftification.]

Repl. Did not I tell you how these men used the ninth Commandment? 1. So far was I from saying that [Mans Righteousnefs is as perfect as Chrifts Righteousnefs in order to Juftification,] that I expresly mention at leaft five respects in which our Righteousnefs is Imperfect, when I ascribe Absolute Perfection to Chrifts. 2. All the perfection that I give our Righteousness, as you may see in the page cited by him, is but these two : 1. A metaphycsiall perfection of being (this he had more brains then to deny.) 2. A perfection of sufficiency in order to its end, *viz.* to be the Condition of our Juftification, &c. this End it shall perfectly attain.] Never did any man question this that vouchsafed me his animadversions, till now. Mr. *Blake,* you may see acknowledgeth it in his book. If our faith be a Means to our Juftification, and be not sufficient in its own place, to the attainment of the End whereto it is a Means, what will follow, but that we muft all perish, and that God hath appointed an Insufficient Means to Juftification, or else that it is not a Necessary Means? Though they that think Infidels are Juftified, take it for no Means, yet Proteftants do.

3. Is it true that he saith, that then [here's a parity?] What if Chrifts Righteousnefs will not juftifie without mans faith, no more then faith without Chrifts Righteousnefs; doth that make any parity in Causality or dignity? The vileft *Causa sine qua non,* may have as much said for it; the nobleft efficient effecteth not without it: and so it is here: when yet the Condition effecteth not at all, so far is it from a parity.

4. Doth he that dare write such a Volume of untruths and railing accusations

as

as this, yet insist on it so confidently that he is perfectly justified? And doth he not voluminously calumniate with the greater audacity, because he supposeth that so long ago he was perfectly justified, from all the sinnes in this world committed. I believe, and shall believe till death, that the most perfect Justification will be at the great Judgment; and that I must be justified in this life from more sinnes, then I was justified from at my first believing, or else perish.

5. He falsly affirms that I say, Works make alive Christs satisfaction as to the attainment of Justification, or that I imply this. And it hath in it more untruths then one. For 1. I never ascribed any Causality to works. 2. I never made them so much as Conditions of our first justified state, but affirm that on our meer Repenting and Believing, *i.e.* Accepting Christ as offered in the Gospel, we are justified before works; and that the Righteousness of ours which consisteth in our fulfilling of the Conditions of the new Covenant, is to be found in faith alone without works, at our first being justified, seeing it alone without works, is the Condition of our first being justified. 3. And though I dare not say, that Christs satisfaction doth justifie without our faith (that is, it justifieth not Infidels) yet I say 1. That this is not through any Insufficiency or Imperfection in it: but because it was never the will of the Father or Redeemer, that any Infidel, or Refuser of Christ, while such, should be justified by his satisfaction. 2. That yet Christs satisfaction is before faith, effectuall to other ends, though not to justifie: viz. to suspend execution of justice, to procure us the new Covenant, and the promulgation of it, and the preaching of the Gospel, and to procure us also Grace to Believe, that so we may be justified: To me, this is not contemptible.

His next words are thus [" 4. That works justifie in the same kinde of causa-
" lity and procurement with faith, not only proving faith to be found, but them-
" selves being in the same obligation with faith, not idle concomitants, only stand-
" ing by while faith doth all (which some fools might imagin that he meaneth,
" when he calls them only Necessary Antecedents of Justification, p. 223.) nay
" they are concomitants with faith, in the very act of procuring it, and in that
" kind of causality which they have, p. 299, 300.]

Rep. 1. Here are many shreds of my words dismembred from that which must manifest their sense; and in all this he conceals that I express and maintain that all this procurement is by no proper Causality, but by meer Conditionality as *Causa fine qua non.* 2. He insinuates untruly in his parenthesis, that I give more to them than to be Necessary Antecedents (that this Section may have somewhat like the rest) whenas I ever took a Condition to be but an Antecedent, though I take not every Antecedent to be a Condition.

His next words are these [" 5. They do all this As they are Works. Even faith
" it self justifieth as it is an act of ours. *Append.p.*80. and As a Morall Duty.
" *Append.p.*102. So do all other Morall Duties *as* they are parts of our sincere obe-
" dience to Christ, *ibid.*]

Repl. Here are in this Section four Propositions, as affirmed by me; and the pages cited where I affirm them. If ever a one of these were ever spoken or meant by me, and if all these Accusations be not downright falshoods of his own devising, then I know not what I have thought or wrote.

For the first [They do all this as they are works] I not only never spoke, but do so expresly affirm the contrary, *viz.* that it is only as the free Donor hath made the Conditions of his Guift, that I even now cast the man by it into such a chafe, that he charged me with [Blessing this *Condition* as the Queen of Heaven,

T making

making it my Idoll, proſtituting all that is called God at the feet of it, making God no God, Chriſt no Chriſt, the holy Ghoſt no holy Ghoſt, and the Goſpel no Goſpel by it:] and yet doth this man in anſwer to the ſame Section, charge me to affirm, that [They do all this, that is, juſtifie and ſave, *As* they are Works.] As if we had given two diſtinct Formal Reaſons of their Intereſt in our Juſtification, or as if, he ſaw not that this is a plain contradiction!

The ſecond Propoſition he citeth my book as affirming. You ſhall hear both, and judge of the mans Credit. He ſaith I affirm [" That even Faith it ſelf juſtifieth *As* it is an Act of ours"] and cites *Append.p.*80. All the words there concerning it that he can refer to, are theſe [*And* we are ſtill ſaid to be juſtified by faith, which is an Act of ours.] This was ſpoken to prove that we may lawfully Act for Life, as well as from Life. This Credible Divine makes nothing to turn [*which is an Act of ours*] into [*As it is an Act of ours,*] and to affirm that I ſay the later when I ſay the former. As if the Matter and form, or the Materiall and formall Intereſt were all one. If I had ſaid that [Mr *Crandon* whoſe word is of ſo little credit, is a Preacher of the Goſpel,] is this all one as to ſay, that [as ſuch a one, he is a Preacher of the Goſpel? Or if I ſay that [he who is a Preacher of the Goſpel ſpeaks un-truths by the hundreds,] it is not all one as to ſay that [As a Preacher of the Goſpel he ſpeaks untruths.]

His third Propoſition which he ſaith I affirm is [that *As* a Morall Duty faith juſtifies.] And the fourth, that ſo do all other Morall Duties as they are parts of our ſincere obedience to Chriſt.] For both theſe he cites *App. p.*102. The words there are theſe [I have fully proved that Morall Duties as parts of our ſincere obedience to Chriſt, are part of the Condition of our ſalvation, and for it to be performed. And even faith is a Morall Duty.] The words are in anſwer to the Marrow of Modern Divinity, which ſaith [when in Scripture there is any Morall work Commanded to be done, either for eſchuing of puniſhment, or upon promiſe of any reward temporall or eternall, *&c.* there is to be underſtood, the voice of the Law] I ſhew that this opinion turns all the ſubſtance of Chriſts Covenant into the Law: and that Morall Duties as they are the Matter of our ſincere obedience to Chriſt, are part of the Condition of Salvation. Do I therefore ſay, that as part of our obedience they juſtifie us? Mark 1. That I ſpeak not here of Juſtification, but Salvation. 2. That I ſpeak not of the Formall Nature of a Condition, but of the Matter of the Condition of Salvation. And ſuppoſing it proved, that ſincere obedience to Chriſt is made by God, part of the Matter of the Condition of Salvation, I conſequently affirmed that ſome Morall Duties, though not *As* ſuch, yet as parts of our ſincere obedience, are part of the Condition, that is, of the Matter of the Condition of ſalvation. I never intended [as] to expreſs the formall reaſon of its Intereſt in our Juſtification, having frequently expreſt the contrary.

And for his third-Propoſition; Is it all one for me to ſay [And even faith is a Morall Duty] which are my words: and to ſay that [even faith it ſelf juſtifieth As a Morall Duty] which he feigneth me to ſay? I cannot believe that ſuch heaps of palpable forgery, are vindications of fundamentall truth, profitable to the Church of God, and worthy the publike view.

His next words are [" 6. That we are juſtified not only by Works, *Aph. p.* " 300. and according to our works, but alſo *for our works,* p.320. That good works are a Ground and Reaſon of it, p.221.]

Repl. 1. Whether the two firſt ſayings be accuſed or no, I know not: If they be, the

the holy Ghost is Accused that useth them. For the third, That we are justified *for our works*, if I had so delivered my minde, he could have interpreted it no otherwise, then so faire as [for] may expresse the Interest of a Condition, seeing I so oft professe to give them no more. But any words which he refers to, are only a question upon *Matth.* 25.34,35. Where Christ gives the reason of his sentence thus] For *I was hungry and ye fed me*, &c.] Now I desire to note, that I never said, that we are justified *For* Works, as the Meretorious Cause, nor that our Constitutive Justification in this Life is *for* them, at all: but I speak only of Justification at judgement, and mention [for] as the Reason of the sentence only: and not as any Cause of our Right in the Blessednesse to which we are sentenced. For that which is but a Condition and no Cause of our Right to the Benefit, yet may be the Reason of the sentence, when the performance of that Condition is the thing questioned. *Luke* saith [*Because thou hast been faithfull in a very little,* &c.] I said not so much as that, nor as many other Scriptures say. But I have to do with such an Accuser, as I have no hope to please without Renouncing the language of Christ, and of all sober Divines. *Paraeus* his exposition is this, which I desire the Reader to compare with my Popery [*Ad Causalem enim dico, significare quidem Causam, verum non Meritoriam Regni, sed Declaratoriam Justae sententiae a judice prolatae) jure ovibus regnum adjudicari, quia operibus se vere oves h.e. fideles esse declaraverint.*] So that in *Paraeus* his judgment it is a Cause of the sentence, though not of their Right to the Kingdom. But because the same opinion is found in other men, which is Popery in me; I will spare mens Names and words, but undertake to prove against any adversary, that sincere obedience is one ground or reason of the sentence of Justification at the last Judgment: and that if any man be accused to be an Infidell or a Rebell against the Lord that bought him, the faith and obedience of that man must be a ground and reason of his Justification, or he shall perish.

Mr Wotton cited in the end, and other of ours say, that we are saved for Works of obedience, though not as Meritorious.

His next words are thus [" 1. That we are Justified For our Works, that is,
" For the Merit of them. Not Merit in the most proper and strict sense, &c.
" [But so farre as it is Possible for a perfect man to have Merited under the Co-
" venant of Works] he may now Merit also under the Covenant of Grace by his
" Works, &c.]

Repl. I have shewed at large before, that *Adam*, or a perfect man under the Covenant of Works, was Capable of a much further Meriting, and in lesse unfitnesse and Impropriety of speech: Never did I speak any such words as the Accuser chargeth me with, either in the place cited by him, or elswhere. The words that are the occasion of his charge I have vindicated before against him, and against Mr. *Eyre:* nor did I ever read to my remembrance one Protestant writer against the Papists on that point, that saith not as much for Merit as I did. I do expect from my great Accuser, the father of Lyes, more malice, then from this man: but I never expect such untruths to be by himself immediately charged upon me, in judgment, as supposing he hath more wit and lesse Liberty.

Thus I have answered, I think, the summe of his book, as to the main matter of Justification by Works; for he contracteth the venime of his charge into these heads: and after his usuall oratory, makes this challenge: [" Let now any of his
" Disciples produce (I will not say one Arminian, but) one Socinian, Papist,
" yea or Jew, that ascribes more to Works then this man, in Derogation from
" Christ and Grace, else let him cease to be a follower of him, or openly and
" ingeniously

" ingenioufly profefs that he followes him as a Jew, Papift or Socinian: and con-
" fequently that he hath made not Mr B. but Mr B' mafters his mafter alfo in the
" doctrine of Juftification: And that in advancing felf fo high, as to affirm
" he Meriteth no lefs fully and properly then Chrift himfelf hath or could have
" done.]

Mr *Caryl* thinks this book worthy the publick view: I think him fo unworthy an Anfwer, that as I will let this pafs without, fo I profefs upon the review I fhould be afhamed that ever I faid a word to him, were it not that I take my felf bound even to do the bafeft work that is lawfull, to fatisfie fuch men as I take Mr. *Caryl* to be: And intreat the Reader to pardon my abufing of his patience with fuch a task, as long as I am thus neceffitated.

Were it not for tyring the Reader and my felf, I might go over the reft of Mr. *Crandons* Book, and fhew them how like it is to this much: but truly I have not fo much time or patience to fpare. Yet a few more tafts let me give you. *Part 2. p. 203.* he faith [1. Then, all the Teftimonies of Dr. *Twiß*, *Junius*, *Paraus*, *Pifca-*
" *tor*, *Aretius*, *Wallet*, Mr. *Burgeß*, are here compiled, to tell them that are no friends
" to the doctrine of Grace, that all thefe Divines confent with him in his do-
" ctrine, firft of a Univerfall Conditionall Redemption and Juftification purcha-
" fed by Chrift, without any more effectual fatisfaction made to the Juftice of
" God, for them that fhall be faved then for them that fhall be damned; and
" 2. That Morall obedience and good works are Concaufes or collaterall Conditions with faith to juftification.],

Repl. Can the wit of man imagin whence this man fhould be occafioned to devife thefe things? Where in all my writings did ever I hint fuch a thing, as that
there is no more effectual fatisfaction made for the faved, then for the damned?
or fuppofe Chrift to die equally for all? Much I am fure I have faid againft it,
but nothing for it. 2. And how can I make faith and works Concaufes, when I
ever deny them both to be any Caufes?

Part 1. p. 73. Becaufe I faid that [fome think the Covenant of Works is re-
pealed to all the world, and the Covenant of Grace alone in force,] he lets fly at
me as a Lyar, with a torrent of reproach faying [" thofe that hold this (moft
" probably.) are fome Utopians, that Mr. *B.* alone and no other either man or
" Angel befides him have had acquaintance with, or the happinefs to know their
" opinion: fo that Mr. *B.* might have done well to have taken a fecond voyage in-
" to the Land of *Eutopia*, either to have joyned with them, or difputed againft
" them on their happy turfe, &c. This Nation among all hath not fuch bug-bears
" and phreneticks, that I know, who maintain fuch an affertion. But it is one of
" Mr. *B*'s fubtilties to feign fuch Ghofts and phantafmes of men to fight againft,
" thereby taking the advantage fecretly and unefpied (as he hopeth,) to erect
" more curfed and monftrous affertions &c.]

Repl. Should a man vex or laugh at fuch a creature as this is? or rather pity him. Muft I (in the midft of fo much bufinefs, and languifhing weaknefs, fpend fo much of my precious time, as I have done, in writing againft that opinion, with moft Learned, Judicious men?) and now muft I and the world be perfwaded that they are but Ghofts, and there is no fuch opinion? I would he could have perfwaded them and me of this fooner, and fpared me all that labour! Have I fuch volumes of it *pro and con.* and now is there no fuch thing? Have I been contend-
ing all this while with Ghofts? They are fuch Ghofts, as write more Reafon in a page, then I have yet feen in all his volume. And I can prove that one of thefe

volumes

volumes that a Reverend, Learned and much honoured Brother wrote to me for that Opinion, was carried to *Oxford* and shewed in more Colledges then one, and to some of Mr. *Crandon*'s friends, or Mr. *Eyre*'s at least: and do those friends of theirs dwell in *Eutopia*? or is this my fiction and subtilty? Methinks this is hard measure.

Part. 1. *p* 300. When I said [I believe that the justified by faith, never do or shall fall away,] as before he flatly affirmed that I say, They do fall away, so here he saith [" What can we think can be his meaning but this, that they that " are sentenced once to Life, in the day of Judgement, and are already Glorified, " neither do, nor shall fall away?]

Methinks still this is hard measure: and if the grand Accuser had used me thus, I should have thought he had dealt more dishonestly with me then with most others.

Pag. 322. *Part* 1. he speaks thus [" *Obj.* Yes he reserves the entire praise of " Merit still to Christs satisfaction alone. *Answ.* Not so: for though in words " he sometime asserteth Christs satisfaction to be the Merit of our Justification, " yet he makes the Worthines of our own Righteousness to be that which " makes both Christs Merit and Justification merited to be ours, and so we out-" merit Christ, deserving not only Justification, but Christ the Meriter, and the " merit of Christ to be made ours In this he is worse then the Papists. They " give the praise of our Merit to Christ: he hath merited (say they) a power to " our Works to Merit: This man contrarywise, that neither Chrsts Merits, nor " Justification the fruit of it, becomes ours till we by our Merits and Worthines, " have put our selves into the possession of it: so according to the Papists the effi-" cacy of mans merits depends upon Christs Merits; according to Mr. *Baxter* the " efficacy of Christs Merits (as to this or that justified person) depends upon a " mans own Merits.]

Repl. All this he dare Print, though I ever renounced mans Merits, never owned so much as the name, much less the thing, never to this day thought or said that man deserved one bit of bread; much less that he deserved Christ, his Merits, and our Justification: never said so much as that faith or any act of mans doth make Christ and his Righteousness ours, but only that they shall not be ours before or without faith, nor continue ours without true obedience: and this very condition I ever maintained to be a fruit of Christs Merits. By this way am I confuted by this man.

Pag. 363, 364. He laies heavy charges on me, unless I will hold that Infants are justified without faith, habitual or actual, thinking in that instance he hath got a proof of Justification before and without faith: When I have so largely in my Book of Baptism, not only given my Judgement, but proofs that the Parents faith is the condition of the Infants Justification, and therefore it is not without faith that they are justified.

Par. 1. *p.* 369. He mentioneth that vain charge which is the summe of much of " his Book, thus, [His meaning is, that it (faith) only so farre justifies as " it fulfilleth the condition. But throughout our whole life according to his " principles, we are but fulfilling, have not fulfilled the condition of the new " Covenant: therefore throughout our whole life we are but in justifying, not " justified, *&c.*]

Repl. In the first moment of our true believing we have fulfilled the whole Condition of our actual Justification from all sinne then committed, and so of our

being

being in a justified state: But we have not then fulfilled all the Condition of our Justification at judgement, if we live longer, nor yet of our non-amission of our justified state.

Part 1. *pag.* 381. he questions, [" How after Mr. *Baxter's* principles can " Chrifts Righteoufnefs be faid to be ours by Divine Donation and Imputa-" tion, when he holds it no otherwife by Gods Donation ours, then the wilde " Goofe is his ? his if he can catch her, and as long as he can hold her : fo his, " as it is every ones elfe, as well as his if they can take and hold her. For fhe is " the worlds Goofe, and proper to none, before one hath taken her, and no longer " that ones then while he holds her ; if he let her go, fhe is the worlds Goofe again. " If Mr.*B's* Righteoufnefs be ftablifhed upon fuch a Law, Donation and Impu-" tation, let it be his not mine.]

Repl. But that God who is found of them that fought him not, may yet be fo mercifull as to give you a part in that Righteoufnefs which you renounce: though not while you renounce it knowingly, yet while you do it ignorantly, and know not what you fay: Yet if a Papift fhould fay, [Let not that imputed Righteoufnefs be mine, which is given by a conditional promife,] I fhould be thought a Papift if I allowed them the charity that I here allow my friend Mr. *Grandon.* Cannot God give us Chrift and his Righteoufnefs by a Conditional promife, without all this reproach and contempt of his gift ? Especially when the Condition is but Acceptance of the free gift according to its nature and ufe ? and when God giveth his Elect the Condition it felf ? To catch his wilde Goofe is a work of Art, and perhaps to moft of natural inculpable impoffibility, nor is fhe fent as a gift to them. To Receive an offered Chrift is an act of meer Confent or Willingnefs, Phyfically impoffible to none, and Morally only through mens own fault ; and Chrift is fent as a gift to all that will Accept him, and grace is given to the Elect to Accept him. Is it a Truth then that he here chargeth me with ? Methinks he fhould have born fo much Reverence, at leaft, to the unanimous Judgement of Proteftant Divines, who maintain that Chrift and his Righteoufnefs is given us by a Conditional promife, as not to renounce the Righteoufnefs that they all look to be faved by, nor to caft in their face this wilde Goofe fcorn.

Pag. 343. he faith [" Mr. *B.* makes and laies his own principles of Religion, " and from them he battereth Chrift and his doctrine, *&c.* 1. How fhall it appear " otherwife then by Mr. *B's* own magifterial dictates that juftifying faith is no-" thing elfe but the receiving of Chrift ?

Repl. 1. Is this a mount to batter Chrift from ? 2. Did I fay it was nothing elfe ? becaufe I faid, It is the receiving of Chrift ? 3. Is this a fit charge from him that feigneth me to comprize all good works as fuch in this faith ? 4. Is it not the words of God, and not my magifterial dictate ? *Job.* 1.12. *As many as received him,* &c. 5. Is it the Affemblies magifterial dictate, to define it, *The receiving of Chrift as he is offered in the Gofpel?* See their proof in the Catechifm from Scriptures.

He addes [" 2. Why elfe doth he make it fimply and only a quality or act of " the foul, without the adjection of its original from above, but to ingenerate into " the mindes of men an opinion, that it hath its emanancy and rife from nature, " from free will, that every man may have and act it, if and when he will, and that " it is not infufed of God, to be, *&c.*]

Repl. Yet no more regard to the ninth Commandment ? O learned Vindication

tion of Fundamental-Truths, by crouds of shameless falshoods! Doth the efficient enter the definition of a habit? or specially the manner of effecting? Do I deny the infusion of faith, or affirm it to be of nature, if I tell you not how God works it, when it nothing concerns the matter in hand, but would be a digression? I suppose Satan himself would not have thus accused me, without a fairer colour then this is.

What he holdeth himself (beside what is said before) you may see *pag.* 357. how farre we are justified by faith, [" Faith is not the *Causa sine qua non* of our " Justification in God, no nor yet in Christs Justification, *&c.* for these are An-" tecedaneous to our faith, and our faith not an Antecedent to it. At the *utmost* " it can be but the *Causa sine qua non* of Gods declaring and evidencing of our selves " to our selves justified.]

Repl. Doth Mr *Caryl* think this a Vindicating Gods Truth? Next, saith he, [" And this Justification Mr *B.* so disdaineth and snuffs at, that he will not own " it, much less mention it. Yet can he not with all his Sophistry name any other " act of Justification in this life, whereof faith can be proved to be the Antece-" dent, *Medium*, or *Causa sine qua non.*]

Rep 1. Do I indeed disdain Gods declaring me to my self to be justified, because I take it not to be the Justification by faith? Good proof of his Accusation! I disdain it not, but beg daily for it as a choise blessing! 2. How can he say [I disdain it] and yet [mention it not:] Was not reason or memory here wanting? 3. Its untrue that I mention it not, for I do give my reasons that it is not [the Justification by faith which Scripture means.] 4. I thought it had been more to Own it, then to Mention it, and not less. 5. Is not here a foul defect of modesty to say, that [with all my Sophistry I cannot name any other Act of Justification, *&c.*] When I did not only name another, but stand more particularly on the explication of it, then almost any one thing in the Book? *viz.* The act of God by his Covenant or Law of grace, conveying to us a Right to Christ, Impunity, and Glory, and so changing our relation; (whether our selves do feel it or not.)

Pag. 341. he saith, when I answer the objection that some make, that faith is a Passive instrument, [" Let him name some one of his [some] that have so " objected a Passive instrument of Justification, or else leave us to conclude, that " the objection is of his own head, partly to take advantage thereby yet further " to take his pastime in his Logical and Metaphysical Learning, which may " possibly please him, but never justifie or save him; and partly by shewing " the weakness of the objection, to gull his unwary Reader with an opinion " of the weaknesse of their Cause, who are forced with such Egyptian " reeds, for lack of better Pillars, to sustain it. It is one of the Jesuites " principles to fetch arms indifferently, either from Heaven or Hell, to storm " the Church and Truth of Christ, and to promote the holy Mother harlot of " *Rome.*]

Repl. 1. The charge is heavy: Do you hear how I am proved to promote the Harlot of *Rome*, as a Jesuite, to fetch armes from Hell, *&c.* and for what? for saying that some object [that faith is a Passive instrument?] And did I lie and feign this? There is but two that I know of, that have wrote against me on that Point, Mr *Kendall* and M^r. *Blake*, and the first most triumphantly disputes for it, though he say, They need it not: and the later owns it, maintains, and soberly disputeth for it: So that it is not the smallest part of my Papers now

in

in the Prefs to anfwer them. Was ever man in the world fo befet as I? that muft be wearied and grieved with writing againft fuch opinions on one fide; and on the other fide, be accounted a Jefuite, that fetches arms from Hell to maintain the Harlot of *Rome*, for faying that any man ever made fuch an objection?

2. Let Mr. *Kendall* and Mr. *Blake* fee how this man befriends their Caufe, that cals it fuch a weak objection and Egyptian Reed.

3. And let the moderate Reader confider by fuch inftances, as this, and a former of the like kinde that I gave him, how impoffible it is for me to pleafe all, or be efteemed Orthodox by all : when one part ufeth thofe objections, which another fends me to *Rome*, if not to hell, for faying that any man ufeth. They muft better agree among themfelves before I can pleafe them all.

Part 2. *p.* 214 he asketh [" Whether is the more arrogant doctrine, the Pa-
" pifts, &c. or Mr. *Baxter's* that faith, Works as Concaufes with, not fruits of
" faith, that flow from no other Grace, but *Pelagius* his Moral fwafion, with-
" out any Phyficall Renovation and change upon the Will, (as for di-
" ftinctions fake fome of our Divines are wont to exprefs themfelves) do fo
" merit ?]

Repl. It is a wonder to me that a man that truly believes that there is a God in heaven, and a day of Judgement, fhould have the heart and face to write fuch things, and leave them on Record againft himfelf to all ages: I thought a man could not have the true fear of God, that had ufed but now and then to fwear in a paffion, or lye for an advantage: but I fee I muft judge better of one that feareth not before God, to ftudy and heap up in fuch a Volume, and publifh deliberately and impenitently to the world, fuch falfe Accufations as a modeft Pagan would fcorn to be guilty of. 1. The firft fentence here is, that I fay [Werks are Concaufes] when I not only never faid it, but denied both faith and Works to be any Caufes. 2. The next is [not fruits of faith:] I ever maintain them to be fruits of faith; but its not poffible that he can hold them to Merit as fruits of faith, that holds them not to Merit at all. 3. The third fentence is that I fay [they flow from no other Grace, but *Pelagius* his Moral fwafion :] I dare challenge him that tempted you to utter thefe words, to prove if he can, that ever I faid them, or any fuch thing. 4. The next words are [without any Phyfical Renovation and change upon the Will.] Shew fuch a word in any Writing of mine, and burn the Book. I confefs I have elfewhere faid this, that *The winde bloweth where it lift, and we hear the found thereof, but know not whence it cometh, or whither it goeth; fo is every man that is born of the Spirit:* and that he that knoweth not how his own members were formed in the womb, knoweth not the myfterious way of the Spirits working on the foul, and therefore what name beft fuiteth it, Morall, Phyficall, or both in feveral refpects, let them tell that know: but that it is fpecial, effectual, infallibly prevailing Grace, on the will, I ever maintained. 5. The next affertion is, that I fay, thefe works [do Merit] yea [fo Merit] as the Papifts affirm; both which are fhamelefs falfhoods, againft my conftant profeffion. But his next words give you the proof of all this.

[" If Mr. *B.* means any thing elfe by Grace, he conceals it as a myftery from
" us, and will not throughout his whole Book give one hint of it : but makes man
" in his own natural and moral qualifications the Meriter of his own Juftification
" by Chrift.]

1. Before

II., Before he writes that [I said it] and now he proves it in that I said not the contrary. Do I deny all that I say, not, when its quite beside my subject? I was writing of no such matter, as the manner of working Grace. 3. Even this is but like the rest, for I do in that Book, maintain a special effectual Grace to the Elect, flowing from Gods absolute decree, and which is the fulfilling of that absolute promise, of taking the heart of stone from us, &c. 4. Is it not enough that I do this in other Books, since, though I did it not in that? 5. Yet doth he in the same-breath here venture to say again, that I [" make man in " his own natural and moral qualifications, the Meriter of his own Justifi- " cation by Christ.] I profess I am ready in charity to hope the man is not well in his witts; for as I had rather he had lost his witts then his consci- ence and common honesty, so methinks a sober man should hardly be so prodigall of his own Reputation, as to publish such a Volume to the world: and it astonisheth me to think that such a man as Mr. *Caryl*, can judge it Profitable to the Church of God, and worthy the Publike view, unlesse it be to shew men, what the Doctrine of this sort of men is by its fruits, and to deterre them thereby from the entertainment of such Opi- nions.

In the next Page he begins a Parellel between me and the Papists: like to the rest:

1. Most of his quotations from them are general, without telling us the par- ticular place: and they may seek it that list, and have nothing else to do.

2. Many of the words of the Papists cited, are the same that our Divines approve of, and ordinarily cite for our Doctrine against the rest of the Papists.

3. He plais with the ambiguity of the word [Justification] and when the Papists are known to mean it of sanctification, he parallels it as the same doctrine with mine, who use it as the Protestants do, for a Relative change: And so he parallels the Papists doctrine of first and second Justification, with mine of our being first justified, and our so continuing, or being justified also at Judgement.

4. Those few sayings of the Papists which particularly he directs us to, are some of them nothing to the purpose, some of them most vilely abused: For example, he doth with unusual exactness quote *Bellarmine*, for these words [" Good works are the Conditions of Justification without which Christs sa- " tisfaction is not applied to us.] Where I intreat the Reader to note the front of the man. 1. This opinion *Bellarmine* mentions as Erroneous, and rejects it. 2. He tels you it is the opinion of *Michael Baius*, whose name is enough to shew that it is mentioned in dislike. 3. It is commonly known that the Pope himself condemned this *Michael Baius*, with a long list of his Opinions (filling divers pages in 4º), as Erroneous or Hereticall, and forced the said *Baius* (as the Jesuites boast against the Dominicans) to recant them all. 4. There is not one word about Justification in the place in *Bellarmine*, but that is falsly added by this man. 5. The second Opinion which *Bellarmine* takes as probable is, that there are two satisfactions, one of Christs, and one of ours; and one de- pending on the other, and this for the honour of man as well as Christ, though one might have sufficed. 5. The third way which *Bellarmine* chooseth as most probable is, [*Quod una tantum sit actualis satisfactio, & ea sit nostra*] that there is but one actuall Satisfaction, and this is ours. Is this my Do- ctrine?

u But

But perhaps you will say, Mr. *Cr.* confesseth *Bellarmine* to different? I answer, He doth so: but hear how: in these words: [" Of this Opinion *Bellarmine* affirmeth some of his fellows to be, and findes no fault with it or them, only himself takes up what seemed to him more probable.]

Rep. O face past blushing! 1. *Bellarmine* talks of no fellows, but saies this is the opinion of some, and names only *Michael Baius*.

2. He addeth these words [*Ita Michael Baius lib. de Indulg. c. ult. Quæ sententia erronea mihi videtur*] which opinion seems to me Erroneous. Is this to finde no fault with it?

3. Yea he thus argueth against it [*Nam Scriptura & Patres passim vocant nostra opera satisfactiones & peccatorum Redemptiones; Deinde si potest homo justus suis operibus mereri de condigno vitam æternam, cur non satisfacere pro pœna temporali, quod est minus?* Is this nothing?

4. If he had found no fault, the name of *Baius* had been disparagement enough.

Should I give you an account of the rest of his quotations of the Papists, I should have small thanks from the Reader, for tiring his patience.

5. Those words which in his parellel he placeth as mine, are some of them none of mine, but his own forgeries; some of them dismembred scraps; some of them intermixt with twice as many of his own, or frequently with some of his own, to pervert the sense; and some of them plain truths confessed by all, with his false interpretations and collections adjoyned. For example, p. 216. he thus citeth my words: [" We are still said to be justified by faith, which is an act of ours. *Append.* pag. 80. Moral duties are part of the Condition of our Salvation; and for it to be performed: And even Faith is a Moral Duty.]

Rep. Was there ever Protestant that denied any of this, or accounted it Popery; But hear his collection how he makes it Popery. [" So that according to Mr. B's doctrine, Moral works and duties, *alone, as such,* are required of us to Justification: and not faith it self this way usefull but *as* a moral work and duty. *Ap.* p. 80.

O hard forehead! He durst put in [alone] and [as such] and that [faith it self is not usefull, but *as* a moral work or duty] out of his own brain, and make it mine, to parellel me with Papists! Well! I have for Mr. *Caryls* satisfaction gone thus farre to shew how he confuteth my Doctrine, and Vindicateth Fundamentals: but my Patience will not hold out, nor my Conscience suffer me to waste my time, in saying much more to such a man. And if any man will judge of his Parellel, without turning to the Authours and to my words, but will believe what this man saith of them or me, without trial, I appeal from him, as a seduced incompetent Judge.

I had thought to have performed the third part of my task, and have shewed you a multitude of his Contradictions; but I'le but give you a very brief taste. You heard before how he made me [as a Jesuite fetching arms from Hell, to promote the Mother Harlot of *Rome*] for saying, that any body doth object that faith is a Passive Instrument. Yet see whether himself do not so, *pag.* 360. in these words, [" Did we hereby make man the *Causa proxima,* yet it is but the *Causa proxima instrumentalis Passiva* of his Justification.

Part 2. p. 22. He complains of mens Galloping after me to the very *Lateran* of *Rome,* and running with head and shoulders thronging who shall be formost. And in his Epistles, what admiration and dolefull complaints finde we, for the success of my doctrine. Yet *pag.* 121. he saith [It is his own, and possibly may continue his own to the worlds end, all men else proving themselves too wise or too foolish to joyn with him in this his speculation] that is, of a two-fold Righteousness, &c.

I am loath it should prove true, that he dare swear an untruth as well as speak it, nor will I affirm it. But let it be considered by the sober, what fear of God is manifested, in the very beginning of his book in the Epistle Dedicatory: In the 5th and 6th pages he comes to clear himself from the charge of Antinomianisme, which he reduceth to four heads: The two first he thus conjoynes [" 1. Justi-
" fication as an Immanent act in God; as actually compleated in the Redem-
" ption which is by Christ and in Christ; both these before we believe.] And concerning this he saith, that so farre as he holdeth and hath declared himself to hold them (a cautelous addition; but I have before shewed how farre that is) [" 1. They are or seem at least to be grounded on Scripture: 2. They are ex-
" presly and boldly asserted by many of the most conspicuous Divines in Piety
" and Learning that any of the Protestant Churches have enjoyed ever since the
" Reformation. 3. And that without the contradiction or exception of any
" Church or Orthodox writer for well nigh a hundred years made against it:
" A great and probable argument that it was the Common Judgment of all the
" Churches.]

Rep. Mark here the height of Immodesty. 1. Would this one man perswade all the sober Divines of *England,* to whom he Dedicateth his Book, that this is true ? Which is the hundred years space that he means ? Not before the Reformation no doubt. Not the last hundred, no doubt, wherein so many have contradicted them. It is most probable he means the first hundred after the Reformation: and if so, who is the man that he hath yet named to us that is for his opinion ? or have his more learned partakers truly cited any orthodox Divine that for a hundred years after the Reformation, did hold it ? I remember not than I have seen any cited. I have observed my self in *Chamier* and *Polanus,* a word or two, sounding expresly for Justification before faith, but I think they were a hundred years after the Reformation begun: much more were *Maccovius,* Dr *Twiss* and Mr. *Pemble.* But let it be when he please that the hundred years begin; doth not the Christian world know, that if not all Churches and Eminent writers, yet some at least ever since the Reformation, have maintained, that none are Justified till they believe ? and without limitation denied that there is any such thing as Justification before faith, either of Infidels, or *non-exiftents* ! much less, a Justification Compleated in Christ ! Must we, can we all believe, that there hath been a hundred years since the Reformation wherein no one orthodox Writer denied Justification before faith ? Yea that others writ for it that while, and no man excepted against it ! Have we not their books at hand to evince the falshood of this ! For my part, according to my small Reading the clean contrary is true, and much more then that : I know not of any man, till *Polanus* on *Ezek.* and *Chamiers Panstrat* were written that, ever let fall a word for their opinion, that I now remember ; (though one or two, words there are in *Zanchy,* and a few more, lyable to misconstruction:) But

I know

I know that it is the currant doctrine of the Proteſtants till that time (and ſince, excepting a few ſuch as aforenamed) that there is no Juſtification of Infidels, or before faith: And if from the Apoſtles dayes till the Reformation he can name any one Orthodox writer, that ever was of his opinion; I will confeſs he hath read that which I never did.

2. But ſuppoſe all this were nothing, let any ſober man tell me, how it is poſſible for this man knowingly to ſay or ſwear, and that abſolutely without the leaſt limitation or exception, that it was [without the Contradiction or exception of any Church or Orthodox writer for well nigh a hundred years, made againſt it] Could this man poſſibly know every Contradiction or exception that any Church in the Chriſtian world, did for nigh a hundred years make againſt it? or hath he read all the books that every Orthodox writer hath written in that time? yea, when he confeſſeth his ſo ſmall reading in the following lines, as I thought few men pretending to Theologie, had been guilty of. It is therefore both unqueſtionably falſe, that there was no contradicting or excepting Divines (when there were any of his way to contradict,) and moſt certain that he could not have known it, if it had been true; there being many a hundred books that he never read or ſaw.

Yet ſee *pag*. 10. of that Epiſt. how he Seals up all with a ſolemn and dreadfull Oath: ſaying [" I have no more to ſay on this ſubject; and what I have ſaid " hath been before him that being omniſcient knoweth that I have ſpoken ſing-" ly the whole Truth, and nothing but the Truth :] Here is an appeal to God, a taking him to witneſs. And if this be the whole Truth, how come we to have ſo much more of his minde afterward on this point?

I will mention but two points more of his vanity: The firſt is in his ſilly aſcribing ſo much humane Learning to me, when Mr. *Kendall* might have given him a truer Information of me: Had I as much Learning as Mr. *Crandon* ſaith I have, and as much Piety as Mr. *Kendall* concedeth, ſure I were ſome excellent perſon, farre better then I am: And if I be not only as unlearned as Mr *K*. doth intimate, but alſo as Impious and damnable a ſeducer as Mr. *Crandon* doth make me, I were one of the unhappieſt men on earth. The teſtimony of theſe two Witneſſes doth ill agree. But the vanity that I mean of Mr. *Crandon* is upon this occaſion, to write ſo laboriouſly againſt the uſe of humane Learning in Divinity: Between eleven and twelve Leaves he ſpends againſt it in his Epiſtle: The ſecond Chapter is much againſt it: The third Chapter is almoſt all againſt it. Alas friend, Learning and I be not ſo neer akin, but that you may ſpare it, and yet be revenged on me, and pour out your gall againſt me to the full.

The laſt vanity that I will ſhew you, is his firſt Chapter (for I thought it fitteſt to read him backward:) I had wrote theſe words in the Epiſtle to my hearers; [who] I hope do underſtand, that to take upon truſt from your Teachers, what you cannot yet ſee in its own evidence, is leſs abſurd, and more neceſſary then many do imagin] Upon theſe words he will prove me to hold the doctrine of Implicit faith. The many ſenſeleſs cavils: the falſe accuſations without the leaſt ground, which are in that Chapter: I will not ſo abuſe the Readers Patience, as to recite. For the thing it ſelf I ſay but theſe two things: 1. My judgement is that all that will be ſaved muſt believe the Fundamentals explicitely: and that as much more as they can reach to know: and

that

that they should use all diligence to know as much as may be, and so should their Teachers to help them to it: and that no Teacher must be believed against the known sense of Gods word: But yet, that they who know the fundamentals by a Divine faith, should as Learners believe their Teachers in the rest with a humane faith, so far as they have no sufficient case of jealousie or unbelief: and that the body of our auditors must take much upon Trust from their Teachers, or they are undone. They that would see more of my thoughts on this point, I refer them to what I have written on it, in my *Method for Peace of Conscience*, and in the second part of my book of *Rest*, and in the Preface to that Part. If they that cannot Read believe not their Teachers, how know they that he reades true, or that there is such a thing as a Bible in the world! How shall others know that the Scripture is true translated, or the same book that is in the Hebrew and Greek? or that there is any at all in the Hebrew and Greek? or that we have now the same books that the Prophets and Apostles did write? or that ever they wrote any?

2. Let me be bold to tell my opinion to my Brethren of the Ministry, that though I deny them to have either Credit or Authority against the known word of God, yet so great is their Credit and Authority, even as Teachers and Guides of the Church in Cases agreeable to the word, and in Cases to the people doubtfull and unknown, and in Cases left by the word to their determination, (the word determining them but Generally) that I think the Ignorance of this Truth, hath been the main Cause of our sad Confusions and schismes in *England*, and that the Ministers have been Guilty of it, partly by an overmodest concealing their Authority, and partly by an indiscreet opposition to the Papists errour of the Authority of the Church: And I think that till we have better taught even our godly People, what Credit and Obedience is due to their Teachers and spirituall Guides, the Churches of *England* shall never have Peace or any good established order: I say again, we are broken for want of the knowledge of this Truth, and till this be known, we shall never be well bound up and healed.

But because Mr *Crandon* is one that I had rather come to a reference with, then to a dispute, if he please our difference may be thus compromized according to our various principles. Because it is agreeable to my Opinions, I shall desire that my hearers would believe me *fide humana* as a faithfull Teacher, when I am shewing them what they know not, that they may learn; and not take me for a Lyar, when ever I speak any word that they know not themselves as well as I, and consequently have need to be taught. But for Mr. *Crandons* hearers or Readers, least they should make a Papist of him, or themselves, let them believe him in nothing that they know not to be true before he told it them, or see not cleer proof of in the evidence which he bringeth. And if they are at any time assaulted with a Temptation, further to believe him; let them but open his book at randome, and read but one page with judgment and tryall, yea half a leaf well chewed and concocted, I doubt not may effectually save them from this Temptation to Popery, and restore them to their Incredulity: *Probatum est*.

And thus I have performed the most unsavoury task that ever I did attempt: If any think I have done it too briefly, I shall desire his own more Patient lungs to traverse the rest by the help of these Informations which I have given him: and so let him judge of it as he findeth cause.

It

It shall suffice me to present these Reasons to Mr *Caryl*, which hinder me from believing, that Mr *Crandon* hath here Vindicated the Truth of God, much less the Fundamentals of a Christians Comfort, or that this his large and elaborate Volume is Profitable to the Church of God, and Worthy Commendation to the Publick View: or that it is likely to add one cubit to the stature of any mans Reputation that shall so Commend it, or to advance that Name which Posterity shall finde affixed, or to give one Grain of solid Peace to the Conscience of any that hath secretly or openly Promoted it. This Judgment I pass, as Impartially as I can, and am somewhat confident the Event will confirm it, and Convince the Incredulous.

FINIS.